THE

INDUSTRIAL RESOURCES, ETC.,

OF THE

SOUTHERN AND WESTERN STATES:

EMBRACING A VIEW OF THEIR

COMMERCE, AGRICULTURE, MANUFACTURES, INTERNAL IMPROVEMENTS; SLAVE AND FREE LABOR, SLAVERY INSTITUTIONS, PRODUCTS, ETC., OF THE SOUTH,

Together with

HISTORICAL AND STATISTICAL SKETCHES OF THE DIFFERENT STATES AND CITIES OF THE UNION—STATISTICS OF THE UNITED STATES COMMERCE AND MANUFACTURES, FROM THE EARLIEST PERIODS, COMPARED WITH OTHER LEADING POWERS—THE RESULTS OF THE DIFFERENT CENSUS RETURNS SINCE 1790, AND RETURNS OF THE CENSUS OF 1850, ON POPULATION, AGRICULTURE AND GENERAL INDUSTRY, ETC.,

WITH AN APPENDIX.

IN THREE VOLUMES.

VOL. I.

BY J. D. B. DE BOW,

PROFESSOR OF POLITICAL ECONOMY, ETC., IN THE UNIVERSITY OF LOUISIANA.

PUBLISHED AT THE OFFICE OF DE BOW'S REVIEW,
MERCHANTS' EXCHANGE, NEW-ORLEANS;
79 JOHN STREET, NEW-YORK; AND EAST BAY AND BROAD STREETS, CHARLESTON.

1852.

Pudney & Russell, Printers.

PREFACE.

The volumes which are here presented to the public, will be found to embrace a vast amount of valuable information in regard to the practical and industrial interests of the country, alike interesting to the merchant and the planter, the manufacturer, the scholar, and the statesman.

Upon all the subjects of Southern life, manners, institutions, and progress, the material is copious and accurate, and has been collected during many years of active researches in the editorial conduct of one of the most widely circulated Journals in the Union. The articles upon Slavery, Slave Laws, and Productions, are from the ablest pens—entirely exhaust the subject, and are worthy the study of the statist and philosopher. Such a study and understanding of the subject, in all its bearings, will do more than all the political essays in the world, to restore peace and harmony between the different sections of our wide and growing country.

Though the aim of the volumes has been to furnish, for the first time, A Complete View of the Industry, Resources, and Wealth of the South, with as full and elaborate statistics of the great and growing West, in the same particulars, as could be obtained, other papers and articles have been added upon the wealth and resources of the North, of the Union, of South and British America, of Mexico, the West India Islands, etc., carefully prepared, and of much practical interest.

Whatever deficiences exist in the minuteness or recentness of the materials of the text, if not corrected, as will generally be done in the appendices of the volumes, will be supplied or corrected in the monthly issues of the work, above referred to, which will at all times furnish the latest and most reliable data.

J. D. B. De Bow.

New-Orleans, Nov. 1, 1852.

The paper on the "Interior Valley of North America," was contributed by our friend Professor Wm. C. Duncan, of the University of Louisiana, as was also the one on "British America," page 16. The other paper on "British America," and the one on "Cotton and Cotton Manufucturing," are contributions from A. W. Ely, M. D. The Hon. Joel R. Poinsett contributed "New Products for the South," and "Indian Corn;" Lieut. M. F. Maury, "Gulf of Mexico, River Basins, Etc.;" Hon. H. Bullard, "Louisiana Early History," page 408: J. S. Duke of St. Louis, "Coffee and the Coffee Trade." The Agricultural Statistics U. S., 1850, were kindly furnished by Mr. Kennedy of the Census Office, and are now first published complete.

INDEX TO VOL. I.

(FOR GENERAL INDEX SEE END OF VOLUME III.)

INDUSTRIAL RESOURCES, ETC.,

OF THE

SOUTHERN AND WESTERN STATES.

AMERICA.—Interior Valley of North America—Boundaries and Appearance—Climate, Natural History, Population, etc.—One of the most useful books, recently published in this country, is the work of Dr. Drake, on the Principal Diseases of our Interior Valley. Its prime object is to detail the ætiology, pathology, and treatment of the diseases prevalent in that valley. Preliminary to the direct consideration of the subject-matter, the author gives a careful and lengthy sketch, geological, hydrographical, climatic, physiological, and social, of the Interior Valley; which, apart from its usefulness to the practical physician and medical student, is rich with matter highly interesting to the historian, geologist, meteorologist, and all who delight in the discoveries of science. Unlike most books, this has a permanent and increasing value. Its true worth will only be known hereafter. It is, in short, a "κτῆμα εἰς ἀεί." The present article is intended as a review, or rather brief condensation of the preliminary sketch, which occupies much the larger part of the volume, being 701 pages in length. The more strictly medical portion is not well fitted for treatment in the pages of this work; and it deserves, too, and will no doubt abundantly receive, the consideration of writers much better acquainted than ourselves with the entire circle of diseases and their ætiology. In describing the Interior Valley we shall follow substantially the order adopted by Dr. Drake, as upon the whole the most natural and convenient. In a treatise so brief, we can have little more to do than condense the subject-matter of the leading topics which he discusses, referring but little, if in any respect, to the observations of other writers, and indulging not at all in original speculations. In accordance with this plan, we proceed to treat of the *Boundaries and Physical Appearance of the Interior Valley.*

This region extends on the north and south, from the tropic of Cancer (lat. 23° 28′ N.) to the north polar circle, the whole length of the north temperate zone; on the east and west, from the Apalachian to the Rocky Mountains, widening as one passes from south to north. Supposing 8,000,000 of square miles to be the area of North America, the valley contains 6,000,000. The northern half is almost uninhabitable; and of the remaining 3,000,000 square miles, only one-third is as yet inhabited, and that but sparsely, by a civilized population. The western boundary of the valley is the Rocky Mountains, which are composed of many chains united by offsets, and run northwest to the Polar Sea. The range varies in height from 10,000 to 14,000 feet above the level of the ocean; and is distant, on an average, about 10° of longitude from the Pacific. The vast inclined plane on the east of the range is 5,000 or 6,000 feet lower than the mountain at the point of recession from the range. Upon this plain are found several tracts of high table land, either projecting from the mountains, or insulated; of which the principal are the Sweetwater Mountains and Black Hills, the *Llano Estacado,* the Ozark Mountains, and the *Coteau des Prairies.* The Apalachian Mountains form the eastern boundary, which run northeasterly, at an average elevation about one-fourth of that reached by the chain on the western margin. The plain which inclines from the Apalachian Mountains to the trough of the valley, is much narrower than that running from the mountain range on the other side. It does not, like it, present elevated ranges of table land, but it is in general more rugged. Nor does the Apalachian chain, like the Rocky Mountains, extend to the Polar Sea, but is interrupted by the lakes and the River St. Lawrence, and finally disappears before it reaches the coast of Labrador. The northern part of the valley is an immense flat, stretching across from the Rocky Mountains to the Labrador coast, deeply indented in many places by the Northern Ocean.

On the north side of the valley lies Hudson's Bay; on the south, the Gulf of Mexico; both penetrating deeply into the land, and each a reservoir of many large rivers, which originate in the centre of this region. Lakes are seldom found in the southwestern part of the valley, but are numerous in the more northern portion. Deserving of particular notice is that remarkable chain which, commencing with Great Bear Lake in the northeast corner of the valley, (lon. 127°,) runs southerly as far as Lake Erie, (lat. 40°, lon. 80°,) and then northeasterly into the River St. Lawrence, through which the waters of nearly the whole series are discharged into the Atlantic. This is the longest chain of lakes in the world. The valley abounds in rivers, on which are situated our largest cities, and between which, in the bottom lands, resides the densest rural population. These rivers have, severally, hydrographical axes, or centres, in which they originate, and by which they are divided into as many distinct groups as there are distinct centres. Of these axes, some lie wholly within the valley; others among the mountains on its eastern and western margins. Those within the valley are: 1. The region west of Lake Superior, (mean lat. 47°, mean lon. 95°,) whose average elevation is 1,500 feet, and from which rivers flow in three different directions. These are, the Mississippi, running southeast through the central trough of the valley; the St. Lawrence, known first as the St. Louis, then by other names, until it flows from Lake Ontario northeasterly into the Gulf of St. Lawrence; the Red River of the north, which flows northward under various titles for 1,500 miles, and empties at last into Hudson's Bay. 2. The country west of Lake Michigan, (mean lat. 45°, lon. 89° to 92°,) which axis, however, is altogether subordinate to the preceding. Its rivers run mostly into the Mississippi; the rest into the lakes. 3. On the other side of the same lake there is another centre, of from five to 1,100 feet elevation, from which streams flow west, north and east. 4. The region occupied by Ohio and Indiana, of greatest elevation in its eastern part, (1,100 feet,) but abounding most in rivers in its western. The waters of this axis flow partly into the lakes and partly into the Ohio. Of the former character the principal streams are, the St. Joseph, Maumee, Sandusky, Cuyahoga, and Grand; of the latter, the chief are the Kankakee, (true head of the Illinois,) Wabash, Great Miami, Sciota, Muskingum, and Big Beaver. 5. Far to the south are the highlands of Alabama and Mississippi, from which centres short tributaries of the Tennessee flow north; to the south are the Yazoo and Big Black, flowing into the Mississippi; the Pearl and Pascagoula into the Gulf of Mexico, and the Tombigbee and Black Warrior flowing into the Alabama, and finally into the same gulf. 6. In the northern part of Texas, a hilly axis, whence flow the Sabine, Trinity, Brazos, Colorado and Nueces, into the Mexican Gulf. 7. The Ozark Mountains, whence descend various tributaries of the Arkansas and of the Missouri; and the Maramac, St. Francis, White, and Washita, (through the Red,) affluents of the Mississippi. 8. The Black Hills, in Missouri Territory, from which all the eastern streams empty in the Missouri directly, and the western mediately by its chief branch, the Yellow Stone. 9. The water table far north, between Hudson's Bay and the lakes, and the St. Lawrence, from which streams descend to the north and to the south. 10. The sterile region still farther to the north and west, east of Great Bear Lake, on the borders of the frigid zone, from which the water is shed from the one side into Great Slave Lake, from the other into the Polar Sea.

The hydrographical axes, or centres, which exist in the western mountain border of the valley, are the two following: 1. The northern Rocky Mountain axis, (mean lat. 51°, mean lon. 115°,) of from ten to 12,000 feet elevation, and the origin of the largest rivers on the continent. It sends down from its west side to the Pacific, Frazer River and the north fork of the Oregon, (Clarke;) from its east side, the streams composing the Mackenzie, which empties into the Polar Sea, the head waters of Saskatchawan, and the Maria, the northern branch of the Missouri. 2. The Southern Rocky Mountain axis, (mean lat. 41°, mean lon. 107,) with an average elevation of 11,000 feet. From the western side it sends down the south fork of the Oregon, (Lewis,) and the Rio Colorado, which latter flows into the Gulf of California. On its east side originate the southern branches of Big Horn, the Platte, and Kansas, tributaries of the Missouri, Arkansas and Red, which flow into the Mississippi; the Rio del Norte emptying into the Mexican Gulf.

The hydrographical axes of the eastern mountain border are these: 1. The elevated region of the White and Green mountains, from which streams flow, on the north and west, into the St. Lawrence and Lake Champlain; on the south, the St. John, Penobscot, Kennebec, and Connecticut, into the Atlantic. 2. The axis between the lakes Ontario and Champlain, from which a number of rivers, chiefly small, flow in all directions. Of these, the chief is the Hudson. 3. The centre, lying in New-York and Pennsylvania, of an average height of 1,800 feet. From this proceeds, on the north, the Genesee and the Oswego; on the east, the western branches of the Susquehanna; on the southwest, the headwaters of the Alleghany. 4. The region in Virginia, between lat. 38° and 39°, and lon. 79° and 80°, of a mean elevation of 2,000 feet. On the east it sends down the Potomac and James; on the north, the Monongahela; on the southwest, the Greenbrier, a branch of the Kanawha. 5. The elevated region, (3,000 feet,) situated mainly in North

Carolina, but extending into S. W. Virginia, the northern parts of South Carolina and Georgia, and the eastern portion of Tennessee (mean lat. 36°, mean lon. 82° ;) from which rivers radiate from the east to the northwest through three quarters of a circle. From the east and south it throws off the Roanoke, Cape Fear, Gadkin, the tributaries of the Santee, and the Savannah. On its west side originate the Kanawha, Big Sandy, Kentucky, Cumberland, Tennessee, Chattahoochie and Alabama. Rising in the outlines and hill lands on the east side, we have the Pedee and Altamaha ; on the west, or valley side, the Guyandotte, Licking, and Green. From these seventeen hydrographical centres proceed nearly all the rivers of North America.

The interior of the valley is traversed by a deep, winding depression, extending from the Mexican Gulf to Hudson's Bay. From either side of this trough arises an inclined plane, each growing more elevated as it approaches its mountain boundary. That on the east is considerably smaller than the western. The Mississippi traverses this trough, or axis, from the Gulf to St. Peter's River, (lat. 44° 52′,) whence it follows the course of that stream to Big Stone Lake, passes thence through Lake Traverse and along Swan Creek and Red River to Lake Winnipeg, and thence along Nelson River to Hudson's Bay, (lat. 57°.) The axis is synclinal, that is, it has a dip in two different directions, to the south and to the north. Its culminating point is the small and narrow tract, (three miles wide,) situate between the lakes Big Stone and Traverse, the elevation of which is about 975 feet. From Big Stone Lake the axis declines to the Mexican Gulf at the rate of twelve inches for every minute of latitude. From Lake Traverse it dips northward but slightly until it reaches Lake Winnipeg, (elevation 750 feet,) whence it falls precipitously to Hudson's Bay. The line of culmination crossing the synclinal axis between Big Stone and Traverse Lakes, extends to the Rocky Mountains on the west, (lat. 49°,) and on the east to Lake Superior, which is set, so to speak, in its eastern extremity.

From the region west of Lake Superior a new culminating ridge begins, running about southeast, nearly at right angles with the last mentioned, around the head of Lake Michigan, until it reaches lat. 41°, whence it proceeds northeast to the northern sources of the Alleghany, (lat. 42° 15′, lon. 78° 30′,) in New-York. From the northern side of this ridge the waters are poured partly into Hudson's Bay by the Red River, but mostly into the Gulf of St. Lawrence by the River St. Louis, the lake chain, and their aqueduct, the River St. Lawrence. The waters running from its southern side are discharged by the Mississippi into the Gulf of Mexico. To this culminating ridge there is a corresponding synclinal axis, which extends from Lake Superior along the lake chain and the St. Lawrence to the gulf of that name, somewhat at right angles to the axis already described. The two axes once had extensive water communication, especially by the river Illinois, along which canoes have passed in high water from one trough to the other. Thus we have formed by the axes, culminating ridges and mountains which have been described, three distinct hydrographical basins. The first, constituting one-third of the whole, is bounded on the north by the culminating ridges already spoken of, on the west by the Rocky Mountains, on the east by the Alleghanies, (Apalachian mountains,) and on the south by the Gulf of Mexico, into which all its superfluous waters are discharged. It is usually known as the *Valley of the Mississippi;* but as that river does not drain the whole of the southern part of the basin, (viz : Texas, Eastern Mexico, East Mississippi, South Alabama, West Georgia, West Florida,) it may be more appropriately called the *Southern* or *Mexican Basin.* The second basin receives the name *St. Lawrence,* because that river conveys all its waters to the ocean. The third is the *Hudson Basin,* extending some twenty degrees in latitude, and lying between 70° and 115° of west longitude. A fourth basin, whose water-sheds have not yet been fully described, includes the whole northern seacoast from Baffin's Bay to the Rocky Mountains, and is denominated the *Polar Basin.* Of these four hydrographical basins, into which the interior valley is divided, the first is, on many accounts, the most interesting.

The geological character of the valley is striking. The soil, or earthy covering of the country, is composed naturally of the disintegrated and decomposed subjacent rocks, and would always be such in the main, were the decomposed materials kept in the place where they are formed. This, however, cannot be ; for the rains are constantly washing down this substance, *alluvion,* as it is called, from the hills into the valleys, whence it is borne along by streams, and gradually deposited in beds, forming alluvial grounds or bottom lands. Owing to the necessary mixture of materials of a vastly different minerological and organic composition, these alluvial grounds form an extremely complicated system. The system is, moreover, so extensive, on account of the vast number of agencies at work in its formation, that every part of the valley may be traversed from north to south, or from sea to sea, without leaving them, except to cross the streams by which they have been deposited.

In the rear of these alluvial bottoms are found, along many rivers, higher deposits of transported materials of less extent than the bottom lands, but evidently made by rivers much deeper and broader than any now existing. Closely related to these formations are the deposits on the general surface of the country, which extend from the sea of the south to an elevation of 1,500 feet on the mountain slopes and higher parts of the valley plain. They vary in depth from a few feet to 100 or more, and are composed of water-worn materials undeniably brought down from the north. These deposits are known as *diluvion*, drift, or post-tertiary. Co-extensive with them are found immense bowlders of granite and other primitive rocks lying at great distances from their parent strata, which were most probably transported, at a remote period, from the north, while imbedded in blocks of floating ice.

A farther description of the geological character of the valley can best be given in the words of Dr. Drake himself: "We must now penetrate the loose, upper coverings, and briefly indicate the nature of the strata below. In doing this, if we begin, as in the study of our physical geography, at the Gulf of Mexico, and proceed up the valley, along its synclinal axis, we shall find that different rocks successively crop out, each to constitute the surface for a certain space, and then to be succeeded by a deeper, which has emerged from beneath it. We shall also find that we pass progressively from the very newest to the oldest; though all the formations which lie between those extremes, in all countries, may not be met with. Thus, around the Gulf of Mexico, we begin on broad and deep alluvial deposits; then rise on diluvial or post-tertiary, and then on tertiary. To these, in Southern Alabama and Mississippi, succeeds a cretaceous deposit, extending into west Tennessee, followed by the coal formations of Illinois and Missouri; then, advancing, we arrive in northern Illinois and Wisconsin, upon the Devonian shales and sandstones which underlie the coal basin; then, upon the silurian or transition limestones, sandstones and slates; and lastly, upon granite and other primitive rocks, which stretch northerly from Lake Superior to the Polar Sea. To the east and west of the line supposed to be traveled over, most of these formations spread out with great regularity and amplitude. Thus, there is a geological, not less than a geographical, unity in the Interior Valley. Not the unity of a single formation, existing everywhere, but the unity of one system of formations, deposited on a scale of vast extent, and subsequently subjected to the same influences, whether conservative or destructive. In no other country, over an equal area, is the geological structure so simple and uniform; in no other does it so decidedly constitute the whole into one natural region.

"It is an obvious truth, that these formations have undergone but few disruptions from any force acting beneath. The Ozark Hills, of primitive rock, in Arkansas and Missouri, have, it is true, been pushed up through the secondary; and, in the former state, there are some volcanic appearances, in the midst of which we find the hot springs of Washita; still further, the great earthquakes of 1811 had their focus in the same quarter. But the whole region is of insignificant extent compared with the entire valley, which elsewhere shows scarcely a vestige of volcanic action. If, however, the rock formations of the interior of the continent still lie in their original position, all that were deposited are not here now. Our best geologists have come to the conclusion that much has been washed away; that vast submarine currents have swept the continent from north to south; scooped out or steepened the valley by cutting down its strata; produced the general levelness of its surface, and finally left upon it the primitive bowlders and other drift or post-tertiary deposits which have been described."

The Southern Hydrographical Basin.—Our limits preclude us giving more than a very brief skeleton of this portion of Dr. Drake's book. The amount of information on the various topics discussed, which he has accumulated from numerous sources as well as personal observation, and his generally logical deductions from a generalization of the same, impart to this division of his work a peculiar value. The nature of the subject first leads to the consideration of the Gulf of Mexico, the position of which, its depth currents, temperature, tides, inundations and coasts, are successively treated. Next comes the special topography of the Mexican coasts, of which we should like, had we room, to present a short sketch, especially of that elaborate part relating to the delta of the Mississippi and its neighboring localities. Above its delta, as high up as the mouth of the Missouri, there lies on each side of the Mississippi a series of low alluvial lands, which are divided into four distinct bottoms; the Tensas, the Yazoo, the St. Francis, and the American. Above the last commences the region described as the Upper Mississippi. The St. Francis bottom is terminated about thirty miles above Cairo by approaching rocky highlands. The alluvial region below is the most extensive of the kind in America, having an area of about 20,000 square miles. It extends from north to south, in a straight line, a distance of 400 miles, but more than 900, reckoning by the course of the river. The major part of these bottom lands are subject to annual overflows, from which, however. they may be, and at some future time will be, reclaimed, by the intelligent application of scientific principles.

Of the country lying between the Mississippi and the Rocky Mountains, not much, comparatively, is known, and the larger part of it is still a wilderness. It possesses, however, not a few claims to the attention of the naturalist, and is destined, in the course of time, to exercise a weighty influence upon the affairs of this republic.

A portion of East Louisiana, all Mississippi, nearly the whole of Alabama and West Florida, and West Georgia, lying east of the Mississippi and south of the Ohio basin, constitute another region of peculiar geological and hydrographical character. Its northeast portion, containing the extreme outlines of the Apalachian mountain range, is mountainous or hilly. The mountains in Georgia and East Alabama are composed of primitive rocks; those further west, of the older secondary limestones, and of sandstones and shales belonging to the coal formations. Coal appears on the surface at certain points of the Black Warrior and the Catawba. South and west of these occurs the most extensive cretaceous formation yet discovered in North America. In the north this formation is hilly; to the south appear frequent and extensive plains. The rivers of this part of the region are subject to inundation. South of the cretaceous formations are tertiary, post-tertiary, diluvial and alluvial deposits, which reach to the Gulf of Mexico. These deposits are even less consolidated than the cretaceous, which latter are friable in texture, of miscellaneous composition, and contain organic remains.

Another, and, in many respects, the most important hydrographical region of the southern third of the valley, is what is felicitously called the Ohio Basin. The central states of this basin are Kentucky and Ohio, which, however, do not lie wholly within it. It includes, also, the most of Tennessee, the north end of Alabama, the N. W. corner of Alabama, the west of North Carolina, western Virginia, the west of Pennsylvania, part of the S. W. corner of New-York, Indiana, and half of Illinois. Its elevation, not reckoning mountains, is more than double (700 to 1,000 feet) that of the regions already described. Some of its mountains rise from 2,500 to 5,000 feet. South of the Ohio the surface is ridgy, and to the east mountainous. In the northwest are tracts of level land resembling, in some respects, the plains of Alabama. Near the mouths of the Ohio and Tennessee are found cretaceous deposits, similar to those of the last described region. Everywhere else, at the surface, the geological formations are older. In the west, south, and east of the region, are extensive coal deposits, and their accompanying sandstones, shales and limestone. Devonian sandstones and shales, of an older date, and also silurian limestone, still older, exhibit themselves in the central part. These rocks are hardened, and the streams cutting through them flow in narrow ravines, except among the deep and extensive diluvial deposits of Ohio, Indiana and Illinois. The waters of this are conveyed to the Mississippi by the Ohio. This latter river runs sluggishly, and in a wide channel, from the mouth of the Tennessee to its own. Above the Tennessee, as far up as the mountains, its banks are more elevated, two terraces of earth being frequently seen, and sometimes three. The lowest bottoms are argillaceous, with a deep soil. The second and third terraces consist of bowlders, pebbles, gravel and sand, over which is a stratum of loam, above which again is spread a thin layer of soil. The bowlders are composed of fragments of every kind of rock yet discovered east, northeast, and north of the Ohio; and they grow larger as one ascends northward. Organic remains are found in all three terraces, imbedded in a tenacious blue clay. Back of the terraces, at an average distance of one mile from the river, a line of hills, about 400 feet high, runs parallel with the stream for 600 miles, where they join the out-crops of the Apalachian coal formation.

The remainder of the Southern Basin is a narrow belt of land, extending 10° of latitude along the east bank of the Mississippi from the mouth of the Ohio. Its southern half lies in Illinois; its northern, in Wisconsin. The general aspect of the region is rolling, but prairies abound in all parts. The southern portion has an elevation of about 800 feet; the northern reaches a height of from 1,500 to 1,800 feet. In the south is the Illinois coal formation; towards the north the older rocks appear, and finally the primitive strata near the sources of the Mississippi.

The remaining three great hydrographical basins of the Interior Valley are quite different in their configuration and general character from that of which we have just given an imperfect, yet, as far as it goes, a correct outline. These three, want of space compels us to pass in silence.

Climate of the Valley.—The axis of the valley runs nearly in the same meridian from the torrid to the frigid zone; and. therefore, it presents every modification which is the effect of the sun's rays in various latitudes. But, though that luminary is the prime cause of all climatic phenomena, its influence is not always immediately asserted. Acting on continents and seas, it imparts heat to the atmosphere in very unequal degrees, affecting its statical equilibrium, and thereby producing winds which in their turn re-act upon the temperature of the atmosphere. Climate is affected by the proportion of watery surface existing in a country; for this vapor is generated and absorbed by the air, which, of course, becomes damper in consequence. Now, in the Southern Basin, the neighborhood of the gulf and delta and trough of the Mississippi are almost the only portions of the surface constantly, or occasionally, covered with water. Except in these portions, then, the surface of the region is but little productive of vapor. The contrary is the fact with regard to the St. Lawrence Basin, which abounds in lakes, as do also the basins situate farther to the north. Forests, by intercepting the sun's rays, retard the heating of the earth's surface by day, and at night diminish the radiation of heat. They lessen, too, the velocity of winds. They possess, therefore, a decided climatic influence. The eastern side of the Southern Basin is much better furnished with forests than the western, which abounds in prairies. The St. Lawrence Basin is generally wooded; the other two have small trees with a limited foliage.

Mountains, again, by giving direction to some winds, modifying some, and cutting off others, exercise an important influence on climate. Thus, the Apalachian chain gives their course to certain winds; and when an easterly breeze prevails, reduces its temperature and condenses its moisture. Hence, in the centre of the valley, a southeast wind is always colder than one from the southwest. The mountains on the west, however, have even a more direct influence on the climate of the valley. In the extreme south the winds of the Pacific find a passage across the Isthmus of Panama into the Gulf of Mexico, and thence, modified of course, into the interior of the valley. Above the isthmus, however, up to the Polar Sea, the elevated Rocky Mountain chain shuts off almost entirely the winds of the Pacific. But the difference of level between these mountains, and the extensive inclined plane running from the eastern side to the trough of the Mississippi, often causes the descent of the cold air from the former, as temporary winds; and then the originally warm breezes of the Pacific come to us deprived, in a great measure, of their caloric and their vapor.

On the south of the valley, running up into it as high as the latitude of 30°, there is situated a large body of warm water, from the surface of which proceed those hot and moist winds from the south which traverse the interior country. The southwest winds, which come from the mountain regions west of the gulf, are colder and less humid. On the north, the valley is subtended by Hudson's Bay and the Polar Sea. Within the latter lies the pole of cold, or point at which the mean temperature of the year is least. No south or southwest wind can reach this region without traversing the snow-covered summit of the Rocky Mountains. Hence, in part, its low temperature. The winds coming from this region are always cold; but they do not blow as frequently as those from the south. Lying, as it does, between the Gulf of Mexico and the Polar Sea, the one very warm and the other very cold, the valley must always be subject to extreme changes of temperature.

Dr. Drake has compiled a number of highly valuable tables, illustrative of the temperature of different places in the valley. We can only give a part of the one registering

THE MEAN TEMPERATURE OF THE MONTHS.

	Mean An.Tem. °	Jan. °	Feb. °	Mar. °	April. °	May. °	June. °	July. °	Aug. °	Sep. °	Oct. °	Nov. °	Dec °	Temp. Obs. Min. °	Temp. Obs. Max. °
Havana	77.34	69.98	71.96	75.74	78.98	83.58	84.12	84.30	85.84	83.04	79.52	75.56	71.78	59	94
New-Orleans	70.19	56.42	59.17	68.60	73.71	88.96	83.09	83.90	33.27	80.23	71.69	60.81	54.38	14	100
Natchez	66.86	52.27	54.51	59.66	69.85	74.52	80·71	81.32	80.85	77.18	67.01	56.98	49.73	0	97
City of Mexico	61.86	54.14	....	....	....	....	67.46	....	....	....	....	....	....	..	..
Nashville	58.46	38.22	40.80	49.43	61.92	68.33	76.48	79.47	75.77	70.80	55.29	45.14	39.63	18	99
Cincinnati	53.36	33.50	33.15	42.94	55.35	63.33	70.86	75.47	73.25	65.46	52.30	41.71	33.09	18	100
St. Louis	55;57	33.19	34.93	44.34	58.99	66.32	73.79	78.43	76.34	68.14	54.92	40.07	33.82	30	105
Montreal	44.90	14.66	18.13	28.43	41.94	58.06	68.12	78.89	69.67	60.23	47.43	33.83	18.96	28	98
Fort Enterprise	14.19	....	....	....	....	....	....	....	55.36	....	....	....	29.12	57	73
Felix Harbor	3.60	26.73	32.02	....	2.54	15.64	34.16	41.25	38.69	25.41	9.07	5.42	22.43	47	70
Melville Island	0.27	....	35.05	....	....	....	....	40.98	....	....	....	....	....	55	60

Among the highest temperatures yet observed in the valley, are: Fort Leavenworth, (latitude 39° 23′,) 105°; St. Louis, 109°; Fort Gibson, (latitude 35° 48′,) 116°. Among the lowest are: Felix Harbor, (latitude 70°,) 47°; Melville Island, 55°; Fort Enterprise, 57°; Fort Reliance, (latitude 62° 46′,) 70°. The mean atmospheric pressure indicated by the barometer, for five years, at the following named cities, are these: Montreal, 29.886 inches; St. Louis, 29.578; Cincinnati, 29.434; Hudson, (N. Y.,) 29.556; Toronto, 29.487. The extreme annual ranges of the barometer and the thermometer bear always the same ratio to each other, as will be seen by the subjoined tabular view:

	N. Orleans.	St. Louis.	Cincinnati.
Yearly Bar. Range.	Inches. 0.790	Inches. 1.760	Inches. 1.620
Ther. Range.	86°	134°	117°

The winds of the valley exercise an important influence on its climate. In changing they follow usually a regular order, veering from the left to the right, the face of the observer being turned to the north or to the south. Their relative prevalence for the entire valley, beginning with the least frequent, is, east, west, north, south. Instead, however, of blowing direct from the cardinal points, they commonly come from between two that are adjacent; and thus their relative frequency is, reckoning as before, southeast, southwest, northwest, northeast. In the whole valley western breezes prevail over eastern in the ratio of 57 to 43; northern over southern in the ratio of 54 to 46.

Plants and Animals.—On the west of the Mexican Gulf, in a low latitude, we observe a striking difference in the nature of the plants of the country as we ascend from the sea-coast to the mountains beyond. At first the productions of a tropical climate abound; but soon only those of the temperate zone are discoverable, and in places only the plants indigenous to high northern latitudes. In a few hours the whole natural scale of vegetation is ranged from the heliconias and the banana, to the resinous and stunted parenchyma. Around the northern curve of the same gulf, we have, mingled with deciduous trees and plants, the long-leaved pine, the live oak, cypress, magnolia, and sweet gum. In the middle latitudes of the valley, (36°–42°) is found the greatest variety of forest trees. But here, the trees are all deciduous, the evergreens having disappeared. Among them may be mentioned the several kinds of oak, the ash, walnut, hickory, dogwood, elm, beech, maple, yellow poplar, and cotton tree. In the eastern extremity of the region the pine is abundant. The forests of these latitudes extend to the further coast of Lake Superior, except certain species which will not flourish so high north. In the northern regions, trees of the temperate zones are found intermingled with those that are peculiar to a colder climate. Most of these species are evergreens; and they nearly cease to appear before we reach the polar circle, beyond which all vegetation is very scarce and stunted. Yet, willows, like those of the Mississippi, grow on the banks and at the very mouth of the Mackenzie River. Of the cultivated plants belonging to the valley, we may mention, in particular, the *banana*, which flourishes on the *tierras calientes* of Mexico; *coffee*, raised, as yet, only in Cuba; the *orange tree*, growing up to lat. 30°; *sugar-cane*, limited to the country south of the 31st parallel; *rice*, produced as far up as 36° 30′; the *fig tree*, reaching to lat. 33°; the *peach*, growing as high as 43°; *cotton*, whose limits are the same as those of rice; *maize*, (Indian corn,) of which three crops a year can be raised in the tropics, successfully cultivated as far as lat. 49°; the *sweet potato*, reaching to the 41st parallel; the *Irish potato*, which, in lat. 43° and 44° attains its highest perfection; *wheat*, most perfect in lat. 43°, but raised as far up as the 60th parallel; and, lastly, the *apple*, which does not succeed well below lat. 33°, but improves as we advance north to the existing limits of cultivation.

A large proportion of the quadrupeds belonging to the valley range across the continent from north to south. Contrary to the analogy of the vegetable kingdom, the larger animals are found in the colder region. This is especially true of the marine mammalia. This provision of nature is just fitted to the circumstances of man in the two extremities of the valley; for, in the north, he draws, or should derive his sustenance, in harmony with the hygienic principles, mainly from the animal kingdom; in the south, chiefly from the vegetable. Of the quadrupeds which are found throughout the valley, may be mentioned the black bear, the grizzly bear, (ranging the Rocky Mountains,) the raccoon, badger, weasel, mink, otter, wolf, fox, (red, swift, gray, not the arctic,) panther, opossum, beaver, mountain goat and mountain sheep, [Rocky Mountain.] and the antelope. Peculiar to the north are the white Polar bear, coming no further south than lat. 55°; the elk, the moose, [seen as low as 54°,] the reindeer, and the musk ox. Confined to the more southern portion are the monkey, [29°,] prairie-dog, gray-squirrel, reaching, however, to the lakes, rabbit or hare, reaching, however, to the limits of the northern woods, common deer, [to Lake Superior,] and the buffalo, [but found as high as 62°.]

The birds of the valley are mostly migratory, moving southward in the autumn, and northward in the spring. Of those ranging over the widest extent, we may particularize the wild goose, wild pigeon, great heron, purple martin, ox-bird, woodcock, rail, and the coot. Among the other birds, some of them ranging over a wide extent of territory, are the turtle-dove, mocking-bird, king-fisher, quail, [partridge,] blue-bird, humming-bird, and the meadow-lark. The purple-grakle belongs especially to Louisiana, though found, in summer, on the northern lakes. The paroquet belongs to the south; the wild turkey to the middle latitudes.

Reptiles and amphibious animals appertain especially to the south. It is the region of venomous snakes, and of the alligator. Fishes are more numerous and more valuable as food in the north. The musquito, once thought to be confined to the south, is said to annoy voyageurs on the Mackenzie River to its very mouth.

Of domestic animals, the hog flourishes throughout the valley. The mule does well in the south; but the horse, coming from the north, has to undergo acclimation. Horses bred around the gulf, or found wild in the southern prairies, are small but hardy. The wool of the sheep degenerates in the south, as do also the milk and flesh of the cow.

Population.—The inhabitants of the Interior Valley are divided into four distinct varieties: the Caucasian, the African, the North American Indian, and the Mongolian. Of these, the first is, and will always be, the most numerous and civilized. They reside in large numbers, especially on the eastern side of the Mississippi, from the gulf to lat. 47°; above which, to lat. 60°, their settlements are sparse. The African variety, chiefly natives, is numerous up to lat. 33°, where they begin to decrease, being found above lat. 39° almost wholly in cities, and ceasing altogether above lat. 44°. The Indians live west of the Mississippi, but are sparse beyond lat. 50°. The Esquimaux, found only in the Polar margin of the valley, represent the Mongolian variety.

The Caucasians of the valley are destined to be, if they are not now, the most mixed race which has ever existed. The commingling of nations in Europe consequent upon the great northern and eastern migration which overwhelmed the Roman empire, bears with this no comparison. The inhabitants of the Atlantic states, by whom the valley has been mainly settled, were originally colonists from Great Britain and Ireland, and from Holland, France, Germany and Sweden. These were descendants partly of the Irish, Welsh, Highland Scotch, Norman and Low Dutch tribes, [*Celts,*] and partly of English, Lowland Scotch, French, High Dutch, Swiss, Danish, Swedish and Norwegian tribes, [*Goths* or *Scythians.*] Both Celts and Goths came at a remote period, from beyond the Black Sea, out of the great northern Asiatic *officina gentium.* Coming to the valley from the east of the Alleghanies, the immigrants have become more and more mixed by continued intermarriages. Add to this, vast numbers of emigrants direct from Europe have been, especially of late years, flocking in and amalgamating with the descendants of the original settlers. They pour in an almost unbroken stream from Germany, Ireland, England, Scotland, Wales, Norway and Poland, into the valley. Here, in a new climate, intermarrying with the people of the country, their physical wants abundantly supplied, and under new moral, social and political relations, their previous habits will, in time, be modified, and their physical peculiarities worn gradually away, until, at last, their descendants will be indistinguishable from the mass of the population. Here, in this valley, is to be the last development of the human race. It is, to use the words of Dr. Drake, "the *last* crucible into which living materials, in great and diversified streams, can be poured for amalgamation. The double range of mountains which separates it from the Pacific Ocean, leaves too little space for an empire on the shores of that sea; and the detached communities which may there grow up, will be but derivatives from the homogeneous millions, with which time will people the great region between the Apalachian and Rocky Mountains, which is thus destined to present the last and greatest development of society."

From the very limited observations made upon the comparative height and weight of the settlers, it results that the mean height of the English, Scotch and Irish, is a little greater than that of the Americans; that of the Germans, French and Jews, is less. In mean weight, the Germans reach the highest figures in proportion to their height; the Americans are next; and after them follow, in descending order, the English, Scotch and Irish. The mean height of the whole is 5 feet 7 inches, 8 lines; the mean weight, 146 lbs. 13 oz.; tallest measurement, 6 feet 2 inches; greatest weight, 192 lbs. Of the native Americans, those living in western Virginia, Kentucky and Tennessee, descendants of English and Irish ancestors, are the tallest, according to the current popular opinion. The people of the country, who are engaged in agricultural pursuits, and exercise much in the open air, are, as a whole, physically stronger than residents of the cities.

The diet of the valley settlers is rich, varied and abundant, consisting, however, almost always of too much animal food in proportion to the vegetable, though the latter is consumed in great quantities. A common fault everywhere, and one that ought to be remedied, is bad cooking. Of the food, thus ill-prepared, too much is eaten, and too hastily, to the great detriment of health. Of liquids used, apart from water, the most common are milk, coffee, tea and alcoholic beverages. The use of the latter, however, is not so prevalent as formerly, and is confined more strictly to public places and bar rooms. Their deleterious effect on the constitution, when employed as constant stimuli, is undeniable. Tea and coffee, though often beneficial, are undoubtedly productive of nervous affections and other chronic diseases. Of the two, tea is least hurtful.

Of water drunk, the different kinds are river, well and spring, cistern, (rain,) and artificial mineral. Though turbid and filled with organic matter, in general, river water seems not to be insalubrious. The water of the muddiest stream on the continent (the Mississippi) is universally deemed healthy, and by some even of medicinal virtue, especially in chronic ailments of the abdominal viscera. Spring and well water of the sandstone formations is nearly free from mineral impregnations, and is healthful. That of the great limestone tract, on the east of the valley, abounds in salts of lime, chiefly the carbonate, and is undeniably salubrious. In the southern tertiary and cretaceous deposits, some of the water is good, but the most is impure. Here is used, in general, rain water, kept in cisterns. It is purer than any other kind. Cisterns, we may remark, should not be lined with lead, as pure rain water, preserved in such, is liable to acquire a poisonous quality. If not pure, but containing saline substances, no danger is to be apprehended. Artificial mineral waters, made by forcing carbonic acid gas into spring or river water, are much used in summer in our towns and cities, and, when rightly taken, are considered healthy.

Another article, used extensively, almost universally, as a stimulant, is tobacco, in the form of snuff, or in smoking or chewing. Snuff-taking is not common, except when used, as it is in some parts of the South, for rubbing the teeth, an operation called "dipping." Smoking and chewing are on the increase. A majority commence one or both these practices while yet boys, some even as early as eight or ten years. The use of tobacco produces a permanent modification of the nervous system, and is demonstrably unhealthy. The habit, once formed, however, becomes in almost every instance inveterate. The narcotic effects of the weed are so soothing, that in most the love of its stimulus "waxes stronger and stronger." There is no probability that any agencies now at work will ever permanently check, much less put a stop to its consumption.

The remainder of the Preliminary View is devoted to a consideration of the clothing, lodgings, bathing, habitations, and shade trees, the occupations, pursuits, exercise, recreations and amusements of the inhabitants of the valley. Each of these subjects is sensibly and practically treated; and, had we space, we should be pleased to glance hastily at all. But we have room only for an extract from the part on amusement, which is so correct in sentiment, and so judicious in expression, that we cannot refrain from quoting it, by way of conclusion to the present article:—

"The rivalries, cares, and misfortunes of civilized life, require to be met with recreations and amusements, to a certain extent their true physiological antidotes. It is well known, however, that in the valley this is not the case. Hence there is no country in which the drudgery and perplexities of business are more pernicious to the constitution. The repugnance of the more rational and moral part of the community to any and all of our fashionable amusements, is founded on their abuses. Most of them run into some form of dissipation, and become repulsive to persons of pure moral taste; while they often prove injurious to the health and morals of those who become devoted to them. This association of sensuality and dissipation with several amusements, keeps the whole in discredit, and repels large classes of the community from participation in any. Public balls have been abandoned by thousands who do not regard dancing as wrong, because of the dissipations connected with them: our theatres are abandoned by the moral portion of the people, on account of their licentiousness and buffoonery; our nine-pin alleys are mere appendages of drinking-houses; our evening parties are scenes of midnight gluttony and drinking; our musical soirees are of feeble and limited interest, from a prevailing want of relish for melody, and the absence of a national ballad music; we are deficient in galleries of painting, and a taste for the fine arts has not yet been generally awakened among us; our public gardens and promenades, few in number, and often in bad order, are generally but marts of intoxicating drinks; finally, to speak of the Anglo-American people of the valley, they have but two patriotic festivals in the year, from both of which, many of the wise and temperate have been repelled, by the outbursts of vulgar dissipation which so often attend their celebration.

"It results, from all that has been said, that the wearied student and careworn business man, night after night, retire to bed without having their imagination and feelings diverted from the pursuits of the day, by any scenes of innocent gayety; and thus their very dreams prey on their nervous systems, prevent the renovation which sleep, preceded by appropriate amusements, would naturally produce, and the reinvigoration which is required to fit them for the labors of the succeeding day."

AMERICA—British; our Relations with, etc.—The subject of our commercial relations with the British North American Colonies, namely, Canada, New-Brunswick, Nova Scotia, Newfoundland, and Prince Edward's Island, is one of immense and increasing importance. It is one, too, that has occupied a large share of the diplomatic attention of our government, and has led to much legislation from time to time, on the part of Great Britain and the United States.

We propose to discuss this important and highly interesting subject under the three following heads:

I. The present state of our commercial relations with the British American Colonies.

II. The present character and amount of our trade with those colonies.

III. How our trade with those colonies can be improved.

I. Immediately after the peace of 1783, by which England acknowledged the independence of the United States, the subject of our commercial relations with the British American Colonies, in the North, began to be agitated by the British government; and if the wise counsels of the great William Pitt, then Chancellor of the Exchequer, had been heeded, our commerce with those colonies would have then been placed on a basis, which, while it secured peace and harmony between the two countries, would have rendered our present commerce immensely greater than it is.

Mr. Pitt contended, in the British parliament, for establishing our intercourse with Great Britain and her colonies on the most liberal and extensive principles of reciprocal benefit to both countries; and for this purpose he actually introduced into parliament a bill, as preliminary to further and more liberal legislation, for abolishing all prohibitions and restrictions of intercourse then existing, and for placing our trade with the colonies on the same footing as that of the mother country with them.

The liberal policy of Mr. Pitt was completely defeated by the shortsighted enemies of America, and of their own best interests, in the British parliament, and the whole subject of the regulation of our trade with England and its colonies was placed at the discretion of the crown. Since that time, England has labored to wrest from us, as much as possible, all the advantages of trade with her colonies, while our government has contended for a fair reciprocity and equal competition.

It is a curious circumstance in the commercial history of England, showing how completely that power is governed by her own selfish interests, and how flexible her policy is, that, in 1807, when our Congress passed the embargo law, England immediately authorized the governors of all the British American Colonies to open their ports to American vessels, thus abandoning in war an interdict which she had promulgated in peace ; for, from 1783 till the time of our embargo in 1807, our vessels had been excluded from the ports of the British colonies. This extraordinary movement on the part of England showed the immense importance, the indispensableness in fact, of our trade to the British colonies.

The first successful attempt to improve our commercial relations with the British American Colonies was made by President Jackson, in 1829, when he instructed Mr. McLane, our minister at St. James's, to open negotiations on the subject, the result of which was, that our ports of entry were opened to British and British colonial vessels, while all *free* colonial ports were opened to ours ; but still the duties in the colonial ports were higher than ours ; and besides, the *free* colonial ports were few in number, compared with those that were not free. Thus, while all of our ports were opened to British vessels, only a few colonial ports were opened to ours. Thus was Mr. McLane completely outwitted by British diplomatists. The advantage was entirely on the side of the British, as was shown by the operation of the new regulations. The increase of British tonnage in our ports was ten times greater than that of our own in the colonial ports ; for British vessels could enter all the colonial ports, while we could enter only a few.

This great disadvantage on our part became a subject of loud complaint among our citizens, and petitions were presented to Congress by the citizens of New-Orleans, Boston, and other ports of the Union, calling for a modification of the regulations governing our trade with the British American Colonies.

Nothing, however, was effected, until the recent changes of the navigation laws of England, in 1849 ; but still, although the effect of Mr. McLane's negotiations was unequal, our trade has steadily and greatly increased, since 1829, in consequence of these negotiations.

At present, all discriminating duties in the British colonial ports are abolished. "American and other foreign manufactures are now admitted into the British North American Colonies, and in many of the West India Colonies, on the same terms as British goods. The tariff of imports, however, in the different colonies varies, each colony being allowed to regulate its own tariff, provided no discriminations are made.

The tariff duties on imports into the different British American Colonies, does not differ much from the following statement :

On agricultural products..........	20	per cent.
Manufactures......................	12½	" "
Raw materials.....................	2½	" "
Groceries, specific..............	18 to 75	" "

The system of free ports, into which ports our vessels are allowed to enter only, is still kept up ; and besides this unfair regulation, there is another equally, if not more, annoying. It is, that while American vessels may enter all the lake and river ports in Canada, west of St. Regis, on the St. Lawrence River, they are not permitted to descend that river lower than Montreal, without special permission from the government. They are not allowed to pass out to sea.

There is also another regulation which appears somewhat whimsical ; it is, that while an American vessel is allowed to sail from a colonial port to any other colonial port, or to Great Britain, with colonial or other produce, and to enter all colonial ports where there is a custom-house officer, loading and discharging its cargo, it is not allowed to sail from one port to another port in the same colony, *except in ballast.*

It is not a little singular, that each of the British American Colonies should have its own separate tariff, thus creating a restraint on the trade of one of them with another. A vessel sailing from Nova Scotia to a port in New-Brunswick, must pay a tariff duty in the latter port, and *vice versa.* The inconvenience and ruinous effects that would attend such a system in the United States, between the different states, is apparent to every American ; and yet the enlightened colonial subjects of Queen Victoria cannot see them. Our perfect freedom from all restraints upon our internal trade, is one of the great sources of our prosperity. If each of our states had its separate tariff system of duties, all our state lines would be studded with custom-houses, and each state would have to maintain an army of custom-house officers ! Smuggling, then, would become a virtue, and the beauties of the tariff system would then be fully developed.

With our prosperous example of perfect exemption from all state tariffs fully before their eyes, it is not a little surprising that our neighbors of the British American Colonies should continue such a system. But some in this world either cannot see, or will not see; and so they have to suffer the consequences.

With this brief account of the present condition of our commercial relations with the British American Colonies, we now proceed to consider—

II. *The present character and amount of our trade with those colonies.*

The first report made to our government, on the subject of our trade with the British American Colonies, was ordered, we believe, by the Hon. Mr. Meredith; and the second by Mr. T. Corwin, from which we derive many of the facts and details which are contained in this paper.

All of our information regarding trade is derived from custom-house returns; but as these returns are, at best, only approximations, and almost invariably far below the real truth, in respect to values, great allowance must be made in determining from those returns the actual amount of trade. It is stated in Mr. Corwin's report, that if 20 per cent. were added to the custom-house returns, in determining the amount of our trade with the British American Colonies, it would not be too great an addition.

It is to be borne in mind that, in this paper, we confine ourselves to the trade of this country alone with the British American Colonies.

The trade of this country, by sea, with those colonies, is carried on chiefly by British vessels, owing to our vessels, by the convention of 1830, being restricted only to a certain number of what are called free colonial ports, while British vessels may enter all ports both of the colonies and of this country.

The total exports to the colonies, from the United States, in 1840, were $6,100,501, which, in 1850, had increased to $9,549,035, an increase of more than 50 per cent. in ten years.

In 1849, our imports to the colonies were as follows:

To Canada	$4,971,420
New-Brunswick	1,058,248
Nova Scotia	1,411,828
Newfoundland	935,400
Prince Edward's Island	65,524
	$8,442,420

We will endeavor to give some details regarding our trade with each of the above colonies.

Canada.—Canada has only two ports for sea commerce, Montreal and Quebec; but these are not free ports, our imports reach them only by British vessels, from the sea, or by American vessels from the lakes.

The articles imported from the United States into Canada, are: tobacco, sugar, molasses, maize, pork, coal, salt, American manufactures of cotton sheetings and shirtings, warp yarn, wadding, batting, plain and printed calicoes, satinets, woolens, cassimeres, kerseys, leather manufactures, doeskins, machinery, paints, oils, edge tools, agricultural implements, India rubber manufactures; also, large quantities of tea, coffee, and other foreign products, under the drawback law, consisting chiefly of sugars, cigars, dried fruits, wines, hides, and hardware.

The exports from Canada to the United States consist of lumber, wheat, flour, vegetables, seeds, ashes, wool, eggs, and coarse grains for distilling. Timber and lumber are, and ever have been, the great staple exports of Canada. The lumber trade of Canada, in 1846, amounted to $6,000,000. Canada now supplies one-third of all the lumber used in the Hudson River markets; and its lumber trade is rapidly increasing.

The inland exports of Canada to the United States, in 1848, were about $3,000,000. These inland exports have been materially increased by the late changes in the commercial policy of England by those in the provincial and United States tariffs, and by the United States draw-back law.

Of these $3,000,000 of exports, $250,000 worth went to New-York for re-shipment to Great Britain, under the drawback law.

The returns of the trade of Canada with this country, for the year ending January 5, 1851, show that the trade is in a highly prosperous condition, and rapidly increasing. They are as follows:

Imports from the United States,	$7,404,800
Exports to the United States,	5,813,500

This shows what certain short-sighted political economists call a "balance of trade" against Canada; but we have no complaints from the Canadians of an "alarming balance of trade," but, on the contrary, the most ample evidence of their rapidly increasing prosperity. It would be a sorry state of affairs, indeed, if the outgoes were greater than the incomes; or if they only just balanced each other; for, in the former case, a decline of prosperity, a ruinous retrogradation, would be manifest; and in the latter, a miserable unprogressiveness in commercial affairs.

The inland trade of Canada with this country has had to contend with the restrictive and unnatural policy of a host of prohibition laws, passed by the British parliament; together with colonial and United States tariffs, which have, to a great extent, checked it, to the injury of both countries,

New-Brunswick.—Next to Canada, our

trade with New-Brunswick is the most important. Bordering on Maine, a species of inland traffic exists between Maine and New-Brunswick, on the Upper St. John, and on the St. Croix River, similar to that carried on between Canada and the Americans in the Niagara district. Since the settlement of the north-eastern boundary question, our trade with New-Brunswick has greatly increased. This trade is chiefly in lumber. The lumber trade of the St. John River, on the American territory, has been about $800,000 during the last five years. The staple exports of New-Brunswick are timber, lumber, the produce of its fisheries, coal, asphaltum, gypsum, grindstones, and manganese. Ship-building is also carried on extensively. Large numbers of vessels, of all sizes, are annually built for foreign markets. Ship-building is the staple manufacture of New-Brunswick. It is said that vessels of the same quality, in every respect, as our best, can be built there for two-thirds of the cost in the United States.

The entire trade of New-Brunswick with the United States may be stated as follows, for 1850:

Imports from the United States,..........	$2,000,000
Exports to the United States,............	200,000

Nova Scotia and Cape Breton.—The exports of these colonies are the same as those of New-Brunswick, with the addition of agricultural products. The amount of their trade with this country annually is nearly as follows:

Imports from the United States,..........	$1,800,000
Exports to the United States,...........	900,000

Ship-building is also extensively carried on in these colonies. In 1849, they manufactured 221 vessels. They have 34 free ports.

Newfoundland.—The staple products of this island are furnished by its fisheries, to which may be added its furs and skins from Labrador, and its seal fisheries. The gross amount of exports from this island, in 1849, to all parts of the world, was about $4,000,000. In 1827, our trade with the island was absolutely nothing. It is now nearly as follows:

Imports from the United States,..........	$1,000,000
Exports to the United States,............	78,000

Prince Edward's Island.—The products of this island are chiefly agricultural; its chief exports being grains, flour, vegetables, beef, pork, and animals. But little fish is exported. Our trade with this island is very small:

Imports from the United States,...............	$100,000
Exports to the United States,..............	6,000

The shores of Newfoundland, Prince Edward's Island, Cape Breton, and Nova Scotia, swarm with fishermen, but Americans are not allowed to fish within three marine miles of the land. Such is the stipulation agreed upon, to exist *forever*, in our treaty of 1818 with England. This arrangement, it was thought by John Bull, would effectually guard him against any intrusions; but it is now found, that either from the superior diligence and skill of the Americans, or because the fish bite better at that distance from the shore, the Americans catch more fish than the English. The latter complain bitterly, and annoy the Americans when they can. As the treaty of 1818 does not specify the points from which the three marine miles shall be measured, the English, wishing to push the Americans as far out to sea as possible, contend that the prescribed distance of three miles should be measured from the head-lands, many of which project a long distance into the ocean. This subject has been several times made a matter of negotiation, and is not yet decided. As late as 1845, it was a subject of inquiry on the part of our minister at St. James, Mr. Stevenson, but nothing was done. The legislatures of Nova Scotia, Newfoundland, and Prince Edward's Island, have petitioned the British parliament on the subject, but without relief.

Nova Scotia furnishes the largest amount of fish to the United States. In 1849 the quantity sent from Halifax alone to the United States was, of pickled fish, 100,800 barrels. In 1847, Halifax exported hither 124,565 barrels of mackerel, besides large quantities of salmon, herring, and codfish.

We will now proceed to consider—

III. *How our trade with the British American Colonies can be improved.*

The great impediment to our commerce with the British American Colonies is that presented by the present foolish and impolitic commercial enactments and treaties both of England and of this country, to which we should also add the colonial tariffs. If these were all swept away, as they should be, the present trade would be immediately greatly increased, and greatly to the profit, of course, of both countries.

The true object of all commercial legislation should be to facilitate commerce; but unfortunately for the world, the progress of trade has always been checked, if not altogether stopped, by the ignorant and intermeddling of governments and legislatures. We say ignorant, because a correct understanding of the principles of political economy and the laws of trade woutd teach legislators that all attempts "to regulate trade" tend only to diminish those very advantages which they hope to acquire by their legislation. They proceed on the false principle that trade is a thing to be regulated, which is the same thing as saying that there are no natural principles which govern trade, and that, therefore, they must be supplied by legislation. Ignorance of political economy, and the selfishness and cupidity of nations, have done more to retard commerce and civilization than all other causes combined. The laws of trade are just as fixed and unalterable as those that preside over the motions of the planetary masses, or that regulate chemical affinities; and it is just as absurd to attempt to modify or regulate the former by legislation as the latter. And yet there are legislators in all countries who believe, that Nature's laws, governing trade, are defective and need patching.

To such a belief must we ascribe all the present tariff laws and commercial restrictions that exist, for the regulation of the trade between Great Britain and this country; and the entire past history of the commerce of the two nations clearly shows, that if these were all swept away, their commerce would soon attain a degree of prosperity which it never can attain under the present system.

Every removal of restrictions on trade has invariably and speedily led to increasing commercial prosperity; whence, we may reasonably infer, that a removal of all restrictions would make our commercial prosperity complete.

It was thought a very wise remark of the great Mr. Canning, when he observed, in 1826, that "to allow foreign ships to enter colonial ports is a boon." A boon, indeed! and quite as great a boon to England as to America, although Mr. Canning could not see how. Great as he was, he never learnt the truth, that a perfectly free trade between two countries could not benefit one without equally benefiting the other. It is not less a truth in trade than in physics, that action and re-action are equal. Of the truth of this, the history of commerce furnishes a thousand striking demonstrations.

The foolish restrictions imposed upon commerce—and we can call them nothing else but foolish—deprive nations of a thousand mutual advantages, and check and distort the developments of humanity and the progress of civilization. The truth of this remark is illustrated by the character of our present commercial relations with Britain and its colonies. Here, neighboring to us, in the British American Colonies, is a population of 3,000,000 of people, industrious, intelligent, enterprising, and occupying a country of more than 500,000 square miles, with a healthy, invigorating climate, and of the most valuable and superabundant agricultural, mineral, and manufacturing resources. Its facilities for river and lake navigation are unparalleled. It is watered throughout by streams affording an unlimited amount of water-power; its fisheries are the most valuable in the world; its sea-coast is indented with numerous admirable harbors. And to these unsurpassed physical capabilities we may add a truly vast and imposing system of internal improvements, projected and completed for the purpose of overcoming the natural impediments of the St. Lawrence River and the Falls of Niagara, and thus connecting the ocean with the great western lakes. These vast improvements, by which a vessel of 300 tons burthen, and capable of carrying 3,000 barrels of flour, and of a draft of nine feet water, can now, but for certain enactments of wise legislators, pass from the harbor of Chicago to the ocean, and thence to any part of the globe, reflect the highest credit on the intelligence, industry, and enterprise of the Canadian people, shackled as they are by the policy and nature of a ruling monarchical government 3,000 miles off. The difference between Canada and this country is striking; and we can only ascribe it to the difference in the form of government, for we have abundant evidence that the energies of the Canadians would have made them a very different people, but for their government.

To gratify her fondness for "regulating trade" and imposing tariffs, England has ever kept the St. Lawrence, the great outlet of Canadian commerce, closed to all but her own vessels. By thus doing, she has inflicted immense evil upon the Canadas and herself, while she has stimulated the energies of *our* people to devise means of overcoming the bar to a more free intercourse, interposed by the closing of that river. The trade of the Canadas is a prize for which our people—we do not say our government—have long contended. They have succeeded at last. The Mississippi valley is not the sole abdomen of plenty that the energies and enterprise of our people have subjected to a commercial paracentesis. The operation of "tapping" the Canadas, as well as the Mississippi valley, has engaged the attention of our people for years; and they have at last succeeded in opening no less than six broad channels, through which the wealth of the Canadas is now flowing, namely,—the Erie Canal, the Champlain Canal, the Ogdensburg and Boston, and the Buffalo and Boston rail-roads and the Erie and New-York Rail-road, and the Montreal and Portland rail-roads.

These outlets to Canadian and Western trade now render the free navigation of the St. Lawrence, below Montreal, a matter of less moment; and the more so, because the St. Lawrence, even though its navigation were free, is closed by ice for several months in the year.

There is but one course now left by which our trade with the British American Colonies can be improved, and that is by reciprocal free trade. The Canadian government has generously taken the first step in this important matter, by proposing to our government to establish reciprocal free trade in certain articles, the products of both countries. This is a liberal offer, and we do not see how our government can refuse to accept it. It recommends itself strongly to our best interests, and we cannot reject the offer without withholding from ourselves the highest commercial advantages.

Although the subject of reciprocal free trade with Canada has long been agitated, we do not know of a single valid objection that can be raised against it, once the measure has been sanctioned by the United States House of Representatives.

It is admitted by all, that the perfectly unrestrained commerce existing between the several states of this Union, has been a very prominent cause of our national prosperity; and from this it is quite natural to infer, that by extending this unrestrained commerce to the British American Colonies, another powerful element of prosperity would be gained. Canada is now willing to withdraw her part of the restrictions; and it now remains for us to say, whether we will deny ourselves the immense advantages that would result to us from a free intercourse with our colonial neighbors. Such an arrangement would make our trade with the British American Colonies only a portion of our home internal trade; and it is admitted, by all political economists, that the home trade of a country is vastly more important than its foreign. This is true, at least of our own country; for our internal trade averages $92 for each individual of our population, while our foreign trade is only $7 for each individual.

Even under the present unnatural restrictive system, the latest returns show that we export more of our domestic manufactures to Canada alone than to any other country. Our exports to Canada alone, in 1850, were equal to the whole amount exported to Sweden, Prussia, Holland, Portugal and Mexico.

Such are the advantages which our great Atlantic cities would afford to the colonial merchants for trade, if the existing tariff restrictions were removed, that the system, heretofore pursued by them, of importing direct from foreign ports, would be abandoned, and they would make all their purchases in our cities. Under our present tariff, however, of 20 per cent., they cannot do this, since the high duties prevent them from exchanging, in our markets, their products for ours. If they buy now in our Atlantic cities, it is only by bank drafts, specie, or their equivalents; but this causes such a drain upon their banks, that their trade with us is very much embarrassed and limited. If we would have the 3,000,000 of our British colonial neighbors trade with us, we must allow them to bring their products into our markets, without paying a duty of 20 per cent., which duty at present amounts to a prohibition. It also leads to a vast deal of smuggling along our entire and extensive northern frontier. It is highly probable, that the amount of goods annually smuggled from both countries across the line, is nearly, if not quite equal to the amount which pays duty; for the frontier is so extensive, and the population so dense, on both sides, that it would require an army of custom-house officers and a fleet of revenue cutters to prevent it. Smuggling is called "a demoralizing traffic;" but as the right of trade is a natural right, and as smuggling is only the natural means of asserting this natural right, it may well be questioned, whether it is not rather the tariff which is "demoralizing," than the business of smuggling. Be this as it may, it is certain that high duties operate as a bounty for smugglers. Mr. J. D. Andrews, the United States Consul at Saint John, New-Brunswick, in his very able report to our government, on the trade, commerce, and resources of the British North American Colonies, from which we take many of the facts contained in this paper, very significantly observes, in speaking of "the necessity of a thorough remodeling of our lake-port custom-houses," as follows:

"To one fact I deem it my duty specially to call your attention, viz.: the practice, in several inland ports, for each collector, on retiring from office, to carry away with him the books and accounts, on the plea, that having paid for the stationery from his private funds, they are private property, the government not making any allowance for this item of public expenditure."

Undoubtedly these "books and accounts," if suffered to see the light, would tell a tale! They would illustrate, in a most striking manner, the "demoralizing effects" of tariffs upon custom-house officers and others.

The entire line of our northern frontier, including Lake Champlain, open for smuggling and bribery of custom-house officers, is nearly 5,000 miles in length.

The system of reciprocal free trade, proposed by the Canadians, is not subject to the objections made to a transatlantic free trade by the friends of protective tariffs. The American protective policy is defended mainly on the ground that we should be protected against the advantages which the European manufacturer has over us, in the abundance and cheapness of his capital and labor; and that we should be relieved from the fluctuations of foreign trade. But none of these reasons will justify a tariff to protect us against colonial producers or manufacturers; for they have not the advantage over us of more abundant and cheaper capital and labor. The prices of labor in the British American Colonies are nearly if not quite as high as in this country. What we want most is a free outlet for our surplus products.

It would be easy to refute the many frivolous objects which the advocates of protective tariffs make to reciprocal free trade with Canada, and the other British colonies. We will only say, that, in considering large commercial questions, it is quite unworthy of a great nation to enter into petty calculations of the advantages it gives and takes in trade. The enlightened and liberal views of Mr. Pitt, in 1782, who contended for an "equal and honest reciprocity" in trade between the two countries, are the only ones worthy of a great nation like ours.

In return for this reciprocity of trade with

us, Canada proposes to open the navigation of the St. Lawrence. This would certainly be a valuable acquisition to us, as is proved by the numerous petitions of our citizens in Michigan, Wisconsin, Indiana, Ohio, and New-York, (who certainly are the best judges,) presented to Congress, praying for the adoption of measures to have that river opened to the shipping of the lakes. If there was no advantage in having that river opened, such petitions would not appear in Congress.

Although the artificial outlets to the upper lakes and Canadian commerce are numerous, yet the St. Lawrence has some important advantages over these. If the navigation of that river was free, all our shipping on all the lakes, from Chicago to Oswego, could pass down to the ocean with full cargoes.

The St. Lawrence is to the North and West, what the Mississippi is to the South and West. The St. Lawrence has a course of 1800 miles, and drains a basin of 1,000,000 of square miles. It is the natural outlet of Michigan, a portion of Wisconsin, Illinois and Indiana, of northern Ohio, northern Pennsylvania, northern and western New-York, and of western Vermont—a vast district of country, comprising the principal portion of the wheat-growing region of the United States. According to Mr. Buel's able report on the free navigation of the St. Lawrence, the trade in wheat in this vast region, in 1841, amounted to 2,780,000 bushels. In 1847 it had risen to 10,688,514, an increase of 17 per cent. per annum. If this same rate of increase were to continue till 1857, the value of the wheat, then, in the valley of the St. Lawrence, at the present prices, would be over $170,000,000.

As commerce always seeks the shortest routes, it may be interesting to consider the advantages which the free navigation of the St. Lawrence would afford in this respect.

A glance at the map will show that the shortest route to Europe, from the heart of North America, is by this river. The shortest route from New-Orleans to Liverpool is up the Mississippi and Ohio to Pittsburgh, and thence to Lake Erie, and down the St. Lawrence. The route to Europe, from all the lake-ports, by way of the St. Lawrence, is several hundred miles nearer than by any other route. This is one important advantage to our north-western trade, which, added to there being no unloading of cargoes in the whole route, renders the free navigation of the St. Lawrence a matter highly desirable to the North-west.

If the St. Lawrence was open to our vessels, it is highly probable that vast quantities of the products of the Mississippi valley would find their way to Europe by that route; for when once on shipboard at Chicago, or at other lake ports, it would naturally and easily take the shortest route. This route, too, would have an advantage over all others, derived from climate and latitude. The pork, bacon, lard, and flour, of the Mississippi valley, would escape the injurious heat of other routes, by taking that of the St. Lawrence.

Another important advantage to be derived from the opening of the St. Lawrence would be, that the vast amount of shipping that is kept idle during the long winters in the lakes, by the ice, could pass down to the ocean, on the approach of winter, and be profitably employed on the ocean.

It is to be hoped that the present session of Congress will take some action on this important subject: for it is one not only of vital importance in a commercial point of view, but also one nearly connected with the maintenance of our present friendly relations with Great Britain. It would be a digression, not contemplated when we commenced this paper, to view our subject in respect to our relation of amity with Great Britain, and we shall, therefore, make but this short allusion to it. In less than a quarter of a century, the population of the great North-west will count millions, where it now counts tens of thousands; and then they will feel more than ever the importance to them of the St. Lawrence, as their natural outlet to the ocean; and they will then begin to regard the free navigation of that river as a "*natural right*," which, if not peaceably granted, might be forcibly taken.

We will conclude this paper by a brief observation on the present indications of public sentiment in Canada, regarding the opening of the St. Lawrence. From certain movements in Montreal and Quebec, it would appear, that the refusal of our government to reciprocate the liberal policy of the Canadian government, would lead to the immediate adoption, by the latter, of measures of retaliation. The tardy movements of our government have already aroused the merchants of Montreal and Quebec, who advocate, in common with the manufacturers of England, the imposition of differential duties against American manufactures. This would probably be the first retaliatory act; and the second would be the closing of all the Canadian canals, now so extensively and profitably used by our lake commerce. It must be admitted, that the offer of the Canadians to establish a system of free trade with us, and to open the St. Lawrence, is highly liberal; and when it is considered that the average Canadian duties on our products is only 12½ per cent., while ours on their products is 23½ per cent., it would seem that our government could not, with any show of liberality and grace, refuse reciprocation, in view, too, of the many advantages our trade would derive from it, and the loud call for it from so many of our citizens.

AMERICA—BRITISH.—Extent of British America—Progress of liberal principles — Destinies — Upper and Lower Canada—New-Brunswick — Nova Scotia —Newfoundland--New-Britain, etc.—The present paper comprises another of the series promised upon the various geographical divisions of the Western world: and the reader will find advantage in consulting them together in the volumes we have published and are now publishing.

British America is in extent equal to about one-third of the whole continent, and is limited by the possessions of Russia on the 141° of longitude, and all other points by those of the United States. The islands of the Arctic sea, and along the Atlantic coast, are claimed as a part of the same empire; and the late treaty negotiations have settled the long agitated Maine and Oregon boundaries.

The northern regions of British America possess no agricultural capacities, but are locked up in frosts and perpetual snows. The fur trade can alone be prosecuted. To the south, the climate becomes genial and the soil fertile. Immense forests prevail here.

British America offers perfect relief, says Mr. Gesner, in his late work upon New-Brunswick, to the overflowing population of the mother-country, whose manufacturing districts and most productive counties have become so overloaded with the humble classes, that the least disturbance in the state of trade produces the greatest degree of misery and crime.

In the same connection Mr. Alison, in his work on Population, remarks :—Nor is there any chance of this prodigious opening for labor in Australia and our North American colonies, being either diminished or lost to this country, except by the folly of internal legislation. The productive land in Canada and New-Holland, exceeds that of all Europe put together. It is so intersected by water through the great chain of the lakes, which flows through its centre, that hardly any part of it is fifty miles from inland navigation, and an immense tract lies on the shores of vast navigable rivers or stupendous inland seas. The climate, severe in Lower, is much more mild in Upper Canada; the vine, the apricot, peach and nectarine, ripen in the open air. The soil is so rich from the falling of leaves during many thousand winters, that it bears the finest wheat crops for three years, without manure. The invention of steam has facilitated indefinitely both the means of getting at this fertile district, and the market for its produce when cultivation has commenced. Nothing is wanted but hands to clear the vast tracts of wood-encumbered plains, and that is precisely what England possesses to superfluity.

The possession of this immense country can in no other sense be considered important to Great Britain, than in offering a vent to her rapidly augmenting population. From its trade and commerce, in consequence of her systems of exclusion and restrictions, she has perhaps obtained less advantage than the continual outlay which has been every year required. One has not to be a deep observer, to mark at a glance the comparative progress of the regions on either side of the St. Lawrence, and there can be no other manner of accounting for it, than the spirit of liberty and attendant enterprise which exist upon the one hand. With equal liberality of laws and government, a very different state of things might early be predicated.

Nor are we to suppose the old colonial policy existing in its full force in British America. Many and marked improvements have been demanded and made since the independence of the American states. The contagion of free institutions is not easily arrested, and a careful study of the colonies now under consideration, will show that they have been gradually gaining power at the expense of the mother-country, and that the concessions made them from time to time, would have been considered treason to demand at the close of the last century.* The influence of the United States is felt all through the British colonies *in their amelioration.* This we regard as the high, holy and peaceful mission of America. We ask no other conquests! Let our neighbors regulate their own affairs in the manner best suitable to them, so long as there shall be no interference with ours. If a "manifest destiny" decree all America to us, it is well to await the falling of the ripened fruit without agency of ours. A better policy would be—"hold, enough!"

British America embraces a territory equal in extent to two-thirds of the whole of Europe. It is divided into the provinces of Canada, (Lower and Upper.) New-Brunswick, Nova Scotia and Newfoundland, and New-Britain,—the latter a cold and barren country, between Hudson's Bay and the

* A well-informed writer, in the last number of the North American Review, July, 1848, shows in strong colors the progress of liberalism in the British colonies. The descendants of the tories of our Revolution who removed to these points, demand yet more than did the whigs of that period, whom they stigmatised as rebels and traitors. Some of the ablest men in the British colonies are of this class. "What do we see," asks the Review, "after the lapse of nine years? The popular will having wholly wrested away the prerogative, now breaks up cabinets and displaces the highest functionaries, without check, accountability or control. We see, too, a minister of the Crown conceding, in express terms, that such a power seems to be a necessary part of representative institutions *in a certain state of their progress!* If a single whig of 1776, in his loftiest mood, even so much as dreamed of obtaining a concession like this, we have yet to be informed of it"

Pacific, thinly inhabited by Esquimaux and other savages.*

The following table shows the area in square miles and population of each, so far as has been specifically ascertained:

	Sq. Miles.	Population.	Pop. to Sq. Mile.
Lower Canada	194,000	700,000	3
Upper Canada	150,000	600,000	4
New-Brunswick	27,700	180,000	6
Nova Scotia	17,000	350,000	18
Newfoundland	50,000	100,000	2
New-Britain	1,861,300	——	–
Total	2,300,000	1,930,000	1

Sebastian Cabot is said to have first discovered Canada in 1497. The French prepared a map of the Gulf of St. Lawrence in 1508, and in 1525 took possession of the country in the name of the king of France. Quebec, the first settlement, was not founded till 1608; after which period the colonists were much annoyed by the native Indian tribes. A friendly compact, however, was ultimately made, and they became auxiliaries against the British. In 1759 Quebec was taken by the British forces under Gen. Wolfe, and the whole territory ceded to Great Britain by the treaty of Paris, 1763. The seignorial rights, the various holdings and tenures under them, and the endowments of the Catholic Church, were left undisturbed; and all the estates, including the unappropriated lands in the provinces, held at the period by the French king, became vested in the British crown. Here began British rule and colonization north of the great American lakes.

We shall notice the provinces separately in the order named in the table.

Lower Canada.—More than two-thirds of the population are of French origin, speak the French language, and profess the Roman Catholic religion. The chief settlements are in the valley of the St. Lawrence, between Montreal and Quebec, a distance of one hundred and fifty or two hundred miles. The following statement exhibits the quantity of lands surveyed, value, &c.:

		Acres.
Jesuits' estates not appropriated		664,080
Indian Reservations and St. Maurice		87,000
Seignorial tenures granted to individuals	7,496,000	
Free and common socage granted to individuals	3,847,629	
Included in the above	1,684,233	
On hand	3,907,000	
		16,934,862
Unsurveyed		107,856,000

Income from the Territorial Fund in 1843, was †$136,000; in 1844, $25,900; due for the sale of Crown lands, $269,600.

Of the unsurveyed lands, 3,907,000 acres are unappropriated; from which $592,293 in government scrip, at the valuation of $1 per acre, must be deducted:

3,314,707 acres, valued by Surveyor General at 60 cents	$2,071,690
8,500,000 unsurveyed, in rear of townships, at 60 cents	5,312,500
6,000,000 north-east part of dist. of Quebec, at 75 cents	4,500,000
750,000 south-east sect. of St. Francis, &c., at 100 cents	750,000
Land Fund	$12,634,190
Which, if invested at 5 per cent. will yield	631,709

This revenue is charged with about $150,000 to common schools, and $20,000 annuity to the Indian tribes.

From an official report in 1845, we collect the following:

Houses inhabited, 106,803; vacant, 4,041; now being built, 1,613—112,487.

Heads of families, 121,441, of whom 76,032 are proprietors of real estate; 37,113 non-proprietors, and 8,296 having votes in towns, &c.

Total resident population, 687,175: of which there are natives of England, 11,886; Ireland, 44,012; Scotland, 13,341; Canada, of French origin, 518,565; Canada, of British origin, 85,075; continental Europe, or otherwise, 2,353; United States, 11,943; aliens not naturalized, 1,505; total, males over 15 years of age, 186,548; females, 188,954; under 15, males, 158,447; females, 157,344. Of those under age, there are 2,111 males married, and 6,705 females married; being a total of 8,816 married minors.

Deaf and dumb persons, 725, of which 447 are males, and 278 females; blind, 523: males, 273; females, 250; idiots, 950: males, 478; females, 472; lunatics, 308: males, 156; females, 152;—total, 2,506.

The proportion of deaf and dumb in Canada to the whole population is as one to about 957, a greater proportion than prevails throughout all Europe, (1 in 1,537,) and the United States, (1 in 2,000,) or the whole world, (1 in 1,556,) and is only exceeded by the solitary cases of Switzerland and Baden, where the proportion is respectively 1 in 503 and 559.

In the whole province there are only 261 persons of color: 140 males, and 121 females.

The Church of Rome has 571,714 of the population within its pale, leaving a fragment for the other fourteen religious sects, the principal of which, in numbers, are the Church of England, 43,274; Scotland, 26,725; Methodist, 15,853; Presbyterian generally, 5,231; Baptist, 4,067.

Occupations are thus stated: Male farm servants, 5,967; other male servants, 5,390; female servants, 11,510; engaged in trade and commerce, 3,739; paupers, 463.

* Labrador, Cape Breton, Prince Edward's Island, Anticosti, may be considered embraced.

† The sterling has been turned into federal money, waiving fractions, as more satisfactory to our readers.

Of the soil, the occupied acres are 7,540,-450, of which 3,083,949 are under cultivation, and 4,456,400 not under cultivation.

The produce of the year 1843 was:—Wheat, 914,909 bushels; barley, 1,221,710; rye, 310,458; oats, 6,688,933; peas, 1,428,-303; Indian corn, 143,947; buckwheat, 375,-744; potatoes, 9,914,639.—Total, 21,365,-913 Winchester bushels.

There are 1,629 educational establishments, including 63 colleges, academies and convents. In all, 56,578 pupils are taught: 31,432 males, and 25,146 females.

The shipping of Quebec, in 1844, consisted of 509 vessels, with a tonnage of 45,351, manned by 2,590 men; that of Montreal at 60 vessels, tonnage 10,097, and 556 men.

Of manufactories, there are 417 grist mills, with 849 run of stones; oat-meal, 111; barley, 48; saw, 895; oil, 30; fulling, 155; carding, 165; thrashing, 451; paper, 7; iron-works, 79; trip hammers, 18; nail factories, 7; distilleries, 37; brewing, 29; tanneries, 305, pot and pearl asheries, 423; all other manufactories, 136. Total 3,333.

The rate of wages of common laborers, for corporation work, is 60 cents per day, and for canal, 75. Mechanics and artisans usually receive in Montreal—masons from $1,25 to $1,75 per day; plasterers, $1,50 to $2; bricklayers, $1,62; painters, $1,62; carpenters, $1,25 to $1,62.

The *Montreal Transcript*, encouraging foreign labor to try its fortunes in Canada, says:

"Our opinion is, that the condition of every industrious mechanic and laborer must be improved by emigration to this colony. There is more elbow-room here—a wider field for energy and exertion. There is, above all, more to hope for. No man need sit down in gloomy despair, toiling on from day to day, and week to week, without the slightest prospect of ameliorating his condition. There is none of that horrible uncertainty—that wavering between starvation and the dread of the workhouse which depresses hundreds of thousands of human beings at home. To the honest, the sober and industrious, the present is more pleasing and the future more bright."

The project of a railroad from the Canada line to Portland, Me., 124 miles, has been introduced, upon estimates of $2,500,000; but the success of enterprises of this kind, in so cold a climate, is much doubted. Mr. Hall says of Canada:—

"I find that falls of snow are frequent in that region—that the quantity of snow on the ground in the winter season varies from two to three feet in depth, but very seldom equals three feet. The snows are light and dry, unaccompanied by rain or sleet moisture. It is the damp, heavy snows, sleet, and frozen rains, which create so much difficulty, and constitute so serious an obstacle to the operations of a railroad. A light, dry snow, of any depth that is known to fall in any one storm, is easily removed by the snow-plough in use. On the seaboard, and farther south, the snow and sleet in their season are occasionally serious obstacles; but the further you go north, and the further you recede from the seaboard, the drier and the lighter the snow, and the less the difficulty in removing it from the track."

Trade of Quebec and Montreal.—Without extending general remarks, we close our statistics of Lower Canada, by a glance at its productions and commerce. The following is a table of the exports by sea, of wheat, flour, oats, and peas, from Montreal and Quebec, for nine years:—

Years.	Flour. Bls.	Wheat. Bush.	Oats. Bush.	Peas. Bush.
1838	59,204	—	—	1,415
1839	48,427	3,330	—	2,855
1840	315,612	142,059	—	59,878
1841	856,210	562,862	—	123,574
1842	294,799	204,107	5,666	78,985
1843	209,957	144,233	3,651	88,318
1844	415,467	282,183	24,574	130,355
1845	442,228	396,252	53,530	220,912
1846	555,602	534,747	46,060	212,339

During the year 1846, 30 vessels, with a tonnage of 19,761, were built at Quebec.

The lumber trade forms a considerable item, as will appear by the following statement of timber measured at Quebec, in the last three years:—

	1845.	1846.	1847.
White Pine	19,111,455 ft.	24,504.375	12,026,294
Red Pine	4,444,515 "	5,247,754	6,516,922
Oak	1,800,446 "	3,429,582	3,484,569
Elm	1,566,915 "	3,455,122	3,035,541
Ash	412,096 "	260,088	122,715
Basswood	37,086 "	82,798	12.693
Butternut	9,664 "	20,782	6,618
Tamarac	199,933 "	593,584	590,619
Birch and Maple	160,007 "	240,787	92,237

Value of exports at Quebec, 1847, $7,067,-900: imports, $3,062,800. Value of imports at Montreal, 1847, $8,479,800, being a decrease of $988,170 from the previous year's imports. Of British manufactures imported, the decrease has been $1,140,000, while the value of foreign goods imported has increased $352,000. The exports from Montreal show an increase in 1847 over the previous year, of $683,000.

PRINCIPAL ARTICLES EXPORTED FROM MONTREAL, 1847.

Ashes—Pot	bbls	11,111
" Pearl	"	4.017
Apples	"	297
Ale	hhds	2
Barley	minots	22,847
Beef	tcs	89
Beans	minots	1,587
Butter	kegs	12,243
Cheese	pkgs	261
Corn, Indian	minots	14,511
Glass	bxs	370
Flour	bbls	281,099
Honey	casks	9
Honey	bxs	28
Honey	cases	2
Lard	kegs	205
Linseed	bbls	624
Indian Meal	"	2,621
Oat Meal	"	10,843
Oats	minots	146,154
Pork	bbls	2,010
Peas	bush	9,046
Seed, Grass	bbls	300
Wheat	minots	2,087,967

The foreign silk trade for 1847 shows a total of imports of 4,425,696 lbs.; consumption, 4,407,908; stock on hand, 1st January, 1848, 2,507,878 lbs.; being a decrease of 409,512 lbs. from the consumption of the previous year.

The number of vessels that sailed from the port of Montreal in 1847, were, for Great Britain, 154; Ireland, 13; the Colonies, 36; Oporto, 1; Quebec, 15.

Internal improvements in all the provinces will appear in a general table.

Upper Canada.—This province is separated from Lower Canada by the Ottawa river, which empties into the St. Lawrence near Montreal. Of Canada generally, it has been said, that the climate is subject to great extremes of heat and cold; the thermometer ranging between 102° above, and 36° below Fahrenheit; the ground being covered five months in the year with snow. The geographical limits are given from 57° to 90° west longitude, and 42° to 52° north latitude; forming an extent of 1,450 miles from Amherstburg, on Detroit River, south-west, to the Straits of Belleisle on the coast of Labrador. This line embraces the settled portions of the country from Lake Huron to Newfoundland; the whole territory is estimated at from 200 to 400 miles wide. Upper Canada is subdivided into seventeen districts or counties, viz:—Eastern, Ottawa, Johnston, Bathurst, Midland, Victoria, Newcastle, Simcoe, Home, Wellington, Gore, Niagara, Talbot, Brock, London, Western, and Huron. The population has increased tenfold in the last forty years, and is still increasing rapidly. From Lake Ontario to Montreal, the St. Lawrence is broken by a succession of rocks and rapids, which render navigation very dangerous. To overcome these obstructions, the Rideau Canal, 135 miles long, affords a passage to boats from the lake, near Kingston, to Bytown, on the Ottawa river, from whence the latter is navigable to Montreal. This canal cost about $5,000,000, and has 47 locks, 142 feet long by 33 wide. Lakes Erie and Ontario are united by the Welland Canal, 42 miles, to avoid the Falls of Niagara. The descent of the canal, 330 feet, is accomplished by 37 locks, 100 feet in length. The whole work, with great natural difficulties to surmount, cost nearly $5,000,000. The Lachine Canal, along the side of the St. Lawrence, to avoid a cascade, and the Grenville Canal, on the borders of the Ottawa, for avoiding its rapids, are minor works, though of great importance to navigation.

The growth of Toronto is evidence of prosperity in Upper Canada. In a statistical work of 1817, by Dr. Thomas Rolph, the writer, describing what was then Little York, (now the City of Toronto,) says:

"Its population is 1200 souls; for five miles round the capital of Upper Canada, scarcely one improved farm can be seen in contact with another. The only connected settlement is about five miles to the north of Yonge street; in other directions, so far as the district goes, you might travel to its utmost limits, and not find more than one farm-house for every three miles."

After quoting the above, in a recent address, the mayor of Toronto proceeded:

"Such was little York about 1835. In 1817, it had no brick houses, no tinned roofs, no planked sidewalks; the stumps remained in the streets, and nothing was more common than to see teams mired in them, requiring all the aid that could be obtained to liberate them. What is now the market was a bay, and the fish-market the resort of wild fowls—unhealthy, liable to fever and agues, and all the distressing catalogue of intermittents. No banks; no markets; a very mean building for a church; no common sewers; scarcely a schooner belonging to it, and few frequenting it; no wharves; not a single importer of British goods; a few, and very few insignificant stores, and a few taverns, offering the worst accommodations. Such was Little York in 1817, now the celebrated city of Toronto. Behold now its 20,000 inhabitants; its rows of splendid brick-built, tin-covered houses, its magnificent churches, and number of places of worship; its banks; its floating palaces; its beautiful schooners; its magnificent stores, some of them rivaling those of the first city in the world, with their plate-glass windows, their spacious areas, and their splendid contents; its hundreds of thousands of annually imported goods; its merchants; its public reading rooms; its Mechanics' institute its Board of Trade; its public baths; its splendid avenue, leading to a noble University; its common sewers; its Macadamized streets; its planked side-walks above a mile, or nearer two, from its magnificent market and City Hall, in every street, and leading to almost to every house. View its export trade, its wharves loaded with produce, and crowded with steamboats and schooners, the daily conveyance of the riches of the neighborhood. Behold its gas-lighted streets at night; and now that greatest of all luxuries—an abundant supply of pure and wholesome water conveyed to every house. Around it and about it, in all directions, fine houses, farms, orchards, villas and roads."

The population of Toronto in 1826 was 1,719, and in 1834, when the city was incorporated, it amounted to 9,654. By the census of 1846, the population is 20,565, of which 8,577 belong to the Church of England, and 4,307 to the Church of Rome. Some twenty other religious denominations divide the balance between them. An increase of ten to one, within twenty years, is almost unprecedented in the population of towns. The city of New-York, which has been regarded as foremost, has not kept equal pace since 1697, when its population was only 4,302. The fertility and healthiness of Upper Canada, and convenient transportation on the lakes and canals, are the chief causes of this prosperity. Much might be said in description of the soil and improvements, together with the general resources of Canada, showing it to be a country capable of sustaining a dense and happy population. Of the Western District, (the peninsula between Lakes Erie and Huron,) Dr. Rolph is enthusiastic in his praise:

"What shall I say?—that there is not in all America a soil so fertile, a climate so pure, scenery more beautiful, properties more reasonable; in fine, where every combination exists to render it the most attractive spot in her Majesty's possessions in America! All this do I say from personal knowledge, and it is a matter of the utmost astonishment that so large a district should remain so neglected and unsettled; for in no portion of Canada could horticulture, floriculture, and agriculture, be prosecuted with more certainty of success than in it. Peaches, plums, peas, apples, melons, grapes, Indian corn, tobacco, and vegetables of every description, grow in an abundance and with a luxuriance that is truly astonishing; and the day cannot be remote when such obvious advantages will attract attention. It is no longer inaccessible from bad roads, and I strongly recommend all who can afford it to pay a visit to it, before they determine where they shall settle when they have resolved on making Canada their home."

The value of imports paying duties in 1846, at Toronto, was $842,385, exclusive of $523,000 specie. Total revenue on importations collected during the year, $162,645. Exports estimated in value, at $1,505,000, of which the following are the principal:

Articles, &c.		Quantity.
Flour	bbls.	194,856
Pork	"	4,133
Beef	"	80
Timothy seed	"	176
Wheat	bush.	108,116
Oats	"	3,000
Peas	"	1,000
Beef	trcs.	65
Hams	tons.	9
Horntips and scraps	"	11
Ashes	casks.	283
Butter	kegs.	200
Lard	"	600
Starch	boxes	600
White Pine Boards	feet	1,680,000
Bricks	No.	1,030,000
Sheep pelts	"	10,750
Woolen cloths	yards	40,000
Blankets	pairs	130
Furs and peltries, value about		£2,000
Fresh fish		£500

The quantity of flour and wheat exported from the Home District, in 1846, was—

	Flour—bbls.	Wheat—bush.
From Toronto	194,356	108,116
" Oshawa	34,630	16,560
" Windsor	55,460	24,300
" Credit	11,450	41,200
Total	296,396	190,176

The increase of exports over 1845 is estimated at $364,840.

Shipping owned on Lake Ontario, and employed in the inland waters of Canada, viz: 57 steamers (two of iron) valued at $1,750,000; 2 ships, 5 brigantines, and 95 schooners of 30 tons and upwards, $750,000; 6 lake propellers, $70,000; 300 barges, $400,000; 7 river propellers, $35,000,—small craft under 30 tons, $85,000. Total, $3,090,000.

Mills, factories, &c., in the Home District and city of Toronto, viz: 87 grist mills, valued $800,000, 196 saw mills, $276,250; 12 oatmeal mills, $16,500; 14 foundries, $100,000; 18 woolen factories, $125,000; 50 carding machines, $15,000; 1 edgetool factory, $10,000; 3 starch factories, $12,500; 28 distilleries, $54,125; 6 soap and candle factories, $21,000; 1 cabinet and chair factory (steam) $12,500; 3 cabinet and piano-forte factories, $7,500; 2 paper mills, $20,000; 36 tanneries, $75,000; 1 snuff manufactory, $2,500; 23 breweries, $66,000;—total value, $1,613,875.

In June, 1844, a steam schooner made the passage from Toronto to Montreal, 470 miles, laden with freight, in two and a quarter days, over the rapids of the St. Lawrence.

The Provincial Government has applied large sums for internal improvement, as the following grants, in 1841, show:

St. Lawrence navigation	$3,458,410
Welland Canal	2,250,000
Light-houses, &c., on Lakes Erie and Ontario	370,000
Lake St. Peter	292,500
Newcastle District navigation	250,000
Burlington Bay Canal	225,000
Bridges between Quebec and Montreal	170,000
Road from Burlington Bay to Port Dover	150,000
Road from Lake Ontario to Lake Huron	150,000
Bridges, slides, &c., on the river Ottawa	140,000
Desjardins Canal Company	112,075
Bay of Chaleur's road	75,000
Cobourg Harbor Company	26,055
Oaksville Harbor Company	18,615
Port Harbor Company	15,375
Tay Navigation Company	7,805
Road from Ottawa to St. Lawrence	7,500
	$7,718,335

Prior to the Union of Upper and Lower Canada, in 1841, the Legislature had expended on the improvement of navigable water courses, and in the construction of canals, the following sums:

Welland Canal	$2,314,280
St. Lawrence Canal	2,200,485
Montreal Harbor	435,000
Chambly Canal	185,000
Trout navigation	116,170
Newcastle District	108,300
Kettle Creek Harbor	37,500
Toronto Harbor	26,000
Trent Bridge	24,000
St. Ann's Rapids	21,540
Paris Bridge	10,000
Brentford Bridge	10,000
Dunville Bridge	10,000
Chatham Bridge	10,000
Steam Bridge, Montreal	7,500
West Gwilliambury Bridge	4,775
(Total, $13,238,885)	$5,520,550

In 1842, the first year after the union, the gross amount of customs collected in Canada was $1,394,650, viz: at Montreal, $727,255; Quebec, $340,000; St. John's, $84,320; Toronto, $40,265; Burlington Bay, $36,315; Kingston, $32,550;—other ports, smaller sums. The increase of revenue from customs over 1841, was $304,453. At Quebec and Montreal alone the increase was $276,630. The tolls on the Lachine Canal produced during the year, $81,610.

The public debt of Canada amounts to $12,000,000; the revenue to about $2,600,000, and expenditures to $3,000,000 annually. Some retrenchment is necessary to equalize the financial system, otherwise it will create an irredeemable liability, draining the people by taxation, as in the mother-country, to pay interest. The government of Canada devotes from $300,000 to $500,000 annually to the support of schools.

New-Brunswick.—The north-east boundary question, which so long agitated the counsels of Great Britain and the United States, concerned the province of New-Brunswick on the one part and the State of Maine on the other. In 1842, it was amicably settled by the Ashburton treaty. The line established does not materially differ from that awarded by the King of the Netherlands. We have seen a calculation of the disputed territory, allowing it to contain 12,027 square miles, of which, by the treaty of 1842, the United States obtained 7,015, and England 5,012. By the line of the King of the Netherlands, the United States would have had 7,908, and England 4,119 square miles. Whatever the claims of either power, they have been adjusted in a satisfactory and honorable manner, so as to admit no future contention.

The province is laid off into twelve counties, of which we subjoin a table, showing the quantity of granted and vacant land in each, and also the number of persons who have squatted on crown lands, to 1842, without authority, the acres occupied by them, and estimated value,—

QUANTITY OF GRANTED AND VACANT LAND, ETC.

Counties.	Granted and located acres.	Vacant acres.	Squatters, No.	Occupied acres.	Value, dollars.
Northumberland	981,000	2,216,000	174	17,400	13,050
York	921,000	1,280,000	142	14,200	10,650
Westmoreland	780,000	532,000	166	16,600	12,450
Kings	605,920	244,000	145	14,500	10,875
Carleton	504,000	2,088,000	122	12,200	9,150
Queens	491,280	470,000	139	13,900	10,425
Sunbury	369,080	413,000	95	9,500	7,125
Kent	354,000	552,400	132	13,200	9,900
Gloucester	324,000	713,440	199	19,900	14,925
Charlotte	303,360	480,000	142	14,200	10,650
St. John	288,720	126,000	62	6,200	4,650
Restigouche	152,000	1,114,560	82	8,200	6,150
	6,077,960	10,129,400	1,600	160,000	120,000

The New-Brunswick and Nova Scotia Land Company have taken 500,000 acres between Nashwach and Miramichi rivers, which they offer in 100 tracts to settlers, at $1 50 per acre, payable in eleven annual instalments, without interest. The lands in general are good, and roads have been opened in different directions across them. It is recommended that emigrants unite, forty or fifty together, and send an agent in advance to select their lands, and make temporary provision for their arrival. Young men usually hire on a farm, or to a lumbering party during the summer, when wages are high, and work on their own land in winter, supposing they have saved money enough in the first two or three years to purchase a tract. Then they marry, and push their fortunes as best they can. Young women find employment both in the town and in the country at two and three dollars per month.

Referring to the necessity and benefits of emigration to New-Brunswick, Dr. Gesner says:

"In the old country, early marriges are discouraged, because they contribute to an increase of numbers, and, consequently, of misery. In the North American Colonies they are viewed as being advantageous, from the accession they make to the population; and the birth of a child in the backwoods is hailed with more than ordinary natural joy, because, by the labor of his offspring, the capital of the colonial settler is increased."

Farther, he remarks:

"A due regard should always be had to the habits and kind of industry the emigrants have been trained to. Serious blunders have been committed, by locating people who had been brought up to fishing, in the forests remote from the sea,—and also by establishing families who had been bred to husbandry, upon a coast or river, where a part of their subsistence must necessarily be drawn from the water. The adopted home of every family brought across the Atlantic should correspond as nearly as possible with their former residence, and their pursuits should deviate as little as possible from those to which they are accustomed."

A number of instances are stated, where individuals, poor and friendless, but with manly resolution, have gone into the forest, and by patient industry have accumulated snug fortunes. Dr. Gesner relates a very interesting case, on a small scale:

"J. G., in the county of Gloucester, took possession of a lot of land on the 16th of May, 1832; in the same season he cleared ground from which he raised eighty bushels of potatoes, ten bushels of turnips, and ten of buckwheat. With these, and the fish he took upon the shore, and five bushels of wheat paid for in labor, he maintained his family, (a wife and two children,) until the second, and a much larger crop was obtained. In the first year he built a log-house and a hovel for a cow, and chopped eight acres; In 1843 he raised eighty bushels of wheat, one hundred of oats, five hundred of potatoes, ten of barley, twenty-five tons of hay, kept ten head of horned cattle and two horses, and was in independent and most comfortable circumstances."

The forests of New-Brunswick constitute much of its trade and wealth. Its position, between 45° and 48° north latitude, is peculiarly suited to the growth of valuable timber trees. Mr. Perley, the government emigrating agent, has described and classified them in a report of much length. We barely have space to enumerate them by their common names, viz: the Oak, two species, gray and red; Maple, white, red-flowering sugar, moose, mountain; Birch, canoe, white, yellow, black; Cherry, wild, northern; Poplar, balsam, American aspen; Beech, white, red; Hornbeam, American, ironwood; Ash, white, black; Willow, black, champlain, shining; Elm, white, red; Pine, red, gray, white; Spruce, black, white, hemlock, American silver fir; Alder, common, black; Walnut; Dog Wood; Cypress or White Cedar.

This variety, found in almost inexhaustible profusion, affords the labor of man a wide field and sure reward. Bonnycastle, speaking of the forests of Canada and New-Brunswick, indulges in some beautiful reflections, which we copy:

"I know of nothing in this world capable of exciting emotions of wonder and adoration more directly, than to travel along through its forests. Pines, lifting their hoary tops beyond man's vision, unless he incline his head so far backwards as to be painful to his organization, with trunks which require fathoms of line to span them; oaks, of the most gigantic form; the immense and graceful weeping elm; enormous poplars, whose magnitude must be seen to be conceived; lindens, equally vast; walnut trees of immense size; the beautiful birch and the wild cherry, large enough to make tables and furniture of. Oh! the gloom and the glory of these forests, and the deep reflection that, since they were created by the divine fiat, civilized man has never desecrated them with his unsparing devastations; that a peculiar race, born for these solitudes, once dwelt amid their shades, living as Nature's woodland children, until a more subtle being than the serpent of Eden crept amongst them, and, with his glittering novelties and dangerous beauty, caused their total annihilation! I see, in spirit, the red-hunter, lofty, fearless, and stern, stalking in his painted nudity, and displaying a form which Apollo might have envied, amidst the everlasting silent woods. I see, in spirit, the bearded stranger from the rising sun, with his deadly arms and his more deadly fire-water, conversing with his savage fellow, and displaying the envied wealth of gorgeous beads and of gaudy clothing."

The fancy sketch, so far as applicable to the Indians of New-Brunswick, will justify a brief allusion to them. They are now reduced to two tribes, numbering 1,377,—the Micmacs, 935, and Milicates, 447. Both inhabit the same district, yet cannot understand each other's language. Fourteen tracts of land, containing 61,273 acres, have been reserved in different parts of the province for their use, and which they are permitted to occupy during pleasure. Like most other red men, they resist all progress. Dr. Gesner says:

"The Indian naturally despises the refinements of civilization; he looks upon the forest as his home, and ever longs for wild adventure. Much pains have been taken to improve the condition of these people. Young children have been taken, with their parents, and educated with much care. They have been instructed in the arts and agriculture; but no sooner were they liberated from their masters, than they returned to the haunts and habits of their forefathers, and became the most depraved of all their race. By associating and laboring with the inhabitants of the Province, they have advanced slowly in agriculture, and a few families may be found who support themselves comfortably by their own exertions. But their intercourse with the whites has always been the introduction to intemperance, disease, and idleness; and if we judge by the rapid decline in their numbers since the country was colonized, there is reason to fear that the day of their arrival at an ordinary degree of civilization will not long precede the day when the names of their races will be blotted from the pages of American history."

In the seven ports of entry,—St. Johns, Miramichi, Dalhousie, Bathurst, Caraquet, Richibucto, and Dorchester, the imports in 1844 amounted to $4,083,710, being an increase of $1,058,135 over the previous year. The exports for 1844, were in quantity, as follows: Timber, 190,320 tons; deals, M. feet, 108,424; boards, M. feet, 844; shingles, Mds., 7,042; staves, 48,612; masts and spars, 5,538; small poles, 8,455; hand-spikes, 273; oars, 3,053; tree-nails, 58,420; lath-wood, 3,424 cords; laths, 1,774 Mds.; pickled salmon, 2,479 bbls.,—6,419 kits; smoked salmon, 406 boxes; mackerel, 24 bbls.; dried fish, 12,405 quintals; alewives, salted, 16,229 bbls.; shad, salted, 117 bbls.; codfish, pickled, 214 bbls.; herring, salted, 1,754 bbls.; herring, smoked, 7,308 boxes; potatoes, 12,782 bushels; lime, 1,470 hhds.; furs, 14 packages; oil, seal, 240 galls.—cod, 5,744 galls.; grindstones, 3,870; gypsum, 388 tons.

Some estimate may be formed of the product of the fisheries, by the exports of fish and oil from the port of St. Johns in 1839, which amounted to $281,545. The yield, however, is fluctuating, as in 1845, it was only $108,485 for the whole province. Many disputes have arisen, as to the right of citizens of the United States to fish within three miles of the coast, under the treaty of 1783, and convention of 1818. The British allege that all fishing by foreigners, within that line, is a trespass; and notes have passed on the subject between the cabinets at London and Washington. In 1841 Mr. Stevenson complained of certain seizures of American fishing vessels by provincial authority. The British Colonial Secretary insisted upon the exclusion, not only from three miles, following the indentations of the shore, but by a line drawn from the headlands, or extreme points of land next the sea. Nothing farther was done, and we presume this construction has been acquiesced in by our government.

The shipping of New-Brunswick in 1844 consisted of 672 vessels, with a tonnage of 92,210, manned by 3,917 men.

Turning from dry details, we beg to amuse our readers with an extract from the book of Dr. Gesner, which shows that even the people of New-Orleans, in musquito time, are highly blessed in comparison with the citizens of New-Brunswick. Dr. G. says:

"A long chapter might be written on the biting and stinging insects that infest the woods during the summer months. In the heat of the day black flies bid defiance to musquito nets, ointments, and every kind of cosmetic. No sooner had we landed than the blood began to flow down our faces from the bites of these merciless tormentors. At sunset the unseen midge commences operations, and the more musical musquito begins to sing and perforate the skin with his blood-pump. A Yankee backwoodsman told us that he could '*stand* the musquitoes and black flies, but as to the midges, he despised them.' We, however, found that our estimation of these sweet creatures had little influence on their biting propensities; the only remedy for them is to stand in a thick smoke of cedar bark. This, it is true, is somewhat inconvenient for those who put a high value upon a fine complexion, as the skin thus smoked soon resembles a piece of Irish bacon. In some of the low, swampy grounds, the musquitoes are so numerous, that they are inhaled by every breath drawn by the traveler. Each of our party was compelled to carry a large torch of cedar bark, and the constant flourishing of these smoking fire-brands around our heads reminded me of the menaces made by an Irish mob with their shillelahs."

With regard to the geology of New-Brunswick, very little is known for want of adequate explorations. Limestone appears to be the prevailing feature. Coal is abundant, and is wrought, near the Grand Lake, by a joint-stock company. Iron and gypsum are also found in large quantities. The climate is similar to that of Canada,—winter lasting from November to April. Agriculture is depressed by the fisheries and timber trade—the latter producing habits of a deplorable kind. The lumberers have been described as the pests of a colony, " made and kept vicious by the very trade by which they live." The population consists mainly of English, Irish, Welsh, and Scotch, with three small settlements of French on the east side of the colony. Besides a regular army paid by England, the native militia is about 25,000 strong.

Education is liberally provided for at the public expense,—there being about 500 schools for elementary instruction, attended by 8,000 boys and 6,000 girls. King's College, at Fredericton, was established by the exertions of Sir Howard Douglas, governor from 1824 to 1831, and is chiefly maintained by an annual grant of $10,000 from the local government.

Nova Scotia.—Of all the British colonies north of the United States, Nova Scotia is the most densely populated. By a low, sandy isthmus, only fourteen miles across, it is connected with New-Brunswick on the west, and separated from Cape Breton on the north by the narrow strait called the Gut of Canscaw. The climate is much like that of Lower Canada, varying from 95°, extreme heat, to 10° below zero, and at times as much as 50° and 60° in twenty-four hours. The warmth of summer occupies about three months, beginning with June. The fair and wet days are in the proportion of eight to five. In most other countries, sudden changes of temperature affect the general health. Not so in Nova Scotia. The complaints most prevalent are rheumatic and inflammatory. Intermittent fevers are wholly unknown; typhus occurs only in a mitigated form, and the ravages of the yellow fever have never been felt.

There is a degree of romance connected with Nova Scotia, which tempts us to give a few particulars. To promote colonization in America, Charles I., in 1625, granted several of his barons large districts of land in Nova Scotia, which should enure to them in fee, on settling a certain number of persons in the colony. These grants subsequently amounted to one hundred and eleven, of 16,000 acres each. The terms were modified by sundry royal acts, and the whole affair seems to have slept for more than two centuries, without any positive fulfilment. At length old dusty parchments were evoked, and in November, 1844, a meeting of the Hereditary Order of New-Scotland took place in Edinburgh. A report was submitted, sustaining the claims of the nobility to the possessions conceded by the crown, and denying all fraud and forfeiture. The speech of Sir Richard Brown on the occasion, is a compact and ingenious defence of the barons. After dealing freely with the industrial and pauper statistics of Great Britain, so far as his object made it necessary, he aims a blow at the United States, accompanied with information entirely new to our people, and we venture to say, unsupported by facts.

Sir Richard is striving to arouse emigration to Nova Scotia, so that the wilderness acres of the nobility may be turned into fruitful fields, with rents fit for the Order! He has quarreled with the British system of labor and compensation, and, as a remedy, points to the new world. There, under the rule of titled proprietors, the working classes are to find plenty, and all the blessings of life, in return for moderate toil. In the effort of Sir Richard, there is such a thorough, bold, and vigorous assault upon the social platform of his own country, that we almost pardon his misguided zeal when directed against our republican form of government. To the charge of combination, which he prefers with pompous particularity, and the secret oath having the overthrow of British dominion in America firmly at bottom, we record as complete a negative as the greatest stickler for certainty could desire. Some experiment must have been made in his imagination. Louisiana is in the catalogue as having eleven lodges at work to accomplish the plot! In the border states—Maine, Vermont, and New-York, it is possible a few sympathizers with Mackenzie may have instituted a league, under obligations, to revolutionize Canada; but the idea that eighteen other states, some of them two thousand miles from the scene of action, engaged in it with solemnity, is too ridiculous to deceive any mind.

We quote from the speech of Sir Richard:

"In the United Kingdom, exclusive of 1,300,000 English paupers who receive legal relief, we have an average of more than one-fifth of the population unable to live by lawful industry—that is to say, 5,400,000 souls. But these figures added together, namely, 6,700,000, exhibit by no means the most revolting features in the social aspect of the present age. Out of a population living by wages—upon the fruit of their daily, aye, and often nightly toil—a large number may be considered paupers in every sense of that term,—their average earnings per head not exceeding eight shillings a week. Are microscopes needed to perceive the filth, the privation, the cold, the hunger, the thirst, the nakedness, the crime, the sickness, the mortality of such a condition as this? 'It has created in the British Islands,' says an intelligent foreign writer who has recently gone through the length and breadth of the land, 'a reality of misery, depravity, and every hideous form of human suffering, which surpasses anything that the imagination of a Dante ever conceived in describing the abode of devils and the torments of the damned!' Turn we then from this great intestinal worm—this *anguis pectoris*—which is living and feeding, and growing daily upon the vitals of the British nation, to consider for an instant that other and scarcely less fearful sources of hostility, centred in our own loins, and ever active in these crowned isles, though chiefly domiciled in what was England's other self, her name-daughter and her glory in the western world—I mean Republicanism. This is the generic title of an aggregate of feelings, each pre-eminently militant to our national security, to our commercial prosperity, to our strength as a maritime and colonial power, and to our very existence as a monarchical state. It has already indicated itself, and it does now indicate itself, by a variety of acts, all aiming at one grand consummation—the breaking up of our territorial supremacy and institutional power. We scarcely sheathed the sword which its development in the Canadas caused us to wield in 1837 and 1838, when it glutted itself with some million acres of our land in the province of New-Brunswick, being one of nine unprincipled concessions of a similar kind which we have progressively yielded since the year 1798. Since then the United States have either founded or multiplied Hunter Lodges as follows: In Massachusetts, 89; in Rhode-Island, 15; in Connecticut, 68; in Maine, 99; in Vermont, 107; in New-York, 283; in Michigan, 54; in Wisconsin, 7; in Illinois, 21; in Indiana, 14; in Ohio, 86; in Pennsylvania, 49; in Kentucky, 11; in Virginia, 21; in Maryland, 16; in Delaware, 2; in New-Jersey, 17; in Missouri, 39; in Iowa, 3; in Louisiana, 11; in New-Hampshire, 78; in Lower Canada, nearly the whole of the French population; in Upper Canada, 84; in New-Brunswick, a few, and in the other parts of the United States not mentioned, nearly 100. The number of members taken at a minimum, may be fairly calculated to be not less than 80,000 able-bodied men; and their objects are exposed in the oath which is administered on their admission. 'I swear to do my utmost to promote republican institutions and ideas throughout the world—to cherish them, to defend them, and especially to devote myself to the propagation, protection and defence of these institutions in North America. I pledge my life, my property, and my honor to the Association. I bind myself to its interests. And I promise until death that I will attack, combat, and help to destroy, by all means that my superior may think proper, and especially never to rest till the British tyrants cease to have any possession or footing whatsoever in North America. So help me God.'"

More than a dozen resolutions were adopted at the Edinburgh meeting, one of which we copy, as indicating the objects to be attained by the whole:

"10. *Resolved*, That with the farther view of combining the influence and exertions of all parties, on either side of the Atlantic, having an interest in, or favorable to, the revival of the rights and objects of the Baronetage of Scotland and Nova Scotia—promoting the systematic colonization of British North America—raising the capital for these national ends—and otherwise superintending and managing the common properties and estates of such Baronets, and other landed proprietors in the Colonies, as shall join it, this meeting sanctions the formation, and approves the principles of 'The Scottish Company for advancing the Plantation of Nova Scotia and Canada;' the Baronets present, and those concurring by letter, agreeing, as soon as 10,000 shares are subscribed for by responsible parties, and the first instalments paid, to vest their lands in it, either in whole or in part, taking shares for the same,—further pledging themselves, on the Company's coming into practical operation, to use every possible means in their power to settle the estates, baronies, and regalities forming its territory, with such of their friends, clansmen, tenantry, retainers, and others, as may be disposed to rent farms of the company under improving leases."

What active measures have been taken to carry this scheme into effect, we are not advised. In a government of classes like that of Great Britain, the system proposed would ameliorate the condition of the laboring poor, by reducing their numbers in the old country, and opening new avenues to emigrants. There is a boundless, teeming field for husbandry in the land to which colonization is invited. Support is easily obtained from forest and sea.

Halifax is the capital of Nova Scotia, and affords the best harbor in British America—a sheet of water equal to ten square miles, completely land-blocked, and capable of containing the whole British navy. The harbor is accessible at all seasons, and its navigation is scarcely ever interrupted by ice. A canal, to which the legislature contributed $75,000, has been finished by a joint-stock company, connecting the harbor of Halifax with Cobequid Bay and the Bay of Fundy. The exports of mackerel, in 1844, amounted to 71,854 bbls., showing a progressive increase over the five years preceding—from 19,127 barrels in 1839 ; 25,010 in 1840 ; 25,031 in 1841 ; 54,158 in 1842, and 64,376 in 1843.

In 1836, the ships entering the ports of Nova Scotia, were 3,404—tonnage 381,133 ; and those clearing were 4,574, with a tonnage of 294,520.

The principal articles exported from Nova Scotia in 1836 were, in quantity and value, the following :

Article	Unit	Quantity	Value
Beef and pork	lbs.	6,880	$ 86,035
Coal	tons	42,587	191,640
Corn and meal			94,900
Fish—Cod, dry	quintals	221,509	595,270
do. wet	"	37,133	150,485
Other sorts of Fish			40,265
Gypsum	tons	31,489	70,825
Oil, train and sperm	galls.	224,967	145,025
Whalebone	lbs.	21,000	3,500
Pine Timber	tons	15,523	73,735
Deals and Planks			266,720
Other sorts of wood			237,645
Miscellaneous			274,445
			$2,230,485

Halifax has a few manufactures, mostly for immediate consumption, such as soap, candles, leather, paper, snuff, rum, gin, whiskey, porter, ale, and refined sugar. There are two private banking companies in the town, and a chamber of commerce of fifteen members. The New-York, Boston, Liverpool and West India steam-packets touch regularly at Halifax.

Nova Scotia has the elements of much wealth,—possessing coal and plaster of paris abundantly, and a fertile soil. The Bay of Fundy is noted for its tides, which rise 50, 60, and even 100 feet, and so rapidly, that cattle feeding on the shore are often overtaken and drowned. About one-fourth of the population is of Scottish origin, and the rest chiefly from England and Ireland, some from New-England.

Newfoundland, the great fishing island of North America, is about 350 miles long, and 150 average width, lying between parallels 46° and 51° north latitude. The surface is broken, wild and rugged, covered, to a large extent, with lakes, marshes and shrubby trees. Only two streams are navigable, the Humber and river of Exploits. Granite prevails, and also limited coal and iron formations, hardly paying the work. Spruce, birch and larch are the principal forest trees. There is but little wood of any value on the island, scarcely enough for its own consumption. The best soil is along the rivers, and at the head of the bays. Grain crops are moderate ; potatoes succeed best. Among the wild animals, are deer, foxes, bears, wolves and beaver, which are mostly hunted by the Indians from Labrador.

What constitutes Newfoundland a place of note, are the immense fishing grounds by which it is surrounded ; it has little or no other resources. The ice fields on the coast, at the close of winter, are of incredible magnitude, often extending 300 miles from the land into the ocean, with peaks resembling mountains covered with snow. These float at random, to the great hazard of vessels, either hemming them in for months, or crushing them by contact. Every spring a number of foreign ships are lost in the ice. Crews have left their vessels locked fast, and walked over the ice for miles to the shore, to avoid perishing.

The seal fishing is prosecuted with much success—800,000 seals being an average taking every spring, on the ice, where they resort in countless numbers. They are usually killed by a blow upon the head—the fat and skin saved, worth from $2 to $3 per animal. In six weeks, a man frequently kills enough to enable him to live a year on the profits. The risk in hunting seals is so imminent, that it has been called a lottery, owing to the ice and other perils. With good fortune, a merchant fitting out five or six vessels, will clear $10,000 upon the cargo of each, in one season.

In the months of June, July, and August, the heat is intense—80° and 90° of Fahrenheit at eight o'clock in the evening. Musquitoes and other biting insects are terribly abundant. A writer who went trouting was so stung, that he kept his bed three days, unable to see, from the effects. His great consolation was, that in six hours he killed thirty dozen of trout with rod and line. He also comforted himself with the privilege of shooting all kinds of game, from the partridge and fox, to the bear and snipe—no laws to the contrary. These are the only amusements in summer. In regard to a colder period, we quote his own words :—

"You can form no idea of a Newfoundland winter —for months, nothing to be seen but frost and snow. We have usually a heavy fall of snow early in January, which will lie on the ground till spring ; this becomes frozen, and is hard as ice. You will see as much snow fall in an hour as will lie six to seven feet deep ; and often, after a few hours' snowing, you will require to dig yourself out of doors. Then is the time for fun in sleighing, the favorite amusement of the country. You may go for miles and miles over fields of frozen show, across ponds and rivers, in your sleigh, without the least fear of danger. The sleighs are drawn by dogs and horses, around the necks of which are hung bells as a preventive for running foul of each other, as they make not the least noise in moving along, and travel at a very rapid rate. The sleighs are usually painted in very gaudy colors, and are covered with furs of various descriptions ; the horses are dressed in like manner. You will see vast numbers of these vehicles running in procession, each one armed with an immense ring of bells."

It has been supposed that the Norwegians

discovered Newfoundland in the eleventh century ; but, if so, it was subsequently forgotten, till John Cabot visited it in 1497, and gave it its present name. In 1500, the Portuguese and French carried on an extensive fishery on the neighboring banks. No permanent colony was established until 1623, when Lord Baltimore took possession of the south-east part of the island, and appointed his son governor. The subject of fishery rights has been a vexed question between the British, French and United States governments ; the people of each occupying at pleasure, especially along the Grand Bank, which affords room enough for millions of laborers, and is not included in any treaty stipulations.

The greatest production of the fisheries in any one year, was in 1814, when the exports amounted to $13,000,000 ; but the English part of the business has since declined, so that for the years 1837–38–39 it averaged only $2,500,000. Number of boats employed, 6,159.

From 1830 to 1843, inclusive, the seal fishery employed the following annual outfit from the port of St. John's :—

Year	Vessels	Tons	Men
1830	92	6,198	1,935
1831	118	8,046	2,598
1832	153	11,462	3,294
1833	106	8,665	2,964
1834	125	11,020	2,910
1835	120	11,167	2,912
1836	126	11,425	2,855
1837	121	10,648	2,940
1838	110	9,300	2,826
1839	76	6,417	2,029
1840	75	6,190	2,058
1841	72	5,595	2,078
1842	74	6,035	2,054
1843	106	9,625	2,175

The value of exports from St. John's, for five years, is given as follows :

Year	Dried Fish	Oils	Seal Skins
1838	$ 2,423,245	1,247,140	152,270
1839	2,540,785	1,226,345	234,680
1840	2,881,225	1,525,985	197,040
1841	3,025,020	1,334,160	149,805
1842	2,809,750	1,666,565	116,000

Year	Salmon	Herrings	Total
1838	66,550	53,615	$3,889,305
1839	59,810	69,200	4,058,620
1840	64,695	45,180	4,714,125
1841	61,510	31,805	5,602,300
1842	68,390	35,595	4,196,300

The imports at St. John's, for 1842, amounted to $3,471,675.

New-Britain, stretching from Labrador on the Atlantic, to New-Archangel on the Pacific Ocean, a greater distance than from New-York to Astoria, is the vast possession of Great Britain, north of the Canadas. It extends from 50° to 70° north latitude. The soil is so rocky and thin, that only moss, shrubs, and a few stinted trees can grow upon it. Numerous lakes and ponds of fresh water are almost everywhere scattered over the surface. Bears, beaver, deer, raccoons, and other animals valuable for their skins and fur abound, and hunting them is the chief employment of the inhabitants. The Hudson's Bay Company have established the only civilized settlements ; Forts Albany, Churchill, Reliance, York, and a few others. This company was incorporated by a charter from Charles II., in 1669. In 1837, the principal furs offered for sale were beaver skins, 82,927 ; marten, 156,168 ; fox, 25,000 ; musquash, 838,550 ; lynx, 31,887 ; mink, 27,570 ; an amount larger than that of several years immediately preceding. The company in the same year exported 1,259,000 goose and swan quills, 461 lbs. sea-horse teeth, besides castor, isinglass, and other articles. The trade at the forts consists in the exchange of blankets, powder, beads and trinkets with the savages for furs, in search of which their agents are sent in every direction.

A country so cold and barren has no improvements worthy of note. The Indian tribes and the fur traders doze away life in camp, animated occasionally by a little traffic with each other. A description of the bays and straits from Belleisle to the mouth of Mackenzie's river, in the Arctic Ocean, would be the most we could furnish our readers relative to this wild desert, a task already better performed by Morse and other geographers.

In the exhibition of facts touching British America, we have endeavored to compress, without groping in the fog of regulations from the mother country, which are about as dense and impenetrable as the atmosphere of the Newfoundland coast, on a calm morning in autumn. While something has been done to improve the condition of her laboring poor, by colonizing, Great Britain has the scope, in her North American provinces, to achieve a hundred-fold more than she has attempted.

AMERICA—SOUTH.—Historical Progress of South America—Revolutions—Spanish Colonial Policy—Declaration of Independence—Reports of U. S. Commissioners upon South America—Mr. Poinsett's Views—South and North American character contrasted—Araucania — Argentine Republic—Bolivia—Brazil—Chili —Colombia—Ecuador—Granada—Venezuela—Paraguay—Peru—Uruguay—Patagonia, etc.—We have had occasion before, to pass under review the historical and statistical progress of the United States, and of those contiguous islands which remain still in the possession of foreign powers, but which it is not too great a stretch of probability to suppose, may ultimately be attached to the government of these states. Our intention is to prosecute these investigations in regard to every other division of America, and furnish the reader as late, as reliable, and as thorough information upon them, as can be had from any or from all sources together. It is important that we, who occupy so large a portion of it, and are so intimately and closely connected with the rest, should know well and minutely everything that concerns or is likely to affect the interests of this western world. It is a theatre, far removed from all the old limits of civilization, upon which a new and somewhat different people are called upon to perform their parts, amid circumstances and influences widely different from those of nations with whom they are most nearly allied. The history of this population, in all its different manifestations, is as unique as it is interesting, and furnishes materials for additional chapters in the history of man, of society, and of human progress.

The cold and inhospitable regions of the north, which are known as BRITISH AMERICA; and those which, amid mountains of ice, slope away to the Pacific and to the ASIATIC POSSESSIONS OF RUSSIA; the intermediate and but lately well-explored divisions of CENTRAL AMERICA and MEXICO, and the vast SEMI-CONTINENT, stretching from the Equator to the South Seas, will furnish abundant fields for investigation.

However important the subjects here announced, it must be said, with great regret, that they have hitherto commanded a degree of interest with our countrymen altogether disproportioned to that importance. We have been pleased to know the states of our own confederation, and even that imperfectly, whilst, as to all the remaining portions of America, they have constituted a far more perfect *terra incognita* than those of a fabulous antiquity. The ancient resources of Greece and Rome, and the modern European states, are far more familiarly known and assiduously studied. To be sure, the difficulties of obtaining reliable information in the one case, have been far greater than in the other. From vain jealousies, indifference or indolence, it happens that little has been given to the world calculated to show, in any adequate manner, the true condition and statistical progress or decadence of these divisions of the Western World. Of their discovery, and of the adventurous spirits who found an arena for the highest romance, there has been no dearth of knowledge. Every one can speak of Cortez and Pizarro. Even travelers, who, in general, do so much in extending information of the countries visited, aid us little here. Books have not multiplied upon these points. In fact, we know of scarcely any sufficiently elaborate and reliable for all the purposes desired. However, a thirst for knowledge has been excited by the contests about Oregon and the wars in Mexico, which will eventually result, we doubt not, in the most complete and perfect developments.

On this occasion, we shall confine our attention entirely to SOUTH AMERICA, a text sufficiently comprehensive for much greater space than that to which we find ourselves necessarily restricted.

The discovery and early settlement of this vast region, whilst it presents little in common with the discovery and settlement of the country to the northward by other European powers, excepting Florida and Mexico, furnishes one of the most romantic and thrilling chapters in the history of mankind:—Valor, endurance, intrepidity in the most trying and terrible exigencies, induced by the basest considerations of rapacity and plunder—the loftiest spirit, and the most criminal and groveling desires. Not all the attractions of poetry or of chivalry can veil the deformities of a picture in which avarice, blood and slaughter, command so prominent a place. No cruelty could be more refined; no tyranny more systematic and heartless.

The Spaniards profited by the feuds existing among the natives at the period of discovery, and made them the instruments of conquest. They sold the Indians into slavery, and destroyed thousands by the harshest abuse. On the suggestion of Las Casas, commissioners were sent from Madrid to inquire into these abuses, and several regulations were made for the protection of the natives, and for the distribution of their labors. These established a less odious but yet perfect system of slavery.

Thousands of these unfortunate people, says the Hon. Joel R. Poinsett, in a paper prepared by him, 1818, at the request of the government of Mr. Monroe, were marched every year to Potosi; and although the period of service was only eighteen months, they were attended by a numerous train of friends and relations, who, on the eve of their entering the mines, sang melancholy dirges, and sounding a horn in solemn strains, mourned over them with all the ceremonies with which they used to evince their sorrow on the death of a relative. Their wives and children remained with the conscripts, who, harrassed by a long march, seldom resisted more than a year the excessive labor and noxious air of the mines.

But with this period we will not long delay, since the reader has been for some time in possession of the valuable works of Mr. Prescott, which entirely exhaust the subject..

Our observations upon South America begin at a period much more modern, and will be brought down as nearly as possible to the present day. They include all the states and provinces, except those of French, English and Dutch Guiana, already considered by us. The contrast furnished by the picture, when viewed in connection with that of the United States of North America, is most striking and instructive.

In the year 1818, the question of South American affairs was brought before Congress by Mr. Monroe, who submitted the correspondence between Mr. Adams and Mr. Aguirre, the agent of the Government of La Plata, in regard to acknowledging the independence of that republic, then in actual revolution against the Spanish authorities.

The papers which were submitted on that interesting occasion, embrace the diplomatic correspondence, the able letter of Mr. Poinsett, and the elaborate returns of a commission, consisting of Messrs. Rodney, Graham and Bland, who were sent on a special embassy to South America, in order to learn the true state of affairs and condition of the country. These, with the able speeches of that liberal and enlightened statesman, Henry Clay, upon the same subject, are upon the table before us. For later information, we are indebted to the Digest of American Statistics, which, with little system, but great labor, the Hon. John McGregor, of London, has lately made and published.

Up to the period of the Revolution of 1790, in France, South America submitted quietly to its European governors in every particular, however arbitrary the exactions or revoltive the principles of government. A hope of liberty would have seemed visionary and absurd in so grinding a despotism. Force and fear, and a sense of weakness and dependence, suppressed every other feeling than that of passive endurance.

Two viceroys were set up by the Spaniards over their American possessions; the *Viceroy of Mexico* and the *Viceroy of Peru*, under whose jurisdiction all things were placed. To these were added, in 1718, the *Viceroyalty of Santa Fe de Bogota;* in 1731, the *Captain Generalship of Caraccas;* in 1768, the *Captain Generalship of Chili;* in 1778, the *Viceroyalty of Buenos Ayres.*

In 1797, disturbances began to occur in Venezuela, induced by the spread of French revolutionary principles. They were succeeded, in the early part of the next century, by the attack of the British army, under General Whitlocke, during the English and Spanish war, most gallantly repulsed by the South Americans, who, in this feat of arms and valor, seem for the first time to have been taught their true strength and importance. Such a lesson was not likely to be lost.

When Charles IV. and Ferdinand VII. of Spain renounced authority in favor of the brother of Napoleon, the act was met with loud protestations in the colonies. Neglected by the mother country in the pressing difficulties which surrounded her, and conceiving themselves abandoned entirely, a *Junta* was established in Buenos Ayres, in 1810, which assumed, in its own hands, the reins of government. In 1815, a Congress, at Tucuman, and afterwards in Buenos Ayres, was employed in framing a republican constitution. A declaration of independence was signed on the 9th July, 1816, and was soon after followed by a similar declaration from Chili.

We are, however, anticipating, and return to a detail of those facts which minutely mark the progress of the revolution. In the first republican government of Buenos Ayres, the executive and legislative powers were vested in the Deputies; afterwards in an Assembly of Deputies from all the chief towns. This assembly having vested its executive powers in a Junta of three, which took the title of the Superior Provisional Government of the United Provinces of the River of the La Plata, in the name of Ferdinand VII., and after dissolving several assemblies, was finally abolished itself, and a supreme director chosen, with regal powers.

The capital and provinces maintained a continual struggle, in which the former preserved the supremacy. Paraguay established an independent government, consisting of a Senate and two Consuls. The eastern shore of the La Plata, comprising the *Banda Oriental*, or Montevideo, refused its adhesion to the capital, and resisted by force of arms. They asserted an independence of Buenos Ayres as well as of Spain. The people of Peru took no active part in the revolution, from causes growing out of the organization, etc. of that province. The power of the church in Chili and its opposition to the revolution, as well as the factions between the powerful families of the Carreras and Larrains, are stated, by Mr. Poinsett, as having been unfavorable to the establishment of independence.

The South American colonies were an object of great interest with Great Britain from a very early period. Their emancipation was a favored project with Mr. Pitt, and proposals are said to have been made by him to the administration of John Adams upon the subject. The first outbreak at Caraccas was encouraged by a proclamation from Trinidad. The expedition of Miranda, and the occupation of Buenos Ayres, in 1806, by Sir Home Popham, were countenanced by the British government. Emboldened by their success, the British now determined upon the entire conquest of South America, as is evinced in the instructions given to Generals Whitlocke and Crawford, whose expedition sailed immediately after, and was repulsed, as we have seen. The expedition of General Whitlocke, says Mr. Poinsett, might have secured the emancipation of these colonies, but was not adequate to tranfer the dominions to the crown of Great Britain.

After the downfall of the Spanish throne, manifestoes were published by the Princess Charlotte of Portugal, and the infant Don Pedro, claiming the Spanish American dominions. The first scheme of revolution was founded upon this pretension, and the delivery of the country to Princess Charlotte, it was thought, would have been soon followed by its absolute independence. The matter, however, made but little progress.

We have already seen the formation of the Junta, and the subsequent revolutionary governments. Years of anarchy and blood were destined to result in the almost irretrievable ruin of the colonies. The monarchical and patriot party, in their dissensions, added no little to the fearful disorders of the times. Civil wars raged between the different sections with various success and carnage. Portuguese and Spanish armies ravaged the country. Everything at times seemed hopeless for the republican cause. The Spanish yoke seemed but too likely to be imposed again. Almost any government would have been a blessing.

Remarking upon this dark chapter, Mr. Poinsett continues: "Their dissensions and ambition render them, in the opinion of some, unworthy to be free; but let us recollect that the virtues that adorn society and brighten the page of history, are the offspring of freedom and science, and that when a people have been for centuries kept in subjection by ignorance and superstition, the first effort to burst their fetters will call into action the most violent of the human passions, and hurry men to commit the greatest excesses. The course of such a revolution will be too often stained by cruelties and crimes, and will almost inevitably terminate in a military despotism."

"In contemplating," said the Hon. Henry Clay, in his speech in the House of Representatives in 1818, on the appointment of a minister to the La Plata, "in contemplating the great struggle in which Spanish America is now engaged, our attention is first fixed by the immensity and character of the country which Spain seeks again to subjugate. Stretching on the Pacific Ocean from about the fortieth degree of north latitude to about the fifty-ninth degree of south latitude, and extending from the mouth of the Rio del Norte (exclusive of East Florida) around the Gulf of Mexico, and along the South Atlantic to near Cape Horn, it is about five thousand miles in length, and in some places near three thousand in breadth. Within this vast region we behold the most sublime and interesting objects of creation; the loftiest mountains, the most majestic rivers in the world; the richest mines of the precious metals, and the choicest productions of the earth. We behold there a spectacle still more interesting and sublime—the glorious spectacle of eighteen millions of people struggling to burst their chains and to be free. When we take a little nearer and more detailed view, we perceive that nature has, as it were, ordained that this people and this country shall ultimately constitute several different nations. Leaving the United States on the north, we come to New Spain, or the vice-royalty of Mexico on the south; passing by Guatemala, we reach the vice-royalty of New-Grenada, the late captain-generalship of Venezuela and Guiana, lying on the east side of the Andes. Stepping over the Brazils we arrive at the United Provinces of La Plata, and crossing the Andes, we find Chili on the west side, and further north, the vice-royalty of Lima or Peru. Each of these several parts is sufficient in itself, in point of limits, to constitute a powerful state; and in point of population, that which has the smallest, contains enough to make it respectable. Throughout all the extent of that great portion of the world, which I have attempted thus hastily to describe, the spirit of revolt against the dominion of Spain has manifested itself. The revolution has been attended with various degrees of success in the several parts of Spanish America. In some it has been already crowned, as I shall endeavor to show, with complete success; and in all, I am persuaded that independence has struck such deep root, that the power of Spain can never eradicate it. What are the causes of this great movement?"

We have frequently had occasion to advert to the absurd and cruel restrictions which are put by the Spanish Colonial System, now greatly moderated, upon the commerce of all its dependencies. From these South America was a principal sufferer, and they have had much influence in paralyzing its industry and arresting its progress. That other causes may be assigned for the relatively unimportant position of the republics which have been established there, and their slow advances in population and wealth, made even under a system of freedom, is not denied. With equal advantages of soil and climate, the inferiority of the Spanish and Creoles tends to place the countries inhabited and administered by them, even under the best possible system, very far behind those in which the Anglo-Saxon element is allowed to rule. Industry and unlimited enterprise are the inheritance of the latter. Indolence and pride hang like an incubus upon the former. The law of one is progress, the other decay. The Anglo-Saxons have been sweeping everything before them on the North American continent, and establishing an empire which is felt, respected and feared, in every quarter of the globe. Their arts, their policy, and their institutions, find imitators where, but a few years ago, it was fashionable to revile. The old thrones of Europe are being shaken down by the young Hercules of America. It is impossible to foresee the ends which are to be ultimately worked out. Will the knowledge of power and resources be followed by their abuse? Will the love of enterprise, and the desire of more extended territory, already so plainly manifested among us, lead to excursions upon the impotent neighbors that surround us upon every hand? Have not results in Mexico taught the *invincibility* of the American arms? What power on this continent is there that can arrest their progress? What army that would not be shattered to pieces in the encounter? What state whose capital would not be occupied? We are not vaunting our prowess in haughty pride, but adducing sentiments and facts *universally* admitted. The time has even passed when Europe can interfere in the movements of the western world. The powers have enough to do in looking after each other, and preventing the overshadowing importance of any particular one. Mr. Calhoun, the other day in the Senate, scoffed with great propriety at the apprehension of English power being unduly exercised upon this continent again. There is no European army that could be brought to this country and landed, large enough to withstand the force that could be brought against it. It is but too evident that the destinies of America are in *our* hands. Wisdom and moderation should induce us to attend to our own peculiar affairs, and leave other American powers to do the same. The Mexican war was in many respects unfortunate, and we hail the peace with gratification. We have territories enough to be peopled for a generation to come. We have states enough formed and in embryo to govern. Let us leave events to take their own course. The North Americans *will* spread out far beyond their present bounds. They *will* encroach again and again upon their neighbors. New territories *will* be planted, declare their independence, and be annexed! We have New-Mexico and California! We *will* have Old Mexico and Cuba! The Isthmus cannot arrest us—nor even the St. Lawrence!! Time has all of this in her womb. *A hundred states* will grow up where now exist but thirty. Let us not anticipate. The end of all of this shall come, and God only can tell what it will be and when.

We condense the leading particulars of the trade of South America, during the colonial state, from the earliest periods.* The alcavala was the most destructive tax upon national prosperity, and amounted to four or six per cent. upon every transfer of property, and every contract of sale.† The government established monopolies in certain taxed articles, extending even to the necessaries of life. The colonial trade was at first confined to particular classes in both countries, afterwards it was opened to all Spaniards, but confined to the single port of Seville, which became the emporium of American trade. In 1720 the monopoly was transferred to Cadiz. Twenty-seven vessels were annually fitted out for the supply of Peru, Chili, and Terra Firma. With other than these fleets the colonists were forbidden to trade, or with any foreigners, or with each other. No colonist could embark his goods to Spain on his own account. A board of trade regulated the periodical fleets from Spain and their cargoes. A license from it was necessary to load or land a cargo. The smallest possible amount of goods was sent to the colonies. The crown exacting the same duties as upon larger shipments, would thus find the collection of them much easier. An impost was levied upon the bulk of the articles shipped, without regard to their value. An *endulto* was levied upon every arrival of produce from America, and was fixed anew on each return of the fleets. Though Spain could not supply all the wants of her colonies, she admitted of no purchases of foreign goods by them except through Cadiz and Seville. The monopolists of these cities realized profits of 170 and 250 per cent. on the colonial trade! Acording to Ulloa, a pound of iron was worth one dollar in Quito, a statement we can hardly credit. Contraband traders very naturally multiplied. In 1740, other expeditions than the periodical ones were allowed to sail from the colonies. but the licenses for this trade constituted a heavy tax upon exports. In 1764, regular packet-boats were established between Corunna and the chief ports of America. Then cargoes were limited in extent, and to Spanish produce. In 1765 the trade of the windward colonies was laid open to several ports of Spain. In 1766 the cotton trade was opened to Catalonia duty free, and in 1772 to other provinces. In 1774 colonial produce, duty free, was admitted into several ports of Spain. The ordinance of 1778 abated some of the enormous duties. The supply of slaves from foreign sources was permitted, first from the French and then from the English by the treaty of Utrecht. There resulted a contraband trade in other things, however, which caused a war between Great Britain and Spain. The slave trade then passed to a private company, whose entrepot was at Porto Rico. The government took upon itself the supply, and a contract was made with a British house for 3,000 annually. In 1789 the slave trade with the colonies was thrown open to all persons whatever. In 1778 the Council of the Indies decreed free commerce, if in Spanish built and owned vessels, with all the officers and two-thirds of the crew Spaniards. The colonial ports were classed with a view to privileges. Articles of the growth and manufacture of the mother country were called free, and paid 9 per cent. duty; those of the manufacture only, paid 12½. Foreign goods, received in the colonies through Spain, paid, including all charges, in all the ports, 33½ per cent. The duties on 74,000,000 reals of imports into America in 1778 was 32,000,000 reals, on 74,000,000 exports from America, 3,000,000 reals vellon. In 1788 the exports to the colonies were 500,000,000 reals; imports from, 800,000,000 reals.

After the British invasion of South America a new era opened in the trade of Buenos Ayres. The most exaggerated notions became prevalent in England with regard to its importance. It was even thought

* Paper by Hon. Joel R. Poinsett; Am. State Papers, 1818.

† The alcavala, according to Adam Smith, was at first a tax of ten per cent.; and afterwards of fourteen per cent. on all sales of property or goods.—Wealth of Nations, Book v. chap. 2.

the loss of the United States might be compensated from this quarter. On the withdrawal of the British troops, the viceroy was obliged to yield to popular clamor and open the ports to neutrals. The duties, however, were too high to attract many from the United States to enter, though British and Spanish capital availed itself of our flag. On the establishment of the Junta in Buenos Ayres, the ports of the Plate were opened to the British flag. A large capital took this direction. The market was overstocked with every article of British manufacture. Even skates and warming-pans were introduced by these sapient traders, like coal into Newcastle. The merchants often lost, not only the prime cost of the articles and freight, but had to pay a further sum for duties. English calicoes were retailed, three hundred leagues from the coast, below the London price—a state of things which has, no doubt, existed during the late Mexican war ; more liberal duties and regulations, however, were the result. In 1818, Buenos Ayres continued to be overstocked with English goods. Vessels were even dispatched from the River Plate direct to China and India. " In the hands of freemen," says Mr. Poinsett, "who were sensible of its advantages, and under an enlightened government, Chili, from the number and variety of its productions, which yield the raw material of every sort of manufacture, has within itself the means of greatness. And from the number of its harbors, and great extent of coast, might carry on an extensive and lucrative commerce with the intermediate ports, with the vice-royalty of Lima, the Philippine Islands, the East Indies, and China.

The following summary, made by Gregorio Tagle, Secretary of State of La Plata, and communicated to Congress by our agent, Mr. Graham, in 1818, is worthy of introduction.

PRODUCTIONS, MANUFACTURES, &c.—REPUBLIC OF LA PLATA.

Buenos Ayres.—Grain, hides, tallow, wool, horns, hair. These are an inexhaustible supply of commercial resources. The trade with the Pampas Indians alone in montas, wool, salt, bridle reins, and feathers, exceeds the sum of $100,000 per annum.

Paraguay.—Wood of a superior quality of many varieties, mani, tobacco, guambe, peasaba for cables, honey and molasses, dried sweatmeats, sugar, rice, cotton cloths, gums, raisins, fancy birds.

Cordova.—Grains, hides, woolen and cotton cloths, mules and herds, lime, minerals of gold and silver.

Mendoza.—Dried fruits, wines, brandy, grain, cattle, woolen, wagons for transportation, minerals of gold.

Tucuman.—Woods, grain, rice, oranges, mani, tobacco, wax, cotton, cheese, woolen, herds, wagons, &c.

Salta.—Herds, mules, grain, sugar, honey, molasses, brandies, wool, woods, minerals of gold, silver, copper, iron, and tin, sulphur, alum, vitriol.

Corrientes.—Hides, hair, cotton, agi, mani, honey, dried sweatmeats, sugar, charcoal, cotton, woolen.

Entre Rios and Banda Oriental.—Ox hides, horse hides, deer skins, otter and chinchilla skins, tallow, dried and salt meats.

Mr. Poinsett thus describes the vice-royalty of Peru :

" The bay of Tumbez separates it on the north from the kingdom of Granada ; the river of Loa on the south, from the desert of Alkama and the kingdom of Chili. The Cordillera of Vilacota in 14° south, separates it from Buenos Ayres. On the east it is bounded by an immense desert, and on the west by the Pacific Ocean. The face of the country is extremely unequal ; bordering on the coast it is a sandy, barren desert ; with a few small but fertile valleys, and in the interior are the lofty mountains and deep valleys of the Cordillera. The temperature varies, therefore, in the same latitude. In the habitable parts of the mountains the thermometer of Reaumer varies from 3° below 0 to 9 degrees above it. At Lima, and generally along the coast, the constant variation of the thermometer is from 13° to 23½°. The productions of Peru follow the nature of its different climates. Wine, oil, and sugar are the most valuable productions of the coast, corn and wheat of the valleys, bark and cocoa of the mountains."

The following, from the same pen, sketches Chili :

" From the Cordilleras de los Andes to the Pacific, the inclination is so great that all the rivers flow with the rapidity of torrents, and are therefore not navigable. They serve to irrigate the valleys, and render them the most fertile in the world. The climate makes this method of cultivation absolutely necessary, for from the Salado to the Stata, that is, from 25° to 36° of south latitude, not a cloud is to be seen above the horizon from the month of November to the month of May. The atmosphere during this period is perfectly clear, and the dews are scarcely perceptible, nor is the heat oppressive. The proximity of the Andes tempers the air, and the mercury fluctuates between 70° and 80° of Farenheit, and rarely rises to 85°. Thunder-storms, so frequent on the east of the Andes, are unknown in this part of Chili. Winter commences in the month of May, the cold is mild, and the rains gentle and unattended with wind. The rains of the winter fertilize the hills, and the plains, which cannot be irrigated during that season, afford pasture for the cattle. The spring commences in September, and the face of nature then in Chili is peculiarly beautiful. The hills are verdant, and covered with innumerable flowering shrubs, and the plains present to the eye a carpet of flowers. The abundance of water and the peculiarity of the climate enable the inhabitants to raise all the fruits of the earth in great perfection. The wheat which is cultivated in the valleys is of excellent quality, and the product seldom less than forty times the seed ; sometimes ninety, and on the the best lands one hundred. Indian corn likewise is cultivated, and on the best land produces abundantly. Barley is raised in great quantities for the use of horses and mules, which in the winter are fed on this grain mixed with chopped straw, as in Arabia and old Spain. Hemp and flax grow abundantly. Cotton is here and there cultivated for domestic manufactures ; and there is one sugar plantation. The climate and soil are well adapted to the culture of sugar, but they have been long accustomed to get that article from Lima, in exchange for their wheat, and are not disposed to change the ancient habits. Rice would likewise grow on the low lands, but it is brought from Lima."*

Mr. Bland, one of the commissioners to South America in 1818, furnishes a picture of the vast *pampas*, or pasture grounds of Buenos Ayres :

---

* Am. State Papers, 1818.

"The pampas, which forms a part of the territory of Cordova and of Santa Fe, and all that of Buenos Ayres, if measured entire in the country of the Patagonian tribes, extends in length 1,500 miles, and in breadth in a direct line, following the southern boundary of the Union, 500 miles, from the ocean to its western confines. Over all this immense space there is not a tree, not a shrub, nor a single perennial plant to be seen, save only those few which here and there lift their heads near a herdsman's hut. There are no hills nor eminences, and the undulations are so gentle, as only to be perceived by taking a long view over its surface; and then the eye passes round and round the horizon as over the face of the undulating ocean in a calm, where there is not a single object to delight or to relieve, or to vary the scene. The keen blast, called the pamperos, sweeps over the houseless and unsheltered plain without the least obstruction, and the fierce rays of the sun are felt in all their unmitigated fervor. You are sometimes in sight of thousands of animals, but they are chiefly horned cattle and horses; and deer, ostriches, wild dogs, &c., fly as you approach. For awhile the pampas presents the mind with an agreeable astonishment, but that soon subsides, and the eye may often be directed in vain in any way to obtain a single glance of society. Surrounded by a boundless, silent sameness, one sensibly feels the value of the voice and variegated scenes of nature. This interminable plain spreads out one of the most expanded and awful solitudes on earth."

These general observations and reflections must, however, be brought to a close, as there will be scarcely sufficient space otherwise for the particular enumeration and description of states intended in this article. We therefore proceed at once to this, the second part of our labors.

POPULATION AND AREA OF AMERICAN STATES IN 1838.

	Sq. Miles	Population.	Whites	Indians & Col'd	Slaves
Araucania	28,000	450,000	—	—	—
Argentine Republic	1,060,000	1,000,000	—	—	—
Bolivia	318,000	1,200,000	300,000	900,000	—
Brazil	2,740,000	6,060,000	843,000	3,130,000	2,086,666
Chili	101,000	602,000	130,000	472,000	—
Colombia	—	—	—	—	—
Ecuador	—	550,000	—	—	—
Granada	—	1,686,000	—	—	—
Venezuela	—	829,000	—	—	—
Paraguay	146,555	600,000	60,000	540,000	—
North Peru } South Peru }	954,000	831,000 } 494,000 }	136,311	729,315	284,773
Uruguay	223,978	175,000	20,000	155,000	—
Patagonia	441,309	150,000	—	150,000	—

Araucania is an unimportant territory north of Patagonia, and included within it on the maps. The inhabitants are ignorant, and are chiefly limited agriculturists and shepherds. There is much curious interest connected with the history of this people.

Argentine Republic, or *Buenos Ayres*.—It formerly included Monte Video and Paraguay, as we have seen. Cattle and agricultural products form the chief source of wealth; wool is also exported, of superior growth. The Argentine Republic is broken up into a number of minor republics, associated together; and Paraguay and Uruguay, or Monte Video, are but nominally included. These states have set up a separate government. The minor republics or provinces are Entre Rios, Santa Fe, Corrientes, Missiones, Bajada de Santa Fe, Cordova, San Luis de la Punta, Mendoza, San Juan, Rioja, Catamarcha, Santiago, Tucuman, Salta. *Buenos Ayres*, the capital, has a population of 80,000, almost entirely of the Spanish race. Its trade is very considerable. The government consists of an Executive, elected for five years, with his appointed council, and a Junta, elected every year. Rosas entirely subverted this constitution, and established a military despotism. The internal trade and navigation is considerable.

EXPORTS—BUENOS AYRES, 1843.

		Value—piastres.	Value—francs.
Hides	1,459,992	65,000,000	21,024,000
" salted	518,381	26,955,000	8,626,000
" of horses	50,238	1,105,000	354,000
Skins, sheep, doz.	94,921	2,848,000	911,000
" goat	39,695	1,191,000	381,000
" calf	6,236	187,000	60,000
" otter, lbs.	312,612	1,094,000	350,000
" deer, doz.	4,658	56,000	18,000
Horse Hair, arrobas.	109,488	4,380,000	1,402,000
Wool	468,790	10,313,000	3,300,000
Tallow	390,216	9,755,000	3,122,000
Ostrich Feathers, lbs	15,500	233,000	75,000
Salt Meat, quintals	162,184	5,676,000	1,816,000
Leather Shavings	9,556	239,000	76,000
Candles, cases	2,394	96,000	31,000
Horns	1,035,325	312,000	100,000
Bones	1,462,500	241,000	77,000
Total exports, in piastres			130,381,000
" " Francs, at the rate of 32 cts. per pias.			41,723,000
" Value, £ sterling			1,649,200
Or about			$8,000,000

In 1828, sixty-four British ships, of 12,746 tonnage, entered Buenos Ayres. In 1836 the whole number of arrivals were 213, of which 37 were from the United States; tonnage 36,117; value of cargoes 39,422,134 current dollars. The number of ships departing were 224—40 to the United States; value of cargoes 29,967,611 current dollars. Contraband trade has been extensively conducted in consequence of the disorders in the republic.

Bolivia, or *Upper Peru*.—More than three-fourths of the inhabitants are aboriginal Indians. The chief manufactures are of cotton, woolens of the hair of the alpaca and llama, glass, silver vessels, fans, &c. Commerce is inconsiderable, growing out of difficulties of transportation. Nearly all the products of Bolivia go to Europe, from the Pacific, after a terrible and rocky land-carriage of a considerable distance. Nothing but the precious metals and the most valued goods can endure the cost. Previous to 1829, Bolivia was included with Buenos Ayres. The independence of the country was then secured under Gen. Sucre. Its present name was taken from the liberator, Boliver, who drew up its constitution. This constitution and code have been abandoned, though the government is still vested in a president, senate, tribunes and censors.

The vast empire of *Brazil* compares with China and Russia in extent; having an Atlantic coast of 4,000 miles, and an area of nearly three millions of square miles. The climate is of consequence very various, though in general mild and regular. Mr. Von Langsdorff, consul at Rio, remarks: "Winter in this country resembles summer in the North of Europe. Summer appears one continuous spring, while spring and autumn are unconsciously lost in winter and summer."

Stern winter smiles on this auspicious clime,
The fields are florid in eternal prime;
From the bleak pole no winds inclement blow,
Mould the round hail, or flake the fleecy snow;
But from the breezy deep the groves inhale
The fragrant murmurs of the *eastern* gale."

All the trees and products of the West Indies abound in Brazil. In the southern provinces, the grains and fruits of Europe succeed. The finest and most valuable woods abound. Scarcely a two-hundreth part of Brazil is in cultivation. "The luxuriance and richness of this vegetable world, is ascribed, by Humboldt, to the great moisture which everywhere prevails, and which gives it an advantage over all other hot countries; forming a more happy and fertile contrast to those parts of Africa which lie within the same parallels of latitude. In many respects the climate, the soil, the varied surface, and the rich vegetation, seem to resemble more some parts of Asia Minor. But in that exuberance of ever-green foliage, which forms the peculiar characteristic of a new continent; in the number of its richly wooded mountains; the sources of countless streams, and the abundance of large springs; in the character, even, of its sandless deserts and indomitable forests, the tropical regions of Brazil are almost pre-eminent to those of any other region."*

Vast quantities of cattle are reared in Brazil, several thousands being common on a single estate.

* McGregor on America, p. 1332.

The mines of Brazil are most prolific of iron, gold and diamonds. The largest diamond in the world was found here. In the search for them, the earth is carefully washed after being taken from the beds of the rivers. The operation is performed by negroes, who receive their liberty when fortunate enough to find a valuable gem. 30,000 negroes have been so employed, and the mines are worked by government. The whole value of diamonds found in the eighty years, ending 1816, was not supposed greater than three and a half millions sterling, little greater than the sugar and coffee export of a single year! After Mexico and Peru, says McCulloch, Brazil has furnished Europe with the greatest quantity of precious metals. The rage for mining has, however, abated, and the people have betaken themselves to the more rational and profitable pursuits of agriculture. There is a large iron foundry belonging to government, which was considered in 1843 a failure.

The population of Brazil are free and slave; the former including Europeans, white persons born in Brazil, mulattoes, aborigines, Africans, &c. There are 83 titles of nobility, viz.: marquises, viscounts, counts and barons. The whole population, in 1844, was 4,450,249, a very inconsiderable number for so vast an empire. McCulloch makes the estimate about 7,000,000. One-half, nearly, are negro slaves, and one-sixth only of Portuguese blood. Mr. Kidder, who lately visited Brazil, says, "the Catholic religion and the priesthood are falling into decay."

Brazil was discovered by the Spaniards in 1500, and soon afterwards by the Portuguese, which gave rise to serious disputes. The Dutch, French and English plundered the earliest settlements. The Dutch held possession of different positions till 1654, when they were expelled. In 1808, the Portuguese sovereign removed his court to Brazil, and threw open the ports to all friendly and neutral powers. A revolution having taken place in Pernambuco, the Portuguese constitution was adopted to arrest its progress. On the king's leaving for Portugal, a struggle ensued, which resulted in the establishment of the *independent* Empire of Brazil, under the son of the Portuguese king, in whose family it still remains.

The cities of Brazil are upon the coast, the harbors fine, and rivers extensive. The Amazon is one of the wonders of the world. It was discovered by Orellana, who, in a frail craft, descended it from the mountains of Peru to the mouth. His description, published in Europe, was exaggerated and embellished in the highest degree, and gave rise to the *El Dorado.* A race of giant female warriors were described, which gave name to the river. These accounts were for a long time credited.

"Considering," says a historian, "the lengthened period during which Brazil has been colonized, its vast extent and fertility, the variety of its productions and its favorable situation for commerce, its progress in the accumulation of population and wealth has been extremely slow. This apparent anomaly may, however, be easily explained. The slow progress of Brazil, like that of the contiguous *ci-devant* Spanish colonies, is entirely owing to the vicious principles on which it was governed by the mother country, and to the rigid exclusion of foreigners from the country; the oppressive restrictions laid on the trade and industry of the colonists, and more than all the rest, to the ignorance of the Portuguese, and their inferiority in respect of science and art to most other nations in Europe. Portugal could bequeath nothing to her colonies but pride, superstition, and intolerance; but since the downfall of the old colonial system, consequent on the emigration of the court to Brazil, the foundations of a new and better order of things have been laid; *novus sæculorum nascitur ordo.* The settlement of thousands of foreigners in Brazil, and the unfettered intercourse she now carries on with all the most civilized countries in the world, have already had the best effects; and though it will require a lengthened period to counteract the joint influence of ignorance, slavery and a debasing superstition, Brazil is rapidly rising, not merely in the scale of wealth and population, but also in that of civilization."

We proceed to notice the most important cities and trade of Brazil.

Pernambuco imports cotton goods from the United States; cod-fish, tea, earthenware, hats, flour, iron, etc., from England, France, and Germany.

EXPORTS PRODUCE FROM PERNAMBUCO—1828–1845.

	Cotton.	*Sugar*					*Hides.*
	Bags.	Cases.	Boxes.	Barrels.	Bags.	W't.—arrob.	No.
1828	70,785	22,870	2,073	31,078	6,771	1,460,628	52,444
1829	54,820	21,984	4,973	28,973	8,222	1,463,332	46,573
1830	61,151	25,335	3,743	38,576	13,849	1,705,614	65,489
1831	53,157	27,970	1,402	42,466	8,429	1,799,986	76,584
1832	31,520	21,708	3,895	42,555	3,640	1,518,300	66,656
1833	58,564	15,507	3,432	54,477	5,444	1,301,612	84,743
1834	42,799	12,148	1,262	27,110	1,143	854,088	86,350
1835	52,142	17,520	2,846	56,996	9,180	1,388,888	91,492
1836	62,832	21,317	4,163	65,337	31,399	1,828,392	90,701
1837	43,847	17,774	1,603	57,346	19,248	1,456,420	93,771
1838	60,648	20,806	1,929	68,812	29,927	1,750,380	105,851
1839	39,173	20,891	3,739	78,800	27,923	1,878,675	111,052
1840	35,854	24,946	3,110	86,247	42,168	2,191,693	132,993
1841	26,990	23,650	2,149	90,256	66,296	2,261,699	136,494
1842	21,357	20,123	1,361	78,739	54,390	1,906,936	125,296
1843	35,906	23,161	1,392	60,613	73,204	2,017,522	104,420
1844	41,385	21,388	772	75,105	96,890	2,146,688	124,074
1845	26,562	19,571	849	61,892	216,015	2,565,824	163,935

Para is situated on one of the mouths of the Amazon, called Para River, 80 miles from the sea. The regular ebb and flow of the tides of the sea are observed for six hundred miles above the mouth of the Amazon. The position of Para is admirable for commerce. Its highways and byways are all by water, on bays, rivers, lakes and creeks. Manufactured goods, silks, hardware, wines, spirits, porter, salt provisions, salt, flour, furniture, oil, gunpowder, iron in bars, lead, cordage, and sail-cloth, are imported to the amount of half a million of dollars. The export, in 1845, reached £147,505 sterling, embracing cotton, rice, rum, India rubber, cacao, cloves, coffee, gums, drugs, cabinet woods, etc. etc. The manufactures are cotton sacks and India rubber shoes.

Maranham is a town of 30,000 inhabitants, and exhibits a general neatness and air of enterprise, said to be uncommon in the other towns of the empire. The imports in 1841 were £359,526, exports £319,833.

Parahiba exported in 1844, 2,134 tons of sugar, valued at £33,493 sterling; 23,172 bags of cotton, valued at £80,765 sterling; 20,583 hides, £9,005 sterling.

Bahia has a population, it is estimated, of 180,000. It was formerly the principal rendezvous of the slave-traders.

EXPORTS AND IMPORTS—BAHIA, 1843.

England	francs,	15,307,047	6,740,242
Hanse Towns	"	1,517,72[illegible]	3,334,472
Portugal	"	2,253,513	1,888,917
Austria	"	553,384	2,654,002
France	"	2,342,336	851,859
Africa	"	262,956	1,455,743
Sweden & Norway	"	109,763	1,550,751
Sardinia	"	586,884	991,926
United States	"	750,353	54,637
Sicily	"	226,302	439,877
Denmark	"	—	411,562
Other Countries	"	342,410	456,536
Fishers	"	404,832	—
Total	francs,	24,687,512	20,130,524

Rio de Janeiro.—"This port," says McGregor, "is much resorted to by vessels in distress, navigating the ocean between the Capes of Good Hope and Horn. Ships of war and merchant vessels, bound round the capes, find this a most convenient place to procure water and fresh provisions. Ships from Europe and North America meet in this great conveying harbor: ships sailing to or arriving from Bombay, Canton, New Holland, New South Wales, Valparaiso, and the various islands of the Pacific, as well as California and Oregon, on the western coast of North America.

"Rio Janeiro has become the chief emporium of Brazilian commerce, and especially of its mining districts. All the ports on the coast south of Bahia, and it may be said to the frontiers of the Banda Oriental, to Monte Video, send most of their produce for exportation to Europe or for home consumption to Rio Janeiro. Farinha, beans, bacon, dried or salt meat, are brought to the metropolis; hides, horns, dried meat, tallow and bacon, with rice and wheat flour, come by sea, chiefly from the provinces of Rio Grande do Sul and San Paulo; the latter furnishes also cheese, the bark of the mangrove tree for tanning, with some gum-woods, sugar, and rum; Santa Catherina sends also sole leather, onions, garlic, dried fish, and pottery. The small harbors to the north of Rio de Janeiro, to wit, Joan do Paraiba, San Salvador, Macahe, Porto Saguro, Caravelhas, Victoria, &c., supply vegetables and fish, beans, planks, hoops, Brazil wood, bark, charcoal, fuel, cocoa-nuts, tobacco, sugar, rum, rice, &c.

"The inland trade is extensive between Rio de Janeiro and the neighboring provinces. From Rio Grande do Sul and San Paulo, many thousands of oxen, horses and mules, are annually driven to Rio de Janeiro. The inhabitants of the remote provinces of Matto-Grosso and Goyaz bring gold in bars and dust, precious stones and smuggled diamonds, (the latter being contraband,) to exchange for European manufactures; to the smaller ports of Brazil, Rio exports all sorts of European goods; to both the western and eastern coasts of America, English and Portuguese goods; to Europe, sugar, coffee, cotton, tobacco, hides, otter skins, horse hair, &c.; and in speaking of trade, we must not omit the abhorred traffic in human beings, which disgraces Rio Janeiro."

IMPORTS AND EXPORTS—RIO JANEIRO, 1842-43.

Imports.

	Milreis *
Great Britain	13,697,638
United States	4,028,471
France	3,985,972
Portugal	1,912,077
Uruguay	1,552,640
Argentine Republic	932,092
Hanse Towns	1,430,875
Spain	618,249
Brazil	1,062,205
Other places	2,045,460
Total	31,265,679

Exports.

	Milreis.
Great Britain	3,920,629
United States	6,005,131
France	1,118,036
Portugal	1,205,100
Uruguay	655,242
Argentine Republic	704,206
Belgium	928,471
Hanse Towns	3,360,950
Austrian Ports	2,050,075
Denmark	544,920
Sweden	469,097
Genoa	389,963
Holland	34,923
Uncertain	834,190
Total	22,220,309

Chili.—Chili stretches in a long, narrow strip upon the Pacific shore of South America. Its rivers have but moderate capacities for navigation. Its agriculture is but slightly attended to. Cattle-raising is a common pursuit. On the coast the fisheries might be prosecuted with great success. The number of copper mines is large, and there are a few of gold and silver. The manufactures are few, and of the coarser kind. Since its separation from Spain the commerce of Chili has increased, which cannot be said of other South American states. The increase has been very great. The trade is chiefly with Great Britain; and exports of foreign goods are made from Chili to other states of South America. The imports from the United States are tobacco, candles, oil, sugar, manufactures: those from Peru, dyes, coffee, sugar, pearls, cacao, tobacco, cotton, rice, salt, and spirits; from La Plata, Paraguay tea, cotton, &c. Exports—bullion, copper, hides, tallow, pulse, wheat, fruits, drugs, and European goods re-exported. Chili is a republic, under a president elected for a term of years. It has a congress of 56 members. The revolution commenced in 1810. It was kept under by the royalists from 1817 to 1818; but in that year secured its independence. The chief commercial town is *Valparaiso.*

* The milreis is worth about 50 cents.

Capt. Wilkes, of the United States Exploring Expedition, writes: "I have had some opportunity of knowing Valparaiso, and contrasting its present state with that of 1821 or 1822. It was then a mere village, composed, with but few exceptions, of straggling ranchos. It has now the appearance of a thickly, settled town, with a population of 30,000, five times the number it had then. Most of the buildings are of one story, and built of sun-dried brick. Santiago contains 60,000 inhabitants, and is increasing in wealth and population."

In 1842, there arrived in Valparaiso 375 vessels, of 101,075 tonnage; 10,000 of these tons were from Great Britain, 7,000 from the United States, and 23,000 from Peru. The departures were 311 vessels of 82,390 tonnage, of which 15,000 were to England, 31,000 to Peru, 10,000 to Brazil, and only 2,000 to the United States. The average annual export of Chilian products, from 1836 to 1840, has been stated at £1,139,913.

TRADE, UNITED STATES AND CHILI—1844.

Exports to Chili.

Fish, Oil, and Sperm Candles	$6,953
Staves, Shingles, Planks	7,535
Masts, Spars, Naval Stores	2,122
Provisions, Beer and Spirits	63,489
Breadstuffs	28,462
Tobacco	6,411
Wax	9,258
Sugar	22,550
Manufactures	703,951
Sundries	5,914
Exports of Foreign Goods	248,576
Total	$1,105,221

Imports from Chili.

Bullion and Specie	$185,117
Copper, pigs, bar, &c	355,842
Dye-Woods	3,445
Leghorn, Straw, &c., Hats	18,833
Wool	19,847
Cocoa	26,431
Hemp	2,234
Manufactures	9,470
Sundries	127,951
Salt	600
Total	$750,370

Colombia.—This territory, in the most northern limit of South America, included in one union the states of Venezuela and New Granada in 1819. The revolutionists, under Sucre and Bolivar, having every where succeeded, Ecuador in 1823 was added. Venezuela separated from the other states in 1829, but rejoined them the following year. This union has, however, been broken up, and the states constitute separate and independent governments, which shall be considered in their order.

New Granada is in the northwest of South America, and includes the Isthmus of Panama. The inhabitants are descendants of Spaniards, Negroes, Mulattoes, Indians, &c., and amounted, at the latest computation, to 1,360,000. Coarse woolens and cottons are manufactured for the consumption of the lower classes. Gold is found in the beds of rivers and in mines; platinum exists on the Pacific shores. The other minerals, of silver, iron, copper, tin, and lead, are not plentiful. Emeralds are abundant in a river north of Bogota; coal occurs on the banks of the Rio Sinu. The average annual value of the trade of Granada is estimated at 40,000,000 francs. The imports in 1840 scarcely exceeded 17,000,000 francs; in 1843 they rose to 23,000,000 francs; in 1844 they fell to 22,000,000 francs. In 1843 the exports were 16,000,000 francs; in 1844, 14,000,000 francs. The contraband trade is very large; the trade is divided in the proportions of

Jamaica and England	13,000,000	francs.
France	3,769,000	"
United States	1,000,000	"
Island of Curacao	820,000	"
Spain	610,000	"
Venezuela and Peru, each	750,000	"

The imports from the United States are flour, salt goods, drugs, &c. The port of Carthagena on the coast is one of the finest harbors in the world. The port of Panama conducts chiefly a coasting trade. A line of steamships carry the English mail from Chagres to Valparaiso. The West India steamers leave the mail at the isthmus to be carried across to that point.

Venezuela.—"The Republic of Venezuela is a vast, fertile and splendid region; magnificent rivers, fertile forests, high mountains, low alluvial districts, and islands, and plains, are its remarkable features. Its name is derived from a fancied resemblance to Venice in the first Indian villages discovered. The republic is divided into thirteen provinces, of which Caraccas is the most important. The provinces have their governors, and send two members to the senate. The government and laws are lodged in a President, Vice-President, Senate, House of Representatives, &c. Caraccas has a population of 50,000. Its port is La Guayra. The inhabitants of the towns and villages of Venezuela are chiefly farmers. The people and government have acted, it is said, since their independence, with more wisdom than any of the Spanish republics, except Chili. The Orinoco River is 1600 miles long, and receives innumerable tributaries. It is navigable for large vessels five hundred miles—it has several mouths. The regions drained by this river are in wilderness. A steam navigation of its waters would work miracles in a short time. Many movements have of late been made to bring about such a result, with which the reader is doubtless familiar."

EXPORTS OF VENEZUELA—1845.

Great Britain and British Colonies	$1,156,751
United States	1,376,596
Denmark and Colonies	441,336
Germany, Bremen, and Hamburg	701,685
Spain and Colonies	1,012,747
France and French West Indies	477,494
Holland and Curacoa	268,135
Mexico	84,554
Granada and Goajiara	6,000
Hayti	540
Sardinia	43,557
Austria	22,000
Other Countries	764,000
Total	$5,592,159
Or in £ sterling	894,745

The imports in the same time, including coin, from all countries, were $4,961,727, or in £793,877.

Paraguay, though nominally included in the Argentine Confederation, has scarcely ever joined the association. It was early under the government of the Jesuits, and on the war occurring between Spain and Portugal, the Indians took sides against the latter. The suppression of the Jesuits in France, and Spain and Portugal, was followed by their banishment from America. The productions of Paraguay are numerous. Quantities of timber are floated down to Buenos Ayres. Tobacco, sugar and cotton are exported; caoutchouc and indigo grow wild; Paraguay tea has been exported to the amount of 8,000,000 lbs. The state of cultivation is superior to that of the neighboring Argentine states. Mr. Robinson saw whitewashed cottages among the trees, surrounded by fields of cotton, yucca, and tobacco, Indian corn, sugar cane, &c. The dictator possessed nearly half the country, in consequence of Jesuit confiscations. It is administered for the state, and agricultural improvements are extended by despotic regulations. Rice, maize, cotton, culinary vegetables are grown, and the breeding of horses and cattle promoted. The Paraguay tea is said to be as much used in Chili, La Plata, Peru, Brazil, as China tea in England. Mr. McGregor remarks, if the war between Buenos Ayres and Monte Video were ended—if these countries were tranquilized, the period will have arrived when a very lucrative trade may be carried on with the fertile region of Paraguay, and the countries drained by the Parana and its affluents. The government of Paraguay is an anomaly in the present times, says McCulloch; it approaches as near an absolute despotism as can well be conceived; the dictatorship of Sylla, in ancient Rome, being the only model with which it may be compared. The second consul, Dr. Francia, had himself declared, in 1817, dictator for life. Under his government the country exhibited great industrial improvement.

Ecuador, since the dissolution of the Colombian union, has formed an independent republic, governed by a president chosen for eight years, and a legislature of two houses. "In the western region of Ecuador, Indian corn, plantains, yams, cacao, tobacco, sugar, cotton, and different kinds of tropical fruits and vegetables are cultivated." From the elevated plains and valleys of the mountain region, wheat is sent down to Guayaquil and other low districts. Towards the southern extremity of the Andes, there are extensive forests. The great plains yield wax, gum, resin, and sarsaparilla. In the mountain region, cattle in large herds, horses, mules, and sheep, are pastured. Turtles are abundant in the Amazon; the *manta* fish abounds on the Pacific coast, and is salted for the Guayaquil market. Pearls were formerly fished; cochineal is collected near Loxa; small quantities of gold, silver, lead, and quicksilver are found. Salt is made on the coast. The manufactures of Ecuador are more important than those of any other of the South American republics; coarse woollen and cotton stuffs are woven at many places in the elevated valleys. There are manufactures of silk, and some tanneries. The city of Guayaquil contains 25,000 inhabitants. It supplies the settlements of the mountain coast with wine, brandy, and the sugars of Peru and Chili, and with European merchandise.*

EXPORTS, GUAYAQUIL—1843–1844.

1843....	Cocoa,....	15,338,970 lbs....	Value,	£170,433
1844....	"	8,565,500 "	"	105,788
1843 ...	Cotton,....	80,000 "	"	1,920
1844....	" ...	256,000 "	"	4,618

Peru.—The constitution of the present government of Peru was framed in 1828, upon the basis of that of the United States. The senate and chamber of deputies are chosen by the people; as also is the president every four years. The Spanish system, which limited supply, forced the inhabitants of Peru to make some indispensable articles. Coarse cotton and woolen stuffs are manufactured. At Lima, arequipa, cuzco, gold and silver vessels, utensils, trinkets, and ornaments are made. The internal trade is impeded from the want of roads. A trade in gums, cotton, resin, wax, sarsaparilla and coarse cottons, called Tucuya, are exported from the eastern districts to those of Brazil, near the Amazon. The maritime commerce of Peru is chiefly with the western coast and other republics of America, with Mexico, Central America, Guayaquil and Chili; to which countries, sugar, wine, brandy, salt and other articles are exported. Gold, silver and saltpetre are also exported. The sugar mills, in the Valley of Huanuco, are made of wood and worked by oxen. On the larger estates, brass rollers are used, but with a single exception, the estate of Andaguaylla, the proprietors adhere to the old practice of working by oxen by day and by night, throughout the year. All accounts agree upon the degeneracy of Peru since its independence. The population has decreased vastly. Von Tschudi, quoted by McGregor, gives a frightful account of prevailing immorality. He says, "the number of newborn infants exposed and found dead, is very great. When a dead child is picked up before the church, or in the street, it is carried without a word of inquiry to the Pantheon. Frequently it is thought not worth while to bury it. Vultures drag about the sweltering carcases of infants, and devour them in the populous streets." The silver mines of Pasco are the richest in South America. There exist quicksilver mines at Huancabelica. Gold-dust and fragments are found in several rivers. Copper, iron, lead and sulphur exist.

Lima is the chief city of Peru, and is elevated 560 feet above the level of the sea. The houses are low, in order to stand the effects of earthquakes. Population, 45,000. Its trade is conducted through the adjacent port of Callao. Capt. Wilkes, of the United States' Exploring Expedition, who visited Lima in 1821 and 1841, marks the change: "Everything betokens poverty and decay; a sad change from its former splendor and wealth. The country has been a scene of commotion and revolution for the last 25 years. The neglected walls and ruined tenements, the want of stir and life among the people, are sad evidences of decay.

Callao, according to Capt. Wilkes, has improved. The streets have been made much wider, and the town has a more decent appearance. Water is conducted from the canal to the mole, and a railway takes the goods to the fortress, which is now converted into a depot. The best idea of the trade of Callao may be formed from the number of vessels that frequent it. The usual number in port is about 40, in the proportion of 9 ships of war and 35 merchantmen.

The progress of Peru has been greatly retarded by its vicious administration of government. Monopolies of every kind have been established. A monopoly of navigating the coasts and ports of Peru in steam vessels has been granted for ten years to Mr. Wheelwright.

* McGregor, 1091.—We have adopted his language.

EXPORTS, PERU—1839, 1840.

	1839.	1840.
Bark	$50,327	117,999
Bullion, &c.	6,554,141	7,810,746
Chinchilla	11,016	9,648
Copper, &c.	91,089	105,210
" in bars	14,637	21,318
Cotton	371,800	429,444
Hides	6,859	19,090
Horns	320	—
Seal Skins	556	—
Saltpetre	299,152	454,712
Sugar	52,150	—
Tin	61,867	64,948
Wool—vicuna	752	910
" sheep's	252,082	295,208
" alpaca	397,650	412,500
Total Exports	$8,164,349	9,741,733

IMPORTS INTO PERU—1840.

From France	$1,450,000
" Great Britain	6,150,000
" United States	1,400,000
" Canton and Manilla	300,000
" Germany	300,000
" Spain and Cuba	300,000
" Italy	200,000
Total	$10,100,000

Uruguay, or Monte Video, has an undulating and fertile soil, with a temperate climate. The rains fall almost entirely during the winter months. Pasturage, rather than cultivation, characterizes the lands. The exports are hides, skins, hair, horns and jerked beef. The city of Monte Video contains 20,000 inhabitants. The chief trade of Monte Video is with Europe and Havana. In consequence of the siege and blockade of the town, no exports were made in 1844, &c.

IMPORTS OF MONTE VIDEO—1835.

	Dollars Currency.
From England	993,954
" France	351,602
" Buenos Ayres	275,935
" Brazil	706,428
" United States	333,811
" Bremen	17,402
" Hamburg	33,472
" Mediterranean	352,245
" Portugal	12,720
" Chili	14,702
" Spain	3,127
Total	$3,095,398

Patagonia and the adjacent islands are in the extreme south of South America. The Indians are tall and bulky, averaging, it is said, six feet, though very exaggerated notions of these tall savages were once circulated and believed. They live under petty chiefs, who are possessed of but little authority. The Spaniards settled, in 1779, Port St. Julian, but speedily abandoned it. The coasts are not often visited by other than whaling ships. Little in this barbarous and almost unexplored country can be worthy of mention.

AMERICA.—CENTRAL.

—— "Declined to dust!
But where they dwelt, the vast and sumptuous pile
Bespeaks the pageant of the splendid trust.
Their sceptre broken and their sword in rust,
Have yielded to the stranger: Empty halls
* * * * * * *
To meditate amongst decay——
—— There to track
Fallen states and buried greatness; o'er a land
Which *was!* ——"

In the antiquities of our own country, how much is there to excite the deepest interest and the most profound speculation. But yet, how prone are we to wander away from the things which are familiar, discarding them as worthless, to fall into ecstacies and wonder in regard to those afar off, and around which the "enchantment" of "distance" hangs alluringly. If we can but wander to Palmyra, or by the Nile, there is at once an acme in the enthusiasm and frenzy of our natures. The noble dead, as of a hundred generations, seem crowding around us; they speak in marble and in monument; in hieroglyphic and in ruin. There comes an inspiration with that language. All feel it.

Alas! the *old* world, with its hallowed associations and memories, has been admired and mourned, and sung by genius and poetry, and romance, for generations and generations. But where is the pen and the pencil that have seized upon the marvels of the *new* world, explored them eagerly, and traced in living colors the memorials of its myriad and *unknown dead*? A gloomy curtain hangs over all the past. We see nothing, and we know nothing behind. We seek in vain to remove that curtain. But fancy, and conjecture, and reason, will not be still. There are monuments which betoken an antiquity, and a far back antiquity, of which all other evidence is lost. We are pointed to men, and heroes, and nations, gone forever from the spots we inhabit! They were not as we, yet were they not less, perhaps, in many exalted characteristics. A giant race of animals were contemporary, of which there remain to us but the fossil bones. Who were these men—whence did they emanate—what is their antiquity—how their civilization, arts and progress—in what manner has the sun of empire and existence set upon them forever? What lessons might this antiquity teach, but what know we of it all? Yet we wander away to Greece and to Rome to hunt after dead men and their works! Dead men and nations, and their works, are scattered every where around us, unheeded, we had almost said, contemned.

With the map of *Central America* extended upon the table, for it is to this particular field we are to confine ourselves now, it would be impossible not to fall into something like the train of thought with which our paper opens. We have only to regret that space and time prevent its indulgence to the extent our humor inclines. The reader will run far beyond the meagre limits of our sketch.

Central America, or Guatemala, extends from about 8 to 18° north latitude, and 82 to 94 west longitude. The area, including the Mosquito territory, previously described by us,* is 120.000 square miles. Mexico, Honduras, New-Granada and the oceans bound it.

We shall sketch the antiquities, as they are called, of this region, and then descending to the present times, describe the appearance of the country, the soil, climate, population and resources.

Central America has been explored by M. Dupaix, Del Rio, M. Waldeck, and our own countryman, Mr. Stephens, whose lately published volumes upon the subject have been received with extraordinary interest throughout the world, and have been universally read and admired. None of these travelers, however, claim to have more than penetrated the crust, whilst the deep bowels remain as for ages undisturbed. Whole regions have been but slightly and imperfectly scanned. What new wonders they may reveal, may be conjectured from past results. Is it improbable the key will yet be found? The pyramids which were dumb to Homer and Herodotus—to the men who gazed stupidly upon them for ages—have been taught to speak a language, at last, a child might understand. The Rosetta stone may exist here too.

In reference to this point, Mr. Stephens relates an extraordinary statement, made to him by a certain *padre*, about the truth of which he does not seem in any degree faithless. The reader may receive it with as much allowance as he pleases.

"The *padre* asserted, that four days on the road to Mexico, on the other side of the great Sierra, was a living city, large and populous, occupied by Indians, precisely in the same state as before the discovery of America. He had heard of it many years before at the village of Chajul, and was told by the villagers that from the topmast ridge of the Sierra, the city was distinctly visible. He was then young, and with much labor climbed to the naked summit of the Sierra, from which, at the height of ten or twelve thousand feet, he looked over an immense plain, extending to Yucatan and the Gulf of Mexico, and saw, at a great distance, a large city spread over a great space, and with turrets white and glittering in the sun. The traditionary accounts of the Indians at Chajul, is that no white man has ever reached this city; that the inhabitants speak the Maya language; are aware that a race of strangers have conquered the whole country around, and murder any white man who attempts to enter their territory. They have no coin or circulating medium; no horses, cattle, mules, or domestic animals, except fowls, and the cocks they keep under ground to prevent their crowing being heard.

"If he is right, a place is left where Indians and an Indian city exist, as Cortez and Alvarado found them. There are living men who can solve the mystery that hangs over the ruined cities of America, perhaps who can go to Copan and read the inscriptions on its monuments. No subject more attractive and exciting presents itself to my mind, and the deep impression of that night will never be effaced.

"Can it be true—being now in my sober senses? I do verily believe there is much ground to suppose that what the padre told us is authentic. That the region referred to does not acknowledge the government of Guatemala—has never been explored—and that no white man ever pretends to enter it, I am satisfied. From other sources we heard that from that Sierra, a large ruined city was visible; and we were told by another person, who had climbed to the top of the Sierra, but on account of the dense cloud resting upon it, had been unable to see anything. At all events, the belief at the village of Chajul is general, and a curiosity is roused that burns to be satisfied."

The ruins of Central America have been thus distributed:

1. *Ruins of Copan.*—These are in a fertile valley, and are on the banks of a small stream called the Copan, tributary to the Motagna. They extend along the river two miles. The temple here discovered is over six hundred feet fronting the river, and from sixty to ninety feet high. It is made of hewn stones, three to six feet long. Ranges of steps rise upon the sides.

"Of the moral effect of the monuments themselves," says Mr. Stephens, "standing as they do in the depths of a tropical forest, silent and solemn, strange in design, excellent in sculpture, rich in ornament, different from the works of any other people—their uses and purposes, their whole history so entirely unknown, with hieroglyphics explaining all, but perfectly unintelligible, I shall not pretend to convey an idea. The tone which pervades the ruins is that of deep solemnity. An imaginative mind might be infected with superstitious feelings. From constantly calling them by that name in our intercourse with the Indians, we regarded these solemn memorials as idols—objects of adoration and ceremonial worship."

2. *Ruins of Quirigua.*—These are a pyramidal structure, similar to the temple, but much smaller, and a colossal head six feet in diameter. Other monuments exist, even larger than those of Copan. Mr. Stephens, quoted by Mr. McGregor, for we have not his work before us, and have not read it for several years, says:

"Of one thing there is no doubt, a large city once stood there; and except for a notice taken from Mr. C.'s notes, and inserted by the Senors Payes in a Guatemala paper after the visit, which found its way to this country and Europe, no account of its existence has ever before been published. For centuries it has lain as completely buried as if covered with the lava of Vesuvius. Every traveler from Yzabal to Guatemala has passed within three hours of it—we ourselves had done the same—and yet there it lay, like the rock-built city of Edom, unvisited, unsought, and utterly unknown."

3. *Ruins of Palenque.*—These, it is said, were first discovered by a party of Spaniards,

* See Commercial Review, vol. v. Art. *West India Islands, &c.*

as early as 1750; but the fact was not known in Europe until the publication of Dupaix's work.

"The Indians and people of Palenque say, that they cover a space of sixty miles. In a series of well-written articles in our own country, they have been set down as ten times larger than New-York; and lately I have seen an article in some of the newspapers referring to our expedition, which represents the city discovered by us as having been three times as large as London!

"The Indians and inhabitants of Palenque really know nothing of the ruins personally, and the other accounts do not rest upon any sufficient foundation. The whole country, for miles around, is covered with a dense forest of gigantic trees, with a growth of bush and underwood unknown in the wooded deserts of our own country, and impenetrable in any direction, except by cutting a way by a *Machete*. What lies buried in the forest, it is impossible to say, of my own knowledge; without a guide, we might have gone within a hundred feet of all the buildings without discovering one of them. Captain Del Rio, the first explorer with men and means at command, states in his report, that in the execution of his commission, he cut down and burnt all the woods. He does not say how far, but, judging from the breaches and excavations made in the interior of the buildings, probably for miles around. Captain Dupaix, acting under a royal commission, and with all the resources such a commission would give, did not discover any more buildings than those mentioned by Del Rio, and we saw only the same; but having the benefit of them as guides, at least of Del Rio, for at that time we had not seen Dupaix's work, we of course saw things which escaped their observation, just as those who come after us will see what escaped ours.

"The palace in which Mr. Stephens resided," he says, "stands on an artificial elevation of an oblong form, 40 feet high, 310 feet front and rear, and 260 feet on each side. The elevation was formerly faced with stone, which has been thrown down by the growth of trees, and its form is hardly distinguishable.

"The building stands with its face to the east, and measures 228 feet front by 180 deep. Its height is not more than 25 feet, and all around it had a broad projecting cornice of stone. The front contains 14 doorways, about nine feet wide each, and the intervening piers are between six and seven feet wide. On the left, in approaching the palace, eight of the piers have fallen down, as also has the corner on the right, and the terrace underneath is crumbled with the ruins. But six piers remain entire, and the rest of the front is open.

"Another portion was inclosed by a richly ornamented border, about ten feet wide and six high, of which only a part now remains. The principal personage stands in an upright position, and in profile, exhibiting an extraordinary facial angle of about forty-five degrees. The upper part of the head seemed to have been compressed and lengthened, perhaps by the same process employed upon the heads of the Choctaw and Flat-head Indians of our own country. The head represents a different species from any now existing in that region of country; and supposing the statutes to be images of living personages, or the creations of artists according to their ideas of perfect figures, they indicate a race of people now lost and unknown. The head-dress is evidently a plume of feathers; over the shoulders is a short covering, decorated with studs and a breast-plate; part of the ornament of the girdle is broken; the tunic is probably a leopard's skin; and the whole dress, no doubt, indicates the costume of this unknown people. He holds in his hand a staff or sceptre, and opposite his hands are the marks of three hieroglyphics, which have decayed or broken off. At his feet are two naked figures seated cross-legged, and apparently suppliants. The hieroglyphics doubtless tell its story. The stucco is of admirable consistency, and hard as stone. It was painted, and in different places about it we discovered the remains of red, blue, yellow, black, and white.

"The piers, which are still standing, contained other figures of the same general character, but which, unfortunately, are more mutilated, and from the declivity of the terrace, it was difficult to set up the camera lucida in such a position as to draw them.

"The piers which have fallen are, no doubt, enriched with the same ornaments. Each one has some specific meaning; and the whole, probably, presented some allegory or history; and when entire and painted, the effect in ascending the terrace must have been imposing and beautiful.

"The whole court-yard was overgrown with trees, and it was incumbered with ruins several feet high, so that the exact architectural arrangements could not be seen.

"About a mile and a half from the village, we came to a range of elevations extending to a great distance, and connected by a ditch, which had evidently formed the line of fortifications for the ruined city. They consisted of the remains of stone buildings, probably towers, the stones well cut and laid together, and the mass of rubbish around abounded in flint arrow-heads. Within this line was an elevation which grew more imposing as we approached—square, with terraces, and having in the centre a tower, in all 120 feet high. We ascended by steps to three ranges of terraces, and on the top entered an area, inclosed by stone walls and covered with hard cement, in many places still perfect. Thence we ascended by stone steps to the top of the tower, the whole of which was formerly covered with stucco, and stood as a fortress at the entrance of the great city of Utalan, the capital of the Quichi Indians.

"This was the first appearance of strangers in Utalan, the capital of the great Indian kingdom, the ruins of which were now under our eyes, once the most populous and opulent city out of the whole kingdom of Guatemala."

In regard to the antiquity of the ruins every where so profusely scattered through out Central America, speculations have multiplied, as is most natural. Different views have been held and abandoned. The subject is as yet involved in doubt and incertitude, though so far as the researches of Mr. Stephens extend, they seem to have satisfied his mind, that the vast cities, and towns, and monuments discovered, were the workmanship and habitations of the people conquered by the Spaniards, and not of any former and obliterated nation. We give his views upon this point:

"My opinion on this question has been fully and freely expressed, that they are not the works of people passed away and whose history is lost, but of the same race who inhabited the country at the time of the Spanish conquest, or of some not very distant progenitors. Some were probably in ruins; but, in general, I believe that they were occupied by the Indians at the time of the Spanish invasion. The grounds of this belief are interspersed throughout these pages; they are interwoven with so many facts and circumstances, that I do not recapitulate them; and, in conclusion, I shall only refer briefly to those arguments which I consider the strongest that are urged against this belief.

"The first is the entire absence of all traditions. But, I may ask, is this not accounted for by the unparalleled circumstances which attended the conquest and subjugation of

Spanish America? Every captain or discoverer, on first planting the royal standard on the shores of a new country, made proclamation according to a form drawn up by the most eminent divines and lawyers in Spain, the most extraordinary that ever appeared in the history of mankind, entreating and requiring the inhabitants to acknowledge and obey the Church as the superior and guide of the Universe, the holy father called the Pope, and His Majesty as king and sovereign lord of these islands and of the *terra firma;* and concluding, 'but if you will not comply, or maliciously delay to obey my injunction, then, with the help of God, I will enter your country by force; I will carry on war against you with the utmost violence; I will subject you to the yoke of obedience to the Church and king; I will take your wives and your children, and make them slaves, and sell or dispose of them according to His Majesty's pleasure; I will seize your goods, and do you all the mischief in my power, as rebellious subjects, who will not acknowledge or submit to their lawful sovereign; and I protest, that all the bloodshed and calamities which shall follow are to be imputed to you, and not to His Majesty, or to me, or the gentlemen who serve under me.'

"The conquest and subjugation of the country were carried out in the unscrupulous spirit of this proclamation. The pages of the historian are dyed with blood; and, sailing on the crimson stream, as master pilot at the helm, appears the leading, stern, and steady policy of the Spaniards, surer and more fatal than the sword, to subvert all the institutions of the natives, and to break up and utterly destroy all the rites, customs, and associations, that might keep alive the memory of their fathers and their ancient condition.

"The graves cry out for the old historian, and the mouldering skeletons of cities confirm Herrera's account of Yucatan, that 'there were so many and such stately stone buildings, that it was amazing. And the greatest wonder was, that having no use of any metals, they were able to raise such structures, which seem to have been temples, for their houses were all of timber, and thatched.' And again he says, 'for the space of twenty years there was such plenty throughout the country, and the people multiplied so much, that men said the whole province looked like one town.'"

Let us now, from the unknown, proceed to the known, and take a practical view of Central America as it is presented at the present day.

The valley countries are fertile, and there are mountain elevations of from 5 to 13,000 feet. The coasts on both oceans are unhealthy. The climate varies. According to McGregor it freezes on the highest table-lands in winter. At Guatemala the dry season extends from November until June. The other months are rainy and stormy. The thermometer ranges between 56° the lowest and 86° the highest. On the Pacific the temperature is hotter and healthier than on the Atlantic. The population has been estimated as 1,500,000: viz., 125,000 European races, 500,000 mixed, 875,000 Indians. There are mines of gold, silver, iron, lead, and mercury. They are much neglected. Jasper and marble are worked. Brimstone and salt are collected. Forests of valuable woods abound. The trees are sometimes 35 feet in circumference, and 90 in height. There are very large lakes. The rivers are numerous, but short. Mr. Stephens has a most interesting description of the *Usumasinta,* the largest river of Central America.

On the banks of the River Dulce is a small town called *Yzabel. San Juan* is at the mouth of the river of the same name, and receives its produce, hides, indigo, &c. *Omoa* receives goods destined for *Guatemala,* and *St. Salvador. Comayagna, Tegucigalpa,* and *Truxillo,* are in the province of Honduras; the last named has 4,000 inhabitants.

New Guatemala, the capital of Central America, is on an undulating plain, 4,961 feet above the level of the sea. The houses are low and stout, from the danger of earthquakes, and contain a population of 40,000. The city is famed for its religious celebrations. "The processions, in honor of the Virgin and others, are frequent. All the streets, through which the processions pass, are strewn with pine leaves, and adorned with arches decorated with evergreens and flowers. From the long balconies and windows are displayed curtains of crimson silk, and flags with various devices. At the corners are erected altars within huge arbors of evergreens, and in these altars pictures and silver ornaments, borrowed from the churches, are conspicuous, and surmounted with flowers. The plain, or the valley of Guatemala, is pre-eminent for the variety and brilliancy of its floral kingdom. These flowers are in profusion devoted to the embellishment of the religious processions."

Old Guatemala is at an elevation of 5,817 feet. It was the capital, but was destroyed by an earthquake in 1773. The old inhabitants and their descendants cling to the ruins, and are in number 15,000.

Mr. Stephens says :—

"On each side were the ruins of churches, convents and private residences, large and costly, some lying in masses, some with fronts still standing, richly ornamented with stucco, cracked and yawning, roofless, without doors and windows, and trees growing inside above the walls. Many of the houses have been repaired. The city is partly repeopled, and presents a strange appearance of ruin and recovery. The inhabitants, like the dwellers over the buried Herculaneum, seemed to entertain no fears of renewed disaster. The great volcanoes of Agua and Fuego look down upon it. In the centre of the plaza there is a large stone fountain, and it is surrounded by magnificent buildings. The former palace of the Captain-General, displaying the armorial bearings granted by the Emperor Charles V., the 'loyal and noble city,' and surmounted by a statue of St. James, on horseback, armed and brandishing a sword, and the roofless and dilapidated cathedral, a vast edifice 300 feet long, 120 broad, nearly 70 feet high, and lighted by 50 windows, are monuments which tell us that La Antigua was one of the most superb cities of America, and to which Alvarado gave the name of '*The City of St. James of Gentlemen.*'"

Totonicapan contains a population of 12,000, and manufactures earthenware, utensils, woolen cloths, &c. *Quezaltenango* contains 140,000, with some coarse manufactures. *Coban* has 14,000. *Salame*, 5,000. *Gualan*, 10,000. Mr. Stephens describes the last:—

"Towards evening we strolled through the town. It stands upon a table of breccia rock at the junction of two noble rivers, and is encircled by a belt of mountains. One principal street, the houses of one story, with piazzas in front, terminates in a plaza or principal square, at the head of which stands a large church with a gothic door, and before it, at a distance of ten or twelve yards, was a cross of about 20 feet high. The population is about 10,000, chiefly mestizoes. Leaving the plaza, we walked down to the motagua; on the bank a boat was in process of construction, about fifty feet long and ten wide, entirely of mahogany; near to it a party of men and women were fording the stream, carrying their clothes above their heads, and around a point three women were bathing. There are no ancient associations connected with this place, but the wildness of the scene, the clouds, the tints of the sky and the setting sun reflected upon the mountains, were beautiful. At dark we returned to our house. Except for the companionship of some thousands of ants, which blackened the candles and covered everything perishable, we had a room to ourselves. Early in the morning we were served with chocolate and a small roll of sweet bread. Towards evening the whole town was in commotion, preparatory to the great fête of Santa Lucia. Early next morning, the firing of muskets, petards and rockets announced the arrival of this lady, one of the holiest saints of the calendar, and next to San Antonio, the most renowned for working miracles."

Realejo is a seaport on the Pacific, and exports mahogany, cedar, &c., to Peru and Chili. The harbor is most capacious. *Leon* is the capital of the State of Nicaragua; and, from a population of 30,000, has greatly declined. The population, in 1820, was 14,000.

"In walking through its streets," says Mr. Stephens, "I observed palaces in which nobles had lived, dismantled and roofless, and occupied by half starved wretches, pictures of misery and want, and on one side an immense field of ruins, covering half the city. I must confess that I felt a degree of uneasiness in walking the streets of Leon that I never felt in any city of the East. My change of dress did not make my presence more acceptable, and the eagle on my hat attracted particular attention. At every corner was a group of scoundrels who stared at me as if disposed to pick a quarrel. With some my official character made me an object of suspicion, for in their disgraceful fights they thought that the eyes of the whole world were upon them, and that England, France and the United States were secretly contending for the possession of their interesting country."

Seba and *Valladolid* are unimportant. In the neighborhood of *Tegucigalpa* are mines of gold, silver, copper and iron. *St. Salvador* has 16,000 inhabitants, who are industrious, and manufacture iron and cotton. In the vicinity of *St. Vincent* are plantations of indigo and tobacco. *St. Miguel* is noted for its fairs. *Sacatecoluca* contains 8,000 inhabitants. Fancy shell-work is manufactured at *Sonzonante*, on the banks of the Rio Grande, and exported. Sugar is also grown in the neighborhood, and exported. *Aguachappa* has 8,000 population. In the vicinity of *Santa Anna* are plantations of indigo and the best sugar; also, iron mines which are worked. *Metapa*, *Managua* and *Masaya* are unimportant. *Granada*, on the banks of the Nicaragua Lake, has 14,000 inhabitants. Cacao is raised about the city of *Nicaragua*. *Segovia* and *Comitan* are small towns.

The roads through Central America are execrable.

The agricultural productions are various. Wheat, barley and fruits abound on the table-lands. Indian corn is the principal article of food. Rice is grown. Sugar-cane, indigo, cochineal, tobacco and cotton are widely cultivated. Mr. Stephens describes a hacienda or estate engaged in producing cochineal.

"In the yard were four oxen grinding sugar-cane, and behind was the *nopol*, or cochineal plantation, one of the largest in the Antigua. The plant is a species of cactus, set out in rows like Indian corn; and at the time I speak of, it was about four feet high. On every leaf was pinned with a thorn a piece of cane, in the hollow of which were thirty or forty insects. These insects cannot move, but breed, and the young crawl out and fasten upon the leaf; when they have once fixed, they never move; a light film gathers over them, and as they feed, the leaves become mildewed and white. At the end of the dry season some of the leaves are cut off and hung up in a store-house for seed, the insects are brushed off from the rest and dried, and are then sent abroad to minister to the luxuries and elegance of civilized life, and enliven with their bright colors the saloons of London, Paris, and St. Louis in Missouri. The crop is valuable but uncertain, as an early frost may destroy it; and sometimes all the workmen of the hacienda are taken away for soldiers at the moment when they are most needed for its culture. The situation was ravishingly beautiful, at the base and under the shade of the Volcano de Agua, and the view was bounded on all sides by mountains of perpetual green; the morning air was soft and balmy, but pure and refreshing. With good government and laws, with one's friends around, I never saw a more beautiful spot on which man could desire to pass his allotted time on earth."

Immense herds of cattle are reared in the pasture lands. Manufactures are, of course, in a primitive state. A cotton factory is described near Realejo, built by an American, and owned by another, from which something was anticipated.

"Of the trade and navigation of this country," says Mr. McGregor, "no statistical account can be obtained. Small vessels from the West Indies and the United States, and occasionally from Europe, frequent the coast, and carry on a trade chiefly contraband in consequence of the pernicious system of high duties, which the government of the day, in some mischievous form or other, has attempted to establish. Vessels from the western coast of America also land various articles. Costa Rica has separated from the other states. Salvador may also be said to act independently. Guatamala is still under the sway of the Indian Carrera. Nicaragua has its separate misrule, and Honduras has published its distinct administration and custom laws. The tonnage duties for anchorage are four reals, or about two shillings per ton for native vessels, and double that amount for foreign vessels. These were the rates established in 1837 for all the other states. Export duties, as well as import, are also attempted to be levied, but at such irregular and changeable rates, that we have not been able to procure correct data to enable us to give tabular statements, or tariff, for any of the states of Central America.

ALABAMA.—Its History, Progress, Resources, etc.—The thrilling and romantice, yet terribly fatal adventures of De Soto, introduced the European for the first time to the wilds of Alabama. After a long and disastrous march through Florida and Alabama, the once splendid cavalcade of this heroic yet fated chieftain arrived by the waters of the beautiful Coosa. The far-famed province of this name extended over three hundred miles, and embraced the present counties of Cherokee, Benton, Talladega, and Coosa. The chief of Coosa met the warrior, riding in a chair, supported upon the backs of several of his people in great state, and extended to him the hospitalities of the town. He even invited the Spaniards to settle in the country, professing a friendship which covered and concealed the most deadly and implacable hostility. From Coosa the expedition advanced towards the Tallapoosa, and eventually to the town of Tallasse. Crossing the Tallapoosa, it advanced towards the residence of the chief, Tuscaloosa, whose son had been dispatched to invite De Soto into his extensive dominions. The haughty chief received the Spaniards without the least expression of admiration or surprise, though with apparent cordiality. His speech was a model of laconic eloquence, and the interview is supposed to have taken place in the present county of Montgomery. The expedition reached soon after the banks of the Alabama, where a fatal disease broke out in the camp, which is said to have been avoided by those who used in their food the ashes of a weed recommended by the Indians. The Mobilian chief was retained in a condition of semi-captivity, but found means with his leading men to plot the destruction of the party of De Soto, which had reached his capital, *Maubilia.* (Mr. Pickett supposes it to have been on the north bank of the Alabama, at a place now called Choctaw Bluffs, about twenty-five miles above the confluence of the Alabama and the Tombigbee.) The description of this town is interesting.

"It stood by the side of a large river, upon a beautiful plain; and consisted of eighty handsome houses, each capacious enough to contain a thousand men. They all fronted a large public square. They were encompassed by a high wall, made of immense trunks of trees, set deep in the ground and close together, strengthened with cross-timbers, and with large vines. A thick mud plaster, resembling handsome masonry, concealed the wood work; while port-holes were abundant, together with towers capable of containing eight men each, at the distance of fifty paces apart. The eastern and western gate opened into the town."

At this place the savages openly threw off the mask, and precipitated themselves upon De Soto, in one of the most terrible and disastrous battles recorded in the annals of history. Ten thousand Mobilians were in arms, with desperate frenzy, and determined, at one blow, to annihilate the ranks of the insolent invaders of their soil. Prodigies of valor were exhibited upon both sides. The Indians fought in the streets, or on the house-tops, and even when hewed down in fearful numbers, uttered no cry for quarter.

"The battle, which now waxed hotter and more sanguinary than ever, cannot be as graphically described as the heroic deeds on either side deserve. Often the Indians drove the troops out of the town, and as often they returned with increased desperation. Near the wall lay a large pool of delicious water, fed by many springs. It was discolored now with blood. Here soldiers fell down to slake the intense thirst created by heat and wounds; and those who were able rose again, and once more pitched into a combat, characterized by the most revolting destruction of human life. For some time the young females joined in the fight, and they now contended, side by side, with the foremost warriors, sharing the indiscriminate slaughter. Heated with excitement, smarting with his wounds, and provoked with the unsubdued fierceness of the natives, De Soto, rushed out alone by the gate, threw himself into his saddle, and charged the town; calling in a loud voice, upon "Our Lady and Santiago," he forced his charger over hundreds of fighting men and women, followed by the brave Wuno Tobar. While opening lanes through the savage ranks, and sprinkling his tracks with blood, he rose, on one occasion, to throw his lance into a gigantic warrior; at that instant a powerful winged arrow went deep into the bottom of his thigh. Unable to extract it or to sit in his saddle, he continued to fight until the end of the battle, standing in his stirrups. Everywhere that mighty son of Spain now gorged upon Alabama blood. His fearless bounds filled the boldest soldier with renewed courage.

"At length the houses were set on fire; and the wind blew the smoke and flames in all directions, adding horror to the scene. The flames ascended in mighty volume! The sun went down, hiding himself from the awful sight! Maubilia was in ruins, and her inhabitants destroyed!"

In this battle, which lasted nine hours, eighty-two Spaniards were slain, or died afterwards from wounds, and forty-five horses perished, an irreparable loss in their condition. The camp equipage, baggage, clothes, medicine, books, armor, pearls, flour, and wine, were consumed in the flames of the burning town. The Mobilians were almost entirely annihilated, their slain being estimated, in one account, at 2,500 ; and in another, at 11,000. The fate of the chief, Tuscaloosa, is involved in doubt.

De Soto had been expecting the vessels of Maldinado to arrive at Pensacola, and learned at Maubilia that they had actually arrived. Notwithstanding this, and the knowledge of a conspiracy among some of the leaders in the camp, to abandon his fortunes, he came to the sudden and desperate resolution, in the crippled and forlorn condition of his followers, to turn his back upon the shipping, and plunge again into the forests of the north. With daring intrepidity he braved the conspirators, and by the mastery of a will and an intelligence, before which the proudest of them were accustomed to bow, he defeated their schemes, whilst yet only in the bud. Thus is it that great natures rise superior to every fortune, making man and the elements alike, and in defiance of rebellious inclinations, subservient to their bidding. Never was a stronger illustration, than that of the heroic De Soto, after the disasters of Maubilia, and in the dense and almost interminable forests of Alabama !

Crossing the Warrior, and interrupted by daily struggles with powerful parties of savages, the expedition reached the Tombigbee, near the county of Lowndes, in the state of Mississippi. The chief of Chickasa met them here, and engaged De Soto to assist him in some of his hostile movements against a neighboring tribe. Quarrels between the Spaniards and the Indians, growing out of the cruelty and oppressions of the former and the cupidity of the latter, soon led to a general outbreak, and an engagement, scarcely less sanguinary and disastrous in its effects than that of Maubilia.

The subsequent fate of De Soto may be briefly told. After the bloody battle of Alabama, which was on the Yazoo River, in the county of Tallahatchie, he crossed the Mississippi, being the first, except, perhaps, De Vaca, to discover its waters —spent a year in wanderings through Arkansas—returning to the Mississippi at the town of Guachaya, below the mouth of the Arkansas River. Here death ended the chapter of his misfortunes, and left history to emblazon his fame, as one of the bravest captains and most extraordinary adventurers that the world has ever known. He sleeps beneath the waters of that great river, which had never before been disturbed by the voices of civilized man, but which has since ministered to the wants of millions and millions of a race more hardy, energetic, and adventurous, than even the Spaniard himself!

"With smiling lips," says Mr. Gayarre, "and serene brow, he cheers his companions, and swears them, one by one, to bear allegiance, in his hands, to Muscoso de Alvarado, whom he designated as his successor. 'Union and perseverance, my friends,' said he, 'as long as the breath of life animates your bodies. Do not falter in the enterprise. Spain expects a richer harvest of glory, and more ample domains for her children.' These are his last words, and then he dies. Blest be the soul of the noble knight, and of the true Christian! Rest his mortal remains in peace within that oaken trunk, scooped by his companions, and by them sunk many fathoms deep in the bed of the Mississippi!"

The aborigines of the Southwest and of Florida are considered by Mr. Pickett as having one common character ; and he has furnished several illustrations, taken from the engravings in the work of Le Moyne. They wore mantles of bark and flax interwoven, ornaments of shell, etc., and in their towns were storehouses, filled with garments of hemp, feathers of every hue, deer, panther, marten, and bear skins, packed in baskets. They strung pearls from the rivers, and shells around their arms, necks, and legs. The chiefs painted their skins in stripes, or punctured with needles and a blackened pigment. Plumes of the eagle feather adorned the head. Their weapons of war, in addition to the bow and arrow, were shields of wood or hides, wooden spears pointed with flint, swords, and Herculean clubs. The declaration of war was made by sticking arrows in the enemy's roads with locks of hair attached. The chief, surrounded by his men, raised the war-cry, which was answered by a thousand voices ; he implored victory from the sun, and sprinkled water, in emblem of the enemy's blood, which was soon to flow. The oracular responses of the people were invoked. The wife of a slain warrior might only marry again after her hair, which she had cut off and sprinkled over his grave, had attained its usual length.

In laying out a town, the Indians first erected a mound, on which was placed the house of the chief and his family. At the foot was a square fronted by the residences of the lesser chiefs. The wigwams of the common people came next in order, etc. The houses were of timber, covered with palm, and straw, or reeds. In the colder latitudes, they were daubed with clay, and summer and winter residences were provided. The chief's house was in one instance 120 feet by 40, and included small buildings like offices. A remarkable temple was found upon the Savannah River at the present Silver Bluff. The length was 100 and the breadth 40 feet. The walls were proportionately high, and the roof covered with a carpeting of split cane. Beautiful plumes, shells, and pearls, were suspended on the inside. The entrance was by three gates, guarded by gigantic and threatening wooden statues, whilst statues of men and women were arrayed around the hill. By the walls were boxes containing the remains of dead chiefs. Chests of valuable pearls, skins, etc., were arranged in the centre, with mantles of feathers, etc. In a storehouse near by was contained copper pikes, bows, arrows, shields, etc., and other implements of warfare.

The Indians planted peas, beans, pumpkins, corn, etc. They made cakes of persimmons, and dug the earth with fish bones, puncturing it with canes for the seed. West of the Mississippi they made fine earthenware and salt. Their canoes were often of the most exquisite workmanship and finish, and were marshaled into fleets. They worshiped the sun, and venerated the moon and certain of the stars, and even the chief, by the cruel sacrifice of the first born male child. The doctor cured his patient by sucking out the blood and spurting it into a bowl from which nursing women were accustomed to drink, if the subject were young and athletic. Sometimes the patient was smoked with tobacco and weeds to produce perspiration.

Should the reader desire to become more familiar with the manners and customs of the southern Indians, and more especially of that extraordinary people, the Natchez, he will find the fullest details in the work of Mr. Gayarre, to which we refer him. The third lecture of the second part of this work is one of the most graphic and eloquent, and deeply interesting contributions to Indian history anywhere to be met with. Indeed, we have often desired to extract it entire in our pages.

At the time of De Soto, Alabama was inhabited by the Coosas, Tallasses, Mobilians, and Choctaws. Being nearly destroyed by his invasion, their places were filled by the Muscogees and Alabamas, who were of Mexican origin, and were driven out of that country by Cortez. Wandering a long time in the wilderness, the Muscogees reached at last and settled upon the banks of the Ohio, almost to the Wabash. They had previously met and vanquished the Alabamas, driving them to the Yazoo, whence they again drove them to the shores of the Alabama, near the confluence of the Coosa and the Tallapoosa. Further pressed by the warlike Muscogees, the unfortunate Alabamas were dispersed a third time, and sought an asylum among the Choctaws and other tribes, whilst the Mucogees overspread Georgia to the banks of the Savannah. Receiving at last into their bosom the relics of the Alabamas, the Tookabatches, the Tuskegees, who were allowed to occupy the forks of the Coosa and the Tallapoosa, the Ozeallies, the Uchees, and fugitives of the Natchez, after the terrible massacre of the French, the Muscogee confederacy increased in strength and power until it became the most formidable in the country, receiving the name of Creek, from the number of beautiful rivers and streams meandering through its limits.

The authorities relied upon by Mr. Pickett for this Indian history are the work of Le Clerc Milfort, who long lived among the Creeks, having married the sister of McGillivray, their great chieftain; the work of Hawkins; Adair's History of the Indians; Notes of Mr Compere, a Missionary among the Creeks; several old manuscripts and conversations with old settlers and traders. The Big Warrior, in 1822, confirmed the accounts to Mr. Compere: "My ancestors were a mighty people. After they reached the waters of the Alabama, and took possession of the country, they went further—conquered the tribes upon the Chattahoochie, and upon all the rivers from thence to the Savannah—yes, and even whipped the Indians then living in the territory of South Carolina, and wrested much of their country from them."

We have only space to note a few of the peculiarities of the Creeks. Before the consummation of marriage, it was necessary that the husband should have built a house, produced and gathered a crop, made a hunt and brought home game, and tendered the whole to the girl; a good rule, which our civilized race might very well adopt. Divorce was *ad libitum*, and both could marry again, though the woman only after the green corn dance was over. Marriage gave no right over the possessions of the wife, or the children she might have. Adultery was punished with many stripes, whoever was the guilty party; the friends inflicting them, also cutting off their ears, nose, etc., and tearing out the woman's hair. When Bartram visited the nation in 1777, he found fifty towns, containing 11,000 inhabitants, the Muscogee being the national tongue. The general council was always held in the principal town, and was held annually, though each town had its separate legislative system, like the federal system under which we live. The walls of the public buildings were daubed with rude paintings and sculptures, which were as insignificant as writing. The green corn dance, a great national festival, is minutely described by Col. Hawkins, whom Mr. Pickett copies at length. The martial arrangements of the Creeks were peculiar. The great chief, on the opening of war, stuck up in public places a partly red stick, and sent to each subordinate as many pieces of sticks as days that must elapse before his presenting himself for service. These latter called up the warriors with the drum, informed them of the rallying place, and the combatants were chosen from those who were the first to arrive, it being some disgrace to arrive too late, to fill up the required number. The warriors then took the "medicine of war," and were supplied by their wives with little bags of parched corn, two ounces being sufficient to make a quart of broth, and satisfy a man for twenty-four hours. This medicine of war was a liquor supposed to possess a virtue in guarding the drinker from all dangers. The "great medicine" secured entire invulnerability, whilst the "little medicine" only diminished the extent of danger. Being purgatives, they may be supposed to have had some slight effect in lessening the danger of wounds. In their marches, each warrior placed his foot in the print of the warrior before him, so as to conceal a knowledge of their numbers, and the last of the party carefully concealed even that print.

Col. Pickett devotes a chapter to the history of the Choctaws, Chickasas and Cherokees. The two former were descended from the Chickemicaws, early emigrants from Mexico, (according to Adair,) who crossed the Mississippi, and inhabited the regions of the Yazoo, the Tombigbee and the Alabama. This account of their origin the Choctaws had lost, believing they had emerged originally from a big hole in a great mound on the road from St. Stephens, in Alabama, to Jackson, Mississippi. The Cherokees were originally settlers of Virginia and Carolina, and can be traced no further, having been driven westward by the whites.

Various relics of the aborigines still exist upon the soil of Alabama. The mounds, though attributed by some to an origin anterior to that of the Indians, our author thinks are chiefly the work of their hands. It is known positively that the Natchez constructed them as late as 1730. In Alabama they are found upon the Tennessee, Coosa, Tallapoosa, Alabama, Cahaba, Warrior, and Tombigbee rivers; and upon being opened, are found to contain bones, stone ornaments, pottery, and sometimes copper and silver ornaments, layers of charcoal, ashes, etc. The practice of erecting a tumulus or mound over the dead has been common to most countries. In some cases, piles of stones were adopted instead, which perhaps accounts for their appearance in many parts of Georgia and Alabama. The ditches which have been discovered at Cahaba, at the falls of Little River, etc., are also thought by Mr. Pickett to be of Indian origin, contrary to the general belief of writers, and intended for purposes of defence. He thinks, at Cahaba there existed an Indian establishment, fortified with palisades, and that the ditch was cut around them. The ditch at Talladega Springs, which formerly had trees growing in it, surrounds an elevation of many acres, embracing a beautiful gushing spring. At Little River are four or five small caves which have been called "De Soto's Rock Houses," from the fact that they exhibit the marks of intelligent occupation. The walls have been smoothed by the hands of man. We give the language of the author:

"It was doubtless a strong Indian fortification, and long used as a safe retreat when the valleys below were overrun with a victorious enemy. The walls were black with smoke, and everything about them bears evidence of constant occupation for years. These caves, or rock-houses, constituted a most admirable defence, especially with the assistance of the walls at the head of the peninsula. In order to get into the first cave, a person has to pass along a rock passage, wide enough only for one man. Below him, on his right, is the awful precipice, and on his left the rock wall, reaching ten feet above his head. A few persons in the first rock-house with swords and spears could keep off an army of one thousand men; for only one assailant being able to approach at a time, could be easily dispatched and tumbled down the abyss below. In regard to the inner walls of the ditches, the author saw no cement among the rocks, although he had heard that that ingredient (never used by Indians) was to be found there."

The cuttings upon rocks, etc., seen in various parts of Alabama, the author attributes also to the Indians, who used the pieces for the fabrication of pipes, mortars, bowls, etc. These cuttings are especially noticeable near the Tallapoosa River, and Elyton, in the county of Jefferson. We shall not undertake to decide such antiquarian questions, but leave the reader to work them out with the volume of Squier before him, which Mr. Pickett appears to have freely consulted.

We now come to the period when the French began to occupy Alabama. Bienville, who is, in truth, the father of Louisiana, and should have a monument at the mouth of its great river, departed with a force from Dauphin Island, sailed up the bay of Mobile, and at the mouth of Dog River commenced to built a fort, warehouse, and other buildings. This was in 1702, and seventeen years before the founding of New-Orleans! The site of Mobile was, however, removed nine years later to the mouth of the Mobile River, higher up the Alabama, where it now stands.

"The high floods having inundated the settlements around Fort St. Louis de Mobile, Bienville determined to place his people upon more elevated ground. All the inhabitants, except the garrison of the fort, removed upon the Mobile River, where, upon the site of the present beautiful and wealthy commercial emporium of Alabama, they established themselves. Here Bienville built a new wooden fort, which, in a few years, was destroyed, to give place to an extensive fortress of brick, called in French times, Fort Condé, and in English and Spanish times, Fort Charlotte. The seat of government was permanently fixed here, and the leading characters of the colony made Mobile their headquarters. Only a small garrison was left at the old settlement at the mouth of Dog River, which, however, continued to guard that point for several years after this period."

The Carolina and Virginia traders began now to penetrate the western wilds, much to the annoyance and jealousy both of the Spanish and French. Upon the backs of packhorses they carried from Charleston stores of goods, "over creeks without bridges, rivers without ferries, and woods pathless and pregnant with many dangers," opening them upon the Coosa and Tallapoosa. To stop these interferences, Bienville fitted out an expedition to locate a fort upon the Alabama. Passing the towns of Selma and Autauga, his boats were moored at the town of Coosawda. The fort was located at Tuskeegee, a most favorable position; and the cannon which guarded it have become a subject of curious history. After remaining in position fifty years, they were spiked and abandoned with the fortress. During the English possession of Alabama, the cannon remained at Fort Toulouse, though the fort was suffered to fall into decay. Some blacksmiths among the Creeks removed the spikes, and the pieces were then used by the Indians for holiday amusements. On the settlement of Montgomery, the inhabitants brought down from Fort Toulouse, then called Jackson, some of these pieces to be used upon festivals, in which service they were in due time burst. A fragment stands now at Pollard's Corner, in Montgomery. One of the cannon still exists at Rockford, and it is thought that the others are in the bed of the river opposite the fort. The reflections which are made by Mr. Pickett upon the labors of Bienville among the savages, we think, detract from, rather than add to the dignity of the narrative.

Passing over the numerous Indian wars of the colonists, and their contests with the Spaniards, including the whole period of the charter of Crozat and the "Mississippi Company," noticing only the arrival at Mobile, loaded with African slaves, of three French ships of war, (1721,) we arrive at a point when the disasters of the colony forced the abandonment of both Mobile and Biloxi, and produced the most terrible sufferings and mutinies at the post upon the Coosa. We also hurry over the chapter upon the Natchez massacre, which, in common with Mr. Gayarre, the author treats with great clearness and elaboration, adopting almost entirely the letter of Father Petit, published among the letters of the Jesuits, in the work of the Rev. Ingraham Kip, of New-York.

Chapters seven and eight of the history of Alabama treat of the English in Georgia, and of the daring scheme of a Jesuit named Priber, who traveled extensively among the Indians, gaining everywhere their confidence, and who pretended to have in view a confederation of all the southern Indians, for purposes of industry, civilization and freedom from the European yoke. Being arrested, he died in prison at Frederika. Dr. Stevens, in his history of Georgia, describes him as "a thorough Jesuit, an accomplished linguist, a deep tactician, far-sighted in his plans, and far-reaching in his expedients."

Referring to the failure of the French expeditions against the Chickasaws, those early natives of Alabama, Mr. Pickett takes occasion to compliment their gallantry, and to urge upon the rising generation of the state, an imitation of their example, *in the maintenance of their rights and their liberties.* We give the passage entire, p. 352:

"The Chickasaws have never been conquered. They could not be defeated by De Soto, with his Spanish army, in 1541; by Bienville, and his French army, and southern Indians, in 1736; by D'Artaguette, with his French army, and northern Indians; by Marquis De Vaudreueil, with his French troops and Choctaws, in 1752; nor by the Creeks, Cherokees, Kickapoos, Shawnees and Choctaws, who continually waged war against them. No! they were the 'bravest of the brave;' and even when they emigrated to the territory of Arkansas, not many years ago, they soon subdued some tribes who attacked them in that quarter.

"Young men of northwestern Alabama and northeastern Mississippi, remember that the bravest race that ever lived, once occupied the country which you now inhabit—once fished in your streams, and chased the elk over your vast plains! Remember, that whenever that soil which you now tread was pressed by the feet of foes, it was not only bravely defended, but drenched with the blood of the invader. Will you ever disgrace that soil and the memory of its first occupants, by submitting to injustice and oppression, and finally to invasion? We unhesitatingly give the answer for you—No, never!"

The first volume of Mr. Pickett concludes with the delivery of Louisiana and Alabama to the English, under the treaty of 1763, and with some account of the expedition of Bossu into the interior of the country. A single extract furnishes a contrast between Alabama as we find it, and the wlderness out of which it has been so soon created:

"Not only were the Creeks and Alabamas at peace with other nations at this time, but gave evidences of warm and generous hospitality. They thronged the banks of the river, which now meanders along the counties of Autauga, Montgomery, Dallas and Lowndes, and as Bossu slowly made his way up the beautiful stream, greeted him with friendly salutations, offered him provisions, such as bread, roasted turkeys, boiled venison, pancakes baked with nut oil, and deer tongues, together with baskets full of eggs of the fowl and turtle. The Great Spirit had blessed them with a magnificent river, abounding in fish; with delicious and cool fountains gushing out from the foot of the hills; with rich lands, that produced without cultivation, and with vast forests, abounding in game of every description. But now the whole scene is changed. The country is no longer half so beautiful; the waters of Alabama begin to be discolored; the forests have been cut down; steamers have destroyed the finny race; deer bound not over the plain; the sluggish bear has ceased to roam through the swamps; the bloody panther does not spring upon its prey; wolves have ceased to howl upon the hills; birds cannot be seen in the branches of the trees; graceful warriors guide no longer their canoes, and beautiful squaws loiter not upon the plain, nor pick the delicious berries. Now, vast fields of cotton, noisy steamers, huge rafts of lumber, towns reared for business, disagreeable corporation laws, harassing courts of justice, mills, factories, and everything else that is calculated to destroy the beauty of a country, and to rob man of his quiet and native independence, present themselves to our view.

"The heart yearns to behold once more such a country as Alabama was, the first time we saw it, when a boy. But where can we now go, that we shall not find the busy American, with keen desire to destroy everything which nature has made lovely?"

Having treated in sufficient detail of the aboriginal and early French history of Alabama, we pass to that period which opens the second volume of Mr. Pickett, and which marks the advent of the British power in the state.

At the conclusion of the long and bloody wars in Europe, and with the adoption of the pacification of Paris in 1763, France had divested herself of her whole North American interests. The western bank of the Mississippi, from its mouth to its source, but including the island of New-Orleans on the other bank, passed into the hands of Spain; whilst Great Britain succeeded to Canada, all of the territories east of the Mississippi as far south as the Bayou Iberville, together with Florida. The whole of Alabama and Mississippi, and that portion of Louisiana north of a line drawn through the Bayou Iberville, the Amite, Lakes Maurepas and Ponchartrain to the sea, and east of the Mississippi River, became thus a British possession, known until 1781 as West Florida and the province of Illinois. Alabama was divided on the parallel of 32° 28′ between West Florida and Illinois, in nearly equal divisions; and Montgomery and Wetumpka, which are but fifteen miles apart, were in different jurisdictions. The Florida portion only was then in European occupation, having Pensacola as its seat of government.

George Johnson, the first English governor, organized the government, garrisoned the fort at Mobile and that of Toulouse up the Coosa; but the government was purely military. Its earliest history was marked by great sufferings among the English inhabitants of Mobile, who died in great numbers from habits of intemperance, exposure, and a contagious disease introduced by one of the regiments. From these disasters the French residents were spared. They lived a regular and abstemious life—refrained from spirituous liquors in summer, confined themselves to spring water, and for a large part spent the sickly months upon their plantations on the Tensaw and Mobile rivers, which were very healthy. Many of them lived to a great old age. The Chevalier de Lucere had a plantation on the first island below the confluence of the Tombigbee and the Alabama. Other islands on the Tensaw and Mobile were cultivated by the French and English, who spent their summers among the hills, and engaged in the product of tar. Lower down than Lucere's plantation, were those of Campbell, Stewart, Andry, McGillivray, Favre, Chastang, Strother and Narbone. Five miles lower still was the site of an old French fort, and eleven miles lower, the plantation of Mr. Lezars, which had once belonged to the French Intendent of Mobile.

The exports of Mobile in 1772 were indigo, raw hides, corn, fine cattle, tallow, rice, pitch, bear's oil, tar, tobacco, squared timber, indigo seed, myrtle wax, cedar posts and planks, salted wild beef, pecan nuts, cypress and pine boards, plank of various woods, shingles, dried salt fish, scantling, sassafras, canes, staves and heading, hoops, oranges, and peltry. Cotton was cultivated in small quantities; and a machine in use for separating it from the seed is thus described by Capt. Roman, (one of them was used by Mr. Crebs, the alleged inventor, who suspended canvas bags between pine trees, and packed in his cotton by treading down to the extent of 300 pounds.)

"It is a strong frame of four studs, each about four feet high, and joined above and below by strong transverse pieces. Across this are placed two round well-polished spindles, having a small groove through their whole length, and by means of treadles are put in opposite motions. The workman sits behind the frame, with a thin board before him, upon which is placed the cotton, thinly spread, which the rollers receive. The lint goes through the rollers, and the seed falls down into a separate pile. The French population have much improved upon this plan, by a large wheel, which turns two of these mills with so much velocity, that seventy pounds of clean cotton can be made every day."

Fearful gales swept over West Florida, inundating Mobile, and running vessels up into the town. The houses of Mr. Crebs' plantation on the Pascagoula were riddled, trees everywhere prostrated, herds scattered, crops ruined. The sea water was driven up the bays and rivers, whilst the coast and shipping suffered frightfully. The Chandelier island came near being entirely swept away; and what was remarkable, the mulberries all produced a second crop of leaves, budded, blossomed, and bore ripe fruit within four weeks after the gale had subsided.

In the summer of 1777, the botanist, Bartram, made an excursion through Alabama. He describes Mobile as extending back half a mile from the river, with a few good buildings, occupied by the French, or emigrants from England, Scotland, Ireland, and the North American Colonies. Swansan and McGillivray conducted the Indian trade, having commodious storehouses. The French buildings were of brick, one story, square, often very large, and including courts within. The common people lived in cypress frames, filled in with plaster. Mr. Farmer resided near the present Stockton, his extensive plantations lying up and down the Tensaw—surrounded by other thriving plantations, and the ruins of many which the French had abandoned on the change of government. In his journeyings, Bartram met a party of Georgians, nine or ten in number, including women and children, who, after passing through the great hardships of the wilderness, are believed to have been the first Anglo-American inhabitants of Baldwin county.

"Returning to Mobile, the botanist presently embarked in a trading vessel, manned by three negroes, and set sail for Pearl River. Passing along the western coast, and reaching the mouth of Dog River, they there landed, and entered the woods for recreation. Here he saw the remains of the old Fort St. Louis de la Mobile, with a few pieces of iron cannon, and also vast iron kettles for boiling tar into pitch. Pursuing his voyage, he again came to the shore, a few miles beyond where resided a Frenchman eighty years of age; he was active, strong and muscular; his mother, who was present, and who appeared to be brisk and cheerful, was one hundred and five years of age. Fifty years previous to this she had landed in Mobile from la belle France."

The effects of the American Revolution began now to be felt throughout the possessions of Louisiana and of Florida; and Mr. Pickett devotes nearly one whole chapter to the biography and adventures of the family of the McGillivrays, who, in conjunction with the Indians, were severely felt in their sanguinary attacks upon the whigs of Georgia. The chapter is in the most finished style of the author, and is evidently his *chef d'œuvre*. A romantic interest attaches to the whole history of the McGillivrays. Lochlan, the father, a Scotch boy of 16, scampered off from wealthy parents at home and sought the Western World. Without money and scarcely clothes, he landed at Charleston, found himself among the Indian traders who quartered in the suburbs, and soon made one in their adventures. For his services he received a *jack knife*, which being converted into skins to be sold at Charleston, constituted the basis of his afterwards extensive fortune. He became, in the event, one of the boldest and most successful traders, extending his commerce to the very neighborhood of Fort Toulouse. Here he had the address to captivate the heart of a beautiful and aristocratic Indian girl, of the tribe of the Wind—Sehoy Marchand, the daughter of a former French captain at Fort Toulouse. Pickett describes her as a second Pocahontas, though we have always received with grains of distrust these descriptions of Indian beauties, prosy as the remark may be. Of the marriage at a trading-house, near Wetumpka, on the Coosa, sprang Alexander McGillivray, and the tradition goes, that his mother, in pregnancy, dreamed of piles of manuscripts, books, papers, &c., as mothers ever will dream, and fathers, too, pending an event like this. The fortunes of the father prospered; he had plantations and negroes in Georgia, large stores in Savannah and Augusta, &c. When the boy Alexander had reached his fourteenth year, he was placed at school in Charleston, and subsequently in a counting-house at Savannah. Commerce pleased him not so much as books, and he forthwith became a hard and diligent student. But even this could not satisfy the wants of a spirit, which, true to the instincts of its mother race, yearned after the sports and life of the *wilderness*. Civilization had lost all its charms. Alexander McGillivray was again among the Creeks, and by virtue of his noble descent, a chief and a leader. He presided at the national council upon the Chattahoochee, received the rank of colonel from the British of Florida, and thenceforward devoted himself to the royal cause. In 1778, he corresponded extensively with the government of Florida and the province of Georgia, and engaged in the task of confederating the Indians against the colonial cause, acting in concert with many royalists who had fled from the colonies, sometimes leading expeditions in person, but generally relying upon Le Clerk Milfort, a bold and daring adventurer, who subsequently published a work, "*Sejour dans la Nation Creek*," from which, and from contemporaneous manuscripts and conversations with the nephew and niece of McGillivray, Mr. Pickett obtains this information.

Before dismissing the McGillivray chapter, we cannot but condemn the introduction of such a passage as the following into it. History should speak in the language of dignity, having no country, no friends, and no party! We give the passage:

"This brought about a collision with John Bull. Spain interposed her friendly efforts to effect a reconciliation, but the *canine* propensities of England were aroused, and that *ungenerous* government declared war against Spain as well as France," &c.

Now, it so happens, by the way, that these very wars which Mr. Pickett refers to in such terms of ignominy, were advocated by the great and pure Earl of Chatham, who came down from his bed to urge them, and who died almost in the very act of speaking these memorable words: "Shall a people, so lately the terror of the world, now fall prostrate before the House of Bourbon? It is impossible. In God's name, if it is absolutely necessary to declare either for peace or for war, and if peace cannot be preserved with honor, why is not war commenced without hesitation? I am not, I must confess, informed of the resources of this kingdom, but I trust it has still sufficient to maintain its just rights. Any state, my lord, is better than despair. Let us, indeed, make one effort, and if we must fall, let us fall like men."

The origin of the name of Murder Creek, in the County of Conecuh, is explained by Mr. Pickett. Kirkland, an English royalist, who had been on a visit to McGillivray, was, on his return, murdered by a band of Indians. One of them was arrested by Milford, under the orders of McGillivray, and carried back to the bloody spot, where he was executed. The place, ever since, has been known as *Murder Creek*.

Chapter XXI. treats of the deep intrigues of McGillivray, in which the author proves that wily chieftain to have been the very Talleyrand of the western wilds. He baffled all negotiations, and generally succeeded in putting them in the wrong. Caressed by the Spaniards in Florida and Louisiana, obeyed by his own people as well as by many of the Cherokees and the Choctaws, and supplicated by the Federal Congress and Washington, it was not remarkable he became haughty and arbitrary. President Washington having at last succeeded in inducing him to visit the seat of government, made with him and other chiefs a permanent treaty of peace, and received a surrender of the Oconee lands claimed by Georgia, about which so much blood had been shed, and so much negotiation exhausted. By a secret treaty, at the same time, McGillivray was given the rank of brigadier-general, and the pay, as Creek agent, of $1,200 per annum. Mr. Pickett is mistaken when he speaks of the terms of this secret treaty being *now* for the first time made public. We were long ago familiar with them.

The treaty of peace with Great Britain had fixed the southern boundary of the United States from a point of the Mississippi in the 31st parallel of latitude; thus giving to the Americans about two degrees of what was known as West Florida, then in the possession of the Spaniards by conquest. The Spaniards refused to deliver this territory, having again come into possession of the Floridas by the same general treaty of peace, and Mr. Pickett justifies them upon the ground that the British had no right to cede territory which was not in their possession. The negotiations were conducted at Madrid by Mr. Jay and Guardoqui. It is sufficient to say, in reply to Mr. Pickett's argument, that when originally in the hands of Spain, the northern limits of Florida were the 31°—they were so considered by the British, who organized a government on that basis, but afterwards saw fit to enlarge it by annexing territory acquired in the French grant of Canada. Now, when by the 8th article of the British and Spanish treaty, it was stipulated that Spain should surrender to Great Britain all the territories conquered by her, except Florida, is not the construction a fair one that the Florida referred to, *was that which had previously existed in the hands of Spain, and which never extended further north than the* 31*st degree of latitude.* The secretary of the French minister, Vergennes, in his correspondence with Mr. Jay, admitted that Spain held nothing beyond this parallel. He says: "She cannot pass beyond Natchez towards the 31st degree parallel of latitude—her rights are therefore confined to this degree—what is beyond is either independent or belonging to England," (i. e., to the United States under England.)

The State of Georgia considering its title now perfect to all of the lands running westward from her limits to the Mississippi, proceeded to grant them out to companies for the purposes of settlement, on a consideration being paid into her coffers. There were two sets of these grants known as the "Yazoo grants," both of which have acquired a great celebrity in history.

By the first, five millions of acres in Mississippi were granted to the South Carolina Yazoo Company; seven millions to the Virginia Yazoo Company; three and a half millions in Alabama to the Tennessee Company: the first paying $60,000, the second, $93,000, and the third, $46,000. The South Carolina and Tennessee companies, in defiance of the opposition of the federal government, attempted to colonize these grants; but they were finally defeated by that opposition, combined with that of the Indians and the Spaniards who held out in their claim of sovereignty over the country. These companies having failed, however, to meet the instalments upon their purchases, the acts were subsequently rescinded by Georgia.

Several years afterwards, other and more considerable grants were made by Georgia, to wit:

For the sum of $250,000, to James Gunn and others, called the Georgia Company, a tract embracing parts of many of the present wealthiest counties of Alabama and Mississippi, eighteen in Alabama and twenty-one in Mississippi.

For $150,000, to the Georgia Mississippi Company, a tract embracing parts or the whole of two or three of the present counties of Alabama, and thirty-one counties of Mississippi.

For $35,000, to Wade Hampton *et al.* of the Upper Mississippi Company, that part of Mississippi now embraced in the counties of De Soto, Marshall, Tippah, Tishimingo, and part of Tunica.

For $60,000, to the Tennessee Company, a tract in North Alabama, embracing most of the present counties of Lauderdale, Limestone, Madison, Jackson, De Kalb, Cherokee, Marshall, Morgan, Lawrence, Franklin, Marion, Walker, and Blount.

This second Yazoo sale was followed by a storm throughout the country. It was denounced in the message of General Washington, and Congress instructed the attorney general to investigate the titles of Georgia to the territory; but the legislature of that state being convened again, and all of the adherents and supporters of the grants having been defeated before the people upon the allegation of bribery and corruption in the terms of the sales, they were declared null and void, and even the papers upon which they were written consumed by fire, drawn direct, as it were, from heaven, through a sun-glass!

When this matter came before Congress, upon an appeal from the grantees, the celebrated John Randolph crowned himself with imperishable fame by his bold and vigorous assaults upon all of the parties connected with it, constituting himself, for a period of ten years, the very scourge of these men. "No, sir," said he, on one occasion, "the orgies of Yazoo speculation are not to be opened to public view. None but the initiated are to behold the monstrous sacrifice of the best interests of the nation on the altar of corruption. When this abomination is to be practised, we go into conclave," etc.

The following passage from Garland's Life of Randolph, vol. i., p. 67, gives many other interesting particulars in regard to the proceedings upon the Yazoo grants:

"On the 7th day of February, 1795, the Legislature of Georgia passed an act authorizing the sale of four tracts of land therein described, and containing a greater part of the country west of the Alabama River, called the Georgia, the Georgia-Mississippi, the Upper-Mississippi, and the Tennesseean Companies, for which they were to pay $500,000. The land contained within the boundaries of the several companies was estimated at forty millions of acres. The sale of a country so extensive, for a sum so far below its value, excited immediate and universal indignation throughout the State of Georgia. The motives of the legislature were questioned and examined. Then corruption was established upon the most indisputable evidence. Upwards of sixty-four depositions were taken, that developed a scene of villany and swindling unparalleled in the history of any country. On comparing a list of the names of the companies with the names of the persons who voted for the land, it appeared that all the members of the Senate and House of Representatives of Georgia, who voted in favor of the law, were, with one single exception, interested in, and parties to the purchase. Every member who voted for the law received either money or land for his vote. The guardians of the rights of the people united with swindlers, defrauded their constituents, sold their votes, betrayed the delegated trust reposed in them, and basely divided among themselves the lands of the people of Georgia. This flagrant abuse of power —this enormous act of corruption, was viewed with abhorrence by every honest man. The press throughout the country burst out into a blaze of indignation. All the grand juries of the state, except in two counties where there were corrupt majorities of the Yazoo men, presented this law as a public robbery, and a deliberate fraud. The convention which met in the month of May, 1795, at Louisville, was crowded with petitions from every part of the state, which, by an order of convention, was referred to the succeeding legislature. The legislature was elected solely with reference to that question. Repeal or no Repeal! Yazoo or anti-Yazoo! was the only subject canvassed before the people. On the 30th of January, 1796, an act was passed with only three dissenting voices, declaring the usurped act of February, 1795, void, and expunging the same from the public records. At a subsequent meeting, this expunging act was engrafted on the constitution, and made a fundamental law of the land."—*Garland's Randolph*, vol. i., p. 67.

At this period, 1792, Alabama was almost entirely in the occupation of the natives. There was a garrison of Spanish troops at Mobile, and also at St. Stephen's on the Tombigbee, with trading posts upon the Oconee, and on other points at the south and west. A settlement of whigs was located on the Tensaw, to which point several Moungers and others from Georgia directed their journeyings, and found already there the Halls, Byrnes, Mims, Kilkreas, Easlies, Linders, etc. Below McIntosh's Bluff they found the Bates, Lawrences, and Powells; whilst above upon the Tombigbee were the Danbys, Johnsons, McGrews, Hockets, Freelands, Talleys and Bakers; with the Moungers were Col. Kimbil Barnet, Sheffield and Hannon. The representatives of many of these may still be found in Alabama. In addition, there lived upon Little River, between the counties of Monroe and Baldwin, intelligent and wealthy families of mixed white and Indian blood; among whom was a sister of McGillivray, a maiden of fair exterior, won in matrimony afterwards by a Huguenot from South Carolina, Benjamin Durant. There was something romantic in the incident of this alliance. Durant had carried away the palm in his feats of strength, when contesting with the young men of Charleston, and came all the way into the Creek Nation in search of one whom the traders represented as his superior. To meet, was to vanquish him, after a vigorous struggle, of which the dark maid of the Coosa was a witness. Women who love power and *masculine* might, whether in courts or in forests, never dispute the claims of youths like Durant, but are carried captive at once. Well said the author of "Yeast," that strange *melange*—"Ay, be as manichean-sentimental as you will, fair ladies, physical prowess, that Eden right of manhood, is sure to tell upon your hearts." "Durant's Bend," on the Alabama, still preserves his memory, and Lachlan Durant, the son, is a resident of Baldwin County even at this day; and it is recorded by Mr. Pickett, of the mother, that when McGillivray was negotiating his treaty at New-York, the Creeks meditated an attack upon the white settlements, which she defeated by a long ride of four days to the camp of the chiefs, where she threatened them with the vengeance of her brother. This was only two weeks prior to her giving birth to twins. In Montgomery County there lived a white woman, the widow of a soldier, who afterwards took up with a chief, and in time acquired a great deal of wealth. She was long known among the traders, etc., as Milly. A little girl who lived with her, and who had been ransomed by her from the Indians, Tenpey Ellis, now an old lady in Pike, Mrs. Frizell, has been seen and conversed with by Mr. Pickett. Two miles east of Lone Creek was located the trading house of Abram Mordecai, a very remarkable character, whose reminiscences of early Alabama history are most interesting.

Another trader named Russell lived here;

while at Mount Meigs were two tories, Love and Dargan, a Dutchman and a horse thief, generally with Indian wives. Charles Weatherford had a house below the confluence of the Coosa and the Tallapoosa, and laid out in the neighborhood one of the earliest race-courses. A not distant neighbor was Savaner Jack, a wretch whose hand had often been steeped in the blood of the frontier settlers.

A sketch of the early commerce of Alabama will interest our readers. Skins, bees-wax, hickory-nut oil, snake-root, medicinal barks, etc., were transported to Augusta and Pensacola on pack horses, and to Mobile and New-Orleans in large canoes. The horses were, generally, the small ones of the wilderness, capable of great endurance. The load was adjusted upon a peculiar saddle, and consisted of three bundles of sixty pounds each. Two of them were suspended so as to come down the sides of the poney, while the third was laid crosswise on the top. Taffai, a mean rum, was carried in kegs. A pack horse-man drove ten ponies in a lead, urging them on with sticks and imprecations. At night, the packs were taken off, piled together, and covered with skins, and the horses belled, and set free to graze. The Indians seldom disturbed these caravans, which pursued their way through a thousand obstacles, swimming creeks, or crossing upon rafts; but if they reached a stream having large cane on its banks, (we quote from Mr. Pickett):—

"These were presently cut, ten feet long, and tied up into bundles about three feet in circumference, which were placed in the water. Across these others were laid, which formed an admirable raft, capable of sustaining great weight. Logs were also often employed in the construction of rafts. Guided by long grape vines, they were generally dragged safely across, where the wet ponies stood ready to receive their packs again. Then all hands drank taffai, and journeyed on with light hearts and laughing faces. The average travel was twenty-five miles a day.

"The route from Pensacola was a well-beaten path, leading up the country, and across the fatal Murder Creek, and thence to within a few miles of Catoma, whence it diverged into several small trails, one of which led to Tookahatcha, along the route of the old Federal Road, the other to Montgomery and Wetumpka, by the Red Warrior's Bluff, now Grey's Ferry, upon the Tallapoosa; this trail continued to the Tennessee river."

The United States having purchased the rights of Georgia in the western wilds, established the Mississippi territory, which extended from the Chattahoochee to the Mississippi, and from the 31° to 32° 28' latitude, appointing Winthrop Sargent governor. Fort Stoddard was established near the confluence of the Alabama and the Tombigbee, and the County of Washington laid out, embracing a space out of which twenty counties in Alabama and twelve in Mississippi have been subsequently carved. Claiborne succeeded as governor; but many of the distant settlers upon the Tensaw remained without laws, and were in the habit of marrying by "pairing off," as it was called—a convenient way of whipping the devil round the stump;—but the condition always was to have *honest marriage* when the preachers or the magistrates came that way. Poor people, what better could they do? Pickett, who seems to relish a good joke, tells us of one of these hard-pressed couples, who repaired to the house of a rather pompous old German, a commandant under Uncle Sam, and demanded nuptials, the parents being in hot chase. The old captain threw down his pipe, and swore that was a thing not to be found in any of the military books. He yielded at last to entreaties, after this fashion—"I, Captain Shoumberg, of the 2d regiment of the U. S. Army, and commandant of Fort Stoddart, do pronounce you man and wife. Go home—behave yourselves—multiply and replenish the Tensaw country!" The happy pair were pronounced by the whole settlement the *best* married people they had known in a long time. A trading-house was located at St. Stephens. The Brothers Pierce settled upon Lake Tensaw, one as a weaver, and the other as the pioneer American schoolmaster. In the neighborhood were the descendants of McGillivray, the Taits, Weatherfords, and Durants, the Linders, the Mims, etc. The Pierces established also one of the first cotton gins in that part of the country, as also did Abram Mordecai.

"Mordecai was a queer fellow. He traded extensively with the Indians, exchanging his goods for pink-root, hickory-nut oil, and peltries of all kinds. These he carried to New-Orleans and Mobile in boats, and to Pensacola and Augusta on pack horses. The hickory-nut oil was a luxury with French and Spanish epicures. It was manufactured by the Indians in a simple manner—by boiling the cracked nuts in water, and skimming off the oil as it floated on the surface. Mordecai bought cotton of the Indians in small quantities, ginning it, and carrying it to Augusta on pack horses, in bags much smaller than those of the present day. He was a dark-eyed Jew, and amorous in his disposition. Tourculla, (Capt. Isaacs,) the Chief of the Coosawdas, hearing of his intrigues with a married squaw, approached his house with twelve warriors, knocked him down, thrashed him with poles until he lay insensible, cut off one of his ears, and left him to the care of his wife. They also broke up his boat, and burned down his gin-house. A pretty squaw was the cause of the destruction of the first cotton gin in Alabama."

Louisiana having been ceded by Spain to France, and re-ceded to the United States, a great controversy arose as to whether it included the country south of the 31°, and between the Mississippi and Pearl river, known as the *Baton Rouge District*, and that south of the same parallel, between the Pearl and the Perdido, known as the *Mobile District*. The Spaniards claimed these as West Florida, and only gave up after long struggles and negotiations. We have frequently spoken of these in our pages.

Mr. Pickett's XXIX. Chapter is a deeply-interesting and graphic one, and recounts the adventures of Aaron Burr, and of his being taken upon the soil of Alabama by the young lieutenant, afterwards General Gaines. We have already published the most of this chapter, excepting the summing up of Burr's character, which we now give; and by which it will be seen that the author has been altogether converted, as we ourselves for the most part were, too, by the interesting biography of M. L. Davis.

"It was not considered treason when President Jackson allowed hundreds of the people of the Southwest to be shipped from Mobile and New-Orleans with arms in their hands, who presently landed upon the coast of Texas, and took that country from the Spaniards; but, for similar designs, Aaron Burr was hunted down, thrown into prison, and tried for high treason. The impartial reader must arrive at the conclusion, that the faults of Burr, of a political and public capacity, were not such as ought really to have placed that odium upon him which still attaches to his name. One of the great secrets of his political misfortunes lay in the prejudice and malevolence of politicians and fanatics. Somebody heard General Washington say, that "Burr was a dangerous man:" thereupon the world set him down as a "dangerous man." He killed Hamilton in a duel, because Hamilton abused him: thereupon the world said he was a "murderer." He was a formidable rival of Jefferson in the contest for the presidency: thereupon a majority of the republican party said he was a political scoundrel. He has always opposed the federal party: thereupon the federal party hated him with exceeding bitterness. A blundering, extravagant man, named Herman Blennerhassett, sought Burr while he was in the West, eagerly enlisted in his schemes, and invited him to his house: thereupon Wm. Wirt said, in his prosecuting speech, that "Burr was the serpent who entered the garden of Eden."

The cultivation of indigo in Alabama beginning to be abandoned for that of cotton, the receipts of the gin-holders came to be held a legal tender, and passed as bills of exchange. The Alabamians having to pay a double duty, viz: at Fort Stoddard to the United States, and at Mobile to the Spaniards, labored under great disadvantages. The neighborhood of Huntsville began to be settled by wealthy emigrants. Mr. Gaines, a brother of the general, was government agent for the Indians at St. Stephen's. Upon the backs of horses, the merchandise was carried from Colbert's Ferry to the Tombigbee, and then floated down to the storehouses at St. Stephen's, to avoid the exactions of the Spaniards at Mobile. So keenly did the people feel these exactions, that an expedition was fitted out, under Kemper and others, to drive them out of the country. It proved a miserable failure, and many of the parties were sent to Havana to be immured for a long time in the Moro castle. At Baton Rouge the Americans were successful in repulsing the Spaniards.

The career of Tecumseh occupies a chapter of Colonel Pickett. That great chieftain made the tour of the South for the purpose of forming a general league of the Indians against the whites, under British instigation. He appeared at Autauga and Coosawda, and after many delays, his great war speech was made at the council of the warriors. Being opposed by the "Big Warrior," he shook his finger in his face, earnestly repeating, "Tustinugee Thlucco, your blood is white; I will go to Detroit—when I get there, I will stamp my foot upon the ground, and shake down every house in Tookabatcha." The conclusion of this fine incident we receive with some grains of allowance, knowing the love of the marvelous which exists everywhere. It was so unlikely that an earthquake should actually have occurred to save the reputation of Tecumseh! though the author says the fact is known to the old settlers. "One day a mighty rumbling was heard in the earth, the houses of Tookabatcha reeled and tottered, and reeled again. The people ran out vociferating, 'Tecumseh has got to Detroit; we feel the shake of his foot.'" *Credat, etc.*

The United States, being now at war with Great Britain, did not deem the occupation of Mobile by so nerveless a power as Spain longer to be consonant with safety to our interest, and by one of those bold strokes of policy, known to nations in trying emergencies, dispatched General Wilkinson from New-Orleans, by sea, to take possession of the country, which he did without striking a blow.

After this event, there followed a series of terrible and bloody Indian wars upon the soil of Alabama. The first of these is known as that of Burnt Corn, and is illustrated in the work before us with a very beautiful plate, entitled "The War in South Alabama in 1813 and 1814." Col. Callis, who commanded in this expedition, had his troops cut to pieces and scattered, the rout being in great disorder. At Fort Mimms, soon after, was enacted one of those bloody tragedies which often marked the early life of the backwoods. The author elaborates upon it with great minuteness, and has written perhaps the only full account the world has ever had of the affair, deriving his information from the manuscripts of Gov. Claiborne and of Dr. Thomas Holmes, of Baldwin county, who was one of the few survivors of the terrible day, and who took notes of it not long after for the purpose of refreshing his memory. He conversed with Jesse Steadham and Lieut. Random, who also escaped. We never read a more thrilling narrative, from beginning to end, or one which would have befitted more the pen of the author of "Wyoming." Out of over five hundred souls, soldiers, officers, negroes, etc., none escaped except a few half-breeds and negroes, and some ten or fifteen others. The disaster was attributed to the fatal and mad security in which the commandant, Beasley, reposed, to which, however, he was one of the first victims. Fort Mimms was situated on Lake Tensaw, not far below the mouth of the Tombigbee. Alarmed by these movements, the settlers began the construction of breastworks on every side. Fort Hawn, at Gallet's Bluff, contained 390 souls; Mount Vernon, where two forts existed, was densely packed; Rankin's fort contained five hundred and thirty;

and families were flocking to Fort Charlotte, at Mobile.

Gen. Jackson, who had joined Gen. Coffee, began now to display against the Creeks those extraordinary qualities as a soldier which have placed him upon a par with the Marlboroughs and Wellingtons of history. He directed Coffee towards Tallasehatchee, where the Indians were congregated in great strength, but where, after a short and terrible action, one hundred and eighty-six were left upon the field, and eighty-four women and children made prisoners: only five Americans were killed and eighteen wounded. Jackson himself forded the Coosa at midnight, and with 1800 troops surrounded the enemy at Talladega. The Indians fought with great desperation, and over 290 bodies were left upon the field, whilst the Americans had 15 killed and 85 wounded. The battle-field of Talladega is now embraced within the limits of the beautiful town of that name, which has a population of nearly 2,000. General Floyd soon after met the Indians in the vicinity of the Tallapoosa, carrying great destruction among them, burning their towns, and leaving two hundred upon the field, including the kings of Tallahassee and Autose. Four hundred houses were destroyed, many of fine Indian architecture.

The canoe fight, on the Alabama, in which Jere Anstill and James Smith displayed the prowess and the chivalry of the heroic ages, though established on incontrovertible evidence, borders almost upon the marvelous. Eight athletic and stalwart Indians were crushed in the most unequal and extraordinary contest, whilst one only of three dauntless Americans received any injury, and that but slight. The canoes interlocked after the fashion of the ancient prows, and that of the Indians after the fight presented a sickening picture of mingled blood and brains and grim carcases. Anstill is still a respectable resident of Mobile, being a South Carolinian by birth. Dale, who was called "Big Sam" by the Indians, was a Virginian, and weighed nearly two hundred pounds, being over six feet in height. He died about ten years ago in Mississippi. In addition to this incident of the canoe fight, Col. Claiborne tells several others of him:

"Some years before he was attacked by two warriors, who shouted their war-whoop as he was kneeling down to drink, and rushed upon him with their tomahawks. He knifed them both, and though bleeding from five wounds, he retraced their trail nine miles; crept stealthily to their camp, brained three sleeping warriors, and cut the thongs of a female prisoner who lay by their side. While in this act, however, a fourth sprang upon him from behind a log. Taken at such disadvantage, and exhausted by the loss of blood, he sank under the serpent-grasp of the savage, and a few moments would have closed the contest. At that instant, however, the woman drove a tomahawk deep into the head of the Indian, and thus preserved the life of her deliverer.

"Some time ago, General Dale, being in Mobile, was held to bail as *endorser* of a note. The debt was in the hands of a *stranger*. Accompanied by an officer, he sought the creditor, and found him in the saloon of Collum's far-famed hotel. 'Sir, said the general, I have no money to pay this debt. The principal has property, make him pay it, or let me go home and work it out.' The Shylock hesitated. '*Very well*,' said the veteran, in tones that rang indignantly through the apartment, '*Very well, sir! Look at my scars! I will march to jail down Main-street, and all Mobile shall witness the treatment of an old soldier!*' These simple words fell like electricity upon that high-toned people. In half an hour the brightest names of the city were on the bond, and before morning the debt was paid, and a full discharge handed to the general. I have seen the manly tears chasing down his cheek, as the aged warrior dwelt on these recollections of the generous citizens."

Econachaca, or Holy Ground, on the bluff to the eastern side of the Alabama River, just below the present Powell's ferry, was fortified in great strength by the Indians. Against this point Claiborne led the advance in person, and was received by Weatherford, who was in command of the Indians, with great gallantry. They soon, however, gave way, leaving thirty of their number dead upon the field. Weatherford, in his flight upon a spirited charger, made his famous leap into the river from a perpendicular bluff ten or fifteen feet deep. This Weatherford, shortly after the decisive battle of Horse Shoe, which we shall mention directly, appeared in the camp of General Jackson. The general rushed out, exclaiming—

"How dare you, sir, to ride up to my camp, after killing the women and children at Fort Mimms!" Weatherford said, "General Jackson, I am not afraid of you. I fear no man, for I am a Creek warrior. I have nothing to request in behalf of myself; you can kill me, if you desire. But I come to beg of you to send for the women and children of the war party who are starving in the woods. Their fields and cribs have been destroyed by your people, who have driven them to the woods without an ear of corn. I hope that you will send out parties who will safely conduct them here, that they may be fed. I exerted myself in vain to prevent the massacre of the women and children at Fort Mimms. I am now done fighting. The Red Sticks are nearly all killed. If I could fight you any longer, I would most heartily do so. Send for the women and children. They never did you any harm. But kill me, if the white people want it done." At the conclusion of these words, many persons who had surrounded the marquee exclaimed, "kill him! kill him! kill him!" General Jackson commanded silence; and in an emphatic manner said, "*Any man who would kill as brave a man as this, would rob the dead.*"

After the battle of Emuckfau, near the creek of that name, in Tallapoosa county, Jackson, who was without provisions, and in force too weak for the emergencies, returned to Fort Strother. On his way, the Indians attacked him again at Enetachopoco, and although in these two battles one hundred and eighty-nine bodies of the Indians were counted on the field, the chieftains always maintained that they had "whipped Captain Jackson, and run him to the Coosa River." The respective forces of the parties are stated by Mr. Pickett: 767 whites, with two hundred friendly Indians, and 500 hostile Creeks, or "Red Sticks," as they were called. In view of this disparity of force and terrible courage of the Indians, the author finds occasion to comment:

"Brave natives of Alabama! to defend that soil where the Great Spirit gave you birth, you sacrificed your peaceful savage pursuits; you fought the invaders until more than half your warriors were slain! The remnant of your warlike race yet live in the distant Arkansas. You have been forced to quit one of the finest regions on earth, which is now occupied by Americans. Will *they*, in some dark hour when Alabama is invaded, defend this soil as bravely and as enduringly as you have done? Posterity may be able to reply."

General Jackson, with two thousand men, passed over the ridge which divides the Coosa and the Tallapoosa, and appeared suddenly before the enemy. We extract the particulars of the battle of Horse Shoe, which followed, and which may be said almost to have put an end to the war:

"Being desirous not to destroy this brave race, Jackson sent out a messenger towards them, who assured them of the clemency of the general, provided they would surrender. They answered by discharges of their guns and with shouts of defiance. The artillery was then effectually brought to bear upon them. The Americans then applied fire to their retreat, which soon forced them to fly, and as they ran, they were killed by American guns. It was late in the evening before the dreadful battle ended. The Red Sticks numbered about one thousand warriors, and out of that number five hundred and fifty-seven were found dead on the peninsula; and many were killed in the river by Coffee's troops while they were endeavoring to swim over. It may be stated that not more than two hundred survived. Some of them long afterwards suffered from the most grievous wounds. Manowa, one of the bravest chiefs that ever lived, was literally shot to pieces. He fought as long as he could. He saved himself by jumping into the water, where it was four feet deep. He held to a root, and thus kept himself beneath the waves, breathing through the long joint of a cane, one end of which he held in his mouth, and while one end came above the surface of the water. When night set in, the brave Manowa* rose from his watery bed and made his way to the forest, bleeding from many wounds. Many years after the war, we conversed with this chief, and learned from him the particulars of the remarkable escape. His face, limbs and body, at the time we conversed with him, were marked with the scars of many horrible wounds. Another chief was shot down among a number of slain warriors; and, with admirable presence of mind, saved his life by drawing over him the bodies of two of them, under which he lay till the darkness of night permitted him to leave the horrible place. The loss of the Americans was thirty-two killed, and ninety-nine wounded. The friendly Cherokees had eighteen killed, and thirty-six wounded. The tory Creeks had five killed, and eleven wounded. Among the killed were Major L. P. Montgomery, and Lieutenants Moulton and Somerville, who fell in the charge upon the breastworks."

The Creeks were now disposed to treat, and it was stipulated that a line should be drawn commencing upon the Coosa at the southern boundary of the Cherokee nation, and continue down that river to Wetumpka and thence eastwardly to Georgia. East and north of that line, containing 150,000 square miles, remained to the Indians; west and south of it was secured to the United States.

* Known by the American settlers as "Old Manorwas."

Apprehending an attack from the British upon Fort Bowyer, at Mobile Point, General Jackson re-garrisoned it under Major Lawrence, who soon after gallantly repulsed the English advance in two sloops of war and two brigs, destroying the Hermes, and killing 162 of the enemy, wounding 70 others. The American loss was but four killed, and four wounded.

The authorities of Pensacola having received the fugitive Indians on the ground of humanity, and allowed the British to occupy their forts of St. Michael and Barancas, in violation of neutral duties, and under pretext of a treaty between the English and the Indians, prior in date to the Spanish occupancy, General Jackson determined upon the occupation of Florida until Spanish troops should arrive in sufficient numbers to protect the neutrality of the territory. Three regiments of infantry, the militia of Tennessee, a battalion of volunteer dragoons and some friendly Indians, took up the march for Pensacola. Governor Manriquez having refused a friendly invitation to surrender, Laval, of the 3d regiment, a South Carolinian, was entrusted by Jackson to lead the "forlorn hope," in the desperate attempt to take a battery which commanded the only approach to the town. This fearful service was performed at the head of 120 men, among whom, and fighting in the ranks, on foot, was the brave Colonel Arthur P. Hayne, of South Carolina. Laval is now a resident of Charleston, and has held many high stations. There was an old story when we were a boy, that after he had received his dreadful wound at the gates of Pensacola, General Jackson came up, and being told by the surgeon that he must die—exclaimed with that ardor and *responsibility* which ever marked him, "*By God, he sha'nt die!*" As Colonel Pickett does not mention the story, we suppose it apocryphal. Manriquez soon after surrendered the town, and the British, after some show of resistance, evacuated the forts.

The British having been defeated at New-Orleans, repaired to Fort Bowyer, near Mobile Point. Twenty-five vessels anchored within a distance of five miles. Thirteen ships approached within three miles, and 5,000 men landed and encamped. The Americans capitulated to a force twenty times their own. This was the last act of the war, as news of the treaty of peace had reached the territory.

Alabama began now its career of rapid progress. Settlers flocked to the Tombigbee, over which, and the Black Warrior, acquired from the Chickasaws, the jurisdiction of the Mississippi Territory was extended. Madison county, in six years, obtained a population of more than 10,000, from the most wealthy planters of the South. In 1816, a cession was received from the Indians of all the territory from the head waters of the Coosa westward to Cotton Gin Point, and to a line running from thence to the Caney Creek, on the Tennessee. The Americans continued to press into the territory, which reached that year 75,000 population, 46,000 of whom were in the counties of Pearl River, in the Tennessee valley, upon the Tombigbee and at Mobile. The following year the limits of the present state of Mississippi were defined and carved out from the territory to be admitted into the Federal Union.

The territorial government of Alabama was at the same time established with the counties of Mobile, Baldwin, Washington, Clarke, Madison, Limestone, and Lauderdale, and a seat of government at St. Stephen's. William Bibb was appointed governor, and the first legislature convened in 1818. The counties of Cotaco, Lawrence, Franklin, Limestone, Lauderdale, Blount, Tuscaloosa, Marengo, Shelby, Cahawba, Dallas, Marion and Conecuh, were laid off:

"The flood-gates of Virginia, the two Carolinas, Tennessee, Kentucky and Georgia, were now hoisted, and the mighty streams of emigration poured through them, spreading over the whole territory of Alabama. The axe resounded from side to side, and from corner to corner. The stately and magnificent forests fell. Log-cabins sprang as if by magic into sight. Never before nor since has a country been so rapidly peopled."

Chapter XLI. contains an interesting account of the modern French colony in Alabama, or the Wine and Olive Company, obtained from the materials of A. B. Meek, Esq., George N. Stewart, Esq., who was agent of the Company, and Armand Pfister, of Montgomery, a descendant of one of the grantees. These Frenchmen, after the fall of Napoleon, from their attachment to his cause, were forced to abandon their country. Congress granted them four townships, at two dollars an acre, on a credit of fourteen years, on condition of introducing the vine and the olive. The land was divided between 340 *allottes*. The region in which they resolved to establish themselves, was an immense forest of trees and canes, interspersed with prairie. Cabins were erected about the White Bluff, in a rude and scattered manner, constituting a town, which was called Demopolis, the city of the people; the site proved, however, not within the grant, and was bought by an American company afterwards from the United States for $52 an acre.

Among the settlers in the wilds of Alabama, were the Count Lefevre Desnoettes, whom Napoleon embraced on departing from Elba, with the words, "I cannot take leave of you all, but will embrace General Desnoettes," etc.; Mr. Peniers, a member of the National Assembly, who had voted for the execution of Louis XVI.; Colonel Nicholas Rooul, who had shared the exile at Elba, but who was at last reduced to the condition of a ferryman on the Alabama. His wife, who shared his fortunes, had been Marchioness of Sinabaldi, and Maid of Honor to Queen Caroline; Colonel Cluis, who had had the custody of Ferdinand of Spain, when imprisoned by Napoleon, afterwards tavern keeper at Greensboro'; Simon Chandon, a distinguished *literatem* and author; General Bertrand Clausel, the commander at Bordeaux, afterwards marketman of Mobile, and finally Governor of Algeria, under Louis Philippe; Henry L'Allemand, a Lieutenant-General of the Imperial Guard; Marshal Grouchy, whose *son* settled the grant; M. Lacanal, head of the Department of Education under the Emperor; General Juan Rico, an eloquent member of the Spanish Cortes, etc., etc. It is needless to say, that from a thousand untoward circumstances, the colony was a miserable failure. Says Colonel Pickett:

"But in the midst of all their trials and vicissitudes, the French refugees were happy. Immured in the depths of the Tombigbee forest, where, for several years, want pressed them on all sides—cut off from their friends in France, surrounded by the Choctaws on one side, and land-thieves on the other—assailed by the venom of insects and prostrating fevers—nevertheless, their native gayety prevailed. Being in the habit of social intercourse, their evenings were spent in conversation, music and dancing. The larger portion were well educated, while all had seen much of the world, and such materials were ample to afford an elevated society. Sometimes their distant friends sent them rich wines and other luxuries; and upon such occasions parties were given, and the foreign delicacies brought back many interesting recollections. Well cultivated gardens, and the abundance of wild game, rendered the common living of the French quite respectable. The female circle was highly interesting. They had brought with them their books, guitars, silks, parasols and ribbons, and the village in which most of them dwelt, resembled in the night a miniature French town. And then farther in the forest others lived, the imprints of whose beautiful Parisian shoes on the wild prairie, occasionally arrested the glance of a solitary traveler. And then again, when the old imperial heroes talked of their emperor, their hearts warmed with sympathy, their eyes kindled with enthusiasm, and tears stole down their furrowed cheeks."

The time had come when, from the rapid increase of the population of Alabama, she might take a place among the states of the confederation, on that truly *American* condition of sovereignty, full and perfect, except as to certain powers, and those only which are delegated to the federal Union. The convention was held at Huntsville, on the 5th of July, 1819, representing twenty-two counties. Many of its members have since been distinguished in the history of the state; and, although their biographies are deeply interesting, we could have wished that the author had devoted less of his space to them and more to the general deliberations of the convention, which are always interesting, and which constitute the land-marks in all subsequent times for the due understanding and administration of government. In a subsequent edition we trust that Mr. Pickett will adopt the suggestion, in which he will do good service to the rising generation of Alabamians.

ALABAMA—HER RESOURCES, AND THE PROPORTION OF WEALTH SHE CONTRIBUTES TO THE NATIONAL WELFARE.—*Natural Advantages.*—Open to the Gulf of Mexico on the south boundary, with a spacious bay, over the bar of which ships drawing twenty and three-quarter feet at low tide safely ride, and into which all of her rivers (with two exceptions) flow—the one invites thither ships of the largest class, and the others bear to Mobile, from the fertile valleys and plains above, their valuable productions—Alabama is watered by the following noble rivers:—

Names of Rivers	Navigable, description, &c	Miles in Alabama	Empties in
Mobile	Largest class steamers	60	Mobile Bay.
Alabama	The same	450	Mobile River.
Tombigbee	The same	540	The same.
Warrior	The same	150	Tombigbee.
Tennessee	do. for 1,000 miles altogether	130	Ohio River.
Chatahooche	The same, eastern boundary	200	Apalachicola.
Coosa	Large steamers below & small above the falls.	170	Alabama.
Cahawba	For small steamers		
Tallapoosa	do	40	do.
Noxuba	do	50	Tombigbee.
Suckernochee	do	35	do.
	Navigation	1945	M'ls in length.

Such are our great and peculiar advantages of navigation that our citizens will never be compelled to abstract from other investments—they may choose largely of their capital for internal improvements. But there is a railroad now in progress, the Mobile and Ohio, that I may properly regard as associated with the natural advantages of the state. The Gulf of Mexico, sweeping up into this division of the continent, continued northerly by the Bay of Mobile, with the Mississippi River inclining from its mouth north-east, throws this river at the mouth of the Ohio within *four hundred and forty-five miles of Mobile*, the commercial emporium of Alabama. The country between those two points being remarkably level, the route unobstructed by a single mountain or river, or any stream of moment, and running in its whole extent through one of great beauty and fertility, and already settled by an active and wealthy population, must throw their great trade, and travel through Alabama into Mobile; and in twenty hours, or less, citizens of Missouri, Ohio, Kentucky or elsewhere, may leave Columbus, in Kentucky, the upper terminus, and arrive at Mobile with their produce in one-fifth the time they could reach New-Orleans.

Before I proceed to the other very interesting portions of this branch of the subject, I will here allude to such internal improvements as are already completed, or are in active progress:

The Muscle Shoals Canal	complete	35¾	miles.
Huntsville Canal	"	16	"
Tuscumbia and Decatur railroad	"	44	"
Montgomery and West Point, nearly	"	87	"
Cahawba and Marion	"	35	"
Canals and Railroads, length		217¾	

A railroad from Selma, or some other points on the Alabama, to the Tennessee river; one connecting the Tuscumbia and Decatur with the Mobile and Ohio road; and another from Blakely, opposite Mobile, to Columbus, Georgia—each of which would add greatly to the traffic and wealth of the state, and pay good dividends—are perhaps the only ones of importance contemplated.

To continue with natural advantages: From Tuscaloosa, on the Warrior, in the direction of Selma, on the Alabama, are bituminous coal-fields and iron ore, with marble, and hard and soft limestone quarries, in rich and inexhaustible profusion, immediately on navigable streams. The lands are covered with splendid forests of white and live oak, cypress, pine, cedar, mulberry, hickory, &c. Water power is unlimited and never-failing. Irrigated by so many streams, as indicated by 1,945 miles of navigation, with the innumerable tributaries thereto, the lands of Alabama are of amazing superiority, as their productions hereinafter noticed will exhibit, and, with a climate temperate and uniform, it is decidedly healthy.

Productions.—To regard alone the ascertained value and extent of the surplus products of Alabama which we ship off, compared with those of other states, omitting an estimate of our own heavy consumption of corn, wheat, hogs, cattle, sheep, timber, cotton consumed in home manufactures, value of negroes raised, and horses and mules raised, which would amount to several millions—confining ourself to the surplus productions, I say we will, I think, do so with some astonishment, as associated with it must be the effort to estimate the vastness of the capital employed to produce it. Her surplus productions are cotton, lumber, staves, turpentine, manufactured cottons, coal, &c.

What is her cotton crop and its value? I will arrive at it in this way, and pardon me for assuring those who read this, that I am quite sure I shall not be far from correct. To the amount of cotton received at Mobile I will add the quantity raised in North Alabama, which is forwarded down the Tennessee, or hauled overland to Memphis. I will also add the quantity which goes down the Chatahoochee to Apalachicola. Adding these together, I will deduct the quantity raised in the eastern counties of Mississippi. This will show the crop of Alabama to result as per following table:

Where received and raised	No. of bales of cotton for years 1846-7	1847-8	1848-9
Alabama and Mississippi, at Mobile	323,462	436,661	530,000
North Alabama to New-Orleans, as per census of 1840, 49,225,474 lbs., at 510 lbs. to the bale, is,	*96,500	*96,500	†96,500
East Alabama shipped to Apalachicola for Chatahoochee	†50,000	†50,000	‡50,000
	469,962	583,161	676,000
Less Eastern Mississippi crop	‡60,000	80,000	80,000
Net crop of Alabama in bales	409,962	503,161	596,000

And the following table will show the value of those crops of cotton, at the average price it sold at, of the respective seasons at Mobile for the three years:

Year	No. bales.	Wt ea. lbs	Total lbs and average price		Total value
1846–7	409,962	510	209,080,620	10⅝	24,570,972 85
1847–8	503,161	510	256,612,110	6¾	17,321,317 42
1848–9	596,000	510	298,760,000	6	17,956,200 00
	1,509,123		764,452,730		59,848,483 30
Av. 3 ys.	503,041		254,817,577		19,949,494 43

Enormous as this is, yet this great interest of Alabama, as well as the whole South, does not yield so profitable a dividend on the capital invested as other investments elsewhere do.

But, to renew the subject, let us glance at her wealth, and what she has done to promote the national welfare.

1st. Of lands, she owns 15,011,520 acres, and, besides, what her citizens have paid for Spanish and French grants and school lands, they have paid into the Land Offices of the Government $17,000,000 for lands in their wild state.

2d. She has paid to Maryland, Delaware Virginia, &c., enormous sums for the three hundred thousand negroes she owns.

3d, The capital invested in foreign and domestic commerce, city and town property, houses, canals, and railroads, manufactures, banking insurance, iron and coal mining, timber trade, steamboats, and shipping, with the increased value of lands by clearing, fencing, &c., value of slaves, live stock, and money hoarded, is very large in the aggregate amount, an estimate of which I scarcely dare mention.

4th. Her liberality expends in trade with the other states a large portion of her income.

5th. The shipping interest is largely benefited by the freighting of her six hundred thousand bales of cotton, and the return cargoes purchased by us.

With such varied and extraordinary advantages for commerce, manufacturing, mining, ship-building, timber-getting, &c., it is not to be wondered at that Alabama is beginning to direct her attention to the advantage of diversifying her pursuits; and, under any circumstances, in time, those vast sources of wealth now reposing within her borders must become transcendently productive. The accumulation of wealth which has been going on, but which has been regularly invested in the purchase of negroes, is now being stayed from that direction, and turned toward other industrial pursuits. It is obvious, however, to every political economist that it is the interest of every interest in the country to promote the value of cotton, as should there be a violent transition of slave labor to the pursuits above alluded to, and which is entirely practicable, a derangement of trade would ensue which would be prejudicial, to say the least of it, to the interests of other sections of the Confederacy. And when cotton sells well, public lands are purchased freely, and the direct interest the government has in this matter will be readily and conveniently demonstrated by the following table, showing the number of acres of land owned by the citizens of Alabama, Mississippi, Louisiana and Arkansas, the amount paid for portions bought of the government, and the number of acres in each remaining unsold:

States	Total No. of acres in	Acres owned	Paid Government for portion bought of it	Acres unsold Jan 1, 1848
Alabama	32,462,080	15,911,520	$16,888,047	17,450,560
Miss	30,174,080	15,811,650	16,402,691	14,326,430
Louis'a.	29,715,840	6,263,822	4,186,394	23,452,018
Ark	33,406,720	5,942,117	3,769,695	27,464,603
			$41,246,837	82,693,611

This table shows some extraordinary facts that are not often considered by those who abuse the South, namely, that besides the government owning 82,693,611 acres of land, which would be sooner purchased up if their agricultural productions could be promoted; these states have paid $41,246,827 for the lands they have alone purchased of the government; and if this sum had been invested at the average time of their payment, say 1835, in six per cent. stocks, payable semi-annually, and such dividends had been reinvested and compounded till now, it would reach a total sum to-day that would equal fully all the bona-fide capital of the North invested in cotton factories and shipping. I allude to this to present a cause why the South may appear behind the North in the progress of her factories, &c.

Cotton factories and iron forges are, however, becoming numerous. Coal mining is attracting great attention, and from the great profits arising from investments in ships, and

* Allowing for each year only what it was in 1840, as per census.

† This year the Alabama shipments by this river may be by some ten to fifteen thousand bags more; but for several years it has been about these figures.

‡ This is as much or more than we received from this river during that season, of Mississippi cotton, as the total receipts out of it were but 122,000 bales; for the other years they are about correct.

our wonderful facilities for building, with our splendid timber on the spot, &c., it is not unlikely we shall ere long enter the lists as competitors with our northern brethren in this exceedingly profitable branch of their wealth. In Alabama our citizens are generally exempt from embarrassment, and in certain quarters large amounts of money are known to be hoarded.

The university and colleges, the high schools and academies, in all the principal towns and cities of the state, are in the highest degree flourishing; and the great increase of the number of churches and membership, the decrease of crime and the orderly character of our citizens, manifest the spreading influences there of religion.

The increase of population of Alabama, Mississippi and Louisiana, is rapid and steady. For example, there were in

	1820	1830	1840
Alabama	127,901	309,527	590,756
Mississippi	75,448	136,621	375,654
Louisiana	153,407	215,529	352,411

And in 1850, a large increase will be found.

In conclusion, I feel the utmost pleasure in announcing to the friends of progress everywhere that, amongst many of those who have violently opposed all measures for encouragement of enterprise and the increase of facilities for the development of our resources more actively and profitably, practical experience has exposed to them their serious errors; and now, in the most cordial manner, the most distinguished as well as many of the masses of their portion of the people, are uniting with the other portion in the most liberal and enlightened disposition to meet the calls of the whole people for the purposes alluded to.

Devoting my remarks to the position, &c., of the one state, I have done so because I am a citizen of it; but the gigantic importance of the whole South may be more justly estimated by a careful consideration of what is here submitted in relation to Alabama.*

ALABAMA—Iron and other Mineral Products of.—At this moment the manufacture of iron is attracting the attention of our citizens, and, as much depends upon a good beginning, these hints are offered with the view of directing inquiry in the proper channel. It is not wise to spend both time and money in working out problems that have been, long ago, solved; if we begin at all, let us do so with the present state of the art.

There are eight bloomeries in the state, two of which are on the Talladega Creek, and the others on the waters of the Cahawba.

Of the two high furnaces, one is in Bibb county; it has but recently been erected, so that its operations are, as yet, confined to the manufacture of pig iron and hollow-ware; the blast is urged by steam power, and the boiler is heated directly from the trundle head. These works are situated within eight or ten miles of the Coosa, and from the convenience and good quality of the ore, and the abundance of fuel, they can scarcely fail of success, under ordinary good management.

* National Intelligencer.

The Benton works are situated on Crane creek, a short distance from the river; they have been for years in successful operation. An extension of the works, the introduction of the hot blast, and various other improvements are contemplated, which, when accomplished, will place this among the most complete establishments in the South. The following brief statement was politely furnished by one of the proprietors:

"Polkville, *Benton Co., Ala.*,
"*Sept.* 26, 1849.

"We have a blast furnace, a puddling furnace, and forge, in operation. We turn out daily about 6000 pounds of iron, 2000 pounds of which are put into hollow-ware and machinery-castings, 2000 pounds into bar iron, and 2000 pounds into pigs. We use 600 bushels of charcoal every 24 hours. Our iron ore beds (some of them) are within 600 yards of the furnace. Our limestone is at the furnace, and in abundance. The nearest stone coal beds that have been worked, are thirteen miles off. We are now preparing to put up a rolling mill, and think that in a short time we will be able to roll iron successfully. Our establishment is five miles east of the Coosa river, opposite the Ten Islands, and eleven miles from Greensport. We ship our iron down the Coosa in flat-boats to Wetumpka, Montgomery, and Mobile. We have found the articles we produce here of a ready sale in either of those markets. We are prepared to make, turn off, and fit up, all kinds of machinery, except fine castings for cotton mills, and will be very soon ready to furnish these."

Red Ochre.—There is a bed of red ochre near Bucksville, which I have had no opportunity of examining in its place, but the specimens that I have seen show that it would require but little preparation to fit it for paint. It is sufficiently rich to be used as an ore of iron.

Lead Ore.—Fragments of sulphuret of lead, or galena, are scattered throughout the state in a manner that would indicate some common origin. Had they been confined to the region of the silurian or carboniferous limestone, one might refer them to the ruins of veins of this ore that are often found in these rocks; but they are equally where this is impossible. I have specimens picked up on the surface of the coal measures, and others from Clarke county, where no such veins can occur. Pieces of considerable size are found in the vicinity of Indian mounds! and the belief is induced that the position of these scattered fragments may be traced to Indian origin.*

However this may be, it is quite certain that much time is unprofitably spent in searching for these mines.

Lead is found in limestone near the iron works in Benton, which is the only place that I have seen it in the state. The ore is granular, and does not occur in a true vein with smooth walls, but is closely attached to the rock, and passes into it in irregular bunches. It may be traced over a distance of ten yards, and although it is not more than an inch or two in the thickest part, it may turn out to be worth the trouble of an examination below the surface. It is a pure sulphuret of lead; the cavities in it are often lined with crystals of the carbonate of that metal. The ease with which lead is reduced allows of considerable expense in mining, and I would recommend the enterprising proprietors of the iron-works, to examine this locality with some care. The existence of veins of calx spar, and sulphate of barytes, are favorable indications.

Peroxide of Manganese.—At the works just mentioned, a fragment of ore, which was brought there for an ore of iron, attracted my attention, and proved, on examination, to be the peroxide of manganese. I have since learned that the bed from which it was taken is probably three or four yards in thickness. This ore is used in the arts for the production of chlorine gas, which is used in bleaching establishments. The gas is combined with caustic lime, by a simple process, and in this form is barreled up and preserved for use. The gas is extricated from the lime by means of water, which absorbs the chlorine, and is then ready for use. As there is lime in abundance where this occurs, chloride of lime may be manufactured. The price of the mineral itself is about $20 a ton. The specimen I examined was quite porous, and mixed to some extent with earthy impurities, but nevertheless it contained 35 per cent. of peroxide of manganese. I trust that when this bed is fairly opened, that it will turn out to be an important acquisition to the resources of Alabama.

Limestones and Marble.—The term marble is applied to any variety of limestone that is susceptible of a polish.

I have mentioned already the occurrence of beds of marble of great thickness on the Cahawba. Many of the beds there afford specimens of great beauty; some are gray with red veins, others are red and yellow, and specimens with greenish veins are not uncommon. There is also a buff-colored marble there, filled with organic remains, that is quite handsome when polished. Beds of white crystaline marble, clouded with red occur. On the opposite side of the river there is a black compact marble, and another on Six Mile Creek, variously intersected by veins of white. A marble of similar quality occurs on the road from Pratt's ferry to Montevallo.

As no quarry of any extent has been opened at any of these places, it is impossible to give a correct view of their value. Marble, to be valuable, must be found in thick beds, that are free from cracks or joints. Of the thickness of the beds there can be no doubt, nor does there appear to be any reason to suppose that the other conditions are less favorable. I look upon this locality as one of great interest, in connection with the industrial resources of the state.

The principal exposures occur near the head of navigation, and on the immediate banks of the rivers.

On the Huntsville road, about 19 miles from Tuscaloosa, ledges are found that would afford pretty good marble.

At Jonesborough, beds of variegated marble, of the red and white variety, occur. The rock is compact, and lies in thick masses, at the base of the red mountain. The same stratum occurs at Village Springs. The magnesian limestone, when compact, is susceptible of a polish, and its peculiar soft gray color I think beautiful; in addition to this, it is extremely durable. The crystalline varieties are also used as marbles.

These rocks, as I have shown, extend from Shultz Creek to the upper end of the valley.

When an outlet to this region is provided, the value of these beds will be appreciated.

At the locality mentioned, on Big Sandy Creek, very good marbles occur, which are, in many respects, similar to those of the Cahawba. As there is abundant water-power at this locality, which has already been turned to account by the enterprising proprietor, who has erected a cotton factory here, may we not hope, before a long time, to find also a saw-mill, for marble, in operation.—*Tuomey's Report.*

ALABAMA.—Coal Lands.—In the first annual report of 1850, of the Geology of Alabama, by M. Tuomey, Esq., State Geologist and Professor in the University of that state, there are the following remarks upon

* All the states from which the Indians have recently departed, have legends of lead and silver mines, that were known to, but afterwards hidden by, them; and the tenacity with which these are believed and retained, is truly suprising. Journeys have been undertaken to the west to ascertain the position of these mines, but hitherto without success. The Indians, being no geologists, located the mines, in the cases that have come to my notice, in the most unpromising positions. The men with mineral rods have been industriously on the trail, and I must do them the justice to say, that where they indicated the presence of "mineral," the excavation was neither expensive nor difficult. The one I last saw was in an Indian mound, on Village Creek, where the miners had reached to within one foot of the vein!

Alabama Coal, which we regard as of great interest:

The earliest notice of the use of Alabama coal that I have been able to find, is contained in Silliman's Journal, vol. xxvi., 1834, in a note by Dr. Alexander Jones, of Mobile, which, notwithstanding unavoidable mistakes, I have thought of sufficient interest to insert here.

This state is very rich in bituminous coal, of a most excellent quality. It is in every respect equal, if not superior to the best English coal. I am using some of it in my little laboratory. It is very heavy, and burns with a good flame, and gives out much heat. It also yields the carburetted hydrogen gas in immense quantity. The vein, or formation of this coal, is very extensive. It is first seen in the bed of the Black Warrior River, near Tuscaloosa, and next appears on the surface of the ground, to the northeast and east of that town, and pursues that course till it crosses the Alabama and Coosa rivers at their falls, or just above them. It passes, probably, for some distance into Georgia, and not improbably, in its southwestern or western direction into Mississippi.

Its principal width is found in Shelby and Bibb counties, where it is forty miles wide; it occupies the whole ground under the surface, and is covered by superficial patches of hard or soft slate stone, or shale, other minerals being rarely found near it. Blacksmiths in its neighborhood dig it up, and work it in their furnaces. It is also used in an iron foundry in Shelby county. The land is smartly broken. The growth consists principally of chestnut, oak and pine, and being more or less poor, it has never, much of it, passed yet out of the hands of the general government, and can therefore be bought by any one who wishes to own it at $1 25 an acre.

In the winter season this coal is brought down the river to Mobile from Tuscaloosa, in flat-bottomed boats, and sold at the same price as the Liverpool coal, or at from $1 to $1 50 per barrel. The strata of this rich and extensive coal bed have an inclination of a few degrees to the S. S. E.

I presume you will, ere long, receive a correct geological account of this extensive and interesting coal formation, from some gentleman of the Alabama University at Tuscaloosa, which is a very favorable point for observing it.

The facts which I have communicated were obtained from an eminent lawyer of this place, who had visited that region, and from a laboring man, who had worked the coal in a blacksmith's shop, which he owned in that region. He informed me, that having worked at the coal mines in Virginia, near Richmond, he considered this coal deposit the richest, and as containing the best coal he had ever seen.

For domestic purposes, the Alabama coal has been sufficiently long in use in the state to have its quality in this relation settled. In Tuscaloosa it is used in the houses, to the almost entire exclusion of wood. The price varies from ten to twelve cents per bushel. It is also used in Mobile for similar purposes, but to what extent I do not know.*

During the months of August, September and October, (1849,) there were about 200 persons engaged in the coal trade of the state; and as only three beds are worked under ground, the rest of the coal raised is taken from the bed of the river, and streams, where of course operations can only be continued during the low stages of the water; and in general, it is only the seasons of leisure that can be devoted to the business by farmers, who are the principal proprietors.

It has already been stated, that the obstruction of the Warrior, which terminates the navigation of that river, is occasioned by the coal measures. Above this point the river is only navigable during freshets, at which times alone coal is carried to Mobile. The boats used are common flat-boats, with gunwales made of solid timbers; the first class have a capacity of about 2,000 bushels, draw 20 to 30 inches of water, and cost $70 or thereabouts. Coal is brought down the river to Tuscaloosa at about four cents a bushel, a distance of 50 miles, and thence to Mobile, a distance of 355 miles, at an additional cost of nearly four cents; the boat being a dead loss in either case, as it brings but a few dollars.

Coal is brought to Tuscaloosa in wagons from those beds exposed five or six miles east of the river, and ten to eighteen miles from the city. When the plank road, at present in contemplation, is constructed, it will greatly facilitate operations in that direction, more particularly as it is intended to reach the iron region of Roup's valley.

It will be seen from the map, that the Warrior runs through the centre of the coal field; and its improvement, 75 or 100 miles above Tuscaloosa, would leave little to be desired in relation to the transportation of coal from this region; for it is supposed by those who have examined it, that with a very moderate outlay, the river below Tuscaloosa may be rendered navigable through the summer for light-draught stern-wheel steamers.

The attempts at improving this river, up to

* Mr. Hanby's account of his attempts at the introduction of Alabama coal into the Mobile market, would furnish an amusing chapter, on the difficulty of diverting any trade from its accustomed channels. The intelligent proprietors of the gas works in that city, however, were not slow to recognize its value as a material for the manufacture of gas; and it has now, where it is known, I believe, a fair reputation. Much of what has heretofore been carried to market, under the name of coal, included everything that resembled it in color; but I know from observation, that those engaged in the business at present, take every reasonable precaution to reject all impurities.

the present time, have been conducted on two different plans, the one in relation to its navigation at low water, and the other to high water navigation. The first and most expensive operations consisted in the construction of jetties, &c., with the view of turning the water into a narrower channel. The plan appears to be good, but the execution was defective. The jetties were, in many cases, not connected with the banks. and not reaching above water, they became dangerous submerged islands, to boats coming down at high water.

Later improvements have been altogether conducted with the view to the removal of obstructions to high water navigation, and consequently, it became necessary to undo, in many cases, what had already been done, at considerable expense.

The work principally consisted in the removal, from the shoals, of prominent points of rock, widening channels, cutting away dead timber, &c. The execution of this was entrusted to sensible men, who knew from experience the dangers and obstructions of the river, and I can bear testimony to the faithful manner in which they have discharged their duties. The clearest proof of this is found in the fact, that formerly, it required four feet rise in the level reaches to produce one on the shoals; now, three feet is sufficient to give the same rise on the shoals.

AGRICULTURE.—South Carolina and Louisiana Agricultural Societies: Proceedings, Reports, etc.—Progress of Agriculture and Agricultural Knowledge at the South—Papers upon Sugar Manufacture — Operations of Hon. P. Rost and J. D. B. De Bow.—In 1784 the first agricultural society of South Carolina was formed, which exists to the present day. In 1823 there were eleven societies in the state—the South Carolina, the Pendleton, the Edgefield, the Barnwell, the St. John Colleton, the St. Helena, the Beaufort, the Beaufort District, the St. Andrew's, the St. Paul's, and the Winyah. In 1826 the St. John's Society invited a convention of all these bodies, which was held in Charleston. In 1827, from the result of this movement, the United Agricultural Society was organized at Columbia. This Association not being productive of the desired results, in 1839 a convention, at Columbia, formed the State Society.

"In perusing," says Mr. Carroll, in his preface to the valuable volume of Carolina Agricultural Reports and Publications,* 1847, "the able documents embraced in this volume, it will doubtless be impressed upon the reader's mind, that South Carolina, though one of the earliest cultivated colonies of the Union, and though the pursuits of its people have been essentially agricultural, yet such is the impoverishment of some of its best lands, that all the helps of science, skill, and industry, are required to save them from barenness, and to restrain her people from that spirit of emigration which is every day depopnlating many portions of the state. Engaged, as four-fifths of her population are, in agriculture; deriving nine-tenths of her treasure from the taxation of our planters; raising, as she does, one twenty-fourth part of all the cotton in the world; producing, too, one-seventh of all the exports of the Union; and paying into the national treasury one million of dollars more than all the New-England states put together, it certainly becomes a question of no little interest, what has been done for the advancement of our agricultural interests. With one or two exceptions legislative aid has done nothing.

"While our planters have, with great forbearance, submitted to this state of things, those of other States have been aroused, and insisting upon their claims have secured many reforms in their agricultural condition. They have been taught to feel, with the rest of the enlightened world, that agriculture is indeed of primary importance to their political economy—that with its prosperity all other branches of industry must flourish; while with its decline they must, just as certainly, languish and decay—in a word, that agriculture is the main shaft around which commerce, and manufactures, and the arts, all cluster, and by which they are sustained in vitality and strength. What, therefore, other States have acted upon, and prosperously consummated, is neither policy nor wisdom for South Carolina to neglect."

In Louisiana, whose resources and progress have been extraordinary, it is scarcely credible how little interest has been taken in the subject of scientific agriculture. Accounts on all hands are agreed that, until within a few years, the rudest systems of tillage were in use, and the most wasteful. Even now it is difficult to convince the planters, as a body, that they have anything to do out of the usual routine. There is not, we believe, at this time, a single Parish Agricultural Society in the state, and but a single society of any sort addressed to these interests! It is almost impossible to induce the planters to attend even this, *a central and general institution*, so remarkable is the apathy which prevails. That there are noble exceptions we admit, but why should not this be a matter of *universal* interest? Surely a little reflection will satisfy any one of the great blessings which may be conferred by these bodies upon a Commonwealth. Whence the extraordinary attention paid to agriculture in Europe? We have hundreds of ponderous volumes of Reports from England and France;* and Russia, which some of us have been wont to call barbarian, has sent a letter to us inviting our agriculturists to co-operate with them in developing the soil. It is but the other day that we were called upon, individually, to furnish the Russian Society with a paper upon tobac-

* Among the papers, &c., in this volume, are the Proceedings of the Society, 1840–45; Orations of Messrs. McDuffie and Seabrook; Essay on Malaria, by Dr. Dickson; Orations of Hammond, O'Neall, Roper, and Poinsett; Memoir on Slavery, by Chancellor Harper; Seabrook on the Cotton Plant; Aliston on Rice—which we have already published; Letters and Reports on Marl, &c., &c., 430 pages. We wish to see the Legislature of Louisiana do this much for the State's agriculture.

* Mr. Vattemare, whose philanthropic mission among nations in inducing exchanges of valuable documents has excited so much attention, presented us, when in New-York, with a large number of works of this kind, relating to France, for the State of Louisiana. Through the same means we can get them all, if willing to reciprocate.

co. Consider, too, the results in our own country. The government is collecting material of this kind, and publishing through the Patent Office. The State of Massachusetts publishes, at its own expense, an annual volume of several hundred pages, including the Reports, &c., of all district societies.* In New-York State they have a great Association, which meets at Albany; and in the city of New-York, every two weeks, is convened the FARMERS' CLUB, of practical and scientific men, who discuss important subjects of agriculture. Having attended several of these meetings, we know their value. We heard discussions on silk, wool, sheep, hemp, etc., etc. There is an annual magnificent fair of the AMERICAN INSTITUTE, of which the Club is a part, held in New-York, and attended by hundreds and thousands of visitors. The published volumes of Reports are worthy of all praise and preservation.

It is now five or six years since the Agriculturists' and Mechanics' Association of Louisiana was organized at Baton Rouge, where it has met from year to year for public celebrations. The attendance, though respectable, has never been large. The exhibition and fair have never been worthy of the state. However, we are inclined to hope much better results hereafter. Experience has been of service—energetic officers have been secured, and the state, by an appropriation, has manifested an interest in the matter. Let us indeed hope that the liberal and enlightened planters of Louisiana are now awake.

The removal of the seat of government to Baton Rouge makes that town a place peculiarly fitted for the meeting of the Institute. It should secure a permanent hall in the new State-house being constructed, and a permanent *salaried* secretary. There should be a library like that of the American Institute, containing all agricultural and mechanical publications, etc. A traveling agent should be appointed. An annual appropriation might be secured from the legislature in furtherance of the work.

But nothing of this kind can be effected without the establishment of *parish* or *district societies*. These are indispensable. Any three or five planters are sufficient to establish one. The monthly meetings will soon have interest to attract others, and thus a valuable system will grow up. These societies will send annually their reports and delegates to the central one. Shall it be asked, how these local societies are to be employed? We will show at a glance.

The Central Society should issue to all the local ones, and to individuals throughout the state, a circular similar to that issued by the South Carolina Society—requiring

1st. An account of the present condition of agriculture, and the changes since the first settlement of the county or parish.
2d. The general aspect of the parish, embracing the nature of the soil.
3d. The principal products.
4th. The kinds of cultivation or tillage in use.
5th. The favorite breeds of horses, mules, cattle, sheep, and swine, and their management.
6th. The agricultural implements in use.
7th. The general value of land.
8th. The agricultural changes necessary to advance the prosperity of the parish.

It is hardly necessary to insist how much Louisiana has to gain by these operations, and what will be secured her by her successes. Let us emulate our sister State of Massachusetts in this. She collects and embodies minutely *all* the statistics of her varied and expanding industry, and publishes them, that every citizen may understand.

We have said nothing of the *mechanical department* of the Institute. We are doubtful here whether Baton Rouge will prove the proper place. The two departments may be separated to advantage, so far as the place of exhibition is concerned. NEW-ORLEANS, the great city of the South and West, presents itself at once. Here the products of the ingenuity, the skill, the manufactures of all the Valley and the South, may be brought annually and presented for inspection. It should occupy a place for these regions like New-York. The city is peculiarly fitted for the purpose. In the immediate vicinity of Texas, Mexico, and Cuba, it must shed the broadest influences over them. We regard this as something worthy of future reflection. The day will yet come when what we have written shall appear prophecy. However, it will take time. The first step has been made in the establishment of the UNIVERSITY OF NEW-ORLEANS.

We have not the data for other southern states, and therefore cannot say what they are doing for agriculture. Will not their citizens favor us with abstract reports? We read the other day a partial geological survey of Alabama, and understand that something of the kind is mooted in Mississippi; indeed, that an agricultural professorship in one of her colleges is talked of. But unless this is an institution of the whole state, and under its patronage, the professorship will be of little service. Mississippi will not be behindhand in this race. She has many distinguished agriculturists, as we know.

Judge Rost on the Culture and Manufacture of Sugar.—In a paper which I had the honor to contribute to the labors of the Association last year, I stated that the modern improvements in agriculture were the result of recent and more accurate knowledge on draining, plowing, manuring, and interchange of crops. I then gave a description of the process of thorough draining, as practised

* We have one of those before us, 200 pages, 1846. It contains an abstract of the proceedings, reports, &c., of ten societies in the state, with extracts from the chief addresses, &c. It is thus that nothing is neglected or lost in Massachusetts.

in Great Britain, and of subsoil-plowing, which is the complement of it. It is unnecessary to revert to the subject here, except for the purpose of stating that this process is being rapidly introduced in the British West Indies, and that it has proved as beneficial there as in Europe; so much so, that although by the present modes of cultivation the average of ratoons and plants is seldom two thousand pounds of sugar per acre, it is confidently believed that in lands thoroughly drained and subsoiled the average will be five thousand pounds per acre. I have no doubt of it, and when that system is introduced here, the produce of a depth of sixteen inches of dry alluvial soil cannot be predicted; nobody knows to what size cane may be made to grow, and how much sugar it can yield. But, sir, the process is expensive, and can only be introduced gradually. We must, for the present, go on with our open drains, and we can do passably well with them, provided we have them not over one hundred feet apart, and not less than three feet in depth. With such drains, made or thorougly cleaned when the land is planted in corn, the hardest clays, if not too low, will be found in the subsequent years to drain as well, to plow as deep, and to pulverize as fine as light soils; they will, moreover, yield greater returns of sugar.

Connected with the subject of draining, is that of draining swamps and low lands so as to render them fit for cultivation—a subject of high importance, since, besides the vast quantity of public lands of that description in Louisiana, there are few plantations on which the proportion of these lands is not greater than that of the cultivated fields.—Some abortive attempts at draining low lands had before been made, but within the last year a few intelligent planters below New Orleans have taken the lead in good earnest. Their draining machines are the most perfect of the kind, and they have succeeded in obtaining solid foundation for their locks. After the heaviest rains they dry their land in an incredibly short space of time, and their crops of corn are now growing in marshes below the level of the tides. Their success establishes the fact, that the low lands may be effectually drained in large tracts at an outlay which, with the Congress price of those lands, would not exceed fifteen dollars per superficial acre.

The food of plants, and their modes of existence, form the subject of a very remarkable work, that of Justus Liebig, upon organic chemistry applied to agriculture.—Others before him had submitted to analysis trees, plants, and the earths in which they grow. Countless results of isolated experiments had been collected, but they were rather perplexing than practically useful, till the master mind of Liebig contructed out of them a rational and simple theory of vegetable life. He had not all the facts necessary to make his theory perfect; he was not aware, for instance, of the action of galvanism and electricity upon growing plants. But he did for agriculture what Lavoisier had done for chemistry; he systematized what was known, and pointed out to his successors the true path of discovery. Taking for granted that the substances which are invariably found in a plant are necessary to its perfect development, he has shown which of those substances were supplied by the earth, by the atmosphere and by rain-water; he has proved that pure vegetable mould, which has been considered as the only agent of vegetation, had in it but a secondary, and not an indispensable agency, and that the results assigned to it were produced by carbonic acid, water, and ammonia, or rather nitrogen, and certain mineral salts which the earth supplies; he has discovered that in sugar-bearing plants carbonic acid is the source of saccharine matter. I cannot enter into a detailed examination of this author's views, but I will attempt to show you some of the results to which his theory would lead in the cultivation of the cane, and you will be pleased to find that the practice of our good planters fulfils all the essential requisites of science.

Sugar-cane, analyzed with great care and in various seasons by Mr. Avequin, a person fully competent to the task, is found to contain in proportions, not material to the present inquiry, the following substances, which, according to Liebig, are supplied exclusively by the earth: acetate of potash, phosphate of lime, silica, sulphate of potash, phosphate of potash, chloride of potassium, acetate of lime. These, as well as carbonic acid, ammonia and nitrogen, are hard names, names new to most of us; we must learn their import. Twenty-five years ago we knew not the meaning of piston and cylinder, of steam-chest and safety valve. We all know it now; and as the application of steam to the mechanical arts has not wrought a greater change than the recent discoveries in agriculture are destined to effect, we will have to sharpen our intellects once more and raise them to the level of the times. Upon this, however, I do not at present insist, and if you are disposed to be very obstinate, take the mineral salts I have mentioned, as things which, being invariably found in the cane and never in the atmosphere, or in rain-water, should exist in the soil in a state fit for assimilation by plants; your lands must contain, in that state, potash, silica, lime, chloride, phosphoric acid, sulphuric acid, and substances yielding ammonia; and should any of these be wanting, they must be supplied by deep plowing or by manure.

As it is well known that cane flourishes equally well on all our alluvial lands, when they are first brought into cultivation, we may assume that all these lands once contained, in a state fit for assimilation, the substances necessary to its growth. There is, therefore, no original deficiency to supply, and wherever the cane has ceased to grow and to ratoon as it once did, it is because those substances have been abstracted from the soil by injudicious cropping.

Knowing the mineral substances which the cane requires, chemists tell us that we might at any time ascertain the deficiencies of our soil, by having it analyzed. The suggestion is plausible, but there is nothing in it; we would be as wise after the analysis as we were before. The learned author already quoted shows that arable lands are the result of the disintegration of rocks during many thousand years; that this process is ever going on at the surface of the earth, and that many thousand years will elapse before it is completed. By this process the alkalies and salts which the earth contains are gradually set free and rendered fit for assimilation by plants; and when all the substances thus set free have been taken up, plants requiring them will cease to grow in the soil where they are wanting: and yet it will require thousands of years to effect a complete disintegration, the quantity abstracted by the cane in Louisiana, during a cultivation of forty years, must be infinitely small in relation to the quantity yet remaining; and accordingly it is found, where land supposed to be exhausted has been analyzed, that it contains the same elements as the fertile soils adjoining it, or found beneath it, united in very nearly the same proportions. It is not the precise quantity of the different elements contained in our soil, which it imports us to know, but that portion of them which is disintegrated and fit for assimilation. This, I apprehend, chemistry cannot tell us.

If we could every year provide a sufficiency of mixed animal and bagasse manure for all the land we plant, it would be idle to inquire about the deficiences of the soil, since that manure contains all the requisite substances. But, compelled as we are by the severities of the climate to plant annually a large portion of crops, we cannot save one-sixth of the quantity of manure required. This should be husbanded with care and placed in rotation on the oldest lands; for the remainder, manure would have to be purchased at an expense which would be under thirty dollars per acre, and the question naturally presents itself—Is it necessary to incur that expense and the extra labor to which it would give rise? Intelligent planters say that it is not, and science justifies their opinion. If in the lands that have been longest in cultivation, the alkalies fit for assimilation are partially exhausted, it should be remembered that the plow has seldom gone beyond the depth of six or seven inches, and that below that depth is a virgin soil, in all respects similar to the original surface soil, and deeper than the plow can ever penetrate. So that if a depth of six inches had yielded a sufficiency of disintegrated alkalies to cane crops during thirty years, there is no reason why the next six inches below should not do the same, provided they can be brought to the surface and kept in good tilth. With the thorough drain system this presents no difficulty, and it can be satisfactorily accomplished with the open drains I have recommended. With those drains, a depth of plowing of ten inches, when the stubble is broken up for corn, will give to the land that cannot be manured all the substances which the cane requires from the earth but one; it will not give a sufficiency of nitrogen. I stated last year that nitrogen or ammonia could only be supplied in large quantities by manure, and I was not then aware that any but animal manure could effect that object. Farther experience and observation have satisfied me that it is supplied in great abundance by a process which has long been followed without any clear conceptions of its mode of action: I mean that of covering the land with peas as early in the summer as the corn crops will permit. One of the advantages of peas as a green crop is, that they take from the land none of the alkalies which the cane requires, while their powerful system of roots has a tendency to accelerate the disintegration of the soil. But their principal action consists in shading the land, thus preventing the escape of ammonia which the rain-water deposits in it, and hastening by shade and humidity the decay going on at the surface, and the formation of nitre, which ever follows it in warm climates. The leaves and seed of the pea are richer in nitrogen than any other vegetable substance, and the result of their decay is the formation of additional quantities of nitric acid. The nitre and nitric acid thus formed, as well as the ammonia retained in the soil, yield to the following crop of cane the nitrogen they contain. The method now generally adopted of plowing in the field-trash, restores to the ratoons, in a state fit for assimilation, most of the alkalies which the plants took up in their growth; and should more ammonia be wanted, by setting fire to the field-trash after rain the top part of it is converted into charcoal, which has the power of absorbing ninety times its volume of ammonia. To facilitate this operation, cane ought not to be planted less than six feet apart. What precedes, and with it such frequent movings of the soil as perpetually keep the young plants in an atmosphere of carbonic acid, is the method pursued in Louisiana by all successful planters, and the only material improvements I would suggest to them are those of thorough draining and subsoil plowing.

There are, however, cheap mineral manures with which it would be well to try experiments. In hard clay lands, for instance, especially if they are too near the level of the swamp to be plowed deep with advantage, quick-lime applied to the corn land at the rate of fifty or sixty bushels to the acre, produces an admirable effect upon the ensuing crops. It is itself one of the substances which the cane requires, and can replace others; aided by a crop of peas, it very much increases the quantity of nitre and acid formed at the surface, keeps the land in the finest state of tilth, causes the rapid decay of the inert vegetable substances which accumulate in it during repeated crops of cane, and is thus an abundant source of carbonic acid. Land I limed four years ago, was planted again last winter, and the cane upon it is the best I have.

Experiments successfully made in Europe induce me to believe that we all have at home a substance possessed of the same qualities as lime, and in a higher degree. That substance is clay when burnt to ashes. I cannot describe the process by which it is prepared; you will find it in a recent publication entitled the "Farmer's Manual." It is sufficient to state that little or no fuel is required, and that one small cart-load of the ashes is said to have a better and more lasting effect than eight bushels of lime. The ammonia which they absorb and retain, more than replaces the nitrification obtained by liming, and the burning disintegrates very large quantities of alkalies. It is to the effect of burning, that the inexhaustible fertility of lands formed by the eruption of volcanoes is to be attributed.

Common salt I have also tried with success, at the rate of ten bushels to the acre. It gives to the cane a deep green color, and seems to prevent the growth of grass.

I observed that covering land with peas caused the formation of nitre. In Europe, nitre and saltpetre are both used upon growing plants, at the rate of about one hundred pounds per acre; it is probable, that sprinked before the plow, here, when the land is first thrown to the cane, their effect would be similar to that of peas.

Much has been said of late on the subject of guano, and experiments made in Jamaica prove it to be a valuable manure for cane. Used there at the rate of one pound to every four feet square, or about twenty-seven hundred pounds to the acre, it caused cane to ripen earlier and yield two hundred pounds more of sugar per acre, than that dressed with common manure. Those who made the experiment seem to think that one-third of the quantity used might have been sufficient. Admitting the fact to be so, and supposing the ratoons to last two years, and to yield an additional quantity of two hundred pounds of sugar per acre, which is not probable, an outlay of nine hundred pounds of guano would, in the next three years, give an increase of four hundred pounds of sugar. Where other manure has to be purchased, as in Jamaica, and costs more guano, this increase of product is a material advantage. But where deep plowing and peas do as well as animal manure, the additional product obtained by the use of guano would not pay for it. An experiment is now going on with it in my neighborhood; if it should make the cane fit for the mill earlier than it usually is, it would on that account be very valuable. In the mean time, I would recommend the use of it to a portion of my audience whom I have, till now, sadly neglected: to you, ladies, within your realm of fruits, flowers, and shrubs. There, as well as in the garden, when applied with intelligence and care, it does wonders, and I beseech you not to neglect the means it affords you of increasing the beauty and the comforts of your homes. When God, for wise purposes, doomed man to waste his energies in conquering physical obstacles, he placed you near him to cheer him in his weary task, to remind him that his toils had a worthy object on earth, and to recall him in his hours of repose to the consciousness of his moral existence. All about his dwelling that has the spirituality of beauty and grace, is by some mysterious tie connected with you, and you have an interest in its preservation. Nurse your flowers, then, as if they were a part of yourselves, and let your favorite plants have a cheerful and happy look. Above all, do not torment them into fantastic and unnatural shapes; remember, that the God who made them, gave each of them, as he gave each of you, peculiar forms of beauty, which knives and scissors cannot improve, and that trimming should be resorted to exclusively with the view to restore and preserve the natural shape of each species, as you resort to the mysteries of the toilet to make the perfections you possess conceal the slight blemishes which may accompany them.

Although, for want of time and of competent knowledge, I have confined myself to the sugar crop, my observations upon draining, tillage, animal manure, and peas, may be considered as applicable to the cultivation of cotton also. I would not recommend any course which would farther extend that cultivation; but, if the same crops could, as I believe, be obtained from half of the land that now produces it, the other half might be employed in raising provisions and other products, such as indigo, hemp, and tobacco.

On the subject of interchange of crops, I have nothing to offer, and I will now direct your attention to the improvements proposed in the manufacture of sugar.

Not less than six new methods have been partially tested, and are now offered for our adoption. We ought to be thankful for every effort of that kind, and encourage to a reasonable extent those persons who, in trying to benefit themselves, desire also to benefit us. But planters cannot be expected to incur the great expense which the adoption of most of those methods requires, till they have satisfactory evidence of their entire success. That evidence is yet wanting; there is in all much room for improvement. The process of my friend, Thomas A. Morgan, of Plaquemines, is thus far considered the best, and he is far from claiming perfection for it. The increase in the quantity of sugar obtained by some of the innovators, is principally owing to the fact that they reboil the molasses. This is done equally well by others in open pans.

A new apparatus, said to embrace all that has been found valuable in the others, is now being constructed at the Novelty Iron Works, in New-York, for Mr. Valcour Aime, of St. James, a gentleman distinguished for his enterprise, as well as for his practical knowledge of the subject. It may do better than the others, but, sir, all these new methods have the original fault of the usual process, their authors being wrong. They commence by creating large quantities of coloring matter in the juice, and then, by a great variety of means, they endeavor to extract that coloring matter first from the syrup, and afterward from the sugar, and in this, by the by, nobody has yet effectually succeeded. Let me explain my meaning.

If you cut in two a sugar-cane, and examine the interior part of it with a magnifying-glass, you perceive the crystals of sugar as distinct and as white as those of double-refined sugar. The object of the operator should be then either to extract those crystals without altering their color, or, if that be found impracticable, to separate them from the impurities mixed with them, while the juice is in its natural state, and yet contains but little coloring matter. Instead of this, the juice is limed while all the impurities are in it. In separating the feculencies from the juice and uniting them in large flakes, lime dissolves a portion of them and forms with them coloring matter, which, we all know, at once discolors the juice, when lime is used in excess. Afterward heat is applied, either in clarifiers or in the *grande;* but most of the impurities found in the juice will decompose and burn at a degree of heat far below the boiling point, say at a hundred and twenty degrees of Fahrenheit. This is shown by the thick scales continually forming in the *grande*. From that degree of heat the decomposition goes on in the clarifier, till the juice is drawn, and continues in the *grande* so long as there are feculencies left. This decomposition greatly increases the quantity of coloring matter, so that, as the juice is being clarified, it loses in color what it gains in purity; and here let me show the relative value of the *grande* and of clarifiers as agents of clarification. In the *grande*, if it is well attended to, the scummings are taken up as fast as they rise. A portion of them is removed before they begin to decompose, and the process goes on, so that before the juice reaches the boiling point, nearly all the feculencies are removed, and the source of coloring matter is removed with them.

Clarifiers reach the boiling point much quicker, and cannot easily be scummed. The general practice is, to bring them to that point without scumming; to let the feculencies separate from the juice by cooling and by rest, and to wash out the clarifiers every second or third time they are filled. Heat and alkalies acting in them upon the accumulated feculencies of one, two, or three charges, dissolve a much larger portion of those feculencies than they can possibly do in the *grande;* the formation of coloring matter continues during the time of rest, and, accordingly, planters, after repeated trials, generally agree that juice well clarified in the *grande* has a brighter and a lighter color, and makes better sugar than that obtained from clarifiers.

But to return to my subject, the first object of research should be to find means of clarifying the juice, without creating coloring matter. It is said that presses, something like those used to represent cotton here, have lately been successfully employed in the West Indies, instead of rollers; that the juice obtained is much purer, and that a much larger quantity of it is extracted from the cane. If so, this will be a great improvement, and the first step of the process I would recommend. From juice thus obtained, or even from our own, I have no doubt that all impurities less soluble than itself, may be separated by mechanical means, before heat and alkalies are applied, or at least with a very small quantity of alkalies. All other liquids, all fatty substances and oils, except cotton-seed oil, are clarified by a very rapid process. Cane-juice can no doubt be clarified by similar means, and if this were accomplished, the process of sugar-making would be very much simplified. The clarified juice might then be placed in an open evaporator, heated by the waste steam of the engine; then be limed and scummed if necessary, and concentrated to fifteen or sixteen degrees of the *pese sirop;* then purified by filtration through animal charcoal, if white sugar was wanted, or by rest for other qualities, and finally concentrated in vacuum pans of great power, such pans as Mr. Thomas A. Morgan now uses, and which he tells me can only be made in America.

The superiority of the vacuum pan is not universally admitted, and we are told that in

France it is superseded by open pans, similar in construction to those called here Mapes' Evaporators. However this may be, I cannot help believing that the vacuum pan has many decided advantages over all others; one is manifest; the sugar may be grained in the pan, and the granulation is completely under the control of the operator. He may accelerate or retard it at pleasure; he may carry it so far that sugar will not run from the pan, and will have to be taken out of it; he may so conduct the operation as to increase almost at will the size and hardness of the crystals. This last is an indispensable requisite, if the practice of draining sugar in pneumatic pans should be adopted. The atmospheric pressure is much too powerful for sugars boiled in any other manner; it breaks and destroys the crystals, and in a very few days sets the sugar to fermenting.

The pneumatic draining of sugar has many things to recommend it; the usual loss by drainage is avoided, sugar is got ready for market day by day, as it is made, and it may be bleached by pouring white syrup over it and forcing it through the mass. It is said that the process is attended with considerable loss in weight; but as all that drains from the pans may be boiled over once or twice, it is not easy to conceive how the loss can occur.

One observation on the subject of our buildings. Houses of unburnt brick are of late much recommended to the working-classes at the North, and to the settlers in the prairies, as being cheaper, drier, and healthier than those built of brick or stone. On reading the description of those buildings, in the excellent Report of the Commissioner of Patents, it struck me that they were substantially the same as the old houses of Louisiana, known by the name of houses *en colomage*. Is it not owing to a change in our mode of building that the present race of our people is not as hardy and as long-lived as their ancestors were? In former days no one ever entered one of those ancient houses without finding in it a brace of octogenarians at least. With our old houses, old people seem to have disappeared; and to you and me, sir, who are not quite as young as we have been, it may be of some consequence to ascertain the cause of this phenomenon. I have no doubt it is in a great measure owing to the dampness of our modern dwellings; and though we may not persuade our ladies to return to the primitive architecture which was the pride of their great-grandmothers, we may at least adopt it for our laborers, and I will make the trial. The brick houses we have built for the purpose of increasing their comfort, are the cause of many of the maladies which afflict them.

After reviewing the means placed at our disposal to increase the value of our products, and to overcome the disadvantages of climate, and the gradual deterioration of the soil, allow me to advert to other disadvantages and dangers, which, in the opinion of many, threaten us with inevitable ruin. Two causes of alarm now exist among a large number of our fellow-planters: the diminution in the value of our lands, which will result from the annexation of Texas, and the destruction of our industry by a reduction of duties on foreign sugars, made before we are in a situation to compete with foreign producers. I am happy to say that I believe we have nothing to fear from either.

A person looking upon the map of America, and perceiving a large portion of Texas south of Louisiana, would naturally suppose that Texas is the better sugar region of the two. But the Louisianian who travels in mid-winter through the prairies of that naked land, exposed to the unmitigated fury of north-westers, soon discovers that he has changed climate indeed, but that he has not come to regions in which tropical plants love to grow. I have it from a gentleman of undoubted veracity, Mr. John C. Marsh, that he has planted cane five successive years in the neighborhood of Galveston, and that he has never obtained ratoons from it. You may then consider it as a well-authenticated fact, that in Texas, as far south as New-Orleans is, cane will not ratoon—the cold of winter destroys the stubble; I do not mean to say that it may not to some extent be cultivated there, but I assert that the competition will be by no means a dangerous one, and that upon trial it will be found that the Red river parishes of this state are better adapted to that cultivation, than the greater part of what has been called the sugar region of Texas.

Louisiana must remain the great sugar region of the United States; her climate and her soil are the best, and her geographical position is unrivaled. Reflect, sir, that almost every hogshead of sugar made here, is shipped without land carriage; that planters can always obtain from New-Orleans, in two or three days, any machinery they want, and that their supplies and their market are both brought to their own door. Compare this situation with that of the Texas planter, and you will admit that there is no room for apprehension.

There is a strong analogy between the cultivation of the vine in Middle France, and that of the cane in Louisiana. During the first centuries of the Christian era, there was no wine produced in France, except Marseilles wine. More Southern Europe and the Isles of Greece were then the wine-growing regions. In the course of time, the monks of Aquitaine, of Champaign, and of Burgundy, God bless them! transplanted the vine to the shelter of their convent walls. Their efforts were for a long time unsuccessful, but they persevered, and the great saints of those dark ages took a conspicuous part in the good work. At last their grapes attained maturity; they tasted the juice, and said it was good. Wine was subsequently made of it, and it is easy to conceive the joy of those holy men, when champaign first sparkled on their board, when the vintages of Medoc and Burgundy replaced in their cellars the rough beverages of Provence. The cultivation of the vine continued to increase and to improve, but the increase was so slow that wine was not exported from Bordeaux to foreign countries, till some time in the twelfth century. And now, sir, the great wine region of the world is that very portion of France, in which the introduction of the vine was the work of centuries.

How is it with the sugar-cane in Louisiana? It was introduced here at an early day from the West Indies, and cultivated to a small extent at Terre aux Bœufs, and in the neighborhood of New-Orleans. Nobody at first imagined that sugar could be made of it. The juice was boiled into syrup, which sold at extravagant prices. In 1796 Mr. Bore, residing a few miles above New-Orleans, a man reputed for his daring and his energy, formed the desperate resolve of making sugar. He increased his cultivation, put up the necessary buildings and machinery, and procured a sugar maker from the West Indies. The day appointed for the experiment was come, and the operation was under way. The inhaabitants of New-Orleans and of the coast had assembled there in great numbers. But they remained outside of the building, at a respectable distance from the sugar maker, whom they looked upon as a sort of a magician. The first *strike* came, and he said nothing; this they thought fatal, but still they remained fixed to the spot. The second strike was out; the sugar maker carefully stirred the first, and then advancing toward the assembled crowd, told them with all the gravity of his craft, "Gentlemen, it grains!" "It grains!" was repeated by all. They rushed in to see the wonder, and when convinced of the fact, scattered in all directions, greeting everybody they met with "It grains!" And from the Balize to the Dubuque, from the Wabash to the Yellow Stone, the great, the all-absorbing news of the colony was, that the juice of the cane had grained in Lower Louisiana. It did grain, it has continued to grain: it has grained the last season, at the rate of two hundred and fifteen millions of pounds, and if no untoward action of government prevents it, in ten years it will grain to the extent of much more than double that quantity. Prepare, therefore, to meet foreign competition. I tell you we can do so, as well as the wine-growers of France, provided we improve the time that is left us, and remain true to the spirit of our national race.

The innate faculty of our people to subdue the physical world, their energy and self-reliance, their habitual disregard of discomfort, difficulties and dangers, have made other nations say of us, that we alone could instil heroism in the common pursuits of life. With heroic determination, then, speed the plow: bear in mind that to go ahead without ever taking difficulties into the account, and by that means to succeed when others dare not undertake, is emphatically the AMERICAN SYSTEM.

Oration by J. D. B. De Bow.—What shall be done for agricultural science? How shall the indispensable wants of man be supplied with greatest facility, and the unwilling earth be made to yield the best and most abundant product for the longest time with the least labor, to satisfy the desires and necessities, and produce the highest amount of comfort to the whole human race? This is the great problem, in the elucidation of which the practical and benevolent minds of all countries are now engaged. Whatever Greek divinity it was that taught the art of culture to mankind, or showed them first how to fashion curious workmanship from the metals, better deserved Olympus than the "cloud-compelling Jove," and performed an act more worthy of a god, than any other fabled by inventive mythology.

The sanguinary and cruel strifes which have desolated the earth in all ages, have been justified in the providence of God as the means of checking the advances of population, and of preserving mankind from the famine and destitution attendant upon a too crowded and overstocked earth. Grave philosophical treatises have been presented to the world, announcing in startling terms this impending calamity. Ingenious moral and political expedients have been proposed to avert it. When Hobbes announced that war was the natural state of man, could he, think you, have much offended Malthus, who conceived that peace has a necessary tendency to starve him? Keep the numbers of the human race, said these philosophers, down to the capacity of the earth to maintain them all. Raise the capacity of the earth, say we, to satisfy all the requisitions of a rapidly augmenting population. Which is the nobler employ? The one is theoretic economy, over wise in its own conceits; the other is practical agriculture, based upon an unwavering confidence in the wisdom and the goodness of the First Cause, and the adaptation of the earth to all the contingencies of the creatures who inhabit it. The great cardinal and fundamental doctrine of an enlightened political economy, may be stated to be the multiplication of product and subtraction of labor. Let two blades of grass shoot up where but one grew before. Let one man conduct the previous operations of two men. With these rules, I doubt whether we shall ever regard much the additional loaf of bread a day, which the neighbor dead leaves to be divided to the neighbor living.

The enlightened Voltaire held it as an axiom, that in the intercourse of nations the benefit of one could only result from the expense or loss of another. A doctrine so mischievous, you will agree with me, ought hardly to have found a convert, and yet we know that for gloomy ages of the world's history—alas! not even excluding our own —its baneful and blighting influences have been suffered to disturb the councils and pervert the actions of mankind. How slowly are we learning the great moral truth, that nations as well as individuals *can* benefit each other—that good is reciprocal—that all free intercourse in fairness must be, and in fact will be, one of the equivalents—that the distresses of our neighbors extend their effects beyond themselves, and that their prosperity is reflected over an equal area. It was Addison, I believe, who thought he could enjoy the beauties of his neighbor's grounds, delight his senses with the varied hues, the exquisite forms, the aroma of their ten thousand flowers, as much, perhaps, and in many cases even more, than the selfish owner who lorded it over them as his "empire sole." The jealousies of nations, as of individuals, are suicidal to the best interests of men. Philanthropy is a higher virtue than patriotism, as patriotism is higher than self-love. That orb which is revolving, and revolving, and revolving forever in a circle which never enlarges, and around a centre which is ever the *individual*, warms never with a genial heat—sunless and cheerless is it course.

The train of thought into which we have fallen originated from two reflections: 1. The indisposition which has sometimes been noted among agriculturists to communicate what great observation, experiment or research may have taught them, and by which they are enabled to realize better returns for their labors, or a superior quality of product for the market. 2. The notion generally current, that a nation ought to be more anxious to receive than to give; and that to be most prosperous is to want nothing whatever of the great world around and beyond us. The first of these levels a blow against industry and cordial reciprocity; the last strikes but too deeply at all commerce and civilization.

When you invited me, fellow-citizens, to address your Association, I was for some time undecided what plan to adopt in the selection and arrangement of subjects. In the first place, I deemed that agriculture was too wide a theme to admit of an indulgence in many details. To discuss almost any one of its numerous divisions, to make anything like a satisfactory exposition of late improvements, even in a particular branch, or to show the results of scientific researches and rigid experiments, would occupy more than the time you allot to this whole address. These matters, too, are usually ably treated in the reports of the practical men who constitute your committees. Need I remark, in addition, that if, from the circumstance of my standing in the presence of agriculturists, any inferences are to be drawn in favor of my capacity as an instructor in the arts they cultivate and advance, these inferences ought to be received, to use a legal phrase, with many grains of allowance. Let them be understood like those convenient fictions of the lawyers, ever raised, ever employed, yet never supposed to be any nearer the truth for all that. Standing near me, however, and your guest upon this occasion,* it is my fortune to recognize one whose voice to-day would have been in your service, as his heart throbs with you, had we been allowed our way in this matter. Let him rest, however, for it is *he* that claims it. A practical citizen, high enough to move with the philosophers, but never so high like them, or like the stars, as Bacon has it, that give little light, because of their so great elevation. An agriculturist to-day, a farmer preparing his stock, perchance, for the market—a statesman to-morrow, a diplomatist —an American senator and patriot, rousing grave senates with resistless eloquence, unmatched since his of yore—that man of Attica, who first

> ———"shook the arsenal,
> And fulmined over Greece,
> To Macedon and Artaxerxes' throne."

I have taken another view of my duties as your speaker. I will regard this Association to be, what it ought to be, and what, to an extent, it is, the representative of the great interests of Louisiana; its prime object being the advancement and permanent welfare of the state. This enables me to take a higher position than I could, were I restrained to the consideration of any one or more of the prominent subjects of agricultural knowledge. In such a view of your Association and my duties, I am sustained by the course of some of the most distinguished similar bodies in the Union. Many of them have their committees upon education, upon the state of the law as affecting the planters' interests, on the condition of slaves, &c., &c. I therefore announce the State of Louisiana as a subject, and in examining into its present condition and future prospects, there will naturally fall under particular divisions, such reflections as may have occurred to me in relation to its agricultural and mechanic interests, and the best modes of advancing them.

I put the question to this respectable assembly, have we sufficiently regarded the

*Hon. Henry Clay, of Kentucky—an honorary member of the Association.

position of Louisiana at the present time, and well considered what may be fairly and reasonably expected from her by the world at large? Has it occurred to us that in the mutation of time, and the sure working out of the problem of American history, Louisiana has ceased to be on the frontiers of the Union, and that in giving up her charge of the boundary, she has relinquished forever the right of being in any respect one step behind the most favored state of the Union? Of what a country has she become, as it were, the centre, and what incalculable influences may be exerted from her position! I care not where the sovereignty of Texas or the Rio Grande, California, Mexico, or Western Indies may reside, by the laws of civil empire or of arms, for I know too well that there are other laws which have been insensibly exerting their secret and mysterious agencies, and giving to our institutions an influence, difficult to be estimated, all over the continent of America. I know that Louisiana, to say nothing of her position at the gate of a great river, which ripples in some of its tributaries almost in the distant Oregon, sits here by the gulf, as it were its sovereign, looking out upon all these immense and fertile countries at her very door—and that the gay metropolis of Louisiana is to be the centre and the heart of all the great movements which, it needs no seer's eye to see, are to be worked out in the course of a generation or two, in the vast region from where the Sabine fixed its boundary, to where the isthmus connects the two Americas. It was a dream of La Salle to connect China with the Gulf of Mexico, through some supposed tributary of the Mississippi; but we, gentlemen, disregarding all rivers and tributaries, shall realize the vision by the amazing power of steam; traverse the country from ocean to ocean, centering in the lap of our already great city much of that Eastern trade which made Venice *what she was*, and left her, when it left her at last, *what she is*.

In such a prospect as is presented us in the view we have calmly taken, is there not enough to rouse the attention of every citizen of Louisiana? Yet, strange as it may seem, the subject in this light does not seem to have presented itself with all its force to those who are most interested. The one great question, as I take it, now for the state is, how shall she be prepared for the new and responsible position she is to occupy?

"Commerce and Agriculture are the two great arms of our state's prosperity, but there must be a will to move those arms, and an enlightenment to will correctly. There must be a Cornelia to produce the Gracchi."

I. *The first duty of Louisiana is the Education of her people.* Has she done this, and is she doing it at this moment? Fellow-citizens, we were told that under our new Constitution there would be another and a better order of things. Let us hope so at least so far as public instruction is concerned, since we have incorporated this in our fundamental law. Can we estimate the hundreds of thousands of dollars that have been prodigally lavished by us in the support of schools and colleges, without any very appreciable advantage? The common school system of the State, with all the aid of parish assessments and legislative appropriations, comes to be regarded as a byword and a reproach. It is not a system from which anything but mortification and defeat can result. I know full well the difficulty with so thin a population as ours is, and as it is generally at the South, to establish and maintain adequate means of public instruction. An indefinite improvement may, however, be made within the limits assigned us. Shall a great and wealthy state pause to consider the difficulties, or enumerate the costs of distributing light and instruction throughout all its extent, and of bringing home to each embryo citizen, even the veriest offspring of beggary and want, the means of becoming a nobleman, in the only sense in which our institutions admit of nobility, and in which the might of intellect can make us all noble? I know of no patriot service more exalted than of that man, who will come forward in our legislative halls, to proclaim and carry out from an enlightened appreciation of the subject in all its bearings, a reform such as the exigencies of the state so loudly demand.

II. If the first duty of Louisiana be found in the development of the minds of her rising population, *the second* is readily suggested, *in the maintenance of a sound and liberal government.* The laws of a people ever reflect their intelligence, though legal systems influence moral progress. I would, therefore, that our legislation be framed upon those safe principles of political science which have their foundations in knowledge and experience. In the utmost simplification is the perfection of government. Every unnecessary restraint is a crime against the principles of civil society. Liberty endures no arbitrary restrictions. National prosperity is secured in governing little and adequately, and not in governing much. Freemen only are the great heralds of civilization and advancement. They only permanently extend the area of knowledge, are found on the outermost verge of thought, daring, and daring, and still daring on in their eagle flight to the sun. The night of civil and political liberty is the dark age of moral, social and intellectual progress. Let us look to it, then, in the administration of our government and our laws, that we elevate to office only the virtuous, the intelligent and experienced; that we reject all rash innovation, and realize, as near as may be, that idea of a perfect government in which the essence is virtue and intelligence. Standing here among you, fellow-citizens, on the site where the sense of the people has decreed the future seat of government to be, I could not but entertain these reflections and give expression to them. As you are made the conservators of the CAPITOL, the citadel of our strength, I would not have you less sleepless in your charge than were those virgins of old, who watched forever, that the sacred fires enkindled on the altars of Vesta might be preserved lustrous and nndimmed.

III. *An enlightened and well-governed people will foster and maintain those enterprises which are the natural results of free institutions; will see that the industry and energies of oll classes are rightly directed and maintained, and that the advances of each important division of human labor are promoted by every legitimate means.*

COMMERCE, AGRICULTURE and ARTS, are the three great divisions under which a thousand minor ones array themselves.

I have said sufficient of the *commerce* of Louisiana on other occasions. It is an interest of our great city, which it does not so much concern us to discuss here. The enlightened men of that city will see to it, that the genius and enterprise of the East keep not so far their dizzy eminence which has in the past dwarfed us in the comparison.

Of our AGRICULTURE we have much to say and in detail. Around me are assembled the men who have collected here from every quarter, to unite in council upon the common interest, and to devise modes of future effectual co-operation. Some of these are the parents of this Association, and I honor the patriot labors which through years of trial and discouragement have been bestowed by them, without one misgiving of a final triumph. I rejoice that there is a spirit abroad now to appreciate these services and to extend their influence.

Fellow-citizens: it is in this view that the appeal is made to you in behalf of the Association of Agriculturists and Mechanics of Louisiana, now convened in this town. It is believed, and can be demonstrated, that an enlightened co-operation of all the minds engaged in these pursuits will tend greatly among us, as it has done everywhere else, to advance the general weal. This much is demanded from us, and will we do our duty?

Agriculture is, without question, THE great interest of mankind. It is the breast, said the celebrated Sully, from which the state derives support and nourishment. Ireland in starvation, and extending her arms for bread, will yet have yielded from her soil an amount in value, which shall exceed the value of all the merchandise which the merchant fleets bear annually away from our shores to all foreign climes together. Without assigning to the agriculturists the rank of being the *only* producers, as the celebrated school of Quesnay sought long to teach the world erroneously, it may still be insisted that the producers of all agricultural wealth are the most numerous and most important of all.

I should be greatly delighted, did time admit, to trace with you the progress which agriculture has made since its first rude incipiency "beyond the verdant walls of paradise," and mark in every age the influence which it has exerted and the relative degrees of perfection it has attained. The limits of this address will yet not exclude us entirely from the field.

To say nothing of the culture of the earth, as mentioned in that ancient record, the Bible, nor to comment upon the beautiful fictions of Ceres, Proserpine and Triptolemus, which poetic fancy created to account for the origin of the arts, we know that the early princes of Greece labored at the plow with their own hands, and that in Homer there are allusions to the soil, its products and its labors, always beautifully conceived and highly colored. The Greek writers, Hesiod and Theophastus, laid down at a very remote period, as then well understood, the principles of plowing, fallowing, irrigation, draining, ditching, manuring, etc.

The Romans interwove agriculture curiously in their religion and their superstitious rites. Their most distinguished statesmen and generals had patronymic names, derived from that of some vegetable, of which their ancestors were the successful producers—for example, Fabius, Cicero, Lentulus, etc. The leading men of the state toiled occasionally in the fields—as Cincinnatus, Curius, Dentatus, Fabricius and Regulus. The farm of Cincinnatus is estimated to have contained four acres of land only. Thus was it, as Pliny held, that the earth took pleasure in being cultivated by the hands of men crowned with laurels and decorated with triumphal honors. Cato, Varro, Virgil, Columella, Pliny and Palladius, renowned names, have been attached to agricultural treatises. Who can forget the graceful and beautiful allusions in the classics to the genial toils of the husbandman? What modern has ever expressed more sententiously the rules of successful culture than Cato? Do you ask, says he, what is first in good tillage?—to plow; what is second?—to plow; the third is to manure; the other part is to sow plentifully, to choose the seed cautiously, and to remove as many weeds as possible in the season.

From the downfall of the Roman empire, until the Reformation, and even much later, industry in Europe was paralyzed, and agriculture, with the other arts of peace, declined, as barbarism and arms usurped the sway. The iron rule of the feudal system resolved the great masses of society into an absolute and hopeless bondage, fatal to all improvement. Fields were converted into forests for the chase. The domain of the king reached over all the lands in his realm, and he distributed them out to his favorites, to be held at his arbitrary will and pleasure. Thus did those lordly chieftains, independent of all the world but their sovereign, and brooking little dependence even upon him, assert their territorial rights, and parcel them out in minor proportions to the vassals, leet men, yeomanry or people, with ingenious tenures, which exhausted the products of labor and enterprise, in the rapacious exactions of a suzerein lord and master. It required centuries to rescue man from this curiously elaborated system of feuds, which, consecrating power and its abuses, imposed upon the senses by its gorgeous concomitants. But where there is insecurity of property, or rather no property at all, there can be no progress nor enterprise. It almost seems in this view that a sixth sense has been added to the constitution of man—*the sense of property*. It is the first to exhibit itself, and the last to disappear. Give us something that we may call our own—no matter what it is—how small soever—how insignificant—the child shows it in his toy—no matter. Is it ours? May we use it, dispose of it, change, direct, alter, destroy it, consulting no other will or pleasure than our own? Oh, there is a luxury in property, and in the rights and privileges of possession and property! Profligacy and avarice are its extremes; industry, order, society, laws, government, are its means. A wise Creator fixes us thus to the earth, of which we are a part, on which we must live, and to which we must return at last, despite the seductions of transcendental dreams.

When the feudal system tottered upon its base, and fell at last in a mighty ruin, scattering its castellated remains over Europe, the world began that rapid stride in the career of progress, which has crowded into a generation the events of a previous thousand years.

In the picture which Europe exhibits at the present day, there is much to gratify every true friend of the race, and in the contrast much to disappoint. The once fertile Campania of Rome has become the resort of beggary, and where the garden of the Hesperides was placed, whole regions of Spain present the aspect of a desert. The country has been parceled out to the nobles and the clergy. "One-third of Spain belongs to the families of the Medina Celi, D'Alva, D'Aceda, and to the archbishops, bishops and chapters of Toledo." The vicious systems of man have destroyed all this fine country. The prospect, however, brightens as we regard Tuscany, which, though two-thirds mountainous, and of but 8,000 square miles surface, contains yet a prosperous populace of 1,300,000; or the Piedmont and the Milanese, the garden spots of the world—vineyards and luxuriant pastures rise upon the delighted senses, amid naked, barren and precipitous rocks.

England and France, within the last few years, have made the most extraordinary progress in agricultural pursuits. We might speak of Britain particularly, where is practised, at the present day, the most liberal, enlightened and scientific husbandry in the world. Every foot of soil capable of production is made to teem with vegetable life, and lands are improved to manifold their former value. In draining, alone, a subject now exciting such deserved attention, there has been conferred almost inappreciable wealth. Dr. Buckland tells us that there are men now living, who can remember when 40,000 acres of land, belonging to the late Lord Leicester, now worth £40,000 a year, were nothing but rabbit warrens and rabbit heaths. And *the secret was draining*. A similar tract of land belonging to Sir Robert Peel, was swampy and altogether barren, until, by the same means, it was made to yield, in the first year, a splendid crop of turnips, in the second, one of barley, so luxurient that the stalks could not support the ears, and fell prostrate to the ground. The expenses were repaid in two years, and a worthless field became a most profitable piece of land.

In the United States, the present may be considered the great age of agricultural reform. It was not singular that with such an abundant country as ours, the soil would be long cultivated without any special care, and with none of that economy which would preserve its vitality. The consequence has been, that lands which were the most fertile in the world, became at last almost irretrievably barren; and the sons, whose fathers grew wealthy, scarcely with an effort, are forced to submit themselves to exile from the paternal estates, sacrificing or abandoning them, to seek in new and virgin soils the support they cannot find at home. Alas! how long has this been so with many of our old southern climes—most particularly Virginia and the Carolinas—and how have their sons been scattered abroad by this reckless system! Taught by sad experience, these ancient commonwealths appear to be now engaged in earnest to recover what they have lost, and their citizens strain every nerve in devising means of regeneration.

In most of the states of the Union, efforts are being made to develop the resources of agriculture, which are proportionate to the subject.* The most usual of these means are the establishment of County and State Agricultural Associations, fruit, flower, and stock exhibitions, etc. Some of these are conducted in the most efficient manner, and exert a degree of influence we can scarcely estimate. There is an emulation excited which never sleeps again. There are essays and reports prepared, and perused by ten thousand readers; there are experiments made, and subjects discussed which are full of light. We have been watching the new spirit of our country, and thank God for it. Legislative appropriations are made for agricultural surveys, and all the mineral characteristics of soil are determined with a degree of precision and certainty which renders it almost impossible to be deceived. What an improvement too in our agricultural publications, standard and periodical. Even the newspaper press finds it necessary to have a department for this subject, while chronicling the events of busy life. Our agricultural periodicals improve rapidly in the nature and value of their material. They have come to be in requisition among the planters, to whom they are addressed, and are liberally sustained; for what planter would be without such means of information? To be without a library of agriculture, is for a planter to be without the implements of his profession.† A lawyer without the civil code, would be in about the same condition and as wise. Then we have the new feature of agricultural schools. We hear of them in different parts of the Union; in Prussia, France, Germany, Russia, Ireland, and Switzerland. A professorship has been endowed in the venerable Harvard; the same has been done in South Carolina, and we trust to see the example followed in every such institution. If we are ever to have the University of Louisiana, of which our constitution speaks, will not the planters look to it, that that institution disseminates the principles of scientific agriculture?* What the government has been doing through the medium of the Patent Office reports, wonld be of inestimable importance, if continued and improved in the manner which so readily presents itself. The Smithsonian Institute may be made, in addition to its other character, a great NATIONAL SCHOOL OF AGRICULTURE.

Fellow-citizens—Gentlemen of the Association: what are WE doing for agriculture, and what do we propose to do? Certainly the state of this science is at a lower ebb here than in other parts of the Union. Our fields have yielded us such abundant fruit, that we deem it impossible they can do otherwise. We do but allow nature her own course, and she enriches without an effort. As Adam Smith used to say of those who rent land in England, we reap almost where we have not sown. But will this continue so always? Does not the human constitution often appear fresh and vigorous, under the most exhausting and destructive habits?—appear, we say, for disease and death almost inevitably close the scene! It must be so with us, if we abuse what God has bountifully given. When Deity proclaimed a sabbatical rest, even to the fields of the Hebrews, he proclaimed, at the same time, a great law, that the earth, like man, demands care and nurture, and that it is piety to exercise them. The economy of agriculture is to plant, that we may plant long, and "hasten slowly," that we may quickly reach wealth. It might be long, very long, before our lands would lose their value, under the worst of all systems of cultivation, but the time must come at last. Why should it come at all? If it be necessary to spend

* Agriculture, from the rude state in which in former times it existed, has emerged, and is becoming every day more and more reduced to the method and precision of science. The profound investigations of Liebig in the vegetable world have already created a revolution; a new and wide field of research is opened, and one that allures from the transcendent interests which are attached to it. The application of chemistry to agriculture, is a farther step in the progress of that Baconian philosophy, which addresses itself to the wants of man. By means of chemical processes, we stimulate nature, we develop and bring into activity latent and inert elements, or neutralize and destroy those which are noxious. We resuscitate soils that are exhausted and dead, and increase without limit those that are already vital and fruitful. Malthus need dread no more a world starving from over population, when the capacities of its soil may be augmented almost indefinitely by means within our control. It is gratifying to mark the new impulse which has been given to agriculture. We cannot refer, without enthusiasm, to the labors of Liebig, Boussingault, Thaers, etc. In our own country we are not without able laborers in the field. Agricultural surveys are being everywhere directed by State legislatures. We may particularly refer to New-York, Virginia, S. Carolina, Alabama, etc. Agricultural associations are rising in dignity with us, and journals devoted to this branch of industry, becoming valuable and complete. The attention of all parties seems to be at length aroused to the importance of the subject.

† While upon an agricultural library, let us be allowed to suggest the best authorities to be consulted by the liberal agricultural student, disposed to perfect himself in the science, and to extend the influences of such knowledge throughout the country. Some of the works may be had in this city, most in our country, and all by foreign order.

Harte's Essays on Husbandry, London, 1770; Works of Arthur Young, 9 in number, from 1771 to 1794, London; Dickson's Husbandry of the Ancients, Edinburgh, 1788; Brown's Treatise on Agriculture and Rural Affairs, Edinburgh, 1811; Loudon's Encyclopædia of Agriculture, London, 1844; Low's Elements of Practical Agriculture, London, 1838; Principles of Tillage and Vegetation, by Tull, London; Kirwan's Manures, London, 1808; Davy's Agricultural Chemistry, London, 1821; Beaton's New System of Cultivation; Chemistry for Farmers, and Treatise on Soils by Sprenghel, 1831; Liebig's Organic Chemistry; Johnston's Agricultural Chemistry; Works of Boussingault, Dumas and Mulder; Gardner's Farmer's Dictionary; Armstrong's Agriculture. To these should be added some of the agricultural periodicals of the country.

* This subject will, we understand, be put in charge of the Professor of Chemistry.

upon the soil a portion of its income, it is a kind parent which repays with abundant interest every act of favor. The state allows eight per cent. interest, and no more; but an enlightened agriculture defies the law and pays you usury, even compound interest. I know there are men around me, who are even more deeply impressed with this truth than I am myself. The state, it rejoices me to say, has many such sons, and her prosperity will grow as their numbers increase.

The society which I address was engendered by these considerations. It has existed several years, and held its annual meetings in this town. Exhibitions have been made, addresses delivered, and legislative aid granted, yet, after all, the association has not flourished, and has had but a small portion of the influence which belonged of right to it. Why is this? Why are we so much in the rear of other communities? Is the fault in the people, or where? I ask in vain. I know not how many of our parishes are represented here in convention, but I know that they should all be; that no consideration should prevent their uniting in a movement which addresses itself to the important interests of a great state. However, gentlemen, we will not despond. Though there is much to be done, it is not impossible to do it. I would even say, *conquer impossibilities*, for in truth there are none such to resolute and determined men. It is not alone our State Association that we want. Let there be such association in every parish. These lesser bodies, consisting of neighborhoods, should often meet in social, though useful union. It would add many a pleasing hour to life. Discussion of practical and agricultural subjects, previously assigned, would stimulate thought and experiment, infuse a liberal spirit, incite research and observation, and much of that emulation which is the secret of success, and which in honorable minds is a beautiful virtue.

Who is there that will lead the advance in these Parish Agricultural Associations. How simple their institution, and how important their results. From the numerous subordinate bodies the central one here would receive its annual delegates, reports, products, etc., for general and mutual interchange and instruction. I say *here*, for now that the legislators of the state are to convene in this town, its importance must be greatly increased, and the meetings of the association and the attendance on the fair will be under more favorable auspices. I would enjoin, then, that we suffer not another year to pass away with the same indifference as the past. It will not be creditable to us. How much more worthy of the human mind is the occasional employment we have suggested, than the listless ease, the unintellectual routine, the torpid life, and even the dissipation of thought and habits, in which the leisure hours of men are often occupied, and planters among the rest. Leisure may always be obtained for liberal pursuits. We never forget the hours which were devoted to them. We never regret a co-operation with our fellow-men for noble purposes. We have *lived* when employed in the study of great truths, valuable in being practicable, but not *because* they are so. There are pleasing memories of the hours we have spent:

> "——— not in joys, or lust, or wine,
> But search of deep philosophy."

The Agricultural Association will therefore aim to induce in our planters something of the true spirit. It will be preserved free from all private or party influences, that have done so much to disturb society. Its *officers* will be selected from the most experienced, intelligent, and worthy. Its *committees*, the most important feature of the organization, will be arranged with special reference to the subjects upon which they are to report, and their opportunities of being acquainted with them. Its *premiums* awarded discreetly, and without a shade of prejudice or partiality. In the first efforts to attain these, and before a very complete system can be arranged, it is not improbable some errors may be made, and some dissatisfaction result. But such can never affect the value and importance of the institution, incident as they are to every similar body, in every shape of its existence, and more espeially in its infancy.

The prominent objects of attention in an organized Society of Agriculturists, may be stated to be *the improvement of the staple crops of the state, and the introduction of new, productive, and profitable ones.* It addresses itself to the fields, and demands an improved and more liberal HUSBANDRY—to the gardens, and bids HORTICULTURE and FLORICULTURE crown our boards, and delight our senses. Nor is it mindless of the condition and improvement of the animal creation—THE STOCK that serve us in our labors, and minister to our wants.

The exhibition made to-day at the Fair of the Association, creditable though it be, is only an earnest of what is intended, and what there are just reasons to predict hereafter. The two staples of sugar and cotton appear to have absorbed all the agricultural capital of the state. The sugar planter may congratulate himself, that from a variety of causes, but chiefly now from the limited range of the sugar region, and the increased demand for the article, from the openings of foreign markets, this staple has enjoyed, and bids fair for a long way in the future to enjoy, unrivaled prosperity. Its production is also on the rapid increase with us, but with no ground for uneasiness that it will ever be too large. The improvements in the culture, in the quality, in the manufacture, so striking and important, are familiar to you all, and need not be dwelt upon here. Though much has been effected in a short time, there are many improvements still indicated. No other branch of agriculture requires more the aid of liberal science than this.

The cotton planters of Louisiana, in the results of the past and previous season, deserve much commiseration. An insect of fearful and voracious appetite has traversed their fields, and in whole regions of country, like the locusts of Egypt, left literally "no green thing alive." The advance in price, in consequence of an average crop in other sections, will not be sufficient to compensate for the reduced quantity, and it unfortunately happens that the advance that has taken place will benefit but the comparatively few who have not been forced early into market. The future, it is thought, will be auspicious to this class of producers, where they can be protected or preserved from the scourge which has visited their fields. It has been made evident that the consumption of cotton is advancing much more rapidly than the production, and of course, gaining upon it. European stocks, that have influenced prices so much, have given way already, and it is not improbable, at the expiration of the present year, they will be reduced very low, and in a few years become nothing. There are new markets for the staple opening on the continent of Asia, in Africa, and in China; even Japan will probably invite us, and the old markets of Europe, as well as of our own country, increase daily in their demands. The competition of the East Indies ceases to be longer named, and one may dare affirm that the discovery in Europe, by which cotton is converted into an agent of detonation is but one among the many uses yet to be discovered, to which this *snowy fleece*, more precious than the "fleece of gold," will be applied.

It is not probable that the agricultural pursuits of Louisiana, will be much diversified for a long time to come. I am by no means persuaded that we have much to gain, by diverting our energies and our capital now into any new channels. Such are the wants of the world, it is reasonable to suppose the day very distant when there shall be a too great production of sugar, and I do not regret that circumstances are tending to make this the one great production of our state. No other staple is likely to yield more abundant returns. But let it not be supposed that any argument can be drawn from this for an exclusive devotion of the planter's life to a single subject to the neglect of all others. A single pursuit, unrelieved, contracts necessarily the views and range of thought of the individual. He becomes a man of one idea—sees, hears, feels, knows, regards nothing else—like a technical lawyer incased in forms and precedents, and forever incapable of reaching that high "vantage ground" of the profession, of which Lord Bolingbroke speaks, and on which he recognized Bacon and Clarendon. It is one of the evils of such extreme division of labor, and devotion of one man to one pursuit, that it degrades a human being into the rank of a machine. It might be very well for trade, that ten men are employed in the manufacture of a pin; but it is a sad account, says Adam Smith, to give to one's Creator, that a whole life-time has been spent in the production of a pin-head.

I would have the planters of Louisiana, as gentlemen and intelligent men, cultivate a knowledge of every department of that profession which they have made their own, though in practice confined to one department solely. Such a study is one of the most liberal and dignified, and tends in a high degree to elevate the whole nature and character of the student. Surely our planters will not complain of a want of leisure for this, and they will not point me to a more appropriate pursuit. I do *not* base the argument upon mere pecuniary considerations, for it is a higher and a nobler one. We are not here to attain wealth simply, but *to make wealth subserve all the great ends of our being*. We do not live to learn only such things as mere living demands. Pythagoras said truly, "He who knows only what he finds it necessary to know, is a man solely among the brutes."

It would employ little if any labor, and draw nothing upon the time of our planters, if they would lay out and cultivate their grounds in orchards of such fruit as will thrive in our genial clime, introduce as means may admit exotics, nurture rare plants, and beautify their estates with vines, flowers, and shades, and exhibit thus the appearances of that true comfort and happiness, ever associated by the virtuous with ideas of rural life. I can conceive of no solitude more cheerless in the world, than an estate in the country, which while inhabited, is neglected and suffered to decay. God has so fashioned us, that we are improved in head and in heart when surrounded and associated with the beautiful in art or in nature.

We have heard it suggested, and believe it to be true, that the culture of the finer qualities of *tobacco* will be found very profitable to those in the state who have proper lands, and whose capital is not large. Indeed, we have seen some very admirable specimens of this growth, both in the city on sale and here. The *olive* has been frequently suggested. The legislature has given encouragement to *silk*, which needs little effort to be successfully produced. And there can be no question that in our abundant waste lands, rice of a superior quality can be made a very considerable crop. Whenever our attention may be given particularly to these subjects, and the time will no doubt ultimately come, we shall find in them sources of great profit and wealth. At present, I suppose, that any attention bestowed will be little more than relief spots in the otherwise monotony of our agriculture.

I cannot dismiss the subject of agriculture without remarking upon its great influences upon the character of society at large. In every country the agricultural classes, or those who have an interest in the soil, in the lands, who are removed afar from the corruption of cities and the adverse influences of courts and power, are the bulwarks of the commonwealth, and the friends and supporters of sound government. They are never radicals They ever deprecate rash innovation. They go for the government, while there is a possibility of preserving it pure, or of reforming it, and they declare only for REVOLUTION in that desperate contingency, when tyranny has overleaped all barriers, when hope has fled, and endurance longer would be a crime.

The poets in all ages have traced the charms of agriculture with touches of exquisite finish. They present us captivating and beautiful, yet not untrue, pictures of its genial labors, its dignity, its repose, and its independence. The finest illustrations in Homer are taken from the husbandmen and their pregnant fields. Hesiod is equally eloquent, when he touches upon rural life. Who could ever forget the graceful and thrilling passages which abound everywhere in the pages of Virgil.

The Romans cherished agriculture as from the gods. Cincinnatus, Dentatus, Regulus, Fabricius, etc., were planters, and devoted their leisure from cares of state to the culture of the soil. The pleasure seats of the leading Romans were their country villas. Hardy independence, sterling patriotism, enthusiastic devotion to liberty and love of country, and all the noble propensities, will be found in the agricultural classes. The virtues, too, of these classes are most likely to be preserved throughout all vicissitudes, and they have ever been conspicuous. The Hon. Daniel Webster, in his speech at Boston, in 1820. contrasted strongly the morals of the farming and other interests, showing an amount of crime in the latter as *twenty to one* greater than in the former. In the preservation of health, true enjoyment and long life, the pursuits of agriculture have the great advantage. Cities hardly counterbalance these by their elegance, refinement, intelligence and luxury. Their frightful waste of life must be supplied from the cradles of the country. Physiologists tell us that in Paris there is scarcely a very old family. If they have not intermarried with new comers they have been lost, and even their names blotted out in a few generations. I am rejoiced, then, from the extent of our great Union, the immense territories, fruitful, and with almost every variety of soil and climate, and of unsurpassed fertility—an immense extent of forests yet unsubdued—I am rejoiced to say, that while our COMMERCE is whitening every sea, and our MANUFACTORIES are seated by every waterfall, the great and predominant influences of our AGRICULTURE will be felt in all time to temper and regulate the whole.

I shall not be thought guilty of any undue eulogy in the reflections which have occurred to so many others than myself. I am willing to leave them with you, and leave you to the enjoyments of the life you are capable of appreciating—to the life for which we might gladly exchange cities, that Cowper well remarks, "God never made"—to the rural retreat, where it will be your own fault if plenty does not smile around ; if true comfort, if refined enjoyment, if contentment and happiness are not realized in the calm hours, with nature for a companion to counsel you from her thousand varied forms :

"For who the melodies of morn can tell,
The wild brook bubbling down the mountain's side,
The lowing herd, the sheep-fold's simple bell?"

Or, lest I should be reminded of a topographical blunder in commending you to the charms of bubbling water-falls, mountains, and sheep-folds, even in this clime of the sun and floral luxuriance, now that your harvests are ended, and you have reaped from your toils sufficient at least for gratitude to an all-bountiful Providence, I will dismiss you with the admonition and counsel of honest and inimitable old Thomas Tusser.*

"In harvest time, harvest folk, servants, and all,
Should make altogether good cheer in the hall,
And fill out the black bowl with blithe to their song,
And let them be merry all harvest time long.

Once ended the harvest, let none be beguiled,
Please such as did help thee, man, woman, and child ;
Thus doing with alway such help as they can,
Thou winnest the praise of the laboring man.

Now look up to Godward—let tongue never cease,
In thanking of him for his mighty increase ;
Accept my good-will—for a proof go and try—
The better thou thrivest the gladder am I."

* In the address as delivered, there were several pages on the mechanic arts, &c., which we now omit. The Louisiana Agricultural Society is dead, but with the formation of the National Society at Washington will it not be revived by our planting citizens. The suggestion made by us in the address, that the Smithsonian Institute should pay tribute to agriculture seems likely to be adopted by Congress.

States and Territories	Acres Improved	Acres Unimproved	Cash value of farms	Value of farming implements and machinery	Horses	Asses and Mules	Milch Cows
Maine	2039596	2515797	54861748	2284554	41721	55	133556
New-Hampshire	2251488	1140926	55245997	2314125	34233	19	94277
Vermont	2591379	1525368	59727731	2790237	61057	218	146146
Massachusetts	2133436	1222576	109076347	3209584	42216	34	130099
Rhode Island	356187	197451	17070802	497201	6168	1	28698
Connecticut	1768178	615701	72726422	1892541	26879	49	85461
New-York	12408968	6710120	554546642	22084926	447014	963	931324
New-Jersey	1767991	984985	120237511	4425503	63955	4089	118736
Pennsylvania	8628619	6294728	407876099	14722541	350398	2259	532224
Delaware	580862	375282	18880031	510279	13852	791	19248
Maryland	2797905	1836445	87178545	2463443	75684	5644	86859
District of Columbia	16267	11187	1730460	40320	824	57	813
Virginia	10361155	15792176	216401441	7021772	272403	21480	317619
North Carolina	5453977	15543010	67891766	3931532	148693	25259	221799
South Carolina	4072651	12145049	82431684	4136354	97171	37483	193244
Georgia	6378479	16442900	95753445	5894150	151331	57379	334223
Florida	349049	1236240	6323109	658795	10848	5002	72876
Alabama	4435614	7702067	64323224	5125663	120001	59895	227291
Mississippi	3444358	7046061	54738634	5762927	115460	54547	214231
Louisiana	1590025	3939018	75814398	11576938	89514	44849	105576
*Texas	639107	14454669	16398748	2133731	75419	12364	214758
Arkansas	781531	1816684	15265245	1601296	60197	41559	93151
Tennessee	5175173	13808849	97851212	5360220	270636	75303	250456
Kentucky	11368270	10972478	154330262	5169037	315682	65609	247475
Ohio	9851493	8146000	358758603	12750585	463397	3423	544499
Michigan	1929110	2454780	51872446	2891371	58506	70	99676
Indiana	5046543	7746879	136385173	6704444	314299	6599	284554
Illinois	5039545	6997867	96133290	6405561	267653	10573	294671
Missouri	[illegible]	[illegible]	[illegible]	3965945	223593	41508	228553
Iowa	824682	1911382	16657567	1172869	38536	754	45704
Wisconsin	1045499	1931159	28528563	1641568	30179	156	64339
California	62324	3831571	3874041	103433	21719	1666	4280
Minnesota	5035	23846	161948	15981	860	14	607
Oregon	132857	299951	2849170	183423	8046	420	9427
Utah	16333	30,516	311799	84288	2429	325	4861
New-Mexico	166201	124,370	1653952	77960	5079	8654	10635
	118435178	184596025	3266925537	151605147	4325652	559070	6391946

States and Territories	Working oxen	Other cattle	Sheep	Swine	Value of live stock	Wheat, bushels	Rye, bushels
Maine	83893	125890	451577	54598	9705726	296259	102916
New-Hampshire	59027	114606	384756	63487	8871901	185658	183117
Vermont	48497	154025	919992	66278	12640248	525925	176207
Massachusetts	46611	83284	188651	81119	9647710	31211	481021
Rhode Island	8189	9375	44296	19509	1532637	49	26409
Connecticut	46988	80226	174181	76472	7467490	41762	600893
New-York	178909	767406	3453241	1018252	73570499	13121498	4148182
New-Jersey	12070	80455	160488	250370	10679291	1601190	1255578
Pennsylvania	61527	562195	1822357	1040366	41500053	15367691	4805160
Delaware	9797	24166	27503	56261	1849281	482511	8066
Maryland	34135	98595	177902	352911	7997634	4494680	226014
District of Columbia	104	123	150	1635	71643	17370	5509
Virginia	89513	669137	1310004	1830743	33656659	11232616	458930
North Carolina	37309	434402	595249	1812813	17717647	2130102	229563
South Carolina	20507	563935	285551	1065503	15060015	1066277	43790
Georgia	73286	690019	560435	2168617	25728416	1088534	53750
Florida	5794	182415	23311	209453	2880058	1027	1152
Alabama	66961	433263	371880	1904540	21690112	294044	17261
Mississippi	83485	436254	304929	1582734	19403662	137990	9606
Louisiana	54968	414798	110333	597301	11152275	417	475
*Texas	49982	636805	99098	683914	10266880	41689	3108
Arkansas	34239	165320	91256	836727	6647969	199639	8047
Tennessee	86255	414051	811591	3114111	29978016	1619386	89163
Kentucky	62074	442763	1102121	2861163	29591387	2140822	415073
Ohio	65381	749067	3942929	1964770	44121741	14487351	425718
Michigan	55350	119471	746435	205847	8008734	4925889	105871
Indiana	40221	389891	1122493	2263776	22478555	6214458	78792
Illinois	76156	541209	894043	1915910	24209258	9414575	83364
Missouri	111268	445615	756309	1692043	19766851	2966928	44112
Iowa	21892	69025	149960	323247	3689275	1530581	19916
Wisconsin	42801	76293	124892	159276	4879385	4286131	81253
California	4780	253599	17574	2776	3351058	17328	—
Minnesota	655	740	80	734	92859	1401	125
Oregon	8114	24188	15382	30235	1876189	211943	106
Utah	5266	2489	3262	914	546968	107702	210
New-Mexico	12257	10085	377271	7314	1494629	196516	—
	1698261	10265180	21621482	30315719	543822711	100479150	14188457

* The County of Lavaca in this state is not included in this aggregate.

States and Territories	Indian Corn, bushels of	Oats, bushels of	Rice lbs	Tobacco, lbs.	Ginned Cotton, bales of 400 lbs. each	Wool, lbs.	Peas and Bns., bsh.	Irish Pts., bushels
Maine	1750056	2181037	—	—	--	1364034	205541	3436040
New-Hampshire	1573670	973381	—	50	—	1108476	70856	4304919
Vermont	2032016	2307714	—	—	—	3410993	104859	4947351
Massachusetts	2345490	1165106	—	138246	—	585136	43709	3585384
Rhode Island	539202	215232	—	—	—	129692	6346	651029
Connecticut	1935043	1158738	—	1267624	—	497454	19090	2689725
New-York	17858400	26552814	—	83189	—	10071301	741636	15398362
New-Jersey	8759704	3378063	—	310	—	375396	14174	3207236
Pennsylvania	19835214	21538156	—	912651	—	4481570	55231	5980732
Delaware	3145533	604518	—	—	—	57765	4120	240542
Maryland	11104631	2242151	—	21407497	—	480226	12816	764939
District of Columbia	65230	8134	—	7800	—	525	7754	28292
Virginia	35254319	10179045	17154	56805218	3947	2860765	521581	1316933
North Carolina	27941051	4052078	5465868	11984786	73849	970738	1584252	620318
South Carolina	16271454	2322155	159930613	74285	300901	487233	1026900	136494
Georgia	30080099	3820044	38950691	423924	499091	990019	1142011	227379
Florida	1996809	66586	1075090	998614	45131	23247	135359	7828
Alabama	28754048	2965697	2311252	164990	564429	657118	892701	246001
Mississippi	22446552	1503288	2719856	49960	484293	559619	1072757	261482
Louisiana	10226373	89637	4425349	26878	178737	169897	161732	95632
*Texas	5926611	178883	87916	66897	57596	131374	179332	93548
Arkansas	8893939	656183	63179	218936	65346	182595	285738	193832
Tennessee	52276223	7703086	258854	20148932	194532	1364378	369321	1060844
Kentucky	58675591	8201311	5688	55501196	758	2297403	202574	1492487
Ohio	59078695	13472742	—	10454449	—	10196371	60168	5057769
Michigan	5641420	2866056	—	1245	—	2043283	74254	2359897
Indiana	52964363	5655014	—	1044620	—	2610287	35773	2083337
Illinois	57646984	10087241	—	841394	14	2150113	82814	2514861
Missouri	36069543	5243476	700	17100884	1	1615860	45974	934627
Iowa	8656799	1524345	500	6041	—	373898	4775	276120
Wisconsin	1988979	3414672	—	1268	—	253963	20657	1402077
California	12236	—	—	1000	—	5520	2292	9292
Minnesota	16725	30582	—	—	—	85	10002	21145
Oregon	2918	65146	—	325	—	29686	6566	91336
Utah	9899	10900	—	70	—	9222	289	43968
New-Mexico	365411	5	—	8467	—	32901	15688	3
	592141230	146533216	215312710	199739746	2468625	52518143	9219642	65781751

States and Territories	Sweet Pts., bushels	Barley, bushels	Buckwheat, bushels	Val. of Orchard Products in dols.	Wine, gallons	Value of Produce, Mkt. Gds.	Butter, lbs.	Cheese lbs.
Maine	—	151731	104523	342865	724	122387	9243811	2434454
New-Hampshire	—	70256	65265	248563	344	56810	6977056	3196563
Vermont	—	42147	208699	315045	659	18853	11871451	8729834
Massachusetts		112005	100095	403993	4688	600020	8071370	7088142
Rhode Island	—	18875	1245	63994	1013	98298	995670	316508
Connecticut	80	19099	229297	175118	4269	196874	6498119	5363277
New-York	5623	3585059	3183955	1761950	9172	912047	79766094	49741413
New-Jersey	508015	6492	878934	607268	1811	475242	9487210	365756
Pennsylvania	52172	165584	2193692	723389	25590	688714	39878418	2505034
Delaware	65443	56	8615	46574	145	12714	1055308	3187
Maryland	208993	745	103671	164051	1431	200869	3806160	3975
District of Columbia	3497	75	378	14843	863	67222	14872	1500
Virginia	1813671	25437	214898	177137	5408	183047	11089359	436298
North Carolina	5095709	2735	16704	34348	11058	39462	4146290	95921
South Carolina	4337469	4583	283	35108	5880	47286	2981850	4970
Georgia	6986428	11501	250	92776	796	76500	4640559	46976
Florida	757226	—	55	1280	10	8721	371498	18015
Alabama	5475204	3958	348	15408	220	84821	4008811	31412
Mississippi	4741795	229	1121	50405	407	46250	4346234	21191
Louisiana	6428453	—	3	22359	15	148329	683069	1957
*Texas	1323170	4776	59	12605	99	12254	2326556	91619
Arkansas	788149	177	175	40141	35	17150	1854239	30088
Tennessee	2777716	2737	19427	52894	92	97183	8139585	177681
Kentucky	998184	95343	16097	106160	8093	293120	9877868	213784
Ohio	187991	354358	638064	695921	48207	214204	34449379	20819542
Michigan	1177	75249	472917	132650	1654	14738	7065878	1011492
Indiana	201711	45483	149740	324940	14055	72864	12781535	624564
Illinois	157433	110795	184504	446089	2997	127494	12526543	1278225
Missouri	332120	9631	23590	512527	10563	99454	7792499	202122
Iowa	6243	25093	52516	8434	420	8848	2171188	209840
Wisconsin	879	209692	79878	4823	113	32142	3633750	400283
California	1000	9912	—	17700	58055	75275	705	150
Minnesota	200	1216	515	--	—	150	1160	—
Oregon	—	--	—	1271	—	90241	211461	36980
Utah	60	1799	332	—	—	23868	83309	30898
New-Mexico	—	5	100	8231	2363	6679	111	5848
	38255811	5167213	8955945	7720862	221249	5270130	312948915	105539599

* The County of Lavaca in this state is not included in this aggregate.

States and Territories	Hay, tons	Clover seed, bushels	Other Grass Seed, bushels of	Hops, lbs.	HEMP Dew Rotted, tons	HEMP Water Rotted, tons	Flax, lbs.	Flaxseed bushels
Maine	755889	9097	9214	40120	—	—	17081	580
New-Hampshire	598854	829	8071	257174	—	—	7652	189
Vermont	866989	760	14996	258513	—	—	20752	939
Massachusetts	651807	1002	5085	121595	—	—	1162	72
Rhode Island	74818	1328	3708	277	—	—	85	—
Connecticut	516131	13841	16608	554	—	—	17928	703
New-York	3728797	88222	96493	2536299	1	3	940577	57963
New-Jersey	435950	28280	63051	2133	—	—	182965	16525
Pennsylvania	1842970	125030	53913	22088	282	2006	528079	41650
Delaware	30159	2525	1403	348	—	570	11050	858
Maryland	157956	15217	2561	1870	63	—	35686	2446
District of Columbia	2279	3	—	15	—	—	—	—
Virginia	369098	29727	23428	11506	90	51	999450	52318
North Carolina	145662	576	1275	9246	—	3	593796	38196
South Carolina	20925	376	30	26	—	—	333	55
Georgia	23449	132	428	261	—	73	5387	622
Florida	2510	—	2	14	—	—	50	—
Alabama	32685	138	547	276	—	70	3841	67
Mississippi	12505	84	533	473	7	—	665	26
Louisiana	25752	2	97	125	—	—	—	—
*Texas	8279	10	—	7	—	—	1048	26
Arkansas	3977	90	436	157	—	15	12291	321
Tennessee	74092	5096	9118	1032	3913	1183	367807	18905
Kentucky	113655	3230	21451	5304	40936	14756	7793123	75579
Ohio	443142	102197	37310	63731	140	50	446937	188880
Michigan	401031	16080	0785	10660	100	37	0994	1421
Indiana	403230	18329	11951	92796	341	1071	584469	36888
Illinois	601952	3427	14380	3551	142	141	160063	10785
Missouri	116743	615	4337	3130	17207	5351	520008	13641
Iowa	89055	342	2096	8242	—	—	62553	1959
Wisconsin	275662	483	342	15930	300	2	68393	1191
California	2038	—	483	—	—	—	—	—
Minnesota	2019	—	—	—	—	—	—	—
Oregon	373	4	22	8	—	—	640	—
Utah	4805	2	—	50	—	—	550	5
New-Mexico	—	—	—	—	—	—	—	—
	12839141	467983	413154	3467514	63588	25380	13391415	562810

States and Territories	Silk Cocoons lbs. of	Maple Sugar lbs. of	Cane Sugar, hhds. of 1000 lbs	Molasses gallons	Beeswax & Honey, lbs	Value of Home-made Manufactures	Value of animals slaught'ed
Maine	252	93542	—	3167	189618	513599	1646773
New-Hampshire	4191	1294863	—	9811	117140	393455	1522873
Vermont	268	5980955	—	5997	249432	278331	1871468
Massachusetts	7	795525	—	4693	59508	205333	2500924
Rhode Island	—	28	—	4	6347	26495	667486
Connecticut	328	50796	—	665	93304	192252	2202266
New-York	1774	10357484	—	56529	1756190	1280333	13573983
New-Jersey	23	2197	—	954	156694	112781	2638552
Pennsylvania	285	2326525	—	50652	838509	749132	8219848
Delaware	—	—	—	50	41248	38121	373665
Maryland	39	47740	—	1430	74802	111821	1954800
District of Columbia	—	—	—	—	550	2075	9038
Virginia	517	1227665	—	40322	880767	2156312	7503006
North Carolina	229	27932	—	704	512289	2086522	5767866
South Carolina	123	200	671	15904	216281	909525	1302637
Georgia	813	50	1644	216150	732514	1838968	6339762
Florida	6	—	2752	352893	18971	75582	514685
Alabama	167	643	8242	83428	897021	1934120	4823485
Mississippi	2	—	388	18318	397460	1164020	3636582
Louisiana	29	255	226001	10931177	96701	139232	1458990
*Texas	22	—	7351	441638	380532	255719	1106032
Arkansas	38	9330	—	18	192338	638217	1162913
Tennessee	1923	158557	248	7223	1036572	3137710	6401765
Kentucky	1301	437345	284	40047	1156939	2456838	6469318
Ohio	1552	4588209	197	308308	804275	1712196	7439243
Michigan	8	2438987	—	19823	359232	340947	1328327
Indiana	387	2921642	—	180325	935329	1631039	6567935
Illinois	47	248904	—	8354	869444	1155902	4972286
Missouri	186	178750	—	5636	1327812	1663016	3349517
Iowa	246	78407	—	3162	321711	221292	821164
Wisconsin	—	610976	—	9874	131005	43621	920178
California	—	—	—	—	—	7000	100173
Minnesota	—	2950	—	—	80	—	2840
Oregon	—	—	—	24	—	—	164530
Utah	—	—	—	58	10	1392	67985
New-Mexico	—	—	—	4236	2	6033	82125
	14763	33980457	247778	12821574	14850627	27478931	119475020

* The County of Lavaca in this state is not included in this aggregate.

AGRICULTURE—ANALYSIS OF CROPS.

THE following table from Johnson's Lectures, exhibits the average produce of nutritive matter of different kinds from an acre of the usually cultivated crops :—

	Gross produce bush	Gross produce lbs	Husk or Woody Fibre lbs	Starch Sugar, &c. lbs	Gluten, &c. lbs	Oil or Fat lbs	Saline Matter lbs
Wheat	25	1,500	225	825	150 to 280	30 to 60	30
"	30	1,800	270	990	180 to 340	36 to 72	36
Barley	35	1,800	270	1,080	210 to 260	35 to 54	50
"	40	2,100	315	1,260	250 to 310	42 to 63	60
Oats	40	1,700	340	1,000	230 to 320	80 to 120	70
"	50	2,100	420	1,054	290 to 400	76 to 150	80
Rye	25	1,300	130 to 260	780	130 to 200	40 to 50	26
"	30	1,600	160 to 320	960	230 to 350	48 to 65	32
Indian corn	30	1,800	100	1,260	216	90 to 170	27
Buckwheat	30	1,300	320	650	100 ?	5 ?	21
Beans	25	1,600	160	640	380 to 450	32 to 48	48
"	30	1,900	190	760	450 to 530	38 to 57	57
Peas	25	1,600	130	800	380	34	48
	Tons						
Potatoes	6	13,500	540	1,400	270	45	120
"	11	27,000	1,080	4,800	540	96	240
Turnips	20	45,000	900	4,000	670	130	300
"	30	67,000	1,340	6,000	1,000	200	450
Carrots	25	56,000	1,680	5,600	840	200	800
Mangel-Wurzel	20	45,000	900	4,950	900	?	450
Meadow Hay	1½	3,400	1,020	1,360	240	70 to 170	220
Clover Hay	2	4,500	1,120	1,800	420	135 to 225	400
Pea Straw		2,700	675	1,200	330	40	135
Wheat Straw		3,000	1,500	900	40	60 to 100	150
"		3,600	1,800	1,080	48	70 to 120	180
Oat Straw		2,700	1,210	950	36	?	135
"		3,500	1,570	1,200	48	?	175
Barley Straw		2,100	1,050	630	28	?	105
"		2,500	1,250	750	33	?	125
Rye Straw		4,000	1,800	1,500	53	?	160
"		4,800	2,200	1,800	64	?	200

The value of this table, in practice, is mainly in the feeding of stock, where the quantity acquired for nutrition can be thrown out, and waste avoided. Sugar, gluten and oil, the highly nourishing properties of grain, are shown by the analysis.

AGRICULTURAL PRODUCTS—NEW ONES FOR THE SOUTH.—First, The vine will flourish wherever the soil is calcareous and the atmosphere not too moist. In small vineries it is easy to add lime or bone manure, so as to furnish the carbonates and phosphorates this plant requires; but in large vineyards the calcareous principle must be in the soil itself, or the culture rarely succeeds, and even if the vines are reared they produce an inferior wine. If we trace the vine-growing region of Europe, we find the best wines are produced in limestone ranges. Indeed, it is not uncommon to find extensive inclosures surrounding a soil suited to the growth of the grape, within which the wine produced is worth two or three dollars a gallon, while that made from grapes grown immediately outside the walls, although attended with equal care, and manufactured with equal skill, is not worth more than ten, or at most twenty, cents a gallon. Volcanic soils, from the peculiar salts with which they are impregnated, are likewise well adapted to the culture of the vine. It will be seen, therefore, that before any attempt is made to establish extensive vineyards the soils should be analyzed by a competent geologist.

A dry atmosphere is likewise important, for it has been found that where great moisture prevails the foot stalk becomes woody before the fruit matures, and the berries in consequence rot or fall off.

It is not our province or our intention to say anything here of the best method of cultivating the vine. There exists many excellent popular treatises upon the vine which contain abundant information on the subject, to which we refer our readers, contenting ourselves with observing, that without judicious trimmings and high manuring, good sound succulent grapes cannot be produced.*

* The vine is indigenous to Persia, but a product of most temperate climates. It was early introduced into Greece and Italy, and into France by the Phœnicians. In North America it was found growing wild, and may be cultivated in most parts south of the 38° of latitude. One of the prominent objects in the colonization of Carolina was the cultivation of the grape, and it was also insisted upon very early in Louisiana, and afterwards in Alabama. See "Locke's Constitution of Carolina," "Martin's Louisiana," "Meeks' Address and Reference to French Colony in Alabama."

Every classical scholar remembers with delight the favorite Falernian and Cecuban wines; the wines of Lesbos and Chios, of which Greek and Roman poets have sung so sweetly, and which they regarded as from the gods. The vine was cultivated in Britain soon after the invasion of Cæsar, and extensive vineyards existed so late as the time of Richard II. It is now found only in hot-houses in that country. Of the native American grapes may be mentioned the Fox Grape, so well known to us, the Little Summer and Chicken Grape, and the Ball

The next article to which we would call the attention of the southern agriculturalist is the cork oak, (*Quercus Suber.*) We have never seen this tree in the interior of the south of Europe, but have frequently observed it on the coast of Spain, Portugal and France, stretching out its long branches in a manner that reminded us very much of the live oak plantations of our own maritime states. The tree begins to yield the cork at fifteen years, and continues to produce to a great age. The stripping of bark which is used in manufacturing corks, does not injure the tree at all; it may be done every five years. Loudon says, "it is taken off in sheets or tables, much in the same way as oak bark is taken from standing trees in England. After being detached it is flattened by presenting the convex side to heat, or by pressure. In either case it is charred on both surfaces to close the transverse pores. This charring may be seen in bungs and taps, but not in corks, which being in the long way of the wood, the charring is taken off in the rounding."

There are many proprietors in the neighborhood of Bordeaux and Bayonne who derive a revenue of twenty-five thousand to thirty thousand livres, (from five to six thousand dollars a year,) from their cork oak groves. The acorns may be procured from thence. They should be packed in wet moss, and allowed to germinate on the passage, after being quite dry, they rarely sprout. They would grow, we believe, throughout the whole region of live oak, and would require very little attention or after-culture, when once well set.*

Another plant which might be introduced at the south, and which would doubtless prove profitable, is the *Laurus Camphora.* The fourth bulletin of our National Institute† contains an admirable report of that distinguished naturalist, J. C. Reinhardt, in which he gives a succinct and useful notice of the principal plants cultivated in Borneo, Sumatra, Japan and China. In speaking of this plant, he says: "Nearly all the camphor exported to Europe and America is obtained from the *Laurus Camphora*, a tree which grows in China, Japan and Formosa. The tree, including the roots, is cut into small pieces and boiled, the sublimed gum being received into inverted straw cones, it is then made into grayish colored cakes of a crumbling consistence, and brought to market.

Grape. This last is a spontaneous product of most of the Southern States. The Scuppernong, which produces a fine wine, is cultivated in North Carolina, and Mr. Sidney Weller, of Brinkleville, attributes the great success of the vine-dressers in North Carolina to the fact that attention has been bestowed solely upon American kinds, and those of approved quality, the first class embracing such as are good and profitable in all respects, and from which not only gallons but barrels of wine are made. The Scuppernong has attained already very high celebrity, is a native of North Carolina, and flourishes south of 37½° latitude. See "Alabama Planter," vol. I., No. 221.

Of the foreign wines principally in use may be named the *Port*, so called from its place of shipment, Oporto. Almost all this wine which is shipped is greatly adulterated with brandy. *Sherry*, a product of Spain, in the vicinities of Cadiz; it is generally much adulterated. *Claret*, the most famous being the Lafitte, Latour, Chateau Margaux and Haut-Brion, the first being in highest esteem. *Champagne*, named from the province making it, the Silery being most esteemed; the trade in this wine is carried on principally at Rheims, Avise and Epernay. *Burgundy* is esteemed as among the best in the world, and extensively grown. The question of preference between it and the Champagne was long and ably discussed. The product of all the vineyards of France was estimated in 1831 at £21,000,000 sterling. *Madeira*, introduced into the island of that name in 1421; it has lost much of its popularity in consequence of frequent frauds practised upon it. The Malmsey is a favorite variety. The *Teneriffe* is an inferior wine. The German are the growth of the country about the Rhine and the Moselle. The *Tokay* is from Hungary, and very costly. The wines from Sicily are principally the *White;* those of Italy have little character as an article of commerce. The wines of Greece and Cyprus had formerly much celebrity.

The quantity of wine imported and received for home consumption in Great Britain in 1835, was 6,420,342 gallons; being of Cape, 522,941; French, 271,661; Portuguese, 2,780,024; Madeira, 139,422; Spanish, 2,230,187; Canary, 56,956; Rhenish, 48,696; Sicilian, 376,455. The import the same year of raisins was 169,366 cwt., and grapes of the value of £16,765. The value of wines imported into the United States 1844–5, was $1,500,000, mostly consumed here, of which the Champagne was largest in value, and claret next. The import of raisins was about $700,000. Vide "Hoar on the Cultivation of the Vine," "Henderson on Ancient and Modern Wines," "McCulloch's Dictionary," "Commercial Review, December, 1846," etc.—EDITOR.

* "The cork is the spongy bark of a species of oak, and abounds in the south of France, Spain, Portugal, Italy and Barbary. The tree attains thirty feet height; its removal does not injure the tree, which lives to very great age. The cork was known to the ancients, and used for stoppers. The Spanish corks are best. The imports of all varieties into Britain are estimated at two to three thousand tons, in value £70,000 to £100,000. Imports into the United States 1845, $90,862. Both public and private interest, according to Michaux, requires the inhabitants of the southern coasts of the United States, and especially of the neighboring islands, to introduce and rear the cork oak in places unfit for the culture of cotton. It will grow wherever the live oak is found.—ED.

† The National Institute has wisely devoted one department to agriculture. In his address at the meeting in 1840, Mr. Poinsett remarked: "This institution has allotted one entire division to Agriculture. This must be considered the most important, as it is the most necessary of the useful arts, as well as the most essential to our existence in a state of civilization. The hunter or the shepherd can do no more than supply himself and his children with his food. Such a people have no surplus for those who follow other pursuits, whereas in an agricultural community a portion of the people only are engaged in raising grain and cattle to supply the remainder with food, who, in their turn, are employed in the useful or fine arts, or in the pursuits of literature and science, and it may be safely asserted that the degree of civilization in any country will be in proportion to the perfection of its agriculture. Cicero says, 'there is no better pursuit in life, none more full of enjoyment, or more worthy a freeman,' and surely there is none which contributes more largely to the wealth and independence of a country."—ED.

It is purified by the Dutch, and offers a profitable article of commerce. The younger Michaux, in addressing the writer, says: "I have frequently and unremittingly urged my friends in Charleston to cultivate the *Laurus Camphora*, camphor tree, which is much less liable to be injured by the cold than the orange tree. It is not in the sandy soil of the environs of that town that this tree ought to be planted, but in the fresh swamp land eight or ten miles in the interior, where the red bay is found, to which it is analogous. The *Laurus Camphora* might very well be grafted upon this tree, but it is commonly found in all the nurseries around Paris, where it is sold at five francs (one dollar) a plant of thirty inches high. This tree reaches the height of forty and fifty feet. What an acquisition it would be to the southern part of Georgia and to Florida!" We hope the experiment will be made and this valuable plant generally introduced into the southern states.*

But the plant which we would recommend most earnestly to the attention of the Southern cultivator, is the New-Zealand flax, (phormium tenax.) It was first brought to Europe by the naturalists who accompanied Captain Cook in his voyage of discovery in the Pacific, in 1775. It is thus spoken of: "One plant in particular deserves to be noticed here, (New-Zealand,) as the garments of the natives are made from it. A fine, silky flax is produced from it superior in appearance to anything we have in this country, (England,) and perhaps as strong. It grows in all places near the sea, and a considerable way up the hills, in bunches or tuffs, bearing yellowish flowers on a long stalk."

Captain Wilkes, in his narrative of the United States Exploring Expedition, says, "The native hemp (phormium tenax) is a most useful plant. It grows in large quantities, and is applied by them (the natives) to many purposes, besides being a principal article of foreign trade It is an important material in the construction of their houses, for which purpose it is made into cords, that are also used for other common uses. It is manufactured into fine fishing lines, which we much admired at Sydney for their strength and beauty."

"The manufacture of the hemp is altogether performed by the women, who cut it, and after it has been dried a little, divide it into strips about an inch in width. The outer green fibres are then scraped off with a piece of glass or a sharp shell. The inner fibres being thus exposed, are easily separated, and the greatest care is taken to keep all the fibres straight as possible, both in this and the following operations. To this precaution the great strength of the cordage the natives make of it is owing. After the fibres are separated they are washed, rubbed, and laid in the sun to bleach."

Captain Wilkes says nothing of the garments of the natives being made of this material, which they are for the most part, and he is mistaken when he attributes the great strength of the cordage to the peculiar manner of dressing this description of flax. If he had referred to the experiments of La Billardiere, he would have seen that the fibre of this plant is much stronger than any vegetable fibre we know of. La Billardiere found that the fibre of the agave americana breaks under a weight of seven; that of flax, eleven and three-fourths; that of hemp, sixteen and three-fourths; that of New-Zealand flax, twenty-three and seven-elevenths, so that the phormium is very much the strongest of known vegetable fibres, and is only exceeded by silk, which reaches twenty-four. The English are well aware of its superiority for cordage, and so long ago as 1831 they imported from New South Wales 1,065 tons of it per annum, the market value of which was from £15 to £25 per ton.

We believe that this plant will succeed best in rich swamp soil, although Captain Cook saw it growing luxuriantly on the hill sides. It may be propagated by the offsets which it throws out at the roots, but no doubt it will produce seed in the southern country which will afford a simple and easy way of propagating it. The phormium has been found to bear the winters of Ireland and the south of England, and is quite naturalized in Provence, France, where it bears seed.

Loudon, in his Encyclopedia of Agriculture, says of this plant, that in New-Zealand, "The phormium tenax answers all the uses of hemp and flax." "There are," he says, "two kinds of this plant, the leaves of one of which are yellow, those of the other, deep red, and both resembling the leaves of flags. Of these leaves they make lines and cordage much stronger than any of the kind in Europe. They likewise split them into breadths, and tying the strips together, form their fishing-nets. Their common apparel, by a simple process, is made from these leaves, and their finer by another preparation

* Camphor is obtained by boiling the *Laurus Camphora* timber of China. The export from China is from 350,000 to 500,000 lbs. Small quantities are exported from Batavia of Japan Camphor. A better quality is produced from the forests of Sumatra, Borneo and Malay, but never reaches European markets. "The camphor tree," says Johnston, "belongs to the same family as the common sassafras of the United States, though in its general character it is most nearly related to the red bay, so common throughout the southern country, both being evergreens of similar height and at a small distance looking so much alike as to be easily mistaken for each other." The value of camphor imported into the United States has increased from $22,000 in 1835 to $143,536 in 1845.—Ed.

from the fibres. This plant is found both on high and low ground, in dry mould and in deep bogs, but as it grows larger in the latter, that seems to be its proper soil. It has lately been found to prosper in the south of Ireland."

The phormium would doubtless succeed in the rich bottoms of the Mississippi Valley, and would add another to the many valuable products of that favored region, and would prove a valuable acquisition to our national and commercial marine.

We recommend its introduction to southern planters, even where it may not be thought advisable to raise it for sale. The leaves form strong and durable baskets, plow lines, and such cords as we daily use on a farm, and may be fabricated by any common laborer. Offsets of this plant may be procured from France at a cheap rate, and from the nurseries in our northern states at from twenty-five to thirty cents a plant.*

We should be much gratified to find this valuable plant added to the staple productions of the South. The prosperity of this portion of our country would be greatly promoted by the introduction of a greater variety of products. A thriving and uninterrupted trade cannot exist without such a variety of articles of exports as will form an assorted cargo at all seasons, and this deficiency cannot be compensated by any single staple however valuable.

We believe that the products of the olive and the vine, the cork and camphor trees, and of the New-Zealand flax, added to our cotton and rice, would furnish all the variety which the most active commerce demands, and that their introduction would largely contribute to the permanent prosperity of the South. We therefore earnestly recommend their culture to our friends south of, 35°.† (Joel R. Poinsett.)

ARKANSAS, AND ITS NATURAL ADVANTAGES.—No part of the United States—climate, soil, and the facilities of getting the products of the earth to market considered—affords so many inducements for the poor man, or one with moderate means, as the northern portion of Arkansas. In using the word northern, I design it in contra-distinction from the southern portion, which is better suited for cotton planters and men of great means. A careful survey of the map will at once demonstrate how abundantly it is supplied with lines of small streams; the river navigable for boats, the small streams capable of driving any kind of machinery.

The great river of northern Arkansas is White River, and when I venture the assertion that it is naturally a better river for navigation than the Ohio, my readers will doubtless at the first blush note me beside myself. But I will prove my assertion without even disparaging the Ohio, or quoting the eccentric and gifted orator of Roanoke, who declared it "dry one half the year and frozen the other."

It is a notorious fact, that for some months in every year boats of even two feet draught find much difficulty in going from Cairo to Louisville. White River, from its mouth to the junction of Black River with it, a distance of three hundred and fifty miles, never has less than three feet of water, and but one bar on which the water gets that low, and for many seasons affords four feet the year round. The Ohio has the advantage of having had thousands appropriated upon it, and the removal of many snags. White River rolls on in silent majesty, just as God made it, the hand of man never yet having done the first thing for it; not one dollar has been spent upon it.

Of its tributaries Black River is the most important, watering the counties of Independence, Jackson, Lowena and Randolph. It is navigable for steamboats nine months in the year to Pocahontas, the county seat of Randolph, a distance of some one hundred miles, and the expenditure of a few thousand dollars would make it navigable the entire year. Little Red River waters the counties of Van Buren and White, and is navigable for steamboats some miles above its mouth. One of its branches is somewhat noted, being the one on which the Whetstone and Cole families reside, and having the soubriquet of the "Devil's Fork." Currant River waters Randolph, and empties into Black; it is navigable for flatboats, as are Spring River and Eleven Points, both emptying into Black.

Steamboats drawing three feet of water could ascend White River ar far up as Bates-

* The New-Zealand flax," says McCulloch, "exceeds every other species in strength of fibre and whiteness, qualities which, if it really possesses them in the degree stated, must make it peculiarly well fitted for being made into canvas or cordage. It has been obtained within these few years at second hand from Sydney and Van Diemen's Land, the imports from them having amounted in 1831, to 15,725 cwt." Attempts are now making, but with what success remains to be seen, to raise it in this country.—ED.

† To the products enumerated by Mr. Poinsett, might be added the *Colza*, a plant extensively cultivated in Flanders and in France. It is admirably adapted for the food of cattle. It also, after expression, yields a cake which is highly prized for fattening animals, or manure. There is a spring variety of this plant which will succeed in almost any part of the United States, and may ultimately become an article of very considerable importance. The oil of the colza is much used in Europe, and highly prized. In France it has been adopted for all the purposes of light-houses. Messrs. Bache & Jenkins, who were sent to Europe by our Government last year, to obtain information upon these subjects, make in their report some remarks which we leave with the reader after referring him for further information upon "New Products" to the paper by Mr. King on the "Olive," in the *Commercial Review*, March, 1847, and the paper of the Hon. Henry Wise on several other subjects in same number.

ville, a distance of four hundred miles from its mouth, every day in the year, were $20-000 judiciously expended upon its improvement, and I am pleased to state that the people interested are becoming aroused to the importance of this work. A recent internal improvement convention, holden at Batesville, took important steps to awake public attention to its vast importance. Ceasing to call on Hercules, to hope for aid from the General Government, the people are going to put their own shoulders to the wheel. That beautiful nest-egg, the bequest to us from the Congress of 1841, in the shape of the five hundred thousand acres donation, will give us a fair start, and then individual enterprise and individual aid will do the rest. Above Batesville, for more than one hundred and fifty miles, there is flatboat navigation, and with money, good steamboat navigation may be had. Our climate is mild; ice is never with us an obstruction to navigation. Our market is New-Orleans, and when we have water we can leave.

Our soil is of every description; the bottom lands of our river are of the very richest character, yielding from fifty to eighty bushels of corn to the acre. Cotton grows well: in Jackson, Monroe, St. Francis, and all the northeastern counties, the yield is from one thousand to two thousand pounds to the acre. Independence, Lowena, Randolph, and Van Buren grow wheat well; all the western counties are well adapted to all kinds of small grain. In most of the counties tobacco does well. It is a fine country for stock; horses, mules and hogs can be raised in any numbers, and with as little cost as in any part of the United States of the same latitude.

The swamps and lowlands of Jackson, St. Francis and other counties, have a never-failing supply of ash and cypress, and immense rafts are taken to New-Orleans annually. White River, above Batesville, abounds with forests of pine, and any quantity of lumber can be procured.

The reader may ask why it is that such a country, possessing such advantages, has been overlooked? When the nature of the American people is changed, I may possibly be enabled to answer. Restlessness is a predominant trait in our character,—a disposition to be ever going towards the setting sun. Men start to move, and for fear there is a better place just beyond them, are never satisfied until their means of traveling are exhausted, or they are brought to a stand by the Rocky Mountains or the Pacific Ocean.

The town of Batesville is one hundred and twenty miles from Memphis; of that distance about ninety miles is as level as any street in New-Orleans, the road passing through the best of timber. A rail-road would be made in yankee land through it in less time than you could say "Jack Robinson." The *progressive developments* of the age may do something towards it, but I fear it will be a long time first. I may as well mention the fact, that about equi-distant from Memphis and this place, but far to the right of the road, herds of buffaloes are still to be found. Every season several are killed; the lakes and swamps are impassable for men and horses, and the buffaloes are there in a great measure protected. We have generally much game in this region, though at this time, from unknown causes, it is scarce. Our rivers abound in delightful fish,—trout that would even make "York's tall sons'" mouth to water.

ARKANSAS—Resources of.—It would please us to be better informed in relation to this prosperous country. It is rich in mineral productions of iron, coal, gypsum, and salt, and is well adapted to cattle raising. In the eastern parts, the climate is regarded unhealthy, but genial in the middle and western parts. It was made a territory in 1819, and a state in 1836. Population in 1840, 97,594, probably now 150,000.

A glance at the map will show that the means of communication to every portion of our state, afforded by the Mississippi on the east, the Red River on the south, and the Arkansas, White, St. Francis, and Ouachita, which, with their numerous tributaries, extend in almost every direction within her territory, give her facilities for the transportation of her produce which are not to be equaled in any other state in the Union. Her mineral resources are incalculable, and the discoveries which are daily being made must soon attract the attention of capitalists. One item of information in relation to the discovery of gold in White county, has come to our knowledge within a few days. A gentleman brought into town a short time since some specimens of the ore, from one pound of which twenty-five grains of pure metal were extracted by the simple process of fusion. The iron trade is destined, at some future day, to occupy a prominent place in the industrial pursuits of our citizens. Inexhaustible quantities of this mineral are found in almost every portion of our state, and many of the deposits are of the finest quality in the world, yielding on analysis ninety per cent. of the pure metal. Coal is abundant. At the junction of the Petit Jean with the Arkansas, near the bank of the first-named river, are very extensive coal hills, where, with the expenditure of a small amount of capital, a large and lucrative trade in the mineral might be commenced. A large bed of fine coal was discovered a few days since, on the Ouachita near Rockport.

ARKANSAS—Geology of.—"I hazard nothing in asserting, that the State of Arkansas has greater mineral resources than any other state east of the Rocky Mountains. I do not mean that it has more of everything than any other state—it has less of some things; for instance, it has less coal than Pennsylvania, yet it has more than the whole island of Great Britain. It probably has not as much lead as Wisconsin, but much of it has two or three times the value of Wisconsin lead, on account of the silver it contains. As to iron, there is no state that has it in greater quantity, or of better quality. Its manganese would supply the wants of the world, as to that article, if there were none any where else. In zinc, it will excel any other state, unless we except New-Jersey. It has more gypsum than all the other states together, so far as is known; and salt is no less abundant than gypsum—it is connected with it. In marble, it does not fall behind any other state; and it contains several very valuable kinds of building materials not found any where else in the Valley of the Mississippi.

"But it is not always that valuable minerals or building materials can be rendered at once available, especially in a new country. This is a matter which requires to be studied, as well as the character of the minerals themselves. Some things can be worked to advantage only after a country has acquired such a degree of development as to create a demand for their use. Such is the case, for the most part, with building materials, gypsum, etc."

ARKANSAS — MINERALS.—The Hazard Mines are in the Choctaw Nation, about six miles west of the state line, opposite the centre of the west boundary line of Polk county in this state, on a little river—"a tributary of the Mountain Fork of Little River," called Buffalo. The vein rock is composed of green stone, porphyry, an inferior article of granite, quartz, felspar, calcareous spar, shale, and argelite; and evidently owes its present contorted state to igneous action. Its width is about forty yards, and from six to seven miles in length. On each side of this range slate is the prevailing mineral; subdivided into clay, mica, shale, and argelite, and after a depth of 20 feet, the interstices are filled with calcareous spar. Nearly every variety of silver and lead ores have been found in this mine; a trace of copper, and in large quantities, the crystalized sulphuret of iron. I have not as yet discovered any specimens of pure galena, or lead ore; nevertheless, I think we have it amalgamated with the ores of silver, and should be designated as "argentiferous galena," or "silver bearing lead ore."

One of the greatest disadvantages to the prosperity of this mine, is its remote distance from navigation, which subjects it to an enormous and injurious expense of one hundred miles land carriage, at twenty dollars per ton.

The great distance of these mines from navigation, produces another hindrance of magnitude—the procurement of necessary supplies. This may be overcome, however, as soon as teams are employed to carry the ore to market. A trifling encouragement from the business men of this place would immediately bring a vast trade to their houses *directly*, and a greater *indirectly*, by creating a cash market in the country for its agricultural products, which would find its way to this market—profiting thereby this trade. You will please pardon this digression, and I will devote a few lines to another, the "Ballah mine." The Ballah mine is in township seven, (7) range thirty-two (32) west, in Sevier county, Arkansas, on the Rolling Fork of Little River, seven miles north of east from Ultima Thule, on the state line. For a description of this mine, and its history, you are referred to the communication of *Locum Tenens*, published in the Herald of the 7th of February last. I will conclude this hasty sketch, by presenting the subjoined note from Geo. G. Shumard, M. D., of this place—in whose judgment I place great confidence. ALFRED PADON.

"*Fort Smith, March* 20, 1851.

"*Dear Sir*—I thankfully acknowledge the receipt of a number of fine specimens of metallic ores from your mines. Having inspected them separately, I am induced to think that the veins from which they have been obtained, will, if properly worked, prove profitable.

"You are, doubtless, well aware of the difficulty always experienced in determining the character of metalliferous veins, from the mere inspection of specimens collected near the surface; but from your description of the associated rock, the character of the matrix, as well the dip and general appearance of the veins themselves, I am strongly of the opinion that you have, in their purchase, made a very safe investment."

ARKANSAS—COAL MINES.—Perhaps it is not generally known that there is coal in Arkansas; and when this is the case, it may not be known whether it exists in such a quantity, or possesses such a quality, as to render it an object worthy of attention. Though the exact limits of the coal field of Arkansas, and consequently its extent, have not been very definitely made out, nor all its varieties brought to light; yet enough is already known, both as to its quantity and quality, to give full assurance to a hundred times more mining enterprise than the wants of the country will soon require.

The coal field of Arkansas commences about forty miles above Little Rock, on the Arkansas River, and extends up the river, on both sides, far beyond the limits of the state. I certainly know of its being from twenty to thirty miles broad, and frequently hear of coal being found to a considerable distance outside of those limits. Its length is more than a hundred miles within the state, extending, I know not how far, into the Indian territory. No coal field could lie more ad vantageously than it does for mining purposes, as the river running lengthwise through its whole extent, must occasion very numerous placers, where it can be mined above the water level. This is a great advantage, as it diminishes the expenses of mining, and renders the mine entirely safe from those disastrous explosions from carbureted hydrogen gas, which often occur in those which lie below the water level.

As yet, very little mining has been done, more than to supply a few blacksmiths in the neighborhood, and to furnish a few boat loads for Little Rock. It is not yet known how many beds there are in the series; nor is it of so much practical importance to know, as one good one is sufficient. The thickness of the veins, so far as it is known, is about the same that it is in the coal fields on the Ohio.

There are three distinct species of coal known, viz., anthracite, bituminous, and cannel coal; but there is an almost infinite number of varieties, occupying every possible shade of difference between the most perfectly formed anthracite, on the one hand, and of cannel on the other. They run into each other by such slight variations, that it is almost impossible to which species certain varieties most properly belong; indeed, they do not belong to the one species more than to the other, but partly to both. Nevertheless, they are none the worse for that.

This is one of the ways by which Providence has shown, as in all His works, the benevolence of His character, by furnishing us with as great a variety in this most important fuel, as there is in the uses to which it is to be applied. There is no one kind of coal that will answer for all purposes, nor is there any kind that is useless, or unsuited to some purpose. It is for the want of knowledge of these facts, that people pronounce certain kinds of coal as poor, or even worthless, because they do not deport themselves in the same manner in the fire, that other coals do with which they are acquainted. Every variety of coal is suited to the production of some specific effect, and requires a corresponding variety in the treatment of its combustion.

It is not pretended that all kinds of coal are of equal value, any more than that all kinds of wood are; yet many varieties of coal are very much undervalued, for want of a proper knowledge to the uses to which they are best suited, or to the best manner of using them. Thirty years ago, anthracite coal was thought to be utterly useless, because it would not burn in the kind of grates then in use; and it was remarked that it never would be burned until the last great conflagration. But a small change in the form of the grate soon showed it to be the most valuable fuel ever known.

Several varieties of the Ohio river coals have been pronounced of little or no value, and could find no market; because they did not, with the same kind of grate and management, succeed equally well with the Pittsburg coal. But afterwards, when their true character came to be known, they have taken their place in the market according to their real merit.

The greater part of the coals in Arkansas is, like that of all other coal fields, bituminous; indeed, this is far the most common kind all over the world. But several *varieties* of bituminous coal have already come to light, and, doubtless, many more will, as its development progresses.

I know not that any true cannel coal has yet been found, but some of the bituminous approaches a little towards it; and there is little doubt that it will be found, as it exists in all our other coal fields.

But anthracite, *well-marked anthracite*, has been found, though not as yet of sufficient thickness to admit of being worked. Yet there is strong ground for believing that it does exist in quantity, and that a proper search would bring it to light. There are two reasons for this belief; one is, that a small quantity, as already stated, has been found; another is, that a portion of the coal field has been disturbed—and the rocks, together with the coal, are highly inclined. Anthracite coal is never found in rocks lying horizontally, though it does not follow that all coals found in highly inclined rocks are anthracite. That portion of the great Pennsylvania coal field only in which the rocks have been very much disturbed, and consequently are highly inclined, produces anthracite. This leads to the conclusion, that the same cause which produced the disturbance, produced also the anthracite; or, in other words, converted bituminous coal into anthracite, by driving off its bitumen. A variety of coal, having very little bitumen, or in other words, almost anthracite, has been found under circumstances which lead to the belief that it exists in inexhaustible quantities.

From what has been said, it would seem that there is no deficiency in the quantity or quality of Arkansas coals. There is little or no doubt that every variety of coal which the multiplied wants of man may hereafter require, will in due time be found to have been laid up there in store for him by the Great Provider, thousands of years before these wants existed, in anticipation of them. And there is no little doubt that this is the best source, and that it will ultimately be the principal source from which the lower portion of the Mississippi Valley will be supplied. B. LAWRENCE, *Geologist.*

ARKANSAS — RIVER LANDS—INFORMATION USEFUL TO EMIGRANTS AND OTHERS— The lands donated to the State of Arkansas by the general government, and known as the "Swamp Land Donation," are just now attracting the attention of the public. When we take into consideration the facts, that they are now being rapidly and permanently reclaimed by a general system of leveeing; that a large proportion of them need no reclamation; that they are the finest and cheapest lands in the Southwest; and are gradually but surely coming into market by the new settlements forming here and there on their borders—it is not to be wondered at, that they should begin to draw a very large share of the public notice.

Four hundred thousand acres of these lands lie in Crittendon county alone, just opposite the county of Shelby. On one side of this immense tract is the Mississippi, on the other the St. Francis River, both navigable at all seasons. Through the centre runs (or will soon run) a plank-road, already partly constructed, and the whole line under contract. And, judging from the indications not only in that state, but here in this city, we may now expect that it will be but a few years before a rail-road will be running alongside the plank-road, all the way to Little Rock. One half of these 400,000 acres never did overflow, and the levees now being constructed will secure all the rest from the highest floods of the Father of Waters.

Mississippi county, just above Crittenden on the river, also contains a very large amount of the lands of this donation—estimated at 450,000 acres. These, we are informed, are mostly choice lands, are as yet wholly unappropriated, and above any overflow without a levee.

Green, Poinsett, St. Francis, Jackson, Monroe, Phillips, De Sha, Chicot, Arkansas, Jefferson, Ashley, Drew, and a portion of many others of the best counties in the state, are subject to the Swamp Land Donation.

In all, the grant is believed to comprise about ten millions of acres, all of which will be exempt from tax ten years in any event; but if not reclaimed within ten years, without tax until reclaimed. Greater inducements were never before offered to settlers, nor to those who wish to make investments in scrip. There is little doubt that these lands can be purchased from the Levee Contractors (who are paid in scrip) much lower than land can be obtained even in Texas. They seem determined to make the levee, and of course, will sell large amounts of scrip to carry on their contracts to successful completion. In Crittenden county alone, there are now 600 hands at work, and in thirty days the principal outlets, through which the overflows have penetrated, will be stopped, thus saving the lands in that county from inundation during the coming spring, and from that time forth. It should, however be distinctly borne in mind, that there are vast bodies and ridges of these lands which are of the class commonly called *second bottom*, and known to be the best and most durable cotton and corn lands in the South.

BREADSTUFFS—Foreign and American Corn Trade.—We shall briefly consider the history of British policy in relation to the subject under discussion, furnish statistics of the foreign corn trade, and exhibit the past and the present condition, as well as the future prospects of our own country, in the same connection.

The first corn system adopted in Great Britain was that of non-exportation. This prevailed for three hundred years prior to the reign of Henry VI. It was not seen here, that to prevent the exportation of a commodity, was to prevent its production above the lowest wants of a country, and increase the danger of famine. In 1436, exportation was tolerated, but only with severe restrictions; and importation, which had hitherto been free, began now to be saddled with conditions. In 1562, exportation was placed on a footing more disadvantageous to it, by requiring the price to be four shillings per quarter higher at home, before it was allowed. In 1571, a duty on grain exports was adopted. This proved so unpopular in time to the agriculturists themselves, that in 1672 it was taken off, and substituted by one more favorable to exportation.

A new system was now introduced utterly at war with those of a previous date. By the statute 1 William and Mary, a bounty was actually held out to exporters of five shillings on every quarter of wheat, while the price continued at or below forty-eight shillings: so singular has been the fluctuation.

For a number of years, under the operation of this system, there were large exports of grain, which, in ten years, drew upon the bounty fund to the amount of £1,515,000. Even this, however, did not have the effect desired. The severe and almost prohibitory restrictions on imports, adopted in an act of 1670, and the great augmentation of population, reduced largely the excess of exportation, and occasioned another important change in the policy of the country. A statute of 1773, admitted foreign wheat free of duty, whenever the price was above forty-eight shillings per quarter. The prices in 1772–3–4, were fifty, fifty-one, and fifty-two shillings.

The liberal toleration of grain imports by the statute of 1773, gave great dissatisfaction to the landed interests, who had weight enough soon to procure its modification, by raising the scale when imports would be allowed, with a nominal duty, from forty-eight to fifty-four shillings. The bounty upon exports was still continued. Thirteen years after (1804), the agriculturists cried out again, and raised the scale of imposts still higher, viz: to 66 shillings, when every kind of soil was at once taken into cultivation, even the poorest. Under this exclusive system, corn rose in 1814 to an unpredented height, and millions of bushels poured into the kingdom, which occasioned new alarm to the landholders. A monstrous bill was prepared, which, had it been adopted in Parliament, would have proved absolutely ruinous to the interests of the poorer classes. Its only object could have been to keep up the prices reached in 1814. Wheat, when under sixty-four shillings the quarter at home, was to be charged with a duty of twenty-four shillings; when it exceeded eighty-six shillings, the duty only then was to be one shilling, or nominal. The nation, almost by one accord, rose up in condemnation of so odious a measure, and the ministers had not face enough to press it into operation.

The following table exhibits the position of Great Britain in relation to the corn trade, for the hundred years preceding the year 1800:

WHEAT AND FLOUR EXPORTED AND IMPORTED FROM 1697 TO 1800—*Winchester Measure.*

Years. England	Wheat and Flour exported Qrs.	Foreign Wheat and Flour. imported. Qrs.	Years. England.	Wheat and Flour exported. Qrs.	Foreign Wheat and Flour. imported. Qrs.	Years Gt. Brit.	Wheat and Flour. exported. Qrs.	Foreign Wheat and Flour. imported. Qrs.
1697	14,699	400	1732	202,058		1766	164,939	11,020
1098	6,857	845	1733	427,199	7	1767	5,071	497,905
1699	557	486	1734	498,196	6	1708	7,433	349,268
1700	49,056	5	1735	153,343	9	1769	49,892	4,378
1701	98,324	1	1736	118,170	16	1770	75,449	34
1702	90,230		1737	461,602	32	1771	10,089	2,510
1703	176,615	50	1738	580,596	2	1772	6,959	25,474
1704	90,313	2	1739	279,542	5,423	1773	7,637	56,857
1705	96,185		1740	54,390	7,568	1774	15,928	289,149
1706	188,332	77	1741	45,417	40	1775	91,037	560,988
1707	74,155		1742	293,260	1	1776	210,664	20,578
1708	83,406	86	1743	371,431	2	1777	87,686	233,323
1709	169,680	1,552	1744	231,984	2	1778	141,070	106,394
1710	13,924	400	1745	324,839	6	1779	222,261	5,039
1711	76,949		1746	130,646		1780	224,059	3,915
1712	145,191		1747	266,907		1781	103,021	159,866
1713	176,227		1748	543,387	385	1782	145,152	80,695
1714	174,821	16	1749	629,049	382	1783	51,934	584,183
1715	166,490		1750	947,602	279	1784	89,288	216,947
1716	74,926		1751	661,416	3	1785	132,685	110,863
1717	22,954		1752	429,279		1786	205,466	51,463
1718	71,800		1753	299,609		1787	120,536	59,339
1719	127,762	20	1754	356,270	201	1788	82,971	148,710
1720	83,084		Gt Bt.			1789	140,014	112,656
1721	81,633		1755	237,466		1790	30,892	222,557
1722	178,880		1756	102,752	5	1791	70,626	469,056
1723	157,720		1757	11,545	141,562	1792	300,278	622,417
1724	245,865	148	1758	9,234	20,353	1793	76,629	490,398
1725	204,413	12	1759	227,641	162	1794	155,048	327,902
1726	142,183		1760	393,614	3	1795	18,839	313,793
1727	30,315		1761	441,956		1796	24,679	879,200
1728	3,817	74,574	1762	295,385	56	1797	54,525	461,767
1729	18,993	40,315	1763	429,538	72	1798	59,782	396,721
1730	93,971	76	1764	396,857	1	1799	39,362	463,185
1731	130,025	4	1765	167,126	104,547	1800	22,013	1,264,520

Average Prices of Wheat in England and Wales, from 1815 to 1824, inclusive.

	£	s.	d.		
1815	3	4	4	64*s.*	per quarter.
1816	3	15	10	76*s.*	"
1817	4	14	9	95*s.*	"
1818	4	4	1	84*s.*	"
1819	3	13	0	73*s.*	"
1820	3	7	11	68*s.*	"
1821	2	16	2	56*s.*	"
1822	2	4	7	44*s.*	"
1823	2	13	5	53*s.*	"
1824	3	4	0	64*s.*	"

In 1815, Parliament having examined leading agriculturists, and they being unanimous in the sentiment that the inferior lands would have to be thrown out of cultivation under the law of 1804, agreed upon a new bill. By this, corn for home consumption was absolutely forbidden to be entered from foreign ports, unless when wheat was selling at eighty shillings per quarter in England, and other grain in proportion. This was intended to raise prices up to eighty shillings, and render them permanent at that. But the signal disappointment of these grinding and greedy interests is exhibited in the preceding table, taken from McCullocb, vol. i. p. 505.

To remedy the new evil of exceedingly fluctuating, and at times low prices, Parliament was again set to work—so strange was the persistence in a course in its nature radically wrong. Importation was, as usual, looked upon as the great evil to be provided against; and the statute 3 George IV., 1822, loaded it with heavy duties, whenever the prices, above seventy shillings at home, appeared likely to stimulate it. But prices, to the regret of agriculturists, remained down provokingly under seventy shillings.

In 1825, wheat was allowed to be imported from British America without any regard to the home prices; a step too liberal to be continued for more than one year.

In 1826, there was a large deficiency in production, and the sovereign was authorized to admit 500,000 quarters foreign wheat, on favorable terms.

In 1827, a general dissatisfaction was exhibited in every quarter, in relation to the corn system. It was discovered to have only been one continued source of evil to the nation, and a permanent benefit to none. Right views began for once to be taken on the subject; and Mr. Canning, the minister, prepared to act on a new principle. He was sustained by the Commons; but the Duke of Wellington, in the House of Lords, tacked on a clause to the bill, which defeated it.

The following year, Mr. Charles Grant proposed a measure, which soon after became a law. It was based upon the principles of Mr. Canning (liberal for the times), but in its details was far less advantageous, we conceive, to the interests of the nation. We furnish the scale of duties provided for in this bill, on the article of wheat:

Whenever the home price is—
62*s*. and under 63*s*. per quarter, the duty shall be for every quarter 24*s*.
Whenever the home price is over—

63*s*. and under	64*s*.	"	"	23*s*.
64*s*. "	65*s*.	"	"	22*s*.
65*s*. "	66*s*.	"	"	21*s*.
66*s*. "	67*s*.	"	"	20*s*.
67*s*. "	68*s*.	"	"	18*s*.
68*s*. "	69*s*.	"	"	16*s*.
69*s*. "	70*s*.	"	"	13*s*.
70*s*. "	71*s*.	"	"	10*s*.
71*s*. "	72*s*.	"	"	6*s*.
72*s*. "	73*s*.	"	"	2*s*.
73*s*. and above				1*s*.
under 62*s*. and over	61*s*.	"	"	25*s*.

This tariff of duties continued in operation for many years, and gave way at last to the present sliding scale, as it is termed, which Sir Robert Peel and the British Parliament have been struggling to maintain against the crying wants of the nation. A proposition to modify it was voted down by an immense majority, only last year, and the Premier declared that no essential modification should ever take place. Events, however, in that country, are now giving a new aspect to the question; and there is no power, which, we think, can be strong enough to resist the influence of popular sentiment.

We extract from the British tariff, as now existing, (1846) its provisions in relation to the corn trade.

Wheat, if imported from Foreign Countries.

Whenever the average price at home, made up and published in the manner provided by law, shall be
Under 51*s*. the duty per quarter shall be .... £1 0*s*. 0*d*.
Over 51*s*. and under 52*s*. the duty per quarter shall be .... 0 19*s*. 0*d*.
Over 52*s*. and under 53*s*. the duty per quarter shall be .... 0 18*s*. 0*d*.

And decreasing progressively 1*s*. duty for each shilling in price to 73*s*. when the duty shall be 1*s*., and continue at that whatever the elevation in price.

In relation to Canadian wheat, a difference is made, which has, to some extent, stimulated our operations with Canada, and occasioned that province to conduct for us our foreign corn trade. Wheat, if the produce of, and imported from, Canada, is allowed to enter English markets at a duty of one shilling the quarter; and flour, at four and one-eighth pence the cwt.

Had England allowed the grain market to regulate itself, she would never have experienced those reverses which have grown out of her unwise legislation; corn would not have ranged from 125s. the quarter in 1812, to 38s. 1d. in 1822, 68s. in 1825, 39s. in 1835, and we scarcely know what in 1845; but she would have had a constant supply, and a scale of prices which would render prosperous both her producers and her consumers. We may suppose that these dear-bought lessons will soon have their proper effect, and that a free grain market will take the place of all restrictions upon either exports or imports. In this way, when there is an expected scarcity, grain will be thrown into her ports from every quarter; and when Providence has abundantly crowned her farmers, they will be able to appear to advantage in foreign markets, should it ever happen that they can more than supply their own.

The increasing population of Great Britain, and the vast amount of it engaged in manufacturing purposes, every year becoming proportionately greater, will, in despite of the improvements in agriculture there, and the supplies which the Irish market may afford, render that country in all future time an immense grain importer. It will be in vain for her to look at home; willingly or not, she must depend to a very great extent upon the world without, for those supplies which are indispensable to her existence. For the fourteen years ending in 1842, her imports were as follows, of foreign and colonial wheat:

1829..	bushels,	11,572,608	1836..	bushels,	240,856
1830..	"	13,822,776	1837..	"	1,979,176
1831..	"	12,053,920	1838..	"	14,787,800
1832..	"	3,062,040	1839..	"	21,693,784
1833..	"	672,208	1840..	"	19,201,488
1834..	"	519,792	1841..	"	21,182,072
1835..	"	228,400	1842..	"	23,917,160

Making an annual average import of 9,625,-378 bushels foreign, and 727,126 colonial. In 1843, the import was 920,800 quarters foreign wheat, and 98,100 cwts. flour, 19,630 quarters colonial wheat, and 294,180 cwts. flour. In 1844, 1.068,570 quarters foreign wheat, 306,000 cwts. flour, and 44,470 quarters colonial wheat, and 774,800 cwts. flour, The average import of the five years preceding 1843, was 20,000,000 bushels wheat and flour. In 1844 the crop was good, and the deficiency felt was only 11,267,000 bushels. In 1845, the last estimate, by a paper of high standing, fixes the enormous deficit of 70,000,000 bushels, supposing that the last annual average consumption, 170,000,000 bushels will be maintained, and the crop to have failed to the extent that it is stated, viz.: two-thirds of the average, neither of which, however, is altogether probable. At all events, the wants of the present year may be stated as out of all proportion greater than of any preceding one; and the question is, how shall these be supplied, and in what manner will the United States be affected by them?

Mr. Peel, not long since, endeavored to make it appear in Parliament, that the United States was not a grain-growing country; but what was policy in the Premier to state, is too remote from fact even to be repeated. Every year exhibits the increasing capacity of our western granaries; and as the tide of population continues to flow in, and new and productive soils are taken into cultivation, we shall see results exhibited, which will prove that our grain market can compete, under a fair system, with that of any other portion of the world.

It has been over and over stated, and sometimes from high sources, that we can only compete with the pauper and serf labor of northern Europe, in seasons of extraordinary scarcity; and that, ordinarily, prices with us, and freights, which we must pay, go entirely to exclude our produce from English markets. We have no confidence whatever in these calculations and estimates. Our convictions are, that the labor and the enterprise of free citizens, in an abundant country, and without grinding taxation, can take care of themselves, and meet and triumph over opposition throughout all the world. We have seen this exhibited in many branches of our industry, and there is no ground for exception in this. Allow a fair trial by removing all obstructions, and we are sure of the result. If it be true that prices are usually lower on the continent of Europe than they are with us, the fact will only stimulate our exertions. Wheat can be afforded in this country, and pay a fair profit to its producers in years of abundance, at prices much lower than any previous quotation. Ten years ago, and our cotton planters would have thought a reduction of a few cents in the prices of their staple, likely to ruin them entirely. Many would have replied, had you interrogated them, that cotton could not be grown in this country at any considerable reduction in prices: yet cotton has been grown, and is still growing beyond all precedent and all expectation, at one-half the price in market which it found ten years ago! Even the poorest soils yet continue its production. The Hon. Dixon H. Lewis stated in Congress, that cotton could be grown profitably in Alabama for five cents. At all events, it will be conceded that many, even at its present value, find cotton-growing no very bad business. Let every one apply these facts to the grain market, and draw his own conclusions: for us, we have no reason to doubt. We say to the grain-growers in every part of the states, go to work actively and cheerfully; develop your soils and reap your harvests, with a perfect surety that, with the staff of life in your hands, you will ever be looked up to with interest, and always find willing buyers and remunerating prices.

The chief grain-growing regions, from which large supplies have in all times past been exported, are Poland, Russia, Denmark, Germany, and the Black Sea. We shall make a few remarks upon the character of each, and then show to what extent Great Britain has been dependent on them and other European sections of minor importance.

Dantzic, as a port, has afforded an outlet for Polish grain; and McCulloch estimates that 350,000 to 450,000 quarters of wheat might be obtained annually from that source. The Dantzic wheat is represented as of superior quality—its "high mixed" sustaining no injury from a comparison with the best English. It is preferred to wheat from the lower Elbe at an advance of 20s. the quarter.

Russia has exported wheat, rye, oats, and meal. She sent to England alone, in 1831, near 500,000 quarters of wheat, but its quality is very indifferent, being small-grained, coarse, brown, and badly prepared; well calculated for keeping, however, in the granary.

Denmark labors under the same disadvantages, as to the quality of grain produced, and her exports have not been very considerable.

Hamburg is the centre of a large grain trade. Corn from the Baltic and the valley of the lower Elbe is deposited there, and also from Bohemia; but, according to McCulloch, the quality is far inferior to Dantzic wheat. In 1830, England received 217,700 quarters hence. Amsterdam has also afforded considerable supplies.

Odessa, on the Black Sea, does all the export business of southern Europe in grain. It is brought there from Polish provinces, mostly by land carriage, a mode of conveyance said to be not very expensive. The quality of wheat is inferior, and commands 8s. a quarter less than British, in the London market. The danger of becoming heated in its passage through warm climates, checks the amount of business done in this grain.

France has never been able to do more than supply her own wants, and she has been resorting to non-exportation and importation systems with little real advantage. The same may be said of Spain, which, though capable of large production, has not yet been able to reach it—her lands being susceptible of abundant development.

In 1831, Great Britain imported from Russia 464,584 quarters ; Prussia, 296,286 ; Germany, 218,507 ; Spain, 154,671 ; Italy, 253,295 ; British Colonies, 218,327 ; United States, 463,418. In 1832, she took from the United States 55,050 bushels wheat, and 95,868 barrels flour ; in 1839, 6,003 bushels wheat, 167,582 barrels flour ; in 1840, 607,108 bushels wheat, 605,778 barrels flour ; in 1842, 143,330 bushels wheat, 204,896 barrels flour.

The following table, taken from McCulloch's Commercial Dictionary, page 507, will show the amount of grain imported into Great Britain from each of the countries named, from 1801 to 1825, both inclusive—(in Winchester Quarterlies.)

Countries.	Annual av'r'ge of 25 years.	Annual average Wheat.	Rye.	Barley.	Do. Oats.	Peas and Beans.	Indian Corn.
Russia	117,902	53,377	9,968	7,112	46,652	785	8
Sweden and Norway	14,397	9,576	960	987	2,446	428	—
Denmark	67,847	16,324	1,123	18,808	30,672	823	97
Prussia	228,584	157,359	5,689	18,718	39,209	7,609	—
Germany	171,103	58,103	5,189	24,839	75,828	7,144	—
The Netherlands	158,078	56,817	1,690	9,500	84,269	5,802	—
France and South of Europe	37,932	24,649	293	1,097	1,953	9,125	816
United States of America	80,712	74,024	2,341	31	9	201	4,022
British North American Colonies	25,627	24,863	—	51	1	697	15
Other foreign countries, Isle of Man and Prize Corn	10,503	4,836	1,438	2,194	1,703	151	41
Ireland	865.968	187,438	253	33,331	639,857	4,922	107

In 1841, her imports were—

om	Russia	bushels	498,205
"	Sweden	"	4,410
"	Denmark	"	1,915,272
"	Prussia	"	7,134,400
"	Germany	"	5,295,674
"	Holland	"	815,964
"	Belgium	"	228,620
"	France	"	1,643,932
"	Italy and Islands	"	901,600
"	United States	"	1,107,840
"	Colonies and other nations	"	3,071,583

For the present year, 1846, her European supplies are likely to be cut off almost entirely. Great scarcity prevails in Holland, so that government has reduced the duty on imports to the smallest point. In Belgium, the same state of things exists. The stock of the Baltic is said to be already in second hands ; and the deficiency in Italy will leave nothing from the Black Sea.

Of course, all eyes must now be turned upon the United States ; and in the remaining pages of this article, we shall confine our attention exclusively to the grain trade, as it has existed with us in the past ; exhibit the prospects of that trade, and the home supplies with which it must be sustained.

The census which was taken in 1840, has been proved to be inaccurate in many particulars ; but we have seen no objection raised to the grain statistics which it affords. It appears that the crop of that year was 84,000,000 bushels wheat, and near 380,000-000 bushels Indian corn. By other information, we have the following table of production :

	1840	1842	1843	1844
Wheat, bushels	84,822,272	102,317,344	100,310,856	95,607,000
Barley	4,161,504	3,871,622	3,230.721	3,627,000
Oats	123,071,341	150,833,607	145,929,666	172,247,000
Rye	18,645,567	22,762,952	24,889,281	26,450,000
Buckwheat	7,291,743	2,483,480	7,959,410	9,710,000
Corn	377,531,875	441,829,246	496,618,305	427,953,000

For the year 1845, we have not the most reliable information ; but the general impression from the best sources is, that the wheat crop will reach the unprecedented yield of 125,000,000 bushels—the State of Michigan alone, with a population of but 400,000, yielding 7,000,000 bushels. Deducting for home consumption 70,000,000 bushels, which, with high prices, will hardly be exceeded, and for seed, there will remain for exportation upward of 40,000,000 bushels wheat. The average exportation of Indian corn, for the last fourteen years, has been 1,500,000 bushels annually, and we cannot have less for the same purpose the present year.

The following table will show the amount of grain which has been exported from our country in the past, and the sources to which it was attracted.

Account of the quantities of Flour and Grain exported from the United States, from October 1st, 1821, to September 30th, 1831, with the prices of Flour at Philadelphia, and of Wheat and Indian Corn at New-York.

Years.	Wheat flour. bbls.	Rye flonr. bbls.	Corn meal. bbls.	Wheat. bush.	Indian corn. bush.	Price of wheat flour per barrel at Philadel'ia.	Price of wheat per bushel at New-York.	Price of Ind. corn per bushel at New-York.
1831	1,805,205	19,049	204,206	405,384	566,761	$- —	$1 19	$0 70
1830	1,225,881	26,298	145,301	45,289	444,190	4 98	0 98	0 57
1829	837,385	34,191	173,775	4,007	897,656	6 35	1 38	0 58
1828	860,809	22,214	174,639	8,906	704,902	5 60	1 08	0 53
1827	865,491	13,345	131,041	22,182	978,664	5 23	0 97	0 65
1826	857,820	14,472	158,625	45,166	505,381	4 65	0 90	0 79
1825	813,906	29,545	187,285	17,960	869,644	5 10	1 04	0 56
1824	996,792	31,879	152,723	20,373	779,297	5 62	1 15	0 47
1823	756,702	25,665	141,501	4,272	749,034	6 82	1 05	0 53
1822	827,865	19,971	148,288	4,418	509,098	6 58	0 90	0 49
1821	1,056,119	23,523	131,669	25,812	607,277	4 78	0 89	0 53

From 1831 to 1843, we have the following, furnished by a writer who looks rather despondingly upon the prospects of our grain trade.

Table of Exports of Wheat and Flour to the principal markets, together with the total Exports to all foreign markets, for thirteen consecutive years.

	England.		*Br. American Colonies.*		*Cuba.*	
Years.	Bush. wheat.	Bbls. flour.	Bush. wheat.	Bbls. flour.	Bush. wheat	Bbls. flour.
1831	362,153	865,744	12,505	150,795	—	97,999
1832	55,050	95,868	20,777	135,640	—	98,248
1833	—	21,707	31,421	168,127	—	119,197
1834	—	19,487	23,247	134,975	—	102,837
1835	—	5,376	—	76,405	—	93,511
1836	—	161	2,082	42,300	—	92,390
1837	—	—	—	23 316	—	55,537
1838	—	8,295	6,076	29,591	—	79,681
1839	6,033	167,582	72,113	149,407	—	90,459
1840	607,108	605,778	1,066,604	432,356	788	69,819
1841	119,854	205,144	695,389	377,806	—	69,387
1842	143,330	204,896	655,503	369,048	4,179	46,846
1843	—	14,214	293,842	190,322	—	29,437
Average	99,502	170,327	221,498	175,391	382	80,411

	Brazil.		*British West Indies.*		*Tot. Ex. to all Foreign Markets.*	
Years.	Bush. wheat.	Bbls. flour.	Bush. wheat.	Bbls. flour.	Bush. wheat.	Bbls. flour.
1831	—	198,870	—	100,382	408,445	1,806,529
1832	—	103,289	—	100,167	83,304	864,919
1833	—	259,536	—	100,057	32,221	955,768
1834	—	152,603	—	95,816	36,948	835,352
1835	—	161,460	—	118,307	47,762	779,396
1836	—	118,470	2,062	70,305	2,062	505,400
1837	—	60,480	—	68,323	17,303	318,719
1838	—	125,275	137	75,524	6,291	448,161
1839	—	177,337	14,129	139,340	96,325	923,151
1840	—	197,823	33,743	232,329	1,720,860	1,897,501
1841	16,457	282,406	41,116	246,465	868,585	1,515,817
1842	—	189,317	14,920	237,478	817,058	1,283,602
1843	—	192,454	17,399	170,577	311,685	841,474
Average	1,266	170,716	9,500	135,005	342,709	997,771

It is to be observed, that during part of this time, a very large portion of wheat entering the British colony of Canada, was intended for the market of the mother country.

BREADSTUFFS. — American Wheat and Corn Trade.—The close of the commercial year, commencing on the 1st September, 1846, and ending on the 31st August, 1847, with the ascertained prospects of the crops of grain for the present year, renders this a favorable time to review the results of the grain and flour trade of the United States for the past year, and enables us to form some opinion of the prospects of the same for the year on which we have entered. Our object will be principally to notice the great staple grains of wheat and Indian corn, and their products of flour and meal, the quantity of other breadstuffs exported from this country being comparatively inconsiderable.

The accounts of exports of produce from the different ports of the United States to foreign countries, are not yet made up in full to the 1st of September, 1847, but the following table is so nearly complete, embracing, within a few days, the exports from the principal ports for the past year, that we adopt it.*

* To Sept. 1, the exports from Charleston were 151,704 bush. corn, 2,287 bush. wheat, 3,000 bbls. flour; 46 bbls. meal; from New-Orleans, to Aug. 27, flour, 1,083,538 bbls.; wheat, 628,599 sacks; corn, 2,222,639 sacks.

Exports of Flour, Indian Meal, Wheat, and Indian Corn, from the Principal Ports of the United States to foreign countries, from Sept. 1, 1846, *to the latest dates received at New-York, up to Sept.* 1, 1847.

Ports.	Bbls. Flour.	Bbls. In. Meal.	Bush. Wheat.	Bush. In. Corn
New-York, to August 30	2,113,166		2,929,878	6,832,164
" to August 10	—	377,177	—	—
New-Orleans, July 31	1,051,474	62,404	1,022,674	5,070,494
Philadelphia, August 13	500,944	313,560	663,082	1,409,720
Baltimore, August 7	652,576	97,148	183,090	1,715,640
Boston, August 10	145,625	30,869	15,173	583,697
Norfolk	39,014	9,018	—	1,298,083
Richmond and Petersburg	49,100	4,105	—	27,164
Alexandria	18,245	1,244	23,542	97,544
Wilmington, Del	420	47,217	—	8,400
Newark, N. J.	91	2,043	—	912
Charleston, S. C.	747	—	6,233	71,643
Savannah	1,807	254	—	70,070
Mobile	1,571	—	—	44,214
Apalachicola	—	—	—	40,000
Gardiner, Me	500	—	—	—
Chicago, Ill	—	—	18,000	—
Cleveland, Ohio	24,449	—	202,962	3,080
Total	4,599,729	945,039	5,065,234	17,272,815

By changing the flour into bushels, allowing 5 bushels of wheat to a barrel of flour, and 4 bushels of Indian corn to a barrel of meal, and adding the same to the wheat and corn, we have the following results:

Exports of wheat...............28,063,879 bushels.
Exports of Indian corn..........21,052,971 "

The estimated value of the above exports is as follows:

Flour	4,599,729 bbls.	*a* $6 00	$27,598,374
Indian meal	945,039 "	*a* 3 25	3,071,376
Wheat	5,065,234 bush.	*a* 1 25	6,331,572
Indian corn	17,272,815 "	*a* 80	13,818,252
Total			$50,819,574

The following comparative table of exports from the United States to foreign countries, of the same articles of breadstuffs for the previous ten years, divided into two periods of five years each, shows the great increase in the trade for the last year:

Year ending	Bbls flour	Bbls In. meal	Bush wheat	Bush In. corn
September 30, 1837	318,719	159,435	17,303	151,276
" 1838	448,161	171,843	6,291	172,321
" 1839	923,151	165,672	96,325	162,306
" 1840	1,897,501	206,063	1,720,860	574,279
" 1841	1,515,817	232,284	868,585	535,727
Total, first period	5,103,349	935,297	2,709,364	1,595,909
September 30, 1842	1,283,602	209,199	817,958	600,308
June 30, 1843 (9 month)	841,474	174,354	311,685	281,749
" 1844	1,438,574	247,882	558,917	825,282
" 1845	1,195,230	269,030	389,716	840,184
" 1846	2,289,476	298,790	1,613,795	1,826,068
Total, second period	7,048,356	1,199,255	3,692,071	4,373,591

TOTAL VALUE OF THE ABOVE EXPORTS.

	First period	Second period	Total 9 yrs 9 mos
Flour	$31,418,999	$34,965,179	$66,384,178
Wheat	2,637,886	3,699,879	6,337,765
Indian corn and meal	4,614,468	5,928,956	10,543,424
Total	$38,671,353	$44,594,014	$83,065,367

It will be observed that the total value of the exports of the above staples for the last year, exceeds the total value of the same for either of the above periods of about 5 years each; and the value of the Indian corn and meal exported the past year, exceeds the total value of the same exported for ten years previously, by about eight millions of dollars.

If we take the annual average of exports of the same staples from September 30, 1837, to June 30, 1846, calling the same a period of ten years, (which is near enough for our purpose,) and compare these averages with the exports for the year ending in September, 1847, we have the following result:

	Exports—1847	Ann av. for 10 yrs previous	Increase
Flour, barrels	4,599,729	1,215,170	3,384,559
Wheat, bushels	5,065,234	640,143	4,425,091
Indian corn, bushels	17,272,815	596,950	16,675,865
Indian meal	945,039	213,455	731,584
Value of Flour	$27,598,374	$6,638,417	$20,959,957
" Wheat	6,331,572	633,776	5,697,796
" Indian corn and meal	16,889,628	1,054,342	15,835,286
Total	$50,819,574	$8,326,535	$42,493,039

The foregoing statements show that the exports of flour, wheat, Indian corn and meal, for the commercial year just closed, exceed in value the annual average exports of the same for a period of ten years previous, by about *forty-two millions* of dollars. It will be noticed that the exports from New-Orleans for the month of August, and from various other ports for a part of the same month, or for a longer period, are to be added to the statement for the last year, which will swell the increase beyond the annual average to a larger amount than we have assumed. It is probable, also, that a considerable amount will be added to the exports of last year, for shipments of flour and grain sent to Europe, via the St. Lawrence, from Detroit and other ports on the lakes.

The destination of wheat, flour, Indian corn and meal, for the two last years, it is well known, has been principally to Great Britain and Ireland. It may be interesting to know where have been our principal foreign markets, for flour, from 1800 to 1840.

The following statement shows the destination of wheat flour exported from the United States for two periods, namely, from 1800 to 1814 inclusive, and from 1815 to 1840, viz:

	For 15 years (1800—14)		For 26 years (1815—40)	
British North America	352,517	barrels	2,873,348	barrels.
West Indies	5,977,716	"	10,016,563	"
South America		"	5,307,607	"
Great Britain and Ireland	1,881,296	"	4,103,205	"
France	36,713	"	347,296	"
Spain and Portugal	4,154,131	"	567,421	"
Other ports of Europe	147,508	"	642,028	"
Asia	—	"	167,431	"
Africa	—	"	82,087	"
Uncertain	1,094,957	"	206,350	"

The large exports to Spain and Portugal during the first period, were principally owing to the wars in the Peninsula. The supply of the allied British and Spanish armies created a great demand for American flour, which caused shipments to be made from the United States from 1810 to 1813, and sustained high prices in this country.

The annual average shipments continue about the same as they were previous to the war with Great Britain of 1812, viz.: nearly 400,000 barrels—while to Great Britain and Ireland the annual average quantity shipped was 125,419 barrels previous to 1815, and 157,815 barrels from the peace to 1840. From the latter year to 1846, our exports of wheat and flour to that kingdom greatly increased, and for the year 1847, of course, much exceed our exports of those staples to all other parts of the world combined.

Previous to the repeal of the British Corn Law, our best and principal trade with Great Britain was through Canada. For seven years previous to 1846, we sent into Canada 12,586,892 bushels of wheat, (reducing the flour to wheat,) while our direct trade to England, at the same time, amounted to only 7,764,588 bushels.

The exports from New-York of breadstuffs other than flour, wheat, Indian corn and meal, from September 1, 1846, to July 31, 1847, (being eleven months,) have been so much larger than usual, that we subjoin them, as follows:

Rye flour	21,028	barrels.
Rye	993,869	bush.
Barley	291,148	"
Peas and beans	177,488	"
Oats	416,147	"
Bread	50,498	barrels.

Crop of Wheat and Indian Corn in the United States.—The last annual estimate of the crops of the United States was made at the Patent Office, for the year 1845. It is known that the crops of grain for 1846 were more abundant than those of the year previous, but we have not the means of forming a calculation on the increase.

The following are the estimates of the Commissioner of Patents, with regard to the crops of wheat and Indian corn for 1845. We have divided the United States into two sections—the first, embracing the Atlantic States and Michigan (as the markets of the latter are principally obtained via the Hudson River and the St. Lawrence)—the second, embracing the Valley of the Mississippi, excluding western Pennsylvania, Virginia and New York:

ATLANTIC STATES AND MICHIGAN.

	Wheat Bushels	Indian corn Bushels
New-England States	2,363,000	11,946,000
New-York	16,200,000	13,250,000
New-Jersey	1,050,000	7,314,000
Pennsylvania	12,580,000	17,126,000
Delaware	440,000	2,713,000
Maryland	4,884,000	3,723,000
District of Columbia	15,000	35,000
Virginia	11,885,000	27,272,000
North Carolina	1,969,000	14,887,000
South Carolina	1,168,000	8,184,000
Georgia	1,571,000	13,320,000
Florida	—	733,000
Michigan	7,061,000	4,945,000
Total—Atlantic States, &c.	61,181,000	125,448,000
" Valley of Miss.	45,362,000	292,451,000
Total—United States	106,533,000	417,899,000

VALLEY OF THE MISSISSIPPI.

	Wheat, Bushels	Indian corn, Bushels
Ohio	13,572,000	57,600,000
Indiana	7,044,000	30,625,000
Illinois	4,563,000	25,584,000
Missouri	1,525,000	15,625,000
Kentucky	4,769,000	54,625,000

	Wheat Bushels	Indian corn Bushels
Tennessee	8,340,000	70,265,000
Arkansas	2,427,000	8,250,000
Mississippi	378,000	2,167,000
Louisiana	—	8,360,000
Alabama	980,000	16,650,000
Wisconsin	971,000	672,000
Iowa	793,000	2,028,000
Total	45,362,000	292,451,000

The above estimates appear to us to be overrated in some instances, and underrated in others. If we assume the aggregate, however, to be about the total amount of the crop of 1845, and add a small increase for that of 1846, we may take the wheat crop of 1846 at 110 millions, and that of Indian corn at 460 millions of bushels.* On this basis it appears that our exports to foreign countries, for the year ending September 1, 1847, amounted in quantity to about 25 per cent. on the crop of wheat, and less than 5 per cent. on the crop of Indian corn.

With regard to the crops of the present year, the accounts received from all quarters of the United States justify the belief that the harvests, both for wheat and Indian corn, will be more abundant than those of last year. Perhaps it would be safe to estimate an addition of 15 per cent. on the quantity of wheat raised over that of 1846, and 30 per cent. on the crop of Indian corn, making about 130,000,000 bushels of the former, and 600,000,000 bushels of the latter.

Should the expectations of these increased quantities be realized with regard to these important staples, and the promise of abundant harvests in Europe be also realized, thus cutting off a large proportion of the great demand from abroad, which has stimulated and sustained prices for nearly a year past, it would seem reasonable to calculate on a much lower range of prices for grain of all kinds than our farmers have been favored with during the recent famine in Europe. A moderate competition, however, from abroad, in the demand for breadstuffs, may enable them to become sensible of the value of the home market.

The importance of the home market for the consumption of the grain crops is shown by the following estimate, made some years since in the Philadelphia Commercial List, with regard to the disposition of the wheat crop of 1840, to which we add a similar calculation respecting the crop of 1846:

	1840. Bushels	1846 Bushels
Estimated wheat crop	80,000,000	110,000,000
Used for seed, starch, &c	7,750,000	10,000,000
Consumed for food in U. S.	60,950,000	72,000,000
Exported to foreign countries	11,300,000	28,000,000

Of the Indian corn crop of 1846, we estimate, that the 460 million bushels raised, will have been thus disposed of:

Exported to foreign countries	22,000,000 bushels.
Sold to and consumed by non-producers	100,000,000 "
Consumed on the farms and plantations of the producers for human and animal food, seed, &c.	338,000,000 bushels.
Total	460,000,000 "

A calculation made, however, upon the basis of the Commercial List, for the last season, we admit, is not by any means a fair one. The foreign demand has increased beyond measure more than the home, from the absolute destitution in Europe and failure of accustomed supplies. High prices at home, too, would operate to check consumption. It stands to reason, however, from the nature of the two demands, that the one originating at home must be many times the greater of the two, though at the same time the foreign may give character to prices, and in general does.

The following table will show the export of Indian corn from the United States for 57 years:

TOTAL EXPORTS OF CORN AND CORN MEAL FROM THE UNITED STATES FROM 1791 TO 1847.

Year	Bushels corn	Bbls corn meal
1791	1,713,214	351,695
1792	1,964,973	263,405
1793	1,233,768	189,715
1794	1,505,977	241,570
1795	1,935,345	512,445
1796	1,173,552	540,286
1797	804,922	254,799
1798	1,218,231	211,694
1799	1,200,492	231,226
1800	1,694,327	338,108
1801	1,768,162	919,353
1802	1,633,283	266,816
1803	2,079,608	133,606
1804	1,944,373	111,327
1805	861,501	116,131
1806	1,064,263	108,342
1807	1,018,721	136,460
1808	249,538	30,818
1809	522,049	57,260
1810	1,054,252	86,744
1811	2,790,850	147,426
1812	2,039,999	90,810
1813	1,486,970	52,521
1814	61,284	26,438
1815	830,516	72,634
1816	1,077,614	89,119
1817	387,454	106,763
1818	1,075,190	120,029
1819	1,086,762	135,271
1820	533,741	146,316
1821	607,277	131,669
1822	509,098	148,228
1823	749,034	141,501
1824	779,297	152,723
1825	869,644	187,225
1826	505,381	158,652
1827	978,664	131,041
1828	70,492	174,639
1829	897,656	173,775
1830	444,109	145,301
1831	571,312	207,604
1832	451,230	146,710
1833	437,174	146,678
1834	303,449	149,609
1835	755,781	166,782
1836	124,791	140,917
1837	151,276	159,435
1838	172,321	171,843
1839	162,306	165,672
1840	574,279	206,063
1841	535,727	232,284
1842	600,308	209,190
1843	672,608	174,254
1844	825,282	247,882
1845	840,184	269,030
1846	1,826,068	298,790
1847	17,272,815	945,039

* This is about the estimate of the Patent Office, an addition of ten per cent. being added to 1845. We rather regard the estimate as much too low.

BREADSTUFFS — Flour Exports.— There has sprung up a much greater disposition to speculate in produce for a rise. Money continues easy for good paper, and the present low prices are looked upon as available, or, as it is tersely expressed on 'Change, "there is money in them." A healthy tone, is, therefore, more apparent. The English duty on flour was 4s., until February, 1849, when it came off, and has since been nominal. We have compiled from Treasury reports the following table of export and destination of flour from the United States. It affords a sort of chart of the direction which the flour export trade has taken at times.

DESTINATION OF FLOUR SHIPPED FROM THE UNITED STATES.

Where to.	1847.	1849.	1850.	1851.
Swed. W. Indies	7,366	7,573	8,757	5,315
Danish do	52,150	49,568	44,802	50,102
Dutch East Indies	1,150	4,625	1,600	1,873
Dutch West Indies	11,387	17,221	18,354	19,217
Holland and Belgium	73,871	727	1,177	594
England	2,457,076	953,815	369,777	1,004,783
Gibraltar	23,974	6,265	2,543	195
British East Indies	3,034	791	1,646	1,600
British West Indies	320,363	303,551	250,776	294,731
British American Colonies	272,299	294,891	244,072	252,380
France	612,641	—	—	—
French West Indies	28,966	5,554	5,480	7,902
Hayti	40,257	10,903	31,504	43,867
Cuba	50,046	7,154	5,584	5,511
Spanish West Indies	17,780	6,429	7,074	2,285
Madeira	4,856	4,358	5,321	7,006
Cape de Verds	1,634	501	455	838
Texas	—	—	—	—
Mexico	5,928	11,633	9,736	14,964
Honduras	10,686	4,125	4,725	5,912
Central America	550	4,180	746	2,573
Columbia	39,403	32,251	41,072	47,477
Brazil	270,473	328,129	295,415	374,711
Argentine Republic	10,684	6,592	4,901	22,612
Chili	5,977	5,129	2,848	4,327
South America	2,128	—	40	200
West Indies	4,902	3,984	1,702	4,079
Africa	25,728	4,617	5,524	5,430
Northwest Coast	764	1,180	858	2,593
Other ports	29,866	35,017	18,949	19,158
Total barrels	4,382,496	2,108,013	1,385,448	2,202,335
Average price	$5.95	$5.35	$5.00	$4.77

The following table gives the aggregate export and official value, showing the yearly average for several years :

AGGREGATE EXPORT OF FLOUR FROM THE UNITED STATES.

	Barrels	Value	Ag. val. bbl
1840	1,893,182	10,143,615	$5 37
1841	1,510,613	7,779,646	5 20
1842	1,283,602	7,373,356	6 00
1843	841,474	3,763,073	4 50
1844	1,438,574	6,759,488	4 75
1845	1,195,230	5,398,593	4 51
1846	2,286,476	11,668,669	5 09
1847	4,382,496	26,133,841	5 95
1848	2,119,393	13,194,109	6 22
1849	2,108,113	11,280,582	5 35
1850	1,385,448	7,098,570	5 00
1851	2,202,335	10,524,331	4 77

The year 1840 was of the largest export for many years ; the following year was also considerable, and the effect of this export was the advance of the average price to $6 in 1842. If the wheat crop was 25,000,000 bbls., the difference was equal to $15,000,000 to wheat growers ; hence agricultural prosperity and improved home markets. In the years 1846 and 1847 the trade was immense. England and her possessions took three-fourths of the whole export of flour, and the result was a yearly increasing average price in the sales of the whole wheat crop. In the above table the average per barrel is given on the export price of the whole quantity ; the prices vary, however, as that sent to the British American colonies averaged $5.25, while that sent to England averaged $6—while that sent to Portugal and Madeira averaged over $7, and that to Mexico $4 50. The exports to France, Belgium, and Holland were considerable, as compared with former shipments, but the corn laws of those countries being suspended, it might have been expected that much larger transactions would have resulted.

In the year 1849–50, central Europe was possessed of a great surplus of wheat, and it poured into England in immense quantities. Of flour, and wheat as qrs. of wheat, France furnished 1,145,000 qrs, out of an importation into England of 4,830,263 qrs., and the United States supplied 537,031 qrs. of that quantity. In that year prices were in Europe very low, under the reaction from the high prices induced by the famine of 1847. The prices in Europe were thus :

PRICES OF WHEAT IN EUROPE.

	Average Price 1829 to 1850	Price 1850
France	45s. 7d.	33s. 2d.
Belgium	46s. 0d.	37s. 2d.
Prussia	34s. 3d.	31s. 6d.

In consequence of these prevailing low prices, England was the recipient of European wheat; nevertheless, the United States supplied in that year more than 10 per cent. of the English consumption. This year the reverse is the case; Europe is short of food, and the production of English is large. It is much to be regretted that our official returns cannot be brought down to a date later than almost twelve months. Since the last official report an entire change has taken place. England is an exporter, instead of being the sole customer, and we have no official guide as to the direction of the trade. Unofficial returns of exports from the United States to Great Britain, from September 1 to nearly the close of April, give the following figures:

EXPORT OF BREADSTUFFS FROM THE UNITED STATES TO GREAT BRITAIN AND IRELAND, SINCE SEPT. 1, 1851.

From		Flour, bbls.	Meal, bbls.	Wheat, bush.	Corn, bush.
New-York	to Apr. 20	448,275	15	1,167,529	488,390
New-Orleans	to Apr. 10	73,595	—	—	301,713
Philadelphia	to Apr. 16	109,137	1,680	291,189	23,583
Baltimore	to Apr. 16	128,353	—	120,121	31,824
Boston	to Apr. 17	27,523	—	18,135	15,021
Other Ports	to Apr. 10	20,925	—	54,544	44,784
Total	1852	807,808	1,695	1,651,518	905,315
About same time	1851	862,378	3,959	844,344	564,805
	1850	281,734	2,552	430,329	2,348,922
	1849	726,979	61,034	956,419	6,751,514
	1848	155,224	83,471	215,139	2,056,053

BREADSTUFFS — Preservation of Wheat and Flour, &c.—Professor Beck's experiments in this department have thus far been confined to wheat and wheat flour, which constitute the subject of the report before us. Indian corn and meal, which have now become such important articles of export, will receive due attention in the course of his researches. In entering upon the subject of his present report, his first object was to ascertain the amount of water in different kinds of wheat and flour, for all contain water in great or lesser quantities Its amount is greater in cold countries than in warm. In Alsace, from 16 to 20 per cent.; England, from 14 to 17 per cent.; United States, from 12 to 14 per cent.; Africa and Sicily, from 9 to 11 per cent.

This accounts for the fact, that the same weight of Southern flour yields more bread than Northern. English wheat yields 13 pounds more to the quarter than Scotch. Alabama flour, it is said, yields 20 per cent. more than that of Cincinnati. And, in general, American flour, according to one of the most extensive London bakers, absorbs 8 or 10 per cent. more of its own weight of water, in being made into bread, than the English. The English grain is fuller and rounder than the American, being in truth puffed up with moisture. All this is accounted for by temperature. The warmer the country, the more is the water dried out of the grain before it ripens; and hence, when made into bread, it absorbs more water again, and is therefore more valuable.

Water also unfits it for *preservation*. The books of a single inspector in New-York city showed, that in 1847, he inspected 218,679 barrels of sour and musty flour. In his opinion, the loss on these was $250,000. Every year the total loss in the United States, from moisture in wheat and flour, is estimated at from $3,000,000 to $5,000,000! To remedy this great evil, the grain should be well ripened before harvesting, and well dried before being stored in a good dry granary. Afterward, in grinding and in transporting, it should be carefully protected from wet, and the flour be kept from exposure to the atmosphere. The best precaution is kiln drying. By this process the wheat and flour are passed over iron plates heated by steam to the boiling point. From each barrel of flour 16 or 17 pounds of water are thus expelled, leaving still four or five per cent. in the flour, an amount too small to do injury. If all the water be expelled, the quality of the flour is deteriorated.

The mode of ascertaining the amount of water in flour is this: take a small sample, say 5 ounces, and weigh it carefully. Put it in a dry vessel, which should be heated by boiling water. After 6 or 7 hours, weigh it carefully until it loses no more weight. Its loss of weight shows the original amount of water.

The next object of Professor Beck, was to ascertain the amount of gluten in the various samples of flour. Gluten is an adhesive, pasty mass, and consists of several different principles, though its constitution has not yet been satisfactorily determined. It is chiefly the nutritious portion of the flour. The remaining principles are mostly starch, sugar, and gum. These three latter, have been thought not to be nutritious, but this is probably an error. On an average, their relative amount in 100 parts are about as follows:

	Average	Kobanka wheat—the best
Water	13	12
Gluten	12	16
Starch	67	60
Sugar and gum	8	9
	100	97

The Professor examined, according to the present report, 33 different samples, from different parts of the United States and Europe, and he gives the preference to the Kobanka variety from the south of Russia. There would probably be a prejudice against it in this country, from the natural yellowish hue of its flour and bread.

The process for determining the relative amounts of gluten, starch, sugar, and gum, is this: put a few ounces of flour, carefully weighed, in a cotton or linen cloth; pour cold water upon it, and work up the dough with the fingers. All except the gluten strains through the cloth. This is then dried and weighed.

The gum and sugar become dissolved in the water, but the starch settles at the bottom of the vessel. This water is poured off, and the starch is thus obtained, and may be weighed. The water is next evaporated, and the gum and sugar also obtained in a dry state for weighing. This is not a perfect method. Other methods, more complicated, give different results; but this is sufficiently accurate in a practical way for ascertaining the relative value of different specimens.

The report contains some valuable remarks on agriculture in general. The inquiry is not simply how productive a field may be made, however important that may be, but concerns also the *cost* of such production. A man may astonish the country by the great abundance of his crops, and yet become bankrupt with his great returns—simply because they cannot repay their cost. The questions, therefore, of economy of measures and economy of treatment, are of the first importance. It should be known, also, that wheat raised on a rich soil is more nutritious, taking the same quantity, than that raised on poor ground.

We hope these inquiries will be continued without delay. As yet, after so few months' labor, they are merely preliminary. Professor Beck has given abundant proof of his ability to pursue the subject, in his noble report on the mineralogy of New-York, and in his valuable works on Chemistry and Botany; and we may reasonably anticipate, that his researches in organic analysis, will be entitled to a place with those of Professor Horsford, of Cambridge, or of Professor Norton, of Yale.

BOSTON—Progress and Wealth of.—*The City of Boston.* In 1738, eight years after its settlement, Boston was said to be rather a village than a town, consisting of no more than twenty or thirty houses. In 1675 the population was 4,000; 1690, 7,000; 1704, 6,750; 1720, 11,000; 1735, 16,000. Slaves in 1754, 989, or one-sixteenth of population. In 1765, the inhabitants were 15,520; 1776, 2,719 whites, the rest having dispersed on account of the revolution; 1789, 17,880; 1790, 18,038; 1800, 24,937; 1810, 33,787; 1820, 43,298; 1830, 61,392; 1840, 85,000; 1845, 114,366. The annual average increase shown by the first six national censuses, was 3.82, 3.54, 2.81, 4.17, 3.84; but the census of 1845 shows an increase of 7 per cent. per annum, during the past five years.

There are in operation 700 miles of railway radiating from Boston, having a capital of $22,202,700, and having cost $26,712,123 57.

RAILROAD BUSINESS DONE IN 1845.

Names	Miles traveled	Income	Expenditures	Dividend
Eastern	218,583	$350,149 55	$116,840 00	8
Maine	194,946	287,063 10	154,099 95	7
Lowell	175,537	356,067 67	179,042 13	8
Nashua (branch)	43,065	112,680 89	48,009 94	15
Fitchburg	167,816	203,996 36	78,333 76	8
Charlestown (branch)	14,800	26,814 04	16,276 77	
Worcester	253,706	487,455 53	249,729 50	8
Norwich (branch)	173,230	204,308 45	134,229 03	3
Western "	530,201	813,480 15	370,621 25	
Connecticut River (branch)	15,268	13,521 06	8,001 26	
Hartford (branch)	14,559	—	—	
Berkshire "	29,359	—	—	
West Stockbridge (branch)	4,410	2,311 20	447 52	4
Providence	175,203	350,628 97	197,827 11	7
Stoughton (branch)	4,232	7,810 00	2,904 76	4
Taunton "	27,988	116,536 99	100,889 95	8
New-Bedford "	48,040	78,211 12	29,353 76	7
Old Colony	2,550	—	—	
Middleborough (branch)	17,800	15,796 72	8,205 83	
Total	2,111,293	$3,426,831 80	$1,694,812 52	

PUBLICATIONS IN BOSTON.

Class of Publications	No. of Publications	Square Inches	Value
Daily subscription	5,075,320	4,786,029,240	$106,076
Daily penny	11,408,000	7,018,617,000	110,400
Semi-weekly	1,462,448	1,442,010,336	58,748
Weekly	11,610,040	8,738,546,856	334,895
Semi-monthly	458,400	216,314,400	31,700
Monthly	2,583,600	1,522,477,200	127,190
Bi-monthly and Quarterly	37,200	143,076,800	24,500
Annual	255,500	265,045,300	31,565
Total	32,890,508	24,132,117,132	$825,074

It thus appears that 32,890,508 publications are issued annually from the Boston press, averaging 109,098 daily, allowing 310 working days to the year, valued at $825,074. These contain 24,132,117,132 square inches, or 3,847 acres of printed sheets, averaging 12 acres each day. Deducting ten per cent. for the margin of the sheets not printed, and there remains 6,926 acres of printed surface which goes out to the public mind, to influence or *educate* it for good or for ill. And it is supposed that the number of sheets printed for books and other publications, not named in the above account, or not periodical, makes a near approach to the same amount.

CHARITIES OF BOSTON FROM 1830–46.

Religious contributions	$1,120,219 75
Instruction	1,161,128 16
General charity	2,272,990 51
Miscellaneous	438,321 39
Total	$4,992,659 81

This not including the private acts of benevolence, which are supposed as much more. Of these donations, $268,753 83 were given in 1845.

COMMERCE OF BOSTON.

Years	Imports	Exports	Revenue
1824	12,828,253	5,036,963	4,193,112 81
1825	15,231,856	6,078,619	5,047,814 25
1826	12,627,449	6,780,577	3,988,378 46
1827	11,591,830	7,322,910	4,179,494 67
1828	12,540,924	7,438,014	4,597,176 86
1829	9,990,915	5,881,717	4,167,199 78
1830	8,348,623	5,180,178	3,662,301 78
1831	13,414,309	5,896,092	5,227,592 00
1832	15,760,512	10,107,768	5,524,839 36
1833	17,853,446	8,062,219	3,895,036 71
1834	15,614,720	7,309,761	2,830,172 69
1835	19,038,580	7,952,346	3,624,771 94
1836	25,897,955	8,475,313	4,470,053 73
1837	15,027,842	7,836,270	2,565,830 67
1838	13,463,465	7,036,882	2,411,155 95
1839	18,409,186	8,013,536	3,294,827 65
1840	14,122,308	8,405,224	2,456,926 22
1841	18,908,242	9,372,612	3,226,441 47
1842	12,633,713	7,226,104	2,780,186 04
1843	20,662,567	7,265,712	3,491,019 82
1844	22,141,788	8,294,726	5,034,954 14
1845	21,591,877	9,370,851	5,249,634 00

PROGRESSIVE WEALTH OF BOSTON.

Years	Real Estate	Personal Estate	Total Valuation	Polls	Tax	Tax on $100
1800	6,901,000	8,194,700	15,095,700	4,543	83,428 75	—
1810	10,177,200	8,273,300	18,450,500	7,764	144,486 72	39
1814	16,557,000	13,859,400	30,416,400	6,636	131,330 00	40
1815	18,265,600	14,647,400	32,913,000	6,457	157,794 00	45
1816	21,059,800	15,448,000	36,507,800	7,755	157,663 70	40
1817	21,643,600	16,373,400	38,017,000	7,497	163,313 50	40
1818	22,321,800	16,879,400	39,201,200	7,699	172,592 04	41
1819	22,795,800	16,583,400	39,379,200	8,030	169,859 10	40
1820	21,687,000	16,602,200	38,289,200	7,810	165,228 30	40
1821	22,122,000	18,671,600	40,793,600	8,646	174,968 32	39½
1822	23,364,400	18,775,800	42,140,200	8,880	167,583 37	36½
1823	25,367,000	19,529,800	44,896,800	9,855	172,423 60	35
1824	27,303,800	22,540,000	49,843,800	10,807	228,181 65	42½
1825	30,992,000	21,450,600	54,442,600	11,660	201,039 10	40½
1826	34,203,000	25,246,200	59,449,200	12,602	226,975 20	35
1827	36,061,400	29,797,000	65,858,800	12,442	242,946 40	35
1828	35,908,000	25,615,200	61,523,200	12,535	235,115 77	35¼
1829	36,963,800	24,104,200	61,068,000	13,495	261,461 10	39½
1830	36,960,000	22,626,000	59,586,000	13,096	260,967 30	40½
1831	37,675,000	23,023,200	60,698,200	13,618	260,184 89	39½
1832	39,145,200	28,369,200	67,514,400	14,184	298,085 84	41
1833	40,966,400	29,510,800	70,477,200	14,898	321,876 60	42½
1834	43,140,600	31,665,200	74,805,800	15,137	374,292 76	47
1835	47,552,800	31,749,800	79,302,600	16,188	408,899 61	48½
1836	53,373,000	34,895,000	88,245,000	16,719	444,656 65	47½
1837	56,311,600	33,272,200	89,583,800	17,182	473,692 00	50
1838	57,372,400	32,859,200	90,231,600	15,615	465,557 34	49
1839	58,577,800	33,248,600	91,826,400	16,561	543,660 66	56½
1840	60,424,200	34,157,400	94,581,600	17,696	546,742 80	55
1841	61,963,000	36,043,600	98,006,600	18,915	616,412 10	60
1842	65,499,900	41,223,800	105,723,700	19,636	637,779 09	57
1843	67,673,400	42,372,600	110,056,000	20,063	712,379 70	62
1844	72,048,000	46,402,300	118,450,300	22,339	744,210 30	60
1845	81,991,400	53,957,300	135,948,700	24,287	811,338 09	57

BALTIMORE—History and Resources, etc.—Baltimore, the most southern of the four great "commercial cities" on the Atlantic seaboard of our country, from its position, the rapidity of its growth, and its prospective greatness, is entitled to a more extended notice than is usually given to the cities sketched in this series. It is the largest and most striking instance yet presented to the world, of the rapid centralization and development of all the elements of commercial greatness which characterize the New World. Barely fifty years old as a city, it already takes rank, in population and trade, with those across the water which have been struggling up toward importance for centuries, and, with all the vigor and elasticity of early youth, is pressing on hopefully to a bright and strong manhood.

It is located upon an estuary, or small bay, which makes up for about two and a half miles on the north side of the Patapsco river, about ten miles from the entrance of this river into the Chesapeake Bay, of which it is for this distance an arm. By ship channel it is about 200 miles from the ocean, in 39° 17′ 23″ north latitude, and longitude 0 26′ east from Washington.

The city contains about 10,000 acres of land, extending about four and a half miles from east to west, and three and a half from north to south. It consisted originally of more than fifty elevations, or hills, separated by abrupt valleys, or ravines, and in a few instances by formidable marshes; while nearly in the centre it is divided by a rapid stream of water, known as "Jones' Falls. This stream has on three occasions—October 5, 1786, August 9, 1817, and June 14, 1837—overflowed its banks and done great damage, both to life and property. The city has, in consequence, been at great pains to remove all obstructions from its bed, and have the numerous bridges by which it is crossed sprung by a single arch, and at such a height as to remove all further danger from this source. The division east of *the falls* is again nominally subdivided into two parts—*Fell's Point* and *Old Town*. *The Point* is the most easterly portion of the city, has the advantage of greater depth of water than the upper harbor contains, is the resort of seamen and immigrants, and the place where the greater part of the ship-building and manufactures of the city are carried on. *Old Town* lies north and west of this, and is principally inhabited by mechanics and laborers.

The portion west of *the falls* is, in like manner, divided into two parts—the *City Proper* and *Spring Garden* section. The former is the centre of trade, and contains most of the residences of the more wealthy of the citizens, while the latter, which is the extreme southwestern quarter, is the residence of many mechanics and laborers. It is the lowest and most unhealthy portion of the city, being subject, to a considerable extent, at certain seasons of the year, to bilious and intermittent diseases. While the uneven and broken nature of the ground, with the exception of this quarter, has severely taxed both public and private resources and enterprise, it has been made to obviate, to a great degree, the necessity of extended sewers, (the whole amount of which is less than two miles,) and greatly conduces to the healthfulness of the city. Indeed, in this important respect, Baltimore will not suffer by comparison with the most highly favored cities of our land.

The first settlers on the shores of the Chesapeake Bay seem to have moved, for a long time, almost at random in the selection of the sites of their future towns, and to have been blindly experimenting with the laws of nature, or attempting capriciously to produce a factitious determination of wealth and population to points never designed for such a fortune by their Maker. Hence, some places for which they mapped out future greatness, and which they tried to nurse up to it, are now almost as much a wilderness as when they were first discovered; while other spots, in which they saw no comeliness, are now thriving marts.

In this way the most unrivaled advantages of the location of Baltimore were long quite overlooked, and when, as late as the year 1729, they attracted attention, and the town was laid out, only a part of it was under cultivation, and that as a farm, while the rest was a wilderness.

The part thus first laid out, (60 acres in extent,) was the central southern portion, about the head, of what is now familiarly called "*the basin.*" Three years subsequent, in 1732, ten acres east of "*Jones' Falls,*" a part of the present "*Old Town,*" were laid out under the name of Jonestown, and the two became united as the town of Baltimore in 1735. For some years its growth was by no means rapid. It was surrounded by older and jealous rivals, and was obliged to contend with all the obstacles which they could throw in its way. An authentic sketch of it, made in 1752, by Mr. John Moale, is in the rooms of the American Historical Society, from which it appears that it then contained about twenty-five houses, four of which were built of brick, while the rest were quite primitive in their structure. Sixteen years later, in 1768, it became the shire town of the county, and arrangements were made for the erection of a court-house and jail, which had been previously located at Joppa, a place now known only in history, Its first newspaper, "*The Maryland Journal and Baltimore Advertiser,*" weekly, was issued on the 20th of August, 1773, and a second, "*Dunlap's Maryland Gazette,*" in 1775. It was not deemed a port of entry till 1780, when first a custom-house was opened, and a naval officer appointed. Until that time all vessels trading to and from the port, entered, cleared, and obtained their registers at Annapolis. None of the streets were paved till 1782, when a commencement was made on Baltimore street, from that day to this the main street of the city. In the same year the first regular communication with Philadelphia—a line of stage-coaches—was opened: watchmen began to be employed in 1784, and, not to enlarge by tedious detail, it began to assume metropolitan airs, and obtained an act of incorporation on the 31st day of December, 1796. The city government was organized in the following year, and from the beginning of 1798, Baltimore may be classed among American cities.

In 1775 a census was taken, at the expense of a few private individuals, and the town found to contain 564 houses, and 5,934 persons. Some idea of its steadily rapid growth since, may be obtained from the following:

Years	Slaves	Free colored	White	Total
1790	1,255	323	11,925	13,503
1800	2,843	2,771	20,900	26,514
1810	4,672	5,671	36,212	46,555
1820	4,357	10,326	48,055	62,738
1830	4,120	14,790	51,710	70,620
1840	3,212	17,980	81,321	102,513

The census of the present year, when it shall be taken, will probably show a population of not less than 135,000, and, it is generally supposed, will considerably exceed that number.

Its increase in wealth has kept pace with the increase of its population. In 1808 the value of taxable property in the city was computed at $2,522,780. The following is the official estimate of the value of the property and number of houses erected in the city for the last six years:

	Real and Personal Property	No. of Houses erected
1844	$53,790,170	609
1845	53,750,496	1,508
1846	54,851,217	—
1847	72,079,322	2,006
1848	74,228,276	1,920
1849	78,252,588	1,894
1850	80,237,960	—

There is, however, every reason to believe that the actual value of the property far exceeds this taxable estimate.

In all the branches of business, in business facilities, and in the public works by which cities are embellished, Baltimore has kept pace with the increase of its wealth and population. It is familiarly known as "*The Monumental City*,"—a name derived from certain monuments which the public spirit of its inhabitants has erected to commemorate worthy men and heroic deeds in their own or their country's history. The largest of these is the one erected to the memory of Washington. This stands upon the highest of the original hills of the city, at the intersection of Charles and Monument streets. The summit of this hill is one hundred and fifty feet above the water in the harbor, and from this the monument, of white marble, rises one hundred and eighty feet. It consists of a base fifty feet square, and twenty feet in height, surmounted by a Doric column, twenty feet in diameter, within which is a winding staircase leading to the top, which is crowned with a colossal statue of Washington, thirteen feet in height. The top commands an excellent view of the city, harbor, river, bay, and surrounding country, for the enjoyment of which it is much visited by strangers. This monument cost upwards of $100,000, which was raised by means of a lottery.

The monument next in importance is "*Battle Monument*," upon Calvert-street, between Fayette and Lexington, erected in 1815, to the memory of those who fell at North Point the previous year, in defence of the city. This monument, also of white marble, is fifty-two feet high, and was erected by the general and voluntary subscriptions of the inhabitants. The base is Egyptian —the column, a bundle of Roman fasces, upon the bands of which are inscribed the names of those it commemorates, and the whole is surmounted by a female figure, emblematic of the Genius of the City, holding aloft a civic crown, the award of those who averted her capture at the expense of their lives.

The city now contains upwards of a hundred churches, three universities, four colleges, and many beautiful and commodious public buildings. To notice these, however, further than they affect the commercial or mercantile character of the city, is no part of the design of this article. The Merchants' Exchange, at the corner of Gay and Lombard streets, is a spacious building, 225 feet long by 141 feet wide, and contains, besides the usual reading-room, and room for the meeting of the merchants, the custom-house, a bank, telegraph offices, a hotel, &c. The room in which the merchants' meetings are held is fifty-three feet square, has upon its east and west sides colonnades, the columns of which are of fine Italian marble, each a single block, and it is lighted by a dome 115 feet above the street.

Building lots in this city are held by a tenure somewhat peculiar. About the year 1747, a practice originated of disposing of lots by leases for long terms—usually ninety-nine years—at a certain specified annual rent, the leases generally containing a covenant for renewal, on the same terms as the original, from time to time forever, at the option of the lessee, or his assigns. This system of "ground rents" has found favor with all classes.

To the wealthy it offers the convenience of a ready and safe investment, with an unalterable and certain return of due interest: while the young tradesman, the successful prosecution of whose business demands the employment of his whole capital therein, and the poor mechanic, who may be unable to purchase a lot for the erection of a shop or residence, it furnishes with a building site without present expense; in other words, it, in effect, gives them a permanent loan to the amount of the value of the building lot, without endorser or mortgage. The buildings, with the lots, are thus held as personal, instead of real estate, and, in consequence, transfers are made with much greater facility.

So convenient has this been found a practice, that, in many instances, nominal "ground rents"—as of one per cent. per lot—are created with an eye to this special convenience. About nine-tenths of the occupied ground of the city is believed to be leasehold property of this nature.

The banking operations of the city are conducted by twelve banks, with a capital of $7,225,794, and a circulation of $2,074,587. The following table will show their condition at the beginning of the current year:

Banks	Capital	Circulation, Jan. 1, 1850.	Deposits, Jan. 1, 1850
Bank of Baltimore	$1,200,000	$230,631	$549,215
Union Bank of Maryland	916,350	160,710	310,170
Mechanics' Bank	591,276	265,706	545,766
Commercial and Farmers' Bank	512,560	196,130	410,936
Farmers' and Merchants' Bank	393,560	110,143	129,138
Marine Bank	310,000	112,170	229,495
Franklin Bank	301,850	84,159	110,568
Merchants' Bank	1,500,000	171,320	369,478
Western Bank	308,280	290,025	363,501
Farmers' and Planters' Bank	600,625	337,653	315,184
Chesapeake Bank	341,293	114,940	331,364
Citizens' Bank	250,000	—	—
Total	$7,225,794	$2,074,587	$3,664,845

The Citizens' Bank, whose operations have been for the last few years suspended, was re-organized, and resumed the regular prosecution of its business on the 15th of April, of the present year. It is for this reason that it is not carried out in the columns of circulation and deposits.

There are ten well-conducted fire and marine insurance companies, and one health insurance company in active operation, while more than this number, incorporated in other states, or in England, have their agencies established, and do a large amount of business. The policy of the state, however, has been to discourage these, and throw the whole business into the hands of the societies of its own creation; and all agents of societies incorporated abroad are compelled to comply with the provisions of the Act of Assembly, passed at the December session, 1846, ch. 357, which provides that "any individual, or association of individuals, or corporations not incorporated and authorized by the laws of this state to make insurances on *marine or fire risks*, or *insurance on lives*, or *other insurances*," &c., shall first pay to the State Treasurer one hundred dollars for a license so to do; and also deposit with him good and sufficient bond in the penalty of five thousand dollars, conditioned for the furnishing to the Treasurer half yearly, on the first Monday in January and July respectively, a true list and account, verified by his oath, of all premiums by him received, and therewith faithfully to pay to the treasurer "the sum of three dollars per centum" of all such premiums.

Difficult as would be the task of enumerating in full the pursuits of the citizens, it would be hardly less difficult to name a branch of business which is not prosecuted to a greater or less degree within the limits of the city, or in its immediate vicinity. Iron and copper-works, woolen and cotton manufactures, flouring, chemicals, white-lead-glass, shot, printers' types, pottery, sugar-refining, distilling, saddlery, agricultural implements, powder, ship-building, ropes, oil, cloth, carpeting, house furniture, hats, leather, are but a part of her manufactures and of the arts which give employment to her people, and bring wealth to her coffers.

The total value of goods shipped from Baltimore during the year ending June 30th. 1849, was $,8,000,600; of which $7,786,695 were of articles of domestic produce, and $213,965 of foreign articles. The exports were in 634 vessels, with a tonnage of 140,028 tons, and employing 6,335 men in their navigation. Of the above, 491 vessels were American, and 145 under the flags of eighteen different foreign nations.

The foreign imports into Baltimore during the same time were valued at $4,976,731; of which $4,613,219 were in American vessels, and $363,512 in foreign vessels. The foreign imports were received in 484 vessels, with a tonnage amounting to 110,068 tons, and manned by 4,581 men.

The total number of vessels owned and registered at Baltimore on the 30th of June, 1849, embraced an aggregate tonnage of 134,025,35 tons, of which 53,624,75 tons were engaged as licensed coasters, and 11,464,28 tons employed in steam navigation. During the same year their were built at Baltimore 63 vessels, viz.:—9 ships and barks, 8 brigs, 41 schooners and 5 steamers, with an aggregate tonnage of 12,199,66 tons.—*See Maryland.*

BALTIMORE—TRADE OF, 1851.

Value of Imports from foreign countries at this port for 1851.

In American vessels	$6,106,106
In foreign vessels	1,137,857
Total value of imports for the year 1851	$7,243,963

Value of Exports for 1851.

Domestic produce in American vessels	$4,460,620
Domestic produce in foreign vessels	1,775,041
Total domestic produce exported	$6,235,661
Foreign merchandise in American vessels	$224,579
Foreign merchandise in foreign vessels	5,925
Total exports of foreign merchandise	230,504
Value of domestic produce exported, as given above	6,235,661
Total exports for 1851	$6,466,165

Value of foreign Imports and Exports at the district of Baltimore, commencing 1st January, 1840, *and ending 30th September*, 1851.

1840	$5,109,274	$5,868,018
1841	6,109,101	4,997,633
1842	4,052,960	4,448,940
1843	3,607,733	4,740,042
1844	4,251,882	1,000,000
1845	3,356,670	6,256,276
1846	4,238,760	6,710,559
1847	4,146,743	9,826,479
1848	5,245,894	7,209,602
1849	5,291,566	8,660,981
1850	6,417,113	8,530,970
1851	7,243,963	6,466,165

Foreign arrivals and clearances, and their tonnage, in 1851.

Arrivals	No.	Tonnage
American vessels	343	90,002
Foreign vessels	147	30,183
Total for 1851	490	120,185
Total for 1850	467	—

Clearances	No.	Tonnage
American vessels cleared for foreign ports	332	81,329
Foreign vessels cleared for foreign ports	152	33,355
Total clearances for 1851	484	114,684
Total clearances for 1850	511	130,587

BANKING.—History of Banking in the United States, from the Earliest Times to the War of 1812, etc.—The first settlers in America had not a sufficient quantity of gold and silver to serve as a circulating medium. Hence other materials, such as *tobacco* and *corn*, were in some of the states occasionally employed as money. In the year 1618, Gov. Argall, of Virginia, ordered "that all goods should be sold at an advance of 25 per cent. and *tobacco taken in payment at three shillings per pound*, and not more or less, on the penalty of three years' servitude to the Colony." In 1641, the General Court of Massachusetts "made orders about payment of debts, setting *corn* at the usual price, and making it payable for all debts which should arise after a time prefixed." In 1643 they also ordered that *Wampomheag*, (an article of traffic with the Indians,) should pass current in the payment of debts at a certain fixed price. In Virginia, young men (and old ones too) bought *wives* payable in tobacco. Maryland also passed an act as late as 1732, making tobacco a legal tender at one penny a pound, and corn at twenty pence per bushel.

Afterwards gold and silver became more plentiful. The *first mint* was established in Maryland in 1652, and coined shillings, sixpences and half-penny pieces. In 1645 Virginia prohibited dealings by *barter*, and established the Spanish piece of eight, at six shillings, as the established currency of that colony. In all the colonies the money of account was English, but the *coin* was chiefly Spanish and Portuguese. But the different colonies established different values to the dollar, which have continued to this day. The first paper money was issued by Massachusetts in 1690, and the first payable bank was established in South Carolina in 1762, and issued £48,000 to be lent at interest, and sunk at the rate of £4,000 per year. Pennsylvania first issued paper money in 1723, but Virginia does not appear to have issued any paper money prior to the Revolutionary War. At the commencement of the war, money was issued upon the authority of Congress. The money was called *Continental money*. The first issue was dated May 10, 1775, but the notes were not actually in circulation until the following August. It slowly increased, and in one year it amounted to $900,000. No sensible depreciation was experienced the first year or two, but the issues began to increase, and it finally became a natural consequence. In April, 1778, it amounted to $30,000,000, and the depreciation was as 6 to 1. About this time the alliance with France was made, and confidence being restored in a great measure, the depreciation was only as 4 to 1, notwithstanding the issues had *increased* to $45,000,000.

From April, 1778, to February, 1779, the issues had increased from $35,000,000 to $115,000,000; and the depreciation as 30 to 1.

The largest amount out was $200,000,000, and although the issues were discontinued, and a part was absorbed by loan officers and taxes, yet the depreciation increased, and was, at the close of the year 1780, as 80 to 1; and when Congress, in March following, acknowledged the depreciation, and offered to exchange the old for the new paper at the rate of 40 to 1, the old sank in one day to nothing, and the new shared the same fate.

On the 31st May, 1781, they ceased to circulate as money, but were afterwards bought on speculation, at various prices, varying from 400 to 1, up to 1000 to 1.

In the year 1781, Congress granted a charter to be called the "Bank of North America." It was accordingly established in Philadelphia, and commenced business on

January 7th, 1782. The charter was given upon the ground that it would offer assistance to the states in carrying on the war. It proved very profitable, and its earliest dividends ranged from 12 to 16 per cent. The state government repealed its charter in September, 1775, upon an allegation that the bank had produced evil effects. But the bank, however, continued its business, claiming the right so to do under the act of Congress. In 1787 the bank was re-incorporated, and thus continued—its operations being confined to Pennsylvania.

The Constitution of the United States was adopted in 1789, and the government was soon after organized. On the 14th December, 1790, Alexander Hamilton reported to Congress the plan of a bank. The bill passed in February, 1791, and was presented to Gen. Washington for his approval, who, after considerable consultation with his cabinet, approved it 25th February, 1791. The idea of this institution was conceived by Alexander Hamilton, the founder of our system of finance. Its continuance was limited by the charter to the 4th March, 1811, at which time it expired, as Congress refused to renew the charter.

Its capital was limited to 10,000,000, in 25,000 shares of $400 each, payable one-fourth in gold and silver, and three-fourths in public securities, bearing an interest of three and six per cent. The corporation was restricted from holding property exceeding $15,000,000 in value.

The subscriptions were filled as soon as opened. The government taking 5,000 shares, equal to $2,000,000; and the bank went into immediate operation. The stock, a large part of which was held abroad, soon rose considerably above par; and during the twenty years' continuance of its charter, the average annual dividend amounted to 8½ per cent.

In June, 1812, war was declared against England, and by August and September, 1814, all the banks South, and not of New-England, had suspended specie payment. The cause of this suspension it is difficult at this lapse of time to fully understand. But the following are probably some of the most important. After the dissolution of the Bank of the United States, in 1811, our country was deprived of more than seven millions of foreign capital, which had been invested in that stock, and which was remitted abroad during the year preceding the war. The great number of banks which were established throughout the interior part of the states, amounting to one hundred and twenty, did not create new capital, but withdrew what might have been lent to government.

The fact, also, that the loans made to government during the war were from the Middle States principally, is important in this connection; for the proceeds of loans (exclusive of treasury notes and temporary loans) paid into the treasury, from the commencement of the war to the end of the year 1814, amounted to $41,000,000; of that sum:

Eastern States lent	$2,900,000
New-York, Pennsylvania, Maryland, and District of Columbia	35,790,000
The Southern and Western States	2,320,000
Total	$41,010,000

The floating debt (not including the above) amounted on January 1st, 1851, to eleven million two hundred and fifty thousand dollars, about four-fifths of what were also due to the Middle States. Almost the whole of the large amount loaned to government by these states was advanced by the cities of New-York, Philadelphia and Baltimore. Another cause which tended to the suspension, was the fact that *large amounts* of British government bills were sent to this country from Canada, and sold at a discount of 20 to 34 per cent. The *average* depreciation on bank bills was about 17 per cent., the banks being perfectly independent of each other, and refusing to take each other's bills. *Coin* was out of the question. Confusion became the order of the day.

Taxes could not be collected by the government without great difficulty. The disorder became so general that it led to the formation of the *Bank of the United States.* This bank went into operation January 1, 1817.

BANKS IN THE UNITED STATES.

COMPARATIVE VIEW OF THE CONDITION OF THE BANKS IN THE UNITED STATES.—JANUARY,

	1848.	1849.	1850.
Number of banks and branches	751	782	829
Capital paid in	$204,833,175	$207,309,361	$217,317,211
Resources.			
Loans and discounts	$344,467,582	$332,333,195	$364,204,078
Stocks	26,498,054	23,571,575	20,006,759
Real estate	20,530,955	17,491,809	20,582,166
Other investments	8,229,682	7,965,463	11,949,548
Due by other banks	38,904,525	33,258,407	41,631,855
Notes of other banks	16,426,716	12,708,016	17,303,239
Specie funds	10,409,822	8,680,483	11,003,245
Specie	46,369,765	43,619,368	45,379,345

COMPARATIVE VIEW OF BANKS—*continued.*

Liabilities.

	1848.	1849.	1850.
Circulation	$128,506,091	$114,742,415	$131,306,526
Deposits	103,226,177	91,178,623	100,536,595
Due to other banks	39,414,371	30,005,366	36,717,451
Other liabilities	5,501,401	6,706,357	8,835,359
Total of current credits, i. e., circulation and deposits	231,732,268	205,922,038	210,953,121
Total of immediate liabilities, i. e., circulations, deposits, and sums due to other banks	217,146,639	236,017,404	277,670,572
Total of immediate means, i. e., specie, specie funds, notes of other banks, and sums due to other banks	112,191,828	98,236,274	114,917,778
Excess of immediate liabilities above immediate means	158,954,811	137,781,130	162,752,974

Specie in the Banks, Circulation and Deposits.

	Specie	Circulation	Deposits	Total of Current Credits
1834	—	$94,839,570	$75,666,986	$170,503,556
1835	$43,937,625	100,602,405	83,034,365	131,773,860
1836	40,019,594	140,301,038	115,104,420	276,495,478
1837	37,915,340	149,135,190	127,397,185	276,533,075
1838	35,184,112	116,138,910	84,691,184	200,830,694
1839	45,132,673	135,170,995	90,240,146	225,411,141
1840	33,165,155	106,986,572	75,696,857	182,665,439
1841	34,818,913	107,290,214	64,890,101	172,180,315
1842	28,440,423	83,734,011	62,408,870	146,142,881
1843	33,515,806	58,563,603	56,163,623	114,732,231
1844	49,898,269	75,167,646	84,550,785	159,718,431
1845	44,241,242	89,608,711	83,020,646	177,629,357
1846	42,012,095	105,552,427	97,918,070	202,465,497
1847	35,132,516	105,519,766	91,792,533	197,312,299
1848	46,369,765	128,596,091	108,226,177	281,732,263
1849	43,619,363	114,743,415	91,178,623	205,922,033
1850	45,379,345	131,366,526	109,586,595	240,953,121

In May, 1837, the banks suspended specie payments. In May, 1838, the New-York banks resumed specie payments, and the other banks attempted to follow their example, so that by January, 1839, there was what was called a general resumption of specie payments, though in many parts of the Union this was merely nominal.

In October, 1839, the banks of Philadelphia again suspended specie payments, and were imitated by the banks of the South and West.

Specie payments were not fairly resumed by the banks of Philadelphia till March, 1842. The banks of the South and West imitated their example; but in September, 1842, there was a tremendous bank convulsion at New-Orleans, the effects of which were felt throughout the country. The consequence was, that by the 1st of June, 1843, the current credits of the banks were reduced to a very small amount. They continued small till May, 1843, when an expansion began, which was at first very gradual.

The great increase in the amount of specie and bank credits in 1848 over 1847, was in consequence of the demand for our breadstuffs in Europe.

In January last, the circulation of the banks was greater than it had been in any previous years, excepting 1834, 1837 and 1839; and the year 1839 may be left out of the comparison, as, in the returns for that year, are included many banks which did not pay specie.

In January, 1850, the banks were more expanded than they were in January, 1848.

The small amount in which the specie in the vaults of the banks varies, when compared with the amount of their circulation and deposits, is not unworthy of observation.

The greatest amount of specie in the banks was in 1844, when it was $49 898,269. The smallest was in 1842, when it was $28 440,423. Difference, $21,457,846.

The circulation was lowest in 1843, when it was $58,563,603; and highest in 1837, when it was $149,185,190. Difference, $90,621,582.

The deposits were lowest in 1843, when they were $56,163,623; and highest in 1837, when they were $127,397,185. Difference, $71,228,562.

The current credits were greatest in 1837, when they were $276,583,075; smallest in 1843, when they were $114,732,231. Difference, $161,850,844.

BANK CAPITAL OF THE SEVERAL STATES.

TABLE SHOWING THE POPULATION IN THE YEAR 1850, THE NUMBER OF BANKS, BANK CAPITAL, BANK CIRCULATION, AND COIN OF EACH OF THE STATES, DECEMBER, 1851.

In those states marked with an asterisk (*) the amounts are, in part, estimated, but it is believed that they approximate the respective amounts at this date.

In Illinois a free banking system has been submitted to the people, and, at a popular election this year, approved by them. In this state there will probably soon be established several banks of circulation, based upon state stocks.

In Florida a law was passed last winter authorizing the establishment of a bank at Tallahassee; but we do not learn that it has been yet organized. In the states of Illinois and Arkansas, the circulation of the Kentucky, Missouri and Indiana banks, is generally used.—*Bankers' Magazine.*

State	Population, 1850	No. of Banks	Bank Capital	Bank Circulation	Bank Coin
Maine	583,000	38	$4,098,000	$3,200,000	$630,000
New-Hampshire	318,000	25	2,586,000	2,120,000	140,000
Vermont	314,000	31	2,685,000	3,377,000	180,000
Massachusetts	994,090	137	43,350,000	17,000,000	3.000,000
Rhode Island	148,000	69	12,338,502	3,000,000	350,000
Connecticut	371,000	47	13,175,675	6,640,000	800,000
New-York	3,090,000	218	58,497,345	27,200,000	7,000,000
New-Jersey	490,000	25	4,019,900	3,500,000	750,000
Pennsylvania	2,311,000	54	18,966,351	12,000,000	6,200,000
*Delaware	91,000	9	1,440,000	1,000,000	250,000
*Maryland	583,000	26	9,287,395	3,700,000	3,000,000
District of Columbia	52,000	4	1,182,300	350,000	300,000
Virginia	1,421,000	39	10,214,600	11,600,000	3,650,000
North Carolina	869,000	22	4,305,000	4,600,000	2,000,000
*South Carolina	669,000	14	11,431,183	7,500,000	2,600,000
*Georgia	906,000	18	5,629,215	4,300,000	1,700,000
*Alabama	772,000	2	2,000,000	3,500,000	1,800,000
Indiana	989,000	14	2,082,151	3,680,000	1,300,000
*Iowa	192,000	1	200,000	100,000	50,000
Kentucky	982,000	26	10,180,000	7,450,000	3,300,000
Louisiana	500,000	5	12,267,120	3,500,000	4,300,000
Michigan	398,000	4	762,000	650,000	150,000
Missouri	682,000	6	1,208,751	2,400,000	1,500,000
Ohio	1,977,000	61	7,866,376	11,635,000	2,800,000
Tennessee	1,003,000	23	8,405,197	5,300,000	1,900,000
*Texas	187,000	1	300,000	400,000	200,000
*Wisconsin	304,000	1	225,000	250,000	100,000
Illinois	858,000	—	none.	none.	—
Florida	87,000	—	none.	none.	—
Arkansas	210,000	—	none.	none.	—
*Mississippi	593,000	1	100,000	100,000	50,000
California	200,000	—	—	—	—
Total	23,144,000	921	$248,803,961	$150,152,000	$50,000,000

BRITISH COLONIAL EMPIRE: WHAT IT EMBRACES.—The following graphic sketch of the British Colonial Empire, on which, it has been well said, the sun never sets, we extract from the first number of that able London publication, the Colonial Magazine, which we commend to the reader.

We will start with *British India.* With that Hindostan will we begin, which, out of a population of one hundred and forty millions of human beings, has ninety millions subjects of Great Britain, forty millions of the subjects of allies, protected however by the British Government, and greatly dependent upon British support, and with but ten millions of subjects of independent states.

Where the Jumna and the Ganges, two rivers destined to give grandeur and fertility to the plains of Hindostan, burst from beneath the eternal snows which no mortal foot hath yet trodden, still in the most elevated recesses of the mountains, Britain has her empire, and the soil is her own. In that India which was one of the earliest seats of civilization, laws, the arts, and of all the improvements of social life, there are we now omnipotent. In that India which is an epitome of the whole earth, extending from the 8th to the 34th degree of north latitude, and from the 68th to the 92nd degree of east longitude, which from north to south is no less in length than 1800, and from east to west 1500 miles, there are we! It has regions that bask beneath the brightest rays of a tropical sun; and others, than which the most awful depths of the polar world are not more dreary. In its vast plains, which present rich double harvests, luxuriant foliage, and even the burning deserts of the torrid zone; in its low heights, enriched by the fruits and grains of temperate and mellow climates; on its upper steeps, clothed with the vast pine forests of the north; and even on the highest pinnacles of its loftiest regions, buried beneath the perpetual snows of the arctic zone;—even there are we! On the great plain of India, between the Brahmapoutra and the Indus, reaching across from the great chain of mountains to the high table land of the southern peninsula, 1500 miles long, and from 300 to 400 broad, there does British influence exist, and there also is the British name respected and revered. Along that plain where the Ganges pours a continually-widening stream, and where the power of vegetation is so great as to render it an entire field of waving grain,—there are we! Where in the east, on the hilly shores of Malabar, the aromatic gales perfume the air of the Oriental Isles—there our name, our power, our good faith, are known, acknowledged and felt. Where the rice, the opium, the indigo, the cotton, grow in the greatest profusion;—there are we! Where nature ever riots in unbounded luxuriance, and covers whole tracts of country with dense, dark, impenetrable masses of foliage and vegetation, crowded and twined together, with trees spreading on all sides their gigantic arms, with thorny and prickly shrubs of every size and shape, and with canes shooting in a few months to the height of sixty feet: there are we! And where in the open plain the banana and other single trees, when full scope is given to their growth, spread out into the dimensions of a considerable forest;—there are we! Amid the wilds of India, where tall and majestic forests of pine, larch, spruce and silver fir, cypress and cedar grow, flourish and decay, still there we are, the owners of the soil, and either the governors of the people, or their protectors and friends.

Where the fruits of the earth luxuriate in abundance and perfection; where the wild rose, the lily of the valley, and the cowslip burst through the green carpet; where the chamois bounds from rock to rock, and the forests are filled with deer and with musks: where the peacock displays his glittering plumage on the lower hills; where the sovereign eagle is descried amid the cliffs; where the bold hawk and the roving kite prey upon their dependents and their victims;—there are we!

In the valleys of the Sutledge and the Jumna; amidst perpetual snows, where, beyond a succession of lofty eminences, a central mass of an enormous chain of mountains exists; by the side of the cataracts which dash down dark ravines unsung by poets, and as yet unpainted by the pencil of man; in those bright and beauteous groves, or in the woods and forests where the gibbon, the wanderoo, the ichneumon, the pangola, the rhinoceros, the nyl-ghau, and the gayall are to be found; and where the finch falcon of Bengal, the hawk-owl of Ceylon, the bulbul, the honey-sucker, the coromandel, and the gigantic stork, walk or fly abroad at liberty and in happiness;—there also are we!

Napoleon once said that "England was a nation of shop-keepers!" We meet the foul libel by pointing to our Indian colonies! A nation of shop-keepers, indeed! What! was that a nation of shop-keepers—a few of whose merchants, with a handful of troops struggling against European rivalry, subdued all the states which had sprung from the ruins of the Mogul empire, and became the arbiters of the destiny of one hundred and forty millions of human beings placed at the opposite extremity of the globe? Was that the effort of men who count coppers on counters, and speculate on short weight and inferior goods for their profits and their fortunes? No! No! the conquest, the retention, the aggrandizement, the improvement, the continued rule and yearly advancement of such a dependency as this, is too mighty a monument of British courage, zeal, perseverance, science and wisdom, ever to be forgotten in the history of the world!

Next in importance to the East Indian possessions of Great Britain, are those of the West Indies. There is *Jamaica*, that "island of springs," with its four millions of acres—with its blue mountains towering to nearly 8,000 feet above the level of the sea—with its dense woods offering a marked contrast to the lower ranges—with its coffee, pimento, cotton, and capsicums—with its numerous ravines and savannahs—with its springs, its harbors, its ports, its beautiful bays, its rich mines, its fine sugar-canes, its coffee plants in the mountains, its dye-stuffs and spices, its arrow-root and cassia. There the bread-fruit tree, the plantain, the banana, the shaddock, the tamarind, the guava, and the star-apple, all arrive at perfection.

There is *Trinidad*, too, presenting one of the most magnificent, variegated, and richly luxuriant panoramas that nature ever formed. The waves of the mighty Orinoco dispute to the east for the empire of the ocean with contending billows, whilst the lofty mountains of Cumana rise from the bosom of the horizon in stupendous majesty. The fecundity of the soil, its gigantic and magnificent vegetation, its beautiful rivers, enchanting slopes, forests of palms, groves of citron and forbidden fruit, and hedges of spices and perfumes—its fine azure skies, deep blue seas, fertile glades and elastic atmosphere, have obtained for Trinidad the title of "the Indian paradise."

There is *Tobago*, once the abode of the Caribs, and named after the first tobacco pipe of the island. It offers a strange contrast to "the Indian paradise," for it is termed the "Isle of Melancholy." At some former period it formed a bold promontory of main land, from which doubtless it was violently dissevered. Though less picturesque than some islands, the fig-tree and the grape yield their fruit twice a year, and the cinnamon and pimento grow wild in different parts of this curious isle.

There is *Grenada*, the most southerly of the Antilles, once a favorite possession of the French; with its mountainous and picturesque scenery, its successive piles of conical hills, its vast forest trees and brushwood, its splendid mount St. Catherine, towering to a height of 3,000 feet, its basaltic rocks, its wondrous cliffs, and its fine cocoa, sugar, and coffee plantations. There is the pretty group of Grenadines or Grenadilloes.

There is *St. Vincent*, the most beautiful of the Caribbee isles, with its bold, sharp, and abrupt mountains, its deep intervening romantic glens, and its lofty and rocky coasts. The delicious valley of Buccament is the admiration of all travellers. The famed botanic garden is the theme of general praise; and the island stands high in reputation as a healthy station.

There is *Barbadoes*, the land of luxuriant fig-trees, and the territory of once as brave a people as ever breathed, with its beautiful bay of Carlisle, and noble square with the statue of Nelson; and there are also the remnants of those primitive forests which formerly covered the whole island.

There is *St. Lucia*, with its sugar-loaf rocks, its fantastic-shaped mountains, its lovely little coves and bays, fringed with luxuriant cane fields; its flotilla of fishing and drogher boats, and its stately trees clothing its noble mountains.

There is *Dominica*, with its lofty rugged acclivities, its fertile valleys, watered by thirty fine rivers—its umbrageous canopy of lofty and magnificent forests, and its romantic and picturesque cascades. The mountains are sulphurous and volcanic; its lofty table rock, Morne Bruce, is one of the finest in the West Indies; its rich parterres of green coffee perfume the whole atmosphere, and its grand savannah is the delight of all who enjoy the murmuring cascades of bubbling brooks which break through the luxuriant vegetation, or roll along the hilly avenues surrounded by piles of rocks, black, bare, or green, with countless traceries of lovely creepers, gigantic ferns, and lofty palms.

There is the fertile island of *Antigua*, with its bays and harbors wholly unrivalled in the West Indies, with its bold and precipitous hills, its innumerable fruits, its aromatic spices, its productive gardens, and its groves of trees of beautiful and refreshing verdure.

There is the delightful little island of *Nevis*, the mother of the English Caribbee Isles. It is a four-mile mountain, yet as green as heart can conceive, perfectly cultivated, and with a forest of evergreens like a ruff round the neck of the high land.

There is *Montserrat*, the Montpelier of the west, with its elastic and healthy atmosphere—its majestic, picturesque, and lofty mountains, and its truly charming and bewitching scenery.

There is *St. Christopher*, (or St. Kitt's,) with its layers of volcanic ashes, its bracing air, its healthy inhabitants, its awful crag of Mount Misery, and its exquisitely beautiful vale of Basseterre.

There is *Tortola*, whose harbor has afforded shelter in time of war to 400 vessels waiting for convoy.

There is the eel-like *Anguilla*, with its little wall of cliffs rising from the beach and protecting a flat and uninteresting surface, but yet producing annually three million bushels of salt from its salt lake; and sugar, cotton, maize, and cattle in comparative abundance.

There are the *Bahamas*, a group of several hundred islets, evidently the work of the coral insect, which, with all its apparent insignificance, has created many beautiful and habitable spots for the dwelling and culture of man. In these numerous isles there are 400,000 acres granted to cultivators, and nearly two millions and a half vacant or unoccupied.

And there are *The Bermudas* or Somers' Isles, exceeding 300 in number, lying like a shepherd's crook, in the Atlantic Ocean, with their coral reefs and shoals, their small cedar groves, their green-clad hills; and that north rock, placed by Nature, or rather by the God of Nature, as a beacon which seems to say, "Hitherto mayst thou come," thou mistaken, billow-tost, deceived, and luckless vessel, "but no further." The Bermudas are the Gibraltar of our West Indian Colonies, and it was therefore that our American enemy, Washington, desired to annex them to the republic, and to make them a nest of hornets to annoy the English commerce.

Yes, there are we; amidst this variegated scenery, these mixed populations, these multiplied products of the West India Islands. There are we, who found the population uncultivated, indolent, ignorant, miserable slaves; and who have rendered them instructed, happy, enlightened, and free citizens. We have doubled the amount of productions by our superior cultivation; we have made their minds, by instruction, as productive as their soil; we have increased their staple products to such an extent, that their exports are now most important; and we have, in nine cases out of ten, so changed the indigenous characteristics of the people, as to have transformed them from dullness, stolidity, and soporific indolence, to comparative activity, brightness, and competition. To the charge that we rendered the Africans slaves, we reply at least with triumph and with truth, that we have purchased their freedom. Yes, noble land of the brave and the good, we can look to our West Indian Colonies with gratitude, dignity, Christian joy, and honest pride; and as the once-captive race point to their broken chains now scattered around, we can say, "Thank God, we bought their freedom."*

Turn we now to *South America*, and to our colonies in that quarter; and the first which presents itself is *British Guiana*. There, on the vast rivers of Essequibo, Demerara, and Berbice, we have possessions which cover an area of one hundred thousand square miles. There its fine savannahs are occasionally interrupted by hill and dale scenery; but the general appearance of the country is similar to the territory of Belgium. Sugar and cotton grow in abundance; and in some districts, though never manured, a single acre has propuced 6,000 lbs. of sugar in one

* Our friend of the Colonial Magazine may be allowed his innocent enthusiasm here, but we think as little as possible ought to be said in England about that "emancipation bubble," which has been such a farce before high heaven. Our readers will refer to Commercial Review, Vol. V., p. 475, in proof.—Ed.

year. In other districts, coffee is not only abundant, but of excellent quality. Although the climate has hitherto been considered one great objection to any vast amount of colonization in that portion of our possessions, yet exercise and temperance are, as elsewhere, the great safeguards to health.

The British settlement of *Honduras*, in Central America, extends along the coast for an extent of 270 miles. That coast is studded with green isles, and the town of Belize is by no means insignificant. The mahogany tree, and logwood, cochineal, indigo, and sarsaparilla, are the great staple produce of Honduras; oranges, shaddocks, melons, pine-apples, and cocoa-nuts, are also abundant. Deeply is it to be regretted that the country is not divided into parishes, and that emigration to that portion of our settlements is not encouraged. Its pine-wood alone would richly compensate all engaged in its cultivation.

The *Falkland Isles* are no less than ninety in number, and the two largest are each nearly one hundred miles in length and fifty in breadth. Though the weather is seldom settled, yet the climate is temperate, and vegetation rapid and productive. There is heard the gentle note of the grele, and the falcon and the heron are by no means rare. There, too, herds of wild cattle would maintain vast numbers of settlers, and the upland geese would delight, by their flavor, even a London or a Parisian gastronome.

Our possessions in *North America* merit a longer and more attentive consideration. First in order of importance comes what was formerly *Lower Canada*. The late settlement of the Maine frontier question has deprived us unquestionably of one of the finest sections of our North American territory, but it is still sufficiently extensive to support in comfort and happiness tens of thousands of our depressed and emaciated agricultural population. Two hundred thousand square miles of territory, with three chief districts—Quebec, Montreal, and Three Rivers—and two of an inferior extent—Gaspé and St. Francis—ought to be far better cultivated and much more thickly populated than they are at present. And are not the natural features of Lower Canada extremely picturesque? Are there not ranges of mountains, noble rivers, magnificent cascades, lakes, prairies, farms and forests, alternating in every direction with sudden and beautiful variety? Who that has seen the eastern parts of the river St. Lawrence, with the high and mountainous districts about it, can forget the noble forests which everywhere meet the eye, and which are lost only in the clouds! And who can forget the Alleghanies, rising abruptly to the lofty elevation of 4,000 feet above the level of the sea? Of cities and towns there are sufficient to assure the minds and remove the fears of settlers; for are there not Quebec and Montreal? And though the winter be somewhat longer than our own, its fine season begins in May and continues until November. When last the census was taken, in seventeen counties there were upwards of 4,100 townships, and a population of nearly 500,000 souls. What forests of timber there invite the industry and the activity of our broad-shouldered and strong-limbed foresters! How many a man whose family now scarcely exists upon the wholly inadequate wages of the mother-country, would there be abundantly compensated for his labor and his toil!

If from Lower, we turn to the position of *Upper Canada*, what a vast territory do we behold embraced in that extensive province! Who can ever think of the Ottawa River—of the Lakes Ontario, Erie and Huron, without strongly feeling what sources of riches are there, in primitive forests as yet untrodden by the foot of civilization? The lakes alone fill us with surprise. Lake Superior is 541 miles long, by 140 wide; and Huron, Erie and Ontario, are from 180 to 250 miles in length. The infant capital, Toronto: Kingston, hitherto the seat of government, with its fine position, but little inferior to Quebec and Halifax; the Rideau Canal, the Welland Canal, the Granville Canal,—all are works of interest to those who exclaim with delight, as we do, when their eyes pass over in succession the various nations of the earth, "Yes, there also we are." And when we think, too, that the people of Canada are among the most favored of the earth, having peace, liberty, security, and abundance—a fertile soil, a beautiful climate, and an almost total exemption from burthens of any kind, how can we do otherwise than desire that swarms of our manufacturing, mining, and wandering poor were there, enjoying at least the comforts, if not the luxuries of life?

Thank God that some districts are colonized by Highland and Lowland Scotchmen, whose prudent, thrifty, hard-working characteristics have fitted them for emigration. There are upwards of eighteen acres of rateable land to each human being, and not more than two acres cultivated. And when it is known that even there, where the advantages are so great, that the proportion of hands cultivating 57,000 acres is as twenty acres to each person, is it not just and right, that we should desire that multitudes of our own starving population should there be transplanted to labor with diligence, but to be well rewarded for their toil?

Nova Scotia is situate between the parallels of 43 and 46 north latitude, and the meridian of 61 and 67 west longitude. It is 280 miles long, embraces upwards of 15,000 square miles, and nearly ten millions of acres. The harbor of Halifax is the admiration of the world, and from its situation being directly open to the Atlantic, and its navigation scarcely ever interrupted by ice, is our chief naval station in North America, and affords safe anchorage for 1,000 ships. Yes, there also the majesty of Britannia rides triumphant on the wave!

Cape Breton and *The Sable Islands*, though forming a part of the government of Nova Scotia, are yet, as it were, a separate colony. They comprise an area of two millions of acres, exclusive of the surface covered by lakes and rivers. How beautiful is the situation of Sydney, the capital, and how enterprising and energetic are the miners! What depths of coal-fields, and what sources of riches are there still hidden! The veins appear to be wholly inexhaustible; and yet, besides all this, timber exists in great abundance, and the fisheries are sources of wealth.

New-Brunswick next invites our notice. It contains no less than nearly 28,000 square miles, and about eighteen millions of acres. Behold its bold undulations, its vale and lowlands, its noble forests, its pleasing settlements, its abundant water communications, its fine extended prairies; and yet, fourteen out of eighteen millions of acres still await the British husbandman to turn the soil of this province with British spades, and to rescue millions of the half-starving population at home from misery and death. The province is healthy, old age is frequent, and sober, industrious settlers cannot fail of being happy and contented.

Prince Edward's Island is no large possession, containing an area of 1,360,000 acres, or 2,134 square miles; but it is delightfully situated for commerce, agriculture and the fisheries. It is a pastoral country: picturesque, admirably adapted for cultivation, and so healthy that many persons live even to one hundred years of age, without ever knowing a day's illness! There, however, the fisheries have been neglected, and hundreds of the famishing fishermen on our eastern and northern coasts would find in the herring fishery of Prince Edward's Island, means for a profitable and satisfactory existence.

Newfoundland and the Labrador Coast are likewise under British dominion, and owe a loyal obedience to our Queen Victoria. Newfoundland is not less than 420 miles long, and at its greatest breadth 300 miles. Little is known of the interior of this vast island; but it would doubtless well repay the toil of those who should decide on exploring it. The longevity of the inhabitants is the best proof of the salubrity of the country. Old fishermen of 90 years of age will be frequently seen, actively occupied in the arduous duties of their calling. How astonishing is British industry and British enterprise! Look at Newfoundland for an example of this! There, in a land certainly "unknown to song," there are nearly a million cwts. of dried cod prepared and exported annually, and from 400,000 to 500,000 seal-skins likewise sent to foreign shores in the same period of time.

The Hudson's Bay Territories occupy no less an extent than four thousand miles. True, the human race is but scanty in this immense region; but the Hudson's Bay Company's settlements are commercially important, and furs are the chief object of their profitable trade.

These are our North American colonies. If the government of this country would direct its mighty energies to their gradual but steady colonization, what beneficial advantages would result, both to the colonies themselves and to our rapidly-increasing, and only partially-employed, home population!

If we turn to that *East* with which we commenced this view of our colonies, we shall find, in addition to India, which we have already noticed, the large *Island of Ceylon*—containing a superficial area of nearly 25,000 miles—but of great importance in all its resources of trade and commerce. There, lofty mountains run in continuous chains, with the most lovely valleys the sun ever shone on, between them. There, the hills are clothed to the very summits with gigantic forests, from which issue magnificent cascades and dashing cataracts. There, the lovely valleys, placid rivers, and rippling brooks are fringed with turfy banks, and all the beauteous verdure of the tropics. Ceylon has been aptly called "the Malta of the Indian Ocean." Its commercial capital, Colombo, is a mile and a quarter in circumference, and is well defended. Its maritime capital, Trincomalee, is, as Nelson described it, "the finest harbor in the world." Its climate is salubrious and delightful; its productions, animal, vegetable, and mineral, are profuse and perfect. Its population, both native and European, is healthful, contented, prosperous, and happy. The state of general education and religious instruction could not well be more satisfactory. The population is upwards of a million souls; and its products are numerous and beautiful, valuable and important. And there are we, respected, honored, and beloved!

Prince of Wales's Island, or Pulo-Pinang, when compared with the mighty Ceylon, of which we have just been speaking, is small indeed; but it is of considerable importance, whether viewed in connection with the Anglo-Eastern Empire, or separately, as containing commercial stations and political maritime positions. The island is picturesque, vegetation is splendidly luxuriant, and the mountain forests are magnificent. Small villages and Malay topes are scattered over the island amidst spice-groves in the valleys, or on beautiful and romantic sites upon the sea-coast. The harbor of Georgetown is capacious and well defended. The trade of Pinang is very considerable; the population is 60,000; and nature is most rich and luxuriant.

Malacca and *Singapore* are also entitled to a distinct notice; but we must hasten to our possessions in *Austral-Asia,* and commence with *New South Wales.*

This vast island of New-Holland, with a width of 3,000 miles, a breadth of 2,000 miles, a superficial area of more than three millions of square miles, and a coast line of 8,000 miles, is one of those of our possessions, the magnitude and importance of which it is impossible for us, at this distance, adequately to comprehend. The rapidity with which this colony has advanced, is one, amongst many proofs, of its admirable climate, situation, and capabilities. It was not until 1788, that the British ensign was hoisted on the shores of Sydney Cove, then thickly wooded and abounding in kangaroos; but the silence and solitude of the forest were soon broken in upon, by the resounding strokes of the woodman's axe, and a few settlers, imbued with that moral and physical courage which Britons possess in so eminent a degree, have erected its Sydney, its Parrametta, its Liverpool, its Windsor, its Richmond, its Newcastle, its Macquarrie, and its Maitland—and month by month its counties within, and its settlements without the boundaries, are becoming increasingly fertile and prosperous. The salubrity of New South Wales is proverbial; the staple products are such as cannot but secure wealth to all engaged in their cultivation and export; the fisheries are varied and valuable, and none of our colonies is so rapidly advancing in population, wealth, and civilization.

Western Australia, or *Swan River,* was founded by four English gentlemen—Messrs. Peel, Vincent, Schenley and Macqueen. Its origin must be dated from the 1st of June, 1829—a period of little more than fourteen years' distance, and through evil and through good report these gentlemen and their followers have proceeded with energy and industry, in their admirable and successful efforts. The seasons are steady and uniform; the rains return in their set time, and there is no drought in the land. The cattle thrive; vegetable matter is productive; the colonists are constantly increasing; the staple products are becoming valuable and numerous; and Swan River is at least a promising colony.

Another portion of New-Holland has been erected into a British colony, termed *South Australia.* Its site is well selected, its climate decidedly fine, its natural products numerous and of a good quality, and several thousands of Europeans are now occupied in establishing a colony which shall one day justify the honest pride of every Englishman.

The quality of the soil, the extent of navigable waters, and the salubrity of the climate, are all most cheering circumstances to those who take an interest in British colonization.

Van Dieman's Land covers an extent of 24,000 square miles, or fifteen millions of acres, and is itself nearly the size of Ireland. The country is mountainous but diversified; the coast is well supplied with bays and harbors. Hobart Town, the capital, is an extensive and well-built place, and its Mount Wellington and Derwent estuary, protect and embellish it. Its exports have, indeed, wonderfully increased in ten years from £14,000 to £420,000 per annum. This is another of those colonies which are satisfactory in their past history, but which present prospects yet far more brilliant—and there are we!

If we turn to *Africa,* we shall find that in that continent of the Sun, where it exercises the most power, and appears to be least congenial to the health and longevity of man, still British colonies, of a grand and imposing character, are to be found. There, too, are we! In *Southern Africa,* the colony of the *Cape of Good Hope* first presents itself to our notice, with a sea-coast of 1,200 miles, and an area of 200,000 square miles. Its chain of mountains are magnificent. The capital, Cape Town, has been built along the shores of Table Bay. Its pastures are of a character highly favorable. It is well wooded with large timber, and watered by upwards of one hundred rivers and streams. The soil is fertile, and it has produced three crops of Indian corn in one year. The Boers have of late, indeed, manifested some dissatisfaction with the Colonial Government; but that has been but a temporary evil, and the population is steadily proceeding in the work of a good and permanent system of colonization. The salubrity of the country admits of no question; and the commerce, staple products, and property, are all in an ascending movement.

The Mauritius, or *Isle of France,* contains 676 square miles, is one of the most picturesque and romantic islands in the Eastern hemisphere, and possesses many bays, arms of the sea, and promontories. Its soil is exceedingly productive; its climate very salubrious; its dependencies numerous and valuable; its population 40,000; and the excess of its revenue over its expenditure gradually improving.

St. Helena contains but 30,300 acres, and is alone celebrated as the grave of a man who could never understand the genius of liberty, and who uttered to the last the most unmerited calumnies against Great Britain.

The inhabitants are healthy, and about 5,000 in number. The climate is salubrious; its soil is watered by clear and wholesome springs; and, before the overland route from India to this country was established, St. Helena was a spot of some note. It is still useful as an English colony, and there can be no question of its abandonment, but it is a heavy annual charge to the mother country, and its revenue bears no proportion to its expenditure.

Ascension is contiguous to St. Helena. It is small, and is of volcanic production: but its turtle is its chief recommendation, except during war, when it is by no means an unimportant possession.

In *Western Africa* we possess that gloomy and unsatisfactory colony, *Sierra Leone*. Let it not, however, be forgotten, that the British colonies on the western coast of Africa are inferior to none in moral, political, and commercial interest. They are, in fact, an indispensable link in the maritime empire of Britain.

Gambia, *Cape Coast Castle*, (celebrated as the grave of the poetess, L. E. L.,) and *Accra*, are likewise to be included in the foregoing remarks; and although we deeply deplore the mortality which from time to time has swept away excellent governors, and admirable merchants and colonists, yet abundant reasons can be supplied why these colonies should never be resigned by Great Britain.

Before we turn to our European colonies, we must not forget our new colony of *New Zealand*, and our more recent settlement at *Hong Kong*. With regard to the former, our sway is but modern, and it is divided; recent events have, of course, excited anxiety and apprehension, and we have yet much to do before we can encourage settlers to proceed in great numbers to New Zealand. But climate, soil, natural productions, are all in favor of this young colony, and we shall watch with intense interest its rise and progress. Of *Hong Kong* we know but little; it is one of the results of our Chinese conquest. Will it be one of the most satisfactory? Is its climate healthy, and suited to our European settlers? This at least appears doubtful. The Chinese evidently regarded it with suspicion, and its cession to England was no proof in its favor. It is by no means impossible that at some future time Hong Kong may be abandoned, and that a new colony may be demanded of the Emperor of the Sun in exchange for that apparently unhealthy settlement.

The British colonies in *Europe* are few, but valuable.

Gibralter is the key to the Mediterranean, and is not the least remarkable possession of the British Crown.

8

Malta, and its adjacent island, *Goza*, are the two colonies most envied by Europe. It is not that the length or breadth of Malta is great—nor that its productions are important—or its population numerous,—but it is commanding in its position, acts as a constant sentinel over European powers, preserves the Mediterranean from becoming the seat of conspiracy and intrigue against British interests, and enables us to assert our power, and to maintain our influence, in the south of Europe.

The same observations will apply to the septinsular cluster of the *Ionian Isles*, extending from the Albanian coast to the southern extremity of the Morean peninsula. The seat of government is at Corfu; the length of the island is about thirty-five, its breadth about twelve miles, and its climate is nearly tropical. But, besides Corfu, there are Cephalonia; Zante, the glory of the Levant; Santa Maura, a mass of mountain; Ithaca, a shapeless combination of huge rocks; Paxo, with a port of good anchorage, and Cerigo, where Ptolemy was once the lord.

And last,—far, far removed from the spicy groves and aromatic odors, from the glowing scenery and the rich forests of the lands of the mountain and the flood, to which, in these observations on our colonies, we have directed the attention of our readers, is situate in the North Sea, our colony of *Heligoland*. There, at only a few miles distance from the mouths of the Elbe, the Eyder, the Weser, and the Jahde, has England placed a sentinel to watch over her commerce and protect her navy. There England has her noble light-house, serving as a beacon to the world; but there she keeps up a good school of pilots, and maintains her supremacy and her glory as still "Mistress of the Waves." Thus it is, and thus may it ever be, that wherever commerce is to be conducted, trade to be carried on, manufactures to be placed, mankind to be civilized, Christianity to be extended, education to be promoted, and the great family of man to be improved—there are we!

We ought, perhaps, to say something of Fernando Po, of Aden in the Red Sea, and of the Island of Socotra; but these are scarcely entitled to notice, and cannot with propriety be denominated colonies. Some, also, would include Guernsey, Jersey, and the smaller contiguous isles, as well as that of Man, where the laws and customs are peculiar. But all of these are rather dependencies of the British Empire, than colonies, in the usual acceptation of the term.

We have said enough. To recapitulate even the titles of our colonies, is a source of honest satisfaction and of national pride;

and to feel that when we carry to a new settlement the British flag, we at the same time plant the standard of science, the arts, letters, civilization, morals and religion, is a motive for exultation and for joy. But as our influence is great, so are our responsibilities to man, to society, to our colonies, and to Heaven. God forbid, then, that when we point to our northern and our southern, to our tropical and to our arctic possessions, and exclaim, "There are we!" it should be supposed we are indifferent to the conditions on which we *are* there. No! if we were there as absolute and tyrannical rulers—as masters indifferent to the happiness and prosperity of our dependents—as colonists sacrificing the welfare of the natives to our love of lucre—as nominal Christians indifferent to the moral and religious education of the people—as mere grinding taskmasters, hard exactors and strong-headed proprietors of the soil—then most heartily would we exclaim, God grant we may soon be there no longer! But it is precisely because in British ships we export British civilization and liberty—the liberty of time-honored institutions, and of a limited monarchy, that we exclaim right joyously and in all sincerity, as we point to our list of noble and glorious colonies—Yes—*there are we!*

COTTON—History and Statistics of.—Of the four great articles of human clothing—cotton, silk, wool, and flax—not one is indigenous to Europe, two only are indigenous to Africa and America, cotton and flax, while all the rest belong to Asia. Cotton is said to possess the advantage over all the materials which the skill of man converts into comfortable and elegant clothing. Its utility is independent of climate. Yielding to many other fabrics in beauty and texture, for health and comfort in the coldest or the hottest regions, the cotton fabric stands unrivaled. The fact is explicable on chemical principles. While linen, a good conductor of heat, condenses the vapor of perspiration into moisture upon the skin, becomes wet, chilled, and unable to absorb what it has condensed; cotton being a bad conductor of heat, on the other hand condenses but little moisture, and absorbs a large portion of what it does condense, leaving the rest to pass off in vapor, and the skin healthy and dry. From these considerations it is said that in cold climates, or in the nocturnal cold of tropical climates, cotton clothing is much better calculated to preserve the warmth of the body than linen. In hot climates also it is more conducive to health and comfort by admitting of freer perspiration. Mr. Leuwenhoeck subjected fibres of cotton and flax to a powerful microscope, and in this way discovered essential organic differences in them. The fibres of cotton are sharp and angular, rendering it unfit for dressing wounds, while those of flax are round and smooth. The corkscrew twist of the cotton fibre is said by Mr. Bauer to be always retained, undergoing no change in spinning, weaving, bleaching, printing, and dyeing, nor in all the subsequent domestic operations of washing, etc., till the stuff is worn to rags; and then even the violent process of reducing these rags to pulp for the purpose of making paper, effects no change in the structure of these fibres. In thickness they are said to vary from 1-800 to 1-3600 part of an inch.

Cotton wool is the down of a vegetable which appears in botanical works under the genus *gossypum*. There are several varieties of the genus. The wool adheres to the seed of the plant, and is incased until maturity in a pod of triangular shape, with three cells. This pod increases to the size of a filbert, becomes brown, bursts and discloses a triple lock of wool. According to Linnæus there are five species of the plant.

1. *Gossypum herbaceum*, or herbaceous.
2. *Gossypum arboreum*, or arborescent.
3. *Gossypum hirsutum*, or hairy.
4. *Gossypum religiosum*, or religious.
5. *Gossypum Barbadenses*, or Barbadoes.

Other writers have varied as to the number of species. The highest number is ten; the *Indicum*, *Micranthum*, *Vitifolium*, *Latifolium*, and *Peruvianum*, being added to the list. But the great and cardinal distinctions of the plant are found in three classes, which we shall hereafter consider.

1. The herbaceous cotton.
2. The shrub cotton.
3. The tree cotton.

We take up our subject now in the order in which it is laid before us:

1. *The earliest history and mention of the Cotton Plant.* The sacred records furnish us nothing satisfactory on the subject. The only word which occurs in them which would lead us to infer that the Jews knew anything of this staple is the word Carpas, translated *green* in the phrase "green and blue hangings."—Esther i. 6.—carpas being an Oriental word for cotton. Herodotus, 400 years before Christ, observed in relation to India, that the wild trees in that country bear fleeces as their fruit, surpassing those of sheep in beauty and excellence, and the Indians use cloth made from these trees. The Greeks knew little or nothing of cotton till the expeditions of Alexander the Great into India. Theophrastus, who lived a little after this time, learned that the trees from which the Indians made cloths have a leaf like that of the black mulberry, and that these trees were set out in rows like vines. His description of the plant is admirably

exact: "The capsule containing the wool is, when closed, about the size of a quince, when ripe it expands so as to admit the wool." Alexander's generals were men of observation, and we have, from two of them at least, clear and indisputable evidence of cotton. Aristobulus instanced the capsule containing seed, and the wool which might be combed out; and Nearchus went into particulars: "There are in India trees bearing as it were flocks or bunches of wool, out of which the natives make garments, wearing a shirt which reaches to the middle of the leg, a sheet folded about the shoulders, and a turban folded round the head."

Carpasus or carbasus were terms without doubt used by the Latin writers to describe the cotton product of the East. Thus Curtius, speaking of the Eastern dress, has the passages *carbasa velant*, "covered with carbasus," *purpurea carbasa*, "with purple carbasus;" and Lucan:

> "Fix
> With colored gems the flowing Carbasus."

As the Greeks and Romans, says our authority, became acquainted with cotton much earlier than with silk, we find that carpas, the proper Oriental name for cotton, was also in use among them at a comparatively early period.

The use of cotton among the Greeks and Romans must necessarily have been of the most limited extent, and only as an article of exquisite luxury. It is not clear that the early Greeks had any knowledge of the fabric at all. The word *carbasinu*, in a Greek play, does not warrant the inference which has been drawn "that 200 years before Christ the Greeks made use of cotton cloths of some kind which were brought from India." The testimony is better for the Romans, but then it goes back at farthest but seventy years before the Christian era.

The luxurious Verres in Sicily protected his tents from the sun's rays by coverings of the *carbasus*. This is the earliest mention of the Roman use of cotton. The following passage has been translated from Livy: "Lentulus Spinther (B. C. 63) is said to have first introdnced cotton awnings in the theatre at the Apollinarian Games. By and by Cæsar the Dictator covered with awnings the whole Roman forum, and the sacred way from his own house even to the ascent of the Capitoline hill, which is said to have appeared more wonderful than the gladiatorial exhibition itself." The word *carbasus* appears in the following translation from Lucretius:

> "As flaps the cotton spread above our heads
> In the vast theatres from mast to beam."

The story of the Vestal Virgin, from another writer of the same period, exhibits her as preserving the last sparks of sacred fire on the altar, by casting upon it her muslin head-dress, *carbasus alba*.

The Roman writers did not always use the word we translate cotton in the same sense, and it requires an understanding of the context and of collateral facts to fix the meaning of the word in any particular instance. Thus, where carbasus in numerous places is mentioned as the material for the sails of shipping, linen is to be understood. In one instance a writer, applying the term to an Indian fleet, undoubtedly meant cotton, for of this from the earliest times sailcloth was manufactured at the East. Virgil uses the word in both senses. Pliny, one of the earliest and greatest naturalists of antiquity, whose volumes are full of light in relation to the vegetable kingdom, appears after all to have had but confused knowledge of the cotton plant. He was the first to affix the botanical name of *gossypion*, and supposed it an Egyptian as well as an Indian product. Mr. Seabrook quotes the passage, which will save us the trouble of a reference: "In Upper Egypt, toward Arabia, there grows a shrub called gossypum, by others xylon, from which the stuffs are made that we call xylina. It is small and bears a fruit resembling the filbert, within which is a downy wool, which is spun into thread. There is nothing to be preferred to these stuffs for whiteness or softness, and beautiful garments are made of them for the priests of Egypt." Julius Pollux, a century later, remarks. "among the Indians, and now also among the Egyptians, a sort of wool is obtained from a tree;" Virgil had said long before—

> "Soft wool from downy groves the Æthiop weaves."

The question then is, was cotton, or the cotton manufacture, known to the Egyptians—that nation of extreme antiquity? and, if known, to what extent as an article of clothing?

There never was any doubt as to the fact of the Egyptians being acquainted at a very early period with the manufacture of various descriptions of cloths. In wool and flax, their works were carried to a high degree of perfection. A word in Herodotus descriptive of the material used for wrappers in preparing and embalming mummies, has given occasion to protracted discussions among the learned. It is not conceived clear what was exactly intended by *byssus*, the word in question. Learned authorities understand cotton, and equally learned, flax. The doubt has even been raised whether a product of the animal, vegetable, or mineral kingdoms, is intended. The contest on this point was waged for many years, and the most elaborate disquisitions given to the world. In the list of disputants are conspicuous the names of

Forster, Blumenbach, Porson, Young, Hamilton, Harris, Wehrs, Voss, Heeren, Gesenius, and Rosenmuller. The world has grown wiser in some respects by the dispute, but would not in all probability have found out, had it been continued to this day, whether the Egyptians of that earlier period of the mummies were acquainted with the uses of cotton. What the learning of philology and the tests of chemistry could not unravel, has been put at rest by that extraordinary achievement of modern science, the microscope.

Mr. Thompson, to whom the world is indebted for the solution of the *vexata questio*, in a paper read before the Royal Society of England, observes that his attention was first attracted to the subject by having presented to him several specimens of mummy cloth. He remarked to Mr. Belzoni that these fabrics scarcely deserved the appellation of "fine linen," which had from all antiquity been bestowed upon the linen of Egypt; to which it was replied by that traveler, that during his researches in Egypt, he had met with mummy cloths of every degree of fineness, from the coarsest sacking to the finest and most transparent muslin. The subject appearing to be sufficiently interesting, Mr. Thompson was induced to examine minutely a variety of specimens of the cloth. The experiments of Leuwenhoeck induced him to apply the microscope as a test of these fabrics; and for this purpose they were sent to Mr. Bauer, who had a powerful instrument at hand. Mr. Bauer's letter in reply was accompanied by a drawing which exhibited the fibres of both raw and unraveled cotton as flattened cylinders, twisted like a cork screw, while those of linen and mummy cloths were straight and cylindrical.

We give the concluding passages of Mr. Thompson's paper before the society, in his own language: "Repeated observations having established beyond all doubt the power of the microscope accurately to distinguish between the fibres of cotton and linen, I obtained through the kindness of various individuals connected with the British Museum, the Royal College of Surgeons, the Hunterian Museum of Glasgow, as well as other public institutions both at home and abroad, a great variety of cloths of human mummies and of animals and birds, which being subjected to the microscope of Mr. Bauer, proved, without exception, to be linen. Nor has he among the numerous specimens we have both collected during many years, been able to detect a single fibre of cotton; a fact since recently confirmed by others, and proving incontestably that the mummy cloth of Egypt was linen. Their form and character the fibres retain ever after, and in that respect undergo no change through the operation of spinning, weaving, bleaching, printing and dyeing, nor in all the subsequent operations of washing, till the stuff is worn to rags, and then even the violent process of reducing those rags to pulp for the purpose of making paper, effects no change in the structure of these fibres." "With Ploessel's microscope," says Mr. Bauer, "I can ascertain whether cotton rags have been mixed with linen in any manufactured paper whatever."

The origin of the word cotton is explained as follows, by Mr. Baines. The pod of the plant had been likened by Pliny to a quince, the Latin name of which is *cotoneum malum*. By a natural and common figure of language, the pod itself, and the fruit of the pod, came to be known by the same designation, and finally *cotoneum* simply, or cotton. The Latins, however, did not themselves apply the word *cotoneum* to this plant. The Arabians called it koton; the Italians of the middle ages, cotone; the Spaniards, algodon.

II. *The culture of cotton* commenced first in the East, and has been handed down for thousands of years. The Chinese have produced large quantities, but not sufficient for the consumption of the country. Importations are made from Surat and Bombay and various other parts of India, into China.

In 1823–4	115,000	maunds.
1824–5	199,000	"
1825–6	177,000	"
1826–7	314,000	"
1827–8	197,000	"
1828–9	125,000	"
1829–30	126,000	"

Being an average of 187,000 maunds of 80 pounds each, or 15,000,000 pounds annually. From Bombay the annual import was at the last period 40,000,000 pounds. The most remarkable fact is, that although cotton was cultivated in gardens from remote antiquity in China, yet this ingenious people never turned it into any account until the end of the thirteenth century, at which time its manufacture among them began.

The following passages from the narratives of those who have visited India, are replete with interesting information on the subject before us. Marco Polo found cotton in Guzerat, in large quantities, taken from a tree about six yards high, and bearing for twenty years. The cotton from a tree of this age is adapted only to quilting, but that taken from trees of twelve years is suitable for muslins and other manufactures of extraordinary fineness. Sir John Mandeville, in the fifteenth century, later by fifty years than Polo, says, that in many places the seed of the cotton in India which we call tree wool, is sown every year, and there springs up from it copses of low shrubs on which the wool grows.

A luxuriant field, says another, exhibiting at the same time the expanding blossom, the bursting capsule and the snowy flakes of ripe cotton, is one of the most beautiful objects in the agriculture of Hindostan. Malte Brun is equally instructive on the point: "The cotton tree grows on all the Indian mountains, but its produce is coarse in quality; the herbaceous cotton prospers chiefly in Bengal and on the Coromandel coast, and there the best cotton goods are manufactured. Next to these two provinces, Madure, Marawar, Pescaria and the coast of Malabar produce the finest cotton. The plant is cultivated in every part of India; the finest grows in the light, rocky soil of Guzerat, Bengal, Oude and Agra. The cultivation of this plant is very lucrative, an acre producing about nine quintals of cotton annually."*

In central Africa cotton has also been a staple growth time out of memory. It is mentioned by travelers as abundant on the banks of the Senegal, the Gambia and the Niger, at Timbuctoo, Sierre Leone, the Cape de Verde islands, on the coast of Guinea and in Abyssinia. In hot climates also, says an authority, the cotton plant grows so abundantly, that this is the cheapest material of which cloth can be made. With such recommendations it cannot fail to continue the staple and universal manufacture of Africa.

Cotton is also of indigenous American growth. On the first landing of the Spaniards in Mexico, they found it in considerable perfection. The Mexicans are said to have been solely dependent upon this product, the wool of rabbits and hares, feathers, and a fibrous plant called maguei, for their clothing materials. They had neither wool, hemp nor silk, and their flax was not used for these purposes. Out of cotton they fabricated webs of exceeding tenuity, and their cloths were woven into beautiful figures. Mantles, bed curtains and carpets they finished elegantly with mingled cotton and feathers. Cortez sent to Charles V. of Spain, "cotton mantles, some all white, others mixed with white and black, or red, green, yellow, and blue, waistcoats, handkerchiefs, counterpanes, tapestries, and carpets of cotton." A peculiar cotton paper was made in Mexico, small cloths of the same material constituted a part of their currency, and their warriors are said to have had cotton cuirasses. The modern Mexicans have lost the perfection of their ancient art of manufacture. The American plant was not confined to Mexico alone; Columbus found it wild in Hispaniola and on the continent of South America, where it had already grown into an article of use for clothing and other purposes. The Brazilians made their beds of it. Columbus, Magellan, Drake, Cavendish, Dampier, Van Noort, all agree that cotton was one of the articles of dress among the American savages, on the discovery of the country. At St. Salvador, the women are described as dressed in cotton coats. Even as far north, says Mr. Seabrook, as the Mes-chacebe, or Mississippi, the earliest explorers of that river and its tributary streams saw cotton growing wild in the pod, and in great plenty. These facts, and they might almost be indefinitely multiplied, are introduced to rebut the opinion founded on the negative testimony of Captain Cook, that the gossypum is not a native of the western hemisphere. That celebrated voyager found no cotton between New Zealand, 36° south, and the Sandwich Islands, 20° north. In addition to flax and the bark of the mulberry tree, in which Captain Cook says that the inhabitants of those regions were habited, the nations all over the continent nearly, used as articles of dress, besides cotton, feathers, the wool of rabbits, the maguei, and silk grass. In 1726, cotton was a staple product of Hispaniola. In 1753, Jamaica exported 2,000 bags. On an average of eight years from 1740 to 1748, the export of cotton from Barbadoes was 600 bags annually. In 1787, St. Domingo, St. Christopher, Grenada, Dominica, Antigua, Montserrat and Nevis, and the Virgin Islands, exported the same commodity. In 1803 there were grown five varieties of cotton in Jamaica, the common, the brown-bearded, the Nankin, the French and the Brazilian. From these facts Mr. Baines draws the conclusion that the manufacture of cotton must therefore be supposed to be coeval with the original settlement of America; but learned men are much divided as to the date of this event, some carrying it nearly as high as the deluge, and others contending for a much later period. The American manufacture may at all events claim a high degree of antiquity.

III. We are now to speak of the *introduction of cotton into Europe;* an event which has had such amazing results, and which has exerted, it is difficult to say how large an influence upon society and upon governments. The wealth and power of Great Britain, acknowledged and felt by all the world, have a nearer connection with the cotton plant and cotton manufacture than with any other branch of industry and enterprise whatever. McCulloch is thrown into ecstasies with the reflection, and is at a loss to find language to express himself. Such, says he, however, has been the influence of the stupendous discoveries and inventions of Hargraves, Arkwright, Crompton, Cartwright, and others, that we have overcome all of these difficulties—that neither the cheapness of labor in Hindostan, nor the excellence to which the natives had attained, has enabled them to withstand the competition of those who buy their cotton, and who, after carrying it five thousand miles to be manufactured, carry

* Pastoral Life and Manufactures of the Ancients, p. 331.

back the goods to them. This is the greatest triumph of mechanical genius, and what, perhaps, is the most extraordinary, our superiority is not the late result of a long series of successive discoveries and inventions; on the contrary it has been accomplished in a very few years Little more than half a century has elapsed since the British cotton manufacture was in its infancy, and it now forms the principal business carried on in the country, affording an advantageous field for the accumulation and employment of millions upon millions of capital, and of thousands upon thousands of workmen. The skill and genius by which these astonishing results have been achieved, have been one of the main sources of our power; they have contributed in no common degree to raise the British nation to the high and conspicuous place she now occupies. Nor is it too much to say that it was the wealth and energy derived from the cotton manufacture that bore us triumphantly through the late dreadful contest; and at the same time that it gives us strength to sustain burdens that would have crushed our fathers, and could not be supported by any other people. But we are intruding upon another division of our subject.

In European history no mention is made of cotton as an article of trade until the fourteenth century. Though silk, woolen, and flax had long been articles of wealth and commerce, cotton had no existence. In Spain, to be sure, small quantities of it were grown and manufactured as early as the tenth century, having been introduced there by the Moors, among other articles of Eastern luxury. The cultivation of the plant at this period would also appear to have been an object of attention in Sicily. In the fourteenth century, a Spanish writer thus glowingly describes his country: "Here you find also the cocus, with which the cotton stuffs are dyed, for there is a great abundance of cotton as well for commerce as for use in manufactures; and the cotton garments made here are said to be far superior to those of Assyria in softness, delicacy and beauty." The Italians had little intercourse with Spain, and did not learn from her the use of cotton. It was not introduced into Venice until the beginning of the fourteenth century. The Turks introduced the use of cotton about the same period in their conquered countries of Romania and Macedonia. The district of Seres in Macedonia, according to Malte Brun, is more fruitful in cotton than any other. The value of the article amounted in one year in Macedonia alone to 7,000,000 piastres.

England was the last to take up this important branch of industry. The precise period of its introduction has not been determined. The first authentic mention of the staple, we are told by McCulloch, is made by Lewis Roberts, in his Treasury of Traffic, published in 1641, where it is stated, "the town of Manchester, in Lancashire, must be also herein remembered, who buy the yarne of the Irish in great quantity, and weaving it, returne the same again into Ireland to sell. Neither doth their industry rest here, for they buy cotton wool in London that comes first from Cyprus and Smyrna, and at home worke the same and perfect it into fustians, vermillions, domestics, and other such stuffs, and then returne it to London, where the same is vended and sold." In the early part of the eighteenth century, cotton from the East and West Indies had become an article of import into Great Britain, to some extent. But of this hereafter.

There is great difficulty in determining the exact period when cotton began to be cultivated in the different cotton sections of the United States. According to Seabrook, the culture of this staple was endeavored to be forced upon the planters of Virginia one hundred and thirty years before the Revolution. Out of this contest of the mother country to prescribe the employment of the colony, and the resistance of the Virginia planters to the encroachments, arose the navigation acts, as they are called, which prohibited the receipt or export of any European commodities other than those carried to them by Englishmen or English-built ships. The act of Charles II. in a similar spirit was calculated to depress the value of tobacco, and the Virginians were driven to other crops, cotton among the rest.

In the historical collections of South Carolina, published by Mr. Carroll, there is an old paper drawn up in the year 1666, entitled "A Brief Description of the Province of Carolina, on the Coast of Florida." This was written and published in England previous to the settlement of Carolina. The object of the paper was to encourage emigrants to go over, and among other inducements it is said that the lands "grow indigo, tobacco very good, and cotton wool." In the same collections Dr. Hewett of the date —— describes the manner of cultivating the cotton plant, and speaks of it as yet not of sufficient importance to attract the attention of the colonists. Wilson, who wrote an account of Carolina in 1782, mentions cotton of the Cyprus and Malta sort, as grown in the state from imported seed. Peter Purry, a Swiss, and the founder of Purrysburgh in the same colony, memorialized the government of George I. in relation to a certain country, extending 33 degrees on either side of the equator, capable of the production of cotton. This individual, in a paper written at Charleston, 1731, observes, that "cotton and flax thrive admirably." The private journal of Miss Lucus, daughter of the Governor of Antigua, and afterward the noble mother of those noble sons, General Thomas and Charles Cotesworth Pinckney, of South Carolina, *par nobile fratrum*, contains this note for July 1, 1739: "Wrote to my father to-day on the pains I had taken to bring the indigo, ginger, cotton, &c., to perfection, and that I had greater hopes from the indigo than any other."

It is a well-authenticated fact, says Mr. Seabrook, that in 1736, as far north as the thirty-ninth degree, cotton on the garden scale was raised in the vicinity of Easton, in the county of Talbot, on the eastern shore of the Chesapeake Bay. About forty years afterward it was cultivated in St. Mary's county, Maryland, and in the northern county of Cape May in New Jersey, also in the county of Sussex, in Delaware. On the breaking out of the American war, General Delagall of South Carolina is said to have cultivated thirty acres of the green seed cotton near Savannah. The Congress of South Carolina, in 1775, recommended the inhabitants to raise cotton. Mr. Jefferson, remarking on Virginia, 1781, alludes to the domestic economy of making cotton goods in families for their own use. The seed from which the cotton of these sections was grown came both from Manilla and Cyprus, according to some authorities, and from Barbadoes, according to others. We may suppose both varieties to be the parent stock of American cotton.

In Louisiana, the subject of cotton would appear to have attracted notice at a very early period of the history of that province. We are informed by the letters from Paris of Mr. Forstall to Governor Roman, that among the archives of the department De la Marine et des Colonies, there is "a most curious report on cotton in 1760, of the great advantages Louisiana might derive from its culture—the difficulty of separating the seed from the wool—its introduction from St. Domingo—a report to M. de Maurepas on that matter, suggesting the importation, from the East Indies, of machinery to separate the seed, &c." These valuable and ancient documents the legislature of the state are taking steps to have introduced into this country—their proper repository.

Tench Coxe, Esq.,* of Philadelphia, called the father of the growth of American cotton, prepared a statement of the arts and manufactures of the United States in 1786. He informs us that the people of the country, south of Annapolis, in Maryland, were not impressed with any belief of their capacity to produce cotton wool in any considerable quantity. From the recollections of cotton as a garden plant in his childhood, Mr. Coxe, in 1785, entertained "the pleasing convictions that the United States, in its extensive regions south of Anne Arundel and Talbot, would certainly become a great cotton producing country." Mr. Madison held the same opinion in 1786. These convictions, together with the fact of a supply of domestic cottons during the Revolution, at Philadelphia, for manufacture, induced a mission to England, on the part of Mr. Coxe, to obtain machinery, etc., for extensive establishments.

The treaty entered into between Great Britain and the United States, in 1792, stipulated against the importation of American cotton, in order to increase the English carrying trade of the West India cotton. We thus infer how great value Mr. Jay attributed to our cotton plant. The Senate refused a ratification of this provision.

Among the exports of Charleston, S. C., in 1748, were seven bags of cotton wool, valued at £3 11s. 5d. a bag. Another small export is stated for 1754. In 1770, ten bales were shipped to Liverpool from the American colonies. The laughable incident of eight bags of American cotton being seized in England on the ground that so much cotton could not possibly be the produce of the United States, occurred in 1784, only sixty-

* The following ancient account of this valuable citizen we extract from Mr. White's memoir of Slater. The first ancestor of the Coxe family, connected with America, was Dr Daniel Coxe, who was physician to the queen of Charles II., of England, and also to Queen Anne. He was the principal proprietor of the soil of West Jersey, and sole proprietor of the government, he having held the office of governor to him and his forever. At the request of Queen Anne he surrendered the government to the crown, retaining the other proprietary rights. A member of the Coxe family was always appointed by the crown, while there was a resident member in the province, a member of the Royal Council of New-Jersey until the Revolution.

Dr. Coxe was also sole proprietor of the extensive province of Carolina, an account of which is extant in an octavo volume, written by his son, Colonel Daniel Coxe, called "The History of Carolina," a copy of which will be found in the library of Congress, the Philadelphia library, and the Athæneum of Philadelphia.

Colonel Coxe intermarried with Sarah, the only child of John Eckley, a judge of the Supreme Court of Pennsylvania, and left issue, among others William Coxe, who married Mary, the daughter of Tench Francis, attorney-general of the province of Pennsylvania, Tench Coxe was the son of William and Mary Coxe, and was born in Philadelphia, 22d May, 1755, and died the 17th July, 1824.

The charter of Carolina was, in the extent of territory and power, the most extensive ever granted by a crown to a subject; the family were therefore obliged to release it to the crown, in consideration of a mandamus of the king, conferring 100,000 acres of land in New-York. Dr. Coxe was also a large proprietor in Pennsylvania, and nearly all the American provinces. To his eldest son, Colonel Daniel Coxe, he gave all his American possessions, and this gentleman was the first of the family who resided in America. He arrived in this country in 1709.

We have thus been particular in our notice of the family of Mr. Coxe, as we shall afterward have occasion to notice this large participator in the earlier operations of our manufacturing system.

two years ago! The export of American cotton to Europe was, in—

1785	14 bags.
1786	6 "
1787	109 "
1788	389 "
1789	842 "
1790	81 "

Of the fourteen bags sent to Europe in 1785, ten were shipped by John Teasdale, of Charleston, S. C., who, it is said, bought, the year before, the first bag of cotton sold in South Carolina. From the period of 1790, from the growth of home manufactures during the war, the improvement in machinery, and the great invention of Eli Whitney, of which we shall afterward speak, to the present day, the growth of cotton has been extending with broader and broader arms, until it embraces at last an immense region of territory, clothes and supports half the world, and affords to be heaped up in warehouses thousands and thousands of bags for future consumption. If, says a writer, the "woolsack" was a significant seal for the Chancellor of the British peers, to remind him of what was the great staple of the empire, the "cotton bag," the staple of the new world, may well be held in equal remembrance by the legislators of the Union. Every member ought to wear it as the girdle of his loins, emblematical of the bulwarks of the agricultural, manufacturing, and commercial interests of the United Republics. Every officer of the government should be clad in the productions of this superabundant article, and every citizen should be enrobed with it in life, and shrouded with it in death. It was protected in its infancy by the administration of Washington; and it has proved in its youth the defence of the beauty and booty of every section of the country.

The French in Louisiana experimented, during the interval between 1786 and 1795, in a species of white Siam cotton, their nankeen cottons being of the Malta kind. Carolina introduced the Bourbon, and Georgia the Pernambuco—the last being received from Havana. The culture of these cottons, we are told, was abandoned on account of their inferiority. The Louisiana cotton of the present day, it is conjectured by Mr. Seabrook, was derived from a species of Sea Island grown at the period of the Revolution, but degenerated in the progress of tillage by intermixing with other kinds. To a cross with Sea Island cottons, large quantities of which were shipped to Louisiana immediately subsequent to its cession to the United States, is perhaps, in part, to be attributed the decided superiority of the New Orleans cotton wool of the present day over all others in North America, of the green seed description.

The cotton cultivated in the United States is of the three great varieties of *herbaceous*, or herb cotton; *hirsutum*, hairy or shrub cotton; *arborescent*, or tree cotton; the two former comprise the green seed, short staple or upland; the latter the black seed, long staple or Sea Island variety. The herbaceum is stated to be of eastern origin clearly, and the hirsutum to be either from the East or West Indies. It will be a proper place to introduce some remarks upon each of the different classes enumerated.

1. The *Herbaceous* Cotton.—This plant grows to the height of eighteen to twenty-four inches, with leaves of dark green, blue veined, and five lobed. The flower is a pale yellow, one pistil, five petals or leaves, purple spotted at the bottom. On the falling of the flower a pod of triangular shape and triple cell is developed. The pod, in course of ripening, bursts, discloses a snow-white or yellowish ball of down, in three locks, inclosing and tightly adhering to the seeds, which resemble those of the grape, though of several times the size. The seed is planted in spring, and the cotton gathered at fall. The rows in the fields are five or six feet apart; the distance of the holes, in which several seeds are deposited, is about eighteen inches. Much care in weeding, thinning, and pruning, is required during the process of culture. This is the course pursued in the United States, which has the advantage over that pursued in India, by producing a cotton vastly more valuable. A field of cotton at the gathering, says Mr. Baines, when the globes of snowy wool are seen among the glossy dark leaves, is singularly beautiful; and in the hottest countries, where the yellow blossom or flower, and the ripened fruit, are seen at the same time, the beauty of the plantation is of course still more remarkable. The herbaceous cotton is reputed the most useful, and said to be cultivated in nearly every country congenial to the gossypum, existing even at Aleppo, in Upper Egypt, Arabia, and Senegal.

2. The *Hirsutum*, or Shrub Cotton.—It is said to grow wherever the herbaceous is found, and to vary according to climate, being biennial or triennial in the West Indies, lasting from six to ten years in India and Egypt, perennial in the hottest climates, and in the mildest cotton regions an annual. The shrub cotton is likened to a currant bush, and is of several varieties. The hirsutum, a low shrub already mentioned, the *Indicum*, attaining ten or twelve feet; the *Vitifolium*, of the south of France and South America; the *Religiosum*, of Surinam and India; the *Latifolium* of the West Indies; the *Barbadense*, of Barbadoes; and the *Peruvian*. The pod of the shrub cotton differs from that of the herb in being egg shaped. The Guiana and Brazil cotton is of this kind, and is said to yield, in the hottest countries, two crops a year.

3. The *Arborescent*, or Tree Cotton.—This remarkable plant is of Indian, Chinese, Egyptian and American growth. The height of the tree varies from fifteen to twenty feet. Marco Polo describes the tree at Guezerat six yards high, and bearing fruit for twenty years. There is a tree described in South America, Indian Isles, West Indies, and on the Guinea coast, of a hundred feet high, bearing a silky cotton, only useful for making quilting and beds. The justly celebrated *American Sea Island cotton* is derived from the Arboreum. Its fibre is long, strong, silky, and of a yellowish tinge. The seed is black, and of Persian origin, though originally introduced into this country from the Bahama Islands, where it had been introduced by the Board of Trade from Anguilla, an island of the Caribbean Sea. This cotton was raised first in Georgia in 1786, and the first bag exported by Alexander Bissel of St. Simon's Island, two years after. The section of country capable of producing this staple is very limited, being confined to the low sandy islands along the coast of South Carolina and Georgia, from Charleston to Savannah. The quantity grown in 1805 and in 1832 was precisely the same.

We condense from Mr. Seabrook's valuable notes on the Sea Island cotton, the most interesting particulars. The region of this cotton in South Carolina is bounded on the north and northwest by a line about twenty miles south of the line that separates Barnwell and Orangeburgh from the neighboring parishes, on the northeast and east by the Santee River, on the west and southwest by the Savannah River, and on the south and southeast by the ocean. The Eutaw Springs, in St. John's, Berkley, is the extreme northern point to which it extends. Williamsburg was for many years embraced in its limit, but that district no longer furnishes a supply of the raw material. In 1812 it was experimented on in Sumpter District, but it was found an unprofitable crop there. Mrs. Kinsey Burden, in 1788, was the first to attempt a crop of Sea Island cotton in South Carolina, her plantation having produced it the preceding nine years in small quantities. This was in St. Paul's parish, and the attempt failed in consequence of the pod not coming to maturity. William Elliott made the first successful crop in the state in 1790, on an island called Hilton Head, out of seed costing 14*s*. a bushel, This crop sold at 10½*d*. per pound. In 1792, a field on the Oakatee yielded 600 pounds, which sold at Savannah for 2*s*. per pound, During 1793 many other planters attempted the culture with various success, and indigo and the Sea Island cotton began to struggle for the mastery.

The enormous prices realized in past times by the planters of Sea Island cotton, have resulted in the accumulation of some of the largest fortunes in South Carolina. In 1799 one gentleman on St. John's, Berkley, realized £78 sterling, or about $350 to the hand, in a single year: another gentleman received 3*s*. per pound for a crop of three hundred acres, and 216 pounds to the acre. William Seabrook, of Edisto, purchased the plantation of Mr. Brisbane, and paid out of the proceeds of two years' crops the whole amount of the purchase money. The price of the cotton in the state ranged at first from 9*d*. to 1*s*., but reached 2*s*. and upward about the year 1806. The staple was found to be of such unusual length, that the English spinners actually thought proper to cut it shorter, thus destroying what is in fact its chief virtue.

The finest and best specimens of Sea Island have been produced by the most finished practical skill on the part of some of the planters, and by an acquaintance with the principles of chemistry and botany. Kinsey Burden, senr., of St. John's, Colleton, S. C., occupies the first place in this list. He succeeded in producing from selected seed a parcel of fine cotton in 1805, worth 25 cents a pound more than that of any of his neighbors. Continuing his laudable labors, his crop of 1826, of 60 bags, brought in market 110 cents the pound, and his crop of the following year 125 cents. Mr. Burden's wonderful success excited quite a sensation, but his secret was kept closely for many years. William Elliott suggested that it might lie in the character of the seed used; and upon the hint several set to work. Hugh Wilson, among the most successful of these, realized the ensuing year 125 cents per pound for his product. Two bags of extra fine cotton raised in 1828, brought $2 per pound, the highest price, says Mr. Seabrook, obtained in this or any other country from which cotton wool is exported. Mr. Burden's secret beginning to leak out, he proposed to divulge it to the Legislature for the sum of $200,000, but afterward changed his mind. William Seabrook, of Edisto, had designed offering $50,000 for initiation into the method, but declined afterward, alleging that "conjecture had yielded to certainty, that to the seed solely was traceable the fine cotton which Burden continued to grow." From that period down to the present day, the Sea Island planters have been constantly improving the quality of their staple at the expense of the quantity, and prices have fallen to but a fractional part of what they were. The result has been, that although particular instances of success are to be found, the planters as a body have been greatly injured by the production of the finest qualities of cotton.

It would be appropriate in this place to introduce a notice of the remarkable progress and improvement in the machinery for separating cotton wool from its fast-adhering seed. The matter was at one time thought a physical impossibility, but mechanical ingenuity in the person of Whitney and others, has been attended with the most triumphant success. We reserve, however, this interesting branch of our subject to be treated of in another article, under the head of *Cotton Manufactures:* it being perhaps better, for the sake of order, to take up in that place the crude cotton as it is spread over the fields, tracing out from thence every interesting change, until it appears at last in the most exquisite specimens of prints or the most delicate varieties of laces and muslins.

V. *The Cotton Trade.*—Notwithstanding our statement, which is sustained by high authority, that cotton was shipped from this country to Great Britain in small quantities in the years 1784–5–6, &c., Mr. McCulloch affirms broadly, that previously to 1790, North America did not supply a single pound of cotton for export, although some inconsiderable quantity had been raised even before the Revolutionary War. There is a discrepancy and difficulty here which Mr. Seabrook has, we think, vainly endeavored to remove. The authorities—Drayton's "Memoirs," Smither's "Liverpool," and a work "On American Husbandry," published in 1775—are of too high a nature to be removed by any merely negative testimony. It is due to Mr. McCulloch, however, to say that the statement he has made is not unsupported from other sources. The subject, cotton, does not appear in the Charleston Prices Current of 1792; and in 1787, an English factor—Mr. Seabrook tells us without giving the authority—replied to a shipment of one or two small packages of cotton from Charleston—"It is not worth producing, as it cannot be separated from the seed." We shall not balance between the authorities, but present simply the most satisfactory explication which could present itself to Mr. Seabrook's mind under all the circumstances of the case. He says the solution was probably this; the cotton was either prepared by hand-roller gins, which were undoubtedly in use even before the War, and sold in small quantities to the merchants, who packed it for exportation; or it was sent in the seed to Philadelphia and New-York, there to undergo the cleaning process. The latter supposition is based on the large amount of cotton shipped from those ports in the years alluded to, and the fact, as will be seen hereafter, that machines to disconnect the seed from the wool were employed in Philadelphia in 1784. Farther, the condemnation of the bags subsequently exported by Wadsworth & Turpin, shows that the previous consignments must have been of clean cotton, and not in the seed, as might be conjectured.

In considering the cotton trade in its origin and progress from the earliest periods to the present day, we shall commence with the year 1790, since before that period and in the best case, the trade in this staple must have been merely nominal. Mr. McCulloch indeed tells us, that from 1781 to 1789, a period of nine years, the whole import of cotton wool into Great Britain was only 150,000,000 pounds, an average of about 15,000,000 of pounds per annum, or 35 to 40,000 bags of the present capacity. For one of these years, 1786, he gives the proportion of each country from which there was any import.

From	pounds
British West Indies	5,800,000 pounds.
French and Spanish colonies	5,500,000 "
Dutch colonies	1,600,000 "
Portuguese colonies	2,000,000 "
Smyrna and Turkey	5,000,000 "
Total	19,900,000

The Secretary of the Treasury, Mr. Woodbury, communicated to Congress in 1836 a paper on the cultivation, manufacture and trade of cotton, to which we refer as authority for many of the statements we are about to make.

1.—GROWTH AND EXPORTS OF COTTON.

	IN THE WORLD	UNITED STATES		
Years	Growth pounds	Growth pounds	Exports pounds	Ex. Value dollars
1790..	—	1,500,000.	250,000.	—
1791..	490,000,000.	2,000,000.	200,000.	—
1792..	—	3,000,000.	143,000.	—
1793..	—	5,000,000.	500,000.	—
1794..	—	8,000,000.	1,667,000.	500,000
1795..	—	8,000,000.	6,000,000.	2,000,000
1796..	—	10,000,000.	6,000,000.	2,000,000
1797..	—	11,000,000.	3,500,000.	1,000,000
1798..	—	15,000,000.	9,000,000.	3,000,000
1799..	—	20,000,000.	9,000,000.	4,000,000
1800..	—	35,000,000.	17,000,000.	5,000,000
1801..	520,000,000.	48,000,000.	20,000,000.	9,000,000
1802..	—	55,000,000.	27,000,000.	5,000,000
1803..	—	60,000,000.	41,000,000.	8,000,000
1804..	—	65,000,000.	38,000,000.	8,000,000
1805..	—	70,000,000.	40,000,000.	9,000,000
1806..	—	80,000,000.	37,000,000.	8,000,000
1807..	—	80,000,000.	66,000,000.	14,000,000
1808..	—	75,000,000.	12,000,000.	2,000,000
1809..	—	82,000,000.	53,000,000.	8,000,000
1810..	—	85,000,000.	93,000,000.	15,000,000
1811..	555,000,000.	80,000,000.	62,000,000.	9,000,000
1812..	—	75,000,000.	29,000,000.	3,000,000
1813..	—	75,000,000.	19,000,000.	2,000,000
1814..	—	70,000,000.	17,000,000.	2,000,000
1815..	—	100,000,000.	83,000,000.	17,000,000
1816..	—	124,000,000.	81,000,000.	24,000,000
1817..	—	130,000,000.	95,000,000.	22,000,000
1818..	—	125,000,000.	92,000,000.	31,000,000
1819..	—	167,000,000.	88,000,000.	21,000,000
1820..	—	160,000,000.	127,000,000	22,000,000
1821..	630,000,000.	180,000,000	124,000,000.	20,000,000
1822..	—	210,000,000.	144,000,000.	24,000,000
1823..	—	185,000,000.	173,000,000.	23,000,000
1824..	—	215,000,000.	142,000,000	22,000,000
1825..	—	255,000,000.	176,000,000	39,000,000
1826..	—	250,000,000.	204,000,000.	25,000,000
1827..	—	270,000,000.	204,000,000.	29,000,000
1828..	—	325,000,000.	210,000,000	22,000,000
1829..	—	365,000,000.	264,000,000.	26,000,000

GROWTH AND EXPORTS OF COTTON—*Continued.*

	IN THE WORLD	UNITED STATES		
Years	Growth pounds	Growth pounds	Exports pounds	Ex. Value dollars
1830..	—	350,000,000	298,000,000	30,000,000
1831..	820,000,000	385,000,000	277,000,000	25,000,000
1832..	—	390,000,000	372,000,000	32,000,000
1833..	—	445,000,000	324,000,000	36,000,000
1834..	—	460,000,000	384,000,000	49,000,000
1835..	—	—	—	61,000,000

Export Sea Island from South Carolina and Georgia........1834..........8,085,000 lbs.
" " " "........1835..........7,752,000 lbs.

Growth of	1791. mil. lbs	1801. mil. lbs	1811. mil. lbs	1821. mil. lb	1831. mil. lbs	1834. mil. lbs
Brazil	22	36	35	32	38	30
West Indies	12	10	12	10	9	8
Egypt	—	—	½	6	18	25
Rest of Africa	45	46	44	40	36	34
India	130	160	170	175	180	185
Rest of Asia	190	160	146	135	115	110
Mexico and S. Amer., except Brazil	68	56	57	44	35	35
Elsewhere	—	15	11	8	4	13

2.—PRODUCE OF AMERICAN STATES, AND VALUE OF THE CROP OF EACH.

	1791. mil. lbs	1801. mil. lbs	1811. mil. lbs	1821. mil. lbs	1826. mil. lbs	1833. mil. lbs	1834. mil. lbs
South Carolina	1½	20	40	50	70	73	65
Georgia	½	10	20	45	75	88	75
Virginia	—	5	8	12	25	13	10
Tennessee	—	1	3	20	45	50	45
North Carolina	—	4	7	10	18	10	9
Louisiana	—	—	2	10	38	55	62
Alabama	—	—	—	20	45	65	85
Mississippi	—	—	—	10	30	70	85
Arkansas	—	—	—	—	¼	¾	½

These tables were compiled by the secretary from the best data within his reach.

3.—PRICE AND VALUE OF THE COTTON CROP IN THE UNITED STATES.

	Price per lb	Val. crop in U. S	Crop elsewhere
1791	26 cents	$333,000	$40,500,000
1801	44 "	8,000,000	39,330,000
1811	15½"	12,500,000	37,000,000
1821	16 "	30,000,000	37,000,000
1831	9¼"	38,500,000	29,225,000
1834	13 "	76,000,000	36,333,000
1835	16½"	—	—

It appears on the authority of the same report of the Secretary of the Treasury, that for every thousand bags of cotton imported into England in 1790, only one bag was received from the United States; only one bag for every 126 in 1792; 1 in every 25 in 1795; and that in 1799 one-ninth of the British cotton imports were from the United States. In 1800, she received sixteen millions of pounds from the United States, six millions from India, one-fifth of a million from Brazil, one-third of a million from the West Indies.

4.—IMPORTS OF COTTON INTO ENGLAND.

	1820. mil. lbs	1825. mil. lbs	1830. mil. lbs	1834. mil. lbs	1835. mil. lbs
From United States	90	140	211	266	253
" India	23	20	12	32	42
" Brazil	29	3	30	19	30
" West Indies, &c	2	8	4	1½	30
" Egypt and Turkey	¼	14	5	1½	—

The United States supplied France in 1821 with 27 millions pounds of cotton, 20 millions in 1825, 75 millions in 1830, 79 millions in 1834, and 91 millions in 1835.

The whole stock taken by France from all the world was 44 millions pounds in 1820, 61 millions in 1825, 84 millions in 1830, 88 millions in 1834, and 94 millions in 1835. Other countries of Europe, says the Report, than those enumerated, import considerable quantities of raw cotton. Holland and Belgium 10 to 12 millions pounds. In 1830, Germany took 12 millions pounds, 19 millions in 1831, and 25 millions in 1832. The Hanse Towns (1835) took from 2 to 6 millions pounds yearly, and Russia 1 million from the United States. Belgium, in 1834, imported 13 millions pounds, and Lombardy 4 millions.

EXPORTS OF COTTON FROM THE UNITED STATES OTHER THAN TO ENGLAND AND FRANCE.

	To Russia lbs	Holland & Belg. lbs	Spain lbs	Trieste lbs	Hanse Towns lbs	Italy & Malta lbs	Other places lbs
1821	304,000	4,186,000	285,000	34,000	748,000	897,000	2,507,000
1822	714,000	1,970,000	—	210,000	2,956,000	1,956,000	40,600
1823	360,000	4,650,000	—	178,000	2,356,000	217,000	833,000
1824	501,000	432,000	—	—	292,000	—	227,000
1825	134,000	1,420,000	—	—	577,000	—	509,000
1826	15,000	4,592,000	—	33,000	2,013,000	—	1,820,000
1827	147,000	5,861,000	8,000	183,000	3,390,000	148,000	1,440,000
1828	650,000	3,781,000	—	980,000	3,386,000	407,000	1,072,000
1829	228,000	9,595,000	—	4,071,000	6,858,000	1,056,000	1,261,000
1830	111,000	8,561,000	32,000	2,814,000	4,123,000	235,000	638,000
1831	762,000	972,000	555,000	2,778,000	2,417,000	306,000	2,243,000
1832	839,000	3,920,000	2,834,000	1,655,000	4,075,000	581,000	2,250,000
1833	1,447,000	2,673,000	758,000	1,107,000	1,871,000	—	1,760,000
1834	1,260,000	6,096,000	892,000	3,805,000	6,613,000	191,000	1,153,000
1835	947,000	5,694,000	878,000	4,943,000	2,788,000	13,000	1,494,000

Out of an import of 31,447,605 pounds of cotton in 1790, Britain exported 944,154 pounds; in 1800, the export was 4,416,610, out of an import of 56,010,732 pounds; in 1805, the export was 804,243, out of an import of 59,682,406 pounds; in 1810, the export was 8,757,109, out of an import of 132,488,935 pounds.

The following table, which we extract from McCulloch, brings down the amount of British trade in this article to 1832:

IMPORTS OF COTTON INTO GREAT BRITAIN, STOCKS, PRICES, ETC.

Years.	Total Imports into Great Britain. Pounds.	Stock in the Ports 31st December. Pounds.	Total Deliveries for Consumption. Pounds.	Amount of Crop in North America. Pounds.	Average Price, Uplands, per Pound.
1814	73,728,000	22,272,000	80,640,000	—	28d.
1815	96,200,000	22,360,000	85,800,000	—	20½d.
1816	97,310,000	22,355,000	88,631,000	—	18¼d.
1817	126,240 000	31,034,000	108,356,000	—	20d.
1818	173,940,000	85,800,000	111,800,000	—	20d.
1819	137,592,000	88,452,000	108,864,000	—	13½d.
1820	147,576,000	103,458,000	125,646,000	160,000,000	17 cents.
1821	126,420,000	106,800,000	126,420,000	180,000,000	16 "
1822	141,510,000	76,362,000	144,180,000	210,000,000	16½ "
1823	183,700,000	105,875,000	147,125,000	185,000,000	11 "
1824	147,420,000	64,428,000	174,174,000	215,000,000	15 "
1825	244,360,000	123,968,000	169,264,000	255,000,000	21 "
1826	170,520,000	100,548,000	164,640,000	350,000,000	11 "
1827	264,330,000	134,244,000	211,167,000	270,000,000	9½ "
1828	222,750,000	120,582,000	217,701,000	325,000,000	10¼ "
1829	218,324,000	84,966,000	221,676,000	365,000,000	10 "
1830	259,856,000	95,350,000	242,000,000	350,000,000	10 "
1831	280,080,000	84,090,000	257,500,000	365,000,000	9¼ "
1832	270,690,000	73,560,000	259,980,000	390,000,000	10 "

STATEMENT OF COTTON IN GREAT BRITAIN.

	1833. Pounds.	1834. Pounds.	1835. Pounds.
Imported	303,656,837	326,875,425	363,702,963
Exported	17,363,822	24,461,963	32,779,734
Left for consumption	286,293,015	302,413,462	330,823,229

Average price in the United States in 1833, 11 cents; in 1834, 13 cents; in 1835, 16½ cents per pound.

From 1822 to 1835, the highest quantity of cotton which France ever took in one year from all the world, was 324,425 bags, and the lowest, 169,845 bags; the mean average for the whole period being about 250,000 bags per annum.

The French, under Bonaparte, attempted to introduce the culture of cotton in France. In 1807, a distinguished agriculturist, Monsieur Lasteyrie, was employed by that government to give instructions relative to the culture of the cotton plant. He published a treatise on the subject, entitled "Du Cotonier, et de sa Culture," in which he gives an account of the various kinds of cotton in different parts of the world, and the modes of cultivating it. The Minister of the Interior also, at the same time, sent a circular letter to the Prefects of all the departments, requesting their particular attention to the cultivation of cotton, and informing them that he had sent for cotton seed to Spain, Italy and North America, to be distributed to the different departments, and offering a premium of one franc* to every killogramme (two pounds English) of cotton raised and cleaned ready for spinning. It is

* A franc is about twenty cents, making a premium of about ten cents for a pound of cotton.

understood that the experiment, if ever made, did not succeed.

The following table, taken from Pitkin's Statistical View of the United States, will exhibit the amount of our exports of Sea Island cotton from 1800 to 1816. We shall in another place bring down the table to the present day.

COTTON—SEA ISLAND.

Whither exported	1805 Pounds	1806 Pounds	1807 Pounds	1808 Pounds
Holland	64,628	—	—	—
Great Britain	8,563,274	6,002,617	8,728,162	941,000
France	156,442	75,451	188,572	—
Average price	—	30 cts.	30 cts.	39 cts.

Whither exported	1809 Pounds	1810 Pounds	1811 Pounds	1812 Pounds.
Russia	67,188	—	113,435	56,700
Sweden	3,023,226	202,771	19,368	1,411
Swedish West Indies	173,257	—	—	—
Denmark and Norway	30,000	109,202	—	—
Holland	—	47,871	—	33,316
Great Britain	2,200,505	4,758,783	7,688,865	3,838,390
France	—	—	—	355,283
Spain	—	50,710	—	—
Spanish West Indies	397,159	—	—	10,500
Portugal	110,444	734,739	—	—
Madeira	1,002,788	—	—	—
Europe (generally)	168,000	138,020	—	7,006
Floridas	852,461	2,510,475	—	52,500
Fayal and the other Azores	372,769	120,512	—	—
Average price	25 cts.	28 cts.	26 cts.	—

Whither exported	1813 Pouuds	1814 Pounds	1815 Pounds	1816 Pounds
Russia	60,000	—	—	—
Sweden	667,219	—	—	—
Holland	—	—	25,953	—
Great Britain	—	—	7,010,753	8,868,054
France	2,304,566	94,975	666,390	989,092
Spain	49,300	—	—	—
Spanish West Indies	228,286	413,412	—	—
Portugal	82,428	—	—	—
Europe (generally)	—	—	96,765	40,430
Floridas	753,050	2,011,951	645,901	—
Hamburg, Bremen, &c	—	—	4,189	—
Gibraltar	—	—	—	2,750
Average price	—	28 cts.	31 cts.	47 cts.

Note—There was not any distinction made between the *Sea Island* and *other* Cotton, until the year 1805.

COTTON—OTHER THAN SEA ISLAND.

Whither exported	1605 Pounds	1806 Pounds	1807 Pounds	1808 Pounds
Denmark and Norway	—	—	272,134	—
Holland	881,584	3,129,146	3,146,209	491,814
Great Britain	24,006,799	18,253,840	44,452,049	7.051,592
Hamburg, Bremen, &c	122,003	955,400	993,342	14,860
France	4,427,887	7,006,667	5,925,786	2,087.450
Average price	—	22 cts.	21 cts.	20 cts.

Whither exported	1809 Pounds	1810 Pounds	1811 Pounds	1812 Pounds
Russia	557,924	3,769,137	9,255,404	727,748
Prussia	—	936,579	231,679	—
Sweden	9,939,934	5,234,293	252,310	303,088
Swedish West Indies	—	168,500	—	—
Denmark and Norway	2,268,827	14,484,922	722,448	—

	1809 Pounds	1810 Pounds	1811 Pounds	1812 Pounds
Holland	1,068,096	100,869	—	115,714
Great Britain	11,099,482	31,413,132	39,083,587	22,248,789
Hamburg, Bremen, &c	1,067,013	976,762	1,836,288	—
France	—	—	—	558,150
Spain	796,496	4,292,055	228,880	—
Spanish West Indies	534,766	55,740	—	79,117
Portugal	1,733,081	2,870,142	—	—

Whither exported	1809 Pounds	1810 Pounds	1811 Pounds	1812 Pounds
Madeira	3,722,280	2,936,738	—	6,153
Floridas	1,059,293	10,339,019	177,200	—
Europe (generally)	771,860	1,922,232	860,993	99,172
Fayal and the other Azores	6,139,263	4,294,091	—	—
Average price	15 cts.	15 cts.	14 cts.	—

Whither exported	1813 Pounds	1814 Pounds	1815 Pounds	1816 Pounds
Russia	307,600	—	676,516	92,344
Prussia	—	—	622,000	—
Sweden	2,545,245	129,166	264,899	113,799
Swedish West Indies	10,909	—	—	—
Denmark and Norway	—	—	156,207	68,878
Holland	202,000	—	5,143,516	1,943,270
Great Britain	—	—	38,658,339	48,925,159
Hamburg, Bremen, &c	41,585	—	1,346,283	1,947,050
France	7,895,782	1,566,110	19,311,753	17,035,475
Spain	1,045,937	—	120,186	20,793
Spanish West Indies	851,381	3,069,577	136,666	—
Portugal	1,085,774	262,336	262,858	48,848
Madeira	5,288	—	—	1,525
Floridas	983,666	10,181,480	3,543,286	—
Europe (generally)	—	—	4,007,189	1,660,302
Average price	..	13 cts.	20 cts.	27 cts.

We have brought down our subject, in most of its particulars, to the year 1835, and discover with regret that it has grown upon us so rapidly that we have nearly exhausted the space which is reasonable to be occupied in a single number of our journal. There yet remain ten of the most interesting years in relation to the cotton trade to be examined, (from 1836 to 1846,) and we have not yet touched upon that wide and prolific field of investigation which was to occupy the sixth head of our article—*the future prospects of cotton.* We are forced into a change of plan, and terminate the statistics of trade here, to resume them in a future number of our journal. The subject will lose nothing of interest or value by the delay which is thus occasioned.

Before coming to a conclusion, however, we will briefly explain the different varieties of cotton which are now brought into competition with that of American growth, or may hereafter be elevated to such competition. These varieties are comprised under the general heads of South American, Smyrna, Egyptian, West and East Indian cottons.

South American.—The climate of this portion of our continent is adapted to the cotton culture in no inconsiderable degree. Brazilian cottons are in high repute in the markets of the world, and receive the different appellations of Pernambuco, Maranham, Bahia, Para, &c. The Pernambuco is of the best description, and it enjoyed for a long period the reputation of being superior to any other than Sea Island or Bourbon. The Guiana, or Demerara, is described as a strong glossy wool of superior length but of unequal fibre, well cleaned and picked, but of only ordinary fineness.

Smyrna.—This is from the Levant, and supplied once almost the whole demand of Europe. For manufacturing purposes it is very inferior, but answers very well, from its inflammable nature, for candle wicks.

Egyptian.—About the year 1823, this cotton, of the long staple species, and of superior fineness, began to be imported into Europe. The Pacha, Mehemet Ali, revived its culture in Egypt after it had been suffered to decline for many centuries and entirely to fall away. The experiment having succeeded on a small scale, and demonstrated the capacity of the soil and climate, the crop from that time began to demand very general attention, and the consequence is, that at the present day it has become one of great importance. The bags are scarcely more than half the size of those made in this country. The Sea Island cotton seed was tested in Egypt in 1827 with signal success. The crops are very irregular.

West Indian.—All of the South American, and most of the West Indian cotton, says Mr. Baines, is long stapled, and is produced from the shrub, not the herbaceous plant. It is supposed that some of the first cotton grown there was in the island of Tobago, by Mr. Robley, between the years 1789 and 1792, but in consequence of a fall in the price of cotton, and a rise in the price of sugar, that gentleman discontinued the cultivation of the former for that of the latter.

East Indian.—The cotton of the East Indies ranges lowest in quality and value. It is imported in large quantities into Europe, but, from want of skill in cultivation, and in picking, excites but little regard. Every effort has been made on the part of the British authorities to improve the quality of this staple, but thus far the efforts have been fruitless, and, although millions have been expended, the desired result seems no nearer attained than at first. The policy of Britain has been to build up her East at the expense of her West India possessions, and ultimately, in the production of cotton at least, at the expense of the United States; and, indeed, if nature did not present an insuperable obstacle, the last would have long since been effected, for there has been no want of capital and enterprise on her part.

COTTON—SEA ISLAND.—This finest of all the varieties of cotton cultivated in the world, it is known, is almost exclusively the product of the islands which stretch along the coast between Charleston and Savannah. The Hon. Whitmarsh Seabrook, in an essay or memoir lately prepared upon the subject, as an appendix to his valuable paper some years ago, examines its history, cultivation, trade, &c.

"The long-staple or black-seed cotton is cultivated in South Carolina to the distance of about thirty miles from the ocean. Of the raw material there are three distinct qualities, designated in the markets as Sea Islands, Mains, and Santees. The first, a pound of the finest of which, manufactured into the finest lace, is now worth from 8 to 15 guineas, and has been sold as high as 100 guineas, is the most valuable grown in any part of the world for exportation. Of descriptions of the plant reared on the seashore, the number is probably much greater than any examinations have yet disclosed. At present we are acquainted with only ten or fifteen varieties. These are distinguishable by certain criteria well known to the observant cultivator, but frequently the eye, unguided by the lights of botany, is unable to detect a difference, until the harvest itself shows the existence of perhaps a very material one. Invariably, fecundity in the plant is counterbalanced by defectiveness in the quality of the fruit; on the contrary, the better the fibre, the smaller is the harvest. This is in conformity with the wisdom of Nature as displayed in all her works. From analogical reasoning alone it may indeed be inferred, that our continued efforts to discover a plant, combining productiveness with superiority of staple, in as high a degree as these properties are separately found in many species of cotton, are utterly hopeless.

"From the time when long cotton was first introduced into this State, to within a recent date, its cultivation was decidedly profitable. Now legal interest on the capital of the grower is rarely ever realized. From 1821 to 1830 inclusive, the aggregate crop was 107,294,930 lbs. In the ten succeeding years it was only 79,041,596 lbs., being a deficit of 28,253,334 lbs. The average annual product from 1805 to 1817, a period of nine years, excluding the four years of the embargo and the war, was greater by 797,033 lbs. than it has been for the last nine years, or since 1832. Although the number of acres at this time in tilth cannot with accuracy be stated, yet it is believed that it is at least one-third greater than it was in 1820, or twice that of 1804. Under the operation, therefore, of decreased and decreasing exports, with a vast augmented population in every part of the world—extraordinary improvements in machinery—greater skill and cheapness in spinning and weaving—lower duties on the importation, and the superior properties of the kinds at present raised, the value of long staple cotton is less now than it was thirty-five years ago.

"Until lately, the Sea Island crop has been confined exclusively to high grounds, as contradistinguished from the marshes. The sagacity and perseverance of two members of the Agricultural Society of St. John's, Colleton, have been instrumental in effecting a change on this head, the ultimate consequences of which it is not easy to predict. There is no soil in South Carolina, if sown in long cotton, that will yield more money in a series of years, than those immense tracts which lie about the points where the salt and fresh waters meet. Nearer to the ocean, the land is low, intersected by numerous small creeks, and too salt for immediate use. Above the line, the total absence of saline ingredients renders the ground fitter for grain, especially rice, than cotton. Of the kind just noticed, there are thousands of acres in the parishes washed by the Atlantic, which to their owners are now barren wastes. This is the great prairie region of the lower country, capable of itself, from its inexhaustible fertility, of producing as much fine cotton as the demands of trade will probably require for a quarter of a century. As these marshes are very level, numerous ditches are required. If this work be faithfully done, such is the richness of the soil, that whether grown on beds or not, the crop, even the first year, will abundantly repay the labors of the cultivator.

"Within three years, other agents than that of human power have been resorted to in separating the seed from cotton. At this time a few planters still depend on the common treadle-gin, but the propeller is steam; others use another machine, distinguishable from the foot-gin chiefly in the length of the roller, to which steam or horse-power is applied. The former produces only about twice the quantity of cotton as the treadle gin when the human foot is employed. Its advantages, therefore, when the outlay and incidental expenses are brought to view, are inconsiderable. The latter gives generally about 200 lbs. per day. On the debit side the items do not subtract materially from the interest of the capital employed. The objections to Farris' gin are: first, that it works irregularly, and that unless the adjustment of the parts to the whole be entirely true, no calculations as to its performance can be made; and, secondly, that from the rapidity of the motion, which, for a profitable daily yield, must be kept up, the staple of the cotton is injured. The first disadvantage is undeniably a strong one, but the last is at least problematical. Steam applied to Farris' gin has so far afforded more satisfaction than any other scheme of accomplishing the object of the planter yet tried. It is, however, certain, that a machine for detaching the seed from Sea Island cotton, without impairing some of its valuable properties, is still a desideratum; and as large expenditures of money and labor have been fruitlessly made in this and other countries to attain an end so desirable to the grower, the task may be pronounced embarrassing and full of difficulties. If, nevertheless, the labor of ginning cotton cannot be essentially abridged, mechanical aid could and ought to be made subservient to the preparing of it for the gin, for the bag, and for packing it. In reference to the last operation, why is not the screw used? This mechanical agent is equal to the power of about twenty men; in other words, with one boy and a mule, it can do in a day as much as twenty men can accomplish in the same time with the pestle. As the pressure of the screw is equal and regular, no damage whatever to the staple can ensue, from its action; on the contrary, the repeated blows of the pestle, always of a wedge-like shape, must in some degree operate injuriously. As it is believed that the ship-owners give a decided preference to the square over the round bale, if there be no weighty objections on the part of the manufacturer, which can easily be ascertained, the planter would consult his interest by substituting the screw for the present clumsy instrument for packing cotton."

EXPORTS SEA ISLAND COTTON, FROM 1805 TO 1842.

Year	Quantity	
1805	8,787,659 lbs.	
1806	6,096,082	
1807	8,926,011	
1808	949,051	—Embargo.
1809	8,664,213	
1810	8,604,078	
1811	8,029,576	
1812	4,367,806	—War.
1813	4,134,849	War.
1814	2,520,388	War.
1815	7,449,951	
1816	9,900,326	
1817	8,101,880	
1818	3,080,838	From S. C. only.
1819	3,442,186	From S. C. only.
1820	6,020,101	From S. C. only.

Year	Quantity	Price	Average
1821	11,344,066	12½ to 30*d*	21¼*d*.
1822	11,250,635	10 to 28*d*	19
1823	12,136,688	11 to 24*d*	17½
1824	9,525,722	11¼ to 27*d*	19¼
1825	9,655,278	15 to 42*d*	28½
1826	5,972,852	10 tc 30*d*	20
1827	15,140,798	9¾ to 20*d*	14¾
1828	11,288,419	10 to 22*d*	16
1829	12,833,307	9 to 21*d*	15
1830	8,147,165	11¼ to 20*d*	16
1831	8,311,762	9½ to 18*d*	13¼
1832	8,743,373	9½ to 18*d*	13¾
1833	11,142,987	10½ to 22*d*	16¼
1834	8,085,935	13½ to 26*d*	19¾
1835	7,752,736	14 to 33*d*	24½
1836	8,554,419	14 to 36*d*	25
1837	5,286,340	12 to 40*d*	26
1838	7,286,340		
1839	5,107,404		
1840	8,770,669		
1841	6,400,000—20,000 bags, at 320 lbs. each.		

COTTON PLANTERS' CONVENTION.—Statistics of Production and Consumption of the Cotton Plant, and how the Planters should combine in their own defence.

—As requested, we cheerfully publish the able address of the Committee of Florida Cotton Planters. We agree entirely as to the importance of a convention of the Planters of the South, and have always advocated such a convention. It would effect much good in many ways, though we are not yet prepared to say how far the plan we now publish may be practicable or achieve the desired results. We are inclined to doubt.

At a meeting of Planters, convened at the Court-House in the city of Tallahassee, Col. Robert Butler was called to the chair, and, after a brief explanation of the objects of the meeting, Col. John Parkhill and Dr. G. W. Holland, were appointed Vice-Presidents, and B. F. Allen requested to act as Secretary.

On motion, a committee of five, consisting of James E. Broome, Edward Houstoun, T. K. Leonard, Richard Hayward and Geo. Whitfield, were appointed by the Chair, to present business to the meeting.

The committee retired for a few moments, and through their chairman, James E. Broome, submitted to the meeting the following report and resolutions:—

Your Committee have had under consideration the subject of a Cotton Planters' Convention, and beg leave to submit the following report:—

There is, perhaps, no interest in the world surrounded with so many difficulties or subject to so many disasters, as the cotton-planting interest. The great irregularity in the production, caused by the seasons, and the appearance or non-appearance of numerous enemies peculiar to this plant, produces fluctuations in the price, such as appear to visit no other great interest. Whether these fluctuations are necessarily incident to the production and sale of this staple, appears to be a question which has, as yet, engaged a very small share of the planter's attention. How far the difficulties which surround us are attributable to over-production, or to irregular production; or how far they result from making our controlling markets too far from our own gin-houses, or how far a remedy for our evils might be supplied by a judicious concert of action among planters, are all questions in which we seem to feel but little concern. These, and many others connected with this subject, might, as your committee believe, be investigated with great benefit; and such a labor would be peculiarly appropriate to a Cotton Planters' Convention.

Having met for the purpose of considering the expediency of calling on our cotton-planting brethren to meet us in convention, it is, perhaps, proper that your committee should present the reasons which induce them to advocate such a call. These will require, to some extent, an examination of the causes of our difficulties and the possibility of applying a remedy. In this examination, the first question which presents itself for our consideration, is the question of over-production.

The depression in price to which we are forced so often to submit, are attributed, generally to over-production. To ascertain whether this has been the cause, aggregates must be looked to, and not the relative production and consumption of any single year. For the purpose of testing this matter, your committee have gone back as far as the year 1825, and find that up to the year 1850, the production has not exceeded the consumption. On this subject, they present the following table, in which is shown the average annual production and annual average consumption of the world, for each period of five years, from 1825 to 1850:

	Production.		Consumption.	
Average from 1825 to 1830	1,231,000	bales per annum	1,187,000	bales per annum.
" 1830 to 1835	1,450,000	"	1,540,000	"
" 1835 to 1840	1,919,000	"	1,943,000	"
" 1840 to 1845	2,561,000	"	2,414,000	"
" 1845 to 1850	2,791,000	"	2,869,000	"
	9,592,000		9,953,000	

These results, multiplied by five, will show that the whole production in twenty-five years, has been 49,760,000 bales, and that the consumption in the same time, has been 49,765,000 bales, or an excess over the production of 5,000 bales, or 200 bales per annum. How much greater the consumption would have been had the raw material been furnished in increased quantity, your committee will not conjecture. Enough is shown by the facts to establish an important point —that the extent of consumption up to this time, has been controlled by the extent of production, and we must, therefore, look to other causes for the ruinous depressions in price, to which we have so often submitted.

The second point requiring investigation, is the capacity of the world for over-production. To this, your committee concede there cannot be a definite answer given; they incline, however, strongly to the opinion, that at fair prices, and with proper organization on the part of the American cotton planters, the capacity for over-production does not, and never can exist.

The extraordinary increase in the production of the world in five years, from 1840 to 1845, averaging 642,000 bales per annum, caused a regular increase in the stock of raw material left on hand in Europe at the close of each year, until, on the 31st of December, 1845, it had reached 1,221,000 bales, estimated as sufficient for twenty-six weeks' consumption. The average increased production in the United States for the next four years (embracing the crops of 1845 and 1848), was 117,000 bales per annum; and yet on the 31st of December, 1849, the stock on hand in Europe was reduced to 646,000 bales, estimated as sufficient for only thirteen weeks' consumption. The crops of 1849 and 1850, not equaling the average consumption of the last five years, it may be safely asserted that the consumption is now being limited and curtailed by a short supply of the raw material. To sustain this view of the case we make an extract from a document read in 1850, by one of the Secretaries of the Board of Trade, before the British Association at Edinburgh. "Great Britain now is, and for many years has been dependent, not at all upon the good-will of the citizens of the United States to sell their produce to us, but very much upon the influence of seasons, for the means of setting to work that large proportion of its population which depends upon the cotton manufacture for the feeding of themselves and their families. In the present condition of our cotton trade, any serious falling off in the amount of the cotton crop in the United States, necessarily abridges the means of laboring among our Lancashire and Lanarkshire spinners and weavers. Such a falling off is, in any year, likely to occur. We have felt its influence twice within the last few years, and are at this time suffering under it, and are threatened with another adverse season, the effect of which must be to deprive of employment a large proportion of those spinners and weavers whose labor is bestowed on the preparation of coarse goods." * * "Our supply of cotton has hitherto been drawn in very fluctuating proportions from British India, Brazil, Egypt, our West India Colonies, and the United States of America. From this last-named country, the quantities were, for a long series of years, in a continual condition of increase. From Brazil, our importations have sensibly lessened, without any reasonable prospect of future increase. From Egypt, the quantities fluctuate violently, and depend greatly upon causes not falling within ordinary commercial considerations. In the British West Indies, the cultivation of cotton has for some time ceased to form a regular branch of industry, and it is hardly to be expected that, having thus ceased to be profitable when prices in Europe were uniformly at a higher level than they have been now for a long series of years, the culture to any important extent will be resumed in these Colonies. From British India, the quantities received depend upon a different set of circumstances, but of such a nature as to forbid any very sanguine hope of great and permanent increase in the shipments." After continuing the argument at some length, attention is called to the immense increased consumption of their cotton mills, showing that in 1800, they consumed 56,010,732 lbs., and in 1849, 775,468,008 lbs., and remark: "It is by no means improbable that the consumption during the last nine years would have gone forward at a constantly accelerated pace, so that it would by this time have gone beyond 1,000,000,000 pounds in the year, but for the check given to it in 1847, and in the present year, through insufficiency in the supply of the raw material." * * * "This increase has been concurrent with, and mainly caused by, a continual reduction in the price of cotton." * * "On the other hand, the continual fall in the price has acted as a stimulus on the producers (American), who have hitherto made up, in general, by the extent of their cultivation, for the diminished price of their crops." Thus it is seen that increased supplies are greatly wanted, but their experience is, that the surest means of stimulating production in the United States, is to reduce the price. Your committee might furnish many authorities to show, that in Great Britain, the great head of manufacturing industry, the idea that markets may not be found for all the cotton goods she can procure the raw material to produce, has long since been abandoned. Even the government is alarmed at the prospect of their industry being seriously checked, not for the want of customers, but for the want of cotton. The most powerful efforts have been made, and are still being made, to stimulate the production of cotton in every country where there is hope of success. How far they have succeeded may be inferred from the fact, that in five years preceding 1850, the production in India and Brazil declined sixteen per cent., and in the same time the supplies of Surat and Madras declined twenty-four per cent. Thus it will be seen that, notwithstanding the extraordinary efforts made to stimulate production in every quarter, the United States is the only country that has continued to furnish increased supplies. But the character of our increase for the last twenty years, must give small consolation to those who apprehend difficulties from a short supply of raw cotton. Our per cent. increase has been regularly and rapidly diminishing, as is shown from the following table, the data of which we take from Hunt's Merchant's Magazine, a work of high commercial character:

		Total.	Per annum.
Increased per cent	in 20 years..	177.....	or 8 85-100
" "	15 " ..	119.....	or 7 66-000
" "	10 " ..	58.....	or 5 95-000
" "	5 " ..	15.....	or 3

Thus it is seen that the per cent. increase in American cotton has been rapidly declining, until we are now down to three per cent. per annum. Not so, however, with American consumption—that is increased in the same time, more than nine per cent. per annum. The per cent. increased production in the world, for the last five years, is down to an average of 1 80-100 per annum; while the per cent. increase in consumption has been 3 80-100 per annum; and leaving out England, France, and the United States, the increase in the balance of the world has been 46 per cent., or more than nine per cent. per annum. This state of things cannot continue; the rate of production must be increased, or the rate of consumption diminished—the equilibrium will be found.

These calculations show, that the area for the consumption of cotton goods is enlarging—that the vast and yet unsupplied population of the earth are rapidly maturing a competition, which, without greatly augmented supplies of the raw material, will at no distant day, be seriously felt by the manufacturers and consumers of England, France, and the United States. The commerce of every civilized nation is opening new markets, and enlarging old ones for our benefit. To what extent now markets already found have been supplied, compared with their wants, or how many others are yet to be opened and supplied, your committee have no means of ascertaining; but an inference may be drawn from the fact, that the largest five years' average production the world has yet furnished, is 2,791,000 bales per annum. That of these, England, France, and the United States require for their consumption, from 2,000,000 to 2,200,000 bales; leaving not more than one-fourth of the annual product to supply the balance of the world, with a population, probably ten times as large as their own. Under such circumstances, it may reasonably be supposed, that with fair average prices, markets will be found for all the cotton which we now have, or ever will have, the ability to produce.

Having now shown that there has been no over-production, in the aggregate, and that there is no reasonable probability that there ever will be, your committee will attempt to show the effects of irregular production on prices and consumption. Here, your committee believe, may be found the source of nearly all the fluctuations to which this great interest has been subjected. To illustrate the effects of irregular production, three simple suppositions will be used, remarking that extreme cases are selected, and a single year used to establish a principle where, in practice, several may be required. Suppose that the crop of 1851 should be 3,000,000 bales—that to manufacture these, $300,000,000 of capital must be invested, and 3,000,000 operatives employed—suppose the capital and operative furnished, the crop manufactured, sold, and consumed. Then suppose the year 1852 yields only 2,000,000 bales; to manufacture these, only two-thirds of this capital and two-thirds of these operatives are necessary. What is to become of the other one-third of each? To retain their position, short-time is resorted to, and this, it is found, starves the operatives and destroys the dividend on the capital. Then fine numbers only are spun; these are found to be unsaleable, and give an unhealthy character to the manufacturing business. These palliatives fail, as they always must, and the equilibrium is restored by driving out one-third of the capital and labor, to seek employment in other pursuits, promising more stability.

Then suppose the year 1853 furnishes another crop of 3,000,000 bales. What is to be done with it? The capital remaining is only sufficient to manufacture 2,000,000, and without manufacturing, it cannot be consumed. The result is inevitable—the crop sells for a trifle, and, at the close of the year, there is a surplus of 1,000.000 bales in excess of the usual supply, and this, perhaps, to be increased by a good crop in 1854.

Under such circumstances, speculators seeing no prospect of improvement withdraw from the market—the manufacturer is left without competition, and fixes the prices to suit himself—the planter becomes discouraged, and forces his cotton off at anything that is offered—unites in the general cry, that the production is immeasurably in advance of the consumption—vies with the manufacturer in fixing the impression and making it universal, that large supplies and low prices are inevitable for all time to come. This impression being fixed, capital flows in rapidly, new factories go up in all directions, old ones are enlarged and improved, trade in Manchester becomes healthy, new and extensive markets are found for the consumption of cotton goods, and in a few years, to the utter astonishment of all the world, it is found that the picture has been reversed—that an unprecedented increase in the consumption has taken place—the surplus is all gone—prices move upward—a short crop is made, and capital is again driven out, to be invited back, by the same process, after another long period of depression in prices.

These, your committee believe, are the natural results of irregular production; and were it possible to obtain such concert of action among planters as would reduce the annual crop one-half, the same principles would govern, and the same results be obtained ultimately.

If it be true, as your committee have supposed, and as a careful examination of the production, consumption and stock remaining on hand for 25 years past, they think will abundantly show, that our difficulties have not been attributable to over-production, but to irregular production, then is it not important that we should apply the remedy, if there is one? Irregular production, it is conceded, cannot be prevented, but your committee think that organized concert of action will control its effects. By way of illustration, suppose that the year 1851 yields 3,000,000 bales, and that it is definitely ascertained that the capital employed is only sufficient to manufacture 2,500,000 of these; now, in the ordinary course of trade, the effects of irregular production would be shown by great depression in price. But suppose the planters refuse to send the crop forward to any greater extent than is actually sufficient to supply the demand for consumption, and retain under their own sheds the other 500,000 bales; such a course would secure them fair prices for the amount sold, and control the natural effects of irregular production for that year. Then suppose the year 1752 furnishes only 2,000,000 bales; the ordinary effect of this, as has been shown, would be to drive capital out of the manufacturing business, and lay the foundation for subsequent low prices. This would be controlled, by adding the 500,000 bales retained from the crop of 1851, supplying the manufacturers' demand, securing good prices for both crops, and preventing the derangement which would have resulted from a withdrawal of manufacturing capital. Thus the principle might be run through any number of years, and admitting that there is no aggregate over-production, every crop would bring a fair price, because offered only in quantities sufficient to supply the demand. Such a system as this would protect us against the consequences of irregular production, but it can never be carried into effect by individual action. There are no means of procuring the necessary concert, to say nothing of other insuperable obstacles.

If we would do anything certainly and effectively, we must organize a Cotton Planter's Association. This should be chartered by the states of South Carolina, Georgia, Alabama, Louisiana, and Florida, with a capital of least $20,000,000, to be increased in the amount, as the wants of the business might require. The Association should erect or purchase extensive warehouses in Charleston, Savannah, Mobile, New-Orleans, Apalachicola, and St. Marks, and establish at each of these points a regular commission business, with a view to the storage and sale of the entire crop of the United States.

For the purpose of securing to themselves the whole cotton commission business, they should establish a minimum price, which, for the purposes of this argument we will fix at 10 to 12 1-2 cents, according to quality and location, and averaging, say 11 cents per pound. This should be guaranteed to all their regular customers, and to all parties holding cotton purchased of them, so long as the said cotton remained in their warehouses. The world should have notice that, whenever the cotton offering was not wanted by others, at or above the minimum fixed, it would be wanted by the Association ; that, when once purchased, it would never be re-sold, until taken at cost, adding storage, insurance, interest on the investment, with a commission for purchasing, and another for selling. This accumulation of charges would induce the manufacturers to take their supplies before the company would be required to take any ; nor is it, indeed, likely that they would ever be purchasers to any iarge extent. Under such a system the planter would not crowd the market with cotton, as is now the case, and speculators at the minimum price would purchase freely, and hold with confidence.

Another inducement for such an organization may be found in its capacity for increasing the consumption, provided the raw material is furnished. The bagging and rope necessary for packing a crop of 2,500,000 bales, would require about 56,000,000 pounds, or about 100,000 bales, of the most inferior part of the crop. This would be 4 per cent. of the entire yield. To insure this large increase in the consumption of the United States, it would only be necessary to erect the machinery for manufacturing these articles —sell them at a trifle above the cost of production, and discriminate in the minimum price fixed, to such extent as might be found necessary, against cotton packed in any other material. This would insure the packing of the entire crop in our own staple, and provide for the employment of a considerable amount of labor in manufacturing the bagging and rope necessary. But this is not the only increase to be effected in the consumption ; the guarantee which the manufacturer everywhere would have, incidentally, that his goods, when made, could never be brought into competition with goods made from cotton at lower prices than his own, would induce the production of a larger proportion of coarse numbers—feeling that there could be no risk in stocking himself heavily, spindles would not be stopped or short-time resorted to, because orders were not in hand for work ahead—the manufacturing business would be characterized by greater regularity, and conducted with greater confidence—the supplies of goods would be better, and the consumption larger. Another inducement for such an organization is the great saving of expense in getting our cotton into the hands of the manufacturers.

The Liverpool market governs the American market ; and it matters not where the planter sells his cotton, he sells in reference to what is the supposed net value in Liverpool ; and the difference between the price in our own sea-ports and the price in Liverpool, is the measure of charges aud expenses paid by deductions from the price of the crop when sold. Taking the period of ten years, from 1840 to 1850, it is found that the average price in Liverpool was 2 95-100 cents per pound higher than the average during the same time in the sea-ports of the United States. Taking this as a measure of charges and expenses, and estimating our production for the next ten years at 2,500,000 bales, of 500 lbs. each, and the expenses may be stated thus :

1,250,000,000 lbs. at 2 95-100 cents per lb		$36,875,000
Add storage in American sea-ports averaging 3 months, at 50 cents per bale on 2,500,000	$1,250,000	
Drayage on do. at 10	250,000	
Mending do. at 5	125,000	
Brokerage, extra labor, &c., at 15	365,000	
Commission on sales at $55 per bale at 2½ per cent	3,437,500	
		5,437,500
		$42,312,500

Thus it is shown that, exclusive of charges in interior towns, the expenses paid by the planter on a crop of the size supposed would be over $42,000,000, or nearly $17 per bale, and this, too, so far as the larger item is concerned, on a range of prices of only 7 cents and 7 mills in the American ports.

How far these expenses may be reduced by concentrating our business in our own ports, and bringing the manufacturer to our own warehouses for his supplies, and thus dispensing with intermediate markets, and intermediate agents, may be seen by reference to the following table :

Total charges now paid on 1,250,000 lbs.		$42,312,500
Deduct for necessary charges, as follows:		
For charges in Southern sea-ports, as per above table	$5,437,500	
For freight from Southern ports to manufacturer's receiving ports, on 1,250,000,000 lbs., at ¾c	9,375,000	
Marine insurance on do. at $60 per bale at 1 per cent.	1,500,000	
Small incidental charges, at 40 cents per bale	1,000,000	
		17,312,500
		$25,000,000

Leaving a balance of $25,000,000, which, if these estimates are correct, must constitute an unnecessary charge on the cotton planter, and might be saved by transacting our business with the manufacturer at our own warehouses. That the organization of such an association as your committee have suggested, would effect such a revolution in the cotton trade, they think may be shown. So long as the cotton remains in their warehouses, it would be under a guarantee that it should bring a certain and fair price; the benefit of this would be lost as soon as it was removed. Under such circumstances, who would ship it? Would the planter or speculator remove a bale? What would be the inducement? Such removal would not only forfeit the guarantee, but render it certain that the cotton must reach the manufacturer with an accumulation of unnecessary charges, by which the net price would be reduced. With strong inducements, therefore, for its remaining, and a certainty of loss on its removal, scarcely a bale would go except to the manufacturer's order. Effect such a revolution, and Liverpool would no longer be the great cotton market of the world, and govern prices for us—our own Southern ports would become the manufacturer's market—our own merchants wou'd be their purchasing agents—we should learn to do our own business, keep our means at home, and this would bring the commerce of all nations to our ports—the gold and produce of all would be brought to our cities to exchange for our cotton. We should become the great importing as well as exporting section of the country. Business would invite capital and population—our property would be greatly enhanced in value—we should be independent of all sections and countries, while all would be tributary to us. In conclusion, your committee will ask, can the necessary capital be raised? Why not? Eight dollars per bale on the production of a single year would be sufficient, while they have attempted to show that ten dollars per bale, per annum, would be saved in expenses, and there can be no doubt that a similar sum would be received by increased price. If so, fifty millions dollars a year would be added to the cotton planters' income. This benefit would be common to all, and is deemed sufficient to justify the subscription of $20,000,000, even if so much would be necessarily sunk in the operation. But your committee can see no reason why the capital should be lost. On the other hand, the cotton commissions, &c., have been estimated to be worth in the sea-ports $5,437,500—the interest on the capital would be equal to at least $1,000,000 more, making $6,437,500, while the back storage, receiving and forwarding, commissions on consignments of other produce, and on vessels, with a great variety of smaller matters, would hardly fail to pay the expenses of conducting the business, leaving the interest and cotton commission business as a dividend of nearly thirty-three per cent. per annum to the stockholders.

Your committee have thus considered, as far as their means of investigation have allowed them, the questions of over-production; and our capacity for over-production, the influence of irregular production, and the possibility of controlling its effects, our ability to increase the consumption, improve the price, and save a large portion of the annual charges and expenses now paid. They have confined themselves to the discussion of a single plan or system of production, not doubting that there are others, aud perhaps, better ones, which will be presented, should a convention of cotton planters be assembled. Accompanying this report they present the following resolutions for the consideration of the meeting:

Resolved, That the great irregularity, and continued tendency to reduction of the price of our great Southern staple, are evils which require investigation, and the application of a remedy, if one can be found.

Resolved, That in the opinion of this meeting, nothing is likely to be accomplished for the benefit of interest, without a reasonable amount of concert of action among cotton planters.

Resolved, That with a view to obtaining such concert of action, we respectfully call on the cotton planters of the Southern states to assemble in Convention at Macon, Georgia, on Monday, 27th day of October next, or at such other time and place as may be most convenient to a majority of those who may desire to be represented, and that this meeting appoint delegates to the same.

On motion of Judge Brevard, the Report was received, and the resolutions taken up *seriatim*, and unanimously adopted.

General Whitfield then offered the following resolution, which was unanimously adopted:

Resolved, That the Secretary of this meeting prepare copies of the foregoing Report and Resolutions, and ask publication of the same in De Bow's Review, the Agricultural papers of the South, and the papers of the city of Tallahassee.

On motion of Mr. Houstoun, it was then unanimously

Resolved, That we form ourselves into a Cotton Planters' Association, to be called the Central Association of the Cotton Planters of Florida.

The following gentlemen were then appointed Delegates to attend the Planters' Convention, to be held in the city of Macon, Georgia, on Monday, the 27th Oct. next:

John S. Shepherd, James E. Broome, Benj. Chaires, George Whitfield, George Galphin, T. W. Brevard, Edward Houstoun, W. D. Moseley, R. K. Call, W. M. Maxwell, F. Chairs, T. K. Leonard, Elijah Johnson, N. L. Thompson, G. W. Holland, John J. Maxwell, W. H. Burroughs, G. A. Croome, Alex. Cromartie, Richard H. Bradford, Edward Bradford, John Branch, Charles Bannerman, R. W. Williams, J. S. Maxwell, Green Chaires, Henry B. Ware, W. L. Thompson, James L. Hart, Thomas Laversage, George T. Ward, Jo. Chaires, Jesse Everett, John Cason, Kenneth Bembry, Wm. Lester, Richard Whitaker, E. M. Garnett, R. H. Hall, Richard Van Brunt.

The officers of the meeting were, on motion, added to the number of delegates above designated.

A committee of three, consisting of Edward Houstoun, James E. Broome and Theodore Brevard, were then appointed, to prepare a constitution and by-laws, for the government of said association, to be reported to their next meeting.

On motion, the meeting adjourned, to meet again on Saturday, at 10 o'clock.

ROBERT BUTLER, *President*.

JOHN PARKHILL, }
G. W. HOLLAND, } *Vice-Presidents*.

B. B. ALLEN, *Secretary*.

COTTON PLANTERS' CONVENTION—EXAMINATION OF THE ABOVE REPORT.—The Convention of Cotton Planters, recently held in Macon, Georgia, as a *substitute* for the report of its Committee of twenty-one, adopted a *printed pamphlet*, purporting to be a report made to a meeting previously held in Tallahassee, Florida, and containing what has been denominated "The Florida Scheme."

More than two hundred names were registered, as members of the Macon Convention; but the question of adopting the substitute was forced upon the meeting, when there were not forty members present. The substitute, therefore, is not a fair expression of the views of the Convention; and deeming it calculated to do injury, I ask permission to state some of my objections; and I do it in the hope that some practical plan will be presented by the next Convention of Cotton Planters.

In reviewing the *pamphlet*, I will suppose its *figures* to be correct; although on this head I have no certain information.

The first thing which presents itself, is the Irish Bull, "That the *consumption* of cotton has exceeded its *production*:" but let this pass. The next of its bold assertions is, that "the extent of consumption up to this time, has been controlled by the extent of production." And this is asserted in the face of the admitted fact, that at the close of every year, a large surplus of cotton has remained in the hands of the sellers, which was not wanted by the manufacturers—a surplus amounting, at one time, to 1,221,000 bales; and at last dates amounting to 646,000 bales. No one will say that the Manchester or American manufacturers have at any time stopped their spindles, "worked short time," or "spun fine," because of short supplies of the raw material. When those measures were resorted to, it was because of limited demand for their goods; or, as the means of depressing the price of cotton. Where, then, are the evidences that "the consumption of cotton up to this time, has been limited by its production?" The quotation from a paper, read in 1850 before the British Association at Edinburgh, is entitled to the same credit, and no more, that would be given to the opinion of any gentleman not concerned in the manufacture of cotton. The paper gives no facts in support of its assertions: and in the pamphlet under review, we have sufficient evidence, that after laborious investigations of the same subject, a gentleman of considerable talent may fall into great mistakes. It is to be remarked, too, that the writer whose opinion is quoted, was urging upon the Association the favored policy of the British Government and British manufacturers, of stimulating the production of cotton elsewhere, so as to render that country independent of this for its supplies of this all-important article. None but one infatuated with some favorite theory, and heedless of facts, can say, that, "up to this time, the manufacture and consumption of cotton have been limited by its scanty production." It may come to pass at some future day, that we cannot produce as much cotton as the manufacturers may want; but it will be well to await the event, or its near approach, before undertaking to provide for it. Meanwhile, our danger is from the opposite quarter; and the object for which the Convention was called, was to devise correctives for the low prices apprehended from an expected large crop.

In each of his speeches, the author of the pamphlet told the Convention, that after supplying the wants of Great Britain, France and the United States our largest crop would not furnish the rest of the world with half a pound of cotton each, for the clothing of its nine hundred millions of inhabitants. Alas! for the poor wretches, who, under this privation, must be shivering with cold, or blistering under tropical suns! How can human beings live under such privation? The speaker, however, had forgotten, that other nations, than ourselves, are producers of cotton. People are clothed with it in China, Hindoostan, Japan, Persia, Africa, and other parts of the world; and long before the first bale of cotton was grown in the United States, our slaves were clothed with coarse cotton cloth, imported from the East Indies. We know, too, that cottons are annually imported into Europe from other countries than the United States; and may reasonably infer, that their exports consist of the *surplus* of their crops, above the wants of their own people.

It is unnecessary to waste words upon the array of figures employed in page 4 of the pamphlet, to show the effects of irregular production on prices and consumption. The figures employed are *assumed* to prove a theory; but are in no way furnished by the history of cotton, either in its production or its manufacture. Any other figures might as well have been assumed. And until some evidence be adduced to prove, that there has at any time been less cotton produced than the manufacturers wanted, all such pretended demonstrations of cause and effect, are, of course, *vox et prœterea nihil.*

In page 5, we find the only valuable paragraph contained in the pamplet. It is the admission, that the evil of over-production may be remedied by the planters withholding a portion of their crops from market. But this simple and common sense remedy is unceremoniously repudiated as impracticable, because "*it cannot be carried into effect by individual action;* there being no means of procuring the necessary concert," &c.

The next two paragraphs contain the grand scheme of the author, the panacea for all our evils. I will quote, and comment upon it, when I shall have noticed two of the subsequent paragraphs. The author says, (page 6,) "Another inducement for such an organization, (meaning his mammoth company,) may be found in its capacity for increasing the consumption, provided the raw material is furnished."* This increased consumption is to be effected by packing the crop in cotton bagging and cotton rope; but it does not very clearly appear how much increased consumption is dependent upon the organization of such a company, unless the company is to become the manufacturer of the rope and bagging, as well as the salesman of the crop. If the planters will agree to use cotton rope and cotton bagging, manufactories of those articles will be erected by individuals.

On same page, we are told that, "the difference between the price in our seaports, and the price in Liverpool *is the measure of charges and expenses paid upon the cotton crop when sold!!!*"

This is a novel discovery, and, if true, the British manufacturer may, with equal justice, say that the difference between the price of his goods at his manufactory, and that for which they are sold to the planters of the South, "*is the measure of the charges and expenses paid, by deductions from the price of his manufactured articles when sold*"!!! And, according to the doctrine of the pamphlet, the manufacturers ought to form a great joint stock company, with warehouses for storage of their goods, until those who want them will come and purchase at the usual consuming prices, less the necessary expense of freight, insurance, &c.

But if, as asserted, the present mode of forwarding our cotton to Liverpool involves a cost of seventeen dollars per bale, why not ship it direct to that market, and, at a cost of only seven dollars per bale, obtain the Liverpool prices?

I will now proceed to the examination of the grand scheme of the pamphlet: that which is to work wonders in curing the evil of irregular and unremunerating prices for cotton. We have the scheme detailed in page 5, in the following words:

"If we would do any thing certainly and effectively, we must organize a Cotton Planters' Association. This should be chartered by the states of South Carolina, Georgia, Alabama, Louisiana and Florida, with a capital of at least twenty millions of dollars, to be increased in amount as the wants of the business might require. The Association should erect, or purchase, extensive warehouses in Charleston, Savannah, Mobile, New-Orleans, Apalachicola and St. Marks, and establish at each of those points a regular commission business, with a view to the storage and sale of the entire crop of the United States.

"For the purpose of securing to themselves the whole cotton commission business, they should establish a minimum price, which, for the purposes of this argument, we will fix at 10 to 12½ cents, according to quality and location, and averaging say 11 cents per pound. This should be guaranteed to all their regular customers, and to all parties holding cotton purchased of them, so long as the said cotton remained in their warehouses. The world should have notice, that, whenever the cotton offering was not wanted by others, at or above the minimum fixed, it would be wanted by the Association—that, when once purchased, it would never be re-sold, until taken at cost, adding storage, insurance, interest on the investment, with a commission for purchasing, and another for selling. This accumulation of charges would induce the manufacturers to take their supplies, before the company would be required to take any; nor is it, indeed, likely, that they would ever be purchasers to any large extent. Under such a system, the planter would not crowd the market with cotton, as is now the case, and speculators, at the minimum price, would purchase freely, and hold with confidence."

Let me examine this scheme, and inquire:

1st. Whether such an Association *can be organized?* and,

2d. Whether, if organized, it would, or could, remedy the evils of short prices?

1st. The company is to be chartered by the several cotton producing states. And the object in obtaining a charter, was avowed by the author of the scheme to be, "the exemption of the stockholders from losses as indi-

* Does any one doubt of a sufficiency of the raw material?

viduals, if, peradventure, the company should become insolvent."

Nor can any man of sense suppose, that under the present state of public feeling, in regard to corporations, any legislature will grant such a charter to a great trading company, which proposes to monopolize all the cotton trade of the United States; and which, according to the showing of its friends, is to divide enormous profits. *Credat Judæus Appellas, non ego!*

If, then, *a charter be necessary* to the organization of the company, the first question may be answered in the negative. But waiving this legislative obstacle, we will suppose a charter obtained; what next? How will the capital of twenty millions of dollars be obtained? Will it be subscribed for, and paid in money? Supposing a willingness to adventure their fortunes in such a scheme, it will not be asserted that its friends have such a sum of money waiting the opportunity of investment; the money must, therefore, be raised by sale of cotton.

It is the general belief that the crop of 1851, which is now being harvested, will prove a large one. It was this belief which induced the meeting of the Macon Convention. The crop is variously estimated at from 2,600,000 to 3 000,000 bales, of 400 lbs. each; and the pamphlet acknowledges a surplus of 646,000 bales of preceding crops. If, then, the crop shall prove equal to the lowest of the estimates, the *supply* of cotton will be 3,200,000, while the *demand* is not estimated to exceed 2,300,000 bales; and under such a state of things, will the price of the article range above 6¼ cents per pound, or twenty-five dollars per bale? At that price it will require a sale of 800,000 bales to raise the proposed capital of twenty millions of dollars. And be it remembered, that these 800,000 bales will go into the hands of the manufacturers, and will supply one-third of their wants for the year. The operation, therefore, will have no tendency to raise prices; on the contrary, it must depress the value of the residue of the crop. Can it be believed that nearly one-third of the cotton crop of the year will be thus disposed of for the purpose of subscribing to the stock of the company? The man who so believes, must have faith in the existence of folly amounting to infatuation.

We will, however, for argument sake, suppose the association to be organized; and proceed to the

Second inquiry,—Whether it would, or could, remedy the evils of short prices?

I will suppose the capital of twenty millions of dollars to have been paid in by stockholders, who had the money ready for investment, when opportunity offered: and will make no deduction from its amount for purchasing, a building, warehouses, salaries of officers, &c., &c.

The company gives "notice to the world, that whenever cotton offering is not wanted by others, at or above 11 cents per pound, it will be wanted by it." Would not cotton be rushed upon it until its capital was invested? At eleven cents per pound, the value of a bale of cotton would be forty-four dollars; and the twenty millions of dollars would purchase 454,000 bales: after which the company would remain dormant, and incapable of action, or life, until some future short crop of cotton should so raise the price, as to enable it to sell what it had purchased. Meanwhile, would this withdrawal from market of 454,000 bales materially raise the price of the 2,700,000 bales left to supply a demand for 2,300,000? I think it would not.

If the capital of twenty millions of dollars was raised by sale of the 800,000 bales before mentioned, the chance for a rise in the price of cotton would be still less; for that sale would have supplied the manufacturers with more than one-third of their wants, and at a minimum price; and they would afterwards dictate the price for the remainder. In this case, too, the capital raised by supplying the manufacturers with 800,000 bales, when invested in cotton at 11 cents, would only withdraw 454,000 bales from market, and leave 1,940,000 bales to supply a remaining demand for 1,500,000 bales.

But the author of the scheme has another way of obtaining his capital of twenty millions of dollars: "The planters will deposit their cotton with the company, and take its stock in payment." Will this plan produce better effects?

The company will not expect subscriptions to its stock, payable in cotton at prices lower than 11 cents; at which rate this plan will place in the company's warehouses nearly the same number of 454,000 bales; after which, as before stated, all capacity for further action ceases; and still no rise in the price of the remainder of the crop will result.

To enable it to raise the price of cotton, the capital of the company should be *forty*, instead of twenty millions of dollars. Such a sum invested, at 11 cents per pound, would place in its warehouses 900,000 bales of cotton; and leave in the market barely a sufficiency to supply the demand. Under such circumstances, prices would certainly advance. But what would be the inducement to such a subscription of stock? *Cui bono?* The advance in prices would benefit only those who were not stockholders; while their 900,000 bales must remain in the warehouses of the company until short crops or increased consumption should cause the *demand* to exceed the *supply*. Where will the author of the scheme find such public-spirited and self-sacrificing stockholders?

This review of the scheme was, however, unnecessary, inasmuch as failure and bankruptcy has been the result of every such attempt at monopoly; and "vanity of vanities" would be the sentence pronounced upon it by every commercial man.

If, as is proposed, another Cotton Planters' Convention be held in April next, at Montgomery, Alabama, it is to be hoped that better judgment will prevail, and some plain and practicable scheme be adopted. G.

COTTON PLANTERS' CONVENTION —THE TRUE REMEDY.—*March*, 1852.—I do not expect to attend the Convention of Cotton Planters, proposed to be held in May next, in Montgomery; and will take the liberty of submitting to you, and, if you think proper, to your readers, the plan which I proposed at the late Macon Convention. It was there submitted in the shape of a few resolutions, which found favor with the committee of twenty-one, who twice recommended their adoption. On the last day, however, when not a fifth of the members were present, the report of the committee was set aside, and the "Florida Scheme," as published in your November number, was adopted as a substitute.

Strange to say, the Macon correspondent of the New-York Courier and Inquirer represented me as the zealous advocate of the substitute. I promptly denied the slander, in a letter addressed to the editor, and received an apology for the mistake, with the offer to publish my plan, if I would forward it. I did so; but as yet have seen no publication of either my denial or the plan.

It would be well if every scheme which may be brought before the Convention should previously be submitted to the view of the planting interest, so as to be maturely considered and well understood. My experience as a member of two such conventions, convinces me of the policy of such a course.

The evils complained of by the cotton planters are, that the prices of their staple productions are *irregular*, and too often not *remunerative*. The first-named evil has at times been disastrously felt by others than growers of cotton; and if a remedy can be devised, the good will not be confined to the cotton planter.

These fluctuations sometimes cause a difference of from *thirty* to *sixty millions of dollars* in the sales of two crops: a difference productive not only of loss to the planter, but which sometimes tells with disastrous effect upon foreign exchanges and banking institutions. These fluctuations are always in the inverse ratio of the production. Thus, while a crop of only 2,200,000 bales of cotton will yield to the producers *one hundred and ten millions of dollars*, a crop of 2,800,000 bales will pay only *sixty millions*; and the bounty of Heaven, in the gift of good seasons, proves more destructive to the planter than seasons of drought, flood, storms and frosts. This loss of fifty millions of dollars falls with its full weight upon the planter, but is also felt by all engaged in, or dependent upon, commerce; and they are equally interested in the discovery of a remedy; yet it is chiefly by such that Cotton Planters' Conventions are jeered at and ridiculed. True it is, that no good resulted from the action of the Convention held in Macon, in the year 1839, and that as little can be expected from that lately held in the same city; but it does not follow that an efficient remedy cannot be found: at any rate, the importance of the object will justify renewed efforts.

The *dogma* "that prices must and will be regulated by the relations of *supply* and *demand*," is by many deemed conclusive refutation of all hope of success. But the question to be solved is, "whether the *supply* cannot be so regulated as to secure *regular* and *remunerating prices?*" If it can, the remedy is found.

If the cotton crop of the United States belonged to one man, the remedy would be obvious. Naming his price, he would sell only so much as is required for consumption, and leave the residue under his cotton shed, to supply deficiency in the crop of next year; and if the surplus was large, he would plant less next year. Such a course would be efficient for the object; and the only obstacle to similar action by the cotton planters generally, is the difficulty of procuring concert of action. The difficulty is great, but I think not insuperable.

Besides the loss attendant upon a large crop, the planter is often subjected to loss upon a small one, because of his ignorance of the extent of the crop of the country. Cotton is the agricultural staple of some eight or ten states, covering a vast extent of country. Seasons are often favorable in some districts, and unfavorable in others. Dealers in cotton take measures to inform themselves, with sufficient accuracy, of the extent of the crop, and are prepared to go into the market with knowledge of its value. It is their interest, too, to exaggerate its extent, and this is annually done by publication of what purports to be extracts of letters written in cotton states, but really fabricated for the purpose. The planter, ignorant of its real amount, and influenced by such statements, disposes of his crop at low prices, before the falsehood is discovered.

For *low prices*, a remedy would be found, in an agreement to plant less cotton; but that would nor prevent *irregularity* in price, because good and bad seasons would still cause irregular production; and although *remunerative*, prices would be *irregular*. A bad season might also so reduce the supply, as to throw out of employment a large portion of capital, and of operatives, now engaged in its manufacture. Such a state of things would be deplorable, and in the end injurious to the grower. His interests, and those of the manufacturer, are best subserved by regular and reasonable prices.

The first thing to be done by the Convention, should be the adoption of a plan for ascertaining the extent of each year's crop. This is essential to all judicious and efficient action. I propose to effect it by the agency of Planters' Societies, to be organized in every county in the cotton states. By districting the counties, and distributing the labor among the members, the crop of each county can be ascertained by the middle of January every year. The county societies should immediately thereafter report the amount of the crop to a committee, or some officer, residing at the seat of the state government, who should report the aggregate crop of the state to a central committee, to be appointed by the Cotton Planters' Convention; upon which central committee should also devolve the labor of obtaining all attainable information respecting the probable demand by manufacturers at home and abroad—the supplies which may be expected from other countries—and, generally, all the information in its power, connected with the production and consumption of cotton.

The information referred to, and the reports from the state committees, may be in the possession of the central committee by the 1st of April in each year, and should be published; and the planters advised what proportion of the respective crops should be sold, and what retained.

But inasmuch as a considerable portion of the crop is annually sold before the report of the central committee could be made, I propose an agreement among the planters, "not to sell more than two-thirds of their respective crops before receipt of said report, and *not to sell any for a price less than agreed upon*." And further, "not to sell more of the reserved one-third than shall be advised by the central committee." For illustration of my meaning: Supposing the crop to be 2,700,000 bales; the sale of two-hirds would amount to 1,800,000—leaving 900,000 bales on hand. If advised that the consumption of American cotton would be only 2,200,000 bales, each planter should then sell only *four* out of every nine bales which had been reserved, and retain the remaining five bales under his cotton shed, to await future demand, or supply deficiencies in future crops.

Experience has shown that a crop of 2,700,000 bales, thrown upon the market, will reduce the price of cotton to about five cents; whereas, a crop of only 2,200,000 bales will raise it to thirteen cents, or more. These are extreme prices; the first not remunerative to the planter, the last tending too much to stimulate production elsewhere. The interests of all parties, producers, manufacturers and consumers, will be best served by moderate and regular prices—say about ten cents per pound. At that price, two-thirds of his crop will put more money into the planter's pocket than would the whole crop, sold at six cents.

I have said that the difficulty of obtaining concert of action among planters, so widely separated from each other, is great; but my confidence in its practicability is based upon their obvious interest and their good common sense. Although less expert at figures than the speculators in the staple, the least informed among them can see that *ten bales* of cotton, sold at ten cents, will yield more money than *fifteen bales*, sold at six cents. And, aided by past experience of the evils resulting from want of organization, it demands no extraordinary faith in their good sense, to believe that concert may be obtained.

The only objection ever made to this plan, is, "that the planters will not act in good faith, but will secretly sell more than their proportion of their crops." Now, without claiming for cotton planters a higher character for honor and integrity, I may say, that they possess as much of those qualities as any other class of our population. And although some may, and will, act basely, the number will be small, and their unfaithfulness will but little affect the result. I may say the same of another small class, found in every community—Solomons in their own conceit, who make it a point of honor never to think or act like their neighbors; and who will, perhaps, refuse to enter into the agreement. But if the plan suggested be tried, breaches of faith will be fewer and fewer every year; and where a sense of honor will not restrain, fear of exposure and shame will. Without some general concert of action, *no plan can succeed*: and that now proposed presents as few objections as any other. It proposes no advance of money—no risk of loss—and no change in the pursuits of the planter. If adopted, it must do good. It can do no harm. You have, in the preceding, my plan for regulating the price of cotton.

There is another subject connected with the cotton interest which I have much at heart; and which, in the shape of a resolution, I submitted to the Convention. I know not whether it was adopted, having left the meeting upon discovery of the determination of the small number present to force the question upon the adoption of the substitute. My resolution recommended the erection of cotton manufactories in every county in the cotton states—these factories to commence with *spinning;* and afterwards connecting the business of weaving the cloth.

Spinning requires little skill in the operatives; and *yarns* sell for double the price of the raw material. The facility of obtaining yarn from neighboring factories would enable our planters to clothe their families and servants better and cheaper than now. There are, upon every plantation, servants who, at times, would be inefficient in the field, while perfectly able to work the loom. This, however, is the least of the benefits which would result from the system of manufacturing. Millions of pounds of cotton yarn are annually exported from Great Britain to the continent of Europe, and to other portions of the world; and the business of *spinning* is said to be more profitable than that of *weaving*. Our southern factories would obtain the raw material at, at least, twenty per cent. cheaper than those of England, and southern yarn and cloth would monopolize both the foreign and the home market. Let each county commence with a factory of one thousand spindles; and let the planters agree to invest, annually, ten per cent. of their crops in the extension of such factories; and in a few years they would manufacture the whole crop of the country, and export it, in the shape of yarn and cloth. Such a course would double the value of our exports, and would add to the prosperity of the country more than the gold mines of California, twice told. Its effect upon the banking institutions and commercial interests of the country cannot be sufficiently estimated. But for the gold of California, these interests would, ere now, have been prostrate, and the country experiencing a recurrence of the scenes of the year 1837. The mines of California may cease to be productive, but not so the proceeds of the cotton fields.

The manufacture of the cotton crop would employ as many operatives as are engaged in its production; and the food and sustenance of this body of operatives would enable our planters so to diversify their agricultural operations, as to transfer one-half of their labor from cotton to the production of breadstuffs.

But this scheme of manufacturing the cotton crop has another aspect, which commends itself to the favor of the patriot, philanthropist and Christian. In the cotton states there is a numerous white population scattered over the pine barrens, and subsisting by hunting and raising stock. From their dispersed condition they cannot have either schools or churches; and their children must grow up without religion, and ignorant of even the alphabet What greater curse can be inflicted upon a republic, than an ignorant and irreligious population? Such, however, must be the fate of large portions of the southern states, unless a remedy can be found. That remedy will be furnished by the erection of cotton factories, around which will be collected our pineywood population; and schools and churches will be supplied.—*J. G. Gamble.*

COTTON TRADE OF THE SOUTH—PRICES—STOCK—SUPPLY—DEMAND—FOREIGN COMPETITION—CONSUMPTION—HOME AND FOREIGN STATISTICS, ETC.—1852.—From year to year, almost without exception, the reports of a short crop are circulated everywhere on this side of the Atlantic; and on the other side, with the same regularity, are heard the tales of ruinous prices of goods, and of bankrupt brokers and manufacturers. These rumors are not, however, peculiar to the dealers in cotton. They are common to all the pursuits of business where the supply and demand are irregular and uncertain. The bulls and bears in Wall street are engaged in the same efforts as the cotton sellers of New-Orleans and the buyers of Manchester. The trade in flour, tobacco, and coffee, as well as wines, spices, and fruits, is subject to the same false reports. They are found everywhere; they are unavoidable, and they cannot be prevented.

These reports sometimes imply fraud and falsehood—but often this is not the case. In a country like ours, where cotton is cultivated in every variety of soil and climate, the drought which is so disastrous to one is often a blessing to another. The frost, the worm, the rust, and the floods, are seldom universal. Partial showers may relieve the general absence of rain. The wet bottoms do not require the same seasons as the thirsty uplands. The early crops do not demand the same supply of rain and sunshine as the late plantings. While thus from numerous localities the rumors of ruin and destruction may be true, they may not be general or universal. Those who meet with calamities make the loudest noise, for it affects them deeply. Those who do not suffer say but little, for they obtain only their wishes or expectations, and there is nothing in this to call particular attention to their condition. The losses affect not only the planter, but the factor, the merchant, and others, and thus many join in the cry of disasters. The good fortune of others has no one to herald it, because few have any particular interest in the result.

But though these false reports may always be expected, and do not of themselves imply fraud and deception, they do nothing but harm to all concerned. Sometimes they appear to help the planter, but this is fully balanced at another time by a loss equal to his former gain. As the profit and loss are thus sure at last to be fairly balanced, the unnecessary fluctuations in price caused by these false reports are a serious and important injury to both parties. It would be a great advantage to all, if greater steadiness could be given to prices. When the planter makes his purchases and expenditures, expecting to receive fifteen cents for his cotton, and sells at last for nine, the loss and inconvenience are greater than the gain and gratification that attend an advance from nine to fifteen. So it is with the manufacturer. If he contracts to deliver his cloth or his yarn, when cotton is low, a rise in the raw material forces him to ruinous sacrifices, perhaps to pay extraordinary interest to the money lender, or close his business in bankruptcy. Goods will not rise immediately with an advance in cotton. They fall sooner with a decline than they rise with an advance. The loss is thus more than the gain. As greater regularity and uniformity would be promoted by correct and accurate knowledge of the crops and markets, the truth, the whole truth, and nothing but the truth, would be of advantage to all.

It is a common opinion among the planters and factors of the South, that a short crop not only brings a higher price, but actually produces a larger amount of money than a large or an average crop. It would be strange if this were true. Fine seasons, instead of being the kind gifts of a bountiful Providence, would then be an injury and a curse. The destructive drought and early frosts would be a positive advantage to the agriculturist. The planter would be acting wisely for his own interests if he should destroy a large portion of what he had produced. These seem like strange propositions, and at first sight, are very improbable. Let us examine them by the history of prices for twenty-five years past.

The receipts for our cotton are constantly changing; they rise and fall like a wave of the sea. At times they go up for several years, and then decline suddenly. At other times the rise is rapid, and the fall gradual. In twenty-five years the value of our cotton exports, according to the official reports of the Secretary of the Treasury, has six times reached the highest point, and five times the lowest. Of these six years of large receipts, three of them were large crops, two an average, and one small. Of the five years of small receipts, four of them were small crops, and one an average. In these eleven years, the rule therefore was true but once.

Perhaps, however, the rule deserves a fuller examination. We have supposed above that the crop and its proceeds were large when they exceeded the amounts of the year before and the year after, and small when they were less than both. It would be fairer, perhaps, to take the average of every five years, both of the crop and of the money it was sold for, and to call that an average crop which was near—say within 5 per cent of this average. Thus, for the year 1847 the number of bales delivered at the seaports was 1,779 000; the average of 1845, '46, '47, '48, and '49 was 2,270,000 bales, so that the receipts were less than the average of 471,000 bales, or 21 per cent. below. This would, therefore, be regarded as a very short crop, because more than 5 per cent. from the average. So with the amounts for which the cotton was sold. In 1848 the value of our cotton exports was $62.000 000. For 1846, '47, '48, '49, and '50, the average of the values was $57,300,000. The real receipts were, therefore, large, being $4,700,000, or 8 per cent. above the average of the five years of which 1848 was the middle one.

If, now, we compare the rule with the facts of the last twenty-five years, the crops were large, according to this definition, in 1827, '30, '31, 40, '43, 45, '48, and '49, and short in 1828, '32, '37, '41, '42, '47, and '50. Of these fifteen years no short crop brought a large value, and only one large one—that of 1831—brought a small value. If we had taken the exports in pounds instead of the crops in bales, there would not have been a single year that the rule would have been found true; so that the only case where the rule appears to hold, in the twenty-five years, occurred when a large crop brought a small price, because a great deal of it was retained at home and unsold. In table I., at the end of this article, may be seen all the crops, values, and exports for the twenty-five years, with the average for each, and every one may examine the facts for himself. In 1827 the exports were 5 per cent. above the average, and the money received for them 32 per cent. above. In 1828 the exports were 15 per cent. below, and the value 17 per cent. below. In 1829 the crop was an average one, and so was the cash received for it. In 1830 both were large, and in 1831 both were small. For the six years, from 1832 to 1837, the exports were about an average, but the values were sometimes large and sometimes small. In 1838 and 1839 the amount exported was first large and then small, and both years brought average values. In 1840 it was large, and the money was large. In 1841 and 1842 we had two very short crops succeeding each other, yet the sales of the second year were 12 per cent. lower than the average. In 1843 the exports were large, and the proceeds were within the average limit. From 1844 to 1851 we have had three large crops—1845, '48, and '49—and each of them brought average values. In the same time we had three short crops—1846, '47, and '50; the first brought a small return—the other two were about the average. And thus, for every year in the whole twenty-five, the rule entirely fails, and cannot therefore be regarded as true.

No doubt it sometimes happens that a small crop brings more money than a large one Thus, in 1847, 1,779,000 bales brought more money than 2,395,000 bales in 1845. But neither year brought large returns—both were an average. The large crop of 1848 brought more money than either; and the very large one of 1849, although it succeeded a large crop, brought still more. The small exports of 1850 were sold for a large amount, but the money received will not exceed the average sales of 1849, 1850, and 1851.

If it be, then, true that short crops are an injury to the planter on account of the diminished amount of money he receives for them, there are other reasons which render the calamity still greater. They stimulate prices to such a high limit that they encourage the production of cotton in India and other places, and thus endanger the monopoly which we now possess in the European market. They discourage the use of cotton in the place of hemp, flax, wool, and silk, and thus put down still further the price of the raw material when favorable seasons have enlarged the supplies. They raise the price of many articles that planters are compelled to buy, and thus lessen the net amount of his income. They increase the price of all kinds of property, so that the gains of the planter with high prices, when invested in anything but money, seldom obtain a larger amount than with low or inordinate prices. They disturb the regular operation of business, tempt the producer to increase his expenditures, to contract debts, to purchase land and negroes on credit, and when the decline comes, as it is sure to do, he is forced to pay for property purchased at high prices, with the sales of his crop at low prices. They lead to the neglect of other products, so that hay is carried from Massachusetts, flour from New-York, corn from Baltimore, bacon from Cincinnati, not only to the seaports of the South, but far into the interior; and when cotton falls, the planter cannot begin at once to supply all his own wants, because he is out of stock from which to raise his hogs, horses, or mules, and some time must elapse before he can obtain them.

These, and many other evils that might be mentioned, show that the interest of the producer is not diverse and opposite to that of the consumer—that the blast and mildew, the drought and the flood, the caterpillar and the boll-worm, which reduce the supply and raise the price to the manufacturer, are also an injury to the planter—that favorable seasons—a proper succession of rain and sunshine, are twice-told blessings, both to him that buys, and to him that sells.

While thus short crops are sources of serious evils to the planter, over-production and ruinously low prices are a still greater injury. How can these be prevented? Not by the combination of half a million of planters scattered over a wide extent of country; not by state conventions and paper resolutions; not by monster schemes of monopoly and governmental interference; not by banks or corporations, or factors or brokers forestalling the markets of New-Orleans, New-York, and Liverpool; not by false rumors—by retaining the crop of the country till the season is far advanced—by publishing in the newspapers every disaster from frost or flood, and withholding the reports of abundance and plenty. These plans are all either useless or injurious. Free trade, unshackled industry, is the motto of the South, not only in commerce and manufactures, but in agriculture. Capital is best employed when let alone. The keen-sightedness of self-interest will discern the proper remedy for over-production, and no one need be concerned lest trade should not regulate itself better than he would do it, if he had full power to manage and control it. God is wiser than man, and the laws he has imposed require no aid from us to adjust and adapt them to the circumstances around us. The proper course for the planter, and the one he is sure to pursue, is to make as much cotton as he can, while the price is fair and remunerative. As soon as it falls below this, he should apply both his capital and labor to other pursuits. By the home manufacture of cotton, wool, paper, iron, and machinery; by producing at the South his flour, corn, bacon, mules, and horses; by the increased planting of the sugar-cane and tobacco; by the introduction of new agricultural products; by devoting his capital to the construction of railways and plank-roads; by building ships and steamers to carry on our own trade with the north and with Europe; by importing directly from abroad our foreign supplies, and by sending our cotton directly to European ports, without the transhipment at New-York; by these, and many other means, his capital and labor can be diversified and rendered profitable, when the price of cotton will no longer bring fair returns. It is the duty of the intelligent and public-spirited men of the South not to attempt to reverse the laws of trade by forcing up the prices to some arbitrary level at which the planter can afford to produce cotton, but to seek out new modes of profitable investment; to undertake new schemes, not yet tried and proved, which promise fair profits to capital; to encourage by words and actions, by legislative enactments, by public and private commendation, every new enterprise calculated to diversify our labor, develop our resources, and divert capital and labor from our great staple.

The prospects of the planter for the present year are by no means gloomy. Though not so bright as last season, they are still cheering and encouraging. Prices have fallen below their average rate ; but with our present moderate crop, with low stocks in Europe and America, with food cheap, money abundant, and labor well employed, a low range cannot be maintaieed. From 1840 to 1851 there have been exported 7,763,000,000 lbs. of cotton, (Table I.,) and the value of this has been $617,300,000. If to these we add, as an estimate for the past year, an export of 800,000,000 lbs., at a value of $88,000,000, we shall have, $8,563,000,000, and $705,000,000, which gives an average of about 8¼ cents a pound.

The price in Charleston for good middling is quoted, October 23d, at 7¾ to 7⅞ ; but so low a rate cannot be maintained—with the present prospect of the supply and the demand.

In South Carolina and Georgia the severe and long-continued drought has cut short the crop very considerably. The rich bottom lands have not indeed suffered. On many plantations partial showers have relieved the general want of rain. The planting has been large ; a great many new hands have been employed on the crop ; but these favorable circumstances will not make up for the damage by the drought in June and July, by the severe storm on the 24th of August, and by the frost on the 23d of October. The receipts, however, at Charleston and Savannah, will not be much diminished, as the deficiency will be made up in part by the extension of the Georgia railroads farther toward the gulf. The decline will not be, probably, far from 10 per cent.

From Florida a slight falling off may be expected. The promise of the crop was very good up to the time of the storm ; but the injury caused by it was very serious. The early frost was also injurious ; but these causes will both be balanced by the increased planting. A slight decline is anticipated in the receipts, because of the diversion of 10,000 or 15,000 bales to Macon and Savannah, by the opening of the South-Western Rail-road.

From Alabama the promise is much better than last year. The drought was not so severe as in Georgia, and the falling off of the forms, when the late rains set in, was not so extensive. They had no worm, no floods, no rust. Last year was disastrous ; and if the new crop may be compared with that, an increase of 10 per cent. may be looked for.

At New-Orleans the receipts will increase very largely. Already 70,000 bales more have been received there than at the same dates last season. From every part of the immense region that sends its productions to that port, the promise of the crop is much better than last year. In Louisiana and Mississippi the worm has done no damage. On Red River they have escaped the floods which did so much harm in 1849 and in 1850. The early frost in Tennessee, near the close of September, did not do as much harm as the frost on the 6th of October last season. The slight drought, which pervaded the entire region, is the only drawback to a large and full crop. The receipts at New-Orleans, instead of ranging near those of the last two years, will probably come up as high as those of 1848 and 1849. The average of these two years may be taken as the probable receipts of 1852. From Texas an increase may also be expected. If we combine these results, (Table II,) the whole crop for 1852 may be estimated at 2,550,000 bales.

The imports from the East Indies will be much less than for the last two years. These are so much affected by the price at Liverpool, that we may be sure a decline in the shipments will follow a decline in the prices. The actual production in India is very large, compared with the exports ; and when the price in England will pay the inland transportation to the seaport and the long voyage round the Cape, a large amount is easily spared for export. The high prices in 1850 raised the English imports from the East Indies up to 308,000 bales, against 182,000 in 1849, and 228,000 in 1848. The present year of high prices witnesses the same increase. The Liverpool receipts on the 3d of October were 164,000 bales against 128,000 bales at the same time in 1850. For the whole year they will reach 350,000 bales for the United Kingdom. For 1852 the decline will be large, but the imports will not probably fall back at once to the figures before 1850. They may be safely estimated at 250,000 bales. (Table III.)

The receipts from Brazil, Egypt, and other places, are small, and nearly stationary. For the last eleven years, the lowest rates were 135,000 bales in 1847, and the highest, 257,000 bales in 1850. The imports into Liverpool have declined from 205,000 bales in 1850, to 138,000 bales in 1851. The average for Great Britain for the last five years, from 1847 to 1851, has been 192,000 bales ; and this may be regarded as the probable amount for 1852. (Table IV.)

If the estimated receipts from all these sources be combined, the result for 1852 will be a probable supply of 3,000,000 bales. (Table V.)

The consumption of cotton during the present year has been seriously affected by the high prices. The American manufacturers have closed their mills to a very large extent. The same check has been felt in France. On the rest of the continent the consumption has not receded. In England, the high prices in the early part of the season reduced the purchases of the manufacturers, but since the decline in prices these deliveries have outrun those of last year, and approached those of 1849. (Table VI.) In fact, as there was an error in the estimated consumption of 1849 of fifty or sixty thousand bales, and as the reported deliveries have been, this year, checked by quarterly examinations of the stocks, the demand for the present year has already equaled the very large demand of 1849. For the whole year, the consumption of Great Britain will probably reach 1,600,000 bales, against 1,515,000 in 1850, 1,590,000 in 1849, and 1,464,000 in 1848. Every element of business favors a still larger demand for 1852. Peace everywhere prevails, the harvest has been gathered from South to North, under favorable auspices. The price of wheat is very low—12 or 15 per cent. lower than last year. Money is abundant; the currency is undisturbed; capital is profitably employed; labor is well rewarded; the export trade, as well as the home market, is in a healthy condition; the manufacturers are not overstocked with goods; the price of cotton will be moderate—25 or 30 per cent. lower than last year. Under these circumstances, the English demand for 1852 must exceed that of any former year. It will probably reach 1,650,000 bales—it may be 1,700,000.

From France, the prospect is not so promising. Political troubles of a serious character will probably accompany the elections for the next president. If the constitution shall be revised, and a Constituent Assembly called for that purpose, the appeal to first principles, and the entire overturning of all that is now established, will endanger the public peace. If the constitution shall not be revised, the re-election of Louis Napoleon will be a signal for revolution, because it will be done in violation of the law, and of his oath to support the constitution. If some new man is elected, uncertainty and distrust will attend all the operations of business, until his government shall attain stability, and secure the public confidence. We may not, therefore, expect a large consumption for 1852, although the prices of cotton will be moderate. For 1851, the French consumption of American cotton will not vary much from 300,000. We have exported 301,000 bales from the 1st of September, 1850, to the 1st of September, 1851, and the stocks in Havre, of American cotton, on the 1st of October, were 26,505 bales against 32,274 in 1850—indicating a probable consumption of 307,000 bales. This was a little higher than last year, but much less than for 1849. Our exports to France in 1850, were 289,000 bales; and a decrease of stocks to the amount of 11,000 bales, showed a consumption of 300,000. In 1849, it was 351,000. In 1852, the distrust, on account of political troubles, will probably neutralize the stimulating influence of low or moderate prices, so that we may estimate the probable wants of France at 300.000 bales.

On the continent, the high prices of the last two years have prevented any increase of the consumption, but they have not reduced it below the average of former years. The exports for 1851, from America and England, will not differ much from 550,000 bales. [Table VII.]

This exceeds every former year except 1849, when the crop was very large and prices very low. For 1852, we may confidently expect an increase, unless political troubles started in France, should excite disturbances and revolutions in the neighboring states on the continent.

In our own country, the large decline in the consumption for 1851, is the most remarkable and singular event in the history of our manufactures. Hitherto, from year to year, almost without exception, our progress has been uniformly onward. High prices of the raw material seem never to have affected us. But for the past year, our consumption is 83,090 bales below 1850, and 114,000 below 1849. It is lower than in any year since 1845.

If this were attributed to the high prices of last year, it might be hoped that the decline we have now experienced would again start our mills, and revive the demand of our home manufacturers. But it is much to be feared that this is not the case, and that the diminished consumption is due, in fact, to other causes. Among these, the tariff of 1846 holds a conspicuous place. The first year after the tariff went into operation, the high price of food in every part of Europe, not only discouraged the foreign manufacturer from entering into competition with us, but, by creating a demand for our breadstuffs abroad, increased our ability to consume all kinds of goods. This home market stimulated the American manufacturer, and the following year our domestic consumption rose from 428,000 to 532,000 bales.

In 1849, the production of foreign looms began to exclude our home-made goods from the market, and the consumption fell off 14,000 bales. The high prices of 1850, gave an increased advantage to the English factories, and the northern manufacturers bought 31,000 bales less than in 1849. The same causes operating for a still longer period in 1851, the American consumption declined still farther, till it had reached the low figure of 404,000 bales.

Another cause that has produced a decided effect, is the increase of manufactories in the South and West. These have not only supplied the Southern and Western demand for yarn and the coarser cloths, but have shipped large and increasing amounts of yarn to the New-York and Philadelphia markets. The high prices of the last year have not, to any considerable extent, checked this consumption. The estimate in the *New-York Shipping List*, of a decline from 110,000 bales to 75,000, appears to be entirely too large. Instead of a decline in Georgia from 20,500 bales to 13,000, there has been probably an increase, on account of the starting of new factories. So also in South Carolina and Alabama. The products of the southern and western mills being consumed principally at home, where general prosperity has not checked the demand, the sales of goods have not been materially reduced. The shipments to the North have been almost as brisk as ever. The coarse yarns can be made as cheap at the South as at the North, and the cost of transportation gives the South the advantage.

These two reasons will help to explain the check given to northern consumption. The low or moderate prices of the coming year will probably set to work more or less of these mills, because when the raw material is low, the advantage of the American manufacturer over the English, in the cost of transportation, is much increased. The demand at the North will not, however, reach the amount of 1850 or 1849, but it will probably exceed that of 1851 by 40,000 or 50,000 bales. (Table VIII.)

If these estimates for the consumption of 1852 be combined, the result will be a demand for 3,000.000 bales. (Table IX.) As this is equal to the probable supply, (Table V.,) the question of price will be much affected by the stocks. These are now lower than they have been for the two preceding years. (Table X.) although the last crop of the United States, and the receipts from India, have very much increased over the amounts of 1850.

It would seem, therefore, very improbable that prices can be kept down below their average. In the first half of the last year, from September, 1850, to February, 1851, the price of good middling in New-Orleans, ranged from 13 to 13½c. From March to August it has regularly declined, being quoted successively, on the 1st of each month, 10¾, 11¼, 10½, 9½, 9½ and 8¼ c., and now (October 29th) it is still lower, being quoted at Charleston, October 23d. at 7¾ to 7⅞ c. The probable supply is not above the probable wants of the world, and with low stocks the present low range of prices cannot be maintained. The crop is large, and can only be consumed at an average moderate price, and this much may be with confidence be anticipated.—*Prof. McCay in Merchant's Mag.*

TABLE I.

UNITED STATES CROP—VALUE AND AMOUNT OF UNITED STATES EXPORTS.

Year	U. States Crop	Average	Large or Small	Value of Exports	Average	Exports in lbs.	Average
1827	757,000	713,000	Large	$29,400,000	$28,000,000	294,000,000	223,000,000
1828	721,000	807,000	Small	22,500,000	26,600,000	211,000,000	255,000,000
1829	858,000	871,000	Average	26,600,000	26,700,000	265,000,000	269,000,000
1830	979,000	917,000	Large	29,700,000	27,200,000	298,000,000	275,000,000
1831	1,039,000	987,000	Large	25,300,000	29,900,000	277,000,000	297,000,000
1832	987,000	1,056,000	Small.	31,700,000	34,500,000	322,000,000	321,000,000
1833	1,070,000	1,111,000	Average	36,200,000	41,600,000	325,000,000	339,000,000
1834	1,205,000	1,175,000	Average	49,500,000	50,800,000	385,000,000	369,000,000
1835	1,254,000	1,262,000	Average	65,000,000	57,000,000	387,000,000	393,000,000
1836	1,361,000	1,409,000	Average	71,300,000	62,100,000	424,000,000	447,000,000
1837	1,423,000	1,540,000	Small	63,200,000	64,400,000	444,000,000	453,000,000
1838	1,801,000	1,725,000	Average	61,600,000	64,200,000	596.000,000	524,000,000
1839	1,861,000	1,780,000	Average	61,200,000	60,800,000	414,000,000	546,000,000
1840	2,178,000	1,832,000	Large	63,900,000	57,700,000	744,000,000	574,000,000
1841	1,635,000	1,947,000	Small.	54,300,000	55,200,000	530,000,000	618,000,000
1842	1,683,000	1,981,000	Small.	47,600,000	53,800,000	585,000,000	668,000,000
1843	2,379,000	2,024,000	Large	49,100,000	51,400,000	817,000,000	694,000,000
1844	2,030,000	2,117,000	Average	54,100,000	49,100,000	664,000,000	697,000,000
1845	2,395,000	2,136,000	Large	51,700,000	50,200,000	873,000,000	686,000,000
1846	2,100,000	2,130,000	Average	42,800,000	52,800,000	548,000,000	685,000,000
1847	1,779,000	2,270,000	Small	53,400,000	55,300,000	527,000,000	757,000,000
1848	2,348,000	2,211,000	Large	62,000,000	59,300,000	814,000,000	709,000,000
1849	2,729,000	2,258,000	Large	66,400,000	66,800,000	1,026,000,000	825,000,000
1850	2,098,000	3,394,000	Small	72,000,000	—	635,000,000	—
1851	2,355,000	2,355,000	Average	—	—	—	—

TABLE II.

CROP OF THE UNITED STATES.

	Receipts.				*Estimate.*
	1848.	1849.	1850.	1851.	1852.
Texas.........bales	40,000	39,000	31,000	46,000	50,000
New-Orleans	1,191,000	1,094,000	782,000	933,000	1,150,000
Mobile	436,000	519,000	351,000	452,000	500,000
Florida	154,000	200,000	181,000	181,000	170,000
Georgia	255,000	391,000	344,000	322,000	300,000
South Carolina	262,000	458,000	384,000	387,000	350,000
Other places	10,000	28,000	24,000	34,000	30,000
Total	**2,348,000**	**2,729,000**	**2,097,000**	**2,355,000**	**2,550,000**

TABLE III.

ENGLISH IMPORTS FROM THE EAST INDIES.

	Bales	Remarks
1830 to 1843, average	81,000	Low prices.
1835 to 1839 “	144,000	High prices.
1840 to 1844, “	232,000	Chinese war.
1844 to 1849, “	177,000	Peace, and low prices
1848, October 6, Liverpool	93,000	Moderate prices.
1849, “ 5, “	69,000	Low prices.
1850, “ 4, “	128,000	High prices.
1851, “ 3, “	164,000	High prices.
1848, whole year, Great Britain	228,000	Moderate prices.
1849, “ “	182,000	Low prices.
1850, “ “	308,000	High prices.
1851, “ estimate	350,000	High prices.
1852, “ “	250,000	Moderate prices.

TABLE IV.

ENGLISH IMPORTS FROM BRAZIL, EGYPT, ETC.

Years		About the 1st Oct Liverpool	Whole year for Gt. Britain	Years		About the 1st Oct. Liverpool	Whole year for Gt. Britain
1846	bales	121,000	155,000	1849	“	178,000	245,000
1847	“	75,000	135,000	1850	“	205,000	252,000
1848	“	94,000	137,000	1851	“	138,000	190,000

TABLE V.

SUPPLY OF 1850, AND ESTIMATE FOR 1851 AND 1852.

	1850	1851	1852
Crop of the United States .... bales	2,097,000	2,355,000	2,550,000
English imports from East Indies	308,000	350,000	250,000
English receipts from other places	252,000	195,000	200,000
Total from these sources	2,657,000	2,900,000	3,000,000

TABLE VI.

DELIVERIES TO THE TRADE AT LIVERPOOL.

	1849	1850	Consumption each week	1850	Consumption each week
May 9 .... bales	562,000	501,000	27,833	453,000	25,165
June 5	688,000	637,000	28,045	619,000	28,137
July 3	835,000	742,000	28,538	644,000	28,616
August 1	993,000	883,000	29,433	887,000	29,568
September 5	1,141,000	981,000	28,028	1,058,000	30,223
October 3	1,220,000	1,086,001	27,850	1,167,000	29,927
October 10	1,287,000	1,116,000	27,900	..	..
Whole year	1,467,000	1,407,000	27,052	1,500,000	29,000

TABLE VII.

CONSUMPTION ON THE CONTINENT—NOT INCLUDING FRANCE—OF COTTON RECEIVED FROM AMERICA.

	Exports from U. States	Exports from Great Britain	Increase of stock	Decrease of stock	Consumption
1846	205,000	194,000	—	53,000	452,000
1847	169,000	215,000	43,000	—	341,000
1848	255,000	194,000	—	29,000	576,000
1849	322,000	254,000	—	20,000	596,000
1850	194,000	272,000	—	—	466,000
1851	265,000	285,000	—	—	550,000
1846 to 1848, average	210,000	200,000	—	—	423,000
1849 to 1851 ... “	260,000	270,000	—	—	537,000

TABLE VIII.

AMERICAN CONSUMPTION.

	North of Richmond	Average for three years	Increase per cent	South of Richmond	Total
1844 ...... bales	347,000	313,000	17 Increase	60,000	407,000
1845	389,000	347,000	11 “	65,000	454,000
1846	423,000	386,000	11 “	70,000	493,000
1847	428,000	413,000	7 “	80,000	508,000
1848	532,000	461,000	12 “	90,000	623,000
1849	518,000	493,000	7 “	100,000	618,000
1850	487,000	512,000	4 “	110,000	597,000
1851	404,000	470,000	8 Decrease	100,000	504,000

TABLE IX.

CONSUMPTION OF EUROPE AND AMERICA.

	1849.	1850.	1851.	1852.
Great Britain, of all kinds	1,588,000	1,515,000	1,600,000	1,650,000
United States	518,000	487,000	404,000	450,000
France, of American cotton	351,000	301,000	310,000	300,000
The rest of the continent	596,000	466,000	550,000	600,000
Total	3,053,000	2,769,000	2,864,000	3,000,000

TABLE X.

STOCKS AT RECENT DATES.

	1849	1850	1851
Liverpool, October 10	582,000	545,000	549,000
Havre, October 1	45,000	32,000	36,000
United States, September 1	155,000	168,000	128,000
Total	782,000	745,000	712,000

COTTON TABLES—I. (*Prof McKay.*)

SUPPLY OF COTTON—IN THOUSAND BALES.

	U. S. crop brought into sea-ports	U. S. consumption in the South	Total U. S. crop	East India imports into G. Britain	Brazil, &c., imports into G. Britain	Brazil, &c., imports into other places	Total besides U. S.	Total of all kinds
1840	2,178n	50	2,228	216h	146h	111	473c	2,701
1841	1,635n	55	1,690	275a	166a	128	569c	2,259
1842	1,684n	55	1,739	255h	124h	166	545c	2,284
1843	2,379n	60	2,439	182h	165h	176	523c	2,962
1844	2,030n	60	2,090	234a	197h	80	511c	2,601
1845	2,395n	65	2,460	155h	201h	105	461c	2,921
1846	2,101n	70	2,171	95b	155a	69	319c	2,490
1847	1,779n	80	1,859	224a	135a	122	481c	2,340
1848	2,348n	90	2,438	228h	137h	36	401c	2,839
1849	2,729n	100	2,829	182h	245h	111	538c	3,367
Ave. from 1825 to 1830	838n	10	848	73h	211h	99	383	1,231
" 1830 to 1835	1,055n	20	1,075	81h	186h	108	375	1,450
" 1835 to 1840	1,440n	35	1,475	144h	196h	104	444	1,919
" 1840 to 1845	1,981n	56	2,037	232a	160a	132	524c	2,561
" 1845 to 1850	2,270n	81	2,351	177a	175a	88	440c	2,791
Inc. p. ct. in 20 years	171		177	142	17		15	117
" 15 years	115		119	118	8		17	92
" 10 years	58		59	23	11		1	45
" 5 years	15		15	24	9		16	

TABLE II.

CONSUMPTION OF UNITED STATES, GREAT BRITAIN, FRANCE, AND OF EUROPE AND AMERICA—IN THOUSAND BALES.

	U. S. north of Richmond	Total for U. S.	Total for G. B.	U. S. cotton in France	Total for France	Total for these three	Total for Europe and America
1840	295n	345	1,171a	374	440a	2,056	2,370
1841	297n	352	1,158a	368	422a	1,932	2,252
1842	268n	323	1,207a	364a	442a	1,972	2,310
1843	325n	385	1,385a	351a	409a	2,179	2,573
1844	247n	407	1,438a	335a	392a	2,237	2,564
1845	389n	454	1,574a	351a	419a	2,447	2,918
1846	423n	493	1,574a	360a	403a	2,470	2,968
1847	428n	508	1,131a	252	293c	1,932	2,296
1848	532n	622	1,491a	376	303c	2,416	2,901
1849	518n	618	1,588a	351	399c	2,605	3,264
Average from 1825 to 1830	117n	127	653h		257	1,037	1,187
" 1830 to 1835	175n	195	876h		269	1,340	1,540
" 1835 to 1840	240n	275	1,069h		349	1,693	1,943
" 1840 to 1845	307n	363	1,292a		421	2,076	2,414
" 1845 to 1850	458n	539	1,472a		363	2,374	2,869
Increase per ct. in 20 years	290	325	125		41	129	142
" " 15 years	161	176	68		35	77	86
" " 10 years	91	96	38		4	40	48
" " 5 years	50	49	14		14	14	19

TABLE III.

CONSUMPTION OF EUROPE AND AMERICA, OMITTING ENGLAND, FRANCE, AND THE UNITED STATES—IN THOUSAND BALES.

	Exports from United States	Exports from Great Britain	Direct imports from Egypt	Stock, January 1	Stock, December 31	Consumption
1840	182m	123a	49	72	112	314
1841	106m	116a	74	112	88	320
1842	132m	138a	88	88	108	338
1843	194m	119a	118	108	145	394
1844	144m	141a	23	145	126	237
1845	285m	122a	37	126	99	471
1846	205m	194a	26	99	26	498
1847	169m	215a	81	26	87	404
1848	255n	192a	9	87	58	485
1849	322n	254a	63	58	38	659
Average from 1840 to 1845						338
" 1845 to 1850						495
Increase per cent. in five years						46

TABLE IV.

STOCKS, 31ST OF DECEMBER—IN THOUSAND BALES.

	Liverpool	Great Britian	Week's consumption in G. Britain	Havre	France	Rest of the Continent	Whole of Europe	Week's cons'ption
1840	366g	464g	18	80d	97d	112	673	17
1841	430g	538g	24	90d	135d	88	761	21
1842	457g	561g	24	109a	138d	108	807	21
1643	654g	786g	29	101a	125d	145	1,056	25
1844	745a	897a	32	53a	78d	126	1,101	26
1845	885g	1,057a	35	52a	65a	99	1,221	26
1846	439g	547a	18	25a	47a	26	620	13
1847	364g	451a	16	43a	53a	87	591	17
1848	393h	498a	17	30a	31a	58	587	13
1849	468h	559a	18	38a	49a	38	646	13

TABLE V.

AMOUNT, VALUE, AND PRICES OF AMERICAN COTTON.

	Exports in millions of pounds	Value in millions of dollars	Price of exports	Whole crop United States	Value of U. S crop	Liverpool prices of Uplands in pence
1840	744r	64r	8·6	891	77	6 h
1841	530r	54r	10·2	684	70	6¼h
1842	577r	48r	8·1	704	58	5⅜h
1843	817r	49r	6·0	988	59	4⅝h
1844	664r	54r	8·1	857	69	4⅞h
1815	873r	52r	6·0	1,009	61	4⅜h
1846	548r	43r	7·9	901	71	4⅞h
1847	527r	53r	10·1	771	78	6¾h
1848	814r	62r	7·6	1,011	77	4¼h
1849	1,027r	66r	6·5	1,174	76	5⅛h
Average from 1825 to 1830	219r	28r	12.8	288	37	7¼h
" 1830 to 1835	312r	34r	10·9	387	42	7¼h
" 1835 to 1840	446r	64r	14·4	560	81	8¼h
" 1840 to 1845	666r	54r	8·1	825	67	5½h
" 1845 to 1850	754r	55r	7·9	079	71	5½h

COTTON CROP OF THE UNITED STATES—STATEMENT AND TOTAL AMOUNT FOR THE YEAR ENDING 31ST AUGUST, 1851.

NEW-ORLEANS.

Export to—	*Bales.*	TOTAL. 1851.	1850.
Foreign ports	844,641		
Coastwise	152,817		
Stock, Sep. 1, 1851.	15,390		
	1,012,848		
Deduct,			
Stock, Sep. 1, 1850.	16,612		
Rec'd from Mobile & Montg'y, Ala.	42,524		
Rec'd from Florida.	11,091		
Rec'd from Texas.	9,252		
	79,479		
		933,369	781,886

ALABAMA.

Export to—	*Bales.*	TOTAL. 1851.	1850.
Foreign ports	321,777		
Coastwise	114,451		
Cons'd in Mobile	685		
Stock, Sep. 1, 1851.	27,797		
	464,710		
Deduct,			
Stock, Sep. 1, 1850.	12,962		
		451,748	350,942

FLORIDA.

Export to—	*Bales.*	TOTAL. 1851.	1850.
Foreign ports	70,547		
Coastwise	111,532		
Stock, Sep. 1, 1851.	273		
	182,352		
Deduct,			
Stock, Sep. 1, 1850.	1,148		
		181,204	181,344

TEXAS.		Total 1851.	1850.
Export to—	*Bales.*		
Foreign ports	2,261,		
Coastwise	43,014		
Stock, Sep. 1, 1851	596		
	45,871		
Deduct,			
Stock, Sep. 1, 1850	51		
		45,820	31,263
GEORGIA.			
Export from Savannah to			
For. ports—Upl	145,150		
S. Islands	8,497		
Coastwise—Upl	160,642		
S. Islands	3,145		
Stock in Savannah, 1st Sep., 1851	4,500		
Stock in Augusta, 1st Sep., 1851	29,511		
	351,445		
Deduct,			
Stock in Savannah and Augusta, 1st Sep., 1850	29,069		
		322,376	343,635
SOUTH CAROLINA.			
Export from Charleston to			
For. ports—Upl	254,442		
S. Islands	13,576		
Coastwise—Upl	138,429		
Sea Islands	2,210		
	408,657		
Export from Georgetown to			
New-York	1,812		
Stck, Charleston, Sep. 1, 1851	10,953		
	12,765		
	421,422		
Deduct,			
Stck, Charleston, Sep. 1, 1850	30,698		
Received from Savannah	3,649		
	34,347		
		387,075	384,265
NORTH CAROLINA.			
Export—			
Coastwise		12,928	11,861
VIRGINIA.			
Coastwise, and manuf. (taken from ports)	20,320		
Stock. Sep. 1, 1851	620		
	20,940		
Deduct,			
Stock, Sep. 1, 1850	1,000		
		19,940	11,500
Rec'd here by the N. Y. and Erie Canal		797	
Total crop of the United States		2,355,257	2,096,706

Increase from last year.....bales..258,551
Decrease from the year before. " 373,339

Crop of	Bales.
1850—1	2,355,257
1849-50	2,096,706
1848—9	2,728,596
1847—8	2,347,634
1846—7	1,778,651
1845—6	2,100,537
1844—5	2,394,503
1843—4	2,030,409
1842—3	2,378,875
1841—2	1,683,574
1840—1	1,634,945
1839-40	2,177,835
1838—9	1,360,532
1837—8	1,801,497
1836—7	1,422,930
1835—6	1,360,725
1834—5	1,254,328
1833—4	1,205,394
1832—3	1,070,438
1831—2	987,477
1830—1	1,038,848
1829-30	976,845
1828—9	857,744
1827—8	720,593
1826—7	957,281
1825—6	720,027
1824—5	569,249
1823—4	509,158

CONSUMPTION.

Total crop of the United States, as before stated		2,355,257
Add—		
Stocks on hand at the commencement of the year, 1st September, 1850—		
In the southern ports	91,754	
In the northern ports	76,176	167,930
Makes a supply of		2,523,187
Deduct therefrom—		
The export to foreign ports	1,988,710	
Less, for'gn included	1,077	1,987,633
St'ks on hand, Sept. 1, 1851—		
In the southern ports	89,044	
In the northern ports	39,260	128,304
Burnt at New-York, Boston and Baltimore	3,142	2,119,079
Taken for home use		404,108

QUANTITY CONSUMED BY AND IN HANDS OF MANUFACTURERS NORTH OF VIRGINIA.

1850—1	404,108
1849-50	487,769
1848—9	518,039
1847—8	531,772
1846—7	427,967
1845—6	422,597

1844—5	389,006
1843—4	346,744
1842—3	325,129
1841—2	267,850
1840—1	297,288
1839-40	395,193
1838—9	276,018
1837—8	246,063
1836—7	222,540
1836—6	236,733
1834—5	216,888
1833—4	196,419
1832—3	194,412
1831—2	173, 800
1830—1	182,142
1829-30	126,512
1828—9	118,853
1827—8	120,593
1826—7	149,513

It will be seen that we have materially *reduced* our estimate of the amount of cotton consumed the past year in the states south and west of Virginia—the capacity of the mills has been very nearly the same as before, but the high prices of the raw material for the greater part of the season, and the low rates obtained for the manufactured articles, have rendered the business unprofitable. The following estimate is from a judicious and careful observer at the South of the quantity so consumed, and not included in the receipts. Thus in—

	Mills	Spindles	Quantity consumed.
North Carolina	30	—	13,000 bales, of 400 lbs.
South Carolina	16	36,500	10,000 " "
Georgia	36	51,400	13,000 " "
Alabama	10	12,580	4,000 " of 500 lbs.
Tennessee	30	36,000	8,000 " "
On the Ohio, &c.	30	100,000	12,000 " "

Total to September 1, 1851	60,000 bales.
" " 1850	107,500 "
" " 1849	110,000 "
" " 1848	75,000 "

To which should be added the stocks in in the interior towns, &c., the quantity burnt in the interior, and that lost on its way to market; these, added to the crop as given above, received at the shipping ports, will show very nearly the amount raised in the United States the past season—say, in round numbers, 2,450,000 bales.

During the year just closed there have been received here, chiefly, it is believed, from Tennessee, 797 bales by way of the New-York and Erie Canal, which we have added in another place to the crop of the country. This route, however, is not a favorite one, and no further supplies of moment are expected.

It may be remarked in this connection, that some of the cotton received overland at Philadelphia and Baltimore is doubtless unaccounted for elsewhere, not being counted in the receipts at New-Orleans; but as we have of late years omitted this item from the crop, in deference to the views of judicious friends, it is not now added, though it may be advisable to introduce it hereafter.

The quantity of new cotton received at the shipping ports up to the 1st inst., amounted to about 3,200 bales, against about 255 bales last year.

The shipments given in this statement from Texas are those by sea only; a considerable portion of the crop of that state finds its way into market via Red River, and is not included in the receipts at New-Orleans.—*N. Y. Shipping List.*

COTTON TRADE OF THE UNITED STATES.—The following table gives the exports of cotton from the United States for a number of years, also the average price per pound:

	Total Pounds	Value	Average price per lb
1821	124,893,405	$20,157,484	16·2
1822	144,675,985	24,025,058	16·6
1823	173,793,270	20,445,000	11·8
1824	142,369,663	21,947,401	15·4
1825	176,449,007	36,846,649	20·9
1826	204,535,415	25,025,214	12·2
1827	294,310,115	29,359,545	10
1828	210,590,463	22,487,229	10·7
1829	264,837,186	26,575,311	10
1830	298,499,102	29,674,883	9·9
1831	376,979,784	25,289,492	9·1
1832	322,215,122	31,724,682	9·8
1833	324,698,604	36,191,105	12·1
1834	384,717,907	49,448,402	12·8
1835	387,358,992	64,861,301	16·8
1836	423,631,367	71,284,925	16·8
1837	444,211,537	63,240,102	14·2
1838	595,952,277	61,556,811	10·3
1839	413,624,212	61,338,982	14·8
1840	743,941,061	63,870,107	8·5
1841	530,204,100	54,330,341	10·2
1842	584,717,017	47,593,464	8·1
1843	792,297,106	49,119,086	6·2
1844	663,633,455	54,063,501	8·1
1845	872,905,996	51,739,643	5·92
1846	547,555,055	42,767,341	7·81
1847	537,219,958	53,415,847	10·34
1848	814,274,431	61,998,294	7·61
1849	1,036,602,269	66,396,967	6·4
1850	635,381,601	71,984,717	11·3

COTTON.—STATISTICS OF COTTON.—Mr. G. R. Porter, one of the Secretaries of the British Board of Trade, recently read a paper on Cotton, before the British Association, from which the following figures are obtained:

CONSUMPTION OF GREAT BRITAIN.

In 1800..................lbs.....	56,010,732
" 1810, incr'd by.... 67,478,203	
" 1820, further "....19,183,720	
" 1830, " 42,287,797	
" 1840, " ...328,526,548	
" 1849, " .1,182,981,008	
Whole consumption in 1849....	775,468,908
400 lbs. to the bale, equal to—bales........................	1,932,692
Importations from Brazil, Surat, and all other parts of the world, in 1849....................	538,000
American kinds consumed in 1849,	1,394,692
Consumed in U. S. in 1849........	600,000
" on the Continent......	1,000,000
Wants of the world from the U. S.,	2,994,692
Average consumption in Great Britain per week, in 1848 and 1849......................	29,346

Mr. Porter proposes to escape from frequent "Cotton Famines," by extending the cultivation and manufacture of Flax, which, he flatters himself, may, by the great improvement in machinery, be made capable of furnishing cheap clothing to the world.

COTTON, AND ITS COST OF PRODUCTION.—The annexed contribution was received from a practical cotton planter in Louisiana:

It has often been observed that many, everywhere, both in Europe and America, have been ready at all times to raise the hue and cry about the high prices of cotton, whenever it bears a value at all *remunerating*, and when it becomes so low as to sink beneath the cost of production, to be ready to congratulate its growers upon the profits they are realizing.

We imagine two prominent reasons may be found sufficiently explanatory of this, and the first is *interest*. This article constitutes the *chief element* of clothing for the whole civilized world, and its cheapness and abundance is as necessary to the millions that consume it, as their bread. The second reason for this general warfare against the planting interest, is, that most of those who have never produced the great staple, which clothes the world at so much less cost than any other good material, is, that they are not familiar with the costs of its production, and generally greatly underrate them.

Having so often observed the erroneous conclusions into which individuals and *communities* have been led, for the want of this knowledge and experience, we propose here to give a short and accurate summary of the *expenses and costs* of producing cotton, as deduced from our experience and observation for fifteen years. When we say *accurate*, we do not mean that standard that a merchant or mathematician observes, but *near enough* to show what is necessary; at least we will not make them greater than they are.

Take a plantation well-improved and properly organized, with good buildings, gins, mill, teams, &c., on which there are one hundred slaves, old and young negroes. Let this be cultivated, *free of rent or hire*, for one year, or a series of years, and left in as good order as it was received; it is a fair calculation that such places, upon rich bottom land, will produce annually seven bales, weighing four hundred pounds, to each hand; but not near so much on "up-lands." On such a plantation, with one hundred slaves, there would generally be found about fifty classified, *average* field-hands—the whole property being worth about *one hundred thousand dollars.*

Thus, 50 hands will produce 350 bales, of 400 lbs.; this, sold at 5 cents per lb., will be $20 per bale—350 bales		$7,000
From which deduct, for sending to market and selling, $2 50 per bale—350 bales	$875 00	
To feed 100 servants, to furnish the hospital, overseer's table, &c..............	750 00	
Deduct bagging and rope per bale—350 bales.........	525 00	
To clothe 100 slaves, shoe them, furnish bedding, sacks for gathering cotton, &c.	750 00	
Wages to competent overseer	700 00	
Such plantation requiring 35 or 40 mules, will need an annual addition of about four or five to sustain the teams..................	400 00	
Annual outlay to keep up farming tools of all descriptions, in wood and iron..	250 00	
Taxes on the whole estate,	300 00	
Medicines, doctors' bills, &c.	250 00	
Annual repairs of gins, mill, press, and purchasing new stands, &c..............	250 00	
Annual outlay for materials to keep in repair all the buildings needed: for nails, lime, plank, and such materials as cannot be had on the place..............	200 00	
Total Expenses above named........		$5,250
Leaves..............................		$1,750

It is to be borne in mind that there are hundreds of *small matters* not enumerated here, which must be annually purchased, and added to the list of expenses; also, that nothing has been allowed for the support of the planter and his family, which should all be charged to the place, as his *supervision is indispensable.* Nor has anything been set down to meet those contingent and incidental losses and costs, to which all such estates are liable. As the loss of servants from epidemics, the loss of *whole teams* from diseases, the frequent accidents to gins and houses from fire, losses from overflows, breaking of levees, &c.; the cost of making *entirely new* all the buildings, gins, &c., on the premises, occur every fifteen or twenty years. If a reasonable charge is made for these things, it will be readily seen the balance of $1,750 will fail to meet them. Thus it appears that it will cost five cents to produce cotton, and if the land is given clear of rent, and the labor without hire, a judicious economy only could save the manager of such an estate from debt, if he be required to surrender the property to the owner, at the end of the year, in good condition.

Nearly half the time, in the last ten years, cotton has been sold for the planters on the *low* lands, for about five cents per pound, which the most superficial observer must see has been ruinous; for it would appear, those immense estates not only pay no *interest* on the large investments, at those rates, but scarcely do the revenues support the charges of cultivating and sustaining them. It would require an extraordinary coincidence of favorable circumstances, to leave the smallest margin of profit to the planters. Their profits begin only when cotton advances above five cents, or the crop reaches beyond the ordinary average of seven bales to the hand; the latter, no one ought to presume on, for he will as often fall below as rise above the average.

We dislike, for those who are utterly unacquainted with the details of its production, to be constantly laboring to produce wrong impressions in the commercial circles, both in Europe and America, and stimulating, under false views, individuals and *nations* to embark in a business, ruinous to themselves and to those already engaged in it. Why should our material be said to be too high, when no other can be found to clothe the world half so cheap, combining the same comfort and utility? Why do people complain of the high prices of cotton, when even at ten cents it will clothe them cheaper and better than anything else by half—and yet only leave 25 or 30 cents per day compensation to the producer of the raw material?

From such calculations as these, it might be easy to show, that all the efforts England is making to succeed in the cultivation of cotton must prove abortive; for her labor is greatly inferior to ours. Her lands and climate have been found to be still more so. (The writer is personally acquainted with some of the planters employed from this country by the English, to try the experiment in India.) The distance from the places of consumption is another impediment to their success; as also, the marked inferiority of the staple. The West Indies, South America, and Egypt, have all failed in the race of competition against us, and have been yearly sinking lower in the amount of product.

Still another reason will forever effectually hinder England from successful competition. We are compelled to employ our labor in the production of this staple, let the price be what it may. We have the labor amongst us; labor of an excellent and superior quality. There is a vast field opened to it. Climate and soil happily adapted to the nature and constitution of the laborer, and to the production of the staple. We may say *peculiarly* to it, for there has not yet been found any other staple to employ so many laborers. Nor do we despair of obtaining remunerating prices, though England may try her India experiments; though manufacturers, merchants and brokers, and every element of selfishness and cupidity may conspire against us; for the world must be clad, and we can do it *cheaper* and *better* than any other people.

Nor do the ravings of abolitionists and pseudo-philanthropists disturb our repose. We well know our domestic institutions will remain as they are, and that we will forever enjoy the advantages of our labor, until *we choose* to dispense with it. We well know that the difficulties in the way of freeing this country of its negro population are insurmountable, and the cost of doing it, even if no compensation were claimed by their owners, would be so enormous, that noisy philanthropists would be the last to advocate the policy.

A national debt of one thousand millions of dollars would be required to *prepare* five millions of our Africans for freedom, in an independent government; to transport them there, and defray their expenses for a season. We cannot but look with confident hope to the future, not only that our domestic institutions will endure, and our labor remain to us, but that it will be hereafter profitable. An article that clothes nine-tenths of the civilized world at such cheap rates, and the laborers who produce it, must be regarded with interest. Destroy either the *material* or the *labor*, and what is the condition of the hundreds of millions of human beings they clothe? What the condition of the millions of poor laborers they give employment to, and supply with daily bread? What becomes of the commerce of the world, that great chain which binds the families of the earth to each other? One general ruin would overwhelm society. Revolutions in trade and society, and with it revolutions in governments, would be unavoidable. If we look for the cause of the extraordinary peace of the world for the last half century, *commerce* solves the mystery. If we ask what gave the impulse to commerce, we answer, *chiefly cotton and its manufactures.* And how such immense quantities of this has been produced at such cheap rates as to enable the peasantry of Europe, who once were ragged, not only to be clad from it, but to be fed by their labor in elaborating it into materials for the rest of mankind,—we answer, by the introduction of Africans into these states: whilst they themselves have been brought up from the depths of ignorance and degradation in which they had been buried for centuries, to a state of comparative civilization and happiness, each generation gradually advancing higher and higher. These are some of the advantages, aided by the skill and capital of the Americans, they have conferred upon mankind. At some future day it may be their destiny to be separated from the patriarchal jurisdiction of those who had been so long their instructors and protectors, when they may be prepared for liberty and self-government.

It seems as if the hand of mercy had conducted them to this land, and placed them in the only possible condition where their moral and intellectual natures could be improved and cultivated. So deep had they been buried in ignorance and degradation, that they could not have mingled with the refined society of European nations, or their descendants, as *equals.* The relation of *master* and *slave,* as it exists here in its *patriarchal character,* is the only conceivable one which could elevate the Africans in the scale of intelligence and morality, while at the same time it has been the means of giving commerce and peace to the world.

COTTON—METEOROLOGY, AND THE COTTON AND SUGAR CROPS.

The following valuable table is taken from Affleck's Rural Almanac for 1852, and was compiled by the editor from the records of the late Dr. Tooley and G. L. C. Davis, Esq., of Natchez, and also from his own records:

	White Frosts				Items of Cotton Crop				
	Latest in Spring		Earliest in Fall						
Year	Date	Temp. at sunrise	Date	Temp. at sunrise	Date of 1st blooms	When killed by frost	Crops of U. States	Consumption of U. States	Sugar crop of United States
1825	Feb. 15	42	Oct. 19	44			Bales.	Bales.	Hhds.
1826	April 11	43	Nov. 18	41			937,000	104,483	(1818, 25,000)
1827	Mar. 19	44	" 30	38			712,000	120,593	(1822, 30,000)
1828	" 17	42	" 12	44			857,744	118,853	88,000
1829	" 22	32	" 1	43			976,845	126,512	48,000
1830	Feb. 14	41	Oct. 20	44			1,038,848	182,142	70,000
1831	Mar. 21	41	" 28	40			987,477	173,800	75,000
1832	" 18	30	Nov. 9	36			1,070,438	194,412	70,000
1833	" 30	44	Oct. 20	44			1,205,394	196,413	75,000
1834	" 30	39	" 20	41			1,254,328	216,888	100,000
1835	" 23	42	" 10	46			1,360,725	236,733	30,000
1836	" 25	43	" 22	44			1,422,930	222,540	70,000
1837	April 9	44	" 26	42			1,801,497	246,063	65,000
1838	Mar. 18	43	" 22	44			1,360,532	276,018	70,000
1839	" 6	37	Nov. 7	42			2,177,835	295.193	115,000
1840	" 31	41	Oct. 25	42	June 6	Oct. 26	1,634,945	297,288	87,000
1841	" 18	45	" 23	38	" 10	" 23	1,683,574	267,850	90,000
1842	Feb. 22	42	" 26	43	May 17	Nov. 1	2,378,875	325,714	140,000
1843	April 1	44	" 28	39	June 9	Oct. 28	2,030,409	346,744	100,346
1844	Mar. 31	38	" 19	41	May 25	" 29	2,394,503	389,000	200,090
1845	" 21	42	" 12	44	" 30	Nov. 3	2,100,537	422,597	186,650
1846	April 14	43	" 19	44	June 10	Oct. 19	1,778,651	427,627	140,000
1847	Mar. 27	40	Nov. 19	42	May 30	Nov. 26	2,347,634	531,772	240,000
1848	" 14	43	—	....	June 1	None.	2,728,596	518,039	220,000
1849	April 16	41	Nov. 8	41	" 6	Dec. 3	2,096,706	487,769	247,923
1850	" 7	40	Oct. 26	36	" 24	Oct. 26	2,355,257	404,108	211,203

COTTON TRADE OF GREAT BRITAIN.—1806–1846.

IMPORTS OF COTTON INTO GREAT BRITAIN FOR 41 YEARS.

	1806.	1807.	1808.	1809.	1810.	1811.	1812.
American	124,939	171,267	37,672	160,180	246,759	128,192	95,331
Brazil	51,034	18,981	50,442	140,927	142,846	118,514	98,704
East India	7,787	11,409	12,512	35,764	79,382	14,646	2,607
West India, &c	77,978	81,010	67,512	103,511	92,186	64,879	64,563
Packages	261,738	282,667	168,138	440,382	561,173	326,231	261,205

	1813.	1814.	1815.	1816.	1817.	1818.	1819.
American	37,720	48,853	203,051	166,077	199,669	207,580	205,161
Brazil	137,168	150,930	91,055	123,450	114,518	162,499	125,415
East India	1,429	13,048	22,357	30,670	120,202	247,659	184,259
West India, &c	73,210	74,800	52,840	49,235	44,872	50,991	31,300
Packages	249,536	287,631	369,303	369,432	479,261	668,729	546,135

IMPORTS OF COTTON INTO GREAT BRITAIN—*continued.*

	1820.	1821.	1822.	1823.	1824.	1825.	1826.
American	302,395	300,070	329,906	352,538	282,371	423,446	395,852
Brazil	180,086	121,085	143,505	144,611	143,310	193,942	55,590
Egyptian	..	..	..	5,624	38,022	111,023	47,261
East India	57,923	30,095	19,263	38,393	50,851	60,484	64,699
West India, &c	31,247	40,428	40,770	27,632	25,537	31,988	18,188
Packages	571,691	491,678	533,444	668,797	540,092	820,883	581,950

	1827.	1828.	1829.	1630.	1831.	1832.	1833.
American	646,776	444,390	463,076	618,527	608,887	628,766	654,786
Brazil	120,111	167,362	159,536	191,468	168,288	114,585	163,103
Egyptian	22,450	32,889	24,739	14,752	38,124	41,183	3,893
East India	73,738	84,855	80,489	35,019	76,764	109,398	94,698
West India, &c	30,988	20,056	18,867	11,721	11,304	8,490	13,646
Packages	894,063	749,552	746,707	871,487	903,367	902,322	930,216

	1834	1835.	1836.	1837.	1838.	1839.	1840.
American	733,528	763,199	704,707	844,812	1,124,800	814,500	1,237,500
Brazil	103,646	143,572	148,715	117,005	137,500	99,300	85,300
Egyptian	7,277	43,721	34,953	41,193	29,700	33,500	38,000
East India	89,098	117,965	219,493	145,174	107,200	132,900	216,400
West India, &c	17,485	22,796	33,506	27,791	29,400	36,000	22,300
Packages	951,034	1,091,253	1,201,374	1,175,975	1,428,600	1,116,200	1,599,500

	1841.	1842.	1843.	1844.	1845.	1846.
American	902,500	1,013,400	1,396,800	1,246,900	1,499,600	932,000
Brazil	94,300	87,100	98,700	112,900	110,200	84,000
Egyptian	40,700	19,600	48,400	66,700	82,000	59,600
East India	273,600	255,500	182,100	237,600	155,100	49,500
West India, &c	32,900	17,300	17,700	17,500	8,800	9,000
Packages	1,344,000	1,392,990	1,744,100	1,681,600	1,855,700	1,134,100

COTTON—EXPORTS, 1850–51.

The total amount of cotton wool exported from the United States, for the fiscal year 1851, compared with the fiscal year, 1850, was as follows:

	lbs.	Value.
1850.		
Sea Islands	8,236,463	$71,984,616
All other	627,145,141	
1851.		
Sea Islands	8,299,656	$112,315,317
All other	918,937,433	

The valuation of the crop of 1850, at the rates obtained for the crop of 1851, would have amounted to $76,951,865

While crop of 1851, at the rates obtained for the crop of 1850, would have amounted but to 92,723,715

Averaging 450 pounds to the bale, the number of bales exported in 1851 were.. 2,060,527

Number of bales exported in 1850........ 1,411,959

Average price per bale in 1851........... $54 50

Average price per bale in 1850........... 45 00

The annexed table exhibits the ports whence the raw material was sent abroad for the past fiscal year, together with the value and amounts of the same:

Port.	*Quality* — Sea Islands.	*Quality* — Other places.	*Value.*
Boston	—	1,131,736	$146,588
New-Bedford	—	37,168	3,350
New-York	787,380	16,010,783	21,148,293
Philadelphia	—	2,094,718	200,544
Baltimore	—	174,041	21,438
Charleston	4,580,310	104,538,658	14,091,931
Savannah	2,927,263	68,473.428	8,878,319
Apalachicola	—	35,611,608	3,858,086
St. Marks	—	451,980	61,685
Mobile	—	159,929,989	18,406,864
New-Orleans	4,703	385,814,458	45,330,084
Galveston	—	646,843	75,422
Vermont	—	21,353	1,808
Genesee	—	1,270	150
Total	8,299,656	918,937,433	$112,315,317

MONTHLY RANGE OF PRICES OF COTTON IN MOBILE FOR 16 YEARS.

SEASON OF	October	November	December	January	February
1835 '36	— a 17	15 a 16½	13½ a 16	13½ a 16½	14 a 17
1836 '37	16 a 20	15 a 19	12½ a 17½	12 a 17½	12 a 17½
1837 '38	7¾ a 12	6½ a 11⅜	6 a 12	7⅛ a 12⅛	6¼ a 12
1838 '39	10 a 11	10 a 12	10 a 14¾	11⅔ a 15¼	12⅓ a 16½
1839 '40	12¾ a 13	11¼ a —	9¼ a 9½	8 a 8½	7¼ a 7½
1840 '41	7½ a 10½	7½ a 10	8½ a 11¼	8½ a 11⅔	7 a 12¼
1841 '42	nominal.	7½ a 9¾	7⅝ a 8⅞	7⅝ a 10⅛	7½ a 10
1842 '43	7⅛ a 8½	6⅞ a 8⅜	5¾ a 7⅔	5¼ a 7⅞	5½ a 8
1843 '44	6 a 8	6⅝ a 8⅛	7⅝ a 9¼	7¾ a 10	7½ a 10
1844 '45	5¼ a 6¼	4⅛ a 6¼	4 a 5⅝	3¼ a 6	3⅝ a 6¾
1845 '46	6½ a 8⅞	6⅝ a 8¾	6⅜ a 8¾	6 a 8½	6 a 8½
1846 '47	8 a 10	9 a 11	8½ a 11	9¾ a 12	9 a 13
1847 '48	8½ a 11½	5½ a 8¼	6½ a 7¾	6 a 7¾	6 a 7
1848 '49	4½ a 6¼	4¼ a 5½	4½ a 6	5 a 7	5½ a 7¾
1849 '50	9 a 11	9¼ a 11¼	9½ a 11	10 a 12½	10⅜ a 12¼
1850 '51	12⅜ a 14¼	13 a 14½	12¼ a 13½	11½ a 13½	7 a 13

MONTHLY RANGE OF PRICES OF COTTON IN MOBILE—*continued.*

SEASON OF	March	April	May	June	Average for season
1835 '36	15 a 20	15 a 20	13½ a 19	13½ a 19	14⅛ a 16⅞
1836 '37	11½ a 17½	6 a 13½	5 a 10	6½ a 11	10⅜ a 16
1837 '38	7⅛ a 12¼	8⅛ a 13½	8¼ a 13½	8½ a 14	7¼ a 12⅝
1838 '39	13¾ a 17½	14 a 17⅝	14¼ a 18	13½ a 17	12⅛ a 15⅝
1839 '40	7 a 7½	7¼ a 7½	7¼ a 7½	7¾ a 7⅞	8¼ a 8⅝
1840 '41	9½ a 12	10 a 12½	9⅝ a 12⅛	9¼ a 11⅛	8⅝ a 14⅜
1841 '42	7 a 10	7 a 10⅝	7 a 10½	7½ a 10⅓	7⅛ a 10
1842 '43	4⅞ a 7⅛	5¼ a 7⅝	5⅝ a 8⅛	5⅞ a 8⅝	5¾ a 8
1843 '44	6⅜ a 9¼	5⅝ a 8¾	5 a 8	4⅝ a 8	6½ a 8⅞
1844 '45	4¼ a 7⅛	5 a 7	5 a 6⅞	5⅛ a 7	4½ a 6½
1845 '46	6¼ a 9	6¼ a 8⅞	5⅞ a 7¾	6 a 7¾	6¼ a 8½
1846 '47	8½ a 11¾	9½ a 11½	9¾ a 12	8¾ a 11	9 a 11½
1847 '48	6 a 7¾	4½ a 7	4 a 6½	4½ a 6¾	5¾ a 7⅞
1848 '49	5⅝ a 7	5½ a 7	5¼ a 7½	6¼ a 8¼	5 a 7
1849 '50	10⅓ a 12	10¼ a 12	11 a 12¼	11 a 12½	10 a 12
1850 '51	6½ a 11½	8 a 11¼	5½ a 9⅞	5¼ a 9	8¾ a 12

COTTON CROPS.

TABLE OF CROPS OF COTTON OF THE UNITED STATES,

With the number of bales imported into Europe, from other countries; also stocks, and consumption of the United States and Europe, for ten years, ending with 1849, divided into two periods, with the aggregate and average of each five years, and the increase or decrease per cent. of one over the other.

Crop of Atlantic Ports—	1840	1841	1842	1843	1844	Aggregate	Average
Savannah	293,000	146,000	222,000	299,000	253,000	1,213,000	243,000
Charleston	312,000	233,000	261,000	352,000	306,000	1,464,000	293,000
Virginia	24,000	24,000	20,000	12,000	14,000	94,000	19,000
North Carolina	10,000	7,000	10,000	9,000	9,000	45,000	9,000
Atlantic ports	639,000	410,000	513,000	672,000	582,000	2,808,000	564,000
Crop of Gulf Ports—							
New-Orleans	954,000	817,000	737,000	1,060,009	832,000	4,000,000	880,000
Mobile	445,000	318,000	318,000	483,000	469,900	2,033,000	407,000
Florida	136,000	90,000	108,000	161,000	161,000	146,000	128,000
Texas and other ports	4,000	....	8,000	4,000	1,000	17,000	3,000
Gulf ports	1,539,000	1,225,000	1,171,000	1,708,000	1,448,000	7,091,000	1,418,000
Atlantic ports	639,000	410,000	513,000	672,000	582,000	2,816,000	564,000
Total crop United States	2,178,000	1,635,000	1,684,000	2,380,000	2,030,000	9,907,000	1,982,000
Crop of India, Brazil, &c. Imp. into Europe	473,000	569,000	545,000	523,000	511,000	2,621,000	524,000
Annual production	2,651,000	2,204,000	2,229,000	2,903,000	2,541,000	12,528,000	2,506,000
Stocks—							
In U. S. 1st Sept. each year	52,000	58,000	82,000	32,000	94,000	....	....
Great Britain, 1st Jan	265,000	464,000	538,000	561,000	785,900	....	....
France and the Continent, 1st Jan	147,000	209,000	223,000	246,000	270,000	....	....
Total supply	3,115,000	2,935,000	3,072,000	3,742,000	3,690,000	....	....
Consumption—							
In Great Britain	1,305,000	1,160,000	1,249,000	1,412,000	1,441,000	6,569,000	1,313,000
In France	434,000	426,000	441,000	406,000	388,000	2,095,000	419,000
On the Continent	276,000	262,000	315,000	337,000	298,000	1,488,000	298,000
	2,105,000	1,848,000	2,005,000	2,155,000	2,030,000	10,150,000	2,030,000
In the United States	295,000	297,000	268,000	325,000	347,900	1,532,000	306,000
Consumption as per tables	2,310,000	2,145,000	2,273,000	2,480,000	2,474,000	11,682,000	2,336,000
Add to each year those quantities which have been exported to foreign ports, and not included in Tables of Consumption, but required to	4,000	6,000	9,000	12,000	17,000	48,000	10,000
Total Consumption	2,314,000	2,251,000	2,282,000	2,492,000	2,491,000	11 720,000	2,346,000

	1845	1846	1847	1848	1849	Aggregate	Average
Crop of Atlantic Ports—							
Savannah	295,000	192,000	243,000	255,000	391,000	1,376,000	275,000
Charleston	428,000	251,000	350,000	261,000	458,000	1,748,000	350,000
Virginia	25,000	8,000	14,000	9,000	18,000	74,000	15,000
North Carolina	12,000	11,000	6,000	2,000	10,000	41,000	8,000
Atlantic ports	760,000	462,000	613,000	527,000	877,000	3,239,000	648,000
Crop of Gulf Ports—							
New-Orleans	929,000	1,041,000	706,000	1,191,000	1,094,000	4,961,000	992,000
Mobile	517,000	423,000	323,000	436,000	519,000	2,218,000	444,000
Florida	189,000	141,000	128,000	154,000	200,000	812,000	162,000
Texas and other ports	....	34,000	8,000	40,000	39,000	121,000	24,000
Gulf ports	1,635,000	1,639,000	1,165,000	1,827,000	1,852,000	8,112,000	1,622,000
Atlantic ports	760,000	462,000	613,000	527,000	877,000	3,239,000	648,000
Total crop United States	2,395,000	2,101,000	1,778,000	2,348,000	2,729,000	11,351,000	2,270,000
Crop of India, Egypt, Brazil, &c., Imp. into Europe	461,000	319,000	481,000	401,000	538,000	2,200,000	440,000
Annual Production	2,856,000	2,420,000	2,259,000	2,749,000	3,267,000	13,351,000	2,710,000
*Stocks—**							
In U. S. 1st Sep. each year	160,000	94,000	107,000	215,000	172,000	....	....
Great Britain, 1st Jan	897,000	1,055,000	145,000	451,000	496,000	....	....
France and the Continent, 1st Jan	204,000	164,000	73,000	140,000	89,000	....	....
Total Supply	4,117,000	3,733,000	2,982,000	3,555,000	4,024,000	....	....
Consumption—							
In Great Britain	1,581,000	1,573,000	1,114,000	1,505,000	1,586,000	7,359,000	1,472,000
In France	418,000	405,000	293,000	303,000	399,000	1,818,000	364,000
On the Continent	357,000	345,000	348,000	351,000	492,000	1,883,000	376,000
	2,356,000	2,323,000	1,745,000	2,159,000	2,477,000	11,160,000	2,212,000
In the United States	389,000	423,000	428,000	532,000	518,000	2,290,000	458,000
Consumption as per tables	2,745,000	2,746,000	2,173,000	2,691,000	2,995,000	13,350,000	2,670,000
Add to each year those quantities which have been exported to foreign ports, and not included in Tables of Consumption, but required to balance	50,000	75,000	115,000	175,000	246,000	661,000	132,000
Total Consumption	2,795,000	2,821,000	2,288,000	2,866,000	3,241,000	14,011,000	2,802,000

☞ By comparing the first period of five years with the second period of five years, it will be seen the *increase* at Atlantic Ports has been 11½, at Gulf Ports, 14 per cent. The production has increased 7½ per cent. The annual consumption in Great Britain has increased 12½, on the Continent 27, in the United States 50; total increase of consumption, 19½ per cent. There has in the same time been a *decrease* of 20 per cent. of India cottons imported into Europe, and 16 per cent. in the consumption of cotton in France.

J. G. Henry, Mobile.

COTTON—Diseases of the Plant and the Remedies.—When the time comes for planting another cotton crop, the mind naturally reverts to the many diseases and disasters which have befallen the plant for the last ten or twelve years. In fact, diseases and disasters have become so numerous, as to cause the planters to look forward to the time when they will be compelled to cease the cultivation of cotton altogether, and pursue some other occupation. My object in this communication is to name them, and to give my planting friends my observations, hoping to obtain from them (through your Review) their views in regard to the same matters, of so much interest to us all, and also to attract the attention of entomologists, In my opinion, the diseases of the cotton plant are always attributable to the variety of insects that feed and live upon its fluids, thereby causing an unhealthy circulation in the plant, and blasting the prospects of rich harvests. The first of disasters by the insect family takes place in the spring, (in this latitude, 34°,) from the 25th of April to the 5th of May. I allude to the "cut-worms," which are frequently so numerous as to destroy whole fields of the young plant, when from five to six bushels have been sown per acre. They are also

* The stocks reported 31st December, 1849, in Europe, are 646,000. To 1st September, 1849, in United States, are 155,000, making 801,000 bales.

† Hamburg, Bremen, Amsterdam, Rotterdam, Antwerp and Trieste, are only included here, while large quantities have been exported to other ports in the South and North of Europe

very destructive in gardens, destroying all kinds of plants, making no difference, when pressed by hunger, as to the properties contained in them; but when surrounded by a variety, they feed upon those that contain the greatest quantity of saccharine matter; consequently, the young "cotton plant" commands their preference. Various experiments have been made to exterminate them from fields and gardens; some, by turning upon them hogs and poultry during the winter season; others by the use of spade and plow, during the same season, that they may experience the effects of freezing—all of which have proved unavailing. I have made an experiment that has proved successful for the last five or six years, both in farm and garden. I plant in my fields a double quantity of seed, say ten bushels per acre, scattering them "broad-cast," with a view to feed the worms and have enough left—the same plan works equally well in gardens. I cultivate my gardens in the usual manner, when, about the 10th of April, I sow upon a garden of one acre, thirty or forty bushels of cotton seed, scattered over walks, among plants, &c. In the course of ten days, the seeds having germinated, the garden presents the appearance of a plant bed. It remains in this condition until about the 5th May, when what cotton is left is cut up, leaving the most of the garden plants unharmed. They are not disposed to travel when they can find any thing green near them. Their term of life is short, say ten days, when they pass into the chrysalis; the same length of time transpires when they pass into the butterfly stage. I would here remark, when I wish to plant a new variety of cotton, and cannot afford to *pay* for seed to be sown so abundantly, I plant seed of the more common kind in the middle of the *row* and *sides* of the bed, giving time for them to sprout, that the worm may begin to feed on *them*. I then mark off the bed, and plant the more valuable seed. In this way, I have been able to get good "stands," of fine varieties of seed, with two bushels per acre. Next to the worm comes the "cotton louse;" they, for the last ten years, (with one exception, 1840, when they made their appearance 20th June, and remained until the 10th of July, yet seasons favored, and fine crops were made,) have made their appearance from the 20th to the 25th May, and remained until the 5th June, when they begin to leave the plant, after killing and destroying from one-third to half that has been left by the hoe for a stand. They have been so regular in their appearance for the last ten years, that my orders to my managers are now, not to reduce "the stand" below, from four to six stacks to the hill, until the 5th of June, at which time you can easily distinguish the plants that have been most injured by their poisonous ravages, whilst the more healthy may remain. They are more numerous in cold, wet springs. How they are brought into existence, is a wonder to all who have examined the cotton fields during their stay upon the plant. Some contend that they are a species of the ant; others, of the lady-bug; others still, that the ants destroy them; but will not pretend to advance an idea as to how they receive their existence. When first discovered, they are mere yellow specks; they soon crawl, and are busy moving about. Next, they assume a black appearance, and become quite dormant; in ten days this black shell opens, and they, like the cut-worm, or caterpiller, fly off, resembling the gnat, or winged ants. My own opinion, from observation, is, that the ant feeds on them; at least, we never see lice on a plant without seeing on the same numerous ants and lady-bugs. Whether the aphis, which emits the honey-dew, is among the crowd, and attracts the ants, we are not sufficiently versed in entomology to decide—we would be gratified to read a treatise on plant-lice, lady-bugs, and aphis, from some of your intelligent correspondents. I have not a remaining doubt that they cause the rust, which at one time I attributed to the want of some chemical property in the soil, and had determined to have it tested by having some of the soil analyzed; before I had an opportunity of testing the matter, however, I was convinced that such was not the case, from the fact that every variety of soil was affected in the same way. The rust is at all times the most fatal of diseases to the plant. It cannot be doubted that the insect poisons the plant by extracting the sap, which leaves it in an unhealthy condition. The rust has no regular time for its coming. I have seen it as early as the middle of May, and from that time till the middle of July, on from one to ten stalks, when it assumes a more formidable shape, spreading over entire plantations in the course of three or four weeks. If produced by insects, might they not be destroyed during the first two months, when they are confined to a few stalks in a place, by sifting lime over the stalks affected, early in the morning, whilst the plant is moist with dew? We have known gardeners to use lime in this way, to drive insects from plants, with great success. It would not cost much labor if taken at the commencement of the disease;—we have bought a few barrels of lime for the purpose of making the experiment; but of course do not intend to apply these remarks to the prairie lands, where the rust is confined to certain spots every year, owing (we suppose) to a want of moisture, as we generally see it on those spots of ground where the limestone rock approaches near the surface. In the flat lands of South Carolina and

Georgia—or "flat woods," as they are called—we suppose the cause to be the same as with us, as there is some similarity between those lands and some parts of the Valley of the Mississippi. Nothing could be of so much advantage to the cotton interest, as the discovery of some remedy, either to arrest or prevent the various diseases to which the plant has of late years become so liable.

Do "cotton lice" belong to the family of "blights" described by Rusticus? He says, (in a letter on "Blights,") "I have taken a good deal of pains to find out the birth and parentage of true blights; and for this purpose have watched, day after day, the colonies of them in my own garden, and single ones which I have kept 'in-doors,' and under tumblers turned up-side down. The increase is prodigious; it beats everything of the kind that I have ever seen or heard of. Insects in general come from an egg—then turn to a caterpillar, which does nothing but eat—then to a chrysalis, which does nothing but sleep—then to a perfect beetle or fly, which does nothing but increase its kind; but 'blights' proceed altogether on another system—the young ones are born exactly like the old ones, but less. They stick their beaks through the rind, and begin drawing sap, when only a day old, and go on quietly sucking away for days; and then, all at once, without love, courtship or matrimony, each individual begins bringing forth young ones, and continues to do so for months, at the rate of from a dozen to eighteen every day, and yet continues to increase in size all the while; there seem to be no males—no drones—all bring forth alike. Early in the year, these 'blights' are scattered along the stems; but as soon as the little ones come to light, and commence sap-sucking close to their mother, the spaces get filled up, and the old ones look like giants among the rest—when all the spare room is filled up, and the stalk completely covered. The young ones, on making their final appearance in the world, seem rather posed as to what to be at, and stand quietly on the backs of the others for an hour or so; then, as if having made up their minds, they toddle upwards, walking on the backs of the whole flock, till they arrive at the upper end of the shoot, and then settle themselves quietly down, as close as possible to the outermost of their friends, and then commence sap-sucking like the rest. The flock, by this means, extends in length every day, and at last the growing shoot is overtaken by the multitude, and completely covered to the very tip. Towards autumn, however, the 'blights' undergo a change in their nature; their feet stick close to the rind—their skin opens along the back, and a winged blight comes out—the summer generation being generally wingless. These are male and female, and fly about and enjoy themselves; and, what seems scarcely credible, the winged females lay eggs; and, whilst this operation is going on, a solitary winged blight may be observed on the under side of the leaves, or on the young shoots, particularly on the hop, and differing from all its own progeny in being winged, and nearly black, whereas its progeny are green, and without wings. These are mysteries which I leave for entomologists to explain. In May, a fly lays a lot of eggs: these eggs hatch and become blights; these 'blights' are viviparous, and that without the usual union of the sexes, and so are their children and grandchildren—the number of births depending solely on the quantity and quality of their food. At last, as winter approaches, the whole generation, or series of generations, assumes wings, which the parents did not possess; undergoes frequently a change in color; and in the spring, instead of being viviparous, lays eggs."

This, description, by a celebrated entomologist, somewhat resembles the kind of insect which, in my opinion, produces the diseases alluded to. Their making their appearance in small quantities in May and June, then in mid-summer extending so rapidly, sustains me in this position.

He also speaks of the skin of the insect opening on the back, and turning to a winged gnat, which is the case with the kind we describe, except that ours open, say in twenty days. May not season and climate cause those changes? I think they may with great propriety be called the cotton blights, as the plant does not recover from their poisonous effects during the whole season, when they have been very numerous; yet with good seasons, by which I mean neither too wet nor too dry, good crops have been made from plants which were, to all appearances, dead on the 10th day of June. To this family of blights, the same author assimilates the "hop-fly" of England, and speaks of their effect as lessening the value of the crop one-half; he says, this little insignificant fly has control of £750,000 of income to the British treasury. The same species of blight draws even a greater proportion from the pockets of the Southern planters.

He also enumerates several varieties of the family of blights, all preying upon the young and juicy parts of the most tender shoots, destroying their form and beauty, and making the best of fruits tasteless and insipid.

The next in turn of disasters from this great family of insects, is the boll-worm, which makes its appearance from the third to the fourth week in July. It seems to be regular in its annual visits, oftener in wet than in dry seasons. Much has been said and written about destroying them. Individuals have traveled over the cotton country professing to have found "the great secret." I have tried several of their plans, one of which is, to top the cotton the fourth week in July, and destroy the bud of the plant. I have no doubt that many of the eggs, or much of the larvæ, are destroyed in this way—but it is ruinous to the plant to top it so early, causing it to throw out many new branches, which are too late to make cotton. Besides, you destroy some three or four branches by taking out the whole bud, which would mature. Another plan has been to build fire lights "to catch the miller." This, too, has its merits, without injury to the plants. Beyond a doubt, the insects commence in the top bud of the stalk, when so very small that they are not able to bore a form of any size, but leave "their mark" on the young form, as a sting. Soon they grow strong, and proceed down the stalk, taking the forms both large and small, until they are able to destroy the full-grown fruit, extracting from every form the whole of the glutinous substance, which causes the very young ones to drop from the stalk, and those nearly ready to bloom to "flare open," plainly showing where the worm is at work. The older ones rot. These marks showed their effects so plainly, that it caused me, with several others, to put our hands in the field to catch them; and in a few days the hands became so expert, that they would catch from three to five hundred per day. If no other good is effected, we may save nearly that number of stalks from ruin. Besides, it is a leisure season of the year, and not so tedious as one would at first suppose. Ten hands will worm upwards of one hundred acres per day. This process should be repeated every three or four days; the "flare," with their excretions, plainly show the plants they are working upon.

The next pest to the cotton planter is the caterpillar, or "cheneille," which makes its appearance from the 25th of August to the 25th of September. When they come early they do the crop a great deal of damage—when late, but little. For the last ten years we can only recollect them as injuring the crop in 1846. Are they not a continuation of the "cut worm?" Having passed through several changes, they pass into the chrysalis and web to the stems of the leaf upon which they have fed. They then pass into the butterfly, or are destroyed by cold. Is it not possible, by watching this numerous tribe of the butterfly family, to destroy them early in the season of their coming? Entomologists describe all these insects at first as few in number, but increasing, from each parent, from fifteen hundred to three thousand in a short time, and making various changes. Could *they* be destroyed, I feel convinced that the plant would be relieved of all its diseases! May we not expect, through your columns, a treatise on these various insects which feed on the plant? You can command such works as Kirby, Spence, Stephens and Curtis, and a host of others, which are not generally possessed by planters; yet no class of mankind could improve themselves more by the study of entomology —for upon our labors the insect world commit their ravages, and destroy the pleasure as well as profits of planting, by changing, in a few days, the most promising harvest fields into absolute poverty.—*M. H. McG.*

COTTON—ITS PREPARATION, PICKING AND PACKING.—Land intended to be planted in cotton should be bedded up as early in the winter as possible, to allow the freezes to pulverize the soil thoroughly and the land to settle immediately under the tap root. The plowing should be done with the best turning plows, as deeply as the nature and depth of the soil will admit, and in the most thorough manner. Especial care should be taken to leave no land unbroken between the furrows. If the soil is stiff and deep, two-horse plowing, to a depth commensurate with that of the soil and ease to the team, is infinitely preferable; this secures a more thorough drainage and greater and freer penetration of the roots of the plant to the most sub-soil, in either wet or dry summers. The rows should be laid off with a scooter plow, at distances suitable to the strength of the soil, say five and a half feet to six feet on bottom land, and four to five feet on upland, or even less than four, if the soil is thin. Stubble land to go in cotton, (which should always follow corn, small grain, or fallow land,) should be broken or bedded up very early in the winter, to allow time for grass seeds and stalks to rot, and the frost to disintegrate furrow slice and clods. A good plan on stubble, corn, or fallow land to go in cotton, is to lay off the rows with a scooter plow; enlarge the furrow with a shovel plow; drag all the grass weeds or stalks into the furrows, and then list two furrows of a two-horse plow upon the soil of vegetable matter, leaving the bulks to be well plowed out with a turning plow about a fortnight before planting. This puts all trash out of the way in chopping out, and provides an absorbent for moisture and a bulk of manure beneath each bed. If a heavy rain or baking wind should run the land together, and form a crust upon the bed, a one-horse harrow run over the bed will pulverize the crust and put the land in good tilth. Cotton should be planted from the fifteenth of March to the tenth of April, as the season or sort of land warrants. Seed should be well saved, and if kept over one year for planting, will ensure a better stand and more vigorous plants, as the imperfect seed perish by keeping over. They should be sown at the rate of one and a half to two bushels to the acre, in direct proportion to the width of the rows (narrow ones requiring more seed) and the stiffness of the soil, the latter case demanding also more seed. Seed on light land may be covered with a board with a notch in it, attached to a scooter stock. But stiff lands should always be covered with a harrow, or two small scooter furrows. The ridge, in the latter case, over the seed, to be scraped off with a board with a notch in it, as soon as the seed cracks the ground in germinating. The board is useful in scraping off the first coat of grass; the first plowing of cotton should begin when the third leaf appears on the young plant, and be done with a sweep, Mississippi scraper, or some similar implement, as no roots are lacerated by this process, and the plant suffers no check in growth; chopping should begin in from four to seven days after running round, and to be done with hoes of as nearly equal size as possible, the stand being more uniform in consequence. From one to four stalks should be left in a stand at this time, and the distance between stands governed by the strength of the soil; though thick planting in moderation on all soils—say six feet by eighteen inches on bottom land, and four feet by twelve inches on good upland—will be found the most productive in an average of years. The second plowing should be done with a sweep next to the bottom, with a mould board next to the plant, to dirt the young cotton, and the balance of the row plowed out with a turning plow to keep up the bed. The stand should then be thinned to one stalk in a place on strong land, but from two to four may be left on being thinned to supply limbs by stalks; all subsequent plowing in ordinary seasons should be done with the sweep, with the mould board to keep up the bed. But in laying by, one or two furrows should be run by a turning plow to drain off the surplus water from heavy rains; bottoms should be plowed every twenty days, and hoed immediately to keep it constantly growing, the earth light and pervious to the sun, air and dews. In very wet seasons, recourse may be had to turning plows with benefit, provided they do not penetrate deeply near the plant, for this checks the plant if it turns off by breaking the roots, and causes it to shed, and forces it too much in growth if rain follows speedily. It is doubtful whether topping cotton is beneficial in the average of years, sometimes doing well, and at others failing in nearly similar circumstances.

Picking should begin as soon as a hand can gather fifty pounds in a day, as the oil is soon evaporated by the sun, wind and rain, and a large per cent. of weight is thereby lost. In full crop years, cotton should be picked as free from leaf as is consistent with good work. But in short crop seasons, too much pains should not be taken with the leaf, as the difference in number of pounds will greatly overbalance that of loss of price per pound, and discrimination does not prevail in the market to any extent comparable with that of the large crop years. Planting seed should be saved from the second picking in general, and from cotton picked from mid-day till night, or that seemed well for the purpose. All other cotton should never be sunned unless wet by rain, but packed in close bulk from four to eight weeks, to allow it to heat; care being taken not to allow it to heat too much and the oil from the seed to diffuse through the lint, imparting to it the tinge so much admired by buyers and manufacturers. Ginning should be carefully done at a moderate speed. Packing should never be done in very dry or windy weather, but always in damp and moderately rainy days, as it packs better, weighs heavier, from the absorption from the air and retention of the oil latent in the lint. The bagging should always be put on loosely to allow for the swelling of the bale, and completely envelop the cotton. The ropes should be put on tightly, to prevent undue expansion of the bale, and be at least six in number.

COTTON BALED WITH IRON HOOPS.—The subjoined letter, written, I have no doubt, in a spirit of perfect candor, and intended fairly and in good faith by the writer, to present a true statement of the relative advantages of rope and iron hoops in the packing of cotton, nevertheless contains objections to the use of the latter article, which I conceive so untenable, that I send the letter to you for publication; hoping it may arrest the attention of R. Abbey, Esq,, of Mississippi, or some one else practically acquainted with the subject, and elicit a reply.

As they are the objections not of the writer of the latter, but of that entire community of cotton sellers and buyers of Mobile, who control the preparation for market of so large a portion of the Southern crop, I hope Mr. Abbey, whose valuable article in your January number, contains so many good reasons for preferring the hoop iron, will not think them undeserving a reply. With several newly invented, and, as I believe, *improved* cotton presses, just coming into use, we can certainly pack our bales within a square of 22 inches, and if we can persuade our mercantile friends in Mobile, that there is no good reason why bales thus packed, *and kept in their square form by the unelastic iron hoop*, should be "*unmerchantable*"—we can certainly avoid the onerous tax of repacking them in Mobile—but as long as we use the hemp rope, which by stretching, allows our bales to lose their compact square shape, and to become enlarged and flattened, so as not to pack close on shipboard, we must submit to the tax of repacking.

MOBILE, SEPT. 8, 1847.

DEAR SIR:

Your favor of the 29th ult., is before us, and contents have had our attention. Cotton compressed is only reduced in *depth*, and the average is about one-third less than the bale before being compressed. A large light bale will be reduced more than a smaller one of the same weight. The presses run them down nearly half the depth; but when the ropes are tied and the bale turned out, it expands, so that it is reduced by compressing about one-third in depth—the length and breadth being the same as before compressing.

A few years ago, a lot of cotton came to this port with iron hoops, but it was pronounced unmerchantable, because, in compressing, the hoops had to be taken off and ropes substituted. The planter discontinued the use of hoops, and none have since been received here put up with them. All cotton is pronounced unmerchantable that has other than good grass or hemp ropes on it.

Could you even put up your cotton in the size of compressed bales, we think it would be the best to use hemp ropes. In loading a ship, the cotton is driven by means of jack-screws so tight that iron hoops would break—where rope would only be loosened and removed a little, and when the cotton is turned out, the expansion immediately fastens the ropes again—even though cotton is compressed as well as it can be done; in stowing the ships it is often driven so hard by means of jack-screws that ropes are loosened, and shippers say that the iron hoops would break.

We can purchase the hoop iron as follows:—at 7 cts. per lb.

Hoop Iron ¾	guage 20,	say 7 ft. 4 in.	weighs 12 oz.
" ⅞	" 20,	" 7 ft. 4 in.	" 14 oz.
" ½	" 20,	" 7 ft. 4 in.	" 1 lb.

Rivets to suit, say 2lb. iron rivets, can be bought at 75 cts. per thousand.

We have stated all that we can learn about this matter, and we think the use of iron hoops instead of ropes is not viewed in a favorable light by dealers, shippers, &c., of cotton.

You will find in the January number of De Bow's Commercial Review, published in New-Orleans, an interesting and well-written article on the mode of putting up cotton in the best manner for market, to which we beg to refer you, if you have not already perused it.

The *average* weight of a compressed bale, we have been told, is 30 lbs. to the cubic foot.

A correspondent of the Review, in the December number, writing from Burtau, Alabama, over the signature of "An Alabama Planter," communicates what purports to be a letter from a mercantile house in Mobile, (without any signature,) on the subject of Banding Cotton Bales with *Iron Hoops* instead of *Rope*, and makes a personal request of me that I would reply to that communication, because he thinks it defective in its reasonings on the subject; and he is pleased to do me the honor to suppose that I am practically acquainted with the question in hand.

I could not consent to make a public reply to the Mobile letter, without expressing an opinion adverse to its authenticity. I suppose your friend in Alabama has been imposed upon by means of a spurious letter. No merchant in Mobile can, upon reflection, entertain the views therein expressed; nor can any man, whether he has ever seen a bale of cotton or not. For instance, the letter says:—"All cotton is pronounced unmerchantable that has other than good *grass* or *hemp* ropes on it." Cotton cordage is used for this purpose to some extent, and it is known to be superior or a least as good as hemp or grass. (It is superior only because if exposed to the weather a long time it will last without rotting much longer.) And I presume it is difficult to conceive why cotton, if offered for sale in Mobile in *cotton ropes*, should be pronounced "unmerchantable."

Again, the letter says that, "in loading a ship, the cotton is driven by means of jack-screws so tight that iron hoops would break." An expansive pressure from the inside of the bale outwards, would, I should suppose, cause the hoops to break if they were not strong enough. But I should hardly think that a pressure on the *outside* of the bale would produce the same effect.

The entire paragraph from which the last quotation above is taken, reads as follows:

"Could you even put up your cotton in the size of compressed bales, we think it would be the best to use hemp ropes. In loading a ship the cotton is driven by means of jack-screws so tight that iron hoops would break—where rope would only be loosened and removed a little, and when the cotton is turned out the expansion immediately fastens the ropes again—even though cotton is compressed as well as can be done; in stowing ships it is often driven so hard, by means of jack-screws, that ropes are loosened, and shippers say that the iron hoops would break."

A very great advantage of iron hoops over rope, in banding cotton bales, is well known and has always been admitted to be, that the bales are much easier handled, particularly in loading and unloading vessels, and the above paragraph from the Mobile letter was intended, I suppose, to set forth, ironically, this advantage. In stowing ships with cotton a great number of bales have to be dragged endwise, upon other bales, half the length of the hold or more; and in finishing, not a few have to be driven, by means of jack-screws, a long distance into apertures scarcely large enough to receive them. The outward pressure of the bale (up and down as it lay in the press, for there is very little sidewise) causes it to swell an inch over the band, on the two sides which may be called the top and bottom. The two other sides of the bale, (of cotton in ropes,) has, of course, a very uneven surface—the ropes on one side and ropes and knots on the other. In driving these bales into a small hole between other bales, with like ropes and knots, they frequently hitch against each other, the knots become torn loose and the ropes dragged off. This is what the letter, in the jesting pleasantry of the writer, alludes to in saying "the ropes are *loosened.*"

All these inconveniences are, of course, avoided by the use of hoops. From conversations I have had with ship-masters and mates, and other authentic information *from them*, I have been surprised to learn that in consequence of the difficulties above alluded to, it is by many said to be double the labor to stow a ship with cotton in ropes that it would be with bales in hoops.

The letter again says: "A few years ago a lot of cotton came to this port with iron hoops, but it was pronounced unmerchantable, because, in compressing, the hoops had to be taken off and ropes substituted."

"*In compressing?*" I thought the principal object in putting cotton in iron hoops, was to put it into *shipment size* at once. It certainly would be very unwise to put iron hoops on bales which would have to be re-pressed.

Your correspondent is certainly correct in supposing we can make our bales in good shipping size on the plantation, and thus entirely avoid the expense of re-pressing. And we can, at the same time, secure other advantages. One of which is the facility in loading vessels, and consequent lessening of freight. I had a conversation with several ship-masters on this subject, the last time I was in Mobile, who were then taking in cargoes of cotton at that port. They expressed the uniform sentiment I have invariably heard from *that quarter*, viz.: an unqualified wish that iron hoops would take the place of ropes upon cotton bales; and a readiness to take cotton in hoops at reduced rates of freight, on account of the greater ease with which they can stow and unload their ships, and the greater security from loss by fire.

If there is a mercantile, or any other, objection to the use of iron hoops on cotton bales, it ought to be fairly and seriously stated, and if there be none, then every planter ought to use them. I am well persuaded there is none, except that it is adverse to the interest of those who are connected, directly and indirectly, by sympathy, friendship, and otherwise, with the steam cotton presses at the import cities.

It ought to be remarked, however, that bales may be so banded with hoops, and no doubt frequently are, as to be unfit for shipment. I once saw a lot of cotton in Yazoo City, banded up in iron bands in so awkward and clumsy a manner, that the cotton ought to have been pronounced "unmerchantable," whether it was or not. When I speak of cotton in hoops, I mean that the bales are to be of the size they come from the steam presses—say 22 to 24 square, and 4 feet 6 inches long—the hoops of proper size and well riveted. The process of putting them on is very simple, and much faster than tying ropes. I would willingly communicate directly with your correspondent on this, or any other subject connected with "*our craft*," and interchange any useful information.

R. ABBEY.

COTTON—COST OF PRODUCING, &c.—We have seen within a short time various statements published in regard to the cost of producing cotton and what should be its natural price. A writer in the Carolinian declares 5 cents will not pay in that state any profit. He takes an estate well managed, inferior to none in productiveness, and affording more than an average yield in the state. The winter but not summer clothing was manufactured at the place. The number of acres was 550, much of which, four years ago, cost $25 per acre, number of slaves forty, one-half field hands. Estimating the negroes at $300 each, and the land at $12, with stock, etc., the investment will be $20,000.

Income 1848.

Bales of cotton 120; 350 lbs. = 42,500 lbs. at 5 cts	$2,100 00
Increase in negroes	200 00
	2,300 00
Deduct expenses, etc.	1,383 00
	917 00
Value planter's superintendence.	417 00
Net income (or 2½ per cent)	500 00

Expenses and loss for 1848.

Wages of overseer,	$300 00
Blacksmith's account, iron included	35 00
Medicine and medical attendance	30 00

Bagging, rope and twine for 120 bales cotton	150 00
Blankets, thirty in number, at $1 12½ each	33 75
Shoes, twenty-five pairs, at $1 25 per pair	31 25
Cotton Osnaburgs, 300 yards, at 8 cents per yard	24 00
Taxes, (state, poor, and bridge,) say	30 00
Salt, six sacks, at $2 each,	12 00
Nails, 100 lbs. at 5 cents per lb.	5 00
Hoes, 1 dozen	4 50
Sugar and coffee for sick, 75 lbs., at 10 cents per lb.	7 50
Annual wear and tear of land, say 5 per cent. upon estimated value (6,600)	330 00
Contingencies, such as re-stocking the place with mules, wear and tear of wagons, etc.	200 00
Cost of transporting 120 bales cotton to market, at 75 cents per bale	90 00
Loss by death of old negro, say	100 00
Whole expenses and loss	$1,383 00

Mr. Solon Robinson, a very observant agriculturist, who has been traveling extensively in the South, furnishes some statistics to the same effect. He presents the case of Col. Williams's plantation, at Society Hill, S. C.

STATISTICS OF A CAROLINA COTTON ESTATE.

Capital Invested.

4,200 acres of land (2,700 in cultivation) at $15	$63,000 00
254 slaves, at $350 each, average old and young	89,900 00
60 mules and mares, and one jack, and one stud, average $60	3,720 00
200 head of cattle, at $10	2,000 00
500 head of hogs, at $2	1,000 00
23 carts and 6 wagons	520 00
60 bull-tongue plows, 60 shaving do., 25 turning do., 15 drill do., 15 harrows, at an average of $1 50 each	262 00
All other plantation tools estimated, worth	1,000 00
	$161,402 00

Crop.

331,000 lbs. cotton, at	
13,500 lbs. of bacon, taken for home place and factory	675 00
Beef and butter for ditto and sales	500 00
1,100 bushels of corn and meal for ditto and sales	550 00
80 cords of tan bark for his tan yard	480 00
Charges to others for blacksmith work	100 00
Mutton and wool for home use and sales	125 00
	2,430 00
331,000 lbs.)	15,464 00
	Cents, 4.7

Expenses.

Interest is only counted on the first five items, $158,620, at seven per cent	$11,103 00
3,980 yards Dundee bagging, at 16 cts., (5 yards to a bale	536 80
3,184 lbs. of rope, at 6 cents	191 04
Taxes on 254 slaves, at 76 cents	193 04
Taxes on land	70 00
Three overseers' wages	900 00
Medical attendance, $1 25 per head	317 50
Bill of yearly supply of iron, average	100 00
Plows and other tools purchased, annual average	100 00
200 pairs of shoes, $175; annual supply of hats, $100	275 00
Bill of cotton and woolen cloth.	810 00
100 cotton comforters, in lieu of bed blankets	125 00
100 oil-cloth capotes (New-York cost)	87 50
20 small woolen blankets for infants	25 00
Calico dress and handkerchief for each woman and girl, (extra of other clothing)	82 00
Christmas presents, given in lieu of "negro crop"	175 00
50 sacks of salt	80 00
Annual average, outlay for iron and wood work for carts and wagons	100 00
Lime and plaster bought last year	194 00
Annual average outlay for gin, belts, etc.	80 00
400 gallons of molasses	100 00
3 kegs tobacco, $60; 2 bbls. of flour, $10	70 00
⅝ of a cent a pound on cotton, for freight and commission	2,069 60
	17,894 48
Deduct other products than cotton	2,430 00
Cost of cotton	$15,464 00

Showing the average cost of producing cotton per lb. a little less than 4 cents and 7 mills. Had this cotton sold at 6 cents, the profits would have been $1,973 68, at 7 cents, $5,385 04, which was about what it brought, being little more than 3 per cent.

STATISTICS ALABAMA COTTON ESTATE.

The following is given by Mr. Robinson

as the results on a plantation in Alabama, in Marengo county, and owned by Robert Montague, Esq.

Expenses.

Interest on capital at seven per cent.	$5,756 80
Cash expenses, taxes, average,	100 00
Blankets, hats and shoes, (other clothing all homemade).	250 00
Medical bill, average not exceeding	40 00
500 lbs. iron, $30; hoes and spades, $30.	60 00
Average outlay for mules over what are raised	100 00
Average expense yearly for machinery repairs	20 00
Bagging and rope.	350 00
	$6,676 00

Capital Invested.

1,100 acres of land, at $25	$27,500 00
120 slaves, at $400	48,000 00
4 wagons	400 00
5 yoke of oxen at $30	150 00
30 mules and horses, at $75	2,250 00
4,000 bushels corn on hand for plantation use, at 35 cents	1,400 00
Fodder and oats, do. do. do.	200 00
40 head of cattle, at $5, do. do.	200 00
70 do. sheep, at $2, do. do.	140 00
250 do. hogs, do. do.	600 00
20,000 lbs. bacon and pork, do.	1,000 00
Plows and all other tools, do.	500 00
	$82.240 00

This crop, 128,000, lbs. at 6 per cent. net, will leave a balance of $1,004.20, which is just about enough to pay the owner common wages of an overseer, which business he attends to himself.

The Columbia South Carolinian, however, makes considerable havoc among the figures of Mr. Robinson, to which they present a very open flank. Referring to Mr. Williams's place, the editor says:

True Profits of Cotton Planters.—Mr. Robinson has included 1,500 acres of land not in cultivation. All the land (4,200 acres) in his estimate of capital was valued at $15 per acre, so that here is $22,500 called "capital" in a business where it is no such thing. It may be said that land for fuel, timber, cattle pasture and range for stock, are necessary to carrying on the business of cotton planting, and so it is; but we think one-half of the residue of the land, say 750 acres, would be a large allowance for these purposes. At the least, then, we make a reduction of the "capital" to the amount of 11,250—leaving the real capital $150,152. But the most glaring inconsistency which our agricultural tourist exhibits in calculating the profits of a business investment, is in adding the item of interest upon capital as expense. A person investing money in any enterprise is justly considered to be doing a fair business if he makes a small percentage over interest and expenses; and the statement which Mr. Robinson furnishes of Col. Williams's plantation, only proves that our fellow-citizen makes about 12½ per cent. on his capital, and that too with the price of cotton placed as low as six cents *in Charleston*—for freight and commission are included in the table of "expenses."

In the first place, the actual capital invested is clearly misstated, as we have shown above. In the second place we deny the principle of adding interest on the capital, as part of the expenses, when the object is to find out the profits upon that capital. In the third place, Mr. Robinson calculates interest upon the cost of the stock of the plantation, which is obviously fallacious and deceptive, where its natural increase must amount to more than the interest. In the fourth place, he omits to add to the income of the plantation the natural increase of the labor employed thereon—an item which is always prominent in the planter's calculation, and which would unquestionably amount to 5 or 6 per cent. per annum upon their original cost. And, in the fifth place, he has entirely neglected the increased value arising from the yearly improvement of a well cultivated plantation. We think the case is fairly stated. The result then, according to our views, will be as follows:

CAPITAL INVESTED, $150,152 00.

INCOME OF THE FARM.

331,136 lbs. cotton, at 6 cents	$19,868 16
Bacon and other provisions	2,430 00
Increase of negroes, say 5 per cent., set down as capital $89,000	4,495 00
	$26,793 16
The annual expenses of the farm, as itemized by Mr. Robinson, a full estimate, including freight and commission,	6,791 48
Net profits of capital invested	$20,001 68

These profits amount to over *thirteen per cent. per annum* over all expenses—the *Charleston* price of cotton being only put down at 6 cents. Suppose the crop averaged eight cents in Charleston, as it would do at the present time, the profits would be $26,614 40, or nearly 18 per cent.

The calculations of the Alabama plantation would, perhaps, show a still greater error but we cannot arrive at correct results, as the whole number of acres, and not the quantity under cultivation, is given; and the statement made, that the plantation having on it 120 slaves, only made about $1,000 over interest and expenses, as Mr. Robinson says, just the common wages of an overseer! We know not what this tourist's object was in giving publication to a statement so much calculated to deceive. We have no doubt, however, that he unwittingly made the mistakes referred to. We have shown that cotton planting, at a moderate price for cotton, pays 13 per cent. profit.

COTTON.—Analysis of.—One hundred parts of cotton wool, on being heated in a platina crucible, lost 85.89 parts. The residuum, on being ignited under a muffle till the whole of the carbon was consumed, lost 12.735, and left a white ash which weighed nearly 1 per cent., or 1.9347. Of this ash, nearly 44 per cent. was soluble in water. Its consituents were as follows:

Carbonate of potash (with a trace of soda)	44.29
Phosphate of lime (with a trace of magnesia)	25.34
Carbonate of lime	8.97
Carbonate of magnesia	6.75
Silica	4.12
Sulphate of potassa	2.90
Alumina	1.40
Chloride of potassium, Sulphate of lime, Phosphate of potassa, Oxide of iron, (a trace,) and loss	6.23
	100.00

Analysis of Cotton Seed.—One hundred parts, treated as before, lost 77.387, and the residuum, after being burnt under a muffle, left 3.986 parts of a perfectly white ash, the composition of which was as follows:

Phosphate of lime (with traces of magnesia)	61.34
Phosphate of potassa (with traces of soda)	31.73
Sulphate of potassa	2.65
Silica	1.68
Carbonate of lime	.47
Carbonate of magnesia	.27
Chloride of potassium	.25
Carbonate of potassa, Sulphate of lime, Sulphate of magnesia, Alumina and oxide of iron, and loss	1.68
	100 00

With respect to these analyses, we may for the present observe, that the seeds yielded nearly four times as much of the ash as the cotton itself did, and at the same time contained a much larger proportion of the phosphoric acid and of lime. In this respect, the quantity of both these substances is greater, as shown by the American analysis, than in that of Dr. Ure. Whether this may be owing to different kinds of wool having been employed, or to differences in the modes of analysis, can only be known when the analysis shall have been repeated by chemists with different kinds of cotton.

In resuming our observations on soils, it is first of all, necessary to observe, that, though no one will dispute the paramount importance of the chemical constituents of the soil, yet these may be considered in some respects to be only of comparative value, as it is equally necessary to attend to the physical state of the soil, and to both, in connection with the climate of particular localities. The mechanical state of the soil, its greater or less degree of porosity or of tenacity, enabling the roots to spread with more or less facility, so as to fix the plant steadily in the earth, at the same time that they supply it with a large portion of its nutriment, is necessarily of great importance. But as a considerable portion of the food of plants is supplied by the air, its different states and due supply require also to be attended to, in addition to climate: no chemical composition or mechanical states will compensate for unsuitableness of climate. We all know that our oaks are as little likely to flourish within the tropics, as South American palms in our meadows; and no one now expects that our rich variety of orchids would flourish, if, supplying them with every requisite of site, of soil, of culture, and even of temperature, we denied them a moist atmosphere. And yet a few years only have elapsed since it was considered a rarity to flower these *air plants*, and also, since mountain rice was attempted to be cultivated here in the open air, because it came from a cool climate, and was said to be cultivated without irrigation. But it was forgotten that, during the season of cultivation in its native mountains, rain falls almost every day, and the air is in a state of continual moisture. So also in the culture of cotton, a certain state of the soil, both with respect to its chemical composition and its mechanical state, may be well suited to one situation, and yet not be desirable in another, chiefly from a difference in the condition of the atmosphere. For instance, a certain degree of porosity of the soil may retain and bring just enough of water within the reach of the roots, and yet if the atmosphere became more damp, the soil may require to be made dryer by drainage. Again, if in another situation the air is more dry, and evaporation necessarily greater, both from the surface of the earth and from that of the leaves, a soil more retentive of moisture will be more suitable than one which is more open, and which thus allows moisture to escape, not only by evaporation, but by drainage. These varieties may be observed, not only in the soil and climate of different localities, but even in the same locality at different seasons of the year, especially in a country like India, which, in the language of meteorologists, is in many parts one of extremes. As plants obtain from the ground their water, holding in solution saline and earthy particles, and are dependent upon the air for the elements of organic matter, it is evidently essential to pay equal attention to both cases, for it is difficult, nay, impossible, in both cases, to say whether the soil or the climate has the most influence upon successful cultivation, and it is nearly as useless, to use the words of Mr. Neill, as "attempting to decide which half of a pair of scissors has most to do in the act of cutting, or which of the factors, 5 or 6, contributes most to the production of 30."

With respect to the practical inferences deducible from the chemical analysis, we may first quote the opinion of Mr. Piddington, that carbonate of lime was essential to good cotton soil. Subsequently, he observed that the American, the Mauritius, and the best Singapore soil, contain a considerable percentage of vegetable matter, and some part of it easily soluble in cold water, while the Indian soils contain very little vegetable matter, and this wholly soluble in water; but that the best contain a far larger proportion of carbonate of lime, and some of them their iron in a different state from the others. The lime, though not indispensable, he supposes may be highly useful; but he ascribes greater value to the presence of vegetable matter. For a soil in Bengal, which contained exceedingly minute proportions of lime and carbonaceous matter, and in which he cultivated cotton, worth from 9*d* to 11*d* per pound, as an experiment, for seven or eight years, during which he had always good, and often abundant crops, he ascribes this effect to the plants having been constantly manured with the black, pesty earth, so abundant in the jheels (pieces of water) of India, and of which an average good specimen contains 26.00 per cent. of vegetable matter, and 15.00 per cent. of carbonate of lime, yielded chiefly by the small shells contained in the above deposits.

Mr. E. Solly, as the result of his analyses, remarks: "that the goodness of the soils from Georgia depended, probably, far more on the mechanical structure than on the chemical composition, and that the presence of lime or any other substance would appear of far less importance than that the soil should be, not too rich, but of a light and porous character, so that delicate fibres of the roots might penetrate easily in all directions." This opinion is probably not far from the truth, wherever the climate is most suitable to the cultivation of cotton.

Dr. Wight, after practical experience of some years, states that where it is in his power to choose, he prefers "a deep, dark-colored, light, almost sandy loam, and if it has been long out of cultivation, so much the better." The black cotton soil, in which so much of the cotton of India is grown, and which is generally considered the best for the purpose, is remarkable for its power of retaining moisture; while of the red soil, he says: "again, I am informed that in some parts of the country, for example, in the Vizagapatam district, the finest cotton crops, both as to quantity and quality, are raised on red soils, and the redder, the better for the purpose." But the suitableness of these several soils, we must consider in connection with climate.

COTTON PLANT—Analysis of the.—At the Farmers' Club of New-York, the Hon. Dixon H. Lewis, of Alabama, remarked that the seed of the cotton made rather more than three-fourths of the plant, and every 1200 lbs. gives 350 clean cotton. "The Club, in accordance with his suggestion, resolved upon having prepared a complete and perfect analysis of the stalk, boll, fibre and seed of the cotton plant." The analysis hitherto made by Dr. Shepard, extended only to the wool and seed. The results as we have them are:—One hundred parts cotton wool lost 86.09 parts in a platina crucible, leaving a charred residuum, "which on being ignited under a muffle until every part of the carbon was consumed, lost 12.985 and left an almost purely white ash whose weight was 0.9247. Of this ash about 44 per cent. was found soluble in water, It contained 12.88 of sand, an adventitious product of harvesting. Deducting the sand, the constitution of the ash is obtained; and abstracting the carbonic acid as the result of incineration, Dr. S. shows that to constitute every 100 parts of the ash, the cotton plant will take from the soil the following important mineral ingredients:

Potassa (with possible traces of soda)	31.09	pounds.
Lime	17.05	"
Magnesia	3.26	"
Phosphoric acid	12.30	"
Sulphuric acid	1.22	"
	64.92	

Or, for 10,000 lbs. cotton wool, there will be taken 64.92 lbs. of these elements.

A table corresponding with the one above is derived from experiments upon *Cotton Seed:*

Phosphoric acid	45.35
Lime	29.79
Potassa	19.40
Sulphuric Acid	1.16
	95.70

In comparing the above table with that afforded by the cotton wool, a marked dissimilarity presents itself. The ash of the cotton seed is fourfold that of the fibre; while the former has also treble the phosphoric acid possessed by the latter, as will the more clearly appear when we present the analysis, under another form, corresponding with the second table under cotton wool.

From the foregoing analysis, it would appear difficult to imagine a vegetable compound better adapted for fertilizing land than the cotton seed; nor can we any longer be surprised at the well-known fact, that soils long cropped with this staple, without a return to them of the inorganic matters withdrawn in the seed, become completely exhausted and unproductive.

Dr. Ure gave in 1825 the following *analysis of Sea Island Cotton.*—1. Matter soluble in water, sixty-four parts, consisting of

Carbonate of potash	44.8
Muriate of potash	9.9
Sulphate of potash	9.3

2. Matter insoluble in water,

Phosphate of lime	9.0
Carbonate of lime	10.6
Phosphate of magnesia	8.4
Peroxide of iron	3.0
Alumina a trace, and lass	5.0
	100.0

COTTON WORM—ITS HISTORY, CHARACTER, VISITATIONS, ETC.—The following are some remarks on the nature of the cotton fly of 1846, being a sequel to a dissertation on the usefulness of a knowledge of the natural history of insects, written last winter. I send you that portion only which treats of the cotton fly, as falling more especially within the province of your periodical. This manuscript would not have sought a place upon your pages, had not my attention been drawn to it by the ill-founded apprehensions of many planters concerning the *present* existence of the cotton worm, an event utterly impossible, for if it makes its appearance at all this season, it most certainly will not do so until the cotton plant has attained its greatest maturity. I see, also, in your Review, a communication claiming to show the means by which the army worm may be effectually eradicated, in which is displayed the greatest ignorance as to the general laws that govern the insect world. The writer states that the chrysalis of the cotton fly may be plowed up, and thus destroyed, &c.! Now, these chrysales never go in the ground at all, but are invariably attached to something above the surface. This is a fact that could not have escaped the attentive observer. I ask how a chrysalis, invariably formed above ground, and incapable of locomotion, is to work its way beneath the soil? As to the insect, on any condition, secreting itself in the earth, beneath the bark of trees, under fallen timber, &c., it is altogether a mistake, if not an absurdity, and easier asserted than proved. In treating of the cotton fly, in the following pages, my aim has been to found my assertions upon general principles, and though the practised entomologist may find some inaccuracies in the detail, yet I insist upon the principles as universal and incontrovertible.

Let us now pass to the consideration of the cotton fly, premising, however, before entering into an examination of this destructive little moth, that my remarks are intended less to enlighten others, than to elicit information from some one who is better able to inform the public mind on this interesting subject. As for myself, I must confess that my limited observations do not justify me in coming to any positive conclusions, nor have they by any means satisfied my curiosity, but my information, such as it is, I give in the following pages, with the hope that, however imperfect it may prove in the main, yet, that some mite of information may be gleaned from it. It is impossible to think for a moment that this species of moth has escaped the observation of entomologists, for the plant upon which it feeds, to the absolute exclusion of all others, (being the great staple production of many countries,) must have brought it into notice at various times and at various places. From its univorous nature, (to coin a word) it must have been coeval with and inseparable from the existence of the cotton plant. My principal motive for broaching this subject, is on account of the frequent remarks made, and fears entertained, that the army worm would become an annual plague. But since I have investigated their nature, I have come to the conclusion that these fears are groundless, and that the cotton fly can never become naturalized in our climate.

The first eruption, as I am informed by an old planter, that this insect made on the cotton fields of Louisiana, was about the year 1820, when its progress was marked with the same utter destruction of the cotton crop, as in the subsequent years of their appearance. It then disappeared until '40, a period of twenty years. There is something singular and unaccountable in the periods of this insect, something vastly different from the periodicities of others which we find with us, for they appear to be governed by some fixed laws; the most of them are annual, very few biennial. Now, the grasshopper, house-fly, and musquito may be looked for at the return of summer, with as much confidence and certainty as we look for the revolutions of the seasons. The cicada septemdecem never fails to make his appearance once in seventeen years. But who can tell whether the cotton fly will appear next year, or fifty years hence? No scourge, whether under the form of a devouring insect, or that of a malignant disease, ever became annual in one particular place. Look at the locust of Egypt: suppose that voracious insect to become annual, the prolific valley of the Nile, once the granary of Asia and Europe, would become a howling desert. Look at the plague that devastates, sometimes, Smyrna and Constantinople, did the cause of that distemper act with the like intensity at each return of the season, those flourishing cities would long since have been numbered with Thebes and Memphis. Let the cholera or yellow fever prevail in New-Orleans every year, as it has at times, and that great emporium of the South-West would become a puny village. Is there not an invisible hand that sways the destinies of the world? a hand that stays the devastations of plague, pestilence, and famine!

The cotton fly belongs to that numerous class of insects known to naturalists under the term of phalena or moth tribe. It resembles the butterfly tribe in many respects, but its chief point of difference is that all moths fly at night, and are attracted by bright lights, and may be seen darting through the flame of a candle, during the summer and fall months, to the great annoyance of those who desire the benefit of its light. Butterflies fly only during the day.

The following are its specific characters, without the technicalities made use of by the naturalist, so far as they could well be avoided:

Antennæ, or little horns projecting from the head, setaceous or terminating a point like a bristle, of a drab color, and five lines in length, being about half of the length of the body.

Wings incumbent, deflexa; under surface of thorax or breast, of a dull silvery white, insensibly terminating on the abdomen and wings in a color tending to a russet; the upper surface of the wings and back varying somewhat in different individuals, but generally of a changeable golden color, with ferruginous zig-zag lines traversing the surface transversely;—posterior margin bordered with a narrow strip of pale pink color, with small denticulations. On the upper surface of the wings there are two black spots, one on each, about the middle of the base; legs white, the four posterior very long when compared with the front ones, which are short and slender; the tail simple. The length of this insect is about nine lines from head to tail. Expansion of the wings at the tips, about the same measurement. To conclude, I will add that the shape of this moth is very much like that of an isosceles triangle, with the line forming the base inflected inwardly about two lines. This peculiar figure is produced by the exterior angle of the upper wings projecting beyond that of the interior angle.

During the present year, the time that my observations commenced for the first time, the cotton fly again made its appearance in the latter part of August, at first making but little progress, but about the middle of September their numbers increased so prodigiously, that in many instances they would eat over a field of several hundred acres in four or eight days.

The number of eggs deposited by the female is uncertain; they are smaller than a mustard seed, and always deposited on the under-surface of the leaf during the night—in a few days their eggs hatch. The worm, at first a minute living point, falls immediately to work to devour the leaf; its growth is rapid, for its labors cease not night nor day until it arrives at maturity, it then winds itself up into a leaf by means of a web resembling *cobweb*, casts its skin and changes into a chrysalis, in which state it remains ten days, then it bursts the thin walls of the chrysalis, and comes forth a perfect insect. In turn, it begins the work of reproduction, deposits its eggs, and in ten more days it dies.

Thus, in every ten days there is an additional generation, and they go on increasing *ad infinitum*. As soon as the leaves were consumed in a field, this great *army* took up its march; some in search of comfortable quarters, where they might repose from their labors; others on a foraging expedition to replenish the means of their subsistence. The first took shelter in the first leaf they met with, but generally they proceeded as far as the fence, a barrier beyond which they never traveled, where they found a plentiful supply of leaves, in which they enveloped themselves. The second division extended their march much farther, sometimes traveling half a mile from the point whence they started, perishing by cart loads for want of food and the many casualties to which their journey subjected them, such as carriage wheels, heat of the sun, and the rapacity of birds.

Here, then, it would appear was an end to the cotton worm, for a season at least, for those which yet remain in chrysalis in the fence corners, will change to the fly in ten days. But where are now the cotton leaves upon which the pregnant female is to deposit her eggs? There is not one left. If they are placed on any other leaf the eggs may hatch, but the worm must perish, as we have just seen them perishing by myriads while wending their way through a various and luxuriant herbage in search of that food intended for them by nature. In ten days from the time that the worm becomes a chrysalis on the borders of the cotton fields, a host of flies are seen issuing therefrom: they go forth in search of food for their forthcoming progeny; now it is to be found their days are numbered, in ten more if they meet with no cotton leaves they themselves must die, and thus put an end to the whole race. But their search is continued, and now when the weary insect is ready to finish its term of days, a tender but sparse foliage crowns the leafless twigs of the cottan plant, on them the eggs are deposited: they hatch, the worm eats, returns again to its chrysalis. The cotton stalk still puts forth new leaves, they grow and expand until the fields again look green; ten days, aye, forty elapses, yet there is not a worm to be found. One would have thought that this second crop of leaves would scarcely have been sufficient for a single repast for them, yet the food that they so lately devoured with such voraciousness is now left untouched. What is the matter! Why don't they eat, their food is spread before them? Read on, the answer will be found in the sequel. Let us examine the cause. In nearly every fourth leaf we find a chrysalis writhing and contorting itself at the touch. Ah! here is the explanation of the difficulty, this is no ten days' chrysalis, but that in which it is to hibernate, possibly for one winter, perchance for twenty. Let us take a pocket full of these home, and place them beneath tumblers, and wait patiently to see what they will produce. If I had found a treasure, my delight could not have been greater than that I experienced at the idea of unraveling this mystery. But man is prone to disappointment, as we shall soon see. About the fifteenth of November the insect appeared, but, *mirabile dictu!* as different from the cotton fly as it is possible to suppose one insect could differ from another. It belonged altogether to a different family, a description of which I give, as follows:

Antennæ filiform; black, six lines in length. Palpi four, two external and two intermediate, the external white, twice the length of the other two, in shape angular, the angle projecting externally. The two middle are straight, scarcely perceptible over a strong light; they are of a dark color. Wings four; hymenopterous; incumbent, extending to and exactly even with the end of the tail; shape of the wings, which are small and extremely delicate, are like that of a fan. Front legs half the length of the posterior, of a uniform orange color; the intermediate legs very little longer than the anterior; the thighs of a deep orange color, the rest of the leg annulated with orange and white. The posterior legs long in comparison to the others; thighs of a deep orange color, the rest of the leg annulated with black and white, the rings being larger than those of the intermediate. The trunk is of a uniform shining black, as would be the upper surface of the abdomen also, were it not for the very narrow white bands which connect the black scales together, giving to the abdomen an annulated appearance; these white lines do not encircle the abdomen, but terminate uniformly on the sides. On the under surface of the abdomen these white rings again commence, which are much larger than those on the upper surface, causing the abdomen to look almost white. The tail terminates in a bifurcated sheath, inclosing a long blunt sting, projecting considerably beyond the tail, and forming a very prominent feature in the general figure of the insect. This is a small slender insect, much longer than the honey bee, but not so thick.

Now, it is evident from its specific character, as well as from its parasitic nature, this insect belongs to that numerous class called *ichneumons,* of which there are upwards of five hundred species. As I am not at present in possession of any practical work on Entomology, I cannot determine the species of this ichneumon, but to show that it differs in some respect from the family to which it belongs, I will quote a paragraph from a work before me, in which are set forth some peculiarities belonging to that class of insects as a genus:

"The whole of this singular genus have been denominated parasitical, on account of the very extraordinary manner in which they provide for the future support of their young. The fly feeds on the honey of flowers, and when about to lay her eggs, perforates the body of some other insect, or its larva with its sting or instrument, at the end of the abdomen, and then deposits them. The eggs in a few days hatch, and the young larvæ, which resemble minute white maggots, nourish themselves with the juices of the foster parent, which, however, continues to move about and feed until near the time of its changing into a chrysalis, when the larvæ of the ichneumon creep out by perforating the skin in various places, and each spinning itself up in a small oval silken case, changes into a chrysalis, and after a certain period they emerge in the state of complete ichneumons."

It will be seen that there is a peculiarity attached to this ichneumon not included in the above description, that of appropriating the chrysalis as well as the larvæ of other insects, to the use of their young. All ichneumons that I ever read of spin their own chrysalis, but this is the prince of parasites, for not content with eating the substance of his neighbor, he seizes also on his house. So far as I have read concerning this curious family of insects, this is a nondescript. As an example of these insects called ichneumons, I may mention the *ichneumon seductor,* or dirt-dauber, well known to everybody as that wasp-like insect which builds its clay houses on the walls, and particularly in the recesses of windows, to the great annoyance of the tidy housewife.

Thus is answered the question why the cotton fly did not again eat up the scant foliage which subsequently appeared on the stalks. This little usurper goes forth in search of "whom he may devour," and as soon as he finds a house built and well provisioned, he seizes upon it for his posterity, which he does in the following manner: when he finds a cotton worm he pierces it with the instrument with which its tail is armed, and deposits an egg; the cotton worm soon spins itself up into its case, there to await the period of its perfection, which never arrives, for soon the egg of the ichneumon hatches, and falls to devouring his helpless companion. This work of extermination continues until there is not a vestige of the cotton fly left. I venture to say, while I am now writing, (first of December,) there is not an egg, chrysalis, or fly, in the confines of the United States. My speculations on the nature and habits of the cotton fly have led me to adopt the following hypothesis: That it is a native of tropical climates, and never can pass a single winter beyond them, consequently never can become naturalized in the United States, or any where else where the cotton plant is not perennial, for nature has made no provision by which they can survive more than ten or twelve days, therefore they must perish wherever the cotton plant perishes during a period of five or six months. That wherever they have prevailed in our cotton growing regions, it is when they have become very numerous and consumed all the cotton in their native climes, and then go in search of their food in more northern climates. It is not to be presumed that this happens often, but the same remark will hold in regard to the cotton fly as it will to many other insects, that owing to some unknown cause they become exceedingly numerous, but at long and irregular intervals. The locust has already been noticed as an example, and many more might be cited. I, however, will mention another to which I was an eye-witness: About eighteen years ago the *green, or blow-fly*, became so numerous that thousands of animals perished by them, as also some human beings. The least spot of blood, the moisture of the mouth, eyes,or nose, was sufficient to cause a deposit of eggs. Sick persons, particularly those who had not proper attention, suffered. Several negro children who came under my notice, fell a sacrifice to them, and it was with difficulty that many others were saved. In these instances the fly deposited the eggs within the nostrils, where they soon caused death by producing inflammation of the brain. This fly is annual, and scarcely ever deposits its eggs on an animal, except it be the victim of a running sore; but at the period alluded to above, it appeared that there was scarcely animal flesh enough to feed the maggots of this numerous host. It is but once within my recollection, that I have witnessed this phenomenon, and neither before nor since have I heard of such ravages of the green fly. Why they should have existed in such incredible numbers at the time referred to is a question not to be easily answered.

There are three circumstances upon which I found my arguments in support of my hypothesis of the cotton fly: First. Nature has made no provision by which it could survive the winter season. Second. The irregularity of their appearance. Third. Their progress from south to north, and from west to east.

It may be remarked on proposition first, that all insects included within the genus *phalena*, hibernate in the state of a chrysalis, therefore it is utterly impossible for the cotton fly to hibernate in that manner, as they remain but ten days in chrysalis. The fly does not hibernate, for the period of their existence is but ten or twelve days. It cannot be in the state of the egg, for it is a law equally inflexible with regard to this tribe, that the egg must be deposited on the leaf on which the larvæ are to feed, and the reason is very plain, for these larvæ, when first hatched, are minute living points, of an exceedingly helpless nature, almost devoid of locomotion, or possessing it in too small a degree to enable it go in search of its food. But let us suppose that the egg does survive the winter, how does it happen that when the worm first makes its appearance it is found on the very summits of the cotton instead of the lower branches: parts that it would reach the soonest if it proceeded from the ground upwards.

The *phalena mosi*, or silk worm, is an insect of the same genus as the cotton fly, and whose habitudes are very much the same as the latter, tropical in its nature, confining itself to a particular vegetable, the different species of mulberry, and being short lived in the chrysalis, remaining in this state but fifteen days. At the approach of winter, when the mulberry trees cast their leaves and remain leafless for many months, these insects, in our climate, would all perish, were they left to themselves. But art in this respect has triumphed over nature, for the silk grower at a certain season gathers a parcel of eggs and places them in a cold dark place until the mulberry tree shall again afford them food in the spring, and in this manner they are perpetuated, and this is the only possible way that they could be preserved here; they are like some tender exotic, which flourishes as long as the warmth of the hot-house affords them a congenial atmosphere, but perishes if left to buffet the rigors of winter.

Proposition Second. Here I contend that when an insect is a native of or naturalized in any country, they are always governed by some invariable laws which determine their appearance. The grasshopper is annual, coming every spring or summer; the locust of our climate septem-decennial, appearing once in seventeen years, but the cotton fly has no regular periods of return, showing that when it reaches our climate it is by some casualty.

In proposition third, I maintain that if the cotton fly sojourned here during the winter or winters, that when it did appear at all, it would do so simultaneously through the whole cotton district, instead of which we see it progressing regularly from south to north, and from west to east.

Such are the speculations that I have entertained concerning the cotton worm, from which I conclude it originates in South America, and reaches us through Mexico, and never can become a denizen of our soil.—*Gorham.*

COTTON CATERPILLAR.—This fatal worm, like the locust of Egypt, threatens to leave no "green thing alive" wherever it finds admission. It is the scourge of the cotton planter, and the devastation of his teeming fields is almost the certain result of its visits. Whoever shall devise a scheme for the extirpation of such an enemy, will confer a benefit upon his country, which nothing could reward. All efforts have hitherto proved unavailing. Mr. Affleck, of Mississippi, that able and practical agriculturist, thus describes the character and habits of the insect.

"The parent insect is a night-flying or owlet moth, I think belonging to the MAMESTRADÆ—of a beautiful greenish gray, with bronze shading: on each outer wing there are two small white spots, shaded with bronze, near the shoulder and in a line with the edge; and lower down, a large kidney-shaped black or brown spot, shaded with white. Several wavy lines of purple crop the outer wing, which has also a fringe of the same color on the inner edge, and a fringe gray and purple at the end. The body is thick, and tapers to the end. The female is larger than the male, but they are otherwise much alike. The female deposits her eggs on the leaf (I am not fully satisfied that they are placed *only* there) in clusters; they are round, and whitish or pale green, and quite small. They are hatched in from two to five days, according to the weather, and immediately commence eating the leaves of the plant. They increase rapidly in size, attaining their full growth of one and a half inches in from three to five weeks. They are of a light green color, with longitudinal stripes of yellow on the sides, and along the back two black ones, separated by a very narrow line of white. Some are without the black stripes. They are also studded with small, distinct black spots, from nearly every one of which a black hair grows. They have sixteen legs—one pair behind, eight in the centre of the body, and six fore-legs. They elevate the front half of the body, when at rest, giving it a continued motion from side to side. They give forth, when in numbers in a field, a peculiar sweetish odor, readily recognizable by the observant planter. During the lifetime of the worm, it casts its skin at least four times. When it has attained its full growth, it places itself near one of the corners of the leaf, spins a few threads of silk, attaching them to the leaf in such a way as to draw up the edge, which it makes fast to the surface of the leaf, forming a scroll, within which it undergoes its transformation to a *pupa*. This it does in thirty-six to forty-eight hours. The pupa is black and slimy. In this state it remains from one to three weeks. I have found the state of the weather influence the change thus far, generally from seven to twelve days—when the perfect insect appears, and proceeds to multiply her species. This, each female will do to the extent of from two to six hundred or more."

In relation to the regions which the caterpillar usually frequents, Mr. Affleck remarks:

"This scourge to the cotton planter is by no means a new thing; nor is it confined to this country alone. In all the West India Islands, Guiana, and elsewhere in South America, it has been the frequent means of greatly lessening the crops. In Georgia, the caterpillar made its appearance as early as 1793. In that year the destruction was complete (from Major Butler's field of four hundred acres, only eighteen bags were made). Seven years afterward they commenced the work of devastation in South Carolina. In 1804, the crops, which would have been devoured by them, were, with the enemy, effectually destroyed by the hurricane of that year. (Between 1804 and 1825, their depredations were only occasional, and then confined to particular fields.) In 1825, the visit of the worm was renewed, and its ravages were universal and complete. In 1827, '29, '33, '34, '40, '41, and '43, the lower parishes generally, or particular locations, suffered greatly by its depredations. (The caterpillar is seldom seen in the upper parishes.) In Guiana the worm is called *chenille*. An interesting account of it is given in the Edinburgh Encyclopædia, article *Cotton*, by Dr. Chisholm, of Clifton. The same account is repeated almost *verbatim*, by Mr. Porter, in his "Tropical Agriculturist." They appear there every year—doing material injury, however, only every second or third year. They show themselves in that mild climate even during the winter, and appear and disappear many times during the year. Some elaborate estimates are made by Dr. C., of the amount of labor which might be profitably expended in destroying the *chenille*, to which I would refer the curious, though they do not apply well to the present value of cotton. He gives one hint, however, which I think a good one. The tobacco growers of Maryland and Virginia have acted upon it for many years, and with much success. "A prudent and economical planter will increase the brood of every species of domestic poultry, particularly turkeys; for this has a tendency to diminish the brood of *chenille* in a very great degree, while profit arises from the augmentation of useful stock. Turkeys are observed to have a remarkable appetite for the larvæ of the cotton moth, and devour prodigious quantities of them." In the Bahamas, between March and September, 1788, no less than two hundred and eighty tons of cotton, on a moderate scale, were devoured by this worm. The same cause produced the abandonment of the gossypium culture in several of the West India Islands. I saw it recently stated, that the destruction of the plant by the caterpillar put an entire stop to the cultivation of cotton, for many years in Egypt. The prospect of a like result in this country seems by no means improbable. The appearance of the worm has hitherto been partial, large districts and even entire states escaping; but this year it seems to be general over the entire cotton growing region."

He concludes with an extract from Seabrook's "*Cotton Plant*," exhibiting a method by means of which Mr. Townsend, of South Carolina, arrested the progress of the worm in his fields:

"1. His people searched for and killed both the worm and the chrysalis of the first brood.

"2. On the appearance of the second brood, he scattered corn on the field to invite the notice of the birds, and while they depredated on the worms on the tops of the stalks and their upper limbs, the turkeys destroyed the enemy on the lower branches.

"3. When in the aurelia state, the negroes crushed them between their fingers.

"4. Some patches of cotton, where the caterpillars were very thick and the birds and turkeys could not get access to them, were destroyed.

"5. The tops of the plants, and the ends of all the tender and luxuriant branches, where the eggs of the butterfly are usually deposited, were cut off.

"By these means, resolutely pursued, although at one time the prospect of checking the depredation was almost cheerless, not the slightest injury to the field was sustained."

We were favored with the subjoined letter, some time ago, from a gentleman formerly resident in Florida, and made an extract from it. We notice since that others have advanced similar views, and the subject is certainly deserving of attention:

"The caterpillar is the origin of the army worm, and as plowing cotton fields is not performed until near the time of planting, they remain undisturbed until they have so far gained maturity, that they are not destroyed by the plow, and at that season they are not apt to be injured by frosts; soon after they begin to feed on tender vegetation, lay millions of eggs, which mature so as to need food, and thus they increase until they deserve the name of army worm. Their effect is only too well known.

"Rainy, cloudy weather, produces them fastest; hot dry weather is not so favorable, but if the heat is too great, they can soon get beyond the heat in the earth, even if they should feed at night. They will find places to spend the winter, not only in the ground, but under wood, in the crevices of the rough bark of stumps or trees. If no remedy is found to exterminate them, they will increase until the cotton country will share the fate of Egypt.

"Now for the remedy. So soon as a field, or part of a field, is relieved of its crop, cut down all the stalks, set fire to them some clear, dry day; and cause the fire to run over the field. If the stalks do not furnish a sufficiency of material to produce a good fire, pine or oak leaves should be added. The stumps and standing trees will take fire, and the deposit of the eggs will be reached by the devouring flames, and the origin of the caterpillar and fly will thus be destroyed. Adjoining woods, and if possible, fences should be removed, and be subjected to the cleansing effect of the fire. This is an easy and will be an effectual process, which will again cause cotton fields to repay the planter by a good product.

"I say to the industrious cotton planter, run fire over your cotton fields, and you will secure your usual product. So soon as the cotton is so far advanced as not to be subject to injury, if hogs are turned into the field they will hunt the caterpillars, eat and get fat on them; will, in fact, take them in preference to corn. The planter will thus turn this destructive insect to profit by fattening hogs."

COTTON WORMS, &c.—There is probably no subject of practical agriculture that will be found on investigation to challenge in the experience of those engaged in its culture such varied and contradictory results as cotton. There is less perceived uniformity of practice observed in the culture of the cotton plant, than in that of any other agricultural staple—and yet with all this diversity of cultivating process, there is no other staple that generally yields such profitable results, exhibiting at the same time an extraordinary adaptation to every variety of soil and climate. So that in your inquiries on the subject, any peculiar mode of culture should not constitute so important an item of investigation, as the ascertainment, if possible, by an appeal to the researches of intelligent planters, of the origin of the whole tribe of destructive insects that habitually infest the cotton crop—I allude particularly to the spring insects called *lice*, that are found to prevail more fatally and *invariably*, irrespective of climate, than any other enemy to the plant. And I venture to assert, that there is no problem in the *modus operandi* of the crop, that will elicit more perplexing controversy. For the last few years I have devoted much anxious and minute attention to the prevalence of this class of insects, with the view to satisfy myself about their origin, and consequently to be enabled to devise some preventive to their recurrence. The result of my observations enables me to assert that no kind of weather nor peculiarity of locality is any guaranty against their existence—and that sudden vicissitudes in the season, a few weeks after the plant gets up, are most favorable to their production. It may also be asserted that they are inherently peculiar to the cotton crop, inasmuch as they are never seen invading any other vegetable growth. There are two opinions most current among the planters as to their origin. The one attributes their existence to some flying insect, that deposits the *larvæ* on the under side of the leaf of the plant—the other holds that famous little model of industry, the ant, responsible for the production of this mischievous nuisance, inasmuch as they are always found existing contemporaneously. I am much disposed to acknowledge myself the advocate of the latter opinion, from the fact that though I have always observed them existing together, I have never detected the ant playing the part of depredator on the lice. An entomological experiment, exposing the procreation of the ant, could at once settle the question. But let either one of these theories be verified by experiment, yet the important desideratum is presented, what remedy or prevention can be devised for this mischievous enemy to our cotton crops? It has recently occurred to me, that inasmuch as plaster of paris has proved a specific for the Hessian fly in the wheat crop of the North, may it not also prove a valuable remedy in the hands of the cotton planters, either by rubbing the seed previously to planting with it, or by using it as a top-dressing to the plant at the time it is most liable to the ravages of this insect. At any rate, I shall make an experimental test of it in my crop the next season. I would call your attention to another somewhat novel opinion recently advanced on intelligent and practical authority, that the cotton plant is destined to a decided, though gradual, improvement in its productive qualities, as it recedes from what has hitherto been considered its favorite climate to a higher latitude—an opinion that is doubtless based on the fact that the cotton crop north of 34 degrees is comparatively exempt from the *desolating* ravages of the worm and caterpillar, so prevalent farther south—and should time continue to verify this opinion, an auspicious influence on the cotton market must necessarily follow, from the decreased production of the article.

COTTON INSECTS, Etc.*—I have read with attention Dr. Gorham's essay on the cotton worm. It might be considered presumptuous in me to dispute any of his statements, from his superior scientific knowledge; but my having been a practical cotton planter for the last fifty years, and one not totally devoid of observation, I hope will be an excuse with you, with him, and with the public, for correcting a few errors that he has fallen into.

We had the worms in great abundance last year, and *consequently* the doctor thinks we shall have none this year, or, if any, not before cotton leaves have attained their full maturity, ("greatest maturity" are his words,) and then goes on to confute some erroneous writings on the subject. Now, like the yellow fever, they would be more likely to return, if no occurrence happened, if no remedy was applied, or means taken to avert both the one and the other. The same local causes which induced the yellow fever one year, would continue to induce it the next year, if not removed or rendered innoxious by some means, either natural or artificial. So would the chenille (the distinctive name of the caterpillar under consideration). I agree with the doctor that we are not likely to suffer by them this year, but from very different causes to those he mentions. It is to the *ants* that we are indebted for making any cotton in this country; they are the great enemies to the chenille as well as other insects. The assistance from the ichneumon is very feeble. Whenever the chenille or other caterpillars appear in large numbers, the ants increase in ratio, from the quantity of food afforded them by these insects. On the first year's appearance of the worms, the ants are thin, but few in number; but the next year they are very numerous, and compose an *army* too strong for the doctor's *army* worm. These insects always begin their depredations in small numbers, and when they are not checked or destroyed, go through all their different metamorphoses in twenty-eight days or one lunar month, each fly or moth depositing eggs, which produce fifteen hundred to three thousand worms, as was completely verified and proved in my presence, about fifty years ago, by an intimate friend of mine. The doctor is wrong in his statement, that 1820 was the first year of the appearance of this insect in Louisiana. I came

* From Phillip Winfree, Esq., Mulberry Creek, Iberville, La.

to the parish of Iberville in 1806, and the cotton fields had been laid waste by them a year or two before. What forcibly impresses this upon my mind is that the inhabitants had applied to their priest, Father St. Pierre, for holy water to drive them away; and I must add, in justice to Mr. St. Pierre, that he told them it would have no effect, but gave them the holy water at their earnest request.

Dr. Gorham thinks we receive the stock from Mexico or South America. If this were the case, it must be in the moth or fly state that the chrysalis is fixed and immovable, and, according to his own showing, the army are easily arrested in their progress, and never reach any existence; the fly, too, it has been noted by hundreds of persons, can only keep on its wing for a few yards, but must alight and rest; a much smaller stream than the Mississippi would stop their progress, and drown them all; they are doubtless indigenous. As to how the stock is preserved through the winter, and for years, I believe no one knows. Their appearance is equally as irregular in the West Indies as here, and from what I have seen of them in the Bahamas, they are much more at home here. On clear, hot days there, they can only feed at night, or early in the morning, or late in the afternoon; I have seen them drop dead from the leaves there, when they have remained too long on bushes, from the heat of the sun; and I have also seen them killed there in immense numbers by the little cold, caused by a north or north-west wind in October or November; here I have seen them feed all day in July and August, with the thermometer five to ten degrees higher, and I have seen them also feeding on leaves covered with frost—*the identical same striped caterpillar*. These worms first made their appearance in the French West India Islands; the inhabitants called them chenille, and hence the general name for this peculiar worm. In 1814, or thereabouts, the chenille made their appearance in great numbers early in June, in Iberville, and eat our cotton close down to the ground. Cotton was then planted in April, and the main stems were so tender, that the worms ate them up. The doctor is mistaken in saying that these worms feed upon cotton bushes alone, for this very year they fed first upon the young tender crab grass, and ate the whole of it up before they attacked the cotton, and in the West Indies they feed promiscuously upon the leaves of a plant there called the salve bush; this plant grows about the height, and the leaves are a good deal like the mullein of this country, having a whitish color, and thick, soft velvety feeling.

Can the doctor tell us how it happens that the tobacco worm finds out every plant of tobacco, scattered in nooks and corners, far from tobacco plantations, and on the first year of planting it? Is it not possible that the same species of worm feeding on different plants may change its appearance?

In the year above mentioned, the chenille made their appearance simultaneously in Iberville, and adjacent parishes, and at Colonel Thomas' on the Bayou Barbara, situated ten miles, on a straight line, from any other plantation. As to the means of destroying them, except by their natural enemies, I conceive we have only one or two ways, and these very equivocal. Their propensity to fly into a light at night is known to every one, where they exist in the fly-state. By kindling blazing fires at night, at a proper distance apart, and keeping them burning briskly, from eight to ten o'clock at night, immense numbers are destroyed. (This is their principal time for flying about, and they will travel about three acres to a fire.) The fly ought to be watched, and as soon as they leave the chrysalis, and before they deposit their eggs, these fires ought to commence. I have known some good result from this, and if the measure had been followed by all the neighboring planters I make no doubt that nearly the whole crop would have been saved. We might do some good by sending all hands into the field and crushing them while in the chrysalis state; but it would be tedious work to destroy them in this way; we could hardly afford the loss of time from other work; fires can be made with much more facility.

COTTON PLANTATION STATISTICS.

Table showing the production of Cotton, its price, &c., on an estate in Ouachita (Louisiana) for eight years, with the amount of supplies purchased.

Date	No. of bales	Price	Net proceeds	Average per bale	Woolen, Negro Clothing, yards	Cottons, yards	Pork used, bls
1839	451	5¾ a 8½	12,386	28.00	750	1,250	75
1840	451	9 a 12½	14,720	37.50	750	1,250	75
1841	334	7 a 9½	10,338	30.33	750	1,250	75
1842	509	4¾ a 7¾	12,057	32.33	750	1,250	75
1843	389	5¾ a 9	12,149	31.00	820	1,600	80
1844	395	4¾ a 6½	8,345	21.00	820	1,600	80
1845	478	6¼ a 7¾	13,630	28.00	820	1,600	80
1846	332	10 a 11	14,474	43.50	820	1,600	80
Total	3,282		98,299	31.40	781av	1,425	77

It will be seen from the foregoing table, that the average amount of cotton raised during the eight years, was 410 bales; average price 9¾ cents per pound; average proceeds per year, $12,287; average per bale, $30 39. The weight of the bales was 400 to 450 lbs. The land cultivated was increased from 400 acres in 1839 to 550 in 1846. The number of slaves was not augmented more than two or three during all the time by purchase, and the land was rather improved by ditching than exhausted.

COTTON.

RECEIPTS AT NEW-ORLEANS.

Year	Date	Bales	
1823	Sept. 20	4	bales.
1824	July 30	1	"
1825	Aug. 28	10	"
1826	Aug. 15	17	"
1827	Sept. 15	33	"
1828	" 7	6	"
1829	" 19	2	"
1830	" 18	13	"
1831	" 10	4	"
1832	Aug. 18	3	"
1833	" 24	1	"
1834	" 28	28	"
1835	" 29	1	"
1836	" 24	1	"
1837	" 20	1	"
1838	" 26	1	"
1839	" 5	5	"
1840	" 9	1	"
1841	July 31	1	or more.
1842	" 25	1	"
1843	Aug. 17	1	"
1844	July 23	4	"
1845	" 30	1	"
1846	Aug. 7	7	"
1847	" 9	2	"
1848	" 5	1	"

COTTON AND ITS PROSPECTS—American and Foreign Product; Demand and Supply of the World; India Cottons and Competition; Future Prospects, &c.—No agricultural staple has ever produced so great an effect upon the civilization of the world as cotton. You cannot civilize man until you first clothe his nakedness. After the knowledge of good and evil, the first thing done by our early parents was to weave fig leaves for aprons. A naked man must necessarily become a savage man. Heretofore, in the history of the world, there has been no cheap and abundant article raised by which the poor and helpless could be clothed on an extensive scale. Hence it is that civilization has had narrow bounds. Before the invention of gunpowder and artillery, those people who acquired the arts and wealth of civilization were constantly overrun by barbarian and brutal numbers, who banded together for plunder and indulgence. Since those inventions, the wealthy and refined portions of the earth have been able to defend themselves against barbarian hordes, and civilization has been nurtured. The tide has been turned and the course of invasion has been reversed. The more cultivated and wealthy nations have overrun those less so. But the difficulty was to civilize after they had conquered. They had no means of extending commerce and its refinements, for want of an abundant and cheap article by which to clothe the nakedness of barbarian life. But the invention of machinery in New and Old England, together with the vast production of cotton by slave labor in the South, have supplied the deficiency.

There is not a battle that England has fought in India, Affghanistan, or China, nor that France has fought in Africa, or that the United States fought on the plains of Mexico, that did not extend the consumption of cotton, and in the results will finally bless the people conquered. It will, in the course of time, introduce trade and commerce, and with them the arts and refinements of life. It is thus that Providence has ever worked upon the destinies of man. When the Lord had selected the firstborn of Egypt as victims to illustrate his power and vindicate his decrees, and left his bloody sign upon the lintels and side-posts, that the destroying angel might pass over his chosen people, this visitation of an awful dispensation was but a part of His providence in working out the redemption of Israel.

And when, in modern times, He chooses to mark the tracks of civilization upon the bloody fields of conquest, it is but to rouse a barbarian people from their stupor and indolence, and quicken a worthless and profligate mass with new enterprise and life, and fit them for that great day of universal light and peace which He has promised for mankind in the millennium. It is by war you conquer an ignorant and barbarian people, and then by commerce and trade with them you introduce the comforts and arts of civilization.

In this point of view, the culture of cotton becomes deeply interesting to the statesman and philanthropist. How far can it be extended, and what can we calculate on as to its production in the future?

The aggregate production for the last ten years in the states of this Confederacy has been 21,370,000 bags, and the average per year has been 2,137.000 bales. We may reasonably infer that it has nearly reached its maximum. In 1839 and '40, the production was 2,177,835 bags; while in 1846 and '47, it was only 1,778,051. In 1842 and '43 the production was 2,378,875, and in 1844 and '45 it was 2,394,503, which is the largest crop ever raised, except the crop of 1848 and '49, which was 2,728,596, while the crop of 1850 and '51 will be about 2,230,000. Thus it would appear it has been little or no increase in production in the last ten years, the crop of 1839–'40 being about equal to the last crop. The reason for this is obvious. The general idea used to be, that the only limitation to the production of cotton was the proper climate and soil, and that of course, then, there was scarcely any limit in the United States. But this is a great mistake.

The great limitation to *production is labor.* Whenever cotton rises to 10 cents, labor becomes too dear to increase production rapidly. When cotton rises, sugar, rice and tobacco also bear a good price, and breadstuffs rise also, so there can be no rapid transfer of labor, it being in good demand elsewhere. By excluding, as well as we can, all those in the cotton states who are engaged in the culture of rice and sugar, as well as those in the mountains of Georgia, Alabama and South Carolina, who produce grain only, and by adding those in North Carolina, Tennessee and Arkansas, who are engaged partially in producing cotton, we estimate the slaves at 1,200,000. And of these we estimate 800,000 as workers, which is probably not excessive, when we consider that the Southwest, the great cotton region, is newly settled, and the number of children out of all proportion less than in negroes peopled by a natural growth of population. There are about 100,000 white laborers, also, engaged in the production of cotton. This, added to the 800,000 slaves, would make 900,000 actual workers in culture. In the real cotton region, perhaps the average number of acres per hand is ten; whereas, high up in Georgia, Alabama, Mississippi, South Carolina, Tennessee, and Arkansas, the average is not three acres white and black per hand. Besides, in these same regions the number of acres in grain per hand will be at least seven. The average per hand in cotton may then be put down at five acres. This would give 4,500,000 acres in cotton. Then take the 2,137,000 bags as the average production for the last ten years, which is a fact, and we have the annual production per acre at a little under half a bale—or a little more than two acres per bale—and to the 900,000 workers it would not be quite two and a-half bags per hand. And all practical men know this is about the production in any given section embracing fifty miles square.

To see that the true limitation upon the production of cotton is labor, and how difficult it is to transfer labor, we have but to estimate the capital engaged in cotton.

The Secretary of the Treasury, in his report, made March 4th, 1836, estimated the capital invested in raising cotton at $771,000,000. But he then estimated the number of acres in cotton at 2,000,000, and the annual product at 300 lbs. net cotton per acre, which was entirely too large an estimate. No doubt he took the estimate of some fine section in Mississippi, made by sanguine young planters as to the production per acre there, and upon that estimated the number of acres necessary to produce the crop as known. He made the number of acres too small and the production too large. By the best calculations from the census of 1840, and other sources, we would estimate the slaves engaged in producing:—

1. Cotton at 1,200,000, which at $500	$600,000,000
2. Land, 4,500,000 acres, at $10	45,000,000
3. Land in grain, 6,300,000 acres, at $10	63,000,000
4. Land in timber, pasture, &c., 14,000,000 at $3	42,000,000
5. Mules and horses, 400,000, at $100	40,000,000
6. Hogs and sheep, 4,500,000, at $1	4,500,000
7. Cattle, 300,000, at $5	1,500,000
8. Plows, 500,000, at $2	1,000,000
9. Wagons and other plantation implements, &c	1,000,000
	$798,000,000
Put the amount of capital vested in the production of cotton at	$800,000,000

Of course this does not embrace the whole capital of the cotton region, commercial, manufacturing, professional, mechanical, and artisan; but I merely mean to calculate the amount actually vested in raising the 2,173,000 bags produced annually for the last ten years, as shown from the tables.

If the 800,000,000 of capital produce an average in ten years of 2,137,000 bales per year, it will take $100,000,000 of capital to produce 267,125 bags. Thus we will see, that to make this a permanent increase in the production of cotton per annum, for the next ten years, it will require a transfer of capital, or an increase of capital, which is the same thing, of $100,000,000. One hundred millions of dollars! This calculation is made upon an estimate of cotton at 10 cents, and whenever it gets over that, the increase in the price of labor is so great, that it would require more than the $100,000,000 to produce the 267,125 bags; and when it gets below the 10 cents, then the inducement is not so great to increase the production. A transfer in capital of $100,000,000 from other departments of labor, to that of cotton, cannot be done immediately, without a shock, or a great rise in those productions from which such capital is abstracted. There may be an increase in a cotton crop from fine seasons and suitable years; but take the average of ten years, and it is the true mode by which to calculate the capacity of the country to produce the article, there is a great mistake as to the supposed capacity of the country to produce any amount of it. Counting-house clerks, who know nothing of the country, make the estimates, and it is taken for granted, in New and Old England, that there is no difficulty in producing any amount. But when you come to calculate that it takes at least $100,000,000 vested capital to produce permanently 267,125 bags, you then see the difficulties. When we calculate again, that the white population of these states now exceeds 20,000,000 of people, and that in twenty years the white population alone will equal 37,000,000; if we allow for emigration here, we will see that the time is rapidly coming, when a great question in society here will be: How is that population to be fed? Heretofore, our population has been so sparse that there has literally been no heed taken as to what we should eat, or wherewithal we should be clothed. But the time is coming when we shall have to consider this matter. Whenever this becomes the case, there will be little room for cotton. Land and labor will be too important in raising breadstuffs. The encroachments of the white population, and the demand for food to supply them, will make a great limitation on the production of cotton. This is another element that has never been calculated. The production of cotton belongs to a sparse population, and the protracted attention of slave labor is essential to produce it on an extensive scale. Besides this, the vast increase of white population, will be pressing down upon the slave population. The law of population is, that where two races come into contact, under one government, and, from density, the great interest in society is to support that population, the race which is the stronger will eat out the weaker. This arises from the necessity of self-preservation. In some instances this has been prevented by amalgamation; but where the races are so distinct as the white and black, and where the union is so loathsome, this is impossible.

In less than fifty years, this struggle for support will be sensibly felt in this country. In fact, the census of 1840 exhibited symptoms of it. From 1810 to 1820, the increase in the slave race in the United States, was 30 per cent.; and from 1820 to 1830, it was 29½ per cent.; and from 1830 to 1840, it was only 22¼ per cent. The last census, as far as I have been able to get any authentic information, seems to be a little over 22 per cent. While the increase of the white population of the United States, since 1840, has been over 35 per cent., the increase of the slave population is but little over 22 per cent. It requires but little foresight to perceive the consequences. To say the least, it will press down upon the cotton region in the next twenty years, and limit its increased production. The real cotton belt is at any rate much more narrow than it was formerly supposed to be. The latitude of 32½° may be said to be its centre in the southern states. The quantity per acre will diminish as rapidly going south of that latitude, as it will going north of it. True, this varies again, according to location. Altitude and distance from the ocean varies climate more than latitude. Our mountains run northeast and southwest, parallel with the sea-coast, and terminate low down in Georgia and Alabama, so that as you pursue the latitude of 32½° west, you come to high lands in both these states, which make it difficult for cotton to mature abundantly; and then as you cross Alabama, and come to the depressed valley of the Mississippi, this parallel we find to be the finest for the heaviest production of cotton.

It is said 270 feet in altitude is equal to one degree in latitude. Soon after you pass the Mississippi Valley, and rise to the spurs of the Rocky Mountains, you get rapidly out of the cotton region. The highlands and "*Northers*" in Texas limit the cotton region in that state to a lower latitude than any other portion of the South.

There are one thousand millions of inhabitants in the world, and of that number not more than five hundred millions, or half the population of the earth, ever use cotton as an article of clothing. The production of cotton throughout tbe world may be estimated at about twelve hundred millions of pounds annually, of which the United States produce 845,000,000 pounds—calculating the average crop of 2,121,000, and each bag at near 400 pounds. The Secretary of the Treasury (Doc. 146, 4th vol. Ex. Doc. 135-36) estimates the production of other countries as follows, viz: India 185,000,000 pounds; rest of Asia 110,000,000 pounds; Brazil 30,000,000; West Indies 8,000,000; Egypt 25,000,000; rest of Africa 34,000,000; Mexico and South America, exclusive of Brazil, 35,000,000, and 13,000,000 pounds elsewhere. If one half the population of the earth (which is doubtful) now use this twelve hundred millions of cotton, it would make two and a half pounds per head. England and the United States now consume about thirteen pounds per head, and so will all highly civilized and commercial people, while those less so will consume less. The Turks, for instance, only use now about three pounds per head. Suppose, then, the thousand millions of people were to consume only three pounds per head, it would make over 7,000,000,000 bags at 400 lbs. as the annual demand, and allow them two and a half pounds, which is now the consumption of only half the population of the earth, and it would make a demand for over six millions of bags. This increasing consumption is going on yearly, as commerce and civilization advance, and the improvements in intercourse will increase it in geometrical ratio; and as nations become more refined and more opulent, its consumption, instead of being only two or three pounds per head, will reach ten pounds in the various forms in which it may be used. How vain and ignorant it is to talk of production outrunning consumption! Such a conclusion implies that commerce and the arts, with their necessary consequences, wealth, comfort, and luxury, will be checked in their triumphant progress, and mankind fall back again into barbarism. This same cry as to production out-running consumption, was made at the increase of the tariff in 1828 and in 1832, when we raised 800,000 bags only, and regularly afterwards, whenever the tariff was to be raised, the same assertions were made. As far back as 1820, a Frenchman, named JUMEL, introduced the culture of Brazil cotton into Egypt. The Pacha ordered it to be extended on a large scale. *Niles' Register*, in October, 1825, raised the alarm, and said "Egypt is our great and fearful rival, and has a capacity to supply much more than we have ever produced." So in 1842, the Northern papers, and particularly the *National Intelligencer*, were full of calculations to prove we were to be overwhelmed by the production of East India cotton. And the same papers could be quoted to prove, from figures, that nothing could save the South from the ruin of this competition, but a *tariff for protection*, the best terms with our kind *task-masters*. We were supposed to be infants who were to be kept in the nursery, and fed on pap by *Northern nurses!*

In a Senator's speech in 1842, we find the following: "While we have heretofore scarcely noticed the existence of that immense country (East India) which would secure to us a *home market*, where we might be allowed to trade on either our domestic calculations or our commercial calculations, all at once we find one of our great staples being supplanted in England, and in great danger of being *driven from our home markets* by its producers." (See Mr. Smith's speech, United States Senate, 1842.) Unless we sink down into stupidity and ignorance, the day is past when such miserable cant is to have any control over us. If we are but true to ourselves, we can command the future, so far as our prosperity is concerned. England is in such a condition, that she must have our cotton. She has $180,000,000 capital vested, and 225,000 persons immediately and actually devoted to the manufacture of cotton as laborers, and 700,000 more dependent upon these factories, and all depending upon the raw material from the United States. Great Britain consumes and manufactures 425,000,000 pounds annually, and the value of her cotton manufactures is estimated at $200,000,000 a year. Her commercial prosperity and credit depend upon this article. In fact, it may be said that her *great Bank* depends upon it, and with it her funded debt itself, and with these, her peace and present civil polity. Withdraw cotton from England, and it would produce a convulsion that would shake all her institutions. Any man can see this from all her movements. She has subjugated all India to extend her commerce and manufactures. She desolated China, and spread havoc amongst a peaceful people by the thunder of her cannon, for the avowed purpose of forcing them to admit opium and eat it, but in reality to penetrate that mighty empire with her trade and manufactures.

By her treaty with China, and her monopoly and power over India, she now commands the great increasing markets for manufactured cottons over the world. These, with her concentrated banking power and commercial credits, give her a great advantage over all other people. It is all idle to suppose she can ever depend upon India for cotton. The length of voyage, freight and insurance alone, would forbid it. The freight on cotton from the United States to Europe, will scarcely ever exceed one cent per pound, and the voyage will not average more than four weeks. Whereas, from Calcutta, Madras, or Bombay, it can never average less than a penny per pound, or near two cents, and the voyage will average four months. The whole expenses of cotton from the United States to Liverpool, and sold there, do not exceed three cents per pound; while from India, the expenses are not less than six cents. Their cotton, from inferiority, is about two cents under ours in price. Suppose "fair cotton" commands in Liverpool 12 cents, ours will, according to the above calculations, yield 9 cents net—while the India cotton will yield only 4 cents net, and a fall in price of 1 per cent. would make it much less in proportion, as the expenses would be stationary.

As to the superior cheapness of Hindoo labor, that appears only on paper. For one well-fed slave with us, managed by the intelligence of our planters, will do more effectual work than five uncertain Hindoos, with their poor diet, and still poorer skill—independent of the extreme vicissitudes of their parching climate.

But there is one thing that will forever prevent India from being permanently a great producer of cotton for a certain supply.

The East India Company is the most stupendous monopoly in the civilized world, and all British India is held in possession by this company. It is a fixed principle with them, never to sell a foot of land in fee-simple, and they only part with it on limited leases, even to the native population themselves. One-half of all that the native population produces is claimed by the East India Company as "land tax;" whether it be indigo, rice, sugar, cotton or opium. This is felt as the heaviest and most grinding exaction, and particularly as to rice, which is so essential to their support. In 1840, it was estimated that 500,000 persons perished in India from starvation and its attendant diseases. Their population is too dense to raise cotton, when food is so essential. If there fall only eleven inches of rain in any year in India, their rice crop falls off, and they have inevitably to encounter famine in its most frightful excess. There can be no calculation made as to the permanent production of cotton to any increased extent, where despotism is so exacting and unlimited as is the case with the East India Company in regard to India—and where food is so scarce, and the vicissitudes of seasons make famine so frequent. The protracted and difficult culture of cotton requires a free government, where those who own labor and capital shall be protected in its free enjoyment. Capital is delicate and sensitive, and will not be invested except where law is fixed, and freedom is a thing beyond the control of government. It takes $100,000,000 of capital in this country to produce annually a little over 200,000 bags of cotton, and here intelligence and enterprise have reached their highest efforts. In India, with their uncertain climate and ill-regulated labor, it would require more than that amount to produce the same. And in such a country, and under such a government, with such uncertain labor, no set of men of any sagacity will invest $100,000,000 of capital in any such enterprise. The importations of cotton from India into England are now actually falling off. In 1837, England imported from India fifty-one millions of pounds of cotton, and in 1838, only thirty-four millions—while she imported the same year, from the United States, three hundred and nineteen millions. In 1849, she imported from India, only thirty-two millions. In 1844, we raised a little more than 800,000,000 lbs., and of that, 660,000,000 went to Europe. And there is still a large portion of the population of Europe who do not use cotton, but consume entirely, hemp, flax and wool.

The population of China may be put down at 252,866,000, and the British possessions in Asia at 121,680,000. These together would make 374,546,000. Allow them only two pounds per head, and it would amount to 749,092,000 pounds of raw cotton—and this, at 370 pounds per bag, which is the East India bale, and it would be about 2,002,600 bales. Put the present growth and consumption of India and China at 600,000 bales, and their exports to all Europe 152,175 bales—and it would then leave a deficiency of 1,250,425 bags in those countries, assuming only two pounds raw cotton per head. But as civilization and trade expand in those thickly populated regions, particularly in China, under the British, French, and United States Treaties, formed within the last few years with that immense Empire, we may safely calculate that they will finally consume at least as much as the Turks now do, which is estimated at three pounds per head. This rate of consumption in India and China would produce a demand in those countries alone for one thousand one hundred and twenty-three million, six hundred and thirty-eight thousand pounds, or near 300,000 bales at 400 pounds—which is 600,000 more than the crop of the United States. We will at once perceive the deep interest that Great Britain has in controlling those countries. They are at present the great outlets for increased manufactures of cotton, and it is the interest and control she has there, which has, for two years, enabled her to purchase cotton at the enhanced prices, and do a good business, while the American manufacturers may be depressed.

Wherever the British or American trade reaches, there the consumption of cotton will be extended. The Caucasian, and of it the Gallic and Anglo-Saxon races, are the conquering and subjugating races of the world; and it may be said, that, wherever the banners of European arms or Christian civilization are unfurled, there will spring up markets for the rapid consumption of cotton.

By the blessing of Heaven, we are enabled to raise the most beneficent product that commerce has ever transported for the comfort of the human family, a product destined to make a new era in the intercourse of nations, and to develop new sources of civilization. And to the *slave-holding* states of the Union, it is the great source of their power and their wealth, and the main security for their peculiar institutions. It is that which gives us our energy and enterprise under a hot climate, and enables us to command the respect of foreign powers. The Egyptian laves in the Nile, and worships it, as the source of his wealth and support. The Hindoo bows with superstitious reverence before the Lotus, under an idea that Vishnu created Bramah from its unfolded flower. And let *us* teach our children to hold the cotton plant in one hand, and a sword in the other, ever ready to defend it as the source of commercial power abroad, and through that, of *independence at home.*

The great difficulty is among ourselves. It is not over-production, or foreign competition, that we have to dread, but the denial of equal rights in the Union, that endangers us. It is the assertion of the right to fetter and restrict us absolutely forever within our present boundaries, that we are called upon to resist. The insulting assumption that the cotton growing states are not good enough to share with the free and pious North in the benefits and rights of the Confederacy, is an outrage and stigma, and if we *bear it in peace,* we shall cover our children with deep degradation.

COTTON CULTURE IN THE EAST INDIES.—The cotton plants belong to the Monadelphia Dodecandria class and order of Linnæus, and are distinguished in botany by the generic name of *Gossypium.* They may be divided into three groups—1st. The herbaceous; 2d. The shrubby; and 3d. The arboraceous.

1. The herbaceous, is a single species of *Gossypium herbaceum* of Willdenow and Roxburgh, although there are many varieties

marked by only slight differences in the eye of the botanist, but of considerable importance in a commercial point of view.

This species is biennial; it is very generally cultivated in India, as well as in North America, China, and elsewhere. Its height varies between six and two feet; leaves, palmate, five-lobed, hairy, dark green, and brown-veined; lobes, sub-lanceolate; flowers, pale yellow, five-petaled; seed-pod or capsule irregularly triangular, ovate, pointed, and three-celled: not longer than a filbert, brown when ripe, and bursting, exposes a globe of cotton, white or yellowish, in three locks, enveloping and adhering strongly to the seeds, which resemble those of the grape in form, but are much larger; stipules, falcate-lanceolate; leaves, of outer calyx dentate. This must not be confounded with the *Gossypium herbaceum* of Pluck. In Hindostan, it is known by various names; it is karpassee in Sanscrit; rewee in Hindostanee; kapass in Bengalee; pati-chitoo in Telinga; upum punthee and upum pirati in Canara; kootu in Arabic; paratti in Malabar; banga in Central India.

Dr. Roxburgh thought that the cotton from which the Dacca muslins are made was produced from a variety of this species, but later information and research certainly raises a legitimate doubt upon the point. At all events, this species is in general cultivation by the natives of Hindostan, and the distinguished botanist just named concluded that there are three principal varieties—the Dacca, the Berar, and the China.

The Dacca variety differs from the common *Gossypium herbaceum* in the following respects:

1st. In the plant being more erect, with fewer branches, and the lobes of the leaves more pointed.

2d. In the whole plant being tinged of a reddish color, even the petioles, and nerves of the leaves, and being less pubescent.

3d. In having the peduncles which support the flowers, longer, and the exterior margins of the petals tinged with red.

4th. In the staple of the cotton being longer, much finer, and softer.

These are the most obvious points of difference, but whether they will prove permanent, I cannot at present say. The most intelligent people of that country (Dacca) think the great difference lies in the spinning, and allow little for the influence of soil.

Berar cotton, I call the second variety; it is in cultivation over the Berar country, and is from thence imported into the Circars, or northern provinces, by Sada, Balawansa, &c., to Yourma-goodum, in the Musulipatam district. With this cotton, the fine Madras, more properly northern Circars, "long-cloth" is made. It differs from the two before-mentioned sorts in the following respects:—1st. In growing to a greater size; in being more permanent, or living longer, and in having smooth and straight branches; 2d. In having the leaflets of the exterior calyx more deeply divided, and the wool of a finer quality than in the first variety.

China cotton is cultivated in the country whence it derives its name, and its wool is reckoned 25 per cent. better than that of Surat. It differs from the former sorts—1st. In being much smaller, with but very few short weak branches; 2d. In being, so far as my experience goes, annual; 3d. In having the leaflets of the exterior calyx entire, or nearly so.

In South Behar, there are four varieties of this species cultivated: 1st. *Rehdhea*, the finest is sown about the autumn equinox, and of this, the Dacca muslins are said to have been made in years gone by, but now, none is exported thither; 2d. *Hewlee*, the next best, is sown in June; 3d. *Jeilowa*, is sown at the same period; 4th. *Kokety*, is yellowish; it makes the best fine thread, and is cultivated chiefly to the north of Tirhoot.

The Guzerat cotton is the produce of this species. The plants are described as differing from the Bourbon perennial species by never exceeding two or three feet in height, by producing few branches, and a smaller number of pods, and by yielding its produce in six months from the time of sowing.

2. The shrubby cottons are—

G. vitifolium, of Willdenow and Roxburgh, vine-leaved cotton, said by some authorities to be a native of Celebes, South America, and the Isle of France; but Dr. Roxburgh considers its place of nativity uncertain. In flower and seed the whole year, but not profitable, because the produce is scanty. Dr. Royle identifies it with *G. Barbadense*, and thinks that the *Sea Island cotton* is produced from a variety of this species.

G. hirsutum (Willdenow and Roxburgh), hairy-branched cotton, found in the hottest districts of South America.

G. religiosum, nankeen cotton (Willdenow and Roxburgh), found in Surinam, Hindostan, and elsewhere. Flower, uniformly yellow; allied to *G. hirsutum*, if not merely a variety. Wool, tawny. This is occasionally grown in Burmah, and is called *wa-nee*.

G. latifolium, broad-leafed cotton, a native of the West Indies, and differing but little from *G. vitifolium*.

G. Barbadense (Willdenow and Roxburgh) is the kind cultivated chiefly in Barbadoes. It is known here as the Bourbon cotton (Roxburgh), and is productive for several years.*

There are two sorts cultivated in the Isle of Bourbon:—1st. *Black-seeded*, which is easily separated from the cotton. 2d. *White-*

* Mr. Hughes, who has cultivated successfully the Bourbon cotton near Tinivelly, says the plant will last a great number of years without falling off in productiveness, if properly managed.

seeded, a whiteness which seems to arise from the ends of the fibres of the cotton remaining adhering to, and requiring to be torn from them with considerable force.

G. Peruvianum a native of Peru.

G. acuminatum (Roxburgh) is easily distinguished by its superior size, and large black seeds adhering firmly to each other, but easily separating from the wool; said to be a native of the mountains to the north and west of Bengal. Dr. Wallich describes a specimen brought from the Nusseerabad, where it seems to be common. He says that it is very productive, and that the cotton is readily and completely separable, milk-white, long staple; and although that grown in the Botanic Garden was harsh and woolly, yet the variety seems improvable by culture, because the specimen from Nusseerabad was soft and silky.

It appears to me that this variety is specifically the same as the *Brazil* or *kidney cotton-tree* recommended to notice by Mr. Rundell in 1819. He describes it as growing to the height of ten or twelve feet; it produces at least six hundred large pods, each containing from six to ten conglomerated seeds, enveloped in very fine and valuable wool. It thrives well on the margin of water; lasts about seven years; requires pruning occasionally of its dead branches, &c.; and, during very hot weather, should be watered at least twice a week. An acre will contain about five hundred trees. Two hundred and thirty pods usually weigh one pound, and yield from four to five ounces of clean cotton.

If this be the *Pernambuco cotton-tree*, (and that town is, we know, in Brazil,) it has an additional claim to attention for cultivation in the interior districts of Hindostan, inasmuch as it is found to improve in quality the farther it recedes from the sea.

Plants of this species differ from the herbaceous not only in stature, but in the form and size of their pods, which are oval and larger. In addition to these distinctions they are longer-lived, for, although in the most temperate climates, capable of growing cotton, they frequently become annuals, yet in the most torrid localities they are perennial; while in the West Indies they are either biennial or triennial; and in Egypt, &c., live for six or even ten years.

The Persian cotton-shrub on the sea-coast lives for twenty or thirty years, but in the interior it is cultivated as an annual.

The influence of climate and soil upon the plant is evinced in another phenomenon, for Mr. Tucker shows that the color of the seed varies with the soil and situation where the plant is grown. The Sea Island cotton has black seeds, but if taken to the back or upland districts the seeds become green, and the staple of the cotton undergoes a great change.

G. obtusifolium, (Roxburgh,) a native of Ceylon, producing a small quantity of ash-colored wool; not cultivated.

G. micranthium (Cavanelles.)—This was raised in the Paris Garden from seed produced in Persia.

3. The arboraceous cotton-plant, *Gossypium arboreum* (Willdenow and Roxburgh), grows to a height varying between twelve and twenty feet. It is indigenous to Hindostan, China, Egypt, and some parts of America and Africa. Dr. Roxburgh says it is not cultivated for its wool, but Dr. Royle states that some produced by this species at Sahanapore was pronounced by a competent judge to be of the best description, as both fabric and staple were good. It appears worthy, he adds, of being the subject of farther trials, particularly to ascertain its productiveness; for of the fineness and silky nature of its staple there can be no doubt, as it is employed by the natives for making the finest muslins only. It was cultivated like the common Indian cotton, and gave its produce, in the first year, during October and November, and a second crop in February.

To ascertain which of the species are best suited to the various soils and climates, is a most important consideration for those interested in the introduction of this sort of wealth into India, because, however judicious the culture, yet, if it be expended upon a species physically unsuited to the climate, it is labor and time uselessly bestowed. My own inquiries lead me to the conclusion that the *Gossypium acuminatum* is in every respect worthy of more attention than it has yet received. It has the advantage of being indigenous, and, therefore, not liable to the changes and difficulties unavoidably incident to acclimating exotics. It most delights in inland localities, and is consequently capable of more extensive cultivation than those species which affect maritime situations, and being a perennial, its culture is attended with very much less expense. To these highly important qualities are to be added those of being far more productive than the sorts usually cultivated, and of producing in the most suitable soils and climate of India, a cotton, long, fine, and silky. I have my suspicions that it will be identified with the perennial species noticed lately at Dacca.

The result of the experiments on the Agricultural Society's farm at Akra warranted the committee of management in reporting very strongly in favor of cultivating in India the Upland Georgia variety. This opinion is sustained by subsequent experiments in various other districts, and there can be no doubt, experience shows, that every effort ought to be made to introduce it generally. There are some districts, however, as the sea-coast and its vicinity, where this variety would not flourish; and in these it is most desirable to try that kind so generally and so advantageously known as the Georgia Sea island cotton.

In mentioning this very superior variety as suitable to maritime districts, I by no means intend to express an opinion that it must be *confined* to such localities; for although it delights and requires to have common salt within reach of its roots, yet this might be supplied by adding that saline manure to soils situated far from the sea. This is no mere theoretical notion, for I have seen strictly maritime plants grown a hundred miles inland by supplying them judiciously with salt, and among the number I would particularize one of the most intractable, the rock samphire (*Crithmum maritimum*).

The kinds which it has been endeavored to introduce here are;—Sea island cotton, Barbadoes cotton, Brazil cotton, Bourbon cotton (both black and green seeded), and China cotton. To this list may be added a variety called "the vine cotton," a very superior kind, from *Jamaica*, the extraordinary fault of which was its having a staple *too long*. The seeds were distributed to Captain Jenkins at Gowhatty, and to a gentleman going to Mirzapore, but with what result does not appear.

Mr. Piddington has ingeniously suggested that new varieties could be raised by cross impregnation, as was successfully practised with the pea by the late Mr. Knight. This might, doubtless, be done in some instances, and is worthy of attention, because, although the kinds at present known are sufficiently excellent if correctly cultivated, yet they are not so perfect as to prohibit the hope of improvement.

Much, observes Dr. Royle, may be effected by introducing into India the different species and varieties which are already successfully cultivated in other countries; and here let us not restrict ourselves to too small a number of varieties, because they happen to be those which at present produce the best kinds of cotton. Not contented in America with possessing already the best kinds, they have tried those of other countries to ascertain if there are any among them suited to the peculiarities of their country and climate.

Districts best suited for Cotton.—As some one of the several species of cotton plants may be found in every district of Hindostan, from Cape Comorin to the Himalayan mountains, it is not an untenable position to assume that no portion of the globe, of similar extent, is capable of yielding so large a quantity of this peculiar produce. Indeed, from the earliest ages, cotton has been mentioned as the special production of India.

Now it is a fact in the history of vegetables, to which I remember no exceptions, that where the wild stock flourishes naturally, there the improved varieties succeed best. Examples occur in the English apples and the French pears; for in no country does the crab abound more than in England, nor the wild pear than in France. The inference I would draw from this observation is, that Hindostan ought eminently to excel in the production of cotton, and the comparatively limited experience we have yet had of the results of applying superior knowledge and superior capital to this object, encourages rather than represses the opinion.

That no part of India has a climate unsuited to the production of superior cotton is demonstrated by the fact that the best samples are produced in Guzerat, at the northwestern extremity; in Behar, the very centre; and at Tinivelly, on the most southern point.

It appears to me that it is the generally dry silicious nature of the soil of Guzerat, as much as the dryness of its climate, that is so extremely favorable to the growth of the cotton plant. It flourishes there even in the most sterile districts, though necessarily not so luxuriantly as in the more fertile soils.

The same observation applies to the neighboring province of Surat, where good cotton is produced; but the best in that part of India is grown in the districts of Jamboseer and Ahmood, and, indeed, throughout the Broach Pergunnah. This is stated, by a government report, to be very superior to the Nagpore or any other cotton grown on the eastern side of India.

Mr. Owen Potter, who was extensively employed in shipping cotton from the above districts in 1837, stated some very interesting relative facts in a paper which he submitted to the Manchester Chamber of Commerce. He says that "the chief cotton ports are Surat, Baroche, Tankaria Bunder, Gogo, and Bownugger." All these ports are within a short distance of each other. The extent of cotton cultivation in their vicinity is very great, as will be seen by the following statement of exports:

	1836.		1837.	
From Baroche..........	42,000	bales..	20,000	bales.
" Tankaria Bunder..	20,000	" ..	12,000	"
" Surat.............	25,000	" ..	15,000	"
" Gogo and Bownugger, including the Dholera cotton..	60,000	" ..	45,000	"
Total...........	147,000	" ..	29,000	"

Each bale weighing about 400 lbs.

Nearly the whole of the cotton here mentioned grows within forty miles of the port at which it is shipped.

At Omrawutte cotton is grown at the rate of two pounds for two pence, in moderately favorable seasons; and did good roads exist, this article could be delivered at Bombay at a handsome remunerating price. It is now carried on the backs of bullocks, and the extra cost thus incurred amounts to a penny a lb. more. This cotton is but little inferior to that grown in Guzerat, which is looked upon as the garden of the western side of India.

In the Deccan the production of superior cotton is not confined to the vicinity of Nagpore, for it can be obtained abundantly much farther to the north, at Calpee, as well as in the districts of Currah, Carah, and Etawah.

Cotton produced in the southern extremity of the Peninsula at Tinivelly and Coimbetore, has been highly approved in the English market.

At Tinivelly, where Mr. Hughes has been long engaged in the cultivation of the Bourbon cotton, that gentleman considers the vicinity of the sea, or situations to which the influence of the sea air extends, are on every account to be preferred. A dry soil, and a dry atmosphere, from March to May, and from July to September, seem almost essential to the good quality of the wool, as well as to the productiveness of the plant. The freest circulation of air and of light windo, are of the greatest benefit to a perfect culture.

On the other hand Mr. Heath, a gentleman also experienced in the cultivation of the same description of cotton, states that his experience differs from that of Mr. Hughes with respect to the influence of vicinity to the sea; for he found the cotton come to perfection at the distance of one hundred and fifty miles from its shore.

I quote these results of experience as evidence that in India local climate is not particularly influential upon the cotton plant. All districts are suitable, but of course this circumstance has no reference to the importance of a free circulation of air, and the penetration of light among the plants.

In Burmah, cotton is cultivated very extensively, chiefly for the China market, though the accounts are too discrepant (varying from 7,000,000 to $37,000,000) to allow of a satisfactory estimate being given of the annual amount. The greatest quantity is produced in the neighborhoods of Ava and Prome; but that produced at Bauksk and that in the Mataban province, (known as Tennasserim cotton,) appears to have the longest staple.

It was even supposed that cotton was conveyed from Burmah to Dacca, to be employed there in the manufacture of its muslins; but this supposition, unsustained even by probability, is contradicted by the Dacca custom-house returns, which show that scarcely more than twenty maunds were imported during the four years, 1828–31.

Soil and Situation.—To arrive at a just conclusion as to the soil and situation best suited for the growth of superior cotton in Hindostan, it is most important to ascertain accurately the nature of those which have been practically found the most favorable in Georgia and elsewhere. This point being satisfactorily settled, and due consideration had as to the object to be obtained by the cultivation, viz: the full development of the parts of fructification, we shall be able, with considerable probability of success, to point out those localities which will be found most productive in the different districts and elevations of India.

Of the nature of the soils where the best cotton is grown, we have information from Mr. Piddington. He describes a specimen of one of the best of the Georgia Sea Island cotton soils, as appearing "like a mixture of fine dark grey sand and charcoal dust, with fragments of shells, wood, twigs, leaves, and even the shells of cotton seeds, the wood being in all states, from dry to charred, as if the rubbish of the cotton bushes had been burned on the spot. Upon sifting nine ounces of the soil, taken fairly from the specimen sent, through muslin, it was found that eight ounces of it was fine sand mixed with dark charcoal-looking dust; and the remaining ounce coarse sand, with a few fragments of sandstone in thin horizontal layers, shells in fragments, with wood and vegetable rubbish as described above.

The wood and twigs were evidently the remains of cotton plants, and suggest that the specimen was taken from the surface. The nature of the subsoil on which it rests was not, unfortunately, made known. The black particles are certainly carbonaceous, and Mr. Piddington states reasons to justify his suspicions that they are finely-divided lignite. The fragments of shells were not sufficiently abundant to entitle the soil to be considered calcareous, but their slow decomposition would furnish a supply for centuries.

The guarded conclusions which are drawn by Mr. Piddington from these researches, are—1st. That the abundance and fineness of good cotton depends on the quantity of carbon in the soil, and the solubility of that carbon. 2d. That the next best soil is one containing carbonate of lime. 3d. That the soil should not be too tenacious. "I have had repeated experience of this," he adds, "in Bengal; and on the Bombay side of India I observed, some time ago, that, a Parsee gentleman, Furdonjee Cowasjee, had partly failed, or experienced much loss, in some experiments in cotton, in consequence of the clayey nature of the soil, which retained too much moisture. In the West Indies, the years of drought are far the most favorable to the cotton crops, and the Singapore soils are instances of cotton growing in what might be called pure sand with vegetable matter; but we must probably make allowances in these instances for the vicinity of the sea." 4th. That it is preferable for the sand to be in coarse particles.

These conclusions, in all of which I cordially agree, sustained as they are by inquiries which I have made, and by a host of concordant testimonies that have been published, concur in establishing one fact beyond controversy, viz: that superior cotton requires a light, porous soil for its production; and resting on a subsoil, permitting the easy escape of superfluous moisture.

The following exhibits in a tabular form the result of experiments upon several specimens of American and India cotton soils:

COTTON SOILS	Vegetable matter	Saline and extractive *geine?*	IRON			Carbon. of Lime	Magnesia	Alumina	Silex	Water and loss	Price of best cottons in Liverpool	REMARKS
			Protox	Deutox	Tritox							
American.											*d.*	
1. Georgia Sea Island.	3.20	0.20	1.00	....	....	2.75	....	0.20	92.00	0.85	24	Vegetable matter, peat, or lignite, partly soluble in cold water, silex in coarse grains.
2. Supposed Georgia Sea Island......	5.00	0.60	1.30	....	....	4.00	....	0.63	88.02	0.45	24	Ditto.
3. Upland Georgia....	4.60	0.10	1.25	....	....	2.90	....	1.00	89.35	0.75	12	Vegetable matter, peat, or lignite, but nothing soluble in cold water; no saline matters.
Indian.												
4. Bundelkund........	2.00	0.33	....	7.75	....	11.90	trac	3.10	74.00	1.00	5	No peat or lignite; nothing soluble in cold water; silex in fine powder; *kunkur* in the gravel.
5. Coimbatore....	2.30	trac	4.00	....	....	7.50	trac	2.80	82.80	0.60	5	Gravel, mostly silex, with some felspar, but no *kunkur*.
6. Bourbon seed cotton (Tinivelly?).	0.15	0.20	....	....	2.88	19.50	0.15	2.00	74.60	1.12	10	Gravel, almost wholly *kunkur;* some carbonate of iron, half the soil of gravel.
7. Mauritius..........	1.75	0.30	9.15	....	....	40.85	trac	2.50	43.60	1.85	12?	Silex mostly coarse grained; gravel, mostly calcareous.
Singapore.												
8. Best soil...........	9.15	0.60	....	0.25	....	1.25	....	...	88.20	0.55	9	Vegetable matter, mostly peaty, and very soluble.
9. Inferior soil........	1.00	....	....	0.71	....	0.071	....	....	98.85	....	4	Vegetable matter, peaty.

Thus, writing from Tinivelly, Mr. Hughes states "that the red and brown looms, or indeed any silicious or calcareous soil, fertile in a moderate degree, is the most suitable and fruitful. That no very rich, heavy, retentive, stiff soils should ever be selected, for though the plants are luxurious, yet they have as much and more tendency to produce redundance of wood and leaf than of fruit buds, besides harboring insects. What is commonly known in many parts of India, under the denomination of black cotton soil, Mr. H. states is to be entirely avoided.

From Persia we have similar information; for there, we learn, that cotton is chiefly cultivated on a silicious soil, containing shells, and consequently supplied with calcareous matter. Again, Captain Robertson reported to the Bombay government that the Bourbon cotton suceeeded very well in the eastern parts of Broach, in the light sandy soils, as recommended by the cultivators of the Isle of Bourbon.

The Agri-Horticultural Society of Bengalore reports that the light brown soil of moderate depth and rather sandy (so prevalent in Mysore) seems to be the soil that suits the Upland Georgia and New-Orleans: but the Sea Island thrives in moist ground that is well drained. Captain Basil Hall says, that for cultivating the New-Orleans cotton, a soil, rich, light, and dry, is to be preferred; but that it is generally thought *new* land does not produce a cotton so fine in *quality* as it does after bearing one or two crops of grain.

Mr. Ewart, speaking of his experience in the cultivation at Guzerat of Bourbon cotton, or a variety nearly akin to it, says, "it requires a dry sandy soil, and no irrigation; water or manure sends it all to leaves and branches."

The failure of the experiments made at the Akra farm by the Agri-Horticultural Society is also a forcible illustration of the unfitness of an over fertile, tenacious soil for the production of cotton. The Committee of the Society, reporting upon the failure, observe, "that it establishes the fact that the cotton of America will not flourish on a rich and moist soil, while its natural basis is for the most part composed of three-fourths of sand and one-fourth of clay." This was evidenced "by the rapidity and luxuriance of vegetation, in the production of abundance of wood, leaf, and flower, but little produce."

These results of experience and observation point out that soils constituted almost entirely of the least retentive of all constituents, silex, carbonate of lime (chalk), and oxide of iron, are best suited to the growth of cotton—in other words, that the soil cannot be too light, whether it is upland or lowland, maritime or inland. This rule applies, I think, to all except the indigenous varieties of the *G. herbaceum*, which are most productive on soils much more fertile and tenacious than are suited to the superior kinds from Bourbon, Georgia, and elsewhere. This opinion is confirmed by the statements of Mr. Heath, who says, "that in the Madras territories two species or varieties of cotton plant are cultivated, and these require very different soils—one is annual (*oopum punthee G. herbaceum ?*) and the other perennial (*madam punthee*). The first succeeds only in the 'black cotton soil,' formed apparently from the decomposition of trap rocks; but the second only in a very light soil, formed from the disintegration of granitic rocks, especially when mixed with *kunkur* or calcareous tufa."

Mr. Heath made his experiments on the Bourbon cotton in the latter kind of soil, which is more abundant than any other in the districts on the Coromandel coast, south of Madras; and he entertains no doubt that the Bourbon cotton plant might be successfully cultivated wherever this kind of soil occurs. In introducing this cultivation, he had to encounter the usual difficulties consequent on the introduction of any novelty in agriculture; but these gave way to perseverance. At the end of four years, Mr. H. had the satisfaction of seeing the experiment completely successful, as in the seasons of 1823–4, he procured from the district of Coimbatore five hundred bales of clean Bourbon cotton, of three hundred pounds each, and the natives were at that time well satisfied that the cultivation of this was more profitable to them than that of the common cotton of the country.

That light soils should be best suited for the production of cotton superior both in quantity and quality, is precisely what our knowledge of vegetable physiology would have suggested. There is an axiom in that science to which I know of no exception; that whatever tends to promote the production of super-luxuriant foliage, and an enlargement of roots, proportionately diminishes the amount and perfection of the parts of fructification. A familiar example is afforded in England by the potato. Its varieties producing early tubers, are characterized by having little foliage, and no blossom; but if the tubers are removed as fast as they are formed, the foliage becomes more abundant, and they blossom as freely as the later varieties.

A soil abounding in moisture promotes the development of leaves and roots, not only by the superfluity of water, but by presenting to the roots the food of the plant rapidly and more abundantly than is done in a drier soil. To explain this, it need only be remarked that the roots of a plant are only capable of imbibing its nourishment afforded by the soil when it is in a state of solution. The roots of a plant in a light, dry soil, are wide-spreading and minutely fibrous; in a wet, tenacious soil they become more massive and fleshy, as do those of a hyacinth grown in water, which suggests that the food of the cotton plant obtained from the soil, should be presented to it very gradually and never in superabundance.

This leads to another important consideration:

Manures.—The facts just stated indicate that rapidly decomposing animal or vegetable remains, if applied in considerable quantities, or even in small quantities, if not well mixed and dispersed through the soil, must be injurious to the crop. On the other hand, if the soil is poor or exhausted, a small quantity of such fertilizing matters may be applied advantageously. In such soil the American cultivators sprinkle a little well-decayed stable compost along the trench where the seed is to be sown.

The best of all fertilizers for cotton will be doubtless found to be peat, saw-dust, or other woody matters that decay slowly. The natives consider that wood ashes are excellent for the purpose, and the opinion is evidently founded on truth, for the carbonaceous matter remaining in them after combustion, is in a state to become slowly available to the plants.

Of animal matters, the only one that could be applied with a prospect of success is *bones*, crushed to fine powder, and sown broadcast in very small quantities.

Mr. Piddington recommends *lignite* (fossil wood) peat, farmyard manure, wood ashes, decayed leaves, mud from old ditches, oil-cake, the cotton seed of the preceding crop, pressed or fomented to prevent germination, and charcoal of all kinds, "excepting, perhaps, the ashes of soondry and other woods near the sea, which may contain too much muriate or carbonate of soda." Why this exception is made I cannot understand, because, of all saline manures, the two just named have been found, in Europe, the most beneficial, if judiciously employed.

So far indeed from agreeing with Mr. Piddington in deprecating the use of common salt (muriate of soda or chloride of sodium) as a manure for the cotton plant, I believe it will be found to be one of the most useful that can be employed in its cultivation, and I would most earnestly urge upon every cultivator to give it a fair and careful trial.

I have seen common salt employed too generally and successfully in England, to come to any hasty conclusion that there is a single crop in India which is incapable of being benefited by its application. Let it be remembered that this manure destroys predatory vermin, abstracts moisture from the atmosphere, thus tending to keep the soil regularly moist; *promotes* the decay of stubborn vegetable remains in the soil, being antiseptic only when present in large quantities, and that it acts as a gentle stimulant to the plant, promoting its health.

I am not driven to advocate the employment of common salt as a manure for the cotton crop, upon conclusions drawn from these general principles alone, for we have direct and satisfactory testimony upon the subject.

Mr. Bolingbroke says that in Demarara, the British settlers found that the cotton plantations succeeded better on the sea-coast than on the banks of the river, a superiority which he attributed to its containing more common salt. This opinion that salt promotes the growth of the cotton plant, is also expressed in the third report of the African Institution, it being stated positively, that the saline air of the sea-shore, though generally destructive to the coffee plant, is favorable to the cotton.

Mr. Bernard Metcalf, remarking upon the cottons of India, observes, "that the Georgia, Sea Island, Surinam, and Demarara cotton plants are all grown on the border of the sea, and the prime qualities only so far inland as the influence of the sea air and tide waters extend."

This fondness of the cotton plant for maritime places, has been observed also in other parts of the world, for Mr. Bruce, who resided many years in Persia, states, that the cotton was always fine in proportion as it was grown nearer to the sea.

It might be objected, that the benefit the cotton plant derives from the vicinity of the sea, arises possibly from some other cause than the saline matter thence obtained, but such surmise is rebutted by the results of direct experiments.

A report, published in 1827, by the Hon. Mr. Seabrook, Corresponding Secretary of the Agricultural Society of St. John's, South Carolina, seems to put beyond dispute the importance, not to say the absolute necessity, of using common salt as a manure, if a superior stapled cotton is desired. His researches were especially directed to ascertain the cause of the fineness of the Sea Island cotton, and the conclusion to which these researches led him was, that *salt mud*, the almost sole manure used by the best planters, was a principal cause of the superiority. "This manure," observes Mr. Seabrook, "is known to impart a healthful action to the cotton plant, inducing it rapidly to mature its produce, and giving it a staple at once strong and silky." One of his relatives, by steadfastly adhering to the application of soft mud, literally converted a barren waste to a soil as fruitful as any of which Edisto Island can boast.

Capt. B. Bailey, a member of the before-named Agricultural Society, demonstrated that one bushel of salt, added to sixty bushels of compost, and spread upon the soil of a cotton plantation, improves most decidedly the quantum and quality of the crop.

This testimony, sustaining the legitimate conclusions deducible from scientific considerations, must justify my urging the importance of attending to the merits, and testing carefully the effects, of one of the cheapest of manures—cheap, from the small quantity required to a biggah; for I believe that half a maund will be found sufficient, and the most beneficial time for applying it (by hand broad-cast), just before sowing the seed.

Let its value be tested fairly; part of the plantation being salted, and part left untreated. Let the produce of an equal number of shrubs on each be brought separately to the scale and to the merchant, and let these decide the question. Let no one be deceived by that suggestion of idleness, "I can see no difference;" for I would impress upon all the result of my own experience, and that of a hundred others, that *common salt promotes the development of the parts of fructification, and rarely or never increases the luxuriance of the plant.* These are precisely the contingencies desirable to be obtained for the cotton shrub; and I would conclude this head of my subject by suggesting as probable, that the use of salt as a manure will enable the Sea Island cotton to be cultivated in inland districts.

It is said that gypsum (sulphate of lime) may be used as a manure to cotton lands not near the sea. Lands so situated usually contain a minute proportion of this earthy salt. It perhaps, therefore, acts beneficially by entering into the constitution of the plant, as is does into that of clover and lucerne; crops which have been ascertained in England never to succeed well on soils in which the salt could not be detected.

Preparation of soil before sowing.—No ground should be cropped with two successive growths of cotton, as the produce of the second is always inferior to the first, both in quantity and quality. This rule applies whether the plants remain in production only one or more seasons. Following and cropping alternately is recommended by some planters: but this is certainly an unnecessarily losing system, for if an intermediate crop of any kind is grown, especially if manure is given, and a strictly clean husbandry followed, the succeeding crop of cotton has never been known to be injured; but, on the contrary, rather improved.

In the south-western parts of Mysore, they cultivate cotton in succession to millet. As soon as the millet is harvested, about the autumnal equinox, they immediately plow the field, and endeavor to cleanse it more effectually by hoeing it twice with the *cuntay*, or bullock hoe. Manure is then put upon the field, which, after the first rain, is again plowed.

In Bundelcund, land which has borne a winter crop, is generally selected for cotton the following year, and the seed appears to be sown upon it without even the previous preparation of plowing.

In other parts of India, although this previous preparation is not quite so neglected, yet in no district is it sufficiently attended to. The cotton plant roots deep, and never succeeds in any soil not permitting the ready extension of its radicle fibres. This circumstance decides the importance of having it brought to a deep and fine tilth before the seed is sown, A Bombay government report of 1811 states, that in Georgia and Carolina incessant labor is bestowed in plowing, harrowing, trenching, and hoeing the cotton fields.

This is confirmed by Capt. Basil Hall, from actual observation in Georgia. "The preparation of cotton land," to use his own words, "requires most particular attention; it must be repeatedly plowed, and frequently harrowed, say twice or thrice, until it is fully pulverized."

The committee, in reporting on the experiments made at the Akra farm, are very particular in enforcing this preliminary cultivation. The success, they say, of a good crop will depend upon the land being dug to a sufficient depth; if less than eighteen inches, the tap-root, which is exceedingly delicate, and extending nearly that length, becomes obstructed, and the growth of the plant is checked.

Choice of Seed.—The employment of seed, possessing its full vegetative power, is a consideration of primary importance, whatever may be the crop under cultivation; but where the seeds are of an oleaginous nature, as is the case with those of cotton,* even extra caution is required, on account of the facility with which their germinating power is injured and destroyed.

Upon this point there are many particulars requiring attention. The seed ought to be selected from the most perfect early stalks, produced on the best soil. Mr. Seabrook adds, "that frequent change of soil and situation is indispensable to sustain the quality of the cotton produced by any particular kind of seed; and employing mixed and bad seed is the origin of the indifferent quality of the produce of many countries. That which is intended for sowing should be known to be new, and ought to be well cleaned previously to sowing. At Surat, this is effected by rubbing it over a kind of sieve, called a *cott*, the bottom of which is made of close and tightly strung coir. The refuse cotton, and a great many of the light seeds, are left upon the coir, and the good seed falls through. But it is best, in order to secure the employment of none but perfect heavy seeds, to put the whole into water just previously to sowing, and reject those which float upon the surface."*

The quantity of seed employed per biggah, varies considerably. In Surat, 5 seers are sown upon a biggah; in Poorneah, 10 seers on a biggah, equal to 3,600 square yards; in the Dooab, 5 seers on a biggah, containing 2,800 square yards. Pierce Butler, Esq., a successful cultivator in the Georgian Island, St. Simon's, says, "that a bushel of seed is required for an acre."

No particular quantity need, however, be assigned, because, if the best mode of sowing is adopted, drills will be made at eight feet apart throughout the field, and the seed inserted in them at three inches distance.

Time for Sowing.—The committee, who reported upon the causes of the failure of the Akra farm, included among them, "positive ignorance of the proper season for sowing;" and, as a more fatal mistake cannot occur than that of performing this operation at a wrong period of the year, it may be well to accord those months which have been selected by the most skilful cultivators.

Mr. Hughes, already mentioned as a grower of Bourbon cotton, at Tinivelly, says, "that there, if the seed can be got into the ground in September, the young plant may be able to resist the continued wet of a heavy monsoon; but little is gained by sow-

* In Burmah, they are burnt in the open air to give light at festivals.

* *Seabrooke's Rep., in* 1827, *on Sea Island Cotton*—We are told that in Burmah they always wash the seed well before it is sown, which must be for the same purpose.

Seed intended for exportation, it may here be remarked, with the intent that it shall retain its vegetating power when it arrives at its destination, should not be at all separated from the cotton. Such separation invariably occasions a loss of the power to germinate during a long voyage. To preserve it, it should remain enveloped in the cotton well dried, and be packed tightly in tin cases, soldered to exclude the air. If casks are employed, it should be kept in a dry situation upon the gun-deck of the vessel, but in whatever manner packed, it must never be subjected to the heat of the ship's hold.

ing in October, November, and December, unless the land is very high, dry, and free from weeds. The clear interval of these months, especially early in October, answers well for transplanting, and the first week of January very well, in general, both for sowing and transplanting.

Mr. Gilder, who has also cultivated the Bourbon cotton successfully, at Guzerat, sowed at the end of July, after the heavy rains had ceased.

In America, Captain Hall says, "The sowing is performed from the beginning of April to the 10th of May."

In central India, Baboo Radhakant Deb relates that the sowing is performed "during the month *Assar* (from mid-June to mid-July), or when the sun enters the sign of Gemini."

In the Dooab and Bundelcund, Mr. Vincent says, "The seed is committed to the ground immediately after the first heavy showers at the end of June, or beginning of July."

In Burmah, the seed is sown in the beginning of the rains in April or May.

In the vicinity of Dacca, the sowing is performed in October or November.

In the district of Poorneah, the seed-time is March and April.

The object to be kept in view is to have the blossoming and harvest-time during the dry season, because heavy rains at such periods of the plant's growth are fatal, both to the quantity and quality of the production.

Sowing.—The best mode of arranging the land for the growth of the cotton plant, is by dividing it into flat beds at least four feet wide, for the smaller kinds separated from each other by alleys about eighteen inches broad. The seed being sown in a single row down the centre of each bed, affords a space of five and a half feet between each two rows.

For the larger kinds, as the *G. acuminatum*, the Bourbon, &c., the beds should be seven feet wide. Mr. Hughes, so often before mentioned, says that the rows ought to be eight feet apart, and the plants thinned in the rows to the same distance. The facility for plowing and hoeing is so great, besides the great advantage of a free circulation of air, that Mr. H. particularly insists on this method, especially as he knows that too close planting is a common mistake.

In Mysore the rows are made two feet apart, and even in some districts of America the intervals are only three or four feet apart; but if there be any increase of quantity obtained by this crowded culture, it is certainly at the expense of quality; and loss is insured by the unnecessary exhaustion of the soil by superfluous plants, and the operations of hoeing, &c., are extremely retarded.

The best mode of sowing is by opening a drill down the centre of each bed by means of a hoe, which insures that the seed shall be buried at a regular, and not too great a depth. The depth should not be more than one inch or one inch and a half.

The seed may be strewed by hand along the drills, about three inches apart, and the earth immediately drawn over it by the hoe. In Mysore, they use a thorny bush for the purpose.

In some parts of America, they open a row of holes with the hoe about a foot apart, sprinkling a handful of seed in each; and in Burmah they adopt the still more slovenly mode of sowing broad-cast.

Preparation of the Seed.—I have already noticed that, in Burmah, the seed is washed before it is sown; but as I am not aware that the cotton plant is liable to the attack of any parasitical plant, I do not see that this operation can be of any benefit beyond removing the seeds which are light and imperfect.

In Central India they wet the seed, and then roll it in powdered cow-dung, waiting until the seed is nearly dry before they commit it to the ground.

About Dacca they merely wet the seed for a few minutes before it is sown; but in Bengal they frequently do not sow until, by keeping it moist, it begins to germinate.

Dr. Anderson tried all these modes, as well as the mixing of various composts with the seed, but could not perceive that there was any difference in the size or strength of the young plants.

Mixing Crops.—Mr. Gilder, who made some successful experiments in cultivating Bourbon cotton in Guzerat, during the year 1816, grew with it *bejaree*, sown in drills as usual, at the same time. Indian corn is similarly mixed with the cotton crop in the Isle of Bourbon, being held to shelter the tender plants from the sun. Mr. Gilder found the bejaree to answer the same purpose; and he says it ought to pay the expense of rent and cultivation the first season, during which the cotton plants yield nothing.

In Burmah they sow brinjalls and other culinary vegetables with the cotton; and in Bundelcund, either urbur, tillil, or motee, are similarly mixed with it. Indeed, it may be considered as the general practice, but this universality is no justification; and, after some years' experience in cultivating plants, I have never yet found two crops which could be grown together without one interfering with the operations that might be usefully performed to the other, or being in some other way prejudicial. In India, neither land nor labor is so dear as to render it desirable in an economical point of view. The plea of sheltering the cotton plants will be found invalid, for the shelter has a more than equivalent drawback by rendering the plants weak and spindled.

After-culture.—The after-culture consists chiefly in hoeing and stirring the soil, not only for the purpose of extirpating the weeds, but to pulverize the surface, so as to facilitate the penetration of the air, and the absorption from it of moisture by the soil. This is particularly beneficial in the dryest periods of the year, when, as is not generally known, the atmosphere is saturated with moisture.

The seedlings make their appearance in three or four days after the seed has been sown, and in two or three more develop two leaves. The thinning and weeding may then at once be commenced, this being at first carefully done by hand, for the young plants are very tender and easily injured. Mr. Butler, who has been more than once mentioned as a distinguished cultivator in the Island of St. Simon's, Georgia, recommends that the hoeing should be repeated at least once every twelve days until the plants flower, or even until they pod, if the ground is foul.

At such hoeing the thinning must be also attended to, which must be done moderately until the third hoeing; the plants will then be out of danger from the worms, and large enough to bear drought.

In Mysore, Dr. Buchanan found that the native cultivators performed the hoeing even still more frequently, drawing the *cuntay* or bullock-hoe between the rows once in every eight days, until the cotton is ripe.

The thinning should keep pace with the growth of the plants, and when they have attained the height of three feet they should be finally thinned to eight feet apart, or whatever less distance may be determined, but the greater the interval the better.

Suckers thrown up about the root must be removed as formed.

Pruning is advisable, if done with judgment.

Mr. Butler says that the Sea Island cotton requires not only the suckers to be removed, but, if the plants are vigorous, to have their tops pinched off once or twice.

Mr. N. Savi goes so far as to say that all who understand the cultivation of the Seychelles and Bourbon cotton agree that, to make them produce a fine quality of down, they should not be allowed to grow higher than three feet, which may be effected by cutting off the tender tops of the stems as soon as the first blossoms appear. This causes them to spread wide in their horizontal growth.

Mr. Higgins, in describing the cultivation of Upland Georgia cotton at Allahabad, says that "topping may or may not be resorted to; it may strengthen the plant, but I think it makes them later in bearing."

Mr. Hughes, who has, as before mentioned, cultivated the Bourbon cotton so successfully at Tinivelly, prunes his shrubs twice in the year, the first and principal, as soon as the heavy rains have passed away, that is from the 15th to the 31st December, when the shrub is cut down, generally to two feet high and two feet wide, only the firm wood being left with the strong white and brown bark. In the fine days of January the plantation is plowed thoroughly three or four times. In less than two months the whole is again in the finest foliage and full blossom, and continues in full bearing all the months of March, April, and May. A good many pods still remain in June, early in which month a second pruning is practiced of the long, straggling, twisted, soft shoots, with diminutive pods. Good produce is yielded from July to September, unless the plants receive damage in these months from rain.

In Persia, after the crop is gathered, and the leaves fed off by sheep, the poor women are allowed to break the shrubs down close for fire-wood. The stumps shoot out again as luxuriantly as ever when the season returns.

Transplanting.—If any vacancies occur in the rows while the plants are young, these may be successfully filled up by removing to these places some of the plants from situations where they may be growing too thickly; otherwise, it is not a practice to be commended, as it renders the plants at least a fortnight later in coming into production.

Watering.—Although the cotton plant requires a light silicious soil, and is destroyed by water remaining stagnant around it, yet excessive dryness of soil is to be avoided. It may even be flooded with advantage, provided that the water is allowed to flow off quickly again.

To preserve the soil in a due state of moisture, considerable attention is requisite during every period of the plant's growth. The object is to keep it soft and damp, so as to allow the free extension of the roots, but at the same time to avoid having the texture saturated with wet; and, much more, never to have so great an excess as to suffer the water to stand in pools upon the surface. The same precaution is requisite at the time of sowing; for water in excess at that time either induces the total decay of the seed, or causes its germination to be weak and unhealthy. When the shrubs are well grown and strong, which they are by the end of October, they seldom require more moisture than they acquire from the heavy dews which then accompany the cold weather. This. however. is not the case if the weather be dry. Particular attention to this point is requisite during the blossoming time.

The flower-buds appear in November, and in the course of five days the blossom is fully open. The flower falls off after being expanded about four days, leaving the pod apparent. Bright weather and heavy dews are to be desired during the blossoming: rain at that time destroys the crop. The pod requires about four weeks for ripening, this period being curtailed or extended in proportion to the heaviness of the dews and brightness of the sunshine at the season. A deficiency of either delays the ripening. If the dews are particularly light, a gentle watering may with advantage be occasionally given. In Peru and Egypt the irrigation of this crop is most carefully attended to, and the results are proportionately beneficial.

Gathering.—The season for gathering differs in India with the place of growth.

Mr. Gilder, at Guzerat, picked his Bourbon cotton from the end of November to the close of January—a second, but more scanty crop occurring in May.

In Central India, Baboo Radhakant Deb says, the pods are ripe in the month Choyte, when the sun enters Pisces (mid-March to mid-April), and that the gathering continues until the close of May.

About Dacca the crop is gathered in April, May, and June; and where the situation is beyond the reach of inundation, a second crop, but inferior in quantity and quality, is obtained.

In Bundelcund, on the poorer soils, the crop begins to be collected about the middle of September, but from those of the richer and more northernly situated soils, not until November and December.

When the pods are ripe, which they are in less than two months after blossoming, three of their sides burst and the cotton protrudes through the fissures. In five or six days after the pods have burst the cotton is usually gathered, though it is often allowed to remain longer. At Surat they wait for ten days, and continue the gathering once after every similar lapse of time until the close of April, by which time the cotton is all gathered.

There is no doubt that the being allowed to remain so long without being gathered after the pods have burst, is not injurious to the quality of cotton, but it is at the same quite as certain that it is no way beneficial. Granting this, however, to be immaterial, the plan of allowing it to remain seems objectionable, upon the plain reason that every day renders the skin of the pod and the leaves of the calyx more brittle, and consequently increases the liability to injure the quality of the crop by their fragments getting intermixed.

I have a strong opinion that it would be found every way advantageous to gather each pod immediately that it shows symptoms of bursting, as enabling the cotton to be separated from it without so much liability to contamination from its fragments. However this may be, experience teaches us that the gathering should be effected very early in the morning while the dew is upon the plant, the calyx is at that time pliant, yielding to the hand without breaking, and consequently keeping the cotton free from leaf.

In gathering, care must be taken to grasp at once all the locks of cotton in the pod, so that they may come away together. If any dry leaves fall upon the cotton before the gatherer has secured it in the bag hanging by his side, they must be carefully removed. This bag must be covered to prevent the admission of pieces of the dry leaves, always to be found about the branches, and which are disturbed by a very slight agitation. It is this admixture of leaf which is so much objected to by the spinner and proportionately lowers the value of the cotton. After gathering, it should immediately be thoroughly dried, whether it is to be stored or at once dressed and packed. A woman in America will generally gather twice as much per day as a man.

The pods which burst the earliest, usually those on the tops of the shrubs, produce the finest cotton; the quality as well as quantity diminishing as the plants decrease in vigor. This is so apparent, that the cotton of the first two gatherings is usually worth three or four rupees per candy more than that of the later gatherings.

Produce.—In favorable seasons a biggah in *Guzerat* will produce 25 maunds of cotton, mixed with the seeds. Where these have been separated by the wheel or cheriah, the cotton will be found to weigh about 9 maunds, and the seed 15 maunds. In the eastern and southern parts of India, two or three maunds of clean cotton is the estimated average of a biggah.

Twenty-seven biggahs in *Broach* produce 44⅜ maunds of clean Bourbon cotton, fully equal to that of the island after which it is named.

In *Poorneah* five maunds of uncleaned cotton are usually grown per biggah.

Dr. Buchanan says, that in *Mysore* the produce varies between 110 and 270 lbs. per acre.

Captain Hall states, that in *America* from 400 to 500 lbs. of cleaned cotton is produced from a similar space of ground.

In Central India, Baboo Radhakant Deb states, that a biggah yields about one maund and three-quarters of cleaned cotton.

The comparative proportion in weight between the cotton and the seed usually varies from one to four and one to three. It is, of course, a great object in the growth of cotton to obtain an increase in the proportion of wood produced above that of the seed. At Shahabad this was effected in the instance of Egyptian cotton. Mr. Seyburne says, its produce there was not only superior in staple, but was half cotton and half seed, while the country plants yielded only one part cotton and three parts seed.

COTTON OF INDIA.—The question of an Indian supply of cotton has, for a long series of years, been discussed with no very great success. The fact appears to be, that the quantity obtained thence has been gradually on the decrease; but those years in which high prices prevailed, through short productions in the article, a stimulus was given to shipments from India, by diverting the cotton from the China market, and induoing greater cultivation. The import of India cotton into the United Kingdom, and the export price in the United States for corresponding years, were as follows:

	Import from India.	Average of prices in the United States.
1847	221,959	10¾
1848	227,572	7⅝
1849	182,079	6⅜
1850	70,838	11¼
1851	118,872	12⅛

The superior quality of United States cotton always enables it to command a higher price (at reduced rates) than the Indian commands; it affords material for all English yarns under twenty, and this may be taken as 50 per cent. of the manufacture. But whenever that price becomes exorbitant, a great stimulus is given to the consumption of the India articles, and a higher price never fails to bring out considerable quantities. The English official tables show the following receipts of cotton to the United Kingdom for two years.

IMPORT OF RAW COTTON INTO THE UNITED KINGDOM.

From	1850	1851	Decrease	Increase
United States	634,504,050	493,153,112	141,350,938	—
India	70,838,515	118,872,742	—	43,034,227
West Indies	944,307	228,913	716,594	—
Egypt, &c	17,369,843	18,931,414	—	1,561,571
Brazil	30,738,133	30,229,982	508,151	—
Other places	1,074,164	2,090,698	—	1,016,534
Total lbs	755,469,012	663,576,861	142,585,683	50,612,332

The average export value of cotton in the United States, for 1849, was 6.4 cents, and for 1850, 11.3, a rise of 80 per cent. This drew from India 70 per cent. more than the usual supply; and the fact presented itself that, at an average of 11 cents, India can supply, at call, 25 per cent. as much cotton as the United States.

For many years the low prices of cotton have gradually discouraged the India production, but occasionally high prices impart a new stimulus to the cultivation in that region, and American cottons feel the reaction. The late accounts from France show that cotton of United States description may be raised very advantageously in the colony of Algiers.

In the United States, little or no India cotton is used; but the latter article, of southern growth, enters into all our cotton fabrics, and the proportion of the crop consumed in the United States increases. Thus, assuming that consumption in the South and West, for the past five years, has been 350,000 bales, then the crops and United States consumption for two periods of five years, will be as follows:

	Crop—Bales	U. S. Consumption Bales
1841-'42	10,585,000	1,951,100
1847-'51	11,304,000	2,719,400
Total bales	719,000	768,300

Thus establishing the fact, that home consumption increases faster than the production, pointing to the speedy control of the value of the crop by the home market. This is more particularly the case, since the export of goods in rivalry with that of Great Britain is now ro rapidly swelling in magnitude.

COTTON CULTURE IN INDIA.—The London Globe of a late date contains an interesting article on the progress of cotton culture in British India, which we extract as follows:

The southern states of America have increased their shipments of cotton to this country since 1800 from 16,000,000 to 600,000,000 pounds, while British India has but swollen her exports from 6,000,000 to 80,000,000 pounds. We cannot avoid wishing for some more explanation of the anomaly. Capital has not been wanting in the East, neither has there been any indifference to the question on the part of the authorities; yet the real progress made is wretchedly small, and we are really at the present moment obtaining less cotton from India than in 1844 and 1842.

As regards the progress of the supply of raw cotton in British India for local use and export to other countries, it is estimated in round numbers to be at the present day 450,-

000,000 pounds annually, of which fully two-thirds are worked up in the country for local purposes. Of the remaining one-third, China takes nearly one-half, leaving about one-sixth of the entire produce of the country at the disposal of Great Britain.

That there are vast tracts of land in each of the three Indian presidencies capable of being brought under cotton cultivation, as also a dense population, at disposal for working such lands, there appears to be little doubt; but the real question to be determined is, whether the manufacturers of Europe really require in larger quantities such cotton as the natives themselves produce and use, and which they can most readily furnish; or whether they want some other kind or condition of cotton than is at present produced in India. The result of the lengthy evidence given by Manchester manufacturers, Liverpool brokers, Bombay merchants and East India civilians, before the committee of the House of Commons on the growth of cotton in India, appears to be, that although a lessening of the cost to the manufacturer of the present quality of Indian cotton would, to a certain extent, enable him to work off larger quantities of it, the greater want is the better quality of article, such a description of produce as shall enable it to be freely worked up in place of much of the present American sorts, and with which it cannot now compete.

Much has unquestionably been done in the way of improving the growth and preparation of Indian cotton; the East India Company has spent largely in importing seed, implements and experienced hands from the cotton-growing states of America, as well as in prizes for the best and largest samples of fine cotton produced within the presidencies, for shipments to England. In 1824, there existed a difference of 2d. per pound between the average price of uplands American cotton and the average price of Indian cotton at Liverpool. In 1836, there was a difference of 3d. per pound in the same qualities, whereas, since 1844, the difference between them has only varied from ¾d. to 1d. per pound.

So long since as 1788, the Court of Directors called the attention of the Indian government to the cultivation of cotton in India, with a view to its encouragement. Two years later, reports were received of the culture carried on, and seed from the Mauritius and Malta were distributed throughout the Indian Peninsula. In 1799 and 1800, plantations were formed on the Malabar coast and in the Circars. From 1801 to 1818, various samples of American, West Indian and Persian seeds were sent out, as also improved gins for cleaning cotton. In 1818, four cotton farms, of 400 acres each, were established at Tinnevelley, Coimbatore, Masulipatum and Vizagapatam. In 1823, Barbadoes and Brazil cotton was grown by Lady Hastings at Barrackpore. Five years later, attention was again called to the subject of cotton culture by Lord Ellenborough, then President of the Indian Board. Between 1830 and 1849, various new cotton farms were established, seed and machinery were introduced from the Brazils and Egypt, and an officer in the company's service was dispatched to America for the purpose of collecting information, and experienced cultivators, with seed and flax.

In 1840, ten American planters arrived under the care of Captain Boyles, and were in the following year stationed in various parts of the three presidencies, to test the practicability of applying the American mode of culture to the soil of India. To the present time these experiments have been continued with varying degrees of success. In the Dooab, at Agra, and at Gorruckpore, the result appears to have been unfavorable; but elsewhere there is good reason to believe that, although no immediate and important improvement in the quality of the crops seems to have taken place, a better system has been gradually introduced amongst a people habitually averse to any changes whatever, whether in their religion, their industry, or their customs.

COTTON CULTURE—EAST INDIA.—Mr. Bright has already presented to the House of Commons, a petition from the Manchester Chamber of Commerce, embodying its views on this subject, and praying for a full and impartial inquiry through the medium of a government commission. The honorable member for Manchester has, also, given notice of his intention to move for the appointment of such a commission; and we are glad to see that active exertions are in progress to strengthen his hands, by an effective representation of the opinions of the mercantile classes of Manchester, on this important subject. A petition now lies in the Exchange, which has already received the signatures of npwards of two hundred of the principal merchants and manufacturers of this district. The following is the petition:

TO THE HONORABLE THE COMMONS OF THE UNITED KINGDOM OF GREAT BRITAIN AND IRELAND, IN PARLIAMENT ASSEMBLED.

The petition of the undersigned, merchants, manufacturers and other inhabitants of Manchester and Salford, and their vicinities,

Showeth—That, for the last four years, the cotton manufacture of this country, which, in a healthy state, supplies nearly one-half of the whole value of British exports, has been subjected to most injurious disturbances through an inadequate supply of the raw material, for which, from its nature, this country is wholly dependent upon imports from warmer climates.

That it is of vital consequence to every interest in this kingdom, that a trade, in which so vast an amount of fixed capital is embarked, which distributes such immense sums, weekly, among a population dependent on them, and which influences the well-being of every consumer in the state, in proportion as it is in a prosperous or a depressed condition, should be as little as possible liable to pernicious fluctuations from a deficient supply of its first requisite.

That, to engender steadiness of supply, it has become of absolute necessity, that the sources whence cotton may be obtained, should be immediately multiplied.

That, in looking to the countries capable of producing cotton, your petitioners first fix their attention upon India, because the plant is there indigenous, and the cultivation of it has been pursued for centuries. They see, however, with regret, that while the use of cotton manufactures has increased with an almost incredible rapidity, in countries which cannot produce the raw material, India, which has so long possessed the raw material and a population adequate to the production of any quantity, has not, from the inferiority and want of improvement of the quality of her cotton, participated with other and younger countries in the supply of it.

That your petitioners believe that the supineness of India, in the improvement of her cotton, has not arisen from the unfitness either of the soil or climate. The government of India, at great cost and with much apparent earnestness, have endeavored to arouse the native population to a sense of their own interest, in this respect; but the experiments have mainly, if not entirely, failed, and the hopes of relief from that quarter, so hopeful by nature, are becoming faint, and the benefits which a more enlarged intercourse with this country would confer upon India, are repressed.

That it is in evidence before your honorable house, that large portions of India are well suited to the production of cotton—your petitioners are anxious to have it ascertained, by means of an inquiry that may leave no doubt, what have been the causes which have restrained India from so improving the quality of her cotton, as to enable her to compete with the cottons of other countries in the British market; and as such an inquiry could not but be most useful in displaying the economical condition of the people of India, and in providing data whereby your honorable house may, at the proper time, be better enabled to consider whether the system heretofore applied to India is such as is best calculated to excite the energies of the people, to lead to industry and well-being, and to develop the resources of the country; and being desirous only that the truth should be made manifest, and that errors in government, if errors exist, should be corrected.

Your petitioners humbly pray, that, for the benefit both of this country and of India, and for the useful guidance of the legislature, your honorable house may address her Majesty to appoint, forthwith, a royal commission, to make strict inquiry within the presidencies of Bombay and Madras into the causes which have prevented the increase of the cultivation and the improvement of the quality of the cotton grown within them.

The capabilities of India, for the growth of any quantity of raw cotton, are unquestioned. The difficulties that impede its cultivation arise from the causes that spring from the very nature of the government, and are remediable only by an entire change in its financial and internal policy. These causes are to be found chiefly in the impoverishment and exhaustion of the material resources of the people—the utter absence of all encouragement, on the part of the government, to any improvement in the means of communication—a wasteful and injurious system of taxation, that strikes at the very root of industrial enterprise, and which denies everything like security or protection to the capital, as well as to the labor, of the cultivator. The government of India assumes to be the landlord of every portion of the soil, and derives the main bulk of its revenue from a direct tax on the produce of the land. Now, if this were a fixed amount, equitably levied, not by any arbitrary assumption on the part of the government, of a right to determine what proportion of the whole produce would constitute a sufficient remuneration for the skill, industry and capital of the cultivator, but on a fair valuation of the intrinsic worth of the mere use of the soil, as an implement of production, this form of taxation would probably be the least injurious in which it could fall upon the tax-payer. But the assessment of the Indian land tax is both arbitrary and capricious. As a rule, it is excessive as well as fluctuating; and the natural consequence is, to deprive industry of all stimulus by destroying the only incentive which can sustain it—the certainty of reaping the full fruits of its own skill and perseverance. Experience sufficiently shows us, in this country, how powerful the tenancy-at-will system has been in checking agricultural improvements, although the great majority of landed proprietors were not disposed to deal harshly or unjustly with enterprising or improving occupiers.

The mere liability to have the fruits of their industry torn from them, has operated like a blight on the energy of our farmers, and maintained the produce of the soil far below its natural capabilities. How, then, must the same principle have worked in India, where the landlord was not the squire of the parish, influenced by local ties and associations, but the government of a huge territory, constantly under the pressure of financial exigencies, and interested in raising the largest revenue in the most summary way? How could industry, capital or cultivation, increase under a system where the amount of produce was invariably made the criterion for determining the tax-paying capabilities of any particular district? For this, unquestionably, has been the practice of the Indian government in most of the collectorates. In the able report of the Bombay commission, made three years ago, the evils of a fluctuating assessment to the land tax are very clearly shown. But a much more important fact is also substantiated by the same document, viz: that a *fixed* assessment, though bearing a larger proportion to the gross *average* produce than a fluctuating one formed on the actual estimates of each year's standing crop, is much more favorable to cultivation and industry. But the facts stated in this report, not only show the advantages of a fixed, over a fluctuating estimate, but prove, most conclusively, that a low *fixed* assessment tends rapidly to increase cultivation, and is more favorable to the revenue than a high one. In the collectorate of Broach, the report informs us that the fluctuating was changed for a high fixed assessment; while, in the Shalopore collectorate, a similar change was made to a fair or low fixed assessment. What was the result of this experiment, in the two districts only, in twelve years, with a *high* but fixed assessment—from 1834 to 1846? In the district of Broach, the total land under cultivation increased only from 590,000 beegas to 610,000; while, in Shalopore, with a *low* assessment, the quantity of cultivated land increased from 409,000 to 1,713,000 beegas: so that, not only was the revenue obtained from the low assessment much greater than it would have been with a high one, but the cultivated surface was increased, in this collectorate, above 400 per cent.

A government commission, dispatched to India, expressly to investigate the operation of the land-tax assessments in all the cotton-growing districts, would supply a vast fund of facts illustrative of the destructive effects of the present loose and arbitrary system of taxation. Whether India can, or can not, successfully compete with the cotton-growing states of America, such an inquiry would, at any rate, conduce most materially to her prosperity, by revealing the real impediments with which our system of government fetters her resources and harasses the industry of her people. The position of Lancashire is every year becoming more critical, and the necessity more imperative for some decisive attempt to ascertain whether or not our possessions in British India can be made conducive to the greater security of our staple manufacture. The accounts, which every successive steamer now brings, from the other side of the Atlantic, with reference to the deficiency of the last cotton crop, and the apparently unfavorable season for the planting of the new one, render it more than ever important that some decisive steps should be taken to render us less dependent upon a single soil and climate for our future supplies. We trust, therefore, that the exertions which are now making will induce the government to accede to the motion of Mr. Bright, and that both the Manchester Chamber of Commerce and the Commercial Association will cordially co-operate to bring the whole weight and influence of the mercantile community of Manchester to bear upon what we cannot otherwise designate than as a great national necessity.—*Manchester Examiner.*

Cultivation of Cotton in India.—As we have repeatedly explained, the transport of cotton from the fields to the port of shipment, as at present conducted, is all but fatal to the character of the staple, and even to the profits of the traders. Until some substitute is found for the miserable bullock-droves, which now supply the only means of carriage, it is quite impossible that a fair trial can be given to the cotton-producing qualities of India. Yet, at this point, also, the personal intervention of English agents might be of infinite service, for their reports would convey authentic information as to facts, and when these facts have been duly appreciated, we are entitled to anticipate with confidence that capital would be no longer wanting to establish all the requisite communications between one port of India and another. At present, the very name of a rail-road has been brought into unfortunate disrepute by the results of improvident speculation and scandalous mismanagement. But these miscarriages should serve rather to guide than to deter, and with warnings so impressive, and so fair a field as India for the revival of enterprise, results of a widely different character might be safely expected. Above all, it must be remembered that our choice is not absolutely free. Cotton we *must* have, and though some aid may be, perhaps, contributed from minor sources, it is evident to all who have considered the subject, that in India alone can be found any permanent or effectual safeguard against such contingencies as have suggested the present remarks.

There is, we fear, little room left for doubting that the apprehensions which have been repeatedly expressed, for the steadiness of our cotton supplies, will receive an unpleasant verification in the imports of the ensuing season. Already have the results of last year's deficiencies become sensible. It is not anticipated that the total shipments to England, from the American ports during the present season, will exceed 1,000,000 bales. They have, hitherto, not reached 950,000; and, indeed, the total exports since the first of last September, have been fully 500,000 bales below those of 1849, and 200,000 below those of 1848. Last year the shipments to England, during the first half of the month of April, were 84,000 bales; this year the return, for the corresponding period, gives an export of only 29,000—showing a decrease of nearly two-thirds. Facts, like these, read us an impressive lesson upon our position and our perils. Cotton is scarcely less indispensable to us than corn; whereas, while in one case we can command the resources of the entire globe, by the immutable laws of demand and supply, in the other we are virtually dependent on the produce of a single state and the variations of a single climate. The cotton plant is as liable to injury as the vine, and a bad crop is as probable an event as a bad vintage; yet, against so disastrous a contingency, in spite of repeated warnings, we have made no provision whatever.

It is true that the attention of the manufacturing districts have been awakened to the hazards of their position, and directed toward the real source of security; but though all parties seem prepared to cooperate in the work, there has been, as yet, nothing effected toward the production of a tangible result. The East India Company has expended vast pains and considerable sums, in testing the agricultural capabilities of their territory; and the Manchester Chamber of Commerce has memorialized government in furtherance of the same ends. It has been ascertained, on one side, that India can unquestionably produce cotton of admirable quality, in abundance, sufficient for all the demands of England; and it is confessed, on the other, that the opening of such a source of supply would be extremely acceptable. To complete the unanimity of purpose, the finances of India are in such a condition that any measure tending to increase the exports and revenue of the country, would be in a high degree opportune and serviceable. If, therefore, certain proceedings would conduce, at one and the same time, to the prosperity of India and the security of Manchester, and are, besides, notoriously practicable, why is the result not achieved without further delay?

The first necessity of a cultivator is food. In this country, as in most parts of Europe, any agricultural produce can find a market and secure a safe return in money; but in India, the cultivator has no such guarantee. He has no certain market within reach, nor has he the means of transmitting his produce, however intrinsically saleable it may be, to markets at a greater distance. Unless, therefore, his crop be of such a kind as will serve in the last resort for his own consumption, he is liable to the extremities of want. Suppose, for example, that he plants his fields with cotton, and that, by aid of a favorable season, he raises a respectable crop, he is, perhaps, hundreds of miles from the cotton markets of the coast, to which he has no means of access. In other countries, such conditions of cultivation would call into being a class of inland merchants, whose trade it would be to purchase the crops on the fields of their growth, and collect them for transmission to the exporters. In India, no such class of agents exist. The inland trader is a man without enterprise, capital or knowledge, who would simply avail himself of such circumstances as we have supposed, to lie in wait for the unfortunate cultivator, and secure his cotton at a nominal price when he was on the verge of starvation. But, by growing edible grains, the ryot escapes such straits as these. In the worst of cases he can pay his modicum of rent in kind, and reserve the remainder of his crop for his own subsistence. By such means, he makes himself independent of merchants or markets—nor can it be any matter of surprise that he adopts them. The consequence is, that in the interior of the Deccan, where the best cotton lands lie, cotton is not grown upon one field in fifty capable of producing it—and thus, no material supplies have ever found their way to England.

The remedy for this is so obvious and simple, that it scarcely needs to be indicated. What is primarily required, is a class of Indian traders, sufficiently intelligent and provided with sufficient means to take the cotton from the ryot, at a money price, which will remunerate him for his labor, and encourage him to renew the experiment. There is no want of acuteness in the native cultivators. The capabilities of various lands, and the values of various descriptions of produce, are computed and known, to a nicety, and the preference would be invariably given to the more remunerative crops, if there were accessible markets for all. At present, grain of the coarsest kind is grown, not because the land will not bear cotton, but because cotton will not yield food. Whenever such arrangements can be made, that cotton becomes readily convertible into money, it will supersede grain to any extent required. As for the land tax, it will be seen how correct were our calculations in attributing no weight at all to this alleged burden on agriculture. With rent and dues of all kinds, at eighteen pence an acre, no man can well complain of taxation.

The Manchester Chamber of Commerce has thus received a very promising, and certainly not an impracticable suggestion. The agents of English mercantile houses are stationed all over the world—in all climates, and under all governments—from Hong Kong to Vera Cruz—from Hudson's Bay to the coast of Africa. Why should not such an element of commercial success be introduced into India?—*London Times.*

COTTON — CULTURE IN BRITISH POSSESSIONS.—The following article appeared as editorial in Wilmer and Smith's European Times:

"The law of supply and demand is the leverage which moves the commercial world. When an indispensable article of consumption becomes scarce, the value, as a natural consequence, rises in the market, just as it falls in value when there is a superabundance. Applying this uncontrovertible fact to cotton, you would imagine, to hear certain sapient persons talk, that they desired a bill of indictment against the whole of the southern planters, because they cannot control the seasons, and furnish abundance of the raw material for all the spindles in the world. These grumblers forget that the grower can no more regulate the price of cotton, than he can mete out the sunshine which feeds, or the frost which kills the plant. The southerners engaged in the cultivation of the staple, might justly retort upon the lords of cottonopolis, in the language of the ancient Briton: 'If Cæsar can hide the sun with a blanket, and put the moon in his pocket, we'll pay tribute to him for light.'

"At the same time, when the equilibrium of prices has been destroyed by an unlooked-for casualty—when exclusive dependence upon a particular country, for an essential article of commerce, is found to interfere with the legitimate course of capital and labor—it becomes not only necessary, but imperative, to look elsewhere for a supply, fully equal to the requirements of the times, so as to be provided for every contingency; and in this spirit we can discern nothing to censure, but, on the contrary, much to commend, in the pains which are now taken to procure a supply of cotton from other parts of the world, to compensate for the unquestionable deficiency of the American crop.

"Much has been said and written about the capabilities of India, to send us as much cotton as we require, and, to a certain degree of faith in the capacity of that country, may be traced the anxiety with which the public has watched the formation of Indian railways, and the eagerness with which the progress and completion have been regarded. The East India Company has partaken largely of this feeling, and has extended a helping hand to two companies which have taken the field, and for which acts of Parliament were passed in the last season. One of these companies will cut a line from Calcutta to Delhi; the other a line from Bombay to Kalliar, in the direction of the great cotton field of Ghauts. These undertakings may be regarded as in practical operation, for the East India Company has guaranteed a dividend on the outlay, which makes their completion a matter of certainty. A third line from Madras to Arcot is also projected; but whether it will struggle into existence is, at present, somewhat questionable. Nevertheless, grave doubts exist whether the best internal communication in the world would enable India to grow cotton in quantities sufficient to affect the price in the home market. At present India grows little more than is required for its own consumption and the export trade to China; and as to quality, it is impossible, under any circumstances, that the cotton of India can ever compete with the long staple of America.

"Port Natal is also mentioned, with encouragement, as a cotton growing district; but the smallness of the population, and the fact that no vessel has ever yet sailed from D'Urban, the only port in the colony, direct to England, shows that a long period must elapse ere its development can produce tangible results.

"The most feasible scheme of the many which has been broached, is one put forward by the owners of property in British Guiana. The West India Association, in their petitions to parliament, as well as in their memorial to the colonial secretary, make out a strong case on behalf of the West Indies generally, and of Demarara more especially. The labor question is at the bottom of all our West India difficulties. Every plan adopted since the emancipation of the black population, to secure a sufficiency of labor, has failed, and the association ask, through Mr. F. Sand, their chairman, permission to engage blacks on the coast of Africa, on the plan which the British factories on the river Bonny adopt with the natives of the Kroo coast—namely, to hire them, say for five years, at the expiration of which they can return, if they desire it, to their native country. In the estimation of many persons, this would be equivalent to a renewal of the slave trade; but if similar arrangements were permitted in the case of the Coolies, and in the one referred to

—that of the Kroo blacks—we can see no sufficient reason why precautions might not be taken on the African coast as well as at Demarara, to protect the blacks who might willingly enter into these engagements, from the possibility of wrong or injury. To no higher practical end could the naval force which excites Mr. Hutt's antipathy be directed, and, under judicious regulation, the moral and physical condition of the laborers, instead of being deteriorated, would, in reality, be improved and elevated, by the boon which the West India Association solicit at the hands of government and the country. If the experiment were tried in British Guiana, it might, if successful, be extended to the West India islands.

"In the mean time, the southern planters of America, stimulated by the prices which now prevail, have every inducement to extend the cultivation of cotton with, if possible, increased power and capital. Probably the next crop may, in its amplitude, compensate for the shortness of the last one, and the outcry which now exists for other fields of cultivation in various quarters of the globe, would, in the event of such a result, correspondingly abate. But at the same time they will read the signs which are every day passing around them very imperfectly, if they do not perceive a fixed determination, on the part of the merchants and the manufacturers of this country, and its government, to rely less exclusively than heretofore on the cotton of the United States."

COTTON—British Competition in Cotton.—The following view of this subject is taken by a leading London journal:

The supply of raw cotton for our manufacturers is every day becoming a subject of greater interest and anxiety in this country; and it is really extraordinary—where cotton is known to grow almost spontaneously in so many regions of the earth, where so many soils and climates are suited to its cultivation—that we should still be dependent upon a small portion of the United States for the greater part of the supply which we require. It is strange that neither Southern nor Western Africa have ever been thought of as countries where this shrub could be cultivated to almost an unlimited extent. Only a few days ago, a specimen of the wild cotton plant of Western Africa, which was plucked within fifty yards of the shore, with full bolls, was exhibited in the Exchange-room, at Liverpool. The *Liverpool Journal* says: "The quality is fine, and this specimen shows that there would be no difficulty in cultivating cotton where it was gathered." We quite believe it. We believe in the possibility of growing cotton *ad libitum* in this district of Africa; indeed, we have reason to think that both cotton and coffee are indigenous along the whole line of coast from 15 deg. N. lat. to the equator. In Prince's Island, lat. 1° 40, and in the Island of St. Thomas, which lies under the equator, coffee grows abundantly, and we think it will be found that the climate, which is suitable to the coffee plant, will also grow the cotton shrub. Indeed, the former island produces not only coffee, but sugar and rice.

The pertinacity with which the manufacturers of Lancashire continue to look to India as the only country which can relieve them from their dependence upon the United States, is, in our opinion, injurious to the object they have in view, as it withdraws their attention from other countries where they would have fewer difficulties to contend with than have hitherto met them in India. It is, however, quite time that they looked more extensively abroad, for there are many reasons why their reliance on America should begin to be on the wane. According to the Liverpool statistics of the cotton trade, which will be found in a recent number of this journal, it appears that the deficiency of cotton in that port, compared with the corresponding period of 1849, is estimated at 100,000 bales, and that an equal deficiency exists in Manchester. The *Liverpool Albion*, from the statistics it presents to its readers, comes to the conclusion that we are beginning this year with a considerable deficiency in the known stock of cotton, while at the same time there is a short crop in the United States. It is certain that, as the manufacture of cotton is annually on the increase in America, there will be a greater home demand for the raw material, less of the article disposable for exportation, and, consequently, an enhanced price put upon it in the country. We think it is evident that the present executive of the States, and the party in office there, wish to encourage their own manufactures. Something of this kind is hinted at in the annual statement of the Secretary of the Treasury, which has lately come to hand. In this document the system of *ad valorem* duties is strongly objected to as injurious to domestic industry, and it is recommended as highly necessary that the present rate of duty should be increased on a variety of articles. Whether manufactured cottons will be included in this category remains to be seen.

We would not discourage the manufacturers from looking to India as one country from which they can be supplied with cotton, but we certainly would discourage their looking to it as the only country for this purpose. The report of the Select Committee of the House of Commons, which sat in 1848, to inquire into the growth of cotton in India, leaves everything in doubt and uncertainty. It does, indeed, conclude with a paragraph expressing an opinion, "that under the continued encouragement now afforded by the government of India, and by taking full advantage of all the resources which are still within reach, there may eventually be opened to the manufacturers of this country a large and regular supply of cotton, of a quality largely consumed by the British manufacturer, which will, by giving them additional sources of supply, render them more independent of the failure of crops, and thus have the double effect of equalizing the price of the raw material, and of lessening those fluctuations in the market which have occurred for some years past, and which have acted so injuriously on the energies of our manufacturing population." There is nothing very encouraging in this, particularly when it is known, as the report says, that—" For sixty years past the Court of Directors have taken an interest in this question, and have expended considerable sums in various attempts to stimulate the growth of cotton in the countries subject to their rule." This may be very true, but, at the same time, it is very depressing. Sixty years, and considerable sums have been almost fruitlessly spent; Americans and American gins have been sent to India; experimental farms have been established there; notwithstanding which, our manufacturers are still without a supply of cotton from that country. "The Court of Directors still adhere to the opinion that the obstacles which are supposed hitherto to have retarded the extension of cotton cultivation in India, may be overcome." We are of the same opinion, but it promises to be a work of time and difficulty, unsuited to the exigencies of the trade, and the anxiety of those engaged in it.

We have said that there are many other countries where cotton may be grown; why, then, wait for the eventuality which is promised by the report of the committee? We should like to see the energies of the manufacturers directed to a country where they would meet with no difficulties, and but little delay; that country is our Australian colonies. In these colonies they have sphere for action which no other country offers, nor even India, to the same extent, and it is a country to which American cultivators of cotton could be easily induced to betake themselves. We believe that the government of India will give every possible encouragement and stimulus to the growth of cotton in that country, but the natives are a people with whom agricultural improvements are of slow growth; nor, in our opinion, are they at all likely to be stimulated by any exertions which our manufacturers can make. In Australia they will have to deal with our own countrymen and our own territory, and we think the rest may be safely left to British energy, aided by British capital: all that is required is to set the machine in motion, when it will be found to work well.

COTTON—GROWING FACILITIES IN CEYLON.—A communication from Badula, in Ceylon, dated 8th July, 1850, gives the following sketch of the cotton growing facilities there:

"I have delayed acknowledging the receipt of your kind letter of 18th March, hoping to have sent you samples of the various qualities of cotton grown in the island, but at this season these are rather difficult to be got, and I must defer sending them till next or following mail. So little is known of the productions of this island at home, that, I dare say, I may as well begin by telling you that the natives have cultivated cotton from time immemorial, but the production has been barely sufficient to supply the native manufacturer. It is grown over the greater part of the island—principally the northern and eastern portions of it. As to cultivation, it gets none, being sown by the natives along with their grain crops, and receives no care or attention; they simply content themselves with plucking the crops as they come to maturity. Samples of a superior quality from Bourbon seed have been raised at Jaffna and Batticalou, but the cultivation was abandoned, and it was found to interfere with that of the cocoa-nut tree. A parcel raised at Jaffna, sent some years ago, sold for, I believe, 6d. per lb.; and a sample I grew at Batticalou was valued in Liverpool at the same price. Mr. Fennie, one of the American cotton planters, who is in the service of the East India Company, with a view to the improvement of the production in Hindostan, and who some time ago visited this island, says, that in every essential—in soil, temperature, and climate—this island is calculated to produce cotton equal in quality and cheaper in price than that of the United States. His words are—'I am of opinion, from what I saw of this climate and soil, that Ceylon will produce the article of cotton equally well, and, when the comparatively small amount of capital required is considered, I doubt not it may even produce the article cheaper than we can in America, where a large sum must be laid out at once for labor, and where the expense of food and clothing is much greater than the imported labor of Ceylon costs, besides the risk of losing the laborers by death after they are purchased.' If any of your friends should think of doing anything with cotton cultivation here, I shall be happy to give them every assistance. I have lands of my own well adapted for its cultivation; and I have no doubt government would be disposed to give every facility for acquiring lands for such a purpose. I believe that more than one-half the island is, by soil and climate, adapted for it; so that there is field enough, the island containing about 24,700 square miles, with a population of only 1,500,000. One great advantage of this island for carrying on cotton cultivation with English capital would be the facilities for obtaining both land and labor cheaply and easily. The former cannot be obtained in Hindostan, where there is a population, at anything like a reasonable price, as there is no unoccupied land, and the natives devoting their fields in the first place to the cultivation of grain, will on no account allow any other cultivation to interfere with that which supplies them food; so that it is only to a comparatively small extent that they cultivate cotton, indigo, or other produce for sale, to enable them to purchase a few superfluities. Now, where plenty of land is to be got, there is no population, or the soil and climate are also unpropitious; and the inhabitants will not emigrate from the rich and over-populated grain districts, to work for a less rate of pay than they can obtain in Ceylon or Mauritius; neither will they cultivate cotton any more than sugar or indigo, unless they obtain advances before even the land is plowed; but in no tropical country can any dependence be placed by European capitalists on the indigenous population, for steady work; for, being all possessed of paddy fields and other lands, they will only work for European capitalists when their own fields do not require their labors. From what I have myself seen—and I believe it is generally admitted—both soil and climate of Ceylon are superior to that of India; whilst from the facility of its communication with China and the east coast of Africa, it possesses the advantage of obtaining cheap and abundant supplies of labor from those countries, as well as from India, from which they emigrate in great numbers, and can at all times be had to work for 15s. to 18s. per month."

COTTON—Production of in Jamaica.—I think I may announce to you now, that cotton cultivation has been commenced with an earnestness from which I augur great success. The press is almost universal in advocating the propriety of it. A company has been formed, including among its members the Chief Justice, with a capital of £2,000, in order to test the question. I have little doubt of a favorable result. A newspaper on the north side of the island,—the *Trelawny*,—whose proprietors speaks from practical experience, stoutly asserts, notwithstanding counter statements have been made, that the article can be produced ready for shipment at two pence per pound, and we have two crops a year, whilst, I believe, in the States they have but one. There is now here a gentleman from Georgia, who is said to understand well the cultivation of the cotton plant, and he has readily afforded information wherever it is sought of him. His name is Williams. The encouragement given to the undertaking by the British press is not without its beneficial effect.

COTTON AND COTTON MANUFACTURES.

"First, with nice eye emerging Naiads cull
From leathery pods the vegetable wool:
With wiry teeth revolving cards release
The tangled knots, and smooth the ravel'd fleece,
Next comes the iron hand with fingers fine,
Combs the wide card, and forms the eternal line;
Slow, with soft lips, the whirling can acquires
The tender skeins, and wraps in rising spires;
With quickened pace successive rollers move,
And these retain, and those extend the rove;
Then fly the spokes, the rapid axles glow,
While slowly circumvolves the laboring wheel below."

DARWIN.

That the ancients were well acquainted with cotton, and used it extensively, cannot be disputed. Theophrastus, the Greek philosopher of Lesbos, wrote a work on botany, entitled Περὶ φυτῶν ἱστορίας. "On the History of Plants," in which he speaks of τα δενδρα εριοφορα the wool-bearing plants, *the cotton plants*. Herodotus also speaks of ἔρια τα ἀπο ξύλου, which evidently means cotton. He is speaking of India, and the whole passage reads as follows: "The wild trees in that country bear fleeces as their fruit, surpassing those of sheep in beauty and excellence; and the Indians use cloth made from these trees. (Book 3, ch. 106.) Also in chapter 47 of the same book he says, that the thorax or cuirass sent by Amasis, King of Egypt, to Sparta, was adorned with gold, and with *fleeces from trees*." What, however, Herodotus says of India, could not be from his own personal observation, since he did not, probably, extend his travels farther eastward than Susa, on the banks of the Choaspes. It is barely possible, too, that the cotton alluded to in the last quotation from that author, was only the down of the *bombax* ceiba*, a tree allied to the cotton plant.

The testimony of Theophrastus, the pupil of Aristotle, leaves no room for doubt. The expedition of Alexander the Great into India, furnished Aristotle and the Greeks with much exact knowledge of that distant region. The entire passage in Theophrastus reads as follows: "The trees from which the Indians make cloths have a leaf like that of the black

* A genus containing many species of very large trees, whose capsules are filled with a fine cottony substance enveloping the seeds. It gives its name to the natural order, *Bombaceæ*, allied to the orders malvaceæ and sterculiaceæ, to the former of which the true *gossypium* belongs. The Bombax is associated with the celebrated Baobab, or Monkey's-bread, of Senegal, (Adansonia digitala,) some of the trunks of which are from sixty to eighty feet in circumference, and with many other of the gigantic tropical trees. The bombax trees are remarkable for forming on their sides huge buttresses, projecting so far from the parent trunk as to be capable of screening many men. The quantity of cotton yielded by these trees is enormous, and often covers the earth around the roots to the depth of several feet; it is unfortunately of too short a staple to be used for manufacturing purposes.

mulberry, but the whole plant resembles the dog-rose. They set them in the plains arranged in rows, so as to look like vines at a distance." (Theoph. Hist. Pl. ch. 4.) In another part of his work on botany, he speaks of the growth of cotton in India, Arabia, and in the Isle of Tylos, in the Persian Gulf. Speaking of this island, he says: "The wool-bearing trees, (δενδρα ἐριοφορα,) which grew abundantly in this island, had a leaf like that of the vine, but smaller. They bore no fruit; but the capsule containing the wool was, when closed, about the size of a quince; when ripe, it expanded so as to emit the wool, which was woven into cloths, either cheap, or of great value." This is evidently an attempt to describe the true cotton plant, the *Gossypium Herbaceum.* Theophrastus wrote about 350 years before Christ.

Aristobulus, one of Alexander's generals, made mention of the cotton plant, as Strabo informs us, under the name of the *wool-bearing tree;* and stated that "its capsule contained seeds, which were taken out, and that what remained was combed like wool."—(*Strabo*, lib. xv. ch. 1.)

The testimony of Nearchus, also another of Alexander's generals, who, on his return from India, sailed down the Indus, and along the coasts of Persia, to the Tigris, is preserved by Arrianus and Strabo. Arrianus quotes him as saying: "That there were in India trees bearing, as it were, flocks or bunches of wool; that the natives made linen garments of it, wearing a shirt which reached to the middle of the leg, a sheet folded about the shoulders, and a turban rolled round the head; and that the linen made by them from this substance was finer and whiter than any other." (*Arriani, Rer. Ind.*) Arrian flourished in the second century. In the above passage from Arrianus, that author uses the term for linen in a general sense, as including all fine light cloths made of vegetable substances.

Strabo speaks of the printed cotton robes used in India, commending them for the variety of their beautiful hues. He also alludes to the cultivation of the cotton plant, and the manufacture of cotton fabrics, in the Persian province of Susiana. What he says, though, regarding cotton, is on the authority of Nearchus. Strabo was contemporary with Christ.

Ctesias, who was contemporary with Herodotus, seems also to have known the fact of the use of a kind of wool, the product of trees, for spinning and weaving, among the natives of India. He lived in the time of Cyrus, and assisted at the battle of Cunaxa, B. C. 401; but it is not known precisely whether he was in the army of Cyrus, or in that of Artaxerxes. He lived many years at Susa, and wrote a history of Assyria, Persia, and India, of which fragments only remain. Servius, quoting Ctesias, says: "*Ctesias ait in India, esse arbores, quæ lanam ferant.*"

Pomponius Mela, also, in his account of India, says that the woods produced wool, used by the natives for clothing. He also distinctly mentions flax, in opposition to cotton, as being a product of India.

Pliny, who flourished about fifty years after Strabo, gives us a more detailed description of the cotton plant in Egypt than any previous writer, which renders it surprising that no trace of cotton cloth has been found on any of the mummies hitherto unrolled. Pliny's account is as follows: "In upper Egypt,* on the side of Arabia, grows a shrub which some called gossypium, others, xylon, from which clothes are made called xylina. The plant is small, and produces a fruit like a walnut, covered with a woolly substance, within which is a soft, silky wool, that is spun into thread. The cloths made of this substance are superior to all others in whiteness and softness. Of these cloths the robes most acceptable to the Egyptian priests were made."

Pliny mentions cotton in four different passages of his Natural History, as abounding in Egypt and in India. He confirms the statement above quoted from Theophrastus, regarding cotton in the isle of Tylos, in the Persian Gulf, and says that there was another island in the same gulf, about ten miles from the former, called the smaller Tylos, which was still more fertile in cotton.

The proper oriental term for cotton was *carpas*, whence the term *carbasus*, used by so many authors for cotton. Cotton was known to the Greeks and Romans much earlier than silk. We might cite a great number of authors who speak of cotton under the name of *carbasus*. Commentators think that the term λίνον or *linum*, was sometimes used to signify cotton. Such is the interpretation which they give to Quintus Curtius, when, in speaking of the Indians, he says, "*Terra lini ferax, unde plerisque sunt vestes*," In another passage, however, he speaks definitely of both cotton and linen: "Corpora usque pedes *carbaso* velant, soleis pedes, capita *linteis* vinciunt."

The earliest author using the oriental name of cotton was Stalius Cæcilius. He has the following line:

Carbasina, molochina, ampelina,

which, as the words are all Greek, are supposed to be taken from some Greek comedy. Commentators infer from this line, that the

* Superior pars Ægypti in Arabiam vergens gignit fruticem, quem aliqui gossypium vocant, plures xylon, et ideo lina inde facta xylina. Parvus est similemque barbatæ nucis defert fructum, cujus ex interiore bombyce lanugo netur. Nec ulla sunt eis candore mollitiare preferenda. Vestes inde sacerdotibus Ægypti gratissimæ.—*Plinius*, lib. xix. c. I.

Greeks made use of muslins or calicoes, or at least of cotton cloths of some kind, which were brought from India as early as 200 years B. C.

In a work entitled *Periplus Maris Erythrei*, supposed to have been written a little before the time of Pliny, by an Egyptian Greek, named *Arrian*, who went on a mercantile expedition down the Red Sea, and along the whole extent of the coast of India, he tells us that the Arabian trading vessels brought India cottons to a port in the Red Sea, called Aduli; and that the port of Barygaza, now Baroche, near the north-western coast of India, was a mart of cotton goods of many kinds, whence common cottons, calicoes and muslins, plain and flowered, of Indian manufacture, were exported to various countries. It appears, moreover, that Massalia, in India, now called Masulipatam, was then famous for its cotton fabrics. Bengal muslins were then celebrated among the Greeks, under the name of *gangitiki*, because they were made near the banks of the Ganges.

The oriental custom of using cotton cloths as a protection from the sun's rays, was adopted by the Romans, cotton being not only more common and cheaper than silk, but better adapted for this purpose from its lightness, beauty and fineness. It is supposed by some learned commentators, that the "white, green and blue hangings," mentioned in the book of Esther, chaps. 1, 6, as adorning the court of the royal palace at Susa, on the occasion of the great feast given by Ahasuerus, were of cotton. Cotton, though cheaper than silk in ancient times, must have been very costly; for Cicero, in enumerating the expensive novelties which contributed to the luxury of Verres, when prætor in Sicily, charges him with using "tents with coverings of cotton" —"*tabernacula carbaseis intenta velis*"—as something very extravagant. At a later period, according to Pliny,* Lentulus Spinther first introduced cotton awnings at Rome, in the theatre at the Apollinarian games, in the year 63 B. C. Afterwards, Julius Cæsar covered with awnings the whole Roman forum, and the Via Sacra, from his own house to the ascent of the Capitoline Hill. Marcellus, the ædile, nephew of Augustus, also covered the whole forum with awnings, to protect from the sun the lawyers and others engaged in law-suits. Lucretius alludes to the cotton awnings, thus:

Carbasus ut quondam magnis intenta theatris
Dat crepitum, malos inter jactata trabeisque.

The poets of the Augustan age, and many subsequent writers, make frequent mention of cotton. The wars against Mithridates and the Parthians, in the first century before Christ, contributed to make the Romans more familiar with cotton and its use, although their chief supply was through Egypt, more than through Persia and Babylonia.

Apuleius mentions *carbasina* in connection with *bombycina* and other kinds of cloth, meaning to designate calico and muslin.

The best account, probably, that has been given of cotton by any ancient writer, is that of Julius Pollux, who wrote about a hundred years after Pliny. He says:

"There is also Byssina, and Byssus, a kind of flax. But, among the Indians, and now also among the Egyptians, a sort of wool is obtained from a tree. The cloth made from this wool may be compared to linen, except that it is thicker. The tree produces a fruit most nearly resembling a walnut, but three-cleft. After the outer covering, which is like a walnut, has divided and become dry, the substance resembling wool is extracted, and is used in the manufacture of cloth for woof, the warp being linen."

Theophilus Presbyter, who wrote about the year 800, A. D., describes the use of cotton paper for making gold leaf. He calls it "*parcamena Græca, quæ fit ex lana ligni*" —Greek parchment made of tree-wool.

We might quote Catullus, Tibullus, and Propertius; and Virgil speaks of cotton five times incidentally in his works; and also add a host of other quotations from a great number of ancient writers, to show that cotton was well known to antiquity; but this will suffice. Those whom we have omitted only allude to cotton incidentally, and often in a manner that leaves one in doubt as to the exact use they intended to make of the terms denoting cotton.

From the travels of the two Arabians who visited China in the ninth century, we learn that, at that time, the ordinary dress of their countrymen was cotton; for they remark, that "the Chinese dress not in cotton, *as the Arabians do*, but in silk." From this, we may infer that cotton was in general use in most of the countries of Western Asia.

The question, so long agitated by the learned, whether cotton was or was not cultivated in Egypt in ancient times, seems to be put to rest by the discoveries of the microscope. Until this instrument was brought to bear upon the subject, the greatest division and uncertainty prevailed among all. The great difficulty was to determine whether the cloths in which the mummies were wrapped were of linen or cotton. All chemical tests failed.

The character of the wrappings of the mummies, that for more than two thousand years had been accumulating in the catacombs of Egypt, was never questioned until about one hundred years ago. All writers,

* Pliny, lib. xix. c. 6.

until then, believed those wrappings to be, as they certainly are, purely of linen. But, in the year 1750, M. Rouelle wrote a dissertation on mummies, which was published in the *Memoires de l'Academie Royale des Sciences*, in which he asserted that the cloth of every mummy which he had examined, even that of the embalmed birds, was *cotton*. This began the discussion, which lasted until the year 1834. Some of the most eminent and learned antiquarians adhered to the opinion of Rouelle; and, indeed, he appears to have been generally followed. Some writers advanced the opinion, that the mummy cloths were a mixture of cotton and linen. Such was that of M. Jomard, one of the authors of the great French work on Egypt, entitled, *Description de l'Egypte*. He founded this opinion partly on the touch and appearance of the cloths, and partly on the testimony of Herodotus, who says distinctly, in his description of the mode of making mummies, that the embalmed body was enveloped in cotton. (Lib. 2, ch. 86.) Herodotus calls the mummy cloth σινδὼν βύσσινος, which may may be translated muslin. It is possible that Herodotus was correct; for, although all mummy cloths now in existence are found, by microscopic observation, to be pure linen, some mummies that have not been discovered, or that have long since perished, may have been, in the time of Herodotus, wrapped in cotton. That writer certainly knew what cotton was; for in the extracts from him, which we have given, he accurately describes it.

M. Costaz, who contributed to the same work on Egypt, the Memoir on the Grotto of El Kab, asserts that mummy cloths were cotton. Dr. Granville, in the Philosophical Transactions for 1825, in describing a mummy which he opened, says: "I have satisfied myself that both cotton and linen have been employed in the preparation of our mummy, although Herodotus mentions only cotton, (byssus,) as the material used for the purpose."

The question, however, was settled by Mr. Bauer and Dr. Ure. The microscope revealed to them a very remarkable and striking difference between the structure and appearance of the ultimate fibres of our modern cotton and those of flax. They found the ultimate fibre of cotton to be a transparent tube, flattened, so that its inward surface is in contact along its axis, and also twisted spirally around it; while that of flax is a transparent tube, *jointed like a cane*, and neither flattened nor spirally twisted. Applying these microscopic results to some 400 specimens of genuine mummy cloth, they were all found to be linen. Mr. Wilkinson, in his *Manners and Customs of the Ancient Egyptians*, considers the observations of Dr. Ure and Mr. Bauer as decisive of the question. Their microscopic observations, too, have proved that the ancient Egyptians made a general application of linen to all the purposes of ordinary life, since the mummy wrappings consist partly of old linen shirts, napkins, and other articles of clothing and domestic furniture.

A vast deal of time and learning has been expended on the question regarding the character of the cloths enveloping the Egyptian mummies; but, as an ingenious writer observes, the microscope has reduced all this learned labor of so many writers "*to the character of old lumber*." There is, doubtless, a vast deal more of this "old lumber" in the world, which some future microscope is destined to sweep away.

In allusions by Greek and Roman writers to cotton fabrics, they are mentioned as expensive and curious productions, rather than as articles of common use. Cotton, among the ancients, must have been far more expensive than linen. It would appear, from all evidence which the Egyptians themselves have afforded us, that they were quite unacquainted with cotton; for it is found on none of their mummies; and, besides, there are no paintings of the cotton shrub on any of the Egyptian ruins. On the other hand, we find upon the tombs of Thebes accurate representations of flax in all its different states of growth and manufacture; also, in the grotto of El Kab. (See Description de l'Egypte, and Hamilton's Ægyptiaca.) Linen was, in fact, the staple article of clothing among all classes of the Egyptians, from the laborer to the monarch and the priest. From them, the Jews first, and afterwards the Greeks and Romans, learned its manufacture.

It is very remarkable, that the proximity of the Syrians and Egyptians to those regions where the cotton plant was indigenous, did lead them to the use of it, the product of which would have furnished them with an article of clothing so much cheaper than flax. Cotton had been manufactured into clothing, and had come into general use in India, many centuries before it began to be used in the west, by the natives about the Mediterranean; and the general use of cotton in India, and its value as an article of clothing, must have been known to the Greeks and Romans, for they were constantly visiting the East, whence they carried away precious stones, silks and spices. We can only ascribe the indifference of the Greeks and Romans to the cotton plant and its fabrics, to their well-known indifference to the arts which contribute to personal comfort. War was the great business of their lives, the all-engrossing subject, the only pursuit thought worthy of a free citizen.

In Cicero's time the mechanical arts, in the Roman empire, were exercised entirely by slaves. In several of the states of Greece the free citizens were prohibited from exercising any mechanical art, became the labor of the mechanic was considered "hurtful to the strength and agility of the human body, rendering it incapable of those habits which their military and gymnastic exercises required, and thus disqualifying it for undergoing the fatigues and encountering the dangers of war." Such occupations were therefore considered fit only for slaves.

For the same reasons, the Greeks discouraged commerce. Many of the states actually prohibited foreign trade altogether. Even in those places where foreign commerce, and the exercise of the mechanic arts were not prohibited, as at Rome and at Athens, the great mass of the people were, in effect, excluded from all the trades and occupations which are, at the present day, exercised by the lower classes. They were carried on by the slaves of the rich for the benefit of their masters, whose immense wealth, power and protection, rendered it impossible for the poor man to find a market for his work, coming, as it did, in competition with that of the slaves of the rich. This state of things also accounts for the utter absence of all progress in inventions of a labor-saving character; for the Greek or Roman slave had no inducement to exercise what inventive genius he might chance to possess. Should a slave propose an improvement, his Roman master, often more ignorant than the slave himself, looked upon it as a suggestion of laziness, and as a desire of the slave to save his own labor at the master's expense. Hence, all inventions or improvements were the work of freemen.

The finer sort of manufactures, among the Greeks and Romans, was excessively dear; nor did a reduction of price begin to take place until after the discovery of the route to India by the way of the Cape of Good Hope. Cotton, indeed, continued to be more costly than linen, until long after the discovery of America. The high price of linens and woolens, among the Greeks and Romans, accounts for the total absence among them of that great but fickle goddess of modern times—*Fashion*. They had gods and goddesses for everything else. Their dress was seldom varied, as is proved by the costumes of the antique statues. A change of costume was too expensive, and their dresses were loose and flowing, so as to last for a long time. It must be admitted, however, that in proportion to the influence which fashion exercises in any country, may its claim to civilization be vindicated, nothing being so characteristic of a rude and barbarous state of existence, as a rigid adherence to the customs of antiquity.

India produces several varieties of cotton, both of the herbaceous and of the tree kinds. Marco Polo, who wrote in the thirteenth century, says, "that cotton is produced in Guzerat in large quantities, from a tree about six yards high, which continues to bear for twenty years; but that the cotton taken from trees of that age is not adapted to spinning, but only to quilting. That taken from trees twelve years old is suitable for muslins and other manufactures of extraordinary fineness." Sir John Mandeville, who traveled in the fourteenth century, fifty years later than Polo, mentions the annual herbaceous cotton, as cultivated in India. "In many places," says he, "the seed of the cotton (cothon,) which we call tree-wood, is sown every year, and there springs up from it copses of low shrubs, on which this wool grows.

Forbes, in his Oriental Memoirs, thus describes the herbaceous cotton of Guzerat: "The cotton shrub, which grows to the height of three or four feet, and in verdure resembles the currant-bush, requires a longer time than rice to arrive at perfection. The shrubs are planted between the rows of rice. Soon after the rice is harvested, the cotton shrubs put forth a beautiful yellow flower, with a crimson eye in each petal. This is succeeded by a green pod, filled with a white, stringy pulp. The pod turns brown and hard as it ripens, and then separates into two or three divisions containing the cotton."

Malte Brun speaks of cotton in India thus: "The cotton tree grows on all the Indian mountains, but its produce is coarse in quality. The herbaceous cotton prospers chiefly in Bengal, and on the Coromandel coast, and there the best cotton goods are manufactured. The cultivation of this plant is very lucrative, an acre producing about nine quintals of cotton in the year."

When Columbus discovered America, cotton was the chief article of clothing among the Mexicans. The Abbe Clavigero says, that of "cotton, the Mexicans made large webs, and as delicate and fine as those of Holland, which were so highly esteemed in Europe. They wove their cloths of different figures and colors, representing different animals and flowers. Of feathers, interwoven with cotton, they made mantles, bed-curtains, carpets, gowns, and other things, not less soft than beautiful. With cotton, also, they interwove the finest hair of the belly of rabbits and hares, after having spun it into thread; of this, they made most beautiful cloths, and in particular, winter waistcoats for their lords." Cortes, the conqueror of Mexico, sent as presents to Charles V., says Clavigero, "cotton mantles, some white, others mixed with white and black, or red, green, yellow, and blue; waistcoats, handkerchiefs, counterpanes, tapestries, and carpets of cotton; and the colors of the cotton were extremely fine." Cochineal and indigo being native products of Mexico, they were well supplied with dyeing materials; but the fact of their having carried the arts of manufacturing and dyeing cotton to such a high stage of perfection, is proof that they must have received their knowledge from India, by way of the west.

Columbus also found the cotton plant growing wild, and in great abundance, in the West India Islands, and on the continent of South America, where the inhabitants were found dressed in cotton, and using fishing-nets of the same material. They also used it for beds. They had probably used cotton for ages.

As we find no traces in any of the Greek and Roman writers, of the culture of cotton in any of the countries bordering on the Mediterranean, until after the Mohammedans had extended their conquests westward, we may infer that Europe is indebted to them for this branch of agriculture. They seem to have carried it into Greece, Syria, Italy, Spain, Sicily, and into every country on the Mediterranean.

The explorations of modern travelers show that the cotton plant is indigenous to Africa, and that in almost every region of that portion of the globe, the inhabitants of every class use it as raiment. The Portuguese made a voyage to South Africa, in 1516, and found the Caffres then wearing cotton dresses. According to Macpherson's "Annals," cotton cloth, woven on the coast of Guinea, was imported into England, in 1590. The colors and designs observed on the cotton dresses of the Africans prove that the manufacture is of high antiquity.

It does not appear that cotton began to be cultivated in the fields in China, as an article of manufacture, until the eleventh century, though it was cultivated by the Chinese, in their gardens, for its flowers, as early as the end of the seventh century. "The whole town is full of cotton flowers," says a Chinese poet of that time, in some lines written on summer.

How so ingenious a people as the Chinese could have known so long the product of the cotton plant and its uses, without making it an article of manufacture, it is difficult to imagine. Indeed, coercion seems to have been necessary before they could be persuaded to undertake its culture. It was not until the dynasty of the Mogul Tartars, who conquered China, in 1280, and held it for eighty-eight years, that cotton began to be cultivated largely. The emperors of that dynasty compelled its extensive cultivation, by imposing an annual tribute of cotton on several of the great provinces. The Chinese objected to its cultivation, on the ground that it interfered with their corn, forest trees, and the manufacture of silk; but their prejudices were finally overcome by the liberality and care of the Tartar emperors, and all of the provinces engaged in its cultivation.

In consequence of a great dearth of provisions in China, about a hundred years ago, an imperial mandate was issued, ordering a considerable portion of the cotton lands to be used for corn; and since that time, the Chinese have imported large quantities of cotton.

We have shown, in the preceding pages, that from a very remote period, the natives of all the tropical countries of Asia, Africa, and America, were well acquainted with the cotton plant; and that in India, some parts of Africa, and in Mexico and South America, it had, at that period, become a common article of clothing. We now proceed to the second branch of our subject, in which we propose to sketch, as briefly as possible, from the earliest period to the present day, the—

History of Cotton Manufactures. — We have the authority of the Sacred Scriptures, for saying, that fig-leaves formed the first clothing used by man; that skins of beasts probably came next, and after these, probably cotton, wool, and silk, in the order in which we here give them. Whether cotton, wool, or silk, was the first natural product manufactured into clothing, is a question which has not been much discussed, and one too which it would be difficult to answer. The earliest historical records throw but little light on the subject. According to the most learned commentators, it cannot be fully determined whether silk is ever mentioned in the Old Testament. It is true, that the word *silk* is found in King James' translation, but it is quite unauthorized. The meaning of the Hebrew word, translated *silk* in the common English Bible, and τρίχαπτον in the Septuagint version, cannot be determined, for τρίχαπτον is in reality as obscure as the Hebrew word itself. Jerome could not make out its meaning, and concluded that the word was invented by the translators. It is found nowhere out of the Septuagint, except in a passage of Pherecrates, a comic poet of Athens, contemporary with Plato and Aristophanes. Braunius, in his *De vestilu Heb. Sacerdotum,* gives the whole question a full examination, and decides that there is no mention of silk in the whole of the Old Testament, and that it was unknown to the Hebrews in ancient times.

Whether cotton was used before wool, depends, we conceive, much upon the question regarding the situation of the Garden of Eden; but this question cannot be determined. If the first inhabitants of the earth dwelt in a region producing cotton as a spontaneous production, it is probable that cotton was the first article manufactured into clothing after leaves and skins; but if the locality of Eden lay in any other region, wool was probably the article used first.

So far as all existing historical records aid us in determining the question, we think that the weight of evidence is in favor of cotton as the first manufactured article of clothing. We know that cotton was an article of clothing in common use in India, in very remote ages, and that the Indians had brought its manufacture to a very high stage of perfection, at a period when neither Egypt nor any of the western nations had any knowledge of its growth or manufacture. Growing, too, as it did, spontaneously, it would naturally present itself as the easiest article for manufacture that could be found. Men would hardly go to the greater trouble of raising sheep for their wool, when the earth presented them, everywhere, with the beautiful pods of silky cotton.

Undoubtedly, the inventive faculty of man began to exhibit itself at a very early period; but the insect world taught man the art of weaving. The *spider*, says an ingenious and learned author, "may be regarded as the earliest practical *weaver* on record;" and he might have said *spinner;* while the much despised *wasp* may claim the honor of being the first *paper* manufacturer, since it produces an undoubted specimen of paper in the material of its nests, of so smooth and hard a surface, as to admit of being written upon with ease and legibility.

The antiquity of the manufacture of cotton cannot be reached by any authentic records. Neither wool, silk, nor linen, can claim a higher antiquity. One thing is pretty certain, that its first manufacture may be traced to India, whence it passed to all the rest of the world. India, indeed, has been the source of many of the arts of civilized life. It was, in all probability, the cradle of mankind, and the source of Assyrian, Egyptian and Persian civilization.

The Indians have, in all ages, maintained an unapproached and almost incredible perfection in their fabrics of cotton. Indeed, some of their muslins might be thought the work of fairies or insects, rather than of man; but these are produced in small quantities, and have seldom been exported. In the same province of India from which the ancient Greeks obtained the finest muslins then known, namely, Bengal, these astonishing fabrics are manufactured at the present day.*

We are told by two Mohammedan travelers, who went to India in the 9th century, "that in that country they make garments of such extraordinary perfection, that nowhere else are the like to be seen. They are woven to that degree of fineness, that they may be drawn through a ring of moderate size." Marco Polo, in the 13th century, mentions Coromandel, and especially Masulipatam, as producing "the finest and most beautiful cottons that are to be found in any part of the world;" and this is still the case as to the flowered and glazed cottons, called chintzes.

The Portuguese adventurers, who went to India immediately after the discovery of the route by the Cape of Good Hope, speak of "the great quantities of cotton cloths admirably painted, also some white and some striped, held in the highest estimation, which were made in Bengal." Cæsar Frederick, a Venetian merchant, who traveled in India in 1563, describes the extensive trade carried on between St. Thomé (a port 150 miles from Negapatam) and Pegu, in *bumbast* (cotton) cloth of every sort, painted, which is a rare thing, because this kind of cloths show as if they were gilded with divers colors, and the more they are washed, the livelier the colors will become; and there is made such account of this kind of cloth, that a small bale of it will cost 1,000 or 2,000 ducats."*

Tavernier, who traveled in India about 200 years ago, speaks of the white calicoes (so called from the city of *Calicut* in India, where they were first seen by Europeans) or muslins woven in Bengal, and rendered so remarkably white by being dipped in lemon juice. He says, "Some calicuts are so fine, that you can hardly feel them in your hand, and the thread when spun is scarcely discernible." The same writer says, that "there is made at Seconge, in the province of Malwa, a sort of calicut so fine, that when a man puts it on, his skin shall appear as plainly through it as if he was quite naked; but the merchants are not permitted to transport it, for the Governor is obliged to send it all to the Great Mogul's seraglio and the principal lords of the court, to make the sultanesses and noblemen's wives shifts and garments for the hot weather; and the king and the lords take great pleasure to behold them in these, and see them dance with nothing else upon them." Speaking of the turbans of the Mohammedan Indians, Tavernier says, "The rich have them of so fine a cloth, that twenty-five or thirty ells of it, put into a turban, will not weigh four ounces."

Eighteen hundred years ago, according to Arrian, author of the Periplus, there were thousands of men, women and children employed at Baroche, in Guzerat, and the adjacent villages, in the manufacture of cotton, from the coarsest sail-cloth to the finest muslins. So that it is a great mistake to suppose that cotton manufactories are of a modern origin. They existed in India, centuries before the Christian era.

The ingenuity of the Hindoo cotton manufacturers, is truly wonderful. The late Rev. William Ward, a missionary at Serampore, says, that "At two places in Bengal, muslins are made so exceedingly fine, that four months are required to weave one piece, which sells at five hundred rupees. When this muslin is laid on the grass, and the dew has fallen upon it, it is no longer discernible." We might cite a great number of creditable authorities, in proof of the fineness of India cotton manufactures, and the ingenuity of the Hindoos, but these will suffice. The oriental hyperbole which describes the muslins of Decca as "*webs of*

* Baine's Hist. of the Cotton Manufacture, p. 55.

* Hakluyt's Voyages, vol. ii, p. 366.

woven wind," is less poetical than is generally supposed. No modern European manufacturer of cotton at all approaches the Hindoos, in respect to the fineness of his fabrics. The extreme of fineness to which yarns for muslins are now spun in Great Britain, is 250 hanks to the pound, though cotton yarn has been spun in England, making 350 hanks to the pound. This was, however, only an experiment, to ascertain how fine cotton could be spun. No such yarn is or could be used in making muslins or for any other purpose. The Hindoos are the only ones who have ever woven such yarn into fabrics.

The cotton manufacture, in India, is not carried on in a few large towns only, or in only one or two districts; it is universal, Almost every village has its weavers. Orme, in his Historical Fragments of the Mogul Empire, says: "At present much the greatest part of the whole provinces are employed in this single manufacture of cotton. The progress of the cotton manufacture in India includes no less than a description of the lives of half the inhabitants of Hindostan."

Dr. Hamilton, in his account of Patna. mentions it as a fact, strikingly illustrating the national character of the Hindoos, that "All Indian weavers, who work for the common market, make the woof of one end of the cloth coarser than that of the other, and attempt to sell to the unwary by the fine end, although every one almost, who deals with them, is perfectly aware of the circumstance; and, although in the course of his life, any weaver may not ever have an opportunity of gaining by this means, yet he continues the practice, with the hope of being able, at some time or other, to take advantage of the purchaser of his goods."

It is a matter of great surprise, that the Hindoos, with such rude materials for manufacturing, should be able to produce fabrics of such exquisite delicacy and beauty, unrivaled by the products of any other nation, even those best skilled in the mechanic arts. This is explained by the remarkably fine sense of touch possessed by the effeminate Hindoos; by their patience and gentleness; and by the hereditary continuance of a particular species of manufacture in families through many generations. It is further observed, that every distinct kind of cloth is the product of a particular district, in which the fabric has been transmitted, perhaps for centuries, from father to son.

The commerce of the Hindoos in cotton fabrics, has been extensive, from the time of Christ to the end of the last century. For many hundreds of years, the Hindoos probably supplied Persia, Arabia, Syria, Egypt. Abyssinia, and all the eastern parts of Africa, together with Europe, with all their cottons and muslins. The great marts of this commerce were at Surat and Calicut, on the west coast of India, and at Masulipatam, Madras, and St. Thomé, on the east coast.

At one time the manufacturers of all Europe, owing to the beauty and cheapness of India muslins, chintzes, and calicoes, apprehended ruin by their competition. In the seventeenth century, the Dutch and English East India Companies imported these goods in large quantities, which importation, in 1678, produced, in England, a loud outcry against the admission of India goods, which, it was maintained, were ruining the woolen manufacture. The interference of cotton with woolen fabrics was greatly dreaded in England. The English regarded the woolen manufacture, for many centuries, with almost superstitious veneration. It was, in fact, the most extensive branch of manufactures in the world, save that of cotton in India, until the commencement of the present century, and the English looked upon it as the palladium of their national prosperity.

The cotton fabrics of India became common in England at the commencement of the eighteenth century, and were complained of as a great evil by a host of pamphleteers. In the year 1700. an act of the British Parliament forbade the importation of India silks and printed calicoes for domestic use, either for apparel or furniture, under a penalty of £200 on the wearer or seller. This was done to "avert the ruin of English manufactures, and revive their prosperity."

The manufacture of cotton, as we have seen, was general in India, and had attained high excellence in the age of the first Greek historian, that is, in the fifth century before Christ, at which time it had already existed for an unknown period; yet eighteen centuries more elapsed before it was introduced into Italy or Constantinople, or even into the neighboring empire of China. Though so well suited to hot climates, we have seen that cottons were known rather as a curiosity than as a common article of dress in Egypt and Persia, five centuries after the Greeks had heard of the δενδρα εριοφορα, the wool-bearing trees of India. In Egypt, the manufacture never reached any considerable degree of excellence, and the muslins worn by the higher classes, have always been imported from India. In Spain, the manufacture, carried thither by the Arabs, flourished for a time, and then became nearly extinct. In Italy, Germany, and Flanders, it maintained only a sickly and ignoble existence.

In the downfall of the Roman Empire, the arts and commerce perished. We have at this period only a few incidental notices of the cotton manufacture in the East. Omar, the successor of Mohammed, is described as "preaching in a tattered cotton gown, torn in twelve places;" and Ali, his fellow fanatic, wore at his inauguration as Caliph, "a thin cotton gown, tied around him with a girdle." Whence, it is inferred that cotton was a common article of dress in Arabia at the time of the Hegira, (A. D. 622,) and had probably been so for many generations.

There is little doubt that the Mohammedans carried along with their conquest into the western world, the art of growing and manufacturing cotton, and that they also introduced into India many improvements in the oriental manufacture of cotton, suggested by their superior intelligence and inventive genius.

In Spain, the cotton manufacture flourished during the thirteenth, fourteenth and fifteenth centuries, and then declined. The cotton plant still grows wild in many parts of Spain. Barcelona was famous for its cotton sail cloth, large quantities of which it furnished to other nations. The Spanish term *fustancroo*, from which comes our word *fustian* denotes manufactures of a stout, substantial kind of cotton goods first manufactured in Spain. Cotton *paper* was also probably first made in Europe by the Spanish Arabs, who brought the art from the East, some say Egypt, others Bucharia. The Arabs also manufactured linen paper at Valencia. The religious antipathy, however, which existed between the Moors of Spain and the Christians, prevented the propagation of the oriental arts in the West; and when the Saracens were driven from Spain, the arts which they had brought to that country perished.

The Portuguese were the first to import into Europe the stuffs and muslins of India, but they did not attempt the manufacture of cotton in Portugal. The Dutch, however, not only imported cotton fabrics largely from India, but also, towards the latter end of the sixteenth century, began to manufacture them at home. Long prior to this period, a manufacture of indigenous cotton had existed in the southern parts of Italy, where, particularly along the gulf of Taranto, the plant had been cultivated since the eleventh century. In Calabria the plant was biennial. The soil of southern Italy is said to have been very favorable to the culture of cotton.

The manufacture of cotton, in England, did not commence until about the beginning of the sixteenth century. They brought their raw cotton from the Levant, Lisbon, and Sicily. The first cotton manufacturers in England were Protestants from the Low Countries, whither they were driven by the religious persecutions of the court of Spain. They commenced the manufacture at Bolton and Manchester.

The cotton fabrics first manufactured in England were partly of linen, owing to the scarcity of cotton. It was not until 1773 that fabrics purely of cotton began to be made in England. These were produced by Messrs. Strull and Need, the partners of the illustrious Arkwright; but no sooner were they produced, than it was discovered that a law existed, expressly *for the encouragement of the arts*, prohibiting the sale of such fabrics. Application was immediately made to the British parliament for the repeal of so unwise a law, but it required much time and expense to convince that legislative body of the propriety of repealing so preposterous an enactment. This it finally did, on condition, however, that three pence a square yard should be paid by the manufacturers on all printed cottons or calicoes.

Men have often complained, that the world has been cursed by physic and false medical philosophy; but it may well be questioned, whether society has not suffered much more from the operations of *stupid laws;* for what step forward has civilization ever made, that has not found a stumbling-block in some stupid enactment, if not in some entire code of laws? Commerce and manufactures especially have suffered, and still continue to suffer by bad laws.

In modern times, cotton has attained to an importance among the vegetable productions of the earth, which could not have been even dreamed of a few centuries ago. The manufacture of cotton, though it now affords employment and subsistence to hundreds of thousands of persons, is almost wholly a consequence of discoveries and inventions, made in England and in this country, since the middle of the last century. Previous to that time the manufacture was confined to the narrowest limits. Owing to the difficulty of separating the wool from the seed, its price, so long as this operation had to be performed by the hand, was necessarily high; while the cost of its spinning and weaving by the wheels and looms in use previous to 1760, added so much to its price, that cotton articles were suited only to the use and demand of the higher classes of society.

It is a very remarkable fact, that no material improvements in the art of manufacturing cotton fabrics took place, during the long period from the earliest historical dates down to the middle of the last century. The Hindoo, at the present day, uses the same rude and simple implements in manufacturing his fabrics, that were used when Herodotus wrote. All the great improvements in the art of manufacturing cotton and woolen were reserved for the present age.

The first great improvement was the invention of the spinning-jenny, by Hargreaves, in 1767, by which one individual could spin 120 threads at once, or in other words, perform, in any given length of time, the work of 120 persons ! Previous to this invention, every thread used in the manufacture of cotton, wool, and flax, throughout the world, was spun singly by the fingers, of the spinner, with the aid of that rude, antique, and classical instrument, the domestic *spinning-wheel*. The jenny of Hargreaves, however, was fit to spin only the softer decriptions of yarn, or that used as *weft*, it being unable to give the thread the firmness and hardness required for *warp*. Two years afterwards, this deficiency was removed by the genius of Arkwright, who completed what Hargreaves had begun, by inventing the *spinning frame*—a wonderful piece of machinery, which spins any number of threads, of any degree of fineness and hardness, leaving to the hand of the operator merely the feeding of the machine with cotton, and joining the threads when they happen to break

Five years later, in 1774, the genius of Compton conceived the happy idea of combining in one machine the inventions of Hargreaves and Arkwright, thus erecting an instrument turning one hundred spindles at once—hundred-handed, like Briareus and his giant brothers of old.

At first this astonishing invention was turned by hand, and Kelly was the first to apply it to the waters of the Clyde. Watt next applied the more potent agency of steam, thus causing two thousand spindles to whirl at once in a single machine.

But the spinning machinery awaited another improvement. By an ingenius contrivance, Roberts succeeded in rendering the hand even of the spinner unnecessary, the machine doing the entire work unaided. Now, in our cotton factories may be seen several thousand spindles, in a single apartment, revolving with inconceivable rapidity, with no hand to urge their progress or guide their operations—drawing out, twisting, and winding up, as many thousand threads, with unfailing precision and indefatigable patience and strength—a scene as magical to the unfamiliarized eye, as the transformations of oriental tales.

Nearly at the same time that the spinning department was thus wonderfully improved, Dr. Cartwright, a clergyman of Kent, England, invented the *power-loom*. But there was still another thing necessary to complete this astonishing career of discovery. Without a vastly iucreased supply of the raw material, and at a much lower price than it had previously brought, the inventions of Hargreaves, Arkwright, Compton, Roberts. and Watt, would have been of comparatively little value. This last, and perhaps, the most important of all, was the work of an American. Mr. Eli Whitney, a native of Connecticut, by the invention of the *cotton-gin*, conferred upon the world a machine which has done more for cotton growers, manufacturers, commerce and civilization, than any other one machine that was ever invented. Without the cotton-gin, all the inventions for spinning would be comparatively useless, and even the steam-engine itself would be stripped of half its value, as a manufacturing engine. Where would now be all our immense exports of raw cotton, all the vast cotton manufacturing establishments of the world, and all the vast commerce of nations in cotton fabrics, if we had not the cotton-gin of our illustrious countryman, Eli Whitney ? We often talk of erecting monuments to perpetuate the memory of our great statesmen and our literary men ; but certainly Eli Whitney deserves a monument whose top would overlook the whole cotton region of North America ; and such a monument should be erected by the cotton planters of the southern states.

Previous to 1790, the United States exported very little of raw cotton. In 1792, we exported the trifling quantity of 138,328 lbs. Whitney's invention came into operation in 1793 ; and in 1794 we exported 1,601,760 lbs. ; and in 1795, 5,276,306 lbs. And so astonishing has been the growth of cotton since the invention of the cotton-gin, and occasioned by it, that in 1838 the United States exported 595,952,297 lbs. Our immense exports since that year need not be given.

A cotton mill is probably, all things considered, the most astonishing triumph of skill and ingenuity ; all the various operations, from the carding of the cotton to its conversion into a texture as fine almost as that of the gossamer, being performed by machinery. Each of the workmen at present employed in a cotton mill, superintends as much work as could have been executed by two or three hundred workmen sixty or seventy years ago ; and yet, instead of the number of workmen being diminished by machinery, it has been vastly increased. It would be curious to investigate how many persons in the world depend directly for subsistence on the inventions and discoveries of Hargreaves, Arkwright, Watt, Whitney, and other founders and improvers of this great manufacture. They certainly amount to several millions ; at the same time that there is hardly an individual on the face of the globe, who is not indebted to them for an increase of comfort and enjoyment. It is impossible to estimate the advantage to the great bulk of mankind arising from the wonderful cheapness of cotton goods. The humblest classes have now the means of dressing as elegantly as did the highest fifty years ago ; and the humblest peasant's cottage may now have as handsome furnituie for beds, windows, tables, &c., as the house of the rich man half a century ago.

The following table will show the early progress of the cotton manufacture in Great Britain prior to the invention of the spinning-jenny by Hargreaves:

Years	Raw Cotton Imported	Value of Goods Exported
1697	1,979,359 lbs	£5,915
1701	1,985,868	23,253
1710	715,008	5,698
1720	1,972,805	16,200
1730	1,545,472	13,524
1741	1,645,031	20,709
1751	2,976,610	45,986
1764	3,870,392	200,354

The spinning-jenny of Hargreaves went into operation in 1767; and Arkwright's improvement was patented and put in operation in 1769. The influence of these, and other inventions and improvements made afterwards, on the manufacture and trade, may be seen by inspecting the following table:

Years	Cotton Imported	Cotton Exported
1781	5,198,778 lbs	96,788 lbs.
1785	18,400,384	407,496
1790	31,447,605	844,154
1795	26,401,340	1,193,737
1800	56,010,732	4,416,610
1805	56,682,406	804,243
1810	132,488,935	8,787,109
1811	91,576,535	1,266,867
1812	63,025,936	1,440,912
1813	50,966,000	—
1814	60,060,239	6,282,437
1815	99,306,343	6,780,392

The importations of cotton into England, from all sources, since 1816, have been as follows, according to the statement of Messrs. Geo. Holt & Co., cotton brokers at Liverpool:

Year	Quantity	Year	Quantity
1816	93,000,000 lbs.	1838	501,000,000 lbs.
1820	143,000,000	1839	388,000,000
1825	222,000,000	1840	583,000,000
1830	261,000,000	1845	721,979,953
1835	361,000,000	1850–'51	800,000,000
1837	408,000,000		

The best portion of the cotton imported into England comes from the United States; the balance from Brazil, Turkey, Egypt, and the British East and West India possessions. England takes the lead of all other nations in manufactures, particularly of cotton. It is estimated that the number of persons employed in this manufacture in Great Britain is not far from 2,000,000. Estimating the state of the cotton manufacture by the number of spindles employed, it stands nearly as follows, at the present time, in the various manufacturing countries of the world:

Great Britain	17,500,000	spindles
France	4,300,000	"
United States	2,500,000	"
Germany	815,000	"
Russia	700,000	"
Switzerland	650,000	"
Belgium	420,000	"
Spain	300,000	"
Italy	300,000	"

Manchester, or rather Lancashire, is the grand seat of the English cotton manufacture; and next to it Cheshire, Nottinghamshire, the West Riding of Yorkshire, and Cumberland, are its principal seats. Glasgow and its vicinity is the seat of the manufacture in Scotland; and Belfast in Ireland, where it is said to be on the decline.

The value of the cotton manufacture of Great Britain is greater, estimating from the last table of spindles of above, than that of all the rest of the world besides. It is difficult to give an accurate estimate of the annual total value of the cotton manufacture of Great Britain. Mr. McCulloch, in his *Commercial Dictionary*, estimates it at about £34,000,000, or $164,560,000. This estimate is considered by Mr. Baines, in his elaborate work on the Cotton Manufacture, as too small.

It would be a pleasant task to trace the history of cotton manufactures in France, Germany, Holland, Russia, and other countries of Europe; but as that would extend this paper much beyond the limits we designed for it, we shall conclude with a brief history of the manufacture of cotton in the United States.

The first cotton-mill of the United States was erected in Pawtucket, Rhode Island, by the late Mr. Samuel Slater, a native of Belper, Derbyshire, England, in 1790. The machinery was that of the Arkwright patent. There is evidence that Hargreave's jennies were in use in this country previous to 1790, but by whom, and when introduced, is not known. They were worked principally by Scotch and Irish weavers, who produced mixed goods of linen and cotton. Great Britain, at that time, used every means to prevent the introduction of her spinning machinery into other countries. Her law expressly forbade its exportation; and every attempt to import the machinery into America had failed. The Hon. Tench Coxe, of Philadelphia, entered into a bond with a person, who engaged to send him, from London, complete brass models of Arkwright's patents. The machinery was completed and packed, but was detected by the examining officer, and forfeited, according to the existing laws of Great Britain. No way remained to obtain the benefit of the British inventions but to manufacture them on our own soil. For this purpose, Mr. Slater came to America. He had been a pupil of Arkwright, and was perfectly familiar with all his patents. He brought with him neither patterns nor memoranda to assist him in his work, but depended entirely on his memory, a thing that the statutes of Great Britain could not reach. The King of England had frequently made proclamations against any tradesman leaving the kingdom, and had called on his officers for their most vigilant watch against it;* but the professions of men leaving the kingdom could not be always detected.

Some of the first yarn made by Mr. Slater, in America, and some of the first cotton cloth made from it, was sent to the Secretary of the Treasury, on the 15th of October, 1791; and it is probably in existence now. It is stated† that Mr. Clay had some of the first yarn in his possession, in 1836. It was as fine as number 40.

Mr. Slater was induced to leave his employment under Arkwright, in England, to come to America, by seeing a premium offered by the Pennsylvania Society for a certain machine to spin cotton.

Mr. Slater labored under the greatest disadvantages for the want of suitable materials, and mechanics of sufficient ingenuity to assist him. The history of his first labors is deeply interesting, for the details of which we must refer the reader to his biographer. His first machine was what is called a water-frame, of only twenty-four spindles. Such was the humble origin of cotton manufacturing in America. From that first machine the advancement of the cotton manufacture has been truly astonishing. It has caused hundreds of populous villages, towns, and even cities, to spring up, as if by magic, where only a few years ago nothing was seen but a barren wilderness.‡

The rapid growth of the cotton manufacture in this country, is unparalleled in the history of industry. The second cotton-mill in America was erected in 1795, at the same place as the first. No more were built until 1803, when a third was erected in Massachusetts, followed by a fourth, in 1804. During the three following years ten more mills were erected in Rhode Island, and one in Connecticut, making in all fifteen miles, with 8,000 spindles, producing 300,000 pounds of yarn annually. By a report made to the government in 1810, it appears that eighty-seven additional mills had been erected by the end of 1809, of which sixty-two were then in operation by horse and water-power, running 31,000 spindles. The cotton manufacture continued to spread, and received a considerable impulse from the war of 1812. In that year there were in Rhode Island thirty-three cotton factories, with 30,663 spindles. In Massachusetts there were twenty mills, with 17,371 spindles.

A report made to Congress, in 1816, gives the following statement of the consumption of cotton by our mills, showing how rapidly the cotton manufacture had advanced. The consumption of cotton was, in

1800	500 bales.
1805	1,000 "
1810	10,000 "
1815	90,000 "

The following statement is also officially made in the same report, showing the state of the cotton manufacture at that time:

Capital employed in 1816	$40,000,000
Males employed over 17 years old	10,000
Women and female children	66,000
Boys under 17 years	24,000
Cotton cloth manufactured	81,000,000 yards
Cost of same	$24,000,000
Raw cotton, 90,000 bales, or	27,000,000 lbs.

The subject of protection was then extensively agitated. The importations of cotton goods, in 1815, and 1816, were immense, and created great alarm among manufacturers. The amount of importations of those two years was about $180,000,000. During the years 1817, 1818, 1819, and 1820, great distress prevailed among the manufacturers, but Congress was not disposed to grant their petitions in full.

Tariff laws were passed in 1824, 1828, and 1832, in each of which the duty upon foreign cotton goods, imported, was 25 per cent. *ad valorem.* These duties, though they did not prevent our markets from being glutted with foreign goods, caused our manufactures to gradually increase.

In 1820, the first cotton mill in Pennsylvania was erected at Manayunk, by Captain John Towers. There were then only two small cottages on the spot. It now contains 500 dwellings, 5 churches, 15 stores, and about 30 mills.

Amongst the numerous towns that have sprung into existence, owing to the influence of manufactures, may be mentioned—Waltham, Paterson, Ware, Fall River, Taunton, Pawtucket, Lawrence, Adams, Newmarket,

* Life of Samuel Slater, by G. S. White, p. 88.

† Idem, p. 89.

‡ Astonishing as has been the increase of the various manufacturing towns and villages in the United States, *Lowell*, in Massachusetts, surpasses everything of the kind that has been witnessed within the memory of man. In 1819 its site was a wilderness, whither sportsmen went to shoot game. The entire population of the territory around it did not exceed 200 souls. It was a poor, barren district, with but a few houses on the spot where the city now stands; and the inhabitants supported themselves principally by fishing in the Concord and Merrimack rivers, at the junction of which Lowell is situated. A company of wealthy men in Boston, seeing the valuable water privileges of the spot, purchased it for manufacturing purposes. The first cotton mill was erected there in 1822; and in 1830, the population of the place had increased to 6,477 persons. In 1840, the population had become 20,796; and the value of property there was $12,400,000. In 1844, the population was 25,000. It is now 35,000. Thus, what only thirty years ago was a wild pasture ground, has become a large and flourishing city; a proof of what water-power, seconded by capital and enterprise, can do for a place. Lowell is a splendid example of an American manufacturing city, and excites the attention, and, in some measure, the jealousy, says McCulloch, of Manchester and Glasgow. We need no better proof what manufactures can accomplish than the history of Lowell. The Lowell cotton-mills, owned by twelve manufacturing companies, extend in a continuous line of about a mile, from the Merrimack to the Pawtucket Falls.

14

Matteawan, Norristown, Pa., and Gloucester, N. J.

In 1840, there were in the United States about 1025 cotton mills, with about 2,112,000 spindles. These mills were distributed as follows:

In Massachusetts	310
New-Hampshire	70
Vermont	30
Rhode Island	130
Connecticut	120
New-York	120
Pennsylvania	80
New-Jersey	55
Delaware	17
Maryland	30
Ohio	10
Virginia	10
Kentucky	10

Many of these were small establishments, with not more than 1000 spindles; there were, also, at that time, numerous small factories in the Western and Southern States, not included in the above statement. In 1840, the

Cotton used annually in our mills was	106,000,000 lbs
Capital invested, was	$80,000,000
Annual value of cotton manufacture	60,000,000

In the same year there were in operation, in the New-England states, 1,590,140, cotton spindles. The whole number of spindles in the United States, in 1850, was 2,500,000, showing an increase of 20 per cent. in the last ten years.

Of the present actual condition of the cotton manufacture in this country, we cannot speak with entire certainty, until the returns of the census for 1850 are published. We are deficient in details, but for the figures given above, derived chiefly from a work on American cotton manufactures, by Robt. H. Baird, 1851, we can speak with confidence.

Of the 2,500,000 cotton spindles now in the United States, 150,000 are in the Southern states, and 100,000 in the Western. A committee of the Manufacturers' Convention, held last year at Richmond, Va., stated, in their report, that there were 20 companies engaged in the manufacture of cotton in that state, with an aggregate capital of $1,800,000. These companies run, when in full operation, 54,000 spindles, producing no yarn, however, finer than No. 20. For some time past, these Virginia mills have had in full operation 22,000 spindles, at a reduction of 25 per cent. on the wages; 7,000 spindles three-fourths of the time, and 8,000 one-third of the time. The remainder of the factories are entirely, or partially, stopped.* In Maryland, affairs are not much better than in Virginia. "Out of 28 mills in that state," says Mr. Baird, "only two are constantly employed; 18 work a part of the time, and eight are entirely idle. The total average product is less than half the capacity of the mills. In Rhode Island, too, we learn from a writer in the Scientific American, for Dec. 7, 1850, some 70, out of the 130 cotton mills in that state, have stopped.

These suspensions and depressions of our cotton manufacturing operations are undoubtedly attributable to the following causes combined:

1. Our present low tariff.
2. The high price of cotton; and
3. Our manufacturing too many coarse goods. Which of these causes is the most potent we leave our readers to decide. The first we cannot discuss without being drawn into the field of politics. The second affects manufacturers by turning capital into other channels; and the third by overstocking the markets with coarse goods, and leaving our citizens dependent on other countries for fine ones. If we could keep the fine goods of other countries out of our markets, we must manufacture that description of goods at home. Nothing but an absolute prohibition of the fine cotton fabrics of other countries would keep them out of our markets, if we did not manufacture them ourselves. If our manufacturers do not supply the demand for fine fabrics, they must and will come from abroad. The real truth of the matter is: England manufactures large quantities of coarse cottons, and our manufacturers make scarcely anything else but coarse; and the consequence is, that the present supply of coarse fabrics is greater than the demand—the markets are glutted. Mills, then, are obliged to stop. We consider this the chief cause of the failures. The other causes mentioned have their weight.

The process of calico printing by machinery is the last invention, and the crowning one, in the manufacture of cotton. Before the introduction of calico printing, the cotton manufacture in the United States was considered to be too precarious to justify one in an attempt to manufacture the finer fabrics; but the introduction of calico printing has placed our cotton manufactures on a permanent basis. Our consumption of domestic calicoes is immense, and all our coarser cotton fabrics have the preference in the markets of South America, China, Siam, the East Indies, and elswhere. on account of their being superior in durability to those of France and England.

The comparative idleness of our cotton factories is to be deplored; but the general government cannot justly be charged with the present state of things, and it is at least questionable whether the evils complained of can be removed by legislation. To succeed, it is evident that our cotton factories must manufacture those fabrics most in demand. If, after glutting the markets with coarse fabrics, they still continue to manufacture

* Baird's Cotton Spinner, p. 25.

them, they must expect to fail, and no legislation could help them. Undoubtedly a higher tariff would help them some, but it would not obviate the necessity of manufacturers adapting their fabrics to the demand and supply of the various markets.

Our cotton manufacturers are at present much affected by the importations of foreign cottons. The value of cotton goods imported into this country, after deducting the amount re-exported, was, in

1844	$13,286,830	1848	$17,205,417
1845	13,860,729	1849	15,182,518
1846	12,857,422	1850	19,685,986

During the year 1850, the value of the cotton goods exported from this country was $4,734,424.

It is a curious fact in the history of the agricultural products of the earth, that cotton, which now yields to this country a profit of from 30 to $40,000,000 annually, was only a worthless plant only sixty-six years ago. Mr. T. Coxe, a writer in Rees' Encyclopædia, says, that in 1786 cotton was only seen growing in gardens in this country. Cotton crops and cotton planters, at that time, were quite unknown. Not a single bale of cotton was exported from this country before 1787, that is, of this country's growth. We find in Smither's History of Liverpool, pages 129, 153, an account of the first exportations of cotton from this country, as follows:

1770......3 bales from New-York.
" ......4 bags " Virginia.
" ......3 barrels from North Carolina.
1784......8 bales " "America."
1785......5 " " "
1786......6 " " "

All of this cotton was from the Spanish Main, or the West Indies. The eight bales marked "America," on arriving in England, were seized, it being presumed that so large a quantity of cotton could not come from America. It would seem that as late as 1794, Mr. Jay, when making the treaty with England at that time, was not aware that any cotton was exported from the United States.* The first export of our own cotton, according to McCulloch, was in 1790. It was in small packages, called "pockets."

The prices of cotton at first were very high. In England, in 1789, it was 22 pence per pound. In America it was as follows:

1790..14½ cents.	1796..36½ cents.	1802..19 cents
1791..26 "	1797..34 "	1803..19 "
1792..29 "	1798..39 "	1804..20 "
1793..32 "	1799..44 "	1805..23 "
1794..33 "	1800..28 "	1806..22 "
1795..36½ "	1801..44 "	1807..21½ "

From 1807 cotton declined until 1814, when it was 15 cents; 1815, 21; 1816, 29 1-2; 1817, 26 1-2, 1818, 34. It then declined to 15 cents in 1824, and in 1825 rose to 21 cents. It then declined to 9 1-2 cents in 1827, and was not over 10 1-4 until 1833, when it became 11; 1834, 13; and in 1835, 16 1-2.

The United States export more raw cotton than all the rest of the world. For the last five years our exports have been as follows:

1846	$42,787,341
1847	53,415,848
1848	61,898,294
1849	66,596,887
1850	71,984,616
1851	112,000,000

Europe paid the United States, in 1851, the enormous sum of $112,000,000, besides what she paid to other cotton-growing nations. Our home consumption is, at present, 539,000 bales; that of England, 1,472,000; that of France, 363,000. All the rest of Europe together consume about as much as France. England, therefore, uses up more than one-half of all the cotton raised on the earth; but all the people of Great Britain and her dependencies do not use as many manufactured cotton goods as the people of the United States. Our home consumption exceeds that of all Europe.

COTTON MANUFACTURES OF THE UNITED STATES.—Historical Sketch of the Rise and Progress of the Cotton Manufactories of the United States.—As early as the year 1787, a society was formed in Philadelphia, under the name of the "Pennsylvania Society for the Encouragement of Manufactures and the Useful Arts," which made some progress in the manufacturing of various kinds of goods, such as jeans, corduroys, fustians, plain and flowered cottons, flax linens, tow linens, &c. But the machinery employed in this manufacture seems to have been of the very rudest kind. A short time before the formation of this society, an attempt to spin cotton yarn by machinery had been made at Bridgewater and Beverly, in the state of Massachusetts. Two mechanics from Scotland, Alexander and Robert Barr, brothers, were employed by a Mr. Orr, of East Bridgewater, to make carding, spinning, and roving machines, which they completed; and on the 16th of November, 1786, the General Court of Massachusetts made them a grant of £200, lawful money, for their encouragement, and afterward added to the bounty, by giving them six tickets in the state land lottery, in which there were no blanks.

In March, 1787, Thomas Somers, an English midshipman, constructed a machine, or model, under the direction of Mr. Orr; and, by a resolution of the General Court, £20 were placed in the hands of the latter, to encourage him in the enterprise.

* Letter of the Secretary of the Treasury, Document No. 146, p. 33.

The above remained in the possession of Mr. Orr for the inspection of all disposed to see them, and he was requested by the General Court, to exhibit and give all information or explanation regarding them. It is believed that the above were the first machines made in the United States for the manufacture of cotton.

The Beverly Company commenced operations in 1787, and are supposed to be the first company that made any progress in the manufacture of cotton goods (that at Bridgewater had been on a very limited scale); yet the difficulties under which they labored—the extraordinary loss of materials in the instruction of their servants and workmen—the high prices of machines unknown to their mechanics, and both intricate and difficult in their construction, together with other incidents which usually attend a new business—were such that the company were put to the necessity of applying to the state legislature for assistance, to save them from being compelled to abandon the enterprise altogether.

In their petition to the Senate and House of Representatives of Massachusetts, presented June 2d, 1790, only three years after they had commenced operations, they state: "That their expenditure had already amounted to nearly £4,000, whilst the value of their remaining stock was not equal to £2,000, and a further very considerable advance was absolutely necessary to obtain that degree of perfection in the manufacture, which alone could ensure success."

Accordingly a grant of £1,000 was presented to them, to be appropriated in such a way as would effectually promote the manufacturing of cotton piece goods in the Commonwealth.

The petition above referred to, and other collateral facts, sufficiently prove than cotton spinning in this country, further that the hand card and one thread wheel, was carried through its first struggles by the Beverly Company in Massachusetts. And from this state the manufacture was carried to Rhode Island—though it must be acknowledged that both states were indebted to foreign emigrants for instruction and assistance in spinning and weaving, as well as in preparing the cotton.

Cotton spinning commenced in Rhode Island in 1788, in which year Daniel Anthony, Andrew Dexter, and Lewis Peck, all of Providence, entered into an agreement to make what was then called "Home Spun Cloth." The idea at first was to make jeans of linen warp spun by hand; but hearing that Mr. Orr, of Bridgewater, and the Beverly Company, had imported some models or draughts, of machinery from England, they sent thither and obtained drawings of them, according to which they constructed machinery of their own. The first they made was a carding machine, which was something similar to those now used for carding wool, the cotton being taken off the machine in rolls, and afterward roped by hand. The next was a spinning frame, something similar to the water frame, or rather the common jenny, but a very imperfect machine. It consisted of eight heads of four spindles each, being thirty-two spindles in all, and was wrought by means of a crank turned by the hand; this, after being tried for some time in Providence, was taken to Pawtucket and attached to a wheel propelled by water: the work of turning the machine was too laborious to be done by the hand, and the machine itself was too imperfect to be turned by water. Soon after, these machines were sold to Moses Brown, of Providence; but as all the carding and roving was done by hand, it was very imperfect, and but very little could be done in this way. Such were the rude machines used for spinning cotton previous to 1790; and the wonder is, not that the manufacturers failed in their undertakings, but rather that they were able to persevere. And we can now perceive that from these small beginnings, the present brightened prospects received their foundation.

Previous to 1790, the common jenny and stock card had been in operation in various parts of the United States; and mixed goods of linen and cotton were woven, principally by Scotch and Irish weavers. Mr. Moses Brown, of Providence, had several jennies employed in 1789, and some weavers at work on linen warps. The jennies were used for making weft, and operated by hand in the cellars of dwelling-houses. During 1790, Almy and Brown, of Providence, manufactured 326 pieces, containing 7823 yards, of various kinds of goods. There were also several other companies and individuals in different parts of the Union, who manufactured goods from linen warps and cotton weft. But, notwithstanding these most laudable and persevering efforts, every attempt failed of success, and they saw their hopes and prospects entirely prostrated. There was no deficiency of enterprise or exertion; no want of funds, or of men ready and willing to engage in the business; and no lack of patronage from the government, they having learned from the privations to which the country was subjected during the Revolutionary War, the absolute necessity of promoting and encouraging domestic manufactures. The great cause of these failures is to be found in the fact, that during all these incipient struggles to establish the cotton manufacture in America, Great Britain had in full operation a series of superior machinery, which the manufacturers in this country had in vain endeavored to obtain.

It is to be remembered that Sir Richard Arkwright took his first patent for an entirely new method of spinning cotton yarn for warps in 1769, at which period his first mill was put in operation in Nottingham, in England; and his second mill, which was much larger, was erected at Cromford, Derbyshire, in 1771. After which his mode of spinning by water-frames extended rapidly all over the kingdom; so that during the period when the most persevering exertions were being made, by various enterprising individuals, in different parts of the United States, to improve and perfect this most important manufacture, England was enjoying all the benefit of Arkwright's patents, by means of which cotton yarn was produced at much less expense, and of a superior quality to any that had ever been made by machinery before that period; and at the same, the British government were using every means in their power to prevent models or drawings of these machines from being carried out of the country. Every effort to erect or import this machinery into the United States had hitherto proved abortive. Much interest had been excited in Philadelphia, New-York, Rhode Island and Massachusetts, but they found it impossible to compete with the superior machinery of England. The difficulties under which these incipient measures, towards the establishment of the business, were pursued, can hardly be conceived at the present day, even by a practical machinest or manufacturer. Besides the difficulties experienced in consequence of imperfect machinery, the period at which the business commenced in this country was also most unfavorable, as from the peculiar state of the manufacture in England at that time, and other causes, many in that country became bankrupts, their goods were sold at auction and shipped to the United States in large quantities, where they were again sold at reduced prices. Agents were also sent from England to the various manufacturing towns with goods, which were sold at low prices and long credit given, extending in some instances to eighteen months. It is likewise said, that British manufacturers formed themselves into societies, for the purpose of sending goods to this country, to be sold on commission, when they could not be disposed of to advantage at home.

Such was the state of the cotton manufacture in the United States in 1790. Every endeavor to introduce a proper system of spinning had been fruitless; and nothing but the introduction of the water-frame spinning, which had superseded the jennies in England, could have laid a foundation for the successful prosecution of the business in America; and that was happily accomplished by one who was personally and practically acquainted with the business in all its details. The individual, here referred to, was Mr. Samuel Slater, who had justly been called the FATHER OF THE COTTON MANUFACTURE OF AMERICA.

Mr. Slater was born in the town of Belper, Derbyshire, England, on 9th June, 1768; and when about fourteen years of age, he was bound an apprentice at Milford, near Belper, to Jedediah Strutt, Esq. (the inventor of the Derby ribbed stocking frame, and for several years a partner with Sir Richard Arkwright in the cotton spinning business). At that time Mr. Strutt was erecting a large factory at Milford, where Slater continued to serve him for some time in the capacity of clerk, but during the last four or five years of his apprenticeship, his time was solely devoted to the factory, as general overseer, both as respected the making of the machinery and in the manufacturing department. After having completed the full term of his engagement, viz., six and a-half years, he continued for some time longer with Mr. Strutt, for the purpose of superintending some new works that were then erecting; his design in doing so was to perfect his knowledge of the business in every department, as previous to this time his thoughts had been directed to America, by various rumors which had reached Derbyshire, of the anxiety of the governments of the different states in that country to introduce and encourage manufactures. A newspaper account of a liberal bounty of £100 having been granted to a person who succeeded in constructing a very imperfect carding machine for making rolls for jennies, and the knowledge that a society to promote manufactures had been authorized by the same legislature, finally determined him to try his fortune in the western hemisphere.

Mr. Slater had a perfect knowledge of the Arkwright mode of spinning; and from the confidential situation he occupied under Mr. Strutt, few enjoyed the same opportunities of acquiring a complete knowledge of all the minutiæ of the business; and being a person of retentive memory, close observation, and attentive to his engagements, it can easily be supposed that he must have been eminently qualified to introduce the cotton manufacture into America upon the same improved scale in which it was then in operation in England, especially as his mind had been for some time directed to that object. For, having once determined to leave his native country, and give to the land of his adoption all the benefit of his practical knowledge and enlarged experience, there is every reason to suppose that he would embrace every opportunity of preparing himself for the great object he had in view. He knew that it was impossible to take any patterns or drawings along with him, as the government restrictions were very severe, and the custom-house officers scrupulously searched every passenger for America. It was therefore necessary that he should be fully qualified to superintend the building and arrangement of the mills, the construction of the machinery, and to direct the details of the manufacture, without the aid of a single individual; as the whole business was new to the people of this country, he could not expect any one to assist him except by his own directions. He, accordingly, stopped with Mr. Strutt until he considered himself qualified to engage in this important enterprise.

He embarked at London for New-York, on the 13th of September, 1789, and landed at the latter on the 17th November, after a passage of sixty-six days. He was immediately after his arrival introduced to the New-York Manufacturing company; but finding that the state of their works did not suit his views, he left that place in the January following for Providence, Rhode Island, and there made arrangements with Messrs. Almy & Brown, to commence preparations for spinning cotton entirely upon his own plan; on the 18th of the same month, the venerable Moses Brown took him out to Pawtucket, where he commenced making the machinery, principally with his own hands; and on the 20th December, 1790, he started three cards, drawing and roving, together with seventy-two spindles entirely upon the Arkwright principle, being the first of the kind ever operated in this country. These were worked by the water-wheel of an old fulling mill in a clothier's building, in which place they continued spinning about twenty months; at the expiration of which time, several thousand pounds of yarn were on hand, notwithstanding every exertion had been used to weave it up and sell it.

Early in 1793, Almy, Brown and Slater built a small mill in the village of Pawtucket —known to this day by the name of the Old Factory—in which they put in operation seventy-two spindles, with the necessary preparations, and to these they gradually and slowly added more and more as the prospects became more encouraging. After a short time, besides building another factory, they considerably enlarged the first.

Such then were the circumstances under which the Arkwright mode of spinning was introduced into this country, and such was the individual to whom belongs the entire merit of its introduction. Previous to 1790, the year in which Mr. Slater arrived at Providence, and which is justly denominated the era of the American cotton manufacture, there had been introduced at various places, particularly at New-York, Providence and Massachusetts, jennies, billies and cards, for spinning cotton weft, to be woven into velverets, jeans, fustians, &c., with linen warp; but the history of those times show the imperfection of the abovenamed machines to have been such, as to preclude the manufacture of cotton cloth, or cotton yarn for warps—that they were defective in their operations —deficient and expensive in their application —and that under such difficulties and perplexities, it was entirely beyond the power of American manufacturers to compete with foreign goods introduced by British agents and American merchants, even though assisted by legislative aid, as was done at Beverly.

The citizens of Massachusetts, perplexed and involved in their incipient and imperfect attempts to manufacture cotton goods, and fully aware of the importance of introducing a better system of machinery, which they knew to be in successful operation in Great Britain, exerted themselves to obtain a model of the Arkwright patent spinning frame; but finding no person able to construct that series of machinery, and unable to obtain one from England, in consequence of the severe penalties imposed by the government on the exportation of machinery, they entirely failed in their efforts. In this gloomy period of the American manufacture, Mr. Samuel Slater, as already stated, then in the employ of Strutt and Arkwright, having seen a premium offered by the Pennsylvania Society for a certain machine to spin cotton, was induced to leave the land of his fathers, where he had every prospect of succeeding in business, and embark for America. After his arrival, being informed that Moses Brown, of Providence, had made some attempts at water spinning, he repaired thither; but on seeing Brown's machinery, he pronounced it entirely worthless, and advised him to lay it aside. At this period, without the aid of a single individual skilled in making machinery, Mr. Slater constructed the whole series of spinning machines upon the Arkwright principle, and put them in operation so perfectly, as to supply all the establishments with cotton warp superior to linen; and in fourteen months, Mr. Brown informed the Secretary of the Treasury, that machinery and mills could be erected in one year, to supply the whole United States with yarn, and thus render its importation unnecessary. Such is the amount of evidence regarding the introduction of the Arkwright machinery into the United States; and if the manufacturing establishments are in reality a blessing, as has been well observed, the name of Slater must be ever held in grateful remembrance by the American people.

Mr. Slater labored under every disadvantage, in the construction of his machinery; for although he had perfect confidence in his own remembrance of every part and pattern, and in his ability to perfect the work according to his agreement, yet he found it difficult to get mechanics who could make anything like his models. But, perhaps, one of his greatest difficulties was to get card sheets made to suit his machines, as the card-makers in this country were entirely unacquainted with the operations of his machinery ; indeed, the first carding machine he put in operation, had almost turned out an entire failure, in consequence of the defective manner in which the card teeth were set. But he persevered until he overcame this, as well as all his other difficulties ; and his case furnishes one other bright example of the never-failing success which always attends patience and perseverance in the pursuit of any laudable object.

In 1798, Mr. Slater entered into partnership with Oziel Wilkinson, Timothy Green, and William Wilkinson ; the two latter, as well as himself, having married daughters of Oziel Wilkinson. He built his second mill on the east side of Pawtucket River; the firm was Samuel Slater & Co., as he owned one-half of the stock. A short time afterwards the hands in the mill revolted, or struck for higher wages ; five or six of them went to Cumberland, and erected a small mill, owned by Elisha Waters and others : from these men and their connections, several factories were commenced in various parts of the country, and, in fact, most of the establishments erected from 1790 to 1809, were built by men who had, directly or indirectly, drawn the knowledge of the business from Pawtucket, the cradle of the American Cotton Manufacture. Some of his servants stole his patterns and models, and by that means his improvements were soon extended over the country ; so that the business has, from that to the present time, been rapidly extending over the United States.

Mr. Slater's business was so prosperous, that about the year 1806, he invited his brother, Mr. John Slater, to come to this country, who, in all probability, brought with him a knowledge of all the most recent improvements made by the English spinners. The now flourishing village of Slatersville in Smithfield, was then projected, in which John Slater embarked as a partner, and in June of the same year, removed to Smithfield as superintendent of the concern. In the spring of 1807, the works were sufficiently advanced for spinning ; and up to the present time, they have been under the management of that gentleman in an uninterrupted state of improvement. This fine estate was owned in equal shares by four partners, but now wholly belongs to John Slater and the heirs of his brother.

Cotton spinning, according to the preceding statements, commenced in the then obscure village of Pawtucket, in 1790, at which time only seventy-two spindles were put in operation. Since that time, the rapid extension of the business in this country has been equaled only by that of Great Britain. According to the report of a committee, appointed by Congress in 1832, to inquire into the progress of spinning and of the manufacture of cotton goods,

The number of mills in twelve states were		795
Spindles in do		1,246,503
Looms in do		33,506
Males employed in the manufacture	18,539	
Females do	38,927	
Total employed		57,466

Previous to 1815, the whole weaving in the United States was done by hand looms, in many of which considerable improvements had been made, and great quantities of cloth were manufactured for home consumption. About 1814, a Mr. Gilmour landed in Boston from Glasgow, with patterns of the power loom and dressing machine, whom Mr. John Slater invited to Smithfield, and made known to him his wishes to construct these important machines ; but not being able to prevail on the whole of the partners to engage in the business, Mr. Gilmour remained some time in Smithfield, employed as a mechanic, where he introduced the hydrostatic press, which proved to be of great advantage in pressing cloth, &c.

Judge Lyman, of Providence, had been endeavoring to construct a power loom, but he failed in the attempt. On hearing of Mr. Gilmour, he, with some other gentlemen, entered into a contract with him, to build a power loom and dressing machine from the patterns he had brought from Great Britain, which he did to the great satisfaction of his patrons, from whom he received a compensation of $1500. These machines were soon after introduced into Pawtucket, where David Wilkinson commenced making them for sale. Gilmour was a man of great mechanical genius, but neglected to turn his talents and opportunities to the advantage of his family, and, consequently, on his death, they were left in poor circumstances.

The hand looms were soon superseded by the others, the introduction of which greatly aided in extending the business in this country, and has enabled the American manufacturers to compete with Great Britain in South America, India, and some other foreign markets.

The preceding historical sketch details the introduction of the cotton manufacture into the United States, and the names of the several gentlemen through whose enterprising exertions it was first established. But in order to know its success, or the extent to which it has arrived, it is necessary to give some account of the various manufacturing districts. As the cotton factories of America, however, are widely scattered over a great extent of country, it is impossible here to take notice of them all. Some observations on a few of the principal districts is all that will be attempted.

It has already been stated in a former part of this work, that Massachusetts is the principal manufacturing state in this country. An act was passed by the Senate and House of Representatives of that state, in 1837, for the purpose of obtaining "Statistical information in relation to certain branches of industry within the Commonwealth." The following table is copied from the report of the Secretary of the Commonwealth, which he prepared from the returns of the assessors in the various towns and cities in the state:

STATEMENT OF THE COTTON MANUFACTURES IN TWELVE OF THE STATES, IN 1831.

States	Capital	Number of spindles	Yards of cloth produced yearly	Pounds of cloth produced yearly	Pounds of cotton consumed yearly
Maine	$765,000	6,500	1,750,000	525,000	588,500
New Hampshire	5,300,000	113,776	29,060,500	7,255,060	7,845,000
Vermont	295,500	12,392	2,238,400	574,500	760,000
Massachusetts	12,891,000	339,777	79,231,000	21,301,062	24,871,981
Rhode Island	6,262,340	235,753	37,121,681	9,271,481	10,414,578
Connecticut	2,825,000	115,528	20,055,500	5,612,000	6,777,209
New-York	3,669,500	157,316	21,010,920	5,297,713	7,661,670
New-Jersey	2,027,644	62,979	5,133,776	1,877,418	5,832,204
Pennsylvania	3,758,500	120,810	21,332,467	4,207,192	7,111,174
Delaware	384,500	24,806	5,203,746	1,201,500	1,435,000
Maryland	2,144,000	47,222	7,649,000	2,224,000	3,008,000
Virginia	290,000	9,844	675,000	168,000	1,152,000
Total	40,612,984	1,246,703	230,461,990	59,514,926	77,457,316

The preceding table shows the extent of the cotton manufacture of the United states in 1831; since that time there has been a considerable increase. The amount of capital invested in manufactures in the State of Massachusetts was then 12,891,090 dollars; in 1836 it had increased to 14,369,719 dollars, being nearly twelve per cent. in the space of only five years; but, allowing the ratio of increase since 1831 to be ten per cent. all over the Union, the amount of capital now invested in the cotton manufacture cannot be less than forty-five millions of dollars, equal to £9,375,000 sterling, being about a fourth part of the capital invested in the cotton manufacture of Great Britain.*

The following table contains the number of mills, rate of weekly wages, and the number of hands employed in the factories in 1831.

States	Mills	Looms	Males employed	Average wages of males weekly	Females employed	Average wages of females weekly	Children under 12 employed	Average wages of children
Maine	8	91	84	$5 50	205	$2 33	—	—
New-Hampshire	40	3,530	875	6 25	4.090	2 60	60	$2 00
Vermont	17	352	102	5 00	363	1 84	19	1 40
Massachusetts	256	8,981	2,665	7 00	10,678	2 25	—	—
Rhode Island	116	5,773	1,731	4 25	3,297	2 20	3,472	1 50
Connecticut	94	2,609	1,399	4 50	2,477	2 20	439	1 50
New-York	112	3,653	1,374	6 00	3,652	1 90	484	1 40
New-Jersey	51	815	2,151	6 00	3,070	1 90	217	1 40
Pennsylvania	67	6,301	6,545	6 00	8,351	2 00	—	—
Delaware	10	235	697	5 00	676	2 00	—	—
Maryland	23	1,002	824	3 87	1,793	1 91	—	—
Virginia	7	91	143	2 73	275	1 58	—	..
Total	801	33,433	18,590	—	38,927	—	4,691	—

COTTON MANUFACTURE IN THE UNITED STATES—Progress of.—We copy from a late number of the "Dry Goods Reporter," the organ of the manufacturing interest, published in New-York, the following condensed and interesting account of the progress of the cotton manufacture in the United States during the last twenty-three years. The reader will perceive that the greatest amount of increase has actually occurred during the existence of the present tariff—thus refuting all the pretences that the cotton manufacturing interest is suffering for want of adequate protection in the shape of a prohibitory tariff, giving it the monopoly of the American market.

Sir—I have thought it might be interesting and important, both to your subscribers and the public generally, to bring before them, at the present time, the following statistical

* This estimate was made several years ago. We shall hereafter give the correct estimate to date.—Ed.

information, comprising the annual consumption of cotton in the United States for the past twenty-three years, and the exports of the domestic manufactured cottons for nearly the same period, which, at one view, shows the progressive increase of these exports, and the far more remarkable increase of the annual consumption of the cotton manufactured goods in the United States. And I propose to add such commentary as the examination of these statistics has brought to my mind.

I begin with the apparent annual consumption of cotton in bales for the years respectively named:

	Bales		Bales
In 1826-27	149,516	In 1838-39	276,018
1827-28	120,593	1839-40	295,193
1828-29	118,853	1840-41	297,288
1829-30	126,512	1841-42	267,850
1830-31	182,142	1842-43	325,129
1831-32	173,800	1843-44	346,744
1832-33	194,412	1844-45	388,006
1833-34	196,413	1845-46	422,397
1834-35	216,888	1846-47	427,967
1835-36	236,733	1847-48	531,772
1836-37	222,540	1848-49	518,039
1837-38	246,063		
Total of 23 years being			6,281,868

These quantities do not include the cotton consumed in the cotton-growing States themselves, which, for the year ending 1st September, 1848, was estimated at 75,000 bales, and 1st September, 1849, 110,000, thus making the real consumption of raw cotton in the United States for the years ending 1st September, 1848, 606,772 bales, 1st September, 1849, 628,039.

Before proceeding to the statistics of exports, let us look at some of the prominent facts exhibited by the foregoing table of annual consumption.

In 1826-27 the consumption stated is	149,516	bales.
1827-28 " "	120,593	"
1828-29 " "	118,853	"
Making	388,962	"
Averaging per annum	129,654	"

In 1846-47 the consumption stated is	427,967	bales.
1847-48 " "	531,772	"
1848-49 " "	488,039	"
Making	1,447,778	"
Averaging per annum	482,593	"

Being an increase of consumption, from the three years first named to the last named, of 280 per cent. in 23 years—or, say the average of 12 per cent. per annum. This, it will be understood, is exclusive of the annual consumption in the cotton-growing States, where the increase may have been even larger.

Again: the consumption of the

Four years, from 1826–27 to 1829–30, was 515,474 bales, averaging 128,869 bales.

Five years, from 1830–31 to 1834–35, was 963,655 bales, averaging 192,731 bales.

Being an annual average increase of 63,862 bales, or 49½ per cent. per annum for the preceding four years.

Five years, from 1835–36 to 1839–40, was 1,276,547 bales, averaging 255,309 bales.

Being an increase on the previous five years of 62,578 bales, or 32 per cent. per annum.

Five years, from 1840–41 to 1844–45, was 1,626,017 bales, averaging 325,203 bales.

Being an increase per annum on the previous five years of 69,894 bales, or say, 27½ per cent. per annum.

Four years, from 1845–46 to 1848–49, was 1,900,176 bales, averaging 475,044 bales.

Showing an increase per annum of 149,841 bales, or say 46 per cent. per annum.

In looking at the ratio of increase annually, by running through the whole period, we find this ratio to be 9 per cent. per annum on the consumption of the previous year, from 1828 to 1836, and 6 per cent. per annum on the consumption of the previous year from 1836 to 1849.

Now, let us look at the table of domestic manufactures of cotton exported from the United States for the years respectively named, which includes white, printed, and colored goods, at the valuations of the time:

For the year ending Sept. 30,	1828, this value was	$1,010,232
" " "	1829, "	1,259,457
" " "	1830, "	1,218,183
" " "	1831, "	1,126,313
" " "	1832, "	1,229,574
" " "	1833, "	2,532,517
" " "	1834, "	2,085,994
" " "	1835, "	2,858,681
" " "	1836, "	2,255,734
" " "	1837, "	2,831,473
" " "	1838, "	3,758,755
" " "	1839, "	2,975,033
" " "	1840, "	3,549,607
" " "	1841, "	3,122,546
Nine months to 30th June,	1842, "	2,970,690
For the year ending Sept. 30,	1843, "	3,223,550
" " "	1844, "	2,898,780
" " "	1845, "	4,327,928
" " "	1846, "	3,545,481
" " "	1847, "	4,082,523
" " "	1848, "	5,718,209

The export for the year ending 30th June, 1849, will be about five millions of dollars, requiring a consumption, therefore, of about 55,000 bales of cotton. The exports consist very much of the heavier fabrics.

If we go into the same analysis as pursued above in regard to the consumption of cotton, we shall find that the annual average increase runs about equal to that of cotton, for the years expressed.

In 1827–28, the export given is	$1,010,232
In 1828–29, "	1,259,457
In 1829–30, "	1,318,183
Making	3,587,872
Averaging per annum	1,195,957
In 1845–46, the amount given is	3,545,481
In 1846–47, "	4,082,523
In 1847–48, "	5,718,205
Making	13,346,209
Averaging per annum	4,448,735

being an increase in 21 years of 272 per cent., or nearly 13 per cent. per annum. Thus, this ratio of increase is about the same as the ratio of the increase of the consumption of raw cotton. Taking, therefore, the average consumption of cotton and the average export of domestics as a basis, we find the export requires of the product of the looms about *one-eleventh*, and the home consumption of the country has required the other *ten-elevenths;* that is, we require, at home, ten-elevenths of all the cotton goods we manufacture, provided the manufacture is just equal to the home and export demands.

It would probably be found, if we could arrive at it with entire accuracy that, taking the coarse and fine goods together, one hundred thousand spindles will work up almost twenty thousand bales of cotton per annum—thus requiring about five hundred thousand spindles to work up one hundred thousand bales of cotton.

If so, then the six hundred thousand bales actually worked up in the United States during the year ending 1st of September, 1849, required the working power of about *three millions of spindles.*

We have seen above, that the ratio of increasing consumption, is, at present, 6 per cent. per annum on the consumption of the previous year. Allowing, therefore, that the export demand and home consumption required, in 1849, the product of three millions of spindles, with their complement of looms, it will be seen, that, for 1850, the ratio of increased consumption, at 6 per cent., demands an addition to the spindles and looms equivalent thereto—say, one hundred and eighty thousand spindles, with their service of looms, and so on annually.

It becomes a very interesting and important inquiry, how these powers of production and consumption stand, at the present time, relatively to each other. To pursue this inquiry intelligibly, we must go back to a period when it was *clearly manifest*, that, for a time, a considerable length of time, consumption was ahead of the out-turn of the spindles and looms, driven to their greatest speed.

I think it will be at once admitted, that this period began to be developed at the close of the year 1843, and that in 1844 and 1845 consumption was fairly ahead of the product of the looms; and that this state of things continued to exist with an abating difference through 1845 and 1846, until, by the combined very large increase of spindles then brought into operation, and the heavy import of long cloths and other cotton fabrics under the tariff of 1846, it became evident, that production was again ahead of the consumption of the country and the demand for export.

During this exciting period, the prices of 37-inch heavy sheetings and drills ranged from 7¾ to 8¾, and even 9 cents. per yard, without any apparent check to the demand. This happening, also, during an interval of low prices of cotton, and from causes beyond control, these years yielded larger profits than any series of years expressed in the foregoing table; and, so far from these high prices being brought about by the manufacturers, the rise in prices was against their wishes, and was mainly brought about by the course pursued by purchasers themselves, who, over the heads of one another, in order to secure their required supplies, offered higher and higher prices for the products of the looms, deliverable ahead, so that, in some cases, a particular kind of goods was secured for six to twelve months before delivery.

These large profits led, of course, to an universal increase of spindles by every manufacturing company, and the creation of many new companies, the influence of which, coupled with a stringent money market and the damaging importations under the tariff of 1846, has been felt by all the manufacturing companies from 1847 to the present time.

The idea prevails, and justly, too, that there has been an immense increase in the number of spindles and looms during the past five years, and, it is supposed by many, that this increase is largely in the advance of the consumption of the country. An examination into the matter, however, does not warrant the supposition, as we shall observe by looking through the following figures:

In 1843–44, when the consumption and export of cotton goods were fairly ahead of the product of the spindles and looms, there were worked up, in this country, without taking into view the cotton consumed in the cotton-growing states, say 346,744 bales. Requiring to spin up the same effective power of 1,733,720 spindles. Now, the cotton consumed in the United States for the year ending 1st September, 1849, including 110,000 bales consumed in the cotton-growing states, we have rated at 600,000 bales, and as being the work of 3,000,000 spindles. If we deduct therefrom the spindles required for the 110,000 bales, say 550,000, we have left for spinning the cotton out of the cotton-growing states, for the year ending 1st September, 1849, 2,450,000 spindles. The spindles required as above, for the year ending 1st of September, were 1,733,720, making the increase in the five years, say, 716,280, spindles, or a little over 41 per cent. in these five years; while the ratio of increase, at 6 per cent. per annum would make it about 34 per cent. The probability is, at the same time, that this ratio of increasing consumption, under the influence of the general prosperity of the country, should be estimated at 7 per cent. per annum, instead of 6 per cent. At 6 per cent. the progressive increase stands at follows:

In 1843-44—Spindles required	1,733,720
6 per cent. increase	104,023
In 1844-45—Spindles required	1,837,743
6 per cent. increase	110,264
In 1845-46—Spindles required	1,948,007
6 per cent. increase	116,880
In 1846-47—Spindles required	2,064,387
6 per cent. increase	123,893
In 1847-48—Spindles required	2,188,682
6 per cent. increase	131,321
In 1848-49—Spindles required	2,320,003
Add to these the spindles required for the 110,000 bales of cotton used up in the cotton-growing states, say	550,000
And we have, by this ratio of increase, a *positive work* for the year ending 1st September, 1849, for	2,870,003

spindles, even if this ratio increase only 6 per cent. per annum; whilst the largest amount of spindles necessary for the consumption of the 600,000 bales of cotton worked up for the same year stands at 3,000,000.

It is pretty evident, from all this, that the consumption and export of cotton manufactures and the power of production are about an equipoise, and, but for the cholera of 1849, this would have been earlier manifested.

If it be true, that the present consumption of the country and the export are about equal to the entire product of the looms (and this is sustained by the fact, that the present stocks of manufactured cottons are very much smaller than a year since), the year 1850 opens with encouraging prospects to the manufacturers, notwithstanding, at this moment, the prices of the manufactured cottons are not equivalent to the present high prices of raw cotton. The power of the country to consume, was never so great as at this time. We have had fine harvests, and some of our staple products—cotton and tobacco for instance—are bringing unusually high prices, and the building of railroads has circulated money through a numerous laboring population, while the state of the money market carries with it a cheering influence into the future.

If there be nothing, therefore, to check the increasing consumption of the country, the years 1850 and 1851 will require an addition, to the present number, of 380,000 spindles, for which, at present, there is no adequate provision made or making, but, the contrary, since it is well known that the present value of the stock of the manufacturing companies generally stands at the average of about 20 per cent. discount, and some shares of new companies are not worth more than 60 or 70 per cent.

We should avoid being sanguine in anything, and particularly so upon so great and ramified a subject as that of comparing accurately the consumption of cotton goods with the product of the looms. Still, we know from experience, that consumptions does overtake production, and even lead it, and that the discovery of it becomes generally known *all at once*, when all the dealers rush to secure their supplies at advancing, and still advancing prices.

Upon the whole, let the manufacturers take courage—let them put their goods at remunerating prices, at the present rates of cotton, and await the result. The present prices of goods are low, and, it would not be surprising, if, in 1850, they shall see swept floors again, and contracts for delivery months ahead.

COTTON MANUFACTURES—CONSUMPTION OF COTTON.

Messrs. Du Fay & Co., of Manchester, have published the following interesting table, giving a comparative estimate of the quantities of raw cotton consumed in the principal manufacturing countries, in millions of weight, from 1836 to 1851. The figures for the United States are much too low.

	1836.	1840.	1845.	1849.	1851.
Great Britain, (millions of lbs.)	350	473	597	627	648
Russia, Germany, Holland, and Belgium	57	72	96	160	118
France, (including adjacent countries)	118	157	158	186	149
Spain	—	—	—	—	34
Mediterranean	—	—	—	—	12
Countries bordering on the Adriatic	28	28	38	47	45
United States of North America	86	111	158	205	158
Sundries	—	—	—	—	11
Total	639	841	1047	1225	1175

COTTON MILLS OF NEW-ENGLAND.—The following returns, based partly on the official census, show the number of mills and spindles in each of the New-England states using cotton wholly, leaving out all of those engaged in the manufacture of warps for satinets, merino shirts, mousselaine de laines, and shawls of mixed materials, of which it forms a component part:

MILLS, SPINDLES, AND LOOMS IN NEW-ENGLAND.

	Mills	Looms	Spindles 1850	Spindles 1840
Maine	15	3,439	113,900	29,736
New-Hampshire	40	12,462	440,401	195,173
Massachusetts	165	32,655	1,288,091	665,095
Vermont	12	345	31,736	7,254
Rhode Island	166	28,233	624,138	518,817
Connecticut	109	6,506	252,812	181,319
Total	507	82,640	2,754,078	1,597,394

This shows a very considerable increase of production, being nearly ninety per cent. in the number of spindles. So rapid a production of yarns in one section of the country could not but swell beyond the increased consumption, and in some degree produce that necessity for "holding up" which has become so obvious.

COTTON MANUFACTURE—FACTS IN.—DECLINE IN THE VALUE OF COTTON GOODS.—Mr. Woodbury, in his report, 1836, made these remarks:

"The value of manufactured cottons, when the quantity of raw cotton in them is the same, differs greatly according to different periods of time in the same country, and according to the quality of the raw material, and the machinery used, and the skill employed.

"Thus, in England, in twenty years after Arkwright's invention in spinning, manufactured cottons fell nearly eight-ninths of their former price. Every ten years since, some have computed their fall in price as equal to 50 per cent. In the American Encyclopedia, article 'cotton,' it is said that, from 1815 to 1829, the coarse cloths fell two-thirds. In 1810, yarn, on an average, was worth $1 12½ per pound. In 1814, it was estimated under $1 per pound by Cox. In 1832, it was said that the cost of making most species of yarn had been reduced, since 1812, about a half, and that of weaving by power looms, &c., still more. Some of the differences as to the whole value of manufactured goods, spring from not adverting to all the fall in prices, though the yarn and cloth have increased in quantity. In 1786 spinning cost 10s. per pound of No. 100, in 1824 only 8d., or only 16 cents instead of 240 cents.

"The best cotton goods are supposed to be made in Switzerland, where the skill and machinery are good, and the climate congenial. But the raw material being carried so far by land is expensive, and the manufacturer cannot compete with England, though 20 per cent. cheaper than in France.

"In France many fine goods are made by skill and experience; but the machinery is poorer, and costs more. Hence the prices in those two countries of the cloth made from a pound of raw cotton exceed, on an average, 50 cents, while in England they are about 50 cents, and in the United States are now somewhat less. In 1806 the cotton was made chiefly into velveteens, nankeens, crapes, muslins, &c.

"But in 1810 our cotton cloths made in houses and manufactories, on an average, were estimated at 33 cents per yard. The prices are now lower, notwithstanding the introduction so extensively of finer cloths and of printing calicoes.

"We make more coarse and substantial cloths of cotton now than England, and they can be afforded cheaper by two or three cents per yard. They are in greater demand abroad. We put more staple into them, the raw material being cheaper here. But the English laces, being made chiefly of Sea Island cotton, with a very little silk, enhance the value of each pound to over $5; and the whole manufacture of it equals nine millions of dollars per annum, and 30¾ millions of square yards.

"The coarse India cottons are made of the worst materials and less smooth, being chiefly spun by hand, and the raw material poorer. But the thread so spun is softer and the cloth more durable. But the power to spin a fine thread there has been carried almost as far as in England."

IMPROVEMENTS IN COTTON MACHINERY—THE SPINDLE.

It will be observed that this was written ten years ago, and must give an inadequate notion. We publish it intending to mark the farther improvements in a subsequent number of the Review.

"With a view to furnish a few more details, which may possess some usefulness and interest, it may be remarked on the power of the spindle, that, by improvements in machinery, it is said that one now sometimes revolves 8,000 times in a minute, instead of only fifty times, as formerly, and that one will now spin, on an average, from one-sixth to one-third more than it did twenty years ago. Indeed, in 1834, it is said that one person can spin more than double the weight of yarn in a given time than he could in 1829. The quantity of raw cotton spun by one spindle depends, of course, on the fineness of the thread and the quality of the machinery. In England, where a considerable portion of the yarn is finer, the average is about 8½ ounces weekly, or from 27 to 28 lbs. yearly; while the average in the United States is about 50 pounds yearly, of yarn number 20 and 25 in fineness, and about 26 pounds of number 35 and 40. In 1808 the average was computed at 45 pounds per spindle, of cotton yielding 38 pounds of yarn. The difference in weight between the cotton and the yarn, by loss from dirt and waste, is usually estimated from one-twelfth to one-eighth. At Lowell, 100 pounds of cotton yield 89 pounds of cloth, though the average here used to be estimated only 85 pounds, when cotton was not so well cleaned and machinery less perfect. One spindle at Lowell produces, through looms, &c., on an average, 1 one-tenth yards of cloth daily; but this result must differ greatly with the fineness of the thread, excellence of the looms, width of the cloth, &c.

"In 1830 it was computed that 37 spindles were necessary to supply one loom; though in 1827, at Lowell, the actual proportion was only 26; at Exeter, in 1831, it was 29, and now at Lowell it is 31. The number of looms in England in 1832 was only one to about 40 spindles, so much more yarn is made and not woven there, and those were mostly hand-looms. But in 1834 the number of them was about 100,000 power-looms and 250,000 hand looms, or in all, about one to 30. One loom formerly wove daily about 20 yards of cloth of the ordinary seven-eighths width, more of the 26 inches in width used for calicoes, and less of the five-quarters wide. The average now is from 30 to 40 yards of number 20. At Lowell, in 1835, it was 38 to 40 yards of number 14, and 25 to 30 yards of number 30. It requires from four to five yards of cloth of numbers 20 to 25 yarn to weigh one pound, and five to six yards of numbers 35 and 40.

"The power of the spindle, as connected with the number of persons actually employed in factories, is, that in making plain cloth of ordinary width and fineness, one person is needed to conduct all the business. from the raw cotton to the finishing of the cloth, for every 20 spindles. If the cloth be colored and printed or stamped, one person will be wanted for every seven spindles. This would be about 250 persons for all purposes in a factory of 5,000 spindles, making plain brown cloth. One person can manage from two to three power-looms.

"The proportion of spindles to a factory was formerly very small, both in England and this country. Before 1806 it was only one or two hundred sometimes, and seldom exceeded 1,000. Soon after that some mills were built containing 4,000 spindles The average in new mills is now from 5,000 to 6,000 In Lowell, 1836, in 27 mills they have 129,828 spindles, or a little under 5,000 to each, though they print, &c., in some.

"A factory with 5,000 spindles must be about 155 feet long and 45 wide, four stories in height, and contain about 140 looms, with other suitable machinery for picking, warping, sizing, &c. Such a one, with a few shops and out-houses appurtenant, and land and water privilege, would cost from $140,000 to $220,000, according to the materials for building, whether wood, brick or stone, and the distance from navigable waters, so as to affect cost of privilege, freight, &c., with other circumstances too numerous for recital. If bleaching or printing cloths be added, more expense will be necessary, and more persons than 250, the average for such an establishment including machinists.

"This would be a permanent investment of capital in buildings, water-power, machinery and all appurtenances, equal to $28 or $44 per spindle, independent of the temporary investment of capital to buy raw cotton, pay wages, &c. It would oftener reach, and even exceed the latter sum, than only the former. In 1810 it was computed that the capital actually invested in machinery and real estate averaged $60 per spindle. It is not proposed here to go into any comparisons of this expense now with former periods, or with other countries, except in regard to the spindle alone, and the machinery as a whole.

"In 1806, when machinery could not by law be exported from England, and the machinists here were unskilful and few, the spindle and its appurtenances, from the picker to the loom inclusive, it is computed, cost $30 each; or 300 to 400 per cent. higher than it cost at that time in England, and over double its present cost in the United States.

"The great fall in its cost and value since, with various improvements in machinery, has been the cause of much loss to many capitalists employed in the manufacture. By A. D. 1820 the machinery cost only about double its then value in England. In 1826 the machinery was made here on an average for about $14 per spindle; and though now lower, it still costs from forty to sixty per cent. more than in England. The whole machinery there, and the mill, cost only $4 16 per spindle. But that includes, probably, no looms, &c., and merely the building, without the water or steam power, and the mule spindle, moved by hand, and costing less than half what the throstle spindle costs, and which is chiefly in use here. In France, in 1832, the spindle alone, which is about half the expense of all the machinery, cost $8. It used to cost there $10. Now the spindle alone costs here about $4½ if of the throstle kind, and $2½ if of the mule kind In some places in the United States, five per cent. higher. The former alone cost here, late as 1826, it is said, $8 each. The spindle used in the filling frame, quite extensively at this time, costs about $6.

"These may constitute useful and sufficient data for farther computations. As a matter of some curious interest it may be added, that *one pound* of cotton usually makes eight yards of coarse muslin, and is then increased in value from the raw cotton eight-fold. But if spun into the finest yarn, it is worth five guineas, and in 1780, if woven into muslin and tamboured, was worth £15. It may now be converted into a piece of lace worth 100 guineas. In India, in 1786, they could spin cotton threads over 115 miles to the pound; in England they have since been spun 167 miles long from a single pound. One pound of cotton spun into number 100 yarn, extends about 84,000 yards in length. The yarn spun yearly in England would reach round the globe 203,775 times, or over 600 times each day.

"They use flour for sizing, &c., in cotton manufactures, 42⅓ pounds to each spindle per annum, or four pounds weekly to each loom. In this country, but one pound weekly to each loom. But at Lowell, 3,800 barrels to 4,197 looms, yearly, or near four pounds each per week. In England three times as many spindles and factories are moved by steam as by water. In the United States not one in a hundred factories is moved by steam. The power to move all the cotton mills in England equals that of 44,000 horses, of which only 11,000 is by the water-wheel. In 1824 the whole power was estimated at only 10,572 horses. Each factory of common size and employment requires from 60 to 80 horse power here, or about 11½ horse power to 1,000 spindles."

Dates of the most important Changes in the Cultivation, Manufacture, and Trade of Cotton.

1730.—First cotton yarn spun in England by machinery, by Mr. Wyatt.

1742.—First mill for spinning cotton built at Birmingham; moved by mules or horses; but not successful.

1756.—Cotton velvets and quiltings first made in England.

1761.—Arkwright obtained his first patent for the spinning frame, though he made farther improvements in 1768. Became free 1784. Baines says his first patent was in 1769. So does Wade, and that his second patent was in 1771.

1779.—Mule spinning invented by Hargrave, or rather perfected by Crompton.

1781.—First imports of raw cotton into England from Brazil; poorly prepared; and in three to nine years after, first from the United States of their own growth; and from India and Bourbon about 1785.

1782.—Watt took out his patent for the steam-engine, though some say in 1769 the first one, and got into general use to move machinery in 1890. He began his improvements in 1764, according to Wade's history of the middling classes.

1785.—Power-looms invented by Doctor Cartwright; though previous to that some similar models had existed which had not been patented or used. Steam engines used in cotton factories. Cylinder printing invented by Bell. Arkwright's patent expired, and a great impulse to manufactures of cotton.

1789.—Sea island cotton first planted in the United States; and upland cotton first cultivated for use and export about this time, or three or four years previous. Some say in 1786.

1790.—First cotton factory built in the United States, in Rhode Island. Water power first applied to the mule spinner, by Kelly.

1793.—The cotton-gin invented by E. Whitney, in the United States. This is often stated to be in A.D. 1795; but the patent is dated in 1794, March 14.

1798.—First mill and machinery erected in Switzerland for cotton.

1803.—First cotton factory built in New-Hampshire. Power-loom, as now used, perfected in England, and patented by Harrock.

1808.—Stamping the cylinders for printing cloth by means of dies, introduced at Manchester.

1810.—Digest of cotton manufactures in the United States, by Mr. Gallatin, and another by T. Cox, Esq., and public attention drawn to their growing importance.

1815.—The power-loom introduced into
1816. the United States first, at Waltham; in 1815, it is said in American Encyclopedia, article "cotton."

1822.—First cotton factory erected at Lowell.

1826.—First exports of American cotton manufactures to any considerable value.

COTTON — Relation between the Price of Cotton and Extent of Cotton Manufactures.—Among the most extraordinary indications of agricultural prosperity, are the returns of produce at New-Orleans for the year ending August 31, 1851, which has been a year of low prices for farm produce generally. In the year 1846 the value of produce arrived at New-Orleans, via. the river, reached 77,193,464, which was the highest figure it had then ever reached. Since then the progress has been, distinguishing the leading heads of articles, as follows:

RECEIPTS OF PRODUCE AT NEW-ORLEANS.

	1846.	1849.	1850.	1851.
Bagging	$917,710	$1,167,056	$816,498	$903,800
Bale rope	255,051	1,119,864	688,832	804,108
Cotton	33,716,256	30,844,314	41,668,250	48,756,764
Molasses	1,710,000	2,288,000	2,400,000	2,625,000
Sugar	10,265,750	8,800,000	12,396,150	12,678,180
Tobacco	4,146,562	3,938,290	6,206,820	7,860,050
All others	26,174,135	33,832,168	32,503,403	33,296,109
Total	77,193,464	81,989,692	96,897,873	106,824,083

Observe the continually increased value in the aggregate, notwithstanding that prices, under the large supply, in some cases have declined. Sugar and molasses are 25 per cent. more, tobacco nearly double, and cotton has increased 50 per cent. in value, affording a rich reward to planters, and laying the foundation of a sound general trade. Cotton has, indeed, borne a very good price in the last two years, and manufacturers, at home and abroad, have been compelled to pay roundly for it. If we take the quantities of cotton exported from the United States, per official reports, and reduce the pounds to bales of 400 pounds, we shall arrive at an annual average export value per bale, per custom-house reports for the whole Union. The following are the results of such a table for several years:

VALUE OF COTTON EXPORTED FROM THE UNITED STATES.

	Bales	Value	Average per bale
1843	1,978,000	$49,119,806	$25
1844	1,659,000	54,063,501	33½
1845	1,892,000	51,739,643	27¼
1846	1,368,890	42,767,341	31⅛
1847	1,318,040	52,514,848	40½
1848	2,356,860	61,998,294	26¼
1849	2,566,250	66,396,967	29
1850	1,588,454	71,984,616	45¼
1851	1,958,710	97,935,500	50

It is here remarkable that the value declined annually in 1844, 1845, and 1846. It then began to rise; and we receive this year $48,000,000, or just double, for the same number of bales as was exported in 1843. If, now, we take the nnmber of bales consumed in the United States in the same year at the same prices, we have results as follows:

COTTON CONSUMED IN THE UNITED STATES.

	Bales	Per bale	Value
1843	325,129	$25	$8,128,225
1844	346,744	33¼	12,629,238
1845	389,006	27¼	10,600,663
1846	422,897	43½	13,250,772
1847	427,967	40½	17,333,633
1848	531,772	26⅓	14,003,358
1849	518,039	29	15,023,131
1850	487,769	45¼	22,071,497
1851	404,108	50	20,205,400

It now appears that the manufacturers in 1851 paid just double what they did in 1845 for the raw material consumed, or in the fourth complete year of the operation of the tariff of 1846, they paid $7,000,000, or 50 per cent. more money for a less number of bales than they bought in 1846, the fourth year of the tariff of 1842. Such a result is very bad for manufacturers, no doubt, but very good for planters, who, the Tribune says, will be ruined by such a course. Now, it is no doubt the case that the advances in the raw material, as is always the case, checks consumption, and that result has taken place in the last year. The low prices of 1848–'49, added to the general prosperity of the country, greatly promoted consumption, and in 1848, 531,772 bales were taken by the manufacturers. As the prices advanced, they bought less freely, but still comparatively very largely in 1850. The cloth made from that high-priced cotton in 1850 has found the shelves of retailers in 1851; but it has encountered diminished demand, owing to the high price in part, and manufacturers have not got back from the cloth the advance of $7,000,000 which they paid out for raw material. The main reason for this, however, is the growth of cotton mills South and West.

It will be understood that the cotton crop is annually made up by the New-York Shipping List from southern local reports of all the cotton which arrives at the seaports, and it is usually very accurate. A few years since, all the cotton came to the seaports; consequently the returns so obtained, embraced all the crop. As, however, cotton mills multiplied in the interior, they obtained their cotton from the plantations, and there exist no means of estimating how much they so take, nor how much their productions displace the cloth of the old eastern factories. The operation of those mills would be to diminish the apparent quantity of cotton taken from the seaports, and by interior competition prevent the rise in prices of the cloth made at the North. The shipping list attempts some estimates of the quantity of cotton taken by the mills South and West, but these guesses are by no means so trustworthy as its crop figures.

The census of 1840 gave the number of cotton spindles in the southern and western states; and since then the number is known to have very much increased. The Shipping List, however, estimated the number in 1850 and 1851, and also the number of bales they consumed. The spindles are given as follows:

	Census 1840 Spindles	Ship. List 1850	Ship. List 1851
North Carolina	47,934	—	—
South Carolina	16,355	36,500	36,500
Georgia	42,589	51,159	51,400
Alabama	1,502	16,960	12,580
Tennessee	16,813	36,000	36,000
Ohio, Pittsburg, Virginia, Indiana, Kentucky, Illinois	32,121	102,000	100,000
Total spindles	157,314	242,830	236,480
Cotton consumed, bales		107,500	60,000

These estimates are apparently arbitrary. The number of spindles in Ohio, &c., is 100,000; yet the consumption of cotton is estimated at 35,000 bales in 1849, and only 12,000 in 1850; that is to say, 12,580 spindles in Alabama are estimated to consume as much cotton as 100,000 in Ohio, &c., and 4,000 bales more than 36,000 spindles in Tennessee. General James calculates that 10,000 spindles require 4,500 bales, 400 lbs. each consequently 286,000 spindles, including North Carolina, allowing that there has been no increase in spindles, will take about 130,000 bales. The reason given for the small consumption of cotton South and West this year—viz.: the high price of cotton—applies with much greater force to the northern factories, distant from market, than to those which are near the plantations. The truth is, that the consumption of cotton South and West has been very large; and the cloth so produced, costing less, has taken the market and prevented the northern articles from realizing an advance corresponding to the rise in raw material. It is the transition of the seat of manufactures from the North and East to the South and West, under which northern manufacturing capital is laboring.—*Kettell.*

COTTON—Present and Future Prospects of Great Britain relative to the Supply and Consumption of Cotton.—At a time when the condition and prospects of the working classes of this country are, fortunately alike for the credit of the age, the future safety of our institutions, and the peace and welfare of the nation, attracting so much attention, it cannot but be of the highest interest and importance, whether viewed in a social, a political, or a commercial light, that a clear, broad and enlarged inquiry should be instituted into the present position and future prospects of the supply of that raw material, upon whtch by far the greatest numbers are dependent in our great manufacturing community. The recent rapid changes in the price of cotton, seem to force this subject more strongly upon us. Lancashire contains a population now little, if anything, short of 2,000,000, who may be said to be directly or indirectly interested in and dependent upon this great article of industry. The West Riding of Yorkshire contains a population of nearly 1,400,000, of whom a large number are also interested in the same industry, either directly in itself, or as intermixed with the woolen trade. Lanarkshire contains a population of more than 500,000, whose chief dependence is the various branches of the cotton trade. In round figures, therefore, leaving out Cheshire and other isolated places, there are in those districts a population of no less than 4,000,000, the great bulk of whom are, directly or indirectly, chiefly interested in this trade. In those districts, too, the greatest demand exists for taste, talent, and ability, connected with all the arts and all the sciences. There, too, is the greatest demand for that class of literature which affords employment to the greatest number of writers. Dependent upon these districts is our chief navigation, our commerce abroad, our trade at home. They exert, according to their condition, a greater influence than any other districts upon the general revenue of the state. Emphatically, the future supply of cotton is "a condition-of-England question." Need we urge any other excuse for the length at which we now deem it our duty to examine it?

The quarters whence Great Britain draws her supply of raw cotton may be classed under five divisions: North America, Brazil, Egypt, India and miscellaneous countries, chiefly our own colonies. On the increase of production in these lands, and on the proportion of that increase which is sent to this country, depends our capability of extending our cotton manufacture, or even of maintaining it at its present level. Let us therefore consider each of these sources of supply in turn, that we may be able to form a fair estimate of our expectations from each. North America, as the most important, we will leave to the last.

Brazil is the chief source whence we draw our supply of long-stapled cottons. Brazil has sent us as follows:

	In five years	Per an.
1830–1834, inclusive	744,784	148,977
1835–1839, "	643,438	128,687
1840–1844, "	471,226	94,245
1845–1849, "	495,685	99,137

In this and the succeeding tables, the imports for 1849 have been found by adding to the *known* imports for the first ten months, the quantity we have yet reason to expect, or that which ordinarily arrives in November and December.

From Brazil, therefore, our annual supply has diminished nearly 50,000 bales; or if we compare the two extreme years of the series, 1830 and 1848, the falling off is from 192,267 bales to 100,244, or 92,000 bales.

Egypt.—Our Egyptian supply, which is long-stapled cotton, has ranged as follows:

	In five years	Per an.
1830–1834, inclusive	99,899	19,899
1835–1839, "	173,031	34,605
1840–1844, "	207,913	41,583
1845–1849, "	224,889	44,918

The supply from Egypt, however, seems to have reached its maximum in 1845, in which year we received 81,344 bales. This year it does not reach half that amount. Moreover, this country, from the peculiar circumstances of its government, is little to be relied upon—the supply having varied from 40,290 bales in 1832, to 2,569 bales in 1833; and again, from 18,245 bales in 1842, to 66,000 bales in 1844.

From other quarters, chiefly the West Indies, the supply has been:

	In five years	Per an.
1830–1834, inclusive	68,873	13,775
1835–1839, "	161,369	32,274
1840–1844, "	117,887	23,577
1845–1849, "	44,833	8,966

East Indies.—Our supply from this quarter varies enormously, from 90,000 to 270,000 bales per annum, inasmuch as we only receive that proportion of the crop which our prices may divert from China or from internal consumption. Our imports thence have been as follows:

	In five years	Per an.
1830–1834, inclusive	403,976	80,795
1835–1839, "	723,263	144,653
1840–1844, "	1,167,294	233,409
1845–1849, "	899,213	179,802

The summary of our supply from all these quarters combined, is:

	In five years	Per an.
1830–1834, inclusive	1,317,632	268,526
1835–1839, "	1,701,101	340,220
1840–1844, "	1,964,320	392,864
1845–1849, "	1,664,310	332,862

The result of this inquiry, then, is, that our average annual supply from all quarters, except the United States, was, in the five years ending 1849, less by 7,358 bales than in the five years ending 1839, and less by 60,000 bales than in the five years ending 1844. Of this diminished supply, moreover, we have been exporting an increasing quantity, viz.: 396,000 bales in the last five years, against 342,000 bales the previous five years.

United States.—We may now turn our attention to our last and main source of supply, America, which has sent us:

	In five years	Per an.
1830–1834, inclusive	3,241,958	648,391
1835–1839, "	4,308,610	861,722
1840–1844, "	5,802,829	1,160,566
1845–1849, "	6,189,144	1,237,619

The last five years, it should be observed, include the three largest crops ever known, one very deficient, and one rather so.

It is a known and admitted fact among those conversant with these matters, that a price of 4*d.* per pound laid down in Liverpool, leaves sufficient profit to the American planter to induce him to grow as much cotton as his negroes can gather; and that, therefore, as the average price has scarcely ever ranged so low as this for any great number of weeks, *possible* increase of the crop of cotton will keep pace with the *actual* increase of the negro population, and cannot do more. Now, the negroes increase at a very regular rate of three per cent. per annum. If, therefore, these premises be correct, it will follow that the cotton crop of each year will surpass that of each preceding year *of equally favorable conditions* (i. e., as to good planting and picking weather, late frosts, freedom from worms, inundations, &c.) by 3 per cent. Accordingly, we find this to have been pretty closely the case, as the following tables will show. The years 1840, 1843 and 1845, were favorable years for the growth and gathering of cotton. Let us see what crop, each of these years, calculated on the above bases, (three per cent. yearly increase,) would give for 1849, also a favorable year:

	Actual crop	No. years	Per cent.	Est. crop, 1849
1840	2,178,000	9	27	2,866,000
1843	2,379,000	6	18	2,807,220
1845	2,394,000	4	12	2,681,280
Average				2,784,833
Actual crop				2,730,000

From the following table it will be seen that, assuming the year 1838 as a starting point, the average increase of the American crop for the last twelve years has not quite reached three per cent., and in fact wherein for a short series of years this rate has been exceeded, it has been attributable simply to an unusual run of favorable seasons:

Years	What the crop would have been with no extraordinary casualties, and increasing at the rate of 3 per cent yearly	Actual crop
1837–1838		1,801,500
1838–1839	1,856,500	1,360,050
1839–1840	1,911,200	2,178,000
1840–1841	1,968,500	1,635,000
1841–1842	2,027,500	1,683,500
1842–1843	2,088,300	2,379,000
1843–1844	2,151,000	2,030,500
1844–1845	2,215,000	2,304,500
1845–1846	2,282,000	2,100,500
1846–1847	2,350,500	1,788,500
1847–1848	2,420,000	2,347,500
1848–1849	2,493,000	3,728,500
1849–1850	2,568,300	2,350,000 est.
Average	1,194,400	2,080,500

It is clear, then, that we shall be sufficiently near the mark, for any practical conclusions, if we assume the average increase of the American cotton crop at three per cent. per annum, barring any *unusual* freedom from or occurrence of disasters, such as sometimes happen. Let us now inquire what proportion of this increase will fall to our share.

The consumption of the United States itself has been steadily on the advance, and now increases at an average annual rate of about 35,000 bales. It is now about 520,000 bales yearly. That of the continent now reaches (of American cotton) about 700,000 bales. America and the continent, therefore, require about 1,200,000 bales at present, and will require more each year. Moreover, they will always take precedence of Great Britain as their margin of profit is larger, and a small increase of price is of less consequence to their manufacturers than to ours, and checks consumption less. The following table, showing the crop of American cotton for five years, together with the imports and exports of Great Britain, and the amount retained for home consumption, will throw much light on this question.

Five years	Crop of Am. cotton	Imp't of Am. cotton into G. Britain	Ex. of Am. cotton from G. Britain	Am. cotton retained for home consump.
1840–1844	9,905,638	5,802,829	295,600	5,507,229
1845–1849	11,349,921	6,188,144	596,640	5,591,504
Increase	1,444,283	385,315	301,040	84,275

From this table it appears, that while the growth of American cotton in the last five years exceeded that of the previous five by the unprecedented quantity of nearly one million and a half of bales, of this increase only 385,000 reached this country, *and of this we had to re-export more than three-fourths*, leaving an annual increase *available for home consumption* of only 17,000 bales. For any augmentation of consumption beyond this, we have been drawing on our stocks.

We will now bring into one view the *whole* supply and the *whole* consumption *of all kinds of cotton* in Great Britain during the last ten years:

Five years	Bales imp'td from all quarters	Bales exported	Retained for home consumption	Supply for home consumption annually	Actual consumption annually
1840–1844	7,767,149	637,650	7,129,499	1,425,900	1,290,480
1845–1849	7,862,454	992,850	6,859,604	1,371,920	1,477,360
Increase	85,305	355,200	—	—	186,880
Decrease	—	—	269,895	53,980	—
Actual consumption weekly, 1840–1844					24,810
" " " 1845–1849					28,410
Increase					3,600

We have taken the actual consumption of 1849 at 1,650,000 bales only, for reasons hereafter stated.

Now, bearing in mind that the figures in the above table are, with scarcely an exception, ascertained facts, and not estimates, let us sum the conclusions to which they have conducted us; conclusions sufficient, if not to alarm us, yet certainly to create much uneasiness, and to suggest great caution on the part of all concerned, directly or indirectly, in the great manufacture of England.

1. That our supply of cotton from miscellaneous quarters (*excluding* the United States) has for many years been decidedly, though irregularly *decreasing*.

2. That our supply of cotton *fro all quarters*, (including the United States,) available for home consumption, has of late years been falling off at the rate of 1,000 bales a week, while our consumption has been increasing during the same period at the rate of 3,600 bales a week.

3. That the United States is the only

country where the growth of cotton is on the increase; and that there, even, the increase does not, on an average, exceed three per cent., or 80,000 bales annually, which is barely sufficient to supply the increasing demand for its own consumption, and for the continent of Europe.

4. That no stimulus of price can materially augment this annual increase, as the planters always grow as much cotton as the negro population can pick.

5. That, consequently, if the cotton manufactory of Great Britain is to increase at all —*on its present footing*—it can only be enabled to do so by applying a great stimulus to the growth of cotton in other countries adapted for the culture.

Within the memory of many now living, a great change has taken place in the countries from which our main bulk of cotton is procured. In the infancy of the manufacture our chief supply came from the Mediterranean, especially from Smyrna and Malta. Neither of these places now sends us more than a few chance bags occasionally. In the last century the West Indies were our principal source. In the year 1786, out of 20,000,000 lbs. imported, 5,000,000 came from Smyrna and the rest from the West Indies. In 1848, the West Indies sent us only about 1,300 bales. In 1781 Brazil began to send us cotton, and the supply thence continued to increase, though irregularly, till 1830, since which time it has fallen off to one-half. About 1822, Egyptian cotton began to come in considerable quantities; its cultivation having been introduced into that country two years before. The import exceeded 80,000 bales in 1845; the average of the last three years has not been a third of that quantity. Cotton has always been grown largely in Hindoostan, but it did not send much to England till about thirty years ago. In the five years ending 1824 the yearly average import was 33,500, in 1841 it reached 274,000, and may now be roughly estimated at 200,000 bales a year.

Now, what is the reason why these countries, after having at one time produced so largely and so well, should have ceased or curtailed their growth within recent years? It is clearly a question of price. Let us consider a few of the cases:

At the close of the years

1836-1839, inclusive.—Lowest price of Pernambuco		9½
1840-1843, " " " "		7
1844-1848, " " " "		5⅞
Fall per cent	36	
1836-1839, inclusive.—Lowest price of Maranham		8¼
1840-1843, " " " "		5⅝
1844-1848, " " " "		4⅞
Fall per cent	42	
1836-1839, inclusive.—Lowest price of Egyptian		10¼
1840-1843, " " " "		7
1844-1848, " " " "		5⅞
Fall per cent	43	
1836-1839, inclusive.—Lowest price of Surat		4⅝
1840-1843, " " " "		3½
1844-1848, " " " "		2¾
Fall per cent	40	

Here, surely, may be read the explanation of the deplorable falling off in our miscellaneous supply. From the four years ending 1839—when the great stimulus was given which procured us so ample a supply during the succeeding period—to the quinquennial period ending 1848, there has been a fall in price, on an average, of 40 per cent. Unless, therefore, we assume either an enormous margin of profit in the earlier period, or an extreme diminution in the cost of producing the article in late years, such a fall in price would be quite sufficient to direct capital and industry into other channels, and to prevent so bulky an article as cotton from being grown or forwarded.

In both Brazil and India, freight and carriage form an inordinate proportion of the price of cotton. In both countries the bales are carried great distances on the backs of mules or other beasts of burden. The deficiency of good roads, convenient vehicles, and safely navigable rivers, in the cotton districts of both countries, swells the expense of bringing the bales to the shipping ports to such an extent, that when prices are low in England, the ultimate net remittance to the planter is quite insufficient to repay the cost of growing, picking and packing. In some years the price of much of the Surat cotton sent to this country was so low as only to remit *one penny* a pound to the shippers at Bombay; and by the time this reached the actual grower, it had probably dwindled away, through the expenses of carriage, to a sum inadequate even to pay the government rent. Our supply from both these countries will depend entirely upon price. In Brazil, where we believe the sugar cultivation is less profitable than formerly, a range of prices of 50 per cent. higher than those of the last few years would probably induce the planters to increase their cotton grounds, and would repay them for so doing. In regard to the East Indies, where large quantities are always grown, our supply thence depends upon two things, first, the demand of China, which is usually supplied before Great Britain ; and secondly, on the question whether the net price at Bombay or Madras will pay for picking, cleaning, packing and transporting to the coast. Under the stimulus of high prices (such as prevail at this moment) large quantities would, we doubt not, be sent forward; and the price that will be requisite to secure such large supplies will diminish as the means of carriage are increased and cheapened. If the prices of the last five years continue, we believe there can be no doubt that the supply will inevitably continue to fall off.

We do not participate in the sanguine expectations which many parties entertain, that even with higher prices the quantity and quality of East India cotton sent to this country can progress so rapidly as to render us at all independent of the American supply. For, in the first place, the absence of good roads or navigable rivers in the cotton districts, the length of time and expenditure of capital needed before the want of those can be supplied by the establishment of railroads, and the languid and unenterprising character of the people, must necessarily cause any material increase of supply (at least over 250,000 bales per ann.) to be a matter of very slow and costly operation. And in the second place, the *quality* of the cotton grown in India is peculiar; and this peculiarity is still traceable, though in a modified degree, in whatever locality, and from whatever seed the plant is grown, even in the best specimens (improved as they unquestionably are) which have of late been sent to this country ; and this peculiarity will always, we fear, prevent it from being substitutable for American cotton, except to a very limited extent.

Our hopes lie in a very different direction: we look to our West Indian, African and Australian colonies as the quarters from which, would government afford every *possible* facility, (we ask and wish for no more,) we might, ere long, draw such a supply of cotton as would, to say the least, make the fluctuations of the American crop, and the varying proportion of it which falls to our share, of far less consequence to our prosperity than they now are.

The West Indies, as we have already seen, used to send us, sixty years ago, about 40,000 bales, or about three-fourths of our then supply. But the enormous profits realized on the growth of sugar, partly caused, and much prolonged by our prohibitory duties on all competing sugars, directed the attention of the colonists exclusively in that direction. As in the analogous case of protected wheat in this country, other cultivation was gradually abandoned in favor of a single article; the cane was grown in soils and localities unfit for it, and into which nothing but the protective system could have forced it; and cotton was altogether neglected. Many parts of the West Indies, St. Vincent especially, which are worst adapted for the cane, are best adapted for the cotton plant, which flourishes in light and dry soils, and especially near the sea-coast. The artificial stimulus which our mistaken policy so long applied to sugar cultivation, having been withdrawn, it must be abandoned in all unsuitable localities; and would be well replaced by cotton. What price would be required to repay its culture there, we cannot say ; but considering at how small a cost it might be placed on shipboard, in all these colonies, and how large a portion this item generally forms of the whole expense of production, we cannot see why cotton should not be grown in the Antilles as cheaply as in the United States, if only the negroes can be relied upon for steady and continuous labor during the picking season. Now the price of West India cotton ranges higher than that of the bulk of the American crop, as being longer in staple. Our belief is, that were the attention of our planters once more energetically directed to this article, they might soon send us a regular supply of 100,000 bales per annum, and thus find a use for many estates that must otherwise be abandoned.—*London Economist.*

COTTON SPINDLES IN GREAT BRITAIN.—The rapid increase in spinning will be apparent from the following:

In 1829, the number of mule spindles used in the cotton manufacture of England, was estimated by our friend, Mr. John Kennedy, at	7,000,000
1832, according to Mr. Bains, and others	9,000,000
1845, our estimate	17,500,000
1850, according to a Government return just published	20,977,017

The following table shows at a glance, the quantity of cotton taken by the trade annually for the last twenty years; we have reduced the deliveries into yarn at the present average weekly production per spindle, and have taken No 40's mule yarn (a much higher No. than the present average production,) as our standard of calculation, in order to show that the present spinning power is fully adequate to reduce the largest annual supply of cotton we have as yet received, into fine numbers of yarns, if required :

Table showing the annual deliveries of cotton to the trade of Great Britain, and the number of spindles required to render such quantities into No. 40's new twist:

Years	Deliveries of Cotton—Lbs.	Spindles required
1831	262,700,000	8,083,076
1832	276,900,000	8,520,000
1833	287,000,000	8,830,769
1834	303,400,000	9,335,384
1835	318,100,000	9,787,692

Years	Deliveries of Cotton—Lbs.	Spindles required
1836	347,400,000	10,689,230
1837	365,700,000	11,252,307
1838	416,700,000	12,821,537
1839	381,700,000	11,744,614
1840	458,900,000	14,120,000
1841	438,100,000	13,480,000
1842	435,100,000	13,387,692
1843	517,800,000	15,932,307
1844	544,000,000	16,738,460
1845	606,600,000	18,664,614
1846	614,300,000	18,901,537
1847	441,400,000	13,581,537
1848	576,000,000	17,741,537
1849	629,900,000	19,381,537
1850	584,200,000	17,975,384

COTTON MANUFACTURE—To what Extent carried.—One of the most important departments of the Great Exhibition was that which was devoted to cotton. It was not particularly attractive to the hasty observer, and was passed with indifference by many. But not so by the careful inquirer, the statesman, the manufacturer, and the political economist. Millions of human beings on both sides of the Atlantic are dependent, directly or indirectly, upon the growth and manufacture of cotton, and an amount of capital truly enormous is invested in this business, in all its various ramifications. The following account of the British importation, connected with the cotton manufacture in the year 1850, is taken from official sources, and will convey an adequate idea of the vast magnitude of this branch of industry:

Import—Raw cotton, 5,934,793 cwt.; cotton yarn, 905,966 lbs., of the declared value of £97,561; cotton manufactures not made up—East India piece goods, 175,010 pieces, of the value of £68,933; of other articles to the value of £297,176; cotton manufactures, wholly or in part made up, to the value of £44,315. Exports—foreign and colonial manufactures—cotton manufactures not made up—East India piece goods, 145,895 pieces, of the value of £58,493; other articles to the value of £93,605; of cotton manufactures, wholly or in part made up, to the value of £23,667; cotton yarn, 777,957 lbs., to the value of £81,014; British cotton manufactures, (exclusive of lace, patent net, sewing-thread, and stockings,) 1,358,238,837 yards, to the value of £20,528,150; other descriptions to the value of £236,058; cotton yarn, 131,433,168 lbs., valued at £6,380,948.

The quantity of raw cotton consumed in the cotton manufacture of Great Britain in the year 1850, was 584,200,000 lbs. The total number of cotton factories in Britain is 1,932, containing 20,977,017 spindles, and 249,627 power-looms. The moving power in these factories is supplied by steam, representing 71,005 horse-power, and water, 11,550 horse-power. The total number of persons employed in these factories amounts to 330,924. If to these we add the persons not employed in factories—such as hand-loom weavers, calico printers and dyers, makers and repairers of machinery, &c., a total of 700,000 would be obtained.

The total value of the cotton goods and yarn exported in 1850 was £28,252,878; and in 1849, £26,775,135. The capital employed in the cotton manufacture of Great Britain is estimated at not less than £45,000,000.

The *London Dispatch*, in noticing the Exhibition, and the display of cotton goods, says:

"The yarns, exhibited as the basis of other products, show to what an extent the ingenuity of man can be carried, when employed in a given direction. There we have specimens of yarn spun by machinery, which is of so delicate a character, that the fibres of cotton can only be discovered in the fabric by a microscope; and so intangible is it that it falls to pieces by handling. This curiosity of manufacture is exhibited by Thomas Houldsworth & Co., of Manchester, and the result of the energy and enterprise of Henry Houldsworth, Esq., of that firm. In the contributions of this house, we find specimens of cotton yarn ranging from No. 100 to No 700 in the single yarn; and No. 100 to No. 670 in double yarn, or lace thread. These figures express the number of hanks to a pound weight, each hank being 860 English yards; and the last named number of 700 in single, and 670 in double yarn, is the triumph of cotton spinning for all practical purposes, since we find that a pound weight of cotton is elongated, in the first instance, to a length of 338 miles, and in the other to a double thread 324 miles, at a cost of £28 as the price of a single pound weight. The most remarkable example, however, is the specimen shown as No. 909, both of yarn and thread, as a curiosity, by which a single pound of cotton is extended 430 miles. This is useless for all manufacturing purposes, being too fine to be serviceable, or even capable of being handled. Still, it is all it professes to be. The fineness of the cotton yarn used for lace-making has always been a great desideratum; and the firm has a world-wide reputation for spinning finest numbers. So late as 1840, 350 was the finest yarn attempted. In 1841, Messrs. Houldsworth spun 450, which was considered as a limit, until the Exhibition stimulated a further trial; and the result is now before the public, as palpable a fact as the building in which it is exhibited. Another still more astonishing specimen exhibited by the Messrs. Houldsworth, is that of No. 2150 yarn, in which we may fairly presume that they have reached the limit at which the fibre will at all cohere. A single pound of this yarn would reach the extraordinary length of 1,026 miles. It is needless to say, that yarn of this character is useless for all practical purposes, though highly significant as illustrative of human skill."

COTTON MILLS BY COTTON GROWERS—Export Duty on Raw Cotton—Price of Cotton, etc.—Cotton is the leading and controlling staple of the South, embracing nine states of the thirty of the United States, and therefore worthy of consideration and study, by all who feel an interest in the prosperity of this end of the Union.

For several years past, the labor of cotton growers has been sacrificed, and the prospect of a fair remuneration for the growing crop, will pass away before another comes into market; leaving the future as a counterpart of the past, with a tendency to get worse unless a remedy be applied.

The only safe and substantial remedy, is to put up the *cotton mills* among the cotton fields. The great bulk of the crops when put into market, is classed as "inferior," "ordinary," and a small portion "middling;"

and these classes have not averaged to the planters more than six cents for seven or eight years past, and some crops have been sold during this period as low as four cents per pound.

A continuation of these prices, will soon create a necessity for a remedy for these low rates, which are not a compensation for the immense labor required in the cultivation of cotton. Under the present plan, the planter's labor, composed of "the sweat of his brow," and the substance of his soil, baled up as *raw cotton*, is shipped off annually four thousand miles to cotton mills, in foreign countries, but chiefly to England, at an expense of eight or nine dollars per bale, which is charged to the grower when the account of sales is furnished from the mill.

If this tax to get to mill was the only evil, it might be yet endured for a while; but there is in reality but one great cotton mill, and that belongs to England, and her agent sits at Liverpool, and sees our labor, in bales of *raw cotton*, piled up around him till it will cover a ten-acre field. The reports of that market will show a stock, sometimes of a million of bales, then stored in Liverpool unsold: with a knowledge of the fact, that it cannot be taken any where else. The grower has no remedy. *There* are the *spindles*, and *there* it must stay; and the agent of this tremendous English mill says, "I will pay you three and half pence per pound for your cotton," and it is sold. An account of sales is sent to the planter, in £ *s. d.*, in red ink, with double entries; and when translated into *English*, he finds that his part is four cents per pound.

Cultivators of this great staple know, that such prices are no compensation for the immense labor required in its growth. They know it is a *sacrifice*, which looks to ruinous consequences, because the substance of their lands is annually wasting away by continued cultivation.

The remedy which is now insisted on is, for the *planters themselves* to "resolve," that the cotton mills shall be brought to the *cotton fields*; that they have been paying toll to the English mills long enough. Make the *resolve*, and the ways and means will be readily pointed out for effecting the end proposed. The cotton fields of the United States, extending from the Atlantic to the Rio Grande, embrace, in their wide extent, 500,000 square miles. The interest of *all planters* in this great cotton field is the same. State lines are imaginary, when the sacrifice of cotton-growing] labor is the question; and old issues in politics may rest in forgetfulness; and the whole South may act as one state, in giving a prosperous direction and division to the labor, of the best trained, most efficient and regular force of workers on the face of the globe. This splendid force of laborers, if directed by skill and wisdom, will yet make brilliant the prospects of the southern end of our Union. But a part of this force must be taken from the soil and put into the mills.

The spindles and looms must be brought to the cotton fields. This is the true location of this powerful assistant of the grower. In the *West*, in the East or in the North, would be better than any foreign country; but the *best* location is the sunny South, where the cotton grows. The next best location is the provision regions nearest the South.

To fix the public eye on the importance of this change, its necessity indeed, and to compel planters to investigate it, it is proposed that they as a body petition Congress to propose an amendment to the 9th article of the constitution of the United States, which prohibits "a duty on exports from any state," and when amended, that they pass a law, that five dollars per bale be paid into the treasury of the United States upon all *raw cotton* shipped after the year 1860.

This would be evidence of a determination among them, and ten years' notice to the world, that they would no longer go four thousand miles to mill with their cotton.

An average crop now of United States is about 2,300,000 bales, which, at six cents, is $55,000,000. The estimated cost of spinning and weaving a pound of cotton is three cents, making two yards to the pound, equal to eighteen cents per pound, at nine cents per yard for Osnaburgs. The crop then, when spun and wove, is worth eighteen cents per pound, making $180,000,000, allowing ten per cent. for waste, instead of $55,000,000, the yield *now*, when sold as *raw cotton*.

The inequality between the labor and capital for growing, and that for spinning, is startling. A pound of cotton, plowed, hoed, picked, ginned, baled, spun and wove, is worth eighteen cents. The spinning and weaving, it is said, can be afforded for three cents cost, which would leave fifteen cents per pound for the labor of the planter, supposing the cotton mill in the cotton field, and the mill to get cost only. But as three cents may be too low an estimate, make it six—and then twelve cents is left for the planter. But now what does he get? Four, five, and six. The question may now be asked, who gets the balance—allowing six cents to the grower and six cents to the spinner, there will be six cents yet unaccounted for? It goes to pay warehouse charges, freight, insurance, drayages, storages, weighages, *pickages*, pressage, commissions, postage, bills of lading, exchange, freight to Liverpool, dock dues, freight on railroad to Manchester, and then it is at the mill, and the same process brings it back, and this will fully account for the six cents per pound. Who pay these charges? The grower.

The growth and production of cotton are

accomplished by the muscles of men and mules, laboring incessantly eleven months in every twelve; exposed to heat, to cold, to winds and rain, and to the malaria of swamps.

The spinning and weaving are done by the iron muscles of the spindle and the loom, driven by the never-tiring engine, waited upon by boys and girls; and this labor is under roof, certain as to *quantity*, free from overflow, from frost, from caterpillar and boll worm. This simple statement is evidence, clear and strong, that it is the grower's labor which is now sacrificed, and greatly sacrificed. A firm and determined resolution among the planters, for they are the men who are suffering, and they must act for themselves, can arrest this policy in a few years. An export duty on "raw cotton," would insure it, but it may be accomplished without it.

Having determined that the mills must come to the *cotton*, which is but one move, whilst sending the cotton to the mills is a heavy annual, perpetual tax, it is proper to inquire if cotton growers can get up the spindles and looms among the fields.

The following facts answer the question in the affirmative, most distinctly. We estimate the crop at 2,300,000 bales. The factories now in the United States require of this 600,000 bales—leaving 1,700,000 for the South to spin. This would require 350 mills with 10,000 spindles each, or 700 mills with 5,000 spindles, or 3,100,000 spindles.

COST OF SPINDLES.

3,500,000 with all machinery necessary, looms, etc., at $12	$42,000,000
700 engines and fixtures at $8,000	5,600,000
Other expenses in and about the machinery	5,000,000
Total	$52,600,000

The machinery, if all purchased in one year, would cost about $50,000,000. This is the only debt of importance necessary to be made, and its payment can be extended into ten instalments of $5,000,000 each, interest added. The difference in the income of the cotton growers when they become spinners, is so great that this debt would never be felt. The 1,700,000 bales intended for the cotton field spindles, now yields an income of $40,000,000 at six cents. The same cotton spun up, by the creation of the above debt by these iron muscles, will give the same growers an income of $120,000,000, less the cost of spinning and weaving, which would give an increase of net gain per annum nearly equal to the cost of the machinery.

One mode here suggested, is, for planters, provision growers, and mechanics of all the cotton states, to send in petitions for manufacturing companies to be chartered, upon applications to the legislatures of their respective states; and also to pass an act for a general charter for all persons who may associate together for manufacturing purposes, so as to avoid partnerships, and limit the liability of stockholders to the loss of their subscriptions as stock.

Spinning may be commenced, with any number of spindles, with or without looms. There is an extensive demand for cotton yarns, and thread is a saleable manufacture. The mills at Lowell average about 6,000 spindles for each building. There is one, however, at Salem, containing 30,000 spindles, the largest in the world, under one roof. The size of buildings, then, will depend upon the quantity of machinery intended to be worked. A mill for 2,500, or 3,000 spindles, for coarse goods, will require, perhaps, three rooms twenty-five by sixty feet long; and a plan suitable for the *cotton field system*, which will be in the country, and where land costs nothing, and manageable by slave labor, at comparatively *no cost*, is for fifteen planters to take $4,000 each in stock, select a site for the mill, near their plantations, detail three men from each, making a building force of forty-five men, besides an overseer and a general manager, one of the stockholders; with this force, and as many teams as may be necessary, they will proceed to put up three rooms of twenty-five by sixty feet, of wood, one story high, of coarse, strong, undressed lumber, such as they can readily prepare from the forest, without an outlay of capital. Add, at convenient distances, fifteen or twenty cabins, and the buildings for the mill are up. This wooden, one story plan, for the cotton field, possesses the advantages of costing nothing, of fixing and running the whole machinery upon the ground, making it more steady, and accessible, and avoiding wear and tear, with better ventilation, less noise, and, perhaps, less risk from fire, because it is not the walls of a mill, but the cotton about the machinery, which is subject to burn.

One-story rooms, running in different directions from the engine, of wood, and without much labor in its preparation, are offered as a substitute for the four story brick and granite palaces of England and of New-England, which are required to be built with thick walls, to avoid motion in the machinery, and therefore expensive, costing from $30,000 to $50,000; and when buildings for the operatives are finished, the bills are often $100,000 in a site and buildings, before a wheel is turned. Whilst the manager and overseer are putting up the wooden mill and cabins, the planters, acting under the charter, have issued their bonds for $40,000, bearing seven or eight per cent. interest, payable in three, four, and five years, in equal instalments, and secured the payment by mortgage on the site and machinery, and a half section of land each, have sold the bonds, and bought the spindles and engine, and are ready for operation in six months from the formation of the company. A man and four boys or girls are taken from the plantation of each stockholder and put in the mill, each getting credit according to the number furnished. These, with eight or ten trained hands as instructors, furnish a mill force which will spin and weave 1,500 bales of cotton; making a million of yards of osnaburgs, worth nine cents per yard, equal to $90,000 gross sales. Tne stockholders being planters, and near the mill, furnish provisions, cotton, and wood for the engine.

Suppose the planters who have put up this mill make 1,500 bales only of cotton, which, at $24, are $36,000. Since the erection of the mill, the same cotton is worth $90,000 per annum. At the end of the three years, they commence paying the debt for machinery by instalments, and before this, the hands are trained to their new employment, and the planting account is raised from six to ten cents a pound for the *field labor*, which had been heretofore shipped off and lost. The mortgage debt is $2,666 each, being fifteen planters associated, to be paid in three instalments of $888, with interest, and that, when they are getting for their field labor, ten cents per pound. What, then, would be a debt of $1,000 a year, on substantial planters, when they have insured ten cents a pound for their crops by incurring the debt.

There are nine cotton states, including Tennessee, which will average about sixty counties to the state. Two mills in every county, of 3,000 spindles each, are sufficient to spin the whole crop, and render the South magnificently rich and gloriously independent. I mention these facts, to show the immediate capability of the cotton growers, to relieve themselves from this blighting system of shipping off the soil in *raw cotton*, and bringing home nothing in return, comparatively speaking. There are twenty counties in Tennessee, South Carolina, Georgia, Alabama, Mississippi and Louisiana, and a less number in Florida, Arkansas and Texas, which can spare the force to erect the buildings and cabins, for ten such mills, in any one year, and make the usual cotton crop besides.

Steam is a regular, portable power, free from freshets, droughts and mill ponds, and can be commanded at will for three hundred days in the year, in any desired quantity, suited to small or large operations. Two sections of land, affording twenty cords of wood per acre, which is a low estimate, will drive an engine for 3,000 spindles, for eighteen years. This also shows that there is a permanent source or power in the cotton states, even when nature has not furnished either suitable streams, or deposited in the earth, beds of coal; in some sections, however, both are found. The difference between the cost of water and steam, is but one item, and that not large; but the only difference now is that of wood and coal; steam power is now considered as cheap as water, all advantages estimated. Among the fields, a site may be often selected, near enough to enable stockholders to haul the seed cotton directly to the mill, the most desirable condition for the mill work—thus saving the labor of ginning and baling, the loss on bagging and rope, commissions for buying cotton and freight, besides saving the work of the picker at the mill.

Cotton growers, who have owned slaves long, know they are capable of making efficient operatives; and when once learned, they are fixed, permanent and valuable. This branch of the business furnishes profitable employment on cotton to a portion of the field force, which relieves the soil to that extent which is now wasting away from over fatigue. It gives scope to all the mechanical talent among the slaves, both males and females—men in the machine shops, and women among the mules, throstles, and looms. The condition of the states now is dependent; that is not the true position of the chivalrous South. A war with Great Britain would prostrate them with one blow. The revolution in France was like an electric shock, though she had but a few cotton mills. The starvation in Ireland, that bright Isle of the Ocean, puts *down cotton*. The Bank of England even, can, and does, press down the price of "*raw cotton*" at Liverpool; and its recoil falls back on the grower. This dependency is unmanly, and does not belong to the American character. The angry ebullition of emancipation sympathy for the happy slaves of the sunny South, among our own northern and eastern friends, is sometimes a source of a moment's uneasiness; in consequence of our dependent condition, and the repeated sacrifice of our field labor. These dependencies should be forthwith severed, by a determination to put up the cotton mills among the cotton fields, and spin and weave by slave labor.

This is the certain, safe, and sure remedy for all the *evils* enumerated above; bringing bright prosperity, humanity, with enlarged sympathies, and an ameliorated condition of the great working force of the South, in its train. Their labor, thus skilfully directed, would increase rapidly the net income of the growers, and slaves take the condition of their owners. Give them large incomes, and you make the negroes rich. As a general rule, (some exceptions, I regret to say,) rich owners have rich slaves.

The true character of the black man in servitude is not understood, except in the South. Negro society, with its amusements and sources of enjoyment, is not organized any where else to the same extent. They are born in servitude, and so were their fathers and grandfathers, and a long line of ancestry, and they have never known any other condition, and but few ever desire to change it. The body is accustomed to daily labor; inured to it from early youth; and it is a habit of his life. The mind is not called into action—they are relieved from all the responsibilities, sufferings, and mental anxiety of freemen, amenable to the laws of the land, and the rules of society.

Out of the general fund, they are fed, clothed and housed; and medical aid and attention and care are furnished when sick: among them, there are no widows or orphans thrown upon the charity of others; no paupers, and no lunatics; no painful anxiety for the future welfare of their wives and children; for a home and competency are left for them when they are dead and gone.

It is the duty of their owners to bring to the aid of this available and efficient corps of regular laborers in the field, the steam-engine, and the iron muscle of the spindle and loom; with these implements, they can put the labor of the field into a consumable shape, which leaves the world open as a market.

No longer will they pile up the cotton bales around the English mill agent in Liverpool, and suffer it to be sacrificed, because they have no remedy. There will be a demand for coarse, heavy, cheap cotton goods, as long as there are laborers in the world to wear them, and in this shape the great bulk of the cotton crops will be consumed. Europe can continue to make the fine goods in which the raw material is no part of the cost; one pound making twenty yards of fine muslins.

South America, Asia, Africa, and the East and West Indies, grow about 470,000 bales of fine cotton, well suited for fine fabrics. This supply Europe could still convert into fine fabrics. New-England to make prints, and all other three to five yards goods, and the cotton fields, in the sunny South, in a warm climate, can work up the bulk of the crop into coarse, heavy goods, which will average not exceeding two yards to the pound. This system, put into operation, would yield to the southern states for cotton alone $150,000,000, and supply the spindles now up in the United States. What effect, such an income, in imports or money, would produce upon the trade and commerce of our southern cities, is suggested for reflection only at present.

Large bodies move slowly; and to insure this result, I suggest an export duty of five dollars per bale on "raw cotton." Corporate companies by growers, and all others. The cheapest buildings which will answer the purpose. Buy the machinery, and mortgage whatever may be necessary to raise the funds by sale of bonds at par. Spin and weave by a part of the field force. Do this, and the fortunes of cotton growers are fixed on a permanent foundation; promising accumulated wealth to the whole South.

The iron establishments in the United States, and the machine shops, generally, may look to the South as an extensive customer in a few years. It is, no doubt, the true policy of the Sonth now, to order the machinery mentioned, worth $50,000,000. This must go to the iron establishments, and the profits might be taken in stock in some of the best mills—and thus lessen the outstanding liability for machinery.

The mild, warm winters in the South, are favorable to cotton spinning in cheap buildings. The passage of the export duty law would turn the eyes of all the spinners and weavers in Europe upon the South, and the country would be benefited for a while, by employing them, until the raw force is trained. These suggestions are made for the study and consideration of cotton growers.

COTTON FACTORY, S. C.—Negro Labor.—We had the gratification recently of visiting this factory, situated on the Saluda River, near Columbia, and of inspecting its operations. It is on the slave-labor, or anti-free-soil system; no operators in the establishment but blacks. The superintendent and overseers are white, and of great experience in manufacturing. They are principally from the manufacturing districts of the North, and although strongly prejudiced on their first arrival at the establishment against African labor, from observation and more experience they all testify to their equal efficiency, and great superiority in many respects. So as not to act precipitately, the experiment of African labor was first tested in the spinning department; since which, the older spinners have been transferred to the weaving-room. They commenced in that department on the 1st of July, and are now turning out as many yards to the loom as was performed under the older system. A weaver from Lowell has charge of this department, and as she reports that, while there is full as much work done by the blacks, they are much more attentive to the condition of their looms. They all appear pleased with the manipulations on which they are employed, and are thus affording to the South the best evidence that, when the channels of agriculture are choked, the manufacturing of our own productions will open new channels of profitable employment for our slaves. The resources of the South are great, and it should be gratifying to all who view these facts with the eye of a statesman and philanthropist, that the sources of profitable employment and support to our rapidly-increasing African labor are illimitable, and must remove all motives for emigration to other countries. By an enlightened system of internal improvements, making all parts of our state accessible, and by a judicious distribution of our labor, South Carolina may more than double her productive slave labor, and not suffer from too dense a population.

COTTON—SOUTHERN FACTORIES.—The number of cotton factories in four of the southern states in 1850 was as follows:

	No. of Factories	No. of Spindles	Capital Employed	Bales Cot. Consumed
Tennessee	30	36,000	$100,000	12,000
Alabama	11	16,962	500,000	6,000
Georgia	36	51,140	121,000	27,000
South Carolina	16	36,500	1,000,000	15,000

Cotton Factories in Alabama.—We were shown last week some samples of cottonades, ginghams, checks and osnaburgs, colored and plain, made at the factory in Huntsville, which, for quality and durability, would compare with goods made in the manufacturing towns of the North. The colored goods were excellent, and, were we not assured to the contrary, we should have pronounced them eastern goods. The factory at Florence is doing a thrifty business. It works forty-six looms turning 1600 spindles, and produces 80,000 yards of cloth per week. Besides this large amount of cloth, it manufactures, also, 6,000 dozen of thread per week. The weekly consumption of cotton is about 6,000 pounds, averaging 750 bales of cotton per year. As an instance of the prosperity of factories in this region, a new one is about being established on the same stream, on the opposite side, which it is calculated will consume 40 bales of cotton per week. The factory in this city is about increasing the number of looms. At this time it works only forty, which are chiefly employed in manufacturing the four qualities of goods. In a few weeks the present number of looms will be increased to seventy-two. The cloths made at this factory are in high repute and meet with ready sales.

Bell factory, in Madison county	2,500	spindles
Florence factory, in Lauderdale county	2,000	"
Decatur factory, in Lawrence county	1,000	"
Tuscaloosa factory, in Bibb county	1,800	"
Clement's factory, in Bibb county	500	"
Fish-pond factory, in Tallapoosa county	600	"
Tallahassee factory, in Tallapoosa co.	1,000	"
Bradford's factory, in Coosa county	600	"
Warrior factory, in Tuscaloosa county	1,000	"
Prattville factory, in Autauga county	2,682	"
Autaugaville " " "	3,080	"
Mobile factory, in Mobile county	3,000	"

The machinery of the Mobile factory has been contracted for, I understand, and that of Autaugaville is now in the mill. D. P.

COTTON AND COTTON MANUFACTURES AT THE SOUTH—COMPARATIVE COST AND PRODUCTIVENESS OF COTTON, AND THE COST AND PRODUCTIVENESS OF ITS MANUFACTURE: BY CHARLES T. JAMES, SENATOR FROM R. I.—The latest official tabular statement, to which we have access, of the amount of cotton produced in the world, is that made in the office of the United States Secretary of the Treasury, in the year 1834, for the use of Congress.

By this table, which is sufficiently correct for all practical purposes, it appears that the total amount of cotton raised in the world was 900,000,000 pounds; of which 460,000,000 pounds, 10,000,000 pounds more than one-half, was the product of the United States. Since that period, the culture of the article in the West Indies has almost ceased. The production in the East Indies rapidly increased during a few subsequent years, owing to the very great efforts of the British East India Company; but, from repeated failures, it has again become stationary, and will probably never be carried to any great extent. In the year 1839, the entire supply of cotton from India was 46,001,308 pounds. It may possibly now reach 50,000,000 pounds. The other cotton growing countries, viz: Brazil, Mexico, Egypt, and other parts of Africa and Asia, other than India, and a few smaller districts, with those named above, made up, in 1834, the balance of the product, say 440,000,000 pounds. Taking all the circumstances into the account, and especially the cheapness of the product in this country, and the known decline in quantity in some others, it is not probable that the foreign product has increased, since 1834, more than ten per cent. This would now give 484,000,000 for all the world, the United States excepted. In the United States, the result has been entirely different. The reduction in the market value of the article has stimulated the planter to make more of it—to compensate for the diminution of price by the increase of quantity. This is a poor policy, to be sure, in most cases, yet it has been extensively practised by the cotton planters of the United States. So greatly have they increased the culture of the article, that their crop for 1848 is estimated, in round numbers, at 1,000,000,000 pounds; and which affords a sure indication, compared with the foregoing statements, that all the rest of the world cannot compete with them, either in quantity or price. Increasing the consumption of the article in Great Britain by ten per cent. from the year 1840 to 1848, the quantity for the latter year would be 584,317,424 pounds; an excess of more than 100,000,000 pounds over the entire quantity produced in, and exported from, all the countries in the world, the United States excepted. France, Germany, and other European nations, require about 300,000,000 pounds; which, added to the consumption in Great Britain, makes the quantity required in Europe 884,317,425 pounds. Of this, only 480,000,000 is supplied by India, Egypt, Turkey, Brazil, the West Indies, &c., and leaving a deficit of more than 400,000,000 pounds, for which Europe is entirely dependent on the United States. To withhold this supply, would enhance the price in Europe; and, though our labor would cost something more than theirs, our cotton would be so much cheaper, that no European manufacturers could compete with us. Almost the only reason why no other country has extended its cotton culture as ours has done, is, because no other one can raise the article at so small a cost. This circumstance has almost annihilated the culture of cotton in the West Indies, and prevented its rapid increase in Brazil. The British East I. Company and the Viceroy of Egypt, with their immense power and resources, have bent their energies to the object, but, hitherto, all efforts have failed, and the cotton planters of the United States still hold and maintain their pre-eminence over all those of the rest of the world. With all these advantages, the United States ought to be, emphatically, THE cotton manufacturers of the world; and the cotton *growing* states should become the *great* cotton *manufacturing* states of the Union. One would think there could be no question that the cotton grower and cotton manufacturer, combined in one concern, with his full supply of the raw material, produced on his own soil, might undersell the European manufacturer, and control, as far as cotton fabrics were concerned, every market in the world. All this may appear chimerical to some, and they may be inclined to make the inquiry, How is all this to be done? The reply is at hand: Manufacture *all* your own cotton. How *can* we do this, is the next query, when we produce so much? Again the reply is ready: Others now do it for you. You have labor, skill and materials—if you wish for more of labor and skill, they are readily obtained in sufficient quantities to manufacture all the cotton in the world. But we produce so much. True, *too* much. Then make a proper distribution and application of labor and skill; produce no more than can be manufactured at home. Cast not yourselves in a foreign market, with a redundancy of an article, begging for a purchaser, on the mercy of foreign brokers, speculators and shavers. But more of this by-and-by. Let us now inquire which, in respect to the article of cotton, has made the best distribution and application of labor and skill, the United States or Great Britain, as far as the creation of wealth is concerned?

We have seen that, according to the best estimates to be obtained, the quantity of cotton imported into the Kingdom of Great Britain, and consumed by her manufactories in 1840, was 531,197,659 pounds; of which, at least four-fifths must have been supplied by the cotton growers of the United States. McCulloch, in his Encyclopedia of Commerce, published in London, for 1847, estimates the increase at about fifteen per cent. This estimate would make the British consumption of cotton at present, 610,877,307 pounds per annum. Allowing only the same proportion, or rather less than we have already stated, say now four-fifths of the quantity, to be supplied from the United States, it will amount to 488,701,846 pounds. The present average value of this cotton in England, is not far from 8 cents per pound; and hence, the aggregate cost, to the British manufacturer, of the above quantity received from the United States, would be $39,096,147 68. At this rate, the highest amount returned to the American cotton planter would be, say 488,701,846 pounds, at 6 cents per pound, $28,922,110 76—for convenience, say, in round numbers, $30,000,000. The best cotton lands will not yield more than three hundred pounds per acre, and the general average from year to year probably does not exceed two hundred pounds. Suppose, however, the quantity to be two hundred and fifty pounds, there is required 1,794,807 acres of land to produce it; and as the product will not average more than 2,500 pounds per hand, it will require about 195,480 hands for its culture. The land, at $25 per acre, is worth $44,870,175. The hands (slaves) at $500 each, are worth $97,740,000. Thus, the land and slaves together, would amount in value to $142,610,000. The cost of other necessary appendages, such as cotton gins, presses, horses, mules, &c., &c., will make up at least, with the above, the sum of $150,000,000, as the capital employed in the production of the above amount of cotton furnished to the British manufacturer. In order to make the estimate high enough for the planter, we will suppose his net receipts to be 6 cents per pound. At that price, the quantity, 480,000,000 pounds, will return him, say, in round numbers, $29,000,000.

According to the estimate in McCulloch's Encyclopedia of Commerce, (English,) the value of British cotton manufactures, for the year 1847, was about £40,000,000. The estimated increase for the seven years, from 1833 to 1840, was 33⅓ per cent. At that rate, the value, in 1848, would have been about £42,000,000, or $186,666,666, nearly. It is estimated also, that the amount of capital invested in the business, is about the same as the amount of value of product per annum. The British manufacturers also employ about 300,000 operatives, and about the same number of hand-loom weavers.

For the above amount of product, it has been seen that the American cotton planter furnishes about 480,000,000 pounds of the raw material, for, at a high estimate, $29,000,000. The cotton thus furnished is four-fifths, nearly, of the entire quantity consumed. The capital invested in the production of the cotton is $150,000,000. That invested in the manufacture of it, viz.: four-fifths of $187,000,000, in round numbers, is $149,600,000. In the ratio of capital, therefore, the planter should receive at least $150,000,000 for his product, whereas he receives but $30,000,000. But the cotton, which returns 6 cents per pound to the planter, costs the British manufacturer 8 cents. At this price, the amount of cost of cotton, 480,000,000 pounds, is $40,800,000. Deduct this amount from $159,600,000, the value of the manufactured product, as above, and you leave $118,000,000, as the value added to the above quantity of cotton, for which the planter receives but $30,000,000 at most, on an outlay of capital very nearly equal to that employed by the manufacturer. So much, as to the productiveness of British capital employed in manufacturing cotton, and American capital in producing it. Again, in respect to the number of hands employed:

We have said that the British employed about 300,000 operatives. To work up four-fifths of the cotton consumed, would therefore require 240,000. Divide the above $118,000,000 among these, and you have $491 69 nearly, as the value of product per hand. Again, divide the net receipts for the planter's cotton, $30,000,000, among the number of hands (195,480) required to produce it, and have but $153 46 per hand—less, by 338 23 per annum, for each hand employed in the production of cotton, than is realized by its manufacture in Great Britain. True, we have seen that, in the process, the British manufacturer employs also 240 hand-loom weavers—making the entire number of persons employed, 480,000. Well, divide the British net product among this whole number, and you have $245 84 per hand, and leaving yet, an excess of $92 38 per hand in favor of the manufacture, against the production of the raw material. But there are other matters to be taken into the account, which will enhance this difference.

In the first place, the planter employs the labor of about half as many horses and mules as field hands. In the second place, the cultivators of his cotton field must be his best, able-bodied hands, while two-thirds, at least, of the operatives in the cotton mills are boys and girls. In the third place, the planter has to employ the labor of such boys and girls many months in the year, to gather his crop in the fields. All these, together with other matters that might be named in connection with the culture of cotton and its preparation for market, would very nearly cancel the demand for the labor of the 240,000 British hand-loom weavers, and, especially, when we consider that the latter are not employed much over one-half their time, and, even then, at rates of wages which, without the aid of public charity, would not prevent starvation.

It may be said, perhaps, that we have not taken into consideration the amount of wages paid by the British manufacturer, while, for slave labor, the planter pays none. True—but, be it remembered, the value of the hand is $500 at least, the interest on which is $30 per annum. Then, the planter feeds and clothes his hands, furnishes them with dwellings and fuel, and with medical attendance in time of sickness; and maintains them when, from old age or other cause, they become unable to labor. Thus, the average cost of labor is probably quite as great to the cotton planter, for a given number of hands, as to the British manufacturer; and, reckoning his entire number, old and young, male and female, and bringing in the amount of labor performed by his mules and horses, he has as many to provide for. True, again, the British manufacturer has to disburse a small portion of his proceeds for other materials than cotton and labor—such as coal, oil, starch, &c. But the planter, on the other hand, has his land to clear, his bagging and bale rope to furnish, his cotton to gin, press and transport to market, &c., &c., which meet a great proportion of all the cost of manufacturing, except cotton and labor. In short, taking everything into the account, the net products and profits of manufacturing cotton in Great Britain, will exceed those from the culture of cotton for that purpose in the United States, by more than one hundred per cent. In other words, in the ratio of the profits made on 480,000,000 pounds of cotton manufactured in Great Britain, the planter should receive, as his net proceeds, at least $60,000,000, whereas, he receives, at most, but $30,000,000. And why is there this enormous difference? Two replies are at hand, each of them satisfactory and conclusive; and each of them plain and simple.

In the first place, the planter sends his cotton abroad to be manufactured, and thus loses the profits of the process, when it might as well be done at home. In the second place, he produces a surplus of the article every year, sends it to Europe in surplus supplies, has to solicit sales, and hence must submit to have purchasers make their own prices, and give him for the article just what they please. This he may know from the fact, that an occasional short crop, or a temporary deficiency in the supply, creates a corresponding advance in prices; while, when the demand has been fully canceled, prices fall again to their usual level, and probably below it. Let us now take another view of this subject, and call the attention of the cotton planter to the principal manufacturing states in our Union; and where, we venture to predict, he will find the balance against him as great in proportion as in Great Britain, although labor is considerably dearer in this country than in that. Could or would the cotton planters of this country employ all the capital and labor now appropriated to the culture of cotton, to a business as lucrative as the cotton manufacturers of Great Britain, they would in the ratio of the present market value of that article now shipped to the British market, realize at least $120,000,000 per annum, instead of $30,000,000 now returned to them. This difference appears enormous, but such is the fact. The entire cotton crop of 1840, as per official statements and returns, was 790,479,275 pounds. Assuming 25 per cent. for the increase since that period, which is probably a near approximation to the truth, the crop of 1848 was 988,099,093 pounds. Assuming, also, 6 cents per pound as the return to the planter, the entire amount realized for the crop was $59,285,945 58. Though persuaded that this estimate is a high one, we will yet increase it, and put it down in round numbers at $60,000,000, for the sake of convenience. Taking our former estimates as a basis, to produce this quantity of cotton would require 3,991,036 acres of land, the value of which, at $25 per acre, would be $99,775,900. There would also be required the labor of 395,200 hands. The value of this number of able-bodied slaves, say as before, $500 each, would be $197,600,000, and which, with the cost of cotton gins, horses and mules, &c , &c., will amount to at least $300,000,000. Let us now inquire what is done by the appropriation of capital, labor and skill, together with the material in the cotton mills of our principal manufacturing states.

In five of the New England States, there are employed, about 75,000 operatives, manufacturing cotton fabrics. The capital employed in the business is estimated at $42,982,120 and the gross product at $40,918,143. Deduct thirty-three and a third per cent. from the latter sum for cost of all materials, labor excepted, say $13,639,381, and you have as net product of labor, $27,278,762. This sum is a trifle less than the entire amount received by the southern planter for all the cotton he ships to Great Britain. Yet this is realized on the employment of a capital of something less than $43,000,000 ; while the planter employs, as has been seen, to produce that cotton, capital in land, slaves and fixtures to the amount of $150,000,000. The difference in the interest on these two sums, per annum, at 6 per cent., is no less than $6,420,000, a very desirable item in favor of the eastern manufacturer. Again, to produce that result, we have also seen that the planter must employ, at least, about 180,000 hands, able-bodied persons, whereas the eastern manufacturer employs only 57,000, being less than one-third part of the number, and who create, by their labor more wealth than the former. In proportion to the capital and labor employed, the planter should realize more than thrice the amount of the manufacturer, but does not, in fact, realize quite as much. Yet, not less than two-thirds of the whole number of operatives in cotton mills are women and children. These are plain and unembellished facts, based on, and borne out by, the most authentic data that can be obtained ; and which we shall, hereafter, attempt to illustrate more fully and verify more substantially by the exhibition of practical details and known results, too simple to be misconstrued, and too well authenticated to admit of doubt. In fact, the superiority in the increase of wealth and population of the manufacturing states, compared with that of the cotton-growing states, affords almost incontestible proof of the fact, that manufactories create wealth with much greater rapidity than the cotton culture—if not, then, whence arises the difference ? for there certainly is a great difference. Labor and skill are more judiciously distributed in the manufacturing states than at the South and more economically applied. With the planter, the object is to work a certain number of hands—to make all the cotton with them that he can, and to sell it for what others may be disposed to give. The market is glutted—cotton must be sacrificed at a low price. Instead of diverting a portion of his means to some other and more profitable object, he exerts himself to produce more cotton this year, that, by increase of quantity, he may make up the loss in price ; instead of which he enhances the supply, reduces the price still lower and still continues at the mercy of foreign brokers. As a general thing, this is not the way with the people of the manufacturing states. Their object is to pursue any certain branch of business no further than it is found profitable. When it ceases to be so they relinquish it and try their hand at some other. For this reason, labor is properly distributed and economically applied. In other words, people are careful that labor should be employed on objects most productive, and in such a way as to insure the greatest result in the shortest time. So, of skill, materials and capital.

Would the northern climate admit of the culture of cotton, and had a Yankee, in either of the New-England states, a cotton plantation, with all the requisites for the prosecution of the business, the moment he found he could make more money by the manufacture of that article, than by its production, it would be farewell to cotton-growing ; and the next thing you would hear on his premises, in the way of business, would be the clatter of the loom and the hum of the spindle. Yankee folks are said to be full of notions ; and such notions constitute the great secret of their prosperity. If southern planters would act on a similar principle, they would much benefit themselves. A gentleman well versed in the statistics of cotton-growing, in the finest cotton regions of the southwest, has calculated that, to supply cotton for a mill of 10,000 spindles, say 1,800,000 pounds per annum, would require the product of ten of the best plantations in the country, which, with their slaves and fixtures, would be worth $738,000. The product, as above, would amount to $108,000; from which, deduct the cost of operating, such as overseers, materials, carriages, &c., which he estimates at $28,000, and you leave to the planters $80,000. The mill to manufacture this cotton will cost, with all its machinery complete, $210,000, and require a working capital of $40,000—or say the entire capital, including mill and machinery, would, at the outside, be $250,000.

To manufacture the above amount of cotton into sheetings of one yard in width, of the fineness of No. 14, will cost, including the cost of the cotton, steam-power, transportation, insurance, labor, and, in fact, every item of expense, a little short of $232,000 ; to which add $15,000, the interest of the capital, at six per cent. per annum, and you have the entire cost of manufacturing the above 1,800,000 pounds of cotton. This cotton will make 4,500,000 yards of cloth ; which, at 7½ cents per yard, (a low price, by the way,) will be worth $337,500, leaving a balance, after having paid every expense, of about $106,000. Thus, you see, by the labor of 275 operatives, mostly women, girls and boys, there will be created, actual wealth to the amount of $106,000, from 1,800,000 pounds of cotton, besides the amount paid to them for labor. To produce that same cotton, worth in market $108,000, required the labor of no less than 600 able-bodied hands, besides one-half that number of horses and mules. The capital employed to produce this result is $738,000. The manufacturer's capital is but $250,000. If, therefore, the planter could by any means remove these plantations into one of the New-England states, with all their slaves, fixtures, &c., and they should continue to produce cotton as abundantly as on the Mississippi or Tombigbee, though now nominally worth toward a million of dollars, the owner of the cotton mill, which cost but $250,000, would not exchange it for them, and would evidently be a loser by the bargain if he should. This will at once appear obvious, when we state that, over and above the cost of working the plantations, already named, there would be expended, for overseers, &c., $20,000 more ; and reducing the net income to $88,000—less, by $18,000, than the net product of the cotton mill. Under these circumstances, the mill owner would much rather keep his mill, and employ his hired operatives, than to take in exchange the plantations with their slaves, &c. The reason: he can make the most money by his mill. But this comparison applies not only to a cotton mill in Massachusetts, New-Hampshire, Rhode Island or Connecticut, but even in the best cotton-growing states, at the side of the best cotton plantation in that state. This statement requires no labored argument to confirm it. Every species of property designed for the creation of wealth, is valuable in the ratio of its productiveness, without respect to its actual cost. One plantation may have cost $50,000, and require an outlay of $20,000 per ann. to work it. Another may have cost $20,000, and be worked at an expense of only $5,000. Without respect to this difference of cost and expenditure, every one knows that, if the cheaper establishment yield a greater profit than the other, it is, of course, of most value to its possessor. Thus, if a planter own cotton lands which cost, with all his slaves and fixtures, $700,000, or more, and yield a net profit of $80,000 per annum, the cotton mill at his side, the capital of which is but $250,000, including the cost of the establishment itself, which yields a net profit of $100,000, is intrinsically worth more to its possessor than the planter's cotton lands and slaves. Every planter knows this common-place statement to be true. But, after having admitted all this, the cotton planters and capitalists of the South raise the inquiry : Suppose we wished to go into the manufacturing business, though we had plenty of the raw material, how shall we obtain the labor and skill qualified for the work, and of both of which we are deficient ?

Up to the year 1767, not a pound of cotton had ever been spun in any part of the world, by machinery. Though a considerable quantity was manufactured in India, and some in England, yet all was done with the aid of the old spinning-wheel and hand-loom, precisely as is now the case with the families of our southern planters. When, therefore, Hargreaves in '67, and Arkwright in '69, brought out the spinning-jenny, only eighty years since, Great Britain possessed neither the requisite labor or skill, trained to the business, nor yet the practical cotton-machine builder, nor the raw material. All these were to be created and inducted into the business. But British enterprise did not falter. The business was taken in hand and prosecuted with vigor. In the course of four years, it was in successful operation. From that time to the present, Great Britain has lacked neither manufacturing labor, skill nor materials. The result of the business, at the present time, we have already seen. About sixty years since, not a solitary cotton spindle had been made or driven in America. It is doubtful if many persons had ever seen one. About that period, an attempt was made, on a small scale, to spin cotton with machinery in Rhode Island, but failed for want of proper skill. This, however, was not long wanting. The arrival in this country of the celebrated manufacturer, SLATER, supplied the deficiency, and we have now only to look around, and to examine the statistics of trade in this country, to learn the great results of the truly wonder-working power of the cotton spindle and the loom. At the time the process of cotton spinning by machinery was first introduced into New-England, the people might have laughed at the idea, and said, how shall we, entirely unaccustomed to building and operating cotton machinery, obtain the skill, and train the labor for the work? But others, far-seeing and shrewd, came to the conclusion, and their conclusion was the correct one, applicable in all cases, that you have but to open a productive field, and there will be labor and skill enough found to cultivate it. The issue has proved the truth of the conviction. These aids have never been required, but they have been at hand. And should the number of mills in the United States be doubled within twelve months, probably not one of them would have to delay, for a day, the commencement of manufacturing operations, in consequence of a deficiency of labor and skill. A vast proportion, if not all required, would undoubtedly be found among us. If not, the first demand would call from Great Britain as many of her now half-starved and starving operatives, as might be required. But, without calling for aid from Europe, a full supply may at all times be obtained in New-England, to manage and supervise the operations of the cotton mill, and there are thousands of persons at the South, who would gladly and gratefully accept such employment to earn a livelihood, much superior to that which their present means can possibly afford; and would quickly become qualified for the work of operatives, under the charge and direction of good superintendents and managers. There is nothing hypothetical in this statement. Experience has shown it to be true to the letter.

As respects all raw materials, especially those of a bulky character, economy dictates that, all other things being equal, they should be wrought on the spot on which they are produced, in order to make the most valuable return. For instance—iron ore, a material abundant in Russia and Sweden. Were that material to be shipped to this country in its crude state, there would be a heavy charge for the transportation of the foreign matter combined with the metal, which must eventually be borne by the original owner. And all that the iron would bring in this market, after having been smelted and manufactured into bars, over and above the cost of the ore, would be so much wealth created here. The extra charge for freight is saved, and the additional value of the iron is retained at home, by its being manufactured on the spot on which the ore is found. Of this, the original owner takes his share, and the balance is distributed for labor, &c., in the community. That community is enriched by so much, therefore, in consequence of the operation. There may be some exceptions to this rule, but, from what we have seen, there is none in favor of the transportation of cotton to a distant market. The rule is founded on a general law. Labor and skill are marketable commodities. These, like all other commodities, will, as a general thing, seek the best market. Suppose all the labor and skill at hand are necessary to the production of a quantity of cotton, sufficient to supply the demand of the manufacturer—the planter then would manufacture his own produce, but lacks the mechanical skill. Let it be known that he is in want of an engineer, managers, overseers, operatives, machinists, carpenters, masons, &c., for the purpose, and you will soon see that, instead of finding it difficult to obtain such, he will, very probably, be overrun with applications. In a comparatively short period, hundreds of factories might be erected and started at the South, and fully supplied with every description of skill and labor wanted. Thousands would resort there with the hope of doing better by a change, induced by the prospects which new enterprises in a profitable business hold out, of permanent employment, with higher wages. Even should the planter, who goes into the manufacture of cotton, find it necessary to import his operatives from Europe at his own expense, he would still be a great gainer by the transaction. In a mill of ten thousand spindles, he would require two hundred and seventy-five persons. Suppose he should procure them in England, and pay the expense of transporting them thence to this country, at fifty dollars each—the transportation of the whole would amount to $13,750. This would be once for all. Another such transaction would never be necessary. His mill will also require, as seen, 1,800,000 pounds of cotton. To place that cotton in a northern manufactory, will cost, including every charge, at least one cent per pound, or $18,000. This amount all comes into the cost of manufacturing in the northern mill, and goes, of course, into the price of the manufactured article. This amount will, therefore, be saved by the southern planters who manufacture their own cotton. It pays, in one year, all the cost of transporting the above number of operatives from England, and leaves a balance of $4,250. But the operation of the transportation of cotton goes on from year to year, at the annual cost of $18,000. We will now go somewhat more into detail on this subject.

The cotton from the planter, reaches the northern manufactory increased one cent per pound in its market value, by the expenses incurred *in transitu*. Allowing the planter's price to be six cents per pound, its cost to the manufacturer will be seven. The pound of cotton, less waste, will make two and eight-tenths yards of sheeting, No. 14, one yard in width, worth, at the present low prices, 7½ cents per yard, or 21 cents per pound. The raw material, however, is subjected to a loss of ten per cent. in the process of manufacturing, so that the weight of the manufactured article from 1,800,000 pounds of raw cotton, will turn off but about 1,600,000 pounds of cloth. Thus—1,800,000 pounds of cotton, at 7 cents, costs $126,000. The entire cost of manufacturing, is $121,000, including labor, and interest on the capital; and making, with the cost of cotton, $247,000. The quantity of the manufactured article will be 1,600,000 pounds at 21 cents per pound, or 7½ cents per yard. This is worth, at that rate, $336,000. From this sum, deduct the cost, as above, and you leave as a balance in favor of the manufacturer, the sum of $89,000. This is the gross income for one year; with the labor of 275 operatives, mostly boys and girls, and a capital of $250,000. From the above amount of $89,000, however, there are certain other expenses to be deducted, such as commissions, guarantees, &c., which will somewhat reduce it; but yet, the amount left will be much greater, taking all things into account, than the net proceeds to the planter from the raw material.

To produce the cotton for the foregoing operation, as already noticed, the planter employs 600 able-bodied hands, and nearly one-half that number of horses and mules, and a capital of at least $730,000. The interest on this capital is $43,800 per annum, or $28,800 more than the interest on the manufacturing capital; and the labor is more than that employed in the manufactory, reckoning that of man and beast on the plantation, by three hundred per cent. Thus, the capital and labor necessary to the production of 1,800,000 pounds of cotton, would be sufficient to erect, furnish and operate three cotton mills, each of which would manufacture into cloth this entire quantity of cotton, and each of which would also return, in the shape of gross income, several thousand dollars more per annum, than is now realized from the entire amount of labor and capital employed to produce cotton for one of them! It must also be borne in mind, that the manufacturer at the north receives his cotton enhanced one cent per pound above the plantation price, which makes the gross amount of the additional cost, $18,000 per annum. This would of course be saved by the manufacture of the article on the spot of its growth, aud would go to increase the profits of the operation.

Were there room for a rational doubt on this subject, the reader might be justified in regarding it with some degree of skepticism. But, when he reflects on the well-known fact, of the much more rapid increase of capital and wealth in the manufacturing community, than in that of the cotton planter, he will be constrained to acknowledge that the effect cannot be without a sufficient cause. That cause he will seek for in vain, unless he find it in the greater profits of manufacturing, compared with those of producing the raw material.

To confirm this statement, we annex a schedule, made up, not from estimates either hypothetical or theoretical, but from authentic data of actually practical results, drawn from a mill now in operation. These results have occurred during the past year, being one of the worst known in the manufacturing annals of the United States.

Cotton—1,800,000 pounds, at 7 cents per pound	$126,000
Cost of power (*steam*)	4,500
" Carding	13,266
" Spinning	14,734
" Dressing and Starch	9,306
" Weaving, including all expenses	26,598
" Repairs, wear and tear, machinists, &c.	17,002
" General expenses, officers' salaries, transportation, &c.	20,642
" Interest on capital of $250,000	15,000
Total	$237,048
Against this sum, which includes the entire cost of manufacturing, we have 4,500,000 yards, of No. 14 sheeting, the product of the mill, worth now 7¼ cents per yard	$326,250
From this last amount, deduct the cost as above	237,048
And you have a balance of	$89,202

As the gross profits to the manufacturer, subject to the deductions for commissions, &c., before named, on 1,800,000 pounds of cotton, after having paid for the cotton, and the cost of manufacturing; while the planter who produced that cotton, receives but $108,000; being more, by only $18,888, than that received by the manufacturer. Yet, from that sum, viz., $108,000, the planter has to pay all the cost of production, together with all incidental expenses, besides the interest on his capital.

Facts like these should fix the attention of the cotton planter, teach him his true interest, and stimulate him to become the manufacturer of the product of his field, instead of permitting others to reap the entire profit. Yet, he acts differently. The small profits derived from his cotton fields, after the deduction from the gross receipts, of a sum sufficient to cover the cost and the incidental expenses, are generally appropriated to the extension of agricultural operations, and the production of *more cotton*—of which there is already *too much*. He neglects the main chance, and delves on, from year to year, to build up European and New-England manufacturing cities, towns and villages, and to enhance their wealth, when he might as well secure a due share of these benefits to himself.

If, say many persons at the South, we had the capital, so abundant at the North, we could then embark in the manufacturing business with some prospect of success; but our means are mostly in lands and slaves, and the money capital is deficient for the purpose. This objection, however plausible, is unsound. It rests on a mistaken view of the subject. What has created the large capital in the manufacturing states? A portion of it is, without doubt, the fruits of agriculture and commerce; but by far the greater part is, either directly or indirectly, the production of manufactures, not only of cotton, but of various other materials. The New-England states, for instance, named in a preceding page, though in a prosperous condition compared with former times, had, at the commencement of the cotton manufacturing era, scarcely money capital sufficient to prosecute their commercial and agricultural pursuits. But they did not hesitate on that account. A rich field for operations presented itself, and, money or no money, people determined to enter and cultivate it. Of course, a portion of capital had to be withdrawn from other pursuits, and some debts to be contracted; but this procedure was fully warranted by the prospect presented, and as fully justified by the result. New England might have hesitated to embark in manufacturing enterprises, on the plea of a deficiency of capital, and continued to this time to devote herself entirely to agriculture and commerce to augment that capital. And what would have been the result? She would not now, as all circumstances past and present go to show, possess one-half the wealth she does, nor probably more than two-thirds of her present population. The truth is, the small means and the credit first embarked were increased; the whole was again enhanced by new operations, and so it has continued, till the amount of capital now invested in manufactures of various descriptions, and the wealth that has been created by them, are probably much greater than the entire value of the now manufacturing states was at the commencement of these operations.

In the year 1839, according to the data appended to the United States census of 1840, there were in operation in Maine, 29,736 cotton spindles; in New Hampshire, 195,173; in Massachusetts, 669,095; in Rhode Island, 518,817; in Connecticut, 181,319—making, in all, 1,590,140 cotton spindles in operation in those five states, at that time. Since that period, the number has been increased twenty per cent. at least, and there can, therefore, not be a less number now than about 2,000,000, nearly. The manufacture of cotton was commenced in Rhode Island about 1791, but its progress, for many years, was extremely slow. We will assume the year 1810 as our starting point, at which time it had begun to put on the appearance of some importance. Thus, reckoning to the close of 1849, we have a range of forty years.

Again, assuming that, in 1810, there were 50,000 spindles in operation, then the medium or average number for forty years would be something over 900,000. Distribute these in 90 mills of 10,000 spindles each, and each mill creating wealth at the rate of $100,000 per annum, or, which is the same thing, adding that amount to the value of raw material, and which is nearly one-third less than the amount stated for the mill before alluded to, and we have $4,000,000 in forty years. Hence, the ninety mills would add, and probably have added, at least $360,000,000 of wealth, or capital, to the community, in forty years, by means of the combined operations of labor, skill, and materials, aided by capital and credit. It is true, there have been fluctuations in the business and occasional failures, as there are, and ever will be, in the most lucrative business ever known. But most persons who have entered into this have made money by it; and, at any rate, failures or no failures, the wealth created by it is in the community—the product of labor, skill, and materials—and if the foregoing estimates are within the limits of truth, and they are believed to be, then, by cotton manufactures alone, the above five states have added to the stock of wealth no less than $360,000,000! Permit us now to inquire; have the whole ten cotton-planting states done as much by the culture of their staple production, or any thing like it, in proportion to the labor, skill, materials, and capital, employed? Let the comparative estimates on the culture of cotton and its manufacture, in the foregoing pages, furnish the reply. Such, as has been stated, is the example set by New England, though commencing with a deficient capital even for her ordinary pursuits, with her system of credit to aid in the production of the most valuable returns from the labor, skill, and real capital, of the country. Can any reason, even a plausible one, be given why southern people should not do the same? Their means are more abundant than were those of New England at the commencement of the cotton-manufacturing business in this country. All that is wanted, is enterprise. There certainly could be no sufficient reason why a number of planters, having available property of the value of half a million of dollars, could not raise, on that property, the sum of two hundred and fifty thousand, to prosecute a business, the profits of which would be almost certain to return one hundred per cent. on the outlay, in the short space of two or three years at farthest. Especially might they do this when known, as known it is by practical experience, that that business would probably enhance the value of the property in possession fifty to one hundred per cent. Southern planters, considered men of wealth, find little or no difficulty in extending their credit, to any desirable amount, in the purchase of land or slaves, or both. It would be quite as easy for them to do so, if necessary, to erect manufactories, and their credit and funds would, in such case, be applied to an object much more productive.

But it is not only the benefit to be derived in a direct manner to the individual manufacturer, that holds out a strong inducement to the South to go largely into the business—nor yet, alone, the prospect of enriching a community as a body. Motives of philanthropy and humanity enter into the calculation, and these should not be disregarded. This is a subject on which, though it demands attention, we would speak with delicacy. It is not to be disguised, nor can it be successfully controverted, that a degree and extent of poverty and destitution exist in the southern states, among a certain class of people, almost unknown in the manufacturing districts of the North. The poor white man will endure the evils of pinching poverty, rather than engage in servile labor under the existing state of things, even were employment offered him, which is not general. The white female is not wanted at service, and if she were, she would, however humble in the scale of society, consider such service as a degree of degradation to which she could not condescend; and she has, therefore, no resource, but to suffer the pangs of want and wretchedness. Boys and girls, by thousands, destitute both of employment and the means of education, grow up to ignorance and poverty, and, too many of them, to vice and crime. This picture is no exaggeration; it is strictly true in all its details. The writer has no disposition to reproach the wealthy for the existence of such a state of things. He is well aware that it is the result of circumstances which have to them been unavoidable. But he cannot resist the conviction that, when a fitting opportunity presents itself to the wealthy men of the South to obviate those evils, at least in a degree, and that even in a way to benefit themselves, they can hardly be held guiltless in case of refusal or neglect to apply the remedy.

The writer knows, from personal acquaintance and observation, that poor southern persons, male and female, are glad to avail themselves of individual efforts to procure a comfortable livelihood in any employment deemed respectable for white persons. They make applications to cotton mills, where such persons are wanted, in numbers much beyond the demand for labor; and when admitted there, they soon assume the industrious habits and decency in dress and manners of the operatives in northern factories. A demand for labor in such establishments is all that is necessary to raise this class from want and beggary, and, too frequently, moral degradation, to a state of comfort, comparative independence, and moral and social respectability. Besides this, thousands of such would naturally come together as residents in manufacturing villages, where with very little trouble and expense, they might receive a common-school education, instead of growing up in profound ignorance. I would, therefore, appeal to the planter of the South, as well as to every other capitalist. Let your attachment to your own interest and the interests of the community, united with love for your species, combine to stimulate you to enter, with resolution, this field of enterprise, and to cultivate it with the full determination not to be outdone. You must succeed.

In a political point of view, the extensive prosecution of the manufacturing business at the South is of vast moment. That the political ascendency of the South, in the councils of the nation, has been neutralized, events plainly show. That it will be greatly overbalanced is a fact as certain as that the increase of population in the North, East and West, shall exceed that of the South. A reference to the official tables, to be sure, will show that, during the last thirty or forty years, the increase in the cotton-growing states exceeds, in some measure, the ratio of that in the five manufacturing states which we have named; and they show an almost unprecedented increase in the new states of Alabama, Missouri, Mississippi and Louisiana. But, as respects the point alluded to, these tables are altogether deceptive. The creation of several new states has, to be sure, increased the number of southern votes in the United States Senate, by adding ten or twelve to the number, but then, there are, to offset against these, Michigan, Indiana, Iowa, Wisconsin, to say nothing of Maine, Ohio, Illinois, and others which will soon follow, so that the balance of power, even in the Senate, will be against the South. The rapid increase of population in the four cotton-growing states named, changes not the relative position of affairs, as to the popular representation in the lower house of Congress—or, at most, changes it in no material degree. Those states have all been settled by persons of other southern states; and scarce a family can be found in them, except here and there a trader in the country, or those in the commercial towns, but such as are emigrants from the Carolinas or other states of the South, or their descendants. Had therefore those states never been settled, the popular representative strength of the South would have been but little less than at present. But how is it with the four manufacturing states named? By the tables their increase of population is less, than that of the South, in proportion. But, if the real increase be the object in view, a large portion of it must be sought for in Ohio, Michigan, Iowa, Wisconsin, Illinois, Kentucky, Tennessee, and the southern trading ports. But we take only the four states of Ohio, Michigan, Indiana and Illinois, for the comparison. The first of these states, Ohio, was originally settled almost exclusively by people from New-England; and the present American-born citizens, now resident within her borders, are mostly New-England people or their descendants. Michigan, Indiana and Illinois, also received a large portion of their original settlers from the same source, together with, probably, a large number of the offshoots of New-England families in Ohio, or elsewhere in the western country. Let us see how the case now stands. The eight following cotton-growing states, viz., North and South Carolina, Georgia, Tennessee, Missouri, Mississippi, Alabama and Louisiana, contained (Mississippi in 1816), in 1810, a population of 1,637,093, including slaves. In the year 1840, the population of the same states amounted to 4,374,362—being an increase of 2,737,269—equal to a fraction less than one hundred and seventy-three per cent. At the former period, the *six* New-England States, after large drafts on their population to settle the new regions of the West, contained a population of 1,471,973. In 1840, with a tide of emigration still flowing westward, the population had increased to 2,245,822—being an increase of 762,849—equal to about fifty-two per cent. In 1810, the population of Ohio, Michigan, Indiana and Illinois, together, was 272,080, which, added to that of New-England, made up an aggregate of 1,744,063. In 1840, those four northwestern states, had a population, in the aggregate, of 2,894,783, which, added to the population of the New-England States at the same period, makes up the aggregate of 5,129,605; and the increase on the ten states being an aggregate increase in those states of 3,385,542—equal to one hundred and eighty-three per cent. on the population of 1810, and in the ratio of ten per cent. over that of the cotton-growing states. We have not sufficient data to enable us to include Arkansas, Florida and Texas, in this calculation, and therefore offset them against Iowa, Wisconsin, and other settlements made by northern people. From the foregoing statements it appears very evident, that the relative political strength of the South must continually decline; or rather, that that of the North will increase in the greatest ratio, until the South shall adopt some method besides that of agriculture to remedy the difficulty. But the case presents itself in a still stronger light, when we reflect, that at least thirty-three and one-third per cent. of the increase in southern population takes place with the slaves, and only two-fifths of which go to increase the representative power. The writer will hazard the assertion, that this state of things will never find a remedy, so long as the South persists in her present impolitic course of purchasing from abroad every manufactured article which she requires, from a penny jews-harp or a yard of shirting, to a steam-engine. We have already shown exclusively, that to manufacture cotton is far more profitable than to produce it for sale. So is the manufacture of almost every other article. Of course, the business can afford better prices for labor and skill; and hence, where manufactures are found, there also these seek employment; and thus is population increased over and above the increase by natural causes. We can further illustrate this fact by reference to the manufacturing states themselves.

In 1820, the state of Massachusetts contained 523,287 inhabitants. Manufactures had received a severe shock by the termination of the war with Great Britain, in 1814, though, at the above period, they had partially recovered from its effect. Little or no onward progress had, however, been made in the business, and cotton mills were few in number, and those of small capacity. During the succeeding period of ten years, the manufacturing business was commenced at Lowell, and some other places in the state, and made rapid advances, though it met with one severe revulsion in 1828 and '29. During these ten years up to 1830, the population of the state had risen to 610,408—an increase of 86,121—equal to about sixteen and one-half per cent. But, as the business continued to increase, notwithstanding the disastrous crisis of 1836 and '37, the population of 1840 was 737,699—an increase of 127,291, or nearly twenty-one per cent. From the year 1820 to 1830, the population of Rhode Island increased fourteen per cent.; but from 1830 to '40, the increase was but about ten per cent. The cause of the difference between the ratios of increase in the last ten years named, in the two states, as far as manufactures were concerned, was owing to the fact, that the water power in Rhode Island had become so far exhausted as to admit of but little extension of the business; while at Lowell, and many other situations in Massachusetts, the manufacturers were, as they still are, extending it on every hand. Besides, Massachusetts is a much larger and better field for agricultural pursuits than Rhode Island; and manufactories having so strong and direct a tendency to enhance the value of agricultural products in their vicinity, this alone helps very much to swell the mass of population. In fact, every interest in the state is promoted. Manufactories increase the demand for agricultural products, and every branch of mechanical industry; and both of which will, therefore, bear remunerating prices. They create a great deal of business for mechanical men and traders of all descriptions. They encourage, foster, and in a great measure pay for, public improvements. They increase the wealth of a community more rapidly than any other branch of business. And, though last not least, they prevent, in a great degree, the evils of extreme indigence and pauperism, by furnishing to all the means of supplying themselves with the comforts of life, through the medium of their own industrial efforts. Most certainly all these benefits are worthy of a trial, by the people of the South, to secure them. The South produces the raw material for the cotton mill in abundance. She has but to say the word, and labor and skill will as readily offer themselves to convert it into cloth on the spot, as ships do to transport it to New-England or to Europe. In the very nature of things, the South ought to become the greatest seat of cotton manufactures in the world.

CHARLESTON—History of, etc.—The city of Charleston is one of the most ancient in the Union. Its foundations were laid in 1672,* and it very soon attracted an additional population, from the planters of Barbadoes and the chivalrous French Huguenots. "On the spot," says Bancroft, "where opulence now crowds the wharves of the most prosperous mart on our southern seaboard, among ancient groves that swept down to the river's banks, and were covered with yellow jasmine, which burdened the vernal zephyrs with its perfumes, the city was begun." Two centuries nearly have passed away since then. Momentous have been the events and changes of this period. In colonial dependence, in Revolutionary conflicts, in republican advancement, it has mattered little for Charleston. Ever unchanged and unchanging; generous, hospitable, and refined; intelligent, patriotic, and enthusiastic; devoted to liberty, and appreciating its advantages on her seat, by the side of the Ashley and the Cooper, the Pinckneys and the Rutledges, the Middletons, Lowndes, and Laurenses, and Elliots—men whose like we shall not soon look upon again—lived, labored, and died. Peace to their sacred manes.

Tho location of Charleston is on a peninsula, washed by the waters of two beautiful streams. The harbor is spacious and secure, and defended by three fortifications—one the famed Moultrie of Revolutionary glory. The bar has some obstructions, but four channels with different degrees of depth; the ship channel being the greatest, and affording seventeen feet at high water and ton at low.

In 1731, we have it on the authority of an old historian, "there were 600 houses in Charleston, five handsome churches, and that out of the city were to be found courtly, stately buildings, noble castles," &c.

The city was incorporated in 1783, and had a population, in 1820, of 24,780, including suburbs, 37,471—very little, if any short of its present population.

Its imports in 1723, were £120,000 sterling. From 1720 to 1729, there were 264,488 barrels rice exported; from 1730 to 1739, the rice exported reached 429,425 barrels. For the year 1728, the export was 26,478 barrels. For 1733 we have the following exports; 36,584 barrels rice, 2,802 barrels pitch, 848 barrels turpentine, 8 chests skins, 60 tons lignum vitæ, 20 tons brazilletto wood, 27 tons sassafras.

In 1744, two hundred and thirty vessels were laden at the port of Charleston. The exports for 1748 were 55,000 barrels rice, 39,308 bushels corn, 296,000 oranges, 6,107 bushels peas, 700 bushels potatoes, 1,700 barrels beef, 150 hogs, 3,114 barrels pork, 10,000 barrels tar, turpentine, &c., 134,118 pounds indigo, 200 pounds beaver skins, 141 calf skins, 720 hogsheads deer skins, 1,700 pounds wax, and a large quantity of lumber, amounting in all to £161,365 sterling.

In 1754, the exports reached £240,000 sterling. In 1799 they were $10,554,842; in 1801, $14,304,045. In 1821 the imports amounted to $3,000,000, and the exports to $8,690,539. In 1824 the imports amounted to $2,030,916, and the exports to $7,143,831. The last consisted of $5,605,948 cotton, 1,114,297 rice; 208,570 other domestic articles; $215,016 foreign articles.

From the commencement of the Federal Government up to 1825, the revenue collected amounted to $22,337,381.

Exports in	1834	$11,119,565
"	1835	11,224,298
"	1836	13,482,756
"	1837	11,138,992
"	1838	11,017,391
"	1839	10,318,822
"	1840	10,036,769

* In 1677 it was called Oyster Point Town; in 1680, New-Charlestown; in 1682, New-Charleston. —*Mills.* It was chartered in 1783.

These were the exports of the whole state, almost the entire part passing through Charleston.

The advantages of Charleston soon made it a place of considerable trade. Its first exports were staves, lumber, furs and peltries, considerable quantities of rice, first planted in 1693, to which were added, in 1747, indigo, in 1782, tobacco—abundant and profitable products—and, in 1790, cotton. In 1723, the foreign import of Charleston was £120,000, over half the foreign import of 1845! The export of the same year was, in rice alone, 26,468 bbls.; and in 1744, two hundred vessels were laden at its wharves. The city was once a considerable ship owner and builder, but we learn from the late report of its chamber of commerce, that there are now very few ships owned there; and the vessels built annually also few, and of the smallest class. In the last seven years, the number of ships owned and sailing from Charleston has decreased from fourteen to six, the number of brigs from sixteen to four, with an increase of three only in schooners, in the same ttme. The revenue collected on the imports of Charleston was very nearly as large under the light tariff of 1789, as under the high one of 1842. But of this again.

"Commerce," said Dr. Ramsay, in 1808, "is of noble origin in South Carolina. Its first merchants were the Lords Proprietors, and such are the superior advantages of trading with Britain, that the Carolinians have been commercially connected with her nearly as much since as before the Revolution. They have a right of trade with all the world, but find it to their interest to trade principally with Britain. The ingenuity of her manufactures, the long credits her merchants are in the habit of giving, the facility of making remittances to her, as the purchaser of the great part of the native commodities of South Carolina, have all concurred to cement a commercial connection between the two countries. From the increased demand for the manufactures of Britain, by the increased inhabitants of Carolina, as a state, the latter is more profitable to the former, than she ever was when a province. Though the trade from South Carolina to Germany has greatly increased, that to the Mediterranean, to France, Netherlands, Spain, Madeira, and Russia, has also increased in the order in which these countries are respectively mentioned. Yet the surplus that remains for Great Britain, far exceeds all she ever derived from the same country, as her colony. It may be confidently asserted that the trade between the two countries for one single year of general peace, free from all interruption, would now be of greater value to Great Britain than all she derived from Carolina for the first half of her colonial existence. The merchants of Charleston do not seem fond of exploring new channels of commerce. There never was but one vessel fitted out for the East Indies; no voyages round the world, to Northwest America, to new or remote countries, have originated there."

In 1844, R. F. W. Allston held the following language to the Secretary of the Treasury:

"The average annual imports of the state for ten years, from 1832 to 1842, were $2,989,463, average annual exports for the same time, $10,291,735. The average annual imports for two years, 1843 and 1844, were $1,213,112; average annual exports same time, $7,597,045. In the year 1800 the produce of the state was exported from her own ports, at which were also received the return cargoes which paid for it. Then trade was brisk. All the interests of the state nourished in a high degree. Then the Imports at the port of Charleston yielded a revenue of $2,203,812; now the duties collected at the same port are $158,405. The great portion of our import business is done in the Northern ports where the chief revenue is collected on them."

REVENUES ON IMPORTS INTO SOUTH CAROLINA.

Year	Revenue	Year	Revenue	Year	Revenue
1800	$2,203,812	1815	$1,400,886	1830	$497,397
1801	2,257,100	1816	1,474,474	1831	505,050
1802	1,206,349	1817	1,145,677	1832	523,031
1803	867,125	1818	1,308,104	1833	401,634
1804	1,061,806	1819	813,829	1834	459,935
1805	1,303,841	1820	613,697	1835	453,391
1806	1,334,517	1821	595,317	1836	682,383
1807	1,352,778	1822	794,004	1837	469,058
1808	452,278	1823	765,899	1838	590,422
1809	537,042	1824	732,076	1839	653,188
1810	697,254	1825	661,327	1840	368,127
1811	386,355	1826	573,707	1841	449,535
1812	457,288	1827	592,025	1842	305,607
1813	272,705	1828	450,967	1843	158,405
1814	149,352	1829	490,750	1844	497,000

Average for first 28 years $928,951
Average for next 17 years 467,993
or a decline of about 100 per cent."

The imports of Charleston, from being nearly half the exports in 1820, are now about one-eighth.

The great exports of Charleston, and products of South Carolina, are cotton and rice. The state produces, of the latter article, three-fourths of the whole crop of the country.

COMMERCE OF CHARLESTON.

We are indebted for the following statistics to the Courier:

COMPARATIVE STATEMENT OF COTTON AND RICE, 1850–51.

Embracing Stock on hand, Receipts and Exports.

	1851			Same time last season		
	Cotton		Rice	Cotton		Rice
	S. I.	Up'd.	Bbls.	S. I.	Upl'd	Bbls.
Stock on hand, Sept. 13	1139	29659	1555	779	23027	1503
Received since August 22	21	1692	1086	—	—	—
" previously	16551	372317	135563	—	—	—
Total receipts	17711	403668	138204	17994	400714	147690
Exported since August 22	188	1509	636	—	—	—
" previously	15598	393174	124536	—	—	—
Total exports	15786	394683	125166	16437	365327	134417
On shipboard not cleared	810	3580	418	100	10265	938
City consumption since Sept. 1	—	—	11250	—	—	11300
Burnt	—	—	310	418	5728	418
Deduct from total receipts	16602	398263	137344	16955	381320	147073
Remaining on hand August 31	1109	5405	860	1039	19394	617

CHARLESTON, S. C.*—Its History, Trade, Commerce, Manufactures, Internal Improvements, Education, Health, Statistics, etc.—The late official publication, by the city council of Charleston, edited by Drs. Dawson and Dessausure, to which we have, on one or two occasions, referred, contains a mass of information, in regard to the population and resources of that city, never before collected, and of inestimable value. We shall present to our readers a digest of the important contents of the volume, regretting, at the same time, that its authors did not go more fully into those comparisons with other cities, and of epoch and epoch, which are among the chief sources of value in these census records.

TABLE OF POPULATION.

Years	White population	Increase or decrease: Total	Increase or decrease: Annual	Increase or decrease per cent.: Total	Increase or decrease per cent.: Annual
1790	8,089				
1800	9,630	1,541	154.1	19.17	1.01
1810	11,568	1,938	193.8	20.12	2.01
1820	10,653	505 dec.	50.5 dec	4.36 dec.	43 dec.
1830	12,828	2,175	217.5	20.41	2.04
1840	13,030	202	20.2	1.57	.15
1848	14,187	1,157	115.7	8.87	.88

SLAVES AND FREE COLORED.

Years	Population	Increase or decrease: Total	Increase or decrease: Annual	Increase or decrease per cent.: Total	Increase or decrease per cent.: Annual
1790	8,270				
1800	10,843	2,573	257.3	31.11	3.11
1810	13,143	2,300	230.	21.11	2.11
1820	14,127	984	98.4	7.48	.74
1830	17,461	3.334	333.4	23.60	2.36
1840	16,231	1.230 dec	123. dec.	7.04 dec.	.70 dec.
1848	12,264	3,967 dec.	396.7 dec.	24.44 dec.	2.44 dec.

The tables show that the largest portion of the population is native, being 58 per cent.; the proportion of foreigners slightly exceeds those born in the United States—but out of Charleston. In Boston, the native born are but 35.92 per cent., and of foreign birth, 23.70 per cent. In Charleston, 17 per cent. of foreign population were not *naturalized*. The white male population of the city has always exceeded the female, except in 1820 and 1830. The reverse is the case in the colored population. The productive class, or those between fifteen and sixty, in Charleston, is as favorably shown as in the other American cities, except Lowell.

The number of dwelling-houses in the city in 1820, was 2,336: in 1830, 2,481; in 1840, 2,804; in 1848, 3,147; of which 358 are stores wholly. The following table exhibits a state of things highly prosperous in Charleston:

* The reader will find, in the first eight volumes of the Review, a great many articles upon Charleston, prepared with much care.

DWELLING-HOUSES.

Class of Houses	Owned by occupant	Number of families	Not owned by occupant	Number of families	Total houses	Total families
Inhabited by one family	784	784	1,482	1,482	2,266	2,266
" " two "	65	130	235	470	300	600
" " three "	12	36	53	159	65	195
Inhabited by four families	0	0	26	104	26	104
" " five "	0	0	5	25	5	25
" " six "	1	6	1	6	2	12
" " eight "	0	0	1	8	1	8
" " ten "	0	0	1	10	1	10
Total	862	956	1,804	2,264	2,666	3,220

The water in Charleston is bad, which makes cisterns generally resorted to. In periods of drought, and when these fail, things are in no enviable state, and fierce conflagrations sometimes rule. An artesian well was attempted in 1823. In 1847 another was bored 323 feet, and abandoned for want of success. It has been re-commenced, but with what prospects we have not learned.

Classes of Population.—The following table exhibits the number and proportions of the different classes. The unmarried men, over fifteen, were 2,571, or 1 in 5.5 of the whole population; the married, 2,053, or 1 in 6.9; and the widowers 180, or 1 in 787. The unmarried women, over fifteen, were 1,760, or 1 in 80 of the whole population; the married 2,119, or 1 in 6.6; and the widowed 887, or 1 in 16:

Ages	Condition	MALES Number	In each 100	FEMALES Number	In each 100	BOTH Number	In each 100
Over 15,	unmarried	2,571	53.51	1,760	37.00	4,331	44.14
"	married	2,053	42.74	2,119	44.56	4,172	43.54
"	widowed	180	3.75	877	18.44	1,057	11.05
15 to 60,	unmarried	2,515	52.36	1,690	35.53	4,205	43.98
"	married	1,910	29,76	2,067	43.25	3,977	41.60
"	widowed	117	2.43	584	12.27	701	7.34
Over 60,	unmarried	56	1.16	70	1.47	126	1.31
"	married	143	2.97	52	1.09	195	2.09
"	widowed	63	1.31	293	6.13	356	3.72

The excess of widows over the widowers is very large, being 887 of the former to 180 of the latter. This, however, does not appear to be peculiar to Charleston, as will appear from Mr. Shattuck's census of Boston.

The tables of *paupers* show that the expense of supporting them has diminished from $100,707 34, for the five years ending 1823, to $38,739 37 in the same period, ending 1849, while the difference in the number has varied little. The labor of these people, employed upon cracking stones for street paving, almost pays the entire expense of their maintenance.

Education.—The list of free-school pupils is 394, amount expended for them, $3,900, average to scholar $10, average attendance five years. These are valuable schools, but they are scarcely adequate to the wants of the city. Private teachers, however, abound. There is an admirable high school, established in 1839, with an average of 130 to 150 scholars. It is endowed with $1,000 per annum, for a hundred years, by council. There are several public libraries in Charleston—the Apprentices', with a fine hall; the Mercantile, and the Charleston Library Society—the last named being the oldest and best.

The old *Charleston College*, for which, from all the associations of our younger years, we entertain an attachment which grows stronger as years advance, was chartered in 1791. For a long time it was but a grammar school. It was reorganized for collegiate purposes, and, having fallen through, was resuscitated in 1837, chiefly, if we remember rightly, through the exertions of Henry L. Pinckney. The common council have taken the institution in hand, and are chargeable with its expenses beyond tuition receipts, which excess has, hitherto, been quite considerable. It is now flourishing, with an able faculty, several new professorships—and the number of students gradually, but steadily, increasing. The annual rates are too high to diffuse the advantages of the college as widely as should be. They are $80 per annum, though the best schools in the city receive even more.*

Commerce.—There are lines of two steamships running to New-York, two to Philadelphia, and one to Havana; eleven sailing ships, two barques, eight brigs, and five schooners, to New-York, three barques and three brigs, to Boston; three barques, three brigs, and three schooners, to New-Orleans; two brigs and nine schooners, to Philadelphia; six schooners to Baltimore, etc. There are eighteen full branch pilots, eight second branch, and nine pilot boats. The tonnage from 1800 to 1805 was:

* This institution has, of late, been greatly improved; extensive and additional wings are about to be added to the main building, and the front to be adorned by a colonnade of Ionic order; another professorship has also been established, entitled the chair of "Intellectual Philosophy and Greek Literature." Its condition is most flourishing.

	Registered foreign trade	Coasting	Total
1800	43,732	7,480	51,212
1801	51,192	8,688	59,880
1802	31,354	8,653	40,007
1803	30,993	9,101	40,094
1804	41,869	8,814	50,683

That from 1843 to 1849, shows a woful falling off—but then the years above were of extraordinary commercial prosperity.

1843	10,013	11,135	21,148
1844	8,394	11,221	19,615
1845	8,516	11,420	19,963
1846	13,732	13,287	37,019
1847	14,992	13,667	28,659

There is a splendid dry dock, Gilbert's patent, owned by James Marsh. The largest vessels, cargoes and all, are taken up in two to three hours, and in four years 169 vessels have been served, 39 being ships and barques, and 42 brigs—charge forty cents the ton without cargo, eighty cents with cargo, ten cents per day per ton for use of dock, etc.

In sixteen years forty-one vessels have been wrecked on the coast of South Carolina and the Charleston bar, of which thirteen were ships and barques.

We have published, as our volumes will show, very full statistics of the exports of rice, cotton, and lumber, from Charleston. We give, however, at the end of this article, the exports of cotton and rice, drawn from the elaborate and laborious tables of the census.

The crops of *Sea Island Cotton* have decreased, from an average of about 35,000 bales in 1820, to an average of 22,000 or 23,000 during the last ten years. Of this, Charleston received about two-thirds, and Savannah the rest. The total rice crop of Carolina reaches an average of 130,000 tierces, of which Charleston receives all, except 1,000 or 1,500 tierces going to Georgetown. The Georgia crop averages 35,000, and the North Carolina 7,000 tierces.

The average importation of corn into Charleston is about 400,000 bushels, of which the railroad now brings one-half from the interior of the state. Importations of oats average 50,000 or 60,000 bushels. Average bales hay 20,000 to 25,000. *Imports* sugar, average hogsheads 8,000, tierces 200, barrels, 2,000, boxes 1,000; molasses, hogsheads 5,000, (of late,) barrels 5,000; average coffee, bags 28,000; salt, sacks about 100,000, and 20,000 bushels.

IMPORTS AND EXPORTS.

	Imports	Exports	Revenue
Year ending 30th June, 1844	$1,131,515	$7,433,282	$497,000
" " 1845	1,143,158	8,890,648	390,276
" " 1846	902,536	6,848,477	284,493
" " 1847	1,580,658	10,431,517	389,553
" " 1848	1,485,299	8,081,917	324,468

BANKS AND INSURANCE COMPANIES.

BANKS	Charter	CAPITAL	Par value of shares	Average rate per cent of dividends 15 years
Bank of South Carolina	1792	$1,000,000	$45	6.09
State bank	1802	1,000,000	100	5.90
Union bank	1810	1,000,000	50	5.82
Planters and Mechanics' bank	1810	1,000,000	25	7.17
Bank of the State of South Carolina	1812	1,123,357	*	..
Bank of Charleston	1835	3,160,800	100	7.44
South Western R. R. bank	1838	869,425	25	5.03
COMPANIES.				
Union Insurance company	1807	†450,000	60	11.11
Ch'n F. & M. Insurance company	1818	†300,000	60	13.15
South Carolina Railroad company	1827	3,112,500	75	4.25
Ch'n Insurance & Trust company	1837	500,000	50	11.68
South Carolina Insurance company	1846	250,000	25	..

* State bank, with no private stockholders. † These companies were broken up by the fire of 1838.

There are four steam cotton presses in Charleston, one cotton factory, six rice-mills, one sugar refinery, fourteen grist-mills, five engine factories, one brass foundry, five saw-mills, five ship yards, one turpentine distillery, &c.

Railroads.—The Hamburg, of 136 miles, was begun in 1831 and finished in 1833, being *then* the longest road in the world. The Louisville and Cincinnati road was chartered in 1837, but failing, the charter was united to that of the Hamburg road in 1844. Two branches have been added—to Columbia 68 miles, and to Camden 37 miles. Two other branch roads are in construction, to Charlotte, N. C., 109 miles, and to Greenville, S. C., over a hundred miles. The number of passengers on these roads has increased, from 26,649 in 1834, to 75,149 in 1848; the gross receipts, all sources, from $166,559 to $800,073; the bales of cotton, from 24,567 to 274,364.

Public Health, &c.—The statistics, here, are very full, and show the most laborious investigation. There are no tables of births, marriages, and deaths, except for a single year, 1848, as no registry system is provided for.

Climate.—"'A variation of eighty-three degrees between the heat and cold of different days of the same year, and of forty-six degrees in the different hours of the same day, in South Carolina, is to be found in its historical records.' This sudden change of forty-six degrees is recorded by Dr. Chalmers as occurring in 1751. In 1813, it is stated that there was a fall of forty-four degrees in a few hours. Dr. Shecut mentions a fall of thirty-three degrees in twelve hours, occurring in 1819. At the present time, however, such great variations are not so common. In Dr. Chalmers' tables for ten years, from 1750 to 1759, the mean annual temperature was sixty-eight degrees; for the period of ten years, from 1809 to 1818, Dr. Shecut gives the mean annual temperature at sixty degrees, or a difference of eight degrees in the mean annual temperature of the city in the space of sixty years. From 1840 to the present time, the mean annual temperature has been sixty-four degrees; showing an increase of the mean temperature of four degrees since 1819."

Yellow Fever.—The inhabitants were exempt from 1750 to 1799, except a few cases in 1753 and 1755. From 1792 to 1801, the westerly winds prevailed, and yellow fever raged every summer except two. In the next ten years, the fever was very fatal in years when this wind most prevailed.

"Yellow fever first prevailed as an epidemic in this city in 1699 or 1700; the exact date cannot now be ascertained. According to the account given of it by Dr. Hewet, it prevailed in that year very extensively, carried off a large number of the inhabitants, including many of the chief men of the province, and was called the plague. The same disease recurred in 1703, and caused as fearful a mortality as at its previous visitation. From this period, no mention is made of its occurrence until 1728, when it again occurred, and was then first called Yellow Fever, although from the description given of the two former epidemics, there can be no doubt of the identity of the last with the two preceding. In this year, also, it caused a great number of deaths. In the year 1732, it commenced its ravages in May, and continued until September or October; during the height of the epidemic, from eight to twelve whites were buried daily. It again appeared in 1739, 1745, and 1748, and is said to have raged as severely in these years as in 1732. The number of deaths which it caused in those years cannot now be ascertained. From 1748 to 1792, no epidemics of yellow fever occurred, although it is stated that in 1753 and 1755, a few sporadic cases were seen. In 1792 a new series of epidemics occurred; it raged in that year, in 1794, 1795, 1796, 1797, 1799, 1800, 1801, 1802, 1804, 1807. The deaths from it, in those years in which any account is to be found, were: in 1799, 239; in 1800, 184; in 1802, 96; in 1804, 148; and in 1807, 162.

"From 1807 to 1817, a period of ten years, there was nearly a complete exemption from epidemics of this disease. In this latter year it reappeared, and caused 270 deaths, of which a large number were children. In 1819, it again prevailed epidemically, causing 176 deaths. In the next year it prevailed slightly, but did not become epidemic. In 1824, another serious epidemic occurred, which carried off 231 persons. From this period, 1824, to 1838, no serious visitation of yellow fever occurred, although several cases of it existed in each of the years 1827, 1828, 1834, 1835. In 1838, the most serious epidemic occurred which has been known in the annals of Charleston, and causing the largest mortality which has ever resulted from the disease in this city. In 1839, it was again epidemic, but to a much less extent than during the former year. From 1839 to the present time, nine years have elapsed, during which the city has been exempt from the visitations of the scourge, and it is a question vitally important to her interests, whether this exemption is to continue, or whether it is but one of those pauses which have occurred at various intervals in her history. This problem can be solved by time only."*

Mortality.—The small-pox has prevailed epidemically several times in the early history of the city, and, in 1738 and 1769, most frightfully. The cholera also raged in 1836. The tables exhibit, in a very favorable light, the health of this city, among the white population, for all ages under fifteen; the proportional mortality being lower, at this age, than either Lowell or Surrey; the former accounted the healthiest city in the United States, the latter the healthiest in all England. Among the black population, the proportional mortality is higher at this age than in Lowell or Surrey, but lower than in the other cities named. In the whole population, under fifteen, the rate of mortality is lower than in any other city named except Surrey. For the ages from fifteen to sixty, however, the comparison is by no means favorable to Charleston; the proportional mortality of this class of her population, both white and black, being higher than in any of the cities named, except Liverpool. For the whole population above sixty, the proportional mortality is higher than in any of the other cities. In the white population, above sixty, the rate of mortality is rather lower than in Liverpool and London, but higher than in the other cities. The cause of this increased mortality in the higher ages is a question of interest. It cannot be the result of climate, for, in unhealthy climates, the mortality among children is always greater, in proportion, than among adults. The source of the greater proportional mortality of the middle ages, must, therefore, be sought for in the habits of the people, as this is the most fruitful cause of sickness and mortality to a population, the effects of climate excepted.

* The yellow fever has again paid a hurried visit to his old friends in Charleston, merely to show he has not forgotten them, 1849.—Ed.

EXPORTS OF COTTON FROM CHARLESTON.

	Exports—Bales Cotton. Foreign		Coastwise		Total Foreign and Coastwise		Total exports	Per cent. Product in 100 bales export		Receipts at Charleston		Stock on hand last day in year		Cotton Crop of the United States.		
	S. Island	Upland	S. Island	Upland	S. Island	Upland	Bales	Foreign	Coast	S. Island	Upland	S. Island	Upland	S. Island	Upland	Total Crop
1st Oct. 1819 to 30th Sept. 1820	..	..	..	..	21,484	125,475	146,959	—	—	—	—	—	—	*33,379	352,397	385,776
" 1820 " 1821	..	..	..	..	24,622	98,673	123,295	—	—	—	—	—	—	35,510	344,089	379,599
" 1821 " 1822	25,510	91,806	"	12,734	25,510	104,540	130,050	"	—	—	—	—	—	36,285	404,317	440,602
" 1822 " 1823	26,747	111,627	"	24,539	26,747	136,166	162,913	"	—	—	—	—	—	37,587	489,656	527,233
" 1823 " 1824	24,632	105,223	"	24,663	24,632	129,886	154,518	"	—	—	—	—	—	34,583	402,557	437,140
" 1824 " 1825	18,253	117,349	"	23,725	18,n53	141,074	159,327	"	—	—	—	—	—	26,016	*505,408	531,434
" 1825 " 1826	12,647	141,806	"	22,737	12,647	164,543	177,190	"	—	—	—	—	—	18,676	691,324	†710,000
" 1826 " 1827	31,828	152,885	"	46,290	31,828	199,175	231,203	"	—	—	—	—	—	46,377	890,623	937,000
" 1827 " 1828	22,750	99,518	"	25,369	22,750	124,887	147,637	"	—	—	—	—	—	34,876	677,124	712,000
" 1828 " 1829	23,047	161,531	"	29,450	23,047	190,981	214,028	86.24	13.76	—	—	—	—	36,776	820,968	857,744
" 1829 " 1830	16,536	165,636	1,172	26,084	17,708	191,720	209,428	86.99	13.01	17,515	191,490	1,704	2,204	27,287	949,558	976,845
" 1830 " 1831	18,597	148,127	1,720	36,854	20,317	184,981	205,298	81.22	18.78	19.516	190,495	903	7,648	27,903	1,010,945	1,038,848
" 1831 " 1832	16.941	165,687	1,302	35,346	18,243	201,033	219,276	83.29	16.71	17,800	195,912	400	2,527	27,907	959,570	987,477
" 1832 " 1833	21,787	143,166	1,102	32,925	22,889	176,091	198,980	82.90	17.10	22,609	175,319	380	1,755	35,054	1,035,384	1,070,438
" 1833 " 1834	17,149	197,959	1,539	40,924	18,688	238,883	257,571	83.51	16.49	19,435	234,888	1,151	2,639	28,144	1,177,250	1,205,394
" 1834 " 1835	15,180	145,649	932	42,358	16,112	188,007	204,119	78.79	21.21	15,265	189,386	301	4,018	24,651	1,229,677	1,254,328
" 1835 " 1836	15,131	180,361	729	47,669	15,860	228,030	243,890	80.16	19.84	16,534	228,548	915	3,298	25,551	1,335,174	1,360,725
" 1836 " 1837	12,152	154,103	269	33,138	12,421	187,241	199,662	83.27	16.73	16,768	188,469	5,179	3,547	22,225	1,400,705	1,442,930
" 1837 " 1838	16,712	229,755	405	56,865	17,117	286,620	303,737	81.14	18.86	12,862	286,866	924	2,245	17,689	1,783,808	1,801,497
" 1838 " 1839	9,975	148,285	537	53,917	10,512	202,202	212,714	74.40	25.60	11,756	203,977	2,168	3,994	16,292	1,344,240	1,360,532
" 1839 " 1840	19,310	228,191	459	59,719	19,769	287,910	307,679	80,44	19.56	18,353	287,317	752	3,401	26,555	2,151,280	2,177,835
" 1840 31st Aug. 1841	12,840	148,208	930	60,589	13,770	208,797	222,567	72.36	27.64	14,063	209,653	1,045	3,507	20,265	1,614,680	1,634,945
1st Sept. 1841 " 1842	14,119	184,705	341	70,442	14,460	255,147	269,607	73.75	26 25	13,731	255,439	316	3,659	20,461	1,663,113	1,683,574
" 1842 " 1843	16,351	257,035	681	78,523	17,032	335,558	352,590	77.54	22.46	17,666	339,233	950	7,334	24,291	2,354,584	2,378,875
" 1843 " 1844	15,043	166,290	1,148	123,023	16,191	289,313	305,504	59.36	40.64	15,680	296,142	439	13,097	19,138	2,011,271	2,030,409
" 1844 " 1845	20,905	288,870	423	111,698	21,328	400,568	421,896	73.42	26.58	21,499	401,221	610	10,269	28,472	2,366,031	2,394,503
" 1845 " 1846	19,527	160,233	476	87,841	20,000	248,074	268,077	67.06	32.94	20,696	145,211	1,303	7,406	20,201	2,070,336	2,100,537
" 1846 " 1847	10,869	179,467	698	156,064	11,567	335,531	347,098	54,84	45.16	14,457	353,587	4,193	25,462	21,105	1,757,546	1,778,651
" 1847 " 1848	15,345	183,501	685	98,061	16,030	281,562	297,592	66.82	33.18	13,506	269,908	1,669	12,416	21,725	2,325,909	2,247,634

* The upland crops of these first six years are the exports from the United States.
† From this period the total crops of the United States are those made up by the "New-York Shipping and Commercial List."

EXPORTS OF RICE FROM CHARLESTON.

	EXPORTS							PER CENTUM						
	Foreign		Coastwise		Foreign and Coastwise		T. exports of Tcs. & R. rice reduced to Tcs at 21 bushels	Proportion in 100 Tcs. exported		*Proportion in 100 Tierces of Clean and Rough exported.		Receipts at Charleston.	† Stock on the last day of the year.	Rice Crops
	Tierces	Bushels R. Rice	Tierces	Bushels R. Rice	Tierces	Bushels R. Rice	Tierces.	In Tierces	In R. R. reduc'n to Tcs at 22 bush.	Foreign.	Coast.	Tierces.	Tierces	Tierces
1st Oct. 1819 to 30th Sept., 1820					64,153		64,153							88,820
“ 1820 “ 1821					75,366		75,366					98,336		115,591
“ 1821 “ 1822	67,131		11,030	“	78,161		78,161			“				100,907
“ 1822 “ 1823	68,014		12,384	“	80,398		80,398			“		90,222		103,252
“ 1823 “ 1824	79,830	106,407	17,273	“	97,103	106,407	102,170			“				125,973
“ 1824 “ 1825	60,750	66,853	19,653	“	89,403	66,853	92,587			“				110,222
“ 1825 “ 1826	76,534	128,750	12,528	“	89,062	128,750	95,193			“				117,248
“ 1826 “ 1827	89,181	170,007	11,266	“	100,447	170,007	108,643			“				132,811
“ 1827 “ 1828	96,618	198,617	15,013		111,631	198,617	121,089			“				145,678
“ 1828 “ 1829	80,620	248,724	31,567		112,187	248,724	124.031	90.45	9.55	74.55	25.45			155,730
“ 1829 “ 1830	78,262	171,834	29,058		107,320	171,834	115,503	92.92	7.08	74.84	25.16	123,101	2,240	145,943
“ 1830 “ 1831	62,176	196,881	30,206		92,382	196,881	101,757	90.79	9.21	70.32	29.68	110,072	1,540	135,586
“ 1831 “ 1832	67,018	268,164	38,212		105,230	268,164	117,999	89.18	10.82	67.62	32.38	127,392	1,891	151,925
“ 1832 “ 1833	75,440	315,202	47,254		122,694	315,202	137,703	89.10	10.90	65.68	34.32	143,473	1,547	178,255
“ 1833 “ 1834	65,715	363,793	31,099	13,719	96,814	377,512	114,791	84.34	15.66	72.34	27.66	118,762	2,084	145,371
“ 1834 “ 1835	60,401	317,594	40,760	41,788	101,161	359,382	118,275	85.53	14.47	63.86	36.14	124,250	1,859	151,000
“ 1835 “ 1836	62,019	356,752	46,438	30,307	108,457	387,059	126,888	85.47	14.53	62.27	37.73	133,533	1,923	168,851
“ 1836 “ 1837	49,384	512,808	39,710	22,999	89,094	535,807	114,608	77.74	22.26	64.40	35.60	119,917	524	150,958
“ 1837 “ 1838	35,493	336,442	29,913	19,399	65,406	355,841	82,351	79.42	20.58	62.55	37.45	90,385	1,936	119,341
“ 1838 “ 1830	41,222	470,312	35,202	22,950	76,424	493,262	99,912	76.49	23.51	63.67	36.33	106,001	913	136,583
“ 1839 “ 1840	48,248	431,506	31,591		79,839	431,506	100,387	79.53	20.47	68.53	31.47	107,108	835	140,243
“ 1840 “ 31st Aug. 1841	53,571	455,592	25,232	15,489	78,803	471,081	101,236	77.84	22.16	74.35	25.65	107,052	452	140,421
1st Sept. 1841 “ 1842	54,516	445,685	34,038	2,870	88,554	448,555	109,914	80.57	19.43	68.91	31.09	117,994	1,332	150,422
“ 1842 “ 1843	57,574	294,018	57,701	6,519	115,217	300,537	129,586	88.96	11.04	55,23	44.77	136,733	1,177	175,049
“ 1843 “ 1844	59,964	483,595	43,265	6,027	103,229	488,622	126,497	81.61	18.39	65.61	34.39	135,561	2,591	176,293
“ 1844 “ 1845	43,351	561,409	40,970		84,321	561,409	111,054	75.93	24.07	63.11	36.89	117,939	1,496	160,597
“ 1845 “ 1846	38,038	346,230	45,666	8,909	83,704	355,139	100,615	83.19	16.81	54.19	45.81	111,407	2,688	156,928
“ 1846 “ 1847	65,970	489,363	48,211	9,395	114,181	498,758	137,931	82.78	17.22	64.72	35.28	146,260	1,017	192,462
“ 1847 “ 1848	44,410	420,419	51,500	1,910	95,960	422,379	116,023	82.66	17.34	55.53	44.47	126,673	915	170,771

* This per centage is calculated on the exports only, the city consumption having been thrown out.
† Exclusive of the stock of Rough Rice at the Mills.

CHARLESTON COMMERCE, 1851.

STATEMENT OF COTTON AND RICE AT CHARLESTON.

Exported to	From Sept 1, 1850, to Aug 31, 1851 S I	Upl'd	Rice	From Sept 1, 1849, to Aug. 21, 1850 S I	Upl'd	Rice
Liverpool	11,244	175,320	4,853	11,858	137,559	8,181
Scotland	11	7,341	1	13	5,549	2
Other British ports	—	10,054	9,260	—	10,644	11,375
Total Great Britain	11,255	192,715	14,114	11,871	153,752	19,558
Havre	2,321	21,034	2,918	2,495	29,695	4,577
Marseilles	—	—	—	—	—	—
Other French ports	—	2,253	2,209	—	892	2,831
Total France	2,321	23,287	5,127	2,495	30,587	7,408
Holland	—	814	2,401	—	2,068	3,268
Belgium	—	3,299	2,500	—	4,130	5,322
North of Europe	—	9,046	17,234	—	2,746	21,571
Total N. of Europe	—	13,159	22,135	—	8,944	30,341
South of Europe	—	85,281	697	—	19,922	260
West Indies, &c.	—	—	19,010	—	—	16,416
Total foreign ports	13,576	254,442	61,083	14,366	213,205	73,982
Boston	10	16,774	8,161	30	22,690	8,182
Rhode Island, &c.	19	2,435	20	18	4,556	157
New-York	2,181	102,004	29,317	2,023	99,863	30,022
Philadelphia	—	11,138	5,848	—	15,564	5,133
Baltimore and Norfolk	—	7,890	5,203	—	9,236	4,405
New-Orleans, &c	—	—	15,284	—	—	12,284
Other U. S. ports	—	—	250	—	152	250
Total coastwise	2,210	140,241	64,083	2,071	152,122	60,434
Grand total	15,786	394,683	125,166	16,437	365,327	134,417

COMPARATIVE EXPORT OF ROUGH RICE AND LUMBER, FROM THE PORT OF CHARLESTON.

Exported to	From Sept 1, 1850, to Aug. 31, 1851 R. Rice, bush	Lumber, ft.	From Sept 1, 1849, to Aug 31, 1851 R. Rice, bush	Lumber, feet
Liverpool	57,902	8,000	42,824	345.059
London	165,015	—	202,960	—
Other British ports	100	68.434	—	124,944
Total to Great Britain	223,017	76,434	245,784	470,003
Havre	75	28,893	2,071	48,422
Bordeaux	21,147	332,725	26,032	15,970
Other French ports	—	4,316	—	—
Total France	21,222	365,725	28,103	64,392
North of Europe	138,133	995,901	254,017	1,328,408
South of Europe	—	654,816	—	1,083,636
West Indies, &c	—	1,536,967	—	1,813,402
Total foreign ports	382,372	3,629,733	527,904	4,759,841
Boston	40,204	647,312	3,733	209,005
Rhode Island, &c	—	2,462,758	—	2,413,760
New-York	21,147	1,033,234	50,195	750,500
Philadelphia	—	5,017,334	—	5,918,304
Baltimore and Norfolk	—	3,321,060	—	1,283,407
Other United States ports	—	2,023,800	—	3,372,168
Total coastwise	61,351	14,505,498	53'928	13,947,144
Grand total	443,723	18,135,231	581,832	18,706,985

CINCINNATI TRADE.

IMPORTS INTO CINCINNATI FOR FIVE YEARS, COMMENCING SEPTEMBER 1ST, AND ENDING AUGUST 31ST, EACH YEAR:

ARTICLES.	1846–'47.	1847–'48.	1848–'49.	1849–'50.	1850–'51
Apples, green, barrels	26,992	28,674	22,109	6,445	16,934
Beef, barrels	186	659	348	801	1,101
Beef, tierces	5	—	27	15	18
Bagging, pieces	5,561	79,228	2,094	324	—
Barley, bushels	79,390	165,528	87,460	137,925	111,257
Beans, bushels	11,688	8,757	3,067	5,565	31,037

IMPORTS INTO CINCINNATI—*continued.*

ARTICLES.	1846-'47.	1847-'48.	1848-'49.	1849-'50.	1850-'51.
Butter, barrels	6,345	6,625	7,721	3,674	8,259
Butter, firkins and kegs	7,090	6,405	7,999	7,487	11,043
Blooms, tons	2,017	2,203	9,519	2,545	2,727
Bran, &c , sacks	14,594	1,941	21,995	49,075	50,976
Candles, boxes	207	133	414	718	697
Corn, bushels	896,258	361,315	344,810	649,227	489,195
Corn, meal	56,775	29,542	5,504	3,688	5,508
Cider, barrels	3,261	2,289	4,346	453	1,047
Cheese, casks	483	164	281	97	74
Cheese, boxes	120,301	138,800	143,265	165,940	205,444
Cotton, bales	12,528	13,476	9,058	8,551	7,168
Coffee, sacks	59,337	80,242	74,961	67,170	91,177
Codfish, drums	292	311	515	464	441
Cooperage, pieces	186,186	179,946	147,352	201,711	146,691
Eggs, boxes and barrels	561	4,035	4,504	2,041	5,956
Flour, barrels	512,597	151,518	447,844	231,859	482,772
Feathers, sacks	2,768	4,467	4,908	3,432	2,858
Fish, sund. barrels	16,836	19,215	18,146	14,527	19,826
Fish, kegs and kits	2,142	725	1,059	1,290	2,694
Fruit, dried, bushels	82,871	27,464	38,317	11,802	41,824
Grease, barrels	482	585	878	1,169	876
Glass, boxes	16,002	20,281	33,868	34,945	37,099
Glassware, packages	17,121	15,025	19,209	25,712	28,619
Hemp, bundles and bales	26,678	15,349	11,161	12,062	13,254
Hides, loose	24,376	33,745	23,766	30,280	8,132
Hides, green, lbs	7,513	10,829	22,774	14,181	25,424
Hay, bales	7,049	8,036	12,751	14,452	12,691
Herring, boxes	1,003	4,191	2,060	3,516	3,832
Hogs, head	38,774	49,847	52,176	60,902	111,485
Hops, bales	1,001	[illegible]	[illegible]	700	756
Iron and Steel, pieces	188,215	197,120	187,864	186,832	225,039
Iron and Steel, bundles	33,463	34,213	29,889	55,168	66,809
Iron and Steel, tons	1,685	827	1,768	2,019	2,570
Lead, pigs	43,675	39,607	45,544	49,197	59,413
Lard, barrels	21,991	37,978	28,514	34,173	36,848
Lard, kegs	22,722	41,714	48,187	63,327	31,087
Leather, bundles	5,069	6,579	3,975	9,620	10,397
Lemons, boxes	2,185	3,068	4,181	4,183	3,379
Lime, barrels	32,016	63,364	61,278	56,482	57,537
Liquors, hhds. and pipes	3,369	3,115	4,476	5,802	1,465
Merchandise and sundry pks	263,940	381,537	68,582	308,523	175,138
" " tons	7,941	7,308	837	4,540	3,370
Molasses, barrels	27,218	51,001	52,591	54,003	61,490
Malt, bushels	12,562	7,999	29,910	41,982	21,356
Nails, kegs	54,918	59,983	55,893	83,073	83,761
Oil, barrels	5,663	6,618	7,427	5,049	6,764
Oranges, boxes and bbls	4,137	5,007	4,317	6,819	9,302
Oakum, bales	1,100	1,486	1,423	1,799	1,739
Oats, bushels	372,127	194,557	185,733	191,924	164,238
Oil Cake, pounds	2,225,988	2,811,793	1,767,421	27,870	194,000
Pork and Bacon, hhds	5,476	4,420	6,178	7,564	6,277
Pork and Bacon tierces	124	140	465	2,358	1,183
Pork and Bacon, barrels	40,581	69,828	44,267	43,227	31,595
Pork, in bulk, pounds	8,027,399	9,643,063	9,249,380	1,325,756	14,631,330
Potatoes, barrels	15,829	22,439	17,269	3,898	19,649
Pig Metal, tons	15,868	21,145	15,612	17,211	19,110
Pimento and Pepper, bags	3,180	3,455	1,257	2,558	2,027
Rye, bushels	41,016	24,336	22,233	23,397	44,308
Rosin, &c., barrels	5,004	11,668	3,298	12,349	12,511
Raisins, boxes	11,990	22,795	14,927	11,936	15,648
Rope, Twine, &c	8,003	7,806	3,950	3,061	2,007
Rice, tierces	1,145	2,494	3,365	3,556	4,783
Sugar, hogsheads	16,649	27,153	22,685	26,760	29,808
Sugar, barrels	7,196	11,175	7,575	13,005	18,584
Sugar, boxes	5,117	2,928	1,847	2,467	3,612
Seed, flax, barrels	25,753	32,060	22,859	15,570	20,319
Seed, grass	4,964	4,968	5,929	4,432	4,104
Seed, hemp	290	214	510	314	58
Salt, sacks	56,292	65,265	76,985	110,650	50,474
Salt, barrels	124,366	94,722	76,496	114,107	79,358
Shot, kegs	1,118	809	818	1,447	1,567
Tea, packages	5,443	2,931	7,412	9,802	7,821
Tobacco, hogsheads	6,200	4,051	3,471	3,213	3,701
Tobacco, bales	822	1,229	1,311	887	1,697
Tobacco, boxes and kegs	9,241	14,815	12,463	17,772	19,945
Tallow, barrels	1,748	2,473	1,829	1,225	3,682
Wines, bbls. and qr. cks	4,006	2,251	2,663	6,874	3,401
Wines, baskets and boxes	1,419	2,272	2,101	4,296	5,060
Wheat, bushels	590,809	570,813	385,388	322,699	388,660
Wool, bales	2,960	1,943	1,686	1,277	1,866
Whiskey, barrels	184,639	170,436	165,419	186,678	244,044
Cotton Yarn, packages	9,271	6,403	5,562	3,494	5,577
Cotton, bales	146,541	288,095	262,893	174,885	124,594

EXPORTS FROM CINCINNATI FOR TWO YEARS.

ARTICLES.	1849-'50.	1850-'51.
Apples, green, barrels	3,519	8,064
Alcohol, barrels	3,302	5,038
Beef, barrels	7,558	19,937
Beef, tierces	6,625	9,356
Beans, barrels	2,469	1,832
Brooms, dozen	7,355	8,735
Butter, barrels	964	3,258
Butter, firkins and kegs	24,393	36,185
Bran, &c., sacks	4,322	5,789
Bagging, pieces	9,353	8,212
Corn, sacks	57,248	26,137
Corn Meal, barrels	1,179	2,148
Cheese, casks	106	25
Cheese, boxes	86,902	121,755
Candles, boxes	67,447	113,412
Cattle, head	30	440
Cotton, bales	1,896	5,132
Coffee, sacks	22,030	38,158
Cooperage, pieces	73,637	63,804
Eggs, barrels	4,246	7,258
Flour, barrels	98,908	390,131
Feathers, sacks	5,380	4,095
Fruit, dried, bushels	1,850	17,480
Grease, barrels	7,597	4,426
Grass, seed, barrels	2,528	2,830
Horses, head	468	599
Hay, bales	504	638
Hemp, bales	1,164	3,112
Hides, lbs.	62,865	48,079
Hides, number	11,225	12,459
Iron, pieces	54,075	108,255
Iron, bundles	36,245	44,110
Iron, tons	5,767	9,776
Lard, barrels	38,192	30,391
Lard, kegs	170,167	71,300
Lard Oil, barrels	16,984	26,110
Linseed Oil, barrels	4,879	7,821
Molasses, barrels	25,878	25,098
Oil Cake, tons	743	963
Oats, sacks	5,023	11,707
Potatoes, barrels	5,283	19,823
Pork and Bacon, hhds	23,529	30,200
Pork and Bacon, tcs	22,477	20,762
Pork and Bacon, bbls	193,581	122,086
Pork and Bacon, bulk, lbs	13,448	2,974
Pork, boxes	2,310,699	4,753,953
Rope, &c., packages	3,151	6,272
Soap, boxes	17,443	21,553
Sheep, head	—	460
Sugar, hogsheads	9,650	13,000
Salt, barrels	29,509	28,585
Salt, sacks	8,301	7,144
Seed, flax, bbls	333	443
Sundry mdze., pkgs	615,641	349,181
Sundry mdze., tons	11,109	10,350
Sundry liquors, bbls	11,798	19,297
Sundry man'fac's, pcs	56,810	22,103
Sundry produce, pkgs	10,327	13,958
Starch, boxes	9,491	14,109
Tallow	4,311	5,927
Tobacco, kegs and boxes	6,905	18,345
Tobacco, hogsheads	4,847	2,856
Tobacco, bales	77	160
Vinegar, barrels	2,404	3,756
Whiskey, barrels	179,540	231,324
Wool, bales	2,156	2,725
Wool, pounds	16,841	4,836
White Lead, kegs	40,294	50,857
Pieces, Castings	54,399	36,266
Pieces, Castings, tons	2,385	1,121

VALUE OF SPECIFIC ARTICLES IMPORTED INTO CINCINNATI FROM SEPTEMBER 1, 1850, TO SEPTEMBER 1, 1851, AND THE CORRESPONDING TIME LAST SEASON.

	1859-'51.			
ARTICLES	Amount	Average price	Total value	Last season
Apples, barrels	16,934	$1 00	$16,934	$11,278
Beef, barrels	1,101	11 00	11,010	7,209
Barley, bushels	111,257	90	100,131	103,443
Butter, barrels	8,259	12	99,198	99,198
Butter, kegs	110,431	10	110,430	59,869
Blooms, tons	2,727	60 00	105,020	152,700
Corn, bushels	489,195	40	195,662	246,706
Cheese, boxes	205,444	2 00	410,888	398,206
Cotton, bales	7,168	40 00	286,720	384,795
Coffee, sacks	91,177	10	91,177	1,310,633
Flour, barrels	482,772	3 50	1,689,702	1,101,329
Hemp, bales	13,254	15 00	198,810	168,868
Hogs, head	334,000	7 50	2,505,000	2,460,000
Lead, pigs	59,413	3 00	207,945	167,208
Lard, barrels	36,889	17 50	64,557	444,246
Lard, kegs	31,087	3 50	108,804	151,984
Molasses, barrels	61,490	12 00	733,880	594,033
Oats, bushels	163,258	35	11,140	57,577
Bacon, hogsheads	6,277	50 00	313,850	249,579
Bacon, tierces	1,183	25 00	29,575	28,296
Pork, barrels	31,595	12 00	37,940	381,350
Pork, pounds	14,637,330	5½	804,723	497,156
Pig Metal, tons	16,110	25 00	402,950	447,486
Rice, tierces	4,783	25 00	119,575	85,344
Sugar, hogsheads	29,808	60 00	1,708,480	1,364,763
Sugar, barrels	18,584	14 00	260,176	195,075
Sugar, boxes	3,612	30 00	108,360	57,208
Wheat, bushels	588,660	70	272,062	302,756
Whiskey, barrels	244,047	8 00	1,952,376	1,680,102

The total value of the above this year is $13,146,348, against $12,668,379 last year.

DESTINATION OF SPECIFIED ARTICLES EXPORTED FROM THE PORT OF CINCINNATI.

COMMODITIES	To New-Orleans	To other down-river ports	To up-river ports	By Canals and Railways	By Flatboats
Beef, barrels	19,319	68	314	236	1,611
Beef, tierces	8,677	8	657	14	96
Butter, barrels	1,850	867	2	539	—
Butter, firkins and kegs	35,200	959	15	8	315
Corn, sacks	15,672	3,519	156	790	—

DESTINATION OF SPECIFIED ARTICLES EXPORTED FROM THE PORT OF CINCINNATI—*continued.*

COMMODITIES	To New-Orleans	To other down-river ports	To up-river ports	By Canals and Railways	By Flatboat
Cheese	69,258	48,432	2,165	1,900	920
Candles, boxes	76,245	20,272	10,695	6,195	522
Cotton, bales	—	10	3,182	1,940	—
Coffee, sacks	10	12,439	7,853	17,856	—
Flour, barrels	281,609	95,943	7,719	4,859	95,877
Iron, pieces	6,608	54,894	6,634	40,119	—
Iron, bundles	1,503	25,281	2,182	15,144	—
Iron, tons	64	1,341	219	8,152	117
Lard, barrels	22,854	117	3,277	4,143	1,821
Lard, kegs	56,380	5,358	5,739	2,823	1,587
Lard oil, barrels	13,617	1,547	3,726	7,220	—
Linseed oil	4,443	1,362	1,042	974	—
Molasses	33	2,665	12,711	9,589	—
Pork, hogsheads	19,044	1,313	8,809	1,054	1,312
Pork, tierces	11,341	18	8,759	644	42
Pork, barrels	112,622	1,055	3,801	4,608	3,781
Pork, pounds	1,345,860	755,860	1,559,280	1,092,953	525,820
Soap, boxes	9,425	6,440	3,600	2,068	375
Sugar, hogsheads	—	1,426	4,378	7,196	—
Whiskey, barrels	140,661	56,164	31,231	3,268	17,980

AVERAGE PRICE NEW-ORLEANS SUGAR AND MOLASSES, RIO COFFEE, CORN, FLOUR, AND WHEAT, AT CINCINNATI.

MONTHS	N. O. Molasses	N. O. Sugar	Rio Coffee	Corn	Flour	Wheat
September	cents 31¼	7	10½	40	$3 55	70
October	35	6¾	12	44	3 57	70
November	33	5⅞	11	33	3 54	68½
December	29¾	6	11½	37	3 68	75
January	28½	6⅛	15⅝	39½	3 67	76
February	29¾	6	12	39⅛	3 52	71¾
March	32	5½	11⅝	37	3 43	67
April	33⅛	6	11⅛	37	3 48	71
May	34	6¼	10¼	37	3 47	70½
June	34	6⅛	9⅝	37	3 35	70¾
July	33	6¼	9½	37	3 15	63
August	33	6	9½	37	3 20	69

CHICAGO INTERNAL IMPROVEMENT CONVENTION—1847.—The following propositions, prepared by the Hon. John C. Spencer, of New-York, were adopted by the Convention:

"1. That the Constitution of the United States was framed by practical men, for practical purposes, declared in the preamble —'to provide for the common defence, to promote the general welfare, and to secure the blessings of liberty;' and was mainly designed to create a government, whose functions should be adequate to the protection of the common interests of all the states, or of two or more of them, which could not be maintained by the action of the separate states. That in strict accordance with this object, the revenues derived from commerce were surrendered to the General Government, with the express understanding that they should be applied to the promotion of those common interests.

"2. That among these common interests and objects, were 1st, Foreign commerce, to the regulation of which, the powers of the states, severally, were confessedly inadequate; and 2d, internal trade and navigation, wherever the concurrence of two or more states was necessary to its prosecution, or where the expense of its maintenance should be equally borne by two or more states, and where, of course, those states must necessarily have a voice in its regulation; and hence resulted the constitutional grant of power to Congress, 'to regulate commerce with foreign nations, and among the states.'

"3. That being thus possessed both of the means and of the power, which were denied to the states respectively, Congress became obligated by every consideration of good faith and common justice, to cherish and increase both the kinds of commerce thus committed to its care, by expanding and extending the means of conducting them, and of affording them all those facilities, and that protection which the States individually would have afforded, had the revenues and authority been left to them.

"4. That this obligation has ever been recognized from the foundation of the government, and has been fulfilled partially, by erecting lighthouses, building piers for harbors, breakwaters and sea walls, removing obstructions in rivers, and providing other facilities for the commerce carried on from the ports on the Atlantic coast; and the same obligations have been fulfilled to a much less extent, in providing similar facilities for 'commerce among the States;' and that the principle has been most emphatically acknowledged to embrace the western lakes and rivers, by appropriations for numerous lighthouses upon them, which appropriations have never been questioned in Congress, as wanting in constitutional authority.

"5. That thus, by a series of acts which have received the sanction of the people of the United States, and of every department of the Federal Government, under all administrations, the common understanding of the intent and objects of the framers of the Constitution, in granting to Congress the power to regulate commerce, has been confirmed by the people, and this understanding has become as much a part of that instrument, as any one of its most explicit provisions.

"6. That the power 'to regulate commerce with foreign nations, and among the States, and with the Indian tribes,' is, on its face, so palpably applicable in its whole extent, to each of the subjects enumerated equally, and in the same manner, as to render any attempt to make it more explicit, idle, and futile; and that those who admit the rightful application of the power to foreign commerce, by facilitating and protecting its operations, by improving harbors, and clearing out navigable rivers, cannot consistently deny that it authorizes similar facilities to 'commerce among the states.'

"7. That 'foreign commerce' itself is dependent upon internal trade, for the distribution of its freights, and for the means of paying for them; so that whatever improves the one, advances the other; and they are so inseparable, that they should be regarded as one. That an export from the American shore to a British port in Canada, is as much foreign commerce as if it had been carried directly to Liverpool; and that an exportation to Liverpool neither gains nor loses any of the characteristics of foreign commerce, by the directness or circuity of the route, whether it passes through a custom-house on the British side of the St. Lawrence, or descends through that river and its connecting canals to the ocean, or whether it passes along the artificial communications and nataral streams of any of the states to the Atlantic.

"8. That the General Government, by extending its jurisdiction over the lakes and navigable rivers, subjecting them to the same laws which prevail on the ocean, and on its bays and ports, not only for the purpose of revenue, but to give security to life and property, by the regulation of steamboats, has precluded itself from denying that jurisdiction for any other legitimate regulation of commerce. If it has power to control and restrain, it must have power to protect, assist, and facilitate; and if it denies the jurisdiction in the one mode of action, it must renounce it in the other.

"9. That in consequence of the peculiar dangers of the navigation of the lakes, arising from the want of harbors for shelter, and of the Western rivers, from snags and other obstructions, there are no parts of the United States more emphatically demanding the prompt and continued care of the government, to diminish those dangers, and to protect the property and life exposed to them; and that any one who can regard provisions for those purposes as sectional, local, and not national, must be wanting in information as to the extent of the commerce carried on upon those lakes and rivers, and of the amount of teeming population occupied or interested in that navigation.

"10. That having regard to relative population, and to the extent of commerce, the appropriations heretofore made for the interior rivers and lakes, and the streams connecting them with the ocean, have not been in a just and fair proportion to those made for the benefit of the ports, harbors, and navigable rivers of the Atlantic ports; and that the time has arrived when this injustice should be corrected in the only mode in which it can be done, by the united, determined, and persevering efforts of those whose rights have been overlooked.

"11. That independent of this right to protection of 'commerce among the States,' the right of 'common defence,' guarantied by the Constitution, entitles those citizens inhabiting the country bordering upon the interior lakes and rivers, to such safe and convenient harbors as may afford shelter to a navy, whenever it shall be rendered necessary by hostilities with our neighbors; and that the construction of such harbors cannot safely be delayed to the time which will demand their immediate use.

"12. That the argument most commonly urged against appropriations to protect 'commerce among the States,' and to defend the inhabitants of the frontiers, that they invite sectional combinations to insure success to many unworthy objects, is founded on a practical distrust of the republican principles of our government, and of the capacity of the people to select competent and honest representatives. That it may be urged with equal force againt legis lation upon any other subject involving various and extensive interests. That a just appreciation of the rights and interests of all our fellow-citizens, in every quarter of the Union, disclaiming selfish and local purposes, will lead intelligent representatives to such a distribution of the means in the treasury, upon a system of moderation and ultimate equality, as will in time meet the most urgent wants of all, and prevent those jealousies and suspicions which threaten the most serious dangers to our confederacy.

"13. That we are utterly incapable of perceiving the difference between a harbor for shelter and a harbor for commerce, and suppose that a mole or pier which will afford safe anchorage and protection to a vessel against a storm, must necessarily improve such harbor, and adapt it to commercial purposes.

"14. That the revenues derived from imports on foreign goods belong to all the people; and the public lands being the common heritage of all our citizens, so long as all these resources continue, the imposition of any special burden on any portion of the people, to obtain the means of accomplishing objects equally within the duty and the competency of the General Government, would be unjust and oppressive.

"15. That we disavow all and every attempt to connect the cause of internal trade and of 'commerce among the States,' with the fortunes of any political party, but that we seek to place that cause upon such immutable principles of truth, justice, and and constitutional duty, as shall command the respect of all parties, and the deference of all candidates for public favor."

CALIFORNIA, NEW-MEXICO, AND THE PASSAGE BETWEEN THE ATLANTIC AND PACIFIC OCEANS.—Having adjusted the great questions of Oregon and California, so long distracting the popular mind, the American people are now setting themselves down, after the usual fashion, to count up their gains and their losses, and strike the balance-sheet. The "pen" with them is "as powerful as the sword," and that is *irresistible.*

Having a thousand miles of coast upon the Pacific, and three times as much upon the Atlantic, subject to our sway, we are naturally solicitous, by some process or other, to narrow the distance between the oceans, and cause them to mingle their commerce, if not their waters, by a readier passage than that through the storms of tbe southern seas, or over many a granite mountain for wearisome months, through the heart of the continent itself.

In Yankee ingenuity there is that which is illimitable, and it is baffled by no combinations or difficulties whatever. That it can discourse at a thousand or five thousand miles with the same facility and rapidity as across a chamber, and without an extra effort of breath, is a mere trifle. Our children shall throw away the telegraph as a plaything and a bauble, with the same contempt that Jupiter's lazy, inert log was trampled upon, in days of yore, by the revellers, at first impressed with such awe at its presence.

There is, perhaps, no better mode of accounting for the extraordinary fact, that, despite of all the glorious achievements of science within the past few years, the moon still continues at the provoking and inapproachable distance of some two hundred and odd thousand miles, than this, that the same science has almost irresistibly demonstrated this satellite "uninhabited and uninhabitable." Had our telescopes, on the contrary, exhibited green fields, and fertile plains, and pleasant water-courses, and broad cultivated acres, and a population evidently in want of cotton goods, clocks, ice, razor-strops, and penknives, some of our indefatigable traders had made explorations thitherward long ago, and ten to one by a new-fangled process in galvanism, magnetism, or any other *ism,* as yet undreamed of in philosophy, because unneeded—discovered a *gap* somewhere, in space, through which a pedlar at least could find his way, and bring back to his countrymen the gladsome news, that their celestial highnesses were willing and anxious for a treaty of reciprocal amity and commerce! A colony, a revolution, annexation, become then but matters of course!

But we have not the time for a lengthened paper, though the subject might be regarded inexhaustible; and we have already fallen into a vein which ill comports with the gravity of the present occasion.

Our object is, to present a few pages upon the proposed connection between the oceans, in addition to what we have so elaborately published in previous volumes of the Review, and also, to furnish the latest and most reliable information in regard to the character, resources, etc., of New-Mexico and California.

We begin by introducing the letter of Lieut. Maury to the Hon. John C. Calhoun, which the writer kindly furnished us some time ago, but which has been delayed for various reasons until now. It is too important, however, to be omitted altogether.

NATIONAL OBSERVATORY,
March 29, 1848.

DEAR SIR:—I have the pleasure of sending you, as you requested I would do, a chart showing the relative distances to Monterey and the Columbia river from some of the principal points on the Atlantic coast. I have added such other information as, in my judgment, is calculated to throw light on the interesting subject, as to the best route across the country for reaching, by railroad, the Pacific coast of the United States.

I am clearly of the opinion that a railroad, through the heart of the country to the most convenient point of our Pacific coast, is greatly more in accordance with the true interests of the United States, than any route by canal or railroad that can be constructed across the narrow neck of land between North and South America.

A chief value of a rail-road or canal consists in its collateral advantages, so to speak, by which I mean the advantages which the country and the people, in the vicinity of the improvements, derive from it; such as the increased value of land and property of various kinds.

The increased value which such property has derived from the rail-roads and canals in the United states, exceeds, I suppose, the original cost of the works themselves. This, therefore, may be considered a permanent value attached to the property of our fellow-citizens, which no reverse of fortune, no enactment of laws, nothing but a destruction of the works themselves, can ever destroy.

A canal between the two continents would not pass through the United States territory, and consequently the citizens of the United States would derive no such collateral advantages from it, nor her statesmen the prerogative of taxing such increased value for the revenues of the country; but they would derive them abundantly from a rail-road running through the heart of the Union, and connecting its Atlantic with its Pacific ports.

In this fact is included one of the many reasons which induced me to favor a rail-road across the country, in preference to a canal out of the country, for connecting the two oceans.

The question, therefore, is: Where shall the rail-road begin on the Atlantic, and where shall it end on the Pacific?

Unfortunately, the present state of topographical information as to the several routes that have been proposed for reaching the Pacific by rail-road, is not sufficient to afford a satisfactory reply to this question. I propose to consider it, therefore, only in a geographical and commercial point of view, leaving the final decision of the question to hydrographers and engineers, after they shall have made the necessary examinations and surveys.

If we continue to increase our tonnage for the next two or three years, at the rate of increase for the last two or three, the shipping of the United States will then exceed that of Great Britain, and the commercial supremacy will be ours, so far, at least, as the business of fetching and carrying is concerned.

If you will examine the accompanying chart, you will observe that I have drawn, *geographically*, the dividing line of commerce between England and the Atlantic ports of the United States. Any point in this line is equi-distant from us and from England; consequently England is nearer to all places, including the ports of Europe, the Mediterranean, and of Africa north of the equator, which are to the east of that dividing line, and *geographically* speaking, therefore, can meet us on that side of it with advantage; whereas, all places on this side of that line, including her American colonies, the West Indies, and the States of Central and South America as far as the equator, are, *geographically*, more favorably situated for commerce with the United States than with England.

Now it so happens, that this dividing line crosses the equator at what may be considered the great thoroughfare of vessels trading to the south of it, whether they be English or American, or whether they be bound around Cape Horn or the Cape of Good Hope. The winds are such as to make this the common and best place of crossing for all such vessels.

Consequently, *geographically* speaking, the ports of Brazil, of the Pacific Ocean, China, and the East Indies, are as convenient to the Atlantic states of the Union as they are to England; and the merchandise of the two countries may be said to meet there precisely on equal terms.

Hitherto, the great channels of trade have led to Europe, yet, notwithstanding that the position of England is much more central than that of the United States with regard to Europe, (the vessels of the former making, in a week, voyages which it takes ours months to accomplish,) we have, under these disadvantages, never ceased to gain on our competitor, and are now about to pass her, with our ships, in the commercial race.

The coasts of Oregon and California are just beginning to feel the energy of American enterprise, and are fast filling up with our citizens. Where they go, there commerce will come. The peopling of these coasts will greatly enlarge the commercial limits of the United States; extending them from lines into a greatly elongated ellipse with its conjugate centres, one on the Pacific, the other on the Atlantic.

Having determined what port on the Pacific offers the most advantages for the commercial focus there, it will then be easy to project the major axis of this new commercial curve; for the line across the country which joins these two centres will show, geographically, the best route for a rail-road between the two oceans.

The shortest distance between two places that are not on the equator, or in the same longitude, is the arc of a great circle included between them; and this arc appears on the chart as a curve. I have drawn such curves on the chart, and called them great circle routes, because they show the route by which a traveler may go from place to place, by accomplishing the smallest number of miles possible, supposing he could follow a line through the air.

You will observe that the great circle, which shows the shortest navigable route between Chili, all the ports of Peru, Ecuador, Central America and Mexico, passes so near to Monterey, that if a steamer bound from Chili to Shanghai, in China, were to pursue the shortest route which it is possible to go, she would make Cape St. Lucas, in Lower California, and might touch at San Diego, Monterey, or San Francisco, by going less than 100 miles out of her way.

But if the point of departure were Panama, then it would be 1,000 miles nearer to take the great circle via California, than to follow the straight compass course by way of the Sandwich Islands.

Monterey or San Francisco, therefore, may be regarded as the great half-way house on the commercial road between Pacific America and the Indies; and this route as the commercial circle of the Pacific Ocean.

It will be observed that Astoria, in Oregon, occupies by no means such a central position with regard to the commerce of the world.

The line, commencing on the Pacific coast midway between Monterey and the mouth of the Columbia river, and drawn to Philadelphia, I have called the dividing line of travel between Monterey and the mouth of the Columbia. It is so drawn through the country, that any given point on it is equi-distant from those two places, so that a traveler who starts from any point to the south of this line is nearer to Monterey; but if he start from a point to the north of it, he is nearer to the mouth of the Columbia.

TABLE OF DISTANCES FROM THE ENGLISH CHANNEL.

To Boston (shortest navigable distance for steamers)	2,670 miles.
Boston, via Albany and the lakes, to Chicago	1,000
Chicago, by an air line, to Columbia river	1,650
Total	5,320
From English Channel, via Philadelphia and Baltimore, to Monterey	5,100
English Channel to Charleston, S. C., (by water)	3,360
Charleston to Memphis (rail-road)	510
Memphis to Monterey (air line)	1,500
Total	5,370

It thus appears that Monterey is quite as central to the European travel as is the mouth of the Columbia, with this advantage, however: the lakes are frozen up half the year, when the Columbia route is impassable; whereas, if the travel from Europe come as far south as Philadelphia, Monterey then is the most convenient port. In truth, Chicago is quite as near to Monterey as to the mouth of the Columbia.

While Monterey is, therefore, altogether as convenient a halting-place as the Columbia river for travelers from any part of Europe to China, it has decidedly the advantage with regard to the travel from three-fourths of the states of the Union, from Brazil, the West Indies, and even from the Pacific ports of South America.

Were a rail-road constructed from Memphis to Monterey, passengers from Chili, Peru, &c., on arriving at Panama, would, instead of continuing on in the Pacific to California, save two or three days by crossing over to Chagres, taking a steamer thence to New-Orleans, and up the river to the Memphis and Monterey rail-road and so across the country.

For this reason, therefore, the route to China, via Charleston or New-Orleans, to Memphis, and thence to Monterey, would, for all the travel to the south of us, be hundreds of miles nearer than the route up to Chicago and thence to the Columbia river; nearer for most of the states of the confederacy, and as near for the rest.

The harbors of San Francisco and Monterey are good, and easy of ingress and egress. The mouth of the Columbia is difficult both of ingress and egress. In 1846, Lieutenant Howison, one of the most accomplished seamen in the navy, was wrecked in attempting to get to sea from that river. He chartered another vessel for himself and crew to get to Monterey, 600 miles; and though in sight of the open sea, and drawing but eight feet of water, he was detained there sixty-two days, waiting for an opportunity to cross the bar. He was wrecked where the Exploring Expedition found water enough to float a 74.*

Vessels in distress off the mouth of the Columbia river, have been baffled in their attempts to enter, and finally, after sundry trials, have found themselves compelled to run down to the ports of California, where they are sure of getting an anchorage.

* "The Cadboro' anchored in Baker's Bay (mouth of the Columbia river), November 17, 1846, where we remained pent up by adverse winds and a turbulent sea on the bar until the 18th January. Her master, an old seaman, had been navigating this coast and river for the last eighteen years, and his vessel drew but eight feet of water; yet in this long interval of sixty two days he could find no opportunity of getting to sea safely. This is, in itself, a commentary upon the dangerous character of the navigation of the mouth of the Columbia."—*Report of Lieut. Niel M. Howison, U. S. N., House of Reps., 30th Congress, 1st Session, Mis. No.* 29.

"I lay at anchor in Baker's Bay, some three hundred yards inside the Cape, from November 17, 1846, until January 18, 1847; and although we were unfortunately destitute of barometer and thermometer, we had a good opportunity of observing, during these two winter months, the wind and weather. The heavens were almost always overcast; the wind would spring up moderately at east, haul, within twenty-four hours, to south-east, increasing in force, and attended with rain. It would continue at this point some twenty hours, and shift suddenly in a hail storm to the south-west; whence, hauling westwardly and blowing heavy, accompanied with hail and sleet, it would give us a continuance of bad weather for three or four days, and force the enormous Pacific swell to break upon the shore with terrific violence, tossing its spray over the tops of the rocks, more than two hundred feet high. A day of moderate weather, with the wind south-east, might succeed this; but before the sea on the bar would have sufficiently gone down to render it passable, a renewal of the south-easter would begin, and go on around the compass as before."—*Ib.*

The railroad to the Pacific should terminate at that port which presents the most advantages for our future dockyard and great naval station on the Pacific. That port is not the Columbia river, for the reasons just stated. Moreover, the mouth of that river will be overlooked by the English from the excellent ports of Vancouver's Island and the Straits of Fuca. While our crippled vessels should be standing off and on, waiting to get in, they would fall an easy prey to inferior British cruizers, which, in safety, could watch their movements from the Straits of Fuca.*

Monterey and San Francisco are beyond the reach of such surveillance; moreover, they are in a better climate, and are midway our line of the Pacific coast. They are in a most commanding position. During the naval operations in the Pacific against Mexico, our men-of-war beat out of the harbor of San Francisco in a gale of wind, so easy is it of ingress and egress.

The harbors of California are convenient for, and are even now visited by, our whalemen. Columbia river is not. There is a fleet in the Pacific of 300 vessels, engaged in this business, manned by six or eight thousand of the best seamen of America.

In money and in kind they expend, annually, among the islands and ports of the Pacific, not less than one million of dollars. The facilities which a railroad to California, would offer in enabling them to overhaul, refit, and communicate with friends and owners in New-England, would attract this whole fleet there; and this vast amount of money would be expended in our own country and among our own citizens, instead of being disbursed broadcast, as it now is, over that wide ocean. As long as there are breakers and a bar at the mouth of the Columbia, there can be in that harbor no attraction for our whale ships.

The coast of California is a favorite place of resort for the whale. They come there to breed.

The chart has two small circles of a radius of 3,000 miles each: one drawn from the mouth of the Columbia as a centre, the other from Monterey. The latter, from its facilities of ingress or egress, is in a geographical position to command the trade with all the places within these circles, except perhaps the ports of British and Russian America. For six months in the year, the difficulties in crossing the bar of the Columbia would place these places nearer to the ports of California by days, if not by weeks and months.

The chart also exhibits the geographical dividing lines of travel and of commerce. The broken line, through the Island of Japan, shows the dividing line of travel from London, by the overland route, to India, and from London through the United States, by railroad from Charleston, via Memphis, to Monterey. The nearest route to London, from all places to the east of this line, is through the United States; but from all places to the west of it, the nearest route is through the Red Sea, and across the Isthmus of Suez. These lines are all drawn without regard to time. They are mere geographical lines, intended to represent distance in *nautical* miles. Were the railroad across the country completed, and the lines drawn with regard to time, they might probably be extended a thousand miles or two further to the westward; for much of the distance to be overcome by the overland route is by water, and there is much less railroad traveling by that route than there would be by a railroad across the United States.

A passenger can accomplish as many miles in two days by railroad, as he can in a week by water.

The other broken line shows the dividing line of travel between London, via the overland route, and this part of the country, via the Atlantic and Pacific Rail-road.

The continuous and most westerly line shows the dividing line of commerce between England, on the one hand, and our Pacific ports on the other, supposing the English ships to pass, as they have to do, the Cape of Good Hope.

This line exhibits many interesting facts, consequences, and significations. Among them, it shows that the United States are now in a position which will soon enable them, *geographically*, to command the trade of the entire east; and that, commercially speaking, our country is in the centre of the people of the earth, and occupies a position for trade and traffic with them which no nation that ever existed has held.

Hitherto, in all parts of the world, except Europe and the West Indies, the ships of the two great competitors on the ocean have met on barely equal terms. An American and a British ship met in India, China, New-Holland, the Islands of the Pacific, or the ports of South America. One was owned in London or Liverpool, the other in some one of our Atlantic ports. To reach home, they both had to pursue the same route and sail the same number of knots. But now that

* "A very snug harbor has, within a few years, been sounded out, and taken possession of by the Hudson's Bay Company, on the south-eastern part of Vancouver's Island. They have named it Victoria, and is destined to become the most important British seaport contiguous to our territory. Eighteen feet water can be carried into its inmost recesses, which is a fine large basin. There is, besides, pretty good anchorage for frigates outside the basin. The Company are making this their principal shipping port; depositing, by means of small craft, during the summer, all their furs and other articles for the English market at this place, which is safe for their large ships to enter during the winter season. They no longer permit them to come into the Columbia between November and March." —*Lieut. Howison's Report.*

Oregon and California are *Americanized,* all of these ports are nearer; and the chief among them, as Bombay, Calcutta, Singapore, the ports of China, Japan, New-Holland, Australia, Polynesia, and the islands of the east, many thousand miles nearer to the United States than to England.

TABLE OF DISTANCES BY SEA.

	To England	To Ports of California
From Persian Gulf	11,300	10,400
" Bombay	11,500	9,800
" Calcutta	12,200	9,300
" Singapore	12,300	7,400
" Canton	13,700	6,100
" Shanghai	14,400	5,400
" Jeddo	15,200	4,500
" New-Guinea	14,000	6,000
" N. W. point of N. Holland	11,800	7,800
" N. E. " "	13,500	6,900
" New-Zealand	13,500	5,600

From Memphis, a centre point in the immense valley of the West, and one on the great natural and national highway from the Gulf to the Lakes, the distance, via Panama and the Sandwich Islands, (the usual route,) to China, is 11,700 miles; but by the proposed rail-road to Monterey and the great circle, thence to China, the distance is but 6,900 miles.

A rail-road across the country, in this direction, would, therefore, it may be observed, shorten the present and nearest practicable route to China near 5,000 miles; it would place us before the commercial marts of *six hundred millions* of people, and enable us, geographically, to command them. Open the needful channels, unbridle commerce, leave it to the guidance of free trade, and who shall tell the commercial destiny of this country?

Rightly and wisely profiting by the advantages which are now opening to us, how long will it be before our sturdy rival will cease to be regarded as such, and when we shall have no competitor for maritime supremacy among nations?

From Monterey to Shanghai is 5,400 miles; midway between the , two, and right on the way-side, are the Fox or Eleutian Islands, with good harbors, where a depot of coal may be made for a line of steamers, for the establishment of which, I understand, Mr. King, the Chairman of the Committee on Naval Affairs, is preparing a bill.

Coal has been found on the surface, at San Diego and San Francisco, and Vancouver's* or Quadra Island. Formosa and the Islands of Japan abound with the most excellent qualities of this mineral. Supposing the vessels to be put upon this line to perform not better than the "Great Western," and that the rail-road from Charleston, on the Atlantic, be extended to Monterey, on the Pacific, you might then drink tea in Charleston within the same month in which the leaf was gathered in China.

The passage from Shanghai, allowing a day for coaling at the Fox Islands, can be made in twenty-six days from Monterey, and thence to Charleston by railroad, at the English rate of forty miles an hour, in less than three days.

Hydrographical surveys, and topographical reconnoissances may show San Diego or San Francisco to be the best terminus for the great railway. I have spoken of Monterey merely from its *geographical* position. San Francisco is a better harbor, and has, in its rear, a more fertile country. But whichever of the three be adopted, the selection will not alter the point I have been endeavoring to establish.

A railroad from Charleston to Tennessee is already completed. Memphis is above the yellow fever region of the Mississippi Valley. It is on the great river, and in a central position. A road thence would cross the head-waters of the Arkansas, the Rio Grande and the Colorado. It would facilitate the overland trade with Mexico, and perhaps be the principal channel of foreign commerce for her people.

Large amounts of bullion are annually shipped from Western Mexico, in British ships of war, for England. Owing to the route, and the uncertainties as to the time when a vessel of war may come for it, it may be assumed that this bullion does not reach England for eight or ten months after it is taken from the mines; during all of which time it is of course idle. Moreover, it pays a freight of two per cent. to the British officer and Greenwich Hospital, for conveying it in one of Her Majesty's vessels. Now, all this bullion would come, as fast as it was taken from the mines, over this road, and would perhaps be coined in our own mints instead of those of Europe.

This route, as compared with one to the Columbia river, is most convenient for a large portion of the citizens of Pennsylvania, all of Delaware, Maryland, Ohio, Indiana, Illinois, Missouri, and of all the states to the south of them; and, considering the present routes, quite as convenient to the people of New England as is the proposed route to the Columbia.

Besides, this last will be obstructed by snow and ice in the winter; the other never. Therefore, California offers the most convenient terminus for the commerce and business of all the states, and the most desirable one for the purposes of the general government.

There is a line of steamers already in operation from Valparaiso, Lima, Guayaquil, and the intermediate ports to Panama.

Under Mr. King's bill of the last Congress,

* Excellent coal has been found here. It is used by the English steamers, and is put on board at a mere nominal price.

contracts have been made for another line to connect with this, to run to the mouth of the Columbia, and touch at Monterey or San Francisco. From Panama to China, via Monterey, is 8,600 miles, and from Panama. by water, to Monterey, is 3,200 miles. Thus it will be observed, that the steam communication has already been provided for more than one-third of the distance from Panama to China.

A railroad to Monterey, and a line of steamers thence to China, would place our citizens only half the distance that they now are, and without such rail-road must continue to be, from Japan and the Celestial Empire.

The most equitable location of a great national railway, to be constructed for the convenience of all the states, from the banks of the Mississippi to the shores of the Pacific, would be along the line which divides the United States territory west of the Mississippi into two equal parts. The main trunk would then be in the most favorable position for receiving lateral branches from all of the states hereafter to be formed out of that territory. But the ports on the Pacific, and the character of the route, do not admit of such a location.

I have endeavored, as you suggested, to determine the geographical centre of the present *states* of the confederacy.

By one method, Memphis is as near that centre as may be; by the other, it falls in Kentucky.

A line drawn diagonally across the states, from the north-east corner of Maine, to the south-west corner of Texas, intersects another from southern Florida to the north-west corner of Iowa, a few miles from Memphis; and Memphis is just about half way between the mouth of the Mississippi and the head of the lakes, counting from Lake Michigan.

But if we take two other lines: one dividing the territory comprehended within the states from north to south, the other from east to west, they will cross each other in Kentucky, and about midway, a line between Nashville and Louisville. These are the two geographical centres of the states of the Union.

Now, if we take a point about midway between Memphis and Louisville, we shall have what, for practical purposes, may be called the territorial centre of the *states* of the Union. I have marked this point A, on the chart. It is near the mouth of the Cumberland. The centre of population is about the same parallel, but considerably to the eastward.

The great circle from this territorial centre to San Francisco, crosses the Mississippi just above the mouth of the Ohio, and crosses the edge of the Kanzas valley. The distance of San Francisco from the Mississippi, at this point, is 1,560 *nautical*, or 1,760 statute miles.

Were the country equally favorable, this would certainly be the most advantageous, because it would be the most convenient route for all the states. It will be the business of the topographer, the engineer, and the hydrographer on the Pacific, to determine the most feasible line, and the precise location of this great national highway.

There is, however, another light in which this subject should be considered. A rail-road to the Pacific is eminently a military road; and in the selection of a route, and a terminus for it, an eye should be had to its bearings as well to the common defence as to the general welfare.

Vancouver's Island abounds in excellent harbors. Coal of superior quality has recently been found there, cropping out in great quantities on the surface. The English steamers on that coast use it, and pronounce it excellent. The *Cormorant* procured it at four shillings per ton, and took specimens of it to England. It is so accessible, that the Indians mine it, and deliver it on board the Hudson's Bay Company's steamers, at a mere nominal charge.

That island is in a position which enables the power that holds it to command the Straits of Fuca and the mouth of the Columbia more effectually, even, than Cuba, in the hands of a rival, would control the mouths of the Mississippi. By treaty, Vancouver's Island belongs to the English. In view of these facts, no one with a military eye in his head would think of fixing the terminus of the great national highway, through which we aim to control the trade of the East, under the very guns of our rival. Vancouver's Island enables England to command both the Straits of Fuca and the mouth of the Columbia.

The mouth of that river can never become a naval station of much importance to us. It is too near Vancouver's Island, which is to be the Portsmouth of England in the Pacific. Its approaches are exposed, and difficult—its egress dangerous. It is too far from the ports of California and the coast to be defended.

San Francisco will probably be the centre of our naval operations there. It is in a central, and therefore commanding position. It offers many facilities which Astoria does not. Suppose Cuba belonged to Great Britain, and we were just beginning with a system of national defences for our Atlantic coast: it would be quite as reasonable to expect our ships from Pensacola to pass Havana and protect the coasts of New-York, in a war with England, as it would be to expect them to come from the Columbia River, overlooked, as it will be, by the English from Vancouver's Island, and give security to the ports and coasts of California.

Our Pacific coast is about one thousand miles in length. San Francisco is midway between its southern boundary and Vancouver's Island, and, in a military point of view, is in a position to command eight hundred of the thousand miles; whereas, Puget's Sound and Columbia River, owing to the close proximity of Vancouver's Island and the dangerous bars of the river, are incapable of commanding so much as their three marine leagues each.

Respectfully, &c., M. F. MAURY.

Hon. JOHN C. CALHOUN,
U. S. Senate Chamber.

CALIFORNIA, ETC.—Col. Fremont, the indefatigable explorer and chivalrous soldier, whose resignation from the army is a subject of so much regret, has lately published a map of this region, accompanied with a sketch of the country, possessing the liveliest interest. The pamphlet is but the pioneer of a more extensive and elaborate work upon the same subject. We design a few extracts, &c.

Colonel Fremont begins with the Sierra, a part of the great mountain range which extends from the peninsula of California to Russian America, with no other gaps than those where the Columbia and Frazer's Rivers find their passage. "That part of the range which traverses Alta California, is called the *Sierra Nevada*, dividing California into two parts, and exercises a decided influence on the climate, soil, and productions of each."

East of the Sierra Nevada, and between it and the Rocky Mountains, is an extraordinary region, termed the *Great Basin*. "It is a singular feature: a basin of some five hundred miles diameter every way, between four and five thousand feet above the level of the sea, shut in all around by mountains, with its own system of lakes and rivers, and having no connection whatever with the sea Partly arid, and sparsely inhabited, the general character of the *Great Basin* is that of a desert, but with great exceptions, there being many parts of it very fit for the residence of a civilized people; and of these parts, the Mormons have lately established themselves in one of the largest and best. Mountain is the predominating structure of the interior of the Basin, with plains between—the mountains wooded and watered, the plains arid and sterile." In this *Great Basin* are situated the vast *Salt* and *Utah Lakes*, besides numerous smaller bodies of water. The *Humboldt River*, within the same limits, is the most important.

"This river possesses qualities which, in the progress of events, may give it both value and fame. It lies on the line of travel to California and Oregon, and is the best route now known through the Great Basin, and the one traveled by emigrants. Its direction, nearly east and west, is the right course for that travel. It furnishes a level, unobstructed way for nearly three hundred miles, and a continuous supply of the indispensable articles of water, wood, and grass. Its head is towards the Great Salt Lake, and consequently towards the Mormon settlement, which must become a point in the line of emigration to California and the lower Columbia. Its termination is within fifty miles of the base of the Sierra Nevada, and opposite the Salmon Trout River Pass—a pass only seven thousand two hundred feet above the level of the sea, and less than half that above the level of the basin, and leading into the valley of the Sacramento, some forty miles north of Nueva Helvetia. These properties give to this river a prospective value in future communications with the Pacific Ocean; and the profile view on the north of the map shows the elevations of the present traveling route, of which it is a part, from the South Pass, in the Rocky Mountains, to the bay of San Francisco."

The winter of 1843, '44, within the basin, says Col. Fremont, was remarkable for the same open, pleasant weather, rarely interrupted by rain or snow. In fact, there is nothing in the climate of this great interior region, elevated as it is, and surrounded and traversed by snowy mountains, to prevent civilized man from making it his home, and finding in its arable parts the means of a comfortable subsistence, and this the Mormons will probably soon prove, in the parts about the Great Salt Lake. The progress of their settlement is already great. On the first of April, of the present year, they had three thousand acres in wheat; seven saw and grist-mills; seven hundred houses in a fortified enclosure of sixty acres, and stock and other accompaniments of a flourishing settlement.

To the westward of the *Sierra Nevada*, and reaching to the sea, is another region of California, considered by Col. Fremont. Its breadth varies between 150 and 200 miles, and the area contained is 100,000 square miles.

West of the Sierra Nevada, and between that mountain and the sea, is the second grand division of California, and the only part to which the name applies in the current language of the country. It is the occupied and inhabited part, and so different in character—so divided by the mountain wall of the Sierra from the Great Basin above—as to constitute a region to itself, with a structure and configuration—a soil, climate, and productions—of its own; and as northern Persia may be referred to as some type of the former, so may Italy be referred to as some point of comparison for the latter. North and south, this region embraces about ten degrees of latitude—from 32°, where it touches the peninsula of California, to 42°, where it bounds on Oregon. East and west, from the Sierra Nevada to the sea, it will average, in the middle parts, 150 miles; in the northern parts, 200—giving an area of above 100,000 square miles. Looking westward from the summit of the Sierra, the main feature presented is the long, low, broad valley of the Joaquin and Sacramento rivers—the two valleys forming one—five hundred miles long, and fifty broad, lying along the base of the Sierra, and bounded to the west by the low coast range of mountains, which separates it from the sea. Long dark lines of timber indicate the streams. and bright spots mark the intervening plains, Lateral ranges, parallel to the Sierra Nevada and the coast, make the structure of the country, and break it into a surface of valleys and mountains—the valleys a few hundred, and the mountains two to four thousand feet above the sea. These form greater masses, and become more elevated in the north, where some peaks, as the Shastl, enter the regions of perpetual snow. Stretched along the mild coast of the Pacific, with a general elevation in its plains and valleys of only a few hundred feet above the level of the sea—and backed by the long and lofty wall of the Sierra—mildness and geniality may be assumed as the characteristic of its climate. The inhabitant of corresponding latitudes on the Atlantic side of this continent, can with difficulty conceive of the soft air and southern productions under the same latitudes in the maritime region of Upper California. The singular beauty and purity of the sky in the south of this region is characterised by Humboldt as a rare phenomenon, and all travelers realize the truth of his description.

The present condition of the country affords but slight data for forming correct opinions of the agricultural capacity and fertility of the soil. Vancouver found, at the mission of San Buenaventura, in 1792, latitude 34° 16′, apples, pears, plums, figs, oranges, grapes, peaches, and pomegranates, growing together with the plaintain, banana, cocoa-nut, sugar-cane and indigo, all yielding fruit in abundance and of excellent quality. Humboldt mentions the olive-oil of California as equal to that of Andalusia; and the wine like that of the Canary Islands. At present, but little remains of the high and various cultivation which had been attained at the missions. Under the mild and paternal administration of the "*Fathers*," the docile character of the Indians was made available for labor, and thousands were employed in the fields, the orchards, and the vineyards. At present, but little of this former cultivation is seen. The fertile valleys are overgrown with wild mustard; vineyards and olive orchards, decayed and neglected, are among the remaining vestiges; only in some places do we see the evidences of what the country is capable. At San Buenaventura, we found the olive trees, in January, bending under the weight of neglected fruit; and the mission of San Luis Obispo (latitude 35°) is still distinguished for the excellence of its olives, considered finer and larger than those of the Mediterranean.

The productions of the south differ from those of the north and of the middle. Grapes, olives, and Indian corn have been its staples, with many assimilated fruits and grains. Tobacco has been recently introduced; and the uniform summer heat which follows the wet season, and is uninterrupted by rain, would make the southern country well adapted to cotton. Wheat is the first product of the north, where it always constituted the principal cultivation of the missions. This promises to be the grain-growing region of California. The moisture of the coast seems particularly suited to the potato, and to the vegetables common to the United States, which grow to an extraordinary size.

Perhaps few parts of the world can produce in such perfection so great a variety of fruits and grains as the large and various region enclosing the bay of San Francisco and drained by its waters. A view of the map will show that region and its great extent, comprehending the entire valleys of the Sacramento and San Joaquin, and the whole western slope of the Sierra Nevada. General phrases fail to give precise ideas, and I have recourse to the notes in my journal to show its climate and productions by the test of the thermometer and the state of the vegetable kingdom.

Valleys of the Sacramento and San Joaquin.—These valleys are one, discriminated only by the names of the rivers which traverse it. It is a single valley—a single geographical formation—near 500 miles long, lying at the western base of the Sierra Nevada, and between it and the coast range of mountains, and stretching across the head of the bay of San Francisco, with which a *delta* of 25 miles connects it. The two rivers, San Joaquin and Sacramento, rise at opposite ends of this long valley, receive numerous streams, many of them bold rivers, from the Sierra Nevada, become themselves navigable rivers, flow toward each other, meet half way, and enter the bay of San Francisco together, in the region of tide-water, making a continuous water line from one end to the other.

The valley of the San Joaquin is about 300 miles long and 60 broad, between the slopes of the coast mountain and the Sierra Nevada, with a general elevation of only a few hundred feet above the level of the sea. It presents a variety of soil, from dry and unproductive to well-watered and luxuriantly fertile. The eastern (which is the fertile) side of the valley is intersected with numerous streams, forming large and very beautiful bottoms of fertile land, wooded principally with white oaks, (*quercus longiglanda*, Torr. and Frem.) in open groves of handsome trees, often five or six feet in diameter, and sixty to eighty feet high. Only the larger streams, which are fifty to one hundred and fifty yards wide, and drain the upper parts of the mountains, pass entirely across the valley, forming the *Tulare* Lakes and the San Joaquin river, which, in the rainy season, make a continuous stream from the head of the valley to the bay. The *foot hills* of the Sierra Nevada, which limit the valley, make a woodland country, diversified with undulating grounds and pretty valleys, and watered with numerous small streams which reach only a few miles beyond the hills, the springs which supply them not being copious enough to carry them across the plains. These afford many advantageous spots for farms, making sometimes large bottoms of rich, moist land. The rolling surface of the hills presents sunny exposures, sheltered from the winds, and having a highly favorable climate and suitable soil, are considered to be well adapted to the cultivation of the grape, and will probably become the principal vine-growing region of California. The uplands bordering the valleys of the large streams, are usually wooded with evergreen oaks; and the intervening plains are timbered with groves or belts of evergreen and white oaks among prairie and open land. The surface of the valley consists of level plains along the Tulare Lakes and San Joaquin river, changing into undulating and rolling ground nearer the foot hills of the mountains.

Bay of San Francisco and Dependent Country.—The Bay of San Francisco has been celebrated, from the time of its first discovery, as one of the finest in the world, and is justly entitled to that character even under the seaman's view of a mere harbor. But when all the accessory advantages which belong to it—fertile and picturesque dependent country; mildness and salubrity of climate; connection with the great interior valley of the Sacramento and San Joaquin; its vast resources for ship timber, grain and cattle—when these advantages are taken into the account, with its geographical position on the line of communication with Asia, it rises into an importance far above that of a mere harbor, and deserves a particular notice in any account of maritime California. Its latitudinal position is that of Lisbon; its climate is that of southern Italy; settlements upon it for more than half a century attest its healthiness; bold shores and mountains give it grandeur; the extent and fertility of its dependent country give it great resources for agriculture, commerce, and population.

The bay of San Francisco is separated from the sea by low mountain ranges. Looking from the peaks of the Sierra Nevada, the coast mountains present an apparently continuous line, with only a single gap, resembling a mountain pass. This is the entrance to the great bay, and is the only water communication from the coast to the interior country. Approaching from the sea, the coast presents a bold outline. On the south, the bordering mountains come down in a narrow ridge of broken hills, terminating in a precipitous point, against which the sea breaks heavily. On the northern side, the mountain presents a bold promontory, rising in a few miles to a height of two or three thousand feet. Between these points is the strait—about one mile broad, in the narrowest part, and five miles long from the sea to the bay. Passing through this gate,* the bay opens to the right and left, extending in each direction about 35 miles, having a total length of more than 70, and a coast of about 275 miles. It is divided, by straits and projecting points into three separate bays, of which the northern two are called San Pablo and Suisoon bays. Within, the view presented is of a mountainous country, the bay resembling an interior lake of deep water lying between parallel ranges of mountains. Islands, which have the bold character of shores—some mere masses of rock, and others grass covered, rising to the height of three and eight hundred feet—break its surface, and add to its picturesque appearance. Directly fronting the entrance, mountains a few miles from the shore rise about 2,000 feet above the water, crowned by a forest of the lofty *cypress*, which is visible from the sea, and makes a conspicuous landmark for vessels entering the bay. Behind, the rugged peak of *Mount Diavolo*, nearly 4,000 feet high (3,770,) overlooks the surrounding country of the bay and San Joaquin. The immediate shore of the bay derives, from its proximate and opposite relation to the sea, the name of *contra costa* (counter-coast, or opposite coast). It presents a varied character of rugged and broken hills, rolling and undulating land, and rich alluvial shores backed by fertile and wooded ranges, suitable for towns, villages, and farms, with which it is beginning to be dotted. A low alluvial bottom land, several miles in breadth, with occasional open woods of oak, borders the foot of the mountains around the southern arm of the bay, terminating on a breadth of twenty miles in the fertile valley of St. Joseph, a narrow plain of rich soil, lying between ranges from two to three thousand feet high. The valley is openly wooded with groves of oak, free from underbrush, and after the spring rains covered with grass. Taken in connection with the valley of San Juan, with which it forms a continuous plain, it is fifty-five miles long and one to twenty broad, opening into smaller valleys among the hills. At the head of the bay it is twenty miles broad, and about the same at the southern end, where the soil is beautifully fertile, covered in summer with four or five varieties of wild clover several feet high. In many places it is overgrown with wild mustard, growing ten or twelve feet high, in almost impenetrable fields, through which roads are made like lanes. On both sides the mountains are fertile, wooded, or

* Called *Crysopylæ* (Golden gate) on the map, on the same principle that the harbor of *Byzantium* (Constantinople afterwards) was called *Chrysoceras* (golden horn). The form of the harbor, and its advantages for commerce, (and that before it became an entrepot of eastern commerce,) suggested the name to the Greek founders of Byzantium. The form of the entrance into the Bay of San Francisco, and its advantages for commerce, (Asiatic inclusive,) suggest the name which is given to this entrance.

covered with grasses and scattered trees. On the west it is protected from the chilling influence of the north-west winds by the *cuesta de los gatos*, (wild-cat ridge,) which separates it from the coast. This is a grassy and timbered mountain, watered with small streams. and wooded on both sides with many varieties of trees and shrubbery, the heavier forests of pine and cypress occupying the western slope. Timber and shingles are now obtained from this mountain; and one of the recently-discovered quicksilver mines is on the eastern side of the mountain, near the Pueblo of San Jose. This range terminates on the south in the *Anno Nuevo* point of Monterey bay, and on the north declines into a ridge of broken hills about five miles wide, between the bay and the sea, and having the town of San Francisco on the bay shore, near its northern extremity.

Sheltered from the cold winds and fogs of the sea, and having a soil of remarkable fertility, the valley of San Joseph (San Jose) is capable of producing in great perfection many fruits and grains which do not thrive on the coast in its immediate vicinity. Without taking into consideration the extraordinary yields which have sometimes occurred, the fair average product of wheat is estimated at fifty fold, or fifty for one sown. The mission establishments of *Santa Clara* and *San Jose*, in the north end of the valley, were, in the prosperous days of the missions, distinguished for the superiority of their wheat crops.

The slope of alluvial land continues entirely around the eastern shore of the bay, intersected by small streams, aud offering some points which good landing and deep water, with advantageous positions between the sea and interior country, indicate for future settlements.

The strait of *Carquines*, about one mile wide and eight or ten fathoms deep, connects the San Pablo and Suisoon bays. Around these bays smaller valleys open into the bordering country, and some of the streams have a short launch navigation, which serves to convey produce to the bay. Missions and large farms were established at the head of navigation on these streams, which are favorable sites for towns or villages. The country around the Suisoon bay presents smooth low ridges and rounded hills, clothed with wild oats, and more or less openly wooded on their summits. Approaching its northern shores from *Sonoma* it assumes, though in a state of nature, a cultivated and beautiful appearance. Wild oats cover it in continuous fields, and herds of cattle and bands of horses are scattered over low hills and partly isolated ridges, where blue mists and openings among the abruptly-terminating hills indicate the neighborhood of the bay.

The *Suisoon* is connected with an expansion of the river formed by the junction of the Sacramento and San Joaquin, which enter the San Francisco bay in the same latitude, nearly, as the mouth of the Tagus at Lisbon. A delta of twenty-five miles in length, divided into islands by deep channels, connects the bay with the valley of the San Joaquin and Sacramento, into the mouths of which the tide flows, and which enter the bay together as one river.

Such is the bay, and the proximate country and shores of the bay of San Francisco. It is not a mere indentation of the coast, but a little sea to itself, connected with the ocean by a defensible gate, opening out between seventy and eighty miles to the right and left, upon a breadth of ten to fifteen, deep enough for the largest ships, with bold shores suitable for towns and settlements, and fertile adjacent country for cultivation. The head of the bay is about forty miles from the sea, and there commences its connection with the noble valleys of the San Joaquin and Sacramento.

The climate of maritime California is greatly modified by the structure of the country, and under this aspect may be considered in three divisions—the *southern*, below Point Concepcion and the Santa Barbara mountain, about latitude 35°; the *northern*, from Cape Mendocino, latitude 41°, to the Oregon boundary; and the *middle*, including the bay and basin of San Francisco and the coast between Point Concepcion and Cape Mendocino. Of these three divisions the rainy season is longest and heaviest in the north and lightest in the south. Vegetation is governed accordingly—coming with the rains—decaying where they fail. Summer and winter, in our sense of the terms, are not applicable to this part of the country. It is not heat and cold, but wet and dry, which mark the seasons; and the winter months, instead of killing vegetation, revive it. The dry season makes a period of consecutive drought, the only winter in the vegetation of this country, which can hardly be said at any time to cease. In forests, where the soil is sheltered; in low lands of streams and hilly country, where the ground remains moist, grass continues constantly green, and flowers bloom in all the months of the year. In the southern half of the country the long summer drought has rendered irrigation necessary; and the experience of the missions, in their prosperous day, has shown that, in California, as elsewhere, the driest plains are made productive, and the heaviest crops produced, by that mode of cultivation. With irrigation a succession of crops may be produced throughout the year. Salubrity and a regulated mildness characterize the climate; there being no prevailing diseases, and the extremes of heat during the summer being checked by sea-breezes during the day, and by light airs from the Sierra Nevada during the night. The nights are generally cool and refreshing, as is the shade during the hottest day.

California, below the Sierra Nevada, is about the extent of Italy, geographically considered in all the extent of Italy from the Alps to the termination of the peninsula. It is of the same length, about the same breadth, consequently the same area, (about one hundred thousand square miles,) and presents much similarity of climate and productions. Like Italy, it lies north and south, and presents some differences of climate and productions, the effect of difference of latitude, proximity of high mountains, and configuration of the coast. Like Italy, it is a country of mountains and valleys: different from it in its internal structure, it is formed for *unity;* its large rivers being concentric, and its large valleys appurtenant to the great central bay of San Francisco, within the area of whose waters the dominating power must be found.

Geographically, the position of this California is one of the best in the world; lying on the coast of the Pacific, fronting Asia, on the line of an American road to Asia, and possessed of advantages to give full effect to its grand geographical position.

New Mexico.—In regard to this extensive region, we shall extract a few pages from the valuable report made by Dr. Wislizenus, attached to the expedition of Col. Doniphan, and printed by order of the Senate of the United States.*

"New Mexico is a very mountainous country, with a large valley in the middle, running from north to south, and formed by the *Rio del Norte.* The valley is generally about twenty miles wide, and bordered on the east and west by mountain chains, continuations of the Rocky Mountains, which have received here different names, as Sierra Blanca, de los Organos, Oscura, on the eastern side, and Sierra de los Grullas, de Acha, de los Mimbres, towards the west. The height of these mountains south of Santa Fe may, upon an average, be between six and eight thousand feet, while near San Fe, and in the more northern regions, some snow-covered peaks are seen that may rise from 10,000 to 12,000 feet above the sea. The mountains are principally composed of igneous rocks, as granite, sienite, diorit, basalt, &c. On the higher mountains excellent pine timber grows; on the lower, cedars, and sometimes oak; in the valley of the Rio Grande, mezquite.

"The main artery of New-Mexico is the Rio del Norte, the longest and largest river in Mexico. Its head waters were explored in 1807 by Captain Pike, between 37° and 38° north latitude; but its highest sources are supposed to be about two degrees farther north, in the Rocky Mountains, near the head waters of the Arkansas and the Rio Grande, (of the Colorado of the west.) Following a generally southern direction, it runs through New-Mexico, where its principal affluent is the Rio Chamas from the west, and winds its way then in a south-eastern direction through the states of Chihuahua, Coahuila and Tamaulipas, to the Gulf of Mexico, in twenty-five degrees fifty-six minutes north latitude. Its tributaries in the latter states are the Pecos, from the north; the Conchos, Salado, Alamo, and San Juan, from the south. The whole course of the river, in a straight line, would be near 1,200 miles; but by the meandering of its lower half, it runs at least about 2,000 miles, from the region of eternal snow to the almost tropical climate of the gulf. The elevation of the river above the sea near Albuquerque, in New-Mexico, is about 4,800 feet; in El Paso del Norte about 300, and at Reynosa, between three and four hundred miles from its mouth, about 170 feet. The fall of its water appeared to be, between Albuquerque and El Paso, from two to three feet in a mile, and below Reynosa one foot in two miles. The fall of the river is seldom used as a motive power, except for some flour mills, which are oftener worked by mules than by water. The principal advantage which is at present derived from the river is for agriculture, by their well-managed system of irrigation. As to its navigation in New-Mexico, I doubt very much if even canoes could be used, except perhaps during May or June, when the river is in its highest state, from the melting of the snow in the mountains. The river is entirely too shallow, and interrupted by too many sand-bars, to promise anything for navigation. On the southern portion of the river the recent exploration by Captain Sterling, of the United States steamer Major Brown, has proved that steamboats may ascend from the gulf as far as Laredo, a distance of 700 miles. Although said steamboat did not draw over two feet of water, yet the explorers of that region express their opinion, that 'by spending some $100,000 in a proper improvement of the river above Mier, boats drawing four feet could readily ply between the mouth of the Rio Grande and Laredo.' Whenever a closer connection between this head point of navigation and New-Mexico shall be considered, nothing would answer but a railroad, crossing from the valley of the Rio Grande to the high table land in the state of Chihuahua.

"The *soil* in the valley of the Rio del Norte in New-Mexico, is generally sandy, and looks poor, but by irrigation it produces abundant crops. Though agriculture is carried on in a

* The reader will find a lengthy and complimentary review of this Report in the July No. of that most interesting western work, published in St. Louis, and entitled the *Western Journal.*

very primitive way, with the hoe alone, or with a rough plow, made often entirely of wood, without any particle of iron, they raise large quantities of Indian corn and wheat, beans, onions, red peppers, and some fruits. The most fertile part of the valley begins below Santa Fe, along the river, and is called 'rio abajo,' or (the country) down the river. It is not uncommon there to raise two crops within one year. The general dryness of the climate, and the aridity of the soil in New-Mexico, will always confine agriculture to the valleys of the water courses, which are as rare as over all Mexico—such, at least, as contain running water throughout the year. But this important defect may be remedied by artesian wells. On several occasions I remarked on the high table-land from Santa Fe south, that in a certain depth layers of clay are found, that may form reservoirs of the sunken water-courses from the eastern and western mountain chain, which, by the improved method of boring, or artesian wells, might easily be made to yield their water to the surface. If experiments to that effect should prove successful, the progress of agriculture in New-Mexico would be more rapid, and even many dreaded 'Jornadas' might be changed from waterless deserts into cultivated plains. But at present, irrigation from a water-course is the only available means of carrying on agriculture. The irrigation is effected by damming the streams and throwing the water into larger and smaller ditches (*acequias*) surrounding and intersecting the whole cultivated land. The inhabitants of towns and villages, therefore, locate their lands together, and alot to each one a part of the water at certain periods. These common fields are generally without fences, which are less needed, as the grazing stock is guarded by herdsmen. The finest fields are generally seen on the *haciendas*, or large estates, belonging to the rich property-holders in New-Mexico. These haciendas are apparently a remnant of the old feudal system, where large tracts of land, with the appurtenances of Indian inhabitants as serfs, were granted by the Spanish crown to their vassals. The great number of human beings attached to these haciendas are, in fact, nothing more than serfs; they receive from their masters only food, lodging, and clothing, or perhaps a mere nominal pay, and are therefore kept in constant debt and dependence to their landlords; so that if old custom and natural indolence did not prevail among them to stay with their hereditary masters, the enforcement of the Mexican laws against debtors would be sufficient to continue their servitude from generation to generation. This actual slavery exists throughout Mexico, in spite of its liberal constitution; and as long as this contradiction is not abolished, the declamations of the Mexican press against the slavery of the United States must appear as hypocritical cant.

"Besides agriculture, the inhabitants of New-Mexico pay a great deal of attention to the raising of stock, as horses, mules, cattle, sheep and goats. Their stock is all rather of a small size, because they care very little for the improvement of the breed; but it increases very fast, and as no feeding in stables is needed in the winter, it gives them very little trouble. There are large tracts of land in New-Mexico, too distant from water to be cultivated, or in too mountainous parts, which afford, nevertheless, excellent pasturage for millions of stock during the whole year; but unfortunately here, as well as in the state of Chihuahua, the raising of stock has been crippled by the invasions of the hostile Indians, who considered themselves secret partners in the business, and annually took their share away.

"A third much-neglected branch of industry in New-Mexico are the *mines*. A great many now deserted mining places in New-Mexico prove that mining was pursued with greater zeal in the old Spanish times than at present, which may be accounted for in various ways, as the present want of capital, want of knowledge in mining, but especially the unsettled state of the country and the avarice of its arbitrary rulers. The mountainous parts of New-Mexico are very rich in gold, copper, iron, and some silver. Gold seems to be found to a large extent in all the mountains near Santa Fe, south of it in a distance of about 100 miles, as far as Gran Quivira, and north for about 120 miles up to the river Sangre de Cristo. Throughout this whole region gold dust has been abundantly found by the poorer classes of Mexicans, who occupy themselves with the washing of this metal out of the mountain streams. At present, the old and the new *Places*, near Santa Fe, have attracted most attention, and not only gold washes, but some gold mines too, are worked there. They are, so far as my knowledge extends, the only gold mines worked now in New-Mexico. But as I have made from Santa Fe an excursion there for the special purpose of examining those mines, I must refer the reader, in relation to them, to that chapter of my narrative. As to the annual amount of gold produced in New-Mexico, I am unable to give even an estimate. But as nearly all the gold of New-Mexico is bought up by the traders, and smuggled out of the country to the United States, I believe that a closer calculation of the gold produced in New-Mexico could be made in the different mints of the United States than in Mexico itself.* Several rich silver mines were, in Spanish times, worked at Avo, at Cerrillos, and in the Nambe mountains, but none at

* At pages 32–3 the author says: "The annual production of gold in the two *Placers* seems to vary considerable. In some years it was estimated from $30,000 to $40,000 per annum; in others, from $60,000 to $80,000, and in latter years even as high as $250,000 per annum."

present. Copper is found in abundance throughout the country, but principally at las Tijeras, Jemas, Abiquiu, Guadelupita de Mora. etc. I heard of but one copper mine worked at present south of the Placers. Iron, though also abundantly found, is entirely overlooked. Coal has been discovered in different localities, as in the Raton mountains, near the village of Jemez, south-west of Santa Fe, in a place south of the Placers, etc. Gypsum, common and selenite, are found in large quantities in Mexico; most extensive layers of it, I understand, exist in the mountains near Algodones, on the Rio del Norte, and in the neighborhood of the celebrated 'Salinas.' It is used as common lime for white-washing, and the crystalline or selenite instead of window glass. About four days traveling, (probably one hundred miles,) south-southeast of Santa Fe, on the high table land between the Rio del Norte and Pecos, are some extensive *salt lakes*, or '*salinas*,' from which all the salt (muriate of soda) used in New-Mexico is procured. Large caravans go there every year from Santa Fe in the dry season, and return with as much as they can transport. They exchange, generally, one bushel of salt for one of Indian corn, or sell it for one, and even two dollars a bushel.

"Not far from these salinas the ruins of an old city are found, of the fabulous '*la Gran Quivira*.' The common report in relation to this place is, that a very large and wealthy city was once here situated, with very rich mines, the produce of which was once or twice a year sent to Spain. At one season, when they were making extraordinary preparations for transporting the precious metals, the Indians attacked them; whereupon the miners buried their treasures, worth fifty millions, and left the city together; but they were all killed except two, who went to Mexico, giving the particulars of the affair, and soliciting aid to return; but the distance being so great, and the Indians so numerous, nobody would advance, and the thing was dropped. One of the two went to New-Orleans, then under the dominion of Spain, raised five hundred men, and started by way of the Sabine, but was never heard of afterwards. So far the report. Within the last few years several Americans and Frenchmen have visited the place; and, although they have not found the treasure, they certify at least to the existence of an aqueduct, about ten miles in length, to the still standing walls of several churches, the sculptures of the Spanish coat of arms, and to many spacious pits, supposed to be silver mines. It was, no doubt, a Spanish mining town, and it is not unlikely that it was destroyed in 1680, in the general, successful insurrection of the Indians in New-Mexico against the Spaniards. *Dr. Samuel G. Morton*, in a late pamphlet, suggests the probability that it was originally an old Indian city, into which the Spaniards, as in several other instances, had intruded themselves, and subsequently abandoned it. Further investigation, it is to be hoped, will clear up this point.

"The *climate* of New-Mexico is, of course, very different in the higher, mountainous parts, from the lower valley of the Rio del Norte; but generally taken, it is temperate, constant, and healthy. The summer heat in the valley of the river will sometimes rise to nearly 100° Farenheit, but the nights are always cool and pleasant. The winters are much longer and more severe than in Chihuahua, the higher mountains are always covered with snow, and ice and snow are common in Santa Fee; but the Rio del Norte is never frozen with ice thick enough to admit the passage of horses and carriages, as was formerly believed. The sky is generally clear, and the atmosphere dry. Between July and October, rain falls; but the rainy seasons are here not so constant and regular as in the southern states. Disease seems to be very little known, except some inflammations and typhoidal fevers in the winter season."

"The whole *population* of New-Mexico was, in 1793, according to a census, 30,953; in 1833 it was calculated to amount to 52,360, and that number to consist of 1.20 Gapuchines, (native Spaniards,) 4.20 Creoles, 5.20 Mestizes of all grades, and 10.20 of Pueblo Indians. In 1842, the population was estimated at 57,026, and at present at about 70,000 souls."

"The *rulers of New-Mexico*, under the Mexican government, used to be a governor and legislative power, (junta departmental,) but as the latter was more a nominal than a real power, the governor was generally unrestrained, and subject only to the law of revolution, which the New-Mexicans used to administer very freely, by upsetting the gubernatorial chair as often as the whole Republic did that of the president. Governor Armijo, the last ruler of New-Mexico, before it was invaded by the Americans, had already received his full share of comment from the public press. He is one of those smart, self-confident men, who, like their prototype, Santa Anna, are aware that the wheel of fortune is always turning, and that the Mexicans are a most credulous and easily deceived people; and although at present he is a fugitive from his country, and subdued, I have no doubt he will, before long, appear once more on the stage, and by some means come into power again. The judiciary power in New-Mexico has always been as dependent as the governor was independent. Besides, that, the clergy, as well as the military class, had their own courts of justice. In relation to the general government of Mexico, New-Mexico ha always maintained greater independence than most of the other states—partly from its distance from Mexico, and partly from the spirit of opposition in the inhabitants, who derived very little benefit from their connection with the Republic, and would, therefore, not be taxed without an equivalent. Several times the general government tried to introduce in New-Mexico the so-called estanquillas, or the sale of tobacco in all its forms, as a monopoly of the general government; but it never succeeded In the same way the introduction of copper coin was resisted. The loose connection with the mother-country will aid a great deal its annexation to the United States, provided that the latter will bestow upon it what the Mexican government never could—stability of government, safety of property and personal rights, and especially protection from the hostile Indians.

"*Santa Fe* is one of the oldest Spanish settlements in New-Mexico; its origin dates, probably, as far back as the end of the sixteenth century. It lies in 35 deg., 41 min., 6 sec., north latitude, and 106 deg., 2 min., 30 sec., longitude west of Greenwich.* Its elevation above the sea, according to my own observations, is 7,047 feet.

"Santa Fe lies in a direct line about twenty miles east of the Rio del Norte, in a wide plain, surrounded on all sides by mountains. The eastern mountains are the nearest; those towards the northeast, the Taos mountalns, the highest; some of their snow-capped peaks are supposed to be from four to five thousand feet higher than Santa Fe. A small creek, that comes from the eastern mountains, provides the town with water, and runs about twenty-five miles south-west from it into the Rio del Norte. There is no timber on the plains, but the mountains are covered with pine and cedar, The soil around Santa Fe is poor and sandy; without irrigation, scarcely anything can be raised. There is no good pasturage on the plains; stock is generally sent to the mountains, and only asses, mules, and goats—the stock of the poorer classes—are kept near the settlements.

"The climate of Santa Fe is rather pleasant; not excessively warm in the summer, and moderately cold in the winter, though snow is a common occurrence. Nearly all the year the sky is clear, and the atmosphere dry. All the houses in Santa Fe are built of adobes, but one story high, with flat roofs; each house in a square form, with a court or open area in the centre. The streets are irregular, narrow and dusty. The best looking place is the 'plaza,' a spacious square, one side of which the so-called palacio, the residence of the governor, occupies. The palace is a better building than the rest; it has a sort of portico, and exhibits two great curiosities, to wit: windows of glass, and festoons of Indian ears. Glass is a great luxury in Santa Fe; common houses have shutters instead of windows, or quite small windows of selenite, (crystalized gypsum.) The festoons of Indian ears were made up of several strings of dried ears of Indians, killed by the hired parties that are occasionally sent out against hostile Indians, and who are paid a certain sum for each head. In Chihuahua, they make a great exhibition with the whole scalps of Indians which they happen to kill by proxy; the refined New-Mexicans show but the ears. Among the distinguished buildings in Santa Fe, I have to mention yet two churches with steeples, but of very common construction.

"The inhabitants of Santa Fe are a mixed race of Spanish and Indian blood, though the latter prevails. The number of inhabitants was, in former times, reported as high as 4,000; at present it contains at most 3,000; and with the surrounding settlements belonging to the jurisdiction of Santa Fe, about 6,000. The manners and customs of the inhabitants of Santa Fe are those of the whole of Northern Mexico; they are indolent, frugal, sociable, very fond of gambling and fandangos, and the lower class, at least, exceedingly filthy. As in most Mexican towns, I was at a loss to find out by what branch of industry the mass of the people support themselves; and I came at last to the conclusion, that if from natural indolence they work as little as possible, their extreme frugality, too, enables them to subsist upon almost nothing."

CALIFORNIA—The New American El Dorado, 1850.—Though the public mind, both in Europe and in this country, has been so much excited within the last two years, upon the subject of California, as to cause every hint or suggestion relating to its condition or prospects, to be greedily sought after and examined, no matter from what source emanating, we have thought it so difficult to sift the truth from the error, where the field for exaggeration was so ample, that our pages have presented little, if anything, to the reader upon the subject. We have preferred to await developments and that settled

* This is the result of the most numerous astronomical observations made by Lieut. Emory, of the engineer corps, during his stay in Santa Fe, and which he has kindly allowed me to refer to. The result of my own observations for latitude, made during my short sojourn in Santa Fe, differs from his but in seconds. Dr. J. Gregg had already determined it as in 35 deg. 41 min. There can, therefore, be no doubt as to the real latitude of Santa Fe. Nevertheless, all the Mexican maps have generally laid it nearly one degree further north. This northern tendency of Mexican maps I observed on many other points where I made observations for latitude.

calm which, sooner or later, is sure to follow in the train of every excitement of the body politic.

Though this period can hardly be said yet to have arrived, it will be admitted the circumstances are far more favorable for a judicious opinion than they have previously been. The embellishments of letter-writers have given place to the more minute and well-considered reports of government agents, selected for their ability, and with few, if any, motives for misrepresentation. We have selected the labors of two of these agents, (T. Butler King and T. O. Larkin,) as a text for the remarks which will follow, and shall embody such facts from other sources as may tend to the further illustration of the subject.

The *political condition* of California may be briefly described. On the treaty of peace, the mail and revenue laws of the United States were extended over the territory, but in every other respect the Mexican system, such as it had previously existed, was left in full force and obligation. Scarcely a single copy of the laws of Mexico were to be found in the country, and, of consequence, a system of rule succeeded, which was exceedingly arbitrary and unequal. Extortion became frequent; land titles were involved in confusion—even injustice was preferable to litigation. The growth of cities carried with it none of the incidents and powers of municipal governments. The Federal authorities, though receiving millions from the customs, paid back nothing toward advancing the condition of the community. Dissatisfaction was the natural and necessary result.

Meanwhile, the tide of emigration, with extraordinary impetus, was setting into the country. The insatiate thirst for gold impelled hundreds and thousands, from every port and haven of the Union, toward the shores of El Dorado. Again was revived the days of Cortez and Pizarro and Raleigh, and, as in the fifteenth and sixteenth centuries, bands of adventurers were organized for distant and perilous voyages, and with the highest hopes and enthusiasm. No class of society escaped the contagion. The more intelligent and enterprising were the first to move, and every gale from the far west wafted the tidings of gold and precious gems, scattered, as it were, upon the surface of this almost fabled region, with greater profusion than they were emboweled in the famed Ophir and Tarshish of antiquity. Enthusiasm grew to higher and higher pitch, and has even at this moment, lost little of its intensity.

It is remarkable of the Americans, that they are an order-loving and law-abiding people, in the strictest sense of these terms. The condition of things found by them in California could not long subsist. *Government* seems to be, with them, an instinct and a passion. Three legislative bodies were organized, respectively, at San Francisco, Sonora and Sacramento, with the prospect of others still, and of much confusion and conflict of laws and institutions. Congress adjourned without extending any relief to the country. The conviction became strong with the people, that the time for action had arrived, and that the remedies were in their own hands. At the call of General Riley, they met in convention in Monterey, and, after protracted discussions, adopted a state constitution and government, and elected two senators and a representative, who now await, at Washington, a seat in the Congress of the nation.

It is not our province now to discuss the political questions which are exciting so much debate in the country, in regard to the admission of this new state. There are many circumstances about which we have never been satisfied in the movement. A military officer takes the lead in ordering a convention of the people. There is no account of any previous census officially taken. What were the qualifications of voters? how many were emigrants from foreign countries, and not naturalized? what proportion had any fixed purpose of domicile in the country? These are important points we have never seen determined. What influences, other than the unbiassed judgment of the people, were brought to bear in giving a turn so novel to their affairs? We have had difficulties in our mind at every step, upon all of these heads, and do not hesitate frankly to confess them.

There is something extraordinary, to be sure, in the whole case, which should protect it from the stringency of general rules. Yet the precedent does not appear the best in the world, to be established. If allowed, it should be only upon its own peculiar exigencies, and upon the express condition of furnishing no rule for future conduct.

We make this remark from nothing contained in the instrument adopted by the Californians, for their government. They had a right to insist upon the exclusion of slavery, if they might make a constitution at all; though there is this, at the same time, to which the South may well object. This territory was acquired by our common blood and treasure. It is no sooner ours, than an effort is made by the free States of the North, to exclude us from occupying it with our property. Such is the strength and power of the northern opposition, that property, which is ever timid, and will seek no hazards, is excluded from the country in the person of the slave, and southerners are forced, willingly or not, to remain at home. Emigrants, meanwhile, crowd from the North. They mould public sentiment in California. Their first act is to confirm the *ex-*

clusion of their southern confederates? Is it well to say that the convention embraced a majority of southerners? Does this affect this case, if true? Public men, the world over, will accord their principles to the doctrines that are *popular*. Elected with a full knowledge of the views of their constituency, we can suppose few of them hardy enough, and independent enough, to brave political death by running counter to the prevailing sentiment. They were not *free* to act in the circumstances of the country. They were but recording a judgment which was previously formed, and for which they had no responsibility.

The population of Upper California was estimated, in 1802, to consist of 15,562 converted Indians, and 1,300 of other classes. In 1831, the number of Indians had increased to 18,683, and the whites, etc., to 4,342, making a total of 23,025 in the whole territory. At the close of the Mexican war, it was supposed there were 15,000 Americans and Californians in the country. By the 1st January, 1850, the number of American emigrants increased 80,000, while those of foreign birth increased 20,000, making a present total population of 115,000 to 120,000, exclusive of Indians. These Indians, who are not converted, inhabit the mountains, are a very low order of beings, and entertain little friendship for our people. Their number has been estimated as high as 300,000.*

We have been accustomed to the most unfavorable reports, in regard to the climate of California. Mr. King goes very full into the subject, and presents many interesting facts. He thinks, upon the whole, it will compare favorably with our northern states, whatever may be the first impressions of settlers, in the novelty of their position. In consequence of the well ascertained results of the currents of air, as influenced by the earth's motion on its axis, the climate of California is divided into two great seasons of *wet* and *dry*, the former embracing the period, at San Francisco, from the middle of November until the middle of May. From the prevalence of cold winds and fogs along the coast, the summer season is more uncomfortable, to strangers, than the winter. As the interior is penetrated, the case is different, the days being by no means so hot, and the nights cool and pleasant, This rule obtains in the valleys of Sacramento and Joaquin. On the Sierra Nevada, the thermometer frequently ranges from 110° to 115° in the shade, during two or three hours of the day. The nights, on the other hand, are cool and invigorating. From meteorological records, kept in various parts of the territory, great variety of temperature is observable, which has, no doubt, given rise to the various and conflicting opinions, so generally current. Mr. King well remarks:

"Those who take up their residence in the valleys, which are situated between the great plain of the Sacramento and San Joaquin, and the coast range of hills, find the climate, especially in the dry season, as healthful and pleasant as it is possible for any climate to be, which possesses sufficient heat to mature the cereal grains and edible roots of the temperate zone.

"The division of the year into two distinct seasons, wet and dry, impresses those who have been accustomed to the variable climate of the Atlantic States unfavorably. The dry appearance of the country in summer, and the difficulty of moving about in winter, *seem* to impose serious difficulties in the way of agricultural prosperity, while the many and decided advantages resulting from the mildness of winter, and the bright, clear weather of summer, are not appreciated. These will appear when I come to speak of the productions of California. We ought not to be surprised at the dislike which the emigrants frequently express to the climate. It is so unlike that from which they come that they cannot readily appreciate its advantages, or become reconciled to its extremes of dry and wet.

"If a native of California were to go to New England in winter, and see the ground frozen and covered with snow, the streams with ice, and find himself in a temperature many degrees colder than he had ever experienced before, he would probably be as much surprised that the people could, or would live in so inhospitable a region, as any immigrant ever has been at what he has seen or felt in California.

"So much are our opinions influenced by early impressions, the vicissitudes of the seasons with which we are familiar, love of country, home and kindred, that we ought never to hazard a hasty opinion, when we come in contact with circumstances entirely different from those to which we have, all our lives, been accustomed."

The valleys of California, parallel to the

* Mr. Larkin says: "1st. The population of California in July, 1846, was about 15,000, exclusive of Indians; in July, 1849, it is about 35,000 to 40,000. The Americans are the lesser half of the people. From July to January, 1850, probably 40,000 Americans, by land and water, will reach this country, and after September, the Europeans will commence arriving here. By January, 1850, we shall number 80,000 to 100,000 people, and in 1851, from 175,000 to 200,000.

"2d. The character of the natives prior to July, 1846, was proverbial for inactivity, indolence, and an unwillingness to learn or improve. They had no wish or desire to indulge, or enjoy themselves, in any new or foreign customs, and they were happy, and kind and hospitable to all strangers. Foreign residents, happily situated among the natives, improving their advantages, gradually became men of property, and many of them have married into some of the principal families in California.

"Very many of our emigrants are Mexicans and South Americans—laborers (*peons*) of the most abject class—mild and inoffensive in their general manners, who are guided with ease. They are, however, slothful, ignorant, and, from early life, addicted to gambling. They will sleep under the canopy of a tree, and enjoy themselves to the full, if they have a blanket, or a sheet, with which to enwrap themselves; and they are content if they have only paper cigars to last them a week, and a mountebank to resort to at will. This class of men are brought, by their employers, from Chili, Peru and Mexico. The employers are men of ease and urbanity, who will, in time, take their departure from this country—most of their laborers, or peons, remaining behind, to live and die here."

coasts, are of unsurpassed fertility, having a deep black, alluvial soil. Many beautiful and abundant valleys exist about the foot hills of the Sierra Nevada. The Colorado, which has not been explored, is supposed, from the color of its deposits, to flow through an alluvial valley. The plains of the Sacramento and San Joaquin, embracing 50 or 60,000 square miles, it is conceived, will support a population as large as Ohio or New York.

Previous to the treaty of annexation, the exports of California were chiefly hides and tallow, and the people pastoral in their pursuits. Wheat, barley and oats were cultivated. An ox was valued at $2, a horse $5 to $10. The former now commands $20 to $30, and the latter $60 to $150. The number of cattle in the country is 500,000. Mr. King argues that, as the population advances, this stock, with its increase, will be found insufficient, and large demands be made upon the western states. He supposes one hundred thousand will be driven annually across the plains and mountains, though, it seems to us, a country possessing such grazing capacities as California, must soon throw off this dependence. Flocks of sheep are, even now, brought from New Mexico.

The cereal grains may be cultivated upon the plains and hills, without the aid of *artificial irrigation*, though, at the missions, this was adopted to the large increase of production. In the rich alluvial valleys, wheat and barley have produced from forty to sixty bushels, from one bushel of seed, *without* irrigation. Irish potatoes, turnips, onions, &c., grow in great abundance and perfection. In the valleys east of the coast hills, Indian corn, rice and perhaps tobacco, will mature. The cultivation of the grape has been carried to great perfection. The same of apples, pears and peaches. Wild oats present almost boundless pastures.

South of 39°, and west of the Nevada, scattering groves of oak and red wood only are found. The rest is entirely bare of forests. This is not attributed so much to defects of soil as to fires continually sweeping over the luxuriant dried grass. North of 39° the country abounds in timber. The farmer's experience will modify his first unfavorable impressions.

"It is soon ascertained that the soil will produce abundantly without manure; that flocks and herds will sustain themselves through the winter without being fed at the farm-yard, and, consequently, no labor is necessary to provide forage for them; that ditches are easily dug, which present very good barriers for the protection of crops, until live fences can be planted and have time to grow. Forest trees may be planted with little labor, and, in very few years, attain a sufficient size for building and fencing purposes. Time may be usefully employed in sowing various grain and root crops, and, therefore, it is not necessary to gather them. They can be used or sold from the field where they grow. The labor, therefore, required in most of the old states to fell the forests, clear the land of rubbish and prepare it for seed, may here be applied to other objects.

"All these things, together with the *perfect security of all crops, in harvest time, from injury by wet weather*, are probably sufficient to meet any expense which may be incurred in irrigation, or caused, for a time, by a scanty supply of timber."

Great confusion and embarrassment may be anticipated in settling the rights of claimants of PUBLIC LANDS in California. Questions will arise as to rights of the Jesuits, under Mexican grants, to the immense and valuable tracts which they claim. Nearly all the territory south of 39° and west of the Sacramento, is covered by Mexican grants, which reserve the minerals to the government. There is great want of precision and certainty as to boundaries under the loose systems which prevailed. It will become Congress, in succeeding to the right of Mexico, to scrutinize very closely the whole of these claims, since the "purchase gives to us, not only all the lands which have not been granted, but all the reserved minerals and metals, and also reversionary rights, which might accrue to Mexico from a want of compliance on the part of the grantees with the conditions of their grant, or a want of perfection in the grants." But few patents have been located in the Sacramento and San Joaquin valleys, where 15 to 20,000,000 acres of valuable land exist.

In regard to the COMMERCIAL RESOURCES of California, we believe Mr. King altogether visionary. Upon the calculation that, in five years, there will be a population in the country of half a million, he argues, their trade with the United States alone will be one hundred millions annually! These estimates, in our opinion, contradict all experience, and are devoid of substantial foundation. The wildest dreams of imagination will not support them. It is from this part of the report only, that our opinions of Mr. King, as an authority to be relied upon, are at all shaken. We believe the calculation safer, that it will require *twenty* years for his figures, either in regard to commerce or population, to be reached. Nothing but a rail-road across the continent, if that be practicable, can produce such results in a shorter period. Discreet men will not suffer their calculations to be disturbed and distorted by the frenzied enthusiasm, which has characterized the first year of California emigration. We believe the destinies of that region to be high and glorious, but time only can bring them about, and things have too much, at present, the aspect of John Law's celebrated epoch, to be altogether encouraging!

But to follow Mr. King. He supposes that San Francisco will be the great mart for supplying South America and all the East with American products. The return cargoes, being inconsiderable in bulk, chiefly gold, &c., freights for other articles will be low, and South American products must seek California ports, as a cheaper mode of reaching the United States. In consequence of the trade winds, vessels for the United States reach San Francisco in about the same time that they do Valparaiso, Callao, &c. The silver of Mexico will seek the mart of San Francisco, for the higher value attributed to it by our laws. The imports of lumber into the country for some time to come, Mr. King estimates at $8,000,000 annually; of clothing, $5,000,000; of coal, supposing the Panama road built, $6,000,000, &c. The whole commerce for 1850 he estimates at $25,000,000. In regard to the China trade we made an extract:

"The countries on the west coast of America have no exports which find a market in China, or other parts of Asia. San Francisco will, therefore, become not only the mart of these exports, but also of the products and manufactures of India, required in exchange for them, which must be paid for principally in gold coin or gold dust. Neither gold coin nor gold dust will answer as a remittance to China. Gold, in China, is not currency in any shape, nor is it received in payment of import duties, or taxes on land, or on the industry of the people.

"The value of pure gold in China is not far from $14 the ounce. Hence, the importer of manufactures and products of India into San Francisco will remit the gold coin or dust direct to New-York, for investment in sterling bills on London. These bills will be sent to London, and placed to the credit of the firm in China, from whom the merchandise had been received, and who, on learning of the remittance having gone forward to their agents, will draw a *six months' sight bill* for the amount, which will sell in China at the rate of four shillings and two pence or *three* pence per dollar.

"I have a statement before me from one of the most eminent merchants and bankers of New-York, who was, for many years, engaged extensively in the India trade, which shows that the profit or gain on ten thousand ounces of gold, thus remitted, would be $34,434 44
And that the loss on the same quantity, sent direct to China, would be 15,600 00

Total difference in profit and loss in favor of the remittance to New-York $50,034 44

It will thus be perceived, that Nature has so arranged the winds and currents of the Pacific, and disposed of her vast treasures in the hills and mountains of California, as to give to the harbor of San Francisco the control of the commerce of that ocean, so far as it may be connected with the west coast of America."

The GOLD REGION of California is between four and five hundred miles long, and from forty to fifty miles broad, following the line of the Sierra Nevada. Many streams penetrate this area, and wash out from the quartz, in which it is found combined, the particles and fragments of gold. These indications are strong that the two were created together. These particles or scales are found in the bars and shoals of rivers, in ravines, and in what are called the dry diggings. When the streams dry up, they are readily collected, and in the dry diggings, the gold and quartz are found combined, cropping out from the hill sides, and requiring the greatest mechanical force to separate them. The following passage from Mr. King will be read with universal interest:

"The rivers present very striking, and it would seem, conclusive evidence respecting the quantity of gold remaining undiscovered in the quartz veins. It is not probable that the gold in the dry diggings, and that in the rivers—the former in lumps, the latter in dust—was created by different processes. That which is found in the rivers has undoubtedly been cut or worn from the veins in the rock, with which their currents have come in contact. All of them appear to be equally rich. This is shown by the fact, that a laboring man may collect nearly as much in one river as in another. They intersect and cut through the gold region, running from east to west, at irregular distances of fifteen to twenty, and perhaps some of them thirty, miles apart.

"Hence it appears that the gold veins are equally rich in all parts of that most remarkable section of country. Were it wanting, there are further proofs of this in the ravines and dry diggings, which uniformly confirm what nature so plainly shows in the rivers.

"For the purpose of forming some opinion respecting the probable amount or value of treasure in the gold region, it will be proper to state the estimates which have been made of the quantity collected since the discovery.

"Gold was first discovered in the south fork of the American River, at a place called Sutter's mill, now Coloma—late in May or early in June, 1848. Information which could be relied on, announcing this discovery, was not received in this city until late in the following autumn.

"No immigration into the mines could, therefore, have taken place from the old states in that year. The number of miners was consequently limited to the population of the territory—some five hundred men from Oregon—Mexicans and other foreigners who happened to be in the country, or came into it during the summer and autumn, and the Indians, who were employed by or sold their gold to the whites.

"It is supposed that there were not far from ten thousand men employed in collecting gold during that season. If we suppose they obtained an average of one thousand dollars each—which is regarded by well-informed persons as a low estimate—the aggregate amount will be $5,000,000.

"Information of this discovery spread in all directions during the following winter; and, on the commencement of the dry season in 1849, people came into the territory from all quarters—from Chili, Peru, and other States on the Pacific coast of South America—from the west coast of Mexico—the Sandwich Islands, China and New Holland.

"The immigration from the United States

came in last, if we except those who crossed the Isthmus of Panama, and went up the coast in steamers, and a few who sailed early on a voyage round Cape Horn.

"The American immigration did not come in by sea, in much force, until July and August, and that overland did not begin to arrive until the last of August and first of September. The Chilinos and Mexicans were early in the country. In the month of July, it was supposed that there were fifteen thousand foreigners in the mines. At a place called Sonoranian Camp, it was believed there were at least ten thousand Mexicans. They had quite a city of tents, booths and log cabins; hotels, restaurants, stores, and shops of all descriptions, furnished with whatever money could procure. Ice was brought from Sierra, and ice-creams added to numerous other luxuries. An inclosure, made of the trunks and branches of trees, and lined with cotton cloth, served as a sort of amphitheatre for bull-fights; other amusements, characteristic of the Mexicans, were to be seen in all directions.

"The foreigners resorted principally to the southern mines, which gave them a great superiority in numerical force over the Americans, and enabled them to take possession of some of the richest in that part of the country. In the early part of the season, the Americans were mostly employed on the forks of the American and on Bear, Uba, and Feather rivers. As their numbers increased, they spread themselves over the southern mines, and collisions were threatened between them and the foreigners. The latter, however, for some cause, either fear, or having satisfied their cupidity, or both, began to leave the mines late in August, and by the end of September, many of them were out of the country.

"It is not probable, that during the first part of the season, there were more than five or six thousand Americans in the mines. This would swell the whole number, including foreigners, to about twenty thousand the beginning of September. This period embraced about half of the season during which gold may be successfully collected in the rivers.

"Very particular and extensive inquiries respecting the daily earnings and acquisitions of the miners, lead to the opinion, that they averaged an ounce per day. This is believed by many to be a low estimate; but from the best information I was able to procure, I am of the opinion it approaches very near actual results. The half of the season, up to the first of September, would give sixty-five working days, and to each laborer, at $16 per ounce, $1,040. It, therefore, we assume $1,000 as the average collected by each laborer, we shall probably not go beyond the mark.

"This would give an aggregate of $20,000,000 for the first half of the season—$15,000,000 of which was probably collected by foreigners. During the last half of the season, the number of foreigners was very much diminished, and, perhaps, did not exceed five thousand. At this time the American immigration had come in by land and sea, and the number of our fellow-citizens in the mines had, as was estimated, increased to between forty and fifty thousand. They were most of them inexperienced in mining, and it is probable the results of their labors were not as great as has been estimated for the first part of the season; and experienced miners, assuming that the average of half an ounce per day ought to be considered as reasonable, it would give an aggregate of about $20,000,000. If from this we deduct one-fourth, on account of the early commencement of the wet season, we have an estimate of $15,000,000; at least five of which was collected by foreigners, who possessed many advantages from their experience in mining and knowledge of the country.

"These estimates give, as the result of the operations in the mines for 1848 and 1849, the round sum of $40,000,000—one half of which was probably collected and carried out of the country by foreigners.

"From the best information I could obtain, I am led to believe, that at least $20,000,000 of the $40,000,000, were taken from the rivers, and that their richness has not been sensibly diminished, except in a few locations, which had early attracted large bodies of miners. This amount has principally been taken from the northern rivers, or those which empty into the Sacramento; the southern rivers, or those which flow into the San Joaquin, having been, comparatively, but little resorted to until near the close of last season. These rivers are, however, believed, by those who have visited them, to be richer in the precious metal than those in the northern part of the gold region.

"There is one river, which, from reported recent discoveries, and not included in the description of those flowing into the great plane west of the Sierra Nevada, is as rich in gold as any of them. That is the Trinity, which rises north of the head waters of the Sacramento, and discharges into the Pacific not far from the fortieth degree of north latitude.

"There are, as nearly as my recollection serves me, twelve principal rivers in which gold has been found; but most of the twenty millions in the above estimate was taken from six or seven of them, where it was first discovered and most accessible.

"Adopting the hypothesis that the gold found in the beds of the streams has been cut or worn from the veins in the quartz through which they have forced their way, and considering the fact that they are *all rich*, and are said to be nearly equally productive, we may form some idea of the vast amount of treasure remaining undisturbed in the veins which run through the masses of rock in various directions over a space of forty or fifty miles wide, and near five hundred miles long.

"If we may be allowed to form a conjecture respecting the richness of these veins from the quantity of lump or coarse gold found in the dry diggings, where it appears to occupy nearly the same superfices it did originally in the rock—its specific gravity being sufficient to resist ordinary moving causes—we shall be led to an estimate almost beyond human calculation and belief. Yet, as far as I can perceive, there is no plausible reason why the veins which remain in the quartz may not be as valuable as those which have become separated from the decomposed rock. This matter can only be satisfactorily decided by actual discoveries.

"The gold region of California having attracted a large share of public attention, it was to be expected that various suggestions and propositions would be made with respect to the proper mode of disposing of it.

"The difficulty in arranging a suitable plan has been the want of accurate information on which a well-considered opinion might be formed. Its distance from the seat of government, the conflicting statements and reports respecting it, served only to bewilder and mystify the public mind, and render a thorough examination of it necessary, to ascertain whether its value is such as to render legislation necessary for its proper protection and management."

Mr. King concludes his report with some important suggestions in regard to the course government should pursue in the control of this extensive and extraordinary mineral domain. In the apprehension that it will be chiefly taken up by capitalists and speculators, if regulated by the usual land system, he advises that Congress retain the proprietary, and issue permits to settlers, etc., Americans only, by birth or naturalization, to collect and take away the gold. A fair price for such a permit, he regards as an *ounce*, or $16 per annum, to each individual. The business of regulating and granting permits to be entrusted to commissioners, who shall have power to lay out towns and dispose of lots, *reserving* the mineral resources. In certain cases, where machinery can be used to advantage, and capital is required in working the mines, he proposes grants, with a certain per centum reserved, etc. The revenue from all of these sources, amounting, perhaps, to several millions annually, is proposed to be applied toward the payment of interest upon the purchase money of California, to create a sinking fund to pay the principal, and to provide for a system of public education and internal improvements in the country.*

The following statistics are taken from the report of the treasurer of the United States mint at Philadelphia, published in the National Intelligencer:

Receipts of Gold in the United States from California.

Total amount of California gold received up to the 28th of February, 1850, as per last report	$8,500,000
Receipts from the 1st to the 15th of March, 1850	825,000
Amount of gold dust on hand, but not weighed, estimated at	150,000
Total	$9,475,000

Branch Mint at New-Orleans.

Total receipts up to 1st January, 1850, as per last report	$666,079
Receipts during January, 1850	376,512
Receipts during February, 1850	561,538
Estimated receipts from the 1st to the 15th of March, 1850	300,000
Total	$1,904,129

Recapitulation.

Receipts at the United States mint, Philadelphia	$9,475,000
Receipts at the branch mint, New-Orleans,	1,904,129
Grand total	$11,379,129

To which may be added say $750,000 worth of gold dust still remaining in private hands.

The extraordinary flow of gold from California, taken in connection with the extreme richness of the lately-discovered mines of Siberia, has given rise to much anxious inquiry and speculation, regarding the probable effects upon the commerce, prices and exchanges, of the world. A few reflections will quiet any uneasiness upon these points.

According to the calculation of Mr. Jacobs, the circulation of the precious metals in Europe, *doubled* in the first fifty years after the discovery of America. In the century ending with 1600, the amount *quadrupled*. In the next hundred years, it did little more than *double*. During the eighteenth century, America alone produced $786,000,000, being an average of nearly eight millions per annum. This average began then to decline, from the exhaustion of the mines, etc.

---

* The *quicksilver mines* of California are believed to be numerous, extensive, and very valuable. There is one near San Jose, which belongs to, or is claimed by, Mr. Forbes, of Tepic, in Mexico. The cinnabar ore, which produces the quicksilver, lies near the surface, is easily procured, and believed to be remarkably productive.

Discoveries of other mines are reported, but no certain information respecting them has been made public. It is, undoubtedly, a fortunate circumstance, that nature, in bestowing on California such vast metallic treasure, has provided, almost in its immediate neighborhood, inexhaustible stores of quicksilver, which is so essential in gold mining.

It is believed that there are many extensive beds of silver, iron and copper ores in the territory; but there is no information sufficiently accurate respecting them, to justify any statement of their existence or value.

Should the California results continue for any long period, their present value, or increase with the progress of settlement, etc.. as was the case for two or three hundred years after the discovery of America, it is inevitable that *a depreciation in the value of the precious metals must again be the result.* Should gold, alone, be the metal discovered and brought into market, reversing the case which occurred with the early Spanish settlers of the continent, the depreciation will *alone* be sustained by gold, and the *proportionate* value it enjoys to silver become more or less disturbed. The extent of this disturbance it is difficult to foresee. It is conceivable that silver might become the more valuable of the two, though the greater *intrinsic* value, for some purposes, of gold, be at the same time admitted. During the fifteenth century, a pound of gold was worth ten to twelve pounds of silver, but the production of the latter metal being so much more considerable than the former, after the opening of the American mines, the gold pound became gradually equal to 13, 14, 15, and even 16 pounds of silver. This difference, however, when the period embraced is considered, about three hundred years, does not appear so striking as at first sight. The fall in the value of silver, as compared with gold, notwithstanding the prodigious amount continually produced, did not average ten per cent. in a hundred years, or *one mill per cent. per annum!*

To determine the decline in the *intrinsic* value of silver in the same period, is a much more difficult operation. We must compare *prices*, say, for instance, of corn and wheat, in the fifteenth and nineteenth centuries. The reduction in the value of precious metals will, of course, be marked in the *rise* of prices. We have not, at present, the data for such computations, which are very intricate, and require much subtile argumentation. Whatever this rise in prices, none can doubt it must be extended gradually over a very long period, and cannot be much appreciated in the lifetime of a single man, unless under circumstances much more extraordinary than anything we can conceive, promised even by California.

It is worthy of remark, too, that the value of silver has not declined in the proportion of its larger production; since, were this the case, as Mr. Jacobs has conclusively shown, its value now would be only one fortieth, or one forty-fifth that of gold, this being the relation of production in the American mines. Nor is this scale of the two metals a *fixed* one the world over. The relation in Japan is 1 to 8 to 9; in China, 1 to 12 to 13; in France, 1 to 15½; in Mexico, 1 to 15⅝; variations depending upon the customs and fashions of countries in the use of jewelry, plate, etc., and in the demands of the arts.

It will also aid us in speculating upon any probable *depreciation* in the value of the precious metals, and *appreciation* in prices, to reflect upon the increasing demand for these metals, which the progress of civilization and society induces, both for currency, and in the arts, and upon the present supply now existing in the world. This supply, upon the estimate of that able economist, Mr. Jacobs, cannot be less now than $5,000,000,000. Of this, perhaps $1,800,000,000 is in currency. Admitting, then, an average from California of $20,000,000 per annum, the whole stock of the world would be increased but one-third of one per cent., and it would require 250 years to double the supply! At fifty millions per annum, one hundred years would be required. It may be inferred how unimportant from year to year these results would be felt upon prices, though it be admitted true, that their rise will be in a much greater ratio than the increase of production.*

We will conclude this paper with an extract from an article prepared by us in 1846, and published in the second volume of the Review. The extract is a quotation from Albert Gallatin's invaluable report upon currency, etc.:

"The total amount of gold and silver produced by the mines of America to the year 1803 inclusively, and remaining there or exported to Europe, has been estimated by Humboldt at about 5,000,000,000 dollars, and the product of the years 1804-30 may be estimated at 750,000,000; if to this we add 600,000,000, the nearly ascertained product to this time of the mines of Siberia; about 450,000,000 for the African gold dust, and for the product of the mines of Europe (which yielded about 3,000,000 a year in the beginning of this century,) from the discovery of America to this day, and 300,000,000 for the amount existing in Europe prior to the discovery of America, we find a total not widely differing from the fact, of 7,200,000,000. It is much more difficult to ascertain the amount which now remains in Europe and America together. The loss by friction and accidents might be estimated, and researches made respecting the total amount which has been exported to countries beyond the Cape of Good Hope; but that which has been actually consumed in gilding, plated ware, and other manufactures of the same character, cannot be correctly ascertained. From the imperfect data within our reach, it may, we think, be affirmed that the amount still existing in Europe and America certainly exceeds 4000, and most probably falls short of $5,000,000,000. Of the medium of $4,500,000,000 which we have assumed, it appears that from one-third to two-fifths is used as *currency*, and that the rest consists of plate, jewels, and other manufactured articles. It is known that of the gross amount of $7,200,000,000, about $1,800,000,000, or one-fourth of the whole in value, and one forty-eighth in weight, consisted of gold. Of the $450,000,000,

* Since writing this paper, and after the first part is in print, it occurs to us we have not spoken in sufficiently decided terms upon the admission of California as a state government. Our opinion has long been fixed. The country should be remanded back to her *territorial* condition, to undergo the usual and regular forms of preparation for state sovereignty. We would constitute no such precedent as to receive her now. If this, however, cannot be, *then the question must be kept inseparable from that of the other territories, and the reduction of the boundaries of the state within proper limits, a sine qua non..* (*1850.*)

the presumed remaining amount in gold and silver, the proportion of gold is probably greater on account of the exportation to India and China having been exclusively in silver, and of the greater care in preventing every possible waste in an article so valuable as gold."

CUBA—STATISTICS OF POPULATION AND INDUSTRY.—The following statistics are taken in part from a pamphlet entitled "Cuba in 1851," and said to be officially correct, and in part from other reliable sources.

Cuba was discovered by Christopher Columbus, on the 27th of October, 1492. It is situated between 23 degrees 12 minutes, and 19 degrees 43 minutes, north latitude. It is about 800 miles long, and in width varies from 25 to 130 miles. According to Humboldt, it contains an area of 43,380 square miles; by others, it is estimated as low as 32,807. Its extent of territory, according to the statistics of 1850, comprises 24,148,509 acres, of which, about one-twelfth is under cultivation. Its soil is one of the most fertile in the world, favorable to the growth of all tropical fruits and productions. The cultivation of sugar-cane was introduced about 1580, and slaves began to be imported four years afterwards. Havana, its most important city, was founded in 1519, and now contains about 200,000 inhabitants, a number just equal to the total Indian population of the whole island when discovered.

The trade of Cuba was very insignificant when the United States declared their independence, and was confined to Santiago de Cuba on the south side of the island. Since then, its advancement in population and commerce has been remarkable, far surpassing the growth of any other Spanish colony. Its population at several periods, commencing with 1775, has been as follows:

1775	170,000
1791	272,000
1817	578,000
1827	730,000
1841	1,007,624
1850	1,247,230

Increase in 75 years, 1,077,230.

Its increase in imports, exports and revenues, has been no less remarkable, as will be seen by a glance at the subjoined table:

Years	Imports	Exports	Revenues
1828	$19,534,922	$13,414,362	$9,086,406
1847	32,389,117	27,998,770	12,808,713
Increase	$12,854,197	$14,584,408	$3,722,307

In 19 years. It will be remarked here, that the principal seat of trade is now on the northern part of the island next to the United States, and not on the southern side as in 1775. So that its growth in both trade and population seems to be identified in a great measure with the development and progress of our government. The value of its agricultural productions in 1849 was $62,781,035. Its exports during the same period were $27,380,921, of which $8,706,224 were to the United States. Its imports during the same period were $26,707,343, of which $7,280,214 were from the United States. The amount of American tonnage employed in the trade of the island, during the same period, was 501,267 tons.

The entries of vessels from the United States, Spain, England and France, amounted in 1847 to 3,493, of which 2,012 were to the United States. Clearances during the same year, 3,043, of which 1,722 were to the United States; thus showing the vast preponderance of trade with this country over any other.

The total amount of taxes levied upon American commerce with the island, in the shape of duties upon imports, tonnage duties, and duties upon exports, exceeds $4,000,000 annually. There are 359 miles of railway in operation upon the island. Of the $27,000,000 of annual imports, according to official documents, $16,000,000 are in provisions, lumber, fabrics, materials, &c., which our country could furnish more readily than any other; but, through the taxes and restrictions imposed by Spanish policy, not more than one-third of it comes from the fields and factories of the United States.

Cuba is divided into three departments—Western, Eastern, and Central. These departments are subdivided into twenty-five jurisdictions. The jurisdiction of Havana is the largest, the Western department, and it contains one city, 60 small towns, 35 villages, 437 sugar estates, 520 coffee plantations, and is inhabited by 454,000 persons. Havana, the principal city of the island, and the capital, as a commercial city, compared with places in the Western world, ranks next to New York and New-Orleans. The value of the exports and imports together, exceed fifty millions of dollars per annum. In 1847, about 644,853 boxes of sugar were exported from this port, and 82,000 quintals of coffee, 32,000 hogsheads of molasses, 198,267,000 segars, and 250,000 quintals of tobacco.

The following is the classification of the population of Cuba in 1850:

Creole whites		520,000	
Spaniards		35,000	
Troops and mariners		23,000	
Foreigners		10,560	
Floating population		17,000	605,560
Free mulattoes	118,200		
Free blacks	87,370	205,870	
Slave mulattoes	11,100		
Slave blacks	425,000	436,100	641,670
Total			1,247,230

Whole number capable of bearing arms, including whites, Spaniards, slaves, &c.. 393,000.

In 1850, the number of sugar estates on the island amounted to 1442; coffee estates to 1618; tobacco plantations to 9101, and 9930 grazing farms, and 223 towns. Wax is produced to the amount of about 800,000 pounds, and honey to the amount of 2,000,000 gallons. Cattle to the number of about 900,000 head are owned in the island, and there are about 200,000 horses and 50,000 mules.

In minerals, the island is very rich; of copper mines, no less than 114 have been discovered in the island, 57 in the Eastern department, 18 in the Central, and 45 in the Western. The mine at Cobre, worked by an English company, has shipped from 27,000 to 43,000 tons per annum. Coal, iron, silver, and amianthus have been discovered.

In 1847, the government revenues amounted to $12,808,713. [See West Indies.]

COFFEE, AND THE COFFEE TRADE. —The march of civilization has introduced among us many luxuries with which the ancients were unacquainted. In the progressive attainments and higher destinies of man in his social capacity, the energies are taxed to produce, superadded to the necessaries, the refinements and elegancies of life. The superfluity of to-day produces the positive want of to-morrow, and thus is man hourly accumulating upon himself habits of a fixed and permanent character. In a primitive state, the calls of nature are readily answered; no wearied exertion, no patient sufferance is demanded, to place within the eager grasp of man the active means of his existence.

COFFEE (Arab. *Bun;* Ger. *Kaffee*, *Kaffeebohnen;* Fr., It. and Port. *Caffè;* Sp. *Café;* Rus. *Kofé;* Turk. *Chaube*) is a shrub indigenous to Arabia, or that part of it called *Yemen*. Prior to the sixteenth century we find no mention made of it, and we are therefore led to infer, that it has only been subsequent to that time made into a decoction and used as a drink. Macpherson, in his annals of commerce, inclines to the opinion that the plant grew wild in Arabia, long before its cultivation as an article of commerce. On this point, all the authorities we have consulted are silent. A German, named Leonhart Rauwolf, is believed to be the first European who took any notice of coffee. His work was published in 1573.

The plant has been very accurately described by Prosper Albinus, in his works *de Plantis Egypti* and *de Medicina Egyptiorum*, published in 1591 and 1592.

In 1652, a coffee-house was opened in London, for the first time. A Turkish merchant named Edwards, having brought several bags with him from the Levant, for his private use, his Greek servant, named Pasqua, was allowed the privilege of making it for public sale.

The use of coffee, says M. de la Roque, was first introduced into France in the period between 1640 and 1660. The first coffee-house was opened in Marseilles, in 1671; and in the following year, one in Paris. Solomon Aga, Turkish ambassador at Paris, in 1669, is said by Lieber to have introduced it into that city. Others give the credit of its first introduction into Paris to the celebrated traveler Trevenot. We will not attempt to reconcile the discrepancies in these statements, or venture an opinion upon the pretensions of either. The fact is not important to us now.

Between 1680 and 1690 the Dutch planted coffee-beans they had obtained from Mocha, in the vicinity of Batavia. In 1714, the magistrates of Amsterdam sent to Louis XIV. a fine tree, about five feet high, in full foliage, with both green and ripe fruit. This plant is said by Du Tour to have been the parent of all since cultivated in the West India islands. In 1732, it is known that coffee was cultivated in Jamaica, and an act was passed to encourage its growth in that island.

Malte-Brun, in his description of the Columbian Archipelago, says, there is but one species of the coffee-tree, and it is supposed to be a native of Arabia Felix. The plant was brought to Batavia, from thence to Amsterdam and Paris, and afterwards transplanted to Surinam and Martinique. It seldom bears fruit before the third season, and sometimes not till the fifth or sixth; it never lasts more than thirty years, and frequently decays long before that time. A single plant may produce from one to four pounds of coffee. We have seen it elsewhere stated, that the plant will produce to the age of forty years, and bears to a considerable extent even in the third year. A difference in soil and climate, doubtless, produces these different results; and this is apparent from the fact of a statement made by Bouissingault, that some shrubs yield from 17 to 22 lbs. of dry coffee beans, though this, he says, is a very large quantity. We can readily conceive the necessity of this qualification.

To thrive, the coffee plant requires frequent rains up to the time of flowering. The fruit bears a strong resemblance to a small cherry, and is ripe when it becomes of a red color, and the pulp is soft and very sweet. As the berries never ripen simultaneously, the harvest takes place at different times; and each requiring at least three visits, made at intervals of from five to six days. A negro will gather from ten to twelve gallons of coffee in the course of a day.

Coffee contains the same active principle as tea, caffein, but in less proportion; the researches of chemists, have shown the presence of a particular acid, called caffeic acid, also a fatty matter, a volatile oil, a coloring principle, albumen, tannin, and alkaline and earthy salts.

LIEBER, in his Cyclopedia Americana, says, he recollects having read in an old sermon, the following passage. We copy it for its quaintness: "They cannot wait till the smoke of the infernal regions surrounds them, but encompass themselves with smoke of their own accord, and drink a poison which God made black, that it might bear the Devil's color."

Beaujour, in his excellent work on Greece, tells of a *theriacophage* (an opium eater) who drank more than sixty cups of coffee in a day, and smoked as many pipes.

Mocha, with a population of, probably, not over 7,000, and situated upon the margin of a dry, sandy plain, probably produces about 12,000 tons of coffee,* universally admitted of the finest quality in the world. Much of it is sent to India, and occasionally large amounts find their way direct to Europe. It is produced in a very dry climate, the best being raised upon mountain slopes and sandy soils. The reasons assigned for the superior excellence of the Arabian coffee are various. The most important, however, are the difference in soil and climate. That part of Arabia where the coffee tree is cultivated is rocky, dry, and hot; and it is found by planters that coffee, grown in a light soil, and on dry and elevated slopes, such as are chosen for it in Arabia, has a smaller berry, with a delicate flavor, while that produced in a low, fertile, and moist soil, has a larger berry, but is comparatively flat and insipid. Rich soils, however, produce the largest quantity. The custom of pollarding the trees, which exists in the French West India islands, has a pernicious effect. The branches are obliged by this operation to take more of a lateral direction, in consequence of which they grow thicker, and afford less access to the rays of the sun. Hence the berries seldom become perfectly ripe. In Arabia, the berries are not gathered till they readily fall off on shaking the tree, when they are received on linen sheets, spread for the purpose, and are then dried in the shade on mats, fitted to imbibe their moisture. The rains in the West Indies cause the berries to fall off; hence this plan cannot be pursued there.

It is said that sugar placed near coffee will, in a short time, so impregnate the berries as to injure their flavor; and Dr. Mosely mentions that a few bags of pepper, on board a ship from India, spoiled a whole cargo of coffee.

Marco Polo describes the territory of Java as very rich, yielding pepper, nutmegs, galanga, cubebs, cloves, and all the richest of spices. Of coffee he says nothing specially, but as, at the period when he returned from his travels in the East, Europe was in a state of profound ignorance, and the regions which he traversed almost unknown, we are at no loss to account for his silence with regard to an article that forms, at the present time, so large a portion of its commerce.

Java promises, under a liberal and enlightened system of government, to become by far the most important of all the Eastern colonial possessions of any European power. The increase in the production of coffee in the island since 1836 sustains us fully in this position. The exports in 1832 amounted to 314,173 piculs, or 42,727,528 lbs., computing the picul at 136 lbs. avoirdupois. We give below the exports from Java, from 1836 to 1845 in piculs and pounds:

Years	Piculs	Pounds
1836	498,077	67,738,472
1837	684,947	93,152,792
1838	59,000	8,024,000
1839	757,476	103,016,736
1840	132,124	153,968,864
1841	961,466	130,759,376
1842	1,013,854	137,884,144
1843	1,018,102	138,461,872
1844	1,239,935	168,631,160
1845	1,005,750	136,782,000

Previous to the negro insurrection in St. Domingo, the exports amounted to near 35,000 tons, and were yearly increasing. It has been supposed that but for the devastation which was created by that melancholy occurrence, they would have reached to 42,000 tons in that year. In 1843, as will be shown hereafter, the whole *production* of the island barely exceeded 19,000 tons. It will scarcely be affirmed that this devoted country is in as prosperous or healthy condition as she certainly was prior to the event we have noticed, nor will we attempt to define the causes which have contributed so powerfully to reduce her from a state of affluence to one of commercial poverty and degradation. The exports of coffee from Hayti were:

In 1791	68,151,180	pounds.
In 1822	35,117,834	"
Decrease	33,033,346	"

The decrease in the exports of sugar, for the same time, are almost beyond conception.

In 1791, she exported	163,405,220	pounds.
In 1822	653,541	"
Decrease	162,751,679	"

Such, then, as we clearly see, is the impoverishment to which this country is reduced, and to account for it we must look a little beyond the measures of her lawgivers,

* We give this estimate upon the authority of Mr. McCulloch.

though to President Boyer is imputed many of the calamities with which the island has been visited.

The labor required for the cultivation of coffee is exceedingly light; the same rule does not apply to sugar; hence the marked and important results to which we are brought by the estimates we have given of the production of these two articles in this island. The legitimate deductions from the acknowledged fact that the inhabitants will not labor beyond that point which their necessities and the absolute calls of nature require, are as clearly exhibited in these figures as though we had the evidence of our visual organs in their confirmation. It has been said that what is called a coffee plantation in Hayti, is nothing more than a large tract of land, throughout which the coffee-tree grows spontaneously. Indeed, the miserable specimens sent to our own markets afford a striking illustration of the truth of this remark. The laws which regulate the industry of the country are urged as another cause of its impoverishment, but to this point we have given but little of our attention, satisfied with the results to which our investigations thus far have led. Her *rural code* is said to be a modification only of the French CODE NOIR.

In Jamaica, results little less satisfactory are forced upon us by a review of her commerce in the article to which our attention has been directed. In 1772, the product was 841,558 lbs.; in 1797, it had increased to 7,931,621 lbs., and in 1802, a still farther increase was manifest to an extent, making the production of that year amount to 17,961,923 lbs. The largest crop was in 1814, which amounted to 34,045,585 lbs. In 1824, it will be remembered Mr. Canning introduced into the British House of Commons his celebrated resolutions for the Emancipation of the slaves in the British West Indies. The effect of that measure upon the agricultural productions and growing commerce of the islands, is a matter, though properly within the sphere of this article, upon which we are not inclined to animadvert. Confining ourselves, then, to plain statements, we find that in 1832, Jamaica *exported* to England 19,811,000 lbs. of coffee, and proceeding still farther, discover the *production* of 1836 to amount to only 13,446,053 lbs. In 1843, the whole production of the British West India islands amounted to no more than 10,000,000 lbs. The decrease in the production and exports of Trinidad, are in much the same ratio with those of Jamaica.

The coffee-tree in Cuba, if left to nature, attains a very great height in the nurseries, and gives off horizontal branches knotted at every joint, which, like the trunk, are covered with a gray bark. The blossom looks like the white jasmine, and forms thick circular clusters around the branches. The berries at first are green, as they ripen they become white, then yellow, and finally red, resembling the cherry in size and appearance. Ninety cherries have been counted on a single tree two feet long, each containing two berries, applied with their flat sides together, having a soft, sweet, mucilaginous pulp between them and the pellicle. From August to December the cherries ripen and are gathered singly by the hand, and as three or four different crops are ripening at the same time on each tree, as many separate pickings are required.

The very quality, says Dr. WURDEMAN, rejected by us, and called *triage*, consists chiefly of the round, small grains produced by old trees, and possesses the finest flavor. It is kept from year to year, and when old, is pronounced equal to the best Mocha coffee. By the end of January, the whole crop is generally sent to market.

The coffee-tree has enemies to contend against in the worm and moths, but the most destructive of all is a small fly that deposits its eggs on the leaf, the caterpillar produced from which destroys all but the vines, leaving a lace-work foliage.

We subjoin a statement of the exports of coffee from Havana, from 1833 to 1845:

Years	Pounds	Years	Pounds
1833	46,428,125	1839	29,374,900
1834	22,890,025	1840	31,820,550
1835	19,832,550	1841	18,564,250
1836	20,998,900	1842	27,036,700
1837	35,244,725	1843	19,326,075
1838	21,612,250	1844	14,481,200

We will not attempt to analyze this table, as we will probably have occasion to draw some deductions from the exports of Cuba, in coming to speak of the trade of our city. A glance will suffice to show the material reduction in the exports of 1844 compared with those of 1833, and to exhibit this fact is sufficient for our purpose here. The exports of 1845, it is assumed, have amounted to 13,983,050 lbs., an amount less by 498,150 pounds than the previous year. In 1831, Mexico prohibited the importation of coffee, and we are not advised that she has ever removed the restriction. Indeed, the Mexican tariff of 1845, published in the *Diario*, places this article in the prohibited list. General Waddy Thompson affirms that she cultivates the article in sufficient quantities to serve the purposes of a very large consumption.

Of the imports into Amsterdam, we were struck with the fact which was presented to us, that about one-third only were from the West Indies. Considerable reductions are made from the weight equivalent to about five pounds per bag, independently of an allowance which is sanctioned by custom. While heavy importations are made into

Holland, she exports to other countries a quantity of old Java, commonly called "government coffee." The extent of the consumption of coffee in Smyrna may be estimated by the fact of 400,000 cups being daily drunk, worth 20,000 piastres, or in our currency, about $1,481 48. The imports are from Mocha, St. Domingo, Havana, and Brazil. The annual consumption is estimated at 3,000,000 okes, or 8,496,094 lbs.

Coffee is imported into Constantinople from Brazil and the West Indies, most of it in American bottoms; the principal importations are from Alexandria, however, as might be very naturally supposed.

The imports of coffee into Trieste have been very large, and this is accounted for on the ground that large quantites are subsequently transhipped by coasting vessels to other places. The duty per hundred pounds is 21 florins, equal to about 49 cents. The imports from the United States in 1830 were 5,159,700 pounds, but subsequent years show a marked decrease down to the present, when we find her imports from this country amounting to no more than 2,019,540 pounds, valued at about $131,000.

The imports into Venice are principally from Trieste, which indeed furnishes nearly the whole of her entire consumption. We might pause here, to pay a passing tribute to a city rendered classic, if from no other cause, from the muse of Shakspeare, of Milton, and of Byron. The recollections of her former opulence and splendor but too painfully contrast themselves in our mind with her present degradation. Where are now the merchant princes who swayed the sceptre of commerce over half the civilized world, and like the good Antonio, though his means were "in supposition," "hath an argosy bound to Tripolis, another to the Indies, a third at Mexico, and a fourth for England?" Where is the Jew, with balances nicely adjusted, to claim with scrupulous exactness the clear fulfilment of the very letter of his bond? Where the Rialto upon which the living mass congregated for purposes of barter and trade? A spirit of desolation seems to have swept away, as with whirlwind force, every vestige of her former greatness; and the modern traveler, his bosom swelling with emotions, which the crowd of long-cherished associations connected with her *past* history excites within him, stands, like Byron,

> "———on the bridge of sighs,
> A palace and a prison on each hand;"

to mourn, perchance, over her "dead doges," her crumbling ruins, and deserted commerce. What a contrast with that state, when

> "——her daughters had their dowers
> From spoils of nations, and the exhaustless East
> Pour'd in her lap all gems of sparkling showers.
> In purple was she robed, and of the feast
> Monarchs partook, and deem'd their dignity increased."

From a late Journal we extract the following:

> "It was recently stated in the French Chamber of Deputies, that the Belgians, a population of four and a half millions, consume twenty-six million pounds of coffee; while the thirty-five millions of French do not consume more than thirty millions of pounds. The French duty on one hundred pounds is more than the common original cost, the Belgian not a tenth part. Were the French consumption proportional to the population, the gain would be material for the venders of French sugar, colonial and indigenous."

The very heavy duty on coffee in Naples,* and on other articles in proportion, is ostensibly for the purpose of encouraging domestic manufactures and for revenue, though all writers agree that it has failed in its object. Our only surprise is, that there should be any legitimate traffic among this misguided people. With a coast stretching some thousand miles in extent, the facilities thus afforded to the smuggler are of a character to enable him to defy the strictest vigilance of the government.

The imports into Barcelona are very inconsiderable. The duty operates powerfully in checking the consumption of coffee, and though this article seems to be so far favored as not to be placed among those prohibited, the import duty is eight reals per quintal, or at a rough calculation, about 2½ cents per pound if imported in Spanish bottoms, or nearly three times that duty if under a foreign flag. In 1831 the imports did not reach 400 bags.

Who can doubt that Spain, without the pressure of duties under which she has so long groaned, would have had a commerce perhaps the most extensive of any European power? Her wheat, brandies, wines and fruits, her wool and iron of the best quality, her lead and quicksilver mines, could scarcely have failed to raise her to a proud position among the commercial nations of the world. But where imports are prohibited, how can you export? All trade is based upon a principle of reciprocity. What does our trade with Cadiz amount to—the principal commercial seaport of Spain? To nothing, absolutely nothing. Wines and salt make up the sum of our principal commodities. Three-fourths of her foreign trade may be said to be carried on in defiance of law.

But let us leave a country which can

* The new tariff of the Papal States, authorized by his holiness the Pope, on the 2d July, 1846, reduces the present duty on coffee about 13 per cent., the modification to take effect from the 7th of the same month. We doubt whether this reduction is of a character to improve materially the condition of the country; it is important, however, as an evidence of the remarkable commercial change through which, it is evident, all the states of Europe are passing.

scarcely be said to have emerged from the superstition and ignorance of the dark ages, so far as the laws which regulate and control the commerce of nations are concerned, and devote our attention for a few moments to England—England, the proud mistress of the seas, the nursery of art, the patron of genius, and, what should be her proudest boast, mother of this infant Hercules, whom she scarcely thought was destined within a brief space to rival her in commerce, arts, and manufactures., The causes which would induce us to extenuate the miserable policy of Spain and of Italy in bringing destruction upon their commerce and poverty to the homes of their people, she would regard as offensive to her pride and insulting to her dignity. But let us see how stands the case, and wherein consists the difference between them.

We subjoin a statement showing the quantity of coffee consumed in Great Britain in each of the years of the census, comparing the consumption with the growth of the population, and exhibiting the influence of high and low duties:

Year	Number of pounds consumed	Rate of duty per pound on British plantation coffee	Population of Great Britain	Average Consumption lb. oz.	Sum contributed per head to the revenue
1801	750,861	1*s.* 6*d.*	10,942,646	0 1.09	1¼*d.*
1811	6,390,122	0 7	12,596,803	0 8.12	4
1821	7,327,283	1 0	14,391,631	0 8.01	6
1831	21,842,264	0 6	16,262,301	1 5.49	8
1841	27,298,322	0 6	18,532,335	1 7.55	10½

Thus it appears, that with a duty of 1*s* 6*d.*, the use of coffee was confined to the rich exclusively, and the amount consumed in the kingdom scarcely exceeded an ounce for each inhabitant. Prior to this there was a duty of 2*s*. During the next ten years a material reduction was made in the duty, and the consumption rose nearly 750 per cent. It is curious to trace out the results of this table, for in going on to the ten years succeeding 1821, we find an addition to the duty of 5*d.*, having the effect materially to check the progressive increase of consumption, and if we take the increased population into account, showing no increase at all. A duty of but 6*d.* was placed upon the article in 1825, and what was the result? An increase in the consumption of nearly 200 per cent., and the revenue considerably augmented. Up to this time there was a discriminating duty in favor of the West against the produce of the East India possessions of 3*d.*, but the consumption having gained so far upon the imports, it was found advisable for the dealer to pay the additional duty upon the East India coffee. So clearly evident was it from this and other facts that the supply from the Western colonies was inadequate to the demand, a modification of the tariff took place, by which the production of the East was admitted at the same rate of duty. Hence we observe a still farther increase in the consumption, and if it does not continue, we can only attribute it to the want of an adequate supply.*

In an article of such primary commercial importance as this has been clearly evidenced to be, it is somewhat surprising, to say the least, that a duty of nearly double the original cost should be placed upon the article.

The following estimate, taken from Porter's Progress of the Nation, exhibits an amount of capital thrown away as effectually as if it had been cast into the sea, in order to take advantage of the privilege of bringing into consumption, at a duty of 9 pence per pound, coffee that was otherwise liable to pay a duty of 1*s.* 3*d.* per pound. Freight, insurance, landing and shipping charges on

7,080 tons, shipped from	Europe,	at £10 6 8	per ton	£73,160
5,060 "	W. Indies	at 4 17 0	"	24,540
5,680 "	Brazil	at 4 10 0	"	25,560
2,030 "	Java	at 2 2 0	"	4,060
				£127,320

tion, eminently disqualify her for any high attainment in manufactures or the arts. To the natural production of her soil must she look for that wealth which is to constitute her future greatness; and hence the palpable

To this amount might be added interest, loss of weight and deterioration of quality, including risk of sea-damage, but the sum is already sufficiently great to convey a just appreciation of the iniquity of a system of high duties, and of discriminations of this character in particular.

Let us turn for a moment to *Russia.* The duty she has imposed on coffee puts to flight the wildest imaginings we could have formed of the folly of restrictions upon an article entering so universally into the consumption of the world. The barbarous and most uncivilized character of her popula-

* The British Tariff of 1842 imposes a duty of 6d. per lb. upon foreign coffees, and 4d. upon colonial productions—to which is to be added 5 per cent. upon the net amount of the duty levied.

injustice of a duty amounting almost to 55½ cents upon every pound of coffee which enters her dominions. The present year has, however, witnessed a great improvement in the Russian commercial system, in the adoption of a new tariff, based upon principles of revenue. By this, articles hitherto saddled with prohibitory duties are admitted into the empire, those with merely high duties lowered, and many commodities previously taxed admitted free.

The Austrian policy differs not materially from that of Russia. While Trieste and Venice are comparatively free ports, and all importations for the consumption of their inhabitants are exempt from the exactions of a high rate of duty, no sooner is it attempted to introduce them into the heart of the country, than the full force of her policy is felt in its operation. A duty of about 9¼ cents is then placed upon the article, and this, *too*, with a view of protecting *domestic manufactures*.

We propose now to direct attention to our own country, and in doing so, we feel no small degree of satisfaction in boldly contrasting the policy by which she has been governed, with those which have for so long a period of years controlled and directed the commerce of the European States. A fertile field is here presented to our view, rich in the promise of a ripe and abundant harvest.

With the view of exhibiting our trade in this article, from an early period, we annex a table, showing the importations into the United States, from foreign nations, and their dependencies, from 1st October, 1806, to 30th September, 1807.

Countries	Pounds
Russia	10
Sweden	1,705,670
Denmark	10,946,411
Holland	10,247,767
Great Britain	2,746,871
France	20,932,324
Spain	9,795,720
Portugal	18,303
Mocha, Aden, and other ports on the Red Sea	1,709,533
China	592,072
All other countries	110,130
	58,804,811

We offer no remark upon this statement, farther than to call attention to the sources whence our imports were derived at that period, and the entire revolution which has since been effected in the trade, so far as production is concerned. Nor can it escape special observation, that those countries to which we were then so largely indebted for our supplies, are at this time, in a measure, tributary to us for their own. Holland, France and Russia are striking examples of this fact, as will be made clearly apparent on a review of the exports from the United States for 1845.

Our imports from China in 1835, amounted to 191,534 lbs., valued at $24,649. In 1842, the assumed value was but $1,968 ; and in 1845, as will appear by the table to which we have already made reference, were but 290 lbs. valued at fifteen dollars. The duty on coffee, in Calcutta, in 1835, was 7½ per cent. if imported on a British, or 15 per cent. if on a foreign bottom. It is asserted, on the authority of Mr. McCulloch, that in 1834 Great Britain furnished about sixty per cent. of the imports into China ; the United States only about 2½ per cent. This may have been true, and doubtless was so at that time, but we are inclined seriously to doubt the existence of such a disparity now. Our exports to China, for three years previous to 1837, were about the same, never exceeding $360,000 till '36–7, when they reached $655,581. But mark the difference in 1844–5. Of manufactured cotton goods alone in that year, we exported to China what was equal in value to $1,496,470, to which, if we add cotton wool, ginseng, lead, and the indefinite number of other articles, which the enterprise and ingenuity of our northern countrymen have thrown into the ports of the "Celestial Empire," amounting by rough calculation to about $1,958,298, we must see the astonishing increase made in that trade within the last few years. The following is stated to be

THE COFFEE CROP FOR 1843.

	Pounds
Brazil (1,170,000 bags)	170,000,000
Java and Sumatra (1,450,000 bags)	140,000,000
Cuba	45,000,000
St. Domingo	38,000,000
Porto Rico, Laguayra, &c	36,000,000
British West Indies	10,000,000
Ceylon	7,000,000
East Indies and Mocha	6,000,000
French colonies	4,000,000
Dutch West Indies	3,000,000
Total	459,000,000

This may be a fair estimate of the crop of 1843, but it strikes us that 1,170,000 bags of Brazil coffee will yield an amount in pounds equal, at least, to 17,000,000 over this calculation. Though with many of our merchants, 160 lbs. is supposed a fair average for a bag of Brazil coffee, there are others who believe 162 lbs. a truer average. Taking the lowest amount then as the basis of our calculation, Brazil must have produced in that year 187,200,000 pounds, instead of 170,000,000, as has been declared. We have alluded to this fact as we may have occasion hereafter to refer to the estimate in the establishment of our positions.

IMPORT, EXPORT, AND CONSUMPTION OF COFFEE IN THE UNITED STATES.

A Statement of the quantity and value of Coffee exported into, and imported from, the United States, in each year, from 1821 to 1844, with the consumption in the United States.

	Import.		*Export.*		*Consumption.*
Years	Quantity—lbs.	Value	Quantity—lbs.	Value	Quantity—lbs.
1821	21,273,659	$4,489,970	9,387,596	$2,087,479	11,886,063
1822	25,782,390	5,552,649	7,267,119	1,653,607	18,515,271
1823	37,337,732	7,098,119	20,900,687	4,262,699	16,437,045
1824	39,224,251	5,437,029	19,427,227	2,923,079	19,797,024
1825	45,190,630	5,250,828	24,512,568	3,254,936	20,678,062
1826	43,319,497	4,159,558	11,584,713	1,449,022	31,734,784
1827	50,051,986	4,464,391	21,697,789	2,324,784	28,354,197
1828	55,194,697	5,192,338	16,037,964	1,497,097	39,156,733
1829	51,133,538	4,588,585	18,083,843	1,536,565	33,049,695
1830	51,488,248	4,227,021	13,124,561	1,046,542	38,363,687
1831	81,759,386	6,317,666	6,051,629	521,527	75,702,757
1832	91,722,329	9,099,446	55,251,158	6,583,344	36,471,141
1833	66,628,900	6,997,051	14,696,152	1,806,583	51,932,748
1834	80,153,366	8,762,657	35,806,861	4,288,720	49,346,502
1835	103,199,777	10,715,466	11,446,775	1,333,777	91,753,002
1836	93,790,507	9,653,053	16,143,207	1,985,176	77,647,300
1837	88,140,403	8,657,760	12,096,332	1,322,254	76,044,371
1838	88,139,720	7,640,217	5,267,087	502,207	82,872,633
1839	106,696,992	9,744,103	6,824,475	734,418	99,872,517
1840	94,996,095	8,546,222	8,096,334	930,398	86,209,761
1841	114,984,783	10,444,882	5,784,536	589,609	109,200,247
1842	110,764,005	8,931,117	5,381,068	483,362	107,383,577
1843	92,295,660	6,346,787	6,378,994	422,860	85,916,666
1844	158,332,111	9,594,877	8,620,291	540,579	149,711,820

The consumption of the United States, as appears from this table, for the ten years previous to 1831, amounted to 257,972,561 pounds, or an average of 25,800,000 pounds per annum. In 1831, the imports were about sixty per cent. over any preceding year, and the exports only about one-half the exports of 1830, one-third of those of 1827, or one-fourth of those of 1825, leaving for consumption, 76,000,000 pounds, an amount more than double the quantity consumed in any previous year. It is not difficult to conceive, that this state of things was produced by some unnatural cause, to which the uniform laws which regulate supply and demand were made subservient. The excess of the imports of 1831 may be properly attributed to the rage for speculation in this article, in the northern cities, during the exciting agitation of the tariff question in that year, which resulted contrary to the expectations which had been formed, in the passage of the act, known as the tariff law of 14th July, 1832. It was assumed as the groundwork and basis of the operation, that as coffee was an article entering so largely into the consumption of the country, it would be found prudent to enhance, rather than to reduce the duty. Of the result, it is unnecessary to speak. The reduction was made; and the prospect which was at one period opened before them of large stores of wealth, proved as delusive as their calculations had been superficial. At this distance of time, we experience no difficulty in arriving at the course of reasoning by which the majority of the members of that Congress were induced to cast their votes in favor of a reduction of the duty on coffee. But as no man, or set of men, may be censured for acts done with the view of protecting their interests, when not in conflict with the true interests of the country, we pass by the argument, having simply called attention to it, with the view of enabling the reader to deduce his own conclusions. With so heavy a speculative demand as was thus created, stocks very naturally accumulated, and were held over. In proof of this, the *exports* of 1832 amounted to nearly ten times those of the year preceding, and 4,000,000 pounds more than the imports of any year previous to 1831. Thus were the surplus imports arising out of the speculative demand of that year driven hence for want of an immediate consumptive demand, and the want of capital necessary to hold it. Not the least important consideration in favor of the very heavy export which was made in this year, was the disposition to avail of the *drawback;* a very important item with those who had embarked in an enterprise so destructive as we can readily imagine this to have been. These two years, 1831 and 1832, we feel bound, therefore, to consider as exceptions to the general and uniform trade of the country, in view of the obvious local causes by which these two years were influenced and controlled.

The remark of Dr. Adam Smith, with regard to drawbacks, that they "do not occasion the exportation of a greater quantity of goods than would have been exported had no duty been imposed," loses some of its force in making an application of it here. Though the general principle is *not* to be controverted, it will scarcely be denied, that the *drawback*, in this case, occasioned "the exportation" of large quantities, which there was sufficient capital in the country to have carried into the consumption of the succeeding year. But this we conceive to be a remarkable exception, particularly in view of the fact, that the money price in both years were about one and the same thing.

The tariff of the 2d March, 1833, commonly known as the "Compromise Bill," admitted coffee free of all duty. The consumption of the United States, for 1833 and 1834, averaged 50,000,000 pounds, or double that of any year in the previous ten years. To what cause, then, are we to attribute the increased consumption of these two years? Coffee was *free!* It surely will not be argued, that the period was not far enough removed to admit of an effect so momentous. We all know that the largest exports from Rio de Janeiro are in the months of September, October and November; and that one month varies but little from the exports of another.

From this date commences the direct, rapid progress of that trade, which at this time forms so large a feature in our commerce. The decline in the price of the article, we may attribute to what cause we please; the fact is evident. This decline induced and increased consumption, which in its turn encouraged the production, as will appear, if we examine the exports from Brazil, and reflect for a moment, that more than half she produces is imported into the United States, and here consumed. In pursuing this train, we discover that the increase in the production caused a farther reduction of prices, till we find coffee at this time ranging in price from six to eight cents, and the *consumption* of the United States for the ten years previous to 1845, amounting on an average, in round numbers, to about 96,600,000 pounds yearly. It is also worthy of remark, that if we take the last *five* years, without regard to the five which preceded them, we will find the average consumption absolutely amounting to over 100,000,000 pounds yearly, or four times the consumption previously to 1831.

In a debate in the House of Representatives of the United States, upon the passage of the tariff bill of 1832, a distinguished member of that body, from South Carolina,* held the following language: "In this estimate," (coffee was proposed to be admitted under a duty of half a cent per pound,) "I regard tea and coffee as being *substantially free*, as the duties retained are scarcely worth the trouble and expense of collecting them." This remark *may* have been true at that time, but it can scarcely be doubted, that a low duty equal to that proposed to be levied under the tariff of 1832, would now add to the revenue an amount probably equal to $700,000. We may concede the point, that even such a duty would have its *effect* upon the consumption of the country, without compromising the position we have assumed; for who can doubt that there are other articles now heavily burthened, that would be in a measure relieved.

For the following tables of the imports and exports of the United States, for 1844–45, we are indebted to the report of the Hon. R. J. Walker, Secretary of the Treasury.

IMPORTS OF COFFEE INTO THE UNITED STATES,

For the year commencing 1st *July*, 1844, *and ending* 30*th June*, 1845.

	Pounds	Value
Danish West Indies	93,320	7,141
Holland	358,723	41,658
Dutch East Indies	3,925,716	259,694
" West Indies	1,270	87
British Guiana	200	16
" West Indies	4,815	312
French West Indies	196,930	25,357
" Guiana	1,658	110
Manilla and Philippine I.	436,705	34,017
Cuba	1,157,794	79,358
Other Sp. West Indies	171,410	11,101
Cape de Verdes	200	16
Hayti	13,090,359	708,855
Mexico	850	68
New-Granada	193,811	13,236
Venezuela	9,450,588	615,115
Brazil	78,553,616	4,401,269
Argentine Republic	11,967	611
Peru	582	50
China	290	15
Asia (generally)	1,040	107
Africa (generally)	208,497	20,036
S. Sea and Pacific	570	42
	107,860,711	6,221,265

To which must be added 272,458 lbs., imported from places other than its growth and production.

EXPORTS OF COFFEE FROM THE UNITED STATES,

From the 1st *July*, 1844, *to the* 30*th June*, 1845.

	Pounds	Value
Russia	149,860	12,204
Prussia	77,891	5,494
Sweden and Norway	6,292	544
Denmark	96,177	5,410
Hanse Towns	1,493,130	87,364
Holland	1,858,355	111,538
Belgium	2,183,627	119,617
England	43,450	2,600
Gibraltar	277,329	15,388
British Honduras	19,765	1,438
British West Indies	38,738	2,438
British American Colonies	524,565	44,170
France on the Medit'n	1,578,745	95,270
France on the Atlantic	528,851	29,665
French West Indies	23,366	1,796
Cuba	670	80
Italy	916,529	66,004
Sicily	394,455	23,695
Sardinia	341,455	22,449
Trieste, etc	2,019,570	131,098
Turkey, Levant, etc	485,367	27,898
Hayti	[illegible]	85
Texas	268,912	18,349
Mexico	147,369	10,954
Chili	8,354	550
Africa generally	1,260	110
S. Sea & Pac. Ocean	22,279	1,531
	13,501,972	840,739

An examination of these tables produces some curious results. They are such, however, as will strike the general reader without the addition of any remarks from us. We

* Hon. George McDuffie.

regard the source whence they are derived as the most reliable.

In one of the leading publications in the United States, giving a "statistical view of the coffee trade," there is a statement of this character—

	1834	1843	Increase
Import of coffee from Brazil	26,571,368	49,515,666	....
Value	$2,819,028	$3,392,960	$573,932
Export U. S. produce to Brazil	1,586,097	2,409,419	832,321

and the following argument upon it: "Now, it is sometimes alleged that the import of foreign goods drains the country of its treasure. Here is the fact, that increased purchase of $573,932 worth of coffee, which added largely to the enjoyments of the people of the United States, resulted in increased sales of American produce to the extent of $823,321, a clear profit of $300,000 besides the coffee."

This is certainly a marvellous conclusion, and one which unquestionably demanded no little exercise of fancy. That directly opposite results should be deduced from the same premises, is the strongest evidence we can have of the diversity of the human mind. Of that diversity there can be no doubt.

Apart from the relative value of the imports into, and the exports from the United States to Brazil in these two separate years, 1834 and 1843, we find the increase in the value of the imports into the United States from Brazil in the latter year, amounting to $573,932 over the former, and an increase in the exports of United States produce to Brazil of $823,321 during the same period. What then are the true facts which result from this state of things? not, certainly, that "*a clear profit of $300,000, besides the coffee*, has accrued to the United States from the trade, but the very opposite. We export an excess of $249,389 to Brazil over our imports, clearly proving, if it proves anything, a loss, instead of a gain. We have noticed this fact, for the reason that it carries with it an air of plausibility at variance with the truth; being based upon the hypothesis, that the greater the excess of our exports over the imports, in just such a degree is our national wealth augmented. This point has been placed in so clear a light by all the writers upon Political Economy, that any attempt to enforce it here is unnecessary.

New-Orleans is destined, unquestionably, to become the great coffee mart of the United States. If we regard her situation and proximate locality to those countries whence our largest imports are derived, or her almost immediate connection with those states, the largest consumers of the article, we cannot well resist this conclusion. Within a few years, the direct imports into this city have increased to an almost incredible extent, while the consumption of that portion of country which it supplies has been enlarged proportionally. With a view to a better understanding of the position of this city, in its relation to the entire trade of the United States, we subjoin a statement of the

IMPORT OF COFFEE INTO THE U. S. FROM BRAZIL, FROM 1821 TO 1844.

Years	Pounds	Years	Pounds
1821	691,536	1833	29,489,224
1822	2,283,280	1834	26,571,368
1823	2,367,778	1835	35,774,876
1824	3,044,587	1836	46,840,219
1825	2,708,775	1837	33,906,246
1826	2,859,075	1838	27,411,986
1827	4,841,943	1839	48,694,294
1828	15,246,299	1840	47,412,756
1829	11,131,936	1841	59,575,722
1830	14,593,232	1842	61,248,942
1831	14,686,986	1843	49,515,666
1832	25,733,532	1844	95,291,484

From this table, it evidently appears, that more than half of the exports of Brazil find their way to our market, and it is fair to infer, are here consumed. In the years prior to 1844, inclusive, with an average consumption of nearly one hundred and twenty millions, the exports of no one year exceeded nine million pounds.

Twelve years ago, and scarcely more than one cargo of Rio coffee was imported direct into our city. Everything now indicates that very nearly, if not the whole of this trade, must very soon be ours. Since there is a very limited demand for this grade of coffee in the northern states, so soon as we import what will be required for the supply of the western trade, this point will have been attained. The western states consume this quality almost exclusively, and ours is found, by experience, to be the best market. The necessity for northern import to supply our trade, in view of these facts, cannot much longer exist.

EXPORTS OF COFFEE FROM RIO JANEIRO.*

	1841.	1842.
	Bags	Bags
To New-Orleans	126,865	112,798
To New-York	125,419	106,617
To Baltimore	120,462	92,562
To Philadelphia	30,199	19,660
To Charleston	3,500	8,130
To Boston	24,271	23,513
	420,716	363,280
To Europe	569,500	793,690
Grand total	1,000,216	1,156,970

Thus we see, that in these two years New-Orleans imported a larger quantity than either New-York or Baltimore, and we may confidently predict for her an import trade that will yearly increase, until she becomes, what it is evident she ultimately must be, the great coffee market of the United States.

* Bahia, among the northern provinces, is, next to Rio, the point whence the largest amount of coffee is shipped.

IMPORTS OF COFFEE INTO NEW-ORLEANS

From all Foreign Ports, from January, 1834, to January, 1845, compiled from the records of the Custom-House at New-Orleans.

	BRAZIL.			CUBA.		
Years	Pounds	Bags	Value	Pounds	Bags	Value
1834	1,722,868	10,768	$181,920	11,326,002	70,787	$1,488,678
1835	5,141,751	32,135	641,542	16,470,199	102,938	1,827,249
1836	6,701,407	41,884	777,575	9,087,344	56,795	1,094,110
1837	3,371,793	21,073	370,977	13,601,687	85,010	1,362,855
1838	2,665,443	16,659	258,243	18,420,610	115,122	1,766,475
1839	12,055,550	75,347	1,101,552	16,143,812	100,898	1,566,178
1840	4,752,806	29,705	441,764	15,921,964	99,512	1,562,646
1841	20,575,177	128,595	1,934,633	10,092,221	63,076	1,017,626
1842	12,255,680	76,598	890,923	6,987,265	43,670	587,634
1843	20,252,460	126,577	1,403,013	9,124,898	57,031	681,155
1844	21,290,561	126.816	1,355,927	6,365,325	39,784	411,454

IMPORTS OF COFFEE INTO NEW-ORLEANS FROM OTHER FOREIGN PORTS.

Years	Pounds	Bags	Value	Years	Pounds	Bags	Value
1834	2,191,748	13,098	$270,598	1840	514,192	3,213	$50,898
1835	1,350,094	8,437	143,544	1841	3,567,757	22,298	338,479
1836	205,522	1,247	28,603	1842	1,912,909	11,956	149,888
1837	103,984	649	12,113	1843	785,583	4,910	56,555
1838	621,991	3,887	57,502	1844	102,000	637	5,758
1839	690,462	4,315	74,094				

[See *New-Orleans.*

COFFEE TRADE.

Production of Coffee in the Brazils.

	Bags	Arrobas	Lbs
1820	95,700	478,500	15,312,000
1825	182,710	912,550	29,201,600
1830	391,785	1,958,925	62,685,600
1835	627,165	3,135,825	100,346,400
1840	1,063,805	5,319,005	170,208,800
1850-51	1,897,231	9,486,155	303,556,960
1851–52, estimate	1,700,060	8,500,000	272,000,000

It would seem from this table that the production of coffee in Brazil doubled every five years up to 1840, since when it has increased 80 per cent. The increase since 1835 has been 200 millions pounds; and of that increase the United States have taken one-half. In the previous number of the *Economist*, we showed that almost all the increased production of sugar in Cuba had found a market in the United States. It now appears that a considerable proportion of the Brazil coffee finds a market here also. This is indicated in the following table, which shows the quantity annually imported into the United States from the four leading countries of production, and also the whole quantity imported into the Union during the past 18 years:

Import of Pounds of Coffee into the United States.

	Brazil	Cuba	St. Domingo	Java	Total
1834	26,571,368	19,536,457	15,141,779	5,307,186	80,153,366
1835	35,774,876	29,373,675	19,276,290	4,728,890	103,199,577
1836	46,840,219	17,850,736	11,772,064	8,850,658	103,790,507
1837	33,906,236	29,503,553	9,252,636	1,779,819	88,140,403
1838	27,411,986	32,051,651	11,375,350	2,423,277	88,130,720
1839	48,694,294	26,181,489	9,726,495	5,628,348	106,696,992
1840	47,412,756	25,331.888	9,153,524	4,343,254	94,996,095
1841	59,575,722	17,198,573	12,547,791	6,794,702	114,948,783
1842	61,248,942	14,321,458	11,530,102	9,781,418	112,764,635
1843	49,515,666	16,611,287	10,811,288	1,638,307	92,295,660
1844	95,291,484	18,628,875	20,781,461	8,740,841	158,332,111
1845	78,553,616	1,157,794	13,090,359	3,925,716	108,133,369
1846	97,353,697	2,326,497	12,734,753	2,819,411	132,812,734
1847	94,916,629	6,673,479	19,085,277	17,819,345	156,716,575
1848	110,927,284	2,258,710	16,990,976	3,037,377	150,559,138
1849	122,581,183	4,000,986	13,384,474	4,208,078	165,334,700
1850	90,319,511	3,740,803	19,440,985	5,146,961	144,986,895
1851	107,578,257	3,099,084	13,205,766	2,423,968	152,453,617

Nearly the whole increase in the import of Brazil coffee was, it appears, at New-Orleans, to supply the Western trade. The import of coffee from Brazil in 1844 was extraordinary, amounting to nearly half the whole product of that country. Coffee, up to 1832, paid a duty of 5 per cent.; since that year it has been free. The effect of this change is seen in the following table:

Imports of Coffee into the United States, with the Export and Quantity retained for Consumption, also the Duty and Average Price.

	Import Pounds	Export Pounds	Consumption Pounds	Duty per lb	Av. cost per pound
1821	21,273,659	9,387,596	11,886,063		20
1822	25,082,390	7,267,119	18,515,271		20
1823	37,337,732	20,900,687	16,437,045	5 cents.	20
1824	30,224,296	19,427,227	19,707,024		20
1825	45,390,620	24,512,568	20,678,062		17
1826	37,319,107	11,584,713	31,734,784		11
1827	50,051,986	21,697,789	28,350,197	5 cents.	11
1828	55,194,697	16,037,964	39,156,733		9
1829	51,133,538	18,083,843	33,049,695	5 cents.	9
1830	51,488,248	13,124,561	38,363,687	2 cents.	8¾
1831	81,747,386	6,056,629	75,702,757		8
1832	91,722,329	55,251,158	40,471,171	1 cent.	10
1833	99,955,020	24,899,114	75,057,906		10
1834	80,150,365	35,806,861	44,346,505		10
1835	103,199,777	11,446,775	91,752,802		10
1836	93,790,507	16,143,207	77,647,300		10
1837	88,140,403	12,096,332	76,044,071		10
1838	88,139,720	5,267,087	82,872,633		9
1839	106,696,992	6,824,475	99,872,633		9
1840	94,996,095	8,698,334	86,207,761		9
1841	144,987,787	5,784,536	109,200,247		9
1842	112,764,635	5,378,068	107,383,567	free.	8
1843	82,295,660	6,378,994	85,916,666		6¾
1844	158,332,111	8,620,291	149,711,820		6
1845	108,133,369	12,501,072	94,631,307		6
1846	132,812,734	8,275,542	124,537,192		6⅜
1847	156,716,575	6,383,583	150,332,992		5⅞
1848	150,559,138	6,998,088	143,561,050		5⅜
1849	165,334,700	14,380,429	150,954,271		5½
1850	144,986,895	15,287,499	129,699,396		8
1851	152,453,617	3,513,126	148,920,491		8

The population of the United States in 1840 was, in round numbers, 17 millions. The ave age consumption for the three years 1839-40-41 was 98½ millions of pounds. which gave a consumption of 5¾ pounds per head. The average for the three years, including the census year 1850, was 143 millions of pounds, and the population was 23 millions, which gave a consumption of 6¼ pounds per head. In 1830 the consumption was only three pounds per head; but the price had ruled nearly double what it did in the three years preceding 1850. In 1821 the consumption, per head, to the inhabitants of the United States was one pound four ounces. In 1830 the proportion had increased to three pounds per head, the foreign price having fallen 50 per cent. After the 31st December, 1830, coffee paid two cents, and in 1831, one cent; after which it was free. The importation in the year 1831, doubled in consequence of the reduced duty; and the consumption, per head, for the four years ending with 1842, averaged six pounds per head, having quadrupled to each inhabitant since 1821. A large portion of the increased consumption, as seen above, is derived from the Brazils; the effect of the production of which country has been to the price of coffee what the products of the Southern States have been to that of cotton. From 1820 to 1840, the Brazilian product increased 1100 per cent., or 155,000,000 pounds. In the same time the consumption in the United States increased 137,000,000 pounds; leaving an increase of 18,000,000 pounds of Rio coffee, besides the enhanced products of all countries, to supply the increased consumption of England and Europe. The result has been, the great diminution in price evinced in the above table. The cost per pound to the consumer was in 1831 further reduced by the removal of the duty; that is, the coffee which cost nine cents in 1830, cost the consumer 16 cents duty and charges. The same coffee now costs seven cents—a reduction of nine cents, which has given the spur to the consumption. In England, foreign coffee paid 16 cents per pound duty, and colonial coffee 8 cents, until 1845. when colonial was reduced to 3d. and foreign to 7d. The consequence is, that while the United States, with a population of 17,000,000, consumed in 1844, 149,711,820 pounds of coffee, Great Britain, with a population of 27,000,000, consumed 31,934,000 pounds only, or less than one-fourth the consumption of the United States. In 1851 the figures remained nearly the same, viz: 148,920,000 pounds in the United States, and 32,564,000 pounds for Great Britain. Now the effect of this increased consumption of Brazil coffee on the American trade, is as follows:

	1834.	1843.	1851.
Import of coffee from Brazil ... lbs.	26,571,368	49,515,666	107,578,257
Do do value	$2,819,028	3,392,960	8,881,104
Export of U. S. produce to Brazil	$1,586,097	2,409,419	3,128,956

This increased export does not appear to suffice for the compensation of the large increase in the value of coffee purchased; and it is time that some movement were made to check English influence in that quarter, and induce Brazil to place her best coffee customer at least on as favorable footing as others.

COINS, CURRENCY, ETC.—It is a very common mode of investigation, first taught by John Locke, to refer back to the origin of society, and of things, and mark their progress thence. We adopt that mode. Certainly there was a period when the man himself was the producer and manufacturer of every article of his consumption—when he did not, as it were, go out of himself—when the germs of every art existed in him, without an idea of their distribution. With few wants, how easy was their gratification. A unit then, an independent existence, man so remained until the development of the social principle sent him into society. In this rude stage, little was there above brute nature. There will be as little again if they are to be heard, whose doctrines, legitimately extended, destroy at "one fell swoop" all the precious results of a *distribution of labor*; results which the Roman poet may well have included in his eloquent passage on the progress of society:

> Inde casas postquam, ac pelles ignemque pararunt
> Et mulier coujuncta, viro concessit in unum
> Castaque privatæ veneris connubia læta
> Cognita sunt, prolemque ex se videre creatam
> Tum genus humanum primum molescere cœpit.

But remove man a single degree from this. Let him perceive how dissimilarly God has endowed us with faculties; how much superior, in certain respects, a neighbor is, and how much inferior in others. Let him mark, too, higher skill in pointing an arrow or a rock than he possesses, or vainly emulates. If his own experience be of service, let him learn that expertness is the offspring of practice, and that practice is a thing of time, toil, and labor, which cannot be given by the same man to all things in the space of a brief life. These will be the first great lessons of political economy. They will break up the unities of which we have spoken—they will amalgamate them, and men henceforward will be found reciprocally employed in each other's service.

Society and civilization, however, are things of slow growth, and we have but arrived at the origin of barter, which will not long suffice. The hunter may find it very well to part with a portion of his venison for a brace of ducks or a handful of fish, but might it not happen that the proprietor of the ducks, or the fisherman, is already supplied with venison sufficient for his wants? What is there for the hunter in this contingency? He must return disappointed, or seize by main force what has been denied his appetite, which we are at liberty to suppose him physically incapable of doing; or finally, or what would be by far the most prudent course, he must acquire something desired and not possessed, or not possessed in sufficient quantities by those with whom he would traffic, and which they would regard as an equivalent for their property. Now the fisherman may be often supposed in the same condition as the hunter. How shall these men meet each other at all times upon common ground, and enjoy their mutual products?

The most obvious reflection which occurs here, is, that some one commodity of universal requisition and demand must be sought to conduct the exchanges, which have become too complicated to be conducted *in kind*. For this each man will barter his wares, because assured that other wares, of whatever description, or at whatever season, may be bartered in turn for it. Is there such a commodity?

Among the Mexicans, when the Spaniards invaded their country, it was discovered that grains of cacao were gaining circulation as a medium of exchange. The grounds of this preference can only be traced in the fact that cacao was a scarce commodity, and one in general estimation. If a mere arbitrary choice were absurdly supposed, why not, then, as well a choice of pebbles or shells?

The early Greeks were wont, as every classical scholar will remember, to estimate the value of their commodities by the number of oxen which they had cost, or for which they could be exchanged. Thus, in Homer, we find the valuation of the arms of Diomedes and Glaucus:

> For Diomed's brass arms of mean device,
> For which nine oxen paid, (a vulgar price,)
> He gave his own, of gold divinely wrought,
> A hundred *beeves* the shining purchase bought.*

It would be easy enough to advance in this manner illustrations from other countries. Thus the Carthaginians adopted leather, which some suppose a kind of substitute for bank-notes, as the precious metals were abundant enough with them; the Lacedemonions adopted iron, and the Romans copper, the Abyssinians salt, the Britons of the time of Cæsar iron and brass, the Saxons live stock, the Maldive islanders cowries, and of later day we find codfish adopted at Newfoundland, tobacco and rice in early Virginia and Carolina, and even pork, horses, etc., in

*Iliad VI. It may be a question, after all, however, whether these were real *bona fide* "beeves," for the Greeks had a coin termed *bous*, ox, an ox being stamped upon it, as we learn from the classics, though coinage in Greece can hardly be deemed as ancient as the wars of Troy. It is a little remarkable, too, that the Latins should have called their coins *pecunia*, from *pecus*, a herd or flock stamped upon them, their word *moneta*, money, being derived, it is thought, from *moneo*, to mark; that is, to mark the fineness or weight.

some of the western states, and the Chinese now coin their money of copper only, and regard gold and silver as articles of mere merchandise.

In each of the cases above stated, the *commodity* so dignified as the medium of conducting the exchanges of all others, became in every sense the *money* of the country, without having lost anything of its character as merchandise. It may have appreciated in value somewhat from the circumstance, but it was impossible at the same time to change its nature.

At the present day the whole civilized world have agreed upon certain commodities, which shall be considered among them, by consent, and from their intrinsic value and usefulness, as equivalents, in due proportions, for all others—*these commodities are gold and silver.* Will any man in his senses maintain that these metals have become by this act in any other sense money, than the Greek five oxen, the Roman brazen *as*, or the Abyssinian salt? And yet this has been done.

We have gained something when we come to regard money as a mere commodity—"*the commodity exchanged most frequently for every other,*" and, like these others, worth only as much as it will sell for in the markets of the world. There is nothing to exempt it from the fluctuations of trade, and to entitle it a *standard* of value, would be the same as to affirm that a thing may be fixed and fluctuating at the same time. A cubic inch of water may be a standard, for we shall find it of the same absolute weight at the equator as at the pole, now as a thousand years before the deluge.*

Regarding money as commodity regulated by the laws of supply and demand, and by all the other laws which regulate other commodities, we discover at once the absurdity as well as the wickedness of all attempts to elevate or depress its value on the mere mandate of an emperor or of a parliament. Canute, the Dane, commanded as wisely the sea to stay its advances. But we discover more, and what will be of great practical value to us, that money, or gold and silver may be in excess in a country from some temporary cause, and, in commercial phraseology, "glut the market," just as we see it glutted occasionally by cotton or any other staple. The same disease will require the same remedy, and the nation will at times be gaining wealth by the exportation of its specie or money, or in the reverse, losing wealth by its absurd retention.

They are mistaken, then, who regard the precious metals as the mere *representatives* of wealth. They are wealth themselves, and no arm of power can cause them for any time to be received for a fraction beyond their intrinsic value; otherwise, we should not so much look to the material as to the "superscription," or stamp.

They are equally mistaken who would regard money as a *measure of value* or wealth; for how can that be a measure which has no fixed value itself, and how can values have a fixed measure when they are merely relative terms?

Were money the representative and measure of wealth, it would follow that the representative and measure must be precisely equal in value to the thing represented and measured, and that the sum total of all the money in any country would exactly express the wealth of that country. Now this is sheerly absurd, since we know that the proportion which money bears to other commodities is but a mere item. Of no other use than to conduct exchanges, how can it at all apply to that immense proportion of every nation's wealth which is consumed without exchanging, or which is exchanged in kind, or finally, exchanged by mere transfers from one side of a ledger to the other? We shall see this more particularly hereafter.

Can all money be regarded as on the same par as the precious metals—for instance, bank notes? Have they *intrinsic* value? Clearly not. They are, then, merely *representatives;* they answer for something else; are not commodities, not values, not wealth,† *not money* in any sense that gold and silver have come

* Adam Smith remarks: The price of gold and silver, when the accidental discovery of more abundant mines does not keep it down, as it naturally rises with the wealth of every country, so it is at all times naturally higher in a rich than in a poor country. Gold and silver, like all other commodities, seek the market where the best price is given for them. Wealth of Nations, vol. I., p. 295.

† If gold and silver be wealth, are they productive wealth? Mr. Tucker considered that the expense of metallic currency, including the wear and tear of metals, the cost of coinage and interest on the value of material, amounted to 5 per cent. on the whole capital of New-York. He, however, included paper as well as metals in the currency. Mr. Webster, in 1838, estimated the whole currency of the Union at $130,000,000; of which, perhaps, $70,000,000 was specie (*Tucker on Money and Banks*, p. 53). The metallic currency of Britain was, at the same period, $150,000,000. The following table, showing the proportion of gold and silver to other currency, and the condition of the banks in 1838, will be found of interest:

Table showing the Number and Condition of all the Banks in the United States, on the 1st January, 1838, according to Mr. Woodbury's Report.

Local Divisions	No. of Banks	Capital	Principal Debts: Notes in circulation	Principal Debts: Deposits	Principal Assets: Specie	Principal Assets: Loans, &c
Eastern States	321	65,257,540	18,307,544	11,412,803	2,902,980	93,575,135
Middle States	213	81,169,776	29,631,248	31,999,806	9,937,187	127,740,077
Southern States	89	32,111,573	20,156,891	9,707,821	6,145,384	55,337,073
South-western States	94	75,048,052	25,194,559	18,874,996	4,984,616	122,305,066
Western States	92	29,049,837	16,080,601	10,178,505	7,443,103	40,492,662
Penn. Bank, U. S.	30	35,000,000	6,768,067	2,617,253	3,770,842	45,181,854
Total	829	317,636,778	116,138,910	84,691,184	35,184,112	484,631,867

to be regarded as money, or that salt or oxen became money in other days. It is their *representative* character which gives them value, and we are yet to learn that that character would be changed in kind, though it might be in degree, if these bank notes *represented* lands or sugar instead of specie; or that their character would not sink altogether and be lost, were it found, as it too often fatally is, that they *represent nothing at all.* Paper bills are the growth of a system of credit, and have much to do with the confidence which man has in his fellow-man. Where they do *not* represent commodities, dollar for dollar, they furnish facilities for making a little wealth control a great deal, and have their convenience and economy, perhaps, in the operations of commerce; which, sometimes, however, they most grievously embarrass and destroy. Of this experience our country has had abundance.

But enough here for the present. It was only necessary to show the origin of money and its true nature, which, we think, have been quite sufficiently done for the satisfaction of every reader, and in the most incontestible manner. We return to the first division of our general subject, which admits of this plain distribution:

I.—*The Material used for Coinage of Money.*

II.—*The History of Coins.*

III.—*The Interference of Government with Coins.*

IV.—*The Value of Ancient and Modern Coins.*

V.—*American Coinage.*

I. There are many reasons to be assigned for the universal preference given to gold and silver, for purposes of coinage and currency. There is not, perhaps, another substance in nature which would meet all the requisitions so well as these. Let us note these requisitions:

1. That the material be durable; *i. e.*, not deteriorate with time.

2. That it possess great value in small bulk.

3. That it exist only in limited quantities, or susceptible only of such gradual increase as the convenience or wants of the world may demand; or in plain terms, that its exchangeable value do not vary as rapidly as that of other commodities. Thus, had gold and silver ever been produced by the alchemists out of base metals, as was the dream of early miscalled science, they must have been abandoned, and the material for money sought from other sources. Or should the working of the Asiatic mines prove as productive as present facts indicate that they will, the proportionate value of gold and silver must be greatly altered, if the last metal do not become ultimately the more valuable of the two. In fact, it has already been stated by a late French journal, that Siberia contains gold in such abundance, that its discovery is likely to produce a financial revolution in Europe, similar to that which took place on the discovery of Peru.* Within fourteen years, the gold product of Siberia has doubled; and all that is required, it is stated, to produce any quantity, is the force to work the mines. Platinum has sometimes been mentioned as an ultimate resort, and the Russians have set the example of coining it, but this metal is liable to the great objection, that the supply may be indefinitely increased should there exist a demand.

4. That the material wherever produced, in all times and in all places, should present the identical same qualities and the identical fineness.

5. That it be capable of division into small portions of the same weight and fineness, so that purchases of all magnitudes may be made with them.

6. That it be readily stamped, marked, or coined, so as not to be easily effaced.

7. That it possess naturally, or may be made to do so by means of alloy, hardness sufficient to resist friction.† This alloy counts, however, for nothing in the value of the coin. In the French silver coins we are told by Say, it is of copper of the value of 1-600 of the whole; the five-franc piece weighing 25 *grammes*, contains 2½ *gr.* alloy. But of alloys and friction hereafter.

Is there then a sufficiency of gold and silver to answer all the purposes of commerce in conducting the exchanges of the world, to say nothing of the immense demand for them in the manufacture of plate and jewels, and for other luxurious uses, and the considerable annual loss by friction? We shall consider this.

1. By an extract from a high authority, approved over and over in our country. "Notwithstanding the apprehensions so frequently expressed among ourselves, lest the United States might not possess a circulating medium large enough for the business purposes of the community, it *is a matter of not the least importance whether this medium be great or small.* Whatever in any country may be the amount of it, if we suppose it to be reduced to the tenth part of that amount, the prices of things will only become one-tenth of what they are; and a hundred dollars will perform precisely the same functions now performed by a thousand."‡ The only inconvenience would be that the divisions

---

* See Bankers' Magazine, No. 2, p. 125, Baltimore.

† Vethake, Pol. Phil., p. 25.

‡ Vethake, Pol. Ec., p. 174. If the thirty-three millions of coins, said Mr. Shields of Alabama, in the Congress of 1841, in the vaults of the banks of this Union were thrown into circulation, and every bank note in the Union burnt up or banished from circulation, it would require but the *one-hundredth* part of the stock of gold and silver now in use in the world, to supply the country with an amount of metallic money equal to that of paper now in circulation.—*Gouge, Journal of Banking*, 106.

might become inconveniently small to satisfy minute values.

2 The quantity of money really necessary for exchanges is much less than is usually imagined. Thus, when 2,200,000,000 francs was the whole currency of France, according to Neckar, the agriculture alone of that kingdom, according to Arthur Young, amounted to 11,000,000,000 francs; and in Great Britain, when the whole capital of the country was valued at £2,300,000,000 sterling, the specie medium was estimated only at £47,000,000. We are told also by Say, that in his time, about the beginning of the present century, England required to effect her sales and purchases, an agent equal only in value to 1,284,000 lbs. weight of gold, or, what is the same thing, 1,200,000,000 lbs. sugar, or what is still the same thing, £60,000,000 sterling.*

The whole gold and silver medium of a country does not, however, exist in coinage. Much of it is melted into the form of bars, assayed and stamped at the mint, which determines their weight and the degree of fineness of the metal. These are entitled *bullion*. In this form it becomes more strictly an article of commerce in an economical manner, and its value may easily be determined. It is, perhaps, to be regretted that the plan in relation to bullion, is not in every case adopted by government, even in the smallest coinage Let the piece be simply stamped by authority, to prevent fraud, without any attempt to fix a value to it, which must ever be changing; and let the world always be supposed wise enough, as it abundantly is, in every instance, to determine that value from the stamp. There is as much wisdom in fixing the price that a barrel of flour shall sell at, as there is in fixing the price of a gold piece, termed an *eagle* or a *sovereign*, of such a degree of fineness and of such a weight.

So soon as gold and silver became articles of exchange or money, some chemical mode of determining their degree of purity became at once necessary.† This much of science must be as ancient, though perhaps in much imperfection, as the first attempt as coinage. These chemical tests, &c., are what is understood as assaying. Let us then determine the antiquity of coins.

II.—*The History of Coins.*—The books of Moses are our most ancient records. They inform us that Abraham "was rich in cattle, *silver* and *gold*," and that he weighed out four hundred shekels of *silver* "according to the currency of the merchants." From this, nothing is learned of coinage; but his great-grandson, Joseph, was sold for twenty *pieces of silver*, and afterward presented his brethren with three hundred pieces. Now were these pieces all weighed out or were they coined? Calmet determines the former, for in his Biblical Dictionary he affirms that in the whole history of the Hebrews, there is not one word of coined money, of any dimension; nothing to show the form of the money or the thing represented upon it.*

Julius Pollux attributes the first coinage to the Queen of Pelops, who went into Greece with her husband, from Phrygia, 1200 years B. C.†

The Lydians, who flourished 500 years B. C., are said by Herodotus to have been the first people who coined money; but fabulous history has ascribed the invention to the reign of Saturn and Janus in Italy.‡

Coins were of common use in Greece, however, we are told, in the time of Solon, B. C. 600; § but it is stated on other authority, that Philip of Macedon first coined in that country, and that his pieces were termed *philippi*.

The Sicilians coined gold and silver, 500 B. C.; and specimens are exhibited at this day in the cabinets of the curious.

It is well ascertained that at the time of Darius, in Persia, there were gold coins

* Vethake, Pol. Ec. p. 174.

† *Gold* is found only in the native state, that is, without ores—crystals irregular, generally octohedron and dodecahedron; dissolves by mixed nitric and muriatic acids; specific gravity 19·3, water being 1; great ductility and malleability; found in rocks, in the beds of streams, and in alluvial deposits, sometimes in iron and other ores; exists in all parts of the world, found sometimes in masses of 20 to 50 pounds, pure. The American gold region, according to *Silliman's Journal*, is a thousand miles square in North Carolina alone. The whole gold region in the United States extends from Canada to the south-western boundary of the Cherokee nation in Georgia, and from the Rappahannock in Virginia, to the Coosa in Alabama, (*Com.'s Chem.*, 236.) The degree of purity of gold is expressed by the number of parts of that metal contained in 24 parts of any mixture; thus gold which, in 24 such parts, termed carats, contains 22 of pure metal, is said to be 22 carats fine.—*Henry's Chem.*, I. p. 134.

Silver.—Found native, also combined with sulphur and mur. acid, also with other metals; crystals, cubes, and octohedrons; soluble in nitric acid; found in South America, Saxony and Suabia, Bohemia, Norway, Ireland, part of England, parts United States, particularly Connecticut, New-Hampshire and New-York; has been found in masses of 100 to 560 lbs.; specific gravity, according to *Henry*, 10.51. The following table is worthy of note:

Product Gold Region United States, from 1824 *to* 1838—15 *years.*

Virginia	$482,000
North Carolina	2,648,000
South Carolina	340,500
Georgia	1,799,900
Tennessee	13,900
Alabama	1,000
Other places	12,400
Total	$5,298,200
Average annually	$353,213.

* Page 678.

† Macpherson's Ann. Com., vol. I., 16.

‡ Br. Encyclopedia, art. Coins.

§ Eschenburg Man. Clas. Lit., p. 73.

termed *darics*, after the monarch; and that with 30,000 of these he bribed Agesilaus, King of Sparta.* Herodotus, also, says of an earlier Darius, that his gold and silver were melted and poured into earthen pots, and that when wanted pieces were broken off.

No Roman coins date farther back than 266 B. C., and these are of silver, though copper had been coined, it is said, before. Seventy years later gold was coined, and the *aureus* of this metal was worth, at the time of Augustus, about 20s. of our money, when the whole coinage of Rome was estimated at £358,000,000 sterling.

A mint was established in Britain, B. C. 14, for coinage of gold, silver and brass, of which coins, we are told by Macpherson, forty specimens have reached our time.

The Franks were permitted, in the sixth century, by the Emperor, to coin their money.

In the age of Charlemagne, 750, such had been the exhaustion of gold and silver from the perpetual wear and tear of the metals, from the inroads of barbarism and the consequent cessation of all kinds of industry, including the working of mines, that the enormous sums mentioned in antiquity, had declined almost to nothing, and there were scarcely any of the precious metals in circulation in Europe. Copper, tin and iron† were the chief substitutes, and the Jews were the only traders and repositories of the finer coins.‡

During the middle ages, the privilege of coining was hereditary in many families, and in England, at the time of Ethelred, 1017, there were about forty petty mints, and the moneyers, whose names appeared upon the coins, numbered two hundred and forty-three. The Bishops and Abbots were licensed coiners—the stamp being sent them from the Exchequer. In the reign of Henry VI. but eight mints remained, in that of Henry VII. four, Edward VI. three, and Queen Elizabeth maintained but a single one in the kingdom, viz.: that of London.§

In the tenth century, so scarce had money become, that the whole amount existing in Europe, is estimated by Jacobs as only about £33,000,000 sterling, and so precious was its value, we are told by Dr. Henry, that prices ranged according to the following table, in money of the present day:

	l.	*s.*	*d.*
Value of a slave	2	16	3
" horse	1	15	2
" ass or mule	0	14	1
" cow	0	6	2
" hog	0	1	10
" sheep	0	1	2
" goat	0	0	4

In the thirteenth century, a ransom of three million crowns was demanded by the English for their prisoner, John of France; in money of the present day, £1,250,000 sterling. The sum was deemed enormous, and the first payment, a *fifth* of the whole, found so great, and France was so exhausted, says Voltaire, that it could not possibly be furnished. The only expedient was to recall the Jews, and sell to them the privilege of trade. The successor of John was forced, on account of this ransom, it is said, to pay for the necessities even of his household, in money of leather, through which a *silver nail* was driven.

As late as 1496, the daughter of Edward III., married to Lord Howard, was allowed by authority £1 1s. per week for her "sustentation and exhibition, and convenient diet of meat and drink," with a farther allowance of £80 12s. per year for eight servants: a gentlewoman, a woman, a girl, a gentleman, a yeoman and three grooms; and £25 10s. 4d. for seven horses.

During this period the delusions of alchemy were at their height, and the great farce of Raymond Lully was enacted. This impostor pretended to have discovered the "philosopher's stone," and being thrown into prison, it is said that he made gold even there, with the inscription upon it: *Jesus autem transiens medium eorum ibat*, intimating that as our Saviour passed among the Pharisees, so *that* gold was made by an invisible and secret art. Many statutes were thereupon passed in England against the *multiplication of gold*, but had this been all we should only have smiled; it is discovered, however, that various acts of parliament were passed from 1307 down even to 1622, against the *exportation* of gold and silver, which were not at all more wise than contemporary statutes against the exportation of wool.

The opening of a new world at last in the fifteenth century occasioned a revolution in the finances of Europe, for the untold mineral wealth, the inexhaustible gold and silver resources of that world were poured bounteously into her lap.

The following table, made up by us from Jacobs (and obtained by him from Ruding's Annals of the Coinage of Britain), and from other authentic sources, will show the great advances in the operations of the English

* This, we are assured, is a mistake, and we stand corrected.—Ed.

† We are told by Voltaire, that copper and iron were in early use among the Swedes, as money: La banque publique, qui est le plus ancienne de l'Europe y fut introduite par nécessité, parceque les payes se faisant en monnaie de cuivre et de fer, le transport était trop difficile.—Histoire de Charles XII., p. 27.

‡ Jacobs on the Precious Metals, 162–165.

§ The standard money was called *sterling* in the reign of the Conqueror—derivation not clear; to say from the Easterling coiners, would be an anachronism.—Macp. An. Com.

mint from the reign of Edward II., 1307, to the present day:

GOLD AND SILVER RECEIVED AT THE MINT.

			Money of that day	Money of this day
Reign of Edward II.,	20	years,	£15,992....	£46,177
" Edward III.,*	50	"	194,079....	473,703
" Richard II.,	22	"	7,095....	15,849
" Henry IV.,	14	"	12,620....	21,927
" Henry V.,	9	"	31,636....	66,148
" Edward IV.,	24	"	70,692....	141,349
" Henry VI.,	39	"	150,493....	240,788
" Henry VII.,	24	"	76,917....	120,328

By comparing these amounts with those which succeed immediately after the opening of the American mines, the great improvement will be marked.

Reign Queen Elizabeth..................	£1,200,000†
" James I., 22 years..............	5,473,666
" Charles I., 35 "	13,241,732
" James II., 4 "	4,228,753
William and Mary, and William III., 12 years..................	9,434,063
Reign Queen Anne, 13 years............	3,102,743
" George I., 14 "	8,725,921
" George II., 37 "	11,966,576
" George III., 61 "	82,750,706
" George IV., 9 "	34,363,868
From 1817-31 14 "	47,000,000‡

From the year 1492, according to Humboldt, to 1500, America alone furnished to Europe £52,000,000 sterling in the precious metals, and up to 1519 the same enormous yield is supposed by Jacobs to have continued. The effects of the rapacity, extortion and crimes of such men as Cortes, Pizarro and others, were such that in fifty years from the discovery of America, the quantity of gold and silver had doubled in circulation in Europe, and reached the amount of £50,000,000.

A new use, however, began to be found for the metals, or one which, during the dark ages, had almost been entirely neglected, viz.: the manufacture of ornaments and plate; these metals began too to be exported to Asia, but notwithstanding all of this, so great did the imports continue, that in the year 1600 the coinage of Europe alone reached £130,000,000, having multiplied *fourfold* in a century.

The seventeenth century brought, with increased wealth, refinement and luxury into Europe, and a more extensive manufacture of the metals and exportation into Asia ensued, so that at the end of it, notwithstanding the steady yield of the mines, the coinage of Europe is not supposed to have exceeded £397,000,000 sterling, or an increase of 150 per cent. in one hundred years.

The products of the mines of America, Europe and Africa, during the eighteenth century, is stated to have been £870,000,000 sterling, of which America alone produced £786,000,000. The estimated coinage of the world in the year 1808 is made by Jacobs, thus:

Coin existing in 1700, reduced by friction....................		£226,000,000
Produce of mines.....	£880,000,000	
Two-fifths exported to Asia................	352,000,000	
	528,000,000	
Two-thirds manufactured...............	352,000,000	
	176,000,000	
Friction for 109 years.	22,000,000—	154,000,000
Stock of coins, 1809..............		380,000,000

From 1809 to 1830 the unsettled and revolutionary condition of Mexico and South America, and the already over-worked and partially exhausted condition of their mines, caused a great declension in the trade of the precious metals. The average annual yield of the whole of this mining country fell from about eight millions sterling to something like five millions. The United States had, however, begun the working of the metals on a small scale in native mines, and also the Russian Empire. The whole coinage, therefore, of 1830, is supposed to have been 313 millions sterling, a reduction of sixty millions in 23 years.

Humboldt calculated in 1804 that there were three thousand mines in Mexico, of which, we are told by Gen. Thompson, not one-fiftieth are worked. The gold of this country is very inconsiderable. We take the following extract from Thompson's Recollections of Mexico, p. 203:

"Mr. Ward estimates the annual produce of the mines, for a few years prior to 1810, at $24,000,000. After that period, from the revolutionary condition of the country, it dwindled almost to nothing—in one year to three and a half millions. The official returns for 1842 show an exportation of gold and silver registered at the custom-house of $18,500,000. The facility with which large values in gold may be clandestinely exported, and the temptation to do so, from the high duties on exportation, (6 per cent,) caused a large amount to be smuggled; to form any accurate estimate of the amount of the exports of specie, a very large addition must be made to this amount. Three or four millions would scarcely cover it. Add to these the amount retained in the country, and it will be very safe to assume the present produce of the mines at from 22 to 24 million dollars per annum. The whole amount coined at the mint in the city of Mexico since the conquest, is $443,000,000; since 1690, $295,968,750. It is risking very little to say, that, if Mexico was inhabited by our race, the produce of the mines would be at least five times as great as it is now. In five years, with such a population, and only of an equal number with that which Mexico now has, I do not hesitate to assert that the mineral and agricultural exports alone would nearly equal the exports of any other country of the world."

It can hardly be supposed, therefore, taking in view all that has been previously remarked, that the whole hard money cur-

* Up to the 18 Edward III. the gold coinage has not been ascertained.

† From Macpherson, who only gives the gold coinage.

‡ McCulloch.

§ Jacobs, on the metals, 200.

rency of the world at the present day, amounts to a much greater sum than *sixteen hundred millions of dollars.* In this view we are sustained by Albert Gallatin, who published twelve or fifteen years ago an admirable paper upon the subject, an extract from which we will now furnish the reader. In a few points it differs slightly from the estimates of Jacobs. Mr. Gallatin says:

"The total amount of gold and silver produced by the mines of America, to the year 1803 inclusive, and remaining there, or exported to Europe, has been estimated by Humboldt at about $5,000,000,000, and the product of the years 1804–30, may be estimated at $750,000,000; if to this we add $600,000,000, the nearly ascertained product to this time of the mines of Siberia; about $450,000,000 for the African gold dust; and for the product of the mines of Europe (which yielded about $3,000,000 a year, in the beginning of this century,) from the discovery of America to this day, and $300,000,000 for the amount existing in Europe, prior to the discovery of America, we find a total, not widely differing from the fact, of $7,200,000,000. It is much more difficult to ascertain the amount which now remains in Europe and America together. The loss by friction and accidents might be estimated, and researches made respecting the total amount which has been exported to countries beyond the Cape of Good Hope; but that which has been actually consumed in gilding, plated ware, and other manufactures of the same character, cannot be correctly ascertained. From the imperfect data within our reach, it may, we think, be affirmed that the amount still existing in Europe and America certainly exceeds $4,000,000,000, and most probably falls short of $5,000,000,000. Of the medium of $4,500,000,000, which we have assumed, it appears that from one-third to two-fifths is used as *currency,** and that the residue consists of plate, jewels, and other manufactured articles. It is known that, of the gross amount of $7,200,000,000, about $1,800,000,000, or one-fourth of the whole in value, and one-forty-eighth in weight, consisted of gold. Of the $4,500,000,000, the presumed remaining amount in gold and silver, the proportion of gold is probably greater, on account of the exportation to India and China having been exclusively in silver, and of the greater care in preventing every possible waste in an article so valuable as gold."

In estimating the loss by abrasion, friction or waste of coins, it is to be observed that with the advance of science the amount has been greatly lessened. That on gold is regarded now as three-quarters less in proportion than upon silver, and Mr. Jacobs, from a series of experiments made by the officers of the English mint in 1816, and previously, deduces the conclusion that of the late issues of British gold the annual loss is one-eight hundredths of the whole value, and of silver one two-hundredths of the whole value. Thus, though the value of silver produced since the discovery of America, be three times that of gold, the loss upon it by wear and tear is fourfold, showing that the relative values of these metals must be naturally undergoing a change, greatly accelerated of late, if what we have seen in relation to Siberia be true. We cannot forbear introducing passages from two of the highest authorities recognized in our country, which show, with some precision, the changes of which we have spoken.

"Before the discovery of the mines of America, the value of fine gold to fine silver was in the proportion, in Europe, of 1 to 10 and 1 to 12. About the middle of the last century, it came to be regulated as 1 to 14 and 1 to 15; that is, an ounce of fine gold was worth 14 and 15 ounces of fine silver. Gold rose in *nominal* value or in the quantity of silver given for it. Both metals sunk in their *real* value or in the quantity of labor they could command, but silver sunk the most.*

"The relative position of gold and silver, in respect to value, is by no means determined by the respective supply of each from the mines. Humboldt states, that silver is produced from the mines of America and Europe, jointly, in the ratio to gold of 45 to 1. Now, the ratio of their value, instead of being 45 to 1, is only

In Mexico	15⅝	to 1
In France	15½	to 1
In China	10 to 13	to 1
In Japan	8 to 9	to 1

"The difference is probably owing to the superior utility and demand of silver for the purposes of plate, &c., as well as of money. This operates most in the east, for gold jewelry is relatively cheaper there than in our part of the world.†"

III.—Under this head we come to consider the *interference of governments with the subject of coins,* and shall be very brief. The history of the world affords nothing more remarkable than this interference, which has been conducted without any regard to the principles of political economy, or even, in some most melancholy instances, to those of faith and justice. The *superscription* which our Saviour referred to upon the coin of Cæsar, the world was taught by its rulers to regard as the secret of the coin's value. It was a notion worthy of those who, under the name of protectors, have been the oppressors of men. There were Cæsars enough in every age to regard the whole currency as their own; and if the affixing of a stamp was the secret of value in a piece of metal, why, then, that piece without a change in weight or quality might be made of any other value at the sovereign's will and pleasure. This was doctrine exceedingly convenient, as we shall see, and it is little better than the *representative* theory which some still strangely prate about. Where governments would thus assume, we agree heartily with Say, that they become *counterfeiters armed with public authority.*‡

* *I. e.,* about $1,650,000,000; Mr. Jacobs estimated it $1,502,000,000.

* Adam Smith's Wealth of Nations, vol. 1, 330.

† Say's Pol. Econ., p. 303. This was written at the beginning of this century. It will be seen that the author, therefore, cannot have considered the effects of African and Asiatic gold upon the proportionate values of the precious metals.

‡ But where the power is delegated to others *for a bounty,* the matter is infinitely worse. "Sire," said the celebrated Helvetius to his master, Frederick the Great, "you need not trouble yourself with reading them through (alluding to petitions for monopolies), they all speak one language—'We beseech your Majesty to grant us leave to rob your people of such a sum; in consideration of which we engage to pay you a certain share of the pillage.'"—*Brougham's Statesmen of the time of Geo. III.*

Philip I. of France substituted four ounces of alloy for silver in the livre of Charlemagne, thus liquidating with his creditors by paying three-fourths of their real dues. Many of his successors performed the same part, and often clandestinely. A French writer declares, that almost all foreign merchants discontinued then their dealings with France, and that French traders themselves, ruined by this system of injustice, withdrew to other countries.* The Roman tyrant Heliogabalus was equally astute in increasing the weight of an *aureum*, after levying a tax to be *paid in that coin*. The *as* and the *denarius* also suffered a similar fate. Even the wise Solon, who we must suppose ignorant here, rather than criminal, by an act for the relief of debtors, *benevolently* raised the value of the *mina* from 73 to 100 drachms.†

King Edward first practically introduced this system into England, in 1301,‡ by coining 3d. less from a pound of silver, which was a small encroachment of one and a quarter per cent., but says the annalist of English commerce, it was a departure from ancient strict and honorable adherence to the integrity of the national money, and a breach once begun was with less scruple enlarged. This sovereign, forty years after, proclaimed a currency which from its too great lightness the people refused to receive, and he was compelled to decree that it should pass only at its bullion value. In seven years he made a further deterioration of the coin in fraud of his creditors. Henry V. and Henry VIII. both decreased the weight of their coin, and deteriorated the quality by alchemy and alloy. Elizabeth restored it to nearer the sterling purity than it had been for the hundred years, whence, according to Coke, her tomb was inscribed *moneta ad suum valorem reducta, etc.*; but James I. and Charles I. proclaimed two standards of fineness. The last-named monarch contemplated another deterioration, by which he was to gain over eight shillings in the pound weight of silver, but the iniquitous scheme was frustrated by the able and enlightened protestations of Sir Robert Cotton. So late as King William, 1696, it was thought advisable to proclaim a penalty of £5 against every one refusing to receive the abraded, mutilated and cracked coin of that period. William found it absolutely necessary to repair his coinage or establish a new one; and the question came before parliament whether, with the same quantity and fineness of material, the crown and silver pieces should not be rated at a a higher value. The discussion was protracted, but ceased at once on the appearance of a treatise upon the subject from the pen of John Locke, the enlightened economist as well as a metaphysician.

Our own country will furnish us with some experience of the same character, particularly the remarkable case of the State of Pennsylvania before the war, which enacted that a pound sterling should thenceforward be received at £1 5s. But of this in another place.

IV. In regard to the *computation of values* mentioned in ancient and modern history, it is to be remarked that many difficulties have occurred, that learned authorities have greatly differed, and sometimes widely erred. These difficulties result from the mutable valuation of the precious metals, and the variations of the quantity of them contained in particular coins.

Thus, according to Say, pure silver was worth in the time of Charles V. four times as much as in the age of Voltaire, which that author not observing, fell into a grievous mistake in estimating the amount settled upon the sons of France by the Emperor. The Abbe Raynal was equally led astray, in regarding the revenue of Louis XII. at 36,000,000, when in fact, in the currency of our day, it would have amounted to 144,000,000 francs.

For more remote periods the difficulties are enhanced. Thus, while La Harpe and Levesque value the pearl presented by Cæsar to Servilius, 6,000,000 sestertii, at 1,200,000 francs, later authorities fix upon 6,072,000 francs as much nearer the truth.

Cæsar laid violent hands upon the Roman treasury, and extracted four thousand pounds of gold and eighty thousand pounds of silver, estimated by Vertot at three million francs in value, and by others at thirty-three millions.

Caligula squandered luxuriously twenty-seven hundred million *sestertii* in a single year, which La Harpe considered as five hundred and forty millions, and Say three thousand millions of *livres*.*

V. We come now to *American Coins and Coinage*. Prior to the Revolution, small pieces of silver and copper, for change, were issued by some of the states, even as we now see the gold dollar of North Carolina. Massachusetts, in 1652, established a mint for the coinage of shillings, sixpences, etc.; Maryland, Virginia, and Carolina, afterward issued pieces of copper. Some of these

* Mathieu Vilani.

† Macpherson's Ann. Com. I., 40.

‡ From the conquest till 20 Edward III., a pound sterling was a pound troy weight of silver, divided into twenty shillings. Edward III. coined 22 shillings, and then twenty-five out of it; Henry V., 30s.; Henry VII., 40s.; Elizabeth, 62s.; George III., 66s. The term troy is said to be derived from a fair of that name.—1 *Black. Comm.*, 208-9, note.

* The reader will pursue this point to advantage, by referring to the tables of Arbuthnot, in his Ancient Coins, Weights, etc., to the article Money, supplemental to the Encyclopedia Britannica, by McCulloch; and to the paper by Mr. Hume, among his Philosophical and Political Essays.

coins may still be found in cabinets. But as soon as the Americans had won their freedom, the want of a uniform and national currency began to be felt, and Congress called upon the Secretary of the Treasury, Robert Morris, to prepare a report of the foreign coins circulating in the country. The report was drawn up by the assistant financier, Governeur Morris, who at the same time presented a system of American coinage. Mr. Morris remarks:

"The various coins which have circulated in America, have undergone different changes in value, so that there is hardly any which can be considered as a general standard, unless it be Spanish dollars. These pass in Georgia at 5s.; in North Carolina and New-York at 8s.; in Virginia and the four eastern states at 6s.; in South Carolina at 32s. 5d.; in all the other states at 7s. 6d. The money unit of a new coin, to agree without a fraction with all these different values of a dollar, excepting the last, will be the fourteen hundred and fortieth part of a dollar. Of these units twenty-four will be a penny of Georgia, fifteen a penny of North Carolina or New-York, twenty for Virginia and the eastern states, forty-eight will be thirteen pence of South Carolina, and sixteen one penny of the other states."*

The following schedule of coins was then proposed:

1 crown or 10 dollars, equal to	......	10,000
1 dollar or 10 bills	"	1,000
1 bill or 10 pence	"	100
1 penny or 10 quarters	"	10
1 quarter	"	1

The value of the quarter to be of the value of one grain pure silver, or 1-1440 of a Spanish dollar. The larger piece only to be of gold, and to receive the unpopular designation of "crown," from the devise upon it, of an Indian with a bow and arrows, and with his foot upon a royal crown. The inscription to be *manus inimicus tyrannis*.†

Governeur Morris' scheme was laid over until 1784, when Thomas Jefferson was appointed by Congress on a committee to consider the question of currency. This great statesman soon prepared a profound and elaborate paper, in which he rejected Mr. Morris' unit of measure as too small for convenience, but adopted his system of decimal notation, with the dollar as a basis, and elaborated a system of his own, which met with the approbation of Congress. That of Mr. Morris was afterward materially modified by its ingenious author, but remained still too complicate and artificial, though in some respects with merits above its more successful rival.

Mr. Jefferson we will allow, however, to defend his own system. He says:

"Let us examine each of the four coins proposed.‡

"1. The *golden piece* will be one-fifth more than a half joe, and one-fifteenth more than a double guinea. It will be readily estimated then by reference to either of them, but more readily and accurately as equal to ten dollars.

"2. The unit or *dollar* is a known coin, and the most familiar of all to the minds of the people. It is already adopted from South to North, has identified our currency, and happily presents itself as a unit already introduced. I know of no unit which can be proposed in competition with the dollar but the pound. But what is the pound? (It varies greatly in different states.) To which state shall we give that pre-eminence of which all are so jealous? Or shall we hang the pound sterling about all their necks as a common badge?

"3. The *tenth* will be precisely the Spanish bit or half pistareen. This is perfectly familiar to us all.

"4. The hundredth or *copper* will differ little from the copper now in use among the states."

The Constitution of the United States, adopted not long after, provides—

1. Congress shall have power to coin money, regulate the value thereof, and of foreign coins.

2. No state shall coin money, or make anything but gold or silver a legal tender. Art. 1, 8, 10.

The act of Congress, 1792, established the mint at Philadelphia. The same act fixed the standard of American coins. Thus, the silver pieces to be 1845 parts fine to 179 copper alloy, or 892.4 thousandths. The dollar to weigh 416 grains. The standard of gold pieces, 11 parts fine to 1 part alloy of silver and copper, or 916⅔ thousandths. Weight of eagle, 270 grains. The President's proclamation, of 1796, fixed the weight of the copper cent. 168 grains.

In 1834, Congress found it necessary to change the standard of gold, and provided that the eagle contain 232 grains pure, or 258 grains standard gold, being 26 grains alloy, or 899.225 thousandths. This was raising the value of gold 6.681 thousandths—the old valuation, as 1 to 15 of silver, being found incorrect. The ratio adopted by the act of 1837, is 1 to 15.9884, or 900 thousandths fineness, virtually adding one-fifth grain fine gold to the weight of the eagle. Under the present American system, it is believed that gold is over-valued from one-fourth to one and one-half per cent. This has been the cause of large exportation of gold to the United States, and could only have been intended to substitute that currency for silver. This will be seen in the increased amounts of gold over silver coined lately at our mint.

With this innovation, it of course became necessary to change the current value of all foreign coins, and the act of 1834 did this also; thus the sovereign of $4.57 was raised to $4.87, and others proportionately. The act declared generally that the gold coins of Britain, Portugal, and Brazil, not under 22 carats fine should have the value of 94 8-10 cts. per dwt.; those of France 9-10 fine, 93¼ cts. per dwt.; of Spain, Mexico, and Colombia, 89 9-10 cts. per dwt. Upon this basis, H. Vethake, Esq., computes a table:

* Life of Governeur Morris, by Jared Sparks, vol. I., p. 275

† Ibid.

‡ Jefferson's Works, pp. 135, 136

COINS OF BRITAIN, PORTUGAL AND BRAZIL.

22 carats.

Value in United States currency*—

Britain—Guinea		$5 11 0
	Sovereign	4 86 9
Portugal—Dobraon (large)		32 70 6
	Moidore	6 55 7
	Milree, 1755	0 78 0
Brazil—Dobraon		32 70 6
	Dobra	17 30 1
	Moidore	6 55 7

GOLD OF FRANCE.—9–10.

Double Louis	$9 15 4
Double Napoleon	7 71 8
New Louis	3 85 9

GOLD OF SPAIN.

Doubloon	15 59 0
Quarter Pistole, 1772	1 01 1

The silver dollar of Mexico, Peru, Chili, and Central America, of the weight of 415 grains, is made current by the act of 1834; and the five-franc piece of France valued at 93 cts. when of the fineness of 10 oz. 16 dwt., in lb. troy.

By the act of Congress, May 22d, 1846, it was declared that foreign coins should be estimated at the custom-house at the following values, to wit:

Dollar of Sweden and Norway, 1.06c.; dollar of Denmark, 1.05c; thaler of Prussia and North German States, 69c.; florins South German States, 40; florin Austrian Empire, &c, 48½; lira, Venetian Kingdom and of Tuscany, 16c.; franc of Austria and Belgium, and lira of Sardinia, 18.6; ducat of Naples, 80; ounce of Sicily, 2.40; pound British Provinces, Nova Scotia, New Brunswick, Newfoundland and Canada, 4.00.

Bullion may be assayed at the mint for a small per centage, or coined, the only charge in the last case being for refining and toughening, when necessary, for alloys, and for the separation of gold and silver when combined. In this our system differs from that of England, where all the gold coinage is done at the expense of government—an erroneous principle, since it happens that foreigners are frequently receiving a premium at the expense of British subjects.† The act of 1835, established branch mints at Charlotte, N. C., Dahlonega, Ga. and New Orleans, the first two being restricted to gold coinage.

CONSULAR SYSTEM.—The Empire of Commerce began its growth in what we are accustomed to call the "dark ages." The flint and steel were in its hand, which struck out the sparks of light that are recognized at that obscure period. The best authorities on international or public law and modern civilization admit, that the stipulations and compacts which commerce induced, were among the first in the order of those influences, which resulted in the resuscitation of letters and arts, and in the entire redemption of mankind. The lordly barons in wresting from King John the rights he had usurped, stipulated at the same time in behalf of the rights of all merchant traders visiting the empire.*

The London chapmen, in losing their insignificance and in growing up to princely wealth, established a third estate in the kingdom; too respectable to be despised, too powerful to be resisted, and bold enough to declare for or against kings and dynasties, for the Henrys or Edwards of the middle ages.

Whether for Britain, for France, or for Russia—for India, for the South Seas and the Pacific, or for republican America—there is but one voice now, and that cries for "trade." "Give us of your labor, and take of ours." "Buy" or "sell" are the pregnant words in every language under heaven. The Rialto is the centre of the world's negotiations. For this navies float upon the ocean, for this grave embassies receive audience from the Tammahamahas of the Pacific, and talk Chinese with the potentates of the Celestial Empire.

What has become *war* in the lexicography of "King Commerce's" subjects? Will men apply torches to the granaries which contain their bread? Will they batter to pieces and sink in the ocean the elements of trade, which are to warm them amid winter snows, and defend them from summer suns? The lines of consolidation between nations and men are verging nearer to each other; and they meet in the unity, the entire "oneness" of us all.

To watch over and protect the great interests of trade, permanent departments of government have been instituted, which, taken together, constitute what is called the Consular System of the world. These *agencies*, representing their sovereign and country, are located at every considerable emporium of traffic, and by the theory of their constitution, are supposed to possess the sleeplessness of Argus, in watching over the rights and privileges and interests of their countrymen abroad, and the many-handedness of Briareus, in providing for their security and defence.

This Consular System was scarcely at all understood among the ancients. Mr. Lester, our able and efficient consul at Genoa, whose work upon this subject is now before us, observes that we get the term *consul* from

* A *minute* difference in mills would result, were the value estimated by the quantum of pure gold in the new eagle, of 232 grains.

† Britain demands a heavy seignorage or charge for coining silver, and realizes a profit of 100 per cent. on copper.

* This provision of the Magna Charta drew from Montesquieu the concession that the people of England, above all other people in the world, understood the value of commerce and liberty.

the Romans; and certainly we get little else. The consuls of the early republic were scarcely less in authority than the kings they superseded. Still the interests of commerce were not neglected in antiquity, but agents were located in different trading states, charged with duties of a similar nature to our modern consuls. The codes of international law, which obtained, for the most part, in those ages even among the most enlightened nations, were such as to speak little for the advancement of mankind. The ships of Athens were characterized as a "piratical fleet,"—"universal spoliation abroad, and cruel oppression at home," is affirmed of Rome, and Phœnicia, Tyre, and Carthage, recognized no rights or duties in their intercourse with foreigners.

Mr. Lester confesses the difficulties of tracing out the origin of the modern system:

"It has long been a disputed point with whom the modern Consular System originated, and what nation first led the way in the establishment of the commercial code, which was finally adopted by modern states, and has in our own times worked itself so deeply into the laws of nations. Nor could it be placed in its proper light without great toil and learning, aided by all the facilities which might be derived from investigations conducted on the shores and islands of the Mediterranean." Pp. 165–66.

When the decayed tree of Rome had fallen and lay massive in its ruins, there grew up on the soil of Italy a few republics of contracted territorial limits, but of genius and enterprise which astonished the world, and of power and influence which made them selves felt among crowned potentates, and extorted from Rome's proud pontiff the confession, that Genoa alone was more "adequate" to the conquest of the Saracens in Africa, than any other power in Europe.

That noble Commercial Code, the *Consolato del Mare*, which has been attributed to the Spaniards, is now said to have originated in the councils of Pisa. The Pisans conquered Amalfi in the 12th century, and carried off the copy of Justinian's Institutes, which had been deposited there—the only copy existing. *Consoluto del Mare* recognizes the existence and regulates the actions of the Consular System.

Venice and Genoa were not long in adopting and carrying out the wise policy of the Pisans. They had commercial agents throughout all the East, and wherever public interests appeared to require it. These officers were held in the highest regard; they were required to be diplomatists; they were sent in public vessels, and were not allowed to participate in any traffic. What were the results?

We are told of Venice—

"Her daughters had their dowers
From spoils of nations; and the exhaustless East
Poured in her lap all gems in sparkling showers."

And Shakspeare says:

"Since that the trade and profit of the city
Consisteth of all nations."

"Venice, which had been founded by a few old men, women and children, who had fled to the marshes of the Adriatic, to escape the rage and devastation of the northern barbarians, who were sweeping over Italy, became, in a few centuries, the first power in Europe. Pisa, which had been obliged to struggle for many years against the most formidable obstacles that can ever impede the growth of new states, with a malaria which annually swept off a multitude of her population, soon made her name feared from the pillars of Hercules to the shores of the Danube and the banks of the Nile, and became the commercial lawgiver of all future ages. Genoa, which stands at the head of the Ligurian sea, hemmed in by almost impassable mountains, the Apennines and maritime Alps (which she could not cross), could not get her bread from the barren and rocky hill-sides, and she was driven out upon the Mediterranean. In the 8th century, the little city of Genoa drove the Saracens from their hold on the continent to the island of Corsica; from Corsica she chased them to Sardinia; from Sardinia, she forced them out upon the open sea, and at last fell upon the seat of their power in Africa, and laid their capital in the dust—seized uncounted millions of treasure, liberated all the Christian captives of all their wars, and dragged back their dreaded chief to an Italian prison, where he died in chains." Pp. 176–78.

It was not till 1845 that England commissioned an agent to reside abroad for the performance of consular duties, and not until the 17th century that these commissions came to be generally granted throughout the European States.

We have alluded to Mr. Lester's letter to Mr. Campbell. This active representative of our merchants abroad complains bitterly of the defects of the American consular system. He regards it, in fact, as no system at all; and trusts that a government such as ours will not long endure its abuses. Surely there needs no elaborate argument at this late day to establish the importance, the absolute necessity, of a proper vigilance over our commerce and our shipping, now scattered over every sea in the world, and over our citizens, who find their way "to the uttermost ends of the earth." If there be any deficiency in the present establishment, an American Congress will look to it—an American people will demand its removal.

We make a few extracts from Mr. Lester, which establish the abuse, and propose the remedy:

"The office of a consul is generally held by American *merchants* or *foreigners*; for, with a few exceptions, no American who is qualified for such a station will ask for or accept an office which is only a bill of expense, except with a view of making his official standing contribute to his own speculations. There are many ports where an American business cannot be supported; and, in such cases, those consulates are filled by foreigners." P. 191.

In regard to the evil of appointing a *merchant* to be consul, Mr. Lester gives the following example in point:

"In 1842 or 1843, (I am not certain which,) an American merchantman arrived at a port in the Mediterranean with a valuable cargo, which the captain was authorized to consign to any house he might select. He addressed himself to the consul, from whom he had reason (as his constituted adviser) to expect safe and disinterested counsel. The consul requested him to go on making the necessary arrangements for discharging his cargo, and call the following day. In the mean time the consul laid a scheme by which he should receive no little profit; although, with an appearance of disinterestedness, the cargo was to be consigned to another man. The captain had never been in the port before, could not speak a word of the language, was ignorant of the customs of the place and the state of the market, which put it out of his power to get the necessary information to guide him in transacting the business for himself. The cargo was just the one which at that moment, if properly sold, would have given the largest profit to the owners. Intelligence had been privately received by the consul the day before, which made his profit large and sure upon his own merchandise and that of the captain. This intelligence, however, he did not communicate to the captain, and his cargo went for the price which then ruled in the market! This intelligence it was the duty of the consul to communicate to the captain, and he would have done it without doubt, had he been disinterested! He kept his own counsel, and made over ten thousand dollars by the speculation!" Pp. 194–5.

Mr. Lester exposes the evils of appointing *foreigners* to our consulates abroad, men without any interest or regard for our institutions, or even, at times, any knowledge of them. He received from one of these consuls, not long since, a letter directed "To his Lordship, the American Consul-General of the United States and its Dependencies."

The following extract illustrates the subject most pointedly:

"For several years the consulate of Trieste has been held by an Englishman, by the name of Moore; and as he has been recently removed, and with very great propriety, I feel no delicacy in calling his name and stating a fact. While the M'Leod case was pending in this country, and a rupture with Great Britain seemed likely to take place, the governor of Malta dispatched a fleet of steamers to the straits of Gibraltar to intercept all our merchant vessels, as soon as the governor of Gibraltar received an intimation of the hostile intentions of Great Britain. At this time there were a large number of our merchantmen in the Mediterranean, and several at Trieste.

"Mr. Andrews, our consul at Malta, immediately sent dispatches to all his colleagues in that sea, communicating this important information, that all American vessels might have warning, and remain in the ports of friendly powers. Mr. Andrews had often enough before had occasion to know that no dependence could be placed upon the consul at Trieste, and he sent a dispatch to Mr. Perdicarus, consul at Athens, requesting him to embrace the earliest opportunity of giving intelligence to our merchantmen in the port of Trieste; and assigned as a reason for adopting this course, that Moore, being an Englishman, no dependence could be placed upon him in such a case. To show how well-grounded was this conviction, Mr. Moore was heard by several Americans (I am informed) to say, that 'Mr. Andrews did perfectly right; for he must have been a great fool to suppose I should do anything that would have a direct tendency to injure my country. The Americans appoint me consul, to do consular business in time of peace; but when war comes that is quite another matter.'"

Mr. Lester proposes, as a remedy, the adoption of the following principles:

Consuls should be paid salaries sufficient to preserve the rank and dignity of the office; should have judicial power to settle differences between citizens abroad; should have a proper library of commerce and diplomacy, and have all their rights and duties particularly defined; should be prohibited from any commercial transactions whatever on their own account; should have no fees beyond their salary; should be divided into grades of office, consuls, vice-consuls, and consuls-general; the consul-general to have served three years in a simple consulate first, and his jurisdiction to extend over several of these consulates. Lastly, Mr. Lester would have commercial agents to gather information abroad for the use of government. At the meeting of the Zollverein, in 1843, Great Britain had thirteen agents present, and the United States had but one—he being accidentally on the spot.

We close with a paragraph which sums up the whole:

"First, there is not an American merchant, nor an American master, nor an American seaman, who is not disgusted with the wretched system, and who would not rejoice in a change.

"Second, there is not an American consul who will not join with them.

"Third, our commerce is laboring under embarrassments which can never be removed until we have organized an efficient and well-regulated Consular Establishment." P. 214.

COMMERCE—Its Origin, Progress, and Influences.—The history of trade carries us back to the primeval history of man himself. Neither science nor art nor any of the institutions of society have anything like the antiquity which of right pertains to this. The first want which was ever felt, the first appetite appeased, were but stimulants offered to new wants and appetites, whose gratification was denied to the unaided labors of the individual. We arrive at barter when we reach a point where the individual want calls into requisition efforts beyond what the individual can exert. When one man has not the thing which he desires, but has that which its proprietor would equally value, there is at once laid a foundation for that system of *exchanges* which is among the first developments in the progress of trade.

Locke, it is, perhaps, who tells us that the hunter of the hills, whom the day's chase has crowned with no other than venison, would be loth to appropriate the whole of it to himself if he knew that his neighbor, whose fire flickered over the way, had a fine stock of grouse and pheasant preparing for the feast, and would be glad enough to smoke upon the embers with it a buck's quarter. If men were the same in those extreme ages as they are now, we are sure that these progenitors of Nimrod partook of each other's good cheer without knowing a word of any of the "laws which regulate exchanges." A shoulder of venison was good for at least a pair of canvas-back ducks. Plain Cudjo, on one of our Southern plantations, proves his connection with the genus homo, by taking half his weekly allowance of rice and bartering it away for a mess of Indian meal.

Anderson, in his History of Commerce, tells of a singular custom which prevailed with several nations of remote antiquity. Happening to have an overplus of any particular commodity or class of commodities, either of these nations would bear the excess to its border limits, and heap it up there. This surplus the neighbor nation drew upon as need be, substituting for the removed deposit so much of its own redundant produce of a different character, as it considered a fair equivalent. Such a system betrays great simplicity of manners and integrity of heart. We would not bespeak for it much favor in an age like ours, when greedy avarice, wily policy, and dollar-and-cent philosophy, take strong hold upon men's propensities. Anderson does not mention, if any frauds resulted from this pristine liberality.

The origin of commerce is a subject which by no means admits of much philosophizing, and we are rather amused than instructed by the wire-drawn theories with which the reader is almost sure to be treated by every writer who sets himself up as instructor in this branch of history; as if traffic of some description were not just as natural, and just as necessary, in the progress of mankind, as the use of language or the powers of locomotion. To explain the origin of the former appears to us as profitless at least as that of the latter.

Nearly six thousand years have passed away since man began to earn his subsistence by the sweat of his brow, and for half of this period we have no other record than that to be found in the Hebrew Bible. Profane history carries us to its extent when we reach the age of Homer, one thousand years before that of Jesus Christ. In Homer's time, navigation had become a system, and the Scion muse sings through his pages of the noble fleet which followed the fortunes of Agamemnon against the strong-walled Troy—

> "What crowded armies, from what climes they bring
> Their names, their numbers, and their chiefs I sing."
> ILIAD, II.

We must go farther back than this to find when trade became first a system.

We take up the Bible and turn to the lamentations and sorrows of Job. Whoever Job might have been, or whoever was the author of the book which chronicles his fortunes, it is certain that it is one of antiquity, equal, if not superior, to any other record in the world. Some have even given it an antediluvian origin. We have depicted in it at least the manners and customs of the patriarchal era. • But the gold of Ophir and the Ethiopian topaz, as articles of commerce, would appear to have been familiar enough at that period to Arabian luxury.

Abraham counted out to Ephron for the burial-place of Macpelah (Gen. xxiii. 16), *silver, current with the merchant*, three thousand five hundred years ago. This evidences, then, a currency and a commercial community. The children whom God has raised up to Abraham—the Hebrews, of all ages and countries from that time to this—have proved themselves, beyond all compare, the most extraordinary nation of traders and traffickers that the annals of mankind have yet recorded. Blackstone fixes upon them the earliest use of that important instrument of commerce, the bill of exchange;* and English historians chronicle how these wealthy Hebrews, ere yet toleration became a virtue, were fleeced of their wares and moneys to satisfy the exorbitant and tyrannical demands of the sovereign purse. Old Isaac, of York, or some other "wealthy Tubal" of his tribe, it was, whose teeth were extracted, one day, by England's king, till he had brought to light from his hidden treasures gold enough to buy him ransom from his hard usage. We are not told whether Isaac came from under the operation toothless, or how many molars and incisors he conceived his treasury to be worth. A modern traveler in Syria pays the same tribute to these descendants of Jacob. "From morning until night," says he, "and from night until morning, in the streets, in the houses, in the public places and promenades, everywhere and for ever, nothing is to be heard in Syria but merchandise and money, money and merchandise."

Abraham went down into Egypt. The Egyptians were a people *sui generis*. They abhorred foreigners on a deep-rooted principle; and these men of yore, of mummies, pyramids, and obelisks, were little qualified for any of the enterprises of trade. They did, however, under one or two sovereigns, exhibit a different characteristic, but the thing was forced. Their traders navigated

* This method is said to have been brought into general use by the Jews and Lombards, when banished for their usury and other vices, in order to draw their effects more easily out of France and England into those countries into which they had chosen to reside. 2 *Black. Comm.*, 269.

for a short season the waters of the Red Sea and Indian Ocean. Long after this, when ancient Egypt belonged to history, and when Alexander the Great had subdued his countrymen and half the world beside, the conqueror fixed upon the site and built the city of Alexandria, midway between the Mediterranean and Indian seas, and commanding the commerce of either. Scarcely a city reached to so great a point of eminence for many centuries as Alexandria, in all the great departments of trade; and it had been to this day as it was in its early existence, but for the skill of Portuguese navigators doubling the "Cape of Storms," and opening a new and better avenue from Europe to the East Indies. From that day to this Alexandria is named "no more."

But we are not done with the Jews. We are to speak of that empire which, in all pomp and splendor and Eastern gorgeousness, David and Solomon raised up and maintained on the shores of ancient Judea. There was a compact, a commercial compact between David and Hiram of Tyre, for the supply of timber and artisans necessary in embellishing the seat of Jewish empire. Solomon carried out the stipulations of his father, and extended the operations of the great co-partnership he had formed. The untold wealth and magnificence of Israel's sapient king stand out boldly in the annals of the nation. Tyrians and Hebrews together toiled on the shores of the Red Sea, at Eziongeber, in fitting out a fleet of ships for their sovereigns. It is certain that this fleet had commercial ends, and that it made a successful adventure somewhere, but where, no one exactly understands. Speculations have multiplied upon the subject. Beawes, in his "Lex Mercatoria," devotes many a page to the inquiry, and labors hard to show that the allied fleet visited the islands of the East Indies, and found, somewhere there, the Ophir and Tarshish, from which the Bible seems to tell us that such abundant gold and treasure were obtained. The periodical winds in these seas explain the success of navigation in the absence of compass or chronometer. Other places, too, these shipping doubtless visited on the coast of Asia and Ethiopia; but as most of this is conjecture, the reader can conjecture as well as ourselves.

Phœnicia, in all antiquity, is without example or parallel. More than twenty-two hundred years before Christ, the Phœnicians had founded the great commercial mart of Sidon. In Sidon were to be found the most splendid developments of arts, manufactures, and commerce, before the Christian era. The Sidonians were an extraordinary people, who marked themselves strongly upon antiquity. Their merchant fleets opened the gates of the Mediterranean, and sailed away beyond the Pillars of Hercules, the *ne plus ultra* of the ancient world. They brought back to the vicinities of the Levant the ore which they obtained in Britain from the miners of Cornwall. With cargoes purchased in Arabia, Ethiopia, and India, these fathers of navigation made their way to Elath, on the Arabian Sea; an overland transportation from Elath to Rhinocolura, and a re-shipment from that port, found their commodities at last safely landed at the quays of Tyre.

Let the rapt visions of Ezekiel describe for us Tyre, in all the georgeousness of Eastern metaphor:

> "O thou that art situate at the entry of the sea, which art a merchant of the people for many isles; thy borders are in the midst of the sea, thy builders have perfected thy beauty. Fine linen with broidered work from Egypt was that which thou spreadest forth to be thy sail; blue and purple from the isles of Elishah was that which covered thee. The inhabitants of Zidon and Arvad were thy mariners: thy wise men that were within thee, were thy pilots. The ancients of Gebal, and the wise men thereof were in thee, thy caulkers: all the ships of the sea, with their mariners, were in thee, to occupy thy merchandise. Tarshish was thy merchant by reason of the multitude of all kinds of riches; with silver, iron, tin, and lead, they traded in thy fairs. Javan, Tubal, and Meshech, were thy merchants; they traded *the persons of men* and vessels of brass in thy market. Syria was thy merchant by reason of the multitude of the wares of thy making: they occupied in thy fairs with emeralds, purple and broidered work, and fine linen, coral, and agate. Judah and the land of Israel, they were thy merchants. Damascus was thy merchant. Arabia, and all the princes of Kedar, in thee, were thy merchants. The ships of Tarshish did sing of thee in thy markets, and thou wast replenished and made very glorious in the midst of the seas. What city is like Tyrus? By thy great wisdom and by thy traffic hast thou increased thy riches, and thy heart is lifted up because of thy riches!"

The fate of this great city we are all familiar with. Sacked and destroyed by Nebuchadnezzar, it was only rebuilt to suffer the same dismal fate at the hands of Alexander. Tyre, the ancient mariner and merchant, has left behind but few traces of his opulence, and the nation of whom Tibullus wrote—"Prima ratem ventis credere docta Tyros," and of whom God decreed, "thou shalt be a terror, and shalt never be any more," fulfilled at last its destiny.

Carthage was a colony of the Phœnicians planted in Africa. The infant settlement, by the extension of its trade and the energy and enterprise of its inhabitants, soon grew up to a stature so great and powerful, that the salvation of the Roman empire admitted but of one voice at its capital—*Carthago delenda esse;* Carthage must be destroyed. This commercial people, through two of the bloodiest and most protracted wars of which history has any mention, met, braved, and defied the "Eagle" and the mailed legions of Rome, and only yielded at last with a struggle worthy of Homer's deities.

Before the Greek states began to send out colonies to the numerous islands of the

Ægean, the Greeks knew little of foreign trade. So soon, however, as these little bands migrated off from the mother country, the influences of their position, free institutions and unrestricted customs began to be felt among themselves, and to re-act upon the parent states. Nearly all of Grecian commerce, prior to the time of Alexander, was confined to this trade with the colonies.

The Romans never were a trading people. Their sympathies were for agriculture, war, and conquest. Trade was held in contempt, and nothing but the sword and the plow were counted honorable. To every person of rank, birth, or fortune, (says Kent,) the Romans prohibited commerce; and no senator was allowed to own a vessel larger than a boat sufficient to carry his own corn and fruits. They were content to receive through Egypt those supplies of Eastern commodities which ministered to their luxury and taste. When the empire was removed to Byzantium, in the fourth century, the commerce of Rome, such as it was, fell almost entirely into decay.

All Scandinavia and the northern hive poured down in the third, fourth, and fifth centuries, upon Rome, their myriads of barbarians. Huns, Goths, Vandals, Attilas, and Alarics—these terrific men swept away all traces of civilization for a gloomy period, and with fire and sword desolated the whole of southern Europe. Commerce received a death-blow in the struggles of this era.

The Byzantian or Greek empire, meanwhile continued its intercourse with Alexandria, and received thence its oriental supplies, until the Arabians, seizing upon Egypt, put a stop at last to this lucrative branch of commerce. We next hear of the Byzantians sailing up the Indus to its highest navigable points, transporting their commerce thence overland to Oxus, and down to the Caspian Sea. Having reached the sea, they made sail into the Volga; transported their commodities across the country to the Tanais, thence to the Euxine, to be shipped there ultimately for Byzantium itself.

It is unnecessary to dwell upon that period of darkness and gloom which settled down upon the seats of ancient letters, civilization, and commerce, when the lights of Rome and Greece had been put out, and bloodshed, anarchy, and fierce discord attained their despotic empire. It seemed as if God had cursed and withered the fair work of his own hand.

There rose at last in Italy, upon these ruins, a community which has been celebrated in every subsequent age. "Pisa was the first republic that rose into power after the dismemberment of the Roman empire," says Mr. Lester in his late work, "and to her, modern times are more indebted for their civilization than to any other people who have flourished since the ancient Romans."

If Italy witnessed the flickering and expiring rays of that light which, in its full blaze, had illumined the ancient world, it was on the soil of Italy that it was re-lit again in the progress of centuries, and it was from thence that darkened Europe caught the first faint beams of morning which broke upon the world. The night of arts, sciences, and commerce, was dissipated by the lights which shone from the Adriatic and the free Italian republics.

We are to speak of Venice and Genoa, who were to modern ages what Tyre and Carthage were to those which had been numbered before the Christian era. Inspired with the recollections of the past, and full of the holy associations of the moment, Byron, standing on the "Bridge of Sighs," and viewing the ruins of Italian glory—

"Where Venice sat in state throned on her hundred isles."

with full heart and impassioned eloquence, lamented over the mistress of the Adriatic, her "dead doges," her perished commerce, her "crumbling palaces" and exhausted treasures—

"In youth she was all glory—a new Tyre;
Her very by-word sprung from victory—
The 'Planter of the Lion,' which through fire
And blood she bore o'er subject earth and sea;
Though making many slaves, herself still free,
And Europe's bulwark 'gainst the Ottomite."

Venice, Genoa and Pisa excelled in genius, spirit, and enterprise, all the nations of Europe. Driven from barbarous invasion to their retreats, these republics, territorially contracted, and little favored in soil, reached to a pitch of opulence and empire which excites our highest admiration. Their rich argosies went out upon the Mediterranean, and their mariners braved the storms of every ocean. Liberty spoke in their halls, and law resumed again its sway. One of the best commercial codes which the world has ever known, we are told, originated in the councils of Pisa.

In the tenth century, Venice had established commercial intercourse with the Saracens of Egypt and Syria, for their staples of sugar and rice, for dates, senna, cassia, flax, linen, balm, perfumes, galls, wrought silks, soaps, etc. She traded, too, for the rich spices and precious stones of India, and with merchandise so rare and rich entered the markets of western Europe, and commanded the whole of its valuable trade.

The Italian republics, when the crusades were firing the brains of knights, kings and beggars, appeared to be inspired too with some portion of the religious frenzy. But the Italians were too good merchants to enter upon enterprises as wild as these without first stipulating for privileges of commerce and trade from the monarchs whom they might serve. They were not such zealots as to give up their ships without prospect of advantage, when their employment in carrying helmets, breastplates, and tall soldiery, was as good as carrying bales of stuffs and merchandise.

We cannot refrain here from introducing a passage from Lester's letter on the "Consular System," which is eloquently descriptive of the progress of one of these republics, and which emanates from a man who was inspired by a residence on its very soil.

"Genoa contributed more powerfully than any other Italian state to the early crusades. The Ligurian* Republic had been able to resist the rush of barbarians from the North, and had, even in the ninth century, nearly destroyed the Saracen empire in the islands of the Mediterranean and on the African coast. More deeply fired with the spirit of maritime adventure than almost any other state in the world, she led the way in the commerce of the east, and closed her magnificent career by the discovery of the New World. Even before the time of Peter the Hermit, she had opened a flourishing commerce with Asia, and she was present at the conquest of Antioch and of Jerusalem. The chivalric leaders of those bold enterprises well knew how much they owed to her valor and commercial activity: and the red cross in the white field, the ensign of the Ligurian republic, was planted on the towers of Antioch and the battlements of Jerusalem. Godfrey and Baldwin ordered the following inscription to be placed over the Holy Sepulchre: '*Stronghold of the Genoese.*' She formed treaties with the Moorish and African princes, and gained, by diplomacy or conquest, a strong foothold in the Black Sea, where she founded a powerful colony that augmented her commercial wealth incredibly."

When Pisa, in those fearful contests which shook the shores of Italy, had yielded to the arms of Genoa, this state eclipsed then even Venice herself.

Whatever may be thought of the crusades in this period of the world's enlightenment, all history attests that they introduced, into Europe, Eastern tastes and customs, and led the way to an extension of commerce, and ultimately to a new era of light, truth and liberty.

In the northern parts of Europe, on the Baltic, and in the island of Gothland, grew up, between the eleventh and twefth centuries, the city of Wisburg. The marine ordinances of this now decayed town are celebrated in the annals of commercial nations. Cleirac gives a glowing account of the wealth and prosperity of the city. He speaks of it then as the most celebrated and flourishing emporium in Europe, where merchants from all parts come to traffic, and had their shops and warehouses, and enjoyed the same privileges as the native inhabitants themselves. Chancellor Kent, in commenting upon this passage from Cleirac, and contrasting with it the Wisburg of the Baltic as we find it now, finds the occasion fitting to indulge the "melancholy admonition of the poet," that "trade's proud empire hastes to swift decay."

Between the years 1164 and 1254, was formed in Europe what is known in history (and famed as known) as the Hanseatic League. The object of this league was protection to the trade of the free cities which formed it, from the robber clans and "roving barbarians" of the North, and the pirates which swarmed in every sea. Lubeck was at the head of the league of Hanse towns, and her first allies in the federacy were Brunswick, Bremen, Hamburg, Dantzic and Cologne. The league extended its influence to embrace most of the trading cities of Northern Europe, and attained to so great power as to form treaties with sovereigns themselves. Its duration was terminated at last by the jealousy of these sovereigns, who withdrew their cities from the alliance.

In coming down to modern times, we tread upon ground so familiar, that any lengthy exhibition of the extenson of commerce will be unnecessary. We all know, familiarly enough, that at the present moment cotton, woolens, silks and French wines have larger influence in making Americans, Englishmen and Frenchmen shake hands over their quarrels, and avow that they have ever loved each other right well, than all the natural affection they might ever be supposed to entertain for each other put together, and all their universal philanthropy in the bargain. We have said before, and repeat it, that the mercantile interests rule the world, and right grateful are we that Providence has imposed so firm a ligament to join together his fractious, headstrong and over-erring children. We sometimes meet with fine treatises on benevolence, disinterested philanthropy, and other things of the same stamp; and once upon a time were fond ourselves of talking about the "dignity of human nature," etc.; but after all, human nature is not without its frailties, and the "stern Saxon," without being anything of a coward either, will never attempt to dictate peace at the cannon's mouth with his neighbor on this side of the water, while he has broadcloths to sell, and a million and a half bags of cotton to buy. And we do not slander the neighbor on this side of the water much by a similar remark.

But Venice, Genoa, Pisa, Wisburg and the Hanse towns, such as they were, have passed away, and the commerce of the world is in other hands. The hardy Portuguese mariners, in discovering the new passage to the East, round the Cape of Good Hope,

* This name, derived from the Romans, was generally used by the Genoese till the downfall of their republic.

struck a blow at the Italian republics from which they never recovered. Spain and Portugal, on the discovery of America, divided the world between themselves, and struggled to establish a magnificent commercial monopoly. The famous treaty of Tordesillas, 1494, entered into between these nations, opened the eyes of England to the schemes which were to exclude her from a participation in the best fruits of either India.

"The progress of commerce," says Robertson, in his admirable chapter introductory to the History of Charles V., "the progress of commerce had considerable influence in polishing the manners of the European nations, and in establishing among them order, equal laws, and humanity. It tends to wear off those prejudices which maintain distinction and animosity between nations. It softens and polishes the manners of men. It unites them by one of the strongest of all ties, the desire of supplying their mutual wants. It disposes them to peace by establishing in every state an order of citizens bound by their interests to be the guardians of public tranquillity. In proportion as commerce made its way into the different countries of Europe, they successively turned their attention to those objects and adopted those manners which occupy and distinguish polished nations."

In the fourteenth century, we are told by Hallam—History Middle Ages, p. 475—that Flanders had become a market for all the world; and that merchants from seventeen kingdoms had their settled domiciles at Bruges, besides strangers from almost unknown countries.

Edward III. was the father of English commerce. Before his reign no advances of any character had been made in that country to extend its foreign intercourse, but Edward set himself in earnest to build up and establish the kingdom. He invited over from Flanders artisans and workmen, who may almost be said to have originated the manufacturing system of England. It is not a little curious to consider the motives which were held out to this enterprising body of men, as they are furnished for us in a venerable record. They were told that in England "they should feed on fat beef and mutton, till nothing but their fullness should stint their stomachs; that their beds should be good and their bed-fellows better, seeing the richest yeoman in England would not disdain to marry their daughters unto them." The products of the labors of these craftsmen, feeding upon "fat beef and mutton" to respectable corpulency, became soon known and famous in the markets of all Europe.

There was little mercantile spirit in England before the time of Queen Elizabeth. True it is, that King John's barons forced the monarch into an acknowledgment of the rights of foreign merchants visiting the empire; but it was long after King John and his barons, ere the English people began to appreciate the advantages of foreign trade. Henry the Eighth was cruel and tyrannical, and taxed illegally the interest he ought to have fostered. Elizabeth had greatness of mind sufficient for the purposes of empire, and had she been as well acquainted with the true principles which regulate trade, as she was desirous of stimulating it in every way, she had been higher praised in history. Her numerous monopolies granted, whether of sweet wines, licenses, or whatever else, were blunders which could only be accounted for by favoritism, were it not notorious that at that period these were considered in themselves to be evidences of sound policy.

In a lecture, delivered by T. W. Tucker, of New-York, on the merchants of the time of Queen Elizabeth, published several years ago in Hunt's Magazine, there is an enumeration of the various monopolies which were granted by that sovereign. We are happy to lay our hands on the address at this moment, as it will save us from farther reference on the point.

The Dutch traders of London, resident at a part of it called the Stilyard, were famous at that epoch, and obtained privileges and immunities from the monarch sufficient to set up the most grinding monopolies.

On the fall of the Dutch traders, the company of English merchant adventurers was formed. This company, too, rose to great wealth and importance, exporting annually English woolen cloths to the amount of £1,000,000 sterling, and maintaining abroad the highest possible credit. The Russia company, about the same time, and the Turkey company existed. The latter traded with India and reached the heart of the Mogul empire. Hard upon these followed the Morocco company, the company of Eastland merchants, the Hamburg company, the Guinea and the East India companies. Sir Francis Drake, in some of his little short of piratical cruisings, first suggested to England the importance of the Indian trade. This trade enriched the sovereign then, and has enriched the nation ever since.

We pass over that stormy season which occupied the larger portions of the reigns of James I. and Charles I. In the disasters of anarchy and civil war which befell the nation at this time, it would have been impossible for commercial enterprise to exhibit itself in any of its higher developments.

Hume, indeed, has informed us that in the reign of James I. the Dutch traded to England with six hundred ships, but England in turn could furnish on her own account but sixty ships in the same traffic. Nine-tenths of the English commerce at this period consisted of woolen manufactured goods.

The administration of Cromwell was crowned with many results favorable to trade. The liberal principles of the Protector could not endure those severe restrictions and monopolies in which the prosperity of the nation had been bound up, and he abolished them all.

When Charles II. was restored to the throne of his father, a new impulse appeared to be given to everything in England, so much so, that Russell affirms in his Modern Europe, "that at no former or subsequent period did England ever make such rapid progress in commerce and riches as during that inglorious one which followed the Restoration, and terminated in the expulsion of the Stuarts."

The present enormous commercial stature of Great Britain is attributed by McCulloch, not to the heaps upon heaps of parliamentary acts for the encouragement of navigation and trade, but to the extraordinary improvements and consequent extension of her manufactures since 1770. Happily seated upon an island girt around by the sea, she finds that the extraordinary influence which she is exerting upon the world, is dependent more upon the immensity of her naval armaments and commercial marine than upon the extent of her territories, or the numerical proportion of her inhabitants. Like Athens of old, she finds strength and safety in her "wooden walls."

The cotton manufacturing system of England has been the offspring, great as it is, of the last seventy-five years. At the commencement of this period it was nothing; at its termination half the entire exports of British produce consists of cotton stuffs and yarn. England looks upon her Hargraves, Arkwrights, Cromptons and Watts, as America does upon her Fultons and Whitneys; but England looks upon her own liberty and enterprise as above them all. In fact, says one of her writers, when these are impaired, the colossal fabric of her prosperity will crumble into dust; and the commerce of Liverpool, London and Glasgow, like that of Tyre, Carthage and Palmyra, will, at no distant period, be famous only in history.

We come at last to consider the subject before us, in connection with the past and present history of America. There is reason enough to dwell upon the ample enterprise, and stubborn, unyielding spirit of the people who fled across the ocean from the tyrannies of the old world, and established, among the deep forests of the new, the germs of a nation which has already become great. What could subdue the spirit of a people like this? Rugged as their own wild homes, the infant colonists braved the seas and the storms. They dug the graves of tyrants with the same implements that brought them bread out of the soil. Struggling with the desperate savage at one moment, they braved at the next the fierce storms and monsters of the deep. There is no adolescence in such a people. They spring into manhood's vigor from the infant's imbecility.

There went up into the high court of Parliament, as early as the year 1670, a grave charge against the colonies which England "protected" across the ocean. Said the ministers, they violate our ordinances of trade with impunity, and our navigation laws, which with infinite pains we have devised, they trample under foot with disdain. Their traders sally out upon the deep, and we find them seeking entrance into all the ports of Europe. "They even encourage"—these are the words of the remonstrance—"they even encourage foreigners to trade with them."

One hundred years after this, Edmund Burke stood up, in the halls of the same Parliament of England, an advocate of freedom and humanity, and a deadly, implacable foeman to their assailants.

This noble Roman found in the wrongs of his countrymen across the ocean a theme worthy of his highest eloquence, and in their daring enterprise that which was too much even for his unmatched powers to portray. Who does not remember his inimitable speech in which the orator found all his country at his heart? We cannot refrain an extract, and we seem to see all the glory of our country shadowed forth in what was but a graphic sketch of the hardy enterprise of the sons of New-England:

"While we follow them," said the orator, "among the tumbling mountains of ice, and behold them penetrating into the deepest frozen recesses of Hudson's Bay and Davis' Straits; while we are looking for them beneath the Arctic Circle, we hear that they have pierced into the opposite region of polar cold; that they are at the antipodes and engaged under the frozen serpent of the South. Falkland Islands, which seemed too remote and romantic an object for national ambition to grasp, is but a stage and resting-place in the progress of their vigorous industry. Nor is the equinoctial heat more discouraging to them than the accumulated winter of both the poles. We know that while some of them draw the line and strike the harpoon on the coasts of Africa, others run the longitude and pursue their gigantic game along the coast of Brazil. No sea but what is vexed by their fisheries—no climate that is not witness to their toils. Neither the perseverance of Holland, nor the activity of France, nor the dexterous and firm sagacity of English enterprise, ever carried this most perilous mode of hardy industry to the extent to which it has been pushed by this recent people; a people who are still, as it were, in the gristle, and not yet hardened into the bone of manhood."*

As early as 1647, as we are informed by Holmes in his American Annals, a flourishing trade was opened by the New-England colonies with Barbadoes and the other islands of the West Indies.

In 1685, a collector of revenues at the port of Charleston, in South Carolina, was appointed by the home government. This was but a few years subsequent to the foundation of the city. Charleston progressed rapidly in commercial importance, and before the Revolution, as an importing and exporting

* Griffith's Notes on American Colonies.

city, maintained an equality with Boston, New-York and Philadelphia.

In 1690 began the hardy enterprise of the whale fishermen of Nantucket. This little island, situated far out from the main land, bleak, sterile, and scarcely inhabitable, with not a tree of its own native growth, and scarcely an inviting prospect to cheer its inhabitants, or minister to their ease and gratification, has yet been enabled to reach to an enviable distinction in commercial wealth. We know not where to affix the limits of the hardihood and daring of these enterprising men. They have planted a garden upon a rock, and they have become rich by hard toil where Nature has been most stinting in her favors. The importance of the whale fisheries it is not difficult to understand, and we shall exhibit, in other pages in the progress of our work, statistics to satisfy all of the magnitude to which they have at last grown up.

The trade of Massachusetts alone, in the year 1717, brought into constant activity and employment four hundred and ninety-two ships, and nearly four thousand sailors.

In 1730, we are informed that there arrived in England from America 154 tons of oil, and 9,200 tons of whalebone; and that in the first fifteen days of July in the same year, 10,000 hogheads of sugar reached the same port from the British American sugar colonies. In the ensuing year, Massachusetts employed six hundred ships and sloops, and five thousand fishermen.

The commerce of New-England, as early as 1742, required for its support upwards of one thousand sail of vessels, while at the South, Charleston alone loaded, in 1744, two hundred and thirty.

The trade of Britain with her American colonies employed, in 1769, 1,078 ships, and 28,910 seamen. The value of her imports from them for that year amounted to £3,370,-900, and of their imports from her to £3,924,606.

The following table, taken from Holmes' Annals, exhibits the progress of this trade for the years named :

		Imports from colonies	Exports to colonies
Annual average,	1700 to 1710	£265,000	£267,000
"	1710 to 1720	392,000	365,000
"	1720 to 1730	578,000	471,000
"	1730 to 1740	670,000	660,000
"	1740 to 1750	708,000	812,000
"	1750 to 1760	802,000	1,577,000
"	1760 to 1770	1,044,000	1,762,000
"	1770 to 1780	743,000	1,331,000

Mr. Burke stated in Parliament in the year 1775, that the trade with America alone, at that time, was within less than £500,000 of being equal to what the great commercial nation of England carried on at the beginning of that century with all the world.

The first year which witnessed peace between England and her colonies, now raised to the dignity of free and independent states, witnessed the opening on their part of a new and lucrative branch of trade with China, which at the present moment, in exports and imports together, is worth annually little short of eight or nine millions of dollars.

Toward the close of the eighteenth century, 1795, we are informed that a vessel sailed from Charleston to the East Indies, the very first enterprise of the kind which was undertaken by that city.

The confederating "articles," which carried the American states through one of the most glorious revolutions on record, were found in every respect inadequate to keep together these states on terms of equal rights and prosperity at the restoration of peace. The conflicting institutions of so many sovereignties, without any head of acknowledged power and influence, tended to paralyze commercial movements, and entirely to arrest those advances which had been already made. One of the most powerful inducements which operated upon the minds of these states to enter upon a new and better compact, was found in the absolute requisitions of commerce, and the immortal constitution under which we now live finds its origin here.

Scarcely more than half a century has elapsed since our federal constitution was adopted, and in that period our advance has already rivaled the dreams of eastern fiction. Every sea and navigable water under the face of heaven witnesses the white wings of our shipping, and hears the bold voices of our mariners. Our flag is upon the deep, and it floats alike at either pole and at the equator, on the uttermost limits of the globe. Great as has been our progress in the past, there is a prophetic voice which tells us that we have but begun to enter upon that bright and glorious "empire of the seas" which is yet to be ours. We have laid the foundations of cities which occupy rank with the Tyres and Carthages of antiquity, and must soon rival the Londons of the present day. To what is New-York indebted for that extraordinary position which she has taken in the republic, but to the centralization of nearly all of its foreign trade in her midst; and New-Orleans, at the other extremity of latitude, is she not marching onward in the same pathway to prosperity ?

It is now, perhaps, full time to bring to a close the interesting subject upon which we have been engaged, and which has been swelling out under our hands to proportions little contemplated at first. So much is there of poetry and romance in the extension, through all ages, of commercial enterprise, that we can easily be excused some enthusiasm and a fond lingering o'er the theme. At the fountain head we recognized commerce in its simplest stage among nature's recent, rude, and unpolished children. We marked its gradual progress. Following the astute Israelite in his bargains for the gold which enriched the temple of Solomon and the streets of Jerusalem, we saw the hardy Phœnician launching out his bark upon the deep, guided only on his perilous voyages by the stars of heaven. We heard the busy voices of Greeks upon the Ægean; we saw the stern Roman curling his lip on his trading neighbor with disdain; and while yet Venice in all its splendor sat mistress of the now "spouseless" and deserted Adriatic, we met with the merchants that congregated at the Rialto from every quarter of the inhabitable globe. We turned our eyes to the Baltic, and contemplated the wonderful "league" which it witnessed, and closing the volume of antiquity and of the middle ages, there remained alone the great maritime and commercial powers of Britain and America. With these the picture closed. What, then, remains of the sketch we designed, but hurriedly to trace some of those effects, most marked, which the empire of commerce over the world naturally and necessarily exerts. These will occupy us but a moment.

When political economy first began to attract the attention of men, and give birth to the erroneous theories with which it so long exerted a control, commerce, as a source of national wealth, was derided. It was asked, where was the creative power which it had ever exerted, or could ever exert? Had it ever developed two blades of grass where but one existed before? Could it ever substantially add a jot or tittle to the *intrinsic* value of a single commodity? With agriculture, said these men, it is directly the reverse. Agriculture is legitimate wealth. It is the creator, the producer of value—it affords something out of nothing. Commerce is mere transportation of agricultural wealth; the laborer hired to carry produce from its maker to its consumer. Can such transportation add anything to the *intrinsic* value of the article transported? If it can, we have only to continue its motion, adding transportation to transportation, without reference to place, and we make accretion after accretion to its value, until, in process of time, it becomes precious beyond all price or compare. Must we be led into such absurdity?

In progress of time it came to be considered, that however plausible the reasonings of these philosophers, there was much of sophistry involved in them, and that the wealthy agriculturists, proud, lordly, and reliant upon their ample acres, were disposed naturally enough to keep up a prejudice so favorable to their interests. The various laws passed in Great Britain, in particular at the period of which we treat, for the benefit of the landholders, and the great jealousy which was exercised toward trading corporations, as, for instance, toward London, all strikingly evince the truth of this.

When commerce began to come more into favor, a distinction was soon set up. It was yielded that foreign commerce might really be of benefit to a nation, and add to its available wealth; but in regard to domestic commerce—merchandising—the home trade—these were regarded as little more beneficial to a community, on the score of new wealth, than ballad singing, or mountebank exhibitions. The last thing which men could be induced to credit was, that the trade intermediate between the importer and consumer, was in any sense productive of wealth. This proposition has, however, become settled in the almost demonstrative reasoning of modern political science; and we may hope that doubts and speculations so inimical to the interests of prominent and useful classes in the community will never be raised again. Freed from these unworthy prejudices, commerce, whether foreign or domestic, comes at once to be admitted as a legitimate source of national aggrandizement.

We have sometimes heard it gravely alleged that the commercial spirit is unfavorable to the existence of true patriotic sentiment and exertion. We have been told that it severs the ties which bind the individual to his native soil, and disposes him to yield much, too much, to the policy of contemporary nations; that the commercial spirit merges the citizen in the cosmopolite, and awakens a keener sensitiveness to national interest than to national honor. Even Burke endorsed the doctrine with the high authority of his name, when he characterized the merchant's desk as his altar, his ledger as his bible, and his money as his god. But is there anything of truth or justice in the charge? Has it appeared in the development of the world's history, that there has been any natural hostility between the merchant and the patriot? Has it been found that commercial communities have been disposed to submit to aggression with easy compliance, and put on the yoke of conquest without a struggle? Was it so with Tyre when the Greek conqueror was thundering at her gates? Did puissant Rome, on her seven hills, ever contend with an enemy bolder, fiercer, and more desperate than the descendants of the Phœnician traders at Carthage? Were the Italian States easy victories to the aggressions of foreign foes, or were they at all less glorious in arms than in enterprise? We shall not pause to answer such questions.

We have no idea that there are in commerce any tendencies like these we have been combating. It disposes nations to be just and liberal in their intercourse with others, but it changes not their own individuality—their own pride of character—in any point that it ought not to be changed. Merchants there have been in all ages and countries who have added to the glory and honor of their states, by the highest and noblest exertions of patriotism. Men enjoying the confidence of their sovereigns, and exhausting their coffers in defence of the realm, have been found in this class, and we shall, upon another occasion, enumerate the most distinguished examples which history furnishes us. The merchants of London were, even in the earliest times, the bankers of the crown, and Elizabeth in particular knew what it was, on many an occasion, in her own exigencies, and in the exigencies of the kingdom, to have her purse replenished by their liberal coffers. In our own country we may be permitted to say that there has on no occasion been ever displayed a truer love of country, and a loftier tone of patriotism than has been displayed by our merchant citizens. They have fallen behind none in the assertion of the rights and the liberties of the republic.

Commerce is a natural guardian of the arts and sciences. Under its influence the highest results have been stimulated. To what, for instance, can the astonishing progress and perfection to which astronomy has been carried be attributed, more than to the ever-arising wants of navigation? The solution of the problem of the latitudes and longitudes has been promised, at different periods, the highest premiums of government. It has set astronomers at toil which only terminated in brilliant discovery. The various problems of navigation even now demand the highest labors of these men in every country, and the mere tables of a nautical almanac—the calculation of eclipses, occultations, and parallaxes—calls into action a degree of scientific skill which can scarcely be appreciated by the uninitiated. The mariner's compass, quadrant, or chronometer, are miracles of art as well as of science. From every nation in the world commerce has brought together her trophies, and laid them at the feet of science. Without leaving his closet, the student of nature may arrive at profound results in the investigation of animals, plants, shells, and minerals, scattered over the whole globe—above the earth, and under the earth, and down to the depths of the sea. Every art and science acknowledges its large indebtedness to the hand of commerce for the influence it is enabled to wield over nature in extending the empire and dominion of man.

Commerce is the parent of civilization. We are acquainted with but one agency which excels it in perpetuating peace and good will among men, and elevating national character, and that agency is Christianity. But even the heralds of the cross, with all their noble and inspiring theme, have not penetrated farther into the depths of savage wildernesses, or among the fiercest islands of the ocean, have not crossed mountains and deserts more desolate and terrific, have not plunged more fearlessly in the midst of horrid idolatry, cannibalism, and semi-demonism, than have these men of bales and merchandises in their search after trade. They have gone hand in hand with the missionary, where they have not acted as his pioneer. It was thus in the early history of America. Marquette and Allouez, fathers in the Roman church, were even distanced in energy by the adventurous La Salle in the first visits which were made by civilized men to the howling wilderness westward of the lakes. It is thus with the hunters and trappers of Oregon and California, who, as far upward as the Russian limit, and south to Mexico, prosecute trade with the savage, as yet ignorant of his soul and of his Maker. It is most strikingly thus in the case of the Sandwich Islands. Commerce, acting as the adjunct or handmaiden of Christianity among the savages there, has transformed them into men and into citizens. We see a trophy won to civilization—a people added to the Christian nations of the earth.

Let us take the extremest limit of the ocean, the stormiest islet of the sea, struggling against a thousand billows, and what do we find? The sailor and the trader have been there, and the return of the "white wings" is hailed by anxious multitudes, who bring out their treasures to be bartered for the veriest trifles of civilization. From the intercourse which arises, new wants are stimulated in their bosoms. They begin to think with the new objects which occasion thought. Their views and ideas are naturally expanded to a wider compass, and they are insensibly moulded in the type of those who have excited their highest admiration and wonder. Mysterious, beneficent and wise are the ways of Providence, when even the interests of men are called into requisition to work out the great problem of their existence.

Commerce, in fine, is what it has been beautifully entitled, "the golden girdle of the globe." It binds together all the great families of men. It teaches that they are creatures of like wants, errors and necessities. It determines them to be component parts of a great and magnificent system which God has devised, and which requires the concurring movements of every part to be preserved in its perfection and duration. It forbids them to treat, like the ancient Roman, the foreigner cast upon their shores, as a barbarian deserving of death, or to confiscate his shipwrecked effects, but urges rather the doctrines of humanity and justice. Even the laws which regulate it are based upon the immutable principles of right, and bind the consciences of men from their very nature. As Mansfield, the most celebrated commercial lawyer of his age, said of them, quoting the splendid language of Cicero: "*Nec erit alia lex Romæ, alia Athenis; alia nunc, alia posthac; sed et omnes gentes, et omni tempore una lex et sempiterna, et immortalis continebat:*"—they are not one law at Rome and another at Athens, they do not fluctuate from extreme to extreme; but among all men, and in all times, the laws of commerce are one and immutable.

COMMERCE—PROGRESS OF AMERICAN.

Commerce, qui fait à la fois la richesse d'un état et les advantages du monde entier.—Voltaire.

The sixteenth century introduced the leading European powers to a minute acquaintance with the Continent of America. Adventurous navigation had rescued a world from savage dominion, and there were adventurous spirits enough to people that world, and identify thenceforward their destinies with it. A hundred years after, and civilization planted her abodes through all this waste. Peculiar, indeed, is the feeling with which these infant days of our country are regarded—so like an illusion does it all seem; so like a dream of glowing imagery. We look back as to a classic era, and the romance of Pocahontas, and of Raleigh, of Fernando de Soto, and Juan Ponce de Leon, do they thrill us less than the beatific visions of the Greek, recurring to ages long ago, when Ilion resisted the shock of Agamemnon's heroes, and the Argo sailed away to distant Colchis? The dim antiquity seems gathered around both of them alike. But let it pass, all—the romance of our history! They imagined not, the men of that day imagined not the stupendous results which have occurred so soon. They saw not the benign and regenerating influences of a virgin land, preserved for countless ages uncorrupted by tyranny, and ignorant of oppression. Could such a soil have nurtured else than freemen? They saw it not, and do we, even we, see other than darkly yet, the great consummation, the mighty destinies of the regions which, three centuries ago, were proclaimed from the mast-head of a crazy ocean bark, a speck upon the distant heaven?

The development of American character is replete with instruction, and solves one of the most remarkable problems in the history of mankind. The untried scenes of a new world, cut off by trackless oceans from contact and communion with the civilization of unnumbered generations, were sufficient to introduce, what might have been predicted of them, results, new, striking and without a precedent. The indomitable will, the stern endurance, the inflexible and hardy spirit of independence, the high daring, the lofty patriotism, the adventurous, unlimited enterprise, the genius resolute, active, intrepid; inexhaustible in resources, elastic in vigor and in freshness, buoyant ever and hoping on, and executing amid every trying scene, every danger, and difficulty, and disaster—triumphing everywhere and in all things. Philosophy could have argued this complexion for the men whose fathers braved so much beyond the ocean, and would philosophy have won less than the fame of prophecy by her judgment?

But we pause not here to lament the causes which have counteracted these genial influences, and left whole regions of America, stagnated as it were, in the very elements of vitality and yet living hopelessly on. Should we refer to Canada, to Mexico, and the South American States? What is there here of progress to chronicle, and how mnch of humiliation? Regions blessed by heaven in everything but in men. Changing ever their dynasties and their despots in revolution and in blood. In motion always, without progress. In arms, without valor. Loving change rather than hating oppressors. Proclaiming civilization and annihilating its advances. The bitterness of Voltaire's sneer has no cruelty or injustice in its application to many of them, "*en pansant les chevaux de leurs maitres ils se donnent le titre d'electeurs des rois et de destructeurs des tyrans!*" Under Heaven, as it was the destiny of the savage aboriginal, incapable of civilization, and with no law of progress engrafted upon his nature, to fade away before the steady advances of European arms and policy, so, the Anglo-Saxon element of America, by its flexibility and its power, by the new elements which it has taken to itself in the trying, yet triumphant scenes through which it has passed, will and must, in the inevitable course of events, preside over the destinies of the continent of America, aiding and directing them, adding life and vitality, rousing dormant and sleeping energies, and developing, upon the theatre of the world, movements in comparison with which all that history can furnish, before the deluge, before the era of Christ, and since, shall dwindle into insignificance! It needs no ardent temperament to draw a stronger picture.

Let our speculations cease, however, for the present. We have a subject before us which looks rather into the past than into the future, difficult though it be not to lift the veil for an instant that shrouds that future. The progress of American commerce is so rich, so fruitful, so limitless a theme, that all our condensation will be required to embrace even the main facts which are presenting themselves to our mind. We will for perspicuity and order distribute the subject under appropriate heads:

I.—*American Commerce in the seventeenth century.*

II.—*From the opening of the eighteenth century to the Revolution.*

III.—*Under the articles of confederation.*

IV.—*Under the Constitution, and until the War of* 1812.

V.—*From that War to the present day.*

A particular reference will afterwards be made to each of the countries with whom our own maintains important commercial relations; commercial changes in the different divisions of the Union will be marked; investigations on the advantages of the South for conducting foreign enterprises made, and the singular and fortuitous events which have unfortunately checked and retarded those enterprises. In conclusion, some remarks may be ventured upon the means of regeneration and the ultimate prospects of the commerce of our country.

I. *Our Commerce in the seventeenth century.* The early colonists were exposed for a fearful probation to the most extraordinary vicissitudes and necessities. With the axe in one hand they reduced the sturdy forests into the farm-yard, and with the knife in the other they resisted the approaches of the stealthy and sanguinary savage. A meagre subsistence rewarded the toils that knew no rest, and the charities of the mother country were invoked for men, whose determined wills grew stronger as they suffered. This period had its different limits. Fifteen years after the landing of Wm. Sale, we find the proprietary government in England complaining to the Carolinas, "we must be silly indeed to maintain idle men."* Thirty-three years after the landing of Bienville in Louisiana, the Western Company threw up their charter in utter hopelessness and despair.†

New-England's rugged soil yielded a too reluctant tribute to the industry of her sons. They went out early upon the ocean by which they were girt, in search of bread that the plow yielded not To this hardy, daring and inimitable people, the boons of Nature were to be found in her apparent denial of them all. Upon the pathless deep they are described in eastern gorgeousness, while yet in infancy, by the oratory of Burke, struggling at either pole amid tumbling mountains of ice; in the frozen recesses of Hudson Bay and Davis's Straits; beneath the arctic circle and engaged under the frozen serpent of the South.

The seventeenth century affords us, however, but a few particulars of the trade which had been started in the colonies. That it was limited can be readily imagined; that it should be worthy of any regard at all, is the only source of surprise. The materials of this portion of our history are meagre. It is sufficient that, in 1647, a trade had been opened from the Northern ports to Barbadoes and others of the West Indies; that a collector of customs was appointed at Charleston in 1685, and that the hardy enterprises of the Nantucket whalemen received their first impulse in 1690. Let us pass then to the second epoch.

II. *Our Commerce from* 1700 *to the Revolution.*—In the year 1731, we find a petition read in parliament from the American colonies that the African trade be thenceforward laid open to them. In the same parliament it was conceded that the whole gain of the mother country from the trade of Virginia and Maryland alone, amounted annually to £180,000. The Pennsylvanians were exporting corn to Spain and to Portugal, and with the proceeds of their ships and cargoes selecting out merchandize in the English markets. To the Dutch alone they sold 5,000 pistoles annually in liquor and provisions. They had their invoices to Surinam, and Hispaniola, the West Indies, Canaries, Newfoundland, and the other colonies, and £150,000 from the proceeds to traffic in Britain. "New-York," says a chronicle of this epoch, "sends fewer ships to England than some other colonies do, but those they do send are richer, as dealing more in furs and skins with the Indians, and they are at least of equal advantage to England with those of Pennsylvania. The soil of New-England is not unlike that of Britain. It employs about 40,000 tons of shipping; and about 600 sail of ships, sloops, &c., about half which shipping sail to Europe." Now began the parent's jealousy of her offspring. Nothing, it was said in parliament, nothing is more prejudicial, and in prospect more dangerous to any mother kingdom than the increase of shipping in her colonies. The only use of colonies, added Lord Sheffield, is the monopoly of their consumption and the carriage of their produce. In 1730, the Commons of England struck an ineffectual blow at the American trade with the French and Dutch colonies, it having been represented to them as greatly detrimental to England and *her* colonies.

In 1732 a writer gravely announced that the convenience of the Americans from the plenty of beavers, hare, coney wool and many other furs, gave them such advantages that, unless restrained, they would soon supply all the world with hats. The Board of Trade of the same year report that there are more trades carried on and manufactures set up in the provinces on the continent of America, northward of Virginia, prejudicial to the trade and manufactures of Great Britain, than in any other of the British colonies. In 1750 the Americans were forbidden to work in iron, and Lord Chatham declared not long after in Parliament that the colonies of North America had not even the right of manufacturing a nail. So stringent had become the restrictive policy!

In 1764 was imposed an onerous burthen upon American commerce by the mother country, grown jealous of its too great extension.* This commerce had greatly en-

* Southern Quarterly Review, 1845. Art. Carolina Political Annals.

† Commercial Review, vol. I. Art. Louisiana.

* The English navigation act of 1660 declared that certain specified articles of the produce of the colonies, and since known in commerce by the name "enumerated articles," should not be exported direct-

riched the home as well as the colonial governments, but the former was too much blinded by erroneous policy to perceive it. She heeded not the annual purchases made in her markets with the avails of lumber, beef, fish, pork, butter, horses, poultry, live stock, tobacco, corn, flour, bread, cider, apples, cabbages, onions, &c., disposed of by our traders to the eager West India planters; and Lord Sheffield, in his observations on the commerce of the American states, tells us that at this time the Carolinians, of their exports to Kingston, Jamaica, took back one-half in the produce of that country, the middle provinces one-fourth, New-England one-tenth, and the balance in specie dollars. The trade of Britain with the American colonies employed in 1769, 1,078 ships, and 28,910 seamen. The value of her imports from them for that year amounted to £3,370,000, and of their imports from her to £3,924,606, showing a large difference in favor of the parent country.*

In 1770 the imports of Carolina were £535,714, those of New-England £564,034, of Maryland, and Virginia £851,140, the exports of Virginia at the same time being double the value of those of either of the others named. Mr. Burke triumphantly announced in the House of Commons, "Our trade with America is scarcely less than that we carried on at the beginning of the century with the whole world! In the six years ending with 1774 there was an average import from the colonies into England of £1,752,142, and an average export to them in turn of £2,732,036. Crippled as our energies were, they could not be repressed. It was a vain effort to confine the enterprise of a people, whose views embraced the world itself, into the narrow compass afforded by English ports, and by portions of Europe southward of Cape Finisterre. When the day of reckoning came, as it did at last, for these reckless abuses of power, and they were solemnly proclaimed in the immortal bill of rights, not the least of the usurpations for which retribution was demanded is to be found in the clause: 'She has cut off our trade with all parts of the world!'"

The following table, compiled by Mr. Hazard from the most authentic sources, will exhibit the trade of the provinces with the mother country during the whole of the periods we have been considering; the table is of great interest, embracing as it does in one view almost the entire commerce of America for seventy-six years.

From these statistics we learn the relative commercial position of the different provinces. Dividing the whole time embraced into periods of twenty-five years each, we observe in the *first* period that Virginia, Maryland and Carolina furnish almost the entire exports, and import much more largely than New-England and New-York. In the *second* period New-York greatly increases her imports, which still fall short of those of New-England, or Virginia and Maryland, while her exports are enhanced but little. The whole exports of New-York, Pennsylvania and New-England combined did not reach the amount of those of Carolina singly. In the *third* period Pennsylvania imports more largely than New-York, but less than New-England; the southern provinces retain their rank as exporters, Carolina being still greater than New-York, New-England and Pennsylvania together; and Georgia, a new plantation, equals New-York. Truly is the empire of trade a fickle and inconstant one. But we pass to another division of our subject—[first giving the Table.]

---

ly from the colonies to any foreign country, but that they should be first sent to Britain, and there unladen before they could be forwarded to their final destination. The act of 1764 provided farther that no commodity of the growth, production, or manufacture of Europe shall be imported into the British plantations, but such as are laden and put on board in England, Wales, or Berwick-upon-Tweed, and in English-built shipping, whereof the master and two-thirds of the crew are English. Such are the amazing lengths to which systems of restrictions and monopoly have been carried by nations claiming enlightenment! Nearly all of North America was doomed, during its colonial dependence upon European powers, to the same senseless and suicidal *régime*. In the instance of Spain it is even yet continued, though much moderated. She levied alike upon exports and imports, the alcavala and other oppressive taxes, and even so late as the middle of the eighteenth century, it was shown that she derived no greater advantages from the possession of Cuba, Hispaniola and Porto Rico, than England or France from the smallest of their dependencies. The course of England, however, was at first of a liberal character, for we find the colonists empowered in the early charter of Pennsylvania to carry on a direct intercourse with foreign states. The permission had but a brief length, as we have seen.

* We very much agree, after all, however, with McCulloch and his school, in relation to these adverse and favorable differences which the world have entitled "*balances of trade*," and made no little hubbub about for the last century or two. "It is difficult to estimate the mischief which the notions relating to the balance of trade, have occasioned in almost every commercial country. The great, or rather the only argument insisted upon by those who prevailed upon the legislature in the reign of William and Mary to declare the trade with France a *nuisance*, was founded on the statement that the value of imports from that kingdom considerably exceeded the value of the commodities exported to it. It never occurred to those who so loudly abused the French trade, that no merchant would import any commodity from France, unless it brought a higher price in this country than the commodity exported to pay it, and that the profit of the merchant or nation would be in exact proportion to this excess of price. The very reason assigned by these persons for prohibiting the trade affords the best attainable proof of its having been a lucrative one, nor can there be any doubt that unrestricted freedom of intercourse between the two countries would still be of the greatest service to both."

AMERICAN TRADE BEFORE THE REVOLUTION.

Years	NEW-ENGLAND.		NEW-YORK.		PENNSYLVANIA.		VIRG. & MARY.		CAROLINA.		GEORGIA.	
	Exp'ts £	Imp'ts £	Exp'ts £	Imp'ts £	Exp'ts £	Imp'ts £	Exp'ts £	Imp'ts £	Exp'ts £	Imp'ts £	Exp'ts £	Imp'ts £
1700	41486	91918	17567	49410	4608	18529	317302	173481	14058	11003	....	....
1701	32656	86322	18547	31910	5220	12002	235738	199683	16973	13908	....	....
1702	37026	64625	7965	23991	4145	9343	274782	72391	11870	10460	....	....
1703	33539	59608	7471	17562	5160	9899	144928	196713	13197	12428	....	....
1704	30823	74896	10540	22294	2430	11819	264112	60458	14067	6621	....	....
1705	22793	62504	7393	27902	1309	7206	116768	174322	2698	19788	....	....
1706	22210	57050	2849	31588	4210	11037	149152	58015	8652	4001	....	....
1707	38793	120631	14283	29855	786	14365	207625	237901	23311	10492	....	....
1708	49635	115505	10847	26891	2120	6723	213493	79061	10340	11996	....	....
1709	29559	120349	12259	34577	616	5881	261668	80268	20431	28521	....	....
1710	31112	106338	8203	31475	1277	8594	188429	127639	20793	19613	....	....
1711	26415	137421	12193	28856	38	19408	373181	91535	12871	20406	....	....
1712	24699	128105	12466	18524	1471	8464	297941	134583	29394	20015	....	....
1713	49904	120778	14428	46470	178	17037	206263	76304	32448	23967	....	....
1714	51541	121288	29810	44643	2663	14927	280470	128873	31290	23712	....	....
1715	66555	164650	21316	54629	5461	17182	174756	199274	29158	16631	....	....
1716	69595	121156	21971	52173	5193	21842	201043	170505	46287	27272	....	....
1717	58898	132001	24534	44140	4499	22505	296884	215962	41275	25058	....	....
1718	61591	131885	27331	62966	5588	22716	316576	191925	46385	15841	....	....
1719	54452	125317	19596	56355	6564	27068	332069	164630	50373	19630	....	....
1720	49206	128769	16836	37397	7928	24531	331482	110717	62736	18290	....	....
1721	50483	114524	15681	50754	8037	21546	357812	127376	61858	17703	....	....
1722	47955	133722	20118	57478	6882	26397	283091	172754	79650	34374	....	....
1723	59339	176486	27992	53013	8332	15992	287997	123833	78103	42246	....	....
1724	69585	168507	21191	63020	4057	30324	277344	161894	90504	37839	....	....
1725	72021	201768	24976	70650	11981	42209	214730	195884	91942	39182	....	....
1726	63816	200882	38307	84866	5960	57634	324767	185981	93453	43934	....	....
1727	75052	187277	31617	67452	12823	31979	421588	192965	96055	23254	....	....
1728	64689	194590	21141	81634	15230	37478	413089	171092	91175	33067	....	....
1729	52512	161102	15833	64760	7434	29799	386174	108931	113329	58366	....	....
1730	54701	208196	8740	64356	10582	48592	346823	150931	151739	64785	....	....
1731	49048	183467	20756	66116	12786	44260	408502	171278	159771	71145	....	....
1732	64095	216600	9411	65540	8524	41698	310799	148289	126207	58298	....	828
1733	61983	184570	11626	65417	14776	40565	403198	186177	177845	70466	203	1695
1734	82252	146460	15307	81758	20217	54392	373090	172086	120466	99658	18	1921
1735	72899	189125	14155	80405	21919	48804	394995	220381	145348	117837	3010	12112
1736	66788	222158	17944	86000	20786	61513	380163	204794	214083	101147	....	2012
1737	63347	223923	16833	125833	15198	56690	492246	211301	187758	58986	....	5701
1738	59116	203233	16228	133438	11918	61450	391814	258860	141119	87793	17	6496
1739	46604	220378	18459	106070	8134	54452	444654	217200	236192	94445	233	3324
1740	72389	171081	21498	118777	15048	56751	341997	281428	265560	181821	924	3524
1741	60052	198147	21142	140430	17158	91010	577109	248582	236830	224270	....	2553
1742	53166	148899	13536	167591	8527	75295	427769	264186	154607	127063	1622	17018
1743	63185	172461	15067	134487	9596	79340	557821	328195	235136	111499	2	2291
1744	50248	143982	14527	119920	7446	62214	402709	234855	192594	79141	....	769
1745	38948	140463	14083	54957	10130	54280	399423	196799	91847	86815	....	939
1746	38612	209177	8841	86712	15779	73699	419371	282545	76897	102809	....	984
1747	41771	210640	14992	137984	3832	82404	492619	200088	107500	95529	....	24
1748	29748	197682	12358	143311	12363	75330	494852	252624	167305	160172	....	1314
1749	39999	238286	23413	265773	14944	238037	434610	323600	100400	164085	51	5
1750	48455	343659	35632	267130	28191	217713	508939	349419	191607	134037	1942	2125
1751	63287	305974	42363	248941	23870	190917	460085	247027	245491	138244	355	2065
1752	74313	273340	40648	194030	29978	201666	569453	325151	288264	150777	1526	3163
1753	83395	345523	40553	277864	38527	245644	632575	356776	164634	213009	3057	14128
1754	66538	329433	26663	127497	30649	244647	573435	323513	307238	149215	3236	1974
1755	59533	341796	28055	151071	32336	144456	489668	285157	325525	189887	4437	2630
1756	47359	384371	24073	250425	20091	200169	337759	334897	222915	181780	7155	536
1757	27556	363404	19168	353311	14190	168426	418881	426687	130889	213949	....	2571
1758	30204	465694	14260	356555	21383	260953	454362	438471	150511	181002	....	10212
1759	25985	527067	21684	630785	22404	498161	357228	459007	206534	215255	6074	15178
1760	37802	599647	21125	480106	22754	707998	504451	605882	162769	218131	12198	....
1761	46225	334225	48648	289570	39170	204067	455083	545350	253002	254587	5764	24279
1762	41733	247385	58882	288046	38091	206199	415709	418599	181695	194170	6522	23761
1763	74815	258854	52998	238560	38228	284152	642294	555391	282366	250132	14469	44908
1764	88157	459765	53697	515416	36258	436191	559508	515192	341727	305808	31325	18338
1765	145819	451299	54959	382349	25148	363368	505671	383224	385918	334709	34183	29165
1766	141733	409642	67020	330829	26851	327314	461693	372548	293587	296733	53074	67268
1767	128207	406081	61422	417957	37641	371830	437926	437628	395027	244093	35856	23334
1768	148375	419797	87115	482930	59404	432107	406048	475984	508108	289868	42402	56562
1769	129353	207992	73466	74918	26111	199906	361892	488362	587114	306600	82270	58340
1770	148011	394451	69882	475991	28109	134881	435094	717782	278907	146273	55532	56193
1771	150381	1420119	95875	653621	31615	728744	577848	920326	420311	409169	63810	70493
1772	126265	824830	82707	343970	29133	507909	528404	793910	425923	449610	66083	92406
1773	124624	527055	76246	289214	36652	426448	589803	328904	456513	344859	85391	62932
1774	112248	562476	80008	437937	69611	625652	612030	528738	432302	378116	67647	57518
1775	116588	71625	187018	1228	175962	1366	758356	1921	579349	6245	103477	113777
1776	762	55050	2318	....	1421	365	73226	....	13668	....	12569	....

III. *American Commerce under the articles of Federation.*—During the Revolution all foreign enterprise was of necessity suspended, and in struggling for liberty, men taught themselves to forget and despise every mere physical want. Leagued together for common defence, the states were able to resist every device of power, and sustain a long and bloody contest. But when that contest was ended and liberty won, the confederation exhibited at once its nervelessness for peace, and for the arts and policy and duties of peace. The fabric which could resist the storm, crumbled away when the sunshine succeeded. So true is it that the necessities of men are the only durable bond of their union, and that without this union there is no strength.

From the close of the war until the adoption of the Constitution there may be considered to have been no great regulating head in America. No uniformity or system prevailed among the states, and their commerce was consequently exposed to the utmost uncertainty, fluctuation and loss. Tonnage duties were levied in different ports as it suited the caprices of the several governments, and as they were more or less desirous of encouraging particular branches of navigation and trade at the expense of others. By a policy more astute than that of her neighbors, New-York managed in this way soon to increase largely her foreign trade, and laid the foundation of the empire she now maintains. From 1784 to 1790 our commerce exhibited the most remarkable results. For seven years consecutively the imports into American cities from Britain were never otherwise than twice the amount of the exports to her, and for several years were three and even five times their value. A drain of specie is said to have been the consequence, a very natural though not necessary one, and great commercial embarrassment and distress.

The following table made up from records of the English custom-house will be found of interest:

	Exports America to Britain	Imports America from Britain
1784	£749,345	£3,679,467
1785	893,594	2,308,023
1786	443,119	1,603,465
1787	893,637	2,009,111
1788	1,023,784	1,886,142
1789	1,050,198	2,525,298
1790	1,191,071	3,431,778

IV. *Our Commerce under the Constitution and until* 1812.—In this crisis the attention of thinking men and patriots in all parts of the nation was aroused, and there was perhaps nothing which contributed so much in urging the states into a general convention, and into the adoption of a constitutional government and union, calculated to preserve their liberties, their fortunes and their glory in all the future. One of the first grants of power conceded to Congress under this Constitution was that of "*regulating commerce with foreign nations, among the several states and with the Indians.*"*

No more, said a memorial from Charleston, on the adoption of this Constitution—no more shall we lament our trade, almost wholly in the possession of foreigners, our vessels excluded from the ports of some nations and fettered with restrictions in others; our materials, the produce of our country, which should be retained for our own use, exported and increasing the maritime consequence of other powers.† With this memorial before them, and others of a similar character, Congress at its first session appointed a committee to report upon "the expediency of increasing the duty upon foreign tonnage, carrying American produce to places in America not admitting American vessels; and to frame a bill placing the same restraints upon the commerce of foreign American States that they place upon us."

By the report of Alexander Hamilton in 1790 it appears that the total tonnage of the United States at that time was as follows:

American vessels in foreign trade	363,093 tons.	
Coasters above twenty tons	113,181 "	
In the fisheries	26,252 "	—502,526 tons.
Total foreign tonnage		262,913 "
United States and British		312 "
United States and other foreign		338 "
Total		766,089 "

The tariff of 1789 was specific and *ad valorem*, and discriminated ten per cent. in favor of the trade conducted by our own shipping. In this we but imitated the navigation acts of European States, by means of which it has been supposed the enormous maritime consequence of some of them was principally secured. We shall not pause to argue a point in political economy so long mooted among writers of the greatest ability. The jealousies of nations have gone and still go very far. Even the philosophical Voltaire thought that their gain could not other-

* Referring to the state of things which existed under the articles of federation, an able writer observes: "Interfering regulations of trade and interfering claims of territory, were dissolving the attachments and the sense of the common interest which had cemented and sustained the Union during the arduous struggles of the Revolution. Symptoms of distress and marks of humiliation were rapidly accumulating. The finances of the nation were annihilated. In short, to use the language of the authors of the Federalist, each state, yielding to the voice of immediate interest or convenience, successively withdrew its support from the confederation, till the frail and tottering edifice was ready to fall upon our heads, and to crush us beneath its ruins. Most of the federal constitutions of the world have degenerated or perished in the same way, and by the same means."—KENT, Vol. 1, 217.

† American State Papers, 1789.

wise accrue than with each other's loss. England long imposed the most onerous restrictions upon all other commerce than her own, and her advances in consequence, or notwithstanding, have been unprecedented. Her tonnage when she commenced this system was less than that of the United States at the adoption of the Constitution!

There was one department of our maritime industry which demanded the earliest attention of government, and we think its general interest will be sufficient apology for any space we may allot to its consideration—THE FISHERIES. Mr. Jefferson, in 1791, then Secretary of State, furnished an admirable report upon the subject, which we proceed to analyze.

As early as 1520 there were fifty ships upon the Newfoundland coasts at a time for cod. In 1577 the French had 150 vessels there, the Spaniards 100, Portuguese 50, and English 15. The French fisheries began early to decline. In 1768 the Americans took but little less than the English, and the French took least of all. In 1789 England obtained double the quantity of America and France together. During the Revolution the American fisheries were almost entirely abandoned, and Mr. Jefferson left it to the wisdom of Congress to decide, whether they should not be restored, by opposing prohibition to prohibitions and high duties to high duties, on the fish of other nations.

The whale fishery was prosecuted by the Biscayans as early as the fifteenth century. The British began its encouragement in 1672 by bounties. The Americans opened their enterprises in 1715. They succeeded early in the discovery in the Southern Seas of the spermaceti whale, which they attacked instead of the Greenland hitherto known to navigators. In 1771 we had 204 whalers. During the war England held out the largest bounties to the trade, and so irresistible were these in the depressed condition of our fishermen, that it is said many of them were on the eve of removing to Halifax, to prosecute the business there, and were only deterred by a letter from Lafayette declaring that France would abate her duties upon oil. The little island of Nantucket is the great heart of these fisheries. A sand bar, said Mr. Jefferson, fifteen miles long and three broad, capable by its agriculture of maintaining twenty families, employed in these fisheries, before the Revolution, between 5 and 6,000 men and boys, and contained in its only harbor 140 vessels. In agriculture then they have no resource, and if that of their fisheries cannot be pursued from their own habitations, it is natural they should seek others from which it can be followed, and principally those where they will find a sameness of language, religion, laws, habits, and kindred.

In 1803 Mr. Huger stated to Congress in his report, that it would seem the cod fisheries had gained ground since the Revolution, but that the whale fisheries on the contrary have been for some time past on the decline. The war of 1812 was most disastrous to the fishermen, but they soon afterward recovered their prosperity, and on the first of January, 1844, we had 644 vessels engaged at sea, of the value, including catchings, of $27,784,-000. On the first of January, 1846, there were 680 ships, 34 brigs, 21 schooners, and 1 sloop; tonnage 233,149; manned by about 20,000 seamen and officers, consuming over three million dollars annually of American produce. Proceeds of whale fisheries $9,000,000 per annum, of which only $2,000,-000 are re-exported.

In 1844, Mr. Grinnell stated in Congress:

> This fleet of whaling ships is larger than ever pursued the business before. Commercial history furnishes no account of any parallel. The voyages of those engaged in the sperm fishery average three and a half years; they search every sea, and often cruise three or four months with a man at each mast-head on the look-out, without the cheering sight of a whale. They are hardy, honest and patriotic, and will, as they did in the last war, stand by their country when in danger; they will man our ships, and fight our battles on the ocean.

Mr. Clayton remarked but the other day (February, 1846):

> We have at this time a commerce of 2,417,000 tons of shipping, England has 2,420,000 tons; so that we are nearly, nay, it is my opinion, we are completely on a par with her. I doubt, sir, whether England has a greater commercial marine or greater interests to protect. We have more than 700 whale ships in the Pacific, an extensive Indian commerce and a great and daily growing commerce with China.*

But we have been anticipating other divisions of the subject, led on by the interest which is so readily excited here. At the close of the last century there were many causes which tended to add a vast importance to the commerce of the United States. For several years this commerce enjoyed unparalleled and almost unmeasured prosperity. Scarcely admitted into the family of nations, we found the whole civilized world engaged in the fiercest and most sanguinary conflict. A wise and indeed "masterly" neutrality was of course the true policy of the nation. The carrying trade of the world fell at once into our hands. We supplied the mother countries with the products of their own colonies. The East and West Indies alike were opened to our shipping. Their rich products filled our warehouses, supplying consumption and re-export. Prosperity such as this however was fated to be brief. The conflicting powers sacrificed everything to their mutual hatred, and minded little the rights of a nation they had not even learned to respect. Protestation ended in war, and

* Browne's Whaling Cruise and Hist. Whale Fishery, 1846, p. 539.

the rights of our glorious sailors were established forever on every sea. With the return of peace in Europe, the carrying trade departed rapidly from us.

In 1791 the king and council of England admitted American unmanufactured goods, except fish, oil, blubber, whale fins, certain naval stores, etc., into Britain at same duties as British American produce. The treaty of commerce of 1794 between the two governments was a reciprocity one, both parties binding themselves to impose no greater restrictions upon each other than they imposed upon others. This treaty regulated our East India commerce, then newly opened and promising a great extension.

From 1790 until 1797 Pennsylvania continued largely the greatest exporter in the Union. In 1791 South Carolina occupied the third rank. In 1797 New-York for the first time took a leading position which she has ever after maintained. The first exports of Tennessee and Mississippi date from 1801, those of Kentucky and Indiana from 1802, of Michigan 1803, Orleans Territory 1804, and Ohio 1806. This we shall see more particularly hereafter. It is sufficient now to indulge the reflections which the facts before us so naturally awaken. Mysterious have been the changes. Old age and premature decay have fallen upon cities once famous for their trade; and the quays, where the flags of all nations floated, have come at last to be comparatively deserted. We look around, and there have started up others like mature creations, full of vigor and stalwart even in their infancy. How hardly can reason realize that these wondrous changes are not all the pictures of a fertile imagination. Where is placed Virginia now, that mother of states, who in 1769 exported to foreign lands four times as much as New-York; and where is Carolina, the land of the "Rutledges, the Pinckneys, and the Sumpters," whose exports at the same time doubled those of New-York and Pennsylvania together, and were equal to five times those of all New-England!* If trade grow to colossal stature, its proud empire, the poet truly admonishes us, hastens also to swift decay.

The difficulties which beset our commerce, in the early part of the present century, when the rival hostile powers of Europe, jealous of our prosperous neutrality, strained every nerve to involve us in their disputes, will be called to mind by every one familiar with history. We were made the victims of the policy and arts of these nations, and even as early as 1793, their depredations upon our commerce were considerable. In five months alone of that year it was stated in the House of Peers, that *six hundred American vessels* were seized or detained in British ports for alleged violations of orders, and decrees claimed as principles under the law of nations. These aggressions upon our rights were long and extensively practised, as the following table will exhibit.

SEIZURES OF AMERICAN VESSELS FROM 1803 TO 1812.

By the British	917
By the French	558
By the Neapolitan	47
By the Danish Tribunals	70
Total vessels	1,592

And this at a time when we were at peace with all the nations on earth.* Indemnity for these spoliations has been the subject of numerous treaties; among others, that of England in 1794, France 1803, and Spain in the Florida treaty of 1819. But this whole period, so interesting in our annals, deserves a minute survey.

On the conquest of Prussia in 1806, Bonaparte conceived the idea of crushing the maritime power of Britain, by prohibiting all the world, in his famous *Berlin decree*, from conducting any trade with her or her numerous dependencies. The retaliatory British *orders in Council* followed at once, and all countries in the world, connected in any way with France, or opposed to England, were declared to be under precisely the same restraints, as if actually invested in strict blockade by British forces. Incensed by so unexpected and ruinous a measure, Napoleon issued the memorable *Milan decree*, making lawful prize of all vessels submitting at any time or in any way to British search or taxation.† It was natural that these illegal and unauthorized proceedings should excite the utmost interest and concern in the United

* See report of the Southern Commercial Convention.

* Seybert.

† The question of blockade has been much discussed by modern publicists; and between ourselves and Europe with no little acrimony. The policy of the United States being that of peace and neutrality, we are induced to insist most strongly upon the rights and privileges of neutral nations. The ordinance of Congress, 1781, required that there should be actually a number of vessels stationed near enough to make the entrance of a port apparently dangerous to constitute a blockade, and we have ever protested against confiscation for ineffectual or fictitious blockades. In our convention with Russia of 1801, a blockaded port was defined "that where there is, by the disposition of the power which attacks it, with ships stationary or sufficiently near, an evident danger in entering." The same is defined in some of our South American treaties, "a place actually attacked by a belligerent force, capable of preventing the entry of the neutral." Kent 1, 146 n. But see this whole subject discussed, *Commercial Review, vol.* 1, art. *Blockade*, by J. P. Benjamin, Esq., p. 498; *International Rights of Peace and War*, p. 192, by the editor. The late proclamation of Commandant Stockton on the Pacific, has been thought opposed to our often declared principles, but it is to be observed that the question of infraction of blockade can only arise on that coast in the cases where our squadron has been found *effectual* in preventing it.

States so materially and even vitally affected by them. We protested in vain. The administration recommended as the sole remaining alternative of peace, an *embargo*, which Congress adopted in 1807. This measure the commercial interests warmly opposed as ruinous to them, and memorials were forwarded from many quarters praying for its repeal. To these it was replied by government, "The embargo, by teaching foreign nations the value of American commerce and productions, will inspire them with a disposition to practise justice. They depend upon this country for articles of first necessity, and for raw materials to supply their manufactures." Such a view of the matter, however, did not occur to the mind of Napoleon, who regarded the embargo as greatly favorable to France, and aiding him in his warfare against English commerce. "To submit," said he to Mr. Livingston, "to pay England the tribute she demands, would be for America to aid her against him, and a just ground of war."

In 1809, a *non-intercourse* with Britain and France was substituted for the embargo, which the latter power regarded as such an evidence of hostility as to justify her in proceeding at once to condemn millions of American property as lawful prize.

The Congress of 1810 determined upon the admission of the commercial vessels of the powers above named, if the act were preceded by a revocation of their hostile and arrogant decrees. The French government pretended to close in at once with the proposal, but it was nearly one year later before her repealing ordinance was officially promulgated, evidencing a disposition on the part of Napoleon, to play with us in bad faith, and to turn the game at any time to his advantage. So humiliating to our pride are the events of this entire era. With England, it was long doubtful what relationship we might expect to sustain. Hostile and peaceable alternately, according to her caprices or her interests, she had provoked in American minds a resentment too deep to be subdued, and forbearance longer was regarded a crime. The orders of Council remaining in force, and the aggressions increasing daily, a non-intercourse act of *sixty days* was resorted to, the prelude only to a solemn *declaration of war*.* Then was the hour of severe retribution, and then was the national honor and dignity of America triumphantly and forever vindicated!

V. We come at last to consider the last general division of the subject, *our commerce since the war of* 1812. This has been an era of prosperity and rapid advance, and the great powers of the civilized world seem to have realized, for once, the rich benefits of a prolonged armistice, or, if another expression be preferred, a protracted, and we hope permanent peace. In commercial rank, the United States of America, subordinate to Britain only, and having outstripped all the world else, is prepared to share a divided sceptre, until that sceptre can be wielded alone by her hand, and the empire of the seas be transferred to her keeping.

But this is not a fit time for such generalizations. The history of our trade for the last thirty years has material enough for many more pages than we can allot to it, even with the greatest condensation. The period has been celebrated by an approach to a more liberal *internationality*, and a *reciprocity* something else than in name. The progress, in the last year or two, has been most strongly marked, toward that *ultimatum* in the minds of every lover of truth and of human advancement, perceived first by Lord Bacon, and ably, though imperfectly presented by his followers—*commerce unfettered as the winds that waft it*—free religion, free government, free press, free traffic—freedom everywhere, and in every righteous thing throughout all the world! When shall nations sacrifice their foolish jealousies, and meet each other on this high, broad and Christian ground? We are no partisan here, but a cosmopolite. We advocate a policy as wide as the earth, and as generous. No single nation can afford to act alone—the movement, if made at all, must be *universal*. Can we expect this cordial and noble co-operation? Alas! the time for it appears as remote, as did the day to Charon, when that empire of truth should be established, for which Hume would have delayed his passage across the fearful river of Styx.*

The condition of Europe now, however, argues little for the early triumph of those principles to which we have been referring. The latest British, French, and Austrian tariffs have been in the highest degree restrictive, though in the case of the first-named nation, her policy would appear about to be radically changed. The German states maintain the exclusive policy, as do also the Spaniards and Portuguese. Russia was latest in adopting the restrictive system, but we see by her last tariff some evidences of improvement, which neither Sweden nor Denmark furnishes. The duties of the Italian States have been generally moderate, except for Rome and Naples, and we recognize a great improvement in these, in the late tariff of his Holiness the Pope. The commercial system of Holland is the most liberal in all Europe, but the South American states appear to be governed by the same spirit as that which dictated the policy of Spain.

In 1824, Great Britain seemed desirous of removing in some degree her restrictions

* The *orders* were revoked five days before the declaration of war. Query, however, whether the intelligence would have prevented the declaration?

* A conceit of the philosopher, who wished the *world* to discover truth, when he himself groped *darkly* hrough it.

upon the navigation of other powers. She entered into reciprocity treaties with many of them, and in this was soon after imitated by the United States, in the treaties of 1825–6–8–9, with Central America, Denmark, Sweden, Hanse Towns, Prussia, Brazil, Austria, Hungary and Bohemia, Mexico, Russia, Venezuela, Greece, Sardinia, Netherlands, Hanover, and Portugal. We also entered into similar, but limited reciprocity treaties with France in 1822, continued afterward, and with England in 1821, 1825, and 1833. These treaties were arranged by Mr. Kennedy, Chairman of the Committee of Commerce in 1842, into three classes.

1. Those securing mutual privileges of export and import of produce, the growth, produce, or manufacture of the stipulating powers, transported in their own vessels, without discrimination on tonnage.

2. Those providing for a levy of duties not less favorable upon the tonnage of either, than are levied upon the tonnage of other powers.

3. Those requiring equality of port charges.

According to our own notions, these conventions have always seemed worthy of all encouragement; but singular as it may appear to us, the fact is nevertheless so, that the Committee of Commerce above referred to, reported against them all, as injurious to our navigation and to our commerce. They urged, that the President give notice of termination to those of them, which extended the reciprocity privilege of trade beyond the limits of articles, the growth, produce, or manufacture of the respective countries. The American tariff passed soon after this; the tariffs of France, Belgium, and the German league of the same year, and the Russian tariff of 1841, were classed in the British Commons as those in the highest degree inimical to the trade of the empire. What new influences, favorable or adverse, are to be exerted by the American tariff of 1846, which has occasioned as well in Europe as in this country so great a sensation, remain to be seen.

Before taking a minute survey of American commerce, as it exists at the present moment, or furnishing in detail its important and elaborate statistics, we will pass hurriedly in review over the chief materials of our export trade. They have been distributed under four great heads.

1. *The Products of the Sea.*—We have remarked amply upon this trade, which was secured to us by the treaty with England in 1783, after great opposition on her part. The treaty of 1815 did not renew the guaranty of the fisheries, which occasioned the convention of 1818; and the discussions of the two powers, resulted at last in the restoration of our rights of fishery, though in a much more restricted manner.

2. *The Products of the Forests.*—By this is understood naval stores, skins, furs,* lumber,† ashes,‡ ginseng,§ bark, &c. Our lumber trade commenced very early, in small quantities, but has grown to large account. Naval stores were encouraged in the colonies by bounties. Furs and peltries exported, reached, even as early as 1770, about half a million of dollars. The average value of these exports before 1833, for thirty years, was for lumber annually near $2,000,000, naval stores, $400,000, ashes, $1,000,000, ginseng, $100,000; what they are at the present day will be seen by and by.

3. *Products of Agriculture.*—To this class belong, have belonged, and will perhaps in all the future belong the great mass of the exports of our country. We have a territory vast and prolific enough to supply with our staples the wants of all the world. There is nothing that we demand but a market. In a fair and open market, all competition may be disregarded. In cotton, it has long been urged upon us, "*you produce too much;*" but such is the growing consumption that this complaint will hardly be again repeated. In rice, our capacities are without limit. Though the product in large quantities of but two states, there are millions of acres of land in Mississippi and Louisiana adapted to its growth. Our wheat and Indian corn crops are making prodigious advances. In sugar, instead of supplying half of our own demand, we shall ultimately grow more than we can consume, and be found soliciting markets throughout the states of Europe. We might remark similarly of tobacco and many other commodities.

Our export trade in wheat, flour, and In-

---

* The American *fur trade* is becoming now of little value. That of the beaver is the most important, but the animal has been very nearly exterminated. The chief supplies of furs are from Russia and North America, but many other countries produce them in limited quantities and of different kinds. There are several great fur companies established:

1. The Hudson's Bay Company of London.
2. The American Fur Company of New-York.
3. The Russian-American Company of Moscow.
4. The Danish-Greenland Company of Copenhagen. The furs are consumed principally in China, Turkey, Russia, England, Germany, Europe generally and America. The China fur trade was begun by the Americans in 1784 and prosecuted at times with great vigor. The exports of furs from British America for the five years before 1832, are said to have averaged about $1,000,000 a year.

† The North American *lumber trade* has ever been of great consequence, and is perhaps the chief value of many of the colonies, which England clings to in this quarter.

‡ Chiefly *pot and pearl ashes*, the latter a calcined preparation. Of great use in the arts for soap, glass, bleaching, &c. The ashes of the United States are the best and purest in the world.

§ *Ginseng*, the root of a plant growing in many parts of North America. Principal or only market, China. The Chinese formerly obtained it from Tartary, and the root is said to be worth in Canton, when prepared, $70 or $80 a picul of 133 pounds. Export from United States to China in 1837, 212,809 lbs., valued at $108,548.

dian corn, commenced early, and was quite considerable before the Revolution. Owing to a growing home demand and foreign restrictions, these exports have greatly varied, and the average annually for flour from 1830 to 1840 are less than from 1810 to 1820. The Indian corn export of 1844 was only half as great as that of 1791. However, this gloom which has hung over our farming interests, is being dissipated, as is shown in the vastly increased exports which are now taking place, and in the liberal modification of the British corn laws. These new laws went into operation 27th June last, and the duties until February, 1849, are as follows:

If imported from any foreign country not being a British possession:

Wheat. Average Price	Duty	*Flour and Wheat Meal.* Per cwt.	Per bbl. of 196 lbs.
Under 48s	10s	3s. 5½d	6s. 6.32d.
48s. and under 49s	9s	3s. 1⅛d	5s. 4.31d.
49s. " 50s	8s	2s. 9d	4s. 9.24d.
50s. " 51s	7s	2s. 4d⅛	4s. 2.17d.
51s. " 52s	6s	2s. 0¾d	3s. 7.10d.
52s. " 53s	3s	1s. 8⅝d	3s. 0. 3d.
53s. and upward	4s	1s. 4¼d	2s. 4.28d.

Oats.

Average Price	Duty
Under 18s	4s. 0d.
18s. and under 19s	3s. 0d.
19s. " 20s	3s. 6d.
20s. " 21s	2s. 6d.
21s. " 22s	2s. 0d.
22s. and upward	1s. 6d.

Rye, Peas, Beans, Barley, Bear or Bigg.

Barley average	Duty
Under 26s	5s. 0d.
26s. and under 27s	4s. 6d.
27s. " 28s	4s. 6d.
28s. " 29s	3s. 6d.
29s. " 30s	3s. 0d.
30s. " 31s	2s. 6d.
31s. and upward	2s. 0d.

Barleymeal, for every 217½ lbs. the duty to be equal to that payable on one quarter barley.

Ryemeal, and flour, for every 196 lbs., the duty to be equal to that payable on five-eighths of a quarter barley.

Peameal and beanmeal, for every 272 lbs. the duty to be equal to that payable on one quarter barley.

Oatmeal, for every 181½ lbs. the duty to be equal to that payable on one quarter barley.

If the produce of or imported from any British possession out of Europe:—

Wheat, barley, bear or bigg, oats, rye, peas, and beans, the duty shall be for every quarter 1s.

Wheatmeal, barleymeal, oatmeal, ryemeal, peameal, and beanmeal, the duty shall be for every cwt. 4½d.

The exports of Indian corn were 825,282 bushels in 1843–4, and 247,882 bbls. meal; in 1844–5, 840,184 bushels, 269,030 bbls. Of flour, 1844, 1,438,574 bbls.; in 1845, 1,195,230; or, estimating each barrel of flour at its equivalent of 5 bushels of wheat, we have nearly six million bushels of wheat for 1845, nearly 1-16 of the whole product. The receipts of corn and flour at New-Orleans alone, in the year 1845–6, trebled in the one instance, and doubled in the other, those of any previous year, as will be seen when we come to treat of this city. The total exports of Indian corn up to May, 1846, were four times as great as in the corresponding months of the previous year. What the whole export of breadstuffs for the coming year from the United States will be, is not easily determined. The estimates are in general high. There can be no doubt that there has been a large crop. We know that on the continent of Europe, in England and in Ireland, the harvest has been disastrous, and that there is a demand far beyond our capacity to export.

It is unnecessary to dwell minutely in this place upon the other articles of our agricultural export. We have published already two comprehensive articles upon *Sugar** by eminent gentlemen, and two also upon *Tobacco*,† to which, with three others upon *Cotton*, *Flour*, and *Indian Corn*,‡ by ourselves, we would refer the reader. The following table contains the growth and home consumption of cotton from 1826 to 1846:

GROWTH AND HOME CONSUMPTION OF COTTON.

	Growth, bales	Consumption, bales
1826-27	937,900	—
1827-28	712,000	—
1828-29	857,744	118,853
1829-30	976,845	126,512
1830-31	1,038,848	182,142
1831-32	987,477	173,800
1832-33	1,070,438	194,412
1833-34	1,205,394	196,413
1834-35	1,254,328	216,888
1835-36	1,360,725	236,733
1836-37	1,422,930	222,540
1837-38	1,801,497	246,063
1838-39	1,360,532	276,018
1839-40	2,177,835	295,193
1840-41	1,634,945	297,288
1841-42	1,683,574	267,850
1842-43	2,378,875	325,129
1843-44	2,030,409	346,744
1844-45	2,394,503	389,006
1845-46	2,110,537	422,597

4. *Products Domestic Manufactures.*—The manufacturing industry of our country began to display itself soon after the Revolu tion, and it has through a great portion of

* Commercial Review, Vol. I., p. 53, *Louisiana Sugar*, by E. J. Forstall, Esq., Vol. II., p. 322, *Cultivation and Manufacture of Sugar in Louisiana*, by J. P. Benjamin, Esq.

† Commercial Review, Vol. II., 42 and 248 pp.

‡ Vol. I., 33, 289, 465 pp. In our article upon *Indian Corn*, we may be thought to have expressed ourselves despondingly in reference to the possibility of its becoming a considerable article of export. But we were arguing a particular and not a general case. What was true for the year of our reasonings, need not be always so in a country capable of indefinite production. What was urged about the home demand, loses little of its force at any time.

of our history, and in different degrees, been an especial favorite with government. We have, indeed, attained to surprising excellence in these branches, and in very many of them may compete with any nation upon earth. For the manufacture of cotton goods we have unrivaled facilities, and it may be doubted now whether this branch is at all dependent upon the favors of government. This will not hold true in many other departments of manufactures, and hence the anxiety manifested in all parts of the Union in relation to the working of the new tariff of 1846. Whatever opinion we may have ourselves upon the subject, this is not the occasion to express them. It is generally concluded, however, that so far as cotton goods are concerned, the manufacture will not be diminished. Abbot Lawrence, Esq., wrote lately to Mr. Rives :

"Our consumption of cotton reached the last year, one hundred and seventy-six millions of pounds, which is equal to the whole crop of the Union in 1825, and equal to the whole consumption of Great Britain in 1826. This is a striking fact, and one that should be remembered. The history of the production and manufacture of cotton is so extraordinary, that I propose to send you some statistics on the subject furnished me by a friend. I hope you will not deem me over sanguine when I tell you that it is my belief that the consumption of cotton in this country will double in eight or nine years, and that it will reach 400,000,000 pounds in 1856, and farther, that we are not only destined to be the greatest cotton growers, but the most extensive cotton spinners in the world. The manufacture of cotton is, probably, in its infancy ; but a moderate portion of mankind have yet been clothed with this healthful and cheap article."

The whole amount in value of domestic manufactures exported from the United States in 1840, was $9,873,462; 1843, $6,777,527 ; 1844, $9,579,724 ; 1845, $10,329,701, according to the exhibits of the Secretary of the Treasury. The exports from Boston for the year ending May, 1846, will give an idea of the accustomed markets.

COTTON GOODS EXPORTED FROM BOSTON IN 1846, TO

(Bales and Cases.)

Hong Kong	650	Honduras	179	Guayma	1
Canton	1,663	California	46	Neuvitas	1
Calcutta	657	Mansanilla	90	Galveston	19
Canton and Manilla	535	St. Peters	146	Aux Cayes	54
Manilla	1,239	Laguayra	164	New-Orleans	5,454
Batavia	152	St. Domingo and St. Thomas	50	Mobile	670
East Indies	5,090	Gonaives	33	Apalachicola	110
Valparaiso	11,080	St. Domingo	90	Charleston	4,530
Sumatra	175	Cape Haytien	39	Richmond	904
Smyrna	656	New-Zealand	31	New-York	22,574
Buenos Ayres	175	Cape Verdis	20	Baltimore	8,254
Palermo and Naples	158	Jamaica	33	Philadelphia	19,669
Rio Janeiro	2,189	West Indies	25	Georgetown	105
Istapa, C. A.	1,138	Bahamas	10	Savannah	15
Sandwich Islands	759	Nassau	10	Hartford	44
Cronstadt	440	Campeachy	25	Salem	50
Gibraltar	132	San Juan	4	Eastport	248
Africa	25	Nova Scotia	8	Norfolk	10
Hobart Town	40	St. Thomas and Maracaibo	58	Pattersonville	5
Zanzebar	576	Fayal	62	Thomastown, Me	6
Matla	146	St. Thomas	147	Belfast	13
South America	164	Porto Cabello	6	Castine	4
Pernambuco	109	Londonderry	2	Portsmouth and Camden	11

Total	91,992
Same time last year	65,971
Increase	26,021

A good market has been afforded by Mexico for these cotton products, and she took in 1835 over one million of dollars, though the amount has fallen off very much since. The Central Republic and Honduras have been regular customers. Chili furnishes the best South American market for cotton goods. Brazil, the Cisplatine Republic, and Buenos Ayres, afford a continually increasing trade. Peru takes nothing ; China has been since 1826 a regular and large purchaser, and took in 1838 half a million of dollars in value. Turkey, the Levant, and Egypt, the South Seas, the Sandwich, and Philippine Islands, Australia and Manilla are small, growing markets. We began to send cotton goods to the Dutch East and West Indies about 1826, and have sent in some years a considerable value. Holland, the Hanse Towns, and Belgium, have taken very little. The amounts sent to the French West Indies, and Russia, are inconsiderable. We exported as early as 1826, $664 cotton goods to England, and there have been annual small shipments ever since ; amount in 1837, $11,889. The British East Indies formerly supplied us with cottons, but since 1827, we have competed with their manufactures in their own market. The African market, since 1826, has progressed with the settlements being made there. Cuba commenced to take in 1826. If we are not mistaken, the Americans will one day supply the world with these fabrics, and why should it not be so? The staple is on the spot, and can be used without expensive costs of shipments. In yarns, of which Britain exports $20,000,000 annually, we ought to stand unrivaled, and in fact, in all manufactures, where the raw material is a large element of cost, or more properly, where the workmanship and processes are less complicated and expensive, and the capital required small.

The chief foreign powers with whom our own has commercial relations, will now demand a minute attention at our hands, and we shall afterward refer generally to those occupying subordinate rank, it being the object of the sketch to furnish as complete a map of American commerce at the present day, as is consistent with our ability and the limited space allotted to us. We begin with—

1. *Great Britain and her Dependencies.*—It has been seen already the struggles that were occasioned in this quarter from the grasping policy of an empire aiming at universal dominion. We have marked, too, a change for the better. Can it be otherwise than that these two great, enlightened and enterprising nations shall be drawn, as time progresses, into nearer and nearer alliance? Do not our great domestic staples supply the very life-blood of English industry? She had as well exclude the rains, and dew, and sun that fertilize and render prolific her soil, as close up for any time her ports to the staples of American growth. Such an exclusion would be the tocsin sounding universal bankruptcy throughout her realms.

With the British West India possessions our trade has been subject to great vicissitudes, as we have previously remarked. We saw the measures of the mother country to arrest it previous to the Revolution. Countervailing systems have been over and over resorted to. The President of the United States in 1816 declared: "The depressed state of our navigation is to be ascribed in a material degree to its exclusion from the colonial ports of the nation most extensively connected with us in commerce." In the same year the restrictions for Canada and Nova Scotia were relaxed, and our trade to them magnified threefold. The retaliatory acts of Congress, 1817, 1818, 1820, upon the navigation acts of England, resulted in so much suffering to the West India planters that they remonstrated to Parliament, and succeeded in having their ports opened to our trade. These ports were again closed in 1826, but in 1830 the United States having accepted the terms of Britain, they were opened. This last arrangement was conceived most beneficial to our commerce, but many have expressed strong doubts. It was thought a triumph of British policy by some of the leading journals there, for "British vessels, it was said, may now proceed from any port in his Majesty's dominions *direct* to the United States, there load a full cargo, either for the West Indies *direct* or *via* the Provinces."

The *British West Indies* consist of Antigua, Barbadoes, Barbuda, Anguilla, Dominica, Grenada, the Grenadines, Montserrat, Nevis, St. Christopher, St. Lucia, St. Vincent, Tobago, Trinidad, Tortola, and Virgin Islands, Jamaica, Bahama, British Guiana, Honduras in Yucatan. The whole export and import trade of these islands with the mother country, according to Porter, amounted in the aggregate to $43,000,000 in 1839.

British North America contains a population of 1,300,000, and its imports from the mother country, in general, largely exceed its exports to her. The divisions are New-Brunswick, with a population of 160,000, and an average annual trade of £1,000,000. Nova Scotia, population 178,000—trade, £1,500,000. Halifax, the capital, has a harbor capable of protecting a thousand ships. Cape Breton, a dependency of Nova Scotia, has a population of 27,000 on the island. Prince Edward's Island, on the St. Lawrence, contains 47,000 inhabitants. Newfoundland, settled chiefly on the coast, contains 74,000 inhabitants. Bermuda has a small trade, and a well-known product, arrow-root. The territories of the Hudson Bay Company are vast, and used chiefly for hunting grounds. The exports of all those colonies are mainly grain, lumber, and fish, and their extensive forests fit them for enterprises in ship building, which render their possessions precious to so maritime a nation as Great Britain.

The following table, showing the official returns, from 1822 to 1845, of American trade with Great Britain and her dependencies, is compiled from the Report of the Secretary of the Treasury.

AMERICAN TRADE WITH BRITAIN AND DEPENDENCIES

	Exports	Imports
1822	$30,041,337	$39,537,829
1823	27,571,060	34,072,578
1824	28,027,845	32,750,340
1825	44,217,525	42,394,812
1826	28,980,019	32,212,356
1827	32,870,465	33,056,374
1828	27,020,209	35,591,484
1829	28,071,084	27,582,082
1830	31,647,881	26,804,984
1831	39,901,379	47,956,717
1832	37,268,556	42,406,924
1833	39,881,486	43,085,865
1834	50,797,650	52,679,298
1835	60,107,134	65,949,307
1836	64,487,550	86,022,915
1837	61,218,813	52,289,557
1838	58,843,392	49,051,181

	Exports	Imports
1839	$68,169,082	$71,600,351
1840	70,420,846	39,130,921
1841	62,376,402	51,099,638
1842	52,306.650	38,613,043
1843	46,091,835	28,978,582
1844	61,721,876	45,459,122
1845	61,044,535	49,003,725

2. *France and her Dependencies.*—Before the Revolution, we had little commerce with France herself. The treaty of alliance formed with her in 1778, was expected to have caused a close commercial union in all the future between the two countries; but this was not realized on the restoration of peace, as it was bitterly complained by French writers. In 1787, our exports to France were $5,000,000, and imports thence $2,500,000. Her commerce with us is second now only to that of Great Britain.

The French West Indies were long governed by the same illiberal policy as the English. The latter was willing that the United States should have the products of the plantations, if her own vessels could carry them, but France monopolized these productions to herself, though willing that the islands should be supplied by America with what she could not herself supply. During the wars of Europe, it was found absolutely necessary to hold out a free trade with the French colonies, and this trade was offered to be guarantied to the United States, on condition, that by a new compact, the islands were guarantied to France. This proposal was at once declined. From 1795 to 1801, our exports to the islands averaged $6,000,000, and imports over $12,000,000. This trade has dwindled away, so that from 1821 to 1833, the exports and imports together, did not average annually over $1,500,000. The estimate is exclusive of Hayti, which averaged 3,500,000.

The French colonies are Martinique, Guadaloupe and its dependencies, viz.: part of St. Martin's, Mariagalante, Desirade les Saints; French Guiana, and Cayenne in America; Senegal, St. Louis, and Goree, on the West Coast of Africa; East of the Cape of Good Hope, the Isle of Bourbon, Mahe, Pondicherry, Karikal, Yanaon, and Chandarnagore; and in North America, the islands of St. Pierre, Miquelon, and Langley, near the coast of Newfoundland.

AMERICAN TRADE WITH FRANCE AND DEPENDENCIES.

	Exports	Imports.
1822	$7,075,332	$7,059,342
1823	9,568,924	6,605,343
1824	10,552,304	9,907,412
1825	11,891,326	11,835,581
1826	12,106,429	9,588,896
1827	13,565,356	9,448,562
1828	12,098,341	10,287,505
1829	12,832,304	9.616,970
1830	11,806,238	8,240,885
1831	9,882,679	14,737,585
1832	$13,244,698	$12,754,615
1833	14,424,533	13,962,913
1834	16,111,442	17,557,245
1835	20,335,066	23,362,584
1836	21,441,200	37,036,235
1837	20,255,346	22,497,817
1838	16,252,413	18,087,149
1839	18,924,413	33,234,119
1840	22,349,154	17,908,127
1841	22,235,575	24,187,444
1842	18,738,860	17,223,390
1843	12,472,453	7,836,137
1844	16,133,436	17,952,412
1845	16,143,994	22,069,914

3. *Spain and Dependencies.*—The period of our greatest trade, from 1805 to 1815, since greatly declined. Chief exports in that direction from us are, fish, flour, oil, rice, tobacco, &c. Imports: wines, brandies, and fruits. With the colonies, during the wars of Europe, we had a most extensive traffic, amounting at times in gross to $20,000,000 annually. The decline, as in other West Indies, has been marked. Exports, principally provisions, lumber, oil, candles, and some foreign products; imports, sugar, coffee, segars. Since 1825, our accounts with Spanish America have been kept separate from those with Spain.

The Spanish possessions are, the Balearic, in the Mediterranean, and Canary Islands, Cuba, Porto Rico, and the Philippines, in the East Indies; but Spain has not now a foot of ground on the *Continent* of America. Of Cuba, McGregor remarks, in 1844, the United States supplied but a small propore tion of the manufactures consumed in th- West Indies, which she has the best means of producing. Nearly all the manufactures entering there from England are in Spanish bottoms, while American manufactures are in United States vessels. Spanish vessels can go to England, take in cotton goods, and carry them to Cuba, on better terms than American vessels can carry them direct. This can only be accounted for on the ground that the paper currency of the United States carries the level of prices too high to admit of profitable shipment to the specie prices of Cuba. The imports and exports of Cuba average about $25,000,000 each annually.

AMERICAN TRADE WITH SPAIN AND DEPENDENCIES.

	Exports	Imports
1822	$8,438,212	$12,376,841
1823	10,963,398	14,233,590
1824	15,367,278	15,857,007
1825	5,921,549	9,566,237
1826	6.687.351	9,623,420
1827	7,321,994	9,100,369
1828	7,204,627	8,167,546
1829	6,888,094	6,801,374
1830	6,049,051	8,373,681
1831	5,661,420	11,701,201
1832	6,399,183	10,863,290
1833	6,506,041	13,431,207
1834	6,296,556	13,527,464
1835	7,069,279	15,617,140
1836	8,081,668	19,345,690
1837	7,604,002	18,927,871

	Exports	Imports
1838	$7,684,006	$15,971,394
1839	7,724,429	19,276,795
1840	7,617,347	14,019,647
1841	7,181,409	16,316,303
1842	6,323,295	12,176,588
1843	3,953,694	6,980,504
1844	6,751,811	13,775,451
1845	7,790,442	10,590,544

4. *Portugal.*—To our trade with Portugal the same stimulus was given during the career of Bonaparte that was given to the trade with Spain, and principally in the periods from 1795 to 1801, and from 1809 to 1814. Since then the trade has greatly decreased. The colonial trade was unimportant until the removal of the home government to Brazil.

Portugal, even before the days of King Emanuel, and of the celebrated Albuquerque, was justly celebrated for the adventurous spirit of its navigators ; its commerce was also extensive. The trade of Portugal, however, has, even when Brazil formed one of her colonies, been greatly overrated, although there is no doubt of its having greatly declined. The foreign trade is chiefly confined to Lisbon and Oporto, and consists in exports, chiefly of wine, salt, and raw produce ; imports, manufactured goods, produce, corn, and flour.*

Portugal has no American possessions, and few in Asia or Africa. In the Atlantic she has the Azores, near at hand, the Island of Madeira, of some importance, and the Cape de Verde Islands.

AMERICAN TRADE WITH PORTUGAL AND DEPENDENCIES.

	Exports	Imports
1826	$313,553	$765,203
1827	357,270	659,001
1828	291,614	433,555
1829	322,911	687,869
1830	279,799	471,643
1831	294,383	397,550
1832	290,218	485,264
1833	442,561	555,137
1834	322,496	699,122
1835	521,413	1,125,713
1836	191,007	672,670
1837	423,705	928,291
1838	232,131	725,058
1839	244,354	1,182,323
1840	321,256	599,894
1841	349,113	574,841
1842	302,964	347,684
1843	168,534	71,369
1844	252,170	257,015
1845	247,180	501,734

5. *Russia.*—Since the age of the Czar Peter, 1689, the advances of this empire have been prodigious. Its population now is, at least, 70,000,000, and its acquisitions from Sweden, Poland, Turkey, Persia, and Tartary, in territory, have been immense. With the enterprise of such sovereigns as the present, Russia must soon take a high rank among the nations of the world. Her late tariff evidences the improvement.

"The empire of Russia, including the greater part of the ancient kingdom of Poland, and the isles of Aland, etc., which formerly belonged to Sweden; the ancient kingdoms of Astrakan and Kazan conquered from the Tartars ; the Crimea, Little Tartary, Bessarabia, and a portion of Moldavia, taken from the Ottoman empire ; the incroachments over the regions of the Caucasus, on the possessions of the natives, and on the dominions of Turkey and Persia; that vast region extending east from the confines of Europe to the Pacific, and to Behring's Strait, and north from the confines of Persia and Tartary to the Arctic Circle; also, a great, valuable and undefined extent of country along the North-west coast of America; occupies altogether even a greater portion of the surface of the globe than the vast but widely spread British Empire."

The American trade with Russia, previous to 1833, seldom exceeded in exports $1,000,000, except in 1810, '11, and '12, when they reached $6,000,000 ; consisting of sugar, coffee, and cotton, a great portion of the last finding its way thence to England. Imports, hemp, iron, duck, and cordage.

AMERICAN TRADE WITH RUSSIA.

	Exports	Imports
1836	$911,013	$2,778,554
1837	1,306,732	2,816,116
1838	1,048,289	1,898,396
1839	1,239,246	2,393,894
1840	1,169,481	2,572,427
1841	1,025,729	2,817,448
1842	836,593	1,350,106
1843	386,793	742,803
1844	555,414	1,059,419
1845	727,337	1,492,262

6. *Sweden, Norway, and Denmark.*—The native products and exports of the first two embrace copper, iron, lumber, naval stores. Highly restrictive tariffs. Our average import from 1820 to 1833, about $1,000,000, and export $3,000,000. At the close of the eighteenth century our trade with Swedish West Indies was quite considerable, and in 1807, during a non-intercourse with other powers, large exports were made to Denmark and Norway, to be re-shipped thence. The Danish West Indies enjoyed a similar privilege. From 1821 to 1841, our imports from Denmark averaged over $1,000,000, and the exports to her about $2,000,000. Since then, both imports and exports have decreased very much, the former about one-half.

AMERICAN TRADE WITH SWEDEN AND DEPENDENCIES.

	Exports	Imports
1836	$700,386	$1,299,603
1837	507,523	1,468,878
1838	355,852	900,790
1839	470,914	1,566,142
1840	652,546	1,275,458
1841	771,210	1,229,641
1842	477,965	914,176
1843	67,762	278,674
1844	295,345	445,553
1845	363,667	640,057

* McGregor.

7. *China.*—Though ever jealous of foreigners, and indisposed to change, the progress of events is bringing the Chinese into nearer connection with the rest of the world. When these hundreds of millions come to understand the advantage and importance of commerce, we expect an extension of the trade of the world in an inconceivable degree. Already have Great Britain and the United States exacted from her more liberal treaties of intercourse, which on a former occasion we published. Should an overland communication be ever established from the United States to China, a thing not unlikely, the trade of that vast empire necessarily falls into our hands, and what it will be may be judged from the fact, that as early as 1830, with Britain alone, it amounted to $41,856,253. Our trade with China began in 1784; two years after, a sloop arrived there from Boston, of 80 tons burthen, and with 7 men; five years after, we had more vessels at Canton than any other nation, except Britain. Imports, tea, silks, nankeens, chinaware, &c. Exports, furs, ginseng, cotton goods, cotton, specie, &c.

A great part of our trade with China is carried on from foreign ports on American account. In 1800 we furnished the Chinese with furs, obtained from North-west America, and seal-skins from the Poles. The imports of tea for the year ending July 1845 and 1846, were:

	1845.	1846.
Green tea	13,802,099	13,355,104
Black tea	6,950,459	3,321,790
Total lbs.	20,752,558	16,676,894

AMERICAN TRADE WITH CHINA.

	Exports	Imports
1836	$1,194,264	$7,324,816
1837	630,591	8,965,337
1838	1,516,602	4,764,536
1839	1,533,601	3,678,509
1840	1,009,966	6,640,829
1841	1,260,816	3,985,388
1842	1,444,397	4,934,645
1843	2,418,958	4,385,566
1844	1,756,941	4,931,255
1845	2,275,995	7,285,914

8. *Italy and the Italian States.*—Their population is estimated at about 21,000,000. The following departments are included under one general head: Lombardo-Venitian Kingdom, including the governments of Trieste, Sardinia, Tuscany, Parma, Lucca, Modena, Papal states, kingdom of Naples. The government, the disunion of the country, the religion, the people themselves, the climate, the soil, the non-division of property in some states, its subdivision in other states, are, one or the other, it is said, ascribed as the causes which have effected all that of good or of evil is presented to us in the existing aspect of Italy, and of the condition of the Italian people.

AMERICAN TRADE WITH ITALY.

	Exports	Imports
1836	$664,059	$1,970,246
1837	623,677	1,827,181
1838	459,893	944,238
1839	438,152	1,182,297
1840	1,473,185	1,157,200
1841	912,318	1,151,236
1842	820,517	987,527
1843	728,221	394,564
1844	576,823	1,096,926
1845	817,921	1,301,577

9. *Netherlands and its Dependencies.*—The Netherlands or Low Countries, now known by the name of Austrian, French, and Dutch Flanders, and the Seven United Provinces forming the Republic of Holland, were anciently known by the name of Lower Germany, or Belgium. They were reduced to a deplorable condition after the fall of the Western Empire, by the ravages of the barbarians. In 1830 the revolution in *Belgium* separated the kingdom of Netherlands into two. That of the Netherlands was reduced to the original Seven United Provinces, with a part of Luxemburg and Limburg added. One of the most prominent sources of the wealth of Holland is the persevering industry in the pursuit of gain continued by each individual during life, and transmitted by each to his successor; and the most extraordinary frugality in the manner of living, joined to the universally governing maxim among the Dutch, that it is a disgrace not to live upon much less than one's income.*

In 1805–7, the exports of the United States to Holland averaged over $15,000,000; but from 1821 to 1833, the average was not above $3,000,000, and the average of imports $1,000,000; the former principally of cotton, rice, and tobacco, of American produce; the latter, woolen, linen, spirits, manufactured iron, steel, lead, &c. With the Dutch West Indies our commerce was greater previous to 1800 than since. We enjoyed at that period, to a large extent, the carriage of her East India produce.

AMERICAN TRADE WITH NETHERLANDS AND DEPENDENCIES.

	Exports	Imports
1822	$5,801,639	$2,708,162
1823	7,767,075	2,125,587
1824	3,617,389	2,355,525
1825	5,895,499	2,265,378
1826	4,794,070	2,174,181
1827	3,826,674	1,722,070
1828	3,083,359	1,990,431
1829	4,622,120	1,617,334
1830	4,562,437	1,356,765
1831	3,096,609	1,653,031
1832	6,035,466	2,358,474
1833	3,566,361	2,347,343
1834	4,578,739	2,127,886
1835	4,411,053	2,903,718
1836	4,799,157	3,861,514
1837	4,285,767	3,370,828
1838	3,772,206	2,194,238

* McGregor, vol. i., p. 802.

	Exports	Imports
1839	$2,871,239	$3,473,220
1840	4,546,085	2,326,896
1841	3,286,741	2,440,437
1842	4,270,770	2,214,520
1843	2,370,884	815,541
1844	3,453,385	1,136,386
1845	3,610,602	1,897,623

10. *The Zollverein.*—The German States cemented a close union with each other, 22d March, 1833, in the celebrated convention, called the Zollverein or Customs Union, consisting of Prussia, Bavaria, Saxony, Wurtemberg, Baden, and other States of the Germanic Confederation, except Austria, Hanover, Oldenberg, Mecklenburg, Holstein, and the Hanse Towns. By this Union is prevented all the inconvenience of Custom-house barriers, and the expense of a multitude of revenue officers. The population of the Union in 1837 was 26,042,338; since augmented by the accession of Brunswick, Schaumburg, and Luxemburg. There is a perfect free trade between the states and their respective commodities exchanged without duties. This, with the opportunities of interchanging ideas, and receiving intelligence, it is said, constitute the greatest material, moral and civilized blessings, ever enjoyed by the German people. The manufacturing industry of this confederation bids fair to be very great, and a large demand for our cottons may be expected. The treaty attempted to be negotiated with these states, a few years ago, will be remembered. Our direct trade with them is yet small; the whole amount of imports from Prussia in 1845, was $31,032, and exports to her $567,-121.

11. *The Hanse Towns.*—Every one is familiar with the antiquity and celebrity of this league, which has from seventy cities diminished to three—Hamburg, Bremen, and Lubec. We export to Bremen in greater quantities than to the others; principally of tobacco, which is distributed thence throughout Germany, Prussia, Austria, and even Italy and Russia. Hamburg is the greatest entrepot for the nations of Europe. The manufacturers of Germany are brought there by the canals, the Elbe and the Weser. Its East India trade is large. In 1797, '98, '99, our trade with Hamburg ranged from 15 to 23 millions a year.

AMERICAN TRADE WITH HANSE TOWNS.

	Exports	Imports
1836	$4,363,882	$4,994,820
1837	3,754,949	5,642,221
1838	3,291,645	2,847,358
1839	2,801,067	4,849,150
1840	4,198,459	2,521,493
1841	4,560,716	2,449,964
1842	4,564,513	2,274,019
1843	3,291,932	920,865
1844	3,566,687	2,136,286
1845	4,945,020	2,912,537

12. *Mexico.*—The continual convulsions of this country have, of course, prevented the growth of any considerable trade. The imports into the republic in 1841 were $12,-300,000 of which the United States supplied but 800,000. The exports were about $20,-300,000, of which $18,500,000 was in specie. The chief ports are Vera Cruz, Tampico, and Matamoras. To the northern provinces of Santa Fé our trade was in rapid progress, and the amount of merchandize sent them in 1843, about half a million dollars. But this is a mere item, compared with the immense amounts which that country requires. Should the present war result in a permanent acquisition of territory beyond the Nueces, and a liberal treaty of reciprocity between the two governments, it is almost impossible to conceive the extension which will be given to our trade in that quarter. The divisions of the Republic are Yucatan, Tobasco, Chiapa, Oaxaca, Vera Cruz, Puebla, Tlascala, Mexico, Queretaro, Guanaxuato, Michoacan, Colima, Jalisco or Xalisco, Zacatecas, San Luis Potosi, Durango, New Leon, Tamaulipas, Cohahuila, Chihuahua, New Mexico or Santa Fe, Occidente.

AMERICAN TRADE WITH MEXICO.

	Exports	Imports
1826	$6,281,050	$3,916,198
1827	4,173,257	5,231,867
1828	2,886,484	4,814,258
1829	2,331,151	5,026,761
1830	4,837,458	5,235,241
1831	6,178,218	5,166,745
1832	3,467,541	4,293,954
1833	5,408,091	5,452,818
1834	5,265,653	8,066,068
1835	9,029,221	9,490,446
1836	6,041,635	5,615,819
1837	3,880,323	5,654,002
1838	2,164,097	3,500,709
1839	2,787,362	3,127,153
1840	2,515,341	4,175,001
1841	2,036,620	3,284,957
1842	1,534,233	1,995,696
1843	1,471,937	2,782,406
1844	1,794,833	2,387,002
1845	1,152,331	1,702,936

13. *Hayti.*—Since the independence of the Island, its trade has sunk almost to nothing, as we may judge from the fact, that in 1791 it exported double the quantity of coffee exported in 1822, and about three hundred times the quantity of sugar!

AMERICAN TRADE WITH HAYTI.

	Exports	Imports
1836	$1,240,039	$1,828,019
1837	1,011,981	1,440,856
1838	910,255	1,275,762
1839	1,122,559	1,377,989
1840	1,027,214	1,252,824
1841	1,155,557	1,809,684
1842	899,966	1,266,997
1843	653,370	898,447
1844	1,128,356	1,441,244
1845	1,405,740	1,386,367

14. *South America.*—The seats of our most considerable trade in this direction, are Venezuela, New Granada, and Equador, Central America, Brazil, Argentine and Cisplatine Republics, and Chili.

TRADE WITH SOUTH AMERICA.

	Exports	Imports
1836	$5,436,559	$10,967,144
1837	4,742,652	8,902,798
1838	5,292,231	6,933,735
1839	5,864,428	9,896,203
1840	5,891,478	9,093,688
1841	6,461,281	11,834,412
1842	5,761,808	11,034,946
1843	4,197,406	7,159,635
1844	5,696,292	11,014,842
1845	5,918,039	10,485,025

These tables will furnish abundant food to the reader for reflection. Our space will not allow a full analysis of them at present. It is sufficient to observe generally, that they exhibit a steady progressive trade with Britain and France, in which the exports to the former are always greatest, and the imports from the latter. For Portugal and Spain we discover the imports to be in general double the exports. Russia and Sweden exhibit the same results, the former falling off in exports from us, and the latter in imports to us. The imports from China range from two to five times the value of exports. Italy takes from us but half the amount we import from her. The exports to Netherlands and Hanse Towns, always exceed the imports thence, sometimes twofold. The imports from Mexico and exports to her, have greatly declined, the former always greatest. The imports from South America and Hayti exceed the exports; in the former case by one-half.

The Austrian Lloyd's List, in an article founded upon official documents, sums up the foreign commerce of Europe. We have taken 10,000, as a unit, and the proportionate parts of which will represent the commerce of each State.

COMMERCE OF EUROPE.

Places not enumerated	55	Sweden and Norway	110	Russia	200
Spain	60	Two Sicilies	120	Hamburg	390
Portugal	70	Austria	140	Holland	500
Bremen	90	Prussia	150	France	1,300
Denmark	100	Belgium	200	Great Britain	6,100
Tuscany	105	Sardinia	210		10,000

It will thus appear that the trade of England is about twice as great nearly as that of all the rest of Europe together. The whole European mercantile marine, without including the coasting trade, comprehends 260,000 vessels, measuring in all 33,493,000 tons. The total amount of merchandize carried in them, $2,387,153,000.

The following tables, founded upon the reports of the Treasury Department and other authentic data, have been prepared with great pains and labor. They will exhibit in one view the entire commerce of our country, from the Revolution until the present day. Previous to 1790, it should be remarked, there was no establishment for obtaining accurately the whole exports and imports of the country; and previously to 1821, the particulars of our trade were scarcely at all given.* During the Revolution we had no trade; nor any with any other nation than Britain, of much consequence, from the close of the war until 1789.

TRADE OF THE UNITED STATES WITH ENGLAND.

	Imports	Exports
1784	£749,345	£3,679,467
1785	893,594	2,308,023
1786	843,119	1,603,465
1787	893,637	2,009,111
1788	1,023,789	1,886,142
1789	1,050,198	2,525,298

IMPORTS AND EXPORTS UNITED STATES FROM 1790 TO 1846.

Years	IMPORTS: Total value of Imports	IMPORTS: Retained for Consumption	EXPORTS: Domestic	EXPORTS: Foreign	EXPORTS: Total
1790	$23,000,000	$22,460,844	$19,666,000	$539,156	$20,205,156
1791	29,200,000	28,687,959	18,500,000	512,041	19,012,041
1792	31,500,000	29,746,902	19,000,000	1,753,098	20,753,098
1793	31,100,000	28,990,428	24,000,000	2,109,572	26,109,572
1794	34,600,000	28,073,767	26,500,000	6,526,233	33,026,233
1795	69,756,268	61,266,796	39,500,000	8,489,472	47,989,472
1796	81,436,164	55,136,164	40,764,097	26,300,000	67,064,097
1797	75,379,406	48,379,406	29,850,026	27,000,000	56,850,206
1798	68,551,700	35,551,700	28,527,097	33,000,000	61,527,097
1799	79,069,148	33,546,148	33,142,522	45,523,000	78,665,522
1800	91,252,768	52,121,891	31,840,903	39,130,877	70,971,780
1801	111,363,511	64,720,790	47,473,204	46,642,721	94,115,925

* We should have been pleased to have introduced, upon our commercial treaties with foreign powers, some observations, but the present article is already too extended. Indeed we have not been able to obtain the work of Mr. Smith, thus alluded to in McGregor's *Legislation, &c.* "In compliance with a resolution of Congress, passed 3d March, 1831, a digest of the existing commercial regulations of foreign countries with which the United States have intercourse, was ordered to be published. The execution of the arduous work was entrusted to a very competent publicist, Mr. John Spear Smith, and the first volume published in 1833, and the whole, as far as information could then be collected, in four volumes, in 1836."

IMPORTS AND EXPORTS UNITED STATES FROM 1790 TO 1846—*continued.*

Years	IMPORTS		EXPORTS		
	Total value of Imports	Retained for Consumption	Domestic	Foreign	Total
1802	$76,333,333	$40,558,362	$36,708,189	$35,774,971	$72,483,160
1803	64,666,666	51,072,594	42,205,961	13,594,072	55,800,033
1804	85,000,000	48,768,403	41,467,477	36,231,597	77,699,074
1805	120,600,000	67,420,981	42,387,002	53,179,019	95,566,021
1806	129,410,000	69,126,764	41,253,727	60,283,236	101,536,963
1807	138,500,000	78,856,442	48,699,592	59,543,558	108,343,150
1808	56,990,000	43,992,586	9,433,546	12,997,414	22,430,960
1809	59,400,000	38,602,469	31,405,700	20,797,531	52,203,231
1810	85,400,000	61,008,705	42,366,679	24,391,295	66,757,974
1811	53,400,000	37,377,210	45,294,041	16,022,790	61,316,831
1812	77,030,000	68,534,873	30,032,109	8,495,127	38,527,236
1813	22,005,000	19,157,155	25,008,152	2,847,845	27,855,997
1814	12,965,000	12,819,831	6,782,272	145,169	6,927,441
1815	113,041,274	106,457,924	45,974,403	6,583,350	52,557,753
1816	147,103,000	129,964,444	64,781,896	17,138,556	81,920,452
1817	99,250,000	79,891,931	68,313,500	19,358,069	87,671,569
1818	121,750,000	102,323,304	73,854,437	19,426,696	93,281,133
1819	87,125,000	67,959,317	50,976,838	19,165,683	70,142,521
1820	74,450,000	56,441,971	51,683,640	18,008,029	69,691,679
1821	62,585,724	41,283,336	43,671,894	21,302,488	04,974,382
1822	83,241,511	60,955,309	49,874,185	22,286,202	72,160,387
1823	77,579,267	50,035,645	47,155,408	27,653,622	74,699,030
1824	80,549,007	55,211,850	50,649,500	25,337,157	75,986,657
1825	96,340,075	63,749,432	66,944,745	32,590,643	99,535,388
1826	84,974,477	56,434,865	53,055,710	24,539,612	77,595,322
1827	79,484,068	56,084,932	58,921,691	23,403,136	82,324,827
1828	88,509,824	66,914,807	50,669,669	21,595,017	72,264,686
1829	74,492,527	57,834,049	55,700,193	16,658,478	72,358,671
1830	70,876,920	56,489,441	59,462,029	14,387,479	73,849,508
1831	103,191,124	83,157,598	61,277,057	20,033,526	81,310,583
1832	101,029,266	76,989,793	63,137,470	24,039,473	87,176,943
1833	108,118,311	88,295,576	70,317,698	19,822,735	90,140,433
1834	126,521,332	103,208,521	81,034,162	23,312,811	104,336,973
1835	149,895,742	129,391,247	101,189,082	20,504,495	121,693,577
1836	189,980,035	168,233,675	106,916,680	21,746,360	128,663,040
1837	140,989,217	119,134,255	95,564,414	21,854,962	117,419,376
1838	113,717,404	101,264,804	96,033,821	12,452,795	108,486,616
1839	162,092,132	144,597,607	103,333,891	17,494,525	121,028,416
1840	107,141,519	88,951,207	113,895,634	18,190,312	132,085,946
1841	127,946,177	112,447,096	106,382,722	15,469,081	121,851,803
1842	100,162,087	88,440,549	92,960,996	11,721,536	104,691,534
1843	64,753,799	58,201,092	77,793,783	6,552,697	84,346,486
1844	108,435,035	96,950,168	99,715,179	11,484,867	111,200,040
1845	117,254,561	101,007,731	99,299,776	15,346,830	114,646,606

EXPORTS AND IMPORTS OF THE PRINCIPAL STATES.

Exports.

Years.	Mass'tts.	New-York.	Pennsylvania.	Maryland.	Virginia.	S. Carolina.	Georgia.	Alabama.	Louisiana.
1791	$2519651	$3505465	$3436093	$2239691	$3130865	$2693268	$491250	—	—
1792	2888104	2535790	3820662	2023808	3552825	2428250	450106	—	—
1793	3755347	2932370	6958836	3665056	2987098	3191867	520955	—	—
1794	5292441	5442183	6643092	5686191	3321636	3867908	263832	—	—
1795	7117907	10304581	11518260	5811380	3490041	5998492	695986	—	—
1796	9949345	12208027	17513866	9201315	5268665	7620049	950158	—	—
1797	7502047	13308064	11446291	9811799	4908713	6505118	644307	—	—
1798	8639252	14300892	8915463	12746190	6113451	6994179	961848	—	—
1799	11421591	18719527	12431967	16299609	6292986	8729015	1396759	—	—
1800	11326876	14045079	11949679	12264331	4430689	10662510	2174268	—	—
1801	14870556	19851136	17438193	12767530	5665574	14304045	1755939	—	—
1802	13492632	13792276	12677475	7914225	3978363	10639365	1854951	—	—
1803	8768566	10818387	7525710	5078062	6100708	7811108	2370875	—	—
1804	16894378	16081281	11030157	9151939	5790001	17451616	2077572	—	$1600362
1805	19435657	23482943	13762252	10859480	5606620	9066625	2394846	—	3371545
1806	21199243	21762845	17574702	14580905	5055396	9743782	82764	—	3887323
1807	20112125	26357963	16864744	14298984	4761234	10912564	3744845	—	4320555
1808	5128322	5606058	4013330	2721106	526473	1664445	24626	—	1261101
1809	12142293	12581562	9049241	6627326	2894125	3247341	1082108	—	541924
1810	13013048	17242330	10993398	6489018	4822611	5290614	2238686	—	1890592
1811	11235465	12266215	9560117	6833987	4822307	4861279	2568866	—	2650050
1812	6583338	8961922	5973750	5885979	3011112	2036195	1066703	—	1060471
1813	1807923	8184494	3577117	3787865	1819722	2968484	1094596	—	1045153
1814	1133799	209670	—	248434	17581	737899	2183121	—	387191
1815	5280083	10675373	4593919	5036601	6676976	6675129	4172319	—	5102610
1816	10136439	19690031	7196246	7338767	8212860	10849409	7511929	—	5602948
1817	11927997	18707433	8735592	8933930	5621422	10372763	8790714	—	9024812
1818	11998156	17872261	8759402	7570734	7016246	11440962	11132096	$96857	12924309

EXPORTS AND IMPORTS—*continued.*

Exports.

Years.	Mass'tts.	New-York.	Pennsylvania.	Maryland.	Virginia.	S. Carolina.	Georgia.	Alabama.	Louisiana.
1819	$11399913	$13587378	$6293788	$5926216	$4392391	$8250790	$6310434	$50906	$9768753
1820	11008922	13163244	5743549	6609364	4557957	8882940	6594623	96636	7596157
1821	12484691	13162917	7391767	3850394	3079209	7200511	6014310	108960	7272172
1822	12598525	17100482	9047802	4536796	3217389	7260320	5484870	209748	7978645
1823	13683239	19038990	9617192	5030228	4006788	6898814	4293666	200387	7779072
1824	10434328	22897134	9364893	4863233	3277564	8034082	4623982	460727	7928820
1825	11432987	35259261	11269981	4501304	4129520	11056742	4222833	692635	12582
1826	10098862	21947791	8331722	4010748	4596732	7554036	4368504	1527112	10284380
1827	10424383	23834137	7575833	4516406	4657938	8332561	4261555	1376363	11728997
1828	9025785	22777649	6051480	4334422	3340185	6550712	3104425	1182559	11947400
1829	8254937	20119011	4089935	4804465	3787431	8175586	4981376	1693958	12386060
1830	7213194	19697983	4291793	3791482	4791644	7627031	5336626	2294594	15488692
1831	7733763	25535144	5513713	4308647	4150475	6575201	3959813	2413894	16761989
1832	11993768	26000945	3516066	4499918	4510650	7752731	5515883	2736387	16530930
1833	9683122	25395117	4078951	4062467	4467587	8434325	6170040	4527961	18941373
1834	1014820	25512014	3989746	4168245	5483098	11207778	7567397	5670797	26557524
1835	10043790	30345264	3739275	3925234	6064063	11338016	8890674	7574692	36270823
1836	10384346	28920438	3971555	3675475	6192040	13684376	10722200	11184166	37179828
1837	9728190	27338419	3841599	3789917	3702714	11220161	8935041	9671401	35328697
1838	9104862	23008471	3477151	4524575	3986228	11042070	8803839	9688244	31502248
1839	9276085	33268099	5255415	4756561	5187196	10385426	5970443	10338159	33181167
1840	10186261	34264080	6820145	5768768	4778220	10036769	6862956	12854690	34236936
1841	11487343	33139833	5152501	4947166	5630286	8043289	3696513	10981271	34387483
1842	9807116	27576778	3776727	4904766	3750386	7525723	4300257	9965675	28404149
1843	4431681	13443234	2071945	2820214	1954510	7754152	4500401	1115160	26653007
1844	9096286	32861540	3535256	5133169	2942279	7433282	4283805	9907654	30498307
1845	10351030	36175298	3574363	5221977	2104581	8890648	4557435	10538228	27157495

Imports.

Years.	Mass'tts.	New-York.	Pennsylvania.	Maryland.	Virginia.	S. Carolina.	Georgia.	Alabama.	Louisiana.
1821	14826732	23629246	8158922	4070842	1078490	3007113	1002648	——	3379717
1822	18337320	35445628	11874170	4792486	864162	2283586	989591	36421	3817238
1823	17607160	29421349	13696770	4946179	681810	2419101	670705	125770	4283125
1824	15378758	36113723	11865531	4551442	639787	2166185	551888	91604	4539769
1825	15848141	49639174	15041797	4751815	553562	1892297	343356	113411	4290034
1826	17063482	38115630	13551779	4928569	635438	1534483	330993	179554	4167521
1827	13370564	38719644	11212935	4405708	431765	1434106	312609	201909	4531645
1828	15070444	41927792	12884408	5629694	375238	1242048	308669	171909	6217881
1829	12520744	34743307	10100152	4804135	395352	1139618	380293	233720	6857209
1830	10453544	35624070	8702122	4523866	405739	1054619	282346	144823	7599083
1831	14269056	57077417	12124083	4826577	488522	1238163	399940	224435	9766693
1832	18118900	53214402	10678358	4629303	553639	1213725	253417	107787	8871653
1833	19940911	55918449	10451250	5437057	690391	1517705	318996	265918	9590505
1834	17672129	73188594	10479268	4647483	837325	1787267	546802	395361	13781809
1835	19800373	88191305	12389937	5647153	691255	1891805	393049	525955	17519814
1836	25681462	118253416	15068233	7131867	1106814	2801361	573222	651618	15117549
1837	19975667	79301722	11680111	7857033	813823	2510860	774349	609385	14020012
1838	13300925	68453206	9360371	5701869	577142	2318791	776068	524548	9496808
1839	19385223	99882438	15050715	6995285	913462	3086077	413987	895201	12064942
1840	16513858	60440750	8469882	4910746	545085	2058870	491428	574651	10673690
1841	20318003	75713426	10346698	6101313	377237	1557431	449007	530819	10256350
1842	17986433	55875604	7385758	4417078	316705	1359465	341764	363871	8033590
1843	16789452	31356540	2760630	2479132	187062	1294769	207432	360655	8170015
1844	20296087	65079510	7217267	3917750	267654	1131515	305634	442818	7826789
1845	22781024	70909085	8159227	3741804	230470	1143158	206301	473491	9354397

EXPORTS AND IMPORTS OF THE OTHER STATES.

		Average Exp	Average Imp		Average Exp	Average Imp
Maine	1820–39	$647,672	$995,231	1839–46	$1,023,930	$685,148
N. Hampshire	"	140,174	212,527	"	27,935	51,806
Vermont	"	441,127	211,568	"	347,477	213,131
Connecticut	"	498,728	452,370	"	615,635	325,881
Rhode Island	"	609,820	839,857	"	255,126	321,343
New-Jersey	"	33,951	159,676	"	33,778	6,334
Delaware	"	51,117	49,846	"	71,913	3,228
Dist. Columbia	"	816,310	229,488	"	554,732	34,325
N. Carolina	"	493,270	259,595	"	342,510	207,159
Ohio	1831–39	114,213	9,299	"	537,969	24,293
Michigan	1830–39	43,311	94,427	"	208,343	110,358

These tables have been drawn up by us with great care and labor. The reader will for himself deduce those conclusions, which a want of space prevents us from introducing into the article. The imports of Florida, previously to 1839, for several years averaged near $200,000, and the exports $100,000; the amounts in 1846 were $107,863 and $1,514,745; Missouri is first named as an importer in 1833, Mississippi in 1836, having exported from the early part of the century; the first imported in 1845, $54,429, the second $738; Kentucky and Tennessee imported in 1845, $17,469 and $6,929, the export in the one having been, in 1802, $626,000, and the other $443,000. Indiana exported in 1804, $17,320.

EXPORTS OF AMERICAN AND FOREIGN PRODUCTS OF THE YEAR ENDING JULY 1, 1845.

AMERICAN.

The Sea.

Cod Fisheries	$803,353
Herring, Mackerel, &c	208,654
Whale, &c., Oil	1,520,363
Sperm Oil	975,195
Wnalebone	762,642
Sperm Candles	236,917

The Forest.

Skins and Furs	1,248,355
Ginseng	177,146
Staves, Lumber, &c	2,351,419
Bark and other Dyes	70,616
Manufactured Wood	677,420
Naval Stores, &c	814,969
Ashes	1,210,496

Agriculture.

Cotton	51,739,643
Tobacco	7,469,819
Flour	5,338,593
Pork, Bacon, Lard, &c	2,991,284
Rice	2,160,456
Beef, Tallow, &c	1,926,809
Butter and Cheese	878,865
Horses and Mules	385,488
Sheep	23,948
Wheat	336,779
Corn and Meal	1,053,293
Rye, Meal, Oats, &c	290,861
Biscuit	366,294
Potatoes	122,926
Apples	81,306
Flaxseed and Hops	172,319
Brown Sugar	11,107
Indigo	70

Manufactures.

Cotton Goods	4,327,928
Soap and Candles	623,946
Leather, Shoes, &c	328,091
Furniture	277,488
Coaches, &c	55,821
Hats	70,597
Saddlery	$20,847
Wax	234,794
Spirits	291,226
Malt Liquor	69,582
Linseed Oil, &c	92,614
Snuff and Tobacco	538,498
Cordage	55,016
Iron, Castings, Nails, &c	845,017
Sugar Refined	164,662
Chocolate	1,461
Gunpowder	122,599
Copper and Brass	94,736
Drugs	212,837
Flax and Hemp	14,762
Clothes	59,653
Combs and Buttons	23,794
Brushes	2,206
Billiard Boards	1,551
Umbrellas	2,583
Skins	16,363
Fire Engines	12,660
Printing Material	26,774
Musical Material	18,309
Books and Maps	43,298
Paper and Stationery	106,190
Paints and Varnish	50,165
Vinegar	14,375
Glass	98,760
Earthenware	7,393
Tin	10,114
Pewter and Lead	14,404
Stone	17,626
Gold and Silver	3,229
Jewelry, &c	10,435
Trunks	3,236
Brick and Lime	8,701
Salt	45,151
Lead	342,646
Coins	844,446
Molasses	20,771
All other articles	2,584,916

Total.

Agriculture	75,409,860
Manufactures	12,832,371
The Forest	6,550,421
The Sea	4,507,124
Total	$99,299,776

FOREIGN PRODUCTS.

Having paid Specific Duties	3,064,439
Having paid *Ad Valorem*	2,107,292
Free	10,175,099
Total	**$15,346,830**

Whole export of the year, $114,646,606, of which the value of $4,782,464 only was in imported articles dutied and entitled to drawback.

IMPORTS OF THE UNITED STATES FOR THE YEAR ENDING JULY, 1845.

Free of Duty		Ad Valorem Duty		Specific Duty	
Gold and Silver Bullion	$107,378	Cotton Manufactures	$13,853,282	Silks	$8,921,780
" Specie	3,962,864	Woolen "	10,057,875	Sugar	4,780,555
Tea	5,730,514	Iron and Steel "	4,291,077	Molasses	3,154,782
Coffee	6,221,271	Silk and Worsted do	1,510,310	Iron Manufactures	4,858,962
Copper in Plates and Sheets	738,936	Other Silks	1,027,541	Wines and Spirits	2,757,904
Copper in Pigs, Bars, &c	1,225,301	Lace, Thread and Cotton	1,122,997	Segars	1,160,644
Dyewood	603,408	Flax, Linen, &c	4,298,224	All other articles	9,280,235
All other articles	3,558,168	Earthen and Stone Ware	2,187,259	Total	34,914,862
		All other articles	21,843,297	" ad val	60,191,862
				" free	22,147,840
				Grand total	**$117,254,564**

The United States have enacted, since the establishment of the government, thirty-one tariffs of duties, general or special in their nature.

The first tariff was that of July, 1789, the *ad valorems* of which were 5, 7½, 10, 12½ and 15 per cent., and a discrimination of 10 per cent. on the gross amount of duty was made in favor of American shipping. The tariff of 1790 was intended as further provision for the payment of our debts; that of 1792, for raising means to defend the frontier, &c.; that of 1794, for adding additional duties; and the *ad valorems*, in some instances, raised to 20 per cent. The tariffs of 1795, 1797, 1800, were of a similar nature to the last. The tariff of 1804 was to protect our seamen and commerce against the Barbary powers, and to impose more specific duties; that of 1812, continued in act February, 1816, imposed an additional duty of 100 per cent. upon the *permanent* duties imposed by law; and that of 1813 taxes salt.

The tariff of 1816 was levied for revenue purposes, its average duties being higher upon other than the articles now called protected; and it was so arranged as to favor as much as possible the manufacturing establishments grown up during the war, and threatened with annihilation at its close. The highest *ad valorems* of this tariff are 30 per cent., and the system of *minimums*, as they are called, was introduced upon certain cotton cloths, raising their value by a *fiction* greatly above the true. These *minimums*, until 1846, have been preserved.

The tariff of 1824 was a high tariff, and intended for the protection of home manufactures. It raised the *ad valorems*, in many instances, to 50 per cent., and extended the *minimums*.

The tariff of 1828 was also general, and it advanced the scale of duties upon most articles much higher than any previous tariff; discriminating widely for protection at the same time. The acts of 1830 reduced the duty on coffee, tea, cocoa, molasses and salt.

The tariff of 1832. The country's debt having been paid, the President suggested to Congress the propriety of reducing the duties. This was done, but the principle of protection preserved. Coffee and teas were for the first time made *free*, and the *ad valorems* now reduced.

The tariff of 1833, or what has been known as the compromise. It was introduced by Mr. Clay in a spirit of conciliation and of true patriotism, to allay the excitement and discontent occasioned in certain sections of the Union. The *protective* character was in effect surrendered, and a gradual reduction of duties toward 20 per cent. substituted in its stead. The system to have effect for ien years.

The tariff of 1842 was destined to a short existence, and substituted by the greatly less-protective one of 1846.

The Secretary of the Treasury in his report estimated the working of the different tariffs adopted previously to 1846, as follows:

Average per cent. on dutiable imports from

1821 to 1829	36.3
1829 to 1833	41.9
1833 to 1843	31.2
1843 to 1844	30.4

Average last year of compromise, 23.9. First year after, 35.1 per cent.

In connection with these statistics and tariffs, the following judicious reflections may be inserted:

"It might have been expected that the effect of the different tariffs which have been enacted from time to time, would be distinctly visible in a table like this; but such is not the fact. There are so many other causes which affect the amount of imports and exports, such as good crops at home, short crops abroad, the state of the currency, and the general prosperity or prostration of business—that the effects of the tariff are not, in all cases, visible on an inspection of the returns. For instance, in the commercial year 1842, when (with the exception of one month) the lowest duties were in force that have existed for 20 years, the amount and proportion of imports and exports were very nearly the same as in 1844, under the tariff which has since gone into operation. Again, it appears that the excess of imports over exports, instead of diminishing with each successive augmentation of duties, as would naturally have been expected, has generally *increased*; having been greater under the tariff of 1824 than under that of 1816, greater still under that of 1828, and greatest of all under that of 1832, prior to any considerable reduction under the Compromise Act. For it must be remembered that only *two-tenths of the excess above* 20 *per cent.* had been taken off, under that act, prior to the 1st of January, 1838. It may therefore be stated, as a general remark, that the greatest excess of imports over exports, has occurred under the highest duties—we say, as *a general remark*, for since the present tariff went into operation, the exports have exceeded the imports. So also they did in 1842, and in 1840, under comparatively low duties. In the last-mentioned year the excess amounted to $25,000,000."

In making a review of all the tables which have been given, the fact is forced upon us, that the South, though furnishing the great aggregate of the exports of the country, has declined in the relative importance of its foreign commerce. This has been accounted for in different ways. That we are a people without enterprise, is in a measure true, though there is no natural reason this should be the case. Almost all the great maritime and commercial people of ancient and modern times have been Southerners; and many, under suns more burning than ours. This has been eloquently shown by Col. James Gadsden in a former number of the Review:

"It was the spirit of enterprise of these south-eastern and luxurious people (the Tyrians, &c.) which reared to greatness and power and wealth the Assyrian, the Egyptian, the Median, Persian, and Arabic empires; extended over Greece and Italy, passed the pillars of Hercules, and explored more distant regions. It was Phœnicia which planted her Carthage on the burning sands of Africa, and which by her commercial power and greatness excited the envy and terror of Rome—a proud military people holding trade in contempt, but who had sufficient instinct to perceive, in the wealth and energy of that southern city, a rival that would overwhelm her, if not controlled and subjected. *Delenda est Carthago*, was the decree which went forth from her oracle. It was, notwithstanding, the commercial resources, the nerve and sinew of Carthage, which, under the lead of a Hannibal passed the Mediterranean sea, overran Spain, scaled the Alps, and descended with the rapidity of her mountain torrents on the sunny plains of Italy, and threatened the mistress of the world under her very walls. It was commercial enterprise in the south that reared Venice, amid the very waters of the Adriatic, and made the silks of Persia and the spices of India tributary to her luxurious grandeur. Alexandria, too, midway between the Indian and Mediterranean seas, though now traced only by its ruins in the sands of the desert, once held its high place among the great commercial marts of the world. Its decline is to be ascribed to the discovery of the passage around the Cape of Good Hope. To adventurous Southern spirits, to Portuguese navigators, is the world indebted for that new avenue to the Eastern ocean and the China seas. Genoa should not be overlooked, or omitted in the enumeration of ancient southern cities, reared by southern enterprise."

The question then presents itself, will the South be content with its present position? If a great centralization of capital at the North be the secret of its vast commerce, have not we to balance against it many other advantages? We are as near to Europe. nearer to the West Indies, to South America, to Mexico, and other important trading points. Thousands of shipping leave our ports, with rich products, annually, and they must return directly to us, in mere ballast, or take a circuitous course back by the way of New-York or Boston. If there are any wares or merchandise to return, for our own consumption, from the cotton, tobacco, rice, sugar, or grain, sent by us to Europe, how natural and proper is it, that these wares and merchandises should return *directly* here, without being saddled with the profits of intermediate hands. That the South should be DEPENDENT upon the North for its imports, is inexplicable upon any sound principle of political economy, and evidences a state of things humiliating in the extreme. We do not want *capital*, but most sadly want *enterprise*, which God, we implore, will give to our children, should it so happen that we are irreclaimable, and past all hope.*

COMMERCIAL STATISTICS—UNITED STATES AND GREAT BRITAIN.—The following tables of the exports from the United States and Great Britain to the countries therein named, during the years 1847 and 1848, we have compiled from official documents. One of the most marked features which they present is the falling off in the British trade to their West Indian and North American colonies, and the increase of the American trade with those places:

	1847.		1848.	
	United States	Great Britain	United States	Great Britain
Russia	$626,332	£1,844,543	$1,047,582	£1,925,226
Prussia	182,259	553,968	145,074	404,144
Sweden and Norway	391,847	348,216	625,972	312,936
Holland	1,885,398	3,017,423	1,595,450	2,823,258
Belgium	2,874,367	1,059,456	1,989,764	823,968
Hanse Towns	4,068,413	6,007,366	3,856,676	4,669,259
British East Indies	237,783	5,470,105	510,289	5,077,247
British West Indies	3,973,252	2,102,577	4,344,536	1,434,477
British American Colonies	5,810,667	3,273,014	6,300,050	1,000,502
France on the Atlantic	17,420,385	2,554,283	14,159,798	1,024,521
France on the Mediterranean	1,172,146		1,215,087	
Spain on the Atlantic	770,748	801,409	597,797	662,710
Spain on the Mediterranean	1,188,340		1,741,474	
Cuba	6,005,617	896,554	6,432,380	733,169
Porto Rico	825,079	16,822	801,722	1,017
Italy	1,056,023	1,811,638	1,101,113	2,212,351
Austrian ports	1,175,375	537,069	1,701,495	494,525
Turkey	61,570	2,363,442	114,830	2,664,281
Mexico	536,641	100,638	2,095,495	945,937
Brazil	2,566,938	2,568,804	3,092,736	2,067,302
Chili	1,461,347	866,325	1,703.625	967,333
Peru	192,978	600,814	124,618	853,139
China	1,708,655	1,503,969	2,063,625	1,445,959
Hayti	1,187,017	192,089	935,586	88,067

For the years ending June 30, 1847 and 1848, the exports of domestic produce from the United States to Great Britain were to

	1847.	1848.
England	$70,223,777	$62,928,024
Ireland	15,397,698	2,452,426
Scotland	3,645,460	2,455,426

The total value of our imports from the same countries for the same year were

	1847.	1848.
England	$65,170,374	$59,763,502
Scotland	1,837,014	1,666,684
Ireland	590,240	415,923

The British exports to the United States during the year 1847 are officially estimated at £10,974,161; and in 1848 at £9,564,909.

---

* We might have remarked at length upon the operation of our system of cash duties, drawback, &c., and the desideratum of a comprehensive WAREHOUSING SYSTEM. Our tables generally will show the comparatively small re-export business done in this country, to what might be done under more favorable auspices, and to what has already been done. Perhaps we have not dwelt sufficiently upon this, but it is now too late. We will leave the reader, however, with one reflection. Mr. Webster stated in his Faneuil Hall speech, in 1820, "that the average value of foreign merchandise re-exported

COMMERCIAL EDUCATION IN UNIVERSITIES.—Several years ago we drew up a plan for a Professorship of Commerce, etc., which we recommended to public attention, and which was adopted by the administrators of the University of Louisiana under an endowment by Col. Maunsel White. The duties of the chair have not yet commenced, owing to interruptions in the organization of the literary department of the institution and the unfinished state of the building. When these impediments are removed and the funds establishing the chair are made available, it will then be in a condition of performing useful service to the community.

We proceed to make a brief exposition of the duties of the professorship, its organization, &c., and give the outline of its labors. In this we are without guide from any quarter, but give our own views, the result of continued reflection upon these matters.

Professorship of Public Economy, Commerce and Statistics.—I. Origin of Society and Government; Theory, Forms, and Ends of Government; Rights, Duties, and Relations of Governments; Sources of National Wealth and Progress, and Causes of National Decline; Production, Distribution, and Consumption of Wealth, with the Laws appertaining thereto.

II. Statistics of Population and Wealth in their application to

COMMERCE,
AGRICULTURE,
MANUFACTURES.

1. History and Progress of COMMERCE, its Principles and Laws; Home and Foreign Commerce; Tariffs, Treaties, Life Insurance, Roads, Canals, Shipping, and Revenue, Systems of Reciprocity; Balances of Trade; Mercantile and Navigation Systems; Colonies and Colonial systems; Banks, Finances, Accounts, Transportation, Book-keeping, Principles of Merchant Law; Commerce of Nations, Ancient and Modern; Geography of Commerce, Commodities of Commerce, etc., etc.

2. Progress and Results of AGRICULTURAL SCIENCE; Principles of Agriculture; Comparative condition of Agricultural, Commercial, and Manufacturing Communities; Statistics of Agriculture, etc.

3. Origin and Progress of the MANUFACTURING SYSTEM; its Relation to the other Pursuits; Invention and Machinery in Manufactures; Condition of the Manufacturing Classes; Statistics of Manufactures, &c.

Text-Books for this Course:

Locke's Essay on Government; Lieber's Political Ethics and Hermeneutics; Montesquieu's Spirit of Laws; Smith's Wealth of Nations; McCulloch's Commercial and Geographical Dictionary; Say's Political Economy; Vethake's Political Economy; Carey on Wealth; Stephen's Progress of Discovery and Maritime Commerce; Heeren's Commercial Researches; Vincent's Commerce of the Ancients; McGregor's Commercial Legislation; Annual Reports American and Contemporary Governments.

It will be seen that the project covers a wide field, and on the most interesting which could possibly be imagined. Of course it would be impossible to treat in detail all of these subjects, but a sufficient view might be taken of them for all general purposes by every student. Some would of course be glanced over, whilst others, being of higher consideration and importance, would receive elaborate notice and exposition. In the successful progress of the University, it might be found, too, at some other day, that the labors of the professorship could be divided, giving to the practical and theroretic, different departments and different professors.

The division we have made of subjects needs little explanation. They run naturally one into the other, and it is necessary to make the beginning in the proper place. For example, of how much importance is it to be understood among merchants, from the constitution, theory, and objects of government, how far they should interfere in the practical and industrial pursuits of life. How many salutary lessons will be learned from a knowledge of the undue interferences which history records! This, with what is generally known as *political economy*, or what we designate *public economy*, are embodied properly in the course.

Political discussions would forever be excluded from the Chair. Whatever may be the views of the professor in relation to any matter or matters connected with commerce or manufactures, and which are involved in the excited controversies of parties, he shall present them only in connection with the views of either side fairly, and refer the student to his own reflections for conviction, after a careful consultation of the text-books and authorities. This can as easily be secured as a professorship of the evidences of Christianity, to be found in many colleges, but excluding rigidly all sectarian views and theological discussions.

It should be required from the professorship to prepare and deliver twelve public lectures each year, free to every one, upon subjects determined in its organization. For example, upon the "*Sources of National Wealth and Decline;*" on the "*History and Progress of Commerce;*" on the "*Foreign Commercial Relations of the United States,*

---

from the United States, from 1795 to 1817, amounted to 42-100 of our whole exportations. In some years *the exportation of foreign had exceeded that of domestic produce.*" From 1822 to 1845, the re-exports have never exceeded one-third of the whole exports, they have been more often a fourth or a fifth of their value, and in 1843 they were *one-twelfth!*

including our Treaties;" upon "Finance;" on the "Results of Agriculture and the Advancement of Agricultural Classes;" on "Manufactures;" the "Science of Statistics;" the "Geography of Commerce;" the "Commodities of Commerce;" the "Literature of Commerce," etc, etc. The lectures to be of a practical character, and perhaps published eventually, under the auspices of the University, as one of its text-books. Such a volume, prepared with all the light afforded in the libraries and collections of the University, would be complete.

For the Library, in addition to all the standard periodicals and the most select journals relative to commerce, commercial pursuits, agriculture, manufactures, statistics, &c., may be mentioned the following works, a very large portion of which we will venture to say could not be obtained at this time in our country, and scarcely any of them in our city. Many other works equally valuable we could enumerate, were it necessary, and we could enumerate maps, charts, etc. etc., which are appropriate to the department. With this catalogue we conclude our observations, in the hope that what has been said will excite public attention, and ensure from our wealthy and enterprising merchants such action as we think they will be proud to take. Now is the time for action; who will take the matter in hand and charge himself with the important service.

Library of the Chair of Public Economy, Commerce and Statistics—Œconomics.—Stewart's Inquiries in Political Economy; Lauderdale on Public Wealth; Smith's Wealth of Nations; Ricardo's Political Economy and Taxation; Malthus' Works on do.; Torens on the Production of Wealth; McCulloch's Works; Dr. Cooper's Treatise on Political Economy; Cardoza's do.; Whateley's do.; Chalmers' do; Scrope's do.; Senior's do.; Carey's Principles of Political Economy; Quincy's Logic of do.; Hume's Essays; West on Land and Capital; Ricardo's Dialogues; Bailey on Values; Jones on Wealth and Taxation; Boileau's Introduction to Political Economy; Young's Political Arithmetic; Foreign Works of Isnard, de Tracy, Say, Garnier, Ganilh, Douffroy, Sismondi, Droz, Blanqui, Rau, Chevalier, Rossi, Verri, Becarria, Gioja, Pecchio, Munoz, Ward, Ortiz, Guarina's Estrado, Dictionaire d'Economie, Scrittori Classici Italiani, di Economia Politica, etc., etc. Mill's Political Economy.

Commerce.—Robertson's Mappe of Commerce; Roberts' Treasure of Trafficke; England's Treasure by Foreign Trade, by Thos Mun; Fortrey's England's Interest and Improvement; Coke's Treatises on Trade, etc.; England's Great Happiness; Britannia Languens; Childs' Discourse of Trade; Dudley North's Discourses on Trade; Davenant on the Balance of Trade; King's British Merchant; Woods' Survey of Trade; Defoe's Plan of English Commerce; Gee's Trade and Navigation of Great Britain; Carey's Discourse on Trade, &c.; Dobbs on Trade of Ireland; Decker on the Decline of Trade; Tucker on the Trade of France and England; Tucker on Commerce and Taxes; Tucker on Trade of Turkey; Bell's Vindication of Commerce and the Arts; Postlethwayt's Dictionary of Trade and Commerce; do. Commercial Interest of Britain; Cantillon's Analysis of Trade; Rolt's Dictionary of Trade; Mortimer's Dictionary of Trade and Commerce; Mortimer's Elements of Commerce; Tucker's Tracts on same subjects; Sheffield on American Commerce; do. on Irish Commerce; Oddy's European Commerce; Mills' Defence of Commerce; M'Culloch on its Principles and History; Pitkin's Commerce of the United States; Hagemeister on Russian Commerce; Macgregor's Commercial Statistics; Melon's Essay on Commerce; Savary's Dictionary of Commerce; Condillac, du Commerce et Le Gouvernement; Ricardo's Traité du Commerce; Arnauld's Balance du Commerce; Sismondi, Laboulinierre, etc., on Commerce; Douglass' North American Settlements; Bacon's Colonization of the Free States of Antiquity; Moseley's Treatise on Sugar; Brougham's Colonial Policy; Edwards' West Indies; Bliss' Colonial Intercourse; Bliss on the Timber Trade; Martin's Statistics of British Colonies; Merivale's Lectures on Colonization and Colonies; Mun on the India Trade; Robertson on Ancient Communication with India, and Modern Trade with it; McPherson's European Commerce with India; Milburn's Oriental Commerce; Chitty on the Laws of Commerce, Manufactures, &c; Hooper on Ancient Measures; Reynardson on English Weights and Measures; Arbuthnott's Coins, Weights, and Measures; John Quincy Adams' Report on Weights and Measures; Gordon's Universal Accountant and Complete Merchant; King's British Merchant; Hertslet's Treaties of England; Evelyn's Navigation and Commerce; Anderson on Commerce; Macpherson's Annals of Commerce; Vincent's Commerce of the Ancients; Stephens' Progress of Discovery, Navigation and Commerce; Cooley's Maritime and Inland Discovery; Heeren's Commercial Researches; Huet's History of Commerce; Depping's Histoire du Commerce; Marin's Commercio d'Veneziani; Petty on Money; Locke's Treatises on Money; Sir Isaac Newton on Coinage; Leake's History of English Money; Harris on Money and Coins; Snelling's Works on Coinage; Murrey on the Coinage of England; Thornton on Paper Credit; Foster's Commercial Exchanges; Liverpool on Coinage; Blake on the Course of Exchange; Rudong's Annals of British Coinage; Gilbert's History of Banking; Gallatin on Currency and Banking in the United States; Gouge's Treatise on do.

Carey's Credit System; Tucker's Theory of Money and Banks; Tooke's History of Prices.

Agriculture, Manufactures, Internal Improvement, and Statistics, etc., etc.—M'Adam's Observations on Roads; Parnell on Roads; Phillips' Inland Navigation; Wood's Treatise on Railroads; Petty's Essays on Political Arithmetic; Works of Arthur Young; Dickson's Husbandry of the Ancients; Chalmers' Comparative Strength of Great Britain; Colquhoun on British Empire; Loudon's Encyclopædia of Agriculture; McCulloch's Statistical Account of British Empire; Porter's Progress of the Nation; Porter's Tables of Revenue, Population, etc.; Tucker's Progress of the United States in Population and Wealth; Holland's History of Coal and the Coal Trade; Fraser's Fisheries of Great Britain; Elking's Greenland Trade and Fisheries; Scoresby's Arctic Regions; Murray's Polar Seas; Babbage's Machinery and Manufactures; Baine's History of Cotton Manufactures; Schrivenor on the Iron Trade; Ure's Dictionary of Arts, Manufactures and Mines; Bischoff on Woolen and Woolen Factories; Slater's American Manufactures; Morgan's Treatise on Life Insurance; Edmond's Tables on do.; Morgan's Essays on Probabilities applied to Life Insurance; Bentham's Defence of Usury; Botero's Cause of the Greatness of Cities; Benjamin Franklin on the Increase of Men; Hume on Populousness of States; Short on Decrease of Mankind; Price, Wales, Malthus on English Population; Summer's Treatise on the Records of the Creation; Saddler's Law of Population; Allison's Principles of Population; Hawkins' Elements of Medical Statistics; Thackrah on the Effects of Arts, Trades and Professions on Health and Longevity; Eden's History of the Laboring Classes and State of the Poor; Walker on Pauperism; Carey on Wages; Farland's Inquiries Concerning the Poor; Pratt's History of Savings' Banks; Prostitution dans la ville de Paris, par M. Parent Duchatelet; Dalrymple on Feudal Property; Maugham on Literary Property; Godson on Copy and Patent Rights; Blair's Slavery Among the Romans; Blandinel on the Slave Trade; Phillips on the National Debts; Saxby on the British Customs; Sinclair on the Revenue of the British Empire; Dr. Hamilton on the National Debts; McCulloch on Taxation; Dr. Davenant's Political and Commercial Works; Beckman's History of Inventions and Discoveries; Jacobs on the Precious Metals; Public Economy of Athens, by Boeckh; Vaughan's Age of Great Cities.

FLORIDA—Its Resources, etc.—The Adventures of Narvaez and the romantic wanderings of Ponce de Leon and De Soto, in search of the perpetual spring and the fabled mines of gold; the buccaneering of the English; the wars waged with Oglethorpe by the Spaniards; and more recently its long and bloody Indian wars, have given to Florida a greater historical interest than attaches to any other portion of our country. But as one of the youngest sisters of our confederacy, but little is known of her topography, resources and productions. Peninsulated from almost all intercourse with other states, she lies out of the great thoroughfare of travel; and while the commerce of the great West sweeps around her shores, they are looked upon but as so many dangerous reefs and rocks, threatening destruction to the mariner. It is our aim, in the following article, to give some idea of the present actual state and condition of Florida.

The peculiar outline of its coast has probably rendered its general shape and position familiar to every one—having been somewhat aptly compared to a reversed boot. It extends at right angles some five hundred miles west and south, and has a length, in its greatest extension, of nearly one thousand miles (?)

The southern portion of the peninsula is covered with a large sheet of water, called the Everglades, of immense extent, filled with islands, and which, it is supposed, may be rendered available by drainage. The central portion of the peninsula is somewhat elevated, the highest point being about 171 feet above the ocean, and gradually declining towards the coast on each side. The portion of the state between the Suwanee and the Chattahoochie rivers, is elevated and hilly; the western portion of the state is level. The St. John's River, of magnificent dimensions, runs from south to north upon the eastern side of the peninsula, and debouches near the northeast boundary of the state; and the Suwanee runs a nearly parallel course on the western side of the peninsula from north to south.

The first settlement of Florida was made at St. Augustine, in the year 1564—it being, by forty years, the oldest settlement in the United States. Pensacola was settled 1696.

The archives of the country during the period of the Spanish rule, prior to 1768, having been removed, it is difficult now to judge to what extent the country was settled previous to its cession to Great Britain. Remains of ancient settlements are found to a considerable extent between the Suwanee and Chattahoochie rivers; the traces of old roads, fortifications, &c., are very distinct; and gun barrels, pottery, ship spikes, &c., are found; but the public opinion of the country is rather inclined to the supposition that these settlements were made by buccaneers, who, about 1660, swarmed in the southern seas; and the quantity of ship spikes, &c., found, seem to render this opinion highly probable.

It is presumable, therefore, from the known inertness of the Spanish character, and the slight progress made by them in the settlement of new countries, that their settlement of Florida was very limited in extent, and that with the exception of establishing a few mission houses, they never ventured far from the coast, and paid but little attention to the tillage of the soil.

In 1763, the Floridas were ceded by Spain to the British crown. The Spanish inhabitants principally left the country, and it soon began to prosper under the energetic impulse communicated by the Anglo-Saxon race. Efforts at settlement on a large scale were immediately undertaken. The British government gave extensive grants of land, upon the condition of their settlement. Dr. Turnbull, in connection with some distinguished gentlemen in England, laid the foundation of an extensive colony at New-Smyrna, and brought from the islands and shores of the Mediterranean some 1500 families. Lord Rolle, Gov. Moultrie, Earl of Beresford and others, established settlements; and upon the breaking out of the American Revolution, large numbers of loyalists came into the country from Georgia and Carolina.

The exports of Florida in 1780, reached 40,000 barrels of naval stores. One of the principal articles of cultivation seems to have been indigo; and it is said that the indigo of Florida brought the highest price in the London market.

The British possession of the country continued but twenty years; but during that period more was effected in settling and improving the country, than its two hundred years of occupation by the Spaniards.

But unfortunately for Florida, in 1783, the province was re-ceded by Great Britain to Spain; and the English population, which in 1778, in East Florida alone, numbered over 13,000, principally left the country and went to the adjoining American states. From that period to its cession to the United States in 1821—a period of about forty years—it languished and struggled along with difficulty; the cultivation of the country neglected; the English settlements having been allowed to go to ruin; and at no time during this period was the population, in both the Floridas, estimated at over 10,000—a large portion of whom lived in town, or were hangers-on of the government.

The Spanish population, to a considerable extent, left the country upon its cession to the United States, and immigration began to flow in rapidly; but the unsurveyed state of the country, the uncertainty of land titles, most injudiciously involved in litigation by the government, militated against its settlement; and the fierce and turbulent Indian race, who had made it a battle-ground for over two hundred and fifty years, and who had never been conquered, and had no egress from their peninsular home, occupied the best lands of the state, rendering it impossible to obtain them. But yet, in spite of all these obstacles, a considerable population planted themselves in the country. The territory was just beginning to reap the fruits of its American occupation, when the desolating Indian war broke out in 1835, and continued for seven long years—rendering all habitations out of the limits of the occupied parts insecure, and destroying all the improvements which had been undertaken. In 1842 this war terminated—and the Seminoles, after a struggle of nearly 300 years, were forced to yield to their destiny, and were nearly all transferred beyond the Mississippi.

Thus the population of Florida had, up to 1842, undergone four entire revolutions; and after having been settled by the European race for two hundred and eighty years, was forced to begin anew the settlement of the country—a series of disasters unparalleled in the history of America.

Since 1842, the actual settlement of the country has commenced, and progressed with reasonable rapidity, the present population being probably about one hundred thousand.

The health of Florida will very favorably compare wlth any other portion of the Union—having no diseases except slight fevers, and that concomitant of all new countries, fever and ague. The ratio of mortality is believed to be unusually small; while many instances of great longevity are presented.

The lands of Florida are almost *sui generis*, and are very curiously distributed, and may be designated as High Hammock, Low Hammock, Swamp, Savanna, and the different qualities of pine land.

High Hammock is usually timbered with live oak and other species of oak, magnolia, laurel, &c., and is considered the best description of land for general purposes. *Low Hammock*, timbered with live oak, water oak, and subject to overflow—usually needing drainage, but when drained, preferred for sugar. Of this description of land, requiring more or less drainage, large bodies exist in the state. *Savanna*, on the margin of streams and frequently in detached bodies—usually very rich alluviums, and susceptible of being cultivated in dry seasons, and yielding largely: ditching and dyking would render much of it available. *Marsh Savannas*, upon the borders of tide streams, when reclaimed, are very valuable for rice or cane—some land of this description, upon the Tomaka, having yielded above three hogsheads of sugar to the acre. First class pine lands are generally preferred by small planters to any other, and they have been found productive and valuable. Indeed, it is believed that the pine lands of Florida are superior to any pine lands in the South for their fertility, yielding good crops in their natural state, and when trodden by cattle, becoming equal to rich hammock land. I have seen, thus early in the season, cane having above twenty joints and well matured, grown upon Florida pine lands; and the sugar made from such lands is generally of superior quality. The hammock lands, when cleared, make excellent crops at all seasons.

The chief staple of Florida, at present, is cotton—the region west of the Suwanee cultivating the upland, and the eastern portion of the state producing sea island, of a quality bringing from 20 to 30 cents per pound the last season, the coast usually producing the first quality.

The sugar cane will, however, in a few years, become the staple of the peninsula, which, from its climate, soil and facilities, is peculiarly adapted for its cultivation. It is now cultivated for home consumption by almost every planter, small and great; but the expense of machinery, and the time required to get under way, has deterred many from abandoning their cotton to raise cane.

Previous to the Indian war, a large number of sugar plantations had been established on the eastern coast of Florida, upon the Halifax, Matanzas, Tomaka and Hillsborough rivers, where the lands are principally the heaviest live oak hammock, and by their advantageous situation upon navigable streams, are very suitable for cane. The cultivation was carried on successfully; and had not the Indian war desolated the country and entirely broken up these establishments, the sugar crop of Florida would now have been a large one. The interior of the peninsula is well adapted to the cane, as is, indeed, the whole peninsula extending southward from lat. 30 to lat. 23; Florida approaching most nearly to the temperature of Cuba of any part of the South. Lands suitable for the cultivation of sugar, may be purchased at the present time at very low prices, from the government price of $1 25, to $5 and $10 per acre, in private hands, according to their situation. Even the old plantations, with their improvements, may now be bought at from $5 to $10 per acre; but as the country becomes settled, of course lands will rise in value.

Cattle are among the most productive sources of income to the Floridian. The vast ranges of unoccupied land give the greatest abundance of perpetual verdure and green pasture, and they double in three years, and may now be purchased in any quantity at $5 per head. Swine are equally profitable, requiring little care or attention. Horses and mules are also raised, without care or expense.

Tar and turpentine, which were in British times extensive articles of export, have been neglected for a long period; but the profitable operations of North Carolina have recently awakened renewed attention to this branch of manufacture, and shipments made from the St. John's last season, it is said, have proved profitable.

Rice has also been neglected, as a staple, since the days of British cultivation, when it was raised to a considerable extent. The lands suitable for its cultivation are abundant along our rivers and streams; and when our population is sufficiently dense to develop all our resources, it will, no doubt, be one of the most important branches of culture.

Fish, oysters and turtle, abound in the greatest profusion, and the Havana fish market receives a large portion of its supplies from the coasts of Florida.

The oak, cedar, and pine of Florida, are becoming valuable for shipment. The navy yards have drawn their supplies of live oak, for many years, from our forests; and the diminution and high prices of pine lumber at the North, are bringing our yellow pine into great demand, and its shipment is rapidly increasing.

Among the various miscellaneous articles which have been found well adapted to the country, may be mentioned the orange, lemon, banana, olive, hemp, palma Christi, benne, arrow-root, cassava, indigo, &c.

Take it all in all, Florida, at the present time, affords as good an opening to the Southern planter desirous of changing his location, as any portion of the Union: and indeed our partiality would lead us to say that, taking into view its splendid climate, tropical latitude, facility of water communication, the fertility of its soil and the low price of its lands, that it affords stronger inducements to the prospective settler, than any other portion of the South, and that capital and enterprise will make it a great state.

FLORIDA—Its Productions.—The climate of South Florida may be at once set down as the most desirable winter climate in the United States, presenting to the invalid of the north, a desirable retreat from the rude blasts peculiar to that region. The Miami, on Key Biscayne Bay and Key West, may be considered as most desirable points for establishing the necessary facilities for the encouragement of visitors of that class, numbers of whom annually go on to Cuba, and other West India Islands, but who would be induced to stop in Florida, were there proper accommodations. No place possesses greater advantages for fishing, boating, &c.,

than those mentioned. At Miami, on Key Biscayne Bay, has been stationed, during the past eighteen months, a company of United States troops, and it has been a matter of surprise to the surgeon, that he has had no case of sickness among the soldiers during all that time. The inhabitants, some of whom have resided there for many years, are all grateful witnesses of the remarkable healthfulness of that vicinity; and although the summers are warm, the air, during the entire day, is fanned by the easterly winds prevailing in that season, and rendering it comfortable for the laborers to pursue their vocations at all times. The writer would here remark, that this class of men, of whom he employs many, are universally more healthy and robust than in any other region he has any acquaintance with. This, in connection with other and peculiar advantages, make it emphatically the home of the man of slender means and enterprising disposition.

Dade County, stretching along the Atlantic seaboard, between lat. 25 and 26 degrees, possesses an excellent harbor for vessels drawing nine feet water, with a light-house at its entrance, on Cape Florida, marking the channel into the bay, (Key Biscayne,) which extends for a distance of thirty miles in a northerly and southerly direction. Numerous streams discharge into it from the Everglades, on all of which is water-power, controlled generally at no great expense, with a fall of about five feet, which may be employed for arrrow root or lumber mills. The necessary supplies for running either, are to be found directly on the banks of the streams. The land on the west side of the bay is gently elevated, commanding a delightful view in many places. An opening directly through the Keys to the Gulf, enables vessels to be seen in their course, north or south. These points are desirable places for building, and in the immediate vicinity is found a spontaneous growth of arrow root, inviting the man of enterprise to avail himself of the water-power so abundant, or of a small steam-engine or horse-power, with which he may, with little difficulty or expense, prepare for market an article yielding one hundred dollars to the acre. This may create a sensation of doubt in the minds of some, and may suggest the inquiry, if such be the case, why has it so long remained unknown, and the country comparatively unoccupied? To this the writer will attempt no reply, further than to allude to the neighborhood of that curse of Florida, the Seminole Indians, and that Dade county has been the scene of bloody encounter and massacre.

The southern portion of this county comprises numerous Keys, stretching along the Florida Reefs, and terminating at Tortugas, in Monroe county; and it may not be amiss here to remark, that the reservation of these Keys by the general government is calculated greatly to retard the growth of that portion of our state. They should be open to settlement, and be subject to pre-emption claims, as all other public lands, and soon a hardy, enterprising people will occupy them, producing plants peculiarly adapted to their light vegetable soil. Those plants are clearly pointed out by nature's unerring hand, wherever the original growth is cleared away, by the spontaneous growth of the bird pepper and the gherkin, in the greatest profusion, both extensively in demand for pickling. On these Keys alone may be raised a sufficient quantity to supply our entire home market, for which large quantities are annually imported from Africa, South America, &c. They are in bearing the entire year, and yield a perpetual harvest.

The palma Christi, the plant from which castor oil is made, peculiarly adapted to this kind of soil and climate, grows continuously for about four years, and becomes a large tree, in constant bearing, ripening its rich clusters of beans in such profusion, that from some experiments made by the writer, he is satisfied that one hundred bushels may be made annually from an acre, and their product of oil two gallons per bushel. An enterprising citizen of Key West is about to establish machinery for engaging in the business, and it may be safely predicted that castor oil will become an important staple product of South Florida, its climate securing to the cultivator so great an advantage over regions where the plant is merely an annual.

The sisal hemp plant is growing throughout these counties, and is natural to the whole southern part of the Peninsula. With the aid of labor-saving machinery, in dressing out the fibre, and manufacturing the hemp, there is no doubt it could be made a profitable pursuit, even in competition with the native labor of Mexico.

The Florida Keys furnish an immense field for the manufacture of that great necessary of life, salt—which is now made upon a large scale by an estimable citizen of Key West, superior in quality to Turk's Island. The plan of evaporation is by solar heat, in large basins, from whence it is pumped by wind-mills into elevated vats, with temporary covers, where it is granulated and made ready for market. Large quantities are annually shipped from Key West to New-Orleans, and other southern markets, where a constant demand exists for all that is made, and at a price that has enabled the proprietor to establish it as a permanent business, that may be largely extended. Many of the Keys in the vicinity present the same advantages as the one referred to, and with the necessary capital, any man of enterprise and perseverance would here find a chance for in-

vestment that could not fail of securing a just reward for his efforts, while to the state the results are of immense importance, in view of the great consumption of an article which may be produced to an extent so unlimited within our borders.

The entire region of pine woods, from Cape Sable to near Indian River, presents a bountiful growth of compty, the root from which the arrow root is made, and it may be claimed that its importance to the state of Florida is second to no other plant adapted to her soil and climate. One of its peculiar characteristics is that of production, without care of planting, as the scattered seeds and the parts of roots left in the earth in the process of digging, shoot forth, and in two years, without any care, present a more bountiful growth than the original. Doubtless the quality and amount of the roots would be improved by cultivation, and as the plant is susceptible of introduction into all the pine lands south of twenty-eight, and perhaps thirty degrees, experiments are recommended, with the view to extend and secure to Florida, at the earliest day, the great advantages promised by the growth of this plant. It is proposed to forward to the Agricultural Board at Tallahassee, for distribution, a sufficient quantity of seed, that each of the middle and southern counties may make the trial, and in the month of April they may be expected, when they may be planted at any period of the summer. The manufacture of arrow root at Miami has now become an established business, yielding to the conductor, with the aid of necessary machinery, three dollars per day as the result of each man's labor, with a ready market for all that is made; and as the production and consumption have greatly increased during the past year, we hazard nothing in predicting that they will continue to do so, until this shall become one of the most important products of the state. Its quality as starch is well ascertained to be superior to that produced from either wheat, corn, or potatoes, vast quantities of all of which are yearly consumed in the manufacture of that necessary article; and when it shall become known that an acre of our poor pine land will produce as much starch from this plant as can be obtained from a similar surface from either wheat, corn, or potatoes, the growth of the best lands of the north, it will be clearly seen that capital and labor must always find a certain and profitable investment in this branch of industry so peculiar to our climate.

In connection with this portion of the Peninsula, the important fact should not be overlooked, that a large portion of the Everglades are within its border; and as that extensive region of swamp land is now the property of the state, it is confidently hoped that measures will soon be taken to redeem from overflow so valuable a portion of tropical territory; and the writer would here remark, that an extensive observation of that region during a long residence at Miami, has convinced him of the perfect feasibility of the project, and that it is only a question of time and money. The Everglade region is of vast importance to our state, covering as it does an area of about one hundred and sixty miles long by sixty broad, and should be at once examined and surveyed with reference to draining. All former reports on that subject have been decidedly favorable; and in view of reclaiming so much tropical territory, early action is very desirable. The writer would suggest that deepening and enlarging the natural outlets, with the opening of some additional ones atfavorable points, would, at no very large cost, as compared with the immense advantage, be the means of preventing any large accumulation of water, as the overflow is believed to be caused entirely by the rains; and so vast is the surface confined to almost a dead level, that the natural outlets are insufficient to drain it off.

Much valuable timber for ship-building and cabinet work is growing in South Carolina, such as live oak, dog-wood, &c., much of which is annually used at Key West, where many small vessels have been built during the past year. Mangrove is of an abundant growth, and furnishes excellent timber for constructing foundations in water for wharves and other structures, while the bark is an excellent substance for tanning leather, or for dyeing. Box-wood, mastic, satin-wood, crab-wood, and lignum vitæ, are all found in quantities throughout the Keys and the southern part of the state generally.

Indigo, of spontaneous growth, is found throughout a large portion of the state, and is extensively manufactured and used in families, but there does not appear to have been any effort made to introduce it as an article of commerce. As the plant is peculiar to our pine-woods soil, its importance deserves some experiment, to ascertain if it may be profitably cultivated and manufactured. Will not some enterprising citizen give the subject the necessary attention?

The various tropical fruits are all adapted to this southern portion of Florida, and many of them can be made profitable for export:—such as the lime, guava, citron, lemon and cocoa-nut. The lime is now an abundant crop, and shipments of them to Charleston and Savannah have netted twenty dollars to the barrel. The product per acre may safely be estimated at thirty barrels. Preserves made from the three first-named fruits are always in demand, and may be prepared for market extensively. The pine-apple is successfully cultivated at India River, and other places, but as it requires a peculiar soil, it is confined to certain localities. Many points of this region are adapted to the plantain, banana, orange, &c., where future efforts, governed by experience and discretion, will doubtless cause them to become established products.

We would refer to the efforts and statements of a lamented citizen of Florida, murdered at Indian Key by the Seminoles, and who was rewarded by Congress for his zeal in introducing tropical plants. From his great skill and experience, he should be considered the best authority as to the future prospect of our state in the production of all these luxuries of life. From long observation, the writer is convinced, that while abundant opportunity exists for employment in producing some of the great staples of commerce, Nature, with a bountiful hand, has also provided a sufficiency of soil, from which to obtain all the necessaries requisite for the wants of the settlement. Gentlemen of worth, who have been long residents of Florida, are well aware that previous to the Indian war, by which our southern counties were depopulated, the sweet orange tree was found in many of those counties: as Orange, St. Lucie, Dade, and Hillsborough, in vigorous growth, and bearing bountifully their peculiarly rich and luscious fruit. These trees were mostly destroyed during that memorable period; and the great uncertainty as to the safety of life and property, has since prevented much attention to that, or any other branch of cultivation. There is now, however, in progress of growth, several young and thrifty orange groves at Indian River, Tampa, Manatee, and other places, proving the soil and climate well adapted to the production of that most profitable, and always desirable luxury.

It is only requisite that citizens should enter the land, clear it, and plant their trees, keeping them clear of all other growth for a space of about six years, and they may enjoy a harvest as rich as a choice vein in California. But it will be asked, what will enable persons to live through these six years without capital? The answer is, that in none of these southern counties is there a spot where the spontaneous products of the earth and water do not afford a very comfortable livelihood, without what may be called labor in obtaining them; and we need not point out to the man of industry and enterprise, the advantage thus conferred, while he, with system and energy, applies himself to some of the various opportunities, holding forth a ready and profitable reward for his labor.

The banana, the plantain, and various other fruits, are being successfully cultivated at various points; and when we take into consideration the fact that the soil of South Florida is so various, presenting here a black vegetable mould, there a yellowish clay soil, and again light sandy loam, or clear sand, it will at once be seen, that where so large a portion of the surface remains untried, it is difficult to attach to separate localities of this great and extended field, the importance which they may justly claim. We will state, however, that where this luscious fruit, the banana, has succeeded best, at New River, Indian River, Miami, Key West, and other places, it has always been a deep, rich vegetable soil, not too dry; and in all such soils, in any county south of 28°, it will undoubtedly become a profitable article of cultivation. In view of the large quantity of this fruit annually imported, it is recommended that more strenuous efforts be made to introduce and extend it wherever it may be done. Too rich a soil cannot be had, and cultivators should look well to manuring wherever there is any deficiency of strength in the soil. The Everglades, whenever drained, will furnish a large amount of soil adapted to the plant; and may we not confidently look forward to the period when so great a luxury shall be furnished to the neighboring cities from our own state?

Officers of the army, employed during the Indian war in the Everglades, report having visited a large island known as Sam Jones, on which was a large and beautiful growth of banana and cocoa-nuts, of the correctness of which there is no room for doubt; and may not this be taken as a test of the importance we should attach to that extensive region, now the property of Florida?

Cocoa-nuts are found to be adapted to nearly all our varieties of soil, and may be raised in the greatest abundance with the necessary care of planting. This article has been sadly overlooked, for the reason that the plant requires some nine years' growth before it yields any fruit. But this should never be considered as a reason why it should be neglected. Let every person who clears a piece of ground, put into it a few of these valuable plants, and in a few years we shall find them important as a source of revenue to the state. Neighborhoods near the salt water are found most desirable for them, and in these locations they will soon, by the rapid unfolding of their elegant fan-like leaves, add beauty to the scene, and at the proper time, a never-failing, and almost never-ending source of profit will be the result.

In regard to the culture of sugar in South Florida, it is well known that the seasons are at least from four to six weeks longer than in the best sugar lands of Louisiana and Mississippi, which had been considered the best in the United States; but owing to the liability of frosts, it has been conceded that they lose at least one crop out of every four; for in what they consider a favorable season, they are compelled to commence grinding their cane early in October, and before the cane matures. In the counties of Levy, Hernando, Orange and Hillsborough, (to say nothing of the counties further south, where the season is still later,) they do not commence grinding until the last part of November; and at the last season, the planters on the Manitee did not finish until the middle of February, giving them three months to gather their sugar crops in. A planter last year made, on the Manitee, thirty thousand pounds of sugar from ten and one-eighth acres. The cane matures and tassels there every season, which is conclusive proof, that no other part of the United States possesses the same advantages for the culture of cane. There is, beyond a doubt, in the counties of Levy, Hernando, Orange and Hillsborough, at least 170,000 acres of the best sugar lands in the United States, entirely uncultivated.

We feel that we have already made this communication of a somewhat lengthy character, yet we are constrained, in justice to two other branches of employment, in prosecution of which South Florida has a large interest, to devote some further space to a cursory glance at their respective merits and advantages. The first is the great interest of cattle-raising. Already has this branch become of great importance, and may be greatly extended, for which there is abundant range in the lower counties. In some of these counties there are no cattle at all, as in Dade, although the range is of the freshest kind during the entire year. A most desirable market for large numbers can be had at the Bahamas and West India Islands, and at Key West. The proximity of Miami (with an excellent harbor) to these places, would give a very great advantage in supplying those markets with beef, not only on account of the distance and expense, but the beef would be in much better condition than after the long passage now made from Tampa, Pensacola, New-Orleans, and other places, from which their supply is now obtained. We make the suggestion, in the hope that persons who now have large stocks in the northern part of the state and in Georgia, may profit thereby, as the price of cattle in those island markets may be estimated at twenty dollars per head for two year old steers, and thirty to forty dollars for those of three years and upwards. It is presumed that at the present session of the General Assembly, an appropriation will be made to open a road from Indian River to that point, when all the difficulties now existing will be removed, and cattle will doubtless soon be driven there; very many of which would find a ready sale to persons settled at that place, who are now entirely without any, owing to the great difficulty of penetrating the hammocks, and crossing the streams which intersect the entire region from the Miami to Hillsborough River.

In a country where the best of pine timber is growing in such abundance, and whose geographical features present such great advantages for transporting it to market, it would be superfluous for us to dwell upon its importance, as furnishing a ready and certain reward for the investment of capital and labor, either in converting it into lumber, or in the production of turpentine. It is remarked, with some degree of pride, that our state is exporting considerable lumber and turpentine; but where one is engaged in either of these branches of business, there should be at least twenty. There is ample room and scope for this increase; and with our ready access to the coast, this should be the greatest exporting state, for these two important articles of commerce, in the Union. There has never been devoted to these important branches of industry anything like the attention they demand; and our state is still sadly in want of saw-mills throughout her length and breadth, save perhaps at one or two points, as at Pensacola and Jacksonville. With the abundant supply of timber, we hope soon to see enterprising men engage in reaping the harvest that is presented everywhere throughout South Florida, where there is not, at this day, within our knowledge, a solitary saw-mill.

Turpentine-making is receiving some attention in the western part of the state, where its profits are so large as to draw off attention from the culture of cotton, even at high prices; and when we consider the enormous consumption of rosin and turpentine, and the large extent to which they may be produced in South Florida alone, we need only look to an accession of laborers in this productive field, for it to become a most valuable and important resource of the state.

We have made industrious researches after some authentic tabular statements in regard to the heat and cold of South Florida, and the only one within access is a series of observations made by the late Dr. Perrine, at Indian Key, during several years following 1830. At that place, in latitude about 25 degrees north, the average range of the thermometer, during a series of years, was found to be 76 degrees, and never descending to freezing point. The entire region, embracing all south of latitude 28 degrees, may be claimed as entirely exempt from frost. Persons now living at Key West, Miami, Tampa, and other places, and who have been many years in Florida, have never known a sufficient degree of cold to injure the most delicate plants. With such mildness of climate, and a widely extended primitive soil, may we not expect, as we have certainly every reason for hope, that South Florida will soon become, what Providence in its wisdom seems so emphatically to have designed it to be, the Garden of America?

In glancing over this view of South Florida, we are forced to one conviction, that with such great and important advantages of climate—such varieties of soil, covered with a spontaneous growth of products of greater value than many that are now being cultivated in other states—with her streams and bays abounding with every variety of fish and turtle—her forests enlivened by all the varieties of game common to the South;—with these and other advantages, we look to the future history of Florida with conscious pride, believing that her course is onward; and that it is only necessary that she arise in her youthful might, and put forth her energies, to show to the world, that within her borders exists that which will make her one of the brightest stars in the galaxy of states. Our citizens have only to employ the means with which they are abundantly provided, for the construction of rail-road and steamboat routes within and around our borders, by which they will remove one of the great obstacles to immigration, and soon we shall find our promising state the recipient of a thrifty and prosperous people. Other states well understand the importance of creating facilities for travel; and knowing its influence in extending to thinly populated regions the benefits of emigration, have made it a prominent policy to encourage all such enterprises; and shall we not profit by their numerous examples? There is much capital now within our state that could be thus very profitably employed. And we would suggest a liberal policy towards the encouragement of all capitalists, who, with the laudable desire to shorten the route between our great northern cities and the Mexican Gulf, propose to construct rail-roads across our state for that object. The speedy accomplishment of such enterprises cannot but result greatly to the prosperity of our state.

FLORIDA—Climate, Etc.—It will be remembered that in 1838, Dr. Henry Perrine, U. S. consul at Campeachy, addressed a number of interesting letters to government relating to the various species of tropical plants of great value, capable of being domesticated and yielding abundant returns in Florida. Some of them were addressed to the committee of agriculture in Congress. Dr. Perrine urged the establishment of a nursery for these plants in the peninsula of Florida, and argued enthusiastically for the ultimate effects upon that territory and the Union. A favorable report upon his memorial was prepared by Senator Lynn, of Missouri.

Without pausing to discuss the matters involved in this transaction, it is sufficient to note some of the points that were chiefly urged. It was stated that the tenderest plants of the tropics would flourish in Florida; that this unimproved territory will sustain productive plants for food, medicine, and art, which grow in air, water, on rocks or trees, in marshes or moving sands; that the tropical regions may be improved for all species of vegetation. Of plants to be introduced, is mentioned caoutchouc, or Indian rubber; the cochineal nourishing species of prickly pear and others; the fibrous agaves, yielding sisal hemp; tea plant, which will thrive in the arid soils of the tropics, and might be produced profitably at one half the rates levied on foreign teas; mulberry tree, of Manilla; indigo, already a wild plant; the grape vine of Campeachy, which on the poorest calcareous soils of Florida might yield fruit to ripen in every month of every year; coffee, tobacco, sugar, black pepper, pimento, cloves, cinnamon, ginger, pine-apple, medicinal roots, etc., etc. Whatever may be thought of Dr. Perrine's views in relation to Florida, whether wild and impracticable, or capable of being at all carried out, one thing is very certain, his letters are most interesting and full of material. We present his tables of temperature and rain, from many observations:

TEMPERATURE.

	Key West Mean	Havana Mean		Key West Mean	Havana Mean
January	69	71	July	82	80
February	70	75	August	81	80
March	73	77	Sept	77	79
April	75	78	October	74	75
May	79	81	Nov	70	72
June	81	81			

January 28–29, 1836, coldest night ever known, thermometer falls to 44 degrees; the greatest heat is 90 degrees.

FALL OF RAIN.

	New-Orleans	Key West
Four years	47.35	31,389

But we give the paper promised in the opening paragraph:

The climate of East Florida will be considered in this place, only in so far as relates to the vegetable productions. In this respect it has been spoken of in extravagant terms, from which it might be supposed that every kind of vegetable growth, indigenous to all regions between Hudson's Bay and Cape Horn, flourish alike, side by side, spontaneously. But the climate has been praised, in an especial manner, as proper for all the tropical staples and fruits. A Mr. Carver is quoted by one writer, as saying: "So mild is the winter that the most delicate vegetables and plants of the Caribbee islands experience not the least injury from that season;" and a Mr. William Stock is made to say, "This country will produce all the tropical plants and staples by the side of those belonging to a northern climate." It is proposed to notice the winter climate of East Florida.

In the year 1765, John Bartram states, that "on the 3d of January, being on the St. John's River, north of Lake George, the thermometer was at 26°, wind N. W., the ground was frozen an inch thick on the banks; this was the fatal night that destroyed the lime, citron, and banana trees in St. Augustine." Williams says: "In 1774, there was a snow storm, which extended over most of the territory. In February, 1822, the cold was so intense in West Florida, that all the fruit trees were killed to the ground; but this season was comparatively mild in East Florida. On the contrary, East Florida suffered exceedingly from a violent frost on the 6th of April, 1828; on this bitter night crops of cotton, corn, and fruits were all destroyed. The thermometer at Six Mile Creek, on the St. John's, stood at 27°, and the ice made an inch thick. The crops of corn and cotton were cut off as far south as Tomoko. During the month of February, 1835, East Florida was visited by a frost, much more severe than any before experienced. A severe north-west wind blew ten days in succession, but more violent for about three days; during this period the mercury sank seven degrees below zero. The St. John's River was frozen several rods from the shore, and all kinds of fruit trees were killed to the ground; many of them never started again, even from the roots. Frost is felt at some seasons in every part of Florida, though not usually below latitude 27°." Vignoles says: "The nipping of the white frost is occasionally felt so far as the extreme capes of Florida, though not an annual visitant." Below, the lowest degrees, in the years mentioned, at several points on the peninsula, are given. In the years omitted, no observations have been published:

St. Augustine, lat 29° 50′; 1826, 33°; 1828, 30°; 1830, 30°; 1841, 24°; Pilatka, lat. 29° 38′; 1840, 28°; 1841, 27°; Fort King, lat. 29° 12′; 1841, 22°. Farry gives the annual range of the thermometer at Fort King, as follows: max. 105°, min. 27°, range 78°. Tampa, lat. 27° 48′; 1826, 28°; 1827, 26°; 1828, 40°; 1829, 28°; 1830, 30°; 1840, 38°; 1841, 30°. Sarrasota, lat. 27° 20′; February, 1841, 30°.

From the above, it is evident that the coast of Florida has a much milder climate than the interior; for Fort King, which is more than half a degree south of St. Augustine, has nevertheless a much more severe climate, as will be still farther shown. In February, 1841, the frost was so severe on Pease Creek, in lat. 28°, for several nights in succession, that thick ice was formed, and the horses' hoofs clattered on the frozen ground as loudly as at the North in the severe cold of November. No observations were made with the thermometer. This frost must have extended several miles lower, or at least to lat. 27°, as it is seen that on the western coast, (in a milder climate,) at Sarrasota, (lat. 27° 20′,) the thermometer was down to 30°. The Atlantic coast has also a much milder winter climate than the Gulf coast, as is evident from the following table, which shows the mean annual range of temperature at the permanent military stations in East Florida:

	Max.	Min.	Range
St. Augustine, Atlantic, lat. 29° 50′	92°	39°	53°
Fort King (interior,) lat. 29° 12′	105	27	78
Tampa, Gulf, lat. 27° 48′	92	35	57

It appears, then, that the winter climate of the coast on the Gulf is more severe than that of the Atlantic coast, and that of the interior is more severe than either. The eastern coast is warmer in winter than the interior, in consequence, no doubt, of the Gulf stream passing northward through the straits of Florida. But whatever the cause, it is certain that the cold of the interior is much more severe than on the coast, and that the winter weather is colder on the western than on the eastern side of the peninsula. Scarcely a year passes at Tampa Bay without ice, and the bodies of the orange trees are all seared from the effects of the cold winds. I trust it has been made apparent that tropical fruits and staples will not flourish above lat. 27°, notwithstanding the stories of Mr. Carver, and the reports floating up and down in the writings of travelers and speculators; and Williams makes the parallel of 27° the limit for tropical productions.

It is only below the 27th degree of latitude, (constituting South Florida "tropical" is a misnomer designed to mislead, for no part of the territory is within the tropics,) if at all, that the tropical fruits can be raised to any degree of perfection. But a small part of South Florida is *entirely* exempt from frosts, except it be the southernmost islands and points, which are, with very little exception, both dry and barren. The guava, plantain, banana, lemon, lime, citron, date, mango, cocoa, &c., can be raised in South Florida, and perhaps the pine-apple and some other West India fruits. But nearly the whole of South Florida is occupied by the Everglades. "South of latitude 28°," says a recent writer, "Florida consists of a vast morass called the Everglades." "That part of the Peninsula of East Florida," says Williams, that "lies south of the 28th degree of latitude, declines toward the centre in the form of a dish, the border of which is raised toward the coast. This vast basin is filled with marshes, wet savannas, intersected by extensive lakes and lagoons, forming a labyrinth, which, taken together, is called the Everglades." Behind Cape Florida it approaches within twelve miles of the coast, it then passes round to near Cape Sable, and up the western coast. All this country, (not including the eastern coast of the peninsula,) containing the district allotted to the Indians, has been officially pronounced by Gen. Worth as of no value; and the only part of the narrow belt of land surrounding the Everglades, which is of the least consequence, is that on the eastern coast. On the narrow strip surrounding the Everglades, allowing for the present that the southern and western portions are of some value, must be raised all the tropical productions of Florida. It can be seen by a glance at the map that the quantity of cultivatable land below the limit of black frost is small indeed. It is said that the Everglades can be drained. It matters not; for if they are, they will be as worthless as before, on account of their insalubrity.

Some space will now be devoted to the general productions of East Florida.

Sugar, where the quality of the land will allow of its cultivation, is undoubtedly the most certain crop among the staples. Florida is superior to Louisiana for the sugar cultivation in this respect—the season is longer, which allows the cane to ripen higher before the occurrence of frost. Vignoles says: "It is perhaps the fact that the exhausting vegetation of this article may not allow a profitable planting of it upon the same lands, more than two or three years in succession; yet, as it may be raised on the pine lands, a change of fields is easy, and attended with but little comparative trouble; and by suffering the lands to lie fallow, or by a judicious succession of crops, it will not require a very extensive tract to establish a sugar plantation. Perhaps it may be thought that Florida presents but little to tempt the large sugar planter: granted, but it is undoubted that if the culture of the cane should be adopted on a small scale, the labor would be amply repaid." The rich swamps and hammocks, after having been properly prepared, will doubtless raise sugar crops in succession, but the pine lands will soon become exhausted and worthless, unless highly manured. The plantations of Generals Clinch and M'Intosh, near Fort Drane, which were never considered of inferior soil compared with Florida land in general, were exhausted at the time they were abandoned. Williams says: "All our *good lands* produce sugar-cane as well as any other crop, and it is more certain and more valuable, in most places. Besides, there can be no danger of glutting the market with sugar." But he is in great error when he says that cane is cultivated with more ease than corn, because it does not require so much hoeing.

Cotton.—So many errors have been propagated in relation to the culture of this article, especially the Sea Island variety, that a more extended notice will be taken of it than would otherwise be necessary. Several months since, a writer in the *National Intelligencer*, with the signature of "A Physician," made use of the following language:

"It is now established beyond a doubt, that the Sea Island, or long staple cotton (the production of which has heretofore been confined to a few small islands in South Carolina and Georgia,) will grow luxuriantly even in the very centre of the peninsula. A superior quality of this article has been produced on the Suwanee, and in the very centre of Alachua, as well as on the eastern coast. This important fact is no doubt attributable to the almost *irregular* position of East Florida. The importance which the production of this valuable staple must give to East Florida, will be duly estimated when it is considered that it can be cultivated there without the fear of *competition*. The few islands in South Carolina and Georgia which yield this staple, are now so nearly worn out, that their average product per acre does not exceed one hundred and fifty pounds, and there is no other portion of the United States, with the exception of East Florida, where it can be produced. Neither can it be produced in Texas, in Egypt, or in India; and it is more than probable that there is in no part of the world a country of much extent, so well adapted, both in climate and soil, to the production of this staple, as East Florida. It is a fortunate circumstance, too, that the northern portion of East Florida, which is the least adapted to the production of tropical staples, is better suited than any other part of the territory to the cultivation of Sea Island cotton."

He says, in another place: "If we cultivate an acre of *second-rate pine land* in Sea Island cotton (a staple which grows everywhere in East Florida), the average product will be three hundred pounds, which, at the average price of twenty-five cents, will amount to seventy-five dollars, which exceeds the yield of South Carolina in this, its most valuable staple."

I deny that Sea Island cotton can be raised in the interior of East Florida at all. Now for my authority. Williams, the eulogist of Florida, whose testimony is therefore the more valuable for my purpose, says:

"Sea Island cotton is peculiarly adapted to our seacoast and islands, and although good crops may sometimes be made at some distance in the country, yet they are uncertain, and always degenerate in proportion to their distance from the sea. Our islands and coast are made up of the debris of sea shells, a small portion of clay and vegetable matter, with a large portion of silicious sand. The larger the proportion of vegetable matter and clay, the larger is usually the crop of cotton, but the less of these matters contained in the soil, the finer and more glossy will be the staple of the cotton, and no kind of manure has been found that will increase the quantity, without, at the same time, injuring the quality of the cotton, except it be sea-weeds, or marsh mud."

The best planters do not average more than three acres of cotton to the hand. The best land will produce, in good seasons, one bale to the hand, but in general half that quantity can be depended on. The value of this crop depends, more than any other, on the manner in which it is handled and put up for market. The crop is liable to many accidents. The caterpillar sometimes destroys whole fields in one night. The red bug pierces the pod and discolors the cotton, and heavy winds destroy the pods; besides, it is a tedious crop to clear and prepare for market. It ought never to be cultivated on lands that will produce sugar or tobacco, but to be confined to light hammock lands within the range of the sea breezes. The Mexican, a green-seed cotton, is still cultivated in the country. High oak land is the only kind which produces this crop to advantage, and at the price now given, it does not, in Florida, pay the expense of cultivation.

SEA ISLAND COTTON can perhaps be cultivated on a few of the Florida islands, and on a narrow strip of land on the Eastern coasts about Indian River. This remains to be determined. It cannot be raised in the other parts of the territory, and least of all in the northern portions of East Florida, which are the least adapted to the production of Florida staples. It cannot be raised in the very centre of the Peninsula. In the cotton market, Florida and Upland cottons are always classed alike, and as bringing about the same price. I do not believe that the "*second-rate pine lands*" will produce "an average of three hundred pounds" of any kind of cotton "per acre." Williams says that "the best lands will produce, in good seasons, one bale to the hand, but in general, one-half that quantity can be depended upon," and that "the best planters do not average more than three acres to the hand." From the "best land," then, in "good seasons," according to Williams, one acre will produce 150 pounds (allowing the bale to contain 450 pounds), which, at 9 cents per lb. (a high price), amounts to $13 50. Allowing 600 pounds to the bale, the product of one acre (200 pounds) is $18. Even if we allow the whole 300 pounds per acre, the product will amount to only $27, and at 8 cents (a fair price, a great one though), to only $24, instead of $75, as set forth by "A Physician." Any one may see by the price current for the last two or three years, that Florida cottons have brought only 7⅜ and 8 cents. So much for Florida Sea Island cotton, which cannot be raised in the interior, and on but a small portion of the coast, if at all.

FLORIDA.—THE EVERGLADES OF FLORIDA, AND THE PROSPECT OF RECLAIMING THEM INTO GARDENS FOR EVERY VARIETY OF THE FRUITS OF THE TROPICS, &c.—We have, upon three occasions, presented to the readers of the Review elaborate sketches of Florida, historically and productively, in almost every interesting particular. Our first paper (vol. iv, 38 p.) was based upon the History by Dr. Monette, and the United States Census of 1840; the second (in the same volume, p. 245), upon the Report to Congress by Dr. Henry Perrine, and private information; the third was the able production of E. R. Fairbanks, Esq., one of the citizens of that state, and is the leading article of our fifth volume. These sketches have left little yet to be presented in regard to Florida that is truly instructive and valuable, except what we have been fortunate enough to find in a volume entitled "Everglades of the Peninsula of Florida," and for which the country is indebted mainly to the efforts of the Hon. J. D. Wescott, jr., who has kindly furnished us a copy.

The volume contains first, a Report from the Committee on Public Lands, urging a donation, by government, to the state of Florida, of the EVERGLADES existing in the southern part of the peninsula, of immense extent, filled with islands and covered with a large sheet of water, on condition that they be drained and reclaimed. The committee present a letter from Mr. Walker, Secretary of the Treasury, approving the suggestion, and from the Commissioner of the Land Office, to the same effect. From this last, it appears that the whole area of the Everglades is about 7,800,000 acres of land and water, of which 4,300,000 are always inundated and incapable of reclamation, 1,000,000 acres only occasionally covered and of doubtful recovery—and the remaining 2,500,000 acres are considered inferior and for a great part valueless, although not inundated.

In the tract proposed to be ceded, lies the grant already made to Dr. Perrine of 23,000 acres, and the Alagon claim, under Spanish grant, covering two-thirds of the territory, but not considered at all valid.

"The project of reclaiming the Everglades," says the Commissioner, "if successful, may reclaim *for cultivation* within the limits of the proposed grant, about *one million of acres* of those lands now covered with water, some *continually*, and the residue occasionally only. It cannot be expected to *reclaim* but a part of the Everglades; a part of the Atscenahoofa, or big cypress swamp, a part of the Halpatiokee swamp, and the skirt of poor lands on the margin of the glades, covered with water some months in every year, and which is very barren. Much of the *subaqueous* lands will still remain inundated, and no one can expect that the parts that are so drained can all be made susceptible of cultivation."

The bill before Congress makes the grant depend upon these conditions: 1. That the state shall, in two years, commence a series of drains and canals for draining purposes; for decreasing the waters of Lake Okeechobee, &c.; for draining the Everglades between that lake and the Atlantic and Gulf coast, so that, if practicable, a communication may be made by such canals for vessels between the Atlantic and Gulf waters, and the whole be completed in ten years. 2. That one thirty-sixth part of the said lands be reserved for public school purposes for the inhabitants thereof. 3. That government shall have alternate sections of such lands south of the line as have been completely surveyed, &c.

The most important point, however, in the

conditions of transfer, is that the surplus of the lands embraced, after defraying all expenses, etc., of reclaiming, shall constitute a perpetual fund for educational purposes, etc. Of this feature we express our warm approval.

The proposed donation to Florida resembles, very much, that which was made to Louisiana, at the last Congress, of a vast body of swamp lands, several millions of acres, supposed to be within the power of recovery without great expense, and to be very valuable for agricultural purposes when so reclaimed. Doubtless, immediate steps will be taken by the Legislature of the state in the premises; and we desire an opportunity of expressing here our ardent hope that the educational feature of the Florida act will be imitated, and that a large tract of the reclaimed lands—one half-million acres, at least—will be reserved forever. The proceeds of this *land fund* will suffice for School and University purposes. The Legislature of Louisiana will then have an opportunity of endowing, in a manner becoming of the noble institution that was in contemplation of the Convention which framed our present Constitution, and which was to be located in the city of New-Orleans. It can make this University one of the proudest and most distinguished seats of learning in America, and thronged with students from half the Confederacy—from the neighboring islands and Mexico—if this scheme be but carried out, and that, too, *without one cent of expense to the state*. The grant from government is a pure gratuity, and it becomes a liberal people like ours to use it for such elevated purposes. Without such endowment, the University must degenerate into a mere grammar school, which its literary and scientific departments are now in great danger of doing, despite of the handsome structures that have been erected, and are in progess. An endowment of one-half or one-quarter million, perhaps, acres of the reclaimed lands would produce an annual revenue of $40,000, the least cost at which a splendid institution can be sustained, including halls, observatories, libraries, cabinets, apparatus, and needy scholars, of whom any number may be instructed *free*. *Louisiana* would have just reason to be proud of such an institution in her great city.*

But to return to Florida, Mr. Buckingham Smith, who was employed by government, in 1847, to "make a *reconnoissance* of the Everglades, etc., makes a report, from which we digest many important particulars. It appears that there is a faint tradition the Spaniards contemplated more than a century ago the draining of the Everglades, and actually undertook it, and some of the works, it is supposed, were discovered in the late Indian war. During the British possession of Florida, De Brahm, an experienced engineer, made surveys of the eastern coast, and some of his maps, notes, etc., are in the collections of Peter Force, Esq., at Washington, and many others among the papers lately brought over from England by Massachusetts.

The Everglades extend from the southern margin of Lake Okeechobee some ninety miles to Cape Sable, the southern extremity of the peninsula of Florida, and are in width from thirty to fifty miles. Their waters are fresh, and are in depth from one to six feet. Lake Okeechobee is a large body of water, thirty miles in diameter, and subject to continual overflow. The geology of the south ern portion of the peninsula comprises oolitic lime rock, filled with shells and corals, porous, easy of excavation, and on exposure to the air hardens and becomes useful for building purposes. It contributes to the fertility of the soil. Along the eastern verge of the glades are spots of wet and black prairie land, and also between them and the sea. Other spots are covered with pine trees, imbedded in a dark soil of vegetable mould. Dryhammocks exist, too, with various descriptions of trees. These lands would all be valuable.

To reclaim the Everglades and the neighboring swamps, it is proposed to tap the Lake Okeechobee by canals, etc., as its waters are supposed to be elevated at least twelve feet above the waters which shall furnish an outlet and a reservoir, and the whole expense at the highest figure is put down about $500,000.

"Whatever may be," says Mr. Smith, "the latent and dormant resources of this region; however great the capability of its being advantageously improved, and however valuable it may be made by the enterprise, energy and industry of the American agriculturist, if encouraged, or even given a fair chance, by the government; yet, hitherto, no proper opportunity has been offered for the development of those resources and capabilities. Whilst in the possession of the savages, even when under the dominion of the Spaniards, who possessed little agricultural enterprise, and whose attention was directed elsewhere; during the short period it was in the hands of the English, suffering not merely from neglect, but pressed down by the most iniquitous policy; from its discovery by Ponce de Leon to the present day, with but brief exceptions, the theatre of savage war, and bloodshed and desolation; in the eighty years preceding its acquisition by the United States, twice changing owners, inhabitants and policy; for some time the resort of the rovers of the sea, or the little less scrupulous cruisers of the many different flags which the revolutions of the present century occasioned; and, when acquired by the United States, assigned as a kind of prison bounds to the Seminoles they failed to remove or subdue, it would have been wondrous indeed, had it become more important, in any respect, than it is now generally regarded."

The action of government has not been favorably felt in the settlement of South Flo-

* The reader will see this educational movement set forth at large under the head of "Commercial Education in Universities."

rida, and the whole number of whites on the peninsula now, below the northern part of the Everglades, does not exceed fifty. At Key West there are about 2000, and occasional settlements on other keys.

During the Florida war, the butcheries of the Indians, the murder of government officers and of Dr. Perrine, drove nearly all the settlers to Key West; and the location since, of some of the Indians in the peninsula, is calculated to deter settlement for a long time.

The government has commenced at Key West and the Tortugas extensive fortifications for the protection of the vast commerce of the country passing in that quarter, and to give us the command of the Gulf, the Straits of Florida, and perhaps, eventually, by our navy, of the Caribbean sea. A numerous population in the vicinity of these fortifications, is much to be desired; and they would, from the character of the country, resort to the seas and the fisheries, and become in the event a nursery of southern seamen. Such a population, it is said, would diminish the dangers of vessels passing along the straits and navigating the Gulf, and prevent losses in property, which are now more than one million of dollars per annum: since more extensive and accurate knowledge would thereby be generally acquired of the reefs and coasts and of their continued changes; and the superior facility of obtaining pilots and other aid, that would be afforded by such settlements, would be valuable safeguards.

The fisheries of Florida, too, would be promoted, which within the last fifteen years have become of some consequence, and are valued at about $15,000 annually. The British have ever eagerly sought a participation in these fisheries for the Bahamians. The salt resources of the islands and keys are equal to the demands of the whole Union.

The Everglades are thus described by Mr. Smith:

"Imagine a vast lake of fresh water extending in every direction, from shore to shore, beyond the reach of human vision—ordinarily unruffled with a ripple on its surface—studded with thousands of islands, of various sizes, from one-fourth of an acre to hundreds of acres in area, and which are generally covered with dense thickets of shrubbery and vines. Occasionally an island is found with lofty pines and palmettos upon it, but oftener they are without any; and not unusually a solitary majestic palmetto is seen, the only tree upon an island, as if to guide in approaching it, or as a place of signal or look out for its former denizens. The surrounding waters, except in places that at first seem like channel ways, (but which are not,) are covered with tall saw-grass, shooting up its straight and slender stems from the shallow bottom of the lake, to the height, often, of ten feet above the surface, and covering all, but a few rods around, from your view. The water is pure and limpid, and almost imperceptibly moves, not in partial currents, but, as it seems, in a mass, silently and slowly to the southward. The bottom of the lake, at the distance of from three to six feet, is covered with a deposit of decayed vegetable substance, the accumulated product of ages, generally two or three feet in depth, on the white sand and rock that underlies it, over the entire surface of the basin. The flexible grass, bending gently to the breeze, protects the water from its influence. Lilies and other aquatic flowers, of every variety and hue, are to be seen on every side, in pleasant contrast with the pale green of the saw-grass; and, as you draw near an island, the beauty of the scene is increased by the rich foliage and blooming flowers of the wild myrtle and the honeysuckle, and other shrubs and vines that generally adorn its shores. The profound and wild solitudes of the place—the solemn silence that pervades it, unless broken by the splashing of a paddle of the canoe or light batteau, with which only can you traverse the Pahayokee, or by the voices of your "compagnons du voyage," add to a wakened and excited curiosity, feelings bordering on awe. No human being, civilized or savage, inhabits the secluded interior of the glades. The Seminoles reside in the region between them and the Gulf. Except for an occasional flight of an eagle or a bittern, startled by the strange invaders of their privacy, or for a view of the fishes in the shallow waters, gliding swiftly away from your boat as it goes near to them, your eyes would not rest on a living thing, abiding in this wilderness of "grass-waters," shrubbery and flowers. Reflections upon the past history of the regions around you, unbidden, force themselves upon the visitor to the interior of the glades. On these islands, in ages that have long since passed away, the haughty and ferocious Carib cacique dwelt.

"He and his people were driven from their homes by more powerful people, who were, in turn, expelled by stronger foes. Here the daring and reckless buccaneer, of later times, came, after his cruise for plunder, to revel in safety upon his unhallowed spoils. Once in this secluded spot, the Catholic missionary pursued the heavenly vocation of teaching the benighted pagan the truths of the gospel; and here he sealed his devotion to his God by yielding up his life to the vengeance of the infidel savage. Part of these glades are now in the allotted district of the wily and intrepid Arpiarka, the chief of those of his tribe that fought so fiercely and so obstinately in resisting the enforcement of the policy of the Federal Government of removing them west, and who finally succeeded in constraining the United States to abandon that policy, and to allow them to remain still longer on the hunting-grounds, and near the graves, of their fathers. The recollection, also, that the sacred name of "Laguna del Espirita Santo" was given to this region by the Spanish discoverers, is not without influence upon the visitor. The effects of such a visit to the Pahayokee upon a person of romantic imagination, and who indulges his fancies on such subjects, it may be presumed, would be somewhat poetic. But if the visitor is a man of practical, utilitarian turn of thought, the first and the abiding impression, is the utter worthlessness to civilized man, in its present condition, for any useful or practical object, of the entire region. A solitary inducement cannot now be offered to a decent white man to settle in the interior of the Everglades! Some of the islands may be fertile, but their inaccessibility, except by small boats, and the entire isolation from society their residents would have to encounter, would deter most men (who did not desire to avoid his fellows either from misanthropy, or fear of justice for crimes committed) from making the glades their homestead."

Whether the Everglades can ever be adapted to the culture of sugar, rice, tobacco, cotton or corn, is undetermined, although many think that they can. Tropical fruits may, however, be cultivated, and the reclaimed swamps will possess advantages for any of the above products. The work of draining would reclaim also the lands for a hundred miles on the Kissime River, and those to the north-westward of the lake. We agree, therefore, with Mr. Smith:

"The citizen, whether in executive or legislative station, or without either, who succeeds in making fit for cultivation, even if but partially, a region equal in extent to either of the three smallest states of this confederacy, now as useless as the deserts of Africa, will earn a rich meed of praise from the people of Florida and of the Union. The Everglades are now suitable only for the haunt of noxious vermin, or the resort of pestilent reptiles. The statesman whose exertions shall cause the millions of acres they contain, now worse than useless, to teem with the products of agricultural industry—to be changed into a garden, in which can be reared many and various exotics, introduced for the first time for cultivation in the United States—whether necessaries of life, or conveniences, or luxuries merely;—that man who thus adds to the resources, wealth and independence of his country—who contributes by such means to the comforts of his fellow-men, will merit a high place in public favor, not only with his own generation, but with posterity."

The views of the same gentleman in regard to the action of government in obtaining valuable seed, etc., we also indorse to the full. It is proper, also, that I should advert in this report to a subject intimately connected with the favorable success of the primary undertaking of draining the Everglades and rendering them capable of being cultivated profitably. It is the adoption of necessary measures by the Federal Government for the procurement of exotic plants, seeds and roots, and such productions as can be reared there for the use of the settlers. Whilst the manufacturing, the commercial, the navigating, the mechanical, and in fine every other interest in society has been encouraged and fostered, by measures adopted with a view of affording them direct aid and protection, is it not astonishing that the agricultural interest of this country has been so entirely neglected. Excepting the limited assistance given by the Patent Office in the procurement and distribution of seeds, scarcely any attention has been bestowed upon this subject by statesmen of later years. The Federal Government, by means of the navy visiting foreign countries, through our ministers and consuls abroad, could obtain and distribute properly many trees, plants and other productions of the forest, field and garden, and introduce them for cultivation in those parts of the United States best adapted to them. It is not doubted that $10,000 per annum properly applied, and the plants, seeds, roots, etc., distributed among agriculturists and horticulturists, rather than theorists—and instead of placing them in nurseries and show gardens in cities, have them sent into the appropriate section of the country, would be a judicious measure. Hundreds of valuable productions from Cuba, West Indies, Mexico, Yucatan, Guatemala, South America, Spain, Portugal, Italy, Sicily, China, East Indies, Africa, now unknown to us, could be introduced and cultivated in South Florida, etc., etc.

In a letter of Col. James Gadsden of South Carolina, to Hon. R. I. Walker, he demonstrates the practicability of draining the glades, and conceives that it will open to the United States the only portion of her territory capable of competing with tropical latitudes in all those productions which enrich them. Gen. Jessup concurs in their views, and adds: The hammocks in this part of the country are all extremely rich, and would soon be converted into sugar plantations. The swamps are generally peat swamps, which, if drained, would be soon converted into olive, lime and orange plantations, and would be cultivated by a numerous white population, interposed between the free blacks of the West Indies and our slaves. Gen. Harney, after some able views upon the matter, declares if it does succeed, in less than five years that region will have, no doubt, a population of one hundred thousand souls and more. Our coast in South Florida is now extremely exposed in time of war. This population would protect it and afford security to the whole commerce of the western country passing along its shores. There are other letters from distinguished officers of the Topographical Engineers, the Army and Navy, to the same effect. Mr. Sewall, who entered the St. Lucie River from the sea, speaks of the settlers there as engaged in the culture of tropical plants, and the turtle fishery. They are endeavoring to get in pine-apple plants, and many were already matured. He saw the cocoa-nut, guava, lemon, lime, orange, banana, tamarind, etc. Sisal hemp is found wild. Sugar cane matures and tassels like corn, a yard long.

A Committee of the Legislature of Florida say: "The United States pay to the West Indies, to South America, to the Azores, to Portugal, and other tropical countries, a large amount annually for their products. South Florida is the only part of the United States where such products can be raised. With the exception of coffee, tobacco, sugar, tea, black pepper, it is believed, with proper encouragement, an amount equal to the entire amount imported into the United States would be raised in South Florida." The arrow root produced is equally as nutritious as that of Jamaica or Bermuda. In 1844, 25,000 lbs. were made in South Florida for shipment. Millions of pounds could be annually produced.

The following in regard to the Fisheries of Florida, is taken from a report to its Legislature:

"Upward of twenty eastern vessels from thirty to sixty tons burthen, with from five to fifteen men each, are now employed in these fisheries. Several vessels owned by resident citizens of Florida are engaged in them. These vessels supply the markets of Havana and Cuba, generally, with not only fresh fish and roes, but also dried and salted fish to an immense amount. The annual amount paid in Cuba to these fishing vessels, it is believed, exceeds $150,000. The retailing of fresh fish in the market is a monopoly sold for a large amount by the Spanish government there. Those who possess the monopoly receive, it is believed, thrice the amount they pay the fishing vessels. At present few dried or salt fish are taken from Florida to New-Orleans for the western country market or to the northern Atlantic cities, as the profits of the Cuba market are much greater, and because those now employed in those fisheries are not more than sufficient to supply that market. It is anticipated, if properly regulated, hundreds of thousands of dollars of such fish could be sold advantageously throughout the whole Union."

WRECKS ON THE FLORIDA COAST.

	Value of vessels and cargo.	Salvage of Court.	Expense.
1844	$725,000	$67,626 76	$169,064 99
1845	737,000	69,591 99	105,709 51
1846	1,624,000	108,992 00	213,423 00

To the pamphlet on Florida, Mr. Westcott has made a concluding note, which we regard important enough to copy :

"It is not a little surprising that, in twenty-seven years since Florida has been held by the United States, no complete nautical survey of the Florida reef has been made. During such time the *British* government has had ships of war, among them the Bustard, engaged for months in such surveys ; and even in surveying the harbor of Key West, and other of our harbors there ! The charts used by our navigators are the old Spanish charts and those made by the British from 1763–1784, and of the recent British surveys alluded to, and compilations of them by Blunt and others, all imperfect in many particulars, and erroneous in others. *We have no original American chart of all the reefs and keys.* That accomplished and scientific officer at the head of the coast survey, Professor Bache, has informed me, that if the means were appropriated by Congress, the entire reef and all the keys, from Tortugas up to Cape Sable, could be surveyed *in one season.* The expense, to enable the work to be finished in one season, might not fall short of $100,000, as to effect it, three or four parties of officers must be employed. But the benefits of such work would greatly outweigh this amount, and it will not cost less to devote two or three years to it."

FLORIDA.—Coasts and Keys of Florida.—S. R. Mallory, Collector at Key West, thus writes to Professor Bache of the Coast Survey :

"I deem it unnecessary to state the character and extent of the immense and increasing commerce, which passes through the narrow strait between the Florida and the Cuba and Bahama shores, as the published statistics of the Treasury Department upon the subject are familiar to you. In the navigation of this passage, and particularly during the summer months, when the trade winds are light and variable, and the rapidity of the gulf stream is believed to be accelerated, vessels bound from the eastward to Cuba and the south-western Atlantic ports, are compelled to hug the Florida shore, not only to avoid the stream, but to find an anchorage in calm weather, which frequently continues several days; and both on their outward and homeward voyages, they keep the Florida shore aboard, regarding the iron-bound coasts of Cuba and the Bahamas as most perilous. The Florida reefs, extending from Cape Florida to the Tortugas, a distance of about two hundred miles, subject to violent storms and the action of wayward currents, have always proved disastrous to navigators in that region. The number of vessels publicly known to strike upon them, including as well those extricated with as without the aid of wreckers, is not less than forty-eight per annum, or one in every seven days nearly ; but it is confidently believed, from reliable sources of information possessed by the people of the coast, that many others strike upon the reefs and get off, of which no accounts are published. Twenty-two vessels, averaging about fifty tons each, are stationed at various points along the reefs, and pursue exclusively the business of relieving stranded property. Many of them are owned by the states of Connecticut and New York; they are expensively and substantially built and furnished, manned by strong crews of from ten to fifteen men, and commanded by skilful pilots, who have devoted their lives to the perilous profession of wrecking. These men are rarely heard of, and seem to be known only to those who have received assistance, or life itself, at their hands; and yet it is thought that few vocations are more essential to the commercial interests of our country, and that the Florida wreckers, in character and conduct, may compare favorably with any other class of seamen in the world. They are licensed by the judge of the United States district court for the southern district of Florida, under the act of Congress of the 3d of February, 1847. Their claims for salvage upon the property saved by them, are adjudicated in this court, and they are held to a strict accountability, not only for the property taken into their possession, but for their personal deportment toward the recipients of their services. The value of the property stranded on the reefs and carried into Key West, during the present year, cannot fall short of one million of dollars. During some years it far exceeds this amount, and the value of all the property which strikes upon them may be safely estimated at two millions of dollars per annum. During the year 1846, there were fifty-five vessels stranded and carried to Key West in distress, the aggregate value of which, with their cargoes, was $1,624,800. The amount of salvage decreed to the wreckers was $108,992, and the total amount of expenditures at Key West by these vessels and cargoes, was $213,423. Of these fifty-five vessels, eleven were owned in New-York, twelve in Maine, seven in Massachusetts, two in Connecticut, two in Rhode Island, five in Pennsylvania, one in South Carolina, five in Florida, and ten in foreign countries.

FLORIDA TOBACCO.—We are gratified to learn that our Gadsden county friends have made fine crops of the valuable tobacco which they cultivate so successfully; and we are also informed that they obtain a good price for the article, purchasers being ready and anxious to buy, which shows that the supply by no means exceeds the demand.

It is not generally known in the United States that the tobacco above referred to, and which has as yet been grown no where to any extent except in Gadsden county, finds a ready market in Germany, being principally shipped to Bremen, and pays the planter as high as twenty-five cents for the first quality.

What makes the culture of tobacco so profitable to the planters, is the fact that it is almost a surplus crop—they being able to make a tobacco crop, and at the same time to make three-quarters of a cotton crop, and enough provisions besides. Fodder cannot well be made with tobacco, but the loss of this crop may be compensated perhaps by the hay, which we learn some of our planters manage to cure from the grass to be found in the fields.

As yet none but new lands have been cultivated for tobacco, the cut-worm prevailing to such an extent in the old lands as to prove very destructive to the plant; we have no doubt, however, but that the skill and energy of onr farmers will enable them to provide a remedy for this evil, and that all rich and strong land, having the right kind of chemical constituents in its soil, will be made to produce good tobacco.

What with sugar, rice, indigo, tobacco, sea island, and short staple cotton, tropical fruits—productions which our soil will yield and our soil will allow of being cultivated with success—the live oak, juniper, cedar and pitch pine, of our forests—our turpentine, and last, not least, our fisheries—our state offers strong inducements to the skillful and industrious agriculturists, not to be surpassed by the much coveted Island of Cuba, nor by any of the most favored regions of the new world. Nature has here been lavish of her bounties—we only need the sweat of man's brow to yield rich fruits to reward his industry.

The vaunted advantages held out by the friends of Texas, turned the tide of emigration away from Florida. Our Indian war did a good deal toward the same result—but we are led to think, from what we have seen and heard, that "sober second thought" has convinced many who passed by Florida to go further West, that they erred in so doing; and we are the more convinced that such is the fact, from having seen and heard of a number of persons, who had been to Louisiana and Texas and "located," but becoming satisfied that Florida afforded better advantages to the planter, have returned and settled in our state.

FLORIDA—CLIMATE, SOIL, AND PRODUCTIONS OF.—It is not merely in the tropical productions that East Florida possesses advantages over every other state in the Union; it is now established, beyond a doubt, that the Sea Island or long staple cotton (the production of which has heretofore been confined to a few small islands in South Carolina and Georgia) will grow luxuriantly even in the very centre of the peninsula. A superior quality of this article has been produced extensively on the Suwanee, and in the very centre of Alachua as well as on the eastern coast. This important fact is, no doubt, attributable to the almost *insular* position of East Florida.

The importance which the production of this valuable staple must give to East Florida, will be duly estimated, when it is considered that it can be cultivated there without the fear of *competition*. The few islands in South Carolina and Georgia which yield this staple are now so nearly worn out, that the average product per acre does not exceed one hundred and fifty pounds; and there is no other portion of the United States, with the exception of East Florida, where it can be produced. Neither can it be produced in Texas, Egypt, or India; and it is more than probable that there is in no part of the world a country of much extent so well adapted, both in climate and soil, to the production of this staple as East Florida.

The cultivation of this valuable staple in East Florida is well worthy the attention of planters in general, but especially of those southern planters who are wasting their energies in the profitless production of the common short-staple cotton, which competition has already reduced to so low a price.

Although the lands of East Florida, which yield on the average three hundred pounds of Sea Island cotton, six hundred pounds of Cuba tobacco, and two thousand pounds of sugar per acre, can at this time be purchased at much lower price than the common agricultural lands of the northern and middle states, or the common short-staple cotton lands of the South, it is not in the nature of things that such can long be the case. It is quite certain, that as soon as the character of these lands becomes generally known, they will sell at a price corresponding with their intrinsic value, which, as has already been shown, is greater than any other lands in the United States.

Besides coffee, cocoa, sugar, Sea Island cotton, Cuba tobacco, rice, indigo, arrowroot, cochineal cactus, silk, Sisal hemp, New-Zealand flax, oranges, lemons, limes, pineapples, olives, grapes, and other fruits and staples too numerous to detail, East Florida produces corn, potatoes, turnips, cabbages, and, in short, all the vegetables that are known in the northern states.

The climate of Florida does not allow corn to be planted so *close* as in the northern states, and there are not, therefore, so many bushels produced to the acre. The good lands in the interior ordinarily produce from thirty to forty bushels per acre, without the aid of manure of any kind: and it is doubtful whether the best corn lands in New-York would produce more under similar culture. Much more might, no doubt, be accomplished by the people of Florida with the aid of manure, rotation of crops, and judicious culture; and it is to be hoped that they will resort to these expedients to preserve the fertility of their lands from deterioration.

With regard to roots, it requires the whole of their summer in the northern states to produce a single crop. In Florida, on the contrary, a crop of Irish potatoes, and a crop of sweet potatoes or yams, can, with great facility, be produced on the same land within the year. If Florida cannot rival the North in the amount of the production of Irish potatoes per acre in a single crop, she accomplishes at least as much by producing two crops within the year on the same land, one crop being planted in January, and the other in July. But admitting that Florida is inferior to the North in the production of *Irish* potatoes, she has still the sweet potato or yam, (a more valuable root,) which ordinarily produces as much per acre as the Irish potato yields in the North.

There is no soil and climate better adapted to the production of turnips and ruta bagas than those of East Florida. It is common to see turnips of eight pounds weight growing in poor, sandy soil. East Florida certainly surpasses the North in the production of turnips and ruta bagas, both as to the amount per acre and the size and quality of the roots.

With very little care and attention, East Florida enjoys every delicacy of vegetable culture at all seasons of the year. Beets, onions, egg-plants, carrots, lettuce, celery, cauliflowers, &c., of a superior size and quality, are produced with the most indifferent culture. Water-melons, cantelopes, pumpkins, cucumbers, and, in short, everything that grows upon vines, come to great perfection in East Florida.

But these are subjects of minor consideration, which serve to convey but a feeble idea of the importance which its geographical position, its climate, and its soil, give to East Florida. The vast amount of soil in the peninsula capable of producing Sea Island cotton, Cuba tobacco, and sugar-cane, (all objects of human consumption, of the most importance not only to the consumer but to the whole country,) and its fine adaptation of climate to their successful production, must form the basis of a degree of prosperity far surpassing that enjoyed by any of the states north of her.

The great advantages to be derived from the culture of the orange, lemon, and lime, in East Florida, is a subject little known or appreciated out of the state. It presents a field for profitable enterprise unequaled in the United States. "The insect," which for eight years had desolated the beautiful groves of these fruits, which adorned the banks of the St. John's, is rapidly disappearing, and the trees are assuming, once more, their healthy vigor and beautiful verdure. The crop of fruit this year, I understand, promises to be an abundant one.

There is no culture in the world by which the foundation for an independent income can be laid, at the expense of so small an outlay, as the culture of the orange and lemon in East Florida. The method of establishing groves, by transplanting the sour orange trees from the hammocks, where they abound in the wild state,—and which has been in successful practice for several years,—is of great importance, in the first place, because it does away with the difficulty and expense of procuring sweet trees; and in the second place, because the sour trees planted and budded will bear much sooner than sweet trees from a nursery.

The sour trees may be dug up carefully in the hammocks at any time from October to June. They should be topped about four feet from the ground, and carefully planted and watered. In about three months, shoots large enough to be budded will grow out. The buds are taken from sweet trees, and carefully inserted into the young shoots, just as peach-trees are budded at the North. It is common for trees to bear the sweet orange in eighteen months from the budding. If the sour trees are selected from the hammock, of good size, (and they can be found at all sizes,) in three years they will be competent to bear a thousand oranges each, and will go on every year increasing in size and production.

This culture is well adapted to persons of small capital, whose health requires a residence in Florida. A suitable piece of land is easily obtained, on which provision can be raised, and an extensive grove established, at a very moderate expense. But to farmers and planters this culture presents also advantages over those of any other southern state; for, without interfering at all with their agricultural operations, they can, gradually and without the outlay of a dollar, plant an orange grove that may ultimately yield more than all their other productions.

The longevity of the orange tree is another thing which invests it with a more permanent character than common fruit trees. It lives and flourishes to a very advanced age. There are orange trees now living in the city of Rome that are known to be more than

three hundred years old! So that an orange grove, when once established, will not only last a man's life-time, but become a valuable inheritance for his children.

FLORIDA.—Sugar Lands of Florida.—In passing the Withlacoochee, in Benton county, we must not fail to notice the large sulphur and iron springs not over a mile from the large hammock we have left (Ten-Mile Creek hammock), and not more than two from the small one on the south side of the river. From these springs to the Crystal River, a distance of ten miles, there are but two small hammocks, and they are not of sufficient size to attract much attention from the sugar planter.

On Crystal River (the most beautiful probably in Florida) there is land enough, it is said, for about four plantations. The land is similar in character, although thought not to be of the first quality, with that of the coast lands before described.

The river is formed by a lake of springs—is wide and deep, and is but eight miles long. A high rolling pine country makes down to its head, and in view of its crystal springs, its lakes and islands, its evergreen woods, its Indian and shell mounds, its high shell islands at its mouth, its harbor and bay, its fish, oysters and turtle, it certainly is a most beautiful and desirable place. There are no planters upon this river.

Between the Crystal and Homossassa rivers, a distance of six miles, it is a prairie, with the exception of one or two hammocks, one of which is owned by the state. It is a question if this prairie would not be a fine sugar land, and the most of it easily brought under cultivation.

The Homossassa is another spring river, about ten miles long, wide enough for steamboats, with rocky islands, shell islands, bayous, cross rivers and salt rivers enough for a person residing upon it to lose his way even in the daytime. It is beautiful, nevertheless, and a person would hardly be satisfied after a month's exploration It abounds in fish, and near it there are fine oysters. On its northern bank there is land enough probably for three or four sugar plantations; and, on the south side the hammock, is about three miles deep, and extends to the Chisewitska River, six miles. Some of these lands are rocky, and this is made an objection to them; but although it may be more difficult to cultivate, yet the crop of corn, potatoes, pumpkins and turnips, and the patches of cane, show that the rocks do not interfere with their growth.

There are three plantations upon this river, but no sugar crop has yet been made. About sixty acres of cane have been planted this year, but it is intended mostly for seed, we presume.

It should be observed that vessels can find safe anchorage off the mouths of these rivers, and there will be but little difficulty in getting the produce to market if once made.

The Chisewitska is another spring river, and is about ten miles long. Most of the lands upon this river, it is thought, will require draining. The hammock upon it extends south, so far as has been surveyed, two miles.

The next twelve miles south to the Weekaiwachee, or Spring C. R., are not much known, as no settlements were made between the two, and there has been no survey. Immediately east of this is the Annuttiliga hammock, containing nearly forty square miles of hammock. This might be termed in Florida "up country;" but I notice it, as no part of this hammock is over sixteen miles from barge navigation on the rivers Chisewitska and Weekaiwachee, and neither river over ten miles long.

This hammock is well dotted around with permit claims, but the majority of those who have settled had not the means to plant extensively, and located there on account of the prospective value of the land. The remainder, with the exception of some few tracts purchased, has been located by the state.

Many remark that the Annuttiliga and Chocochata country is as fine and as desirable as any in the state; and if we think rich lands, a high rolling country and beautiful places for residences a desideratum, it should certainly claim as much attention as any part with which I am acquainted.

Chocochata hammock will not probably claim much attention from sugar planters, although the average distance from the Weekaiwachee River would not be upwards of fifteen miles.

On the Weekaiwachee River there are good lands, but they are mostly unsurveyed. This is another spring river, rising in the high rolling country, about two miles long, and emptying into the Gulf. South of Weekaiwachee there are no rich lands north of Tampa Bay, a distance of fifty miles, with the exception of one or two small hammocks; but it is a very desirable country for raising stock. My estimate of the lands adapted to sugar culture, in Benton county, is seventy-five square miles unoccupied. This, with the amount in Levy county, will make two hundred square miles.

I have not estimated in this the small detached hammocks, nor any pine lands that may be used profitably for this crop. I have mentioned sugar, as I believe it will be the principal product of this section of the country, most of which is further south than Lake George, and a portion below Lake Monroe. These lands are as well adapted to cotton, corn and tobacco, as any other in the South.

The state owns most of these lands. What is the best course to pursue to have them settled and to enhance their value ? I propose to consider this in a future communication.

FIRES—Statistics of.—In every city in the Union, the fire department has come to be of leading importance, and comprises the most active, energetic, and valuable citizens. They are a surety to our property and our lives—the watchmen who snuff the first approaches of danger.

It is true that their institution is of modern date. Other ages had little of the kind. The conflagration raged at will, and mocked the undisciplined efforts of mere crowds, awing them into blind dismay or stupid resignation !

The fire or forcing engine is ascribed to the inventive genius of Ptolemy Philadelphus. It is supposed the Romans were acquainted with some such invention, for the letter of Pliny to Trajan complains that Nicomedia was destroyed by a neglect in using it. The ancients, however, must have made little use of the engine, since it is ascribed as the independent invention of a German. In 1518, it was used in Augsburg, Germany. Engines began to be built in 1657 extensively by Hantsch, and were introduced into Paris, 1699. These were very rude, and it was long after that the air chamber was appended. Small engines of this construction, weighing sixteen pounds, and carried by one man, threw a jet of water thirty feet, and this was the model ! The hose was invented by two Dutchmen at Amsterdam, and it is said that before its introduction the city lost 1,024,130 florins in ten years, and afterwards but 18,355 florins in five years, by fire. Mr. Perkins added the rivets, instead of seams. Of the subsequent impovement in the engine, the text has sufficiently spoken.

It would be a very interesting paper that traced the history of great fires in our own and foreign countries. What extraordinary statistics of ruin, death, misery, and devastation ! Our friend has referred to several instances, but what are they ; the frightful losses that have thus been sustained, who can chronicle ?

Professor Olmstead, of Yale College, we have learned, has collected together many interesting materials upon this head, in the design, perhaps, of contributing a volume to the press. The facts and inferences may have much practical value. We regret our inability to communicate with the professor, who might have furnished some interesting hints for our note.

It would not be difficult to determine with some degree of accuracy the annual losses which are sustained in the United States by fires, and the whole expenses of the fire department. In many of the cities records are kept. The books of insurance companies will show how much they are called upon to pay, and some estimate may be made of the ratio of insured and uninsured. Statistics of this sort would be of great value to our insurance companies, and we marvel that some one has not collected and arranged them in a permanent form.

Having fallen into something like this train of thought, it occurred to us that an hour or two might be spent, not unprofitably, in calling to mind some of these noted catastrophes which have befallen mankind. Of course it would require volumes to go back very far.

The great fire of London comes in first, and has furnished Mr. Ainsworth the groundwork of an interesting romance. Much of mystery hangs over it. Houses, towers, palaces, and temples were reduced to ashes at a blast. Two-thirds of the capital of Europe lay smouldering ! 200,000 inhabitants fled to the fields to make their beds or collect their scattered and miserable rags !

However, we must be satisfied with a glance at the losses of the past fifteen or twenty years, for these are more within memory. They show that even yet, with all our art and science, the despot reign of fire has not been checked, but mocks and baffles the impotent efforts of man.

In the memory of almost every reader, are many terrible conflagrations. We shall introduce some of the more notable of those which have occurred since 1833 in our own country and abroad, taking no notice of the thousands of minor losses.

In 1833, two tremendous and unparalleled fires swept over Constantinople within a week of each other, destroying, the one 2,500, and the other 850 houses !

In 1835, a great fire destroyed 50 or 60 houses in Charleston, S.C., and the famous old church of St. Philip, consecrated by so many memories of olden time.

In 1835, 15th December, the memorable 15th—a little spark performed its mission, and fifty two acres, closely and compactly built, of great and towering houses and stores were swept away in New-York—648 buildings ! Who will forget the dismay and ruin—Eighteen Millions of Dollars in a few hours—the earnings of years of toil and enterprise are gone for ever, and beggars created by thousands !

But we have no time for these reflections. With some pains and labor we have collected together the chief fires that occurred between the years 1836, and September, 1846, ten years. Such of them where the loss is under $50,000 we omit; and it is probable many have escaped our observation, we mean in our own country, for it is to this we particularly confine ourself, where the loss has been greatly more.

STATISTICS OF FIRES.

1836—Bowery Theatre, New-York, burnt; loss $100,000
" Fire in Quebec, 16 buildings 300,000
" TEA WAREHOUSES, LONDON 1,800,000
" Washington Post-Office, Patent Office; all models, &c.; loss not given—at least, we suppose 500,000
" All fires in Boston together this year 151,000
" St. John's, New-Brunswick, 150 buildings; loss not given; could not have been less than $2,000 the building 300,000
" London, all fires this year 2,400,000
1837—Bowery Theatre, N. Y., third time 75,000
1838—CHARLESTON ONE-THIRD DESTROYED, 1,200 houses; insurance companies break 4,000,000
" Nantucket 150,000
" Hudson, N. Y. 200,000
" Boston, 1829....128 fires .. $112,000
" 1830.... 85 " 58,000
" 1831.... 51 " 34,000
" 1832....133 " 54,000
" 1833....144 " 94,000
" 1834....103 " 38,000
" 1835....155 " 200,000
" 1836....208 " 151,000
" 1837....136 " 167,000

9 yrs. 1,143 900,000 900,000
Insurance effected $470,000
1838—Mobile, 100,000 100,000
1839—Port Gibson, Miss., $300,000; Eastport, Maine, half the property of town, $24,000; Cincinnati, $40,000; St. Johns, N. B., $800,000; St. Louis, extensive fire, say $100,000; New-York, theatres, churches, &c., $400,000; Natchez, $70,000; PHILADELPHIA FIRE, $1,500,000; New-York, $1,000,000; Aiken, S. C., $80,000; MOBILE, awful fire, 500 BUILDINGS; loss of property not given; we estimate $1,000,000; another, 11 squares, $120,000 5,424,000
" CONSTANTINOPLE, 5,000 HOUSES 23,000,000
" Prussia, $500,000, Quibdo, on Spanish main, merchandise alone $1,000,000—other property perhaps $500,000 more; Chicago, 19 buildings, value perhaps $80,000; Newton, N. Y., $70,000 2,150,000
" In the month of October, this year, there were no less than 24 fires, and $4,000,000 property destroyed in the United States!
1840—New-York, $500,000; Yazoo, Mississippi, half the town burnt—loss not stated, must have been at least $300,000; steamer Lexington, 200 lives lost on the Sound; New-York, $1,000,000; Wilmington, N. C., ONE-THIRD OF THE TOWN, 500 buildings, $500,000; New-Orleans, St. Louis Exchange, and other property, over $2,000,000; Louisville, Ky., $300,000; New-Orleans, $300,000; Penn Yan, N. Y., $80,000; Louisville, several fires, $70,000 5,050,000
" Salenchez, Switzerland, 250 houses, all but four on fire; 100 lives lost .. 1,000,000
" San Fernando, Cuba, ENTIRELY DESTROYED, estimated 1,000,000

23

1841—New-York, $355,000; Georgetown, S. C., $500,000; New-York, $200,000; St. Johns, N. B., vessels and buildings, $1,200,000; Harrisburg, ENTIRELY DESTROYED, say $500,000 .... $2,755,000
" TOWER OF LONDON BURNT, built by James II., 300,000 stand of arms in it; value unknown, suppose 3,000,000
" ONE-THIRD OF SMYRNA DESTROYED, 10,000 houses, 40 persons killed, 20,000 destitute; loss unknown, suppose 6,000,000
1842—Baton Rouge, La., $100,000; Detroit, Michigan, $150,000 250,000
" In the four years preceding this, there were in London, 2,464 fires, 300 being by bad fire-places, 386 by candles.
" New-York, 40 or 50 houses, unknown, suppose $500,000; Columbia, S. C., $200,000; Norwich, Conn., $100,000; Boston, year to 1st Sept., $93,000; Philadelphia, year to 1st June, $362,000, 189 alarms in all; American theatre, New-Orleans, loss not known, say $100,000; Richmond, $800,000; Morrisville, Indiana, town nearly destroyed, say $200,000; New-York, $250,000 1,885,000
" HAMBURG, GERMANY, FOUR DAYS' FIRE—61 streets, 120 lanes, 1,992 houses, 498 small houses, 468 cellars, 3 churches, 300,000 volumes, 4,000 machine models; fire seen 100 miles; total loss estimated over 30,000,000
" Koseger, Germany, 179 houses, unknown, suppose 1,000,000
" Kamenz, Germany, nearly destroyed, suppose 500,000
" Liverpool, great warehouse 2,700,000
" Rheinback, Germany, half destroyed, suppose 500,000
1843—Newbern, N. C., $100,000; Tallahassee, Fla., $500,000, EVERY STORE AND SHOP; Fall River, $400,000; Valparaiso, Chili, $915,000; Baltimore, whole year, 153 fires, say $100,000; Boston, whole year, $140,000 2,155,000
" Mimordia, France, town destroyed, suppose 600,000
" Kingston, Jamaica, 1,340 HOUSES, besides out-houses; loss not stated, must be at least 2,000,000
1844—New-Orleans cotton press and cotton 700,000
" Canton, China, 1,500 HOUSES; loss not stated, must be 5,000,000
" Resched, Persia, DESTROYED 2,500,000
" New-York, whole year to 1st Aug., $78,000 in buildings, $173,000 in furniture, &c.; in 1843, it was $72,000 by first and $173,000 by last 500,000
" Guadaloupe 1,000,000
" Ship and cargo, New-Orleans 120,000
1845—GREAT PITTSBURGH FIRE — 22 squares, 1,000 houses, a mile of surface, one-third of city, 56 acres of buildings 3,479,950
" Pittsburgh, 30 to 40 buildings }
" New-York, 100 buildings } 500,000
" QUEBEC, GREAT FIRE—1,630 houses, 46 human beings destroyed ....
" St. Johns, N. B. 300,000
" Mantanzas, Cuba 1,200,000
" Fayetteville, N. C., IN RUINS 500,000
" Quebec, ANOTHER GREAT FIRE two months after last, 2,000 houses; losses by both fires 8,000,000
" New-London, Conn., $500,000; Barbadoes, W. I., $2,000,000 2,500,000

1845—GREAT FIRE IN NEW-YORK, 546 buildings $6,000,000
" New-York, $100,000 100,000
" Another GREAT FIRE IN SMYRNA—one mile and a half of town destroyed; loss, estimate 2,000,000
" Canton, China, 1,259 PERSONS DESTROYED by the burning of theatre.
" Bordeaux, France, in Brandy 600,000
1846—Theatre, Quebec, 50 lives; La Prairie, Canada, $250,000 250,000
In three months, 1845, the losses in U. S. by fire were $15,000,000!

Total in 10 years $137,362,950

Thus, from an imperfect view of a period of ten years, hurriedly collected, and taken only from important points, regardless of thousands of minor losses, we have *one hundred and thirty millions of dollars* in property and effects, committed to the devouring element. But this cannot be supposed more than half the truth, considering Europe, Asia, and America, throughout all this period, and taking into account the smaller losses, and that immense class of losses not noticed at all in our calculations, viz.: those which grow out of the interruption of trade, etc., etc. We have, then, in a fair estimate, $275,000,000. *Two hundred and seventy-five millions of dollars* lost to the world from 1836 to 1846, by the ravages of fire alone—an average of $27,000,000 a year! sufficient to pay all the expenses of the American government in the same time; equal to the whole foreign commerce of the United States for one year; one fifth of the whole annual product of the United States in agriculture, manufactures and commerce; more than our whole banking capital from Maine to Louisiana; sufficient to purchase the absolute necessaries of life one year for all the inhabitants of the Union; double the cost of all the railroads in our country; more than the total of all state indebtedness! Who shall limit the ravages of this amazing influence.

It will be observed of the catalogue of fires before given, that $37,000,000 of loss occurred in our country, being an average of $3,700,000 a year, which might be considered a fair average calculation annually for every period of ten years. Now, when it is considered, as before remarked, what numerous losses, direct and indirect, have not been chronicled by us; to which, were the whole expense of the fire department added, and all expenses of engines and machinery, and police, the average loss by fire during the last ten years will not be rated lower than $8,000,000 or $9,000,000 annually, and the average losses for years to come not less than $5,000,000 or $6,000,000, an amount sufficient to carry on the railroad proposed from Lake Michigan to the Pacific Ocean, as fast as labor could urge it!

In the tables we have given it must be regarded extraordinary that fires have, as it were, a contagious character, and occur at times almost simultaneously in different parts of the country, and often in the same place. Thus, we have two vast conflagrations in 1832 in Constantinople; two great fires in 1839 in Mobile, within a few days of each other; $9,000,000 of loss in the single month of October, 1839, in different parts of the Union; two enormous fires in Quebec, 1845, almost the same month, and in three months, in the United States, in 1845, upward of 13 or 14 millions of dollars destroyed! In cities, too, certain districts appear to be fated. We have known a square burnt three times to the ground in four or five years. Doubtless these are not all remarkable coincidences and inscrutable providences. The hand of man is not always idle!

The great fire of London is said to have been predicted long before by zealous soothsaying enthusiasts, and occurred almost in the terms of the prediction.

But this interesting subject we must leave to the reader. It is capable of great extension, and we should be pleased if some one would resume it in our pages. For example, could we have the statistics of losses by fire since the Revolution, or in the history of our great cities, the loss of life, etc., how interesting and valuable this may be, and then the results of insurance companies, the losses and profits, the fire department, the fires at sea and by lightning—what a wide subject is there here.

GEORGIA* — SITUATION, BOUNDARIES, SOIL, PRODUCTIONS, MINERALS, RESOURCES, &c., &c.—Georgia extends from the Blue Ridge Mountains, on the north, to the Okeefenokee Swamp on the south, and from the Chattahoochee River on the west, to the Savannah on the east. From South Carolina, on the east, it is separated by a line running from the mouth of the Savannah River up that stream to the confluence of Tugaloo and Keowee, and thence along the most northern branch of the Tugaloo until it intersects the northern boundaries of South Carolina. From North Carolina and Tennessee on the north, it is separated by a line commencing on a summit of the Blue Ridge, where the same is crossed by the 35th degree of north latitude, and terminating at Nickajack. From Alabama, on the west, it is separated by the Chattahoochee, running from its southern boundary up to a position near West Point, and then by a line running thence directly to Nickajack. Several attempts have been made by commissioners to settle the line between Georgia and Florida on the south. All attempts at a definite settlement have, as yet, failed. This

* "Statistics of the State of Georgia," by George White

line, however, is somewhere near a direct course from the mouth of the Flint River to the source of the St. Mary's, thence along that stream to the point where it empties into the ocean.

Georgia is situated between 30° 21′ 39′, and 35° north latitude, and 81° and 84° 53′ 38″ west longitude from Greenwich, and 3° 46′ and 7° 39′ 26″ west longitude from Washington City.

Its length from north to south is........272 miles.
Its breadth from east to west is..........256 "
Square miles........................63,397½ "
Acres..........................40,574,400 "

"No state in the Union presents a richer field for the geologist than Georgia. With a territory embracing the southern extremity of the great Atlantic chain of mountains, extending across them to the N. W. into the valley of the Mississippi, running to the S. W. into the cretaceous slope of the Gulf of Mexico, and occupying along its eastern boundary a wide belt of territory, it contains most of the important geological formations.

"Commencing at the Atlantic Ocean, and spreading out from 100 to 150 miles to the west, an extensive plain of a *tertiary formation* rises from the level of the sea, and gradually swells up to a height of about 500 feet, at a line passing near the head of navigation of the rivers Savannah, Ogeechee, Oconee, and Ocmulgee, where it meets a primary formation. Between the Ocmulgee and Flint rivers it leaves the primary formation to the right, and rests on the cretaceous from a point nearly midway between Macon and Knoxville, by a line running in a S. W. direction to another point between Petanla Creek and Fort Gaines on the Chattahoochee river.

"Bounded by the last mentioned line to the S. E., and by the southern edge of the primary, as indicated by the heads of navigation in the Flint and Chattahoochee rivers, the *cretaceous* formation extends from Alabama into Georgia, forming an acute triangle. The *primary*, or non-fossiliferous, bounded on the east by the tertiary and cretaceous formations, as described above, crosses the state from N. E. to S. W., with a width of 160 miles at the northern limit, and 100 at the southern. The Blue Ridge range of mountains passes near its western edge, and forms the most elevated land of the state, varying in height from 1,200 to 4,000 feet. From this crest there is a gradual descent to the east, by a series of parallel and undulating ridges, until the tertiary plain is reached. On the west the descent is much more precipitous. The western boundary of the primary is not very accurately established, but is believed to be not far from a line running nearly north and south through the centre of Gilmer county, and continued in the same direction to near Canton, in Cass county; thence to the western base of the Allatoona Mountain on the Etowah River, where it turns to the S. W., and, passing near Van Wert, in Paulding county, and along the northern base of the Dugdown Mountain to the Alabama line.

"The north-west part of the state, bounded to the east and south by the western limit of the primary, consists of a *transition*, or older fossiliferous formation, except the extreme N. W. corner, where the *carboniferous* occurs."—*White's Statistics*, pp. 14 and 15.

Georgia embraces every variety of soil, climate and productions. While the inhabitants of Southern and Middle Georgia are being parched with heat, frequently so intense as to prevent comfortable rest, even at night, the more northern climate, among the mountains, is such as to render necessary a blanket in order to comfortable repose by sleep. The sky is of a deep blue, and it is said by those who know, that a more lovely heaven does not smile upon the classic land of Italia than upon the highly favored inhabitants of Georgia. The light sandy soil of the cordon of islets which border the sea-coast of this state produces the fine and valuable description of cotton known as the "Sea Island." In the south are the tide swamp lands producing immense quantities of rice. The soil of these lands vary as they are situated upon the sea-shore, or upon larger or smaller rivers. On the Savannah they are very extensive, and are cultivated more than twenty miles from the brackish marsh up the river, and are considered the most valuable lands in the state. Next to these lands are those on the Altamaha River, which, in width, are equal to those of the Savannah. They do not extend from the marshes up more than sixteen miles. Beyond this, the freshets render them valueless, except for timber. Their soil has more of vegetable mould than the lands on the Savannah, and they are more easily cultivated. Their products are rice, black-seed cotton, Indian corn, and sugar-cane. Next come the tide lands of the Ogeechee, extending ten miles up from the marshes, which produce rice, but are not very well adapted to cotton. The tide lands of the great St. Illa are not as broad as the others, but are productive and fertile twenty miles up from the marshes, yielding good crops of rice and cotton. They are not so much liable to freshets as some others.

The inland swamp lands produce abundantly, but unless there be contiguous a reservoir of water, the produce is uncertain. Black-seed cotton is produced on the oak lands adjoining the inland swamps, though these lands are said to be of inferior quality. About sixty or seventy miles from the coast begin the pine lands, or, as they are some times called, "the pine barrens," which have heretofore been chiefly valuable for the immense quantity of timber which has been annually prepared for market. Within a short time past the attention of people has been turned to the manufacture of tar, pitch and turpentine, from the pines growing on these lands, and the time is at hand when these pine barrens will not afford the least source of wealth and prosperity to the citizens of Georgia. The middle region of the state contains land of a red, loamy soil, producing tobacco, cotton, and all the grains. It was once very productive, but owing to the system of cultivation adopted by our planters who have raised upon it year after year, with scarce any intermission, large crops of cotton, it has become, in many counties, much impoverished. Large gullies, and red barren hill-sides, often greet the eye in places which were once as fertile as any under the sun. Our planters are becoming awake to the folly of their past course, and hill-side ditching, manuring, and a judicious rotation in crops, together with occasional rest to the land, is doing much to restore the soil to its virgin fertility. Much still remains to be accomplished, and he who will do most towards setting the example of improving our land, will be our greatest benefactor. We now have our yearly agricultural State Fair, which is doing a great deal to stimulate our planters to an honorable emulation in producing upon Georgia soil, in the largest quantities, every thing needful to our peace, prosperity and happiness.

We cannot agree with our author in the assertion that the lands in the south-western part of the state, between the Chattahoochee and Flint rivers, "are of inexhaustible fertility." Our observation, which is confirmed by the assurance of many intelligent and respectable planters, teaches us, that although these lands when first cleared are very productive, they are not very durable. Being of a light, sandy soil, they produce fine crops of cotton, and sometimes sugar-cane, for a few years, and then become exhausted, when resort must be had to improvements to render them fertile again. These lands are cheaper in proportion to their fertility than any others in Georgia.

Let us turn now to the most interesting part of the state, known as Cherokee Georgia. This is in the north. The valleys here are exceedingly rich, producing wheat, corn, Irish potatoes, beans, peas, onions, &c. In some places cotton is extensively raised, but the crop is not so certain as in other parts of the state. This part of the territory of Georgia is peculiarly a grain country, so far as the valleys are concerned, while the mountains yield the more valuable minerals, gold, iron, marble, granite, lime-stone, &c. The land here is more costly than in any other part of the state, ranging from ten to thirty dollars per acre, while in south-western Georgia lands of equal fertility range from three to ten dollars per acre. The difference in the price is traceable to the fact that the lands of Cherokee Georgia are much more durable than those in the south-western part of the state—it being the fact, that in the former portion there is land which was cultivated by the Indian before the white man's axe ever echoed back from the hills the sound of the march of civilization, which now produces from fifty to seventy-five bushels per acre. Cherokee Georgia is not the place to raise cotton, but it is to be the granary and the work-shop of the balance of the state. Its fields will produce corn to feed the operatives who are to direct its water-power in manufacturing the cotton which is raised in the more southern parts of the state, and in digging out from the bowels of the earth the minerals which are to regulate the inland commerce, and form the implements of husbandry, life and peace, and, in case of necessity, of war, death and destruction.

Mr. White says, "In the country bordering on the Savannah River, as far up as Elbert, and extending across to Broad River, the land, though long cultivated, is still productive; and we know of bodies of land in this section of the state, particularly in Oglethorpe county, which have been cultivated for more than half a century, and which still produce 700 and 800 pounds of cotton to the acre." P. 38.

Our author enumerates upwards of fifty streams in the state of Georgia which deserve and wear the name of rivers. A very cursory glance at the map of the state will show that her water resources are immense. The streams of this state alone, which pour the volume of their waters from the mountain springs into the bosom of the Atlantic and the Gulf, would supply sufficient power in the eligible sites, to manufacture all the cotton grown in the world, or to grind all the grain produced in Uncle Sam's wide dominions. In addition to this, the Savannah, the Altamaha, the Oconee, the Ocmulgee, the St. Mary's, the Ogeechee, the Flint, the Chattahooche, the Coosa, and various others, bear upon their bosoms steamboats, sloops, cotton, and flat-boats, laden with the productions of Georgia soil, and going to swell the tide of commerce upon which depend the wealth, power and prosperity of our nation.

Mr. White has in his book some interesting extracts from the MSS. of the late Col. Benjamin Hawkins, many years agent of the United States Government in its transactions with the Creek Indians, formerly residing in this state. We give the following in reference to the origin of this tribe, as being most interesting:

"The origin of the name Creek is uncertain. The tradition is, that it was given by white people, from the number of creeks and water-courses in the country. The Indian name is Muscogee. The Creeks came from the West. They have a tradition among them that there is, in the Fork of the Red River, west of the Mississippi, two mounds of earth; that at this place the Cussetuhs, Conetuhs and Chickasaws found themselves; that being distressed by wars with red people, they crossed the Mississippi, and directing their course eastwardly, they crossed the falls of Tallapoosa above Tookaubatche, settled below the falls of Chattahoochee, and spread out from thence to Ocmulgee, Oconee, Savannah, and down on the sea-coast towards Charleston. Here they first saw white people, and from thence they have been compelled to retire back again to their present settlements."—P. 28.

"According to the census of 1840, the population of Georgia amounted to

210,634 white persons, males.
197,161 white persons, females.
1,374 free colored persons, males,
1,379 free colored persons, females.
139,335 slaves, males.
141,609 slaves, females.

Total...691,492

"Of this number 574 are computed to be engaged in mining, 209,383 in agriculture, 2,428 in commerce, 7,984 in manufactures and trades, 262 in navigation of the seas, 352 in navigation of canals, lakes and rivers, 1,250 in the liberal professions."

COMPARATIVE VIEW OF THE POPULATION FOR FIFTY-FIVE YEARS.

1790.	1800.	1810.	1820.
82,548	162,686	252,433	344,773
1830.	1840.	1845.	1850.
516,823	691,392	774,325	920,000

The Central Rail-road is the longest in Georgia. It connects Savannah with Macon, being 190 miles and 3,900 feet in length. The experimental survey of this route was first made in 1834, under the direction of Col. Cruger, at the cost of the city of Savannah. In 1836, the company was formed, and preparations made for commencing the work without delay. The road was completed to Macon on the 15th of October, 1843.

The work on this road is done in a superior manner. The arrangements for the comfort of passengers are surpassed by few roads in the United States.

The conductors, some of whom have been in the service of the company since its commencement, have acquired an enviable reputation for their courtesy and attention to the passengers. R. R. Cuyler is President of the road, and L. O. Reynolds, Chief Engineer.

The Milledgeville and Gordon Rail-road was chartered in 1847, and organized the same year. It is now in progress of completion, and will probably be finished during the present year. The work has not progressed with that rapidity which has characterized similar works in other parts of the state. The road is only 17¼ miles long, and should have been finished long ago. To the discredit, however, of some of the wealthy capitalists of Baldwin county, who could have sped the work on with the assistance of a little finger only, it has been suffered to labor on under great disadvantages and many doubts as to its final completion. No doubt now remains that it will be finished this year, however.

The Georgia Rail-road is 171 miles long, connecting Augusta with Atlanta. The charter was granted in 1833, and amended in 1835. A portion of the road was put in operation on the 1st of November, 1837, and was finished to Atlanta on the 15th of September, 1845. The whole cost of the road, and its equipments up to April 1st, 1849, has been $3,551,975. John P. King, Esq., is the President.

The Macon and Western Rail-road was chartered in 1833, under the name of the Monroe Rail-road and Banking Company. In 1835 the company was organized, and the work commenced. The road was first chartered from Macon to Forsyth, in Monroe county. In 1836, by an amendment of the charter, the company was authorized to extend the road in a westerly direction, to some point on the Chattahoochee River, between Alabama and Georgia. The company went forward with the work and with banking, too fast for their means, so that by the time the road reached Griffin, in Pike county, there was a grand blow up, and the road was finally sold, in 1845, under a decree of court, for $155,000. At the session of the legislature for this year, the purchase was confirmed, and a change to its present name granted to the road. The work was pressed forward with vigor and energy, and the total cost of the road to its present owners has been about $628,091. Daniel Tyler, Esq., is the President. In 1847 the legislature conferred upon the present company all the privileges of the old one, except banking privileges. The right to construct a road from Griffin to West Point, a village built on both sides of the Chattahoochee River, was also given.

The public are aware that the trains of this road have been run with a regularity unsurpassed by any rail-road in the United States; and the President of the Company, in his report for the last year, says: "The entire credit of which is due to the superior skill and management of Mr. Emerson Foote, the general superintendent."

The South-Western Rail-road is to connect the city of Macon with some point on the Chattahoochee, to the south-west. It is also to connect with a contemplated rail-road from Pensacola,—meeting the South-Western at its terminus on the above river The charter was granted in 1845, and the company organized in 1847. The road has been nearly completed to Oglethorpe,—a new town which has sprung up at the present terminus of the road, so far as constructed, distant fifty-one miles from Macon. It is to be hoped that the work will be speedily prosecuted to its termination on the banks of the Chattahoochee.

The Western and Atlantic Rail-road, otherwise called the State Road, from its belonging to the state, commences in Atlanta, at the terminus of the Georgia Rail-road, before mentioned, and terminates in Chattanooga, in Tennessee. The most remarkable feature of this road is its tunnel through an arm of the Blue Ridge Mountains, running through the upper part of Georgia. This tunnel is 1,477 feet long, 18 feet in height, and 12 feet in width. It is one of the grandest achievements that grace the annals of the human family. It is cut in a great measure through solid rock. The lateral walls are of rock, six feet thick at the base, and five feet at the top. The approaches to the tunnel are protected on both sides by massive masonry. This road passes through a portion of the most interesting country in the world. The chief engineer, in his report of 1848, says:

"The watering-places along our line of road, and convenient to the same, are becoming very popular, and they may be expected to attract large crowds every summer, and thus contribute to swell the income of the road. Indeed not only these mineral and medicinal waters, but also the Saltpetre Cave near Kingston, the Tunnel beyond Dalton, the rich and varied scenery along our whole line, the mountainous ridges, the long fertile valleys and beautiful streams, together with the bold features around Chattanooga, are all objects to interest and attract summer visitants."—P. 93.

Since the above was written, we find in the Macon Journal and Messenger, a table of the rail-roads in the state.

		MILES.
1.	Central Road, from Savannah to Macon, completed	191
2.	Georgia Road, from Augusta to Atlanta, completed	171
3.	Macon and Western Road, from Macon to Atlanta	101
4.	Western and Atlantic Road, from Atlanta to Chattanooga	140
5.	South-western Road, from Macon to Oglethorpe, nearly completed	51
6.	Muscogee Road, from Columbus to Fort Valley, on South-western, in progress	71
7.	Atlanta and West Point Road, from Atlanta to West Point, in progress	85
8.	Milledgeville Road, from Gordon to Milledgeville, in progress	18
9.	Eatonton Road, from Milledgeville to Eatonton, in progress	22
10.	Wilkes Road, from Double Wells to Washington, in progress	18
11.	Athens Branch, from Union Point to Athens, completed	39
12.	Burke Road, from 80-mile Station on Central Road to Augusta, in progress	56
13.	Rome Branch Road, completed	17
	Total completed and in progress	980

The Journal has not taken into consideration the road in progress leading from Dalton to the Huvassee River, in East Tennessee, sometimes called the Hiwassee Branch Road, and sometimes the East Tennessee and Georgia Road. We do not know the exact length of this road, but believe it is over twenty miles within the limits of this state. So that in Georgia there are now completed, and in progress together, one thousand miles of rail-road! an amount of internal improvement of this kind unsurpassed, if we are correctly informed, by that of any other state in the Union, save New-York. An article devoted exclusively to internal improvements in Georgia, would be as interesting a chapter of exploits for the public good as could be anywhere found. Our citizens are making some experiments in plank roads; and others are only waiting the result of these experiments, if favorable, to go ahead in this department of internal improvements.

Mr. White says, speaking of canals: "The only works of this description in Georgia, are the Savannah, Ogeechee and Altamaha Canals, and the Augusta Canal, an account of which is given in this work. Turning to pp. 503–5, an interesting description is found of this canal, whose object is commerce, the affording of water to turn factories, mills, &c., &c. We would like to give a farther account of this canal, but our limits forbid us.

Revenues.—General tax, viz., capitation-tax on free white males, (from 21 to 60)—slaves—free persons of color—lawyers—physicians—factors and brokers—tax on land, per acre, according to its classification as to quality—on town lots, merchandise, ferries, toll-bridges and turnpikes, the returned value—on money at interest—capital of manufacturing companies—capital of banks of other states employed in this, and sales of merchandise by factors, amount returned—and on pleasure carriages and billiard tables, the number returned.

Net amount, 1848, about	$265,000
Tax on bank stock, special	19,300
Dividends on bank stock, "Education Fund," $262,300	19,250
Miscellaneous sources (say)	10,000
	$313,550

GEORGIA AND HER RESOURCES.

Her Population; Internal Improvements; Productions; Enterprise; Minerals; Manufactories; Mineral Springs.—It is an undeniable fact, that no state in the Union possesses, in so great a degree, the elements of national and individual wealth as Georgia. All that we need, is legislation looking to their development and the enterprise of a few public-spirited individuals to give direction to our energies. Our citizens want to feel *secure* from innovations in our institutions—they want no legislation which is designed as experiments to catch popular favor. Hence *relief* laws, the election of judges by the people, and all that class of demagogue-like measures, are only clogs which fetter public enterprise and deter the prudent, thoughtful, energetic man from embarking his capital and his labor in pursuits which add to the permanent prosperity, security and advancement of our state. We think there has been enough of the demagogue in Georgia already, working only mischief and ruin; and it is to be hoped that the intelligence and patriotism of older heads of all parties will unite to check innovation, and give security and permanency to our institutions and consequent fame and wealth to our people.

Georgia has always been a mighty workshop, in which her citizens have been operatives, whose labor has gone to build up and add to the wealth of other states. We have always needed capital to sustain the enterprise and to furnish the exchanges in the sale of our products. Hence other states have furnished us the money, and our people have sent their labor, in the shape of money, to pay to strangers dividends on their bank stock and interest on their advancements. This has been so much yearly taken from our pockets, we have been made so much the poorer, and strangers have been made so much the richer. A wise economy, therefore, says to our people, keep these dividends and interest at home to enrich yourselves. This can be done by increasing our banking capital. New banks should be established, and located at such points as their capital was needed. Macon, Columbus, Atlanta and Griffin, four of the most important interior commercial points in the state, have not a dollar of banking capital of their own. All the interest made upon advances to buy cotton and other produce, is paid to banking institutions in other cities and states, instead of being kept where it legitimately belongs, *where it is made*, and where it should stay, to help to build up its own community. The next legislature should create new banks at each one of these points, as well as increase the capital of those of the city of Savannah. This is the first step in the noble and patriotic scheme of developing the resources of the state. *It would be the taking care of what we made*—it would be *laboring for ourselves* and *not for strangers*. Thus far, Georgia has been only a great plantation for the benefit of the Charleston banks.

The completion of the Georgia, Central and Macon rail-roads, the partial completion of the Western and Atlantic road, has thus far stimulated the enterprise of our state, far beyond the most sanguine expectations of the advocates of those works. The completion of the state road to Chattanooga, the construction of a branch to Rome, and the improvement of the Coosa River, will pour the produce of Tennessee and North Alabama into our state. The construction of the south-western rail-road will give us the control of the entire products of our own state in that direction, that of Western Florida and of all Southern Alabama. The construction of the rail-road from Columbus eastward will give us the control of Middle Alabama. Through all these channels an immense amount of commerce must pour itself to enrich our state. Let us be prepared to meet it, and let not a want of *means* within our own state drive it into other markets in other states. *Georgia must appropriate her own improvements to the building up and enriching her own people.* These are some of the elements which must stimulate the enterprise of our people. But we have within ourselves elements of wealth far greater than any derived from foreign commerce.

The pine lands of the state, including one-sixth at least of all its territory, is now unproductive. That opens a vast field for enterprise. We consume annually many millions of pounds of wool, in coarse satinets, linseys, blankets, flannels and baizes. That wool may all be grown profitably there. Vermont finds her wool a source of immense profit. Her rigorous climate compels her to feed her sheep six months in the year; we need not feed them *two* months in the year. Why not, then, produce *all* the wool we use? and why not establish factories in the pine region, driven by steam power, to manufacture all the articles we need? Again, the finest beef range in the world is in the pine woods. Hides, tallow, beef, horns and bones, are items of great wealth to be drawn from that region. And no small item of commerce must be the production of turpentine itself. There is no business which promises such a return for the capital employed, as the raising of sheep and beef cattle and the making of turpentine. *Energy alone* is wanting to develop the immense resources of Georgia in this one respect.

We consume in Georgia annually some three millions of dollars worth of leather, shoes, saddles, harness, and other manufactures of leather. This might be supplied at home. In the middle and upper counties, within reach of the bark, tanneries might be established for the tanning of all the hides which are grown in the state; factories united for the production of shoes, harness, and the like, and thus this immense sum be saved at home. But more—we can and will manufacture for other states. This is a business which never can wear out; for, so long as the descendants of Adam have souls, they must have soles to their feet. A mistaken notion has prevailed, that our *climate* is not adapted to the manufacture of leather. The truth is, our tanneries have been hitherto erected by men of limited capital; they could neither afford to furnish the materials in proper quantities, nor could they afford to wait sufficiently long for the tanning of the leather. Hence the cry, *the climate don't suit*.

Georgia is the greatest cotton *growing* state in the Union, and she is destined to be the largest *manufacturing* state, because she can manufacture cheaper and as well as any other state. It costs at least twenty per cent. upon the price of the raw material to transport it from Macon, Ga. to Lowell, Mass. This is no small advantage to start with. Then, a given number of spindles can be put in operation *here*, with all necessary appendages, for much less cost than a like number can be put in operation in any of the northern states, because of the difference in the value of land, water-power and buildings. They can be kept in operation for much less, because of the difference in the price of labor, provision, clothing and fuel. This must necessarily give us the advantage in the markets of the whole world; and this advantage will soon cause factories to spring up in almost every county—not to supply alone the local demand, but that of foreign markets. It will not be long—so soon as we acquire a little more skill—before we shall see Georgia sheetings, shirtings, calicoes and muslins, as common in northern, western and foreign markets, as we now find those of Lowell. Georgia in a few years will be a large exporter of all cotton fabrics. At corresponding prices, the Georgia factories must pay a profit largely increased over those of any of the northern states.

Georgia has minerals of vast amount and value; and her legislature should appoint a geologist to explore and develop them. Our mountains are filled with inexhaustible beds of the very best iron ore, sufficient to supply ourselves and a large portion of our Union. In the May number of the "Merchants' Magazine" there is an article on the subject of Manufacture of Iron in Georgia, by the geologist of the State of New-York; and, after speaking of its inexhaustible supply, says: "The iron is of superior quality, resembling that made of the best hematiles in other localities. It is suitable both for foundry and forge purposes, inclining particularly to the best No. 1 iron. From the abundance both of ore and charcoal, cheapness of living and labor, and great profits in this region on store goods, the expenses of manufacture are extremely low, while the iron, both that made into castings for the supply of the country around and of the bar, are what would be considered, at northern works, remarkably high." This is sufficient inducement to capitalists to embark in this most lucrative business. Lime, coal and marble all abound throughout our mountain regions, and would prove sources of great wealth when developed, as they must be in a few years.

In agricultural products no state can boast a greater variety or value. With the long staple cotton on the coast, and more than two-thirds of her whole territory adapted to the successful growing of the short staples—with her whole limits suited to the production of corn, and more than half to the successful growing of wheat, rye and barley—with a considerable part adapted to the production of sugar—and her mountains to the raising without limit the finest of winter apples and pears—Georgia has within herself a diversity of soil and climate which will amply repay the labor bestowed upon it for the production of every staple best suited to it. If the enterprise of our people is but properly directed, it will be but a few years before Georgia brands of flour will command the highest price in other states, while her superior fruits will rank without a superior in the markets even of England. Nor will the products of the dairy, in our mountain regions, prove a source of less profits to our dairy-men, than an equal capital invested in any other pursuit.

These are some of the more prominent resources of Georgia, which need development, and which must amply repay the enterprise of those who engage in their development.

The rail-road improvements of Georgia are obliged to give her the position of the Keystone State of the South; and their effect must be to open up new enterprises never before thought of. The man who is insensible to the future greatness of our state must indeed be stultified; and he whose sagacity will enable him to appropriate future developments to his own profit will be singularly blest!

Casting the eye over the direction of our rail-roads, the city of Macon strikes it as the great central depot of the state. Situated just at the point where the oak and pine lands divide, within immediate reach of the facilities which each afford for manufacturing purposes, her citizens and those of the adjacent country, must be singularly unfortunate if she does not in a few years become the centre of a great manufacturing population, producing woolen and cotton fabrics, leather and all its manufactures, with extensive flouring mills to manufacture the wheat of a fertile region of country.

We repeat: the improvements of Georgia must create new and greater facilities to labor of every sort, that must diversify and increase the amount of labor—it becomes more profitable and consequently more in demand. The effect at once is the improved state of our agriculture. This ties our people to the soil, and instead of a roving population, we have one fixed and prosperous. Each branch of industry improves the other, and we advance step by step, unconscious of the approach, to wealth and fame and power.

Georgia has the resources—she may develop them slowly, but yet they will surely be developed. All that our people need, is to be told what they can do, and how it should be done; and as knowledge pours in upon them, so will their energies be stimulated and aroused.

Georgia need take but a lesson from the conduct of her sister, South Carolina, which, in the midst of her political vagaries, she has steadily pursued—and that has been to build up *herself*, and by her enterprise and capital to make her sisters contribute their share in the work.

The idea may be regarded as somewhat visionary, but we hesitate not to declare a sentiment, long since entertained, that the child is now born who will see the commerce of all India and China reach the Atlantic through the improvements of Georgia!

Steam power will carry the products of these countries some three hundred miles up the Sacramento River; from thence to head of navigation on the Mississippi by railroad; then by steamboats to Chattanooga, and from thence to Savannah by rail-road. If there is *one spark* of state pride in the Georgia legislature, the whole benefits of this immense trade—the advantages resulting from our state works—will be made to account to our interests, and not to those of other states. The only link of communication now wanting to connect Savannah with China, is the rail-road between the Sacramento and the Mississippi. The Federal government will construct that link in the next ten years. Look at the immense region of fertile country which will become tributary to Georgia so soon as *our own* road is completed to Chattanooga, and the South-western road finished! West Florida, Alabama, southern and northern Mississippi, upper Louisiana, Tennessee, Kentucky in part, Arkansas, northern Texas, Missouri, Iowa, Minnesota and western Virginia. Why then should Georgia raise cotton and hides, to be sent North to be woven, and factured, and returned through her borders to be supplied out West? Why should she not manufacture them *herself*, and make the profits of the transportation and re-transportation.

But still more: open the transportation to the Pacific, and who is there so short-sighted as not to see the inducements to our people to grow and manufacture these articles for further consumption?

In despite of every obstacle, man's interests will prompt him to seek an investment the most profitable; and the position of Georgia, her location on the coast, and her facilities for reaching the West, will make *her* the great manufacturing emporium of the South. And she will see her benefit in so doing. Every branch of trade will receive a new impulse. The canvas of all Europe will gladden our own port. Let us be prepared to reap the benefits which this mighty change in our condition will bestow. (*See Savannah.*)

GEORGIA—Resources and Progress of.—We were much delighted with the annexed remarks made in Congress by Mr. Stephens, one of the representatives from Georgia. They exhibit a state of things in that commonwealth, which must provoke the admiration, as it should the emulation, of every southern state. It is thus we can be respected and feared, and thus only.

" Georgia was the youngest of the old thirteen states that formed the Union. At that time she was the weakest of the fraternal band. Twelve years have not yet passed since the last remnants of the aborigines were removed from her limits, and since she had complete jurisdiction over her entire domain. Of course the comparison would be with great odds against her if matched against Massachusetts, New-York or Virginia, which were wealthy and powerful communities before the infant colony of Georgia was planted in the wilderness. Boston, New-York and Richmond, were nearly as old as Georgia now is when Oglethorpe first landed at Savannah. But notwithstanding all this, I will not shrink from the comparison, let it be instituted when and where it may.

" Georgia, too, we tell that gentleman, has her beds of coal and iron; her lime, gypsum and marl; her quarries of granite and marble. She has inexhaustible treasures of minerals, including gold, the most precious of metals. She has a soil and a climate suitable for the growth and culture of almost every product known to husbandry and agriculture. A better country for wheat and corn and all the cereal plants, to say nothing of cotton and tobacco, is not to be found in an equal space on this continent. There, too, grow the orange, the olive, the vine and the fig, with forests of oak and pine sufficient to build and mast the navies of the world. She has mountains for grazing, rivers for commerce, and waterfalls for machinery, of all kinds, without number. Nor have these great natural advantages and resources been neglected. Young as she is, she is now the first cotton-growing state in the Union. Her last year's crop will not fall short of six hundred thousand bales, if it does not exceed it. She has, I believe, thirty-six cotton factories in operation, and a great many more hastening to completion —one of them has, or soon will have, ten thousand spindles, with two hundred looms capable of turning out eight thousand yards of cloth per day. Her yarns are already finding their way to the markets of the North and foreign countries; and the day is not distant when she will take the lead in the manufacture, as well as the production, of this great staple. She has also her flour mills and paper mills—her forges, foundries and furnaces, not with their fires extinguished, as the gentleman from Pennsylvania said of some in his state, but in full blast. Her exports, last year, were not less than thirty millions of dollars—equal to, if not greater than those of all New-England together. She has six hundred and fifty miles of rail-road in operation, at a cost of fifteen millions of dollars, and two hundred more in the process of construction. By her energy and enterprise, she has scaled the mountain barriers and opened the way for the steam-car, from the southern Atlantic ports to the waters of the great valley of the West. But this is not all. She has four chartered universities—nay, five, for she has one devoted exclusively to the education of her daughters. She was the first state, I believe, to establish a female college, which is now in a flourishing condition, and one of the brightest ornaments of her character. She has four hundred young men pursuing a collegiate course; a greater number, I believe, than any state in the Uinon in proportion to her white population. Go, then, and take your statistics, if you wish—you will find not only all these things to be so, but I tell you also what you will not find. You will not find any body in that state begging bread or asking alms. You will find but few paupers. You will not find forty thousand beings, pinched with cold and hunger, demanding the right to labor, as I saw it stated to be the case, not long since, in the city of New-York. And when you have got all the information you want, come and institute the comparison, if you wish, with any state you please; make your own selection; I shall not shrink from it, nor will the people of that state shrink from it. Other gentlemen from the South can speak for their own states; I speak only for mine, and in her name and in her behalf, as one of her representatives upon this floor, I accept the gauntlet in advance, and I have no fears of the result of a comparison of her statistics, socially, morally, politically, with any other state of equal population in this confederacy. I know gentlemen of the North are in the habit of laying great stress upon the amount of their population, as if numbers were an index of national prosperity. If this principle were correct, Ireland should be considered one of the most prosperous countries in the world, notwithstanding thousands of her inhabitants die annually for want of food. The whole idea is wrong. That country has the greatest elements of prosperity, where the same amount of human labor or exertion will procure the greatest amount of human comforts; and that people are the most prosperous, whether few or many, who, possessing these elements, control them, by their energy and industry and economy, for the accumulation of wealth. In these particulars, the people of Georgia are inferior to none in this or any other country. They have abundant reason to be content with their lot—at least none to look to you to better it. Nor have they any disposition to interfere with the affairs of their neighbors. If the people of Massachusetts, New-York or Ohio like their condition better, they are at perfect liberty to do so. Georgia has no desire to interfere with their local institutions, tastes or sentiments, nor will she allow them to interfere with hers. All she desires is to let others alone and to be let alone by others, and to go on in her own way in the progress she has commenced, prosperous and to prosper.

"The six hundred and fifty miles of railroad now in operation, to which I have alluded, were built by Georgia capital. One hundred and thirty-six miles, from Atlanta to Chattanooga, on the Tennessee River, which is one of the greatest monuments of the enterprise of the age, was built by the the state. But her public debt is only a little over *eighteen hundred thousand dollars*, while that of the State of New-York is over twenty millions, besides the fourteen millions owed by the city alone; and the debt of Pennsylvania is forty millions of dollars. The bonds of the State of Georgia are held mostly by her own people. You do not see them hawked about in northern or foreign markets at a depreciation. But they, as well as the stocks and securities of the private companies, are held mostly by her own citizens, and are commanding premiums at home."

GEORGIA — Topography of Middle Georgia.—We take the following from a contribution made by Dr. Pendleton to Fenner's Medical Reports of the South:

That region of country properly known as *Middle Georgia*, and to which this paper relates, is bounded on the south by an isothermal line, running diagonally through the state, about 30° south of west from Augusta to Columbus, varying but little in a direct route through Milledgeville and Macon. The northern line may be considered as running parallel with this from Elbert county on the Savannah River, through Walton, to Heard county on the Chattahoochee. This forms the true isothermal line between Middle and Upper Georgia—the one being suited to the production of cotton, the other almost exclusively restricted to grain.

A latitudinal line running west from a point on the Savannah, would strike nearly a degree higher on the western boundary of the state; but the southern termination of the Alleghany Mountains assumes this diagonal line in Upper Georgia, and I have no doubt impresses itself on all the region below, even to the Atlantic—hence Augusta, in the east, is about as warm as Columbus in the west. This isothermal line runs directly parallel with the shore of the ocean, which seems to be conformed to the general geological aspects of the country. Thus, we perceive a granite ridge extending along the above-mentioned line between Lower and Middle Georgia, over which all the waters of the state and the adjoining states pour themselves in shoals or cataracts, and thence glide on by a gradual and easy course to the ocean. The Savannah, at Augusta, Oakmulgee at Macon, and the Chattahoochee at Columbus, all have impassable reefs, constituting these cities the heads of navigation. The same line crosses Hancock county at the shoals of the Ogeechee, and by Garnett's Mills on Buffalo Creek; and I doubt not every tributary of all these rivers presents the same shoaly appearance in running over this granite ledge, which separates the Plutonic and Metamorphic regions of Georgia from the alluvial or tertiary. No granite is found below this line to the ocean, few rocks of any kind, and no shoals of water ; all is a vast pine forest, with a gray, silicious soil, abounding in tertiary fossils, mostly Eocene and Pliocene.

Following the line of this Plutonic ridge, which is about fifteen miles in width, we find numerous deposits of kaolin, of a beautiful white variety, which will some day be brought into requisition for the manufacture of porcelain ware. This is, doubtless, a decomposition of sepentine or felspathic rock, which, not being able to stand the ravages of time like the everlasting granite, have dissolved to form another mineral of more value to man. In some places, as in Richmond county, these deposits form high cliffs, marking distinctly tho ancient shore of the Eocene Sea, which once swept solitarily over the vast plain below.

Above this ridge there seems to have been an ancient valley, now filled with metamorphic rocks, through which the rivers glide with a much more gradual descent than they do higher up the country, where another and another granite ridge rises successively, on one of which rests, in beautiful and majestic proportions, one of the wonders of the new world, the *Stone Mountain of De Kalb.* Beyond this ridge the culture of cotton ceases in Georgia, except in small patches for domestic use, and perhaps more extensively in the valleys of the Coosa, on the western borders of the state.

The native soil of Middle Georgia is a rich, argillaceous loam, resting on a firm clay foundation. But the face of the country being hilly, and in some places semi-mountainous, much of this good soil has long since been washed into the valleys beneath, under the wretched system of agriculture at first adopted in this country. In some of tho richer counties, nearly all the lands have been cut down and appropriated to tillage, a large maximum of which has been worn out, leaving a desolate picture for the traveler to behold. Decaying tenements, red old hills stripped of their native growth and virgin soil, and washed into deep gullies, with here and there patches of Bermuda grass, and stunted pine shrubs, struggling for a scanty subsistence on what was once one of the richest soils in America.

The water-courses have received the same tincture of the hills, especially after heavy rains, holding in solution a large proportion of alumina and the red oxide of iron, and presenting a muddy and forbidding aspect to one accustomed to the clear, pellucid streams of many portions of our country, especially the pine regions. There are no lakes, and but few lagoons or native ponds in this region of Georgia. Art, however, has not failed to make up the deficiency in this respect, by improving many of the thousands of mill-seats on the numerous streams that water this favored region, thus forming artificial ponds enough to produce a good crop of autumnal fevers for the anxious sons of Esculapius to reap an annual harvest from. These, however, when decidedly pernicious, have in some instances been abolished by law, to the no small comfort and health of the inhabitants within reach of their deadly borders. Agriculture also has come to the aid of suffering humanity, of late years. Many creeks and marshy lands are being drained for purposes of cultivation, which adds no little to the health and wealth of the country. The improved method of hill-side ditching also is helping much to protect the soil from washing into the bottoms, and at once enrich and beautify the country.

The native growth of this country is oak and hickory, interspersed with the short-leaf pine, poplar, gum, &c., all indicating a good soil. It is a little singular that when the lands are exhausted and turned out to rest, they invariably spring up with the long-leaf pine. It is accounted for on the chemical principle of rotation in crops. The first growth had exhausted all the richer elements in conjunction with the cultivation, and now no forest tree but the pine could find sufficient nourishment in the soil to cause it to spring up and become a tree ; partly from the fact, that it does not require so many of the salts, but mainly because it sends its roots deep in the earth, and brings them up whence they had filtered away from the surface for ages But this is a digression.

It is unnecessary for me to say a word in regard to the population. They are strictly an agricultural people, inhabiting what is properly a rural district, and are made up of two distinct classes, the white and the black. Formerly, when the country was in its pristine strength and glory, they averaged, probably, some twenty inhabitants to the square mile. Now it is reduced to about sixteen, and in some of the older counties it has been even lower than this, but they have, in the last ten years, been showing a gradual increase. The proportion of whites to blacks is considerably in favor of the latter, especially in the lower belt of counties, where cotton is a more lucrative article of produce.

GULF OF MEXICO—Military and Naval Defences of—In March last, (1846,) Major Wm. H. Chase, United States Engineer, published a memorial in relation to this important subject, and, although his suggestions were thought to be on too expensive a scale for the wants and resources of the country, his remarks are deserving of serious attention. We would recommend the memorial, from the great ability with which it is drawn up, to general perusal, and at the same time would call attention to the admirable paper of Lieut. Maury, on a similar subject, first published in the Southern Quarterly Review, and lately republished in the Southern Literary Messenger. Mr. Chase says:

"The military defence of the Gulf coast within our limits commenced when Mr. Calhoun was Secretary of War, and urged forward by that distinguished statesman, has not been disregarded by the government, especially since the present able Chief Engineer has been its military adviser. The approaches to New-Orleans and Mobile have been occupied by strong works. The naval position at Pensacola is already surrounded with fortifications, the completion of which rests with a small redoubt in the progress of construction."

We give the following other extracts from the body of his memorial:

"Considering that war steamers would enter largely, if not exclusively, into our naval forces in the Gulf of Mexico, it is important that convenient depots for coal should be established. Deposits of coal could be made at Bahia Honda and at Key West. At Tortugas a three years' supply for thirty steamers could be constantly maintained. A position for a coal depot on some point on the western coast of Florida is certainly necessary. Tampa Bay would probably afford the requisite depth of water for heavy steamers, and convenient sites for the depot and its defence. Thus held, it would also give protection to vessels seeking refuge from an enemy. A coal depot would be established at Pensacola and at Mobile Point, under the protection of Fort Morgan. Another depot for coal would afford great facilities to steam operations if established at Ship Island. A strong battery, but not costly, would protect the harbor. This depot would be easier of access than the one at Fort Jackson, on the Mississippi, and would afford supplies not only to the light steamers cruising along the coast, but to those of the heaviest class. A depot at Fort Jackson would be necessary to enable the steamers descending from Memphis to take in a full supply of coal before proceeding to sea.

"It is in place here to exhibit a statement near the truth of the cost of the public works, military and naval, already completed within the Gulf of Mexico, and those necessary to be executed:

At Fort Livingston (may be completed in one year)	$300,000
" Jackson (in course of repairs)	700,000
" St. Phillip, (do.)	51,000
" Bienvenue	20,000
" Dupré	25,000
" Pike	400,000
" Wood	410,000
" Morgan (in course of repairs)	1,100,000
" Pickens	740,000
" McRee	335,000
At Fort Barrancas	$334,000
Advanced redoubt of do. (in course of construction)	150,000
Amount for fortifications	$4,564,000
Probable amount expended at Navy Yard, Pensacola	600,000
Sundry additions and improvements, exclusive of docks	1,000,000
For three Dry Docks	2,100,000
Total for Pensacola	$3,700,000
A Dry dock at Key West is indispensable	500,000
Store-houses in connection therewith	200,000
Two floating docks of some description must be arranged for Tortugas, say of iron	300,000
Store-houses in addition to what may be afforded by the works	500,000
Establishment at Memphis	1,000,000
Total of naval fixtures indispensable and necessary to be accomplished as soon as possible	$6,200,000
To which add, in time of war, 30 steamers of war of 2,500 tons burden, built at St. Louis, Cincinnati, Memphis, New-Orleans, and Pensacola, roughly but of great strength and speed, completely armed and equipped, at $400,000	12,000,000
Grand total of naval means	$18,200,000
The defence of Key West will cost	1,500,000
That of Tortugas,	1,500,000
That of Bahia Honda, (probably,)	200,000
That of Tampa Bay, (do.)	200,000
That of Ship Island, (do.)	100,000
Grand total of military means necessary to be applied	$3,500,000
Total of military means already applied	4,564,000
Grand total of naval means, of which $12,000,000 are for a movable force, and belongs as much to the Atlantic coast as to the Gulf	18,200,000
Total of naval means already applied	600,000
Grand total for Gulf defence, part of which can be applied directly to the protection of the Atlantic coast, while the whole acts indirectly in accomplishing the object	$26,264,000

"This large sum (though not too large for the interests to be protected) would be applied to more than one-half the surface and population of the United States, if considered geographically and dependently of the country west of the Alleghany mountains. But its consideration involves every section of the country, and none more so than the extreme sections of the north-east—Maine having as direct interest in the defence of the Gulf of Mexico as if it were applied to her own coast: her ships and carrying trade requiring it as much as the safe transit of the vast productions of the West. So that, while the consideration of defensive points at the north and south Atlantic coasts has for the most part a local tendency, that of the Gulf of Mexico embraces the interests of the country at large. A quotation from a letter of a distinguished gentleman, formerly at the head of the War Department, is apposite to the subject: 'And it must be borne in mind, that the evils which would result from the temporary occupation of the delta of the

Mississippi, or from a successful blockade of the coasts of the Gulf of Mexico, would not only injure the prosperity of these states, but would deeply affect the interests of the whole Union. No reasonable expense, therefore, ought to be spared to guard against such a casualty.'"

GULF OF MEXICO—River Basins of the Gulf and Caribbean Seas; the Gulf Stream; the Mississippi and Amazon Rivers; Rivers of the Old and New World; Bounties of Nature to America; Influence of Rivers and their Courses upon Commerce and the Destinies of a People; Connection between the Pacific and Atlantic Oceans.—A line from the Delta of the Orinoco to the east end of Cuba is but a thousand miles long; and yet, to the west of it, lies this magnificent basin of water, locked in by a continent that has on its shores the most fertile valleys of the earth. In the midst of these valleys, ships may sail thousands of miles on the largest rivers that bring tribute to the ocean. They contain the elements of dormant wealth, of national power and greatness, which it requires facility of communication with the Pacific to begin to develop, and which, when fully developed, will astonish the world. An era and an epoch in the affairs of nations will date from the opening of this communication. All, and more, too, that the Mediterranean is to Europe, Africa and Asia, this sea is to America and the world.

A sea is important for commerce in proportion to the length of the rivers that empty into it, and to the extent and fertility of the river basins that are drained by it. The quantity and value of the staples that are brought down to market depend upon these. The Red Sea is in a riverless district; few are the people and small the towns along its coast. Its shores are without valleys, not a river emptying into it; for there is no basin for it to drain. Commercially speaking, what are its staples in comparison to those of the Mediterranean, which gives outlet to rivers that drain and fertilize basins containing not less than one million and a quarter of square sea miles of fruitful lands?

Commercial cities have never existed on the shores of the Red Sea. Commerce loves the sea, but it depends for life and health on the land. It derives its sustenance from the rivers, and the basins which they drain, and increases the opulence of nations in proportion to the facility of intercourse which these nations have with the outlets of such basins.

The river basins drained into the Gulf and Caribbean Sea, greatly exceed, in extent of area and capacity of production, the river basins of the Mediterranean. The countries in Africa, Asia and Europe, which comprise the river basins of the Mediterranean, are, in superficial extent, but little more than one-fourth the size of those which are drained by this sea in our midst. It is the Mediterranean of the new world, and nature has laid it out on a scale for commerce far more grand than its type in the old—that is, about 45° of longitude in length, by an average of 7° of latitude in breadth. Ours is broader, but not so long; it is, therefore, more compact; ships can sail to and fro across it in much less time, and gather its articles of commerce at much less cost.

The two seas cover each about the same superficial extent; but from one extreme to the other of that of the old world, the route is tortuous and the voyage long; it cannot be accomplished without sailing a distance quite equal to that between Europe and America. Whereas from the most remote point in the Caribbean Sea to the furthest port in the Gulf, a straight line may be drawn on the water, and the distance, from one extremity to the other of it, will be little more than two thousand miles.

From the ports of the Levant and Black Sea to the ocean, a vessel, under canvas, requires a month or more; but from any point on the coast of this central sea of America, a vessel may be out upon the broad ocean in a few days. Winds and currents, with all the adjuvants of navigation, are here much more propitious to the mariner than they are in any other part of the world.

There is a system of perpetual currents running from the ocean into this sea, and from this sea back into the ocean. They are literally rivers in the sea, for they are as constant and almost as well marked as rivers on the land.

Had it been left to man to plan the form of a basin for commerce on a large scale—a basin for the waters of our rivers and the products of our lands—he could not have drawn the figure of one better adapted for it than that of the Gulf, nor placed it in a position half so admirable.

The shores of the Mediterranean are indented by deep bays and projecting points of land, which greatly lengthen the sailing distance from port to port. The sinuosities of shore lines add to the expenses of commercial intercourse. By land, the distance from Genoa to Venice is that only of a few hours travel; but by water they are more than a thousand miles apart. There are no such interruptions to navigation in the Gulf of Mexico. The shortest distance from port to port there, as from New-Orleans to the ports of Texas and Mexico, to Pensacola, Havana, and the like, is by water.

The windings of the Mediterranean shore line, exclusive of its islands, measure twelve thousand miles, whereas those of the Gulf and Caribbean Sea do not mete out half that distance.

Ships, therefore, which go into the Mediterranean have—to gather the produce which is brought down from its river basins, containing less than two millions of square miles—to wind along a coast line twelve thousand miles in length; whereas those which go into the Gulf of Mexico may, by sailing five thousand miles, reach the mouths of rivers that drain, of water and surplus produce, more than four millions of square miles of fruitful plains and fertile valleys.

Easy access, by sea, to the mouths of rivers which drain extensive basins of rich land, has always been regarded as the best basis upon which the foundations of commerce can be laid. The character and extent of the back country which supplies such outlets, are the true exponents of the commercial prosperity of the cities, and of the condition of the people who live there. The closer these outlets are together, and the greater the diversity of the climates drained by them, the more numerous are their products, and the more active is their commerce. Hence, the commercial importance of every bay, gulf and sea of the ocean, may be considered as in direct relation to the extent, variety and fertility of their river basins.

Because the Red Sea is in a riverless region it has no markets; consequently it has, in the eye of commerce, ever been regarded as valueless in comparison to the Bay of Bengal and the Mediterranean Sea, with their broad basins and beautiful tributaries.

Every one who takes the trouble to examine is struck with the fact, that the greatest commercial cities of the world are, and ever have been, those whose merchants have been most advantageously situated with regard to the outlets, natural or artificial, of great river basins and producing regions.

Rightly to perceive how admirably located and arranged for the purposes of commerce are the Gulf and Caribbean Sea, and duly to appreciate the advantages arising therefrom, let us, before comparing the river basins of America with those of Europe and Asia, or before tracing further the effects which the course of the rivers of a country has upon its commerce, take a glance at the geographical position of this our central sea.

Curtained on the east by a chain of fruitful islands stretching from Trinidad to Cuba, it is, on the north, and the south, and the west, land-locked by the continent which has bent and twisted around this sea, so as to fold it within its bosom, and hold it midway between the two semi-continents of the new world.

In this favored position, it receives, on one side, the mountain streamlets of a sea of islands; on another, all the great rivers of North America; and, on the others, the intertropical drainage of the entire continent.

The Atlantic Ocean circulates through this our Mediterranean. Its office in the economy of the world is most important. It not only affords an outlet for the great American rivers, but it makes their basins habitable by giving them drainage, and sending off, far away into the ocean, the drift and the overheated waters which the rivers bring down. It also, through its system of cold and warm currents, makes its own shores habitable to man, tempers the climate of Europe, and, by its genial warmth, makes productive the soil there.

The Amazon, rising in the Andes, and emptying into the ocean under the line, also finds its way through the magnificent llanos and pampas of the tropics down to the margin of this sea.

In consequence of the Gulf Stream, the mouth of the Mississippi is really in the Florida Pass. The waters of the Amazon flow through the same channel. The great equatorial current of the Atlantic sweeps across the mouth of this river, and carries its waters into the Caribbean Sea; from the Caribbean Sea they flow into the Gulf of Mexico, and thence by the Gulf Stream back into the Atlantic. Such is the channel through which the waters of the Atlantic complete their circuit, and are borne back into the ocean again. The distance, in a straight line, from the mouth of the Amazon to the Florida Pass is only twenty-four hundred miles; therefore, the Amazon may very properly be regarded as one of the tributaries, and its basin as a part of the back country, to this our noble sea.

The connection is even more close; for one mouth of the Amazon is that of the Orinoco, which empties directly into the Caribbean Sea. These two streams present the anomaly of two great rivers having sources that are common. A person sailing up the Amazon may cross over into the Orinoco, and re-enter the sea through that river, without having set his foot on shore, or disembarked once. The Rio Negro takes its rise from the eastern slope of the Andes, and, after having run several hundred miles, it divides itself into two streams, one of which flows into the Amazon, the other into the Orinoco. This is nature's canal between them.

The Mississippi and the Amazon are the two great commercial arteries of the continent. They are fed by tributaries, with navigable length of channel, more than enough to encircle the globe.

This sea, therefore, is like a heart to the ocean. Its two divisions of sea and gulf perform the office of ventricles in the system of ocean circulation. Floating bodies from the region of Cape Horn, from the coast of Africa and the shores of Europe, are conveyed into the Caribbean Sea, and thence into the Gulf of Mexico, whence its waters, supplied anew with heat and motion, are again sent forth, through their channels of circulation, over the broad bosom of the Atlantic. To western Europe, the heated currents of this sea distribute their warmth, and then return back to their sources through the invisible channels of the deep.

We have seen that the river basins of the Mediterranean cover but little more than one-fourth the area which is drained by the streams which empty into the central sea of America.

That we may realize the extent of these river basins of America, let us add to those of the Mediterranean the chief river basins of western Europe and southern Asia, and see then if they can out-measure the valleys drained by our Mediterranean alone.

Before doing this, however, we will take a glance at the geographical features and physical condition which regulate the size of the river basins to be considered.

It is a remarkable feature in the formation of this continent, that there are no great basins in the interior without sea-drainage, and no rainless districts of any considerable extent. With one or two exceptions, as the inland basin of the city of Mexico and the Salt Lake, which comprise but small districts of country, all the water courses of America empty into the sea. The extent of country for sea drainage here, is far greater than in any other part of the world. Hence, we have larger valleys, valleys that are longer and broader than any in the old world. Consequently, they collect more water, call for more drainage, and hence give rise to more and larger rivers. In the old world, there is a region of country, 80° of longitude by 17° of latitude in extent, in which it never rains. Here, between the Andes, and the Atlantic, there is no such rainless region. The annual fall of rain, between the tropics, in the old world, is six feet; in the new world it is eleven; and it is greater here than there in the temperate zones also. More than one-half of all the fresh water in the world is on the continent of North America. In facts like these, is found the explanation as to the cause of the surprising length and volume of many of the American rivers. Big rivers are required to drain broad valleys.

In Europe and Asia, the great continental declivities are such as to leave no room for any remarkable length of river or breadth of valley.

In North America, there is an immense valley between the Alleghany and the Rocky Mountains. The great lakes form the northern edge of this valley, the entire drainage of which is, therefore, carried off toward the south, into the Gulf of Mexico.

This is the basin of the Mississippi.

In South America, the Andes skirt the western coast very closely, and send off to the east a chain of mountains from Bolivia to the Atlantic coast of Brazil. These mountains divide South America into two great systems of river basins; the drainage of one is to the north and east, of the other to the south.

In the broadest part of the continent, therefore, which is its northern portion, the continental slope gives rise to the first mentioned system. The district of country included in it is an immense one, the rains are heavy, and the drainage great. Hence, the direction and volume of the Para, the Amazon and Orinoco. The basin which slopes to the south is much less in extent; it is drained by the La Plata. In one part of Europe the drainage is, in all directions, toward the Black Sea, which is sunk down in a sort of a basin of its own, and receives the drainage from several quarters. But the longest slope on the sides of this basin runs up west, toward the centre of the continent. Here the Danube and other draining streams, which empty into the Black Sea and thence into the Mediterranean, take their rise.

On the shores of this last, we have the drainage to the south, which gives rise to the Rhone, etc. Europe has its Atlantic slope also, and there the rivers, as the Tagus, the Rhine and the Elbe, run west. Thus we see that the geographical features of Europe leave no room for a hydrological expression like that of the Amazon and the Mississippi, with their valleys.

In the interior of Asia there is a grand continental basin 85° of longitude in length. It is spread out over the middle of the continent, and extends from the borders of Europe to the eastern districts of China. It embraces a region of country more than four millions of square geographical miles in extent, which has no ocean drainage. In the midst of the old world, it is surrounded by steppes and mountain ranges which shut it out from the world of waters beyond. It gives rise to many large rivers, as the Volga and the Oural; but they empty into the Caspian, and other continential seas, which have no visible outlet or communication with the ocean. For all the great purposes of commerce, this immense and fertile basin is as blank as the desert of Zahara. Of course, then, the rivers above this basin must run north into the frozen ocean, which also is a blank as white as snow, in the book where commerce records her statistics. They embrace nearly four millions of geographical square miles.

On the south side of this inland basin, the inclination of the continental level is toward the China seas and the Indian ocean. Here, then, we must look for those river basins, and the origin of those streams, which give rise to the commerce of the East, and here, accordingly, we find the teeming valleys drained by the Euphrates, the Ganges and the Yangtse Kiang—all of which descend from fruitful plains, and all, except the last, are open to trade and traffic with "Outside Barbarians."

The distance from the Bay of Bengal and Arabian sea, to the southern edge of this great inland basin, varies from 3 to 10 degrees of latitude, consequently the climates, through which the rivers of India flow, are limited to 10 degrees of latitude; the produce that comes down these streams, for market, has no greater range of climate than that which is due a north and south line of five or six hundred miles in length. Neither can the rivers themselves be very long, nor their basins very broad, nor their volume of waters very great. Their valleys may vie, in fertility, with those of the Mississippi and the Amazon, but as for diversity of climate, variety of productions and navigable capacity of water-courses, there is no comparison.

Let us now return to the comparison as to extent of river basins of the old world with those under consideration in the new.

According to one of the most remarkable works of the age—Professor Johnson's Physical Atlas—the river basins in the old world contain, in geographical square miles, stated in round numbers as follows, viz.:

of Mediterranean Europe	1,160,000	square miles.
Nile	520,000	"
Euphrates	196,000	"
Indus	312,000	"
Ganges	432,000	"
Irrawady	331,000	"
Others of India	173,000	"
Those of Western Europe, as Rhine, &c	730,000	"
Total Mediterranean, India and Western Europe	3,854,000	"

AREA IN GEOGRAPHICAL SQUARE MILES OF RIVER BASINS DRAINED INTO THE GULF OF MEXICO AND CARIBBEAN SEA.

Basin of Mississippi River	982,000	square miles.
Basins in Florida and Texas (estimated)	529,000	"
" Mexico and Central America (estimated)	300,000	"
" Amazon	1,796,000	"*
" Orinoco and all others of Caribbean Sea	700,000	"
Total Gulf and Caribbean Sea	4,298,000	"
Total Mediterranean, India and Western Europe	3,854,000	"

Difference—call it nothing, though it measures an area containing nearly half a million of square miles.

From this statement, we are led to the very remarkable conclusion—and it is an important physico-commercial fact—that the area of all the valleys which are drained by the rivers of Europe which empty into the Atlantic, of all the valleys that are drained by the rivers of Asia which empty into the Indian ocean, and of all the valleys that are drained by the rivers of Africa and Europe which empty into the Mediterranean, does not cover an extent of territory as great as that included in the valleys drained by the American rivers alone, which discharge themselves into our central sea. Never was there such a concentration upon any sea, of commercial resources. Never was there a sea known with such a back country tributary to it.

The produce which comes down the rivers of Europe, has, when it arrives on the shores of the Atlantic, to be transported 15 or 20,000 miles, to be exchanged for that which comes from the river basins of India. From the mouth of the European rivers discharging into the Atlantic ocean, the voyage to the mouth of the Asiatic rivers which run into the Indian ocean, often occupies 200 days; consequently, it requires a ship more than a year to take on board a cargo from the river basins of Europe, go with it to India, exchange it, and return with the proceeds thereof to the place when she started—so great the distance and so long the period of time which separate these two fountains of commerce.

One ship, therefore, trading between the American system of river basins, may fetch and carry, exchange and bring back, in the course of one year, as many cargoes as ten ships can, in the same time, convey between the remote basins of the system in the old world.

The products of the basin of the Mississippi, when they arrive at the Balize, may, in 20 or 30 days, be landed on the banks of the Orinoco and Amazon. Thus, in our favored position here in the new world, we have, at a distance of only a few days' sail, an extent of fruitful basins for commercial intercourse, which they of the old world have to compass sea and land and to sail the world around to reach.

On this continent, nature has been prodigal of her bounties. Here, upon this central sea, she has, with a lavish hand, grouped and arranged in juxtaposition, all those physical circumstances which make nations truly great. Here she has laid the foundations for a commerce, the most magnificent the world ever saw. Here she has brought within the distance of a few days, the mouths of her two greatest rivers. Here she has placed, in close proximity, the natural outlets of her grandest river basins. With unheard-of powers of production, these valleys range through all the producing latitudes of the earth. They embrace every agricultural climate under the sun; they are capable of all variety of productions which the whole world besides can afford. On their green bosom rests the throne of the vegetable kingdom. Here commerce, too, in time to come, will hold its court.

The Mississippi comes down from the grain producing regions of the North, bearing vessels deeply laden with produce; freighted with all varieties of the fruits of the temper-

* Including the basin of Para.

ate zones; they convey to the sea large cargoes of merchandise, gathered from the products of the field, the forest and the mine. Hills of iron, mountains and valleys filled with coal, are found on its banks. Its waters are mingled, in the Gulf, with those of the Amazon and Orinoco, which run between the tropics. From their basins they are ready, at the bidding of civilized man, to place on this sea, in all variety and abundance, the products of the torrid zone. Arrived in the Gulf with these goods, the mariner then finds a river in the sea to speed him on with its favoring currents to prosperous voyages. Through the Gulf stream, the productions of this grand system of river basins will be distributed over the world, passing by and enriching as they go, Norfolk, Philadelphia, New-York and Boston, all the Atlantic slope, and all the Pacific slope, too, of the United States.

From 50° north to 20° south, the Mississippi and the Amazon take their rise. A straight line from the head-waters of one to those of the other, measures a quadrant of the globe. They afford outlets to all the producing climates of the earth. Upon this Gulf and sea, perpetual summer reigns; and upon their shores, climate is piled upon climate, production upon production, in such luxuriance and profusion that man, without changing his latitude, may, in one day, ascend from summer's heat to winter's cold, gathering, as he goes, the fruits of every clime, the staples of every country.

To gather such things in the old world, commerce must first plume her wings and sail in search of them through all latitudes and climates, from the extreme north to the furthest south.

In the small compass of the West India sea, are crowded together the natural outlets of the ocean, from mountains, plains and valleys, that embrace every variety of production, every degree of latitude and climate, from perpetual winter to eternal spring. The largest water courses of Europe and India, do not run through more than 10° or 15° of latitude. The greatest variety of climate possessed by the river basins of India, the Mediterranean and Atlantic Europe, is included between 10° and 55° of north latitude. Only forty-five degrees of latitude there against 70° here. They are all in the same hemisphere, and when it is seed time in one basin, it is seed time in all; and short harvests there produce famine. Here, in the American system, we include both hemispheres—and therefore, when it is seed time in one basin, it is harvest in the other.

With this blessed alternation of seasons, so near at hand, and so convenient to our seaport towns, and avenues of trade, famine on these shores is impossible. With this American sea between the two hemispheres, and in the lap of both, nature has endowed it with commercial resources and privileges of infinite variety. Here come together and unite in one, the natural highways to the ocean, from mountains, plains and valleys teeming with treasures from the mineral, the vegetable and the animal kingdoms—nature's most princely gifts to man.

Were it given to us of this day to look down through future generations, and to see the time when the valleys of the Mississippi, the Orinoco and the Amazon shall be reclaimed, and peopled and cultivated up to their capacities of production, we should behold in this system of river basins, and upon this central sea of ours, a picture such as no limner can draw, no fancy can sketch. All the elements of human greatness which river, land and sea can afford, are here crowded together. For their full development, easy access to the Pacific is necessary.

The course of a river exercises important bearings upon commerce. A river that runs east or west, has no diversity of climate, its basin is between two parallels of latitude, and there is no variety of production from source to mouth, except such as is due to elevation. The husbandman who inhabits the banks of such a stream, when he descends it with his surplus produce for exchange or barter, finds, on his arrival at its mouth, that he has but come to Newcastle with coal only. He is there offered duplicates in exchange for what he has brought to sell; all sellers and no buyers never can make commerce brisk. Such a river may have a staple, it may be corn, it may be oil, but whatever it may be, it is all they who dwell in its valley have to sell, and whatever they buy, they buy with that staple. The commerce of such a basin therefore must be with other latitudes, with other climates and with regions which afford *variety*.

On the contrary, one who descends a river that runs north and south, finds his climate changing day by day; at every turn new plants and strange animals meet his eye. He brings with him from its head-waters the furs, the cereal grains, and a variety of articles—the productions of the north—to exchange for the coffee and sugar and the sweets of the south, which are gathered on its banks below.

It is the business of commerce to minister to the fancies as well as the necessities of man; she therefore delights in variety of climate and assortments of merchandise. It is owing to the diversity of climate and production afforded by the States of this Union, and to the facilities of intercourse with them, that the trade of a single state, as Massachusetts, with the rest, exceeds in value the entire foreign commerce of the whole country with all the world besides. The pursuits of commerce abound in secrets of high import to the happiness of man; an easy communication from the Gulf to the Pacific is the key to some of them.

The products of seventy degrees of latitude are to be found in the river basins drained by this central sea. All nations want of them; but the 600 millions of people who live on the shores that are washed by the Pacific ocean, are excluded from them. They are barred out from this great *cornucopia* of the world, by a strip of land but a span in breadth. From the mouth of the Amazon, and the Delta of the Mississippi, to the Isthmus of Panama, the distance in each case is less than two thousand miles. Shall this barrier forever remain in our way to the markets and the wants of six hundred millions of people? Let those who study the sources, and understand the elements, of true national greatness, ponder this question, while we consider the effects which the course of a river has upon the character of the people who inhabit its basin.

The most superficial observer remarks the effect which the course of a river has upon the flora and fauna that inhabit its banks; as the traveler ascends an east or west stream, he finds all the way up, the same fish, the same beasts, birds and reptiles. There is as little variety among those as there is among the plants and herbage upon which they feed. But along rivers whose beds lie north and south, he sees, as he descends from source to mouth, entire changes in the families, species and genera, both of plants and animals.

Can it be, that climate which, with its multitudinous influences, so strongly impresses itself upon the vegetation of a country, upon its beasts, birds and fishes—upon the whole face of organic nature—should produce no effect, either upon the outer or the inner man? His habits depend, in an eminent degree, upon climate and soil, and these upon latitude; they operate upon his organization, and affect his appearance; else, whence the difference between the Caucasian and the Ethiopian? the Esquimaux of the north, and the Aztec of the south?

The frigid zone is a niggard, yielding scanty returns to labor; there, man is a beggar, and from the cradle to the grave, he has a hard struggle to snatch from the land and water the bare means of animal subsistence. He has no time for moral developments; his severe climate, with its consequently barren soil and stunted vegetation, taxes all his energies to make provision for the night of his long and dreary winter. It should not be forgotten that man, in the climate of severe cold, requires more food for sustenance than he does in the temperate regions; while, on the other hand, nature is much less generous in her sources of supply. These are based on the vegetation, which goes on decreasing in perfection and development from the equator—where its energies are most active—to the poles, where they are most torpid. The torrid zone is most favorable for the development of vegetable as well as for purely animal life. But for man, in the true nobleness of his being, the temperate zone is the place. Here he is neither pinched with hunger, nor starved with cold, as in the frigid, nor surfeited to plethora, as in the torrid zone. Extremes are closely allied, the abundance of one and the scarcity of the other of the zones, each tends rather to the development of the animal passions than of the moral attributes. The temperate zone is the happy middle for these. Here nature is not the severe task-master of the polar regions, nor the prodigal host of the tropics. She lures man to labor, and in the wholesome necessities of labor, he finds exercise and incentive to the intellectual being. Here he is surrounded with all the physical conditions most favorable to progress and improvement. Within the tropics he is enervated by the climate. Nature does not impose the necessity of severe toil there, but invites to luxury and repose; and in so doing, stimulates and excites the animal propensities at the expense of moral advancement.

The facts are curious and ought to be mentioned. Not only the temperate zones, but certain places in them, seem to be best adapted as the nurseries of civilization and Christianity, and therefore for the development of those faculties, attributes and qualities, which distinguish and ennoble the human race most of all.

These favored spots are secluded places; they have been, for the most part, surrounded by mountains, and separated from the world beyond by barriers difficult to pass. They are inland basins, the most striking peculiarities of which are, that they have no ocean drainage; their streams all empty into closed seas or lakes which have no visible connection with the great salt seas that cover two-thirds of the earth's surface.

When man was created in God's own image, he was placed in the garden-spot of the earth, near one of these basins, and on the banks of a river that crosses parallels of latitude and runs through varieties of climate. Here he waxed strong and became wicked, and caused God to repent of the work of creation. Then the condition of things was changed; the earth was cursed for man's sake, and, after the flood, the ark was landed within an inland basin, which has since had no connection by water with the ocean.

The promised land of the Israelites is another inland basin. It is so good that, as a special mark of Divine favor, Moses was permitted to look down upon it and die. It is drained by the Jordan and other streams which are shut out from the ocean. Here Christianity had its birth.

For the want of natural barriers to make their country an inland basin, and to exclude them from liability to incursions from the savage hordes without, the Chinese built a wall, and under the shelter of that they attained the highest degree of civilization known among the ancients. Intercourse with the world, during the primitive ages, seems to have been unfavorable to the well-being and advancement of civilization.

It is remarkable that in the new world there should be but two inland basins, and they the spots where the aborigines had attained their highest degree of civilization. When compared with the whole continent, the area which these basins occupy is found to be quite inconsiderable as to size. Grants of land of larger extent, on the continent, have been made to single individuals. The Incas of Peru and the Aztecs of Mexico, each dwelt in inland basins. The basin of the sealed lake Titicaca is the only inland basin of South America; and, with the exception of the great salt basin, the basin of Mexico is the only one in North America from which there is no outlet to the ocean. Each of these basins is partly within the tropics, but their elevation above the level of the sea is such as to give them the climate, the flora and the fauna, with all the advantages and conditions of the temperate zones. More striking examples as to the effect of geographical conditions upon the character of man could be scarcely mentioned.

But civilization has now attained a growth which no longer requires the shelter of the mountains and their fastnesses to protect it from the rude shocks of savage man and his blighting passions. It now delights in free intercourse among nations, and flourishes best where commerce is most active and institutions are most liberal. The history of civilization in its early stages is that of a tender plant, which, while young, requires the protection and shelter of the hot-bed; but which, after it has attained a certain degree of vigor, thrives best in the open air. Since the transplanting of civilization from its secluded valleys, it has attained a vigorous growth; under its shadow liberty finds shelter, man safety, and nations freedom of intercourse. Its seeds and its fruits have been borne to distant lands on the wings of commerce. Its branches reach all parts of the habitable globe.

There is this further analogy: as the plant which has been nurtured in the green-house acquires the power to withstand the vicissitudes of the open field, the conditions of the nursery become less and less adapted to its habits and the promotion of its vegetable health. It cannot, therefore, after having acquired in the grove the magnitude and habits of the forest tree, flourish in the green-house again. It will pine away there and die, or at least it will cease to thrive. So with the moral and the intellectual culture of man. These inland basins seem to have been not only most favorable to its early development, but, after civilization acquired the strength to advance beyond its green-house in the mountains, it seems to have acquired organs and powers, for the unfolding and growth of which the conditions of secluded valleys were altogether unfavorable.

The people who now inhabit the river basin of the Jordan have fallen back into a semi-barbarous state. Neither can the basin of Mexico nor the shores of the Peruvian lake, any longer be considered as the seat of the highest degree of civilization in the new world.

Considering the small area of these inland basins in comparison with the extent of the whole earth, it cannot be that chance should have made them the nurseries of civilization. Effects here, as elsewhere, must have their causes; mere coincidences would be miraculous. It would be interesting, and profitable too, to trace out those physical conditions, cosmical arrangements and terrestrial adaptations peculiar to those places, and which must have been especially favorable for the development of those traits and attributes of man which, when fully matured, are destined, perhaps, to make him only a little lower than the angels of heaven.

"As the external face of continents," says Humboldt, "in the varied and deeply-indented outline of their coasts, exercises a beneficial influence upon climate, trade and the progress of civilization, so also in the interior, its variations of form in the vertical direction, by mountains, hills and valleys and elevated plains, have consequences no less important. Whatever causes diversity of form or feature on the surface of our planet — mountains, great lakes, grassy steppes, and even deserts surrounded by a coast-line margin of forest—impresses some peculiar mark or character on the social state of its inhabitants."

Our lofty mountain chains and majestic water courses have served, according to the same great philosopher, to furnish a more beautiful and rich variety of individual forms, and to rescue the face of the continent from that dreary uniformity which tends so much to impoverish both the physical and intellectual powers of man. Had the Missouri River, after taking its rise under the Rocky Mountains and uniting with the Mississippi, held its course eastward until their waters were emptied in Long Island Sound, how different would have been the present condition of these United States; had the drainage of the country been in this direction, the Gulf of Mexico would have been as a stagnant pool, and we should have been as indifferent to New-Orleans and the purchase of Louisiana, as we now are to Merida and Yucatan. Because the Mississippi River runs from the north to south, it is one among the strongest of the bonds which holds this union of states together.

All the great rivers of the United States lie wholly within the temperate zone. Their basins are spread out under climates which call for the highest energies of man. Dwelling in such regions, he is constrained to be diligent; to labor; to be prudent; to gather into barns; to study the great book of nature; to observe her laws; and whilst it is summer to take thought for winter.

The perpetual summer of the tropics presents no such alternatives. On the same tree may be seen the bud, the flower and the ripe fruit. Here, therefore, nature urges no such necessities, imposes no such tasks, and savage man is as careless of the morrow as are the lilies of the field. The people of the two climates are therefore different. Frequent intercourse between them will improve the character of each, and the most ready channels for such communication are afforded by the rivers that run north or south. With the exception of the Nile, the general direction of all the rivers of Africa is east or west; and not one of their valleys, except the valley of the Nile, has ever been the abode of civilized man.

Civilized society cannot be stationary. Vacuity is not more abhorrent to nature, than is a state of rest, either in the moral or the physical world. The materials of the latter she has divided into ponderables and imponderables, and invested them with antagonistic principles. By the action of light, heat and electricity, upon ponderable matter, "the morning stars were first made to sing together," the earth is clothed with verdure, the waves lift up their voices, and the round world is made to rejoice.

She has divided the former into animal and spiritual, and they are antagonistics; the one elevating, the other depressing man in the scale of being. When his course ceases to be upward and onward, the spirit yields to the animal, virtue gives way to vice, the force of evil prevails, and the course of men in their social state is no longer onward and upward, but backward and downward. The sphere that lags behind in its course is hurled from its orbit. History bears witness to the fact, that when nations cease to rise, they begin to fall. The laws of nature are her agents; they cannot be active and be still: action implies motion; nature herself is all life and motion—she knows no rest, brooks no pause, either for her moral or her physical agents. Wise men say that she has attached a curse to standing still. This is German philosophy; but the idea is beautiful because it is true. We want the stimulants to energy, the incentives to enterprise, which a highway across the isthmus is to give, to urge us on to the high destinies that await us. The energies of the country are great; they require some such highway to the Pacific to give them scope and play.

It is for time, and time alone, to decide the question, as to whether the highest degree attainable by man in the social scale, will not first be reached by those people who, with the blessings of free institutions, live on rivers that run north or south through the temperate zone.

On account of this central sea and its system of winds and currents; on account of the course of the rivers which run into it, and of the direction of mountain ranges that traverse the continent; and on account of the character and extent of the river basins, and other geographical features with us, the old world affords no parallel, either in history or example, by which to judge of the destinies of this country. Our mountain ranges are longer, our rivers are more majestic, our valleys are broader, our climates are more varied, our productions are more diversified here, than they are there.

The wheat harvest on the Lower Mississippi commences in June, and in the upper country Christmas is at hand before the corn crop is all gathered in. Thus we have, in the valley of this majestic watercourse, a continued succession of harvests during more than half the year. In the other hemisphere the seasons are reversed; and on the banks of the southern tributaries to our central sea, reapers are in the field during the remainder of the year. A sea which is the natural outlet to market of the fruits of regions where seasons are reversed, and the harvest is perennial, is no where else to be found.

Such advantages, both moral and physical, such means of power, wealth and greatness, as have been vouchsafed to us, no nation has ever been permitted to enjoy. We have already more works of internal improvement, a greater length of rail-road and canal, built and building, and of river courses open to navigation, more of the buds and blossoms of true greatness, than all the world besides.

In these facts we see the effect of geographical features, as well as of free institutions.

As a general rule, our rail-roads and rivers are at right-angles in their courses. In the New-England states, where the rivers run south, the rail-roads run east and west; in the Middle and Southern States, where the water-courses run eastwardly, the rail-roads take a more northwardly direction. Rivers run from the mountains to the sea. Rail-roads run across the mountains; they go from valley to valley.

In calculating the sources of national wealth, prosperity and greatness which are contained, for this country, in river basins, central seas, mountain ranges, water-courses and geographical features, the lights of history are of no avail. The canvas is prepared and the easel ready, but colors that are bright enough for the picture cannot be found. The exceeding great resources of our Mediterranean beggar description.

We know that other places, with the elements of commerce in far more scanty proportions, with facilities less abundant and obstacles far greater, have grown opulent and obtained renown in the world: while one calls to mind the history of such places, he feels that here is room and scope enough for individual wealth far more dazzling, for national greatness far more imposing, and a renown far more glorious.

From all this, we are led to the conclusion, the time is rapidly approaching, if it has not already arrived, when the Atlantic and Pacific *must* join hands across the isthmus. We have shown that there is no sea in the world which is possessed of such importance as this southern sea of ours; that with its succession of harvests there is, from some one or other of its river basins, a crop always on the way to market; that it has for back country a continent at the north and another at the south, and a world both to the east and the west; we have shown how it is contiguous to the two first, and convenient to them all. The three great outlets of commerce, the Delta of the Mississippi, the mouths of the Hudson and the Amazon, are all within two thousand miles, ten days' sail, of Darien. It is a barrier that separates us from the markets of six hundred millions of people—three-fourths of the population of the earth. Break it down, therefore, and this country is placed midway between Europe and Asia; this sea becomes the centre of the world and the focus of the world's commerce. This is a highway that will give vent to commerce, scope to energy, and range to enterprise, which, in a few years hence, will make gay with steam and canvas, parts of the ocean that are now unfrequented and almost unknown. Old channels of trade will be broken up and new ones opened. We desire to see our own country the standard-bearer in this great work.—*M. F. Maury.*

GOLD AND SILVER.—U. S. MINT, &c.—It is difficult to realize at first thought the great accession to our metallic currency, since the discovery of gold in California. When the first few thousand dollars of the glittering dust were landed here from the Pacific coast, the whole city was excited, and specimens were everywhere objects of great curiosity. It is hardly three years since, and yet semi-monthly arrivals are now regularly bringing us at the rate of fifty millions per annum, and we receive it all as a matter of course, scarcely asking what effect it is likely to have upon the wealth and prosperity of the nation. Various estimates have been made upon the entire production of the California gold regions, and we have several times prepared tables in which the amount was given as far as it could be ascertained. For many of our items, however, we have been obliged to take estimates in the place of official returns, as the latter were frequently wanting, or so published as to be unreliable. We have been for some time preparing tables which should give the receipts at all of the mints down to a given point, from which our readers could begin, and complete the record for themselves. The monthly statements, hastily made up, of the deposits of gold at the mint, must of course be partially estimated, as a large quantity is continually under the process of assay, and its exact value can only be determined when the work is complete. In the statements annexed the figures are official, and can be relied on as strictly correct. For this, as well as our former table, we are much indebted to the courtesy of Robert Patterson, Esq., of Philadelphia, son of the late director of the mint.

The following statement embraces the total coinage of gold, silver and copper, at the mint and branches, from their organization to the 1st October, 1851. The coinage at the Philadelphia mint was commenced in 1793; at the branches in 1838. The Dahlonega (Georgia) and Charlotte (North Carolina) mints issue only gold coins, and the New-Orleans only gold and silver, all of the copper coins are struck at Philadelphia. The table also includes a statement of the total deposits at the mint of gold produced from California and other sources within the limits of the United States:

I.—STATEMENT OF THE COINAGE OF THE MINTS OF THE UNITED STATES, FROM THEIR ORGANIZATION TO SEPTEMBER 30, 1851.

Philadelphia Mint.

Periods	Gold	Silver	Copper	Total Coinage
To the close of 1847	$52,741,350 00	$62,748,211 90	$1,145,591 21	$116,635,153 11
Year 1848	2,780,930 00	420,050 00	64,157 99	3,265,137 99
1849	7,948,322 00	922,950 00	41,984 32	8,913,266 32
1850	27,756,445 50	409,600 00	44,467 50	28,210,513 00
Nine months, 1851	35,426,513 00	283,874 00	85,442 43	35,795,829 43
Totals	126,653,570 50	64,784,685 90	1,381,643 45	192,819,899 85

STATEMENT OF COINAGE (I.)—*continued.*

New-Orleans Mint.

Periods	Gold	Silver	Total Coinage
To the close of 1847	$15,189,365 00	$8,418,700 00	$23,608,065 00
Year 1848	358,500 00	1,620,000 00	1,978,500 00
1849	454,000 00	1,192,000 00	1,646,000 00
1850	3,619,000 00	1,456,500 00	5,075,500 00
Nine months, 1851	7,500,000 00	206,000 00	7,706,000 00
Totals	27,120,865 00	12,893,200 00	40,014,065 00

	Charlotte Mint.	*Dahlonega Mint.*	*At all the Mints*
Periods	Gold	Gold	Gold, silver & copper.
To the close of 1847	$1,656,060 00	$3,218,017 50	$145,117,295 61
Year 1848	364,330 00	271,752 50	5,879,720 49
1849	361,299 00	244,130 50	11,164,695 82
1850	347,791 00	258,502 00	33,892,306 00
Nine months, 1851	217,934 50	190,152 00	43,909,915 93
Totals	2,947,414 50	4,182,554 50	239,963,933 85

II.—STATEMENT OF THE AMOUNT OF GOLD, OF DOMESTIC PRODUCTION, DEPOSITED AT THE MINTS TO SEPTEMBER 30, 1851.

	Philadelphia Mint			*New-Orleans Mint.*		
Periods	From California	Other sources	Total	From California	Other sources	Total
To the close of 1847	—	$7,797,141	$7,797,141	—	$119,699	$119,699
Year 1848	$44,177	197,367	241,544	$1,124	11,469	12,593
1849	5,481,439	285,653	5,767,092	669,921	7,268	677,189
1850	31,667,505	122,801	31,790,306	4,575,567	4,454	4,580,021
Nine months, 1851	31,300,105	98,340	31,398,445	6,310,462	885	6,311,347
Totals	$68,493,226	8,501,302	76,994,528	11,557,074	143,775	11,700,849

	Charlotte Mint.			*Dahlonega Mint.*		
Periods	From California	Other sources	Total	From California	Other sources	Total
To the close of 1847	—	$1,673,718	$1,673,718	—	$3,218,017	$3,218,017
Year 1848	—	370,785	370,785	—	271,753	271,753
1849	—	390,732	390,732	—	244,131	244,131
1850	—	320,289	320,289	$30,025	217,673	247,698
Nine months, 1851	$12,805	202,256	215,061	70,925	129,376	200,301
Totals	12,805	2,957,780	2,970,585	100,950	4,080,950	4,181,900

At all the Mints.

Periods	From California	Other sources	Total
To the close of 1847	—	$12,808,575	$12,808,575
Year 1848	$45,301	851,374	896,675
1849	6,151,360	927,784	7,079,144
1850	36,273,097	665,217	36,938,314
Nine months, 1851	37,694,257	430,857	38,125,154
Totals	80,164,055	15,683,807	95,847,862

The total production of California gold since its first discovery must be considerably over one hundred millions of dollars; thus being equal to one-half the total coinage of the country since its separation from the British empire. To the $80,000,000 received at the mint, as shown above, must be added large amounts received here, and consumed by dentists and jewelers; considerable amounts shipped from San Francisco directly to other countries; the whole amount of the gold coinage and circulation of California itself, including the $50 pieces stamped by the United States assayer; the shipments received since the 1st of October, amounting at this port to nearly or quite $5,000,000; and all the gold dust now in the hands of miners and merchants on the Pacific side. It will not be too large an estimate probably to put down the entire production, so far, at $120,000,000.

The production of gold has appreciated the value of silver in comparison, and that too at a time when the relative value of the latter had been increased by a series of financial movements in Europe heretofore fully explained, so that we are fast losing our silver coin. The only remedy which appears feasible, and likely to be generally acceptable to the country, seems to be for Congress to authorize a seignorage to be taken from all the new issues of silver coin. It cannot obtain a free circulation at its present value, as it is worth about three per cent. premium, and all large pieces are quickly taken for export. There are many objections to alloying the coin with the baser metals, which would not apply to reducing the weight. Let seven per cent. be taken by the Government from the present value of the silver coin, and gold made the sole legal tender for all amounts above three or five dollars, and the export of coin would at once be stopped, while no one could be wronged. The present coins would be worth their full value to the holders; the new coin could be obtained at par for the convenience of change; and the Government would be reimbursed for all the expenses of the mint.

HOG BUSINESS OF THE WEST.—We are indebted to the Cincinnati Prices Current and to Mr. Cist's valuable work, entitled "Cincinnati in 1851," for the following statistics of this most important western crop, which will interest our readers everywhere. The figures show that whatever may be the merits of other places in this particular, and we speak it deferentially, the palm, after all, will have to be accorded to Cincinnati, of being, beyond comparison, in that sense only in which it is no discredit, the most *hoggish* place in all the West.

Mr. Cist says, that Cincinnati is the principal pork market in the United States, and without even the exception of Cork and Belfast, the largest in the world. The business dates back twenty-six years, but has only been important since 1833.

PACKING OF LOWER KENTUCKY AND TENNESSEE AND KENTUCKY RIVER.

	1849-'50.	1850-'51.
Bowling Green and vicinity	15,000	9,000
Clarksville	15,000	6,000
Canton	5,271	1,700
Nashville, Tenn	13,476	5,382
Gallatin, Tenn	6,800	895
Woodsonville, Ky	4,000	1,000
Owensboro, Ky	3,500	none
Brandenburgh	2,100	600
Rock Haven	5,300	1,300
Salt River, in flatboats	6,000	1,200
On Kentucky River	15,000	7,000
	91,447	34,077
	34,077	
Deficiency	57,370	
To which add deficient weight of fully 22 lbs. per hog, equal to (hogs)	3,950	
Total deficiency	61,320 hogs.	

HOGS KILLED IN THE WEST.

	1850-'51.	1849-'50.
Ohio, exclusive of Cincinnati	64,027	152,900
Indiana	329,549	380,174
Kentucky	205,414	201,000
Cumberland Valley	30,000	40,000
Cincinnati	310,000	401,735
	938,990	1,175,809
		938,990
		236,819
Deduct 10 per cent. for light weight		93,899
Total deficiency		142,920

COMPARISON OF THE NUMBER OF HOGS DRIVEN SOUTH FROM KENTUCKY AND TENNESSEE.

	1849-'50.	1850-'51.
Through Cumberland Gap	43,000	21,000
Through Asheville, N. C., embracing Tennessee hogs	81,000	40,000
	124,000	61,000
	61,000	
Deficiency	63,000	
To which add deficiency in weight	6,300	
Total	69,300 hogs.	

RECAPITULATION.

Deficiency in hogs driven	69,300
Deficiency in hogs packed in Lower Kentucky, Tennessee, and on Tennessee River	61,320
Deficiency in weight around the falls equal to	1,180
Total deficiency in hogs	131,800
Deficiency in barrels of pork around the falls	1,705
Deficiency in pounds of lard around the falls	519,227
Equal in barrels to	2,360

Pork Packing in Kentucky and Tennessee.—The Louisville Courier says: We subjoin the following statistics in regard to the product of the hog, which have been accurately and carefully compiled from authentic sources, and will prove serviceable to the mercantile community. It gives the exact number of hogs slaughtered around Louisville for the last two years; also, the actual weight of hogs, the weight of lard, and the quantities of pork made; together with the deficiencies and gains, here and elsewhere. The list embraces full returns from Kentucky, Tennessee, and the hogs driven South, and shows a total deficiency of 131,800 hogs this season. This table will be valuable for future references:

PACKERS 1849-'50	Hogs Slaughtered	Aggregate Weight, (lbs)	Aggregate Weight of Lard	No. of bbls Pork
Adams & Co	41,545	8,852,398	1,732,210	19,755
A. S. White & Co	34,017	6,494,040	1,360,680	12,984
Huffman, Maxcy & Co	30,363	5,772,288	775,919	10,863
M. D. Walker	35,600	6,831,900	1,479,213	13,820
McDonald & Day	11,000	2,068,600	352,000	2,815
Clifton, Atkinson & Co	26,580	5,200,000	625,000	8,200
R. Ernst	none	—	495,000	none
Bailey	none	1,225,000	154,000	none
Total	179,105	36,442,726	6,974,022	68,437

PACKERS 1850-'51.	Hogs Slaughtered	Aggregate Weight, (lbs)	Aggregate Weight of Lard	No. bbls Pork
Jackson, Owsley & Co	41,752	8,056,015	1,484,236	14,439
A. S. White & Co	31,773	5,535,900	1,048.409	10,952
Huffman, Maxcy & Co	24,600	4,568,238	586,986	8,757
W. Jarvis & Co	25,691	4,878,349	975,179	9,102
Brannin, Bacon & Co	27,550	5,219,760	927,669	9,541
Clifton, Atkinson & Co	25,178	4,657,950	553,816	8,360
McDonald & Day	13,370	2,366,490	361,000	3,681
Key & Garner	5,500	962,500	147,500	1,900
R. Ernst	none	—	370,000	none
Total	195,414	36,245,182	6,454,795	66,732

We extract the following entire from Mr. Cist's work:

HOG BUSINESS OF CINCINNATI.

Year	No. of Hogs	Year	No. of Hogs
1833	85,000	1843	250,000
1834	123,000	1844	240,000
1835	162,000	1845	213,000
1836	123,000	1846	287,000
1837	103,000	1847	250,000
1838	182,000	1848	498,160
1839	199,000	1849	310,000
1840	95.000	1850	401,755
1841	160,000	1851	334,529
1842	220,000		

Year	Hogs packed in Ohio	Per cent. in Cincinnati
1844	560,000	43
1845	450,000	47
1846	425,000	68
1847	325,000	70
1848	742,212	66
1849	600,316	71
1850	563,645	80
1851	388,556	80

"The hogs raised for this market, are generally a cross of *Irish, Grazier, Byfield, Berkshire, Russia and China*, in such proportions as to unite the qualifications of size, tendency to fat, and beauty of shape to the hams.

"The slaughter-houses of Cincinnati are in the outskirts of the city, are ten in number, and fifty by one hundred and thirty feet each in extent, the frames being boarded up with movable lattice-work at the sides, which is kept open to admit air, in the ordinary temperature, but is shut up during the intense cold, which occasionally attends the packing season, so that hogs shall not be frozen so stiff that they cannot be cut up to advantage. These establishments employ, each, as high as one hundred hands, selected for this business, which requires a degree of strength and activity that always commands high wages.

"The slaughterers formerly got the gut fat for the labor thus described, wagoning the hogs more than a mile to the pork-houses, free of expense to the owners. Every year, however, enhances the value of the perquisites, such as the fat, heart, liver, &c., for food: and the hoofs, hair and other parts for manufacturing purposes. For the last two years, from ten to twenty-five cents per hog have been paid as a bonus for the privilege of killing.

"The hauling of hogs from the slaughter-houses to the packers, is itself a large business, employing full fifty of the largest class of wagons, each loading from sixty to one hundred and ten hogs at a load.

"The hogs are taken into the pork-houses from the wagons, and piled up in rows as high as possible. These piles are generally close to the scales. Another set of hands carry them to the scales, where they are usually weighed singly, for the advantage of the draught. They are taken hence to the blocks, where the head and feet are first struck off, no blow needing its repetition. The hog is then cloven into three parts, separating the ham and shoulder ends from the middle. These are again divided into single hams, shoulders and sides. The leaf lard is then torn out, and every piece distributed with the exactness and regularity of machinery, to its appropriate pile. The tenderloins, usually two pounds to the hog, after affording supplies to families, who consume probably one-half of the product, are sold to the manufacturers of sausages.

"The hog, thus cut up into shoulders, hams and middlings, undergoes further trimming to get the first two articles in proper shape. The size of the hams and shoulders varies with their appropriate markets, and with the price of lard, which, when high, tempts the pork packer to trim very close, and, indeed, to render the entire shoulder into lard. If the pork is intended to be shipped off in bulk, or for the smoke house, it is piled up in vast masses, covered with fine salt, in the proportion of fifty pounds of salt to two hundred pounds weight of meat. If otherwise, the meat is packed away in barrels, with coarse and fine salt in due proportions—no more of the latter being employed than the meat will require for immediate absorption, and the coarse salt remaining in the barrel to renew the pickle, whose strength is withdrawn by the meat, in process of time.

"The different classes of cured pork, packed in barrels, are made up of the different sizes and conditions of hogs—the finest and fattest making clear and mess pork, while the residue is put up into prime pork or bacon. The inspection laws require that clear pork shall be put up of the sides, with the ribs out. It takes the largest class of hogs to receive this brand. Mess pork—all sides, with two rumps to the barrel. For prime—pork of lighter weight will suffice.

Two shoulders, two jowls, and sides enough to fill the barrel, make the contents. Two hnndred pounds of meat is required by the inspector, but one hundred and ninety-six pounds, packed here, it is ascertained, will weigh out more than the former quantity in the eastern or southern markets.

"The mess pork is used for the commercial marine, and the United States navy. This last class, again, is put up somewhat differently, by specifications made out for the purpose. The prime is packed up for ship use and the southern markets. The clear pork goes out to the cod and mackerel fisheries. The New-Englanders, in the line of pickled pork, buy nothing short of the best.

"Bulk pork is that which is intended for immediate use or for smoking. The former class is sent off in flatboats for the lower Mississippi. It forms no important element of the whole, the great mass being sent into the smoke-houses, each of which will cure a hundred and seventy-five thousand to five hundred thousand pounds at a time. Here the bacon, as far as possible, is kept until it is actually wanted for shipment, when it is packed in hogsheads containing from eight hundred to nine hundred pounds, the hams, sides and shoulders put up each by themselves. The bacon is sold to the iron manufacturing regions of Pennsylvania, Kentucky and Ohio—to the fisheries of Pennsylvania, Maryland and Virginia, and to the coast or Mississippi region above New-Orleans. Large quantities are disposed of, also, for the consumption of the Atlantic cities. Flatboats leave here about the first of July, and they all take down more or less bacon for the coast trade.

"Of five hundred thousand hogs cut up here during that season, the product, in the manufactured article, will be:

Barrels of pork	180,000
Pounds of bacon	25,000,000
" lard	16,500,000

"These are the products, thus far, of the pork-houses' operations alone. That is to say, the articles thus referred to, are put up in these establishments, from the hams, shoulders, sides, leaf lard, and a small portion of the jowls—the residue of the carcasses, which are taken to the pork-houses, being left to enter elsewhere into other departments of manufacture. The relative proportions, in weight of bacon and lard, rest upon contingencies. An unexpected demand and advance in price of lard would greatly reduce the disparity, if not invert the proportion of these two articles. A change in the prospects of the value of pickled pork, during the progress of packing, would also reduce or increase the proportion of barreled pork to the bacon and lard.

"The lard made here is exported in packages for the Havana market, where, besides being extensively used, as in the United States, for cooking, it answers the purpose to which butter is applied in this country. It is shipped to the Atlantic markets, also, for local use, as well as for export to England and France, either in the shape it leaves this market, or in lard oil; large quantities of which are manufactured at the east.

"There is one establishment here, which, beside putting up hams, &c., extensively, is engaged in extracting the grease from the rest of the hog. Its operations have reached, in one season, as high as thirty-six thousand hogs. It has seven large circular tanks—six of capacity to hold each fifteen thousand pounds, and one to hold six thousand pounds —all gross. These receive the entire carcass, with the exception of the hams, and the mass is subjected to steam process, under a pressure of seventy pounds to the square inch; the effect of which operation is to reduce the whole to one consistence, and every bone to powder. The fat is drawn off by cocks, and the residuum, a mere earthy substance, as far as made use of, is taken away for manure. Besides the hogs which reach this factory in entire carcasses, the great mass of heads, ribs, back-bones, feet, and other trimmings of the hog, cut up at different pork-houses, are subjected to the same process, in order to extract every particle of grease. This concern alone turned out, the season referred to, three million six hundred thousand pounds lard, five-sixths of which was No. 1. Nothing can surpass the purity and beauty of this lard, which is refined as well as made under steam processes. Six hundred hogs per day pass through these tanks, one day with another.

"We follow now to the manufacture of lard oil, which is accomplished by divesting the lard of one of its constituent parts—stearine. There are probably thirty lard oil factories here, on a scale of more or less importance. The largest of these, whose operations are probably more extensive than any other in the United States, has manufactured, heretofore, into lard oil and stearine, one hundred and forty thousand pounds monthly, all the year round.

"Eleven million pounds of lard were run into lard oil that year, two-sevenths of which aggregate made stearine; the residue, lard oil, or in other words, twenty-four thousand barrels of lard oil, of forty to forty-two gallons each. The oil is exported to the Atlantic cities and foreign countries. Much the larger share of this, is of inferior lard, made of mast-fed and still-fed hogs, and the material, to a great extent, comes from a distance, making no part of these tables. Lard oil, besides being sold for what it actually is, enters largely, in the eastern cities, into the adulteration of sperm oil; and in France, serves to reduce the cost of olive oil. The skill of the French chemists enables them to incorporate from sixty-five to seventy per cent. of lard oil with that of the olive. The presence of lard oil can be detected, however, by a deposit of stearine; small portions of which always remain with that article, and may be found at the bottom of the bottle.

"We now come to the star candles, made of the stearine expressed from the lard in manufacture of lard oil. The stearine is subjected to hydraulic pressure, by which three-eighths of it is discharged as an impure olein. This last is employed in the manufacture of soap. Three million pounds of stearine, at least, have been made, in one year, into star candles and soap in these factories, and they are prepared to manufacture thirty thousand pounds star candles per day. The manufacture of 1847–48, embracing stearine from foreign lard, probably reached one-half that quantity.

"From the slaughterers, the offal capable of producing grease, goes to another description of grease extractors; where are also taken hogs dying of disease or by accident, and meat that is spoiling through unfavorable weather or want of care. The grease tried out here, enters into the soap manufacture. Lard grease is computed to form eighty per cent. of all the fat used in the making of soap. Of the ordinary soap one hundred thousand pounds are made weekly, equal at four cents per pound, to two hundred thousand dollars per annum. This is exclusive of the finer soaps, and of soft soap, which are probably worth twenty-five per cent more.

"Glue, to an inconsiderable amount, is made of the hoofs of the hogs.

"At the rear of these operations, comes bristle dressing for the Atlantic markets. This business employs one hundred hands, and affords a product of fifty-five thousand dollars.

"Last of all is the disposition of what cannot be used for other purposes, the hair, hoofs, and other offal. These are employed in the manufacture of prussiate of potash, to the product of which, also, contribute the cracklings or residuum left, on expressing the lard. The prussiate of potash is used extensively in the print factories of New-England, for coloring purposes. The blood of the hog is manufactured into Prussian blue.

"A brief recapitulation of the various manufactures out of the hog, at this point and date, presents:

Barrels pork	180,000
Pounds bacon	25,000,000
" No. 1 lard	16,500,000
Gallons lard oil	1,200,000
Pounds star candles	2,500,000
" bar soap	6,200,000
" fancy soap, etc.	8,800,000
Prussiate of potash	60,000

"Five hundred thousand hogs exhibit, including seven pounds of gut-fat to each, one hundred millions pounds, carcass weight, when dressed. This is distributed thus:

180,000 bbls. pork, 196 lbs. net is	35,280,000
Bacon	25,000,000
No. 1, or leaf lard	16,260,000
Common lard or grease for oil, stearine and olein	6,000,000
Inferior grease for soap	1,200,000
Evaporation, shrinkage, waste, cracklings, and offal for manure	16,260,000
	100,000,000

"The value of all this depends, of course, on the foreign demand. In 1847 the pork, bacon, lard, lard oil, star candles, soap, bristles, &c., exceeded six millions of dollars in value. For 1848, it had, probably, reached eight millions. But for the reduced prices which a greatly increased product always creates, it must far exceed that value.

"The buildings in which the pork is put up, are of great extent and capacity, and in every part thoroughly arranged for the business. They generally extend from street to street, so as to enable one set of operations to be carried on without interfering with another. There are thirty-six of these establishments, besides a number of minor importance.

"The following are specimens of hogs and lots of hogs, killed in Cincinnati, this season and the last.

Hogs.	Average weight lbs.
7	722
5	640
22	403
52	377
50	375

Of these were nine—one litter—weighing respectively, 316, 444, 454, 452, 456, 516, 526, 532.

320 hogs	325
657 "	305

"Few, if any of these hogs, were over nineteen months old. The last lot is extraordinary—combining quantity and weight—even for the West. They were all raised in one neighborhood in Madison county, Kentucky, by Messrs. Caldwell, Campbell, Ross, and Gentry, the oldest being nineteen months in age.

"The value of these manufacturing operations to Cincinnati, consists in the vast amount of labor they require and create, and the circumstance that the great mass of that labor furnishes employment to thousands, at precisely the very season when their regular avocations cannot be pursued. Thus, there are, perhaps, fifteen hundred coopers engaged in and outside of the city, making lard kegs, pork barrels, and bacon hogheads: the city coopers, at a period when they are not needed on stock barrels and other cooperage, and the country coopers, whose main occupation is farming, during a season when the farms require no labor at their hands. Then there is another large body of hands, also agriculturists, at the proper season, engaged getting out staves and heading, and cutting hoop-poles, for the same business. Vast quantities of boxes of various descriptions, are made for packing bacon, for the Havana and European markets. Lard is also packed to a great extent, for export in tin cases or boxes, the making of which furnishes extensive occupation to the tin-plate workers.

"If we take into view, farther, that the slaughtering, the wagoning, the pork-house labor, the rendering grease and lard oil, the stearine and soap factories, bristle dressing, and other kindred employments, supply abundant occupation to men, who in the spring, are engaged in the manufacture and hauling of bricks, quarrying and hauling stone, cellar digging and walling, bricklaying, plastering, and street paving, with other employments, which, in their very nature, cease on the approach of winter, we can readily appreciate the importance of a business, which supplies labor to the industry of, probably, ten thousand individuals, who, but for its existence, would be earning little or nothing, one-third of the year.

"The last United States census gave 26,301,293, as the existing number of hogs at that date. The principal increase since, is in the West, owing to the abundance of corn there; and that quantity may be now safely enlarged to forty-five millions. This is about the number assigned to entire Europe, in 1839, by McGregor, in his Commercial Dictionary; and there is probably no material increase there since, judging by the slow advance in that section of the world, in productions of any kind.

"The number of hogs cut up in the valley of the Mississippi, will reach, for recent years, as an average, one million seven hundred thousand; of this, it will be seen, that twenty-eight per cent., or over one-fourth of the whole quantity, is put up for market in Cincinnati alone."

Hogs Packed in the West.—The Cincinnati Price Current of last week compares the returns of hog raising for the past year as follows: 1849–'50, 1,652,200; 1850–'51, 1,332,867, thus showing a deficiency in number of 319,353.

The deficiency in weight was 10 per ct. Last year the hogs averaged 205 lbs., while this year the average was only 185 lbs. According to this, the product of the two years would be as follows in pounds:

1850, lbs	349,140,010
1851, lbs	243,779,640
Deficiency	105,777,640

This deficiency is equal to 552,839 hogs of this year's average, and the total is a fraction less than two-thirds of the number packed last year.

The deficiency in the whole West, including number and weight, may therefore, we think, be put down with safety at one-third.

In addition to the falling off in the number packed in the West, there is a deficiency of 60,000 in the hogs driven South.

INDIANA—PROGRESS AND RESOURCES OF.—The Territorial Government of Indiana was formed in 1800; in 1805, the Territorial Legislature was organized; and in 1816, the state was admitted into the Union, and the present State Constitution formed, by a convention assembled at Corydon, for that purpose.

Population in 1800, 4,651; in 1810, 24,520; in 1820, 147,178; in 1830, 341,582; in 1840, 684,868; in 1845, about 766,034.

The earliest settlement in the state was made at Vincennes, by a French colony, who called the place Port Vincent. The principal towns now in the state are New-Albany, Madison, Vincennes, Terre Haute, Lafayette.

The State of Indiana exhibits, in the extent and fertility of its territory, as well as by the facilities of transportation by which it is almost surrounded, extraordinary agricultural and commercial advantages. There is embraced in the state a territorial domain of about thirty-seven thousand square miles, in which is represented a soil of unusual fertility; and from more than half the counties that compose the state, the produce of the agriculturist may be transported from his farm by steam or flat-boats.

The southern portion of the state is generally of a broken and uneven surface. A range of hills runs nearly parallel with the Ohio River, through the greater part of the state, alternately approaching and receding from the river, leaving frequently immense tracts of bottom-land of a rich alluvial soil. The south-western portion is exceedingly broken and hilly, abounding in abrupt rocky and precipitous cliffs. As we advance toward the interior, the hills disappear, and the surface assumes a more level and unbroken appearance, the soil partakes considerably of a clay nature, but is productive of the ordinary crops. As we approach nearer the centre of the state, we find a still more level region. The White-water valley is considered unsurpassed in the fertility and productiveness of its soil. Approaching north, the country is considerably rolling; a number of counties are, however, of a low and wet soil, composed of too much clay, which renders it cold and uncertain in its crops.

The north-western portion of the state consists of several species of soil, and is characterized by a marked difference of scenery. A part is heavily timbered, consisting principally of walnut, maple, beach, buckeye, &c. A considerable part of this country is what is denominated "prairie." The soil composing this species of land is a deep vegetable mould, of exhaustless fertility. This soil is perhaps the most productive of any found in this part of the state, yielding very plentiful crops of the grain usually raised in the western states; corn, however, is the more abundant and favorite crop. Many of these prairies are exceedingly beautiful; the surface extends as far as the vision reaches, in sweeping undulations, interspersed with numerous groves, and delightfully variegated with rivers and small streams. In the spring and summer they are covered by a varied and luxuriant growth of herbage and fragrant wild flowers, of every tint and hue, which gives them an appearance of beauty beyond description.

There is a species of land, differing from any yet mentioned, called "barrens," comprising a rolling country, with a dry, sandy, gravelly soil, with large trees growing from ten to fifty feet apart, then densely covered with an undergrowth of stunted oak, bushes, hazel, and other shrubbery. The soil is better adapted to the culture of wheat than any other species of soil in the state; it is both surer and more abundant in crops.

The north-eastern portion of the state consists of heavily-timbered lands, interspersed with occasional small prairies and barrens. Some parts are low and marshy, too wet for cultivation, but could be reclaimed without great labor or expense, and be rendered arable, and susceptible of the highest improvement.

There are numerous small lakes in the northern part of the state, the water of which is deep, clear, and exceedingly transparent, abounding with fish of different kinds.

The mineral resources of Indiana are but partially developed; coal is found in different parts of the state in great abundance. There are also great quantities of iron ore. In 1840 there were about 57,700 dollars invested in the manufacture of iron.

There are numerous salt springs of a superior quality. In 1840 there were about 6,400 bushels of salt manufactured in the state.

The agricultural interests of the state are rapidly advancing. There have been of late years agricultural societies formed in the different counties of the state, by which, with the laudible efforts of many enterprising individuals, a more efficient and systematic mode of farming will be introduced.

No better idea can be given of the agricultural resources than by exhibiting a table of the annual products of 1844.

There were raised:

Wheat	5,419,000	bushels.
Corn	24,500,000	"
Oats	11,587,000	"
Potatoes	3,573,000	"

Also, 3,200,000 pounds of tobacco; 2,027,000 tons of hay; 500 tons of flax and hemp; 7,365,000 pounds of sugar. The productiveness and opulence of the state will better appear by knowing the comparative standing with other states. In wheat and oats, Indiana is the sixth in the Union; in corn, the fifth; in potatoes, the ninth; in hay, the third; in flax and hemp, the fourth; in tobacco, the sixth; in sugar, the third. The increasing facilities for transportation of produce, in addition to the advantages already mentioned, operate as a great incentive and stimulus to the agricultural interest. The Wabash and Erie Canal, the Madison and Indianapolis Railroad, (a company has been incorporated this winter to extend it to intersect the Wabash and Erie Canal,) with the Central Canal, make an almost perfect internal communication, and must tend to realize, in various ways, the great commercial and agricultural prosperity that position and soil would indicate, and ultimately develop her yet hidden resources.

The whole amount of foreign debt is as follows:

Bonds, on which the State has to pay interest	$11,090,000	
Bonds on which the bank pays interest	1,390,000	
Interest due January 1, 1846	2,777,320	
		$15,257,320

The whole amount of the domestic debt is as follows:

Six per cent treasury notes outstanding	$491,435	
Interest now due on six per cent. treasury notes (estimated)	147,000	
Five per cent. treasury notes outstanding	441,325	
Interest now due on five per cent. treasury notes (estimated)	69,000	
Loan from the bank, under act of January 15, 1844	56,000	
		1,204,760
Total amount of state debt		$16,462,080

The value of the taxable property in the state is estimated at $118,537,965: by which it will be seen that the faith of the state stands pledged for the ultimate payment of a debt nearly equal to one-seventh of the value of all its taxables.

The amount of interest to be paid, annually, on the foregoing debt is as follows:

Interest on bonds, as above stated	$556,220	
Interest on six per cent. treasury notes	29,486	
Interest on five per cent. treasury notes	22,066	
		$607,772

It will be seen by this table, that the annual interest accruing upon the state debt (without including the interest falling due on the bank bonds) is equal to one-half of one per centum of the value of all its taxable property.—(1846.)

INDIANA—HER RESOURCES AND PROSPECTS—HISTORY OF SETTLEMENT—ADVANCE OF POPULATION; DEVELOPMENT OF RESOURCES; EXTENSION OF PRODUCTS; INTRODUCTION OF MANUFACTURES; FACILITIES FOR MANUFACTURES; COAL AND IRON OF INDIANA COMPARED WITH GREAT BRITAIN; UNLIMITED NATURAL RESOURCES OF INDIANA; POWER OF MANUFACTURING NATIONS; THE WEST MORE FAVORABLE TO MANUFACTURE THAN NEW-ENGLAND.—At the commencement of the present century, the *Territory* of Indiana, including what is now Illinois and Michigan, numbered less than 5000 people, whose labors were impeded by 100,000 hostile barbarians. At the close of the first quarter of the century, the State of Indiana contained a population of 200,000, and the census at the termination of the half century will enumerate more that one million of free people within her boundaries. Yet her extended surface will be but dotted here and there with improvements. In most of her counties there will be then thousands of acres as still and wild as when the foot of the white emigrant first pressed the northern shore of the Ohio. Tens of thousands of strong arms with fire and steel are filling her forests, yet the results of their labor are barely perceptible.

In 1825 the emigrants to Indiana were chiefly from the eastern states; their journey was made after long preparation and was toilsome, slow and expensive. They were compelled to bring their heavy tools and bulky implements of husbandry, their kitchen utensils and fragile furniture, by a difficult navigation and over heavy roads; several years were required to make a small clearing, rude improvements and enough coarse food for domestic use. Yet, despite all these difficulties, the population of the state has already quadrupled since that period.

Now, the emigrant from beyond the Alps gathers and sells his summer's crop, crosses the ocean, passes the Alleghanies, selects his farm, erects his cabin, and puts in his plow in the following spring; he has wasted neither time nor money on the way; he comes with his means and health and energies unimpaired—he becomes at once a producer and is at once an addition to the productive capital of the state.

In view of these points of difference; of the removal of the causes of disease; of enlarge d social, educational, and religious advantages; of greater facilities of intercommunication, and of the greater attraction presented to all classes of emigrants, what limit can we fix to the increase of the state during the remaining half of the century? We cannot rely on ordinary rules in the computation; we have not only to ascertain what number the state can employ and sustain, but the comparative profits to be made here and elsewhere by labor and capital. In the valley of the Mississippi are very many millions of acres yet unoccupied, while Oregon and California present real and unreal attractions to the restless of older countries. The overtaxed and underfed masses of eastern Europe long for our cheap food. The capital of eastern and central Europe is insecure and highly taxed, and its possessors would place it under our stable and inexpensive government. On our seaboard, land, compared with ours, is dear and unproductive; the hills of New-England, the sandy plains of the Carolinas, and the worn out soil of Virginia, offer few inducements to the generations rising upon them.

The eyes of all are turned westward, and hundreds of thousands are now carefully studying the guide-books and maps of this West, and gathering and collecting all the attainable facts by which their future course and location will be determined.

During the present year, the number of emigrants to the United States will probably exceed 300,000. Of these not over 50,000 remain on the seaboard, and our accessions from the Atlantic States probably exceed the emigrants who remain there. The natural increase of the population of the countries from which we receive most of these emigrants is about two millions a year, and, as the facilities of emigration are yearly enlarged, it will not be considered as too high an estimate, if we set down one-fifth of that increase, or 400,000, as the yearly average of emigrants to this country during the next quarter of a century. This number and their natural increase will be, during that period, not less than thirteen millions; we shall have in 1850, about 12,000,000, and their increase will be over 10,000,000, giving an aggregate population, in 1875, to the valley of the Mississippi of 35,000,000. The larger proportion of this increase will, for obvious causes, be north of the Ohio River.

If Indiana will now ascertain and develop and publish her resources; if she will fairly describe her mines of wealth, and fully and truly set forth the advantages she possesses —twenty-five years will give her a population of five millions, and at the close of the century the constituents of her representatives in the councils of the nation may outnumber the present population of the United States.

As to the actual capacity of the state to sustain such numbers, there can be no question. It has 20,000,000 of acres susceptible of high cultivation, and under the present best modes of husbandry, these acres can be made to yield not only enough substantial food for 100,000,000 of people, but flowers to decorate the dressing table of every female, and fruits to furnish a dessert to every family for every day throughout the year.*

* By Mr. Wakefield's estimate, an acre is capable of supporting more than five persons with food.

Indiana has forty miles of lake coast; the Ohio, for 370 miles, washes her southern border; the streams intersecting her interior counties give over 2,000 miles of flatboat navigation at a season when her produce is ready for shipment. By the Wabash and Maumee, passing diagonally through the state, she is connected with the "Father of Waters" and the lower series of the great lakes; by Lake Michigan, she can conveniently exchange products with the vast country bordering on Lake Superior; the surface of the state is so level, and the materials for the construction of rail-roads are so abundant, that her people can quickly and cheaply connect themselves with each other and with adjacent states, and can thus obtain ready and cheap facilities for transporting what they desire from abroad and the surplus for foreign markets, while their central position in reference to the valley of the Mississippi will give them, to the end of time, controlling advantages in imports and exports of which we now have an indistinct conception.

To descend from generalization to known facts, and give reason for the faith that is in us, let me refer to the causes of the agricultural wealth of the state.

In a report that does but partial justice to Indiana, simply because the examination on which it was based was too limited, Dr. Owen says, and most justly:

"The fertility of the soil of Indiana is universally admitted, yet few are aware that this arises mainly from its geological position. It is well known to geologists that that soil is most productive which has been derived from the destruction of the greatest variety of different rocks, for thus only is produced the due admixture of gravel, sand, clay and limestone, necessary to form a good medium for the retention and transmission of the nutritive substances, be they fluid or aeriform, to the roots of the plants. Now, Indiana is situated in the middle of the great valley of North-western America, and far distant from the primitive range of mountains; and, accordingly, her soil is formed from the destruction of a vast variety of rocks, crystaline and sedimentary, which have been minutely divided and intimately blended together by the action of air and water. It has all the elements, therefore, of extraordinary fertility."

Here we have the reason not only why the prairies and alluvials of Indiana are so peculiarly adapted to the culture of the cereals and the grasses, but why the hilly and the rolling lands between the eastern fork of White River and the Ohio bear such a weight of forest growth? This may be said without further commentary, that nearly all the products of the temperate zone, necessary or desirable for the sustenance of man and useful beasts, will reach perfection in quality and abundance within the limits of the state, which is, in respect to food, nearly independent of the rest of the world.

But, although agriculture is the foundation of a nation's wealth, it is but the foundation; other interests and employments must rest thereon, to complete the fabric of a nation's glory. To eat, drink and die, is the destiny of a grade in creation lower than our own.

The more fertile the soil, the less labor required in the production of food, the more labor is demanded in the supply of other wants. We call those wants artificial; but, although the forms of supply are artificial, the wants themselves are as natural as the cravings of appetite.

Here but one working hour out of five is required for the production of food. We have four-fifths of our population to be employed in other pursuits.

Now how shall these spare hours and this surplus labor be employed with most profit to individuals, and with the greatest advantage to the whole?

Indiana is now emphatically agricultural. Up to 1843, its supply of agricultural staples was, on the whole, within her home demand. Since that period it has had a large and a largely increasing surplus, and its producers now look anxiously over the world for consumers.

Its neighboring states are in the same condition; all of our staples are superabundant. Dearths and floods at home, and wars and famine abroad, afford us but insufficient relief—he is most fortunate who can first reach a deficient market. As we cannot hasten the rise of our streams, through which our produce finds a natural outlet, we are all entering into competition with each other in making canals and rail-roads toward the great markets of the world. When these are completed we shall find ourselves precisely as we were; away from home, on expense, and bidding against each other for the dollars of foreign hucksters. We shall then, as now, be fleeced on the way, plundered at the market, and, if we have anything left, run the risk of being robbed on our return. The longer the road, the more numerous the dangers; the further from home, the fewer the chances of detecting imposition, and of bringing those to justice by whom we have been injured.

Even with rail-roads and canals, with every possible facility for transporting our provisions and breadstuffs to Eastern Europe, with far less profits on our capital, and with far lower wages for our labor, can we compete in France and England with the fifteen millions of serfs between the months of the Vistula and the Dnieper who grow similar products for exportation? The noble landholders of Poland, Podolia and Volhynia do not allow their slaves to eat what can be sold. These districts, almost as fertile as our own, are now producing as much grain as will supply the deficient markets of Europe, and yet the traveler through them can hardly procure a wheaten loaf. Bring what it will, this grain must be exported and sold. The crop is like that of cotton—useless at home. Until then, we can send our wheat and flour to Liverpool, at a less cost than the transportation of the same article to that port from Dantzic and Odessa, and then, until we reduce its price at home to zero, it is useless for us to enter the field of competition with Russian nobles and Polish slaves.

But we have one certain and speedy mode of relief. We have a labor-saving process by which we can avoid the waste of time and money now employed in carrying over the world the bulky and perishable articles we produce and the heavy fabrics we consume. We need not continue to pay strangers for watching our corn-cribs and meat-houses in foreign countries, for we can bring the mouths to our food.

The makers of anvils at Birmingham, of trace-chains at Sheffield, of plates in Staffordshire, of cotton cloth at Manchester, would come here and eat twice as much food as they do now, if they only knew that they could make anvils, chains, plates and cloths, as cheaply and well here as there. It is cheaper to pay the freights on advertisements than on axes and scythes. Pay some trifling bills to the printer, and these foreign consumers will soon hasten to our well-filled granaries. As fast as they come, they will do our shop work and help pay our taxes. If they do not come fast enough, we must encourage our carriers to learn the use of the awl and hammer. If the men who are now, directly and indirectly, engaged in the export of our bulky products, such as corn, and in the import of such heavy articles as trace-chains, were employed here in the fabrication of what should be made at home, we should save more every year than the amount we yearly receive for our entire exports. Should we, in process of time, make more plates and plows than we need at home, we can send the excess to Odessa if there is no market nearer. The products of skill will bear transportation and pay high wages.

But combine our food with cotton, wood, hemp and iron, and you can send it to Moscow ; to the sources of the Nile ; and to the foot of the Himalaya Mountains ; and while we grow rich, we can pay high wages to every intermediate agent.

Let me now illustrate how this change can be effected ; how our wealth can be increased ; and how our independence can be established. And let me say that, in effecting all this, no law is required but the law of liberty ; the liberty of associating labor, skill and capital, so that the many can accomplish what would be beyond the power of the few. No bounties are necessary, but those which result from a business well conceived, and prudently conducted, in security and without exactions. No state expenditures are called for, save the wages of the schoolmaster, and the printer, and their co-workers, the engineer, the geologist and the chemist. The parent state best discharges her duty to her children by affording them such an education as will enable them most wisely to select, and most efficiently to pursue, their respective employments. This educational care should not be limited to the village school. The same purposes in view when establishing common schools, are embraced in any system by which we may furnish our adult population such information as will enable them to use their time and positions most productively.

The information referred to, the motives to influence action, the employment to attract labor, should chiefly emanate from the capitol. The ruler there is but the teacher, and there, knowledge can be made the most effective power that rulers ever possessed. Whatever change of pursuits ; whatever great work is there conceived, illustrated and clearly shown to be of profit—the people, with their irresistible force, will speedily accomplish.

Legislators, then, have far more power than Cheops. He could, by his arbitrary will, direct the masses to build a pyramid for the dead ; but the pyramid was not reproductive. They, by imparting the knowledge of profitable employments, can influence the masses to construct workshops for the living, which will be reproductive until man shall have ceased to accumulate.

In nothing is progress more clearly shown than in industrial associations, and in nothing have we so marked our advantage over other countries as in the case with which our associations can be organized, and the perfect security with which they can be carried on. They ask no monopoly, yet they can effect all that is desired. Elsewhere, and in other times, the few have determined what direction the labor and capital of the many should take. To say nothing of the innumerable schemes undertaken by government, or by chartered monopolists, ostensibly for the public good, but in reality as an excuse to levy taxes and support the powerful, we find that nearly all the great changes that have been effected in industrial pursuits, called for by the circumstances of the times, have been effected by the representatives of the state, whether king, parliament or ministers. It was the proudest boast of Henry the Great, that he had introduced the culture of silk among a people who lacked profitable employment. Edward III., when he brought over to England the spinners and weavers from Flanders, and thus laid the foundation of England's power and greatness, did more for his country than any king of his line. The states of Holland showed their practical wisdom when they reclaimed so many thousands of acres from the sea.

We, in the freedom of action, and in the aggregate of individual power, are effecting far more than governments could ever do. In the State of Massachusetts individual capital and labor began to associate, in 1833, to construct rail-roads. The emperor of Russia put his laborers to the same work in 1836. The little state has made a network of rail-roads through all her valleys, while the single line of the Autocrat is yet incomplete. Since 1836, our twenty millions of people, by their associations, have made over 7,000 miles of rail-road. Europe, with her population of 233 millions, has, in the same time, constructed less than 10,000 miles; and the largest part of these have been the work of individual companies.

But while the government need not be called to aid in the construction of a rail-road, the building of a manufactory, or the opening of a mine, it is not less its duty to gather and publish all the facts bearing on the road, the profits of the manufactory, the importance and position of the mine. The individual hesitates to incur the expenses of surveys and experiments, because the road may not come near him, and the ore may be of a better quality on his neighbor's lands. The association cannot be got up without a fair prospect of success. But the state has broader lines, and the expenses of her surveyors, geologists and chemists, divided among the many, are not felt.

It will be granted that, if neither old markets are enlarged, nor new markets opened, for our agricultural staples, these must fall in the ratio of the increase of production; and it will not be very wide of the mark to say, that the aggregate value of these staples will not be very much enlarged, whatever the increase may be. The history of the cotton crop shows frequent instances of this, when our production has materially lessened its average value. The throwing a large quantity of spices in the Zuider Zee, raised the value of the remainder to an amount far above what the whole would have brought, when the supply was greater than the demand.

Now, suppose the average increase of population in Indiana, for the next few years, should be 120,000 per annum, and that, of these, only 40,000 are productive, and are directed to new employments in which the average remuneration for labor would be seventy-five cents per day; the product is $9,000,000, or two-thirds of the entire export of the state. Suppose, further, that manufacturing employments were provided, suitable for female labor, giving 25 cents a day for 200 days in the year; the operatives being chiefly from the ages of 15 to 19; and the remaining 100 working days in the year being spent by these operatives at common schools. Fifty thousand females, whose labors are now almost entirely unproductive to themselves and the state, would gladly avail themselves of such opportunities of providing themselves with a dowry. The product of their labor of the year, would be two and a half millions of dollars.

It is beyond our power to calculate the effect that such an amount of earnings, such a saving of money and of such a home market, would have on the values of land and labor within the state.

The premises, that over production lessens the value of the product, being granted, it cannot be said that withholding the product of the surplus labor will lessen the value and quantity of commodities from abroad, or our ability to pay for what we should import, or the ability of foreigners to pay for our produce, which they require. Indeed, both parties would divide the savings made in the avoidance of the unprofitable carriage. Let the carriers, if too abundant, engage themselves in the production, instead of the transmission of wealth.

To illustrate my idea, let me suppose that we make our axes and import our watches. The whole manipulation about the axe may require two days of labor. That about the watch may require the labor of two hundred days. The one worth one dollar and the other one hundred dollars. The carriage of the least valuable is one-half of its cost, that of the most valuable, including insurance, is not one hundredth part of its cost. Now the savings on our axes and such heavy commodities, will enable us to buy and import the watch and such light and less bulky commodities. In buying the axe we support the foreign labor of two days. In the watch we buy, we give the equivalent of two hundred days. Thus, in precisely the same ratio that we save carriage and make our coarse fabrics at home, we have the means, and we furnish foreigners with whom we trade with the means, to render mutual exchange profitable; and in this way only can we keep up the prices of our labor, and take every possible advantage of the cheap labor of other countries; and thus arises the axiom, that a country that does not procure at home the necessaries of life, has but a very limited ability of procuring the conveniences and luxuries of foreign fabrication.

The leading principle of political and productive economy in civilized countries, is independence and the substitution of domestic for foreign exchanges. Progress is most rapid in that country which possesses and uses the elements for producing exchangeable commodities at home.

This is the age of steam, and coal is now the chief element of physical power. Let coal, and its near neighbor, iron, be combined and operated by the hand of skill, and the woman and the child can laugh at the hands of

Briareus and the strength of the Titans. The chain of Otus and Ephialtes can no longer hold a god. Mind now asserts her full supremacy over matter.

With all these elements of power, with every facility for obtaining the rich results of skill, the people of Indiana will not long compete in the Liverpool market with the white woman of Poland, shrinking under the lash of her overseer, nor with the naked Fellah of Egypt, nor with the degraded Riot of India, in commodities which the earth yields in abundance and without the instruments of skill.

In reference to this power the geological map of the world affords a most interesting study.

The most important and available coal formations are those of the United States, of northeast British America, of Great Britain, Belgium, and France. Of the areas of coal, now known, those in the United States comprise one-seventeenth of the whole, or over 133,000 square miles. British America has 18,000 square miles, Great Britain about 12,000, Belgium 518, France 1,719. Of the 133,000 square miles of coal in the United States, about one-half is the field of the central west, a part of which underlies about one-fifth of Indiana. This state, then, has thirteen times as much as Belgium, four and half times as much as France, and two-thirds as much as Great Britain. The map, however, gives but a very imperfect idea of the respective values of these coal fields. In heavy and bulky articles *position* is everything. The first boat made by Robinson Crusoe after his shipwreck was admirably adapted to his purpose, could it be moved to its point of use. There is coal on the borders of the Arctic Ocean, and there it will be until the last conflagration.

The coal of Europe is on the whole inferior to our own in quality, and its position averages five hundred feet "under the grass." The amount of labor and capital required to dig and raise this coal, is greater than that which would be required to dig that of Vigo county and transport it to Indianapolis. But, coal derives its greatest value from its juxtaposition to other minerals and materials with which it is to be combined, such as iron, copper, lead, timber, and the fibres of which cloth is made. The nearer these materials are to each other, the more valuable each becomes if they are there combined, and they impart a corresponding value to the nearest food and labor.

If we institute a comparison between England and Belgium, and Indiana, in reference to the positions of their respective coal fields and to the source of supply of materials to combine with the coal, the result may be full of encouragement to us.

Great Britain now produces yearly, 31,500,000 tons of coal, worth, at the points of production, about $46,000,000, and at the points of consumption, chiefly within the kingdom, about $100,000,000. The value of the iron manufactured by a part of this coal, is estimated at $80,000,000 per annum. The value of her exports, produced mainly through the agency of her coal and iron, now reaches the enormous sum of $250,000,000 per annum.

Her cotton mills, alone, give employment to 1,500,000 operatives, whose yearly wages are $43,000,000.

Of the materials used in combination and produced in the kingdom, the iron stone of Wales yields but 18, and that of Northumberland but 20 per cent.; the copper ore of Wales yields about 8 per cent.; the tin of Cornwall has to be protected from foreign competition by an impost duty of 80 per cent.; the lead mines are falling into decay; the quantity of flax, wool, and hides, is vastly insufficient for the demand; while the value of her food may be estimated by the price of wheat in her manufacturing districts, which will average over one dollar and ten cents the bushel.

For foreign materials, Great Britain sends to Japan, Cuba, and Lake Superior for copper ore, to China for tin, to South America for hides, and to Spain for wool.

Her nearest food market is on the Baltic, and her chief supply of cotton is from this valley. She is now using our coal to cheapen the cost of Indiana pork and Tennessee cotton on its way to Manchester to be combined with her inferior coal. A singular anomaly! But the most mortifying feature of the process is, that she pays us with the products of our own pork, cotton and coal; she takes five bales of cotton and balances the account with one of cloth; she pays us one barrel of flour for ten bushels of wheat; as to coal, she is more liberal, for she allows us 7 cents a bushel and only charges 14 cents.

Belgium produces coal and iron at about the same cost as Great Britain. She has no domestic material to combine with the coal, but iron, wool, flax, and food, and can only compete with England in manufactures, while her food is equal to the demand, and while her government is less expensive.

In the fifteenth century, the cities of Belgium were the most important seats of the commercial and manufacturing world. Bruges and Antwerp contained each 200,000 people; the Scheldt, at Antwerp, often contained 2,500 vessels waiting their turn of approach to the wharves, and her exchange was attended twice a day by 5,000 merchants. Ghent contained 50,000 weavers. Progress in all the arts and sciences kept pace with the increase of business and wealth. The decline of Belgium, in the fifteenth and seventeenth centuries, was the consequence, first, of foreign dominion, and next, of the use of coal, and the introduction of labor-saving machinery by English manufacturers. But within the present century, she has advanced with wonderful rapidity. Her mines have given vitality to her work-shops, and her miners and artisans have so stimulated her agricultural industry, that her sandy and clayey soil has become the most productive in continental Europe, and, while it sustains a population of 350 to a square mile, furnishes large quantities of food, flax and wool for export. Her rail-roads, which are the instruments of her artisans and agriculturists—as much as their tools of trade, as the hammer and the plow—now connect every portion of her territory; her people are busy and well paid, and notwithstanding they labor under some oppressive exactions, they have been scarcely affected by the recent revolutions around them.

Let us now turn to the twenty-two counties of Indiana which give an area of 7,700 square miles of coal—of that power which has proved so potent in England and Belgium. It is safe to say that this area will average 50,000,000 of bushels to the square mile. Here we have the enormous quantity of 385,000,000,000 bushels, or an amount equal to eleven hundred times the yearly production of Great Britain. It will be remarked that *this power is just where it is wanted*, at and near the confluence of important streams. Nature has been very kind, and in the course of years, has worn down convenient roads to and through these coal strata. The "adit levels" are the Ohio, the Wabash, and the White rivers, and the natural is far more efficient than the artificial drainage. These streams, thus cutting the coal, extend through and to almost every county of the state, and afford cheap facilities of transporting bulky products to points where they can be combined with the power into forms of less bulk and weight, and of greater value, and thus fitted to bear transportation to the best market.

It will be observed that, on the edges of this coal field, there is iron ore of greater yield and purity than that of England or Belgium; potter's clay equal to that of Staffordshire; lead, silicious earth and alkalies, to compare with any in Bohemia; here, also, is the best of marl, the best stone for building and manufacturing purposes; here, besides, is the soft freestone water, and below the surface is, doubtless, brine of sufficient strength to justify boring through the superincumbent sandstone and the construction of salt works.

Although no copper has yet been discovered in this district, the coal approaches within one hundred and ten miles of Lake Michigan, and a railroad on this route will, before long, be used in transporting to the coal the richest copper on earth—that of Lake Superior. Unless the coal basin of Michigan should prove of more value than is now expected, this copper must, of necessity, be smelted either on the north-east edge of the central coal field, or on the north-west edge of the Apalachian coal field, back of Cleveland and Erie; on the whole, the advantage in distance and in the superiority of a food-producing district, is with the former.

In Wales, the copper ores average about eight and a half per cent. of metal, and require nearly twice their weight of coal in the smelting process. The ore of Lake Superior, which is of astonishing richness, will require a larger proportion of fuel, and it will be brought here for use as well as for fuel. From present indications, the copper refineries and manufactories of the Upper Wabash will eventually be the most important in the world, if, indeed, they do not distance all competition. And that day is not far remote, when this copper will be largely used in sheathing vessels built on the Wabash, of Indiana timber.

This, at the first view, may seem strange; but when it is borne in mind that the merchant marine of almost every country is now built of fresh water timber, we may be disposed to inquire why our produce cannot as well be borne to the ocean by ocean craft, as well as in unsafe and perishable arks.

The English dockyards are, to a great extent, supplied from the forests of St. Lawrence and its tributaries, and from points far above tide water.* The seaboard of France is nearly denuded of oak, and she draws her supplies far from the interior. The Russian navy may be said to be built entirely of fresh water timber. The Memel oak, probably the best in the world, can hardly be affected by any ocean peculiarity, as the water high up the Baltic contains less than one part in a thousand of saline substances, and is so pure as to be used by the sailors. The shipyards of our seaboard, north of the Chesapeake, are now supplied by forests on the streams in the interior; and, in New-England, land ten and twenty miles from tide water, and well covered with oak, will sell from one to five hundred dollars per acre. A single fresh water oak tree will often sell for one hundred dollars to the shipwright. The oak on the Indiana coal field is of a very superior quality; it has been of slow growth; it has on the hills been exposed to the sun, and its roots have been forced to spread near the surface, and thus affords the best "knees and arms." These pecularities are well understood by all who have examined the subject. The ship "Minnesota," built at Cincinnati, and sent to sea last spring, is pronounced by the most competent judges

* British America furnishes three-fourths of the timber imported into Great Britain. See tables in McCulloch's Com. Dict.

equal to any ship afloat, in the quality of her materials.

Indiana millwrights can furnish two-inch oak plank at ten dollars per thousand, while its price in the eastern ship-yards ranges from thirty-five to sixty dollars per thousand. Pine masts can be floated from the Alleghany, Kanawha and the Cumberland rivers, at half their eastern prices. Other timber, such as black locust for ribs, poplar and chestnut for keels, black walnut for ornamental work, can be had at vastly less than eastern rates. We have the soft iron ore for fastenings, anchors and cables; hemp for cordage; cheap food for the builders and riggers; and then we have downward and outward freight for any port where the best market for ship and cargo can be found. As high as the falls of the Ohio and the falls of the Wabash and White rivers, ships of four hundred tons, and drawing, when fully laden, seventeen feet, can be towed to sea one hundred days in the year, and at the time when the flatboatmen are guarding against the dangers of snags, sawyers and winds, which could not harm the vessel.

I dwell the longer on this subject because I regard this business as one of very great importance to our agriculturists who are now subjected to high freights and insurances—who are delayed in getting their produce to an uncertain market—and who are yearly subjected at New Orleans, to high charges and to the losses attending the exposure of perishable articles on the levee of that city during the time occupied in effecting sales and making reshipments. All that is wanted to bring the ship-builders to us is to inform them of the quality of our materials, the conveniences where these materials abound, the capacity of our streams, and the abundance of our freights.

Bring the ship-builders, and the speculators in produce from New-York and New-Orleans will come here and buy and ship our produce; we shall receive the money at home, and not be compelled to risk foreign markets and foreign agents.

This business requires but a moderate capital, and it would afford immediate relief. Had it been introduced ten years ago the farmers in the Wabash valley would have since saved, on their shipments of produce, enough to have constructed their railroads from Terre Haute, Lafayette and Vincennes, to their eastern termini in the state.

There are very many other articles of which wood is the chief material, and in the aggregate, costing a large amount of money, which should be made at home, and are now imported from most unnatural sources. For instance pails and tubs; almost every steamboat which touches at the southern parts of Indiana brings nests of these articles made in the interior of New-England.

Black-walnut is now cut on the banks of our rivers, floated to New-Orleans, shipped to Boston, sawed into veneers, and often brought back to us as the covering of bulky and fragile furniture. The tree which leaves us at a price of a few hours' labor, comes back at the cost of five hundred days' labor.

In the productions of the forest, then, we have incalculable advantages over England and Belgium. The materials are much more convenient for combination with the power.

The same remark is true of our minerals, of which iron is the most important.

Of the iron stone, and argillaceous iron ore, we have inexhaustible quantities in the south-western counties, and bog-iron ore, as is said, in the north-western counties of the state—none of this is regarded as valuable unless it is at least equal to the best English ore—while much of ours will yield double the per centage of that of England and Belgium.

Iron stone in South Wales is now raised with the coal 1800 feet, and the coal must be coked before it will smelt the ore. By improved modern processes our ore, found on the surface, can be smelted by the coal itself. In the production of iron the wages of labor could not be lowered to English rates, simply because the miner and iron worker here can produce two or three times the quantity that their competitors in Wales or Northumberland could produce.

Indiana now sends abroad her bulky and perishable corn and meat, which can be produced equally cheap by the ignorant Russian serf, to the extent of over one million of dollars a year in exchange for coarse fabrics of iron—such as axes, scythes, spades and hoes, which are made of ore and by coal far inferior to her own; and the loss on the carriage both ways is a self-imposed tax on her labor and capital. She not only sends the tree to New-England, but she sends a thousand miles for the axe to cut down the tree, and across the ocean for the chain to drag the tree to the river. She is a producer and a consumer, and, as such, pays the freights and loses the profits.

Of potter's clay she has enough of all the ordinary qualities to supply the world, and yet she sends to Staffordshire for her common plates, pays a duty of 33 per cent., a freight of over 50 per cent., and an extra profit corresponding with the distance of over 20 per cent., on an article, which, considering the price of food and the difference in taxes, can be made cheaper on the White River than in Staffordshire.

There is now a new-born town on the upper Ohio, called Liverpool, where coarse potter's ware is now made, and sold at half the cost of the imported article; and this is now forcing its way into common use, despite the opposition of dealers in such goods;

who, like other merchants, make the highest profits on the most costly and distant-made fabrics. The further the source of supply, the less chance has the consumer of detecting imposition.

By the way, this traffic in goods is a curious study. Our retail merchant is familiar with the cost of staple goods made near home; by the prices of these he judges of the fairness of the wholesale dealer; these staples are often put at cost by the jobber, to obtain the favorable opinion of his customers. Where, then, are the profits of the New-York and Philadelphia jobbers? They must live and make enough to pay enormous rents. Why, on sleazy calicoes, made in England; on German trinkets; on French silks so very changeable that the tint of the rose on them will last but a summer's morning—with these distant-made fabrics our retail merchant and his customers are semi-annually imposed on; and so will ever be while our policy is to consume what we do not produce, and to produce what we do not consume.

Another of our great staples is wool. Now, our bags of wool, and imported bales of woolen cloths and carpets, are meeting and crossing each other on routes of a thousand miles, connecting us with eastern mills, operated by power more than five times as expensive as our own. Here again we are producers and consumers, and pay the freights and lose the profits.

The price of wool here, in its various grades of preparation, will average, perhaps, not over fifteen cents a pound, and when it reaches the eastern mill will average twenty-five cents; it is spun and woven into carpets, for instance, and becomes worth eighty cents; on its return to us it has advanced to one dollar. Here distance has added ten cents to the value of the material which has been combined with seventy-five cents of foreign labor.

For the yard of carpet we pay first the one and a half pounds of wool, at twenty-two and a half cents; to make up the seventy-seven and a half cents we send to the carder, spinner and weaver of the carpet factory, a bushel and a half of wheat, or five bushels of corn, they paying the carriage.

Now, on good land, an industrious man will produce an average of two and two-thirds bushels of corn a day, and wheat is the proportion of one and half to five. For this yard of carpet, then, we exchange nearly two days labor and one and a half pounds of wool. The actual capital employed to produce the former is actually less than that required to produce the latter. The carpet weaver has spent no more time at the power loom in learning the trade than our farmer's daughters have at the house loom; her labor is not as severe, and the quantity of labor employed by the girl in the fabrication of the yard of cloth is not one-half that employed by the man in the production of the five bushels of corn. Our wool, in the eastern market, is in competition with the wool of South America, and our wool-growers are competing with the wool-grower of South America, who pays nothing for land or pasturage, and has to support neither preacher nor teacher. He can produce as much wool without as we can with the schoolmaster; but he has neither the power nor the skill to make cloth. We can combine a single pound of wool with the power, skill, food, wood and iron, and send the yard of cloth to Brazil, and bring back in exchange for it, fifteen pounds of wool, and enough coffee to pay all the expenses.

The southern section of Indiana is admirably adapted to the cultivation of hemp. That which is now grown is put chiefly into coarse bagging and rope, because we cannot send it to the seaports of the world, where are the manufactories of cordage and sails. The Russian slaves will forever keep it out of the markets of Glasgow and Liverpool, and generally will undersell us in New-York. But the Russian slaves are too ignorant to make "duck" and cordage, and they have no available power. If we will put up the proper machinery, we can rig our ships at home and export sail cloth to Riga and St. Petersburgh.

Room will not admit of the enumeration of very many other productions of the state which should, and eventually must be manufactured within its limits. I pass to the consideration of a staple, which, in its rude and perfect forms, now nearly controls the commerce, the exchanges, and the policy of the commercial world. The field of production of this staple extends to within a few hundred miles of our inexhaustible power and well supplied granaries. The coal of Great Britain and Belgium and the water power of New-England have attracted the cotton of the South, from three to seven thousand miles, and the consumers of cotton goods have not only paid the expense of its removal, but also freights on distant shipments, of subsistence, the commissions of numerous factors, the dividends on costly roads, and the taxes of expensive governments. The food producers of the upper, and the cotton producers of the lower, sections of this valley are depressed, because the product of their joint labors is combined at such a cost in distant workshops; because it has to support too many carriers, too many roads, too many navies and armies. On investigation, these producers are just beginning to find that capital and skill are easily transported, and that our home power is vastly more convenient and less costly than that to which we have so long been tributary. Further investigation will show to the producers, the propriety and profitableness of associating their own materials, capital and labor, in such proportion and at such positions as will render the joint product so cheap, that a demand commensurate with its supply will arise, and afford satisfactory profits and wages to all who have been employed in its combination.

Indiana now offers the very best positions for effecting this combination; where the aggregate values of power, materials, subsistence and transportation, are the lowest known; where health is secure, and social wants can be fully supplied. When Kentucky has become emancipated from her slaves, she will offer a few positions equal to ours, but she now lacks a most attractive element to productive labor.

Illinois has nearly 44,000 square miles of power, but nearly all the points at which her coal rises above the plane of high water, and where it is very accessible, are now unhealthy.

There are obvious reasons why the cotton planters on the Lower Mississippi cannot profitably work up their staple at home. The reasons are almost equally obvious why they should manufacture in Indiana, if they are encouraged so to do, and shown that they can do so with profit. But, perhaps there is not one cotton planter in a hundred, who is aware that Indiana has the cheap power; and the ninety-nine yet see no chance of avoiding the expensive transportation of their staple to expensive workshops. These planters are now receiving less than four per cent. on the estimated value—and, indeed, actual amount of their capital. Our farmers are not making as large a per centage on their investments. The English spinner is in distress and poverty, and his employer is in failing circumstances; the carriers say that their business is unprofitable, and the shipwright is begging for employment. Is not the reason of all this obvious? The cost of transportation is absorbing the profits of capital and the wages of labor.

To extend the consumption of cotton cloth, we must diminish its cost. This can be done by lessening the amount and cost of transportation. Then its joint producers can grow rich. The cotton crop is, say, 2,200,000 bales; over 1,000,000 of these bales are required for coarse fabrics. 1,000,000 spindles and corresponding machinery will make these coarse fabrics. This machinery can be set in motion for $75,000,000.

Were these fabrics made in Indiana, and at the most convenient positions, the savings in carriage of cotton, cloth, food, &c., to say nothing of taxes, would exceed *twenty millions* of dollars a year. The incidental advantages to the West, attending such a change, would be expressed by a sum vastly larger. This would be the result of our manufacturing only the coarser, least expensive and least profitable goods, and the result is susceptible of proof in which there can be no uncertainty. Indiana could spare all the labor, and the South and the West could now easily furnish the capital, even if that capital was money. But if we made the machine shops and furnaces, and the rolling mills, the money we should need would be merely the amount required to import our tools and patterns; the remainder would be but the representative of labor, and the product would be the investment made by labor.

Let us review the comparison between the relative power of Indiana, England and Belgium, and take in that of New-England.

The most important coal field of Belgium commences in the province of Namur, traverses Liege, and extends to the centre of Rhenish Prussia; including the portion which passes by Valenciennes to Douai, in France; its whole length is about 150 miles.

The coal fields of England and which lie under her chief manufacturing districts, commence near Worcester, north of the British Channel, and extend north about 150 miles.

The water power of New-England worthy of notice, is at perhaps 150 different positions, and they all may represent a line of 150 square miles of power equal to those of Indiana.

The power of England, and Belgium is at the mouths of pits along its lines, and used at the positions where mills and tenements can conveniently be erected. The power of New-England must be used precisely where it is found, and irrespective of the cost of access to it.

The power of each is in a country naturally barren, and the most expensive instruments are required to make it available; its first cost is in money at least four times that of ours; measured by labor, the difference is much greater.

The surface of the countries, and the respective advantages in this respect, may be measured by the cost of railways in each. In Belgium, their cost of construction has averaged over $35,000 per mile. The English manufacturing district is connected by roads at an average cost of over $150,000 per mile, and receives its materials, and sends its products over roads of a still higher cost. That from Manchester, for instance, has cost about $170,000 per mile. In New-England, the rail-roads which connect her power with raw materials and markets, have cost over $50,000 per mile.

The roads which may be required to connect the power of Indiana with the Ohio, the lakes and the markets afforded by the state, will not average over $15,000 per mile, and, from the cheapness of fuel, the low grades and the straight routes over which they will pass, they will be operated with much less expense, and with a greater saving of time than those in the other districts referred to.

In England, Belgium and Indiana, the coal fields present nearly equivalent geological formations, and almost every mineral earth and stone, specially useful to the manufacturer, can be found on each formation. In the two former, the coal, stone, iron and earth, are deeply buried in the bowels of the earth; in the latter, they meet the hand of the traveler on the surface. New-England has very few of these auxiliaries to her power. She has been enabled to compete with her rivals, by exemption from government exactions, and by comparative nearness to certain materials and markets.

Indiana, like the other districts, has also a line of power. This line extends from the Ohio in Perry county, to Perryville in Vermilion county, or about 150 miles. There is probably another line through Spencer, Warwick, Pike, Knox and Sullivan, but as this has not yet been clearly defined, we limit this review to that section of the lower stratum of coal and above the plane of high water. This will average about four miles in width, and give an area of 600 square miles of power. In most of these square miles there is an average of 50,000,000 bushels of coal, at least, and if we allow an average of four and a half feet thickness to the stratum, over 125,000,000 bushels. The smaller quantity will give an amount of power, for hundred of years, equal to the average of 150 places of water power in New-England.

The coal and auxiliary minerals of Belgium have concentrated population, created immense wealth, constructed rail-roads, drained morasses, leveled hills, made barren wastes fertile, and while all this has been done, the people have paid high prices for food (so high that farming land often brings $300 per acre), and enormous expenses of government.

The same materials have given Central England wealth beyond computation, and an influence that affects the world.

Power alone, of another character, and of a more costly kind, has made sterile New-England the garden of America. One of its results is the construction, in one state alone, and within fifteen years, of 700 miles of rail-road, at a cost of $35,000,000. Another exhibition of its value is found in the investments made by that single state within two years and a half, and in stocks and public works, of over $50,000,000.

Now, is there any possible reason why like causes here should not produce like results? If our power is cheaper, our ores more pure, our food more abundant, our taxes lighter, our instruments of labor more convenient and less expensive than in those of other countries, are we not reasonably to expect developments and progress, corresponding to such advantages? and are we not imperiously called on by our own interests to ascertain the full extent of these sources of wealth and independence?

When we shall have sent men of high scientific acquirements, to explore our hills and plains, and to analyze our ores, to examine our forests and mines, and have their full reports, we can safely challenge the world to show 23,000,000 of acres in one body, capable of sustaining and employing as large a population as can those of Indiana.

In truth, compare fact with fact, advantage with advantage, and there cannot be found, the sun does not shine upon,36,000 contiguous square miles of hill and dale, so highly favored by nature, and which contains so many physical elements of prosperity as those within the limits of Indiana. (1849.)

INDUSTRY—Opening of New Branches.—Among the two or three hundred thousand vegetables and animals that God has created to satisfy our natural and artificial wants, there are very few that we have yet acclimated or domesticated, or know how to employ. However few they may be, we continue to increase them, and our power to make acquisitions would appear to have no limits but those of creation. A considerable number of the plants which grow among us have been brought very recently from climates quite different from ours. It will be useful to notice this fact.

Thus, Asia has given us hemp, the cherry, the peach, the French bean, the tarragon, the onion, rhubarb, mint, the mulberry, the citron, the lime, the orange, the chesnut, the pine of Siberia, the pine of Jerusalem, the plane tree of the East, the aloe, the rose of Provence, the mallow rose, the millet, the cypress, and so forth. Grain and buckwheat we got from the Levant, and the olive from Africa.

Europe has borrowed from America the potato, the maize, the tobacco, the banana, the love-apple, the strawberry, the medlar tree, and a hundred other trees, fruits, plants, and flowers.

Within three or four centuries, Europe and America have been literally invaded with vegetables from all parts of the globe. We live almost entirely upon what has been borrowed from other countries; and it is but the advance guard of the immense quantity and variety which science, and the rapid intercommunication between the different parts of the world, will give us. We are at liberty to choose from the general herbal of creation all that suits us.

I cannot give an inventory of all the riches that we can appropriate. It would almost be an endless labor to give such a catalogue of creation. I will but glance at a few among the alimentary plants—the *artocarpe*, (so precious to the inhabitants of Tahiti,) the *sagotier*, the palm-cabbage, the bamboo of Celebes, (of which the young sprouts have a delicious flavor,) the cocoa tree, (of which the fruit is both meat and drink,) the gum tree, the bread fruit, the sugar palm, the plantain and banana, the tamarind, the *papayer*, the mangosteen, &c. Among the textile plants

I might mention a great variety; but I will notice only the New Zealand flax, and the abaca, (*artica utilis*)—a kind of flax in the Philippine Islands and China, of which the Chinese make the most superb stuffs. Of the trees for cabinet-making, for building, and for the masts of vessels, a thousand might be taken from the pines, the cedars, the ebony, the sandal, and the satin wood. Then there are the trees which yield us gums, rosin, tinctures and medicines; the spice and tea trees; and a number of others not so useful, perhaps, but which would delight us with their beauty and fragrance.

To speak of the animal kingdom: how many more kinds might we domesticate than we have? Mr. Jeffroy St. Hilaire cites several in his memoir upon the utility of a menagerie of acclimation—those great antelopes, which would furnish an abundance of healthy food; the Peruvian sheep, of which the wool is so fine and soft; the tapir, larger than the pig, and as easy to feed, the flesh of which is very agreeable and wholesome, and which might be made useful as a beast of burden; the lama, the alpaca, and a number of others.

And thus, among birds, if we direct our attention to the subject, we shall discover many other kinds worth introducing or domesticating for their flesh, their eggs, or their beauty.

With respect to fish also, our rivers or streams, and small lakes, could be peopled with a vast multitude and variety of the finny tribes. Fish increase very abundantly, and science will teach us to transform those of the sea into fresh water fish. Carp did not appear in England till the sixteenth century, and the plaice of the North Sea have multiplied infinitely in the ponds of the Old World.

INTERNAL IMPROVEMENTS BY FEDERAL GOVERNMENT.—Distribution of Public Money in Internal Improvements, from 1790 to 1847.—The following is the amount of appropriations that have been made by Congress to internal improvements, specifying the amount to each State:

Maine	$276,575
New-Hampshire	10,000
Vermont	101,000
Massachusetts	526,148
Rhode Island	32,000
Connecticut	160,407
New-York	2,632,115
New-Jersey	28,963
Pennsylvania	207,981
Pennsylvania and Delaware	38,413
Delaware	1,038,356
Maryland	55,000
Maryland, Pennsylvania, and Virginia	1,901,228
Virginia	25,000
North Carolina	370,377
Georgia	243,043
Alabama	204,998
Florida	287,713
Mississippi	46,500
Louisiana	717,200
Arkansas	486,065
Tennessee	11,920
Kentucky and Tennessee	155,000
Missouri	75,000
Missouri and Arkansas	100,000
Illinois	993,601
Indiana	1,270,734
Ohio	2,617,662
Michigan	645,724
Iowa	75,000
Wisconsin	167,500
States through which the Ohio, Missouri, Mississippi, and Arkansas rivers run	1,698,000
Total	$17,199,223

INDIAN CORN.—This grain was named by Linnæus *Zea Mays*, and classed *Monœciæ Triandria*. It is now conceded to be a native of America, and appears to have been by the first conquerors and earliest settlers, from the north-eastern part of North America to the southern provinces of Chili on the southern continent. Maize, or Indian corn, was first introduced into Spain about the beginning of the sixteenth century, from whence its cultivation spread into Africa and Asia, where it has ever since been a favorite article of food. From Asia it was probably carried back to Europe, for we find it called in France *Bla de Turkie*, (Turkish corn,) and in Italy *Gran Turco*. At the present day Indian corn has been introduced and is cultivated in almost every part of the universe where the summers are sufficiently long and warm enough to ripen the grain—in France and in Germany, as far north as 48° north latitude. In the south of France, on all the shores of the Mediterranean, in Spain, Italy, the countries of the Levant, in many other portions of Asia and of Africa, and in North and South America, it is the food in most common use. The English Quarterly Journal of Agriculture says: "It is that which, next to rice, supplies food to the greatest number of the human race; and it may be held to be the most valuable gift of the old world to the new." This grain adapts itself to almost every variety of climate, and is found growing luxuriantly in the low countries of tropical Mexico, and nearly equally well on the most elevated and coldest regions of the table land; in the rich valleys of the Cordilleras or the Andes, and on the sandy heights of those mountains, wherever a rill of water can be brought to nourish its roots. In short, it ripens under the sun of America, in every part of both continents.

Like other grains that have been long cultivated, Indian corn abounds in varieties. In Spain they count no less than one hundred and thirty, and here in the United States we might safely state the number at upward of forty. The differences consist in size, color, period of maturation and hardness and weight of grain. Of size, there exists a considerable variety, from the Zea Curagua, of Chili, and the Egyptian or chicken corn, both extremely diminutive, to the large white flint and gourd seed corn of these southern states. The differences in color are the red, yellow and white. The period of maturation varies, apparently, very considerably; but it is questionable whether this variation is real and independent of climate. In the North, corn ripens in a shorter period of time than it does with us in the South, owing, possibly, to the greater length of the summer day in those latitudes. It is true, if seed be brought from the North, it will ripen earlier the first year than corn raised from seed grown here; but it is found the second year to require a longer term, and soon loses altogether its habit of early maturation. On occasions, therefore, when it is desirable to plant late in the season, seed corn raised at the North ought to be used, as it will mature in much less time than that raised at home. In the French catalogues, *mais en poulet* and the *quarantaine*, chicken and forty-day corn, are recommended as the earliest; but we have no means of judging the effect of climate upon these varieties. In selecting varieties, some experienced and judicious farmers prefer that which yields the greater number of ears, without regard to their size or number of rows. Others prefer that which furnishes one or two large ears, having from twelve to twenty-four rows. At the North, the yellow corn bears the highest price in the market, and in our country it is considered the most prolific and best suited to feed cattle and hogs. For bread, the white dutton is preferred at the North, and the white gourd seed is used for that purpose in the upper part of this state. We have a valuable variety cultivated in our interior, having rarely less than eighteen rows on the cob. We think, however, preference ought to be given to white flint corn, as it is unquestionably the heaviest and contains the greatest proportion of farina. We believe that it would be advisable to purchase and sell Indian corn by weight instead of measure, as there can be no doubt the heaviest corn contains the greatest amount of nutriment.

The method of cultivation varies very much in this country, and in other parts of America and Europe. In Europe, generally, as well as in the northern states, it is sown much closer than our climate and the size and growth of the corn will permit, and the product is, in consequence, frequently greater. In Lombardy, where corn is sown in close drills, and still nearer proximity in the drill, the produce varies from fifty to seventy-five bushels to the acre. The land is highly manured, and the corn sowed after flax, rape seed, or on clover seed. In other and poorer districts of Italy, and in the south of France, the average does not exceed twenty-five bushels of corn and five of beans. In Mexico and throughout Spanish America, Indian corn is sowed about three feet and a half between the rows, and two feet apart in them. The average produce can hardly be estimated in so extensive a country, possessing such an infinite variety of soil and climate; but the product is abundant, especially in the south, where the lands are irrigated—much greater than with us in the Atlantic states. The fresh, strong and fertile lands of the West will compete, however, with the best in the world. The largest crops throughout that region, and indeed everywhere, appear to be made upon fresh turned sod; and next, wherever the earth, besides being enriched with an abundant supply of manure, is deeply stirred. In addition to what has been said by our President on the subject of subsoil plowing, in the subjoined letter, we find the following observations in a memoir, published by one of the best practical farmers of Delaware: "To obtain the greatest possible quantity of Indian corn from the least allowed quantity of land, the soil should be as deep as the farmers can make it—if possible, twelve inches. Admitting the same quality in each acre, it will, I think, be found on trial, that if one acre of land, the soil of which is four inches deep, and which has been plowed for the crop no deeper, will produce twenty bushels of corn, the same acre, extending the soil and plowing eight inches, will produce forty bushels; and if twelve inches, eighty bushels, with the same labor."

In the preparation of the land by manuring, we are inclined to the opinion that it is always better to spread the manure evenly over the surface, if the farmer has enough; next, to spread it in the ridges and bed over it; and, last and least, to put the manure in the holes where the grain is to be deposited. In the first method, where the manure is spread over the whole surface of the field, the lateral rootlets—which in good soil extend five or six feet from the stalk—receive abundant nourishment throughout the whole period of the growth of the plant, which is not the case where the manure is confined to the furrow or to the hills. In the dry summer of 1846, the difference in the crops of corn, treated in these several different ways, was very remarkable—the first yielding a fair average, while the others were burnt up and produced nothing.

Various methods are practised of preparing the seed, both to preserve it from the devastation of birds and insects, by rendering it nauseous and repulsive to them, and by hastening its germination. For these purposes, the most common practice is to soak the seed corn in a weak solution of coal tar, separating the grains by means of sand or ashes. Another is to use an infusion of nitre with the coal tar, separating the grains as above. Others again recommend soaking the seed for eight and forty hours before planting, in a solution of muriate of ammonia—one pound of this salt being dissolved in a sufficient quantity of water to soak a bushel of seed corn. Thus prepared, the grains germinate more rapidly, and are said to maintain their superiority, *ceteris paribus*, throughout the growth of the crop. We have known a solution of sulphate of ammonia tried with equal success. It may be prepared by adding an infusion of gypsum (plaster of Paris) to a solution of carbonate of ammonia.

Your committee agree entirely with the president of this society, in his recommendation to cease the use of the plow, in cultivating Indian corn, early enough to permit the rootlets to attain their full growth, and to clear and to lay by the crop with the cultivator and hoe. To shorten these feeders is to diminish the produce of the crop, as his well-conducted experiments will show.

In many parts of our state it is the practice to top the corn, and in all, to strip the blades at the period when the grain is considered sufficiently ripe; but in the north-eastern and western states it has been found, by experience, more profitable to cut the corn off at the surface, and stack it in small stacks in the field, until the grain is sufficiently hardened to admit of its being hauled in. It is then stripped from the stalk and shucked at the bin. With us in the low country, the shucks are left on the stalk and both exposed to rot for manure, and not unfrequently both are piled up and burnt. This must be regarded as a wasteful process. The stalk, when properly cured, contains a great deal of saccharine juice; so much, that in many parts of Spanish America, sugar was made from the stalk of maize before the introduction of the sugar cane. The shuck is always cured and put away, in the upper country, and the best farmers there throw a few handfuls of salt upon each layer of shucks. This provender would be found very useful on our plantations, and prove a wholesome and nutritious food for working cattle and mules.

As the experience of more than a quarter of a century proves the superiority of cutting off corn at the ground, and stacking it in the field, over the method practised by us, the gain being no less than ten per cent., we will, at the risk of being a little too tedious, describe a very common method of performing this operation. A laborer, walking between the second and third rows, counts to the eighth hill, and ties or locks together the stalks on the four centre hills, above the ears, which four hills are not to be cut, but left as a support to begin the stack. He then counts on sixteen hills further, and ties the four hills in the same manner; and so on through the whole field. Two cutters follow between the first and second, and third and fourth rows, cutting the corn close to the ground, and casting it forward; the carriers take it, and set it up straight, in equal proportions, round the four stalks left standing. For security against the high winds, these stacks may be bound round two-thirds of their height from the ground. Others, again, simply cut all the corn and stack it in the field, thirty or forty stalks to the stack, binding the stalks together near the top. After the corn and stalks are hauled home, and the latter stripped, they may be stacked in the form of our potato houses, with two crotchets at each extremity, a ridge pole, and a few laths. The first row of stalks is placed with the butts on the ground, and the succeeding rows with the butts uppermost, so as to allow the water to drip along the leaf blade. The interior of such stacks serves to store pumpkins, turnips, &c., and preserves them from the frost.

Your Committee will conclude this report by giving the opinion of the celebrated agriculturist, Arthur Young, in relation to this plant. He first met with Indian corn in France, and at once appreciated its full value. He says: "For the inhabitants of a country to live on that *plant*, which is the preparation for wheat, and keep their cattle fat upon the leaves of it, is to possess a treasure for which they are indebted to their climate." "Planted in squares, or rows, so far asunder that all imaginable tillage may be given between them, and the ground thus cleansed and prepared at the will of the farmer, is an invaluable circumstance; and finally it is succeeded by wheat. Thus a country whose soil and climate admit the course of 1st, Indian corn, and 2d, wheat, is under a cultivation that perhaps yields the most food for man and beast that is possible to be drawn from the land."

The superiority of this rotation is to be accounted for, not only by the reasons assigned by Arthur Young, that the successful cultivation of Indian corn requires that the land should be highly manured, thoroughly and frequently stirred, and kept clean from grass and weeds, but because, through the medium of its broad leaves, this plant derives a large portion of its nourishment from the atmosphere, and, possessing less gluten than other cereals, extracts from the earth materials not required for the growth of wheat. In consequence of this eulogium, and of the subsequent publications of Cobbett on the same subject, several attempts were made in England to cultivate Indian corn, but hitherto without success. It is to be seen there only in gardens, where it is raised and brought to maturity by forcing it forward in the early spring, and transplanting it into the open beds after the frosts are over. Wherever seen, it is an object of admiration: and its lofty stem, broad leaves, silken tassel, and tall waving flower, justly entitle it to be considered the most beautiful, as it is the most bountiful, of all the cereal grasses.—*J. R. Poinsett.*

INSURANCE OF CHARACTER.—While insurance companies are daily taking risks against fire, life, and the dangers of the sea, there is still one important branch of the business, heretofore overlooked in this country, which would materially contribute both to their own profits and the advancement of the industrial interests of the people—we mean that of affording securityship on the bonds of applicants for public offices, banks, &c., or any situation of responsibility,—or the extension of the present system of insurance, so as to embrace the *character* as well as the *life* of the insured party.

The advantages of such companies are twofold, the benefits resulting not being confined to the party more immediately interested. Relief is at once afforded to many liberal-hearted friends, who have experienced the inconvenience of being often called upon to assume for others, who become candidates for office, a heavy weight of pecuniary responsibility. Here is, of itself, no small inducement to such unlucky wights to become members of an association of the kind, and thereby diminish their own personal liabilities. The individual insured, by paying a premium for the benefit, is saved either the unpleasant condition of dependence and indebtedness, to which the boon which he is compelled to ask gratuitously from an individual invariably subjects him, or else the humiliating mortification of a refusal. The insurer, instead of becoming individually in danger of suffering from his agency in the matter, throws his annual contribution into the general fund, and shares with a hundred others, not the risk of loss, but the *certainty of a handsome dividend.* To illustrate what may appear to some an extravagant conclusion, let us suppose for a moment that every bank officer, (to say nothing of officers in various grades and departments of labor, who are required to give security for the faithful discharge of their duties,) instead of having been compelled to incur obligations to individual friends, had been in the habit of paying to an insurance company, annually, a per centage on the amount of securityship for which those individuals have been hitherto *nominally* liable. What a large amount of revenue might have been accumulated to add to the funds of the company, and what an immense disproportion would this be to the losses incurred,—if any of consequence have been incurred during the last ten or fifteen years. Losses by fire, shipwreck, and other casualties, are not only *frequent,* but absolutely *certain* and *inevitable* in the common course of nature. Our banks and corporations, on the contrary, exhibit little or no evidence of the danger to be apprehended from responsibility for the character of their officers. Individual securityship (admitting, of course, some occasional exceptions) has been so far in a great measure nominal. Indeed, so great is the disproportion between the amount of security required in many instances, and the largest possible amount for which the officer can ever become a defaulter, (admitting him to be the very quintessence of knavery!) that the *apparent* responsibility is, to a great extent, nominal, and merely for effect. Still the obligation conferred is not the less binding, as the security is sometimes compelled to prove himself, on oath, to be worth double the already extravagant sum demanded on his client's bond.

To the poor man, especially, such an institution is most desirable. It is chiefly in subordinate situations, where the salaries are moderate, and the amount of security disproportionately large, that the benefits of insuring character are experienced. A man, with a family dependent upon him for support, would cheerfully appropriate, every year, a certain portion of the proceeds of the office which he may seek, in order that he may obtain, for a consideration, that guarantee of character which he would be reluctant to purchase at the expense, perhaps, of his own independence, or, at any rate, of incurring obligation to a friend or patron.

There is but one institution of the kind that we know of in the world, and we have been at some difficulty to ascertain definitely the precise *modus operandi* by which its movements are regulated. The Guarantee Society of London was established in 1840. This society is empowered to give security for the fidelity of persons holding situations of trust where securities are required, on the annual payment of a stipulated rate per cent. Security is granted to all approved persons employed by public companies, by the great trading and banking interests in London and the country; also to persons in any capacity, either at home or abroad, who may be called upon to furnish security to their employers for honesty and the faithful performance of their duties. No demand is made for stamps, legal charge or otherwise, in addition to the premium. Forms of proposal, or other information, are furnished by the secretary, Thos. Dodgson—office, 19 Birchin-lane, and by the society's agents in all the principal cities throughout the kingdom. These forms embrace all necessary particulars relative to the condition of the applicant—age, residence, occupation, standing in respect to character and habits, relations in life, and extent of responsibility attached to the office. The premium which the office-holder pays is graduated in reference to these attendant circumstances; so that, instead of the applicant obtaining accommodation in proportion to his means, it is rather according to the estimated risk which the company undertakes in becoming responsible for the honesty of the insured. One whose character is above suspicion in the community in which he resides, would thus become entitled to be insured at a lower rate of premium than his less circumspect neighbor—a decided improvement upon the policy of banking privileges, which often reverses the picture.

The salutary effect of such an enlargement of the benefits of insurance, would, it is natural to suppose, be soon felt in the more favorable tone which it would impart to the general aspect of business, and the influence which it would exert in placing the poor man, without means or friends, and him who is blessed with both, on the same footing. Many worthy and capable men, whose qualifications would confer dignity upon the offices to which they may be chosen, are deterred from offering their names for office, through an indisposition to place themselves in situations where they must become indebted for favors; and instances have often occurred, where persons who have been unanimously called to fill such positions have been compelled to decline for the same reason. The per centage of insurance in such cases may be graduated in reference to the known and acknowledged character and standing of the applicant; and the risk incurred (at least in the community where we have enjoyed the most opportunities of observation) would be far less than that involved in any other contingency provided against by associations now in existence.

There are many in every community who feel deeply the embarrassment of being frequently called upon to assume the responsibilities of securityship. Unbounded as may be the confidence reposed in the integrity of a friend whom he may desire to serve, the individual insurer of character feels it to be an investment which yields no premium, and may, one day or other, through some accident by no means affecting his friend's integrity, reduce him and his family to beggary. A single loss of a few thousands, by fire or any other catastrophe, may break an individual, but would be an every-day trifle to a wealthy corporation. The advantage of association, for any object, cannot, of course, be questioned in this age of the world. To both the insurer and insured, then, the system proposed would appear to be a blessing. The former is subjected to far less risk, the latter is relieved of his unpleasant position of dependence. Such an improvement in the financial condition of society is worth striving after. No better mode of investment can be devised, whether for capitalists or every citizen who has the means of purchasing a single share. Many of our citizens with very moderate means would willingly unite in such an organization, if those more able, and possessing the requisite means and influence, would only take the lead. We have had occasion before, at the suggestion of others, to present this subject for consideration through the medium of the press, and now would most respectfully invite the views of our friends with regard to it in these columns. The proposition strikes us as especially adapted to the interests of the industrial pursuits of our times—one of the great objects which it is the province and duty of the press to watch over and foster. An association such as it contemplates would be one of general public utility, inasmuch as the plan involves the encouragement of industry and economy, and the equitable division of labor—two essential elements in the politico-economical organization of wealth.—*Heriot.*

IRON INTERESTS OF U. S.—The United States census returns, for the decennial periods, 1840 and 1850, show a vast increase in the make of iron in the United States. If we take the returns by states, the result is as follows:

PRODUCTION OF PIG IRON IN THE UNITED STATES.

States	1840	1850
Maine	6,122	1,484
New-Hampshire	1,320	200
Vermont	6,743	3,200
Massachussetts	9,332	12,287
Rhode Island	4,126	—
Connecticut	6,495	13,420
New-York	29,088	23,022
New-Jersey	11,114	24,031
Pennsylvania	98,395	285,702
Delaware	17	—
Maryland	18,876	43,641
Virginia	18,810	22,163
North Carolina	968	400
South Carolina	1,250	—
Georgia	494	900
Alabama	30	522
Louisiana	1,400	—
Tennessee	16,128	30,420
Kentucky	29,206	24,245
Ohio	35,236	52,658
Michigan	601	660
Indiana	810	1,850
Illinois	158	2,700
Missouri	180	19,250
Wisconsin	3	1,000
Total in tons	286,903	564,755

The census of 1840 did not distinguish quite accurately the making of cast iron itself, from making "iron castings." The census of 1850 has been more definite, giving the quantity of iron made from the ore, and quantity of the raw or pig iron made into castings and into bar iron. This accounts for the apparent decrease in the make of cast iron in the New-England states. In Maine, for instance, there was only one blast furnace in 1840, producing three hundred tons. If, however, we allow the whole quantity in 1840 to be cast iron made, and take the quantities of pig iron imported, we shall have the apparent consumption of pig iron in the United States, at both periods, as follows:

MAKE AND IMPORTATION OF IRON INTO THE UNITED STATES.

	1840.	1850.
Quantity made	tons 286,903	564,755
Quantity imported	" 5,515	74,874
Supply	tons 292,418	639,629

This gives a result rather more than double for 1850, what was consumed in 1840. If, now, we take the weight of iron articles imported for the same years, the result will be as follows:

IMPORT OF CERTAIN IRON ARTICLES INTO THE UNITED STATES BY WEIGHT.

	lb. 1840.	1846.	1850.
Wire, iron and steel, cap and bonnet	3,543	26,990	8,342
All other	184,259	72,828	2,123,481
Manufactures of Iron—			
Tacks, brads and sprigs	4,234	11,644	—
Wood screws	—	64,177	—
Nails, cut and wrought	715,191	770,240	2,656,786
Spikes	104,134	10,306	51,311
Chain cables	2,114,760	2,374,925	10,990,355
Chains and other cables		66	
Wrought iron, for ships, locomotives and steam engines	—	54,621	—
Malleable iron	—	17,599	—
Anchors	154,227	49,755	960,482
Anvils	324,698	1,270,451	1,423,408
Blacksmith's hammers and sledges	35,279	103,411	133,979
Castings of vessels	444,388	631,194	264,468
All other	3,180,100	656,678	2,806,936
Glazed or tinned hollow ware	—	363,386	32,615
Sad irons, hatters' and tailors' irons	—	43,968	—
Cast iron butt hinges	—	634,065	—
Axletrees, or parts thereof	—	71,910	—
Braziers' rods, from 3-16 to 10-16th inch diameter	433,620	305,883	4,470,040
Nail or spike rods, slit, rolled or hammered	1,108	8,471	654,124
Sheet and hoop iron	5,529,585	10,087,507	33,753,714
Casement rods, band, scroll, etc	34,470	6,754	1,297,767
Old and scrap … cwt.	110,314	47,247	202,090
Bar, manufactured by rolling … "	656,574	482,176	4,959,022
Bar, manufactured otherwise … "	576,381	426,569	294,132
Steel … "	44,506	103,141	127,517
Total tons	75,351	61,007	366,640

This gives an immense increase—nearly all of which is railroad bars and boiler plates, contributing to locomotion. If we embrace these figures in the make and importation, the consumption will be as follows:

SUPPLY OF CAST AND WROUGHT IRON IN THE UNITED STATES.

		1840.	1850.
Make of cast-iron	tons	286,903	564,755
Import	"	5,515	74,874
" wrought iron	"	75,351	366,640
Supply	tons	367,769	1,006,069

The weight of nails and domestic iron articles exported is about 5,000 tons, and with the foreign re-exported, leaves the consumption of iron in the United States at about 1,000,000 tons, nearly the whole of which is the raw material, for manufactures and hardware, which have struggled manfully against English competition, driving out nearly all the leading articles formerly imported, although they have had to pay such exorbitant prices for the raw material, as compared with the English manufacturers. The manufacturers of iron paid last year three and a quarter million dollars tax on the raw material they used; notwithstanding which, the shelves of our hardware stores show constantly increasing proportions of American goods. In very many cases, as in wood screws, butt hinges, scales, etc., the American articles are much superior in quality, and cheaper in price, than the English articles, consequently the importation has gradually ceased. The importation and cost of iron has been as follows for several years:

	BARS—ROLLED IRON.			HAMMERED IRON.			PIG IRON.			HOOP & SHEET IRON.		
Year	Quantity Tons	Value	Av. cost per ton	Tons	Value	Cost	Tons	Value	Cost	Tons	Value	Cost
1843*	15757	$511282	$33 50	6254	$327550	$52 37	3873	$48251	$12 46	1202	$134206	$111 70
1844	37891	1065582	28 12	11822	583065	49 32	14944	200522	13 42	2010	152771	76 00
1845	51188	1691748	33 05	18176	872157	47 99	27510	506291	18 40	5344	409528	190 00
1846	24188	1127418	46 76	21328	1165429	54 65	24187	489573	20 24	4508	481828	106 80
1846†	8098	434316	53 63	10413	588322	56 50	4478	82398	18 40	641	70660	109 20
1847‡	32085	1695173	52 83	1998	266386	53 30	23477	472088	20 11	5345	399042	74 80
1848	81589	3679598	45 10	20156	975214	48 38	51632	815415	15 79	9730	729955	75 00
1849	173457	6060068	34 93	10598	525770	49 61	105632	1405613	13 30	11500	543256	47 35
1850	247951	7397166	29 83	14706	744735	50 64	74874	950660	12 69	15150	835995	55 19
1851	254301	7324283	28 80	20198	900026	44 50	67248	787524	11 71	21520	960802	44 62

* Nine months to June 30. † Seven months to Nov. 30. ‡ Jan. 7.

In all these articles the reduction in price has been very great, particularly in hoop and sheet. It is in this lessened cost of the raw material that we find the main cause of the stimulus given to the manufacture of hardware and cutlery in the country—as the raw material was obtained on better terms, the import of manufactured articles declined. The census returns show the following result:

IRON PRODUCED IN THE UNITED STATES.

	Pig Iron	Castings	Wrought Iron
Value of raw material	$7,005,289	$10,346,355	$9,698,109
Value produced	12,748,777	25,108,155	16,747,074
Net product	$5,743,488	$14,761,800	$7,048,965
Hands employed	20,448	23,589	13,257

Thus the raw material purchased for the employment of 36,846 men cost $20,044,464, and pays about $5,000,000 tax to those who employ 20,448 men. In consequence of this tax, the manufacturers of iron require 30 per cent. protection, against imported articles, on the $41,855,229 of iron articles that they produce, and which, in the state to which they have brought it, becomes the raw material for cutlery, plow, machine, factory, locomotive, rail-road, steamboat, house and ship builders, and tool makers, and every employment of life—all these persons have to contend against the importation of the articles they make, and they do so with this heavy load upon their backs for the raw material. Where there are 20,000 men employed making pig iron, there are 36,846 men who purchase it, and advance it to a state which employ about 30,000 men, in hardware and iron industry: that is to say, the industry of over 66,000 men is heavily clogged, in order that the employers of 20,000 men may make inordinate profits. England, and even France in some cases, have seen the wisdom of placing raw materials, to the best advantage, at the disposal of industry. Thus the British government, seeing that Swedish steel-iron was essential to the manufacture of British steel, reduced the duty from $30 per ton in 1825, making it free in 1845. France charged $84 per ton duty on that steel iron, until a commission discovered that, in order to make steel in France, it was necessary to have Swedish steel-iron, and it is made free of duty. With us the iron manufacturers are very slow of discovering that, in order to make their wares as cheap as the English, they should have raw material on as favorable terms. The above table shows what an immense development the use of iron has undergone as the prices here declined, but even at the present rates the difference in favor of the English manufacturer is as follows:

PRICE OF IRON PER TON IN LIVERPOOL AND NEW-YORK.

Price July 17	Scotch Pig	English Bar	Sheet	Hoop
Liverpool	$11 75	$23 50	$34 80	$31 70
New-York	20 00	38 00	78 40	67 20
Excess in N.-York,	$8 25	$14 50	$43 60	$35 50

We may now glance for a moment at the development which the internal trade has reached, as indicated by the returns of the Ohio public works.

POUNDS OF IRON AND NAILS CLEARED ON THE OHIO AND MIAMI CANALS.

	Cleveland	Portsmouth	Cincinnati	Toledo	Total
1841	4,195,970	6,587,019	2,389,306	—	13,172,295
1842	3,351,235	5,148,527	1,653,890	—	10.153,652
1843	457,021	7,115,650	1,930,318	860,234	10,363,223
1844	365,764	5,864,941	2,403,725	962,710	9,597,340
1845	450,367	6,787,378	3,026,385	785,522	11,049,652
1846	1,281,533	8.479,749	3,696,200	1,112,273	14,569,755
1847	1,552,171	7,856,287	4,945,800	1,320,068	15,674,326
1848	2,030,305	12,564,243	6,301,364	1,528,365	22,424,277
1849	5,503,505	12,768,527	8,781,467	1,396,435	28,449,934
1850	16,990,795	13,558,228	10,823,804	2,955,604	44,328,431
1851	11,713,594	14,782,000	19,345,053	17,296,040	63,136,687

This has been an increase of over 20,000 tons in Ohio alone, within five or six years, and that iron is so distant from the sea-board as to be little affected by the imported article, which costs in New-York 80 per cent. more than in Liverpool, as follows:

	s.	d.	s.	d.
Cost of one ton pig iron in Liverpool			44	0
Insurance, 1½ per cent	0	9		
Interest, 60 days at 3 per cent	0	3		
Duty on 44s. with 2½ per cent. added by the Custom-house at New-York, say 45s. at 30 per cent	13	0		
Freight	20	0		
Commission and charges at New-York, 5 per cent	4	4		
Brokerage 10s., weighing 21 cwt.	1	5½	40	3½
Cost in New-York	$21 2 or		84	3½

At Constantia, New-York, the expense of iron making is thus stated by the manufacturers:

One hundred and fifty bushels charcoal, 5c	$7 5
Two tons ore, $1 75	3 5
Flux	0 25
Labor	2 00
Interest and repairs	3 00
Product 2,000 tons per annum	$16 25

To get the imported iron to the Constantia furnace would cost $2 more, making $7 in favor of the domestic manufacture—and it will be observed that this is *charcoal* iron, which is more expensive than coal iron. In Pennsylvania, where all the materials for iron are favorably situated, an extensive furnace owner states it can be delivered in Philadelphia at $15 per ton. In Poughkeepsie, New-York, the same iron will cost $19 per ton, because the materials are brought to the furnace from a distance. If a duty is graduated to the wants of a disadvantageously situated furnace, great injustice is done to consumers in order to sustain a blundering projector, and those more skilfully located reap inordinate profits. The shipping interest suffers materially from this course of legislation. A ship of 500 tons will require 20 tons of iron-work, 10 tons cables, 2 tons anchors, say 32 tons. The tonnage built in the Union last year, 298,203, would require in round numbers 20,000 tons of iron, which cost at least $600,000 more than it would have cost English shipping.—*U. S. Economist.*

KENTUCKY—DESCRIPTION OF THE COUNTRY; EARLY HISTORY AND MANNERS; SCHEMES FOR SEPARATION FROM VIRGINIA AND FROM THE UNION; MR. BURR, WILKINSON, &C.; CAUSES OF WESTERN EXCITEMENT; POPULATION AND PRODUCTS OF KENTUCKY; AGRICULTURE OF KENTUCKY; DANIEL BOONE; MINERAL SPRINGS OF KENTUCKY; THE MAMMOTH CAVE; LEXINGTON, FRANKFORT, MAYSVILLE, LOUISVILLE; INTERNAL IMPROVEMENTS; EDUCATION AND SLAVERY IN KENTUCKY.—The fame of "Old Kentucky," whose hardy hunters and warriors have been celebrated so much in national patriotic songs and legends, from the time when George Rogers Clark made his descent upon the savage tribes of the Wabash to that which saw, in all his "martial pomp," "John Bull" in the "low and murky places" of Louisiana, is not likely soon to be lost among the generations that are now passing upon the board. If the romance of hunter and border life has given way to civilization, scattered log huts and villages to mansions and crowded cities, dense forests to cultivated fields, Daniel Boone to Henry Clay—still is Kentucky famed for her hardy independence and fearless intrepidity, for her stalwart men and her handsome women, for her fruitful soil, her benign climate and the general and uninterrupted prosperity of her people.

"The country is in some parts nearly level; in others not so much so; in others again, hilly, but moderately—and in such places there is most water. The levels are not like a carpet, but interspersed with small risings and declivities which form a beautiful prospect. The soil is of a loose, deep and black mould, without sand, in the first-rate lands about two or three feet deep, and exceedingly luxuriant in all its productions. The country in general may be considered as well timbered, producing large trees of many kinds and to be exceeded by no country in variety. Those which are peculiar to Kentucky, are the sugar-tree, which grows in all parts, and furnishes every family with great plenty of excellent sugar. The honey-locust is curiously surrounded with large thorny spikes, bearing long and broad pods in the form of peas, has a sweet taste and makes excellent beer. The coffee-tree greatly resembles the black-oak, grows large and also bears a pod in which is inclosed coffee. The pawpaw tree does not grow to a great size, is a soft wood, bears a fine fruit, much like a cucumber in shape and size, and tastes sweet. The fine cane, on which the cattle feed and grow fat, in general grows from three to twelve feet high, of a hard substance, with joints at eight or ten inches distance along the stalk, from which proceed leaves resembling the willow. There are many canebrakes so thick and tall that it is difficult to pass through them. Where no cane grows there is an abundance of wild rye, clover and buffalo-grass, covering vast tracts of country, and affording excellent pasture for cattle. The fields are covered with an abundance of wild herbage not common to other countries. Here are seen the finest crown imperial in the world, the cardinal flower, so much extolled for its scarlet color, and all the year, excepting the winter months, the plains and valleys are adorned with a variety of flowers of the most admirable beauty. Here is also found the tulip-bearing laurel tree, or magnolia, which is very fragrant and continues to blossom and seed for several months together. The reader, by casting his eye upon the map, and viewing round the heads of Licking from the Ohio, and round the heads of Kentucky, Dick's River, and down Green River to the Ohio, may view, in that great compass of above one hundred miles square, the most extraordinary country on which the sun has ever shone."*

In the geology of Kentucky the *blue limestone* occupies a conspicuous place. It forms the surface rock in a large part of the state, and is used for building purposes. Among the cliffs of the Kentucky River, is found an excellent *marble*, capable of fine polish. The cliff limestone is the base of the Ohio falls

* "Filson's Kentucky" in a supplement to "Imlay's," 1784; see Collins.

at Louisville. The *slate*, or shale, is very common, bituminous, and supports combustion and contains iron pyrites and ores, giving rise to mineral springs. The sand, or *freestone*, extends from Danville to Louisville, etc., is used for purposes of art and even the construction of grindstones. The *cavernous limestone*, as its name imports, gives rise to many caves, the most famous of which, the *Mammoth*, we shall hereafter describe. The *conglomerate* or pudding stone, consists of quartz pebbles, rounded, and united with fine sand by a kind of natural cement. It underlies the coal formation. The *coal beds* of Kentucky are known as those of the Ohio and Illinois. They cover ten or twelve thousand square miles. The coal is very accessible, but very little is mined, not perhaps, annually, more than 4 or 5,000,000 bushels. *Iron* is equally abundant in the state, but mostly neglected. It is commanded by navigable streams and must produce future wealth. An estimate of the quantity embraced has been fixed at 38,000,000 tons, "a quantity sufficient to supply a ton of iron annually to every individual in the United States, estimating them at 15,000,000, for 2,560 years." Small quantities of *lead* are traced in Kentucky. *Salt springs* abound in the sandstone formation, and a million bushels of salt is annually worked. *Saltpetre* and *plaster of Paris* are found in the caves. The mineral springs are numerous, embracing sulphur, blue lick, epsom, chalybeate, etc. The most fruitful soil of the state is that of the blue limestone formation —the country about Lexington and toward the Ohio is said to be the garden of the state.

It was not until the middle of the eighteenth century, that the Saxon foot-print was traced in Kentucky. The state was one great hunting-ground and battle-field for the savages of the North and the South. Among the earliest American explorers were Boone and Knox, and these, after incredible perils, returned to Virginia and Carolina, spreading everywhere the fame of the back-woods. Then came Thomas Bullitt, James Harrod and Richard Henderson. The foundation of Boonesboro' was laid by Daniel himself, who had brought to the banks of the Kentucky the first white women—his wife and daughters. Kenton, Calloway and Logan arrived. Kentucky was now made a County of Virginia, and, in 1777, the first court was held at Harrodsburg.

We pass over the bloody strife with the Indian tribes, the invasion from Canada, of Du Quesne, the expedition of Clark against Vincennes, the perils and the heroism of the Kentuckians, during all of which adventurers were still crowding to their midst. "The rich lands of Kentucky," says a chronicle, "were the prize of the first occupants, and they rushed to seize them with a rapacity stronger than the fear of death."

In the early manners of the settlers of Kentucky, there is much that will interest our readers. We have, on another occasion, referred to the peculiarities of border life in the Great West,* and shall only add now to what we have already written—basing ourself upon the authority of "Doddridge's Notes."

The Kentuckian was altogether self-dependent, being excluded from intercourse with his Eastern neighbors. His table furniture was of wood, but never larder furnished better meats and butter, or stimulated keener appetite. With his guest he freely divided. He wore a hunting shirt—sometimes of skins—and a wallet for his provender and amunition. The tomahawk and scalping-knife adorned his belt. A fur cap, leggins and deer-skin moccasins, completed his costume. His residence was a log cabin without floors, defended by walls, stockades and block-houses, from the fierce savages. He married young and needed no fortune but his unerring rifle. His wedding was an epoch in the settlement. The ladies flaunted in their linsey petticoats, brogans and buckskin gloves. The marriage procession was unique. The whisky bottle performed its important part. The ceremony being performed, dinner followed, and then the dance, reels and jigs, until morning.

"About nine or ten o'clock, a deputation of young ladies stole off the bride and put her to bed. This done, a deputation of young men, in like manner, stole off the groom and placed him snugly by the side of his bride. The dance still continued, and if seats happened to be scarce, every young man, when not engaged in the dance, was obliged to offer his lap as a seat for one of the girls, and the offer was sure to be accepted. In the midst of this hilarity, the bride and groom were not forgotten. Pretty late in the night some one would remind the company, that the new couple must stand in need of some refreshments; 'black betty,' which was the name of the bottle, was called for and sent up stairs, but often 'black betty' did not go alone. Sometimes as much bread, beef, pork and cabbage, were sent along with her, as would afford a good meal for half a dozen hungry men. The young couple were compelled to eat and drink more or less of whatever was offered them."

Soon the whole neighborhood unite in building for the happy pair the needful log cabin; and thus, as log cabin after log cabin appeared, began the peopling of Kentucky. A race of hunters and yeomen and *freemen* sprung from that early stock, whose *epitha-*

---

* See Vol. IV., Com. Rev., Art. "Great West."

lamium was sung by wild forests, and whose morning slumbers were cheered by the melody of nature's choristers.

A review of the political history of Kentucky presents but few prominent landmarks. The war of the Revolution closed, but left the Kentuckians in constant fear of an Indian invasion. The citizens assembled at Danville, which became afterward famous for Conventions west of the mountains, soon discovered they were without the means of defence, and that a government at Richmond was too far off to be relied upon. Two other Conventions at Danville recommended a peaceable and constitutional separation from Virginia. The third Convention sent a petition to Richmond, and, in 1786, an act was passed complying with the wishes of Kentucky. This act made some unfortunate provisions which caused great delays, as well as danger to the country. The Kentuckians looked upon the old federal government with great distrust, as being too weak to defend them from the Indians ; and it was notorious, that the New-England states, entirely at peace themselves, were desirous, for commercial considerations, to yield up the navigation of the Mississippi for twenty years, to Spain. Congress, from the fear of a standing army, would send no men to protect the frontier from savage warfare. Virginia could give no relief. Can it be wondered, then, that there was a deep feeling in Kentucky of self-defence, which sought a *separation by any means*, from such a federation, and *entire independence?*

A fourth Convention at Danville was attended with no better result than the three others, and Virginia had prolonged the time two years when Kentucky might be independent. To add to the ill-feeling occasioned by this, it was announced that John Jay was actually ceding the navigation of the river. Then were formed committees of correspondence, and the name of Jay was every where odious in the West.

A fifth Convention met, and on petition, a delegate to Congress was allowed by Virginia ; but the Constitution of the United States having been adopted, Congress turned over to the new government all action upon the claims of Kentucky. The whole state was again in a ferment, and, at this early period, the refusal of Congress was attributed, by able minds, to the jealousy of New-England of any increase of *southern power*. This jealousy was expected to continue under the new government.

Taking advantage of such a state of things in the West, Spain proposed clandestinely through her minister, peculiar commercial favors and facilities to Kentucky, if she would erect herself into an *independent government*. At the very moment of the proposal, Gen. Wilkinson returned from New-Orleans, where he had been on a mercantile adventure, with intelligence that he had secured the right of landing, selling and depositing tobacco there. He proposed to purchase all the tobacco, and gave out that Kentucky might command the trade of the river and of the South West, if she would be true to herself and her position. Then were party politics at their height, and the risks to the Union imminent.

A sixth and seventh Convention met at Danville. A separation, by violent means, from Virginia, was proposed. Wilkinson read a manuscript essay upon the navigation of the Mississippi, for which the Convention tendered *unanimous* thanks. Constitutional measures prevailed, and an address by Wilkinson was voted to Congress. An eighth and a ninth Convention assembled, and on the 4th of February, 1791, Kentucky was admitted into the Union.

Indian wars continued frequent on the frontier, and complaints of the inefficiency of the federal government was again heard. The whiskey tax, too, became oppressive. The American policy toward the republicans of France was denounced in every cabin west of the mountains. Enthusiasm was at its height, and the agents of the mad minister Genet were received in triumph in the West. It was proposed to raise an army in Kentucky, to descend upon New-Orleans. The people were rife for the movement. " Democratic clubs" were extending everywhere. Even the Governor could write to the Secretary of State: "I shall feel but little inclination in restraining or punishing my fellow-citizens, etc., to gratify or remove the fears of a minister of a prince who openly withholds from us an invaluable right, and who secretly instigates against us a savage and cruel enemy." The old idea of *independence* was mooted again, but the storm passed over.

In the ten or twelve years which succeeded, and which included the period of negotiation for the navigation of the Mississippi, and then for the purchase of Louisiana, Kentucky was destined again to be agitated to her very centre.

The treaty of 1795 with Spain, gave to the United States a deposit at New-Orleans for merchandise, and the freedom of the river. Pending negotiations, the Governor of Louisiana had approached some leading citizens of Kentucky, with the view of a different treaty ; but the matter was checked in its bud by the action at Washington. Judge Sebastian, it is said. was willing to go on, believing the regular treaty would not be ratified, or being, as is most probable, in the interests of Spain.

The faithlessness of the Spaniards was soon evident. An agent again appeared in Kentucky with the offer of artillery, small arms and munitions of war, money in large quantities, etc., if inflammable documents were circulated calling for a separation of the Union—

independence, etc.; if Fort Massac were seized, the federal troops everywhere dispossessed, and the northern boundary of Louisiana on the east of the river extended to the mouth of the Yazoo. This scheme of course received little countenance, for Kentucky had already achieved her darling object.

Seven years now passed in comparative quiet and prosperity, when the whole nation was excited by the intelligence that the Spaniards had violated the treaty by a denial of the right of deposit at New-Orleans, without assigning any other point for that purpose. It was even announced that Louisiana had been ceded to France.

The purchase of Louisiana by the United States, would at once and forever have composed the turbulent elements of the West, but for the appearance there, at this period, of a man whose genius was of the most profound character, whose popularity had been wide, but whose career and ambition had been prematurely arrested. Aaron Burr was prepared for any great or desperate enterprise, and the West seemed to promise the widest field for his abilities. What the designs of Burr were, have never, perhaps, been fully divulged. The probabilities are that they have been exaggerated. We have little, if any, faith in the affidavit of Eaton, about the assassination of the President, corruption of the Navy, and violent overthrow of Congress.* The policy, if not the ambition or virtue of Burr, was opposed to this. The material that he could rely upon was entirely *in the West;* and within the bounds of a not very clearly ascertained national policy or duty, at that period, an army of adventurers might be found to precipate themselves upon the Spanish colonies in the southwest, and entirely revolutionize them. The success of citizen Genet a few years before evinced this, but now the times were even riper, as Spanish troops, in the first heart-burnings of Spain after the cession of Bonaparte, had been ordered to our frontier, and an American army under Gen. Wilkinson was ready to check their advances—war with Spain was daily apprehended.†

Thus far the design of Col. Burr, though *unlawful*, was in no respect *treacherous*, and without even the knowledge of its unlawfulness, thousands were enlisted in the enterprise. Had he stopped here, it would be difficult to show in what respect he was more guilty than the men who raised armies among us for Texan independence, or entertained favorably the "*Sierra Madre*" *scheme*. Mr. Burr would then have appeared only *in advance of his times*, and with profound genius recognizing the necessity of a *more southern extension* of our territories, perceived long after by the statesmen who originated the Mexican war, and the people who almost universally applauded and approved *its results*. The rapacity of the American mind was so early perceived.

This southern republic or empire which loomed up so magnificently in the diseased mind of Col. Burr, was not intended to dispossess Spain, only. A part—it is difficult to say how much—of the territory lately purchased by our government was to be included—*certainly, New-Orleans.* This territory had been purchased in the face of a violent opposition from a powerful party. The Americans had no knowledge of the importance of the purchase and had no love for it. In the event of war with Spain, was there no chance of a re-cession? The free navigation of the river, and the right of deposit, being all that was desired, would Congress care who exercised the sovereignty? Was there no hope that government, despite of the cost of Louisiana, might acknowledge its independence, should a sufficient power be established there? We have heard, even in our day, leading statesmen speak with complaisance of ceding back the purchased territories in New-Mexico and California; without equivalent we must suppose—for what could Mexico pay?

We throw out these views, not so much to exonerate Mr. Burr, (a defence of whom we have never read, who was, without doubt, not very scrupulous in the pursuit of his ends, or in the character of them, but who has, it is not at all improbable, been abused far more than he deserves, a common fate with most intriguers,) as to rescue the fame of many who were disposed to favor and co-operate with him.

It is difficult to fix precisely the position occupied by Gen. Wilkinson in all these matters. From his first appearance in Kentucky, he took an active part in its politics, and being an able and ambitious man, was calculated to have a wide influence in the then forming society. He found the Kentuckians restive under the rule of Virginia, and readily united with them in the legitimate purpose of separating from her. Ardent, impulsive and impatient of results, which, from various causes, were tediously protracted, and which appeared at times not likely to be realized at all, he took an active part with many leading citizens in favor of separation at once and by any means. The patriot was not so much at fault here. Kentucky was not unwilling, on many occasions, to *acknowledge the patriotism* and *adopt the services* of General Wilkinson.

After the question of Kentucky's separate existence from Virginia became complicated by the new and exciting questions of the navigation of the Mississippi and the deposit at New-Orleans, the enterprising spirit of Wilkinson led him into a commercial adventure to

* On his dying bed, thirty years after, he solemnly protested to Dr. Hosack, he had never meditated the dissolution of the Union.

† Mr. Burr owned a large share of the "Bastrop grant," originally made by the Spaniards in the South West, and held out an intention of colonizing it. He often told his daughter she should be "Queen of Mexico."

Louisiana, where, without doubt, he listened to overtures from the Spanish authorities, and perhaps about the same period began to think not unfavorably of the plan, entertained by many, of a complete separation of Kentucky from the Union. Before visiting with bitter denunciation this conduct, there are many things which ought to be considered. The old confederation, during its existence, was utterly impotent in affording protection to the West. The republicans of the West, like those of some of the eastern states, looked with great jealousy upon the consolidating character of the *new* and federal and *constitutional* Union of 1789. Many of the states refused, for a long time, to come into such a Union at all. The course of some of the eastern states, in disregarding the interests of the West, had excited disgust and alarm. Would the new government be more propitious to the West, whose wants it could scarcely understand or appreciate? In those days many good and wise men all over the country doubted of the success of the federal experiment. In the difficulties, the almost impossibilities of communication between the eastern states and those beyond the mountains, was it not at least improbable that a *federal* system, then so little understood, could have included them all under a sound, equal and republican government? Men might well have doubted, as they now doubt, whether Oregon and California can be retained under our system, should there be any very powerful adverse temptatations. If such a doubt can be expressed now, how much more probable when the power of steam by land or by water lay dormant, and a passage from New-Orleans or Louisville to Washington was even more hazardous, protracted and expensive, than to Francisco or to China, perhaps, when our *rail-road* shall be completed!

Whilst Wilkinson was listening to the overtures of the Spaniards at New-Orleans, it is probable he lent an ear also to those of Col. Burr, whose schemes were of course the very opposite. In neither case is it evident that he took a very decided and active part, and, although there is little doubt that the independence of the West occupied a place in his mind, we have not been able, from the history of the times, to find him committed in any criminal manner. In the condition of the country, it was natural to look anywhere for relief. A far-seeing man might well have deemed it important to conciliate the Spaniards, in the then infant state of the West, and to give an under show of countenance to the designs of Burr, to keep the Spaniards in check. If Wilkinson *coquetted*, he did only what a late President of Texas boasted; and if he went too far on either side, it should be reflected how almost impossible is the *mean*, and how difficult, and even dangerous, the game to be played. We will not go further than this with the evidence before us, and accuse the old soldier of any want of high and patriotic regard for his country, or of any act which he believed would in the slightest degree redound to her injury.

Having thus gone more at length into the discussion of the early and stormy politics of Kentucky, and the West, than was intended or might be justified, we shall now proceed to consider the physical characteristics, agriculture, commerce, and wealth of this state.

I. POPULATION OF KENTUCKY.

Years	Blacks	Total Population
1790	12,430	73,677
1800	43,344	220,959
1810	80,560	406,511
1820	120,732	564,317
1830	165,350	688,844
1840	182,258	779,828
1850, approx.	—	881,863

Of the blacks, in 1840, 7,317 were free. The whole number of blacks in Kentucky is perhaps not much greater than in 1840.

II. POPULATION OF CHIEF TOWNS OF KENTUCKY.

	1810.	1820.	1830.	1840.	1847.
Louisville	1,357	4,012	10,352	21,210	40,000
Lexington	4,226	5,279	6,104	6,996	8,000
Maysville	335	1,130	2,040	2,741	5,000
Frankfort	1,099	1,679	1,680	1,916	2,500
Covington	—	—	—	—	6,000

III. REVENUE STATISTICS OF KENTUCKY.

In 1845, land, acres, 17,879,148; value of lands, $109,991,650: lots, $21,266,249; slaves, $52,372,139; jennies, $86,410; mules, $684,504; cattle, $1,290,216; stores, $6,363,359; horses, $10,294,922.

In 1846, land, acres, 18,502,903; value of lands, $116,785,543; lots, $23,270,561; slaves, $55,003,861; jennies, $91,897; mules, $898,603; cattle, $1,584,994; stores, $6,855,863; horses, $10,598,042.

The number of slaves had increased 1,840 in one year; the number of horses and mares increased from 358.567 to 361,828; number of mules from 21,277 to 28,806; jennies, from 2,169 to 2,276; cattle, from 435,956 to 457,403; stores, from 2,498 to 2,759.

The whole value of the above articles, including the effects of the equalization law, about 27 millions, was, in 1846, estimated in taxation at $242,388,967. The whole revenue from taxes, $383,283. The average value of land in the state was estimated at $6 31 per acre.

IV. VALUE PRODUCTS BY CENSUS OF 1840—MANUFACTURES.

Machinery product	$46,074
Hardware	22,350
Precious metals	19,060
Other metals	164,080
Granite	8,820
Brick and lime	240,919
Woolens	151,246
Cottons	329,380
Silk manufactures	819
Flax manufactures	7,519
Mixed manufactures	127,875
Tobacco	413,585
Hats, etc	201,310
Tanneries, etc	732,646
Liquors (capital invested)	315,308
Soap and candles	28,765
Glass, earthenware, etc., pro	24,090

Confectionary	36,050
Powder (cap. invested)	42,000
Drugs, etc	16,630
Cordage, product	1,292,276
Paper	44,000
Printing and binding (cap.)	86,325
Carriages and wagons, pro	168,724
Mills—their product	2,437,947
Household furniture, product	273,350
Houses built, val. in 1 year	1,039,172
Other manufactures	697,029

V. ESTIMATED PRODUCT AGRICULTURE, 1846.

Bushels wheat	4,769,000
" Barley	15,400
" Oats	13,091,000
" Rye	2,548,000
" Buckwheat	14,000
" Corn	54,625,000
" Potatoes	1,508,000
Tons hay	123,000
Tons flax and hemp	22,500
Pounds tobacco	63,310,000
" Cotton	1,400,000
" Rice	17,000
" Silk cocoons	6,970
" Sugar	2,100,000

The chief agricultural products of Kentucky, it will be perceived, are Indian corn, tobacco and hemp, and these are in sufficient quantities to give the state character as a great agricultural producer. In this is centred her chief source of wealth. Her cattle and stock, we have also seen, are important interests.

We have desired to furnish the readers of our Review a paper upon the most improved methods of cultivation and manufacture of tobacco and hemp in the western states, and applied, not long since, to the Hon. Henry Clay for the desired information. Mr. Clay, with the true characteristics of his high and generous nature, and unlimited public spirit, handed us a copy of a publication, entitled "*Essays* on Practical Agriculture," &c., by Adam Beatty, Vice-President of the Kentucky Agricultural Society. Among these essays are several prize papers upon the subjects desired, as also upon several others of the first importance. As space admits, hereafter, we shall make large extracts from the volume.

According to an authority, the first English cattle brought to Kentucky were from the stock of Mr. Patton, of Virginia, who imported, in 1782, bulls of the long-horned or beef breed, and also a cow of the short-horned or milk breed. The first stock of Kentucky was, therefore, a cross of the milk and beef breed, and this constitutes the basis of most of the English cattle now in the state. Mr. Beatty controverts the statement, and maintains " the cows of Mr. Patton's stock were only *part* blooded, without the admixture of short-horned or milk breed. In 1803, a bull of the Miller stock was introduced from Virginia, which, with the cows from Patton, produced unquestionably the best milkers that have ever been in Kentucky, little inferior in form to the present most approved stock, and of greater size." It was not before 1817 that English cattle were imported directly from England into Kentucky. Mr. Sanders introduced four short-horned bulls, the same number of cows, and also two bulls and two cows of the long-horned. Mr. Clay, on his return from Ghent, brought over some Hereford cattle, esteemed by some superior to the short-horned Durham. The importations came now to be very frequent, and the result is the splendid and unrivaled cattle of Kentucky. The Merino breed of sheep was introduced into the state by Seth Adams, in 1809; and in 1829, Mr. Clay brought from west Pennsylvania a flock of fifty full bloods.

Mr. Beatty gives this view of the progress of agriculture in Kentucky:

"The first settlement of Kentucky may be regarded as the hunter state. Though cattle could easily have been raised by grazing them on the natural pastures in the summer and upon the extensive canebrakes in the winter, if the inhabitants had been living in a state of peace, yet such was not their condition. Surrounded by a savage foe, who was ever on the watch to seize upon the property or take the lives of the settlers, if they had raised cattle to any extent, it would only have been for the use of the enemy, and the better to enable him to prolong his predatory incursions, and thereby do them the greater mischief. Thus situated they could rear no more cattle than they could secure within their stockade forts in time of danger. A few cows for milk and butter, and as many of the young as were necessary to keep up the stock, and to supply the emigrants, were as much as they could aim at, in the early period of our history. But game was plenty, and the same rifle which was necessary for their protection, was amply sufficient to afford an abundant supply of bear, deer, and buffalo meat. The whole system of husbandry, at the first settlement of the country, was to raise a little Indian corn for bread or hominy, around the fort and within the protection of the garrison. But when the population had so far increased as to enable the settlers to act on the offensive, as well as the defensive, they could embody and meet the Indians in their advance, or pursue them in their retreat, and frequently inflict severe retaliation upon them. This had the effect of making the enemy embody in larger parties, and to diminish the frequency of their predatory expeditions. As the settlers began to feel their strength, they enjoyed a greater sense of security, and consequently extended their efforts in raising supplies of agricultural products, for the use of their families, and to supply the wants of the emigrants to the country. But a considerable period elapsed before anything of the grain kind was raised, except Indian corn. The want of mills to grind wheat was an obstacle to the cultivation of that crop. But the great fertility of the soil and the demand for corn, as an article for subsistence for the settler and his stock, as well as to supply the wants of the emigrant, held out strong inducements for its cultivation. It was not until a commercial communication was opened with the Spaniards, at New-Orleans, that wheat and tobacco began to be objects of importance. From this period the culture of those articles began to assume some importance. But there was, as yet, little or no system in the husbandry of the country. A part of the corn ground might be sowed broad cast, among the standing corn in the fall, and reaped in July following, and the balance of the cleared ground cultivated in corn the succeeding year, and that sowed in wheat the following autumn. The wheat stubble the year after the harvesting of the wheat, might be plowed for corn, and so on in succession, whilst some new ground cleared for tobacco would serve for that crop. Others again cultivated corn only, in continued succession, without any change. Such was the system (if system it could be called) of cropping that generally prevailed, until a late period of the history of our state. As fertile as our soil naturally is, it began at length, to show the effects of a bad system of husbandry. To remedy this deterioration of soil, something better deserving the name of system began to prevail among the more judicious farmers of the country."

We shall now remark briefly upon the prominent objects of interest in the different counties of Kentucky, and begin with the *mammoth remains*, at the Big Bone Lick, near the Ohio River.

"In 1773 the Lick was first visited. There were no trees or herbage, but large numbers of mammoth bones scattered over the ground. Since then large quantities have been exhumed. Some of the teeth weigh near ten pounds, and expose a chewing surface seven inches long and four broad. Some of the tusks were eleven feet long, and at the butt seven inches in diameter—thigh bones four or five feet in length—ribs four and five inches broad, and distance apart sometimes five feet. These ribs were formerly used for tent poles. Distance across the forehead of a supposed young animal and between the eyes two feet; depth of tusk sockets eighteen inches; length of tusk eight feet. The first collection of these fossil remains was made by Dr. Goforth, in 1803, and in 1806 was entrusted by him to the English traveler Thomas Ashe, to be exhibited in Europe, who, when he arrived in England, sold the collection and pocketed the money. The purchaser afterward transferred part of this collection to the Royal College of Surgeons, in London, to Dr. Blake of Dublin, and Professor Monroe of Edinburgh; and a part was sold at auction. The next collection was made by order of Mr. Jefferson, while he was president of the American Philosophical Society, about the year 1805, and was divided between that society and M. Cuvier, the distinguished French naturalist. A third collection was made in 1819, by the Western Museum Society. In the year 1819 a fourth collection was made by Mr. Finnell. This was first sold to a Mr. Graves, for $2,000, and taken by him to the eastern states, and there sold for $5,000. The mammoth is considered by geologists the last animal destroyed *before the creation of man*."

The name of Boone county is from the famous pioneer of that name, whose romantic history is familiar to most persons, and was traced by us in the fourth volume of the Review, when treating of the great West. The following letter from Boone to Judge Cobren will evince that not letters only give immortality.

"The Later I Recd from you Respecting Squire Boones Surtivaté Was Long Coming to hand and my Not being able to go to St Lowis I Dunn the Bisness before Col Keebby and Sent it on by Lewis Bryan in Closed &c &c. If that Will not Dow pleas Wright to me &c. I am well in halth But Deep in Markury & Not able &c. I Shall Say No thing about our petistion &c.

"Youres DANIEL BOONE."

In Boyle county there is at Danville a deaf and dumb asylum and a college which has since 1819 educated about 1,200 students. In Cumberland county, on the bank of Cumberland River, an *oil well* was discovered in 1830. The oil spouted up to fifty feet above the surface when struck; and, covering the surface of the river for miles, was, by the application of a torch, made to present the singular spectacle of a river on fire. It was found to be useful only medicinally, and is bottled and exported for that purpose. In Edmonson county is that extraordinary curiosity, the MAMMOTH CAVE. It is situated midway between Louisville and Nashville, and is a fashionable place of resort. The cave is approached through a romantic shade. At the entrance is a rush of cold air, a descent of thirty feet by stone steps, and an advance of one hundred feet inwards brings the visitor to the door, in a solid stone wall which blocks up the entrance of the cave. A narrow passage leads to the great *vestibule* or antechamber, an oval hall, two hundred by one hundred and fifty feet, and fifty feet high. Two passages, of one hundred feet width, open into it and the whole is supported without a single column. This chamber was used by the races of yore as a cemetery, judging from the bones of gigantic size which are discovered. "Far up, a hundred feet above your head, you catch a fitful glimpse of a dark, gray ceiling, rolling dimly away like a cloud, and heavy buttresses, apparently bending under the superincumbent weight, project their enormous masses from the shadowy wall. The scene is vast and solemn and awful. A profound silence, gloomy, still and breathless, reigns, unbroken by even a sigh of air, or the echo of a drop of water falling from the roof. You can hear the throbbings of your heart, and the mind is oppressed with a sense of vastness and solitude and grandeur indescribable." In *Audubon Avenue*, leading from the hall, is a deep well of pure spring water. It is surrounded by stalagmite columns from the floor to the roof. The *Little Bat Room* contains a pit two hundred and eighty feet deep, and is the resort of myriads of bats. The *Grand Gallery* is a vast tunnel many miles long and fifty feet high, and as wide. At the end of the first quarter of a mile is found the *Kentucky Cliffs* and the *Church*, one hundred feet in diameter and sixty-three feet high. A natural pulpit and organ-loft are not wanting. "In this great high temple of nature, religious service has been frequently performed, and it requires but a slight effort to make the speaker heard." The *Gothic Avenue* is reached by a flight of stairs, and is forty feet wide, fifteen high and two miles long. The ceiling is smooth and white Mummies have been discovered here, which have been a subject of curious study to science. In the Gothic Avenue are also stalagmites and stalactites, *Louisa's Bower* and *Vulcan's Furnace.* On the walls of the *Register Rooms* are inscribed thousands of names. The *Gothic Chapel* is "one of surprising grandeur and magnificence, and when brilliantly lighted up by the lamps, presents a scene inspiring the beholder with feelings of solemnity and awe." At the foot of the *Devil's Arm Chair* is a small basin of sulphur water. Then we have *Napoleon's Breastwork*, the *Elephant's Head*, *Lover's Leap*, *Gatewood's Dining Table*, and the *Cooling Tub*, a basin six feet wide and three deep, of the purest water—*Napoleon's Dome*, etc.

The *Ball Room* contains an orchestra fifteen feet high; near by is the row of cabins for consumptive patients—the atmosphere being always temperate and pure. The *Star Chamber* presents an optical illusion. "In looking up to the ceiling the spectator seems to see the firmament itself, studded with stars, and afar off a comet with bright tail." We pass over the *Salts Rooms*, *Black Chambers*, *Fairy Grotto*, &c., and come to the TEMPLE.

"The temple is an immense vault, covering an area of two acres, and covered by a single dome of solid rock, one hundred and twenty feet high. It excels in size the cave of Staffa, and rivals the celebrated vault in the Grotto of Antiparos, which is said to be the largest in the world. In passing through from one end to the other, the dome appears to follow the sky as in passing from place to place on the earth. In the middle of the dome there is a large mound of rocks rising on one side nearly to the top, very steep, and forming what is called the *mountain*. When I first ascended this mound from the cave below, I was struck with a feeling of awe, more intense and deep than anything I had ever before experienced. I could only observe the narrow circle which was illuminated immediately around me; above and beyond was apparently an unlimited space, in which the ear could not catch the slightest sound, nor the eye find an object to fasten upon. It was filled with silence and darkness; and yet I knew that I was beneath the earth, and that this space, however large it might be, was actually bounded by solid walls. My curiosity was rather excited than gratified. In order that I might see the whole in one connected view, I built my fires in many places of cane which I found scattered among the rocks. Then taking my stand upon the mountain, a scene was presented of surprising magnificence. On the opposite side the strata of gray limestone breaking up by steps from the bottom, could scarcely be discerned in the distance by the glimmering. Above was the lofty dome, closed at the top by a smooth oval slab, beautifully defined in the outline, from which the walls slope away on the right and left into thick darkness. Every one has heard of the dome of the Mosque of St. Sophia, of St. Peter's and St. Paul's; they are never spoken of but in terms of admiration, as the chief works of architecture, and among the noblest and most stupendous examples of what man can do when aided by science; and yet, when compared with the dome of this temple, they sink into comparative insignificance."

"The RIVER HALL descends like the slope of a mountain; the ceiling stretches away, away before you, vast and grand as the firmament at midnight. Proceeding a short distance, there is on the left a steep precipice, over which you can look down by the aid of blazing missiles upon a broad, black sheet of water, eighty feet below, called the Dead Sea. This is an awfully impressive place, the sights and sounds of which do not easily pass from memory. He who has seen it will have it vividly brought before him by Alfieri's description of Filippo. Only a transient word or act gives us a short and dubious glimmer that reveals to us the abysses of his being—daring, lurid and terrific as the throat of the infernal pool. Descending from the eminence by a ladder of about twenty feet, we find ourselves among piles of gigantic rocks; and one of the most picturesque sights in the world, is to see a file of men and women passing along those wild and scraggy paths, moving slowly—slowly, that their lamps may have time to illuminate their sky-like ceiling and gigantic walls — disappearing behind high cliffs—sinking into ravines—their lights shining upward through fissures in the rocks—then, suddenly emerging from some abrupt angle, standing in the bright gleam of their lights, relieved by the towering black masses around them. As you pass along you hear the roar of invisible waterfalls; and at the foot of the slope the river Styx lies before you, deep and black, overarched with rocks. Across, or rather down, these unearthly waters, the guide can convey but four passengers at once. The lamps are fastened to the prow, the images of which are reflected in the dismal pool. If you are impatient of delay or eager for new adventure, you can leave your companions lingering about the shore and cross the Styx by a dangerous bridge of precipices over head. In order to do this you must ascend a steep cliff and enter a cave above, over three hundred yards long, from the egress of which you find yourself on the bank of the river, eighty feet above its surface, commanding a view of those in the boat and those waiting on the shore. Seen from the heights, the lamps in the canoe glare like fiery eyeballs; and the passengers sitting there, so hushed and motionless, look like shadows. The scene is so strangely funereal and spectral, that it seems as if the Greeks must have witnessed it before they imagined Charon conveying ghosts to the dim regions of Pluto."

The Mammoth Cave is said to be explored to the distance of ten miles without reaching its termination, whilst the aggregate width of all the branches is over *forty miles !* Next to Niagara it is the wonder of nature in the western world, or perhaps throughout all her domains.

The city of Lexington is situated in Fayette county, and was incorporated in 1782. It is handsomely laid out, and in the midst of a beautiful country. The taxable property is $3,039,000. Hemp is extensively manufactured here, and there are fifteen establishments for the purpose, working six hundred hands, running ninety looms, making annually 2,500,000 yards bagging and 2,000,000 lbs. rope. In the suburbs and neighboring country there is as much more manufactured. Here is situated the *State Lunatic Asylum* and *Transylvania University*. The latter contained a literary department once of great influence, but now fallen very much to decay. The medical and law schools are still in successful operation. Here is published the *Gazette*, the oldest paper except that at Pittsburgh west of the mountains. In the suburbs is *Ashland*, the seat of Henry Clay.

Frankfort is sixty miles above the mouth of the Kentucky River, making a beautiful appearance as we approach. This is the capital of the state, and the government was located here in 1792. Here, also, is the state penitentiary, containing an average of about 170 inmates. It is farmed out and the keepers pay over to the state two-thirds of the profits, guaranteeing that these profits will not fall short of $5,000 annually. The heaviest business of the convicts is the manufacture of bagging and rope. In the public cemetery of Frankfort were lately deposited the remains of *Daniel Boone*, brought from Missouri by act of legislature and interred with great funeral pomp.

Louisville, the metropolis of the state, is well laid out, is an important mart, and contains some of the finest private residences in America. We were struck with the shaded beauty of the streets and the general elegance of structure. There are thirty churches, a medical institute which attracts over 300 students, an asylum for the blind, a university still in its infancy, but containing a law department, a hospital, several banks, mercantile and historical library, &c. The export and import of the place is estimated at $50,000,000 annually. There are numerous bagging, cotton and wool factories, flouring mills, foundries, tobacco stemmeries, paper mills, &c., twelve newspapers and periodicals. The town was originally laid off by Captain Thomas Bullitt, of Virginia. The *Canal* round the falls of the Ohio is at Louisville. As early as 1804, a company was chartered to build this canal, but nothing was done until 1825 and the canal only finished in 1833. Its effect on commerce was supposed prejudicial to Louisville. The government of the United States owns stock in the company, which is said to pay good dividends. The charge for toll is enormous and the canal too small for its purposes. For further and more full description of Louisville, the reader will consult the first volume of our Review, 1846.

Maysville is situated on the Ohio, sixty miles above Cincinnati, and was established in 1788 and incorporated in 1833. It is a thriving town, the largest hemp market in the country, and an important depot for the commerce of north-east Kentucky.

The *Harrodsburg Springs*, 35 miles from Frankfort, is now the most famous fashionable watering place in all the West. The accommodations are extensive and splendid, and the country around possessed of every natural beauty.

The *Blue Lick Springs*, near Carlisle and 58 miles from Frankfort, have also a wide fame. The waters are highly medicinal and are an extensive article of commerce, in barrels, throughout the West. They are strongly purgative. The main hotel is an extensive and magnificent structure, and thousands are annually attracted here. There are also sulphur springs in Grayson county, said to be the purest and best in the

United States, and also at Drennon's Lick, 70 miles from Louisville. In Hart county, natural curiosities are said to abound, as the following description will evince.

"There is a large spring near Green River, which, at certain hours of the day, rises twelve or fifteen inches above its level and then gradually recedes again, resembling the ebb and flow of the tides. The flood occurs at the hour of twelve each day—recurs at the same hour every day, and is marked by the utmost uniformity in the time occupied in the ebb and flow. Near Munfordville a circular hole, sixty feet in diameter, runs down into the earth in funnel shape. Thirty feet below the surface its diameter is about ten feet. The depth is unknown, and on throwing down a rock it will ring against the sides, fainter and fainter without appearing to strike bottom. A hundred cart-loads of rocks have been thrown in by visitors, without the least effect. There is another hole, called 'Frenchman's Knob,' which has been explored 275 feet, by men descending with ropes, without reaching bottom."

GEORGETOWN, in Scott county, is the seat of a flourishing college with over 100 students. There is also a female institute here, and a military institute under Colonel Johnson. We understand that they are both prosperous, and regret that circumstances have not yet allowed us to visit them, so as to form any opinion.

Kentucky has but few *public works* except her turnpikes and the "lockings" of some of her rivers, of much value. The state owns about 400 miles of turnpike road stocks, 29 miles of rail-road and 290 miles of slackwater navigation, yielding in all about $135,000. Her public debt is $4,608,735 86. A rail-road is now in course of construction between Louisville and Lexington.

The subject of *public education* as in other southern states is not very perfect. Although the number of academies and colleges is considerable throughout the state, complaints of the school system are heard. We have before us the report of Mr. Breckenridge the superintendent, for 1849. It appears the question was submitted last year, to the people, if they would be taxed the *one-fifth* of *one mill to the dollar*, on all taxable property, for the establishment of a common school system, and decided in the affirmative by a large majority. Including this tax, the whole revenue for school purposes is estimated at $120,000 per annum. The report of the superintendent is very imperfect and shows that out of 183,458 children, 31,501 only are reported in attendance. We cannot infer how many attend without being reported. Despite of all these difficulties, however, Kentucky has given many eminent citizens to the republic of native birth or adoption. Among these are twenty governors and lieutenant-governors of other states, thirteen ministers and charges to foreign powers, one president of the United States, (Taylor,) one vice-president, ten cabinet officers, three major-generals of the army, eleven judges United States and other state courts, nine senators, eight presidents of colleges in other states, &c.

The state, as we have seen, has nearly 200,000 SLAVES—about one-fourth of the population. The question of *emancipation* is now (1849) in agitation, and a convention will pronounce upon the subject. What the result will be we are very clear. Although it it be demonstrable that free labor would be more advantageous to Kentucky than slave labor, which we are not prepared to admit, but which might be true without affecting the question in the more southern states, yet Kentucky is by no means prepared for emancipation; with such a proportion of blacks it is impossible that she can be. She would not incur the perilous risk of retaining in her midst such an army of lazy, worthless *free negroes*, as would result. It would be a blight upon the prosperity of the state not easily to be overcome—an army of paupers which no wealth could sustain. To send them off by colonization is a scheme altogether impracticable in such magnitude. Kentucky "*must be free*" we admit, but it will be when the superior southern demand shall draw off by degrees her slaves, and the continued increase of white population shall make the relative proportion of colors but a fraction of what it now is, and altogether unimportant.

KEY WEST—WRECKERS OF FLORIDA.—A correspondent of the Charleston News gives many interesting particulars in relation to the wild life of the wrecker among the Florida Keys. "The wrecking business, as it is called, is a source of very considerable revenue to the government, and is the principal support of Key West; there are generally from six to eight vessels engaged in it.

They are fine large sloops and schooners, each officered and manned by eight or ten persons. The crews generally are not on wages, but on shares. The owner furnishes the vessel with all necessary materials, provisions, etc.; and in the event of a wreck one half the amount of salvage is taken by the vessel, the other is divided among the officers and crew; that is to say, the captain receives three shares, the mate two, and each of the crew one. These vessels are generally stationed at different points of the reef, where a constant look out is kept for vessels which may perchance get ashore upon any part of it, when they immediately proceed to their assistance. Sometimes two or more wreckers will unite in saving the goods from wrecked vessels, in which case an equal share is allotted to each, in the proportion that they may save. At times, when vessels are not damaged to such an extent as to prevent them from continuing their voyages, an agreement is made between the captain and the wrecker for the payment of a stipulated price, as compensation for the services rendered. In most cases where a vessel has been relieved, she is taken down to Key West, where there is a port of entry and an Admiralty Court; in the absence of the court, the case is generally determined by arbitration, which has been so often arranged, as to have enabled the parties interested to defraud owners and underwriters of very large amounts. In many cases, the captains of the vessels shipwrecked, for certain weighty considerations, allow the wreckers to appoint the arbitrators, who, of course, are in their interest, and would give any amount which they were required to do. I hesitate not to say, that in a very large majority of instances where owners and underwriters have been swindled, the fault has been with the captain of the vessel shipwrecked, consigning to irresponsible agents. From what I can learn, there has been a better condition of things latterly, and a state of moral feeling in the community of Key West calculated to repress the evil practices which formerly existed.

Key West being an isolated place, and having no back country, is not likely to become a town of any considerable size; the resources consisting principally of the wrecks which are almost constantly occurring on the Florida Reef; and of the *Salt Ponds*, which are now in full operation, and of sufficient extent to furnish a very large quantity of salt for consumption. The income derived from shipwrecks is very considerable, as will be seen by the following statement:

1831	$39,487 00	1839	$90,797 00
1832	46,555 00	1840	85,113 00
1833	58,128 00	1841	71,173 00
1834	32,040 00	1842	38,103 00
1835	87,249 00	1843	83,811 00
1836	174,132 00	1844	88,369 00
1837	107,495 00	1845	63,981 00
1838	34,578 00		

This gives an average of very nearly $80,000 per annum, besides the expenditures *incidental*, such as repairs, lading and unlading of vessels, cartage, storage, etc., all of which, added together, amount to a very considerable sum, and furnish employment to the laboring classes of the community.—(*See Florida.*)

LOUISIANA—Early History, Etc.—To minds exclusively devoted to the pursuit of wealth, and bending all their energies to that simple purpose, it would seem a startling proposition, that there could be any thing either of interest or utility in inquiries into the history of the first discovery and settlement of Louisiana by Europeans; in rescuing from threatened oblivion the records of its first colonization; in efforts to bring to light and to perpetuate by means of the press, all such documents as would form the elements of an authentic history of our multiform population, and the successive changes in the forms of colonial government, and the progress of its settlement under the different sovereigns who have successively ruled this country. But the time has arrived, I trust, when pursuits of a character purely literary, will have their value among us; when those who engage in researches, having only truth for their object, although barren of immediate results, will be regarded as contributing in some measure to the public good, by adding something to the stock of our national literature. As contemporary history is liable to be discolored by interest, by prejudice and passion, each generation as it passes away, is under obligation to its successors to furnish them those authentic materials by which alone its true character can be known to posterity, and to perpetuate the public documents and correspondence which accompany and explain every public transaction. But we, who are enjoying the fruits of the labors, and fatigues and sufferings of our predecessors, owe it also to their memory, to snatch from oblivion the record of their actions, and no longer to leave their fame there to rest on the loose and garbled and exaggerated narrations of contemporary writers, or catchpenny authors of what the world calls history. History, as it is generally written, is at best but an approximation to truth, I had almost said, an approximation to probability. It is true, the exaggerated and marvelous statements of travelers, ior discoverers and settlers, as to the physical features and productions of a new country, and the character of its aboriginal inhabitants, may be corrected by subsequent observation and experience. The width of the Mississippi, for example, below this capital, has dwindled from a league to less than a mile; St. Louis is no longer in latitude 45° north, and 276° longitude; quarries of emeralds, silver mines and gold dust, are no where to be found in Louisiana. But the narratives of events and transactions, by real or pretended eye-witnesses, or by the authors of histories and memoirs, can only be tested by reference to authentic records, or by their own intrinsic evidence of falsity or truth. This latter is not always to be relied on, for the true is not always probable. Tradition, ornamented and colored by fiction, has proved from the earliest records of our race, a large ingredient in the composition of history. Hence the origin and early annals, not only of the people and states of antiquity, but of many of comparatively modern date are involved in mystery and fable.

But it would be a matter of just reproach, if a people, whose first lodgment on the continent was made long since the discovery of the art of printing; whose entire annals embrace a period of the highest civilization; if such a people, I say, should suffer to perish the monuments of its early history, and the mists of fiction to settle on its origin and progress.

In many of the states of this Union, of British origin, historical societies have been organized, whose labors have been eminently successful. A mass of materials has been accumulated and preserved by means of the press, which excludes the possibility of future misrepresentations in regard to the true history of the country, and the times to which they relate. It is singularly interesting to look at the conduct and character of our ancestors through such a medium. We see them as they were; we hear them speak the language of their own age, we are brought in immediate contact with the founders of our rising empire; we trace the gradual progress of their settlement, from the sea-board to the interior; we witness their privations, their sufferings, their unflinching purpose and constancy of purpose. At a more recent period, we are introduced into the primitive assemblies of the people; we observe the gradual development of those opinions and principles, which at this day lay at the foundation of our free popular institutions; the first discussed, when the threatened encroachments of power upon right were met and resisted, and the blood of the Barons of Runymede cried out for Magna Charta, in the wilderness of a new world.

The field of research which we propose to explore, is vast and in a great measure new. It is proposed to extend our inquiries into the history of all that country formerly possessed by France and Spain, under the name of Louisiana; to endeavour to bring to light and perpetuate by means of the press, all authentic papers relating thereto; to collect interesting traditions, private histories and correspondences, and pictures of manners; to investigate the progress of our jurisprudence; the state of religion, and the condition of the Indian tribes in that whole region. It is obvious that many of the original documents and records, relating to the settlement and colonization of that extensive region, must exist in the public archives at Paris, Madrid, and Seville, as well as the Havana; some in the archives of the former government of this city, at St. Louis and Natchez; others again at notaries' offices here; in the parochial records of the different posts in the interior, and much interesting matter in possession of the families of some of the earlier settlers of the country. It is becoming more and more difficult every day, to bring together from sources so various and so widely dispersed, such memorials as may yet exist. It is time, therefore, to begin the work in earnest and methodically.

Before I proceed to make a few remarks on the several heads into which the programme of our proposed researches is naturally divided, let us pause and take a momentary survey of the population of the country as it exists, whose origin and first establishment it will become us to investigate more minutely in the progress of our labors. Like the rich soil upon our great rivers, the population may be said to be alluvial; composed distinctly of colored strata, not yet perfectly amalgamated; left by successive waves of emigration. Here we trace the gay, light-hearted, brave chivalry of France: the more impassioned and devoted Spaniard; the untiring industry and perseverance of the German, and the bluff sturdiness of the British race. Here were thrown the wreck of Acadie, and the descendants of those unhappy fugitives still exist in various parts of this state. Little colonies from Spain, or the Spanish islands on the coast of Africa, were scattered in different parts of the country. Such were New Iberia in Attakapas, Valenzuela in Lafourche, Terre aux Bœufs and Galveston. They still retain to a certain extent, their language, manners and pursuits. There are, in the Western District, some families of Gipsy origin, who still retain the peculiar complexion and wildness of eye that characterize that singular race. The traces of the Canadian hunter and boatmen, are not yet entirely effaced. The Germans, I believe, have totally lost the language of their fatherland. The country of the German coast is, perhaps, the only existing memorial of the celebrated John Law, the author of the most stupendous scheme of banking, and stockjobbing, and fraud, that was ever practised on the credulity of modern times. Among the earliest concessions of land in the province, was one in favor of Law, situated on the Arkansas, and prior to the settlement of New-Orleans; he had sent over a small colony of Germans to take possession and improve it; but on the downfall of the grantee, his colonists broke up the establishment, and returned to this city, where they obtained each for himself, a small grant of land on the Mississippi, at a place which has ever since been called the German coast. The little colonies of Spaniards at New Iberia and Terre aux Bœuf, never had any written concessions, they were put in possession by the public surveyor, and it was not until long since the change of government, that their descendants obtained an authentic recognition of their title from the United States. But time does not permit me to pursue this subject any farther; these few hints are intended merely to direct your attention to it, as one of curious interest.

I proceed to submit a few remarks on some of the several heads of our proposed plan. First, The general history of the province from its first discovery to the present day. Second, The progress of our jurisprudence and state of religion; and Third, the condition of the Indian tribes. It is by no means my purpose to attempt to give you a full view of the present state of our knowledge on these topics, much less to collate or criticise the various histories and memoirs which have appeared, even if I were capable of the task. But let us see in what particulars our knowledge is clearly defective, and whether it be probable that by proper diligence the deficiency may be supplied, and errors or misrepresentations corrected.

The successive changes of government form, naturally, the epochs of our history. The first extends from the discovery of the mouth of the Mississippi by La Salle, in 1681, from the interior, by way of the Lakes, until the grant to Crozat in 1712. 2d, Under the monopoly of Crozat, until 1717. 3d, Under the administration of the Western Company, until the surrender of their grant, 1732. 4th, Under the direct authority of the crown of France, until the final delivery of the province to Spain, 1769, in pursuance of the treaty of Paris. 5th, Under the government of Spain, until the treaty of cession in 1803; and lastly, as an integral part of the United States, whether as a territory or state.

I. I think it cannot be controverted that Robert Cavalier de la Salle first discovered the mouth of the Mississippi on the 7th of April, 1681. Accompanied by the Chevalier de Tonti and a few followers, he descended from the mouth of the Illinois to the Gulf of Mexico, passing through numerous tribes of Indians, not in hostile array, but his most effectual arms, the calumet of peace. De la Salle was, without doubt, a man of great energy and enterprise, ardent and brave, sagacious and prudent, and of conciliatory manners. He appears to have been, at the same time, feared, respected, and even beloved by the natives. I should not have considered it necessary to mention this fact of the first discovery, as one well settled, if attempts had not been made to create doubts about it, if not to deprive him of that honor, and to confer it upon Father Louis Hennepin, a missionary of the order of St. Francis. In the first volume of "The Condensed Geography and History of the Western States, or the Mississippi Valley," published a few years ago at Cincinnati, under the particular head of "history," not a word is said of De la Salle having explored the course of the river as far as the Gulf, and of his having taken formal possession of the country in the name of the King of France. On the contrary, it is asserted, that in the spring of the previous year, Hennepin, who had been instructed, in the absence of De la Salle, to explore the sources of the river, finding it easier to descend than ascend, had proceeded down, and reached the Balize in sixteen days—"if his word can be taken for it," says the author—from the time of his departure from the mouth of the Illinois. In the next place, the author represents that De la Salle, in 1683, after laying the foundations of Cahokia and Kaskaskia, left M. de Tonti in command of those establishments, returned to Canada, and thence made all haste to France, to solicit the co-operation of the French Ministry in his views. In addition to the utter improbability of this whole story, it is completely refuted by the testimony of the Reverend Father himself. His first publication was after his return to France, and the first edition of it is now in my possession. It was published on the 5th of January, 1683, the author being then in Paris, and was dedicated to the King of France. The work is entitled, "Description de la Louisiane nouvellement découverte au sud-ouest de la Nouvelle France." He gives a minute account of his voyage from the mouth of the Illinois to a considerable distance above the Falls of St. Anthony; of his captivity, during eight months, among the Indians of the Upper Mississippi; and finally, of his return to some of the French posts in Canada about Whitsuntide, (May,) 1681. The "Privilége Du Roi," for the publication of this work of Hennepin, was granted on the 3d of September, 1682. Not only is the author silent as to any voyage by himself down the river as far as the Gulf of Mexico, or of his having descended below the mouth of the Illinois, but the concluding paragraph shows conclusively that he at that time set up no such pretensions. He says, in conclusion—"They sent me word, this year, (1682,) from New France, that M. de la Salle, finding that I had made peace with the tribes of the north and north-west, situated more than five hundred leagues above, on the river Colbert, (Mississippi,) who were at war with the Illinois and the nations of the south, this brave captain, governor of Fort Frontenac, who, by his zeal and courage, throws new lustre on the names of the Cavaliers, his ancestors, descended last year, with his followers and our Franciscans, as far as the mouth of the great river Colbert, and to the sea, and that he traversed unknown nations, some of whom are civilized. It is believed he is about to return to France, in order to give the court a more ample knowledge of the whole of Louisiana, which we may call the delight and terrestrial paradise of America. The king might there form an empire, which, in a short time, will become flourishing in spite of the opposition of any foreign power."

In another part of the same work the good Father says: "We had some intention to descend as far as the mouth of the river Colbert, which probably empties into the Gulf of Mexico, rather than into the Vermillion

Sea; but those natives who had arrested us did not allow us time to navigate the river both above and below." Here is a formal disclaimer of any discovery made by Hennepin, and an announcement that the discovery had been made by another; and yet the author of the *Condensed* History and Geography of the Western States, represents Hennepin, I know not on what authority, as having reached the Gulf of Mexico on the 25th of March, 1680, a period when, according to his own account of himself, he was struggling in a frail canoe against the ice and currents above the mouth of the Missouri. One is tempted to repeat the reflection of Voltaire, "c'est ainsi que l'on écrit l'histoire."

Father Hennepin did not certainly much overrate the great natural fertility and resources of Louisiana. But it is not a little remarkable how slow and lingering were the first attempts to colonize it, although made under the immediate auspices of the crown of France. The most superficial reader of history cannot have failed to remark the different spirit which characterises the colonization of this continent by Spain, France and England. The Spaniard came for conquest and for gold, regarding the aborigines as enemies to God. No alternative was left them but the cross or the edge of the sword: even submission did not save them from the most abject and oppressive servitude. France, on the contrary, cultivated the good-will of the natives, and was in general eminently successful in gaining their friendship, so far at least as relates to Louisiana;—commerce with them, in the natural productions of the country, seems to have been their primary object. Trade, in fact, was the basis of her colonial policy—trade, too, not open to all her subjects, but in the hands of monopolists, by grants from the crown, and maintained in the enjoyment of it by naval and military power. The first establishments of the French were rather trading-houses than colonies. The English colonies, on the contrary, were, for the most part, the offspring of individual enterprise. The basis of their system was agriculture combined with commerce. They brought with them their household gods—they sought a permanent abiding place for themselves and their posterity. Many of them, far from enjoying the patronage and protection of the crown, fled from persecution and intolerance. They came, and, as soon as private interest began to operate freely, on a soil comparatively sterile, and in a rigorous climate, the country was converted into a garden. The English colonists brought with them the germ of popular self-government. At very early periods they made laws for themselves—sometimes in assemblies purely democratic, generally through their representatives—laws suited to their condition and their wants. In the colonies of France and Spain, on the contrary, except in matters of mere local police, all laws and regulations came over the ocean. Trade, in its most minute ramifications, even domestic trade, was fettered with precise tariffs of prices and profits, instead of being left open to free competition. According to a regulation established by the Western Company, 1721, the price of a slave sold to the colonists by the proprietary company was fixed at six hundred livres, on a credit of one, two, and three years; tobacco, in leaf or twist, was bought at their warehouses at the rate of twenty-five livres per hundred; rice, at twelve livres the quintal; peltries and furs had their fixed prices. French goods were sold at Biloxi, Mobile and New-Orleans, at five per cent. advance on the invoice price in France; at Natchez and Yazoo, at seventy per cent. profit; at Natchitoches and Arkansas, at eighty per cent., and at one hundred per cent. in Illinois. The price of wine was one hundred and twenty livres the *barrique*.

There sprung out of this spirit of petty traffic, a class of characters, altogether unique and unknown elsewhere, called "*coureurs des bois*," half peddlers and half hunters, with a little finish of the broker. It was through their agency that goods imported from France were pushed into the most remote settlements of the country and the Indian villages, and exchanged for the productions of the country. When I first came to this country, I knew some old decrepit men of that class; crippled, frost-bitten, and yet at an extreme old age retaining a singular predilection for that wandering, half savage life, and still dressed in skins, with leggins and moccasins.

Appended to the regulations of the Western Company, to which I have alluded, was a strong recommendation, which I mention to show how singularly it has been neglected up to the present day. The company earnestly recommend to the colonists to cultivate silk, to plant out mulberry trees, and offer as high a price for raw silk, as it now bears in the best market. They were sensible that perhaps no country on earth was better suited to that branch of industry; that the mulberry is indigenous in every part of the province and grows with great luxuriance, and is among the first trees to put forth its foliage in the spring. This recommendation seems to have been totally neglected, until more lucrative staples were introduced, which now engross the whole industry and capital of the country. But the time may yet come, when the raising of silk, a beautiful branch of industry, which in fact would not interfere with more heavy crops, will become extensive, as it could not fail to become lucrative in this country.

The first colonists made two or three successive selections of a capital for their new colony, that were injudicious in the extreme; Dauphine Island and the two Biloxis, all sandy barrens. More than twenty years after the establishment, they depended almost exclusively on France, Vera Cruz and the Havana, for a supply of provisions, and in the vicinity of the richest soil in the world, the people were threatened with famine. It was not until those places were finally abandoned, after the surrender of his charter by Crozat, and a change of system under the administration of the Western Company, that the great resources of the country began to develop themselves; numerous grants of land were then made, and agriculture began to take a start. On this part of our early history, little need be said at this time; but I should be wanting to myself, as well as the occasion, if I failed to make honorable mention of the production of our best historian, whose labors have thrown important light upon every part of our history, without omitting many minute and interesting details on this part in particular. Historical literature is deeply indebted to my learned and distinguished friend and colleague, Judge Martin. His work, while it evinces great labor and research, proves at the same time how scattered and fugitive are the materials employed by him in its composition, and how difficult, if not impossible, it would be for a reader to satisfy his curiosity by resorting to original sources of information from which the author drew. *He appears to have had access to manuscripts which have never been published, but which it is not, perhaps, too late to wrest from oblivion.**

It must be confessed, that at the breaking out of the war of 1756, France possessed on this continent the basis of a splendid empire. Her possessions embraced on the South the mouth of the Mississippi, and on the North that of the St. Lawrence, stretching through the heart of the continent, and covering the great central valley of the Mississippi and the northern lakes. Louisiana, though by far the most important and interesting portion of her domain, had made but little progress, and was regarded as an appendage to Canada. That war, it is well known, was disastrous to the arms of France, and at the pacification in 1762, she was stripped of all her possessions in North America, except that part of the ancient province of Louisiana, west of the Mississippi, together with the Island of Orleans. Simultaneously with the treaty of peace, France ceded to Spain the remnant of her possessions on this continent. With this treaty commenced a new era for Louisiana. Its ancient forms of administration, and its entire system of laws were changed. This transition was attended by afflicting events to the ancient population of the province, attached as they were to the land of their origin. Such was the delay attending the delivery of the province to Spain, that the people began to entertain a hope, that the transfer itself was a mere simulation, for the purpose of securing Louisiana to the crown of France, against the hazard of future wars. It was not until 1766, that Don Antonio de Ulloa was sent over, to receive possession, in pursuance of previous instructions given by the King of France to D'Abbadie. There hangs over the conduct of Don Antonio, an extraordinary mystery; although he remained two years in the province at the head of a military force, he appears never to have taken formal possession of the country, and was finally compelled to withdraw, on his refusal to furnish the council his powers and instructions from the King of Spain. I am not aware that his report to his government has ever been made public. We are, however, fully warranted in believing that such a report was made, and that it formed the motive or pretext for the sanguinary orders subsequently given to his successor, and led to the fatal catastrophe which ensued. If such a document exists, as we have every reason to suppose, a copy might be procured from Spain, and would throw great light on an obscure and interesting crisis in our annals. The bloody tragedy which followed on the arrival of Don Alexandro O'Reilly the next year, the total abolition of the council, and the introduction of the laws of Spain, as over a conquered people, are well known. Until recently, however, the extent of O'Reilly's powers was a matter of conjecture; and although the courts have uniformly considered the whole body of the Spanish law as in force from the date of his proclamation, and the French jurisprudence as abrogated, yet they were compelled in a great measure to judge of the extent of his authority by his official acts. Within a couple of years, documents have come to light through the agency of our minister at Madrid, which go to prove not only his original powers, but the approbation of the court of Spain of all his proceedings. Among other documents thus procured is a copy of a royal order of the 28th of January, 1771, in which the king declares that he had in 1765 appointed Don Antonio de Ulloa to proceed to the province of Louisiana and take possession as governor, making, however, no innovation in its system of government, which was to be entirely independent of the laws and usages observed in his American dominions, but considering it as a distinct colony, having even no commerce with his said dominions, and to remain under the control of its own administration, council and other tribunals. But he goes on to say, the inhabitants having rebelled in October, 1768, he had commissioned Don Alexandro O'Reilly to proceed thither and take formal possession, chastise the ringleaders, and to annex that province to the rest of his dominions. That his orders had been obeyed, the council

* There are reams of manuscripts *in Europe*, even now, materially relating to our history. Will we have them here?—Ed.

abolished, and a cabildo established in its place, and the Spanish laws adopted. He proceeds to ratify and confirm all that had been done, and directs that Louisiana shall be united, as to its spiritual concerns, to the Bishopric of the Havana, and governed conformably to the laws of the Indies. It was made a dependency of the captain-generalship and royal hacienda of the Island of Cuba, and as relates to the administration of justice, a special tribunal was created, consisting of the captain-general as president, the auditors of war and marine, the attorney of the hacienda, and the notary of the government. To this tribunal appeals were to go, and from it to the council at Seville, without resorting to the audiencia of St. Domingo.

O'Reilly appears to have made a detailed report of his proceedings, consisting of six distinct statements. These statements have never, probably, been made public *in extenso*, but another document, procured at the same time at Madrid, contains a minute analysis of them. I allude to a report made to the king by the Council and Chamber of the Indies, to whom the whole matters had been referred. It is filled with the most extravagant encomiums upon O'Reilly. The profoundness of his comprehension, the sublimity of his spirit, the correctness of his judgment, the admirable energy displayed in his provisions for the civil, economical and political government, his delicate knowledge and acute discernment of the laws of both kingdoms, as well as of the practical and forensic styles of the courts—all these are set forth in the most pompous and sonorous phraseology of choice Castilian. By way of finish to this picture, and in the spirit of the most sublime bathos, the council adds, "that by the admirable arrangement of pay and distribution which he has proposed in the military and political classes, the treasury has gained (how much do you suppose?) one hundred and thirty dollars! which advantage is due to the comprehensive and indefatigable genius of the commissioner!" Miserable, cold-blooded, heartless calculators! at that very moment O'Reilly was the object of the just execration of the whole population of Louisiana. They had seen some of their best citizens, the élite of the country, immured in the dungeons of Moro Castle, others shot down without mercy, without necessity, without a crime, unless it was a crime to love the land of their birth, the land in whose bosom repose the bones of their ancestors—all entrapped at a moment of profound security and submission, under circumstances of the most infamous treachery and duplicity, and mocked with the forms of a trial, under a statute written in a foreign langaage, and never promulgated in the province. Does no one yet survive, in this whole generation—no one yet lingering on the stage—who was an eye-witness of those transactions, from whom we could hope to obtain a vivid picture of the grief, consternation and despair which smote the heart of the country, while the place d'armes of New-Orleans was reeking with its best blood, that we might hold it up to remote posterity as a comment on the specious bombast of the Council of Seville?

The commercial regulations proposed by O'Reilly, and which form the subject of his first statement, were undoubtedly liberal and calculated to advance the prosperity of the province. They contemplated a wide departure from the rigorous monopoly with which the commerce of the Spanish colonies had been shackled: a free trade between Havana and Spain, the productions of Louisiana to pay no duties when imported into that port, and no duty to be levied on exports from Havana to Louisiana; the admission of all Louisiana vessels into all the ports of Spain as well as the Havana, provided that none but Spanish or Louisiana bottoms should be employed in that trade. This system met the entire approbation of the council, except that the exemption from the payment of duties should be considered only as temporary.

The second statement relates to the propriety of subjecting Louisiana to the same system of laws which prevailed in the other Spanish colonies, of carrying on legal proceedings in Spanish, the establishment of the new appellate tribunal, of which I have already spoken, with a direct appeal from it to the council. These arrangements were sanctioned by the council with this proviso: that the intendents of hacienda and marine should have a voice and vote in the proposed tribunal.

The third and fourth statements relate to the organization of the cabildo, and the appointment of Don Louis de Unzaga as civil and military governor of the province.

The fifth details the new ecclesiastical and economical arrangements.

The sixth and last statement of O'Reilly, informs the king that he had appointed a lieutenant-governor for the district of Illinois and Natchitoches, incloses copies of his instructions, and proposes that the governor alone should have the power to grant lands, and that concessions should be made according to certain regulations which he had adopted on the advice of well-informed persons. This is the well-known ordinance of 1770, of which I may have occasion to speak hereafter.

It cannot be denied, that in many respects the new government was liberal and even paternal. Lands were distributed gratuitously to meet the wants of an increasing population, and direct taxation was unknown in the province. If the ratio of increase of the population be an index of its prosperity, Louisiana was certainly flourishing and prosperous. In sixteen years from the year 1769, the population was more than doubled by the ordinary means, independently of small colonies from Malaga and the Canary Islands. In 1711 it amounted only to four hundred, including twenty slaves. During thirty-four years of Spanish domination in this country, its resources were considerably developed, and Louisiana has been regarded, perhaps with justice, as the favored pet of Spain.

It does not enter into my plan to go into any historical details relating to the different periods of our history; but my object is simply to call your attention to them, as worthy of minute investigation in the progress of our researches. Much interesting matter might yet be brought to light, illustrative of the characters of many distinguished persons who figured, and some who suffered, in the crisis I have already alluded to. What has become of the memorials and correspondence of Mihlet, who was dispatched by the Louisianians to France, to entreat the king not to compel his loyal subjects to pass under the yoke of Spain? Who, that has read our earlier history, does not desire a more intimate acquaintance with the spirit of the times, and with the enterprising men who laid the foundation of the colony, and to investigate more minutely its graduel development.

II. I proceed to make a few remarks upon the second head of our proposed inquiries, to wit: the progress of our jurisprudence. The most important part of the history of a state, is that of its legislation. Upon that depend its prosperity and the character and pursuits of its people. It is not a little remarkable, that although successively an appendage of the monarchies of France and Spain, Louisiana never knew anything like a right of primogeniture, and a privileged class. No part of feudality was ever known here, neither inequality in the distribution of estates, nor fiefs, nor seignories, nor mayorazgos. The grants of land were all allodial, and under no other condition than that of cultivation and improvement within limited periods; in fact, essentially in fee simple. The colonists brought with them, as the basis of their municipal law, the custom of Paris. By the charter in favor of Crozat, the laws, edicts and ordinances of the realm and the custom of Paris, are expressly extended to Louisiana. To this custom, which we all know was a body of written law, may be traced the origin of many of the peculiar institutions which still distinguish our jurisprudence from that of all the other states in the Union. I allude especially to the matrimonial community of gains, the rigid restrictions on the disinheritance of children, and the reserved portion in favor of forced heirs, the severe restraints upon widows and widowers, in relation to donations in favor of second husbands or wives, by the *Edit des Secondes Noces;* the inalienability of dower and the strict guards by which the paraphernal rights of the wife are secured against the extravagance of spendthrift husbands. The community of acquests and gains between husband and wife, is altogether a creature of customary law, unknown to the jurisprudence of Rome, and even in those provinces of France formerly governed by the written law. It is said to be of German or Saxon origin, and during the régime of the two first races of the kings of France, the share of the wife was one-third, instead of one-half of the property acquired during marriage, as regulated by the existing code. The introduction of the Spanish law in 1769, produced but slight changes on most of these points. The general rules of descent, as regulated by the law of Spain, did not vary materially from those of the custom of Paris; a perfect equality among heirs, was the essential characteristic of both codes. The points of discrepancy will form a curious subject of investigation to any one desirous of pursuing the inquiry. The existing code of this state has maintained, to a certain extent, those peculiarities, and they have become deeply rooted in the public mind.

O'Reilly, when he introduced by proclamation the whole body of the Spanish law, published a Manual of Practice. How far the practice was changed in substance, by that regulation, from what existed before, I am not prepared to say. It is to be presumed, from the character of those who had been previously engaged in the administration of the laws, that the practice was very simple, and, perhaps, rude, and the records of judicial proceedings at these early periods, are extremely meagre. The order of the commandant, after hearing the stories of both parties, was the decree to which all submitted.

Until the cession of the country to the United States, the writ of habeas corpus and the trial by jury, were of course unknown here. Of the first, it is sufficient to say, that without it there can be no genuine personal security. Whatever we may think of the trial by jury, as a test of right or law, as a tribunal to decide upon the disputed rights of the citizens in civil cases, there is one point of view in which it may be regarded as above all price, namely, as the means by which the citizens become insensibly instructed in the great leading principles of the laws, and the foundation and extent of their rights. It is the best school of the citizen. The people assemble at stated periods to attend the sessions of the courts; the discussions are public, the neighbors of the parties are called on to act as jurors; they hear the laws commented on by counsel, they receive the instructions of the court, and retire to deliberate on their verdict. Each juror feels the responsibility under which he acts. Thus, the citizens in rotation, are called on to perform highly important functions in the administration of the laws, and after serving a few terms, cannot fail to become pretty well acquainted with the great leading principles of the laws of their country, and more vigilant in maintaining their own rights. My own opinion is, that the trial by jury, in the interior of this state, has done more to enlighten the people, than all the means of education which have been provided by the munificence of the legislature. Many men who can neither read nor write, are yet capable of deciding, as jurymen, a question of disputed right between two of their fellow-citizens, with admirable discrimination. I think I can perceive, in this respect, a singular improvement in the general intelligence of the people since I came to reside here, twenty-two years ago, especially among that class of our population to whom the trial by jury and the publicity of judicial proceedings, were novelties. A friend of mine used to relate an anecdote, which illustrates this position. Two honest creoles were disputing about a point of law; said one of them, "How, do you think I don't know, Sir? I am a Justice of the Peace?" "And I," said the other, "I ought to know something about it, I have been twice foreman of the Grand Jury."

If I were to dwell longer upon the subject of our jurisprudence, this address would swell into a dissertation. Permit me recommend this subject to your attention, and particularly an inquiry into the practical operation of the laws above referred to, which regulate the great relations of social and domestic life. Whether an equal participation of the wife in the property acquired during marriage; a right growing originally out of the presumed collaboration of the parties in a rude primitive state of society, ought still to exist in the present age of refinement and extravagance. Whether such a system be not productive of more frauds and injustice to creditors, and disruption of families and litigation, than of public good and domestic tranquillity, are questions more proper for discussion in the halls of legislation than here; they belong rather to the legislator than the historian.

III. I should hardly be pardoned, if I dwelt long on the next subject embraced in our plan, the state of religion. I will confine myself to a single remark. Fortunately Louisiana was ceded to Spain after the Inquisition had, even in that country of bigotry, been disarmed of its terrors, and although in this country the Catholic religion was the only one openly tolerated, yet an attempt to introduce that most infamous of all human institutions, was indignantly put down by the people and the local authorities.

IV. The condition of the Indian tribes comes next. The Indians! the Indians! whether subjects of history or heroes of romance, or mixed up in the miserable, ephemeral, dramatic trash of the day, always exaggerated, disfigured, caricatured. They have been represented by some as brave, high-minded, and capable of sustaining extraordinary privations; sometimes as cold, stern, taciturn; sometimes as gay, lively, frolicksome, full of badinage, and excessively given to gambling, sometimes as cruel, and even man-eaters, delighting in the infliction of the most horrible tortures. Some will tell you that they have a simple natural religion; or as the poet has it:

"His untutored mind
Sees God in clouds, and hears him in the wind;
His soul, proud science never taught to stray,
Far as the solar walk or milky way.
Yet simple nature to his hope has given,
Behind the cloud-topped hill, an humbler heaven,
Some safer world, in depth of woods embraced,
Some happier island in the watery waste.
To be content, his natural desire,
He asks no angel's wings, no seraph's fire,
But thinks, admitted to that equal sky,
His faithful dog shall bear him company."

Some of the earlier historians represent the Natchez as worshipers of the sun, or worshipers of fire; as having a temple dedicated to the sun, keeping up a perpetual, a vestal fire. They conclude, of course, that those Indians must have been allied at least to the Peruvians or Mexicans, if not descended from the fire-worshipers of the East. The truth probably was, that in some miserable cabin or wigwam, a few chunks were kept burning, as is the case in every Indian encampment, and indeed in every well-regulated kitchen. The fact is, that neither the pen of Cooper, nor the more eloquent and fascinating style of Chateaubriand, can inspire the slightest interest for their Indian heroes and heroines, in the mind of a man who has been much among the aborigines, and knows something of their real character and habits. With respect to those nations which yet exist, we are able to see for ourselves, and correct the false impressions which earlier writers may have produced. It is melancholy to look over the list of tribes, which were once scattered over the surface of lower Louisiana at early periods of the colony. How many of them are totally extinct! How many have dwindled down to a mere shadow, and their feeble remnant confounded with some neighboring tribe! The Attakapas, the Carancuas, the Opelousas, the Adayes, the Natchitoches, the Natchez, where are they, and what monuments have they left us, by which any trace of their history may be known? Of the Natchitoches, only a single individual exists, and he has been adopted by the Cados. Who knows anything of the language of these nations? Their language, certainly among the most curious of the remnants of erratic tribes, and by which an acute philology might perhaps trace some affinities with other existing people, is known only to a few; and they are not of that class from whom the republic of letters might expect some account of it. The powerful tribe of the Natchez is totally extinct; its last miserable remnant took refuge among the Chickasaws. There remain a few degenerate (if such beings can degenerate) descendants of the Tunicas, Chitemachas, Pascagoulas, Apalaches, and Biloxis.

Neither the French nor the Spanish governments recognized, in the Indians, any primitive title to the land over which they hunted, nor even to the spot on which their permanent dwellings were fixed. They were often grants of lands for very limited extents, not exceeding a league square, covering their village. They were sometimes permitted to sell out their ancient possessions; and had a new locality assigned them. Many titles of that kind exist at the present time, and have been subjects of judicial decision. But the policy of extinguishing the primitive Indian title, as it is called, by purchase, which prevailed universally among the English colonists, appears to have been wholly unknown to the French and Spaniards in Louisiana. The massacre of the French at Natchez, which led to the extermination of that tribe, was provoked, by the atrocious attempt, by the commandant, to destroy their village at St. Catherine's, in order to annex the land to his own plantation.

There are many indications here, as well as in upper Louisiana and Ohio, of a race of men, long since extinct, who had probably made considerable advances in some of the useful arts, and perhaps the art of defence. In Sicily Island, in the parish of Chatahoula, there is a curious circle of mounds, regularly disposed, embracing a large area of alluvial soil, but little elevated above high-water mark. I believe the dwelling-house of the present proprietor, Mr. Matthews, is built upon one of them. There are others equally curious on Black River; and near the village of Harrisonburg may yet be traced an extensive elevation of earth, strongly resembling breastworks. The enemy against which these works were thrown up, was probably the Mississippi, whose waters once flooded the whole of that region at certain stages. The study of Indian mounds has heretofore led to no important discovery upon which much reliance can be placed. It is worse than idle to indulge in conjectures upon the origin of these monuments. A few sculls, picked up here and there, may indicate, perhaps, to the professed phrenologist, the former existence of a race more civilized than the present Indians, more capable of combination, having the organ of constructiveness more amply developed; but no general conclusions can be safely drawn from indications so feeble and equivocal. It would be, in my opinion, equally philosophical to conclude with the poet:

> "The earth has bubbles as the ocean has,
> And these are of them."

That there are, among the existing race of aborigines, instances of extraordinary capacity and power of combination, a few individuals, infinitely superior to the common herd, is undoubted. What was the boasted Cadmus of antiquity, who introduced into Greece a few letters of Egyptian or Phœnician origin, when compared with that poor, crippled Cherokee of our own day, who, by the unaided efforts of mind, by the simple power of induction, invented, perhaps, the most perfect alphabet of any existing language?

In these hasty and imperfect glances over the wide field of our proposed inquiries, I have purposely omitted to touch upon the last, or rather the present, era of our history, commencing with the annexation of Louisiana to the Federal Union, by far the most brilliant and important, and marked by great and interesting events. In relation to Louisiana, this may be properly designated as the epoch of constitutional, popular self-government, and of steam, as applied to navigation. The documents which illustrate this part of our history are within our reach, and ought to be collected and preserved. Forty years ago what was New-Orleans—what was Louisiana? The mighty river which sweeps by us then rolled silently through an extended wilderness, receiving the tribute of its vassal-streams from the base of the Rocky Mountains on one side, and the Apalachian chain on the other; its broad and smooth surface, occasionally ruffled by the dip of an Indian's paddle, or a solitary barge, slowly creeping up stream to the feeble settlements in the interior. What are they now? This city has become the greatest mart of agricultural products on the face of the globe; and yonder river traverses a double range of states, peopled by freemen, who, by the miracles of steam, are brought almost in contact with the great market for the productions of their industry. That river is literally covered with floating palaces, which visit its most remote branches; and along the extended levee fronting our port, a dense forest of masts exhibits the flags of every commercial nation in the world. At her annexation to the Union, the destiny of Louisiana became fixed—admitted at once to a participation in the great renown of the republic, connected with it by bonds of a common interest, she sprung forward, as it were by a single leap, from colonial dependence, to the glorious prerogatives of freemen, and to the enjoyment of the most luxuriant prosperity.

Let us endeavor to make a wise use of this

prosperity, and do something for the cause of letters. Colleges are springing up under the generous patronage of the legislature, which promise soon to be amply sufficient for the education of the rising generation. The Medical College of this city, the offspring of private enterprise, and sustained by the devotion of a few medical gentlemen to the cause of science, deserves public encouragement, and I trust will receive it. The Lyceum of this city promises to unite utility with all that is agreeable in the public discussion of interesting topics. Let us turn aside, occasionally at least, from the worship of mammon, devote some of our leisure moments, stolen from mere sordid and engrossing pursuits, to the cultivation of liberal studies. Who does not sigh, sometimes, amidst the bustle and struggle of active life, to retreat upon the studies of his youth? To fly to his early friends; friends who never deceived him, and never weary; to the society of the philosophers, poets, historians of past times, and to bask in the mild radiance of those great luminaries of the intellectual world, to renew again those studies—which, if you will allow me to paraphrase the splendid eulogium of the great master of Roman eloquence—studies which form the generous aliment of youthful mind; the hoped-for delight of declining years; the best ornament of prosperity; in adversity our surest consolation and refuge; inexhaustible source of the purest pleasure, whether at home or abroad, whether engaged in the bustle of the city, or enjoying the sober tranquillity of rural life.

LOUISIANA—History and Progress of.—"Si je réglais mes conditions sur ce que ces vastes territoires vaudront aux Etats-Unis, les indemnités n'auraient point de bornes," said Napoleon, when, pressed by the times and by the exigencies of his treasury, he called Barbé Marbois to his side, and instructed him immediately to open negotiations with Mr. Livingston for the sale of Louisiana to the Americans. "I want fifty millions," the First Consul continued, "and for less than that sum I will not treat: I would rather make a desperate attempt to keep these fine countries."

We have opened with this extract from Marbois' history of the negotiations, which Mr. Gayarré has felicitously adopted as the motto of his work on Louisiana. Bonaparte, with that decision of character which made him superior to every emergency, and with that political foresight which was only second to his great military genius, seized upon the first breathing moment which the conflicts of Europe would admit, to fix the destiny of Louisiana on the best possible basis for the interests of France. On the 10th April, 1803, he summoned to his presence two ministers well acquainted with French continental possessions, one of whom was M. Marbois. He told them that he was aware of the vast importance of Louisiana, which had just returned to the possession of France, after having been abandoned since 1763 to Spain, by the fault of the French negotiator. That the British had taken from France Canada, Cape Breton, Newfoundland, Nova Scotia, and the richest portions of Asia, but that he had solemnly resolved the Mississippi, which they coveted, should not be theirs. "The conquest of Louisiana would be easy, if they would only take the trouble to make a descent upon it. If there is yet time they shall see that it is no longer within their reach. I will cede it to the United States. These republicans ask of me only one town in Louisiana; but I already consider the colony as entirely lost; and it appears to me, that in the hands of this growing power it will be more useful to the policy and even to the commerce of France, than if I should attempt to keep it." This was making virtue of an imperious necessity, on the part of a man who understood the vast value of the territories which were slipping from his grasp, which could not possibly be retained, but for which he would not consent to treat, even then, on a lower basis than fifty million francs.

But Louisiana has passed into the hands of the United States. All the heart-burnings of those who opposed the measure, all the exultations of its friends, have long since subsided, and the sober and enlightened judgment of the whole country, and of the world at large, has admitted the wisdom of a purchase which has brought us a great and a fertile country, commanding the gates of the Mississippi, open to the Gulf of Mexico, limitless in resources, and destined, in the hands of God, to be the right arm of American wealth, liberty and power.

Out of this vast domain has been carved Texas.* We shall not pause here to speak of this virgin country, which we have hardly yet learned to appreciate, either in its elements of wealth or influence—Texas, which in an evil hour we sacrificed to Spain, but which was watched over by a ruling and benignant Providence, and brought back with its gallant populace to the homestead of its republican brotherhood across the Sabine, in defiance of the armies of Mexico, the wiles of European diplomacy, and the infatuation of a large portion of our own countrymen.

We confine ourselves here to Louisiana proper. We are acquainted with the interest she excites, necessarily, in every portion of the Union, and know how desirable it is that a general understanding should be had

* We hold to this interpretation of the treaty of purchase, whatever may be urged to the contrary, and though M. Marbois, one of the negotiators, confesses an intentional ambiguity in the boundary clause. Hist. Louis., p. 286.

abroad of the peculiar structure of her society, her government and her laws, in so many respects without parallel in any other portion of the states. It could not but be expected that the policy of a state would be largely influenced by the vicissitudes through which she has passed, and by the admixture of races or of people who have found a home upon her soil, and shared empire and dominion over her. And such indeed is the case, as we shall have abundant evidence hereafter.

To understand fully the constitutional and legal, and the general history of the state, it will be necessary to refer over and over again to several standard works. These are now upon the table before us, and we shall, *in limine*, make a few reflections upon them in their order.

I. *Histories of Louisiana.*—Major Amos Stoddard published, in 1812, a work entitled "Sketches, Historical and Descriptive, of Louisiana." It embraces a most interesting collection of material, and discusses, in an enlightened and liberal spirit, the policy and history of the state. Mr. Stoddard had full opportunity to inform himself of his subject. He had taken possession of the country for the United States, under the treaty of cession, and had had access to all the public records. He also resided several years in the state, and tells us that respectable men in most of the districts, furnished him with such local and other information as they possessed.

In 1827, François Xavier Martin, judge of the Supreme Court of Louisiana, published a work, in two volumes, on the state. Judge Martin's work embraces a very extended field, and might, with much propriety, have been entitled, Outlines of the History of America since its Discovery. He is learned and elaborate; but there is nothing in his work which would warrant us to believe that he considered history as a science, and the facts with which it is conversant only important as they indicate principles of universal use and application. Judge Martin, when speaking of Louisiana, loses himself in his details, and we have scarcely a comprehensive view throughout the whole work. His history is chiefly important as a storehouse of valuable material, out of which another might rear a beautiful structure. The style, too, of the production, is frequently dry and inelegant; but of this it is ungenerous to complain, since the author has candidly informed us that as he does not write in his vernacular tongue, elegance of style is beyond his hope, and consequently without the scope of his ambition. He also tells us that the labor of twenty years has been spent in the collection of materials, and that age has at last crept upon him, and the decay of his constitution has given more than one warning, that if the sheets now committed to the press were longer withholden, the work would probably be a posthumous one.*

In 1828, the Marquis de Marbois, a peer of France, and a man deeply conversant with the history of his own and of other countries, enriched the world with a volume upon Louisiana, conceived in the most liberal, enlightened and philosophic spirit. Marbois had been intimately connected with the transactions he was to discuss. He tells us that the treaty of cession of Louisiana had given rise to regrets in France, and that these could not be better dissipated than by a clear and dispassionate view of the whole transaction. No man was better qualified for the work. For more than fifty years M. de Marbois had watched our national progress with an eye evidently partial to our interests, and gratified at our success. His writings bear ample testimony to this declaration. As a sound and judicious exposition of the nature of our government, the present work is valuable; but its peculiar interest consists in the history of the Louisiana treaty, in which he held a conspicous part. In whatever light it is considered, we cannot point to a single historical work more worthy of a place in every American library.† This noble Frenchman had filled the highest stations in his country. He was secretary of legation to the Empire in 1769. At Dresden and Bavaria he was chargé d'affaires, and afterward a councilor at the parliaments of Metz. In 1779 Marbois was recognized as secretary of legation under the Chevalier de la Luzerne, minister of France to the United States; and five years afterward as chargé d'affaires to the same gov-

---

* Let us not be charged with injustice to Judge Martin. His late retirement, at a ripe old age, from the bench of the Supreme Court, which he has occupied for over thirty years, is an event which furnishes us an opportunity, as a lawyer, to pay a deserved tribute to his pre-eminent legal character. One cannot refer to his voluminous decisions without admiring the depth of learning, the cogency of reasoning, and the clear appreciation of right and justice which characterize them all. We admire Judge Martin, the jurist. More than fifty years ago, he commenced his mission as a lawyer. By industry and application, more than by adventitious circumstances, he succeeded in acquiring his elevated position, and with it a fortune scarcely equaled by any professional man in the country. Besides his history of Louisiana, he has contributed to the world a digest of its laws, and twenty volumes of reports. He is also the author of a history of North Carolina. Possessing a retentive memory and a readiness of application, joined to astute reasoning powers, he has rendered, in the language of the Louisiana Law Journal, decisions on important and difficult questions which possess undoubted merit, and will stand the test of time. The same journal throws some doubt upon the authorities which he consulted in his History of Louisiana; as, for instance, Tonti and Vergennes; but we think without any great effect; for Tonti might have been quoted though he never wrote the work, and yet be authority; and the memoir of Vergennes is several times referred to in the English edition of Marbois.

† North American Review, 1830.

ernment. He married an American lady, returned to France in 1790, was entrusted with important missions by Louis XVI., was imprisoned by Robespierre, made president of the Council of Ancients, banished by a revolutionary faction, restored by Bonaparte, made counselor of state and director of the treasury, and finally minister plenipotentiary on the part of the French republic to treat for the cession of Louisiana. Marbois, after filling other high honors under the Consulate and Empire, was made a peer on the restoration of the Bourbons, secretary of state, and keeper of the seals. He was a man of letters and a philosopher; and in addition to the work before us, has contributed works on morals, on finance, and on history.*

In 1830, Charles Gayarré, a native of Louisiana, and now the secretary of state, was induced to publish, in the French language, a manual of the history of his state, as he modestly terms it: Essai Historique sur la Louisiane. He pleads that this was a youthful production, and that having lately had access to valuable documents from France, he was induced to attempt a more extended and elaborate history of the state. The first volume of this undertaking is before us, written in French, and printed in the most beautiful style by a New-Orleans publisher. We have placed the work as a text for our article, and shall have frequent occasion to refer to it hereafter.

That a work should be published in the United States and for the use of American citizens, in the French language, has been thought not a little singular by many with whom we have conversed. In this category we were found ourselves, up to the period of the publication, and even now, after having given full hearing to the ingenious apologies of the author, our doubts have been shaken only, and by no means removed. Such a work can only be intended for the people of Louisiana, for those of France have long since lost all interest in their ancient possession. The Louisianians of French origin, or even of French birth, as a general rule, have acquired a sufficient knowledge of English to be able to read and speak it with ease and fluency, we mean the enlightened portion of them, for it is only in this class that Mr. Gayarré could expect readers at all. Why then write an elaborate work for these in a language, though consecrated by the tenderest associations of our nature, rather than in another, with which, as American citizens, it is their best interest, as well as their highest duty, to be familiar? We would have proposed this query before seeing Mr. Gayarré's work, and really after the best reflection have not been able to pursue a different course, however much we may be disposed to do full justice to the motives of the writer and to his work.

Mr. Gayarré tells us that, comparing the historian to the artist about to execute a portrait, there are but two methods for him to adopt. He may strike out with a bold pencil the main outlines, the leading traits, the grand points of resemblance—se contentant de saisir les principaux traits et ce jeu de physionomie qui constitue la ressemblance; or he may adopt what is called the anatomical method,—appeler de la peinture anatomique, and descend to the minutiæ of his subject, omitting not the slightest and most delicate shades and touches; n'omettant ni une mêche de cheveux ni une ligne veinuèse. Mr. Gayarré has chosen the latter method, because it was a family portrait on which he was engaged, to be kept with the old family mansion and all the heirlooms of a venerated ancestry. Louisiana he can only regard as a tender mother. All the affections of his heart are entwined around her, and the most trifling incidents connected with her history are treasured up in his memory. The language of the historian here is so beautifully tender, and betrays so much of the best feelings of our nature, that we cannot refrain from giving the whole passage as he has written it.

> "Mon cœur me dit que c'était notre mère à nous Franco et Hispanio-Américains, qui était là devant moi. Mon cœur me dit que dans le portrait de l'objet aimé, on regrettait toujours l'omission de la moindre minutie, d'un signe, d'une marque presque imperceptible pour un œil indifférent, même d'un pli de vètement. Ainsi, j'entrai dans des détails qui nuiront peut-être à l'effet de l'ensemble. Je sentis que je travaillais, non pas seulement pour satisfaire le goût ou l'esprit, mais le cœur. J'avoue donc que je me suis plu à contempler la Louisiane avec un microscope, et à la reproduire comme je l'avais vue. C'est-à-dire que, pour le moment, c'est un portrait de famille que j'ai voulu faire, et, je le répète, je suis entré dans des details qui ne seront nullement interessants pour l'étranger. Mais j'ai jugé mes compatriotes d'après moi-meme, et j'ai pensé que, dans l'inventaire que j'ai fait des souvenirs laissés par leurs ancêtres, ils me sauraient gré de n'en avoir pas omis même les plus insignificants et d'en avoir par là complété la série. De là, des redites et des longueurs."—*History of Louisiana*, p. 5.

It is in this view of his undertaking that Mr. Gayarré has entered upon its execution. His first volume, an octavo of 400 pages, is employed in the discussion of the affairs of Louisiana from the earliest period to the year 1743—the expeditions of De Soto, Marquette, La Salle—the settlements of Iberville and Bienville, Crozat's Charter, the Western Company, arrival of the Jesuits in Louisiana, Indian war, etc., etc.—the authorities for all of which are papers brought over from France by Mr. Magne, of New-Orleans, private family papers, the work of Garcillasso de la Vega, and the history by Judge Martin. The second volume, we understand through another source, is nearly

* Marbois' History of Louisiana, pp. 9, 10, 11, 12.

complete, and only delayed in anticipation of important information, which, it is thought, a search in the records of Spain will furnish, and without which, it appears to us, a history of Louisiana must necessarily be very imperfect. This volume will be brought down to 1803. The American history of Louisiana will occupy a third volume.*

There is one reason which Mr. Gayarré has given for adopting the French language, of which it would not be fair to omit a notice. He is employed upon characters who thought and spoke in that language, and as far as possible he deems it necessary that these should be allowed to give accounts of the scenes and events of which they formed a part. He has, in the spirit of the skilful dramatist, thought it proper to retire himself behind the scenes, and let the characters on the stage divulge and develop the plot. A better idea of M. de Bienville, for example, can be formed from a single sentiment he may utter, than from any elaborate description. We would far rather, however, admit the justness of Mr. Gayarré's last apology, which he had almost forgotten, but which is very refined and chivalrous. The "fair Louisianians" will appreciate the passage. "Je dirai donc que, sachant que la plupart de nos Louisianaises ne lisent guère l'anglais, j'ai pense qu'en écrivant dans la langue qui leur est familière, elles seraient tentées, par un sentiment de curiosité, de jeter les yeux sur les pages de cette histoire, et peut-être de les lire jusqu'au bout. Comment pouvais-je résister à cette considération? C'était pour moi plus qu'une raison. C'était une seduction."*

II. *Discoveries.*—The legends of De Soto, Marquette, and La Salle, shall not arrest our attention. These wild and daring passages belong rather to the romancer than the historian. Louis XIV. seized upon the proposal of Iberville, and addressed himself in earnest to a new and vast country which dazzled his ambition. Iberville, and Bienville his brother, founded a colony of Frenchmen on the shores of Louisiana in 1699. Hard was their struggle against nature; "the buzz and sting of the musquitoes, the hissing of snakes, the croaking of frogs, and the cries of the alligators, incessantly asserted that the lease the God of nature had given these reptiles had still a few centuries to run." This is the earliest era in the history of Louisiana.

III. *Crozat's Charter.*—In 1712, the King of France granted to M. Crozat a charter which covered the whole province of Louisiana. The aims of both parties were commercial, and included the whole of the Mississippi and its tributary bays, lakes, rivers, and bordering territories. M. Crozat, for twenty years, was endowed with exclusive privileges of trade in these countries—to work mines for gold and precious stones, with a large share of the results. The laws, edicts, and ordinances of the realm, and the customs of Paris, were extended over Louisiana.

A word about this custom of Paris. France, in ancient times, was governed by the usages of the different provinces. These were unwritten, and of consequence conflicting. Charles V., in 1453, ordered them to be reduced to writing by commissioners. So far as the customs of Paris were concerned, the edict was not executed till 1510. These customs were embraced under sixteen heads and three hundred and sixty-two articles. The heads are fiefs, quit-rents, movables and immovables, complaints, actions, prescription, redemption, arrests and executions, servitudes, community of goods, dower, guardianship, donation, testaments, successions,

* This volume, we are to judge, will be in English, since, as Mr. Gayarré infers, the Americans are only interested in this portion of the history of Louisiana. We are not to expect a translation of the first two volumes, for our author hates translations as he does prefaces: "Je hais les préfaces." He hints to us, however, that he will re-make the work in English hereafter.

* The above-named, Stoddard, Martin, Marbois, and Gayarré's are all the historical works proper that we have upon Louisiana. The reader, if disposed to extend his investigations into every department, will find material enough within reach. We would name the memoirs of Charlevoix, Hennepin, and Tonti, upon which Mr. Sparks comments at large in his Life of La Salle; also Vergennes' memoir, Dupratz' History of Louisiana, printed in 1758, and the files of the colonial gazettes. Of later days we have "Views of Louisiana," by Wm. Brackenridge, 1814, a work singularly accurate in its delineations of country and in its geographical particulars. Mr. Wm. Darby, formerly of this city, a distinguished geographer and practical man, has also published a work upon the physical character of the state, &c. Flint's "Valley of the Mississippi," will also be referred to with advantage. There is also a small volume upon Louisiana prepared by some one at the North, and now in the hands of the teachers and scholars of the Second Municipality. The early documents of Louisiana, such as Charlevoix and others, are in Mr. French's library, and might be published as Louisiana Historical Collections. [Now being published 1852.] Seriously, a good English history of the state, brought down to the present time, is a great desideratum, but it is a work that few can execute, though many may attempt it. [Now being published by Chas. Gayarré, Esq., 1852.] We dismiss our note by referring, as other sources of valuable information upon the subject before us, to the Louisiana Law Journal; to the second volume United States Land Office Papers; to Hall's Law Journal, where the discussions of Jefferson and Livingston on the Batture case are to be found; to the frequent decisions upon that case in the Reports of the Supreme Court of Louisiana, and particularly the great case of 1840, and the able arguments of Hunt, Mazureau, Soule, Preston, Peirce, Hoffman, and Roselius, occupying with the decisions of the court, upward of a thousand pages of matter; to Bullard & Curry's Digest of the Laws of Louisiana, and the debates on the adoption of the Constitution of 1846. We also refer to the Digest of the French Colonial Papers, which Mr. Forstall has published in the Review, and to the papers copied in France by John Perkins, Esq.

seizures and sales.* The customs of Paris extended to all the French colonies.†

The privileges allowed to Crozat were ample; but so vain are the calculations of men when employed upon novel enterprises, they satisfied not one of his greedy desires after wealth in the western world. The grant was surrendered, after five years, into the hands of the king, with the bitter complaint, that, from the imbecility of the colony, the strength of the Indians, the presence of the British, and the sterility of the soil, it had proved of no kind of value whatever to him, but rather a ruinous expense.

IV. *The Western Company and Law.*—There settled in Paris about this period a man from Scotland, by the name of John Law. He was a singular character, a restless projector, a daring financier, high-minded, and full of enterprise. This extraordinary man soon succeeded in gaining a ruling influence over the Duke of Orleans, then Regent of France, obtained a charter for a bank of $1,200,000, substituted paper for specie, and set the whole French nation mad with magnificent schemes of creating wealth, as it were, by the wand of a magician. The Chancelor d'Aguesseau opposed this daring scheme with infinite peril to himself. To the royal bank of Law was attached a great commercial company, in which were to be concentered all the rights, privileges and possessions of all the trading companies then chartered in France. To this company was granted the great territory of Louisiana, as it was surrendered up by Crozat. All Paris was in commotion—every man, woman and child became a financier; the boot-black and the collier of to-day were the grandees of to-morrow, and their splendid equipages dazzled the Parisian populace. The Royal Bank stock went up to six hundred times its par value, and dividends were rendered of two hundred per cent. The exhaustless mines near the Mississippi would reimburse any investment, it was said. In three years, John Law was a bankrupt and a beggar. The government of France received a terrible shock; the deluded votaries of stock-jobbing were undone; the magnificent Western Company—the Mississippi scheme—became a by-word; the banking bubble, when inflated to the skies, had burst!

The charter of the Western Company was granted for twenty-five years. It was to have exclusive privileges of trade, and of the purchase of beaver skins for exportation. The company might make all Indian wars and treaties, work all mines, grant lands, construct fortifications, nominate governors, and appoint inferior judges. Its vessels and crews to be of the French nation. The descendants of European parents, born in Louisiana, to be counted natural-born subjects of France. The inhabitants of Louisiana are exempted from taxes, and the company's goods from duty. The company engage to bring into Louisiana six thousand white persons and three thousand negroes. The issue of its stock is not limited in amount, but the shares are to be five hundred francs each. The holder of fifty shares will be entitled to a vote in the affairs of the company, which are to be managed for the first two years by directors appointed by the king, and then by those appointed by the stockholders every third year.

There are different accounts of the condition of Louisiana during the fourteen years it remained under the Western Company, who enjoyed the privileges granted to Law. Dupratz and Charlevoix, quoted by Marbois, represent everything in the most deplorable condition; while Judge Martin, on a comparison of all the authorities, has concluded that these were the best years which Louisiana knew under the dominion of France, the white population having increased from 700 to 5,000, and the black from 20 to 2,000: "a vast number of handsome cottages lined both sides of the river at the German coast, the culture of rice, indigo, and tobacco, and a regular administration of justice, were provided for."

The Western Company, in despair of finding the gold they had anticipated in Louisiana, from mineral researches turned their attention to agriculture. To promote their aims, large grants of the soil were made to powerful and wealthy individuals. To Law, they granted a plot of twelve miles square. These grantees were to introduce settlers; but they succeeded to an extent far less than was anticipated, while sanguinary Indian wars desolated the colony. The company, in utter hopelessness, threw up their charter in April, 1732, which the king accepted, and declared the commerce of Louisiana thenceforward free.

V. *French Colonial Government.*—The commissioner Salmon took possession for the king. He found property, to which the company had sold out their rights to the monarch, amounting to two hundred and sixty-three livres: among this property was found 8,000 barrels of rice. The new government established consisted of a superior council, of the governor-general of New France, the governor and commissary of Louisiana, the king's lieutenant and the town mayor of New-Orleans, six councillors, an attorney, and a clerk.*

A war broke out between Great Britain and France in 1760, whose influences were felt throughout all America. We know the particulars of this conflict, in which our own Washington had so conspicuous a part. Cana-

* Louisiana Law Journal, pp. 15, 46.
† Marbois' History of Louisiana.

* Martin's History of Louisiana.

da fell into the hands of the English at last, and, rather than submit to the consequences, large numbers of its inhabitants sought a home in southern climes, fixing themselves on the Acadian coast of Louisiana, or taking their course westward of the river, to form the settements of Attakapas, Opelousas, and Avoyelles.

VI. *The Cession of Louisiana to Spain.*—France looked to Spain in her emergencies, and the Duke of Choiseul, the minister, entered into a family compact with the Spanish king, on the 15th August, 1760, and on the 3d November, 1762, a secret treaty between the two governments ceded the territory of Louisiana, west of the Mississippi, with New-Orleans, to Spain.

The bad system of government under which Louisiana long suffered, was attended with the consequences which were to be expected from it, and the sovereignty of the finest country in the world, says Marbois, a country which might have become another France, was of no use to the parent state, but was even a charge to her. After the experience of several years, the government, wearied with a possession which its faults and ignorance had made burthensome, felt disposed to abandon it.

In 1763, Great Britain, France, and Spain, entered upon the treaty of Paris, and terminated their difficulties. France abandoned to Britain Nova Scotia, Acadia, Canada, Cape Breton, and all the islands and coasts of the gulf and river of St. Lawrence, the whole of Louisiana east of the Mississippi, except the town of New-Orleans. The navigation of the Mississippi is declared free to the subjects of either nation. Thus did France, by her cession to Britain and Spain, divest herself of every foot of territory she held in North America.

The private treaty of cession to Spain was long held secret, and it was not until 1764 that D'Abadie was ordered by Louis XV. to announce the fact to the colony. D'Abadie was heart-broken at the intelligence, and died before he could communicate it. The duty devolved upon his successor, Aubry. A day of lamentation and sorrow had dawned upon the unfortunate Louisianians, and they heard their fate with settled gloom. A general meeting of the leading inhabitants of all the parishes assembled hastily in New-Orleans, and entreaties were sent up to the throne that this painful treaty might not be made to go into effect. Louis XV. declared the cession irrevocable.

Ulloa.—Don Antonio de Ulloa arrived in Louisiana in 1766, appointed, as he professed, by Charles of Spain, to take possession of the province. His powers, being demanded by the colonists, were not shown. This man was a scholar, a mathematician, and an astronomer, but was held in detestation by the Louisianians, and the more particularly that Aubry, the governor, exhibited towards him, in appearance, the most humiliating obsequiousness. The council, over the head of the governor, notified the Spaniard to produce his powers, or to depart the province. He determined on the latter alternative, and in a few days made sail for Spain, amid the universal acclamations and rejoicings of the people.*

O'Reilly.—Scarcely had the colony breathing time before it was announced that a Spanish frigate and transports were upon the coast, and approaching the town. Notwithstanding some threats of resistance on the part of the inhabitants, Don Alex. O'Reilly, commander of the Spanish forces, landed, and sent up a message to the governor, informing him that he was prepared to take possession of Louisiana; that he would not publish more of his orders until put in possession; and that any show of opposition would be signally punished. The inhabitants returned a deputation to the Spaniard, declaring their intention to abandon the colony, and requesting two years' delay to effect the arrangement. O'Reilly consented with apparent cheerfulness, and with the warmest professions of regard. He soon after landed at the city, and took formal possession in the name of the king.†

But this display of clemency and virtue was a scheme to ingratiate himself into the confidence of the inhabitants, and then, by a single stroke, to bring down upon their heads the worst excesses of tyranny. Some of the first citizens were arrested and thrown into prison. They were declared guilty of treason against a government which they had never acknowledged, and which could not, in fact, be considered as established. The prosecution was based upon the statute of Alphonso VII., (*Partidas, vii.,* 1.) making it death to incite insurrection against the king. Villere was murdered in cold blood, Marquis and De Noyant, French officers, La Frenière, the attorney-general, Milhet and Caresse, merchants, after the form of a trial, were sen-

---

* In a statement by Governor Ulloa, of the events in Louisiana, a paper of 300 pages, now among the colonial records of Paris, Mr. Forstall conceives it clearly demonstrated that Aubry was at the bottom of the plot, the principal informer; and that the design of the colonists in the whole transaction was not for the purpose of remaining under a kingly dominion, but that the end was freedom. But this was Ulloa's statement, which, after all, ought not to be too much relied upon in the circumstances of the case.—*Com. Review,* vol. i., No. 4, p. 257.

† The trade of Louisiana at this time, 1769, was not inconsiderable. The following were a few of the items:—

Indigo, annually	$100,000
Rice, Peas, and Beans	4,000
Deer Skins	80,000
Lumber	50,000
Naval Stores	12,000
Tallow	4,000

The population of New-Orleans was 3,190, and of Louisiana 13,539.

tenced and executed. Posterity, says the historian Martin, the judge of men in power, will doom this act to public execration; and posterity, we add, has already regarded it as one of the blackest which it is the shame of history to record.*

What was the precise character of the powers conferred upon O'Reilly has never yet been satisfactorily determined; and it is almost equally uncertain how far he construed these powers, and how far, in one particular, he exerted them—we mean in relation to the change of government. This question has, within the last forty years, been extensively discussed in Louisiana, both in the forum and out of it, and opposite opinions held.

The question was first opened in 1809, during that famous discussion of those remarkable men, Edward Livingston, of Louisiana, and Thomas Jefferson, on the Batture case. Mr. Jefferson maintained that the proclamation of O'Reilly in November, 1769, introduced only a specific, and not a general change in the polity of the colony; that it neither abolished nor was it intended to abolish the whole system of French jurisprudence then in force. Mr. Livingston, on the contrary, held:†

1. That though the transfer of a country does not in general change its laws, yet this is not to be understood in relation to those fundamental laws which affect the perogative of the sovereign, which are of necessity changed by the cession, because the transfer releases the inhabitants from the allegiance due to the former sovereign, and makes them the subjects of another, toward whom it places them in the same relation as all his other subjects.

2. That O'Reilly's proclamation changed not only the form of government, but the administration of justice, and with it all the laws of the province.

3. That Spain had promulgated a code for the government of all her colonies, and this code declares that the laws it contains shall govern not only all the present colonies of Spain, but such as it may acquire hereafter. A great point in this celebrated controversy was to discover by what law the Batture was to be governed at the period when Louisiana passed into the hands of the United States—by the law of France or by that of Spain.‡

The king of France, in writing to D'Abadie at the period of the cession, conceded that the laws, forms and usages of the colony would be preserved, que les juges continuent, ainsi que le conseil superieur à rendre la justice, suivant les lois, formes et usages de la colonie; but this does not appear to have been inserted in the treaty of cession to be found in the senate document for 1837. O'Reilly, as soon as he was at ease in his government, made a proclamation to the people. He declared himself empowered by the king's letters patent, issued at Aranjuez, to establish that form of government, dependence, and subordination, which should accord with the good of his service and the happiness of his subjects in the colony. He therefore proceeded.

1. To establish a cabildo or city council for the administration of justice, &c., with six perpetual regidors who shall elect alcaldes or judges, &c., &c.

2. To prepare an abstract of the Spanish laws, in the form of a code, which should have effect until a more general knowledge of the Spanish tongue would admit of the introduction of the whole body of that law. This code to be applied unless the pleasure of the king of Spain be expressed to the contrary. The code occupies some sixty closely printed pages, and may be found in the second number of the Louisiana Law Journal, a work which, for the sake of sound jurisprudence, we wish could have met with a far better and more deserving destiny.

Whatever may have been the powers of O'Reilly, we think it on the whole clear that the laws of Spain were gradually extended by him over Louisiana, and afterwards by his successors, so that, in the end, but little trace of French legislation remained. La Frenière and Doucet, the only French lawyers at the time, had been dispatched by O'Reilly, who acknowledges himself, by his proclamatiom, the want of advocates in the colony. The inhabitants were compelled, through necessity, to apply for legal advice to the Spanish lawyers that had accompanied the expedition. The Supreme Court of Louisiana have also, on several occasions, arrived at the same conclusion. In Beard *v.* Poydras, 4 *Martin's Reports*, Derbigny, J. said, this publication, (O'Reilly proclamation,) followed from that moment by an uninterrupted observance of the Spanish law, has been received as an introduction of the Spanish code in all its parts, and must be considered as having repealed the laws formerly prevailing in Louisiana. The court afterward, in Malpica *v.* McKown, 1 *Louisiana Reports*, p. 255, declared that the laws of Spain having been in force in Louisiana need not be proved as facts. The laws of Spain, said Judge Martin, when he had laid aside the gown and taken up the pen as the historian, became the sole guide of the tribunals in their decisions. The transition was not perceived before it became complete, and very little inconvenience resulted from it.

* The reader should consult the second volume of Gayarré's (English) History, now being published, which puts rather a new face upon this whole matter. (1852.)

† Hall's Law Journal, vol. v.

‡ Law Journal, No. iv., p. 89.

It is unnecessary to analyze minutely the government of Louisiana at this period. The inhabitants were compelled to submit with the best grace when abandoned by France, and when resistance would have been fruitless. Excepting a few acts of tyranny, O'Reilly's government was not intolerable. He displayed, on some occasions, higher and better principles, but had given such offence in general, that on returning to Spain, he was prohibited from appearing at court. Louisiana lost largely during this administration, by the emigration of numbers of her best citizens.

To exhibit the liberality of the Spanish colonial policy, it may be remarked, that in 1778, Mercier's Law, deux mille quatre cent quarante, was prohibited from being read in in Louisiana, and also Robertson's History of America, for which the king thought he had just reason.

When the American revolution, with its deeds of high daring and patriotism, had progressed, and Spain, in an endeavor to mediate, had failed, the Catholic king prepared himself for war. Galvez, governor of Louisiana, with the first intelligence, threw himself upon the British garrison at Baton Rouge, and captured it. An American minister was sent to Madrid to negotiate a favorable treaty for his countrymen, and to obtain for them, if possible, the free navigation of the Mississippi to the sea. The French minister had previously intimated that the exclusive right to the navigation of that river would be a *sine qua non* on the part of Spain, and pressed by the exigencies of affairs, Congress was at one time (1782) disposed to make the concession, and instructed its minister to do so, if a favorable treaty could in this way be negotiated.*

Spanish Treaty of 1783.—The treaties between Great Britain, France, Spain and the United States, concluded in 1783, opened the navigation of the Mississippi without restrictions to the United States; ceded the Floridas to Spain, and bounded the possessions of the two countries by a line eastward of the 31° parallel on the Mississippi to the Apalachicola river, through the middle of that river to its junction with the Flint, on the Flint to the head of St. Mary's river, down the St. Mary's river to the Atlantic. These treaties were soon followed by embarrassing disputes, in which the Spaniards laid claim to a large tract of country, and an exclusive right to the navigation of that portion of the Mississippi which passed through their territories, against both of which claims the United States protested.

Spanish Scheme for Dividing the Union.—It may be remarked that very little, if any, intercourse was tolerated by the Spaniards, through the Mississippi, with the people of the United States. Any attempts to navigate the river, or to introduce merchandise into New Orleans by boats, were resisted, and the property seized. About the year 1787 General Wilkinson, a revolutionary officer, conceived the design of making a settlement of American families in Louisiana, for which he expected to receive some commercial favors from the Spaniards. He descended the river to New-Orleans with a small adventure of tobacco and flour, &c., and by an artifice, so worked upon the fears of Miro the governor, that he was disposed to listen to the proposal of opening a traffic with the people of the Western states. Miro flattered himself that a division might in this way be insured of the States of the American Union, and those westward of the Alleghany mountains attached to the interests of Spain. His suggestions were favorably received at Madrid, and the court, according to Marbois, consented, in 1788, to cede the free navigation of the Mississippi to the states founded on the left bank of that river, on the condition that they determined to form an empire distinct from that of the Atlantic states. The people of these states, however, having ceased to feel the grievances they suffered under the articles of American confederation, and having passed under the admirable federal constitution of 1789, forgot their dissensions, and treated every proposition of the Spaniards with contempt.

Freedom of the Mississippi.—In 1790, it was again attempted to procure from Spain the navigation of the Mississippi for the United States, also the island on which New-Orleans is situated, and the Floridas. For these concessions Spain was to be guarantied the rest of her possessions in the difficulties which threatened her with England. The proposition was not assented to, but five years after the American plenipotentiaries signed at St. Lorenzo a treaty stipulation for the freedom of the river to their countrymen, and a freedom to use for ten years the city of New-Orleans as a depot for their merchandise.

Carondolet's Plot.—Spain had no sooner signed the treaty than she began to display the utmost regret for her liberality. Her alliance with France, and the position of the United States, determined her by all means to hold on to the territory in Upper Louisiana, which she had agreed to cede. In vain were officers sent on the part of the United States to take possession of the posts and settlements In vain did the settlers themselves protest against the delay. A magnificent scheme had been planned, and was in progress, the design of which was to prevent Louisiana forever from falling into the hands of the American government. The Baron

* Marbois.

de Carondolet endeavored to sound General Wilkinson on the subject, and to bring him over to the plan by flatteries and by the most liberal offers. Wilkinson dismissed the messenger with an expression of views little favorable to the success of the project which was opened to him. We shall not on this occasion indulge ourselves with any reflections on the course and character of this officer, or pronounce any opinion as to the extent of his innocence or blame in these transactions.*

The face of European affairs in May, 1798, influenced the American people to put on their armor. Washington was again appointed to the head of the army; and the difficulties with regard to Louisiana, and consequent losses to the government, forced upon all minds the absolute necessity for the acquisition of New-Orleans, whatever might be the hazard.

Schemes for the Possession of Louisiana.—Louisiana indeed occupied an unenviable position at this time. She had been abandoned by the French in an evil hour, and contrary to her strongest remonstrances. Hardly had the cession been made, however, when it came to be regarded in France with a mortification and regret which increased the more the subject was regarded. So strong was this feeling, that, on the breaking out of hostilities with the Spaniards, Mr. Genet, the young and rash minister from France to the United States, employed himself immediately after his arrival in devising and carrying out a comprehensive scheme for the invasion of Louisiana, with troops and arms procured in the United States. In vain did General Washington oppose the duties of neutrality, and the principles of our government. Mr. Genet appealed from the President to the people, and though his course was condemned by the French government, the Committee of Public Safety immediately instructed Mr. Barthelemy, the ambassador of the French republic, to demand from Spain the restoration of Louisiana. In other respects was the position of Louisiana remarkable. The United States had been long regarding with a jealous eye the existence of a territory in the hands of a foreign power, capable of influencing, and of determining and controlling the destiny of the immense regions of country embraced in the Mississippi valley. A plot had been laid too by an American citizen, Blount, then governor of Tennessee, the object of which was to throw down upon Louisiana, during the wars between England and Spain, in 1797, through the medium of the western waters, large numbers of British troops from Canada. The plot was discovered, Blount degraded by the Senate, and the English government exonerated from the charge of any knowledge of his proceedings.

The eyes of Spain were not closed to the difficulties of her position; she could not be heedless of the "warnings" so often repeated, and so full of meaning. Bonaparte had by this time assumed the reins of government, and he cherished the idea of bringing back to the parent country a province which he conceived had been unnaturally severed from her. He conceived too that it was possible by this means to restore the ascendency which France had in former periods occupied in America. The consul entered at once upon negotiations, and worked upon the court of Madrid by his representations "that Louisiana restored to France would be a bulwark for Mexico, and a security for the tranquillity of the Gulf."

VII.—*Spanish Treaty of Cession.*—On the first of October, 1800, was concluded, between the Catholic King and French consul, the treaty of Ildefonso, the third article of which was, that His Catholic Majesty promises and engages to retrocede to the French republic, six months after the full and entire execution of the conditions therein stipulated in relation to the Duke of Parma, the colony and province of Louisiana, with the same extent that it had in the hands of Spain, and that it had when France possessed it, and such as it should be after the treaties subsequently entered into between Spain and the other powers. The stipulation in relation to the Duke of Parma was, that he should be put into possession of Tuscany. Another stipulation in the treaty provided for a preference to Spain, in the event of Louisiana passing again out of the hands of France.

French Government.—Bonaparte took immediate steps to enter upon his new possession, to establish a government over it, and to promote, by judicious steps, the health of its capital city. General Victor was appointed commissioner for accepting the transfer. Laussat, the colonial prefect, arrived in Louisiana, and issued a proclamation denouncing the previous separation of the province from France as the fruit of a corrupt government, an ignominious war, and dishonorable peace. "The French still remembered that a portion of the inhabitants of Louisiana were their descendants, with the same blood running in their veins; but as soon as France, by a prodigious succession of triumphs in the late revolution, had recovered her own freedom and glory, she turned her eyes towards Louisiana, the retrocession of which signalized her first peace." The Louisianians prepared an address in reply, in which, after a compliment to their late governors, they declared

* We have not within reach the memoirs of Wilkinson. In the difficulties of his time, his conduct was often open to mistrust. The question is a delicate one, but Congress, after a hearing, dismissed the charges that were brought against him. On another occasion we shall refer to the subject.

that the proclamation had filled the people with gratitude for its parental care, and that they already felt the happiness of their union with the French republic. The happy selection of some of her most virtuous citizens to govern them, and her choicest troops to protect them, were such sure pledges of their future happiness and prosperity. They offered in return their love and obedience, and would endeavor to prove themselves worthy of the title of French citizens."*

Everything seemed now prepared for the re-establishment of French dominion in Louisiana. The Spanish commissioners had issued their proclamation, announcing the cession, the good-will of their sovereign toward the colonists, his ardent desires that the privileges of the clergy and of the people, and the laws of the province as then administered, would be preserved and perpetuated by the king of France, and, according to to Martin, every one was ready to mount the tri-colored cockade, when a vessel from Bordeaux arrived at the Levee, announcing that Louisiana had become a part of the United States, by an act of Napoleon Bonaparte. But we are anticipating.

Uneasiness of the American People.—As soon as it became known in the United States that France had again come into possession of her old province, the greatest anxiety and uneasiness were manifested on every hand. The West was suddenly in a flame. New-Orleans was about to escape, and with one deep and pervading sentiment they exclaimed, "The Mississippi is ours. Its mouth is the only issue which nature has given to our waters. If our liberty be disputed nothing shall prevent our taking forcible possession. If Congress refuses us effectual protection, we shall adopt the measures which our safety requires. No protection, no allegiance!" It was everywhere taken for granted that France would entirely exclude American citizens from the province, and Congress itself, and the President, Mr. Jefferson, shared in the general uneasiness.†

Mr. Monroe was dispatched to Paris. Mr. Livingston, the minister there, had already displayed some temper upon the subject, and had advised his government to extreme measures. Hasten to France, said Mr. Jefferson to Mr. Monroe, if we cannot by a purchase of the country ensure a perpetual peace and friendship with all nations, then, as war cannot be far distant, it behooves us immediately to prepare for it. We saw, said a memorial of the territory of Mississippi, in January, 1803, to Congress—we saw our trade prospering, our property rising in value, and we felicitated ourselves. A recent order of the government of Louisiana, prohibiting intercourse between the Louisianians and Americans, has embarrassed our trade, and breathes a spirit of enmity to the United States. Mr. Monroe was directed to offer two millions of dollars for the city of New-Orleans, and Mr. Rost, of Pennsylvania, proposed in the Senate to place five millions of dollars at the disposition of the president, and to raise fifty thousand men to take possession of Louisiana by force.

French Views of Louisiana.—Napoleon was informed of all of this. He saw a thick cloud impending over France and another fifteen years' war with England, as he expressed it, on the eve of breaking out. He pondered deeply upon the crisis, and summoned two of his ministers to his side with the language with which we opened our article. With these he consulted, and was advised to opposite measures. We should not hesitate, said one, to make a sacrifice of that which is slipping from us. The efforts of France to form colonies in America have always been fruitless. Commercial establishments are better than colonies. "We must retain Louisiana," said the other; "*there does not exist on the face of the globe* a single port, a single city, susceptible of becoming as important as New-Orleans. All the productions of the West Indies suit Louisiana. If we must abandon St. Domingo, Louisiana will take its place. Attempts have been made there to introduce the vine, the olive and the mulberry tree, and these experiments have but too well succeeded. If the colony should become free, Provençe and our vineyards must prepare for a fearful competition with a country new and of boundless extent." Napoleon yielded to the former opinion, and Barbé Marbois opened negotiations at once.

French and American Negotiations.—Mr. Monroe arrived in France. Mr. Livingston met him with the expression—"I wish that the resolution offered by Mr. Rost in the Senate had been adopted. Only force can give us New-Orleans." Mr. Livingston had no confidence in the overtures of M. de Marbois. The three negotiators met together. They deliberated. The question came before them in every possible point of view, and the terms of a treaty sufficiently liberal, but indefinite in an important particular, was agreed upon at last, and presented to the First Consul, who approved it on the spot, with the remarkable words—

* We have followed Martin, but there is another version to be found in the pages of Marbois—"Every one will be astonished (*Hist Louis.*, p. 207) to learn that a people of French descent have received, without emotion, and without any apparent interest, a French magistrate, who comes to us accompanied by his young and beautiful bride, and preceded by the public esteem. Nothing has been able to diminish the alarm which his mission causes. His proclamations have been heard by some with sadness, and by the greater part of the inhabitants with the same indifference as the beat of the drum is listened to which announces the escape of a slave, or a sale at auction."

† Mabois' Hist. Louis., p. 221.

"Let the Louisianians know that we separate from them with regret, that we stipulate in their favor everything that they can desire; and let them, hereafter, happy in their independence, recollect that they have been Frenchmen, and that France in ceding them has secured for them advantages which they could not have obtained from any European power!"

VIII. *Purchase of Louisiana by the Americans.*—The treaty of Paris, 13th April, 1803, ceded to the United States forever and in full sovereignty, the province of Louisiana, with all its rights and appurtenances in full, and in the same manner as they had been acquired by France from the Catholic King. Eight stipulations exist in the treaty. The first and second provided for the full surrender of the province, the third for its privileges under the Constitution of the United States, the seventh for privileges of trade to the province for twelve years to French and Spanish vessels. The United States agreed to pay sixty millions of francs and to discharge certain claims of their citizens on France.

Ceremonies of Delivery.—No sooner had the treaty of Paris been signed than a new difficulty arose. The King of Spain protested against the transfer, and his minister at Washington was authorized to declare that no alienation of the territory by France could be considered valid after her express promise never to alienate to other than Spain. Bonaparte had appointed Laussat to receive the territory from the Spanish government and deliver it over to the Americans. The Spanish flag descended from its staff in the public square at New-Orleans, and the tri-colored one of the French republic ascended in its stead. The banner of the French republic, said Mr. Laussat, now displayed, and the sound of her cannon announced the return of French dominion; but it is only for an instant. I am here to deliver possession of the colony to the United States. Wilkinson and Claiborne appeared in New-Orleans on the part of the American government. On the 20th December the American eagle occupied the staff where the tri-colored flag had waved for twenty days, and amid the roar of cannon and the shouts of the citizens, the province passed forever from its allegiance to France. A group of the citizens of the United States, says Martin, who stood on a corner of the square, waved their hats in token of respect for their country's flag, and a few of them greeted it with their voices. No emotion was manifested by any other part of the crowd. The colonists did not appear to be conscious that they were reaching the *Latium sedes ubi fata quietas ostendunt.* Marbois relates a beautiful incident here, strikingly illustrative of the enthusiastic patriotism of the French. When the French colors were lowered and received in the arms of the French who had guarded them, their regrets were openly expressed, and to render a last homage to this token, which was no longer that of the sovereignty of the country, the sergeant-major wrapped it round him as a scarf, and after traversing the city, proceeded toward the house of the French Commissioner. The little troop accompanied him; they were saluted in passing before the lines of the Americans, who presented arms to them, and they finally delivered the banner into the hands of Laussat.*

Ambiguity in the Treaty.—The treaty of cession left the boundaries of Louisiana in some ambiguity in consequence of the great difficulty in coming to correct conclusions as to where the province might be conceived to terminate on the east and west and north-west. Marbois predicted that difficulties would arise out of the ambiguity, and warned the other negotiators; but no method of obviating them could present itself. The fear of opposition on the part of Spain prevented the court of Madrid from being consulted; and indeed the pressing exigencies of the time did not admit of delay for such consultation. Napoleon thought the ambiguity proper enough, and that it would have been good policy to have placed one in that part of the treaty, whether it existed there or not. The prediction of M. de Marbois was verified. We all recollect the embarrassing questions which were agitated in the diplomatic correspondence of Mr. Adams and Don Louis de Onis, in 1810, on this very subject of conflicting American and Spanish boundaries, and the resulting treaty which transferred to us Florida, and fixed the Sabine as our western boundary. The course of Mr. Adams in this particular has been so much mixed up with politics, that we decline discussing it.

Opposition of Spain.—The Spanish court were not informed of the proceedings in relation to Louisiana until the treaty was concluded, which, as we remarked before, gave great and perhaps just offence. For upwards of a year it was regarded with sullen dissatisfaction; and it was not until February, 1804, that the Spanish minister gave notice to Mr. Pinckney that the benevolence and friendship of Spain toward the United States, had overcome her opposition.

Action of Congress.—In the meanwhile all was not quieted at home. Mr. Jefferson called together Congress earlier than usual, and submitted the compact for their confirmation. All the bitterness of party was at once enkindled. It was denied in the Senate that the constitution permitted the

* Marbois' Hist. Louis., p. 335.

acquisition of foreign territory, and more particularly without the consent of its inhabitants. It was denied in the House that the indemnity was at all reasonable or just. But the administration was in too powerful a majority to render opposition other than futile in the extreme.

IX. *Territorial Government of Louisiana.*—The first act of Governor Claiborne was to settle the judiciary system of the territory, which he did by establishing a court of pleas, consisting of seven justices.

The act of Congress, 20th March, 1804, established the territorial government. Louisiana was divided into two sections, of which that which now constitutes the state of the same name was to be known as the Territory of Orleans. The act provided for a governor, appointed for three years, unless sooner removed by the president; a secretary for four years; a legislative ceuncil of thirteen freeholders; a judiciary, according to the regulations of the legislative council, but to be appointed by the president.

The period which elapsed between the act of Congress of 1804 and the one of March 2d, 1805, which set up another territorial government of Louisiana, was one of dissatisfaction and uneasiness to the people of that section. They complained of the governor, that he was unacquainted with their language, their laws and their interests, that he exhibited favor only to those of his own country, that the English language was attempted to be set up in all judicial proceedings, that the division of the country postponed almost indefinitely the prospect of its becoming a state, and that it suffered greatly from the want of a circulating medium. The citizens held a meeting in the city, and unanimously resolved upon memorializing Congress in relation to their grievances. The council, as established in the meanwhile, passed several acts bearing upon the proper organization of the territory, dividing it into twelve counties, with inferior courts in each, instituting the modes of procedure, defining crimes, etc., according to the common law, chartering the city, and establishing (but only on paper) a university. The council also appointed a committee to prepare a civil and criminal code, with the aid of two professional gentlemen, whose remuneration was fixed by law.

Territorial Government of 1805.—The effect of the dissatisfaction in New-Orleans produced the territorial act of 1805, by which Congress set up a government in Louisiana similar to that of the Mississippi Territory, and provided for its admission into the Union as a state as soon as 60,000 inhabitants could be afforded. This act gave to the people the election of a legislature, and to the legislature the election of a legislative council, or upper house. In these the property qualification was insisted on. The first acts of this new legislative body were the adoption of the black code, or *code noir*, for the government of slaves, and the appointment of two lawyers, Messrs. Lislet and Brown, to prepare a civil code, based upon the former laws of the country.

Burr's Plot.—Having settled these points, Louisiana prepared to meet the position of things which was forced upon her in relation to Spain, and in the anxieties which arose in relation to boundaries, and the opposing claims of the two nations, it is likely that hostilities would have occurred, had not the intimation of a vast scheme on foot for the separation of the western country from the Union, at the head of which, it was said, was Col. Burr, influenced Gen. Wilkinson and the Americans to compromise matters with the Spaniards, and concentrate everything to meet the anticipated danger. The reports which reached Louisiana each day in relation to this plot were alarming; military preparations were being urged on all sides, and Burr himself, after a reward offered for his arrest, was taken at Fort Stoddard, and conveyed to Richmond.

Old Civil Code of 1808.—Messrs. Moreau, Lislet and Brown reported to the legislature of 1808 a civil code for the government of the territory, which was adopted, and is known as the old civil code. It purported to be a digest of the civil laws then in force, with such alterations and amendments as were necessary to the present form of government. The compilers did not refer solely to the Spanish colonial law, the partidas and the recopilacion, but drew largely upon the code Napoleon, the *projet* of which, inferior in many respects to the code itself, having only at that time come to hand. This digest, a volume of 500 pages, was printed in French and English, divided into three books on persons, on things, on the acquisition of things; including subdivisions of titles, chapters and articles. It forms the basis of the present civil code of Louisiana, and is to a large extent identical with it. The digest repealed only all laws irreconcileable with it, and therefore did not set up a new and independent system of jurisprudence, which Judge Martin much regrets, but only furnishes an "incomplete digest of existing statutes, which still retained their empire, and threw out thus a decoy instead of a beacon to the people."

Imperfections of the Law.—The jurisprudence in Louisiana at this period presented a singular jumble of various and in many respects opposing systems, scarcely, if at all, harmonized in their important particulars, or perhaps understood by legislators, lawyers or people, The Fuero Viejo, Fuero Juezgo, Partidas, Recopilaciones,

Leyes de las Indias, Accordados and Royal Schedules, being unrepealed, and of course in effect were yet not to be found complete in a single library; and of some of the laws, according to Martin, there was not a copy in the territory. The Spanish commentators upon these were relied upon, the Roman civil law, and the works of Pothier, D'Aguesseau, Demoulin, etc. The trial by jury, too, was lamentably deficient, and even ridiculous; the arguments of counsel on one side or the other being in a language which the jurors did not understand.

Spanish Difficulties. — The conflicting claims of the United States and Spain to the strip of territory east of the Mississippi River, and south of the parallel 31° to the Perdido River, being upward of two hundred and fifty miles in length and fifty in breadth, were brought to something like a crisis in 1810, by the inhabitants seizing upon the Spanish post at Baton Rouge, holding a convention at St. Francisville, declaring their independence and setting up a constitution; and by proclamation of the President of the United States, taking possession of the territory. The event was peaceable, and the parishes of Feliciana, East Baton Rouge, St. Helena, St. Tammany, Biloxi and Pascagoula, were soon after established.

On the 11th February, 1811, an act of Congress was passed to enable the inhabitants of Louisiana to form a constitution and state government, if the same should be the desire of the people, signified by the calling of a convention. This body being called, assembled in November, at New-Orleans, and prepared and unanimously signed a constitution, based upon that of Kentucky, on the 22d of January, 1812.

X. *State of Louisiana.*—The constitution of 1812 remained the organic law of the state until the present year, but as it is now superseded* we shall defer any comments upon its provisions until, in future sheets of our article, it will be appropriate to compare and contrast the two systems of law. We also postpone to the same place the consideration of the judiciary system at that time established.

War of 1812.—The share which Louisiana took in the English and American war of 1812, though signalized in history, is so familiar that it will detain us but a moment. Wilkinson took possession of the country west of the Perdido River, then in the occupation of Spain. The English colonel, Nichols, arrived at Pensacola, and made proclamation to all Englishmen, Spaniards and Frenchmen, to join his standard and resist the encroachments of the United States. To the people of Kentucky this ridiculous officer proposed similar terms. To the privateer Lafitte and his followers, at Barrataria, he was most prodigal in his offers. The overtures, says Marbois, were rejected with indignation, and the men who saw no degradation in enriching themselves by plunder, had a horror of treason. The course of General Jackson in relation to the Spaniards and English at Pensacola is familiar to all.

Battle of New-Orleans.—An attack upon New-Orleans was every moment expected; the most extraordinary preparations were being made to raise forces, and provide fortifications and armaments to meet the impending danger. The city was all excitement. "The people were preparing for battle as if for a party of pleasure," says the historian: "the streets resounded with martial airs, the several corps of militia were constantly exercising; every bosom glowed with the feelings of national honor." The West was pouring down upon the city—martial law was proclaimed.* The battle of New-Orleans, of 8th January, 1815, was fought and won to the high honor of the American people, and the lasting laurels of the great man who commanded, and who, whatever his faults, is becoming every day more and more honored in the memory of his grateful and admiring countrymen.

Rapid Advances of Louisiana.—The history of Louisiana, since she has become a state, and been incorporated in the Federal Union, has yet to be written. The uninterrupted prevalence of peace in our country takes away from this chapter those lively features which characterize anterior periods. The records of revolution, of changing dynasties, of deeds of arms and high renown, are not presented here, and, perhaps, to the avidity of general readers, the whole is a hopeless blank. But to those seeking higher views of individual good and national destiny, the onward march of the arts of peace, the extraordinary development of industrial resources, the unmatched augmentation of population and wealth, the erection of an opulent state, with laws, government and order, in a former French and Spanish province, are events worthy of the highest efforts of the historian, replete with interest, and deserving of careful study.

In the remaining sheets of our article, we shall be confined almost wholly to the ex-

* The new Constitution of 1845 is about to go by the board, and we are to have another one of 1852.

* General Jackson ordered—

1. Every individual entering the city shall report himself at the attorney-general's office, and on failure be arrested and held for examination.

2. None shall be permitted to leave the city or bayou St. John without such a passport, or that of the commodore.

3. No vessel, boat, or craft shall leave the city or bayou St. John without such a passport, or that of the commodore.

4. The lamps in the city to be extinguished at nine o'clock, after which every person found in the streets, or out of his usual place of residence, without a pass or the countersign, to be apprehended as a spy and held for examination.

amination of the constitutional and legal history of the state, not so much, perhaps, for the advantage of its inhabitants as for those abroad, who, we believe, are not yet clearly informed upon the subject. In fact, we have it on the authority of Judge Porter, a distinguished jurist of our sister state, that he has discovered, in Alabama especially, a prevailing opinion that the law of Louisiana is alone the *corpus juris civilis*, and that even the erudite author of law studies has committed the same error.*

Code Noir, or Black Code.—We have alluded to the old civil code of 1808, and expressed our views upon it. This, with the exception of the digest of O'Reilly, and the code for the government of the blacks, or code noir, was the first codified body of laws in Louisiana. The black code was adopted in 1806, and has received frequent amendments almost up to the present day. Most of the harshness of its original character has been taken away, and although in some points still defective and requiring legislative reform, we will venture to say, that in no slave state can there be found a system of law for the government of this class, more fair, equitable and humane, and tenderly regardful of the rights of those whom nature has decreed shall be inferior, subservient and ruled. If sick and disabled, or old, the act of 1806 provides that they shall be maintained by their owners, under a penalty. If well and not amply supported, a justice shall supply the deficiency at the cost of the master. But these are vain laws; for who has ever heard, except, perhaps, a northern abolitionist, of a negro suffering from old age or want? The 16th and 17th sections of the same act provide even for the most minute injuries inflicted upon slaves beyond moderate and reasonable chastisement. Their hours of rest and meals, and their clothing are regulated; Sundays are to be theirs: if old or disabled, they cannot be sold from their families, and the mother cannot be separated from her young children. The code noir applies also to free negroes. This class are especially favored. They have served the state on some occasions in time of peril, and have been rewarded. It was only the other day that the present legislature granted a pension to two veterans of this class. Mr. Marigny, who stood up in the State Convention of 1845 for the rights of these people, went back, in memory, to the good old days "when slaves were allowed to assemble and enjoy themselves every Sunday in such games as they pleased;" which was justified by the king's commissioner, by reading to Jean Paul Lanusse, a passage of sacred history, where it was laid down that St. Madeline, tired and weary from six days' labor, applied to the Lord for the privilege of dancing on Sunday, and he granted it. It would appear that our town council now are not quite so accommodating! Mr. Marigny's speech is full of allusions to the public services of the free blacks.*

New Civil Code of 1825.—In 1825 the new civil code prepared by order of the legislature, was enforced in Louisiana. Experience had shown, says the Law Journal, that the old civil code had omitted to provide for cases of frequent occurrence, and that some of its provisions, borrowed chiefly from the Spanish law, were not in harmony with the spirit of the time, and required amendment. Messrs. Livingston, Derbigny, and Moreau Lislet, were charged with the performance of this duty, and it would certainly have been difficult to select three individuals more competent. This code is still in force, with the amendments to it, and with a vast number of decisions of the court, explaining and applying it. We have read in connection with it, a little book published in 1840, by Mr. Eyma, examining the doctrines of succession by the lights of foreign jurists; and it is understood that a new edition of the code, with notes by that able lawyer Mr. Mazureau, taken from the experience of a long and distinguished practice at the bar, will soon be presented to the public.† The civil code is embraced in a volume of some 600 pages, published in French and English. It is also said to be the intention of the present legislature to modify and change the code in many important particulars, in order to suit the state of things under the new constitution. This is a delicate undertaking, and will be no doubt effected, with a full sense of its responsibility. We are always suspicious of change, though admitting the present code deficient in many particulars. The Supreme Court declared in Flower *v.* Griffith, that it does not repeal such parts of the old code as are not retained in it; and in Ellis *v.* Prevost, 13 Louisiana Reports, 237, expressed broadly their opinion of the work:—"Our codes were prepared by lawyers, who mixed with the positive legislation definitions seldom accurate, and points of doctrine always unnenecessary: from this circumstance, as well as from the inherent difficulty of the subject, the positive provisions of our code are often at variance with the theoretical part, which it was intended to elucidate."

The Code of Practice.—The present code of practice went into operation in September, 1825, and repeals all former rules of practice. With reference to these former rules, it may

* Commercial Review, vol. i. No. iv., p. 378.

* Reports of Convention, p. 321.

† We have heard it rumored that Judge Martin and Mr. Greiner have in preparation a new edition of the Code.

be well to observe that they are to be found in the acts of Assembly, 1805 and 1813, 2 Martin's Digest, and in the pleadings of the French and Spanish lawyers, particularly in the Curia Felipica, a work in two volumes, by Juan de Hevia Bolanos, an edition of which, printed at Madrid in 1825, is before us. The first volume is divided into five parts, and the second into three, discussing minutely the organization of courts, and conduction of suits. Of the present code of practice some complaint is made. It was constructed by the same jurists as the civil code. As a system of pleading, it is lamentably deficient, in the opinion of almost all parties ; and frequent amendments have been made to it without altogether curing the evil. Composed, says the Law Journal, without sufficient knowledge of the theoretical principles of practice, and with very inadequate acquaintance with the practical difficulties which occur in the administration of the law, it has been the source of much error and embarrassment. There have been several editions of this code, a small volume in itself, published, with copious references to adjudged cases, and a new one seems now to be required by the bar, with such additions and amendments as are required to meet the advance of legislation in the state.

The Roman, French, and Spanish law was abolished in Louisiana in 1828. The Supreme Court explained the act in Bell's case, 13 L. R. 198, by declaring that it applied only to the positive, written or Spanish laws of those nations and of this state, which opinion has been somewhat criticised.*

Jurisprudence of Louisiana.—We are naturally led to ask the particular complexion of the two codes we have been discussing, and to what extent they are felt in the infinite variety of cases which arise in the state ? How far are the civil and the common law admitted in their elements ? Do the codes constitute the whole body of the laws of Louisiana, or how much of them ? We shall indulge a few remarks here.

In former pages it was shown how multifarious are the sources of the laws of Louisiana. Rome, Spain and France, have all contributed from their best repositories to the completion of her system, and the most distinguished minds which have been felt in the jurisprudence of Europe are acknowledged here with scarcely less authority. Any one who has studied the reports of the Supreme Court of the state, will have discovered this upon almost every page. The celebrated Batture case is most strongly in point, a case which called into action all the energies, and developed all the resources of the bar, and was argued and adjudged almost upon the same principles and in the same manner as it would have been in a court sitting upon the banks of the Tiber, at Madrid, or in Paris. The laws of Louisiana have but little in common with those of England, except so far as enlightened reason and experience may have brought two great systems, the civil and the common law, to similar results. In many respects the principles of correct jurisprudence are universal, and the jealousy which has existed between the common and civil lawyers has little to sustain it that is at all commendable. Both are great and wonderful systems which they cherish ; both have upon their sides a venerated antiquity, and the influences of names so high and holy that we dare not approach their presence without some emotions of awe. Both systems have their perfections and their deficiencies, their points of contrast favorable and unfavorable ; and it has appeared to us, the more we have reflected, that, upon the soil of Louisiana, more than any place else in the whole world, is to be found the spot where the problem of jurisprudence can be solved with most advantage, and where can be elaborated, from the joint wisdom and perfection of the common and the civil law, a new and a better system than either, and one which cannot but shed a broad influence upon the whole body of American law. We see this work already going on, and it only needs a careful hand and an enlightened judgment to complete it ultimately by a process so gradual as almost to be unfelt. Even now we have the common law pure and unmixed in the whole of our criminal proceedings, and the trial by jury and the *Habeas Corpus*, those bulwarks of liberty, have lost nothing by their juxtaposition with Roman institutes. In the rules of evidence, we follow the wise principles of the common law, and commercial jurisprudence in Louisiana is what it is with slight modifications all over the Union and in England, and what it should be all the world over ; for, as Lord Mansfield expressed it, "among all men and in all times the laws of commerce are one and immutable." The work of amalgamation must go on with the elements at work which are presented in the state. We have among us able civil lawyers, educated in Europe, and enlightened advocates from all the states of the Union have been crowding in upon us, flattered by a prospect which, though bright, cannot be conceived as ample enough to gratify them all. Minds so differently educated, brought into collision, must develop intermediate results, and the compromises and amalgamations of which we have already spoken. We recollect that the late Mr. Legare, who was scarcely less eminent as a common lawyer, than as a profound civilian, entertained views similar to our own He cherished fondly the idea of harmonizing rival systems which he

* Louisiana Law Journal, vol. i. No. iv., p. 150.

venerated, dissipating the jealousies of their adherents, and developing for America, out of the great process, a legal polity infinitely higher than that of any other nation on earth. But Mr. Legare fell into an untimely grave; and his great idea, which was to some extent to have been exhibited in his contemplated edition of Heineccius, will continue to influence minds equal to his own. The late Judge Story declared that the jurisprudence of Louisiana presents the most valuable means of improving the science of the common law. "I have always read the Louisiana Reports," said Judge Kent, "as fast as they appeared, and considered them the most learned and interesting decisions in the United States."*

Doctrine of Codes.—The experiment of a code of laws has not succeeded so well in Louisiana, we think, as to make it a source of emulation on the part of those states of our Union which have not fallen into the idea. The theory of codification is beautiful enough, but always carries along with it an air of impracticability. It supposes jurisprudence to have arrived or to be able to arrive at perfection, at some one point where the code fixes it. If this be not so, why take the infinite pains to elaborate a code when a slight modification of society, a new phasis, a new institution growing up, a new interest in a few weeks or months, will demand corresponding changes, however slight, yet changes in the law which is to be applied to them. Fix society, and you may fix the law. The metaphysician, John Locke, *abstracted* a constitution for the ancient colony of Carolina, which was to be unchangeable, because perfect; and this whole constitution was so visionary, that hardly a trace of it remained in the colony in twenty years. Away with your ever-changing codes—an absurdity in terms! Our codes have proved themselves to be such. Every session of the legislature has altered or amended them. Hundreds and hundreds of judicial determinations have been required to explain them, and extensive amendments are even now contemplated. What, then, have we gained? Is our law any clearer, and more certain and fixed than it is in other states? Are legal proceedings less costly and less dilatory? Have we done away with the reporters and their ponderous volumes of decisions? None of all this. We have not advanced anything in these particulars, if it be admitted, and we are disposed to admit, that we have not fallen anything behind. In the matter of pleading, we have, perhaps, gained something in simplicity of process, for this is as far removed from complication with us as anything can be; but then how many judicial decisions, even upon these points? We have no partialities for codes from what we have seen of them in this and in other states of the Union; nor, however, any great aversion to their use. If we must have them, let us understand what they are, and not cherish any idea of political perfection, which they clearly do not possess. They are modes of law with advantages and disadvantages; and living in a state where they exist, we would have them improved, as far as possible, just as we would have the law improved in every state even where a code was never thought of, and where, if we lived, we should certainly not be in favor of its introduction.

We have in past sheets exhibited how it happened that codification forced itself upon Louisiana, and how we think it could not well have been otherwise. All the parent systems of her youth were based upon this model, and when she passed into the hands of the United States, it was necessary to know what her laws were, so as to know what they should be under the new aspect of things. This gave rise to the old codes, and the new are but modifications and improvements of them. Mr. Livingston, who played a large part in the compilation, a profound and enlightened jurist, entertained notions of their possible perfection, which almost made him an enthusiast in the cause. His labors we may applaud and admire, though hesitating to agree with him in his conclusions. By act of Assembly of Louisiana in 1820, it was resolved that some person learned in the law be appointed to prepare for consideration a code of criminal law for the state. Mr. Livingston received the appointment, and on the 21st March, 1822, presented his system of penal law, a volume of eight hundred pages, which was approved and published at the public expense. We say approved, because nothing more was ever done in the

* The following is a list of the statutory works and legal reports now used in the state (1846):—

Martin's Reports of the Decisions of the Supreme Court, commencing in 1809—old series	12	volumes.
Martin's New Series, commencing 1823	8	"
Miller's Louisiana Reports, commencing 1830	5	"
Curry's Louisiana Reports, commencing 1833	14	"
Robinson's Louisiana Reports, commencing 1841	11	"
Benjamin and Slidell's Digest of the Decisions of the Supreme Court to 1840	1	"
P. J. Deslix's Supplement to do. to date	1	"
Christie's Digest of the Supreme Court, published about 1835	1	"
Deslix's Analytical Index of all the Decisions of Supreme Court, 1846	1	"
Harrison's Condensed Reports	4	"
Moreau Lislet's Digest of the Statutes of Louisiana up to 1828	2	"
Martin's Digest of the Statutes of Louisiana up to 1816	2	"
Bullard and Curry's Digest of the Statutes of Louisiana up to 1841	1	"
Robinson's Penal Law of Louisiana	1	"
	64	"

matter, and the code remains now in the State House, and in private libraries never consulted, except in merely speculative matters. Little probability is there for its adoption in the future, since the prejudice in favor of codes is rapidly on the decline in the state. Mr. Livingston made a great book, but one of little practical utility. It consists of five divisions—a code of crimes and punishments, a code of procedure, a code of evidence, a code of reform and prison discipline, a book of definitions, &c., &c. In the undertaking, Mr. Hoffman* has said he has shown himself a philosophical legislator, possessed of all the capabilities of the late Jeremy Bentham, but without any of his objectionable peculiarities, together with all the wisdom of Montesquieu, and the animating and ennobling philanthropy of Beccaria. Mr. Livingston's labors were highly applauded in Europe, and the Emperor Nicholas of Russia thought proper to open a correspondence with him in 1826 on the subject. Eminently successful in these undertakings, which had placed him at the head of the school of modern reformers and of philosophical digesters or codifiers, he prepared voluntarily, as we presume, a very elaborate and admirable system of penal law for the United States of America, which was presented to the national legislature, and by order of that body printed and published at Washington, in 1828, in one volume, folio. It consists of three codes or books, viz.: of crimes and punishments, of procedure in criminal cases, and of prison discipline, to which is added a book of definitions of all the technical words used by him in the foregoing codes.†

Supreme Court of Louisiana.—Before completing our sketch of the jurisprudence of the State of Louisiana, it will be necessary to indulge some reflections upon its highest judicial tribunal—the Supreme Court. This was substituted in 1813, in place of the old superior court established in 1805. The superior court consisted of three judges, either one of whom constituted a quorum for business, on which account it is said to have had little influence in the development of the laws of Louisiana. The reports of its decisions, by Judge Martin, are highly esteemed. The Supreme Court of Louisiana was organized in 1813, and had appellate jurisdiction only, and that in no other than civil cases. The new constitution, as we shall see hereafter, has essentially changed its organization. The first three judges of the Supreme Court were Dominick A. Hall, George Matthews, and Pierre Derbigny. Hall soon resigned, discovering his knowledge of civil law too limited for the office, and his place the year after (1815) was filled by Judge Martin. These jurists were all eminent in their way; of Martin we have already spoken; Derbigny, it is said, "united with all the learning and science requisite to place him in the first rank of jurists, the sterling integrity and unsullied honor which made him an ornament of the bench;" Matthews was a most excellent man, characterized by the sincerest rectitude and love of justice.

Judge Derbigny resigned his seat in 1820, in favor of Judge Porter. This latter jurist, during the fourteen years of his administration, attained a most brilliant aud enviable reputation. He was learned, comprehensive, deep, powerful in argument and illustration, impartial, clear and convincing; some of his opinions are referred to as masterly productions.* Henry A. Bullard was appointed in 1834, in place of Judge Porter, resigned; and Henry Carleton, in 1837, in place of Judge Matthews, deceased. In 1839, Messrs. Bul-

* Legal Outlines, p. 439.

† Hoffman's Legal Study, vol. i., p. 440.

It cannot be doubted that, were codification desirable, America would present a fine field for its exercise. Our laws are at best but in a nascent state, and are thus more susceptible of being thrown into form than they would be at a more advanced period. Several states have been induced to revise and codify their laws, in particular Massachusetts and New-York, the last named having innovated with the boldest strokes upon the common law, and struck, as it were, at its very heart. This change was in a measure brought about by the labors of a Mr. Sampson of that state, who devoted himself with unsparing zeal and earnestness to the great reform. Mr. Sampson published a volume on the subject in 1826, containing, among other things, a series of letters upon codification, which passed between himself, Dr. Cooper, and Gov. Wilson, of South Carolina, Charles Watts, Esq., of New-Orleans, and Judge Workman, of Louisiana. The attention of South Carolina was called to the subject of Codes in 1827. Mr. Grimke, a most eminent leader of the bar there, published an address in advocacy of the reform, which was followed by an able speech in the Senate of that state, by the Hon. John Lide Wilson, and by an elaborate report on the part of that body, but nothing farther was done. Among the law tracts of Lord Bacon, there is one proposing to compile and amend the laws, which, it is said, had he undertaken and executed, would have placed him above his rival Coke, as a lawyer. Jeremy Bentham has been looked upon as the great high-priest of codification. On the continent of Europe, these systems have been extensively admitted from the Code Justinian, of Rome, through the codes civil, penal, commercial, and practical of Spain, France, Prussia, Austria, Russia, and Sweden. The code controversy has been agitated for many years in Europe, and resulted in distinct orders or classes of jurists, in view of it. Mr. Hoffman classes them into the Practical School, the Philosophical School, the Historical and the Legistic, all battling for their various views. We should rather, in view of all the difficulties of the subject, agree with Chancelor Kent, that there is a peculiar and inherent difficulty in the application of the new and dazzling theory of codification to such intricate doctrines which lie wrapped up in principles and refinements remote from the ordinary speculations of mankind; and that no system of law can be rendered free from such imperfections, and the extent of them will necessarily be enlarged and the danger greatly increased, when there have been entire and radical innovations made upon the settled modifications of property, disturbing to their very foundations the usages and analogies of existing institutions.—4 Kent. Com. 352.

* See Louisiana Law Journal, No. iv. Art. Sup. Court.

lard and Carleton resigned, and were replaced by Hon. P. A. Rost and George Eustis, who also resigned the following year, and G. Strawbridge and A. Morphy were appointed in their stead, the former consenting only to serve temporarily. In 1840 the judges of the Supreme Court were increased to five—Martin, chief justice; associates, Bullard, Morphy, Simon and Garland. In 1846, the re-organization of the court, under the new constitution was effected—Hon. George Eustis, chief justice; associates, King, Rost, and Slidell. Two of them are well-tried jurists, and we have it on high authority that it is impossible to peruse many of their decisions without admiring the sagacity as well as comprehensive knowledge of our legislation which they display. The other two carry to the bench a high standing acquired in the profession.*

The City of New Orleans.—The charter of this now opulent corporation was granted in 1805. Forty years only have passed in the history of New-Orleans, and from a population of six thousand souls it has attained already one hundred and fifty thousand, and is pressing on in a ratio amazing and almost incredible. What New-Orleans will be we can only conjecture. It is already great. Standing on the heights of the Alleghany, and looking westward to the Rocky Mountains—tracing the mighty waters of the Ohio, the Missouri, the Mississippi, the Tennessee, and the Arkansas—standing on the Gulf coast, as the waters of Texas and Mexico roll into it and mingle themselves with those of the Northwest and the West, and marking at the moment a city seated, as it were, in the lap of all these magnificent developments of nature—the fiat of New-Orleans has already been sealed, and language confesses its impotence! We sigh not for the mere greatness of a monster, however—the giant's arms and will—the mighty, misshaped, inorganized proportions. We wish for the head, the heart, and the soul, to control our great resources. Who does not mark the changes that are working already? We have a literature growing up; literary men are settling in our midst; our libraries, public and private, are increasing; we have just closed a course of brilliant public lectures by distinguished citizens; we are talking of scientific societies; our common-school system is not surpassed in the country; we have a medical college of high reputation, and a medical journal of brilliant fame; we are to have a university—if the legislature carries out the will of the people—with departments of law, physic, literature and science; our bar and our pulpits are filled with eminent men; and temples for the worship of the most high God are growing up all around us; we have an efficient police; and Providence appears in the act of crowning us with uninterrupted health—the last, but the best boon of all. How little does the world know of New-Orleans.

In 1836 it was thought advisable to divide the city into three separate municipalities by act of assembly, each with distinct municipal powers. These municipalities extend backward six miles to the Lake Pontchartrain, and are divided from each other by streets and lines running from the river to the lake. The first municipality is divided into five wards, the second into four, and the third into four. Each municipality has a recorder and twelve aldermen, except the third, which has but seven aldermen. A mayor and twelve aldermen preside over the whole city, called the general council, who are elected by general ticket from the city at large, four from each municipality. The mayor has a qualified veto. There are different courts established throughout the city for the settlement of small demands for and against citizens in a summary manner, and which are so strikingly defective as to have given great cause of complaint. Some important changes will doubtless be attempted in the city charter so as to accommodate it to the new state of things under the present constitution. The division of the municipalities will, however, not be touched. It has worked well in the past, and though we have our doubts as to the propriety of divisions and subdivisions, yet change, perhaps, is worse than these. A single body, as in other cities, would doubtless possess more efficiency, but would be liable to more abuses. As the city enlarges, this subject will present itself more and more to the minds of those intrusted with its administration. (That period has already arrived, 1852.)

LOUISIANA.—MINERALS.—Dr. J. Holliday has made a large collection of the minerals in the region surrounding Harrisonburg. The collection is now in New-Orleans in charge of J. D. B. De Bow, Esq., editor of the "Southern Review," which gives a good exposition of the mineralogy of this section of the state. Before his collection was formed, a very limited knowledge was obtained thereof. For nine years past he has been industriously engaged in procuring every specimen he could, being anxious to elucidate, as far as possible, the minerals of the state: he has so far succeeded as to form a nucleus, which every addition thereto may increase its interest, and add new light to the mineralogy of Louisiana. As yet there has been no discovery made of the precious ores, though, from very credible information, silver has been found in the bed of a creek, six miles from Harrisonburg. Stone coal has been found abundant in a certain locality.

* See Louisiana Law Journal, number 4, Art. Sup. Court.

Dr. Holliday chiefly predicates interest in his collection, from their applicability to ornate purposes. Subject to the manipulations of a lapidary, a great number of them could be made quite pretty.

1*st*, *Quartz.*—Perfect crystalizations of this mineral occur on the Geode; some of which are found as large as the double fist; when fractured, exposing internally colorless crystalizations of a primary form, six-sided prisms, terminated by six-sided pyramids. Colorless pebbles of quartz, of the size of a hen's egg, and as small as a shot, abound in many localities here. When first taken out of the water, gives somewhat the appearance of sparkling dewdrops. There is one specimen of the size and form of a hen's egg, perfectly transparent. These pebbles, no doubt, originally possessed the primary form of crystalization; but water, or other agencies, have thus worn out their angles, and thus rounded them.

2*d*, *Agate.*—If the agate could be made by art to look as beautiful as when immersed in limpid water, they would, indeed, be splendid. Their color then shows to advantage, and each imperceptible line is then distinctly seen. This region is prolific in agates, from those as large as the double fist to others no larger than the finger nail. The fortification agates are the most numerous, but we have several other varieties. There is one which exposes on its surface a number of concentric lines parallel to each other, a number of which is seen here and there on the face of the agate. A second variety presents a mammillated appearance—a third resembles the moss agate; this variety has only been found on the bar of the Ouachita, opposite Harrisonburg. It is small, but a beautiful gem. The predominant color of our agates is yellow, but we find them of many other colors—*i. e.*, green, brown, chesnut, red, pink, purple, nearly black, and a cream color. They are all susceptible of a high polish, and specimens are found in this locality which would form handsome ornaments.

3*d*, *Jasper.*—There is a great variety of jasper found in this region—1st, dark red; 2d, dark brown; 3d, jasper combined with quartz and cacholong; 4th, ribbon jasper. These are also all susceptible of a high polish, and would make very pretty ornamental stones.

4*th*, *Sardonyx.*—They are found also on the same bar, and the only locality where I have met with them. A number of the specimens that I have met with are very beautiful. Dr. H. sent to Gen. Downs a specimen of sardonyx, of a crimson color, translucent with parallel lines of cacholong encircling it at the top.

5*th*, *Red Cornelian* abounds on the same bar. In the collection now in New-Orleans, here, are many superior specimens, which bear comparison with any in the jewelry stores of the city. Yellow quartz or yellow cornelian is found also on the same bar in small amorphous masses.

6*th*, *Onyx.*—Several specimens of this gem have been collected in the same locality.

7*th*, *Fossil Wood.*—Found in great variety in the pine hills, as large as nearly a whole tree, and broken fragments of hickory, pine, ash, and other kind of woods. These petrifactions are all silicious, and susceptible of a very fine polish, and would be adapted to many ornamental purposes; they are of different colors, nearly black, yellow, green, and dusky white.

8*th*, *Selenite* is found in the alluvial land, where the pine hill encroaches near the river, in small masses, which, no doubt, was detached from considerable masses in the hills. I was informed, that, in digging a well in Catahoula prairie, that, twenty feet below the surface, the workmen observed a large formation of the selenite, and raised a mass of it weighing two hundred pounds. Could this not be used as a manure?

9*th*, *Feldspar*, of splendid quality, is found in several different places in rounded masses. By the light reflecting on its surface, it gives the appearance of burnished silver.

10*th*, *Alumine* in great abundance.

11*th*, *Mountain Wood*, of a mahogany color.

12*th*, *Chalcedony* abounds here, of a muddy white color.

13*th*, *Encrenite* abounds here, and frequently impressions of the encrenite are found here upon rocks and stones, although a perfect encrenite has not been met with.

14*th*, *Orathera* are frequently found here in different locations.

15*th*, *Oolite.*—Specimens of it have also been found.

Volcanic Remnants.—There are many evi dences seen here of volcanic action, as manifested by the specimens of fused iron ore, which, whilst in a fluid state, and when cooling, sand and pebbles become combined with it, and is firmly adherent to the mass, some of which are very large. There are *geodes* of the same mineral, that seems to have been fused also; and whilst in a liquid state, and in violent ebullition, being suddenly cooled, has taken the form of a *geode.* Being porous, the moisture of the atmospheric air has oxidized its internal surface, and has given rise to a deposition of a red and yellow oxide of the metal. These will rattle when shaken. They are seen in immense quantities in the western part of the parish.

Another variety presents the appearance of bubbles on the surface, having suddenly cooled whilst in a state of ebullition.

Great quantities of lava stone are found on Sicily Island, up in the high pine hills, near Mr. Knapp's academy.

Meteoric Stones have been picked up at different places in the parish, specimens of which can be seen in the collection of Doctor Holliday.

On digging wells in the pine hills, and also in Catahoula prairie, beds of oyster shells have been found twenty feet below the surface.

Two feet below the surface, on the bluff lands of Sicily Island, is found a hard pan of amorphous iron ore, mingled with pebbles about six inches thick. It is pretty uniformly diffused, and constantly found on digging ditches.

LOUISIANA.—GEOLOGY AND HYDROGRAPHY.—Professor Forshay, who was one of the gentlemen employed, several years ago, to make a geological exploration of this state, which was never published, but lost in manuscript, has been lecturing in New-Orleans upon the general subject. We give the substance of one of these lectures.

The state presents but a limited geological field. It is divided into the leading grand divisions of tertiary, diluvial and alluvial. The tertiary beds occupy two-fifths of the state, as is shown upon a chart delineated by Prof. Forshay.

"The tertiary lies north of a waving line, commencing on the Sabine, near the mouth of the Neches, crossing Red River twenty miles north of Alexandria, and the Ouachita, ten miles north of Harrisonburg. Its beds contain coal (aluminons brown coal), salt, iron, ochre, gypsum and marls. The coal was inferior to Pittsburgh coal, and would not compete with it in market, but was worth developing for use, in those portions of the state, where the better coal would not bear the expense of transportation. It abounded in Sabine, Natchitoches, Caddo and De Soto, and all the parishes thence east to the Ouachita River. Salt springs were common in Natchitoches and Rapides, and had been wrought in earlier times. A saline bed seemed to underlie the tertiary bed generally. Iron was found in great quantities in most of the tertiary parishes, and is well worth the attention of those who would develop the state resources. Ochre, gypsum and marls, too, were found—the first in the native form, and the others coextensive with the tertiary beds. The gypsum was very fine—equal to any known to commerce; and the marls very rich, in the regions where they will be most needed.

"We were trying to control the Mississippi River, and keep him within bounds. He once usurped the whole alluvion, and yearly kept it under water. Our barriers were mere child's play as yet. We must build greater ones, not higher, but stronger and further back—and give room to the steamboat waves and the abrading power of increased currents, produced by leveeing.

"The river did not rise higher now than before levees were used. This he proved *a priori*, and then illustrated by history and observation; but the most powerful proof adduced was, that there were many alluvial banks higher than our present highest waters, and the levees do not differ in average height for 500 miles up the river. Of course, the river was once high enough to deposit the highest alluvial grounds. Therefore, levees, by confining the water, enabled the river to keep open its own channel. Nothing else kept open such a channel, 100 feet deep, ten miles above the S. W. Pass, but the abrasive force, and nothing else could keep the bars as they are, fifteen to eighteen feet. Divide the river by outlets, and you divide the channel-making power—you weaken the attack upon the bars at the mouth, and destroy the river's navigability. The river belonged to the commerce of the valley, not to Louisiana. Have a care what experiments you try—for, once divided, you never could restore it to its channel."

LOUISIANA HISTORICAL SOCIETY.—FOREIGN DOCUMENTS AND RECORDS RELATING TO THE HISTORY OF LOUISIANA.—Several years ago there was formed in New-Orleans a Society, of which Judge Martin was made the President, succeeded by Judge Bullard, for the preservation of the material of the state's history. The editor of the Review, as secretary of the association, has collected some manuscripts and books, which are in his possession, and has received from John Perkins, Esq., two splendidly bound volumes, of five or six hundred pages each, of transcripts from the records of the French colonial offices at Paris.

Mr. Perkins, having visited Europe for his health, and being one of the most active members of the Society, as well as one of our most estimable citizens, received the appointment of agent, with full powers to collect whatever he regarded as important to the proper knowledge of our history in England, France, or Spain. His excellency, Gov. Johnson, was pleased to make him, officially, and by letter, a similar request. With these he has complied in a spirit and manner at once creditable to his patriotism, public zeal and literary sympathies, and at great pecuniary cost and sacrifices to himself.

The material included in the two volumes received, embraces a summary or index of all French documents relating to Louisiana, from the earliest epoch to the year 1803, when the transfer was made to the United States. Mr. E. J. Forstall had previously made some references to many of these papers, and Mr. Magne, of New-Orleans, had copied some hundred pages, which were purchased by the legislature, and were of material use to Mr.

Gayarré in the preparation of his history of the state.

Searches are even now being prosecuted in Spain, under an appropriation made by us of three thousand dollars, and although much has come to light, none of the material has yet reached the state.

Mr. Perkins concludes his letter to Governor Johnson, which will be laid before the legislature, with the following

RECAPITULATION.

There are 17 cartons in the Department Marine, averaging....1,000 pages		=17,000	pages
40 volumes dispatches and royal orders, averaging................	300 "	12,000	"
3 volumes memoirs, averaging..............1,000	"	3,000	"
Indian accounts..........................		2,000	"
The personal commissions, &c.		2,000	"
Concessions		1,000	"
Indirect documents...................		10,000	"
In the National Library, Rue Richelieu..................................		3,000	"
" Ancient Archives of the Kingdom ..		200	"
" Archives of the Cour des Comptes..		3,000	"
" Ministry of War.......		6,000	"
" Ministry of Foreign Affairs.........		3,000	"
Total..........................		61,200	"

This is probably a calculation rather large.

As to the expense of having these documents copied, there are three points to be considered: 1, the payment for copies of the documents; 2, the cost of the paper; 3, the selection and revision and general superintendence of the work. The cost of copying may be rated at ten cents the page. This is what New-York and Massachusetts paid. The paper of the kind required to copy on will cost about thirty francs the thousand pages. For 60,000 pages, say from $300 to $600. As to the salary of the person who shall compile the papers and direct the copyists, it must depend upon circumstances and the merit of the individual. It is difficult to assign a sum.

The labor of securing all the documents will require two years, perhaps more time. A hundred pages a day is all that can be relied upon, and it is proper to allow for many delays. The above estimate supposes that the state would desire copies of every document touching its history. There are, however, many of these unimportant. Should a selection be made, those of real value would not exceed 35,000 pages.

The person commissioned to superintend this compilation should receive his instructions from the Historical Society, and have his commission signed by the Governor. He would then have every facility extended to him.

I need not dwell upon the importance of securing at once the documents I have sketched. Their possession, in a degree involves the honor of the state. They are rich in material, and will fully repay investigation. No one can rise from their study without a higher opinion of those who first settled in Louisiana. They were, like all other colonists, influenced by varied motives, but a perusal of the reports made to the Home Government shows that they carried with them into the forests much of the romantic enthusiasm for liberty that has since characterized the French nation. They appear to have been kind and just in their dealings with the natives. We read nowhere of cruelty. They conciliated when it was possible, and their priests met with a success scarcely equaled in any other part of America.

With the hope that you will deem it consistent with your duty to advise an appropriation by the approaching assembly, for securing the historical materials referred to,

I am, with great respect,

JOHN PERKINS, JR.

(*See New-Orleans.*)

LOUISIANA.—WELL WATER IN THE LOWLANDS OF LOUISIANA.—Professor Riddell, of the United States Branch Mint at New-Orleans, made the following experiments and reflections, in relation to the subject before us. The well from which the water examined was drawn, was situated at No. 328 Camp-street, and ten feet in depth, lined with boards.

The result of an experiment on the 22d of September, was, that by evaporation, a yield was obtained of one part of solid residue to 1,200 of water by weight.

The result of an experiment from the same well, on the 29th of December, yielded one part solid to 1,094 of water.

"The residue was an olive-colored powder of sharp taste, nearly one-fourth appearing to be organic and organized matter, such as the sporules or germs of algæ (plants like frog spittle), microscopic animalcules, and their ova."

By chemical analysis, Professor Riddell was enabled to determine the presence of the following "acids and bases, which may be regarded as the mineral impurities of the water:" carbonic acid, muriatic acid, lime, oxide of iron, magnesia, soda.

"These various ingredients may be supposed to constitute the following saline substances: bi-carbonate of lime, bi-carbonate of iron, muriate of lime, muriate of magnesia, muriate of soda."

This water was not adapted for washing in consequence of the presence of iron in the condition of a protoxide, combined with carbonic acid; and clothing, upon being washed or boiled in it, acquired a permanent yellowish hue.

Professor Riddell farther remarks, that "the use of the water is objectionable, not on account of the mineral impurities, but in consequence of the presence of the organic and organized matters; most of which, it is probable, may be got rid of by very careful filtering."

"If a bottle of crude water be corked up, the process of putrefaction commences in a few weeks; after which, when uncorked, it exhales a fetid and peculiar odor."

We have long wondered that among the many wealthy planters whose fortunes are staked in the lowlands, there is not an individual in this entire district who has had the enterprise to try the experiment of boring for water after the Artesian plan that has been so successfully tested in Alabama and other parts of the Union.

The belief is induced, by the contiguity to highlands of this strip of valley, having for 400 miles an average width of about thirty, that good water can be procured at a very moderate depth. The hills bounding the lowlands are precipitous, and in height varying from eighty to two hundred feet; those on the left, the bluffs of Mississippi, are familiar to all our readers, while the right is bounded throughout its course with the high pine hill region of the Ouachita, being a continuation of the smaller ranges of mountains in the western and southern portions of Arkansas.

This range of hills is composed of immense beds of freestone, and abounds in springs of water equal to any in the world—the reservoirs that feed those springs, we doubt not, having their hundred shoots spreading in all directions, seeking the lowest level, might be tapped by the process suggested—the prospect of success is, we think, certain, and we are satisfied that an effort would well repay the enterprise of him who first attempts the experiment in the lowlands of Louisiana.

LANDS.—PUBLIC LANDS OF UNITED STATES.—ORGANIZATION AND HISTORY OF THE LAND OFFICE—VALUE OF LANDS SOLD—LANDS GRANTED TO STATES AND TERRITORIES—RELIEF TO PURCHASERS—COST OF THE PUBLIC LANDS—AREA OF THE LAND, STATES, AND LANDS REMAINING — PRE-EMPTION RIGHTS—WAR BOUNTIES—MINERAL LANDS, ETC.—The General Land Office, as a bureau of the Treasury Department, is more extensive and complex in its details than any other at Washington. A late report from the Commissioner, published by order of Congress, has just been received. On examination, highly interesting facts appear, and we propose to aid in spreading them more generally before the people. A glance at the machinery of the system may be proper, if only to impress the reader with a fair conception of the wisdom and labor which contrived and sustains it.

Whether Mr. Crawford, Secretary of the Treasury from 1817 to 1825, or some other distinguished adviser of Congress, first recommended the public lands to be laid off on the present plan, we have no evidence at hand to justify an award of credit. It is enough that a masterly, practical mind furnished the idea.

Before proceeding further, we beg to show the confusion which must have existed in land titles under the old method of surveying, to suit government scrip holders or bounty claimants. The case of Virginia is illustrative. This state had immense limits, which enabled her to make liberal provision for her troops in the Revolutionary War. Of these, she had two separate and distinct classes—one in the continental line, subject to the orders of Congress, and the other under the exclusive control of her own state authority. To both she promised lands. Congress engaged likewise to those who served during the war. Hence, that portion of the Virginia troops on the continental establishment became entitled to double bounties. By deed of 1784, ceding the north-west territory, Virginia reserved a district in Ohio, containing upwards of 4,000,000 acres, to satisfy the claims for which she was liable. These lands were surveyed at random, so as to include the best for each holder. Frequently the lines crossed, and returns were made in favor of two or more conflicting parties for the same lots. This created litigation, which has continued for half a century to jeopard the property of thousands, and inflict enormous costs. The investigation of each case involved the acts of Virginia, the regularity of the original claim and survey, and of all subsequent titles resting on this foundation. Besides such proof, difficult to make after a long interval, the identity of boundaries had to appear in court. This could not always be established by the plat and field-notes. Oral testimony had to be invoked to show the beginning and marks of each survey. Who does not see the endless confusion and hazard of this state of things? It was a fortunate suggestion, which led to the simplicity afterwards engrafted by Congress on the land system, the beneficial results of which are so widely felt and acknowledged. We will briefly state the merits.

Say that a district is owned by the government, to be surveyed and sold. It is divided by a meridian line, running north and south, with base lines east and west. On each of the latter, ranges, six miles wide, parallel with the meridian, are thrown, and checked at the same distance, forming townships of thirty-six sections of 640 acres, or a square mile, numbered from the north-east corner backward and forward. These are subdivided into halves, quarters, eighths and sixteenths, subject to private entry, after having been offered at public sale, without commanding $1 25 per acre, the minimum price. Purchasers obtain government titles designating the entire section, the half, quarter, half-quarter, or half-of-the-half-quarter, ranging from 640, 320, 160, 80 to 40 acres, as the case may be. This is the form in which divisions are expressed, varying to suit the compass for the lot selected. At the entering, certificates are issued by the receiver for the proper quantities, and duplicates registered in the office. Maps, on a scale of one mile to the square inch, are usually kept, on which, as sales take place, a mark signifies the fact. The vacant lands are thus represented. Persons wishing the information can obtain it from the maps; or, if they prefer, a plat of any township, duly scored, will be prepared instantly, and sold for a small fee, say fifty cents or a dollar to the clerk in charge.

The land office papers are truly voluminous. Some idea may be formed from the report of the Commissioner in 1840, when the number of certificates had reached 810,-667. Offices in three states had returned over 100,000; viz., Indiana, 152,655; Illinois, 132,890; and Alabama, 114,802. On each of these, a patent had to be issued at Washington, with the signature of the President. There was great justice in the relief afforded by Congress to General Jackson and his successors, by deputing another to sign patents. The returns from receivers, annually, are about four hundred to be adjusted. In addition to the space occupied on the books by every certificate and map of sale, and the business entries, each patent is recorded at large. All these duties form only a part of the work.

The correspondence of the land office, of whatever description, is copied on the books. Instructions to registers, receivers, deputy surveyors, and all the agents employed, are likewise preserved in duplicate. In ten thousand controversies between claimants, the Commissioner has to decide, and often on the advice of the Attorney-General, to whom the facts are submitted in writing. The arguments for and against each pretension are spread out freely. Whoever will examine the many volumes printed on this subject, will see the propriety and extent of the practice. They serve as guides in similar cases, and furnish the law of each appeal. In this branch of its functions, the land office is something more than a routine of mechanical labor. A degree of intelligence is required equal to that of any bureau at Washington second to the heads of department. In proof, we refer to the 2,537 entries which have been confirmed by the Secretary of the Treasury, Attorney-General and Commissioner, under the act of 1846, respecting controverted claims. The aggregate thus adjusted was 332,870 acres, of which the largest proportion is in Louisiana; say 525 pre-emption entries, embracing 80,080 acres. The next from Missouri, 492 entries, and 61,450 acres. In Mississippi, 242 pre-emption entries embraced 20,600 acres, and 473 private entries about 44,560 acres. In the nine other states litigating, the quantity was much less.

Having viewed the machinery of the land office in defining the public domain, granting title and preserving the evidence, we proceed to facts more statistical.

RECEIPTS AT THE TREASURY—VALUE OF PUBLIC LANDS SOLD FROM 1833 TO 1840.

States and Territories	1833	1834	1835	1836	1837	1838	1839	1840	Total
Ohio	$692426	$600561	$826224	$1663116	$588564	$303945	$315559	$27146	$5017544
Indiana	693522	842170	2075571	4061492	1564653	753419	773998	114157	10878986
Illinois	450242	439613	2604698	4000294	1266118	987170	1445766	387304	11581209
Missouri	296522	320978	828121	2071204	830095	642087	1304718	587152	6880880
Alabama	565818	1444299	1985449	2377573	477219	204935	152728	43442	7251460
Mississippi	1531390	1470323	3835625	2531282	320660	339060	22234	18395	10068973
Louisiana	111809	104813	407445	1099323	288692	216330	822080	189875	3240369
Michigan	563,264	643,826	2271575	5241228	969071	121929	175008	24340	10010245
Arkansas	52324	213020	787927	1204544	353063	197587	188710	113199	3110377
Wisconsin	—	—	316709	808932	223479	109416	819909	127197	2405644
Iowa	—	—	—	—	—	343664	373180	590798	1307643
Florida	14963	48364	60455	108839	125907	86018	70660	29191	516408
Total	4,972,284	6,099,981	15,999,804	25,167,833	7,007,523	4,305,564	6,464,556	2,252,202	72,269,749

This table is derived from the report of Mr. Whitcomb in 1840, and introduced to show the rise in three years from $5,000,000 to $25,000,000 in sales under the paper system, and the sudden decline of $18,000,000 after the specie circular of President Jackson in 1836. It is given as a record of the times. Previous to 1833, the sales were comparatively small. From a Senate report in 1832, we learn that the sales for 1828 amounted to $1,108,308; in 1829, $1,517,175; in 1830, $2,329,356, and in 1831, $3,000,000. That the sales never exceeded the latter sum in any one year is proved by the annual report of the Secretary of the Treasury in 1831, in which he says:—"The receipts from the public lands during the present year, it will be perceived, have likewise exceeded the estimates, and, indeed, have gone beyond any former example." How rapidly this column ascended within the next five years, and then gradually sank below its ancient level!—A striking illustration of the agency of banks in expanding and contracting the business of the country.

Grants to the States.—Without expressing an opinion on the power of the government to apply the public lands to other than national objects, we annex a statement from official sources:

WHOLE QUANTITY OF LANDS GRANTED TO THE STATES AND TERRITORIES.

States and Territories	Colleges and Academies	Internal Improvements	Seats of Government	Salines	16th Sections	Total	Amount at $1 25 per acre.
Ohio	69,120	1,050,287	—	23,680	678,576	1,822,663	$2,278,328
Indiana	46,080	783,209	2,560	23,040	556,184	1,411,073	1,763,841
Illinois	46,080	689,085	2,560	121,629	977,477	1,836,751	2,295,938
Missouri	46,080	500,000	2,449	46,080	1,086,639	1,681,248	2,101,560
Alabama	46,560	500,000	1,620	23,040	722,190	1,293,410	1,616,742
Mississippi	46,080	500,000	1,280	—	635,884	1,183,244	1,479,055
Louisiana	46,080	500,000	—	—	873.973	1,420,053	1,775,066
Michigan	46,080	500,000	13,200	46,080	543,893	1,149,253	1,436,566
Arkansas	46,080	500,000	10,600	46,080	950,258	1,553,018	1,941,272
Florida	46,080	500,000	1,120	—	877,484	1,424,684	1,780,855
Wisconsin	46,080	171,200	—	—	*1,310,424	1,527,704	1,909,630
Iowa	46,080	500,000	640	—	469,832	1,016,522	1,270,690
Total	576,480	6,693,781	36,029	329,629	9,682,814	17,318,623	21,648,279

* The 16th section for Wisconsin and Iowa estimated according to the area of those states.

Relief to Purchasers.—While tracing the action of Congress in behalf of the states, we notice, that for the relief of individuals who had become indebted to the government for lands previous to 1820, the minimum price was $2, and large sales had been made over that sum, even to $50 and $70 per acre, on credit, after a trifling cash instalment. In this year, however, the price was reduced to $1 25, at which it has since remained. Debtors saw their condition, and asked relief, which was granted by sundry acts of Congress to 1832. They were permitted to relinquish the lands purchased, and receive back their bonds, upon forfeiting what they had already paid to government.

TABLE SHOWING THE QUANTITY RELINQUISHED, AMOUNT OF PURCHASE MONEY, AMOUNT ABATED BY GOVERNMENT, AND AMOUNT FORFEITED BY PURCHASERS.

	Acres relinquished	Original purchase money.	Abated by Government	Forfeited by Purchasers
Ohio	432,954	$1,038,932	$1,155,128	$666 28
Indiana	704,315	1,427,465	823,108	2,480 21
Illinois	697,334	1,401,512	603,288	3,288 85
Missouri	709,346	2,004,698	1,256,206	818 43
Alabama	1,842,535	8,649,400	8,020,297	7,141 64
Mississippi	188,990	377,980	298,081	1,456 25
Louisiana	1,898	3,797	18,407	—
Michigan	25,196	79,844	59,569	—
Total	4,602,573	14,983,631	12,234,086	15,853 66

From this showing, the government was very little profited by the forfeitures. The lands relinquished, (4,506,418 acres,) at $1 25, would yield 5,633.022, which would be so much refunded. Whatever the loss, it was better that the government should bear it than individuals, who would have been deceived by the transaction. The cash system having been adopted since 1820, there has been no other occasions for appeals to Congress to rescind contracts for land.

Cost of the Public Lands.—The Register of the Treasury, in answer to a resolution of Congress, reported the following in 1832:

Payment on account of the purchase of Louisiana:—

Principal	$14,984,872 28	
Interest on $11,250,000	8,529,353 43	
		23,514,225,71

Payment on account of the purchase of Florida:—

Principal	$4,985,599 82	
Interest to 30th September, 1831	1,265,416 67	
		$6,251,016 49
Payment of compact with Georgia		1,065,484 06
Payment of Yazoo claimants		1,830,808 04
Payment of contracts with the several Indian tribes, (all expenses on account of Indians,)		11,852,182 56
Payment of commissioners, clerks, and other officers, employed by the United States for the management and sale of the western domain		3,563,834 54
		$48,077,551 40

Amount of money received at the Treasury as the proceeds of public lands, to 30th September, 1831.....$37,272,713 31

Since 1832, several treaties have been made with the Indians, for the extinguishment of their title, the cost of which we have not the means of ascertaining. But, within the last sixteen years, the expenditures of the government have been about $30,000.000, on account of public lands; and their whole cost, up to 1848, as stated in Congress by Gov. Brown, of Mississippi, was $77,130,498. We have seen nothing official on the subject later than 1832, as quoted. The whole amount received for sales to 1848, is $130,-280,156, leaving a clear gain to the government of $53,149,428, according to Gov. B., who, no doubt, had proper data. The lands unsold, to which the Indian title has been extinguished, amount to 242,342,802 acres. By a table from the commissioner, showing the area of the states holding public lands, it will be seen that the government has about

800,000,000 acres unsurveyed in the north-west territory.

Sales of Lands in 1846 *and* 1847.—Merely to post up, we annex a table showing the receipts at the treasury for lands sold in 1846, and in the three first quarters of 1847, together with the amount of incidental expenses in each state, where offices are open, for the same period.

UNITED STATES LAND OFFICE SALES, ETC.

	1846	3 qrs. 1847	Expenses
Ohio	$150,827	$107,081	$12,042
Indiana	127,596	193,182	23,052
Illinois	548,650	410,226	53,391
Missouri	181,142	240,213	20,859
Alabama	104,106	127,042	21,743
Mississippi	47,907	26,994	16,882
Louisiana	61,221	69,932	19,178
Michigan	38,593	47,202	10,640
Arkansas	17,748	92,560	20,040
Florida	44,317	24,735	10,170
Iowa	284,897	298,311	27,562
Wisconsin Territory	798,861	600,224	41,929
Total	$2,405,871	$2,337,684	$287,565

As to the incidental expenses stated in the report, we are at a loss to conjecture the items which constitute them. We presume that registers, receivers, and agents, to whom a fixed compensation is allowed, are not embraced, but that surveys, and other objects which necessarily involve an expenditure, form the basis. The footing up shows a fraction over five per cent. on $2,904,637, the gross amount of purchase money in 1846. Of this sum, $2,713,648 was paid in cash, $20,816 in treasury notes, $300 in forfeited land-stock, $19,460 in military scrip, and $150,412 in Choctaw certificates—in all, $290,988, which, with expenses deducted, left the balance paid into the treasury.

For three quarters of 1847, as stated, the receipts were nearly equal to the whole of 1846. If the last quarter was in proportion, the receipts for 1847 fall very little short of $3,000,000—an average requiring forty-three years to make the sum total received by the government. By reference to a preceding table of sales, from 1833 to 1839, inclusive, it will appear that in those seven years the sum of $70,017,547 accrued to the treasury from the public lands—more than half the whole amount since the origin of the government.

Area of the Land States.—In the table furnished by the commissioner, is an estimate of the area of the states and territories containing public lands, the quantity surveyed, that in process of survey, and the number of acres not yet surveyed, or put under contract.

PUBLIC LANDS REMAINING IN THE STATES.

		Entire Area	Surveyed	In process of Survey	Unsurveyed
Ohio	acres,	25,361,593	25,361,593	—	—
Indiana	"	23,411,431	23,411,431	—	—
Michigan	"	38,426,294	27,097,900	900,000	10,428,388
Iowa	"	16,913,972	12,803,351	1,730,000	2,380,621
Wisconsin	"	47,175,292	12,455,825	1,500,000	33,219,467
Illinois	"	35,235,209	35,235,209	—	—
Missouri	"	43,169,028	39,838,171	650,000	2,680,857
Arkansas	"	33,086,548	31,565,908	1,200,000	320,640
Mississippi	"	30,153,054	30,153,054	—	—
Louisiana	"	28,297,602	19,906,897	325,000	8,065,705
Alabama	"	32,499,872	32,465,746	—	34,126
Florida	"	34,423,055	13,106,045	1,650,000	19,667,010
N. W. Territory east of the Rocky Mountains and west of Miss. River, exclusive of ceded lands in Iowa	"	478,549,708	—	—	478,549,708
N. W. Territory, west of the Rocky Mountains	"	218,536,320	—	—	218,536,320
Emigrant Indian lands west of Mississippi and Arkansas	"	132,295,680	—	—	132,295,680

Connected with this subject, it may be curious to pursue the calculation. Estimate the vacant lands to which the title of the government is complete at 240,000,000, and the domain north-west, more or less incumbered by the Indian tribes, at 800,000,000, and the aggregate is 1,040,000,000 acres, which, at fifty cents per acre, would yield five hundred and twenty millions of dollars to the treasury! Add New-Mexico, say 500 miles in length, and 200 in width, the area will be 100,000 square miles, or 64,000,000 acres; and California, 600 miles long and 300 wide, will amount to 180,000 square miles, or 115,000,000 acres—both together about 180,000,000. Suppose the whole population of the United

States, 20,000,000, were destitute of land, the government could supply each man, woman, and child, white and black, with sixty acres of the public domain. Reduced into families of five persons, the share would be 300 acres to each head of a family,—enough, with diligent cultivation, to produce ample support. This, however, is a mere speculative view, without any disposition to forward a grant on such a scale; yet we believe that the more liberally government acts in behalf of settlers, the happiness of the people and the prosperity of the Republic will be increased. It may be urged against too free a use of the public lands, that they should be retained for emergencies, so that the government may establish a sufficient credit on this security, should occasion require a loan, especially if revenue from imports be cut off by a war with European powers. This necessity can never arise. In case of war, the people will cheerfully submit to taxation in any form to sustain our flag; and such are the admitted resources of the country, and willingness to contribute, that government bonds will be at par value in all parts of the world.

Besides, the sooner government can dispose of its lands the better for all parties. So long as they remain a subject of political discussion, the public mind will be influenced by appeals alike unworthy a high standard of statesmanship, or of an intelligent constituency. It is right that every man who desires should have a domicile;—and we go farther in public policy—that domicile, with acres enough for industry to live upon, should be inalienable. The best hold government can have upon the affections of the citizen is reciprocity of interest; the one rewarding with kindness the sacrifices which the public service may at any time demand, and the other performing with alacrity, because, if disabled or slain, provision will be made for his relief, or for those dear to him. In this spirit of mutual obligation the Republic has its safest guarantee.

Pre-emption Rights.—The commissioner advises a course toward actual settlers in which we fully concur—the law to be so modified as to embrace every family who may, in good faith, seek a home on the public lands, whether surveyed or not, provided the Indian title has been extinguished. We cannot find better expression than the reasoning of the Report, p. 29:

"A policy thus liberal towards a very large class of our fellow-citizens cannot fail to produce the most beneficial results. It will facilitate the settlement and improvement of the frontier portions of the country, raise up a hardy race of backwoodsmen for its protection against the encroachments of our Mexican and Indian neighbors, afford them the means of improving their condition in many respects, and, above all, to educate their children, and will impress those patriotic frontiersmen with deeper feelings of regard for their government, when they find that they are no longer in danger of losing their hard-earned improvements, by being brought into competition with a more wealthy class of citizens at the land sales."

Graduation of Price.—The views of the commissioner on this head are sound and expedient, viz.: that the refuse lands, for many years culled over, should be reduced in price so as to find sale, thereby aiding the treasury, and relieving it proportionably from interest on loans; and also to enable the states within which the lands lie to impose the necessary tax to which other lands are subject, after five years, from sale.

War Bounties.—Any objection to grants of land to the soldiers who fought our battles, should rest for validity on some ground other than loss of revenue. With a national domain exceeding ten hundred millions of acres, the quantity, even a section to each man, would be a trifle. Say that 40,000 soldiers were in Mexico at different stages of the war, all entitled to 160 acres, the aggregate would be only 6,400,000 acres—scarcely to be felt in the administration of this interest. If allowed half a section, (320 acres,) the result would be twice, and if a section, (640 acres,) four times the quantity,—total, 25,600,000 acres. This may appear extravagant, and, compared with former legislation, is somewhat startling. If soldiers would settle upon their bounty lands, and thereby reap the full benefit, we should defend the liberality we have suggested; but as nine-tenths barter off their scrip for a trifle, from 25 to 40 cents per acre, merely serving as prey to speculators, without any solid advantage to themselves, we cannot justly advocate such an appropriation by Congress. A direct pecuniary grant, which shall produce to the holder par value in any market, is preferable, and government stock would be laudably issued for this object.

The bounty lands granted by Congress to soldiers of the Revolution and the war of 1812, in lieu of money, amounted in the aggregate to 9,750,000 acres.

Mineral Lands.—The report includes much information from Lake Superior, and from Wisconsin and Iowa, respecting ores on the public lands. Dr. Jackson, a learned geologist, has explored the Lake region with a sufficient corps, and, in summing up his discoveries, says:

"We certainly have the most wonderful veins of native metals there that have ever been seen in the world. * * * * * *

"With regard to the government, it will certainly be considered a liberal and enlightened policy to explore each new region, and to lay before the public a true account of what may be expected in the rocks and soil. The settlement of the country by emigration from more populous districts, and from Europe, will be the necessary result, and an active business will be created along the line of our great lakes, communicating with our mineral lands. Mining will cause a settlement of that district by our active population of miners, mechanics and farmers, when, if only agricultural lands were sought for, no one would think of going to the shores of Lake Superior, while so many fertile lands offer their attractions elsewhere."

Dr. Owen, U. S. Geologist for Wisconsin and Iowa, furnished an interesting narrative of his labors, from which we should be glad to extract passages if the limits of this article were not already too extended.—(1848.)

UNITED STATES PUBLIC LANDS, 1851.

The following table shows the area of each state and territory wherein the land office is operating, with the amount of its surveys and the work yet to be done:

	Areas of the states square miles	Acres	Surveyed to September 30 1850	Unsurveyed to September 30 1850
Ohio	39,964	26,576,960	16,770,984	None.
Indiana	33,809	21,637,760	21,488,658	None.
Illinois	55,405	35,459,200	35,455,469	3,731
Missouri	67,380	43,123,200	42,613,273	509,927
Alabama	50,043	32,027,490	31,993,813	33,677
Mississippi	37,337	23,895,628	23,895,628	None.
Louisiana	46,431	29,715,840	19,152,523	10,563,317
Michigan	56,243	35,995,520	30,629,076	5,866,444
Arkansas	52,193	33,406,720	33,201,425	205,295
Wisconsin	53,924	34,511,360	16,169,498	18,341,862
Iowa	50,914	32,584,960	19,196,106	13,388,854
Florida	59,268	37,931,520	21,907,314	16,024,206
Minnesota Territory	83,000	53,120,000	237,227	52,882,773
N. West Territory	587,564	376,040,960	—	376,040,960
Nebraska	136,700	87,488,000	—	87,488,000
Indiana	137,171	119,789,440	—	119,789,440
New-Mexico	210,744	134,876,160	—	134,876,160
Utah	187,923	120,270,720	—	120,270,720
California	188,981	120,947,840	—	120,947,840
Oregon	341,463	218,536,320	—	218,536,230
Total	2,526,462	1,616,935,598	312,710,994	1,295,269,526

The above table shows that in a few years all the lands in the new states will be surveyed and opened to settlers and pre-emption claims.

The following statement of the amount of lands, sold and located by Military Land Warrants, &c., in 1848 and 1849, and first three quarters of 1850, exhibits the decrease in cash receipts, and the increase for 1849 in the amount of funds disposed of:—

	Acres		
Sales in 1848	1,887,553 : 04	equal to	$2,621,615 26
Mexican war warrants	2,288,960 : 90	"	2,861,200 00
State selections, act 1841	378,058 : 57	"	472,573 21
Improvements rivers, &c	321,188 : 33	"	401,485 51
Choctaw certificates	57,249 : 10	"	71,571 37
Total acres	4,933,009 : 04	"	$6,428,435 35

	Acres		
Sales in 1849	1,329,902 : 77	equal to	$1,757,890 42
Mexican war warrants	3,405,510 : 00	"	4,256,900 00
State selections, act 1841	259,806 : 60	"	324,758 25
Improvements rivers, &c	135,246 : 21	"	169,057 76
Choctaw certificates	53,935 : 33	"	67,419 16
Total acres	5,184,410 : 91	"	$6,575,025 59

	Acres		
Sales in the three quarters in 1850	869,082 : 32	equal to	$1,129,186 50
Mexican war warrants for 1st, 2d, and part of 3d quarter	1,520,120 : 00	"	1,900,150 00
State selections, for 1st, 2d, and part of 3d quarter	379,803 : 59	"	474,754 47
Choctaw certificates	46,360 : 52	"	57,950 65
Total acres	2,815,366 : 42	"	$3,562,041 62

From this statement it will be perceived that the aggregate amount of land disposed of in 1849 considerably exceeds that of 1848. There is a falling off in the current fiscal year, caused probably by emigration to the Pacific, the extensive reservations for the rail-road from Chicago to Mobile, and the fact that most of the military warrants have been located, and the state selections disposed of.

Since the last annual report, over six millions of acres of lands have been brought into market, and about seven millions are now prepared for sale, and will be offered early in the ensuing season.

By careful examination, it is ascertained that the entire area of the public domain, exclusive of the lands in Oregon, California, New-Mexico, Utah, the Indian and Nebraska Territories, was 424,103,750 acres.

About one-fourth of these lands has been sold, and the purchase money received for it amounts to		$135,339,092
The cost of the whole of these lands, including the amount paid to France for Louisiana, to Spain for the Floridas, and amount paid for extinguishing the Indian title, was	$61,121,777	
A portion only of these lands has been surveyed, the cost of which, including salaries of surveyors-general and clerks, and expenses attending the surveys, was	6,369,838	
Less than half the land surveyed has been sold, and the whole cost of selling and managing the same, including every expense not previously charged, is	7,466,324	
Aggregate outlay of every kind		74,957,879
Net profit to the Government		$60,381,218

Or an average of nearly one million and a quarter of dollars annually for the last fifty years.

If to this should be added the value of $1 25 per acre of the land granted in bounties for military services and internal improvements, donations, &c., it would amount to nearly double that sum. This will be more fully appreciated when it is understood that the average cost to the government of acquiring title to the Public Lands, including the extinguishment of the

title, is	14 41	cts. per acre.	
Do. of survey	2 07	"	"
Do. of selling and managing	5 82	"	"
Total average cost	21 4-5	cts per acre;	

while for each acre sold the government gets $1 25, or a net profit over and above every cost and expense of $1 03 15.100 per acre.

Statement showing the condition of the State selections under the Act of 4th September, 1841, on 30th day of June, 1850.

States	No. of acres to which each State was entitled under the 8th Section of the Act of September 4, 1841.	No. of acres approved up to 30th of June, 1850.	No. of acres to which each State was entitled on the 1st July, 1850 and to be selected and approved.
Illinois	209,085,50	208,980,05	105,45
Missouri	500,000,00	449,317,62	682,38
Alabama	97,499,17	none	97,469,17
Mississippi	500,000,00	498,835,53	1,164,47
Louisiana	500,000,00	355,870,41	144,129,59
Michigan	500,000,00	494,513,43	5,486,57
Arkansas	500,000,00	499,889,03	110,97
Florida	499,990,09	45,567,94	454,422,15
Iowa	500,000,00	172,394,86	327,605,14
Wisconsin	360,364,01	285.648,42	74,715,59
Aggregate	4,166,908,77	3,061,017,29	1,105,891,48

The several grants to the state of Indiana for the construction of the Wabash and Erie Canal, amounting to about 1,400,000 acres, have all been selected, the grants certified to the state, and closed upon the books of this Office.

LAKES.—Great Lakes of the United States.—"Extending from east to west over nearly fifteen and a half degrees of longitude, they seem, regarding them upon the map, to rest like a crown of waters upon the head of the Union, their centre of gravity; the island of Mackinac, balancing upon the meridian which separates Indiana and Ohio, equi-divides Kentucky and Tennessee, and passes between Georgia and Alabama, and East and West Florida, in the Gulf of Mexico. The difference in the latitude of the northern and southern extreme points of the lakes is not far from eight and a half degrees. The estimated area of country draining into them is 400,000 square miles; the extent covered by the waters of the whole is 93,000 square miles, divided as follows: Ontario, 6,300; Erie, 9600; St. Clair, 1,060; Huron, 20,400; Michigan, including the bay, 24,400; Superior, 32,000. The waters of the 'Father of Lakes' (Superior) are 568 feet above the level of the sea; which elevation is attained by unequal gradations, each lake rising above the previous one from Ontario to Superior. The surface of the waters of Ontario is 232 feet above the tide-water of the St. Lawrence; Erie rises 333 feet above Ontario; St. Clair 6 feet above Erie; Huron and Michigan are 13 feet higher than St. Clair; and Superior rises 44 feet above those.

"The St. Clair is by far the shallowest of any of the lakes, the average depth being about 20 feet; Erie averages in depth about 85 feet: Ontario 500; Superior 900; Huron and Michigan 1,000, as nearly as can be arrived at. The deepest soundings are found in Lake Huron: off Saginaw bay, we are told, leads have sunk 1,800 feet, or 1,200 below the level of of the Atlantic Ocean, without reaching the bottom.

"Great difference is observable in the transparency and purity of the waters of the several lakes. Those of Ontario, Erie, and the southern part of Michigan have no peculiar excellence—while those of the northern part of Lake Michigan and Lake Huron surpass in clearness and flavor any waters of which we have ever drunk, though a still greater purity and a higher relish is said, by those who have visited that lake, to distinguish the waters of Superior.

"So completely transparent are the waters of Huron, that the rays of the sun are said to pass through them as through the cloudless atmosphere, without meeting with solid matter in supension to elicit their heat. Thus Dr. Drake accounts for the fact, which he himself ascertained by experiment, that the water on the surface, and that 200 feet below the same spot, had precisely the same temperament, 56 degrees.

"Through the Welland Canal the navigation of the Lakes is uninterrupted for the distance of 844 miles from east to west; the distance north and south is, of course, various, ranging from 347 miles as the extreme distance. The country to which these waters are the great highway of transport has often been the theme of high-wrought eulogium, for the variety and richness of its soil, and the extent of its resources. The justness of these praises, as well as the extent to which this fertility has been subjected to the hand of culture, and the rapidity with which these resources are being developed, under the life-bringing touch of the enterprise which peculiarly characterizes its inhabitants, is gathered from the bare glance at the fact, that the commerce of the four great Lakes, including all capital afloat, during the year 1843, was estimated by the Topographical Bureau at 65,000,000 dollars. The total amount expended by the General Government of the United States on these lakes, for the improvement necessary to protect and convenience this commerce, is stated by Mr. Whittlesey, of Ohio, at $2,100,000.

"When the projected ship-canal around the Falls of Ste. Marie, shall be completed, the wide expanse of Lake Superior will be added to the present extent of the lake navigation, allowing the adventurous commercialist to crowd some 175 miles still farther north, and several hundreds farther west. The length of the road proposed to be cut by this canal is said to be but *three-fourths of a mile*, and the whole expense of the improvement is estimated, if we rightly remember, at 230,000 dollars. By this comparatively small outlay, access is at once obtained to the whole country tributary to Lake Superior—a tract so rich in timber and mineral wealth, that it has not been unaptly termed 'the Denmark of America.'

"The following is a most accurate statement of the length, width, and depth of the respective Lakes, which cannot fail to be interesting to our readers:

THE GREAT LAKES.

	Greatest length. Miles.	Greatest breadth. Miles.	Aver. depth. Feet.
Ontario	180	40	500
Erie	270	80	200
Huron	250	100	900
Superior	350	150	900

"Of these, the surface of Lake Superior has been calculated to be 1,048 feet above the level of the high tide of the sea; Lake Huron is 570 feet above ditto; Lake Erie is 330 feet above Lake Ontario, and 566 above the Hudson at Albany. The Ontario is 218 feet above the St. Lawrence and Three Rivers."

There are several important canals connected with the Lakes, which may be briefly noticed. Erie canal, 363 miles, in the State of New-York; Welland canal, uniting Erie and Ontario, and avoiding the Falls of Niagara, 42 miles; Rideau canal, 135 miles; Greenville canal; Lachine canal, from Montreal to Upper Lachine.

In relation to the Falls of Niagara and the river of St. Lawrence, the following from the same source is valuable:

FALLS OF NIAGARA.

Extent of the Horse-shoe Falls, on the British side	2,200	feet.
Breadth of Goat Island, between it and the American	980	"
American Falls in breadth	1,140	"
The whole extent, or full three-quarters of a mile	4,200	"
Height of the Horse-shoe Falls	150	"
Height of the American Falls	160	"
Extent of the cave beneath the Horse-shoe Falls, from the outside of the Termination Rock	153	"
Height of the cave is estimated by Captain Hall at	100	"
The estimated quantity of water discharged over the Falls is calculated at 48,524,000 cubic feet, or 113,510,000 gallons, per minute		
Depth of the river above the Falls, as near as can be approached, about	200	"
Breadth of the river at the ferry	1,170	"

THE ST. LAWRENCE.

Lake Superior being the real head of this river, the distance from Cape Chat, which is 100 miles above Cape Rosier, where its mouth may in reality be deemed to commence, to the head of that Lake, is calculated to be no less than	2,120	miles
Breadth of the mouth of the river at Cape Rosier	80	"
Breadth at Kamouraska, where its waters are perfectly fresh, and its average depth twelve fathoms	20	"

LAKE AND WESTERN RIVER TRADE, ETC.—The net money value of the *lake commerce* for the year 1846, was $61,914,910; having nearly doubled in five years. For the same year the total amount of American lake tonnage was 106,836 tons, and of merchandise 3,861,088 tons. British, 30,000 tons. Estimates from highly intelligent authority make the cost of constructing this tonnage $6,000,000. The passenger trade is also an important item in the lake commerce. The number of passengers, in all directions, is stated at 250,000; which, at $5 each as average charges, gives for its value, $1,250,000. The number of mariners employed was 6,972.

The aggregate population depending on the lakes for means of communicating with a market, in 1846, was 2,928,925.

Of the *Western rivers*, i. e. the Mississippi, and its direct and indirect tributaries, it appears from the official returns of the treasury department, that the steamboat tonnage for the year 1842, was 126,278; and for 1846, 249,055. It is supposed that there are 300,000 tons of other boats (not steamboats) employed on these rivers, which, added to the steamboat tonnage, gives for the year 1842, an aggregate of 426,278 tons. The flat-boat navigation is supposed to carry to market, in one year, 600,000 tons of produce, while the steamboat freight amounted to 1,262,780 tons, or a total merchandise transported to and from New-Orleans on the Western rivers, (exclusive of the way-trade,) for 1842, of 4,862,780 tons. The probable money value of this commerce, for the same year, can be stated at $50,506,903; and for 1846, according to a statement from the treasury department, $62,206,719. This includes, of course, only the *direct* river commerce, and not that immense amount of commodities interchanged between place and place on the Western rivers, and which forms no part of the New-Orleans commerce. Of this latter, the total *net* value can be stated for 1846, at $148,306,710—the *floating* value cannot be less than double this amount. The passenger trade, too, is very great, and is supposed to have yielded for 1846 $3,191,982, making the total commerce of the Western rivers, $151,498,701. The steam tonnage for 1846, is stated at 249,054 tons.

The total cost of the river craft, engaged in this trade, was $12,942,355, and sustained at an expense of $20,196,242 per annum. The nnmber of hands employed (not shore employées) was 25,114. These amounts the Bureau considers too small, or at least not at all exaggerated; and that if $183,609,725 be assumed as a reliable exposition of Western commerce for 1846, instead of $151,498,701, it will more nearly approximate to the truth.

The total *population* depending upon the Western rivers as a means of communication with a market for the year 1846, was 6,576,027—the rate of increase 1840 to 1845 having been about 5 per cent. The Mississippi, with its tributaries, which traverse every section of this immense valley, furnish 16,674 miles of good steamboat navigation, thus affording great natural facilities for the development of its unlimited resources.

These facts, in reference to the commerce of the lakes, (says the Report,) and Western rivers, justify the following conclusions:

1st. That the net moneyed value of the commerce of the lakes and Western rivers, including the passenger trade, amounted, for the year 1846—

Of the lakes, to	$63,164,910
Of the Western rivers	183,609,725
Aggregate	$246,774,635

2d. That the population depending upon the lakes and upon the Western rivers as a means of communicating with a market, was, for the year 1846—

For the lakes	$2,928,925
For the Western rivers	6,576,027
Aggregate	$9,504,952

3d. That the number of hands employed in this commerce as mariners, exclusive of shore hands, for the year 1846—

For the lakes	6,972
For the Western rivers	25,114
Aggregate	32,086

And it may be added that the total amounts which have been appropriated and expended for lake harbors, and for the improvement of the Western rivers, from the year 1806, when these appropriations by the general government commenced, up to, and including the last appropriations of 1845, are—

For the lake harbors	$2,790,500
For the Western rivers	2,758,800
Aggregate	$5,549,300

The tonnage of Lake Champlain is stated at 3,182 tons, and the value of the export and import trade for 1846, $11,266,050. The total amount appropriated for the improvement of its harbors is $191,500. The tonnage of Lake Ontario is stated to be 65,636, of which 42,325 tons are British, and 25,311 American. The export and import trade for 1846 is stated at $14,025,907, and the total amount expended for its harbors, $608,902. On Lake Erie, the total amount expended for harbor improvements is $1,348,249, and the total amount of its commerce (exports and imports) in 1846, $94,358,350. The total amount of expenditures on Lake Michigan for harbor improvements, is $604,447; amount of commerce not known. For Chicago, however, it amounted, in 1846, to $3,027,150.

The total amount of American lake tonnage is 106,836 tons. The total of British lake tonnage is 46,675, making a combined tonnage of 153,411 tons.

LAKE AND VALLEY TRADE.—Extent of our Inland Trade; Trade and Tonnage Lakes, 1846, 1850, and 1860; Steam Tonnage, Trade and Navigation, Western Rivers; Population of Lake Country, and Communication with Mississippi and the Atlantic; Extent of Lakes; American and British Maritime Power on Lakes, etc. 1850.—At the last session of Congress, Colonel Albert, being called upon to report such information as could be had by the Engineer's Department, in regard to the lakes, presented a document of great interest and value, which, being official and of latest date, will form the groundwork of our present remarks.

The value of lake commerce in 1841, was:—

Imports	$33,483,441
Exports	32,342,541
	$65,826,022

Or, dividing this amount by two, since the exports of one place are the imports of another, we have $32,913,011, as the floating value of lake commerce in 1841.

TRADE OF LAKES, 1846—EXPORTS AND IMPORTS.

Oswegatchie District	$180,555
Champlain.	
Whitehall	6,327,489
Plattsburg District	1,160,844
Burlington "	3,777,726
Ontario.	
Sackett's Harbor District	2,735,091
Dexter Port	484,575
Port Ontario	423,724
Oswego	9,502,980
Big Sodus	39,206
Rochester	212,926
Pultneyville	20,342
Niagara	606,863
Erie.	
Buffalo	48,989,116
Conneaut	380,475
Ashtabula	715,467
Fairport	819,584
Cleveland	12,559,110
Sandusky	5,943,127
Monroe	9,519,067
Detroit	8,706,348
Erie	6,373,246
Black River	215,040
Vermilion	137,770
Michigan.	
Chicago	3,927,150
Total commerce, 1846	$123,829,821

Or, dividing, as in 1841, by two, we have a total of $61,914,910, having nearly doubled in five years, or, to be more accurate, increased seventeen and a half per cent. per annum. The registered, enrolled, and licensed tonnage of the lakes, was:—

TONNAGE, 1846.

Champlain District	3,192
Sackett's Harbor District	4,279
Oswego "	16,046
Niagara "	75
Genesee "	769
Oswegatchie "	2,058
Buffalo "	24,770
Cape Vincent	2,230
Presque Isle	2,993
Cuyahoga	18,526
Sandusky	2,864
Maumee	3,163
Detroit	24,804
Mackinaw	1,067
Total tonnage	108,836

having increased, since 1841, in very nearly the precise ratio of the exports and imports. The whole number of clearances and entries upon the lakes, was, in 1846, 15,855, and the number of tons of merchandise carried, 3,861,088, also an increase of over seventeen and a half per cent, per annum, since 1841.

It ought to have been observed above, that in the list of lake ports, and the amount of their trade, the following were omitted as not ascertained:—Black Rock, Silver Creek, Irving, Portland, Huron, and Dunkirk, on Lake Erie; St. Joseph, Grand River, Kalamazoo, New Buffalo, Michigan City, Mouth of Calumie, Little Fort, Southport, Racine, Milwaukie, Sheboygan, and Manitowoc, upon Lake Michigan.

In addition to the American tonnage, the British have upon the lakes 46,575 tons, of which 30,000 tons are employed in the American trade—making the whole amount of tonnage in the American trade in 1846, 136,-836 tons.

The value of this American shipping, in 1846, is estimated by one account $5,341,800, and by another, $6,000,000. It may be safely put down at $7,000,000, including the value of British vessels employed by us. The annual expenses upon all this shipping, including interest and insurance, is very near $2,000,000.

The passenger trade of the lakes amounts to about 250,000 per annum in numbers, and cost of carriage, perhaps, $1,250,000. The number of mariners employed, 6,972.

If we suppose that the same ratio of increase has been observed since 1846, we may state the commerce of the lakes, as compared now with 1841, as follows:—

COMMERCE OF THE LAKES, 1849–50.

Exports and imports, increase 4 yrs. at 17½ per cent. per annum	$105,255,347
Tonnage, increase 4 yrs. at 17½ per cent. ... tons	185,017
Tons merchandise carried	6,536,844
British commerce employed	51,000
Value American shipping	10,200,000
Expenses "	3,400,000
Passengers carried	425,000
Receipts from passengers	2,335,000
Mariners	10,500

The Buffalo Advertiser has, however, furnished the following as the—

TONNAGE OF THE LAKES, 1849.

Ports	Steamers and Propellers	Barques and Brigs	Schooners	Sloops and Scows	Total	Tonnage
Buffalo	42	31	85	5	163	42,265,40
Presque Isle	5	4	14	—	23	6,237,07
Cuyahoga	10	23	55	17	105	22,949,86
Sandusky	7	4	34	3	48	8,458,25
Miami	4	—	11	2	17	2,921,27
Detroit	43	9	109	36	197	23,609,83
Chicago	2	13	55	1	71	11,387,42
Michilimackinac	3	—	21	1	25	1,671,51
Lewiston	1	—	8	—	9	753,11
Rochester	2	—	6	1	9	1,298,00
Oswego	13	9	80	—	102	17,813,01
Oswegatchie	4	—	4	—	8	2,215,63
Cape Vincent	—	1	8	—	9	1,708,63
Sackett's Harbor	2	4	33	—	102	5,484,12
Champlain	2	—	25	63	90	4,653,51
	140	98	548	129	915	153,426,62

British Tonnage on Lake Ontario.—The comparative increase of steamers, propellers, and other vessels, owned on Lake Ontario, and employed on the inland waters of Canada, during the season of 1846 and 1847, was as follows :—

	1847.	1846.
Steamers	67	57
Propellers (lake and river)	14	13
Ships	2	2
Brigantines (30 tons and above)	5	5
Schooners	110	94
Barges	300	300
Total	498	471
Tonnage (aggregate)	63,346	56,380
Valued at	$2,750,000	$2,472,00

There were built on Lake Erie, during 1848, and to be in commission in 1849, the following *steamers*, viz. : At Sandusky, the Alabama of 1,200 tons ; at Buffalo, the Keystone State, of 1,354 tons ; at Detroit, the May Flower, of 1,300 tons ; at Cleveland, the ———, of 1,300 tons ; at Newport, the Atlantic, of 1,000 tons. And the following *propellers*, viz. : at Cleveland, the ———, of 450 tons, and the Troy, of 350 tons ; at Buffalo, the ———, of 450—in all, 7,404 tons.

TOTAL TONNAGE AND VALUATION.

45,067	tonnage of steamers, valued at	$3,380,000
15,685	" propellers, "	950,000
101,080	" sail vessels "	3,538,000
161,832		$7,868,000

In order to form any estimate of what the value of the lake commerce, ten years hence, say in 1860, will be, it is necessary to consider the nature of the country which is tributary, "the region whose intercourse is facilitated by this commerce, the productiveness of the soil of the adjacent states ; the extent of that soil, and extent of lands yet unoccupied ; the population depending upon the lakes, as a means of communicating with a market already great and daily increasing ; the agreeableness of the climate and its general salubrity ; the character of the population, and the foreign emigrant, to whom the lake region is so great a favorite ; the cheapness of the land," etc. etc. With these elements of progress at work, it cannot be unfair to argue that the increase for the next ten years will not be materially less than in the years from 1840 to 1846. Upon this basis we construct the following table :—

COMMERCE OF LAKES, 1860.

Value of exports, imports, and passengers	$213,507,365*
Amount of tonnage on Lakes	367,085
Value of American shipping on Lakes	14,208,000

If we compare the results as furnished with those from the western rivers, some instructive comparisons may be made.

STEAMBOAT TONNAGE—WESTERN RIVERS.

	1842.	1846
New-Orleans	80,993	—
St. Louis	14,725	—
Cincinnati	12,025	—
Pittsburg	10.107	—
Louisville	4,618	—
Nashville	3,810	—
Total	126,278	249,055

In addition, it is estimated that in 1842 there were 4,000 boats of other kinds, flatboats, etc., employed, with an aggregate tonnage of 300,000 tons, making the whole tonnage for that year 426,278 tons. It is supposed that the flatboats carried about 600,000 tons, and the steamboats 1,262,780 tons, making a total of merchandise transported on the western rivers, in 1842, of 1,862,780 tons. Estimating these tons as equally valuable with those of the lakes, and it is thought they are more so, and we have lake tonnage both ways, or duplicate enumeration, 3,861,088, divided by two, 1,930,544, worth $64,913,910, or $32 07 per ton : therefore the 1,862,780 tons of the river trade with New-Orleans will be $69,739,354, for 1842. This is Col. Albert's calculation. The New-Orleans returns, however, show a receipt at that city, in 1842, of 45,716,045, and in 1846–47, of 90,033,256 tons, being a little less than double in four years ; but taking the average receipts from

* The net value is alone involved in this amount, that is, half the aggregate value of the exports and imports ; since the exports of one place are imports of another.

1842 to 1845, viz.: 54,184,484, and comparing them with average receipts from 1845 to 1848, 76,051,248, we have an increase of very nearly ten per cent. per annum. Col. Abert makes the per centage only about five and three-fourths per cent.—clearly an important mistake. A very respectable committee in Cincinnati, in 1842, estimated the aggregate trade on western rivers, exclusive of that of New-Orleans, at $70,000,000. Supposing this to have increased at the same rate as New-Orleans trade, we would have, for 1849, $111,000,000, and the whole western river trade, in 1849, $190,777,151 net; or a floating trade of double that sum, the exports of one town being the imports of another, viz.: $381,554,362. If the passenger earnings be added, the *net* result of river trade will be swelled to nearly $195,000,000 The value of all the boats in 1842, was $10,522,240. If they have increased in the same proportion as the trade of New-Orleans, the present value per annum of boats afloat would be $20,000,000 nearly. The working expense of this craft, and sustaining it, is over one hundred per cent., on its cost per annum, or on $20,000,000, about $25,000,000. The boatmen on western rivers, in 1842, were 20,418: at ten per cent. increase, we have, in 1849, nearly 20,000.

By another estimation, based upon the increase of tonnage upon western rivers, which, from 1842 to 1846, was twenty-four per cent., and supposing the same increase preserved since, we would have the value of river trade in 1849, $218,400,000, or, including passengers, about $225,000,000 net, or a floating trade of $450,000,000 annually; that is, adding up the exports and imports of all the various towns.

The whole population dependent *entirely* upon these lakes, Col. Abert estimates at 6,191,555 in 1846, or in 1849, probably 7,000,000; but this is evidently much below the figure, since the West increases faster than the Union, and should rather be 8,000,000.

What the future population of the Mississippi valley may be, and what the amount of its commerce, are questions of some importance, but in the discussion of which the imagination is not unapt to run wild and become bewildered. Even sober reason seems elevated upon the wings of fancy. Upon the calculation of Col. Abert, the valley contains 666,666 square miles of good arable land. To people this region with the average of the fertile parts of Europe, 110 to the square mile, there would be a total of 73,333,260 inhabitants; with the density of France, 165.1 to the mile, it would be 110,066,556; and of Great Britain, 222.6 to the mile, 148,399,851. Immense periods may be required to produce this, but the result is more than practicable, even with *great* prosperity. If however, the advances for the next twenty years are equal to those of the last six or eight, five per cent., we shall have, in 1870, 17,775,272 inhabitants in the great valley.

The productions of these people will follow some fixed relation to their numbers; and if the productiveness of the region be considered, Col. Abert's calculation, upon the basis of Professor Tucker, will appear reasonable, viz.: as 8 is to 5: i. e. to every five per cent. increase in population, there will be an 8 per cent. increase in production, reversing Mr. Malthus' rules. Taking the mean of the figures, found by the two estimates of western commerce we have given for 1849, the amount for 1850 will be at least $250,000,000. Col. Abert estimates $274,000,000, and calculates the increase at eight per cent., viz.:

Commerce Great West,	1850	$274,459,816
" " "	1860	494,027,668
" " "	1870	889,249,802

The figures seem prodigious, but, governed by the light of the past, it may be questioned whether we have a right to doubt. The most sober-minded and skeptical reader will not, however, venture to fix the population of the valley, in 1870, at less than 15,000,000, and its commerce at 500,000,000, being little less than the whole Union now. The probable navigation by steam on the western waters of the Mississippi, is estimated by Col. Long, of the engineers:

MILES WESTERN STEAM NAVIGATION.

Mississippi and Branches.	
Mississippi proper	2000
St. Croix	80
St. Peter's	120
Chippeway	70
Black	60
Wisconsin	180
Rock	250
Iowa	110
Cedar	60
Des Moines	250
Illinois	245
Maramec	60
Kaskaskia	150
Big Muddy	5
Obion	60
Forked Deer	195
Big Hatchee	75
St. Francis	300
White	500
Big Black	60
Spring	50
Arkansas	603
Canadian	60
Neosho	60
Yazoo	300
Tallahatchee	300
Yallabusha	100
Big Sun Flower	80
Little Sun Flower	70
Big Black	150
Bayou de Glaze	90
Bayou Carre	140
Bayou Lafourche	60
Bayou Rouge	40
Bayou Plaquemine	12
Bayou Teche	96
Grand River	12
Bayou Sorrele	12
Bayou Chêne	5

Missouri and Branches.	
Missouri proper	1500
Yellowstone	300
Platte River	40
Kansas	150
Osage	275
Grand	90

Ohio and its Branches.	
Ohio proper	1000
Alleghany	200
Monongahela	60
Muskingum	70

Kanawha	65	*Red River and Branches.*		Tensas	150
Big Sandy	50	Red River proper	1500	Lacke Bistenaw	60
Scioto	50	Wachita	375	Lake Caddo	75
Kentucky	62	Saline	100	Sulphur Fork	100
Salt River	35	Little Missouri	50	Little River	65
Green	150	Bayou D'Arboune	60	Kiamichi	40
Barren	30	Bayou Bartholomew	150	Boggy	40
Wabash	400	Bayou Boeuf	150	Bayou Pierre	150
Cumberland	400	Bayou Maçon	175	Atchafalaya	360
Tennessee	720	Bayou Louis	30		
				Total	16,674

The population which depends upon the lakes for a market, is embraced within eight states, viz.:

Vermont	177,278
New-York	608,116
Pennsylvania	126,094
Ohio	723,119
Michigan	212,267
Indiana	250,263
Illinois	93,069
Wisconsin	23,045
Total, 1840	2,313,251
Add increase since	1,256,625
Total, 1850	3,569,876

The estimate is made upon an annual increase of five per cent. per annum, which was about maintained from 1840 to 1846.

The number of American steamboats on the upper lakes, above Niagara, was in 1847, 62; propellers 18, barks and brigs, 59; schooners, sloops and scows, 319—the average tonnage of steamers being 400, propellers 328, brigs and barks 230, schooners 152, sloops, etc., 46. There were on Lake Ontario, at the same time, 8 steamers of average 877 tons, 10 propellers of 275 tons, 186 sailing vessels of 114 tons; on Lake Champlain 3,192 tons, not enumerated.

The whole amount expended by government, from 1806 to 1845, upon improvements of the

Lake Harbors	$2,790,500
Western Rivers	2,758,800
	$5,549,300

The great lakes are connected with the Valley of the Mississippi by—

1. *Illinois and Michigan Canal*, 96½ miles long, 60 feet wide, and 6 feet deep; locks, 17; total lockage, 158 feet. It connects the Chicago, which empties into Lake Michigan, with the Illinois at La Salle, 213 miles from the Mississippi. The Illinois is navigable all the year in flatboats, and four months by steam (the ice season being excluded.)

2. *Wabash and Erie Canal.*—This extends from Lafayette, about 378 miles above the Wabash mouth, where it enters the Ohio, to Toledo, on the Maumee, adjacent to Lake Erie, and is 187 miles long. It is intended to complete the canal from Lafayette to the Ohio River. At a place called Junction, this canal intersects the Miami Canal from Cincinnati. It is probable the Wabash and Erie Canal is now complete to Terra Haute, on the Wabash. The Muskingum improvement extends to the Muskingum River, at or near Zanesville, and is 91 miles long.

3. *Sandy and Beaver Canal*, connecting the Beaver River with the lake from the Ohio.

4. *Mahoning Canal*, being a cross canal of 83 miles long. There is a canal called the Beaver and Erie, 136 miles long, connecting with the Ohio 28 miles below Pittsburgh The connection with Lake Ontario is by the Welland Canal in Canada, and with Ontario and Champlain by the New-York canals. The points of union of these canals, then, with the Mississippi, are as follows: mouth of Illinois on the Mississippi, 40 miles above St. Louis; mouth of Wabash on the Ohio, 130 miles from the Mississippi; Cincinnati, on the Ohio, 550 miles from Mississippi; Portsmouth, on the Ohio, 589 miles from Mississippi; mouth of the Hocking, on the Ohio, 756 miles from Mississippi; Marietta, on the Ohio, 783 miles from Mississippi; at mouth Little Beaver, on Ohio, 924 miles from Mississippi.

In addition to these numerous canals, there is a rail-road in partial completion from St. Joseph's, on Lake Michigan, to Detroit, 200 miles long. The Mad River and Erie road extends from Sandusky on the lake to Dayton, Ohio. The connection of this road with the Little Miami at Springfield, completes the line from Cincinnati to Sandusky.

The great Erie Canal connects Buffalo on Lake Erie with Albany on the Hudson, and is 363 miles long, etc. There are several branches. The branch from Syracuse to Oswego on Lake Ontario; the Black River Canal; the Champlain Canal, to Whitehall, at the head of Lake Champlain, 65 miles long. Thus is the Hudson River at Albany connected by this canal and its tributaries, with Lakes Erie, Ontario, and Champlain. The canal also connects with the Atlantic by the Chenango Canal from Utica to the Susquehanna, and thence by Pennsylvania canals, or from Rochester, by the Genesee Valley Canal, to the head of boat navigation on the Alleghany River, and thence to the Mississippi.

From Montezuma, on the Erie Canal, 205 miles west of Albany, there is a connection with Philadelphia by the Seneca Lake and Canal, Chemung Canal, Williamsport Railroad, 73 miles, Susquehanna Canal, Harrisburg, etc., rail-roads, 107 miles. Total distance, 360 miles.

From the Erie Canal at Montezuma, there is a connection with Baltimore by the Cayuga Lake, by the Ithaca and Oswego Rail-road, by the river Susquehanna, thence by rail-road or water, etc., to Baltimore.

A rail-road is now in operation from Buffalo

to Albany, from Albany to Boston, and also to New-York. The Philadelphia and Pittsburg Rail-road connects the Atlantic with the Ohio, and of course with the lakes. It consists of

The Columbia Rail-road to Harrisburg on Susquehanna	82	miles.
Centre Division Pennsylvania Canal	172	"
Rail-road from Hollidaysburg to Johnstown	36	"
Western Division Pennsylvania Canal	104	"
Total	394	"

In reference to the application of the commercial means of the lakes to the purposes of defence, Col. Abert calculates the present commercial marine of the upper lakes, is adequate to supply, without injury to the commerce of a state of war, as an auxiliary to a national fleet, means of transporting ten thousand men and all their supplies—means of creating, at short notice, ten heavily-armed steamers, and of furnishing 1,500 mariners. Though, in cases of emergency, the whole commercial marine of the upper lakes could be make tributary to their defence.

In regard to the lower lakes, or those below the Falls of Niagara, it may be remarked, that the British have greatly the preponderance on Lake Ontario, our mariners there being 1,300 available for war, four heavily armed steamers, and 15,000 tons shipping. On Champlain, however, the American power is supreme. The dimensions of the Welland Canal are not such as will admit the naval supremacy of the British on Ontario to be felt on the upper lakes. Their force is as follows, compared with ours:

BRITISH MARINE ON LAKE ONTARIO.

57 steamers, averaging	200	tons.
6 lake propellers	300	"
7 river "	75	"
2 ships averaging	500	"
6 brigantines, "	150	"
94 schooners, "	150	"
300 barges, "	40	"
30 small craft, "	20	"

AMERICAN MARINE, LAKE ONTARIO.

8 steamers, averaging	277	tons.
10 propellers, "	275	"
204 sailing vessels, averaging	114	"

By means of locking the St. Lawrence, heavy-armed steamers can be passed into the Lake from Montreal; and although the Welland Canal will not admit large armed vessels, every supply from the St. Lawrence may be dispatched to the upper lakes through it.

The entire line of lake coast is about 5,000 miles, 2,000 of which are the coast of a foreign power.

CAPACITY OF LAKES.

	Length.	Greatest Width.	Average Width.
Lake Champlain	105	12	8
Lake Ontario	180	52	40
Lake Erie	240	57	38
Lake St. Clair	18	25	12
Lake Huron	270	105	70
Lake Michigan	340	83	58
Lake Superior	420	135	100

In the greatest width of Lake Huron, is not included the extensive Bay of Georgian, 120 miles long, and 45 miles wide on the average.

These lakes are connected throughout. Champlain with Ontario by the river Richelieu, the lock and dam navigation of St. Lawrence, the river Ottowa, the Rideau Canal through Canada, and the Champlain and Erie canals of New-York. Ontario is connected with Erie by Welland Canal and Oswego and Erie canals, through New-York; Erie with St. Clair by navigable and deep Strait of Detroit; St. Clair with Huron by navigable Strait of St. Clair; Huron with Michigan by Strait of Mackinaw, and with Superior by Strait of St. Mary. Some slight obstructions remain to be removed.

Lake Champlain lies almost exclusively in New-York and Vermont, and government has been at most expense upon the harbors of Burlington and Plattsburg.

Lake Ontario.—Its ports are Sackett's Harbor, used in the last war as a naval depot; Port Ontario, Oswego, Little Sodus Bay, Big Sodus, Harbor of Genesee, Oak Orchard, etc., being nine good harbors, all requiring, however, work of improvement. "The whole of this coast being a southern coast, is exposed to the violence of the prevailing northern winds, and in consequence requires whatever protection can obtain."

Lake Erie.—On the New-York coast of this lake are Black Rock, Buffalo, Cattaraugus, Dunkirk and Portland harbors. Buffalo is the greatest of all, and has a commerce of $60,-000,000 or $70,000,000. On the Pennsylvania coast is Erie Harbor, of great capacity, which caused it to be adopted in 1812, as a principal naval station. It is now the principal place of outfit for naval vessels, and winter quarters. The Ohio coast of Erie includes Conneaut, Ashtabula, Grand River, Cleveland, Black River, Vermilion, Huron, Cunningham Creek, Sandusky Bay, of which Cleveland and Sandusky are the most important in point of trade, and are rapidly advancing. The Michigan coast includes Monroe and Toledo, which last, though used by Michigan, is in the state of Ohio. Upon all of these harbors, works have been in progress by the government.

Lake Michigan has 320 miles of coast in Wisconsin, 560 miles in Michigan, 40 miles in Indiana, and 60 miles in Illinois. There are three good harbors in Michigan; one in Indiana, Michigan City; three in Illinois, of which Chicago is chief; several in Wisconsin, of which Milwaukie is most important. Besides all this coast, there are several hundred miles of coast, of which but little is known, and which is known as the upper peninsula of the State of Michigan.

With these remarks we dismiss the subject, regretting that the most clear and explicit information has in so few instances been obtained; and with a confiding hope, that the labors begun by Mr. Burke, the late Commissioner of Patents, in collecting the statistics of our internal trade, will be continued by the home department, and that the states themselves will soon establish bureaux of statistics in connection with their several governments. As we obtain information from time to time upon these subjects, it shall be furnished to our readers in De Bow's Commercial Review.

LAKE COMMERCE OF UNITED STATES—1851.

Lake Erie. Names of Ports	Imports	Exports	Total value of Exports and Imports
Buffalo	$22,143,404	$37,996,658	$60,140,062
Silver Creek	212,819	107,081	312,905
Barcelona	217,789	121,394	339,183
Dunkirk	903,341	486,398	1,389,734
Erie	1,300,897	2,531,955	382,833
Conneaut	389,050	240,405	599,455
Ashtabula	307,757	421,007	729,665
Fairport	343,658	450,850	794,508
Cleveland	7,030,957	6,855,556	13,886,513
Black River	203,345	154,529	557,845
Vermilion	150,000	207,200	357,200
Huron	469,807	790,201	1,260,089
Sandusky	7,010,304	3,099,939	10,110,048
Lower Sandusky	189,163	108,300	297,463
Port Clinton	38,978	24,755	63,733
Kelley's Island	7,852,021	11,679	11,679
Toledo	1,050,915	5,263,464	13,115,486
Monroe	3,502,660	812,105	4,863,023
Brest	~~13,495~~	18,956	18,956
Gibraltar	54,043	13,816	13,816
Detroit	~~7,325~~	2,781,192	6,283,858
Lake and River St. Clair.			
Algonac	13,495	198,793	212,288
St. Clair	51,043	71,524	132,567
Trenton	7,325	25,553	32,878
Mount Clemens	84,000	187,790	271,790
Lake Huron.			
Sault St Marie	151,134	340,800	491,934
Mackinac	143,400	212,818	356,218
Lake Michigan.			
Green Bay	151,537	80,830	232,367
Manitowoc	49,129	13,719	62,848
Sheboygan	571,800	12,191	583,991
Port Washington	278,311	48,267	326,579
Milwaukie	3,828,650	2,098,469	5,927,119
Racine	1,452,750	650,950	2,103,700
Southport	629,791	583,608	1,213,399
Waukegan	69,081	283,107	352,188
St. Joseph's	672,892	543,894	1,216,787
Michigan City	28,915	369,168	398,083
Chicago	7,751,872	4,151,905	11,903,777

Lake Erie Districts.

District		
Buffalo Creek District—	Tonnage	44,744 49 cwt
	Value tonnage	$722,400
Presque Isle "	Tonnage	7,419 27
	Value	$328,000
Cuyahoga "	Tonnage	22,047 30
	Value	$936,640
Miami "	Tonnage	2,920 00
	Value	$94,000
Sandusky "	Tonnage	8,366 80
	Value	$379,335
Detroit "	Tonnage	34,067 19
	Value	$1,847,710

Total value of exports and imports.............$115,785,048
Value of tonnage in aggregate.............5,308,083

Lake and River St. Clair.

Mt. Clemens District—Tonnage...... —
Value......... —

Total value of exports and imports........... $639,524
Value of tonnage in aggregate........... —

Lake Huron.

District of Mackinac—Tonnage.......1,919 77 cwt.
Value...........$75,000

Total value of exports and imports...........$848,152
Total value of tonnage in aggregate........... 75,000

Lake Michigan.

Chicago District—Tonnage..........15,890 86 cwt.
Value...........$564,435

Total value of exports and imports........... $24,320,481
Value of tonnage in aggregate........... 564,435

RECAPITULATION.

Aggregate value of exports..............$72,341,612
" " imports............. 69,251,955

Total value of exports and imports on all lakes..........$141,593,567
Aggregate tonnage on all lakes......... 137,466
" value of tonnage on lakes.... 5,647,520

The foregoing figures are for the lakes enumerated, exclusive of Lake Champlain, Superior and Ontario. The returns for the latter I must present you in a consolidated form, as follows:

	Valuation
Lake Superior—exports and imports...	—
Lake Ontario " "	$28,141,000
Lake Champlain " "	16,750,700
	$44,891,700
Add lakes previously enumerated........	141,593.567
	$186,485,267

Thus it appeared that the aggregate valuation of the lake trade of the United States amounts to the enormous sum of $186,485,-267, or more by $40,000,000 than the whole foreign export trade of the country.

Add also the tonnage of Lake Superior......	—
" " " Ontario.......	60,829
" " " Champlain....	4,746
With the previously given.....................	137,466
And we have.....................................	203,041

as the aggregate tonnage employed on the lakes of the United States, of which 35,904 tons are foreign. To the valuation of the tonnage on the previous lakes append, for Lakes Superior, Champlain and Ontario, and we have the subjoined summary of aggregates:

Export and import trade of the lakes...		$186,485,267
Value of American tonnage ..	$7,251,247	
Value of passenger trade..............		1,000,000
Gross aggregate........................		$187,485,267

TONS.

Tonnage	American.........167,137	Foreign.......... 35,904	203,041 tons.
Hands employed in the American trade......			10,907
Steam tonnage..............................			61,701
Sailing "			105,904

I will endeavor to give you the Western River trade in full in my next. Meanwhile I furnish you with the aggregates:

	1840.
Net valuation of the commerce of the Western rivers......................	$256,233,820
Value of vessels.......................	18,661,500
Number of hands employed on craft....	35,047

RECAPITULATION.

Gross* valuation of lake commerce......	283,187,134
Western rivers..........................	512,467,640
Aggregate valuation of internal commerce of the U. States................	795,654,774

LOUISVILLE COMMERCE.—In answer to your inquiries as to the imports and exports of Louisville, the following statement is submitted as the best statement I can procure, as no records have been kept other than our import tables. We have neither a Merchants' Exchange nor a Chamber of Commerce to regulate these matters. The receipts annnexed are chiefly by the river, and the total imports into Louisville will of course exceed these amounts.

IMPORTS FOR THE YEAR 1850.

Sugar—hhds..................................	13,320
" bbls....................................	9,200
" boxes...................................	755
Molasses (plantation)—bbls..................	13,010
Coffee—bags..................................	34,572
Rice—tierces.................................	752
Bagging—pieces...............................	65,250
Rope—coils...................................	56,300
Twine—bales..................................	2,056
Hemp—bales...................................	15,354
Cotton—bales.................................	7,857
Cheese—boxes.................................	20,378
Flour—bbls...................................	75,350
Whiskey—bbls.................................	39,897
Liquors and Wines—casks, &c..................	5,988
Nails—kegs...................................	45,261
Tobacco—hhds.................................	7,425
" boxes..................................	6,530
Salt—Kanawha, bbls...........................	112,250
" Turks Islands, bags.....................	40,525
" Liverpool, bags.........................	10,350
Merchandise—boxes, bales, and packages...	105,750
Drugs, dyes, &c., &c.—packages...............	14,378
Hides—doz....................................	18,891
Merchandise--crates and casks................	5,132
Hogs—number slaughtered for packing......	197,750
Pork—bbls. by packers........................	75,500

In addition to this quantity of pork, there are annually received thousands of tons of bacon by wagons, &c., which is packed by our merchants into casks, and large quantities exported.

The imports of Kanawha salt in 1849 were 95,000 barrels. In addition to the receipts of this year, there were 23,500 sent on to St. Louis.

In the article of flour this exhibit falls far short of the actual receipts, as there are six large flouring mills in the city and environs, the product of which is not included in the receipts. The same remarks are applicable to various other articles, including baggage and rope.

The exports of Louisville cannot be accurately estimated, as no record whatever has been made. The tonnage of this district is a fair guarantee of the exports. There are at least ten boats leaving this port daily, and we have some six or seven daily packets, all of which are well patronized in freight and passengers.

For several years past the river has not been entirely obstructed by ice for a greater length of time than two or three weeks altogether. During some three months of every year, navigation has been much restricted by low water, which has enhanced freights, and been considerable annoyance and loss to our merchants, but to what extent I cannot calculate.

* The net valuation is assumed as half the gross valuation, for what are the exports of one place are the imports of another.

APPENDIX.

AGRICULTURAL STATISTICS, U. S.—We are informed by J. C. Kennedy, Superintendent of the Census Office, that the agricultural returns which he was good enough to furnish for the present volume, in anticipation of their publication by Congress, do not include the number of horses, mules, &c., in the cities and towns, as they were not embraced in the schedules.

BOSTON—EXPANSION OF.—A peninsula less than one square mile in extent was soon found insufficient for Boston; and the state annexed to her Dorchester Point, a peninsula containing six hundred acres. To this she is wedded by four bridges. At a later period, ferries were established to Noddle's Island, an area of hundred acres, and this island now forms a ward of the city. Some hundred acres have also been reclaimed from the sea; but these narrow limits, less than two miles square, prove entirely inadequate, and have been long exceeded.

The population of Boston, outside of her chartered limits, already equals the population within. We should do injustice to Boston, were we to confine her to such narrow bounds, or within such arbitrary lines. Her true limits as a commercial metropolis are those marked out by her business men for their stores, piers, shops, and dwellings—the space occupied by those who resort daily to her banks and warehouses, or meet at her exchange. How is it with her sister cities? Philadelphia, by the last census, embraced within her chartered limits less than half her inhabitants; the residue were diffused through the extensive districts of Spring Garden, Moyamensing, and Northern Liberties. She virtually extends, under different charters, from Richmond, six miles down the Delaware.

New-York reaches fourteen miles from King's Bridge to the Battery.

New-Orleans embraces three distinct municipalities, on the crescent of the Mississippi.—[Now one government.—ED.]

London, the queen of commerce, contains but six hundred acres, and less than one hundred and thirty thousand people in her chartered limits; but her streets stretch eight miles on the Thames. Within her metropolitan districts are eighteen square miles of buildings, and three millions of people.

Boston, with less scope than New-York, has, like New-Orleans, Philadelphia and London, overstept her sea-girt isles. She has attached herself to the main by one wide natural avenue, the Neck, paved and planted with trees; by one granite structure, the Western Avenue, a mile and a half in length; by six bridges, seven railways, and three ferries, one terminating in a railway. Seven railways branch into sixteen, and ten avenues divide into thirty within the first nine miles from her Exchange. These diverge like a fan, and on the streets thus made is found a large population under separate municipalities. As land rises in value, hotels, offices, and blocks of stores usurp the place of dwellings. The old residents, leaving the low and reclaimed land to foreign laborers, plant themselves in the suburbs. There they build tasteful houses, with flower plots and gardens; availing of the frequent omnibuses, or of special trains, run almost hourly, and commuting for passage at $20 to $40 a year, they reach their stores and offices in the morning, and at night sleep with their wives and children in the suburbs. No time is lost, for they read the morning and evening journals as they go and return. Some of the wards appropriate for stores thus rise in value, but diminish in population. The suburbs extend, and the commercial community grows in a widening semicircle.

Taxes of Boston.—The amount assessed for taxes has been as follows:

Years	Amount of Tax assessed*	Rate on $1.000	Property Assessed
1846	$931,998	$6 90	$141,839,600
1847	1,014,674	6 00	162,360,400
1848	1,131,821	6 50	167,728,000
1849	1,174,715	6 50	174,180,200
1850	1,236,030	6 80	179,525,000
1851†	1,350,000	7 00	187,000,000

Foreign Commerce of Boston.

Year	For. Arrivals	Imports	Exports
1846	2,090	21,284,800	8,245,524
1847	2,739	28,279,651	12,118,587
1848	3,009	23,388,475	10,001,819
1849	3,111	24,117,175	8,843,974
1850	2,885	29,909,376	9,332,306

Population of Boston.

	Population	Real Estate	Personal	Total
1845	114,366	81,991,400	53,957,300	135,978,700
1850	138,788	105,093,400	74,907,100	180,000,000

Miles of Rail-road in 1845	512
" " 1850	1,130

"The principal cause of the growth of Boston has undoubtedly been the construction of railways, and the establishment of a semi-monthly steam-line to Europe. These have given great facilities to her commerce, enlarged her market, attracted merchants, stimulated every branch of manufacture, created a demand for houses and stores, and advanced the value of real estate. September 30th, 1839, there were but one hundred and sixty-seven miles of railway radiating from Boston." In 1851, Boston is wedded to more than one thousand miles of railway in Massachusetts, more than eighteen hundred in the five other states of New-England, and six hundred and fifty more in New-York. "In all, three thousand miles. In September, 1839, her railway horizon was bounded by Salem, Bradford, Nashua, and Providence. It now encircles a web spreading over Massachusetts, and extends to the Kennebec, the St. Lawrence, and the Lakes. This great system of railways has been principally planned and directed by her sagacity. Boston invested largely in lines to the North, and in distant railways,—the Michigan Central, Mad River, Reading, and Wilmington; and she also expended five millions in an aqueduct, and as much more on factory cities. The aqueduct has been in operation three years. Her last investments promise to be remunerative, and will bring with them a strong current of trade from newly acquired territory. Railroads have become the great interest of Boston, and her investment in them exceeds fifty millions of dollars.

CHARLESTON COMMERCE, 1851–52.

Receipts cotton year ending 31 Aug.		457,254 bales.
" Sea Island	"	19,379 "
Exported to G. Britain	"	207,220 "
" France	"	43,950 "
" other foreign	"	38,265 "
" northern ports	"	202,910 "
Rice—received to Sept. 1852		137,497 trcs.

---

* The amount of tax assessed includes the Poll Tax.

† Approximately.

CINCINNATI—EXPORTS FOR YEAR ENDING AUGUST 31, 1852.

Articles	'51-'52	Articles	'51-'52
Apples..... bbls.	7223	Lard oils....bbls.	24830
Alcohol..........	7607	Linseed oil..	9377
Beef.............	20015	Molasses.......	48866
Do.........tcs..	9023	Oil Cake.... tons	1601
Beans ......bbls.	1611	Oats.........sks.	2718
Brooms......doz.	7934	Potatoes.... bbls.	23844
Butter.......bbls.	3006	Prk.&bacon,hhds.	43933
Do. firks. & kegs	31395	Do..........tcs..	34398
Bran, &c...sks..	10543	Do..........bbls.	131560
Bagging.....pcs..	12918	Do. in bulk..lbs.	3912943
Corn........sks..	51231	Pork.........bxs.	2372
Corn meal.. bbls.	928	Rope, &c...pkgs.	9365
Cheese......csks.	71	Soap........bxs.	28033
Do...... .bxs..	150689	Sheep.......head.	45
Candles..........	121727	Sugar.... ..hhds.	20360
Cattle.......head	1840	Salt.........bbls.	27022
Cotton......bales	8810	Do.........sks.	16314
Coffee.......sks.	43654	Seed, flax...bbls.	3520
Cooperage...pcs.	64279	Sundry mdz.pkgs	656793
Eggs........bbls.	9160	Do. mdze...tons.	11241
Flour......	408211	Do. liquors.bbls.	49348
Feathers.....sks.	7876	Do. manf's..pcs.	66200
Fruit, dried.bush.	6413	Do. pr'dce.pkgs.	42333
Grease......bbls.	4732	Starch ...... bxs.	18293
Grass seed.......	7587	Tallow...........	3039
Horses......head	944	Tobacco,kgs&bxs	24761
Hay.... ....bales	554	Do........hhds.	10821
Hemp	3616	Do........bales.	629
Hides.......lbs..	142823	Vinegar.....bbls.	5965
Hides.......No..	31775	Whiskey....bbls.	276124
Iron.........pcs..	172409	Wool.......bales.	3404
Do....... .bdls.	36368	Do..........lbs.	2972
Do....... ..tons.	11329	White lead...kgs.	65514
Lard........bbls.	47862	Pieces castings..	33942
Do.........kgs.	115845	Do........tons.	1629

CANADA IN 1852—THE HISTORY, CONDITION, AND RESOURCES OF—EXTENT OF THE COUNTRY—EARLY HISTORY UNDER THE FRENCH—THE PROVINCE UNDER THE RULE OF THE ENGLISH—CANADA UNDER "RESPONSIBLE GOVERNMENT"—GEOGRAPHICAL DIVISIONS, CLIMATE AND SOIL—ANIMALS AND NATURAL PRODUCTIONS—AMOUNT AND CHARACTER OF THE POPULATION—AGRICULTURE—MANUFACTURES AND SHIPPING—EXPORTS AND IMPORTS—INTERNAL IMPROVEMENTS—REVENUE AND PUBLIC DEBTS—BANKS—EDUCATION, ETC.—The British possessions on this continent constitute about one-third of North America: occupying an area of some 2,300,000 square miles, a space two-thirds as large as that covered by the whole of Europe. These territories lie immediately north of the United States, including eastwardly the islands of Newfoundland and Breton on the Atlantic coast, and extending on the west to the possessions of Russia. This immense area is divided into five provinces, Newfoundland, New-Brunswick, Nova Scotia, Canada, and New-Britain; of which Canada, the second in size, is, and probably always will be, the first in importance. It contains about 350,000 square miles, and is bounded on the north by a range of hills, which separates it from the territory of the Hudson's Bay Company; on the east, by Labrador, the Gulf of St. Lawrence, and New-Brunswick; on the south, by the United States; and on the west, by Lake Superior, and a line running northwardly from this lake to Hudson's Bay. It may be represented in general terms as lying between the meridians of 57° 50′ and 90° west, and the parallels of 42° and 52° north, and stretching about 1,300 miles from east to west, and from 300 to 700 from north to south.

Early History under the French.—Five hundred years before Columbus reached the western world, America was discovered by *Biorn Heriolson*, a native of Iceland; and from this time, (1001,) during two centuries, repeated visits were made to its northern coasts by Scandinavian voyagers. Civilized Europe, however, knew not of the discovery. After the expiration of that period, these Scandinavian voyages ceased, and thenceforth North America was visited by no European until the 24th of June, 1497, when John Cabot, an enterprising navigator of Venice, then in the employ of Henry VII. of England, discovered the coast of Labrador. Soon afterwards, in 1500, Gaspar Cortereal, a Portuguese, discovered the Gulf of St. Lawrence; of which Jean Denys, a Frenchman, prepared a map in 1506. France began now to take an interest in the new world; and under the patronage of its king, Francis I., Verazzano, a Florentine, surveyed (1523–24) nearly all the eastern coast of North America. In April, 1534, the same monarch sent out *Jacques Cartier* with a colony to make a settlement in the unexplored coast. In July following he entered the Gulf of St. Lawrence, and in the same month formally took possession of the country in the name of the French king. No settlement, however, was then made; yet this was the beginning of the French rule in the province of Canada. In October of the following year, Cartier ascended the St. Lawrence as far as the Indian village of Hochelaga, the site of the present city of Montreal; and here, for the first time, a European heard, from the natives, of the great lakes and of the mighty Mississippi. The contests of Francis I. with Charles V., of Germany, and the civil wars which desolated France during the latter half of the 16th century, put an effectual stop to all efforts on the part of that kingdom to effect a settlement in Canada, or to prosecute its discoveries in America. But the spirit of enterprise was again revived under the sway of Henry IV.; and again Canada was sought by French adventurers. Trading companies and private individuals, eager for gain, fitted out expeditions for carrying on the fur trade; and this was prosecuted with success. Efforts were now made to establish trading posts; and on the 3d of July, 1608, *Samuel de Champlain*, the lieutenant of Sieur de Monts, arrived at the site of Quebec, where he at once determined to lay the foundation of the French empire in the west. Such was the origin of *New France*, for so the settlement was afterwards designated by its original founders. Twelve years subsequently the Pilgrims made their landing at Plymouth.

The origin of the appellation *Canada* is a subject of dispute. Some derive it from the Spanish "*aca nada*"—*here is nothing;* in which they follow an old Castilian tradition; according to which the Spanish visited the country before the French, and finding no mines, as they had hoped, in their disappointment uttered this exclamation. The natives having caught the sound, repeated it to the next Europeans who arrived; and they took it to be the proper Indian appellation of the country. The derivation is evidently fanciful. Other explanations of the term equally improbable are given by historians. The most likely derivation is that adduced by Charlevoix in his *Histoire de la Nouvelle France*, (vol. 1., p. 13, note,) who says: "D'autres dérivent ce nom du mot Iroquois '*Kannata*,' qui se prononce *Canna da*, et signifie *un amas de cabanes*." The word meant, then, in the Indian tongue, *a collection of cabins*, i. e., *a village;* and it is so used in Brandt's translation of Matthew's Gospel into the Mohawk language. The early discoverers hearing the term frequently employed by the natives, naturally thought it the name of the country; though it is not likely that at this early period Canada was distinguished by any general appellation.

After the founding of Quebec, the French applied themselves to extending their knowledge of the country in which they had effected a settlement. The main objects of those who controlled the infant colony, were trade with the natives and their conversion to the Christian faith. The cultivation of the earth was not only considered of secondary importance, but was attended to only so far as was necessary to the supply of the immediate wants of the settlers. Nor in these respects did there afterwards take place any material change in the policy and habits of the colony, until it passed, in the following century, from the hands of the French to the rule of the English. From the first, Jesuit missionaries were engaged in propagating the Catholic religion among the Indians of Canada; and they received much aid and sympathy in their undertaking from the pious and charitable of their native land. Alone, or in pairs, agreeably to the directions given by Christ to the Seventy, they traversed the lone wilderness bearing with them the tidings of salvation. In 1634, two priests of this order made a settlement on the shores of Lake Huron; and, in 1641, others had advanced as far as the Falls of St. Mary. Meanwhile, the Jesuit influence had been increasing in Quebec. A college was founded in that city in 1635 by De Rohaut, and placed under their control; and soon after, an Ursuline convent was established, and a hospital for the sick and poor, both of which were under Catholic direction. In a few years the exercise of any religion but the Catholic was prohibited by law. As early as 1665, a house of worship was erected by Father Allonez, near the west end of Lake Superior; and here he preached to the Indians in the Algonquin tongue.

What success these missionaries met with in a religious point of view, cannot be readily determined. It is certain, however, that they acquired great influence among the natives by their prudent and conciliatory conduct; and to this influence are attributable in no small degree, it is thought, the ravages which were made by hostile Indians during the first part of the 18th century upon the people and territory of New-England. The policy of the Jesuits, therefore, was political as well as religious. They were influential, accordingly, in persuading the native tribes to acknowledge the supremacy of the French monarch. In 1671, a large number of chiefs from the sources of the Mississippi, Red River and St. Lawrence, met the deputies of the king at the Falls of St. Mary, and, by common consent, placed themselves and their people under his protection. Seeking to extend their dominions still farther, the French government commissioned Marquette and Joliet, in 1673, to discover the Mississippi. How they did so, and what adventures they met with in their descent of that river as far as the mouth of the Arkansas, has been often told with eloquent pen. Somewhat later, the French found their way by sea to the mouth of the river; and on this discovery, and the exploration of Marquette, was founded the claim which they subsequently urged to the valleys of the Mississippi and Ohio, and all the territory lying to the northwest of that region.

For nearly one hundred years after the discovery of the Mississippi, there occurred no change of importance either in the political or social affairs of Canada. The Indians, who had been at first annoying, were at length conciliated, and united with the French against the colonists from England. Few immigrants came over from France; whilst those who were already settled in the country were occupied either as missionaries, in hunting, in fishing, or in the cultivation of small feudal farms. From these farms their occupants derived just enough to afford them subsistence. There was little prospect of advantage held out to emigrants from the mother country. The land of the province was granted to subjects by the king upon feudal tenure, as was customary in Europe at the time of the discovery of Canada. Tracts of land of all sizes, from one square mile to one hundred or more, were conferred by the king on private individuals, and these were styled seigniories. The seigniors were bound to concede land to immigrants, on application, on condition that they would pay a small rent and perform certain feudal duties and services. On the tenant's death, his children inherited his land in equal shares, subject to the same conditions; and so, when the seignior, or lord, deceased, his territories descended to his children, one-half to his eldest son, while the other half was distributed in equal shares between him and his brothers and sisters. A seigniory might be sold; but the king was entitled to one-fifth of its price, one-third of which, however, was relinquished in case of immediate payment. Besides the lands thus owned, there were others which constituted endowments for the established Catholic Church; and yet these were reserved for state purposes. All the grants of land made in Canada, while it continued a French province, were made upon this uniform plan; and the system was, very unfortunately, maintained among the French population even after the conquest by the British. The influence of this feudal tenure was highly injurious to the prosperity of the colony, for it operated, among the French settlers, as a check upon industry and enterprise. Since that conquest, however, the new lands granted have not been given upon this plan, but a clear title has been made to the purchaser. It has happened, consequently, that the portion of the territory which has been settled since the transference of the province to England, has advanced much more rapidly than the other in prosperity and internal improvement. Public opinion has long been opposed to these feudal tenures; and such as now exist will, no doubt, at an early period, be superseded by titles more in accordance with the progressive ideas of the age.

The Province under the rule of the English.—From the beginning of the 18th century the French and English colonies in America struggled for pre-eminence in North America, as their parent nations were doing on the battle-fields of Europe. English villages were attacked and destroyed by the Canadians and their allies the Indians, and these acts were retaliated in kind by the English colonists. Mutual invasions were made with various success, until, finally, on the 14th of September, 1759, Quebec was taken by the British under General Wolfe. In September of the following year, the surrender of Montreal completed the subjugation of Canada, and the whole territory was formally ceded to England in 1763, by the treaty of Paris. Such was the end of the French domination in the northern part of North America. During the continuance of her power, France had ruled the province with maternal sway. Her resources and treasures were spent upon the colony, and her best officers were sent out to administer the government. Yet was she unsuccessful in developing the hidden resources of the country; for she had adopted a policy which, though kind and in many respects beneficial, was upon the whole unfitted for drawing out the strength of an infant colony. Military governments were fixed at Montreal, at Three Rivers, and at Quebec, upon which, subject to the control of the French minister of marine, devolved the administration, civil as well as military, of the province. A governor and an intendant were the heads of the government. Free admission was granted to colonists from every country; a policy more liberal than that adopted by other European states, which then controlled settlements in America. Commerce, however, was fettered, because it was confined to chartered monopolies. Popular rights, too, were wholly unacknowledged. All power was centred in the government. The state was all, the people nothing; and hence, when the state fell, the people passed without a murmur from the power of France to the control of her hereditary enemy.

From the time of the conquest until 1774, Canada was ruled by an English governor and council, with *English law*, administered solely in the *English language*; but from 1774 to 1791 the province was governed by the same functionaries, administering English *criminal* but French *civil* law. In 1791, owing to troubles experienced in carrying on the government, Canada was divided by the so-called Constitution Act (31st Geo. III., c. 31) into two provinces, Upper and Lower. A similar form of government was established in each, but its administrations differed in some particulars. In the upper province, where the English colonists were most numerous, the new constitution worked well, and was not specially complained of until a comparatively late period in its history. In the lower province, however, where the French settlers were stronger than the English, the new arrangement was a source of disquiet and turmoil from its first institution. The government was composed, according to the act of parliament, of a governor, and an executive council of eleven members appointed by the crown; a legislative council, consisting of 15 members, (afterwards raised to 40,) also appointed by the crown; and an assembly, or house of commons, composed of 50 members, (subsequently increased to 88,) elected by the people of the province upon the basis of population. At the first meeting of the assembly, (Dec. 17, 1792,) it was found that 35 of its members were French and only 15 English, a minority which was, at a later period reduced to *three*. Of course, French influence was predominant in the assembly. The other two estates, however, were thoroughly English. Hence arose, almost from the outset, a most violent contention between the different branches of the legislature, the council striving to retain the power with which it had been vested by parliament, and the assembly straining every nerve to circumscribe the privileges of the council and governor, and make itself independent of their control. It would be tedious to trace the progress of this struggle from its commencement to the catastrophe in 1837, when Lower Canada broke out into rebellion. Suffice it to say, that the assembly obtained by degrees some of the powers which had been granted to the other estates of the government, and from time to time had its demands for increased privileges complied with by the mother country, and always with apparent readiness and liberality. Finally, however, tired of concession, the home government refused to yield any further to the increasingly clamorous, and, in some respects, unreasonable demands of the assembly. To have yielded would have been in effect to have surrendered the whole government of the province; a step which England was not prepared to take, and which, considering the limited education of the French Canadians, and their general want of preparation for self-government, and considering also the equitable rights of the English colonists who (or their ancestors) had settled in the province under the distinct assurance of being ruled *according to the laws of England*—would not, all things taken into account, have been either prudent or just The assembly refusing, during several years, to make appropriation for administering the government, and persisting to do so after repeated remonstrances from the mother country, the English parliament passed resolutions providing for the current civil expenses independent of and contrary to the action of that branch of the provincial legislature. Rebellion followed; but in a short time it was put down by military force, the power of England triumphing in the contest.

There can be no question that England, when matters had reached the crisis just noticed, followed the only course which could have preserved her dominion over Lower Canada; yet it is equally certain that all the troubles which for so many years agitated that province, were due to the unwise act passed by the British parliament of 1791, by which a representative assembly was established. The act was unwise in the first place, because, if the province was to be preserved as a British possession, it should have been ruled by English laws and in the English language, in order that the French and English inhabitants might, in time, have become a united and homogeneous people. The consequence of the course which was followed was inevitable; the two races by which the colony was inhabited, having no powerful bond of union, were kept by the force of previous prejudices distinct from, and hostile to each other, as they are to the present day. It was unwise, furthermore, because it was impossible that an assembly chosen by a people, the great majority of whom were French by descent, by habits and by education, could act for any length of time, or on any important subject, in harmony with a legislative council composed mainly of English settlers and nominated by the crown. It was unwise, finally, because the French Canadians had no experience in the art of self-government, and were at that time, if they are not now, unfitted for so important a trust. "They were, without doubt," says Halliburton, the most ignorant inhabitants of any portion of America; but few of them could either read or write. They were even unacquainted with the common operations of husbandry, preferring the listless idleness engendered by a fertile soil, that yielded its productions without the aid of art, to the laborious operations of the enterprising Anglo-Saxons. Accustomed to implicit obedience, they saved themselves the trouble of thinking, and yielded their judgment to their leaders and their conscience to their priests. Yet to such a people was entrusted the power not only of making laws, but of governing the English. The experience of all ages was against the experiment." Nor was "the experience of all ages" fallacious in this instance. The French, though ruled with a more than paternal sway, became more and more dissatisfied with the home government, and, as each demand was complied with by the parliament, and each alleged grievance redressed, became more and more clamorous for still further concessions. Warned by her experience in the case of the United States, England treated Canada with more mildness than any other colony had up to that time experienced, resigning the right of taxation, (1788,) though compelled to contribute of her own means to the support of the province, and leaving all its internal affairs, commerce excepted, to the regulation of the provincial legislature. Complaints were listened to with respect by the British parliament, and honest efforts made to remove every cause of dissatisfaction, real or imaginary; and it was only when the whole machinery of government was thrown into disorder, and its movements stopped by the provincial assembly, that the parliament interposed to save the country from anarchy and civil war.

The rebellion which had been partially communicated to Upper Canada having been put down with little effort, the British parliament attempted anew the construction of a government. What the Canadians had failed to gain as malcontents, they now gained as rebels reduced to subjection. After various preliminary investigations and discussions, the two provinces of Canada were united in 1841, chiefly through the representations and influence of the viceroy, Lord Durham, into one government, under one legislature. By this *Act of Reunion*, as it is called, important changes were made in the constitution, and a "responsible government" introduced. The governor was deprived of the patronage which had pertained to his office under the old *régime*, and this patronage was transferred to the leader of the assembly, while the governor's veto was made of little or no effect; the legislative council was made "a mere duplicate of the assembly." and the laws passed by the provincial legislature thus constituted, were subjected no longer, as before, to a rigid examination in England before they received the sanction of the king, but only to a merely nominal surveillance. In a word, the legislature was made independent in all but the name. A government more democratic, in fact, than that of the United States, was established; while that admirable system of checks and balances which regulates our institutions had no counterpart in the new administration.

Canada under "Responsible Government."—Having gained the object for which they had for years been striving, or what was equivalent to it, the French party, which, of course, was predominant, under the working, and according to the provisions of the new constitution, ceased to fill the province with confusion and alarm. And now a singular and yet not an unnatural phenomenon occurred. The English settlers, who had previously been the staunchest loyalists, and had continued steadfast and unshrinking in their adherence to the mother country, began to murmur against the conduct of the home government. They asserted, and not without reason, that they were in effect not represented in the new legislature; for the majority of the French party was too overwhelming to allow of successful resistance, on their part, to any measure which their enemies might please to propose, or to any law they might please to enact. Before, they could appeal to the king or to the parliament; but now, they declared they had, though nominally free, no voice in managing the affairs of their country, and no means of redress when oppressed by the unjust and one-sided enactments of their political opponents. It was vain to appeal to the governor, for his veto was virtually powerless. To ask redress of the legislative council was equally vain, for it was but an echo of the assembly, and this latter body was under the control of the French representatives. Vain was it, finally, to appeal to the monarch or to parliament, for to such petitions one uniform answer was returned: "You have a responsible government; we cannot interfere. It is a local matter; you must settle it yourselves."

He knows but little of the science of political economy, who supposes that government is established for the good of the majority solely. It is founded for the greatest good, not of the greatest number, but *of all*—the minority as well as the majority. Unquestionably, when in a state it becomes necessary that some of its members should lie under disabilities, it is better, other things being equal, that the minority rather than the majority should suffer. But if the interests of all *can* be secured, and yet only those of the greater number *are* actually regarded, irrespective of the feelings and rights of the minority, then and there, call the state by what name you please, a monarchy or a democracy, you have a despotism. Situated as they were under the new constitution—a helpless minority ruled by an inconsiderate majority—the English residents despaired of obtaining a just influence in the management of their country's affairs. Thrown off, as they seemed to be, by the mother country, they looked elsewhere for support. No means of relieving themselves from French control appeared so likely to succeed, as the project which they, though loyalist before the Union, started a few years since, (1849,) and which was then discussed, as it is even now, with not a little feeling, as well by the press of this country as by that of Canada and England. The proposed plan is *the annexation of Canada to the United States.*

Among the Canadians, the idea of annexation to this country arose among, and first found favor with the English settlers; but the proposition is not countenanced by them alone. Their opponents, the French, entertain, it is ascertained, a similar wish, though of course their motives are different. They fear a threatened league of all the British North American provinces, which, if made, would deprive them of their power, and, rather than this, they would have annexation. Thus affairs stand in Canada, unsettled, and, to a strong though not the dominant party in the state, highly unsatisfactory. A change of some sort must come at no very distant day. England, it is probable, cannot, and, if the wishes of some of her statesmen be followed, *will not* long continue to exercise even the small remnant of authority which she has retained over the province. Whenever she withdraws her supervision, Canada will either form a separate and distinct government in North America, or it will become a constituent element of our Union. But, will England surrender her claims without a struggle? If she should do so, can Canada escape civil convulsion, in case she make the attempt to form herself into an independent power? If she should apply for entrance into this already overgrown confederacy, can she be received without endangering the whole framework; the very existence of our government? These, it will be seen, are momentous questions, and upon their correct solution may depend, before many years have passed away, the most momentous consequences.*

Geographical Divisions, Climate and Soil.—The province of Canada is now divided, geographically, into Canada East and Canada West, corresponding respectively to the Upper and Lower Canada of the period preceding the Union. Canada East is comprised between the parallels of 45° and 52° north, and between the meridians 59° 50′ and 80° 06′ west, and contains about 160,000,000 of acres. That part of it which lies east of the River Chaudiere and south of the St. Lawrence, is the least fertile of the whole, much of it being unfit for cultivation. That part, on the other hand, which lies west of the Chaudiere as far as St. Regis, is composed of excellent land, and, bordering as it does on the United States, is improving, and is being settled more rapidly than any part of the lower province. That large tract, moreover, which is situated north-west of Montreal and east of the Ottawa, (the western boundary of the province,) is said to be even more fertile. The climate of this division is colder than that of the western under the same parallel, the mercury sometimes falling in winter at Quebec to 30° below zero. The winter beginning in November, lasts five months, during which time the snow is usually four feet deep in the woods. When it does break up, the approach of summer is very rapid, and vegetation, commencing early, advances rapidly to perfection. All kinds of grain come to maturity, though the crops of most are not so abundant as they are in more southern climates. The common fruits are readily raised as high up as Quebec where, however, cold as the winters are, the thermometer sometimes rises in summer as high as 100° above zero.

Canada West is comprised between the parallels 41° and 49° north, and the meridian 74° and 117° west, and contains about 64,000,000 acres. The true period of the settlement of this province was 1783, at the close of the American war of independence, when a number of British loyalists from this country took refuge here, and had lands assigned them, on highly favorable terms, by the home government. In 1791, it was created, as has been seen, a separate province, at which time it contained, by computation, 10,000 inhabitants. York, now the flourishing city of Toronto, on Lake Ontario, was founded three years afterwards, and made the seat of government, and colonists from Great Britain were encouraged to come into the province and make a settlement. Emigration did not commence on a large scale till 1803, since which time it has continued to flow in without cessation, this division being naturally preferred by Englishmen to Canada East, in which French influence was predominant. In 1811, the province contained 9,623 persons who paid taxes, from which it is estimated that the entire population was then about eighty thousand. The climate is not so cold as in the eastern division, and the province contains both a larger extent of fertile land, as well as tracts more productive. Most of the soil equals the best lands of New-York and Ohio, and some of it is even superior. Near Toronto, 100 bushels of wheat have been raised upon a single acre. It is stated on good authority, that the lands lying between the lakes, of Huron on the one side, and Erie and Ontario on the other, are sufficiently productive to supply all Europe with grain, "besides producing cattle and sheep, hemp and flax, and yielding iron, copper, lead, lime, mar and gypsum; and that they are capable of support ing, by agricultural pursuits alone, at least five mil lions of additional inhabitants." Of this tract, and of the western district generally, a somewhat enthusiastic writer, speaking after personal examination, remarks: "In no portion of Canada could horticulture, floriculture, and agriculture, be prosecuted with more certainty of success than in it. Peaches, plums, pears, apples, melons, grapes, Indian corn, tobacco and vegetables of every description, grow in abundance, with a luxuriousness that is truly astonishing; and the day cannot be remote when such obvious advantages will attract attention."

Animals and Natural Productions.—Among wild animals found in Canada may be enumerated the elk, fallow deer, bear, wolf, fox, wild-cat, raccoon, beaver, marten, otter, hare, squirrel, and in the south the buffalo and the roebuck. Some of these, however, are being rapidly exterminated by hunters, and by the advance of civilization. Among birds are found wild ducks, geese, and other water-fowls, pigeons, the quail, partridge, turkey, and various kinds of grouse. Fish abound in the rivers and lakes, among which are the sturgeon, salmon and herring.

* An interesting article on the subject of Canadian Annexation appeared in De Bow's Review, Oct., 1850. It may be consulted with advantage, though the writer does not seem to have written from reliable information respecting the relation of the British to the French party in the lower province previous to the rebellion of 1837, nor to have been correctly informed as to the origin and cause of that melancholy outbreak.

Canada is covered with forests, among the trees growing in which are firs, pines, the white cedar, maple, birch, ash, bass wood, hickory, cherry and the oak. Among the smaller plants are found a kind of rice, called *zizania aquatica*, which grows in the swamps, ginseng, various species of wild berries, and the lily, violet, and other flowers. The live oak, which is produced in the southern part of the country, is said to be adapted to ship-building; but not the other kinds of the same tree which are found in Canada. Such trees as are useful for no other purpose supply material to the pot and pearl-ash manufactories. The maple tree (*acer saccharinum*) is abundant, and yields an excellent sugar, of which large quantities are yearly raised in the province. The sugar is obtained by inserting a small cane-shoot into an incision, made by an axe or with an auger, in the bark of the tree, in the spring, when the sap is rising; along which tube the sap is conducted, and from which it falls into a wooden trough placed beneath. The tree continues to flow about a month. The sap is boiled twice, during the last process being carefully skimmed and cleared from whatever impurities may rise to the surface. It is then left to cool, by which means it is formed into hard cakes, ready for use or for the market. The amount of maple sugar manufactured in Canada West in 1848, is stated to have been 4,160,667 lbs., or about six pounds to every inhabitant. Valued at the average market price, this year's production was worth more than $200,000.

Amount and Character of the Population.—Previous to the year 1760, all those who emigrated to Canada were of French origin, and they came principally from Normandy. In 1676, Canada East contained about 8,000 inhabitants; in 1700, 15,000; in 1714, 26,904; and in the year 1760, the year above mentioned, when the French immigration ceased, about 65,000. The census of 1784 gave 113,000; of 1825, 423,630; of 1831, 511,917; of 1844, 699,806; of 1848, 768,344, an increase in twenty-three years of 334,704; at which rate the population would be doubled in thirty years. The greater part of this increase was due to births alone, for there has been comparatively little immigration into this division of the province since the control of the country passed from the hands of France. In 1787, a number of English loyalists came in from the United States; and, at a subsequent period, there took place still further emigration from this country, particularly from Vermont. It is by these men that the resources of Canada East have been chiefly developed; they possess the best cultivated farms in the district, are owners of at least half of the more valuable seigniories, and are the main conductors of the retail trade, and of the internal and foreign commerce. The other, and much the larger portion of the inhabitants, are of French descent, and retain the habits and modes of thought of their ancestors. Neither the conquest, nor the time that has since elapsed, nor the example of their more enterprising fellow-citizens, has wrought any essential change in their character. They are, as a people, frugal, honest, industrious, and hospitable; cheerful in temperament, social and polite in their manners, but uneducated, tenacious of old customs, and unprogressive. There are but few of them who are wholly dependent on wages for their support; the most own small farms upon which they labor with the same kind of implements used by their ancestors a century ago. Only a few families own any large amount of property, and even then it is not very valuable. Yet the people live happy and contented, neither wanting nor abounding. Their religion is the Catholic, and the education which they receive is acquired under the direction of Catholics, the clergy among whom are supported by endowments and tithes granted before the conquest, and guarantied by express stipulation in the treaty then made between England and France.

In 1845, according to the census then taken, the Church of Rome included within its pale 571,714 of the population; the Episcopalians had 43,274; the Scotch Presbyterians, 26,725; other Presbyterians, 5,231; the Methodists, 15,853; the Baptists, 4,067.

The time of the settlement of Canada West, and its population in 1811, have already been mentioned. The number of inhabitants which it contained, in 1825, was 158,027; in 1835, 336,000; in 1848, 723,292; an increase in twenty-three years of 565,265, the population doubling itself once in about eleven years. Of this population 166,340 belonged to the Church of England; 119,810 to that of Rome; 148,182 were Scotch or other Presbyterians; 137,752 Methodists; 28,053 Baptists; 7,186 Lutherans; and 115,969 belonged to no denomination. One seventh of the ungranted lands in this district have been set apart for religious purposes, and are called "Clergy Reserves." The income thus arising is apportioned to the Church of England two-fifths; to the Church of Rome, that of Scotland and the Wesleyan Methodists, each one-fifth. Other sects are supported by their congregations, as the Church of England is in Canada East. Thus the joint population of the two districts amounted in 1848 to 1,491,626, or in round numbers, one and a half millions; of whom 600,000 are descendants of the French; 550,000 come from Great Britain; 250,000 from Ireland, 60,000 from the United States; and 60,000 from the Continent of Europe. If the relative rates of the increase of population in the two districts have continued unchanged up to the present time, Canada West has now a population of 859,000; Canada East of 840,000, making a total of 1,699,000. From this it would seem that the western province is now ahead of the eastern. At the same rate of increase, Canada West will contain, in 1862, 1,259,000; while Canada East will contain only 1,015,000. Indeed, taking into account the continued increase of immigration into the western province, it is highly probable that in the year 1862 it will have one million and a half of inhabitants, or about one-third more than Canada East.

Comparing the increase of the population in the two provinces of Canada during ten years with that of Great Britain and that of the United States, we have in Great Britain (1831–41) an increase of 1.11 per cent.; in the United States (1830–40) 3.26 per cent.; in Canada East (1834–44) 3.18 per cent.; in Canada West (1832–42) 8.61 per cent. The proportion of deaf and dumb among the inhabitants of Canada is about as one to 957, which is higher than anywhere else in the world where censuses have been taken, except in Switzerland and Baden. If we count lunatics and idiots, the proportion afflicted in this way added to those suffering under the other calamities just mentioned, is one in 370 against one in 533 in the United States. The causes of this phenomenon have not yet been discovered. The ratio of females to males in the two provinces is 88 to 100. The number of paupers in Canada East was, in 1831, one in 399; in 1844, one in 151—a strange and alarming increase. In Canada West there is only one pauper to every 1,469 inhabitants, against one to 318 in New-York in 1835. The number of colored persons settled in the province of Canada East up to 1845, only reached 261, of whom 140 were males and 120 females. Since that time, especially within the last two or three years, there has been a considerable augmentation of this class from the United States.

Agriculture.—In 1845, the amount of soil occupied in Canada was 7,540,450 acres; of which 3,083,949 were under cultivation. The amount of land surveyed in the eastern province up to 1845, was 17,685,942 acres, of which 3,928,100 were unappropriated; in the western, up to 1848, the amount surveyed was 15,902,006 acres, of which 1,597,123 were unappropriated. Vast quantities in both provinces are yet unsurveyed. The average price of this public domain was, in 1840, 11s. 2d. per acre for crown lands; 12s. 8d. for clergy reserves; and 12s. 6d. for school lands. The cultivated land is for the most part divided into small farms, which, where the feudal tenure does not operate, are almost always owned by those who reside on them; by whom, assisted sometimes by hired laborers, they are tilled. The condition, therefore, of the mass of the people is one of happiness and contentment. If great wealth is rarely concentrated upon a single individual, poverty, on the other hand, is but little known. The agriculturists are becoming every year more prosperous; and though they may not accumulate rapidly, they do it surely.

The amounts of agricultural and other kinds of property assessed in Canada West in 1825, was £2,256,874; in the year 1848 it had reached £8,567,001. During the same time, the number of acres under cultivation had increased from 535,212 to 2,673,820; of houses, from 8,876 to 42,957; and of horses, oxen, milch cows, and young cattle together, from 121,206 to 481,417. Thus, we perceive, Canada West, seventy years after its settlement, had 3¾ acres of ground under cultivation for every unit of its population; whereas New-York, it would seem, had, in 1835, two hundred and twenty-one years after its settlement, only 4½ acres to every unit of its population. The number of neat cattle and horses, possessed in 1848, was equal to one head for every one and three-quarters of the population; or, if we take another estimate of their number, which puts them down as 717,234 instead of 481,417, the ratio is very nearly as one to one; while New-York, in the same particular, only possesses one head to every unit of her population. The estimate made of the crop of Canada West for 1847, was, of wheat, 7,558,773; barley, 515,727; oats, 7,055,730 rye, 446,293; maize, 1,137,555; buckwheat, 432,573; peas, 1,753,846; potatoes, 4,751,331; the value of the whole of which was supposed to be about £2,676,285 currency. Taking the per centage, the quantity of each of these articles per inhabitant was, of wheat, 10·45 bushels; barley, 0·71; oats, 9·75; rye, 0·62; buckwheat 0·60; maize, 1·57; potatoes, 6·57; peas, 2·52. To oppose to this, we have in the United States for the same year, the following per centage: wheat, 5·50; barley, 0·28; oats, 8·09; rye, 1·42; buckwheat, 0·56; maize, 26·01; potatoes, 4·86. This estimate shows that Canada West raised in 1847 as much again of wheat as we did, in the ratio of population. She even outstripped our best wheat-producing states; for, in the same year, New-York raised only five bushels to each person; Virginia ten; Pennsylvania seven; Indiana eight; Ohio ten; while Canada West raised ten and a half. During the year 1848, there were produced in the province 2,339,756 lbs. of wool, an increase within six years of more than 50 per cent.; of tobacco, 1,865 lbs.; flax, 41,599; beef and pork, 99,251 barrels.

The statistics of Canada East are not so full nor so reliable as those of its sister province. In 1844, its whole produce in bushels amounted to 21,325,596, which is equal to 30 bushels for each unit of the population, a ratio about one-fourth less than that of Canada West for 1842. Taking into account the fact that the most of those who engage in the lumber trade are found in the lower province, and the additional fact that it contains the two largest cities in Canada, the disproportion between its agricultural products and those of the upper province is not so great as might have been expected. In 1831, there were raised here 3,404,756 bushels of wheat; in 1844, only 942,835, owing to the devastations of the wheat-fly which occurred at this period. Since that time, partly owing to the introduction of new seed-wheat, and partly from other causes, the crop has very materially increased. The produce of 1843 was, wheat, 914,909 bushels; barley, 1,221,710; rye, 310,458; oats, 6,668,933; peas, 1,428,303; maize, 143,947; buckwheat, 375,744; potatoes, 9,914,639; total, 21,365,913 bushels.

Manufactures and Shipping.—The statistics of manufactures in Canada are very imperfect, and are worthy of little reliance. There were in the country in 1848, 661 fulling and carding mills; 130 breweries; 174 distilleries; 389 tanneries; 1,740 asheries; 10 paper mills; 19 trip hammers; 14 oil mills; 9 nail factories; besides other less important factories and mills. There were produced in the same year, by factories in Canada West alone, 624,971 yards of fulled cloth; 71,715 of linen; and 1,295,172 of flannel. In 1846, the value of the various kinds of factories situated within the Home District and city of Toronto, in Canada West, was estimated at $1,613,875.

In shipping also, Canada is advancing. The lower province had in 1844 a tonnage of 55,448; of which 45,351 belonged to Quebec, and 10,097 to Montreal. The number of vessels employed was 569, worked by 3,146 men. The upper province had in 1838, 4,505 tons; in 1840, 8,630 tons. The shipping owned on Lake Ontario, and employed on the inland waters of Canada in 1845, was valued at $3,090,000. Steamers now go from Chicago, down the St. Lawrence to the ocean, without breaking bulk.

Exports and Imports.—The prosperity of Canada is shown by the consistent increase of its trade. In 1840, the exports amounted to $1,475,000; in 1850, $13,290,000. In 1838, the exports were valued at £2,612,851 currency, (four dollars to the pound,) of which £772,432 came to the United States; the imports for the same year by sea alone, at £2,107,264. In 1850, the exports were valued at £2,990,428, of which £1,237,789 were for the United States. Classified, the articles exported were: produce of the mines, £9,145; fisheries, £36,512; lumber, £1,360,734; vegetable food, £1,046,034; other agricultural produce, £13,439; manufactures, £6,676; shipping, sold abroad, £320,430. The imports during the same year amounted to £4,245,517; the duties paid on which were £615,645.*

The trade between the United States and Canada is becoming increasingly important. In 1840, our exports from that province were estimated at $162,741; our imports thither at $398,356. In 1850, the exports reached $5,813,000; the imports, $7,404,000. Of this excess of imports over exports the greater part consists of "foreign merchandise," goods intended for foreign markets which pass through the canals of the United States in preference to passing out by the River St. Lawrence. In 1840, the value of imports of lumber, animal and vegetable food, was $28,507; in 1849, $2,561,416; an increase in ten years of $2,532,907. In 1840, the value of our exports of the same articles was $204,683; in 1840, $445,344; an increase of $320,661. From this it will be seen, that while both imports and exports have increased, our exports from Canada, in 1846, were nearly eight times greater than our imports thence; but that ten years later, in spite of our higher duties, our imports were nearly six times greater than our exports. In 1847, there were imported into Canada 27,137,234 lbs. of sugar and molasses, about 18¼ lbs. to each person; of coffee, in 1848, there were imported 11 oz. per head; of tea, 2 lbs. 4 oz. to each inhabitant. In the United States, in 1848, coffee was imported to the amount of 6½ oz. a head; tea, 5 oz. a head. This comparison would seem to indicate that the people of Canada understood the art of living comfortably; rather too comfortably, perhaps, for in 1848 they consumed about two gallons of wine and other spirits; the greater part of it being whiskey distilled within the province.†

Internal Improvements.—The provincial government has expended liberally of its funds in effecting internal improvements. In 1841, the year of the Union, it appropriated to this object $7,718,335. Previous to this time the legislature had expended, in constructing canals and in improving navigable water courses, $5,520,550; making in all up to 1841, $13,238,885. Since that time other liberal grants have been made. The canals which have been dug in Canada have proved of immense advantage. The longest and most important of these is that called the Rideau Canal, which connects the northern end

---

* For further information on this, and some of the preceding heads, see an article in the present volume on "British America."

† The subject of our commercial relations with Canada is well discussed in a number of De Bow's Review, March, 1852; and in the North American Review for January, 1852.

of Lake Ontario at Kingston, with the Ottawa River at Bytown, a distance of 128 miles. It was constructed in order that vessels might avoid the dangerous rocks and rapids which are found in the St. Lawrence between lake Ontario and Montreal. The Ottawa, from Bytown to Montreal, on the other hand, is navigable and perfectly safe. This canal is 142 feet long by 33 wide, contains 47 locks, and cost about $5,000,000. Farther west and south we have the Welland Canal, which unites the Lakes Erie and Ontario, avoiding the Falls of Niagara. Its length is 42 miles; its descent, 330 feet, accomplished by 37 locks; and its cost was nearly $5,000,000. The Canadians have, besides these, the Chambly Canal, eleven miles long, connecting Lake Champlain with the St. Lawrence near Montreal; the Grenville Canal, on the Ottawa, to avoid its rapids; and several short canals on the St. Lawrence, to avoid falls in that river, which measure altogether about 90 miles. By means of these canals, direct navigation has been opened from Lake Michigan down the St. Lawrence to the sea. In 1850 there passed through the canals on the St. Lawrence 7,166 vessels and steamers, of which 6,827 were British and 339 American, with an aggregate tonnage of 547,322 tons. Through the Welland Canal there passed, the same year, 4,671 vessels and steamers, 2,692 British and 1,799 American, with a tonnage of 587,100.

Public attention has of late been directed in Canada to the making of rail-roads, several of which are being constructed and others are projected. Two or three short roads only have as yet been completed; the Champlain and St. Lawrence, 36 miles long, connecting the St. Lawrence opposite Montreal with the Sorel River at St. John's, and therefore with Lake Champlain; the Lachine, 7 miles; the Atlantic, 12; Saunay and Industry Village, 12; in all 84 miles, in Canada East. In the other province there are two short lines above Bytown on the Ottawa; and another extending from Queenstown below to Chippewa above the Falls of Niagara, used, however, only in summer, and employing only horse power.

Two very important rail-roads have recently been projected, and a part of each has been constructed. One is called the Atlantic and St. Lawrence Railroad. Leaving the south shore of the river, just below Montreal, it is to pass through a part of Canada East, the north-east corner of Vermont, New-Hampshire, north of the White Hills, and through Maine to Portland. The Montreal end is finished and in use as far as Skipton, a distance of about 80 miles; at which place it is expected it will be joined by a rail-road from Quebec. On the other end, some ninety miles are finished and in operation, from Portland to Gorham, in New-Hampshire. The other proposed road, called the Great Western, will be about 230 miles long, extending from Niagara Falls westwardly, at some point 40 or 50 miles north of Lake Erie, through some of the most fertile land in America, as far as Windsor, opposite Detroit, in Michigan; where it will connect with a line passing through Michigan to the Far West. At its eastern end it will connect with the line leading from Buffalo to the Hudson River, and thence, by separate routes, to New-York and New-England. Thus, when this road is completed, a traveler will be enabled to go by rail-road from Portland, Maine, to the Mississippi.*

Revenue and Public Debt.—The revenue of the province for 1842, the year after the Union, was £365,505; in 1847, £506,826. The customs during the first-mentioned period amounted to £265,386; during the last, to £381,063. The impost of one per per cent. on the circulation of notes of chartered banks rose from £10,277 in 1842, to £16,006 in 1847. The net revenue derived from the canals, in 1842, was 16,369; in 1847, it had risen to £42,557. The gross revenue from this source for the latter year, was £83,335; the unusual amount of £31,307 having been spent this year in making repairs. The gross revenue of the canals from 1842 to 1847, inclusive, was, respectively, £24,232; £34,604; £44,429; £41,039; £61,486: £83,335; an increase in six years of 240 per cent. The tolls of the State of New-York, during the six years preceding 1842, increased only 36 per cent. The interest on the whole public debt of Canada was, in 1847, £148,264; 42 per cent. of which would, it is computed, be paid by the proceeds of the public works. The expenditures of the government reach about $3,000,000 annually. The taxes for the same time amounted, a few years since, to £429,044; about 5s. 8d. per head. They are comprised in the following items: customs, excise, light-house, and tonnage duties, bank imposts, militia commissions, and various fines and forfeitures.

Banks.—There are eight banks in operation in Canada, the most important of which, that of Montreal, had a capital of £750,000 in May, 1851; the smallest, the Gore Bank, a capital of £80,000. Between these there are the Bank of British North America, £640,000; Commercial Bank, M. D., £411,300; Bank of Upper Canada, £381.192; City Bank of Montreal, £221,793; Quebec Bank, £100,000; and Banque du Peuple, £200,000. Their combined capital, in May, 1851, was £2,784,285. Their circulation at the same time was £1,623,435; coin, £413,420; deposits, £1,691,630; loans, £5,574,280. There was an increase within twelve months of capital, £8,405; circulation, £313,503; specie, £29,289; deposits, £167,369; loans, £1,199,382.

Education.—The future of Canada, especially of the western province, is promising with respect to education. A system of instruction for the whole people has been adopted, which gives indication of the most useful results. As yet, however, its successful working is confined to Canada West. As long ago as 40 years, the legislature of Canada West made an appropriation for common schools; and this was renewed annually till 1841. These grants, however, were expended to little advantage. In 1841, a provincial statute was enacted, granting money to each county for the support of common schools, provided that the county would raise, for the same object, an equal amount by taxation. This statute has several times since been altered and improved; and in 1850, all the provisions of former laws respecting education, which had been found to work well, and others which seemed necessary, were united into one statute by the legislature. The sum of £25,000 ($100,000) was set apart as an annual donation by that body to the school fund. This fund is apportioned annually by the chief superintendent among the townships of the province, according to the population of each. The local superintendents distribute these apportionments among the several sections of each township, according to the average attendance of scholars. Each section is obliged by law to raise a sum at least as large as that received from the treasury. Every section appoints three trustees over its public schools; and each county council appoints a local superintendent for the county, or for one or more townships, a superintendent having the charge of no more than 100 schools. These trustees and the local superintendents constitute the local board of public instruction. It is the business of this board to examine candidates for the office of teacher. The local superintendents are required to visit, at stated intervals, all the schools under their charge; and clergymen, recognized as such by law, members of the legislature, and all magistrates, are also authorized to make visits to them, and to inquire into their condition. Provision is made for libraries by the county and township councils. At the head of the whole system are placed a chief superintendent and a council of public instruction. The duties of the chief superintendent are substantially the same as with us. The council has the management of the provincial, normal, and model schools; prescribes to them rules and regulations; examines and classifies teachers; recommends text-books; and has entrusted to it the establishment and care of the school libraries. The schools are said to be man-

* See a good article on the "Condition and Prospects of Canada," in the North American Review, for April, 1852.

aged with a view to the best interests of the state and of society, apart from all political party advantage.

The number of schools in Canada West, in 1851, was 3,059, with 151,891 pupils. Massachusetts had, in 1849, when it contained 150,000 inhabitants more than Canada West has now, 3,749 public schools, with 200,000 scholars. This comparison is very favorable to our Canadian neighbor. A normal and model school was established last year at Toronto. It is designed to accommodate 200 teachers in training in the normal, and 600 pupils in the model school. The legislature has granted £15,000 ($60,000) to carry the measure into execution. Similar liberality has been shown, we believe, by no legislature on this side of the Atlantic.

Such are the educational prospects of Canada; and such as we have previously described, are the indications of her approaching commercial, manufacturing, and agricultural prosperity. A glorious, and, what is better, a happy destiny, may yet await her in the future.

COTTON CROP—Cost of Transportation from the Plantation into the European Market.—A correspondent of the "Cotton Plant" is authority for the following. As an illustration of the charges on a crop before it reaches Manchester, I give you an account of sales of 100 bales in Liverpool, in 1844, when the price was about what it is now:

100 bales of cotton		
Draughts per bale		42,000
Tare 4lb. per cwt.	100	
	1,500	
		1,600
Net weight		40,400
At $4\frac{3}{8}$ per lb.—$8\frac{3}{4}$ cents		$3,535,00

Charges in United States and Liverpool.

Baggage, twine, mending and making	$14 50	
Wharfage, $4; cartage, $10; storage, $8	22 00	
Fire insurance, $3 81; postage, &c., $3 50	7 31	
Marine insurance, 1 per cent. on $3,578 81	35 79	
Policy	1 25	
		$80 85
Dock dues, £4 6d.; town dues, 16s. 8d.		23 32
Duty 35d. per cwt., on 360 cwt. 2 qrs. 24 lbs.		252 50
Cartage, porterage, weighage, £3 14s. 1d.		17 78
Canvas, twine, and mending, £2 9s.		11 76
Warehouse rent, for 12 weeks, £5		24 00
Postages and small charges, 10s. 6d.		2 52
Brokerage, $\frac{1}{4}$ per cent.; insurance, $\frac{1}{8}$ per cent.; 3 mo. 10 days interest; discount, $\frac{1}{4}$ per cent.—$1\frac{5}{8}$ on £731 9s. 2d.		66 26
Freight, at $\frac{1}{2}$d. per lb., on 40,400 lbs.		404 00
Five per cent. primage on freight		20 20
Commission and guaranty, 3 per cent. on £736 9s. 2d.		106 05
Three months' interest on cash charges, £974 70		14 62
Total charges		$1,023 14 nearly one-third.

COTTON CROP, 1851-2.—From the statement of the cotton crop, prepared for the New-York *Shipping and Commercial List and Prices Current*, it will be seen that the

	Bales.
Total crop, 1851-52, is	3,015,029
Total export	2,443,646
Taken for home use at the North	603,029
Taken for home use at the South and West	75.000
Quantity of *new* received to 1st inst.	5,125

Showing an *increase* in the crop of 659,722 bales, in the export of 454,936, in the consumption at the North, of 198,921; and South and West, of 15,000 bales.

Comparative Statement of Growth.

Crop of	Bales.		Bales.
1851—2	3,015,029	1842—3	2,378,875
1850—1	2,355,257	1841—2	1,683,574
1849-50	2,096,706	1840—1	1,634,945
1848—9	2,728,596	1839-40	2,177,835
1847—8	2,347,634	1838—9	1,360,532
1846—7	1,778,651	1837—8	1,801,497
1845—6	2,100,537	1836—7	1,422,930
1844—5	2,394,503	1835—6	1,360,725
1843—4	2,030,409	1834—5	1,254,328
		1833—4	1,205,394

QUANTITY CONSUMED BY AND IN THE HANDS OF MANUFACTURERS.

North of Virginia.

	Bales.		Bales.
1851-2	603,029	1842-3	325,129
1850-1	405,108	1841-2	267,850
1849-50	487,769	1840-1	297,288
1848-9	518,039	1839-40	295,193
1847-8	531,772	1838-9	276,018
1846-7	427,967	1837-8	246,063
1845-6	422,597	1836-7	222,540
1844-5	389,006	1835-6	236,733
1843-4	346,744	1834-5	216,888

Consumption.

			Bales.
Total crop of the United States, as before stated			3,015,029
Add—			
Stocks on hand at the commencement of the year, Sept. 1, 1851:—			
In the southern ports	89,044		
In the northern ports	39,260		
			128,304
Makes a supply of			3,143,333
Deduct therefrom—			
The export to foreign ports	2,443,646		
Less—foreign included	543		
		2,443,103	
Stocks on hand Sept 1, 1852:			
In the southern ports	31,098		
In the northern ports	60,078		
		91,176	
Burnt at Savannah, Charleston and Providence		6,025	
			2,540,304
Taken for home use			603,029

We give below our usual table of the amount of cotton consumed the past year in the states south and west of Virginia, and not included in the receipts at the ports. We have increased the estimate somewhat from the year previous, though the number and capacity of the mills have been about the same, but give it only for what it purports to be, an *estimate* which we believe approximates correctness. Thus, in—

	Quantity consumed.		
North Carolina	15,000	bales,	of 400 lbs.
South Carolina	10,000	"	"
Georgia	22,000	"	"
Alabama	5,000	"	of 500 lbs.
Tennessee	7,000	"	"
On the Ohio, &c.	16,000	"	"
Total to Sept. 1, 1852	75,000	"	
" " 1851	60,000	"	
" " 1850	107,500	"	
" " 1849	110,000	"	
" " 1848	75,000	"	

To which, if we add the stocks in the interior towns, &c., the quantity burnt in the interior, and that lost on its way to market, to the crop as given above, received at the shipping ports, the aggregate will show very nearly the amount raised in the United States the past season—say, in round numbers, 3,100,000 bales, against 2,450,000 bales the year previous.

During the year just closed, there was received at an eastern port, 175 bales by way of the New-York & Erie Canal, which we have added in another place to the crop of the country.

It may be remarked in this connexion, that some of the cotton received overland at Philadelphia and Baltimore is doubtless unaccounted for elsewhere, not being counted in the receipts at New-Orleans, but as we have of late years omitted this item from the crop, it is not now added.

The quantity of new cotton received at the shipping ports up to the 1st inst. amounted to about 5,125 bales against about 3,200 bales last year.

The shipments given in this statement from Texas, are those by *sea* only; a considerable portion of the crop of that state finds its way to market via Red River, and is included in the receipts at New-Orleans.

EXPORT TO FOREIGN PORTS, FROM SEPT. 1, 1851, TO AUG. 31, 1852.

From	To Great Britain.	To France.	North of Europe.	Other Foreign P'ts.	Total.
New-Orleans—bales	772,242	196,254	75,950	134,657	1,179,103
Mobile	306,002	97,753	8,826	18,265	430,846
Texas	1,388	3,202	2,695	—	7,235
Florida	48,638	1,560	9,840	4,454	64,493
Georgia	109,378	12,593	2,483	—	124,454
South Carolina	207,220	43,950	16,240	22,025	289,435
North Carolina	419	—	5	—	424
Virginia	—	35	—	—	35
Baltimore	71	—	100	—	171
Philadelphia	4,619	55	—	422	5,096
New-York	218,772	65,973	50,536	4,491	339,772
Boston	50	—	2,200	333	2,583
Grand total	1,668,749	421,375	168,875	184,647	2,443,646
Total last year	1,418,265	301,358	129,492	139,595	1,988,710
Increase	250,484	120,017	39,383	45,052	454,936

FISHERIES OF THE UNITED STATES.—It may be interesting to state (says the Courier and Enquirer) that of so much consequence did Massachusetts, as early as 1790, consider the fisheries to her foreign trade, that she had nearly $2,000,000 invested in salt works alone. She had

Works in number—supply fishery	80
Capital invested	$1,754,576
Persons employed	679
Bushels salt annually manufactured	503,689

Recently the assessors of each town in that state, by act of the legislature, were directed to make return to the Secretary of the Commonwealth of all the branches of the manufacturing industry of the state. The return comprehended the fisheries, and exhibited the following result for Massachusetts alone:

	Value.	Hands employed.	Cap. invested.
Fisheries	$7.592,290	20,168	$12.484,078
Oil	2.030,321	145	1,135,500
	$9,622,611	20,313	$13,619,578

Such is the state of the Massachusetts fisheries, involving a capital of over thirteen and a half millions of dollars, and producing annually near ten millions dollars worth of property! Latest statistics on the subject show that we have, for the entire country, fishing interests at stake as follows:

Capital invested	$27,000,000
Hands employed	40,000
Product of the fisheries	$20,000,000

On the coast of Labrador, according to the Quebec *Star*, the statistics of the fisheries for 1829, were:—

	Vessels.	Men.	Fish, Cwt.	Oil, Hhds.
United States	1,500	15,000	1,100,000	11.000
Newfoundland	400	4.000	350.000	3,500
Nova Scotia	100	800	70.000	700
England, &c.	80	4,000	240,000	2,400
Lower Canada	8	150	5,000	50
N. Brunswick, Magdalen Isds.	20	160	8,000	80

But the more attractive feature with which we are presented in this review, is the increase of the fisheries since 1675. The annexed statement exhibits this increase:

Years.	Cod—Tons.	Mackerel—Tons.	Total—Tons.
1675	25,650	—	—
1795	30,933	—	—
1828	74,947	—	—
1840	76,035	28,629	104.304
1849	73,882	42,992	116,876

The distribution of tonnage in the cod fisheries in 1797 and 1848, was respectively as subjoined.

The United States, down to a recent period, was the great supplier of fish to the world. Our principal markets were the West Indies and the Mediterranean; but we also exported large quantities to other sections Going back to 1821 we exported fish amounting to—

Dried or Smoked.

Domestic	267,305 quintals.
Foreign	14 do.

Pickled.

Domestic	76,429 bbls.
Do.	4,162 kegs.
Foreign	none.

The figures now present a totally different result. Steadily but surely has England and her American possessions been pursuing this fishing interest, until, at this time, besides being a partial supplier of our own markets, they have almost superseded us in the foreign The estimate of the value of the fish sent abroad from the ports of the two Canadas from 1840 to 1850, were $7,000,000. The exports of a single year from Halifax were 275,000. And as our trade declines, and that of rival states is augmented, a source of national wealth, national revenue, (from the duty on salt,) and national prosperity, is lost to us, or unjustly embarrassed. We have but to adduce official figures in support of the remark that our fishery trade is being gradually wrested from us. In 1790 we exported fish to the West Indies, valued at $700,000. Last year our exportations of fish to the same localities did not exceed $167,000. With Europe our fishery transactions have also vascillated and declined:

A Statement, showing the Exports of Fish from the United States to Foreign Countries, in 1790 *and* 1851.

	1790.	1851.
To West Indies—value	$685.001	$166.679
To Europe, Africa, and Asia	253.554	6,376
Decline		$765,100

GOLD AND SILVER — Production of, from 1492 to 1852. — An officer of the United States Treasury Department at Washington, in answer to a semi-official inquiry made at the department, has presented an elaborate report, estimating the production of the precious metals from 1492 to 1852. The writer, after an examination of the standard authors upon the subject, Humboldt, McCulloch, and Jacobs, estimates the total product of the world, exclusive of Australia, as follows:

America, excl. of the United States		$6,077,833,800
California, received at Mint	$98,408,000	
California, foreign exports, manufactured, &c	51,592,000	
Other United States gold at mint	15,855,000	
Ditto not brought to mint	1,145,000	
Total United States	167,000,000	
Total America		7,044,833,800
Europe and Asia, exclusive of Russia		1,755,000,000
Russia		213,581,000
Total production, 1492 to 1852		$9,013,414,800

The present annual product of the precious metals, the writer estimates as follows:

All South America	$30,710,000
Add for any probable increase, according to the best authorities	3,290,000
Hungary, Saxony, and Northern Asia	4,000,000
Russia, at the highest estimate of years	20,000,000
Africa and South Asia (a rough estimate	1,000,000
Carolina, Georgia, &c	500,000
California	64.500,000
Total	$124,000,000

The compiler of the estimate remarks:—"It is not clearly expressed by any of the authorities quoted, whether the amounts of the precious metals stated to have been produced at different periods, applies to the amount coined or to the entire production, but the inference is strongly in favor of the latter.

"The limited production of gold and silver in the last years of the 15th century, may be very naturally accounted for in the limited number of people who at first ventured to explore the New World, and in the scarcity of those metals in the lands first occupied by Columbus; but it will, perhaps, excite surprise to find that the first deposits of California gold in the mints of the United States, in the year 1851, exceed the highest annual production of gold and silver in Mexico and South America by nearly 40 per cent."

ESTIMATES OF ENTIRE GOLD PRODUCT—CALIFORNIA.

Official report of deposits of gold from California.

At the various United States mints in 1848			$44.177
" " " " 1849			6.147,509
" " " " 1850			36.074.062
" " " " 1851			55,938.232
Manifested shipments to U. S. ports in December, 1851, which did not reach the mints in 1851			2,910,214
Importations into Chili in 1851, by official returns from that country		$2,372,000	
Shipments per steamers in 1851, on freight to Europe and various countries, (not including Chili,) via Panama, so far as destination was declared on manifests	$3,600,000		
Add estimate of shipments by same course and to same quarters in 1851, for which the destiuation beyond Panama was not declared—50 per cent. of above	1.800.000	5,400,000	
Known shipments by sailing vessels in 1851, to various foreign ports	1,000,000		
Add for amount not manifested, believed to be as large	1,000,000	2,000,000	
Total estimate of exportation to foreign countries in 1851		9,772,000	
The early foreign trade to this was very large, particularly in 1849, from Pacific ports. Remittances in this early trade were made chiefly in gold dust. The aggregate shipment to foreign countries for 1848, 1849, and 1850, is therefore assumed for the three years to be as large as that of 1851		9,772,000	
Total estimate of exports to foreign countries to December 31st, 1851, which would not reach U. S. mints			19,544,000
			120.658
Estimated amount taken overland to Mexico and by passengers to Europe, East Indies, Australia, South America, (exclusive of Chili,) manufactured in California and United States and otherwise, retained by individuals leaving the country, and therefore not represented in the mint deposits, say 5 per cent. on above			6,032,909
In hands of bankers, merchants and traders in San Francisco, per tabular statement prepared December 31st, 1851			5.000.000
In hands of bankers or traders, in other parts of California and Oregon, Dec. 31st, 1851			2.500.000
Estimated half month's yield at mines not brought forward December, 1851—say			2,500,000
In circulation—gold dust and California private coin, estimated at $20 per individual, and population estimated at 212,000			4.240.000
Estimated product to December 31st, 1851			$140,931.103
Do. do. from January 1 to June 30, 1852			33.849.774
Total do. do. to June 30, 1852			$174.780.877

Circular Hussey, Bond & Hale.

DEPARTMENTS OF THE REVIEW.

The different departments of the REVIEW will be kept up faithfully from month to month, so as to preserve, in a convenient form for study or for reference, everything that particularly appertains to them, or that may be of value to the country.

Commercial Department.—Its statistics are full and complete upon every crop or community—the trade of every city and state of the Union, and of foreign countries. Here are included *Treaties and Tariffs, Shipping and Steam Navigation, Mercantile Laws and Decisions, Finances and Banking, Commercial Literature and Biography.* To Merchants and Bankers in particular these statistics are invaluable.

Agricultural Department.—Every staple product of the Southern and Western Country, under this head receives its appropriate place, and everything tending to their advancement is carefully embodied and presented. The pens of practical planters are employed, who contribute their own experience for the benefit of their fellows. The agricultural information is thus specially adapted to our own localities, an advantage not possessed by works published abroad, which we have been hitherto supporting. Practical and scientific papers upon agriculture are included from the best authorities in our country and in Europe. The cotton planter finds the most interesting monthly summaries of information relating to the plant—*the estimates of crops, the mode of cultivation, extent of consumption, circumstances influencing prices, comparative tables of production and consumption, diseases affecting the growth, etc.* The SUGAR PLANTER finds a chronicle of all the latest improvements at home and abroad, *descriptions of machinery, modes of culture, productions of other countries, demand and supply, competition, etc.; the latest and best experience of planters and manufacturers, etc.; reprints of leading foreign works on sugar, with engravings.* The HEMP and TOBACCO grower, the *Farmer* and the *Horticulturist*, and, in fact, every agricultural interest, find equal sources of information.

Manufacturing Department.—Already cotton mills are multiplying on the banks of the Ohio, in Tennessee and Kentucky, throughout Virginia, Carolina, Georgia and Alabama. In a few years more they will extend through every part of the South and the West. In the infancy of our efforts we shall need the light of experience from abroad, and from each other. We must know what our neighbors are doing as well as ourselves, and their success. There is no other work in the Union devoted in such a degree to the *manufacturing interest*—none which has contained in the past such an immense amount of manufacturing information, and no work shall excel it in this respect in the future.

Internal Improvements.—The South and the West have entered upon a great era of progress in RAILROADS. Our *necessities* demand much, and we have thousands of miles in contemplation or in progress. Our people require information, collected from the experience of others. They must have all the facts and figures to aid their action. This has been our favorite field of labor, and will be. We entered the vineyard among the very first, and have never deserted it. The reports and results of every road are chronicled; the cost of construction; the amount of travel, freights, passage and profits—the extent of lines in this country or abroad, etc.; proceedings of rail-road conventions throughout the South and West; resolutions, etc. Every rail-road stockholder, or officer, or person seeking investment or benefits in roads, will find the Review of very great advantage.

Miscellaneous.—Under this head will be included statistics of *population*, and of *health and diseases, public wealth and progress;* relative condition of *whites and blacks;* condition and operations of SLAVERY AT THE SOUTH; *slave laws and statistics* of the South and of other countries; management and amelioration of slavery; *origin, history, and defences of slavery and slave institutions;* standard treatises upon slavery from all the highest authorities. In this department the South will be fairly presented and vindicated before the world, and her interests maintained and protected. A large volume might already be made up from the extremely valuable papers, like those of Hammond, Harper, Dew, and many others which have appeared in the Review. This information is valuable to the planters in too many ways to be enumerated; and to the citizens of the free states honestly seeking information, the value will be even higher.

Literary Department.—Under this head, will be included Sketches of Fact and Fancy, Original Poetry, Critical and Historical Essays, Reviews and Notices of Late Books, Literary Movements at Home and Abroad, papers upon Education and Southern Schools and Colleges, Incidents and Notes of Travel, etc. Able pens will at all times be elicited, and no effort will be spared to give to this department of the Review as much of the character of the light MISCELLANY as will secure it a place in the parlor as well as upon the shelves of the library.

Biographies, Portraits, Engravings, Maps, etc.—The object here is to select from all of the states, men who have been, or are active in promoting the progress of enterprise and industry, and thus advancing their fellows. Handsome steel engravings will accompany these. Occasional views of cities will be furnished, wood-cuts and charts representing machinery-improvements, etc.

Advertising Department.—This will furnish an important part towards the completion of the work. A few pages at the end will be included, or a chart folded in.

Brief cards and announcements will be inserted—illustrated, where necessary, with wood-cuts. Thus the planters throughout the country may be informed of the names and places of business of the merchants: the merchants may know of the professional men in the interior: and those desirous of investing in estates may find a record of those in the market. We design entrusting this department, which may be made very valuable, to the management of a special person. The terms will be moderate to advertisers; and, now that we have over five thousand subscribers throughout the southern and middle states, of the best classes, the Review is the very best medium for them.

NOTICES OF THE PRESS.

De Bow's Review.—This Review is an able one. We anticipate and realize invaluable information from its pages, as to the progress and industry of the flourishing districts of which it is the herald and organ.—*Simmond's Colonial Magazine, London.*

De Bow's Review.—We need hardly say that we are charmed with this Review, when we add that we read it through at a heat.—*Skinner's Farmer's Library, New-York.*

De Bow's Commercial Review contains much valuable matter of Commercial and Miscellaneous character. Success to our namesake. The paper in it which interests us the most, is that entitled "COMMERCE AND AGRICULTURE SUBJECTS OF UNIVERSITY INSTRUCTION," from the pen of the accomplished editor of the Review, in which he submits the plan of a Professorship of Public Economy, Commerce, and Statistics for our Colleges and Universities. The plan has our hearty approval, and will, we trust, ere long be adopted by some of our higher institutions. The article on "CHARLESTON AND ITS RESOURCES," we shall endeavor to find room for in a future number of the Magazine.—*Hunt's Merchants' Magazine.*

De Bow's Review is one of the most useful of the monthly publications, accumulating at such periods a large and valuable body of statistics and opinions, such as we rarely find in any other form of publication. The editor is a person of rare industry and enthusiasm. His work is particularly important to the commercial community of the South.—*Southern Quarterly Review, Charleston.*

De Bow's Review. We are exceedingly pleased to hear of the success of this work, so important to the South, and so creditable to its literary enterprise. It comes to us monthly, freighted with the most valuable and reliable information, in relation to the sources of that section of the country, and ought not to be missed from any northern library.—*Democratic Review, N. Y.*

De Bow's Review.—It gives us great pleasure to state, that J. D. B. DE BOW, editor of the Commercial Review, has been selected to fill the chair of Commerce and Statistics in the new University. Mr. D has, in the columns of his popular and widely circulated journal, shown himself to be familiar with the commerce and statistics of the South and West, and also a zealous advocate for disseminating widely accurate information upon these important heads. We want more educated merchants, a more intimate knowledge of the history of commerce, and of the principles and theory of political economy, trade and manufactures.—*Bankers' Magazine, Boston.*

De Bow's Review.—Suppose one should desire to keep himself advised of the state of our domestic and foreign trade, and also of the commerce of all nations, where else would he find this information in a form so convenient, satisfactery and cheap, as in Hunt's Magazine. Should he desire to combine with commercial information a knowledge of the great interests of the South, her agriculture, manufactures, and internal improvements, where else could he find so much information in so small a compass, and at so cheap a rate, as in De Bow's Review?—*Western Journal, St. Louis.*

De Bow's Review.—This Review, now in its sixth year, has not as yet received the attention which it deserves at the North. It is amply supported, we learn, at the South; and for this reason, as an accredited organ of the commercial interests of that great region of our country, should find its readers in all circles. We should be more anxious to learn what views are taken of our great producing interests, and of the natural questions which agitate the country at headquarters.—*Literary World, New-York.*

De Bow's Review.—The statistics are collected with great care and industry; and the work presents more useful information in relation to the great staples of the South, than can be found in any other periodical. As these staples form the basis of a great part of all our leading commercial transactions, the above work is an indispensable part of every business man's library.—*Rail-Road Journal, N. Y.*

De Bow's Review.—We are persuaded that no more useful publication than this emanates from the American press. Its range of topics is, indeed, a wide one, but it is always filled with valuable statistical papers, and its literary department is highly interesting. Mr. De Bow is well known as a scholar and a writer. A recent address delivered by him before an agricultural society, has pleased us so much, that we could find it in our heart to quarrel for not contributing more frequently in *propria persona* to the pages of his magazine.—*Southern Literary Messenger, Richmond, V.*

De Bow's Review.—The work is printed in a style creditable to the press, and its contents are such as to render it a valuable adjunct to the similar work devoted to the commerce of the United States, published by Hunt, of New-York, &c.—*Boston Daily Adv.*

De Bow's Review.—This periodical performs for the South and West the same office which the Merchants' Magazine performs for this part of the country. We learn that its circulation is rapidly increasing. The present number contains many valuable articles, among which is one by the Editor, on the "Progress of the Great West," full of interesting statistical information and speculations. It is to the credit of the mercantile class that works of this kind find encouragement among them.—*N. Y. Evening Post.*

De Bow's Review.—We rejoice that so good a work has been established at New-Orleans, and apparently well established. It can hardly fail to secure patrons in every part of the country.—*N. Y. Tribune.*

De Bow's Review. This is the title of a monthly journal of trade, commerce, commercial policy, agriculture, manufactures, internal improvements, and general literature, published at New-Orleans by J. D. B. De Bow, and is well worth the attention of the merchant and the statesman. It is second to no other work of the kind in this or any other country, and must soon become authority for everything relating to matters of which it treats. We notice among its contributors some of the most distinguished writers in the Union.—*N. Y. Herald.*

De Bow's Review has been upon our table for several days. This work is well worthy of attention, not only in the section of country in which it is published, but at the North, as it contains a great amount of very valuable information which cannot be found elsewhere. It is properly the complement of Hunt's Magazine, and in connection with that work, forms a complete record of mercantile and commercial facts. We commend it to the notice of our readers, and to the favor of all who are interested in the commerce of the South.—*N Y. Courier and Enquirer.*

De Bow's Review.—Much as we had heard and read of this celebrated New-Orleans publication, it was not till the present week that we had an opportunity of making ourselves acquainted with its great merits. We were wholly unprepared to find in this magazine a work evincing so much ability and industry, and containing such a mass of information—commercial, statistical, historical, political and philosophical. The number before us (for September) contains 142 closely printed pages of reading matter. Such a work, the reader will readily conceive, must be one of universal interest, deserving of unlimited circulation.—*N. Y. Sun.*

De Bow's Review.—We have received from the proprietor the May number of the above popular periodical, and find it one of the most interesting that has yet been issued. The various departments of Agriculture, Commerce, Manufactures, and Internal Improvements, have each appropriate articles and statistics, and besides these, the present number is embellished with two remarkably fine steel-engraved portraits. This is a new and pleasing department, and we are gratified to notice that it is the intention of the proprietor to follow it up, in each succeeding number, with a portrait of some leading and practical business man of the South or West.—*New-Orleans Price Current.*

De Bow's Review.—This number contains several valuable essays, especially those upon Georgia and Turkey. That on Turkey is extremely valuable and interesting. The biography of Mr. Gregg, which accompanies the engraving, is worth more than all the Carolina lectures on political economy.—*New-Orleans Crescent.*

De Bow's Review.—We have received from the editor, the March number of this periodical, the advance of which in popular favor is so rapid. We think the present number improves even on its predecessors. The articles are germane,—they are written with force and judgment, and an excellent feature of them is, that they are not too long or tedious.—*New-Orleans Delta.*

De Bow's Magazine.—We have read the April number of this excellent review, with a great deal of satisfaction. It comprises a number of miscellaneous articles, of interest to the general reader, besides a mass of valuable statistics. The worthy editor is a devoted friend of the South, and is acting the part of a true patriot, by giving our people reliable facts, going to show the extent and value of our inexhaustible resources. This magazine should hold the same rank (as it is fully entitled to) in the South, that *Hunt's Magazine* does at the North; and with a clear conscience, we can commend it particularly to our commercial friends, as a work in every way deserving of their patronage.—*New-Orleans Bulletin.*

De Bow's Review.—We received the March number of this excellent monthly. The contents are of their usual highly-interesting and useful character. A literary department has been added to the Review, thereby adding greatly to its previous enviable reputation and high standing. Every western and southern man should subscribe to it.—*Picayune, New-Orleans.*

De Bow's Review.—The editor, Mr. De Bow, is now well known throughout the South, and the manner in which he has conducted this periodical through all its vicissitudes, amply demonstrates his entire competency for the task.—*South Carolinian.*

De Bow's Review.—Mr. De Bow's acute mind and indefatigable industry, have long since deserved popularity, and we trust is destined to obtain it, as a faithful worker for southern interests.—*Evening News, Charleston.*

De Bow's Review.—The great and growing value of the work will not be questioned, when it is remembered what a reputation it has already acquired in every portion of the Union. Its practical information and statistics are full upon every subject which relates to the agriculture, manufactures, commerce, etc. of the South. Nothing escapes the vigilance of the work which can make for the industrial independence of the whole South.—*Charleston Cour.*

De Bow's Review.—Professor De Bow has, amid the cares and toils of a multiplicity of other important duties connected with the University and Bureau of Statistics in New-Orleans, devoted a vast amount of time, talent and research to the enriching of its pages with voluminous articles, many of them from his own pen, and a mass of statistics in every department of labor, gleaned with care and discrimination from the best sources of the country. It has secured the aid of contributors, men of sound sense, experience and means, who feel a deep interest in the publication.—*Charleston Courier.*

De Bow's Review.—Ex-Governor HAMMOND says, if the *Review* should fail it would disgrace the South. Let every merchant, planter and reading man, subscribe. Place this work on a firm basis, and your interests will be well advocated.—*Charleston Courier.*

De Bow's Review.—The March number has been received. It contains an unusual amount of the industrial and commercial progress of the South, besides several well-written articles on more general subjects. The work does not cease to establish higher and higher claims to the patrons and confidence of the southern people.—*Mercury, Charleston, S. C.*

De Bow's Review.—The editor is a native southerner, and has made noble efforts to develop the mental and physical resources of the South, and his work, which abounds in instructive, useful and entertaining matter, deserves the most liberal encouragement.—*Huntsville (Ala.) Democrat.*

De Bow's Review—The editorial and literary department is exceedingly interesting for its variety and ability. We commend the Review most heartily to a southern public. The subscription price is five dollars.—*Mobile Advertiser.*

De Bow's Review.—It holds up to our commerce a light which shows the way to great ends—concentrates attention on important works of internal improvement, and furnishes to agriculture those facts which direct it to its best sources of profit. The results thus secured are invaluable—no valuation can be made of them, and we are disposed, therefore, to estimate the one who, like Mr. De Bow, has shown a capacity for his office, far above others who may reap honors, and whom we run after and shout for from day to day.—*Mobile Herald.*

De Bow's Review.—One of the chief merits of the work, at all times, has been the earnest devotion and efficient support it gives to the institutions of the South. We have, now, highly interesting articles as to the States of Mississippi, Maryland and Texas, embracing notices of their history, climate, soil, productions and resources, from the pens of well-informed and accomplished writers.—*Register, Mobile.*

De Bow's Review.—We commend the work to the attention of persons who are desirous of subscribing to a Southern Commercial Magazine of the highest character.—*Nashville, Ten., Union.*

De Bow's Review.—As an able and elaborate record of the current facts affecting the great staple of the South—setting forth to the latest dates and from the most varied sources the stocks on hand in the several ports of America and Europe, the quantities necessary to meet the wants of the consumers, the probabilities of prices at different periods, etc., etc., De Bow's Review is absolutely essential to the intelligent action of every man concerned in cotton, from the broker to the planter. As a journal of internal improvement, showing all the facts of railroad progress, and guiding our young enterprise here by the teachings of experience in the older states, this periodical is at the present moment particularly valuable to the citizens of Western Tennessee and Northern Mississippi.—*Enquirer, Memphis, Ten.*

De Bow's Review.—It abounds, as usual, with able articles on the commercial, social and political questions of the South and West, and in statistical information. It is a work that ought to be cherished with liberality by the southern people, and it ought to be consulted by all statesmen, who aspire to the distinction of nationality.—*Southern Press, Washington.*

De Bow's Review.—It is conducted by a man of rare capacities and qualifications for such a work, as its pages abundantly attest. In addition to the editor, it has among its contributors some of the ablest and most distinguished writers of the South and West.—*Washington Union.*

www.ingramcontent.com/pod-product-compliance
Lightning Source LLC
LaVergne TN
LVHW020931110826
845150LV00004B/826

9781425552848